CHRYSLER FULL SIZE 1967-88 REPAIR MANUAL

CHILTON'S

Covers all U.S. and Canadian models of
Dodge A-100, A-200, A-300, B-100, B-150, B-200,
B-250, B-350, MB-250, MB-350, Cutaway Van,
Mini-Motor Home Chassis, Plymouth PB-100,
PB-200 and PB-350

by Todd W. Stidham, A.S.E.

CHILTON *Automotive Books*

PUBLISHED BY **HAYNES NORTH AMERICA, Inc.**

Manufactured in USA
© 1997 Haynes North America, Inc.
ISBN 0-8019-9063-7
Library of Congress Catalog Card No. 97-67982
3456789012 9876543210

Haynes Publishing Group
Sparkford Nr Yeovil
Somerset BA22 7JJ England

Haynes North America, Inc
861 Lawrence Drive
Newbury Park
California 91320 USA

ABCDE
FGHIJ
KLMNO

Contents

Contents

SAFETY NOTICE

Proper service and repair procedures are vital to the safe, reliable operation of all motor vehicles, as well as the personal safety of those performing repairs. This manual outlines procedures for servicing and repairing vehicles using safe, effective methods. The procedures contain many NOTES, CAUTIONS and WARNINGS which should be followed, along with standard procedures to eliminate the possibility of personal injury or improper service which could damage the vehicle or compromise its safety.

It is important to note that repair procedures and techniques, tools and parts for servicing motor vehicles, as well as the skill and experience of the individual performing the work vary widely. It is not possible to anticipate all of the conceivable ways or conditions under which vehicles may be serviced, or to provide cautions as to all possible hazards that may result. Standard and accepted safety precautions and equipment should be used when handling toxic or flammable fluids, and safety goggles or other protection should be used during cutting, grinding, chiseling, prying, or any other process that can cause material removal or projectiles.

Some procedures require the use of tools specially designed for a specific purpose. Before substituting another tool or procedure, you must be completely satisfied that neither your personal safety, nor the performance of the vehicle will be endangered.

Although information in this manual is based on industry sources and is complete as possible at the time of publication, the possibility exists that some car manufacturers made later changes which could not be included here. While striving for total accuracy, the authors or publishers cannot assume responsibility for any errors, changes or omissions that may occur in the compilation of this data.

PART NUMBERS

Part numbers listed in this reference are not recommendations by Haynes North America, Inc. for any product brand name. They are references that can be used with interchange manuals and aftermarket supplier catalogs to locate each brand supplier's discrete part number.

SPECIAL TOOLS

Special tools are recommended by the vehicle manufacturer to perform their specific job. Use has been kept to a minimum, but where absolutely necessary, they are referred to in the text by the part number of the tool manufacturer. These tools can be purchased, under the appropriate part number, from your local dealer or regional distributor, or an equivalent tool can be purchased locally from a tool supplier or parts outlet. Before substituting any tool for the one recommended, read the SAFETY NOTICE at the top of this page.

ACKNOWLEDGMENTS

The publisher expresses appreciation to Chrysler Corporation for their generous assistance.

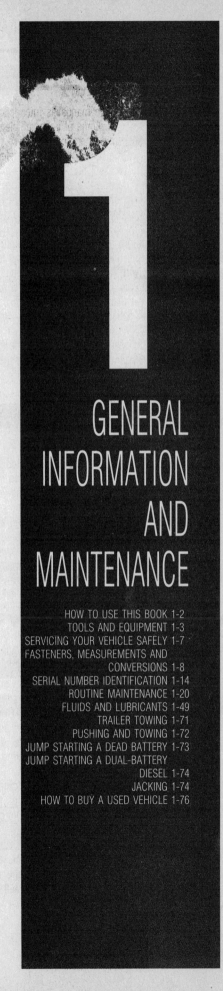

1

GENERAL INFORMATION AND MAINTENANCE

HOW TO USE THIS BOOK

Chilton's Total Car Care manual is intended to help you learn more about the inner workings of your vehicle while saving you money on its upkeep and operation.

The beginning of the book will likely be referred to the most, since that is where you will find information for maintenance and tune-up. The other sections deal with the more complex systems of your vehicle. Operating systems from engine through brakes are covered to the extent that the average do-it-yourselfer becomes mechanically involved. This book will not explain such things as rebuilding a differential for the simple reason that the expertise required and the investment in special tools make this task uneconomical. It will, however, give you detailed instructions to help you change your own brake pads and shoes, replace spark plugs, and perform many more jobs that can save you money, give you personal satisfaction and help you avoid expensive problems.

A secondary purpose of this book is a reference for owners who want to understand their vehicle and/or their mechanics better. In this case, no tools at all are required.

Where to Begin

Before removing any bolts, read through the entire procedure. This will give you the overall view of what tools and supplies will be required. There is nothing more frustrating than having to walk to the bus stop on Monday morning because you were short one bolt on Sunday afternoon. So read ahead and plan ahead. Each operation should be approached logically and all procedures thoroughly understood before attempting any work.

All sections contain adjustments, maintenance, removal and installation procedures, and in some cases, repair or overhaul procedures. When repair is not considered practical, we tell you how to remove the part and then how to install the new or rebuilt replacement. In this way, you at least save the labor costs. Backyard repair of some components is just not practical.

Avoiding Trouble

Many procedures in this book require you to "label and disconnect . . ." a group of lines, hoses or wires. Don't be lulled into thinking you can remember where everything goes—you won't. If you hook up vacuum or fuel lines incorrectly, the vehicle will run poorly, if at all. If you hook up electrical wiring incorrectly, you may instantly learn a very expensive lesson.

You don't need to know the official or engineering name for each hose or line. A piece of masking tape on the hose and a piece on its fitting will allow you to assign your own label such as the letter A or a short name. As long as you remember your own code, the lines can be reconnected by matching similar letters or names. Do remember that tape will dissolve in gasoline or other fluids; if a component is to be washed or cleaned, use another method of identification. A permanent felt-tipped marker can be very handy for marking metal parts. Remove any tape or paper labels after assembly.

Maintenance or Repair?

It's necessary to mention the difference between maintenance and repair. Maintenance includes routine inspections, adjustments, and replacement of parts which show signs of normal wear. Maintenance compensates for wear or deterioration. Repair implies that something has broken or is not working. A need for repair is often caused by lack of maintenance. Example: draining and refilling the automatic transmission fluid is maintenance recommended by the manufacturer at specific mileage intervals. Failure to do this can ruin the transmission/transaxle, requiring very expensive repairs. While no maintenance program can prevent items from breaking or wearing out, a general rule can be stated: MAINTENANCE IS CHEAPER THAN REPAIR.

Two basic mechanic's rules should be mentioned here. First, whenever the left side of the vehicle or engine is referred to, it is meant to specify the driver's side. Conversely, the right side of the vehicle means the passenger's side. Second, most screws and bolts are removed by turning counterclockwise, and tightened by turning clockwise.

Safety is always the most important rule. Constantly be aware of the dangers involved in working on an automobile and take the proper precautions. See the information in this section regarding SERVICING YOUR VEHICLE SAFELY and the SAFETY NOTICE on the acknowledgment page.

Avoiding the Most Common Mistakes

Pay attention to the instructions provided. There are 3 common mistakes in mechanical work:

1. **Incorrect order of assembly, disassembly or adjustment.** When taking something apart or putting it together, performing steps in the wrong order usually just costs you extra time; however, it CAN break something. Read the entire procedure before beginning disassembly. Perform everything in the order in which the instructions say you should, even if you can't immediately see a reason for it. When you're taking apart something that is very intricate, you might want to draw a picture of how it looks when assembled at one point in order to make sure you get everything back in its proper position. We will supply exploded views whenever possible. When making adjustments, perform them in the proper order; often, one adjustment affects another, and you cannot expect even satisfactory results unless each adjustment is made only when it cannot be changed by any other.

2. **Overtorquing (or undertorquing).** While it is more common for overtorquing to cause damage, undertorquing may allow a fastener to vibrate loose causing serious damage. Especially when dealing with aluminum parts, pay attention to torque specifications and utilize a torque wrench in assembly. If a torque figure is not available, remember that if you are using the right tool to perform the job, you will probably not have to strain yourself to get a fastener tight enough. The pitch of most threads is so slight that the tension you put on the wrench will be multiplied many times in actual force on what you are tightening. A good example of how critical torque is can be seen in the case of spark plug in-

stallation, especially where you are putting the plug into an aluminum cylinder head. Too little torque can fail to crush the gasket, causing leakage of combustion gases and consequent overheating of the plug and engine parts. Too much torque can damage the threads or distort the plug, changing the spark gap.

There are many commercial products available for ensuring that fasteners won't come loose, even if they are not torqued just right (a very common brand is Loctite®). If you're worried about getting something together tight enough to hold, but loose enough to avoid mechanical damage during assembly, one of these products might offer substantial insurance. Before choosing a threadlocking compound, read the label on the package and make sure the product is compatible with the materials, fluids, etc. involved.

3. **Crossthreading.** This occurs when a part such as a bolt is screwed into a nut or casting at the wrong angle and forced. Crossthreading is more likely to occur if access is difficult. It

helps to clean and lubricate fasteners, then to start threading with the part to be installed positioned straight in. Then, start the bolt, spark plug, etc. with your fingers. If you encounter resistance, unscrew the part and start over again at a different angle until it can be inserted and turned several times without much effort. Keep in mind that many parts, especially spark plugs, have tapered threads, so that gentle turning will automatically bring the part you're threading to the proper angle, but only if you don't force it or resist a change in angle. Don't put a wrench on the part until it's been tightened a couple of turns by hand. If you suddenly encounter resistance, and the part has not seated fully, don't force it. Pull it back out to make sure it's clean and threading properly.

Always take your time and be patient; once you have some experience, working on your vehicle may well become an enjoyable hobby.

TOOLS AND EQUIPMENT

Naturally, without the proper tools and equipment it is impossible to properly service your vehicle. It would also be virtually impossible to catalog every tool that you would need to perform all of the operations in this book. Of course, It would be unwise for the amateur to rush out and buy an expensive set of tools on the theory that he/she may need one or more of them at some time.

The best approach is to proceed slowly, gathering a good quality set of those tools that are used most frequently. Don't be misled by the low cost of bargain tools. It is far better to spend a little more for better quality. Forged wrenches, 6 or 12-point sockets and fine tooth ratchets are by far preferable to their less expensive counterparts. As any good mechanic can tell you, there are few worse experiences than trying to work on a vehicle with bad tools. Your monetary savings will be far outweighed by frustration and mangled knuckles.

Begin accumulating those tools that are used most frequently: those associated with routine maintenance and tune-up. In addition to the normal assortment of screwdrivers and pliers, you should have the following tools:

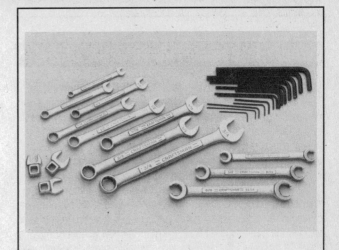

In addition to ratchets, a good set of wrenches and hex keys will be necessary

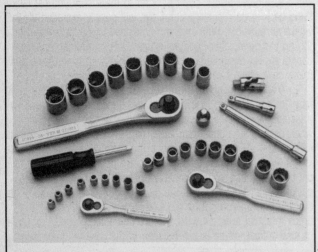

All but the most basic procedures will require an assortment of ratchets and sockets

A hydraulic floor jack and a set of jackstands are essential for lifting and supporting the vehicle

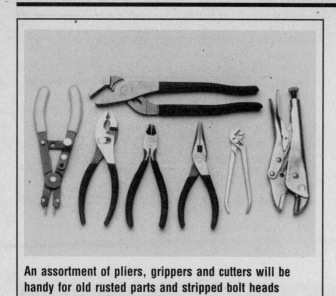

An assortment of pliers, grippers and cutters will be handy for old rusted parts and stripped bolt heads

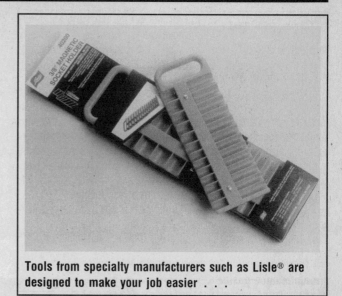

Tools from specialty manufacturers such as Lisle® are designed to make your job easier . . .

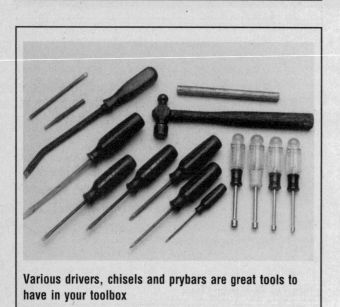

Various drivers, chisels and prybars are great tools to have in your toolbox

. . . these Torx® drivers and magnetic socket holders are just 2 examples of their handy products

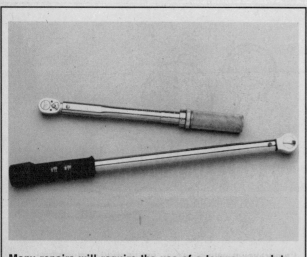

Many repairs will require the use of a torque wrench to assure the components are properly fastened

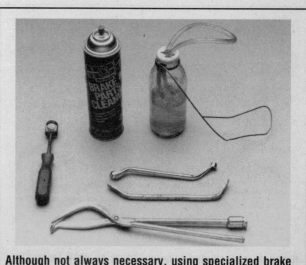

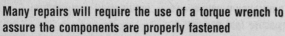

Although not always necessary, using specialized brake tools will save time

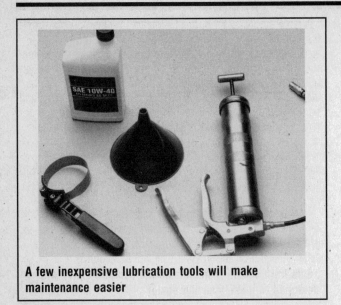

A few inexpensive lubrication tools will make maintenance easier

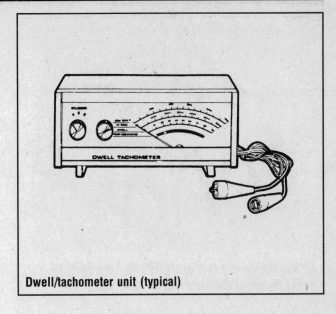

Dwell/tachometer unit (typical)

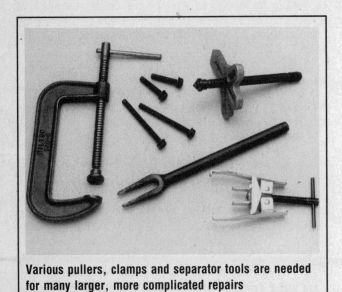

Various pullers, clamps and separator tools are needed for many larger, more complicated repairs

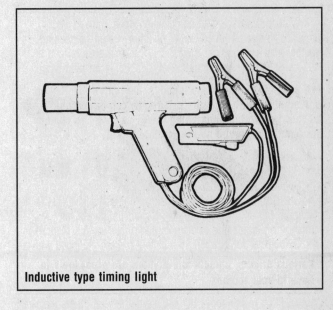

Inductive type timing light

A variety of tools and gauges should be used for spark plug gapping and installation

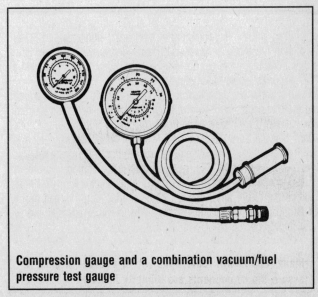

Compression gauge and a combination vacuum/fuel pressure test gauge

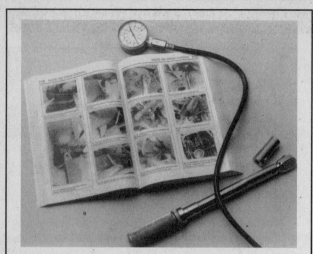

Proper information is vital, so always have a Chilton Total Car Care manual handy

• Wrenches/sockets and combination open end/box end wrenches in sizes from 1/8–3/4 in. or 3mm–19mm (depending on whether your vehicle uses standard or metric fasteners) and a 13/16 in. or 5/8 in. spark plug socket (depending on plug type).

➡**If possible, buy various length socket drive extensions. Universal-joint and wobble extensions can be extremely useful, but be careful when using them, as they can change the amount of torque applied to the socket.**

• Jackstands for support.
• Oil filter wrench.
• Spout or funnel for pouring fluids.
• Grease gun for chassis lubrication (unless your vehicle is not equipped with any grease fittings—for details, please refer to information on Fluids and Lubricants found later in this section).
• Hydrometer for checking the battery (unless equipped with a sealed, maintenance-free battery).
• A container for draining oil and other fluids.
• Rags for wiping up the inevitable mess.

In addition to the above items there are several others that are not absolutely necessary, but handy to have around. These include Oil Dry® (or an equivalent oil absorbent gravel—such as cat litter) and the usual supply of lubricants, antifreeze and fluids, although these can be purchased as needed. This is a basic list for routine maintenance, but only your personal needs and desire can accurately determine your list of tools.

After performing a few projects on the vehicle, you'll be amazed at the other tools and non-tools on your workbench. Some useful household items are: a large turkey baster or siphon, empty coffee cans and ice trays (to store parts), ball of twine, electrical tape for wiring, small rolls of colored tape for tagging lines or hoses, markers and pens, a note pad, golf tees (for plugging vacuum lines), metal coat hangers or a roll of mechanics's wire (to hold things out of the way), dental pick or similar long, pointed probe, a strong magnet, and a small mirror (to see into recesses and under manifolds).

A more advanced set of tools, suitable for tune-up work, can be drawn up easily. While the tools are slightly more sophisticated, they need not be outrageously expensive. There are several inexpensive tach/dwell meters on the market that are every bit as good for the average mechanic as a professional model. Just be sure that it goes to a least 1200–1500 rpm on the tach scale and that it works on 4, 6 and 8-cylinder engines. (If you own one or more vehicles with a diesel engine, a special tachometer is required since diesels don't use spark plug ignition systems). The key to these purchases is to make them with an eye towards adaptability and wide range. A basic list of tune-up tools could include:

• Tach/dwell meter.
• Spark plug wrench and gapping tool.
• Feeler gauges for valve or point adjustment. (Even if your vehicle does not use points or require valve adjustments, a feeler gauge is helpful for many repair/overhaul procedures).

A tachometer/dwell meter will ensure accurate tune-up work on vehicles without electronic ignition. The choice of a timing light should be made carefully. A light which works on the DC current supplied by the vehicle's battery is the best choice; it should have a xenon tube for brightness. On any vehicle with an electronic ignition system, a timing light with an inductive pickup that clamps around the No. 1 spark plug cable is preferred.

In addition to these basic tools, there are several other tools and gauges you may find useful. These include:

• Compression gauge. The screw-in type is slower to use, but eliminates the possibility of a faulty reading due to escaping pressure.
• Manifold vacuum gauge.
• 12V test light.
• A combination volt/ohmmeter
• Induction Ammeter. This is used for determining whether or not there is current in a wire. These are handy for use if a wire is broken somewhere in a wiring harness.

As a final note, you will probably find a torque wrench necessary for all but the most basic work. The beam type models are perfectly adequate, although the newer click types (breakaway) are easier to use. The click type torque wrenches tend to be more expensive. Also keep in mind that all types of torque wrenches should be periodically checked and/or recalibrated. You will have to decide for yourself which better fits your purpose.

Special Tools

Normally, the use of special factory tools is avoided for repair procedures, since these are not readily available for the do-it-yourself mechanic. When it is possible to perform the job with more commonly available tools, it will be pointed out, but occasionally, a special tool was designed to perform a specific function and should be used. Before substituting another tool, you should be convinced that neither your safety nor the performance of the vehicle will be compromised.

Special tools can usually be purchased from an automotive parts store or from your dealer. In some cases special tools may be available directly from the tool manufacturer.

SERVICING YOUR VEHICLE SAFELY

It is virtually impossible to anticipate all of the hazards involved with automotive maintenance and service, but care and common sense will prevent most accidents.

The rules of safety for mechanics range from "don't smoke around gasoline," to "use the proper tool(s) for the job." The trick to avoiding injuries is to develop safe work habits and to take every possible precaution.

Do's

- Do keep a fire extinguisher and first aid kit handy.
- Do wear safety glasses or goggles when cutting, drilling, grinding or prying, even if you have 20–20 vision. If you wear glasses for the sake of vision, wear safety goggles over your regular glasses.
- Do shield your eyes whenever you work around the battery. Batteries contain sulfuric acid. In case of contact with the eyes or

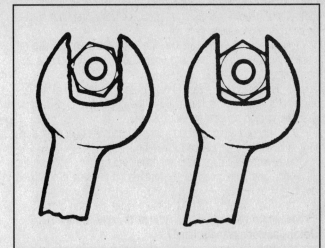

Using the correct size wrench will help prevent the possibility of rounding off a nut

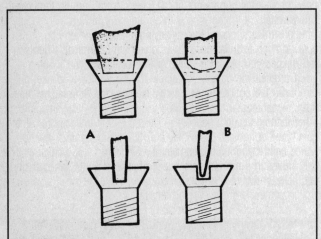

Screwdrivers should be kept in good condition to prevent injury or damage which could result if the blade slips from the screw

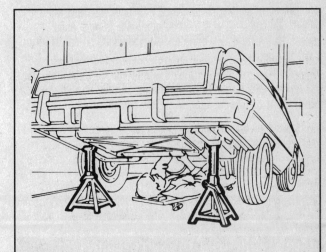

NEVER work under a vehicle unless it is supported using safety stands (jackstands)

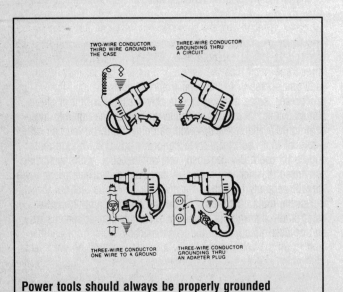

Power tools should always be properly grounded

skin, flush the area with water or a mixture of water and baking soda, then seek immediate medical attention.

- Do use safety stands (jackstands) for any undervehicle service. Jacks are for raising vehicles; jackstands are for making sure the vehicle stays raised until you want it to come down. Whenever the vehicle is raised, block the wheels remaining on the ground and set the parking brake.
- Do use adequate ventilation when working with any chemicals or hazardous materials. Like carbon monoxide, the asbestos dust resulting from some brake lining wear can be hazardous in sufficient quantities.
- Do disconnect the negative battery cable when working on the electrical system. The secondary ignition system contains EXTREMELY HIGH VOLTAGE. In some cases it can even exceed 50,000 volts.
- Do follow manufacturer's directions whenever working with potentially hazardous materials. Most chemicals and fluids are poisonous if taken internally.

• Do properly maintain your tools. Loose hammerheads, mushroomed punches and chisels, frayed or poorly grounded electrical cords, excessively worn screwdrivers, spread wrenches (open end), cracked sockets, slipping ratchets, or faulty droplight sockets can cause accidents.

• Likewise, keep your tools clean; a greasy wrench can slip off a bolt head, ruining the bolt and often harming your knuckles in the process.

• Do use the proper size and type of tool for the job at hand. Do select a wrench or socket that fits the nut or bolt. The wrench or socket should sit straight, not cocked.

• Do, when possible, pull on a wrench handle rather than push on it, and adjust your stance to prevent a fall.

• Do be sure that adjustable wrenches are tightly closed on the nut or bolt and pulled so that the force is on the side of the fixed jaw.

• Do strike squarely with a hammer; avoid glancing blows.

• Do set the parking brake and block the drive wheels if the work requires a running engine.

Don'ts

• Don't run the engine in a garage or anywhere else without proper ventilation—EVER! Carbon monoxide is poisonous; it takes a long time to leave the human body and you can build up a deadly supply of it in your system by simply breathing in a little every day. You may not realize you are slowly poisoning yourself. Always use power vents, windows, fans and/or open the garage door.

• Don't work around moving parts while wearing loose clothing. Short sleeves are much safer than long, loose sleeves. Hard-toed shoes with neoprene soles protect your toes and give a better grip on slippery surfaces. Jewelry such as watches, fancy belt buckles, beads or body adornment of any kind is not safe working around a vehicle. Long hair should be tied back under a hat or cap.

• Don't use pockets for toolboxes. A fall or bump can drive a screwdriver deep into your body. Even a rag hanging from your back pocket can wrap around a spinning shaft or fan.

• Don't smoke when working around gasoline, cleaning solvent or other flammable material.

• Don't smoke when working around the battery. When the battery is being charged, it gives off explosive hydrogen gas.

• Don't use gasoline to wash your hands; there are excellent soaps available. Gasoline contains dangerous additives which can enter the body through a cut or through your pores. Gasoline also removes all the natural oils from the skin so that bone dry hands will suck up oil and grease.

• Don't service the air conditioning system unless you are equipped with the necessary tools and training. When liquid or compressed gas refrigerant is released to atmospheric pressure it will absorb heat from whatever it contacts. This will chill or freeze anything it touches. Although refrigerant is normally non-toxic, R-12 becomes a deadly poisonous gas in the presence of an open flame. One good whiff of the vapors from burning refrigerant can be fatal.

• Don't use screwdrivers for anything other than driving screws! A screwdriver used as an prying tool can snap when you least expect it, causing injuries. At the very least, you'll ruin a good screwdriver.

• Don't use a bumper or emergency jack (that little ratchet, scissors, or pantograph jack supplied with the vehicle) for anything other than changing a flat! These jacks are only intended for emergency use out on the road; they are NOT designed as a maintenance tool. If you are serious about maintaining your vehicle yourself, invest in a hydraulic floor jack of at least a 1½ ton capacity, and at least two sturdy jackstands.

FASTENERS, MEASUREMENTS AND CONVERSIONS

Bolts, Nuts and Other Threaded Retainers

Although there are a great variety of fasteners found in the modern car or truck, the most commonly used retainer is the threaded fastener (nuts, bolts, screws, studs, etc). Most threaded retainers may be reused, provided that they are not damaged in use or during the repair. Some retainers (such as stretch bolts or torque prevailing nuts) are designed to deform when tightened or in use and should not be reinstalled.

Whenever possible, we will note any special retainers which should be replaced during a procedure. But you should always inspect the condition of a retainer when it is removed and replace any that show signs of damage. Check all threads for rust or corrosion which can increase the torque necessary to achieve the desired clamp load for which that fastener was originally selected. Additionally, be sure that the driver surface of the fastener has not been compromised by rounding or other damage. In some cases a driver surface may become only partially rounded, allowing the driver to catch in only one direction. In many of these occurrences, a fastener may be installed and tightened, but the driver would not be able to grip and loosen the fastener again. (This could lead to frustration down the line should that component ever need to be disassembled again).

If you must replace a fastener, whether due to design or damage, you must ALWAYS be sure to use the proper replacement. In all cases, a retainer of the same design, material and strength should be used. Markings on the heads of most bolts will help determine the proper strength of the fastener. The same material, thread and pitch must be selected to assure proper installation and safe operation of the vehicle afterwards.

Thread gauges are available to help measure a bolt or stud's thread. Most automotive and hardware stores keep gauges available to help you select the proper size. In a pinch, you can use another nut or bolt for a thread gauge. If the bolt you are replacing is not too badly damaged, you can select a match by finding another bolt which will thread in its place. If you find a nut which threads properly onto the damaged bolt, then use that nut to help select the replacement bolt. If however, the bolt you are replacing is so badly damaged (broken or drilled out) that its threads cannot be used as a gauge, you might start by looking for another bolt (from the same assembly or a similar location on your vehicle) which will thread into the damaged bolt's mounting. If so, the other bolt can be used to select a nut; the nut can then be used to select the replacement bolt.

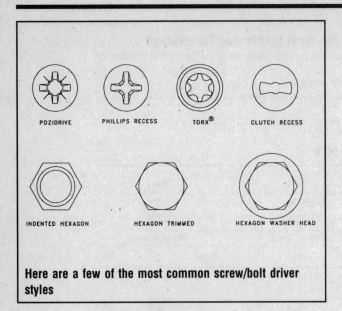

Here are a few of the most common screw/bolt driver styles

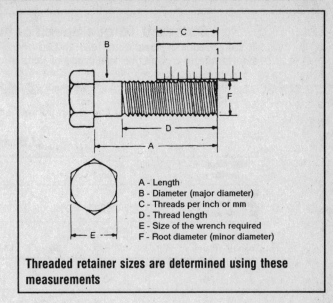

A - Length
B - Diameter (major diameter)
C - Threads per inch or mm
D - Thread length
E - Size of the wrench required
F - Root diameter (minor diameter)

Threaded retainer sizes are determined using these measurements

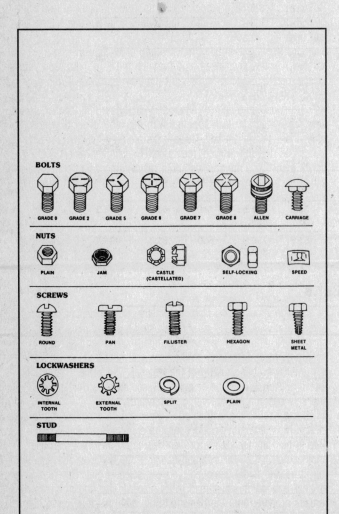

There are many different types of threaded retainers found on vehicles

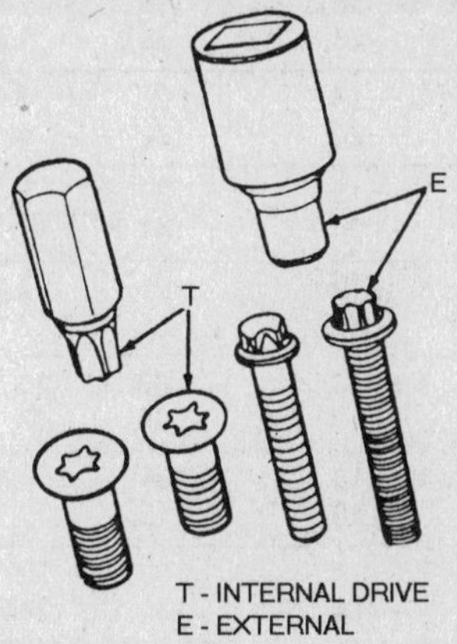

Special fasteners such as these Torx® head bolts are used by manufacturers to discourage people from working on vehicles without the proper tools

In all cases, be absolutely sure you have selected the proper replacement. Don't be shy, you can always ask the store clerk for help.

� WARNING

Be aware that when you find a bolt with damaged threads, you may also find the nut or drilled hole it was threaded into has also been damaged. If this is the case, you may have to drill and tap the hole, replace the nut or otherwise repair the threads. NEVER try to force a replacement bolt to fit into the damaged threads.

Torque

Torque is defined as the measurement of resistance to turning or rotating. It tends to twist a body about an axis of rotation. A common example of this would be tightening a threaded retainer such as a nut, bolt or screw. Measuring torque is one of the most

Standard Torque Specifications and Fastener Markings

In the absence of specific torques, the following chart can be used as a guide to the maximum safe torque of a particular size/grade of fastener.

- There is no torque difference for fine or coarse threads.
- Torque values are based on clean, dry threads. Reduce the value by 10% if threads are oiled prior to assembly.
- The torque required for aluminum components or fasteners is considerably less.

U.S. Bolts

SAE Grade Number	1 or 2			5			6 or 7		
Number of lines always 2 less than the grade number.									
Bolt Size (inches)—(Thread)	**Maximum Torque**			**Maximum Torque**			**Maximum Torque**		
	Ft./Lbs.	Kgm	Nm	Ft./Lbs.	Kgm	Nm	Ft./Lbs.	Kgm	Nm
¼—20	5	0.7	6.8	8	1.1	10.8	10	1.4	13.5
—28	6	0.8	8.1	10	1.4	13.6			
⁵/₁₆—18	11	1.5	14.9	17	2.3	23.0	19	2.6	25.8
—24	13	1.8	17.6	19	2.6	25.7			
³/₈—16	18	2.5	24.4	31	4.3	42.0	34	4.7	46.0
—24	20	2.75	27.1	35	4.8	47.5			
⁷/₁₆—14	28	3.8	37.0	49	6.8	66.4	55	7.6	74.5
—20	30	4.2	40.7	55	7.6	74.5			
½—13	39	5.4	52.8	75	10.4	101.7	85	11.75	115.2
—20	41	5.7	55.6	85	11.7	115.2			
⁹/₁₆—12	51	7.0	69.2	110	15.2	149.1	120	16.6	162.7
—18	55	7.6	74.5	120	16.6	162.7			
⁵/₈—11	83	11.5	112.5	150	20.7	203.3	167	23.0	226.5
—18	95	13.1	128.8	170	23.5	230.5			
¾—10	105	14.5	142.3	270	37.3	366.0	280	38.7	379.6
—16	115	15.9	155.9	295	40.8	400.0			
⅞—9	160	22.1	216.9	395	54.6	535.5	440	60.9	596.5
—14	175	24.2	237.2	435	60.1	589.7			
1—8	236	32.5	318.6	590	81.6	799.9	660	91.3	894.8
—14	250	34.6	338.9	660	91.3	849.8			

Metric Bolts

Relative Strength Marking	4.6, 4.8			8.8		
Bolt Markings						
Bolt Size Thread Size x Pitch (mm)	**Maximum Torque**			**Maximum Torque**		
	Ft./Lbs.	Kgm	Nm	Ft./Lbs.	Kgm	Nm
6 x 1.0	2–3	.2–.4	3–4	3–6	.4–.8	5–8
8 x 1.25	6–8	.8–1	8–12	9–14	1.2–1.9	13–19
10 x 1.25	12–17	1.5–2.3	16–23	20–29	2.7–4.0	27–39
12 x 1.25	21–32	2.9–4.4	29–43	35–53	4.8–7.3	47–72
14 x 1.5	35–52	4.8–7.1	48–70	57–85	7.8–11.7	77–110
16 x 1.5	51–77	7.0–10.6	67–100	90–120	12.4–16.5	130–160
18 x 1.5	74–110	10.2–15.1	100–150	130–170	17.9–23.4	180–230
20 x 1.5	110–140	15.1–19.3	150–190	190–240	26.2–46.9	160–320
22 x 1.5	150–190	22.0–26.2	200–260	250–320	34.5–44.1	340–430
24 x 1.5	190–240	26.2–46.9	260–320	310–410	42.7–56.5	420–550

Standard and metric bolt torque specifications based on bolt strengths—WARNING: use only as a guide

common ways to help assure that a threaded retainer has been properly fastened.

When tightening a threaded fastener, torque is applied in three distinct areas, the head, the bearing surface and the clamp load. About 50 percent of the measured torque is used in overcoming bearing friction. This is the friction between the bearing surface of the bolt head, screw head or nut face and the base material or washer (the surface on which the fastener is rotating). Approximately 40 percent of the applied torque is used in overcoming thread friction. This leaves only about 10 percent of the applied torque to develop a useful clamp load (the force which holds a joint together). This means that friction can account for as much as 90 percent of the applied torque on a fastener.

TORQUE WRENCHES

In most applications, a torque wrench can be used to assure proper installation of a fastener. Torque wrenches come in various designs and most automotive supply stores will carry a variety to suit your needs. A torque wrench should be used any time we supply a specific torque value for a fastener. A torque wrench can also be used if you are following the general guidelines in the accompanying charts. Keep in mind that because there is no worldwide standardization of fasteners, the charts are a general guideline and should be used with caution. Again, the general rule of "if you are using the right tool for the job, you should not have to strain to tighten a fastener" applies here.

Beam Type

The beam type torque wrench is one of the most popular types. It consists of a pointer attached to the head that runs the length of the flexible beam (shaft) to a scale located near the handle. As the wrench is pulled, the beam bends and the pointer indicates the torque using the scale.

Click (Breakaway) Type

Another popular design of torque wrench is the click type. To use the click type wrench you pre-adjust it to a torque setting. Once the torque is reached, the wrench has a reflex signalling fea-

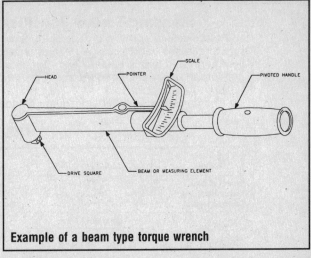

Example of a beam type torque wrench

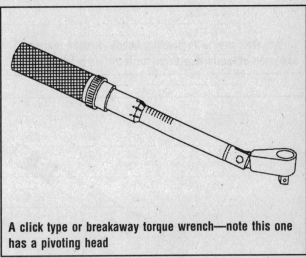

A click type or breakaway torque wrench—note this one has a pivoting head

ture that causes a momentary breakaway of the torque wrench body, sending an impulse to the operator's hand.

Pivot Head Type

Some torque wrenches (usually of the click type) may be equipped with a pivot head which can allow it to be used in areas of limited access. BUT, it must be used properly. To hold a pivot head wrench, grasp the handle lightly, and as you pull on the handle, it should be floated on the pivot point. If the handle comes in contact with the yoke extension during the process of pulling, there is a very good chance the torque readings will be inaccurate because this could alter the wrench loading point. The design of the handle is usually such as to make it inconvenient to deliberately misuse the wrench.

➡ **It should be mentioned that the use of any U-joint, wobble or extension will have an effect on the torque readings, no matter what type of wrench you are using. For the most accurate readings, install the socket directly on the wrench driver. If necessary, straight extensions (which hold a socket directly under the wrench driver) will have the least effect on the torque reading. Avoid any extension that alters the length of the wrench from the handle to the head/driving point (such as a crow's foot). U-joint or Wobble extensions can greatly affect the readings; avoid their use at all times.**

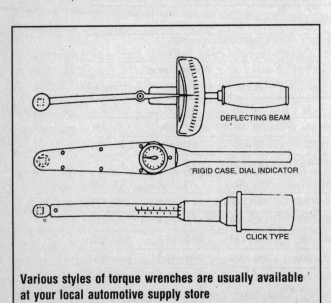

Various styles of torque wrenches are usually available at your local automotive supply store

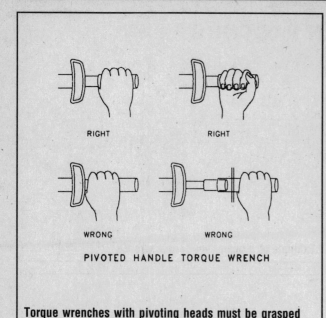

RIGHT   RIGHT

WRONG   WRONG

PIVOTED HANDLE TORQUE WRENCH

Torque wrenches with pivoting heads must be grasped and used properly to prevent an incorrect reading

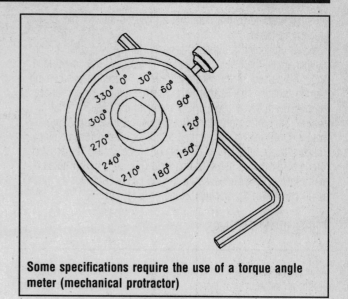

Some specifications require the use of a torque angle meter (mechanical protractor)

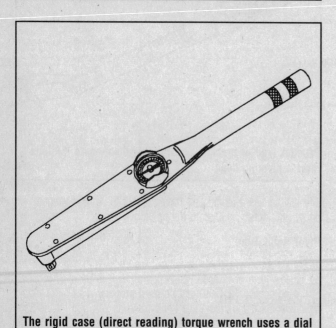

The rigid case (direct reading) torque wrench uses a dial indicator to show torque

Rigid Case (Direct Reading)

A rigid case or direct reading torque wrench is equipped with a dial indicator to show torque values. One advantage of these wrenches is that they can be held at any position on the wrench without affecting accuracy. These wrenches are often preferred because they tend to be compact, easy to read and have a great degree of accuracy.

TORQUE ANGLE METERS

Because the frictional characteristics of each fastener or threaded hole will vary, clamp loads which are based strictly on

torque will vary as well. In most applications, this variance is not significant enough to cause worry. But, in certain applications, a manufacturer's engineers may determine that more precise clamp loads are necessary (such is the case with many aluminum cylinder heads). In these cases, a torque angle method of installation would be specified. When installing fasteners which are torque angle tightened, a predetermined seating torque and standard torque wrench are usually used first to remove any compliance from the joint. The fastener is then tightened the specified additional portion of a turn measured in degrees. A torque angle gauge (mechanical protractor) is used for these applications.

Standard and Metric Measurements

Throughout this manual, specifications are given to help you determine the condition of various components on your vehicle, or to assist you in their installation. Some of the most common measurements include length (in. or cm/mm), torque (ft. lbs., inch lbs. or Nm) and pressure (psi, in. Hg, kPa or mm Hg). In most cases, we strive to provide the proper measurement as determined by the manufacturer's engineers.

Though, in some cases, that value may not be conveniently measured with what is available in your toolbox. Luckily, many of the measuring devices which are available today will have two scales so the Standard or Metric measurements may easily be taken. If any of the various measuring tools which are available to you do not contain the same scale as listed in the specifications, use the accompanying conversion factors to determine the proper value.

The conversion factor chart is used by taking the given specification and multiplying it by the necessary conversion factor. For instance, looking at the first line, if you have a measurement in inches such as "free-play should be 2 in." but your ruler reads only in millimeters, multiply 2 in. by the conversion factor of 25.4 to get the metric equivalent of 50.8mm. Likewise, if the specification was given only in a Metric measurement, for example in Newton Meters (Nm), then look at the center column first. If the measurement is 100 Nm, multiply it by the conversion factor of 0.738 to get 73.8 ft. lbs.

CONVERSION FACTORS

LENGTH–DISTANCE

Inches (in.)	x 25.4	= Millimeters (mm)	x .0394	= Inches
Feet (ft.)	x .305	= Meters (m)	x 3.281	= Feet
Miles	x 1.609	= Kilometers (km)	x .0621	= Miles

VOLUME

Cubic Inches (in3)	x 16.387	= Cubic Centimeters	x .061	= in3
IMP Pints (IMP pt.)	x .568	= Liters (L)	x 1.76	= IMP pt.
IMP Quarts (IMP qt.)	x 1.137	= Liters (L)	x .88	= IMP qt.
IMP Gallons (IMP gal.)	x 4.546	= Liters (L)	x .22	= IMP gal.
IMP Quarts (IMP qt.)	x 1.201	= US Quarts (US qt.)	x .833	= IMP qt.
IMP Gallons (IMP gal.)	x 1.201	= US Gallons (US gal.)	x .833	= IMP gal.
Fl. Ounces	x 29.573	= Milliliters	x .034	= Ounces
US Pints (US pt.)	x .473	= Liters (L)	x 2.113	= Pints
US Quarts (US qt.)	x .946	= Liters (L)	x 1.057	= Quarts
US Gallons (US gal.)	x 3.785	= Liters (L)	x .264	= Gallons

MASS–WEIGHT

Ounces (oz.)	x 28.35	= Grams (g)	x .035	= Ounces
Pounds (lb.)	x .454	= Kilograms (kg)	x 2.205	= Pounds

PRESSURE

Pounds Per Sq. In. (psi)	x 6.895	= Kilopascals (kPa)	x .145	= psi
Inches of Mercury (Hg)	x .4912	= psi	x 2.036	= Hg
Inches of Mercury (Hg)	x 3.377	= Kilopascals (kPa)	x .2961	= Hg
Inches of Water (H_2O)	x .07355	= Inches of Mercury	x 13.783	= H_2O
Inches of Water (H_2O)	x .03613	= psi	x 27.684	= H_2O
Inches of Water (H_2O)	x .248	= Kilopascals (kPa)	x 4.026	= H_2O

TORQUE

Pounds–Force Inches (in–lb)	x .113	= Newton Meters (N·m)	x 8.85	= in–lb
Pounds–Force Feet (ft–lb)	x 1.356	= Newton Meters (N·m)	x .738	= ft–lb

VELOCITY

Miles Per Hour (MPH)	x 1.609	= Kilometers Per Hour (KPH)	x .621	= MPH

POWER

Horsepower (Hp)	x .745	= Kilowatts	x 1.34	= Horsepower

FUEL CONSUMPTION*

Miles Per Gallon IMP (MPG)	x .354	= Kilometers Per Liter (Km/L)
Kilometers Per Liter (Km/L)	x 2.352	= IMP MPG
Miles Per Gallon US (MPG)	x .425	= Kilometers Per Liter (Km/L)
Kilometers Per Liter (Km/L)	x 2.352	= US MPG

*It is common to covert from miles per gallon (mpg) to liters/100 kilometers (1/100 km), where mpg (IMP) x 1/100 km = 282 and mpg (US) x 1/100 km = 235.

TEMPERATURE

Degree Fahrenheit (°F)	= (°C x 1.8) + 32
Degree Celsius (°C)	= (°F – 32) x .56

Standard and metric conversion factors chart

SERIAL NUMBER IDENTIFICATION

Vehicle

▶ **See Figures 1, 2 and 3**

The vehicle data plate containing the Vehicle Identification Number (VIN), on 1967–69 models is located on the top inside surface of the left wheel well opening. On 1970–80 models, the plate is located on the rear face of the driver's side door. On 1981–88 models, it is located on the upper left corner of the instrument panel, near the windshield.

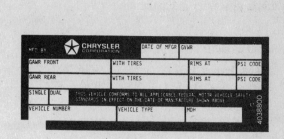

Fig. 3 Safety certification label from 1979–88 vehicle

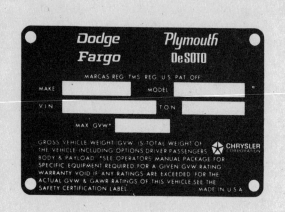

Fig. 1 Example of a 1974–88 vehicle identification plate

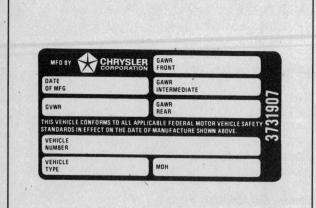

Fig. 2 Safety certification label from 1974–78 vehicle

1967–69 VEHICLES

A typical serial number for these years might be 2082-158000. The first 2 digits indicate the model code.
The third digit indicates the number of cylinders; 6-6 cylinders and 8-8 cylinders.
The fourth digit indicates the assembly plant, as follows:
- 1 or 2 Warren Truck Assembly
- 6 Windsor Truck Assembly
- 7 Missouri Truck Assembly
The fifth to tenth digits are the sequential serial number.

1970–73 VEHICLES

The vehicle identification number consist of a combination of 13 digits. The first seven characters identify the model, body type, GVW, engine model year and assembly plant. The last 6 digits are the sequential serial number, always starting from 000001. A typical serial number might be B24AE3U000001.
The first letter indicates the model
- B = van
The second character indicates the series
- 1 = 100 (½ ton) series
- 2 = 200 (¾ ton) series
- 3 = 300 (1 ton) series.
The third number is the body code
- 1 = Tradesman van
- 2 = Sportsman wagon
- 3 = Custom Sportsman wagon

- 4 = Royal Sportsman wagon
- 5 = Tradesman Maxivan
- 6 = Sportsman Maxiwagon
- 7 = Custom Sportsman Maxiwagon
- 8 = Royal Sportsman Maxiwagon
- 9 = Kary Van

The fourth character indicates the GVW

- A = 6,000 lbs. or less
- B = 6,000–10,000 lbs.

The fifth character indicates the engine

- B = 225-1
- C = 225-2
- E = 318-1
- F = 360
- G = 318-3

The sixth digit gives the model year

- 0 = 1970 F series
- 1 = 1971 G series
- 2 = 1972 H series
- 3 = 1973 J series
- The seventh digit gives the assembly plant.
- J = Windsor
- N = Burt Road
- S or V = Warren
- U or X = Missouri
- The last six digits are the sequential serial number

1974–78 VEHICLES

Dodge and Plymouth VIN's are interpreted in a similar manner. An example follows:

Element 1 - Model Designation

- B1 = B100 Dodge
- B2 = B200 Dodge
- B3 = B300 Dodge
- BA = PB100 Voyager
- BB = PB200 Voyager
- BC = PB300 Voyager

Element 2 - Body Type

- 1 = Tradesman van
- 2 = Sportsman wagon
- 3 = Mid-Line wagon
- 4 = Hi-line wagon
- 5 = Tradesman Maxivan
- 6 = Sportsman Maxiwagon
- 7 = Mid-line Maxiwagon
- 8 = Hi-line Maxiwagon
- 0 = Kary Van

Element 3 - GVW Class

- A = 6,000 lbs. or less
- B = 6,001–10,000 lbs. (1974–77)
- C = 6,001–11,500 (1978)

Element 4 - Engine Type

- A = 440
- B = 225
- C = 225

- D = 440
- E = 318
- F = 360 2-bbl.
- G = 318
- H = 243 Diesel
- J = 400
- K = 360
- T = 360 4-bbl.
- X = Special 6
- Y = Special 8

Element 5 = Model Year

Indicates the last number of the model year. Example "4" indicates 1974.

Element 6 = Assembly Plant

- J = Windsor
- S = Warren Plant 1
- T = Warren Plant 2
- V = Warren Compact
- X = Missouri Assembly

Element 7 = Sequential Serial Number

Every year this number starts at 000,001.

1979–80 VEHICLES

Element 1 = Model Designation

- B1 = B100 Dodge
- B2 = B200 Dodge
- B3 = B300 Dodge
- BA = PB100 Voyager
- BB = PB200 Voyager
- BC = PB300 Voyager

Element 2 = Body Type

- 1 = Vans
- 2 = Wagons
- 5 = Extended body vans
- 6 = Extended body wagons

Element 3 = GVW Class

- A = 6,000 lbs. or less
- J = 6,001 = 8,500 lbs.
- K = 8,501 = 10,000 lbs.
- C = 10,001 = 14,000 lbs.

Element 4 = Engine Type

- B = 225
- E = 318
- F = 360
- H = 243 Diesel
- K = 360

Element 5 = Model Year

Indicates the last digit of the model year. Example: "9" indicates 1979.

Element 6 = Assembly Plant

- C = Jefferson
- J = Windsor
- K = Windsor
- T&S = Warren
- X = Missouri

Element 7 = Sequential Serial Number
Every year this number starts at 000,001.

1981–88 VEHICLES

The vehicle identification number consists of a combination of 17 elements (numbers and letters). Use the following example as a key:

1 B 4 F 5 1 3 E 1 B K 000001

Element or Position 1 - Country of Origin
- 1 = U.S.
- 2 = Canada
- 3 = Mexico

Element or Position 2 - Make
- B = Dodge
- P = Plymouth
- E = Fargo

Element or Position 3 - Type of Vehicle
- 4 = Multipurpose
- 5 = Bus
- 6 = Incomplete
- 7 = Truck

Element or Position 4 - GVWR (lbs.) and Hydraulic Brakes
- D = 1,000–3,000
- E = 3,001–4,000
- F = 4,001–5,000
- G = 5,001–6,000
- H = 6,001–7,000
- J = 7,001–8,000
- K = 8,001–9,000
- L = 9.001–10,000
- M = 10,001–14,000
- W = Bus or Incomplete Vehicle

Element or Position 5 - Truck Line
- B = Wagon/Van/Bus

Element or Position 6 - Series
- 0 = 100
- 1 = 150
- 2 = 250
- 3 = 350

Element or Position 7 - Body
- 1 = Wagon
- 3 = Van
- 7 = Step van
- 8 = Front Section

Element or Position 8 - Engines (CID/Liters)
- E = 225/3.7L 1-bbl.
- X = 238/3.9L EFI
- P = 318/5.2L 2-bbl.
- M = 318/5.2L 4-bbl.
- Y = 318/5.2L EFI
- S = 360/5.9L 2-bbl.
- T = 360/5.9L 4-bbl.
- U = 360/5.9L 4-bbl. Heavy duty, Single exhaust
- V = 360/5.9L 4-bbl. Heavy duty, Dual exhaust
- W = 360/5.9L 4-bbl.

Element or Position 9
Check digit

Element or Position 10 - Model Year
- B = 1981
- C = 1982
- D = 1083
- E = 1984
- F = 1985
- G = 1986
- H = 1987
- J = 1988

Element or Position 11 - Assembly Plant
- K = Pillette Road (Windsor)
- M = Lago Alberto
- S = Dodge City
- T = Sherwood
- X = Missouri

Element or Position 12 through 17
Sequence Number

Equipment Identification Plate

The Equipment Identification Plate is located on the inner surface of the hood or the front surface of the air conditioning or Heater housing. It contains the model, wheelbase, V.I.N., T.O.N. (Truck Order Number) and all production or special equipment on the vehicle when it was shipped from the factory.

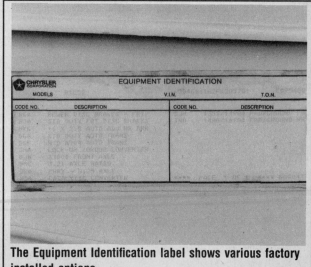

The Equipment Identification label shows various factory installed options

Engine

♦ See Figures 4, 5, 6 and 7

The engine that the factory installed can be identified by one of the digits of the Vehicle Identification Number, as explained earlier. The engine itself can be identified by the engine serial number. The cubic inch displacement is given by the second, third, and fourth, or the third, fourth, and fifth digits of the engine serial number, depending on the year and engine.

Inline 6-cylinder engines have their serial number stamped on the joint face of the block, just below the number six spark plug.

318 and 360 cu. in. V8s have the number on the front of the block, just below the left cylinder head.

The 238 cu. in. V6 has the serial number stamped on a pad on the right side of the block.

400 cu. in. V8s have the number on the right side of the block ahead of the base of the distributor.

440 cu. in. V8s are numbered on the left bank front tappet rail. 318 and 360 cu. in. (small block) V8s can quickly be identified as having the distributor at the rear of the engine, while the 400 and 440 cu. in. V8s have it at the front.

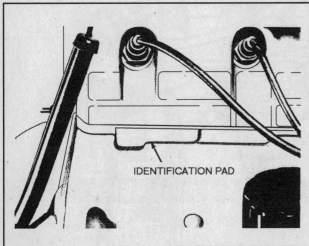

Fig. 4 Engine serial number location on inline 6-cylinder engines

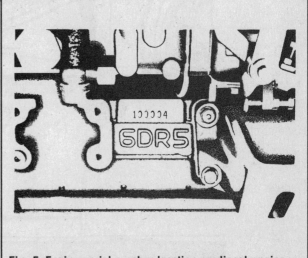

Fig. 5 Engine serial number location on diesel engine

Fig. 6 Engine serial number location on 1967–84 V8 engines

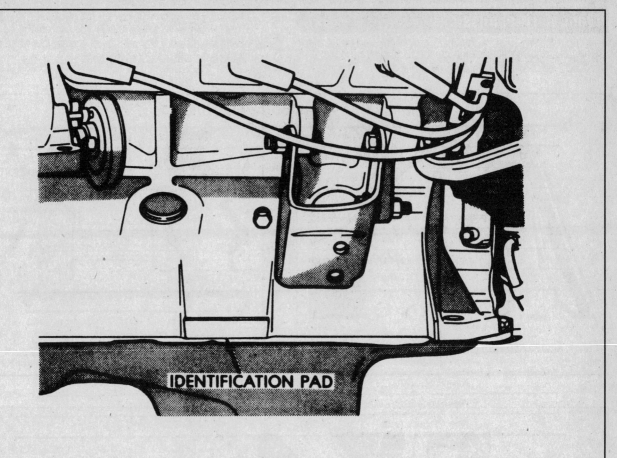

IDENTIFICATION PAD

Fig. 7 Engine serial number location on 1985–88 V6 and V8 engines

Engine Identification Chart

No. of Cylinders and Cu. In. Displacement	Actual Displacement			Fuel System	Type	Built by	Engine Code	Years
	Cu. In.	CC	Liters					
6-170	169.96	2,785.2	2.8	1-bbl	OHV	Chrysler		1967–69
6-198	198.29	3,249.4	3.2	1-bbl	OHV	Chrysler		1970–72
6-225	224.48	3,677.8	3.7	1-bbl	OHV	Chrysler		1967–87
				2-bbl	OHV	Chrysler		1978–79
								1982–83
6-238	238.46	3,907.7	3.9	EFI	OHV	Chrysler		1988
6-243	243.31	3,987.1	4.0	Diesel	OHV	Mitsubishi		1978–79
8-318	317.95	5,210.3	5.2	2-bbl	OHV	Chrysler		1967–87
				4-bbl	OHV	Chrysler		1981–83
				EFI	OHV	Chrysler		1988
8-360	359.90	5,897.7	5.9	2-bbl	OHV	Chrysler		1972–87
				4-bbl	OHV	Chrysler		1972–88
8-400	400.01	6,555.0	6.6	2-bbl	OHV	Chrysler		1974–79
8-440	439.72	7,205.7	7.2	4-bbl	OHV	Chrysler		1974–79

Manual Transmissions

The transmission identification number is located on a tag secured by 2 bolts to the power take-off cover.

Manual Transmission Application Chart

Transmission Types	Years
New Process A-230 3-sp	1970–79
New Process A-250 3-sp	1970–74
New Process A-390 3-sp	1976–79
New Process A-745 4-sp	1967–69
New Process A-903 3-sp	1967–69
New Process NP-2500 5-sp	1988
A-833 "Overdrive-4" 4-sp	1976–88

Automatic Transmission Application Chart

Transmission	Years	Models
New Process A-727	1967–88	All models
New Process A-904T	1981–88	Models w/6-225 and 8-318
New Process A-999	1981–88	Models w/6-225 and 8-318

Axles

The drive axle code is found stamped on a flat surface on the axle tube, next to the differential housing, or, on a tag secured by one of the differential housing cover bolts.

Drive Axle Application Chart

Axle	Model	Years
Chrysler 8⅜ in. SF	100	1972–79
	150	1980–88
Chrysler 8¾ in. SF	100	1967–78
Chrysler 9¼ in. SF	100	1979
	150	1980–88
Chrysler 9¼ in. HD SF	250, 350	1984–88
Dana 60 9¾ in. FF	200	1967–80
	250	1981–88
Dana 60HD 9¾ in. FF	200	1972–79
	300	1980
	350	1981–88
Dana 70 10½ in. FF	300	1967–80
	350	1981–88

SF: semi-floating
FF: full-floating

ROUTINE MAINTENANCE

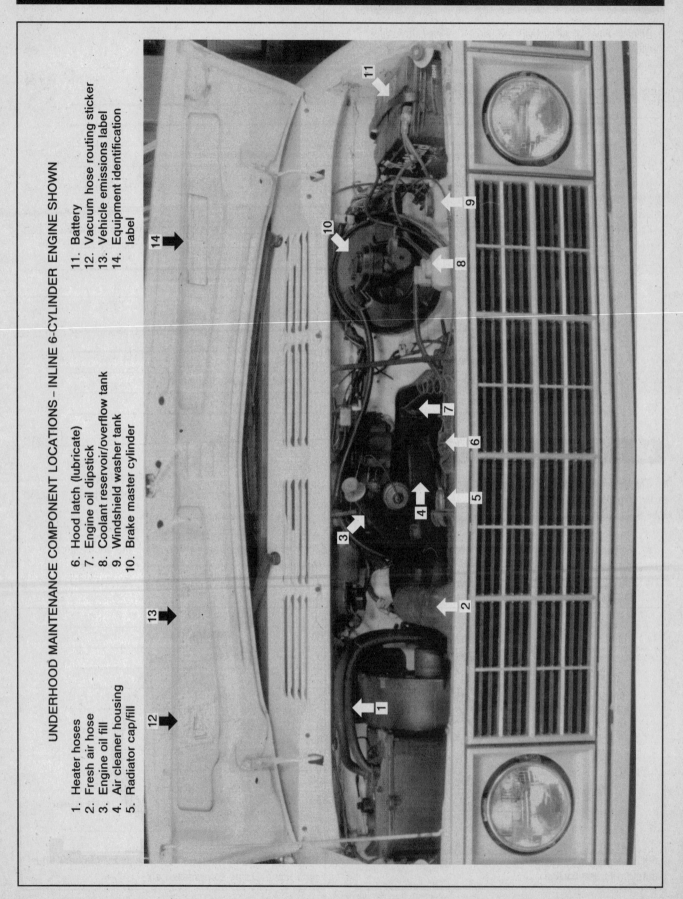

UNDERHOOD MAINTENANCE COMPONENT LOCATIONS – INLINE 6-CYLINDER ENGINE SHOWN

1. Heater hoses
2. Fresh air hose
3. Engine oil fill
4. Air cleaner housing
5. Radiator cap/fill
6. Hood latch (lubricate)
7. Engine oil dipstick
8. Coolant reservoir/overflow tank
9. Windshield washer tank
10. Brake master cylinder
11. Battery
12. Vacuum hose routing sticker
13. Vehicle emissions label
14. Equipment identification label

Air Cleaner

Different types of air cleaners are used. The standard type is the traditional dry paper element, but an oil bath air cleaner could be included on the vehicle as special equipment.

SERVICING

Dry Type

▶ **See Figures 8, 9, 10, 11 and 12**

Remove the top from the air cleaner and remove the element and wrapper (if equipped). If the filter is equipped with a wrapper, remove and wash it in kerosene or similar solvent. Shake or blot it dry. Saturate the foam wrapper (through 1973) in 10W-30 oil

Remove the wingnut securing the lid to the air cleaner housing and lift off the lid . . .

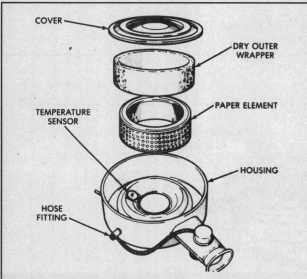

Fig. 8 Exploded view of the air cleaner components with the optional outer filter wrapper shown

. . . then remove the air filter from the air cleaner housing

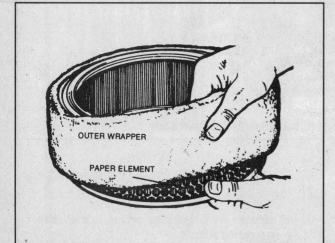

Fig. 9 Simply pull the outer wrapper off of the filter element to service it

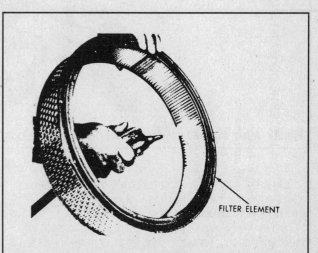

Fig. 10 You can sometimes clean a paper element filter with low pressure compressed air

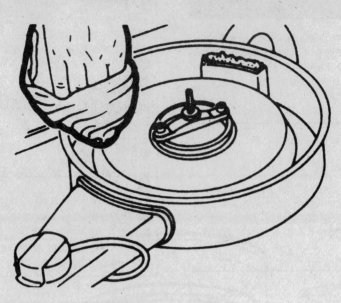

Fig. 11 Clean out the air filter housing before installing the new filter

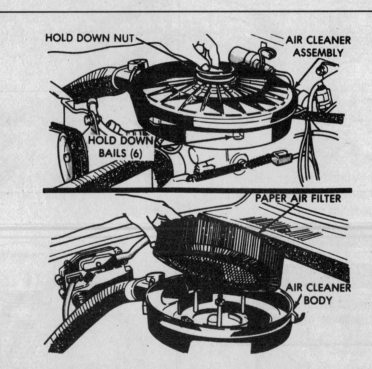

Fig. 12 A fuel injected engine's air cleaner assembly looks different, but is serviced the same way

and squeeze it tightly in an absorbent towel to remove excess oil. Leave the wrapper moist. 1974 and later models use an optional white polyester outer wrapper, which is to be left dry.

Clean the filter element by blowing it out with compressed air (from the inside out). Do not immerse the paper element in liquid. If the paper element is saturated for more than ½ of its circumference by oil from the wrapper, the element should be replaced and the rest of the crankcase ventilating system checked for proper functioning.

Wash the top and the air cleaner housing in solvent and wipe it dry.

➡**Do not immerse the temperature sensor, located in the housing, in cleaning solvent.**

Replace the paper element and wrapper (if equipped) and replace the air cleaner cover.

Oil Bath Type
▶ See Figure 13

Oil bath air cleaners are recommended for use in extremely dusty or off-road areas. When the vehicle is operated in extremely dusty areas, more frequent service is required. Under extreme conditions, the filter may have to be serviced each day.

To service the air cleaner, remove the cover and empty the old oil from the reservoir. Thoroughly clean all parts, paying particular attention to the sump in the reservoir. Refill the reservoir to the arrow with SAE 10W-30 engine oil and install the cover.

Diesel Engine

The diesel engine air filter should be cleaned every 6,000 miles and replace every 18,000 miles. Remove the air cleaner assembly and remove the paper element and the outer wrapper, if so equipped. Wash the wrapper in kerosene and shake it dry. Blow compressed air through the paper element to remove any dirt. If the filter element is saturated with oil for more than one half it circumference, replace the filter element and the wrapper.

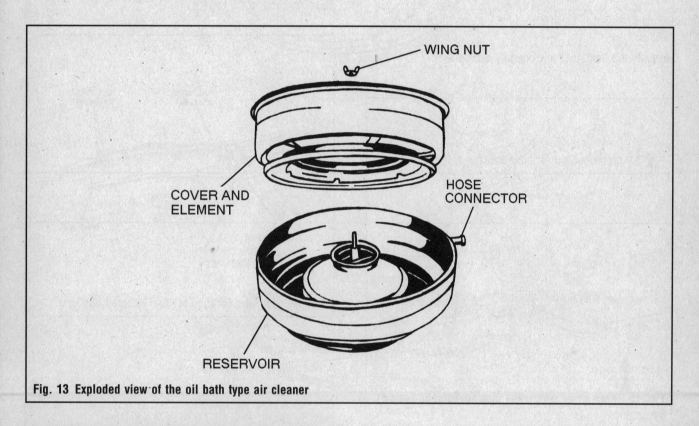

Fig. 13 Exploded view of the oil bath type air cleaner

Fuel Filter

❊❊ CAUTION

Never smoke when working around gasoline! Avoid all sources of sparks or ignition. Gasoline vapors are EXTREMELY volatile!

REMOVAL & INSTALLATION

Carbureted Gasoline Engine
CANISTER TYPE FILTER
▶ See Figure 14

Some 1967–78 models had a cartridge type filter enclosed in a canister located in the fuel line. To replace the filter, unscrew the body of the canister, discard the gasoline safely and install a new cartridge. Screw the canister body on securely.

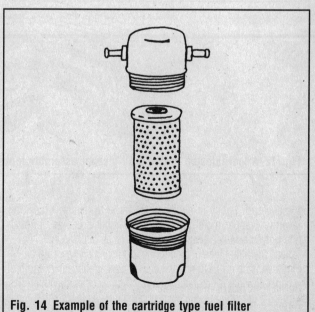

Fig. 14 Example of the cartridge type fuel filter

THROW-AWAY TYPE

▶ **See Figure 15**

On some 1967–78 and all carbureted models thereafter, the fuel filter is a disposable type sealed paper element located in the fuel line.

On 1967 models, the filter is located in the line just before it enters the carburetor. In all other years, it is located in the line near the fuel pump. Later models also have another filter located on the fuel tank in the end of the fuel suction tube. This filter does not normally require service, although it is replaceable.

To replace the filter, remove the two hose clamps and discard the old filter. Install a new filter in the line and attach with new clamps.

➡**Position a container to catch any spilled fuel.**

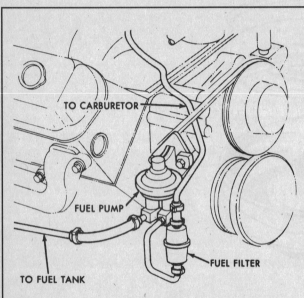

Fig. 15 Throw-away type inline filter location on most V8 engines

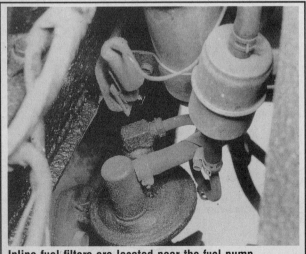

Inline fuel filters are located near the fuel pump. Remove the fuel hoses to change the filter

Fuel Injected Gasoline Engines

▶ **See Figure 16**

The fuel filter is located inline on the inside of the left frame rail just ahead of the crossmember. To change the filter:
1. Relieve the fuel system pressure as described in Section 5.
2. Remove the filter retaining screw and remove the filter from the frame rail.
3. Loosen the fuel hose clamps, wrap a shop towel around the hoses and disconnect the hoses from the filter.
4. Installation is the reverse of removal. Tighten the filter mounting screw to 75 inch lbs.

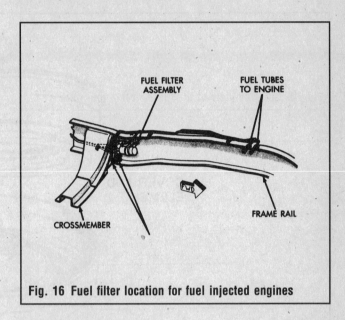

Fig. 16 Fuel filter location for fuel injected engines

Diesel Engine

▶ **See Figures 17 and 18**

A gauze filter, located at the inlet port of the fuel feed pump, is designed to catch large particles of dirt in the fuel line. This filter must be cleaned every 12,000 miles in kerosene.

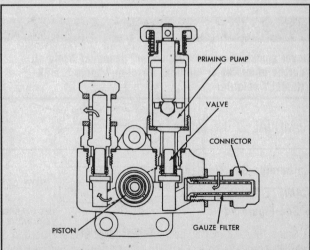

Fig. 17 Gauze fuel filter location on the diesel fuel feed pump

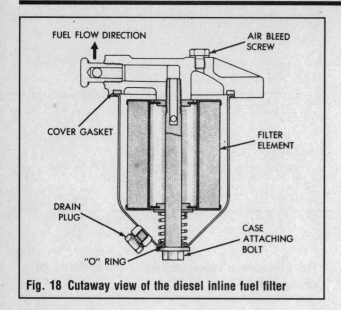

Fig. 18 Cutaway view of the diesel inline fuel filter

Another in-line fuel filter must be inspected every 12,000 miles. Loosen the drain plug at the bottom of the filter and drain the fuel. Loosen the case attaching bolt and detach the filter case from the cover. Replace the element if it appears dirty or clogged, or at least every 24,000 miles.

Positive Crankcase Ventilation System

◆ See Figures 19 and 20

The Positive Crankcase Ventilation (PCV) system is used in two forms, the standard and closed types. The standard type is used in all states except California for 1967 models, while the closed type is used exclusively in 1967 California models. Beginning in 1968, the closed type is used in all states.

Blow-by gases or crankcase vapors must be removed from the crankcase to prevent oil dilution and to prevent the formation of sludge. Traditionally, this was accomplished with a road draft tube. Air entered the rocker arm cover through an open oil filler cap and flowed down past the pushrods, mixing the blow-by

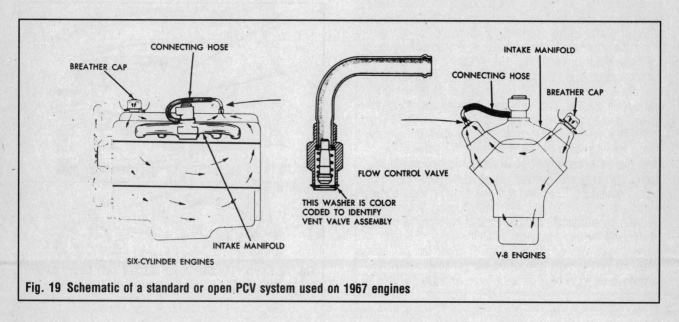

Fig. 19 Schematic of a standard or open PCV system used on 1967 engines

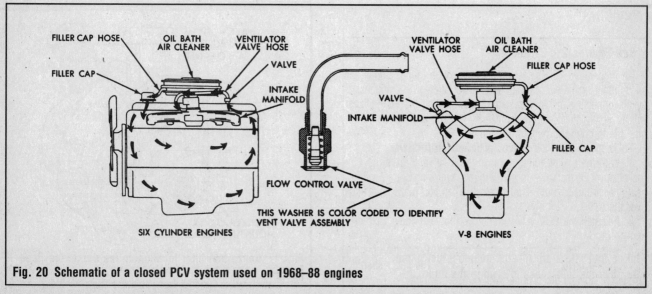

Fig. 20 Schematic of a closed PCV system used on 1968–88 engines

gases in the crankcase. It was finally routed into the road draft tube where a partial vacuum was created, drawing the mixture into the road draft tube and out into the atmosphere.

The open PCV system replaced the road draft tube and engine manifold vacuum was used instead of the action of a moving vehicle to create a low pressure area. Air flowed into an open oil filler cap, which is characteristic of an open PCV system, and mixed with crankcase fumes. This was then drawn into the intake manifold and burned in the combustion chamber. However, under heavy acceleration, manifold vacuum decreases and crankcase pressures build up. When this happened, a portion of the crankcase vapors were forced back out of the oil filler cap, creating a system which was only about 75% efficient.

The closed PCV system operates in a similar manner as the open system, except for the following:

• In place of a vented oil filler cap, an air intake line is installed between the carburetor air filter and a crankcase opening in the valve cover.

• A sealed oil filler cap and dipstick are used.

• A separate PCV air filter is used when the intake air hose is connected to the "dirty" side of the carburetor air cleaner. The filter is located where the intake air line connects to the valve cover.

Under normal engine operation, the closed PCV system operates the way an open system does except that air enters through the intake line from the air filter. Under heavy acceleration, any excess vapors back up through the air intake line and are forced to mix with incoming air into the carburetor and are burned in the combustion chamber. Back-up fumes cannot escape into the atmosphere, creating a closed system.

The PCV valve is used to control the rate at which crankcase vapors are returned to the intake manifold. The action of the valve plunger is controlled by intake manifold vacuum and the spring. During deceleration and idle, when manifold vacuum is high, it overcomes the tension of the valve spring and the plunger bottoms in the manifold end of the valve housing. Because of the valve construction, it reduces, but dies not stop, the passage of vapors to the intake manifold. When the engine is lightly accelerated or operated at constant speed, spring tension matches intake manifold vacuum pull and the plunger takes a mid-position in the valve body, allowing more vapors to flow into the manifold.

SERVICING

◆ **See Figures 21, 22 and 23**

An inoperative PCV system will cause rough idling, sludge and oil dilution. In the event erratic idle, never attempt to compensate by disconnecting the PCV system. Disconnecting the PCV system will adversely affect engine ventilation. It could also shorten engine life through the buildup of sludge.

To inspect the PCV valve, proceed as follows:

1. With the engine idling, remove the PCV valve from the rocker cover. If the valve is not plugged, a hissing sound will be heard. A strong vacuum should be felt when you place your finger over the valve.

2. Reinstall the PCV valve and allow about a minute for pressure to drop.

3. Remove the crankcase intake air cleaner. Cover the opening in the rocker cover with a piece of stiff paper. The paper should be sucked against the opening with noticeable force.

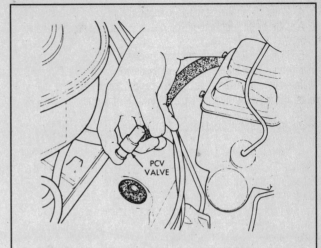

Fig. 21 Check for vacuum at the PCV valve with the tip of your finger

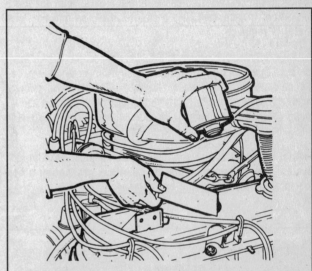

Fig. 22 Cover the valve cover opening with heavy paper to check for vacuum

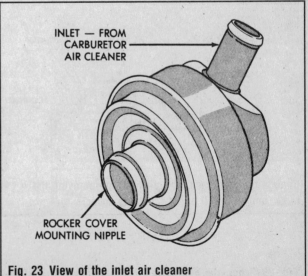

INLET — FROM CARBURETOR AIR CLEANER

ROCKER COVER MOUNTING NIPPLE

Fig. 23 View of the inlet air cleaner

4. With the engine stopped, remove the PCV valve and shake it. A rattle or clicking should be heard to indicate that the valve is free.

5. If the system meets the tests in Steps 1, 2, 3, and 4, no further service is required, unless replacement is specified in the Maintenance Intervals Chart. If the system does not meet the tests, the valve should be replaced with a new one.

➡**Do not attempt to clean a PCV valve.**

6. With a new PCV valve installed, if the paper is not sucked against the crankcase air intake opening (see Step 2), it will be necessary to clean the PCV valve hose and the passage in the lower part of the carburetor.

7. Clean the line with Combustion Chamber Conditioner or similar solvent. Do not leave the hoses in solvent for more than ½ hour. Allow the line to air dry.

8. Remove the carburetor and HAND turn a ¼″ drill through the passages to dislodge solid particles and blow clean.

➡**It is not necessary to disassemble the carburetor for this operation. If necessary, use a smaller drill, so that no metal is removed.**

9. Clean the crankcase air intake filter. Inspect the hose from the crankcase intake air cleaner and clean if it necessary. Remove the crankcase intake air cleaner and wash it thoroughly in kerosene or a similar solvent. Lubricate the filter by inverting it and filling with SAE 30 engine oil. Position the filter to allow excess oil to drain thoroughly through the vent nipple.

➡**After checking and/or servicing the Crankcase Ventilation System, any components that do not allow passage or air to the intake manifold should be replaced.**

Evaporative Canister

SERVICING

◗ **See Figures 24, 25 and 26**

The Vapor Saver Evaporation Control System was originally used in 1970 on those vehicles sold in California, and thereafter on most vehicles.

This system prevents evaporated gasoline vapors from escaping into the atmosphere.

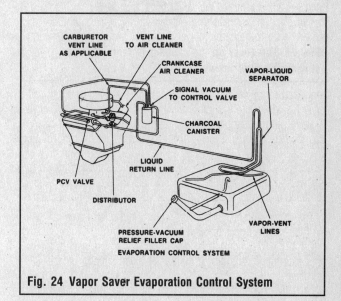

Fig. 24 Vapor Saver Evaporation Control System

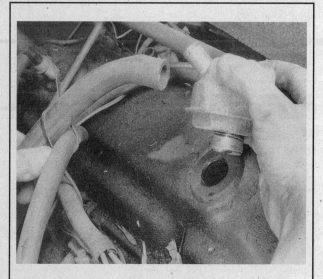

Change the crankcase inlet air filter by removing the hose, and pulling it out of the valve cover

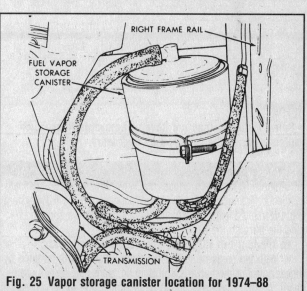

Fig. 25 Vapor storage canister location for 1974–88 vehicles—some vehicles may have two canisters

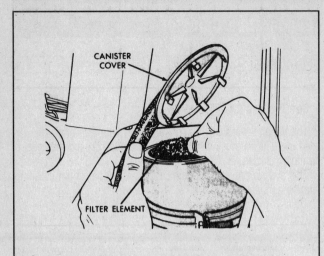

Fig. 26 The cover on the canister is removable to service the filter inside

The carburetor is either vented internally or through the charcoal canister. Vapors are routed to the canister which is filled with activated charcoal, providing temporary storage.

On fuel injected engines, a bi-level system is used in which vapors are drawn into the engine at idle and off-idle as well. The source of idle vacuum is a tee in the PCV system.

The vapor storage canister is located on the left frame rail behind the steering gear through 1973.

On 1973–87 models it is located under the van, next to the right side frame rail, behind the transmission support crossmember.

On 1988 models, the canisters for all engines are located in the wheelwell area of the engine compartment.

Some models are equipped with two storage tanks. These are identical and should be serviced together.

The only service associated with the system is a replaceable filter element inside the canister. If necessary for access, unfasten the retaining bracket, disconnect the hoses, and remove the canister. Open the cover and pull out the filter element. Install a new filter element and close the canister. If applicable, reconnect the hoses and install the canister.

➡**Some canisters may not have a removable filter. Such canisters should be replaced as necessary.**

Battery

GENERAL MAINTENANCE

All batteries, regardless of type, should be carefully secured by a battery hold-down device. If this is not done, the battery terminals or casing may crack from stress applied to the battery during vehicle operation. A battery which is not secured may allow acid to leak out, making it discharge faster; such leaking corrosive acid can also eat away components under the hood. A battery that is not sealed must be checked periodically for electrolyte level. You cannot add water to a sealed maintenance-free battery (though not all maintenance-free batteries are sealed), but a sealed battery must also be checked for proper electrolyte level as indicated by the color of the built-in hydrometer "eye."

Keep the top of the battery clean, as a film of dirt can help completely discharge a battery that is not used for long periods. A solution of baking soda and water may be used for cleaning, but be careful to flush this off with clear water. DO NOT let any of the solution into the filler holes. Baking soda neutralizes battery acid and will de-activate a battery cell.

✳✳ CAUTION

Always use caution when working on or near the battery. Never allow a tool to bridge the gap between the negative and positive battery terminals. Also, be careful not to allow a tool to provide a ground between the positive cable/terminal and any metal component on the vehicle. Either of these conditions will cause a short circuit leading to sparks and possible personal injury.

Batteries in vehicles which are not operated on a regular basis can fall victim to parasitic loads (small current drains which are constantly drawing current from the battery). Normal parasitic loads may drain a battery on a vehicle that is in storage and not used for 6–8 weeks. Vehicles that have additional accessories such as a cellular phone, an alarm system or other devices that increase parasitic load may discharge a battery sooner. If the vehicle is to be stored for 6–8 weeks in a secure area and the alarm system, if present, is not necessary, the negative battery cable should be disconnected at the onset of storage to protect the battery charge.

Remember that constantly discharging and recharging will shorten battery life. Take care not to allow a battery to be needlessly discharged.

BATTERY FLUID

✳✳ CAUTION

Battery electrolyte contains sulfuric acid. If you should splash any on your skin or in your eyes, flush the affected area with plenty of clear water. If it lands in your eyes, get medical help immediately.

The fluid (sulfuric acid solution) contained in the battery cells will tell you many things about the condition of the battery. Because the cell plates must be kept submerged below the fluid level in order to operate, maintaining the fluid level is extremely important. And, because the specific gravity of the acid is an indication of electrical charge, testing the fluid can be an aid in determining if the battery must be replaced. A battery in a vehicle with a properly operating charging system should require little maintenance, but careful, periodic inspection should reveal problems before they leave you stranded.

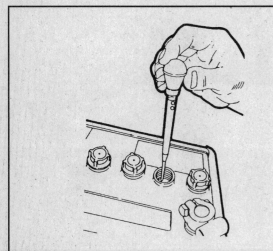

On non-maintenance free batteries, the level can be checked through the case on translucent batteries; the cell caps must be removed on other models

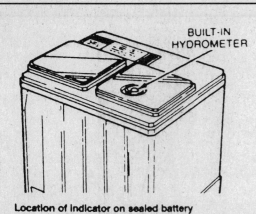

Check the specific gravity of the battery's electrolyte with a hydrometer

Fluid Level

Check the battery electrolyte level at least once a month, or more often in hot weather or during periods of extended vehicle operation. On non-sealed batteries, the level can be checked either through the case on translucent batteries or by removing the cell caps on opaque-cased types. The electrolyte level in each cell should be kept filled to the split ring inside each cell, or the line marked on the outside of the case.

If the level is low, add only distilled water through the opening until the level is correct. Each cell is separate from the others, so each must be checked and filled individually. Distilled water should be used, because the chemicals and minerals found in most drinking water are harmful to the battery and could significantly shorten its life.

If water is added in freezing weather, the vehicle should be driven several miles to allow the water to mix with the electrolyte. Otherwise, the battery could freeze.

Although some maintenance-free batteries have removable cell caps for access to the electrolyte, the electrolyte condition and level on all sealed maintenance-free batteries must be checked using the built-in hydrometer "eye." The exact type of eye varies between battery manufacturers, but most apply a sticker to the battery itself explaining the possible readings. When in doubt, refer to the battery manufacturer's instructions to interpret battery condition using the built-in hydrometer.

➡**Although the readings from built-in hydrometers found in sealed batteries may vary, a green eye usually indicates a properly charged battery with sufficient fluid level. A dark eye is normally an indicator of a battery with sufficient fluid, but one which may be low in charge. And a light or yellow eye is usually an indication that electrolyte supply has dropped below the necessary level for battery (and hydrometer) operation. In this last case, sealed batteries with an insufficient electrolyte level must usually be discarded.**

Specific Gravity

As stated earlier, the specific gravity of a battery's electrolyte level can be used as an indication of battery charge. At least once

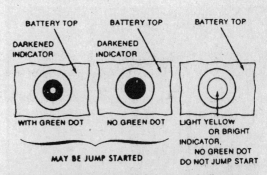

Check the appearance of the charge indicator on top of the battery before attempting a jump start; if it's not green or dark, do not jump start the car

A typical sealed (maintenance-free) battery with a built-in hydrometer—NOTE that the hydrometer eye may vary between battery manufacturers; always refer to the battery's label

a year, check the specific gravity of the battery. It should be between 1.20 and 1.26 on the gravity scale. Most auto supply stores carry a variety of inexpensive battery testing hydrometers. These can be used on any non-sealed battery to test the specific gravity in each cell.

The battery testing hydrometer has a squeeze bulb at one end and a nozzle at the other. Battery electrolyte is sucked into the hydrometer until the float is lifted from its seat. The specific gravity is then read by noting the position of the float. If gravity is low in one or more cells, the battery should be slowly charged and checked again to see if the gravity has come up. Generally, if after charging, the specific gravity between any two cells varies more than 50 points (0.50), the battery should be replaced as it can no longer produce sufficient voltage to guarantee proper operation.

On sealed batteries, the built-in hydrometer is the only way of checking specific gravity. Again, check with your battery's manufacturer for proper interpretation of its built-in hydrometer readings.

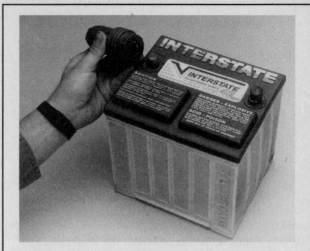

The underside of this special battery tool has a wire brush to clean post terminals

CABLES

Once a year (or as necessary), the battery terminals and the cable clamps should be cleaned. Loosen the clamps and remove the cables, negative cable first. On batteries with posts on top, the use of a puller specially made for this purpose is recommended. These are inexpensive and available in most auto parts stores. Side terminal battery cables are secured with a small bolt.

Clean the cable clamps and the battery terminal with a wire brush, until all corrosion, grease, etc., is removed and the metal is shiny. It is especially important to clean the inside of the clamp (an old knife is useful here) thoroughly, since a small deposit of foreign material or oxidation there will prevent a sound electrical connection and inhibit either starting or charging. Special tools are available for cleaning these parts, one type for conventional top post batteries and another type for side terminal batteries.

Before installing the cables, loosen the battery hold-down clamp or strap, remove the battery and check the battery tray.

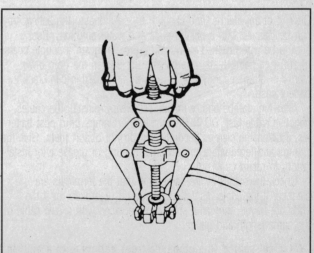

Place the tool over the terminals and twist to clean the post

Maintenance is performed with household items and with special tools like this post cleaner

A special tool is available to pull the clamp from the post

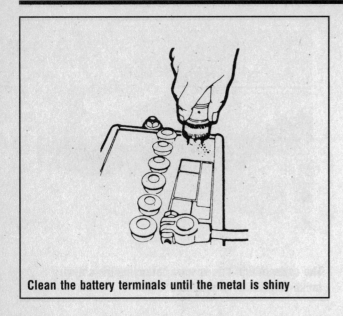

Clean the battery terminals until the metal is shiny

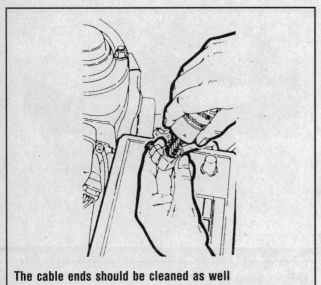

The cable ends should be cleaned as well

Clear it of any debris, and check it for soundness (the battery tray can be cleaned with a baking soda and water solution). Rust should be wire brushed away, and the metal given a couple coats of anti-rust paint. Install the battery and tighten the hold-down clamp or strap securely. Do not overtighten, as this can crack the battery case.

After the clamps and terminals are clean, reinstall the cables, negative cable last; DO NOT hammer the clamps onto post batteries. Tighten the clamps securely, but do not distort them. Give the clamps and terminals a thin external coating of grease after installation, to retard corrosion.

Check the cables at the same time that the terminals are cleaned. If the cable insulation is cracked or broken, or if the ends are frayed, the cable should be replaced with a new cable of the same length and gauge.

CHARGING

✳✳ CAUTION

The chemical reaction which takes place in all batteries generates explosive hydrogen gas. A spark can cause the battery to explode and splash acid. To avoid serious personal injury, be sure there is proper ventilation and take appropriate fire safety precautions when connecting, disconnecting, or charging a battery and when using jumper cables.

A battery should be charged at a slow rate to keep the plates inside from getting too hot. However, if some maintenance-free batteries are allowed to discharge until they are almost "dead," they may have to be charged at a high rate to bring them back to "life." Always follow the charger manufacturer's instructions on charging the battery.

REPLACEMENT

When it becomes necessary to replace the battery, select one with a rating equal to or greater than the battery originally installed. Deterioration and just plain aging of the battery cables, starter motor, and associated wires makes the battery's job harder in successive years. The slow increase in electrical resistance over time makes it prudent to install a new battery with a greater capacity than the old.

Belts

INSPECTION

▶ **See Figure 27**

Inspect the belts for signs of glazing or cracking. A glazed belt will be perfectly smooth from slippage, while a good belt will have a slight texture of fabric visible. Cracks will usually start at the inner edge of the belt and run outward. All worn or damaged drive belts should be replaced immediately. It is best to replace all drive belts at one time, as a preventive maintenance measure, during this service operation.

Once a year or at 12,000 mile intervals, the tension (and condition) of the alternator, power steering (if so equipped), air conditioning (if so equipped), and Thermactor air pump drive belts should be checked, and, if necessary, adjusted. Loose accessory drive belts can lead to poor engine cooling and diminish alternator, power steering pump, air conditioning compressor or Thermactor air pump output. A belt that is too tight places a severe strain on the water pump, alternator, power steering pump, compressor or air pump bearings.

Replace any belt that is so glazed, worn or stretched that it cannot be tightened sufficiently.

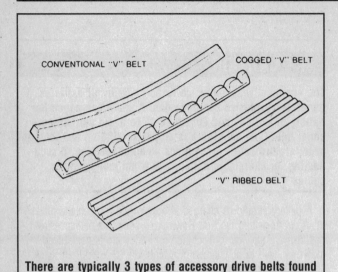

There are typically 3 types of accessory drive belts found on vehicles today

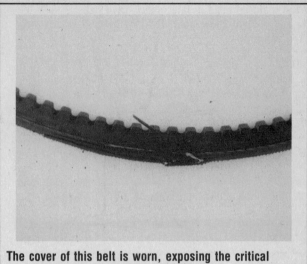

The cover of this belt is worn, exposing the critical reinforcing cords to excessive wear

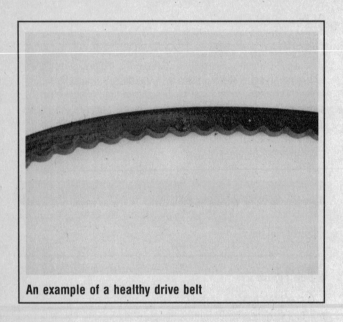

An example of a healthy drive belt

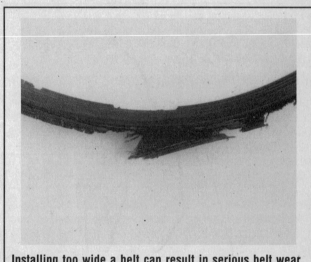

Installing too wide a belt can result in serious belt wear and/or breakage

Deep cracks in this belt will cause flex, building up heat that will eventually lead to belt failure

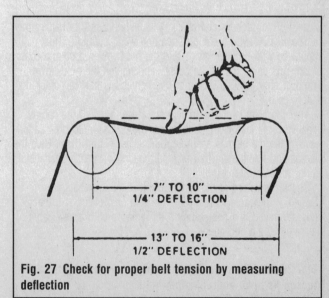

Fig. 27 Check for proper belt tension by measuring deflection

➡The material used in late model drive belts is such that the belts do not show wear. Replace belts at least every three years.

On vehicles with matched belts, replace both belts. New 1/2", 3/8" and 15/32" wide belts are to be adjusted to a tension of 140 lbs.; 1/4" wide belts are adjusted to 80 lbs., measured on a belt tension gauge. Any belt that has been operating for a minimum of 10 minutes is considered a used belt. In the first 10 minutes, the belt should stretch to its maximum extent. After 10 minutes, stop the engine and recheck the belt tension. Belt tension for a used belt should be maintained at 110 lbs. (all except 1/4" wide belts) or 60 lbs. (1/4" wide belts). If a belt tension gauge is not available, the following procedures may be used.

ADJUSTING

Except Serpentine (Single) Belt

◗ **See Figures 28 and 29**

On models equipped with an electric cooling fan, disconnect the negative battery cable or fan motor wiring harness connector before replacing or adjusting drive belts. The fan may come on, under certain circumstances, even though the ignition is off.

ALTERNATOR (FAN DRIVE) BELT

1. Position the ruler perpendicular to the drive belt at its longest straight run. Test the tightness of the belt by pressing it firmly with your thumb. The deflection should not exceed 1/4".
2. If the deflection exceeds 1/4", loosen the alternator mounting and adjusting arm bolts.
3. Place a 1" open-end or adjustable wrench on the adjusting ridge cast on the body, and pull on the wrench until the proper tension is achieved.
4. Holding the alternator in place to maintain tension, tighten the adjusting arm bolt. Recheck the belt tension. When the belt is properly tensioned, tighten the alternator mounting bolt.

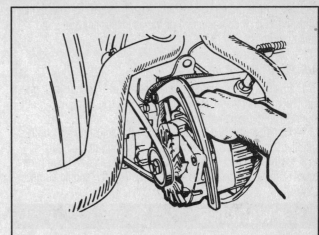

Fig. 29 Pull or push on the component until the proper belt tension is reached, then tighten the adjusting and pivot bolts

POWER STEERING DRIVE BELT—INLINE 6-CYLINDER ENGINE

1. Hold a ruler perpendicularly to the drive belt at its longest run, test the tightness of the belt by pressing it firmly with your thumb. The deflection should not exceed 1/4".
2. To adjust the belt tension, loosen the adjusting and mounting bolts on the front face of the steering pump cover plate (hub side).
3. Using a prybar or broom handle on the pump hub, move the power steering pump to ward or away from the engine until the proper tension is reached. Do not pry against the reservoir as it is relatively soft and easily deformed.
4. Holding the pump in place, tighten the adjusting arm bolt and then recheck the belt tension. When the belt is properly tensioned tighten the mounting bolts.

POWER STEERING DRIVE BELT—V6 AND V8 MODELS

1. Position a ruler perpendicular to the drive belt at its longest run. Test the tightness of the belt by pressing it firmly with your thumb. The deflection should be about 1/4".
2. To adjust the belt tension, loosen the three bolts in the three elongated adjusting slots at the power steering pump attaching bracket.
3. Turn the steering pump drive belt adjusting nut as required until the proper deflection is obtained. Turning the adjusting nut clockwise will increase tension and decrease deflection; counterclockwise will decrease tension and increase deflection.
4. Without disturbing the pump, tighten the three attaching bolts.

AIR CONDITIONING COMPRESSOR DRIVE BELT

1. Position a ruler perpendicular to the drive belt at its longest run. Test the tightness of the belt by pressing it firmly with your thumb. The deflection should not exceed 1/4".
2. If the engine is equipped with an idler pulley, loosen the idler pulley adjusting bolt, insert a prybar between the pulley and the engine (or in the idler pulley adjusting slot), and adjust the tension accordingly. If the engine is not equipped with an idler pulley, the alternator must be moved to accomplish this adjustment, as outlined under Alternator (Fan Drive) Belt.

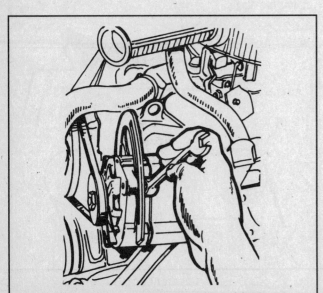

Fig. 28 To adjust the belt tension on any accessory, loosen its pivot and adjusting bolts

3. When the proper tension is reached, tighten the idler pulley adjusting bolt (if so equipped) or the alternator adjusting and mounting bolts.

AIR PUMP DRIVE BELT

1. Position a ruler perpendicular to the drive belt at its longest run. Test the tightness of the belt by pressing it firmly with your thumb. The deflection should be about 1/4".

2. To adjust the belt tension, loosen the adjusting arm bolt slightly. If necessary, also loosen the mounting belt slightly.

3. Using a prybar or broom handle, pry against the pump rear cover to move the pump toward or away from the engine as necessary.

✳✳ WARNING

Do not pry against the pump housing itself, as damage to the housing may result.

4. Holding the pump in place, tighten the adjusting arm bolt and recheck the tension. When the belt is properly tensioned, tighten the mounting bolt.

Serpentine (Single) Drive Belt Models
▶ **See Figure 30**

Most models feature a single, wide, ribbed V-belt that drives the water pump, alternator, and (on some models) the air conditioner compressor. To install a new belt, loosen the bracket lock-bolt, retract the belt tensioner with a prybar and slide the old belt off of the pulleys. Slip on a new belt, then release the tensioner and tighten the lockbolt. The spring powered tensioner eliminates the need for periodic adjustments.

✳✳ WARNING

Check to make sure that the V-ribbed belt is located properly in all drive pulleys before applying tensioner pressure.

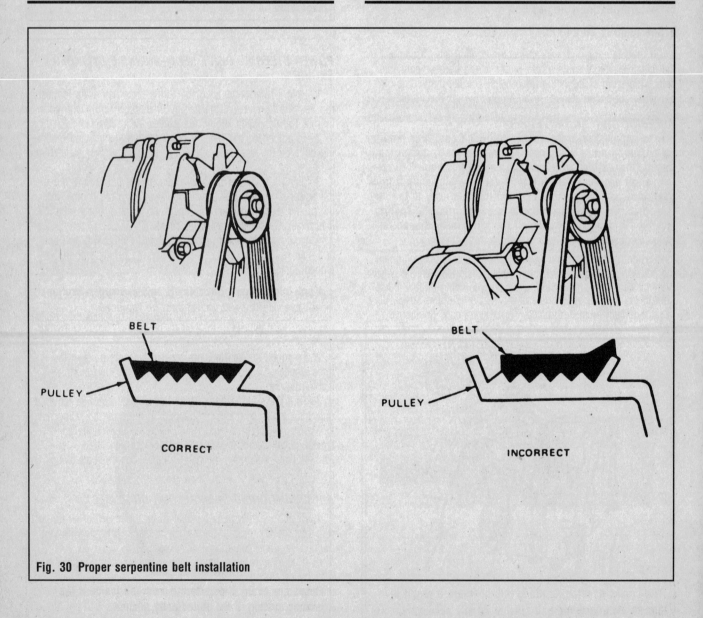

BELT

PULLEY

CORRECT

BELT

PULLEY

INCORRECT

Fig. 30 Proper serpentine belt installation

Hoses

INSPECTION

Upper and lower radiator hoses along with the heater hoses should be checked for deterioration, leaks and loose hose clamps at least every 15,000 miles (24,000 km). It is also wise to check the hoses periodically in early spring and at the beginning of the fall or winter when you are performing other maintenance. A quick visual inspection could discover a weakened hose which might have left you stranded if it had remained unrepaired.

Whenever you are checking the hoses, make sure the engine and cooling system are cold. Visually inspect for cracking, rotting or collapsed hoses, and replace as necessary. Run your hand along the length of the hose. If a weak or swollen spot is noted when squeezing the hose wall, the hose should be replaced.

REMOVAL & INSTALLATION

1. Remove the radiator pressure cap.

✱✱ CAUTION

Never remove the pressure cap while the engine is running, or personal injury from scalding hot coolant or steam may result. If possible, wait until the engine has cooled to remove the pressure cap. If this is not possible, wrap a thick cloth around the pressure cap and turn it slowly to the stop. Step back while the pressure is released from the cooling system. When you are sure all the pressure has been released, use the cloth to turn and remove the cap.

2. Position a clean container under the radiator and/or engine draincock or plug, then open the drain and allow the cooling system to drain to an appropriate level. For some upper hoses, only a little coolant must be drained. To remove hoses positioned

A hose clamp that is too tight can cause older hoses to separate and tear on either side of the clamp

A soft spongy hose (identifiable by the swollen section) will eventually burst and should be replaced

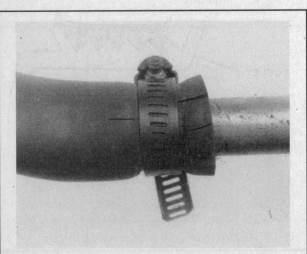

The cracks developing along this hose are a result of age-related hardening

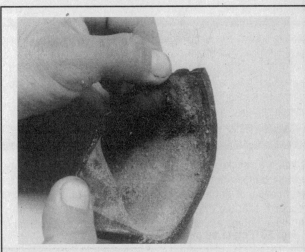

Hoses are likely to deteriorate from the inside if the cooling system is not periodically flushed

lower on the engine, such as a lower radiator hose, the entire cooling system must be emptied.

✳✳ CAUTION

When draining coolant, keep in mind that cats and dogs are attracted by ethylene glycol antifreeze, and are quite likely to drink any that is left in an uncovered container or in puddles on the ground. This will prove fatal in sufficient quantity. Always drain coolant into a sealable container. Coolant may be reused unless it is contaminated or several years old.

3. Loosen the hose clamps at each end of the hose requiring replacement. Clamps are usually either of the spring tension type (which require pliers to squeeze the tabs and loosen) or of the screw tension type (which require screw or hex drivers to loosen). Pull the clamps back on the hose away from the connection.

4. Twist, pull and slide the hose off the fitting, taking care not to damage the neck of the component from which the hose is being removed.

➡**If the hose is stuck at the connection, do not try to insert a screwdriver or other sharp tool under the hose end in an effort to free it, as the connection and/or hose may become damaged. Heater connections especially may be easily damaged by such a procedure. If the hose is to be replaced, use a single-edged razor blade to make a slice along the portion of the hose which is stuck on the connection, perpendicular to the end of the hose. Do not cut deep so as to prevent damaging the connection. The hose can then be peeled from the connection and discarded.**

5. Clean both hose mounting connections. Inspect the condition of the hose clamps and replace them, if necessary.

To install:

6. Dip the ends of the new hose into clean engine coolant to ease installation.

7. Slide the clamps over the replacement hose, then slide the hose ends over the connections into position.

8. Position and secure the clamps at least ¼ in. (6.35mm) from the ends of the hose. Make sure they are located beyond the raised bead of the connector.

9. Close the radiator or engine drains and properly refill the cooling system with the clean drained engine coolant or a suitable mixture of ethylene glycol coolant and water.

10. If available, install a pressure tester and check for leaks. If a pressure tester is not available, run the engine until normal operating temperature is reached (allowing the system to naturally pressurize), then check for leaks.

✳✳ CAUTION

If you are checking for leaks with the system at normal operating temperature, BE EXTREMELY CAREFUL not to touch any moving or hot engine parts. Once temperature has been reached, shut the engine OFF, and check for leaks around the hose fittings and connections which were removed earlier.

Heat Riser

SERVICING

▶ **See Figures 31 and 32**

Every 30,000 miles, the heat riser valve should be checked for free operation and lubricated with penetrating oil. The valve is located on the exhaust manifold near the point that the exhaust pipe attached to the manifold. Try to turn the valve counterweight by hand. If it's stuck, tap the end of the shaft a few times with a hammer. Apply penetrating oil to the shaft ends and work the valve back and forth a few times. If the valve is still stuck and can't be loosened with oil and/or heat, it will have to be replaced.

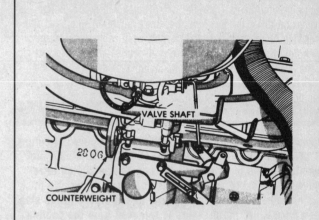

Fig. 31 Manifold heat control valve on inline 6-cylinder engines

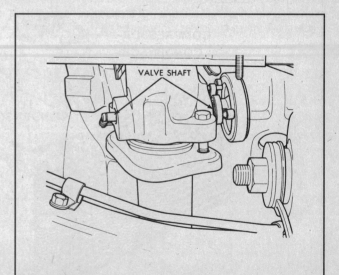

Fig. 32 Manifold heat control valve on V8 engines

Air Conditioning

♦ **See Figure 33**

➡ **Be sure to consult the laws in your area before servicing the air conditioning system. In most areas, it is illegal to perform repairs involving refrigerant unless the work is done by a certified technician. Also, it is quite likely that you will not be able to purchase refrigerant without proof of certification.**

SAFETY PRECAUTIONS

There are two major hazards associated with air conditioning systems and they both relate to the refrigerant gas. First, the refrigerant gas (R-12) is an extremely cold substance. When exposed to air, it will instantly freeze any surface it comes in contact with, including your eyes. The other hazard relates to fire. Although normally non-toxic, the R-12 gas becomes highly poisonous in the presence of an open flame. One good whiff of the vapor formed by burning R-12 can be fatal. Keep all forms of fire (including cigarettes) well clear of the air conditioning system.

Because of the inherent dangers involved with working on air conditioning systems and R-12 refrigerant, these safety precautions must be strictly followed.

• Avoid contact with a charged refrigeration system, even when working on another part of the air conditioning system or vehicle. If a heavy tool comes into contact with a section of tubing or a heat exchanger, it can easily cause the relatively soft material to rupture.

• When it is necessary to apply force to a fitting which contains refrigerant, as when checking that all system couplings are securely tightened, use a wrench on both parts of the fitting involved, if possible. This will avoid putting torque on refrigerant tubing. (It is also advisable to use tube or line wrenches when tightening these flare nut fittings.)

➡ **R-12 refrigerant is a chlorofluorocarbon which, when released into the atmosphere, can contribute to the depletion of the ozone layer in the upper atmosphere. Ozone filters out harmful radiation from the sun.**

• Do not attempt to discharge the system without the proper tools. Precise control is possible only when using the service gauges and a proper A/C refrigerant recovery station. Wear protective gloves when connecting or disconnecting service gauge hoses.

• Discharge the system only in a well ventilated area, as high concentrations of the gas which might accidentally escape can exclude oxygen and act as an anesthetic. When leak testing or soldering, this is particularly important, as toxic gas is formed when R-12 contacts any flame.

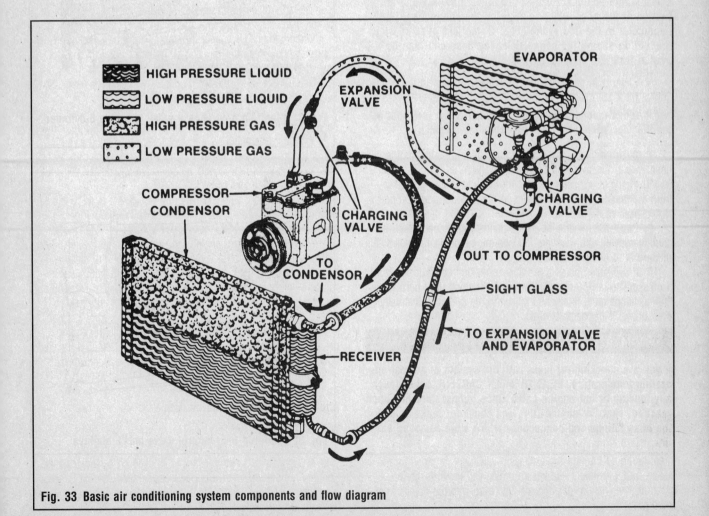

Fig. 33 Basic air conditioning system components and flow diagram

• Never start a system without first verifying that both service valves are properly installed, and that all fittings throughout the system are snugly connected.

• Avoid applying heat to any refrigerant line or storage vessel. Charging may be aided by using water heated to less than 125°F (50°C) to warm the refrigerant container. Never allow a refrigerant storage container to sit out in the sun, or near any other source of heat, such as a radiator or heater.

• Always wear goggles to protect your eyes when working on a system. If refrigerant contacts the eyes, it is advisable in all cases to consult a physician immediately.

• Frostbite from liquid refrigerant should be treated by first gradually warming the area with cool water, and then gently applying petroleum jelly. A physician should be consulted.

• Always keep refrigerant drum fittings capped when not in use. If the container is equipped with a safety cap to protect the valve, make sure the cap is in place when the can is not being used. Avoid sudden shock to the drum, which might occur from dropping it, or from banging a heavy tool against it. Never carry a drum in the passenger compartment of a vehicle.

• Always completely discharge the system into a suitable recovery unit before painting the vehicle (if the paint is to be baked on), or before welding anywhere near refrigerant lines.

• When servicing the system, minimize the time that any refrigerant line or fitting is open to the air in order to prevent moisture or dirt from entering the system. Contaminants such as moisture or dirt can damage internal system components. Always replace O-rings on lines or fittings which are disconnected. Prior to installation coat, but do not soak, replacement O-rings with suitable compressor oil.

GENERAL SERVICING PROCEDURES

➡**It is recommended, and possibly required by law, that a qualified technician perform the following services.**

The most important aspect of air conditioning service is the maintenance of a pure and adequate charge of refrigerant in the system. A refrigeration system cannot function properly if a significant percentage of the charge is lost. Leaks are common because the severe vibration encountered underhood in an automobile can easily cause a sufficient cracking or loosening of the air conditioning fittings; allowing, the extreme operating pressures of the system to force refrigerant out.

The problem can be understood by considering what happens to the system as it is operated with a continuous leak. Because the expansion valve regulates the flow of refrigerant to the evaporator, the level of refrigerant there is fairly constant. The receiver/drier stores any excess refrigerant, and so a loss will first appear there as a reduction in the level of liquid. As this level nears the bottom of the vessel, some refrigerant vapor bubbles will begin to appear in the stream of liquid supplied to the expansion valve. This vapor decreases the capacity of the expansion valve very little as the valve opens to compensate for its presence. As the quantity of liquid in the condenser decreases, the operating pressure will drop there and throughout the high side of the system. As the R-12 continues to be expelled, the pressure available to force the liquid through the expansion valve will continue to decrease, and, eventually, the valve's orifice will prove to be too much of a restriction for adequate flow even with the needle fully withdrawn.

At this point, low side pressure will start to drop, and a severe reduction in cooling capacity, marked by freeze-up of the evaporator coil, will result. Eventually, the operating pressure of the evaporator will be lower than the pressure of the atmosphere surrounding it, and air will be drawn into the system wherever there are leaks in the low side.

Because all atmospheric air contains at least some moisture, water will enter the system and mix with the R-12 and the oil. Trace amounts of moisture will cause sludging of the oil, and corrosion of the system. Saturation and clogging of the filter/drier, and freezing of the expansion valve orifice will eventually result. As air fills the system to a greater and greater extent, it will interfere more and more with the normal flows of refrigerant and heat.

From this description, it should be obvious that much of the repairman's focus in on detecting leaks, repairing them, and then restoring the purity and quantity of the refrigerant charge. A list of general rules should be followed in addition to all safety precautions:

• Keep all tools as clean and dry as possible.

• Thoroughly purge the service gauges/hoses of air and moisture before connecting them to the system. Keep them capped when not in use.

• Thoroughly clean any refrigerant fitting before disconnecting it, in order to minimize the entrance of dirt into the system.

• Plan any operation that requires opening the system beforehand, in order to minimize the length of time it will be exposed to open air. Cap or seal the open ends to minimize the entrance of foreign material.

• When adding oil, pour it through an extremely clean and dry tube or funnel. Keep the oil capped whenever possible. Do not use oil that has not been kept tightly sealed.

• Use only R-12 refrigerant. Purchase refrigerant intended for use only in automatic air conditioning systems.

• Completely evacuate any system that has been opened for service, or that has leaked sufficiently to draw in moisture and air. This requires evacuating air and moisture with a good vacuum pump for at least one hour. If a system has been open for a considerable length of time it may be advisable to evacuate the system for up to 12 hours (overnight).

• Use a wrench on both halves of a fitting that is to be disconnected, so as to avoid placing torque on any of the refrigerant lines.

• When overhauling a compressor, pour some of the oil into a clean glass and inspect it. If there is evidence of dirt, metal particles, or both, flush all refrigerant components with clean refrigerant before evacuating and recharging the system. In addition, if metal particles are present, the compressor should be replaced.

• Schrader valves may leak only when under full operating pressure. Therefore, if leakage is suspected but cannot be located, operate the system with a full charge of refrigerant and look for leaks from all Schrader valves. Replace any faulty valves.

Additional Preventive Maintenance

USING THE SYSTEM

The easiest and most important preventive maintenance for your A/C system is to be sure that it is used on a regular basis. Running the system for five minutes each month (no matter what the season) will help assure that the seals and all internal components remain lubricated.

ANTIFREEZE

In order to prevent heater core freeze-up during A/C operation, it is necessary to maintain a proper antifreeze protection. Use a hand-held antifreeze tester (hydrometer) to periodically check the condition of the antifreeze in your engine's cooling system.

➡**Antifreeze should not be used longer than the manufacturer specifies.**

RADIATOR CAP

For efficient operation of an air conditioned vehicle's cooling system, the radiator cap should have a holding pressure which meets manufacturer's specifications. A cap which fails to hold these pressures should be replaced.

CONDENSER

Any obstruction of or damage to the condenser configuration will restrict the air flow which is essential to its efficient operation. It is therefore a good rule to keep this unit clean and in proper physical shape.

➡**Bug screens which are mounted in front of the condenser, (unless they are original equipment), are regarded as obstructions.**

CONDENSATION DRAIN TUBE

This single molded drain tube expels the condensation, which accumulates on the bottom of the evaporator housing, into the engine compartment. If this tube is obstructed, the air conditioning performance can be restricted and condensation buildup can spill over onto the vehicle's floor.

SYSTEM INSPECTION

➡**R-12 refrigerant is a chlorofluorocarbon which, when released into the atmosphere, can contribute to the depletion of the ozone layer in the upper atmosphere. Ozone filters out harmful radiation from the sun.**

The easiest and often most important check for the air conditioning system consists of a visual inspection of the system components. Visually inspect the air conditioning system for refrigerant leaks, damaged compressor clutch, compressor drive belt tension and condition, plugged evaporator drain tube, blocked condenser fins, disconnected or broken wires, blown fuses, corroded connections and poor insulation.

A refrigerant leak will usually appear as an oily residue at the leakage point in the system. The oily residue soon picks up dust or dirt particles from the surrounding air and appears greasy. Through time, this will build up and appear to be a heavy dirt impregnated grease. Most leaks are caused by damaged or missing O-ring seals at the component connections, damaged charging valve cores or missing service gauge port caps.

For a thorough visual and operational inspection, check the following:

1. Check the surface of the radiator and condenser for dirt, leaves or other material which might block air flow.

2. Check for kinks in hoses and lines. Check the system for leaks.

3. Make sure the drive belt is under the proper tension. When the air conditioning is operating, make sure the drive belt is free of noise or slippage.

4. Make sure the blower motor operates at all appropriate posi-

An antifreeze tester can be used to determine the freezing and boiling levels of the coolant

tions, then check for distribution of the air from all outlets with the blower on **HIGH**.

➡**Keep in mind that under conditions of high humidity, air discharged from the A/C vents may not feel as cold as expected, even if the system is working properly. This is because the vaporized moisture in humid air retains heat more effectively than does dry air, making the humid air more difficult to cool.**

Make sure the air passage selection lever is operating correctly. Start the engine and warm it to normal operating temperature, then make sure the hot/cold selection lever is operating correctly.

DISCHARGING, EVACUATING & CHARGING

Discharging, evacuating and charging the air conditioning system must be performed by a properly trained and certified mechanic in a facility equipped with refrigerant recovery/recycling equipment that meets SAE standards for the type of system to be serviced.

If you don't have access to the necessary equipment, we recommend that you take your vehicle to a reputable service station to have the work done. If you still wish to perform repairs on the vehicle, have them discharge the system, then take your vehicle home and perform the necessary work. When you are finished, return the vehicle to the station for evacuation and charging. Just be sure to cap ALL A/C system fittings immediately after opening them and keep them protected until the system is recharged.

Windshield Wipers

ELEMENT (REFILL) CARE & REPLACEMENT

For maximum effectiveness and longest element life, the windshield and wiper blades should be kept clean. Dirt, tree sap, road tar and so on will cause streaking, smearing and blade deterioration if left on the glass. It is advisable to wash the windshield carefully with a commercial glass cleaner at least once a month. Wipe off the rubber blades with the wet rag afterwards. Do not attempt to move wipers across the windshield by hand; damage to the motor and drive mechanism will result.

To inspect and/or replace the wiper blade elements, place the wiper switch in the **LOW** speed position and the ignition switch in the **ACC** position. When the wiper blades are approximately vertical on the windshield, turn the ignition switch to **OFF.**

Examine the wiper blade elements. If they are found to be cracked, broken or torn, they should be replaced immediately. Replacement intervals will vary with usage, although ozone deterioration usually limits element life to about one year. If the wiper pattern is smeared or streaked, or if the blade chatters across the glass, the elements should be replaced. It is easiest and most sensible to replace the elements in pairs.

If your vehicle is equipped with aftermarket blades, there are several different types of refills and your vehicle might have any kind. Aftermarket blades and arms rarely use the exact same type blade or refill as the original equipment. Here are some typical aftermarket blades; not all may be available for your vehicle:

The Anco® type uses a release button that is pushed down to allow the refill to slide out of the yoke jaws. The new refill slides back into the frame and locks in place.

Some Trico® refills are removed by locating where the metal backing strip or the refill is wider. Insert a small screwdriver blade between the frame and metal backing strip. Press down to release the refill from the retaining tab.

Other types of Trico® refills have two metal tabs which are unlocked by squeezing them together. The rubber filler can then be withdrawn from the frame jaws. A new refill is installed by inserting the refill into the front frame jaws and sliding it rearward to engage the remaining frame jaws. There are usually four jaws; be certain when installing that the refill is engaged in all of them. At the end of its travel, the tabs will lock into place on the front jaws of the wiper blade frame.

Another type of refill is made from polycarbonate. The refill has a simple locking device at one end which flexes downward out of the groove into which the jaws of the holder fit, allowing easy release. By sliding the new refill through all the jaws and pushing through the slight resistance when it reaches the end of its travel, the refill will lock into position.

To replace the Tridon® refill, it is necessary to remove the wiper blade. This refill has a plastic backing strip with a notch about 1 in. (25mm) from the end. Hold the blade (frame) on a

Bosch® wiper blade and fit kit

Pylon® wiper blade and adaptor

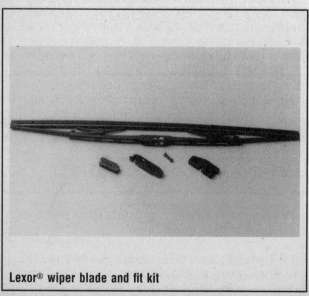

Lexor® wiper blade and fit kit

Trico® wiper blade and fit kit

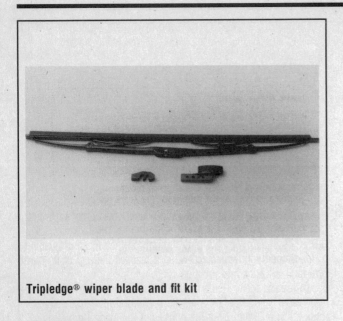

Tripledge® wiper blade and fit kit

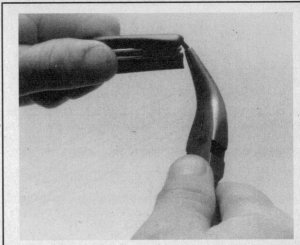

On Trico® wiper blades, the tab at the end of the blade must be turned up . . .

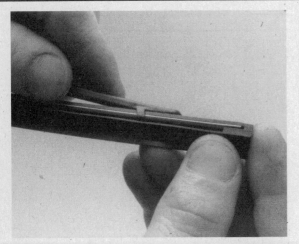

To remove and install a Lexor® wiper blade refill, slip out the old insert and slide in a new one

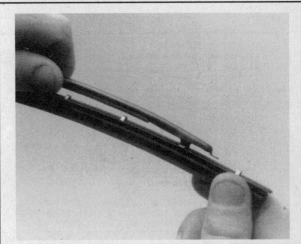

. . . then the insert can be removed. After installing the replacement insert, bend the tab back

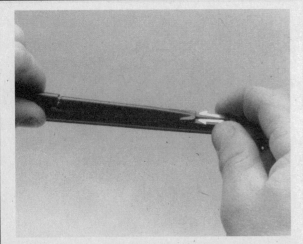

On Pylon® inserts, the clip at the end has to be removed prior to sliding the insert off

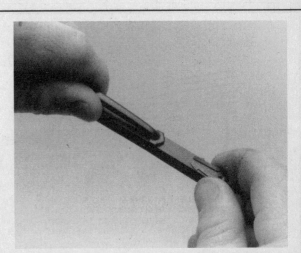

The Tripledge® wiper blade insert is removed and installed using a securing clip

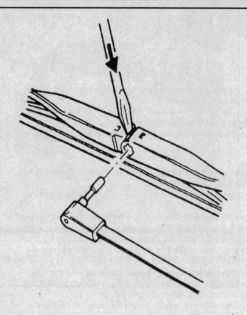

BLADE REPLACEMENT

1. CYCLE ARM AND BLADE ASSEMBLY TO UP POSITION- ON THE WINDSHIELD WHERE REMOVAL OF BLADE ASSEMBLY CAN BE PERFORMED WITHOUT DIFFICULTY. TURN IGNITION KEY OFF AT DESIRED POSITION.

2. TO REMOVE BLADE ASSEMBLY, INSERT SCREWDRIVER IN SLOT, PUSH DOWN ON SPRING LOCK AND PULL BLADE ASSEMBLY FROM PIN (VIEW A)

3. TO INSTALL, PUSH THE BLADE ASSEMBLY ON THE PIN SO THAT THE SPRING LOCK ENGAGES THE PIN (VIEW A). BE SURE THE BLADE ASSEMBLY IS SECURELY ATTACHED TO PIN

VIEW A

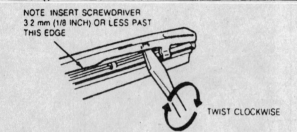

NOTE INSERT SCREWDRIVER 3.2 mm (1/8 INCH) OR LESS PAST THIS EDGE

TWIST CLOCKWISE

ELEMENT REPLACEMENT

1. INSERT SCREWDRIVER BETWEEN THE EDGE OF THE SUPER STRUCTURE AND THE BLADE BACKING DRIP (VIEW B) TWIST SCREWDRIVER SLOWLY UNTIL ELEMENT CLEARS ONE SIDE OF THE SUPER STRUC- TURE CLAW

2. SLIDE THE ELEMENT INTO THE SUPER STRUCTURE CLAWS

VIEW B

4. INSERT ELEMENT INTO ONE SIDE OF THE END CLAWS (VIEW D) AND WITH A ROCKING MOTION PUSH ELEMENT UPWARD UNTIL IT SNAPS IN (VIEW E)

VIEW D

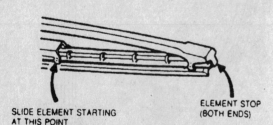

SLIDE ELEMENT STARTING AT THIS POINT

ELEMENT STOP (BOTH ENDS)

3. SLIDE THE ELEMENT INTO THE SUPER STRUCTURE CLAWS, STARTING WITH SECOND SET FROM EITHER END (VIEW C) AND CONTINUE TO SLIDE THE BLADE ELEMENT INTO ALL THE SUPER STRUCTURE CLAWS TO THE ELEMENT STOP (VIEW C)

VIEW C

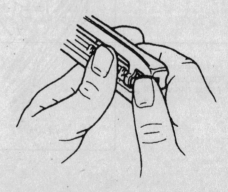

VIEW E

Trico® wiper blade insert (element) replacement

BLADE REPLACEMENT

1. Cycle arm and blade assembly to a position on the windshield where removal of blade assembly can be performed without difficulty. Turn ignition key off at desired position.
2. To remove blade assembly from wiper arm, pull up on spring lock and pull blade assembly from pin (View A). Be sure spring lock is not pulled excessively or it will become distorted.
3. To install, push the blade assembly onto the pin so that the spring lock engages the pin (View A). Be sure the blade assembly is securely attached to pin.

ELEMENT REPLACEMENT

1. In the plastic backing strip which is part of the rubber blade assembly, there is an 11.11mm (7/16 inch) long notch located approximately one inch from either end. Locate either notch.
2. Place the frame of the wiper blade assembly on a firm surface with either notched end of the backing strip visible.
3. Grasp the frame portion of the wiper blade assembly and push down until the blade assembly is tightly bowed.
4. With the blade assembly in the bowed position, grasp the tip of the backing strip firmly, pulling up and twisting C.C.W. at the same time. The backing strip will then snap out of the retaining tab on the end of the frame.
5. Lift the wiper blade assembly from the surface and slide the backing strip down the frame until the notch lines up with the next retaining tab, twist slightly, and the backing strip will snap out. Continue this operation with the remaining tabs until the blade element is completely detached from the frame.
6. To install blade element, reverse the above procedure, making sure all six (6) tabs are locked to the backing strip before installing blade to wiper arm.

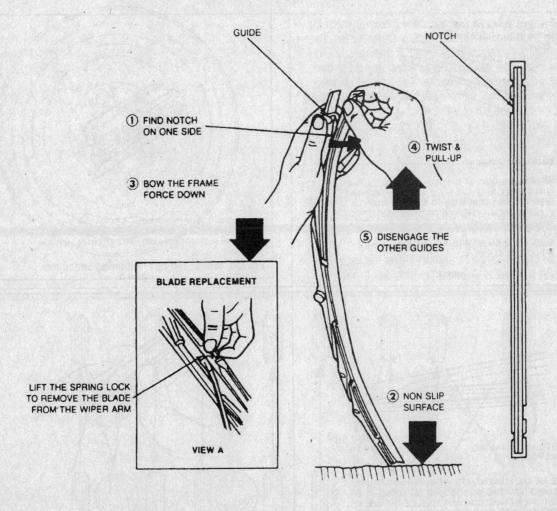

Tridon® wiper blade insert (element) replacement

hard surface so that the frame is tightly bowed. Grip the tip of the backing strip and pull up while twisting counterclockwise. The backing strip will snap out of the retaining tab. Do this for the remaining tabs until the refill is free of the blade. The length of these refills is molded into the end and they should be replaced with identical types.

Regardless of the type of refill used, be sure to follow the part manufacturer's instructions closely. Make sure that all of the frame jaws are engaged as the refill is pushed into place and locked. If the metal blade holder and frame are allowed to touch the glass during wiper operation, the glass will be scratched.

Tires and Wheels

Common sense and good driving habits will afford maximum tire life. Fast starts, sudden stops and hard cornering are hard on tires and will shorten their useful life span. Make sure that you don't overload the vehicle or run with incorrect pressure in the tires. Both of these practices will increase tread wear.

➡**For optimum tire life, keep the tires properly inflated, rotate them often and have the wheel alignment checked periodically.**

Inspect your tires frequently. Be especially careful to watch for bubbles in the tread or sidewall, deep cuts or underinflation. Replace any tires with bubbles in the sidewall. If cuts are so deep that they penetrate to the cords, discard the tire. Any cut in the sidewall of a radial tire renders it unsafe. Also look for uneven tread wear patterns that may indicate the front end is out of alignment or that the tires are out of balance.

TIRE ROTATION

◆ **See Figure 34**

Tires must be rotated periodically to equalize wear patterns that vary with a tire's position on the vehicle. Tires will also wear in an uneven way as the front steering/suspension system wears to the point where the alignment should be reset.

Rotating the tires will ensure maximum life for the tires as a set, so you will not have to discard a tire early due to wear on only part of the tread. Regular rotation is required to equalize wear.

When rotating "unidirectional tires," make sure that they always roll in the same direction. This means that a tire used on the left side of the vehicle must not be switched to the right side and vice-versa. Such tires should only be rotated front-to-rear or rear-to-front, while always remaining on the same side of the vehicle. These tires are marked on the sidewall as to the direction of rotation; observe the marks when reinstalling the tire(s).

Some styled or "mag" wheels may have different offsets front to rear. In these cases, the rear wheels must not be used up front and vice-versa. Furthermore, if these wheels are equipped with unidirectional tires, they cannot be rotated unless the tire is remounted for the proper direction of rotation.

➡**The compact or space-saver spare is strictly for emergency use. It must never be included in the tire rotation or placed on the vehicle for everyday use.**

When installing the wheels on the vehicle, tighten the lug nuts in a crisscross pattern. Lug nuts should be torqued to the following figures:

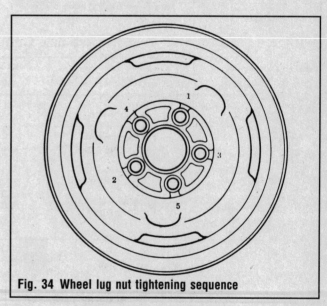

Fig. 34 Wheel lug nut tightening sequence

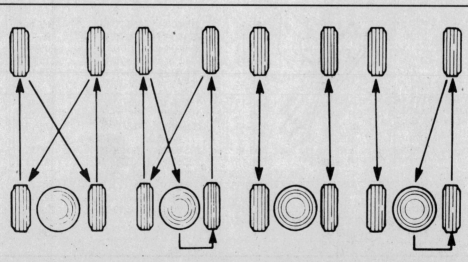

Common tire rotation patterns for 4 and 5-wheel rotations

Unidirectional tires are identifiable by sidewall arrows and/or the word "rotation"

- 1967: 65 ft. lbs.
- 1968–69: 75 ft. lbs.
- 1970–71: 80 ft. lbs.
- 1972–74: 65–85 ft. lbs.
- 1975–84: 85–125 ft. lbs.
- 1985–88: 85–110 ft. lbs.
- 1982–88 350 w/H.D. axle (cone nut): 175–225 ft. lbs.
- 1986–88 350 w/H.D. axle (Flanged nut): 300–350 ft. lbs.

TIRE DESIGN

✵✵ CAUTION

Radial tires must not be used on 1975 and earlier 16.5 x 6.75 wheels! The 1976 and later design wheels can be used with radial tires.

For maximum satisfaction, tires should be used in sets of four. Mixing of different types (radial, bias-belted, fiberglass belted) must be avoided. In most cases, the vehicle manufacturer has des-

Tire Size Comparison Chart

"Letter" sizes			Inch Sizes	Metric-inch Sizes		
"60 Series"	"70 Series"	"78 Series"	1965–77	"60 Series"	"70 Series"	"80 Series"
			5.50-12, 5.60-12	165/60-12	165/70-12	155-12
		Y78-12	6.00-12			
		W78-13	5.20-13	165/60-13	145/70-13	135-13
		Y78-13	5.60-13	175/60-13	155/70-13	145-13
			6.15-13	185/60-13	165/70-13	155-13, P155/80-13
A60-13	A70-13	A78-13	6.40-13	195/60-13	175/70-13	165-13
B60-13	B70-13	B78-13	6.70-13	205/60-13	185/70-13	175-13
			6.90-13			
C60-13	C70-13	C78-13	7.00-13	215/60-13	195/70-13	185-13
D60-13	D70-13	D78-13	7.25-13			
E60-13	E70-13	E78-13	7.75-13			195-13
			5.20-14	165/60-14	145/70-14	135-14
			5.60-14	175/60-14	155/70-14	145-14
			5.90-14			
A60-14	A70-14	A78-14	6.15-14	185/60-14	165/70-14	155-14
	B70-14	B78-14	6.45-14	195/60-14	175/70-14	165-14
	C70-14	C78-14	6.95-14	205/60-14	185/70-14	175-14
D60-14	D70-14	D78-14				
E60-14	E70-14	E78-14	7.35-14	215/60-14	195/70-14	185-14
F60-14	F70-14	F78-14, F83-14	7.75-14	225/60-14	200/70-14	195-14
G60-14	G70-14	G77-14, G78-14	8.25-14	235/60-14	205/70-14	205-14
H60-14	H70-14	H78-14	8.55-14	245/60-14	215/70-14	215-14
J60-14	J70-14	J78-14	8.85-14	255/60-14	225/70-14	225-14
L60-14	L70-14		9.15-14	265/60-14	235/70-14	
	A70-15	A78-15	5.60-15	185/60-15	165/70-15	155-15
B60-15	B70-15	B78-15	6.35-15	195/60-15	175/70-15	165-15
C60-15	C70-15	C78-15	6.85-15	205/60-15	185/70-15	175-15
	D70-15	D78-15				
E60-15	E70-15	E78-15	7.35-15	215/60-15	195/70-15	185-15
F60-15	F70-15	F78-15	7.75-15	225/60-15	205/70-15	195-15
G60-15	G70-15	G78-15	8.15-15/8.25-15	235/60-15	215/70-15	205-15
H60-15	H70-15	H78-15	8.45-15/8.55-15	245/60-15	225/70-15	215-15
J60-15	J70-15	J78-15	8.85-15/8.90-15	255/60-15	235/70-15	225-15
	K70-15		9.00-15	265/60-15	245/70-15	230-15
L60-15	L70-15	L78-15, L84-15	9.15-15			235-15
	M70-15	M78-15				255-15
		N78-15				

Note: Every size tire is not listed and many size comparisons are approximate, based on load ratings. Wider tires than those supplied new with the vehicle, should always be checked for clearance.

ignated a type of tire on which the vehicle will perform best. Your first choice when replacing tires should be to use the same type of tire that the manufacturer recommends.

When radial tires are used, tire sizes and wheel diameters should be selected to maintain ground clearance and tire load capacity equivalent to the original specified tire. Radial tires should always be used in sets of four.

✳✳ CAUTION

Radial tires should never be used on only the front axle.

When selecting tires, pay attention to the original size as marked on the tire. Most tires are described using an industry size code sometimes referred to as P-Metric. This allows the exact identification of the tire specifications, regardless of the manufacturer. If selecting a different tire size or brand, remember to check the installed tire for any sign of interference with the body or suspension while the vehicle is stopping, turning sharply or heavily loaded.

Snow Tires

Good radial tires can produce a big advantage in slippery weather, but in snow, a street radial tire does not have sufficient tread to provide traction and control. The small grooves of a street tire quickly pack with snow and the tire behaves like a billiard ball on a marble floor. The more open, chunky tread of a snow tire will self-clean as the tire turns, providing much better grip on snowy surfaces.

To satisfy municipalities requiring snow tires during weather emergencies, most snow tires carry either an M + S designation after the tire size stamped on the sidewall, or the designation "all-season." In general, no change in tire size is necessary when buying snow tires.

Most manufacturers strongly recommend the use of 4 snow tires on their vehicles for reasons of stability. If snow tires are fitted only to the drive wheels, the opposite end of the vehicle may become very unstable when braking or turning on slippery surfaces. This instability can lead to unpleasant endings if the driver can't counteract the slide in time.

Note that snow tires, whether 2 or 4, will affect vehicle handling in all non-snow situations. The stiffer, heavier snow tires will noticeably change the turning and braking characteristics of the vehicle. Once the snow tires are installed, you must re-learn the behavior of the vehicle and drive accordingly.

➡**Consider buying extra wheels on which to mount the snow tires. Once done, the "snow wheels" can be installed and removed as needed. This eliminates the potential damage to tires or wheels from seasonal removal and installation. Even if your vehicle has styled wheels, see if inexpensive steel wheels are available. Although the look of the vehicle will change, the expensive wheels will be protected from salt, curb hits and pothole damage.**

TIRE STORAGE

If they are mounted on wheels, store the tires at proper inflation pressure. All tires should be kept in a cool, dry place. If they are stored in the garage or basement, do not let them stand on a concrete floor; set them on strips of wood, a mat or a large stack of newspaper. Keeping them away from direct moisture is of paramount importance. Tires should not be stored upright, but in a flat position.

INFLATION & INSPECTION

The importance of proper tire inflation cannot be overemphasized. A tire employs air as part of its structure. It is designed around the supporting strength of the air at a specified pressure. For this reason, improper inflation drastically reduces the tires's ability to perform as intended. A tire will lose some air in day-to-day use; having to add a few pounds of air periodically is not necessarily a sign of a leaking tire.

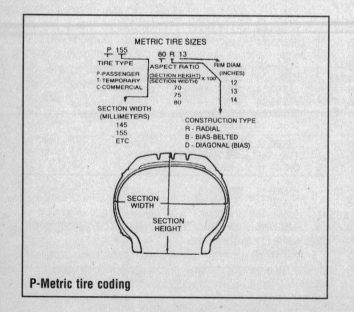

P-Metric tire coding

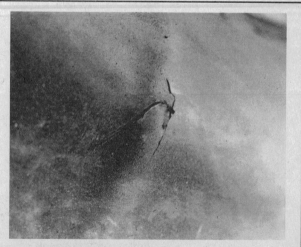

Tires should be checked frequently for any sign of puncture or damage

Tires with deep cuts, or cuts which show bulging should be replaced immediately

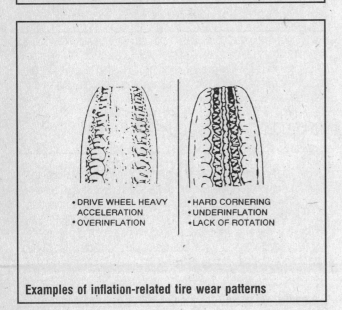

- DRIVE WHEEL HEAVY ACCELERATION
- OVERINFLATION

- HARD CORNERING
- UNDERINFLATION
- LACK OF ROTATION

Examples of inflation-related tire wear patterns

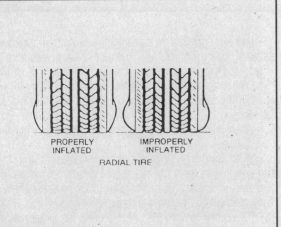

PROPERLY INFLATED   IMPROPERLY INFLATED

RADIAL TIRE

Radial tires have a characteristic sidewall bulge; don't try to measure pressure by looking at the tire. Use a quality air pressure gauge

Two items should be a permanent fixture in every glove compartment: an accurate tire pressure gauge and a tread depth gauge. Check the tire pressure (including the spare) regularly with a pocket type gauge. Too often, the gauge on the end of the air hose at your corner garage is not accurate because it suffers too much abuse. Always check tire pressure when the tires are cold, as pressure increases with temperature. If you must move the vehicle to check the tire inflation, do not drive more than a mile before checking. A cold tire is generally one that has not been driven for more than three hours.

A plate or sticker is normally provided somewhere in the vehicle (door post, hood, tailgate or trunk lid) which shows the proper pressure for the tires. Never counteract excessive pressure build-up by bleeding off air pressure (letting some air out). This will cause the tire to run hotter and wear quicker.

✳✳ CAUTION

Never exceed the maximum tire pressure embossed on the tire! This is the pressure to be used when the tire is at maximum loading, but it is rarely the correct pressure for everyday driving. Consult the owner's manual or the tire pressure sticker for the correct tire pressure.

Once you've maintained the correct tire pressures for several weeks, you'll be familiar with the vehicle's braking and handling personality. Slight adjustments in tire pressures can fine-tune these characteristics, but never change the cold pressure specification by more than 2 psi. A slightly softer tire pressure will give a softer ride but also yield lower fuel mileage. A slightly harder tire will give crisper dry road handling but can cause skidding on wet surfaces. Unless you're fully attuned to the vehicle, stick to the recommended inflation pressures.

All tires made since 1968 have built-in tread wear indicator bars that show up as ½ in. (13mm) wide smooth bands across the tire when ¹⁄₁₆ in. (1.5mm) of tread remains. The appearance of tread wear indicators means that the tires should be replaced. In fact, many states have laws prohibiting the use of tires with less than this amount of tread.

You can check your own tread depth with an inexpensive gauge or by using a Lincoln head penny. Slip the Lincoln penny (with Lincoln's head upside-down) into several tread grooves. If you can see the top of Lincoln's head in 2 adjacent grooves, the tire has less than ¹⁄₁₆ in. (1.5mm) tread left and should be replaced. You can measure snow tires in the same manner by using the "tails" side of the Lincoln penny. If you can see the top of the Lincoln memorial, it's time to replace the snow tire(s).

CARE OF SPECIAL WHEELS

If you have invested money in magnesium, aluminum alloy or sport wheels, special precautions should be taken to make sure your investment is not wasted and that your special wheels look good for the life of the vehicle.

Special wheels are easily damaged and/or scratched. Occasionally check the rims for cracking, impact damage or air leaks. If any of these are found, replace the wheel. But in order to prevent this type of damage and the costly replacement of a special wheel, observe the following precautions:

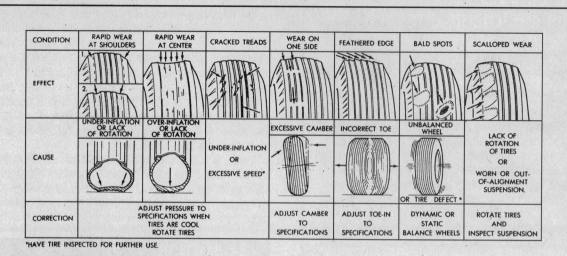

CONDITION	RAPID WEAR AT SHOULDERS	RAPID WEAR AT CENTER	CRACKED TREADS	WEAR ON ONE SIDE	FEATHERED EDGE	BALD SPOTS	SCALLOPED WEAR
EFFECT							
CAUSE	UNDER-INFLATION OR LACK OF ROTATION	OVER-INFLATION OR LACK OF ROTATION	UNDER-INFLATION OR EXCESSIVE SPEED*	EXCESSIVE CAMBER	INCORRECT TOE	UNBALANCED WHEEL — OR TIRE DEFECT *	LACK OF ROTATION OF TIRES OR WORN OR OUT-OF-ALIGNMENT SUSPENSION.
CORRECTION	ADJUST PRESSURE TO SPECIFICATIONS WHEN TIRES ARE COOL ROTATE TIRES			ADJUST CAMBER TO SPECIFICATIONS	ADJUST TOE-IN TO SPECIFICATIONS	DYNAMIC OR STATIC BALANCE WHEELS	ROTATE TIRES AND INSPECT SUSPENSION

*HAVE TIRE INSPECTED FOR FURTHER USE.

Common tire wear patterns and causes

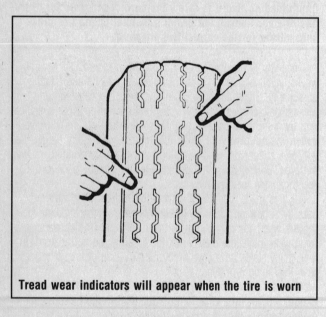

Tread wear indicators will appear when the tire is worn

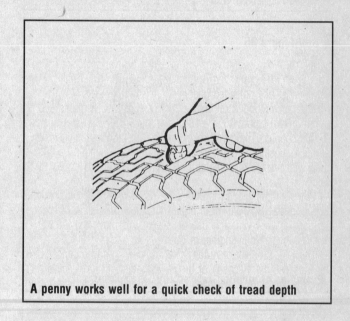

A penny works well for a quick check of tread depth

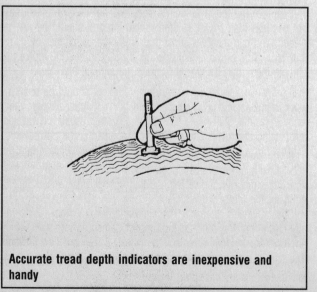

Accurate tread depth indicators are inexpensive and handy

• Use extra care not to damage the wheels during removal, installation, balancing, etc. After removal of the wheels from the vehicle, place them on a mat or other protective surface. If they are to be stored for any length of time, support them on strips of wood. Never store tires and wheels upright; the tread may develop flat spots.

• When driving, watch for hazards; it doesn't take much to crack a wheel.

• When washing, use a mild soap or non-abrasive dish detergent (keeping in mind that detergent tends to remove wax). Avoid cleansers with abrasives or the use of hard brushes. There are many cleaners and polishes for special wheels.

• If possible, remove the wheels during the winter. Salt and sand used for snow removal can severely damage the finish of a wheel.

• Make certain the recommended lug nut torque is never exceeded or the wheel may crack. Never use snow chains on special wheels; severe scratching will occur.

FLUIDS AND LUBRICANTS

Fluid Disposal

Used fluids such as engine oil, transmission fluid, antifreeze and brake fluid are hazardous wastes and must be disposed of properly. Before draining any fluids, consult with the local authorities; in many areas, waste oil, etc. is being accepted as a part of recycling programs. A number of service stations and auto parts stores are also accepting waste fluids for recycling.

Be sure of the recycling center's policies before draining any fluids, as many will not accept different fluids that have been mixed together, such as oil and antifreeze.

Oil and Fuel Recommendations

GASOLINE ENGINES

▶ **See Figure 35**

All 1967–74 Dodge vans are designed to run on leaded gasoline. From 1975, any van originally equipped with a catalytic converter must use unleaded gasoline.

The recommended oil viscosities for sustained temperatures ranging from below 0°F (–18°C) to above 32°F (0°C) are listed in this chapter. They are broken down into multiviscosities and single viscosities. Multiviscosity oils are recommended because of their wider range of acceptable temperatures and driving conditions.

When adding oil to the crankcase or changing the oil or filter, it is important that oil of an equal quality to original equipment be used in your van. The use of inferior oils may void the warranty, damage your engine, or both.

The SAE (Society of Automotive Engineers) grade number of oil indicates the viscosity of the oil (its ability to lubricate at a given temperature). The lower the SAE number, the lighter the oil; the lower the viscosity, the easier it is to crank the engine in cold weather but the less the oil will lubricate and protect the engine in high temperatures. This number is marked on every oil container.

Oil viscosities should be chosen from those oils recommended for the lowest anticipated temperatures during the oil change interval. Due to the need for an oil that embodies both good lubrication at high temperatures and easy cranking in cold weather, multigrade oils have been developed. Basically, a multigrade oil is thinner at low temperatures and thicker at high temperatures. For example, a 10W-40 oil (the W stands for winter) exhibits the characteristics of a 10 weight (SAE 10) oil when the van is first started and the oil is cold. Its lighter weight allows it to travel to the lubricating surfaces quicker and offer less resistance to starter motor cranking than, say, a straight 30 weight (SAE 30) oil. But after the engine reaches operating temperature, the 10W-40 oil begins acting like straight 40 weight (SAE 40) oil, its heavier weight providing greater lubrication with less chance of foaming than a straight 30 weight oil.

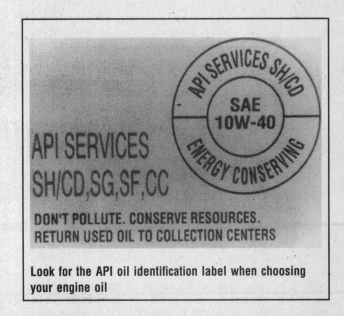

Look for the API oil identification label when choosing your engine oil

The API (American Petroleum Institute) designations, also found on the oil container, indicates the classification of engine oil used under certain given operating conditions. Only oils designated for use Service SF heavy duty detergent should be used in your van. Oils of the SF type perform many functions inside the engine besides their basic lubrication. Through a balanced system of metallic detergents and polymeric dispersants, the oil prevents high and low temperature deposits and also keeps sludge and dirt particles in suspension. Acids, particularly sulphuric acid, as well as other by-products of engine combustion are neutralized by the oil. If these acids are allowed to concentrate, they can cause corrosion and rapid wear of the internal engine parts.

❊❊ WARNING

Non-detergent motor oils or straight mineral oils should not be used in your gasoline engine.

RECOMMENDED SAE VISCOSITY GRADES							
20W-40, 20W-50, 30							
20W-20							
15W-40							
10W-30, 10W-40, 10W-50							
5W-30, 5W-40							

| °F | –20 | –10 | 0 | 10 | 20 | 32 | | 60 | 80 | 100 |
| °C | –29 | –23 | –18 | –12 | –7 | 0 | | 16 | 27 | 38 |

TEMPERATURE RANGE ANTICIPATED
BEFORE NEXT OIL CHANGE

RF 68 A

Fig. 35 Gasoline engine oil viscosity chart

DIESEL ENGINES

♦ **See Figure 36**

Diesel engines require different engine oil from those used in gasoline engines. Besides doing the things gasoline engine oil does, diesel oil must also deal with increased engine heat and the diesel blow-by gases, which create sulphuric acid, a high corrosive.

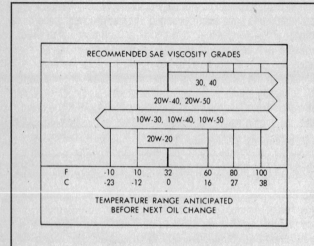

Fig. 36 Diesel engine oil viscosity chart

Under the American Petroleum Institute (API) classifications, gasoline engine oil codes begin with an **S**, and diesel engine oil codes begin with a **C**. This first letter designation is followed by a second letter code which explains what type of service (heavy, moderate, light) the oil is meant for. For example, the top of a typical oil can will include: API SERVICES SF, CD. This means the oil in the can is a superior, heavy duty engine oil when used in a diesel engine.

Many diesel manufacturers recommend an oil with both gasoline and diesel engine API classifications.

➡**Chrysler Corp. specifies the use of an engine oil conforming to API service categories of both SF and CD. DO NOT use oils labeled as only SF or only CD as they could cause engine damage.**

Fuel makers produce two grades of diesel fuel, No. 1 and No. 2, for use in automotive diesel engines. Generally speaking, No. 2 fuel is recommended over No. 1 for driving in temperatures above 20°F (−7°C). In fact, in many areas, No. 2 diesel is the only fuel available. By comparison, No. 2 diesel fuel is less volatile than No. 1 fuel, and gives better fuel economy. No. 2 fuel is also a better injection pump lubricant.

Two important characteristics of diesel fuel are its cetane number and its viscosity.

The cetane number of a diesel fuel refers to the ease with which a diesel fuel ignites. High cetane numbers mean that the fuel will ignite with relative ease or that it ignites well at low temperatures. Naturally, the lower the cetane number, the higher the temperature must be to ignite the fuel. Most commercial fuels have cetane numbers that range from 35 to 65. No. 1 diesel fuel generally has a higher cetane rating than No. 2 fuel.

Viscosity is the ability of a liquid, in this case diesel fuel, to flow. Using straight No. 2 diesel fuel below 20°F (−7°C) can cause problems, because this fuel tends to become cloudy, meaning wax crystals begin forming in the fuel. 20°F (−7°C) is often called the cloud point for No. 2 fuel. In extremely cold weather, No. 2 fuel can stop flowing altogether. In either case, fuel flow is restricted, which can result in no start condition or poor engine performance. Fuel manufacturers often winterize No. 2 diesel fuel by using various fuel additives and blends (no. 1 diesel fuel, kerosene, etc.) to lower its winter time viscosity. Generally speaking, though, No. 1 diesel fuel is more satisfactory in extremely cold weather.

➡**No. 1 and No. 2 diesel fuels will mix and burn with no ill effects, although the engine manufacturer will undoubtedly recommend one or the other. Consult the owner's manual for information.**

Depending on local climate, most fuel manufacturers make winterized No. 2 fuel available seasonally.

Many automobile manufacturers publish pamphlets giving the locations of diesel fuel stations nationwide. Contact the local dealer for information.

Do not substitute home heating oil for automotive diesel fuel. While in some cases, home heating oil refinement levels equal those of diesel fuel, many times they are far below diesel engine requirements. The result of using dirty home heating oil will be a clogged fuel system, in which case the entire system may have to be dismantled and cleaned.

One more word on diesel fuels. Don't thin diesel fuel with gasoline in cold weather. The lighter gasoline, which is more explosive, will cause rough running at the very least, and may cause extensive damage to the fuel system if enough is used.

Engine

OIL LEVEL CHECK

Check the engine oil level every time you fill the gas tank. The oil level should be above the ADD mark and not above the FULL

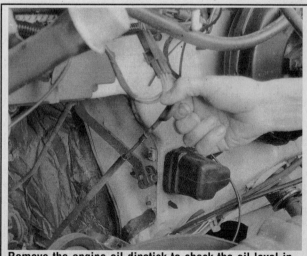

Remove the engine oil dipstick to check the oil level in the engine

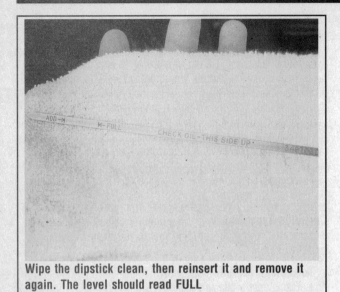

Wipe the dipstick clean, then reinsert it and remove it again. The level should read FULL

If oil is to be added to the engine, remove the cap on the engine oil fill tube . . .

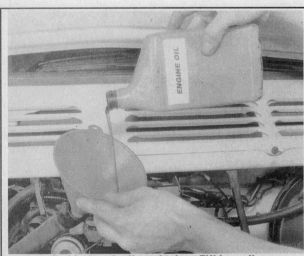

. . . and add enough oil to obtain a FULL reading on the dipstick. Check the level often when filling

mark on the dipstick. Make sure that the dipstick is inserted into the crankcase as far as possible and that the vehicle is resting on level ground. Also, allow a few minutes after turning off the engine for the oil to drain into the pan or an inaccurate reading will result.

1. Open the hood and remove the engine oil dipstick.
2. Wipe the dipstick with a clean, lint-free rag and reinsert it. Be sure to insert it all the way.
3. Pull out the dipstick and note the oil level. It should be between the **SAFE** (MAX) mark and the **ADD** (MIN) mark.
4. If the level is below the lower mark, replace the dipstick and add fresh oil to bring the level within the proper range. Do not overfill.
5. Recheck the oil level and close the hood.

➡**Use a multi-grade oil with API classification SF.**

OIL & FILTER CHANGE

▶ **See Figures 37, 38 and 39**

✳✳ CAUTION

The EPA warns that prolonged contact with used engine oil may cause a number of skin disorders, including cancer! You should make every effort to minimize your exposure to used engine oil. Protective gloves should be worn when changing the oil. Wash your hands and any other exposed skin areas as soon as possible after exposure to used engine oil. Soap and water, or waterless hand cleaner should be used.

➡**The engine oil and oil filter should be changed at the same time, at the recommended intervals on the maintenance schedule chart.**

You should have available a container to hold a minimum of 7 quarts of oil; 9 for the diesel!

The oil should be changed more frequently if the vehicle is being operated in very dusty areas. Before draining the oil, make sure that the engine is at operating temperature. Hot oil will hold

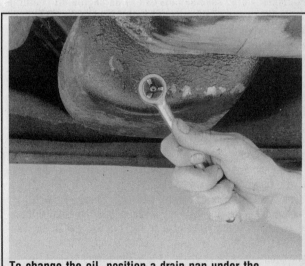

To change the oil, position a drain pan under the engine, loosen the oil drain plug on the oil pan. . .

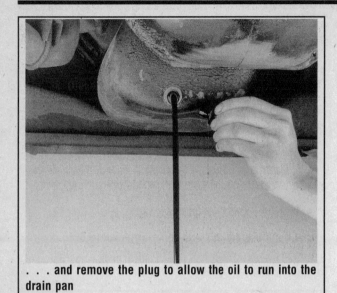

. . . and remove the plug to allow the oil to run into the drain pan

more impurities in suspension and will flow better, allowing the removal of more oil and dirt.

Loosen the drain plug with a wrench, then, unscrew the plug with your fingers, using a rag to shield your fingers from the heat. Push in on the plug as you unscrew it so you can feel when all of the screw threads are out of the hole. You can then remove the plug quickly with the minimum amount of oil running down your arm and you will also have the plug in your hand and not in the bottom of a pan of hot oil. Drain the oil into a suitable receptacle. Be careful of the oil. If it is at operating temperatures it is hot enough to burn you.

For longest engine life, the oil filter should be changed every time the oil is changed.

Cartridge Type Filter

Some early models were equipped with a cartridge type filter located in a canister on the side of the engine.

To replace the filter element:
1. Place a drain pan under the filter housing.
2. Remove the filter housing bolt and lower the housing containing the cartridge.

✱✱ CAUTION

The housing is full of hot oil! Be careful!

3. Remove the cartridge from the housing and dispose it.

➡There are springs and washers located on the bolt. Be careful to avoid losing them.

4. Insert the new cartridge in the housing. It's a good idea to replace the housing O-ring or gasket.
5. Position the housing on the base and install the mounting bolt.
6. Fill the crankcase, start the engine, let it idle for a few minutes, shut it off and recheck the oil level.

Spin-On Type Filter

To remove the filter, you may need an oil filter wrench since the filter may have been fitted too tightly and the heat from the en-

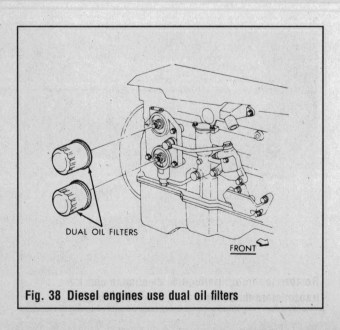

Fig. 37 Engine oil filter removal on V6 and V8 engines

PLATE
OIL FILTER
TOOL

Fig. 38 Diesel engines use dual oil filters

DUAL OIL FILTERS
FRONT

The spin-on type oil filter on an inline 6-cylinder engine is located on the right side of the vehicle

gine may have made it even tighter. A filter wrench can be obtained at an auto parts store and is well worth the investment, since it will save you a lot of grief. Loosen the filter with the filter wrench. With a rag wrapped around the filter, unscrew the filter from the boss on the side of the engine. Be careful of hot oil that will run down the side of the filter.

➡**The diesel has 2 oil filters. Change both at the same time.**

Make sure that you have a pan under the filter before you start to remove it from the engine; should some of the hot oil happen to get on you, you will have a place to dump the filter in a hurry. Wipe the base of the mounting boss with a clean, dry cloth. When you install the new filter, smear a small amount of oil on the gasket with your finger, just enough to coat the entire surface, where it comes in contact with the mounting plate. When you tighten the filter, rotate if only a half turn after it comes in contact with the mounting boss.

Before installing a new oil filter, lightly coat the rubber gasket with clean oil

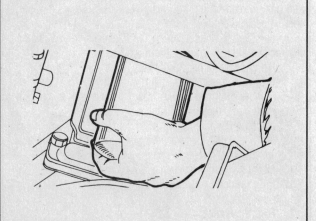

Fig. 39 Install the new filter by hand to avoid overtightening it

Transmission

FLUID RECOMMENDATIONS

Manual Transmissions
- New Process A-230: Dexron®II ATF
- New Process A-250: Dexron®II ATF
- New Process A-390: Dexron®II ATF
- New Process A-745: Dexron®II ATF
- New Process A-903: Dexron®II ATF
- Overdrive-4 4-sp: Dexron®II ATF
- New Process 2500: Dexron®II ATF

➡**If gear noise or rattle is experienced with the A-230/A-250/A-390/A-903/Overdrive-4, SAE 90 gear oil may be used in place of the ATF.**

Automatic Transmissions:
All types: Dexron®II ATF

LEVEL CHECK

Automatic Transmissions

It is very important to maintain the proper fluid level in an automatic transmission. If the level is either too high or too low, poor shifting operation and internal damage are likely to occur. For this reason a regular check of the fluid level is essential.

1. Drive the vehicle for 15–20 minutes to allow the transmission to reach operating temperature.

2. Park the van on a level surface, apply the parking brake and leave the engine idling. Shift the transmission and engage each gear, then place the gear selector in **P** (PARK).

3. Wipe away any dirt in the areas of the transmission dipstick to prevent it from falling into the filler tube. Withdraw the dipstick, wipe it with a clean, lint-free rag and reinsert it until it seats.

4. Withdraw the dipstick and note the fluid level. It should be between the upper (FULL) mark and the lower (ADD) mark.

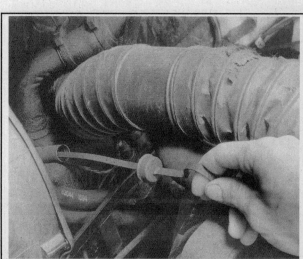

Remove the transmission fluid dipstick to check the transmission fluid level

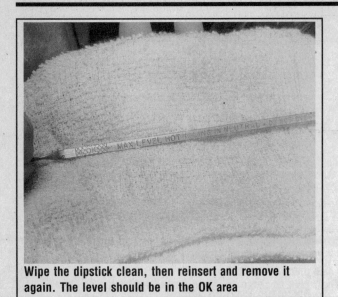

Wipe the dipstick clean, then reinsert and remove it again. The level should be in the OK area

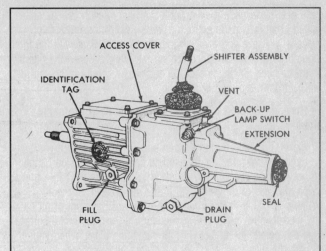

Fig. 40 Common manual transmission details—NP-2500 shown, other models similar

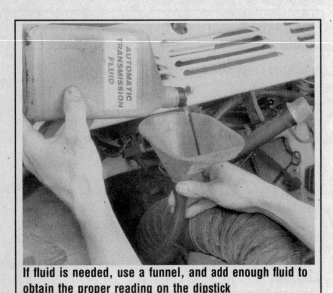

If fluid is needed, use a funnel, and add enough fluid to obtain the proper reading on the dipstick

5. If the level is below the lower mark, use a funnel and add fluid in small quantities through the dipstick filler neck. Keep the engine running while adding fluid and check the level after each small amount. Do not overfill.

Manual Transmission
♦ See Figure 40

The fluid level should be checked every 6 months/6,000 miles, whichever comes first.

1. Park the van on a level surface, turn off the engine, apply the parking brake and block the wheels.
2. Remove the filler plug from the side of the transmission case with a proper size wrench. The fluid level should be even with the bottom of the filler hole.
3. If additional fluid is necessary, add it through the filler hole using a siphon pump or squeeze bottle.
4. Replace the filler plug; do not overtighten.

DRAIN & REFILL

Automatic Transmission

➡A running production change was made in January, 1977, which eliminated the converter drain plug from the automatic transmission. This means that the transmission must be removed in order to drain the converter on models manufactured after this date.

WITH CONVERTER DRAIN PLUG
♦ See Figures 41 thru 46

➡To drain only the transmission (not the converter), use the procedure labeled "without drainplug."

1. Jack up the front of the vehicle and support it on jackstands. Place a large drain pan under the transmission.
2. Remove the converter access plate and turn the converter using the starter, until the converter drain plug is accessible.
3. Remove the converter drain plug and allow the converter to drain completely. Late 1972 and 1973–77 models use a 5/16" hex head bolt, instead of the previously used 7/16". A six-point socket must be used in the 5/16" head.
4. Remove the bolts securing the transmission pan and carefully remove the pan to drain the fluid.
5. Reinstall the drain plug.
6. Clean the transmission pan thoroughly.
7. Remove the three screws from the fluid filter in the bottom of the valve body; remove the filter and discard it.
8. Install a new filter using three screws.
9. Install the pan using a new gasket. Tighten the pan screws to 150 in. lbs. of torque in a criss-cross pattern.
10. Install the torque converter access plate.
11. Pour 6 quarts of DEXRON®II automatic transmission fluid through the filler tube.
12. Start the engine.
13. Let the engine idle for 2 minutes and move the gear selector through all the drive positions, pausing momentarily in each position.

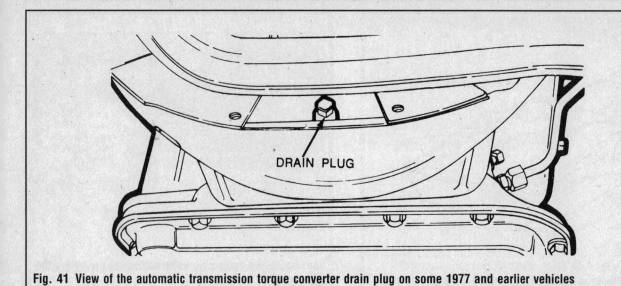

Fig. 41 View of the automatic transmission torque converter drain plug on some 1977 and earlier vehicles

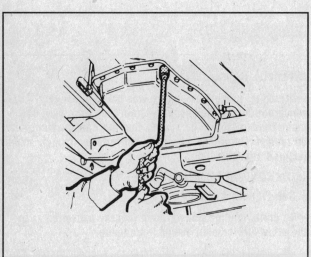

Fig. 42 Remove all but two transmission pan bolts, then loosen them and allow the transmission fluid to drain

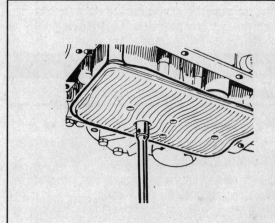

Fig. 44 Remove the filter attaching bolts and discard the old filter

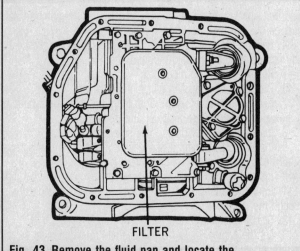

Fig. 43 Remove the fluid pan and locate the transmission filter

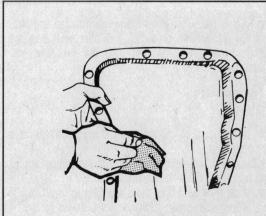

Fig. 45 Clean the transmission pan thoroughly and dry it before installing

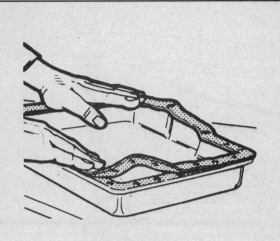

Fig. 46 Position a new gasket on the transmission pan

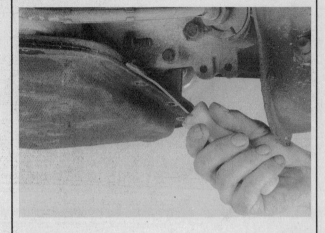

Loosen the two remaining bolts and tap or gently pry the pan loose . . .

14. Leave the gear selector in Neutral and check the fluid level. If necessary, add enough fluid to bring the level to the "ADD ONE PINT" mark on the dipstick.

✳✳ WARNING

Do not overfill the transmission!

15. Make sure the dipstick is fully seated and lower the vehicle.

WITHOUT DRAIN PLUG

1. Raise the front of the van and support it on jackstands. Place a large drain pan under the transmission.
2. Loosen the pan attaching bolts and tap the pan at one corner to break it loose.
3. Allow the fluid to drain into the drain pan.
4. After most of the fluid has drained, carefully remove the attaching bolts, lower the pan and drain the rest of the fluid.
5. Remove the filter attaching screws and remove the filter.

. . . and allow the fluid to drain. Remove the two remaining bolts and the transmission pan

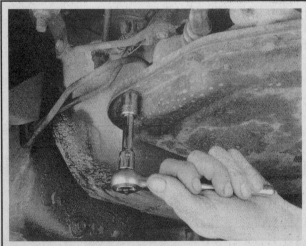

Place a large drain pan under the transmission and remove all but two of the pan bolts

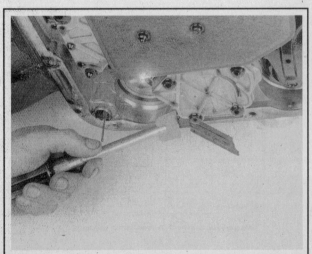

Remove any traces of the old transmission pan gasket from the mounting flange and the pan

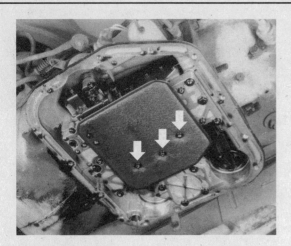

The transmission filter is held to the transmission by three attaching screws

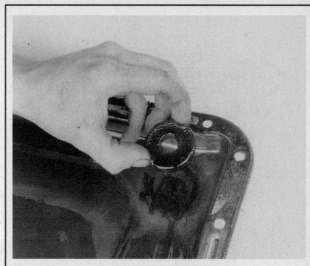

Clean the pan and its magnet before installing

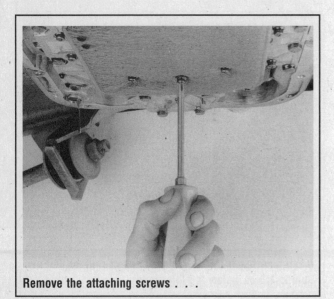

Remove the attaching screws . . .

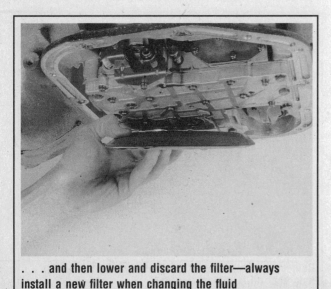

. . . and then lower and discard the filter—always install a new filter when changing the fluid

6. Install a new filter. Tighten the screws to 35 in. lbs.

7. Thoroughly clean the fluid pan with safe solvent and allow it to dry.

8. Using a new gasket, install the pan to the transmission. Tighten the attaching bolts to 150 in. lbs.

9. Pour four quarts of DEXRON®II automatic transmission fluid in through the dipstick tube.

10. Start the engine and allow it to run for a few minutes. With the parking brake set, slowly move the gear selector to each position. Return it to the Neutral position.

11. Check the fluid level. Add more fluid as necessary to bring it up to the "ADD ONE PINT" level.

12. Drive the van to bring the temperature up to normal operating temperature. Check the level again. It should be between the "Add" and "Full" marks.

Manual Transmission

1. Position the van on a level surface.

2. Place a pan of sufficient capacity under the transmission and remove the upper (fill) plug to provide a vent opening.

3. Remove the lower (drain) plug and allow all of the fluid to drain from the transmission. On the A-390 top-cover three speed, remove the lower extension to case mounting bolt to drain the transmission.

4. Reinstall the drain plug.

5. Pump in sufficient lubricant to bring the level to the bottom of the filler plug opening.

➡ **Chrysler Corporation has used a variety of transmission lubricants through the years covered in this manual. Please refer to the owner's manual for the proper Lubricant.**

Drive Axle

FLUID LEVEL CHECK

◗ **See Figure 47**

To check the axle lubricant level, remove the axle filler plug with the van level.

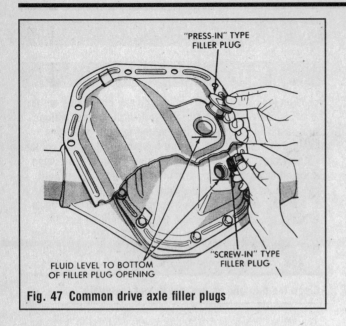

Fig. 47 Common drive axle filler plugs

"PRESS-IN" TYPE FILLER PLUG

FLUID LEVEL TO BOTTOM OF FILLER PLUG OPENING

"SCREW-IN" TYPE FILLER PLUG

➡**1976–80 9¾" and 10½" axles (300 series) have a pressed in rubber filler plug instead of the usual screw in plug.**

You can use a finger for a dipstick, being careful of sharp threads, and add lubricant with a suction gun. The lubricant level should be ½" below the filler plug hole on 8¼", 8⅜", 8¾" axles, and at the bottom of the filler plug hole on all the rest. Multipurpose gear lubricant meeting API GL-5 requirements or MOPAR hypoid lubricant can be used in conventional differential axles. Limited slip units, except in the 9¾" and 10½" axles, must use MOPAR hypoid lubricant. A MOPAR friction modifier additive is available to cure chatter and noise in these units.

9¾" and 10½" limited slip units must use MOPAR Sure-Grip lubricant. Gear lubricant viscosity depends on the anticipated temperatures: SAE 140 for above 90°F, SAE 90 for normal conditions (−10°F to 90°F), and SAE 80 for below −10°F. The factory fill is normally SAE 90. Multiviscosity lubricants may be used. Refer to the Rear Axle Identification Chart to find out which axle you have.

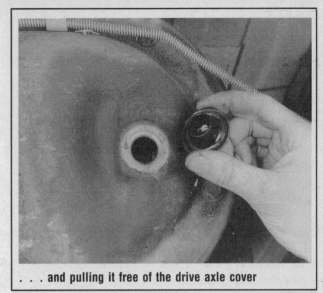

. . . and pulling it free of the drive axle cover

Insert your finger into the filler hole and confirm that the fluid is 1/2 in. below the filler hole

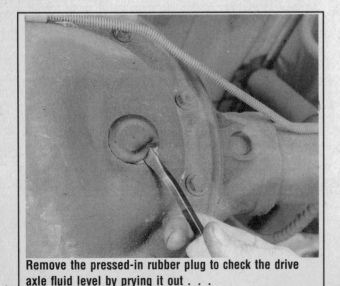

Remove the pressed-in rubber plug to check the drive axle fluid level by prying it out . . .

If the level is more than 1/2 in. below the filler hole, add gear oil to correct the level

DRAIN & REFILL

➥**Axles on Dodge and Plymouth vans are not equipped with drain plugs. The old lubricant must be drained by removing the differential housing cover.**

Most 1972 and later models no longer use a paper gasket under the rear axle cover. Instead of the paper gasket, a bead of RTV silicone sealant is now used in production. The sealant is available for service. The sealer should be applied as follows:

1. Scrape away any remains of the paper gasket.
2. Clean the cover surface with mineral spirits. Any axle lubricant on the cover or axle housing will prevent the sealant from taking.
3. Apply a 1/16–3/32" bead of sealant to the clean, dry cover flange. Apply the bead in a continuous bead along the bolt circle of the cover, looping inside the bolt holes as shown.
4. Allow the sealant to air dry.
5. Clean the carrier gasket flange and air dry. Install the cover. If, for any reason, the cover is not installed within 20 minutes of applying the sealant, remove the sealant and start over.

Cooling System

✳✳ CAUTION

Never remove the radiator cap under any conditions while the engine is running! Failure to follow these instructions could result in damage to the cooling system or engine and/or personal injury. To avoid having scalding hot coolant or steam blow out of the radiator, use extreme care when removing the radiator cap from a hot radiator. Wait until the engine has cooled, then wrap a thick cloth around the radiator cap and turn it slowly to the first stop. Step back while the pressure is released from the cooling system. When you are sure the pressure has been released, press down on the radiator cap (still have the cloth in position) turn and remove the radiator cap.

At least once every 2 years, the engine cooling system should be inspected, flushed, and refilled with fresh coolant. If the coolant is left in the system too long, it loses its ability to prevent rust and corrosion. If the coolant has been diluted with too much water, it won't protect against freezing.

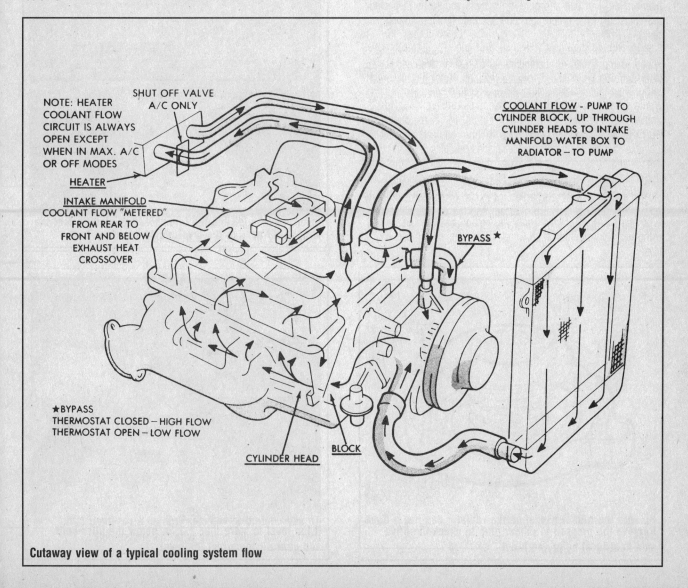

Cutaway view of a typical cooling system flow

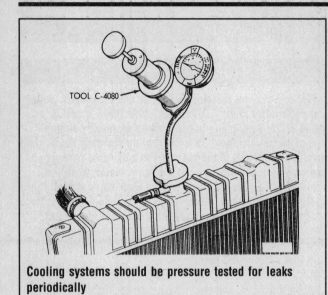

TOOL C-4080

Cooling systems should be pressure tested for leaks periodically

To add coolant to vehicles with a reservoir tank, remove the reservoir cap . . .

The radiator cap should be looked at for signs of age or deterioration. Fan belt and other drive belts should be inspected and adjusted to the proper tension (See Belt Tension Adjustment).

Hose clamps should be tightened, and soft or cracked hoses replaced. Damp spots, or accumulations of rust or dye near hoses, water pump or other areas, indicate possible leakage. This must be corrected before filling the system with fresh coolant.

CHECK THE RADIATOR CAP

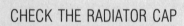

While you are checking the coolant level, check the radiator cap for a worn or cracked gasket. If the cap doesn't seal properly, fluid will be lost in the form of steam and the engine will overheat. Replace the cap with a new one, if necessary.

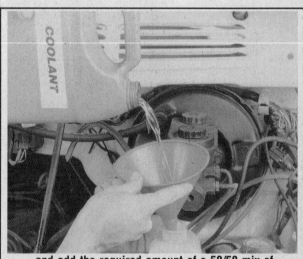

COOLANT

. . . and add the required amount of a 50/50 mix of water/antifreeze to the level indicated on the tank

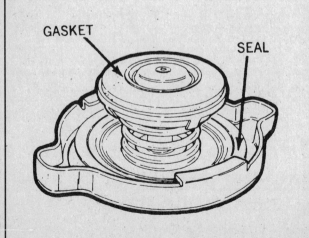

GASKET

SEAL

Be sure the rubber gasket on the radiator cap has a tight seal

To add coolant to vehicles without a reservoir tank, remove the radiator cap with the engine cold . . .

. . . and add a 50/50 mix of water/antifreeze until the level is 1/4–1/2 in. below the opening

CLEAN RADIATOR OF DEBRIS

Periodically clean any debris—leaves, paper, insects, etc.—from the radiator fins. Pick the large pieces off by hand. The smaller pieces can be washed away with water pressure from a hose.

Carefully straighten any bent radiator fins with a pair of needle nose pliers. Be careful—the fins are very soft! Don't wiggle the fins back and forth too much. Straighten them once and try not to move them again.

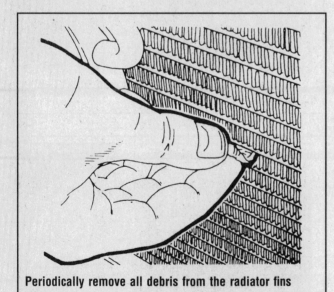

Periodically remove all debris from the radiator fins

DRAIN & REFILL

♦ See Figures 47a and 47b

Completely draining and refilling the cooling system every two years at least will remove the accumulated rust, scale and other deposits. Coolant in late model vans is a 50/50 mixture of ethylene glycol and water for year round use. Use a good quality anti-

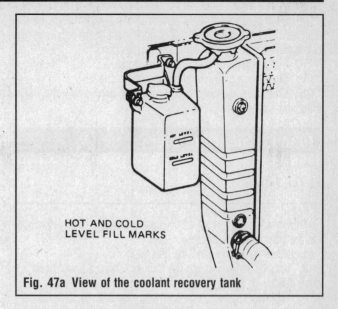

HOT AND COLD
LEVEL FILL MARKS

Fig. 47a View of the coolant recovery tank

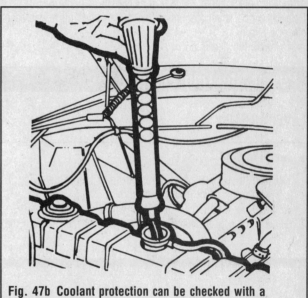

Fig. 47b Coolant protection can be checked with a simple float-type tester

freeze with water pump lubricants, rust inhibitors and other corrosion inhibitors along with acid neutralizers.

1. Remove the radiator cap. Drain the existing coolant by opening the radiator and engine drain petcocks, or disconnecting the bottom radiator hose at the radiator outlet.

➡**Before opening the radiator petcock, spray it with some penetrating lubricant.**

2. Close the petcock or re-connect the lower hose and fill the system with water.

3. Add a can of quality radiator flush.

4. Idle the engine until the upper radiator hose gets hot.

5. Drain the system again.

6. Repeat this process until the drained water is clear and free of scale.

7. Close all petcocks and connect all the hoses.

8. If equipped with a coolant recovery system, flush the reservoir with water and leave empty.

9. Determine the capacity of your cooling system (see the Capacities Chart). Add a 50/50 mix of quality antifreeze (ethylene glycol) and water to provide the desired protection.

10. Run the engine to operating temperature.

11. Stop the engine and check the coolant level.

12. Check the level of protection with an antifreeze tester, replace the cap and check for leaks.

Manual Steering Gear

LEVEL CHECK

This check is only required on models through 1973; later models are permanently lubricated.

1. Clean the area around the filler plug.

2. Remove the filler plug. The level of lubricant should just cover the worm gear.

3. If it is necessary to add lubricant, use SAE 90 Gear Oil. In extremely cold weather use SAE 80 Gear Oil or dilute SAE 90 Gear oil with a small amount of SAE 10W engine oil to decrease steering effort.

4. Install the filler plug.

Power Steering Pump

LEVEL CHECK

▶ **See Figure 48**

1. Clean the outside of the reservoir cover before removing it.

2. Remove the cover from the reservoir.

3. When the fluid is HOT, the level will be approximately ½–1″ below the top of the filler next or at the level indicated on the dipstick.

4. If the fluid is at ROOM TEMPERATURE (approx. 70°F), the level will be about 1½–2½″ below the top of the filler neck.

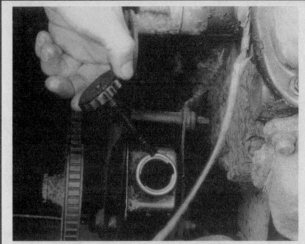

To check power steering fluid level on this V8 equipped van, remove the reservoir cap . . .

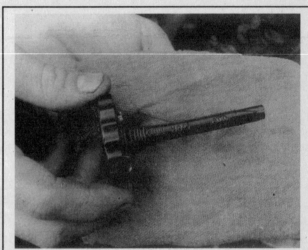

. . . and read the dipstick—it should read Full-HOT if the vehicle has been driven recently . . .

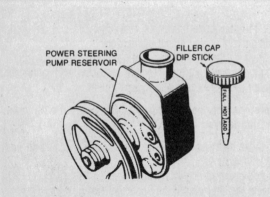

Fig. 48 View of the power steering pump reservoir and the filler cap

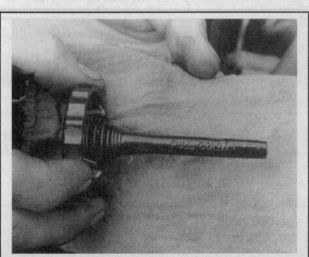

. . . or Full-COLD if the vehicle has been sitting for a while

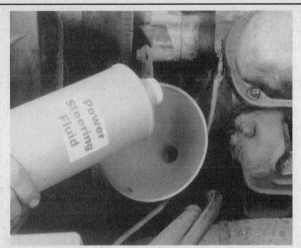

A funnel will help avoid any messy spills if topping off is necessary

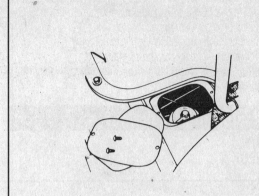

Fig. 49 Brake master cylinder access plate for the A-100 and A-108 models

The power steering pump location on an inline 6-cylinder engine (arrow) is similar to that of a V8 engine

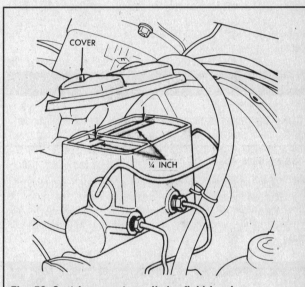

Fig. 50 Cast iron master cylinder fluid level

5. If it is necessary to add lubricant, use Chrysler Power Steering Fluid or its equivalent.

✳✳ WARNING

Never add gear oil or automatic transmission fluid!

Brake Master Cylinder

LEVEL CHECK

▶ **See Figures 49 and 50**

The master cylinder reservoir is located under the hood, on the left side firewall. Before removing the master cylinder reservoir cap, make sure the vehicle is resting on level ground and clean all dirt away from the top of the master cylinder. Pry off the retaining clip or unscrew the hold-down bolt and remove the cap.

Remove the cap(s) on the brake fluid reservoir. The level should be within 1/4 in. from the top

If fluid is needed, add the proper amount of DOT-3 brake fluid to correct the level

The brake fluid level should be within ¼″ (6mm) of the top of the reservoir.

If the level of the brake fluid is less than half the volume of the reservoir, it is advised that you check the brake system for leaks. Leaks in the hydraulic brake system most commonly occur at the wheel cylinder.

There is a rubber diaphragm in the top of the master cylinder cap. As the fluid level lowers in the reservoir due to normal brake shoe wear or leakage, the diaphragm takes up the space. This is to prevent the loss of brake fluid out the vented cap and contamination by dirt. After filling the master cylinder to the proper level with heavy duty brake fluid, but before replacing the cap, fold the rubber diaphragm up into the cap, then replace the cap in the reservoir and tighten the retaining bolt or snap the retaining clip into place.

Clutch Master Cylinder

LEVEL CHECK

The hydraulic fluid reservoirs on these systems are mounted on the firewall. Fluid level checks are performed like those on the brake hydraulic system. The proper fluid level is indicated by a step on the reservoir. Keep the reservoir topped up with DOT-3; do not overfill.

✳✳ CAUTION

Carefully clean the top and sides of the reservoir before opening, to prevent contamination of the system with dirt, etc. Remove the reservoir diaphragm before adding fluid, and replace after filling.

See the illustration of the hydraulic clutch assembly in Section 7.

Chassis Greasing

▶ **See Figure 51**

The lubrication chart indicates where the grease fittings are located. The vehicle should be greased according to the intervals in the Preventive Maintenance Schedule at the end of this chapter.

Water resistant EP chassis lubricant (grease) conforming to GM specification 6031-M should be used for all chassis grease points.

Every year or 7,500 miles the front suspension ball points, both upper and lower on each side of the van, must be greased. Most vans covered in this guide should be equipped with grease nipples on the ball joints, although some may have plugs which must be removed and nipples fitted.

✳✳ WARNING

Do not pump so much grease into the ball joint that excess grease squeezes out of the rubber boot. This destroys the watertight seal.

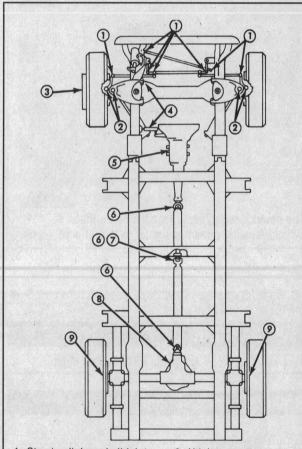

1. Steering linkage ball joints
2. Front suspension ball joints
3. Front wheel bearings
4. Clutch torque shaft
5. Transmission
6. U-joints
7. Slip spline (if equipped)
8. Rear axle
9. Rear wheel bearings

Fig. 51 Common chassis lubrication points

Jack up the front end of the van and safely support it with jackstands. Block the rear wheels and firmly apply the parking brake. If the van has been parked in temperatures below 20°F for any length of time, park it in a heated garage for an hour or so until the ball joints loosen up enough to accept the grease.

Depending on which front wheel you work on first, turn the wheel and tire outward, either full-lock right or full-lock left. You now have the ends of the upper and lower suspension control arms in front of you; the grease nipples are visible pointing up (top ball joint) and down (lower ball joint) through the end of each control arm. If the nipples are not accessible enough, remove the wheel and tire. Wipe all dirt and crud from the nipples or from around the plugs (if installed). If plugs are on the van, remove them and install grease nipples in the holes (nipples are available in various thread sizes at most auto parts stores). Using a hand operated, low pressure grease gun loaded with a quality chassis grease, grease the ball joint only until the rubber joint boot begins to swell out.

STEERING LINKAGE

◊ See Figure 52

The steering linkage should be greased at the same interval as the ball joints. Grease nipples are installed on the steering tie rod ends on most models. Wipe all dirt and crud from around the nipples at each tie rod end. Using a hand operated, low pressure grease gun loaded with a suitable chassis grease, grease the linkage until the old grease begins to squeeze out around the tie rod ends. Wipe off the nipples and any excess grease. Also grease the nipples on the steering idler arms.

PARKING BRAKE LINKAGE

Use chassis grease on the parking brake cable where it contacts the cable guides, levers and linkage.

TRANSMISSION LINKAGE & DRIVESHAFT

◊ See Figures 53, 54 and 55

Apply a small amount of clean engine oil to the kickdown and shift linkage points at 7,500 mile intervals. The driveshaft and U-

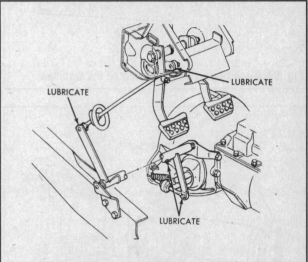

Fig. 53 Manual transmission clutch linkage lube fittings

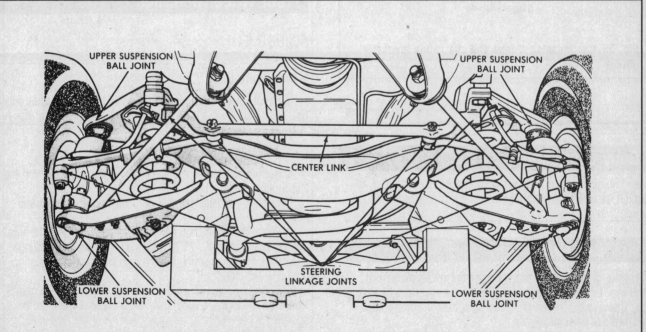

Fig. 52 Independent suspension steering linkage lube fittings

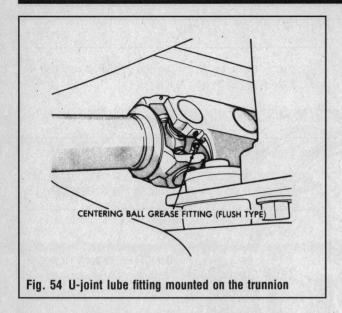

Fig. 54 U-joint lube fitting mounted on the trunnion

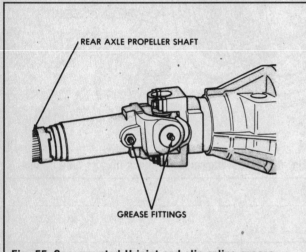

Fig. 55 Cap mounted U-joint and slip spline grease fittings

joints have grease nipples like the steering linkage and, therefore, are greased in the same manner.

Body Lubrication

HOOD LATCH & HINGES

Clean the latch surfaces and apply clean engine oil to the latch pilot bolts and the spring anchor. Also lubricate the hood hinges with engine oil. Use a chassis grease to lubricate all the pivot points in the latch release mechanism.

DOOR HINGES

▶ **See Figure 56**

The gas tank filler door and van doors should be wiped clean and lubricated with clean engine oil once a year. The door lock

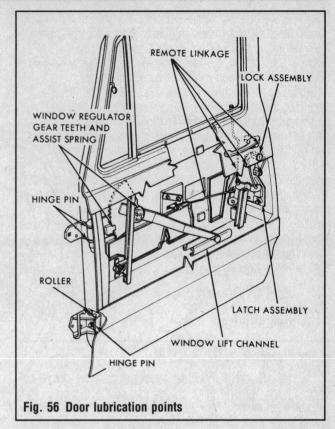

Fig. 56 Door lubrication points

cylinders and latch mechanisms should be lubricated periodically with a few drops of graphite lock lubricant or a few shots of silicone spray.

Front Wheel Bearings

ADJUSTMENT

▶ **See Figure 57**

The front wheels each rotate on a set of opposed, tapered roller bearings as shown in the accompanying illustration. The grease retainer at the inside of the hub prevents lubricant from leaking into the brake drum.

1. Raise and support the front end on jackstands.
2. Remove the grease cap and remove excess grease from the end of the spindle.
3. Remove the cotter pin and nut lock shown in the illustration.
4. Rotate the wheel, hub and drum assembly while tightening the adjusting nut to 17–25 ft. lbs. in order to seat the bearings.
5. Back off the adjusting nut ½, then retighten the adjusting nut to 10–15 inch lbs.
6. Locate the nut lock on the adjusting nut so that the castellations on the lock are lined up with the cotter pin hole in the spindle.
7. Install the new cotter pin, bending the ends of the cotter pin around the castellated flange of the nut lock.
8. Check the wheel for proper rotation, then install the grease cap. If the wheel still does not rotate properly, inspect and clean or replace the wheel bearings and cups.

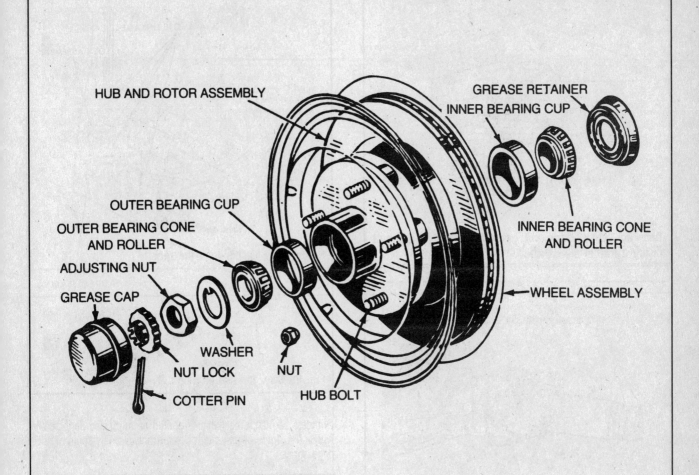

HUB AND ROTOR ASSEMBLY

GREASE RETAINER
INNER BEARING CUP

OUTER BEARING CUP

OUTER BEARING CONE
AND ROLLER

ADJUSTING NUT

GREASE CAP

INNER BEARING CONE
AND ROLLER

WASHER

NUT LOCK

NUT

COTTER PIN

HUB BOLT

WHEEL ASSEMBLY

Fig. 57 Exploded view of the front hub and bearing—models with disc brakes

REMOVAL, REPACKING, & INSTALLATION

▶ See Figure 58

Before handling the bearings, there are a few things that you should remember to do and not to do.

Remember to DO the following:

• Remove all outside dirt from the housing before exposing the bearing.

• Treat a used bearing as gently as you would a new one.

• Work with clean tools in clean surroundings.

• Use clean, dry canvas gloves, or at least clean, dry hands.

• Clean solvents and flushing fluids are a must.

• Use clean paper when laying out the bearings to dry.

• Protect disassembled bearings from rust and dirt. Cover them up.

• Use clean rags to wipe bearings.

• Keep the bearings in oil-proof paper when they are to be stored or are not in use.

• Clean the inside of the housing before replacing the bearing.

Do NOT do the following:

• Don't work in dirty surroundings.

Pry the dust cap from the hub taking care not to distort or damage its flange

Once the bent ends are cut, grasp the cotter pin and pull or pry it free of the spindle

Remove the washer from the spindle

If difficulty is encountered, gently tap on the pliers with a hammer to help free the cotter pin

With the nut and washer out of the way, the outer bearings may be removed from the hub

Loosen and remove the castellated nut from the spindle

Pull the hub and inner bearing assembly from the spindle

Use a small prytool to remove the old inner bearing seal

Thoroughly pack the bearing with fresh, high temperature wheel-bearing grease before installation

With the seal removed, the inner bearing may be withdrawn from the hub

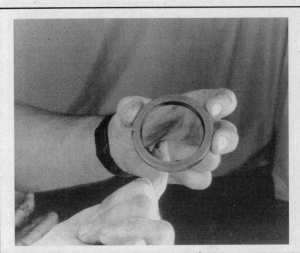

Apply a thin coat of fresh grease to the new inner bearing seal lip

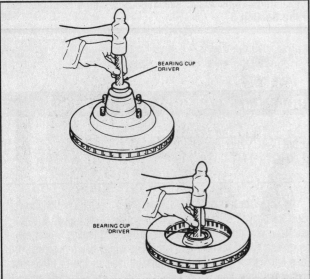

Fig. 58 If new bearing cups are to be installed, use the proper tool to avoid damaging the bearing surfaces

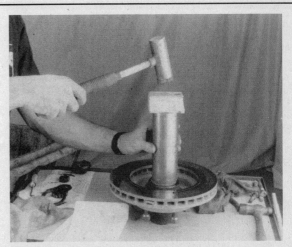

Use a suitably sized driver to install the inner bearing seal to the hub

With new or freshly packed bearings, tighten the nut while gently spinning the wheel, then adjust the bearings

After the bearings are adjusted, install the dust cap by gently tapping on the flange—DO NOT damage the cap by hammering on the center

• Don't use dirty, chipped or damaged tools.
• Try not to work on wooden work benches or use wooden mallets.
• Don't handle bearings with dirty or moist hands.
• Do not use gasoline for cleaning; use a safe solvent.
• Do not spin-dry bearings with compressed air. They will be damaged.
• Do not spin dirty bearings.
• Avoid using cotton waste or dirty cloths to wipe bearings.
• Try not to scratch or nick bearing surfaces.
• Do not allow the bearing to come in contact with dirt or rust at any time.

1. Raise and support the front end on jackstands.
2. Remove the wheel cover. Remove the wheel.
3. Remove the caliper from the disc and wire it to the underbody to prevent damage to the brake hose. See Section 9.
4. Remove the grease cap from the hub. Then, remove the cotter pin, nut lock, adjusting nut and flat washer from the spindle. Remove the outer bearing assembly from the hub.
5. Pull the hub and disc assembly off the wheel spindle.

6. Remove and discard the old grease retainer. Remove the inner bearing cone and roller assembly from the hub.
7. Clean all grease from the inner and outer bearing cups with solvent. Inspect the cups for pits, scratches, or excessive water. If the cups are damaged, remove them with a drift.
8. Clean the inner and outer cone and roller assemblies with solvent and shake them dry. If the cone and roller assemblies show excessive wear or damage, replace them with the bearing cups as a unit.
9. Clean the spindle and the inside of the hub with solvent to thoroughly remove all old grease.
10. Covering the spindle with a clean cloth, brush all loose dirt and dust from the brake assembly. Remove the cloth carefully so as to not get dirt on the spindle.
11. If the inner and/or outer bearing cups were removed, install the replacement cups on the hub. Be sure that the cups seat properly in the hub.
12. It is imperative that all old grease be removed from the bearings and surrounding surfaces before repacking. The new lithium-based grease is not compatible with the sodium base grease used in the past.
13. Install the hub and disc on the wheel spindle. To prevent damage to the grease retainer and spindle threads, keep the hub centered on the spindle.
14. Install the outer bearing cone and roller assembly and the flat washer on the spindle. Install the adjusting nut.
15. Adjust the wheel bearings by torquing the adjusting nut to 17–25 ft. lbs. for 1967–76 or 30–40 ft. lbs. for 1977–88, with the wheel rotating to seat the bearing. Then back off the adjusting nut ½ turn. Retighten the adjusting nut finger-tight. Install the locknut so that the castellations are aligned with the cotter pin hole. Install the cotter pin. Bend the ends of the cotter pin around the castellations of the locknut to prevent interference with the radio static collector in the grease cap. Install the grease cap.

✴✴ WARNING

New bolts must be used when servicing floating caliper units. The upper bolt must be tightened first. For floating caliper units, see Caliper Assembly Service in Section 9. For sliding caliper units, see Shoe and Lining Replacement in the Section 9.

16. Install the wheels.
17. Install the wheel cover.

Dana 60 or 70 Rear Axle Bearings

REMOVAL, REPACKING, INSTALLATION & ADJUSTMENT

The wheel bearings on the 200 and 300 series full floating rear axles are packed with wheel bearing grease. Axle lubricant can also flow into the wheel hubs and bearings; however, wheel bearing grease is the primary lubricant. The wheel bearing grease provides lubrication until the axle lubricant reaches the bearings during normal operation.

➡**Refer to Section 7 for these procedures.**

TRAILER TOWING

General Recommendations

Your vehicle was primarily designed to carry passengers and cargo. It is important to remember that towing a trailer will place additional loads on your vehicles engine, drivetrain, steering, braking and other systems. However, if you decide to tow a trailer, using the prior equipment is a must.

Local laws may require specific equipment such as trailer brakes or fender mounted mirrors. Check your local laws.

Trailer Weight

The weight of the trailer is the most important factor. A good weight-to-horsepower ratio is about 35:1, 35 lbs. of Gross Combined Weight (GCW) for every horsepower your engine develops. Multiply the engine's rated horsepower by 35 and subtract the weight of the vehicle passengers and luggage. The number remaining is the approximate ideal maximum weight you should tow, although a numerically higher axle ratio can help compensate for heavier weight.

Hitch (Tongue) Weight

Calculate the hitch weight in order to select a proper hitch. The weight of the hitch is usually 9–11% of the trailer gross weight and should be measured with the trailer loaded. Hitches fall into various categories: those that mount on the frame and rear bumper, the bolt-on type, or the weld-on distribution type used for larger trailers. Axle mounted or clamp-on bumper hitches should never be used.

Check the gross weight rating of your trailer. Tongue weight is usually figured as 10% of gross trailer weight. Therefore, a trailer with a maximum gross weight of 2000 lbs. will have a maximum tongue weight of 200 lbs. Class I trailers fall into this category. Class II trailers are those with a gross weight rating of 2000–3000 lbs., while Class III trailers fall into the 3500–6000 lbs. category. Class IV trailers are those over 6000 lbs. and are for use with fifth wheel trucks, only.

When you've determined the hitch that you'll need, follow the manufacturer's installation instructions, exactly, especially when it comes to fastener torques. The hitch will subjected to a lot of stress and good hitches come with hardened bolts. Never substitute an inferior bolt for a hardened bolt.

Recommended Equipment Checklist

Equipment	Class I Trailers Under 2,000 pounds	Class II Trailers 2,000-3,500 pounds	Class III Trailers 3,500-6,000 pounds	Class IV Trailers 6,000 pounds and up
Hitch	Frame or Equalizing	Equalizing	Equalizing	Fifth wheel Pick-up truck only
Tongue Load Limit**	Up to 200 pounds	200-350 pounds	350-600 pounds	600 pounds and up
Trailer Brakes	Not Required	Required	Required	Required
Safety Chain	3/16" diameter links	1/4" diameter links	5/16" diameter links	—
Fender Mounted Mirrors	Useful, but not necessary	Recommended	Recommended	Recommended
Turn Signal Flasher	Standard	Constant Rate or heavy duty	Constant Rate or heavy duty	Constant Rate or heavy duty
Coolant Recovery System	Recommended	Required	Required	Required
Transmission Oil Cooler	Recommended	Recommended	Recommended	Recommended
Engine Oil Cooler	Recommended	Recommended	Recommended	Recommended
Air Adjustable Shock Absorbers	Recommended	Recommended	Recommended	Recommended
Flex or Clutch Fan	Recommended	Recommended	Recommended	Recommended
Tires	***	***	***	***

NOTE The information in this chart is a guide Check the manufacturer's recommendations for your car if in doubt

* Local laws may require specific equipment such as trailer brakes or fender mounted mirrors Check your local laws
   Hitch weight is usually 10-15% of trailer gross weight and should be measured with trailer loaded

** Most manufacturer's do not recommend towing trailers of over 1,000 pounds with compacts Some intermediates cannot tow Class III trailers

*** Check manufacturer's recommendations for your specific car trailer combination
   —Does not apply

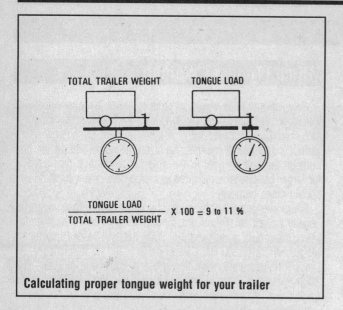

TOTAL TRAILER WEIGHT   TONGUE LOAD

$$\frac{\text{TONGUE LOAD}}{\text{TOTAL TRAILER WEIGHT}} \times 100 = 9 \text{ to } 11\%$$

Calculating proper tongue weight for your trailer

Cooling

ENGINE

Overflow Tank

One of the most common, if not THE most common, problems associated with trailer towing is engine overheating. If you have a cooling system without an expansion tank, you'll definitely need to get an aftermarket expansion tank kit, preferably one with at least a 2 quart capacity. These kits are easily installed on the radiator's overflow hose, and come with a pressure cap designed for expansion tanks.

Flex Fan

Another helpful accessory for vehicles using a belt-driven radiator fan is a flex fan. These fans are large diameter units designed to provide more airflow at low speeds, by using fan blades that have deeply cupped surfaces. The blades then flex, or flatten out, at high speed, when less cooling air is needed. These fans are far lighter in weight than stock fans, requiring less horsepower to drive them. Also, they are far quieter than stock fans. If you do decide to replace your stock fan with a flex fan, note that if your vehicle has a fan clutch, a spacer will be needed between the flex fan and water pump hub.

PUSHING AND TOWING

Pushing

Dodge and Plymouth vans equipped with manual transmission can be push started, although this is not recommended if you value the appearance of your van.

To push start, make sure that the bumpers of both vehicles are in reasonable alignment. Bent sheet metal and inflamed tempers are both predictable results from misaligned bumpers when push

Oil Cooler

Aftermarket engine oil coolers are helpful for prolonging engine oil life and reducing overall engine temperatures. Both of these factors increase engine life. While not absolutely necessary in towing Class I and some Class II trailers, they are recommended for heavier Class II and all Class III towing. Engine oil cooler systems usually consist of an adapter, screwed on in place of the oil filter, a remote filter mounting and a multi-tube, finned heat exchanger, which is mounted in front of the radiator or air conditioning condenser.

TRANSMISSION

An automatic transmission is usually recommended for trailer towing. Modern automatics have proven reliable and, of course, easy to operate, in trailer towing. The increased load of a trailer, however, causes an increase in the temperature of the automatic transmission fluid. Heat is the worst enemy of an automatic transmission. As the temperature of the fluid increases, the life of the fluid decreases.

It is essential, therefore, that you install an automatic transmission cooler. The cooler, which consists of a multi-tube, finned heat exchanger, is usually installed in front of the radiator or air conditioning compressor, and hooked in-line with the transmission cooler tank inlet line. Follow the cooler manufacturer's installation instructions.

Select a cooler of at least adequate capacity, based upon the combined gross weights of the vehicle and trailer.

Cooler manufacturers recommend that you use an aftermarket cooler in addition to, and not instead of, the present cooling tank in your radiator. If you do want to use it in place of the radiator cooling tank, get a cooler at least two sizes larger than normally necessary.

➡**A transmission cooler can, sometimes, cause slow or harsh shifting in the transmission during cold weather, until the fluid has a chance to come up to normal operating temperature. Some coolers can be purchased with or retrofitted with a temperature bypass valve which will allow fluid flow through the cooler only when the fluid has reached above a certain operating temperature.**

Handling A Trailer

Towing a trailer with ease and safety requires a certain amount of experience. It's a good idea to learn the feel of a trailer by practicing turning, stopping and backing in an open area such as an empty parking lot.

starting. Turn the ignition key to ON and engage high gear. Depress the clutch pedal. When a speed of about 10 mph is reached, slightly depress the gas pedal and slowly release the clutch. The engine should start. Never get an assist by having the vehicle towed. There is too much risk of the towed vehicle ramming the towing vehicle once it starts.

Vehicles equipped with automatic transmission cannot be started by pushing or towing.

Towing

Tow only in Neutral and at speeds not over 30 mph and distances not exceeding 15 miles. If either the transmission or rear axle is not functioning properly, or if the vehicle is to be towed more than 15 miles, the driveshaft should be disconnected or the van towed with the rear wheels off the ground.

JUMP STARTING A DEAD BATTERY

Whenever a vehicle is jump started, precautions must be followed in order to prevent the possibility of personal injury. Remember that batteries contain a small amount of explosive hydrogen gas which is a by-product of battery charging. Sparks should always be avoided when working around batteries, especially when attaching jumper cables. To minimize the possibility of accidental sparks, follow the procedure carefully.

✳✳ CAUTION

NEVER hook the batteries up in a series circuit or the entire electrical system will go up in smoke, including the starter!

Vehicles equipped with a diesel engine may utilize two 12 volt batteries. If so, the batteries are connected in a parallel circuit (positive terminal to positive terminal, negative terminal to negative terminal). Hooking the batteries up in parallel circuit increases battery cranking power without increasing total battery voltage output. Output remains at 12 volts. On the other hand, hooking two 12 volt batteries up in a series circuit (positive terminal to negative terminal, positive terminal to negative terminal) increases total battery output to 24 volts (12 volts plus 12 volts).

Jump Starting Precautions

• Be sure that both batteries are of the same voltage. Vehicles covered by this manual and most vehicles on the road today utilize a 12 volt charging system.
• Be sure that both batteries are of the same polarity (have the same terminal, in most cases NEGATIVE grounded).
• Be sure that the vehicles are not touching or a short could occur.

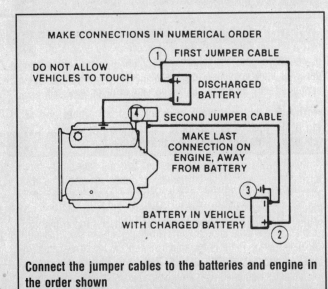

MAKE CONNECTIONS IN NUMERICAL ORDER

DO NOT ALLOW VEHICLES TO TOUCH

① FIRST JUMPER CABLE

DISCHARGED BATTERY

SECOND JUMPER CABLE

MAKE LAST CONNECTION ON ENGINE, AWAY FROM BATTERY

③

BATTERY IN VEHICLE WITH CHARGED BATTERY

②

Connect the jumper cables to the batteries and engine in the order shown

• On serviceable batteries, be sure the vent cap holes are not obstructed.
• Do not smoke or allow sparks anywhere near the batteries.
• In cold weather, make sure the battery electrolyte is not frozen. This can occur more readily in a battery that has been in a state of discharge.
• Do not allow electrolyte to contact your skin or clothing.

Jump Starting Procedure

1. Make sure that the voltages of the 2 batteries are the same. Most batteries and charging systems are of the 12 volt variety.
2. Pull the jumping vehicle (with the good battery) into a position so the jumper cables can reach the dead battery and that vehicle's engine. Make sure that the vehicles do NOT touch.
3. Place the transmissions/transaxles of both vehicles in **Neutral** (MT) or **P** (AT), as applicable, then firmly set their parking brakes.

➡**If necessary for safety reasons, the hazard lights on both vehicles may be operated throughout the entire procedure without significantly increasing the difficulty of jumping the dead battery.**

4. Turn all lights and accessories OFF on both vehicles. Make sure the ignition switches on both vehicles are turned to the **OFF** position.
5. Cover the battery cell caps with a rag, but do not cover the terminals.
6. Make sure the terminals on both batteries are clean and free of corrosion or proper electrical connection will be impeded. If necessary, clean the battery terminals before proceeding.
7. Identify the positive (+) and negative (−) terminals on both batteries.
8. Connect the first jumper cable to the positive (+) terminal of the dead battery, then connect the other end of that cable to the positive (+) terminal of the booster (good) battery.
9. Connect one end of the other jumper cable to the negative (−) terminal on the booster battery and the final cable clamp to an engine bolt head, alternator bracket or other solid, metallic point on the engine with the dead battery. Try to pick a ground on the engine that is positioned away from the battery in order to minimize the possibility of the 2 clamps touching should one loosen during the procedure. DO NOT connect this clamp to the negative (−) terminal of the bad battery.

✳✳ CAUTION

Be very careful to keep the jumper cables away from moving parts (cooling fan, belts, etc.) on both engines.

10. Check to make sure that the cables are routed away from any moving parts, then start the donor vehicle's engine. Run the

engine at moderate speed for several minutes to allow the dead battery a chance to receive some initial charge.

11. With the donor vehicle's engine still running slightly above idle, try to start the vehicle with the dead battery. Crank the engine for no more than 10 seconds at a time and let the starter cool for at least 20 seconds between tries. If the vehicle does not start in 3 tries, it is likely that something else is also wrong or that the battery needs additional time to charge.

12. Once the vehicle is started, allow it to run at idle for a few seconds to make sure that it is operating properly.

13. Turn ON the headlights, heater blower and, if equipped, the rear defroster of both vehicles in order to reduce the severity of voltage spikes and subsequent risk of damage to the vehicles' electrical systems when the cables are disconnected. This step is especially important to any vehicle equipped with computer control modules.

14. Carefully disconnect the cables in the reverse order of connection. Start with the negative cable that is attached to the engine ground, then the negative cable on the donor battery. Disconnect the positive cable from the donor battery and finally, disconnect the positive cable from the formerly dead battery. Be careful when disconnecting the cables from the positive terminals not to allow the alligator clips to touch any metal on either vehicle or a short and sparks will occur.

JUMP STARTING A DUAL-BATTERY DIESEL

Vans equipped with the diesel engine utilize two 12 volt batteries, one on either side of the engine compartment. The batteries are connected in a parallel circuit (positive terminal to positive terminal, negative terminal to negative terminal). Hooking the batteries up in parallel circuit increases battery cranking power without increasing total battery voltage output. Output remains at 12 volts. On the other hand, hooking two 12 volt batteries up in a series circuit (positive terminal to negative terminal, positive terminal to negative terminal) increases total battery output to 24 volts (12 volts plus 12 volts).

✳✳ WARNING

NEVER hook the batteries up in a series circuit or the entire electrical system will go up in smoke, including the starter.

In the event that a diesel pickup needs to be jump started, use the following procedure.
1. Turn all lights off.
2. Turn on the heater blower motor to remove transient voltage.

3. Connect one jumper cable to the passenger side battery positive (+) terminal and the other cable clamp to the positive (+) terminal to the booster (good) battery.

4. Connect one end of the other jumper cable to the negative (−) terminal of the booster (good) battery and the other cable clamp to an engine bolt head, alternator bracket or other solid, metallic point on the diesel engine. DO NOT connect this clamp to the negative (−) terminal of the bad battery.

✳✳ CAUTION

Be very careful to keep the jumper cables away from moving parts (cooling fan, belts, etc.) on both engines.

5. Start the engine of the donor van and run it at moderate speed.
6. Start the engine of the diesel.
7. When the diesel starts, remove the cable from the engine block before disconnecting the positive terminal.

JACKING

Your vehicle was supplied with a jack for emergency road repairs. This jack is fine for changing a flat tire or other short term procedures not requiring you to go beneath the vehicle. If it is used in an emergency situation, carefully follow the instructions provided either with the jack or in your owner's manual. Do not attempt to use the jack on any portions of the vehicle other than specified by the vehicle manufacturer. Always block the diagonally opposite wheel when using a jack.

A more convenient way of jacking is the use of a garage or floor jack.

Never place the jack under the radiator, engine or transmission components. Severe and expensive damage will result when the jack is raised. Additionally, never jack under the floorpan or bodywork; the metal will deform.

Whenever you plan to work under the vehicle, you must support it on jackstands or ramps. Never use cinder blocks or stacks of wood to support the vehicle, even if you're only going to be under it for a few minutes. Never crawl under the vehicle when it is supported only by the tire-changing jack or other floor jack.

➡ **Always position a block of wood or small rubber pad on top of the jack or jackstand to protect the lifting point's finish when lifting or supporting the vehicle.**

Small hydraulic, screw, or scissors jacks are satisfactory for raising the vehicle. Drive-on trestles or ramps are also a handy and safe way to both raise and support the vehicle. Be careful though, some ramps may be too steep to drive your vehicle onto without scraping the front bottom panels. Never support the vehicle on any suspension member (unless specifically instructed to do so by a repair manual) or by an underbody panel.

Jacking Precautions

The following safety points cannot be overemphasized:
• Always block the opposite wheel or wheels to keep the vehicle from rolling off the jack.
• When raising the front of the vehicle, firmly apply the parking brake.
• When the drive wheels are to remain on the ground, leave the vehicle in gear to help prevent it from rolling.
• Always use jackstands to support the vehicle when you are working underneath. Place the stands beneath the vehicle's jacking brackets. Before climbing underneath, rock the vehicle a bit to make sure it is firmly supported.

Jacking Points

1967–69 VEHICLES

An axle type jack is provided for emergency road service. When raising the front end of the vehicle, place the jack under the front spring, forward of the axle. When raising the rear end, place the jack under the axle next to the spring hanger.

✳✳ CAUTION

Do not attempt to raise one side of the van with a floor jack midway between the front and rear wheels. This will result in a permanent damage to the body.

1970–88 VEHICLES

A jack may be used under the rear axle at the spring U-bolts or under the front suspension crossmember in the reinforced area inboard and next to the lower control arm pivot.

Place the jackstand near the lower control arm pivot point, beneath the crossmember . . .

. . . or under the front frame rail

Raise the front end of the vehicle by jacking under the center crossmember

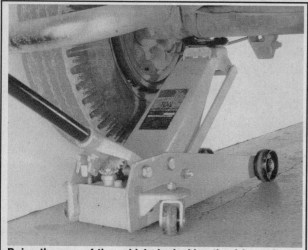

Raise the rear of the vehicle by jacking the drive axle at the spring U-bolts

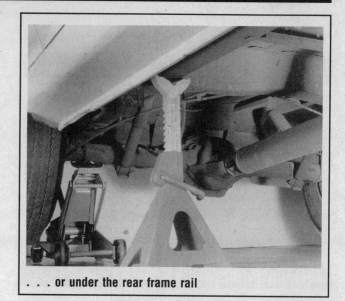

. . . or under the rear frame rail

Place the jackstand under the axle tube . . .

✳✳ CAUTION

Never use a floor jack under any part of the underbody. Do not attempt to raise one entire side of the vehicle by placing a jack midway between the front and rear wheels. This may result in permanent damage to the body!

For models supplied with a bumper jack, notches are provided in the bumper for raising the vehicle.

HOW TO BUY A USED VEHICLE

Many people believe that a two or three year old used car or truck is a better buy than a new vehicle. This may be true as most new vehicles suffer the heaviest depreciation in the first two years and, at three years old, a vehicle is usually not old enough to present a lot of costly repair problems. But keep in mind, when buying a non-warranted automobile, there are no guarantees. Whatever the age of the used vehicle you might want to purchase, this section and a little patience should increase your chances of selecting one that is safe and dependable.

Tips

1. First decide what model you want, and how much you want to spend.
2. Check the used car lots and your local newspaper ads. Privately owned vehicles are usually less expensive, however, you may not get a warranty that, in many cases, comes with a used vehicle purchased from a lot. Of course, some aftermarket warranties may not be worth the extra money, so this is a point you will have to debate and consider based on your priorities.
3. Never shop at night. The glare of the lights make it easy to miss faults on the body caused by accident or rust repair.
4. Try to get the name and phone number of the previous owner. Contact him/her and ask about the vehicle. If the owner of a lot refuses this information, look for a vehicle somewhere else.

A private seller can tell you about the vehicle and maintenance. But remember, there's no law requiring honesty from private citizens selling used vehicles. There is a law that forbids tampering with or turning back the odometer mileage. This includes both the private citizen and the lot owner. The law also requires that the seller or anyone transferring ownership of the vehicle must provide the buyer with a signed statement indicating the mileage on the odometer at the time of transfer.

5. You may wish to contact the National Highway Traffic Safety Administration (NHTSA) to find out if the vehicle has ever been included in a manufacturer's recall. Write down the year, model and serial number before you buy the vehicle, then contact NHTSA (there should be a 1-800 number that your phone company's information line can supply). If the vehicle was listed for a recall, make sure the needed repairs were made.

6. Refer to the Used Vehicle Checklist in this section and check all the items on the vehicle you are considering. Some items are more important than others. Only you know how much money you can afford for repairs, and depending on the price of the vehicle, may consider performing any needed work yourself. Beware, however, of trouble in areas that will affect operation, safety or emission. Problems in the Used Vehicle Checklist break down as follows:

• Numbers 1–8: Two or more problems in these areas indicate a lack of maintenance. You should beware.

• Numbers 9–13: Problems here tend to indicate a lack of proper care, however, these can usually be corrected with a tune-up or relatively simple parts replacement.

• Numbers 14–17: Problems in the engine or transmission can be very expensive. Unless you are looking for a project, walk away from any vehicle with problems in 2 or more of these areas.

7. If you are satisfied with the apparent condition of the vehicle, take it to an independent diagnostic center or mechanic for a complete check. If you have a state inspection program, have it inspected immediately before purchase, or specify on the bill of sale that the sale is conditional on passing state inspection.

8. Road test the vehicle—refer to the Road Test Checklist in this section. If your original evaluation and the road test agree—the rest is up to you.

USED VEHICLE CHECKLIST

➥**The numbers on the illustrations refer to the numbers on this checklist.**

1. Mileage: Average mileage is about 12,000–15,000 miles per year. More than average mileage may indicate hard usage or could indicate many highway miles (which could be less detrimental than half as many tough around town miles).

2. Paint: Check around the tailpipe, molding and windows for overspray indicating that the vehicle has been repainted.

3. Rust: Check fenders, doors, rocker panels, window moldings, wheelwells, floorboards, under floormats, and in the trunk for signs of rust. Any rust at all will be a problem. There is no way to permanently stop the spread of rust, except to replace the part or panel.

➥**If rust repair is suspected, try using a magnet to check for body filler. A magnet should stick to the sheet metal parts of the body, but will not adhere to areas with large amounts of filler.**

4. Body appearance: Check the moldings, bumpers, grille, vinyl roof, glass, doors, trunk lid and body panels for general overall condition. Check for misalignment, loose hold-down clips, ripples, scratches in glass, welding in the trunk, severe misalignment of body panels or ripples, any of which may indicate crash work.

5. Leaks: Get down and look under the vehicle. There are no normal leaks, other than water from the air conditioner evaporator.

6. Tires: Check the tire air pressure. One old trick is to pump the tire pressure up to make the vehicle roll easier. Check the

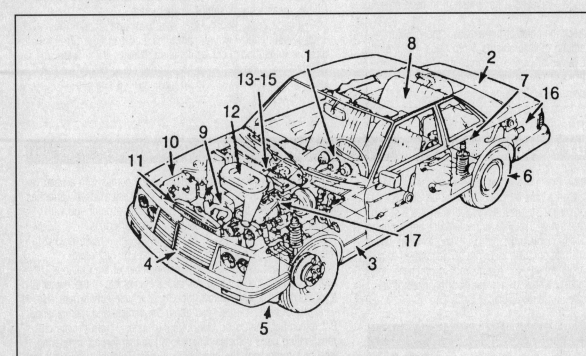

Each of the numbered items should be checked when purchasing a used vehicle

tread wear, then open the trunk and check the spare too. Uneven wear is a clue that the front end may need an alignment.

7. Shock absorbers: Check the shock absorbers by forcing downward sharply on each corner of the vehicle. Good shocks will not allow the vehicle to bounce more than once after you let go.

8. Interior: Check the entire interior. You're looking for an interior condition that agrees with the overall condition of the vehicle. Reasonable wear is expected, but be suspicious of new seat covers on sagging seats, new pedal pads, and worn armrests. These indicate an attempt to cover up hard use. Pull back the carpets and look for evidence of water leaks or flooding. Look for missing hardware, door handles, control knobs, etc. Check lights and signal operations. Make sure all accessories (air conditioner, heater, radio, etc.) work. Check windshield wiper operation.

9. Belts and Hoses: Open the hood, then check all belts and hoses for wear, cracks or weak spots.

10. Battery: Low electrolyte level, corroded terminals and/or cracked case indicate a lack of maintenance.

11. Radiator: Look for corrosion or rust in the coolant indicating a lack of maintenance.

12. Air filter: A severely dirty air filter would indicate a lack of maintenance.

13. Ignition wires: Check the ignition wires for cracks, burned spots, or wear. Worn wires will have to be replaced.

14. Oil level: If the oil level is low, chances are the engine uses oil or leaks. Beware of water in the oil (there is probably a cracked block or bad head gasket), excessively thick oil (which is often used to quiet a noisy engine), or thin, dirty oil with a distinct gasoline smell (this may indicate internal engine problems).

15. Automatic Transmission: Pull the transmission dipstick out when the engine is running. The level should read FULL, and the fluid should be clear or bright red. Dark brown or black fluid that has distinct burnt odor, indicates a transmission in need of repair or overhaul.

16. Exhaust: Check the color of the exhaust smoke. Blue smoke indicates, among other problems, worn rings. Black smoke can indicate burnt valves or carburetor problems. Check the exhaust system for leaks; it can be expensive to replace.

17. Spark Plugs: Remove one or all of the spark plugs (the most accessible will do, though all are preferable). An engine in good condition will show plugs with a light tan or gray deposit on the firing tip.

ROAD TEST CHECKLIST

1. Engine Performance: The vehicle should be peppy whether cold or warm, with adequate power and good pickup. It should respond smoothly through the gears.

2. Brakes: They should provide quick, firm stops with no noise, pulling or brake fade.

3. Steering: Sure control with no binding harshness, or looseness and no shimmy in the wheel should be expected. Noise or vibration from the steering wheel when turning the vehicle means trouble.

4. Clutch (Manual Transmission/Transaxle): Clutch action should give quick, smooth response with easy shifting. The clutch pedal should have free-play before it disengages the clutch. Start the engine, set the parking brake, put the transmission in first gear and slowly release the clutch pedal. The engine should begin to stall when the pedal is ½–¾ of the way up.

5. Automatic Transmission/Transaxle: The transmission should shift rapidly and smoothly, with no noise, hesitation, or slipping.

6. Differential: No noise or thumps should be present. Differentials have no normal leaks.

7. Driveshaft/Universal Joints: Vibration and noise could mean driveshaft problems. Clicking at low speed or coast conditions means worn U-joints.

8. Suspension: Try hitting bumps at different speeds. A vehicle that bounces excessively has weak shock absorbers or struts. Clunks mean worn bushings or ball joints.

9. Frame/Body: Wet the tires and drive in a straight line. Tracks should show two straight lines, not four. Four tire tracks indicate a frame/body bent by collision damage. If the tires can't be wet for this purpose, have a friend drive along behind you and see if the vehicle appears to be traveling in a straight line.

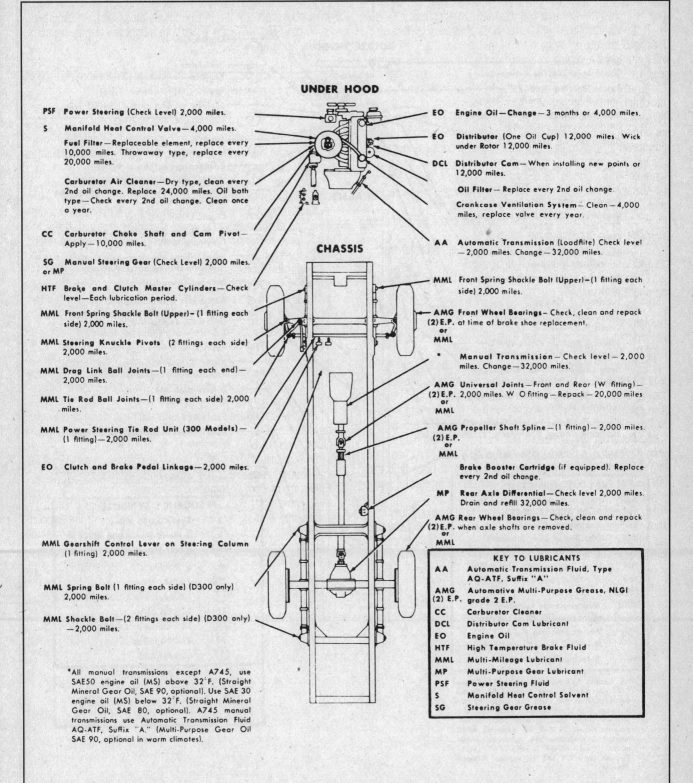

UNDER HOOD

PSF   Power Steering (Check Level) 2,000 miles.

S   Manifold Heat Control Valve—4,000 miles.

Fuel Filter—Replaceable element, replace every 10,000 miles. Throwaway type, replace every 20,000 miles.

Carburetor Air Cleaner—Dry type, clean every 2nd oil change. Replace 24,000 miles. Oil bath type—Check every 2nd oil change. Clean once a year.

CC   Carburetor Choke Shaft and Cam Pivot—Apply—10,000 miles.

SG   Manual Steering Gear (Check Level) 2,000 miles.
or MP

HTF   Brake and Clutch Master Cylinders—Check level—Each lubrication period.

MML   Front Spring Shackle Bolt (Upper)—(1 fitting each side) 2,000 miles.

MML   Steering Knuckle Pivots (2 fittings each side) 2,000 miles.

MML   Drag Link Ball Joints—(1 fitting each end)—2,000 miles.

MML   Tie Rod Ball Joints—(1 fitting each side) 2,000 miles.

MML   Power Steering Tie Rod Unit (300 Models)—(1 fitting)—2,000 miles.

EO   Clutch and Brake Pedal Linkage—2,000 miles.

MML   Gearshift Control Lever on Steering Column (1 fitting) 2,000 miles.

MML   Spring Bolt (1 fitting each side) (D300 only) 2,000 miles.

MML   Shackle Bolt—(2 fittings each side) (D300 only) —2,000 miles.

*All manual transmissions except A745, use SAE50 engine oil (MS) above 32°F. (Straight Mineral Gear Oil, SAE 90, optional). Use SAE 30 engine oil (MS) below 32°F. (Straight Mineral Gear Oil, SAE 80, optional). A745 manual transmissions use Automatic Transmission Fluid AQ-ATF, Suffix "A." (Multi-Purpose Gear Oil SAE 90, optional in warm climates).

CHASSIS

EO   Engine Oil—Change—3 months or 4,000 miles.

EO   Distributor (One Oil Cup) 12,000 miles Wick under Rotor 12,000 miles.

DCL   Distributor Cam—When installing new points or 12,000 miles.

Oil Filter—Replace every 2nd oil change.

Crankcase Ventilation System—Clean—4,000 miles, replace valve every year.

AA   Automatic Transmission (Loadflite) Check level—2,000 miles. Change—32,000 miles.

MML   Front Spring Shackle Bolt (Upper)—(1 fitting each side) 2,000 miles.

AMG   Front Wheel Bearings—Check, clean and repack
(2) E.P.   at time of brake shoe replacement.
or
MML

*   Manual Transmission—Check level—2,000 miles. Change—32,000 miles.

AMG   Universal Joints—Front and Rear (W fitting)—
(2) E.P.   2,000 miles. W O fitting—Repack—20,000 miles
or
MML

AMG   Propeller Shaft Spline—(1 fitting)—2,000 miles.
(2) E.P.
or
MML

Brake Booster Cartridge (if equipped). Replace every 2nd oil change.

MP   Rear Axle Differential—Check level 2,000 miles. Drain and refill 32,000 miles.

AMG   Rear Wheel Bearings—Check, clean and repack
(2) E.P.   when axle shafts are removed.
or
MML

KEY TO LUBRICANTS	
AA	Automatic Transmission Fluid, Type AQ-ATF, Suffix "A"
AMG (2) E.P.	Automotive Multi-Purpose Grease, NLGI grade 2 E.P.
CC	Carburetor Cleaner
DCL	Distributor Cam Lubricant
EO	Engine Oil
HTF	High Temperature Brake Fluid
MML	Multi-Mileage Lubricant
MP	Multi-Purpose Gear Lubricant
PSF	Power Steering Fluid
S	Manifold Heat Control Solvent
SG	Steering Gear Grease

Fig. 59 Lubrication interval and location chart for 1967 100 thru 300 models

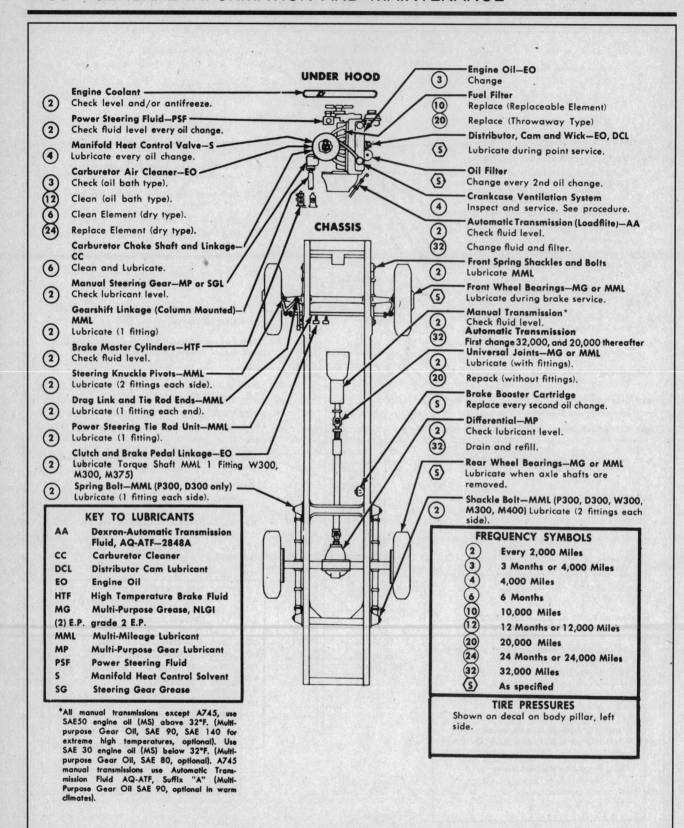

UNDER HOOD

Engine Coolant
(2) Check level and/or antifreeze.

Power Steering Fluid—PSF
(2) Check fluid level every oil change.

Manifold Heat Control Valve—S
(4) Lubricate every oil change.

Carburetor Air Cleaner—EO
(3) Check (oil bath type).
(12) Clean (oil bath type).
(6) Clean Element (dry type).
(24) Replace Element (dry type).

Carburetor Choke Shaft and Linkage—CC
(6) Clean and Lubricate.

Manual Steering Gear—MP or SGL
(2) Check lubricant level.

Gearshift Linkage (Column Mounted)—MML
(2) Lubricate (1 fitting)

Brake Master Cylinders—HTF
(2) Check fluid level.

Steering Knuckle Pivots—MML
(2) Lubricate (2 fittings each side).

Drag Link and Tie Rod Ends—MML
(2) Lubricate (1 fitting each end).

Power Steering Tie Rod Unit—MML
(2) Lubricate (1 fitting).

Clutch and Brake Pedal Linkage—EO
(2) Lubricate Torque Shaft MML 1 Fitting W300, M300, M375)

Spring Bolt—MML (P300, D300 only)
(2) Lubricate (1 fitting each side).

CHASSIS

Engine Oil—EO
(3) Change

Fuel Filter
(10) Replace (Replaceable Element)
(20) Replace (Throwaway Type)

Distributor, Cam and Wick—EO, DCL
(S) Lubricate during point service.

Oil Filter
(S) Change every 2nd oil change.

Crankcase Ventilation System
(4) Inspect and service. See procedure.

Automatic Transmission (Loadflite)—AA
(2) Check fluid level.
(32) Change fluid and filter.

Front Spring Shackles and Bolts
(2) Lubricate MML

Front Wheel Bearings—MG or MML
(S) Lubricate during brake service.

Manual Transmission*
(2) Check fluid level.
Automatic Transmission
(32) First change 32,000, and 20,000 thereafter

Universal Joints—MG or MML
(2) Lubricate (with fittings).
(20) Repack (without fittings).

Brake Booster Cartridge
(S) Replace every second oil change.

Differential—MP
(2) Check lubricant level.
(32) Drain and refill.

Rear Wheel Bearings—MG or MML
(S) Lubricate when axle shafts are removed.

Shackle Bolt—MML (P300, D300, W300, M300, M400) Lubricate (2 fittings each side).
(2)

KEY TO LUBRICANTS

AA	Dexron-Automatic Transmission Fluid, AQ-ATF—2848A
CC	Carburetor Cleaner
DCL	Distributor Cam Lubricant
EO	Engine Oil
HTF	High Temperature Brake Fluid
MG	Multi-Purpose Grease, NLGI (2) E.P. grade 2 E.P.
MML	Multi-Mileage Lubricant
MP	Multi-Purpose Gear Lubricant
PSF	Power Steering Fluid
S	Manifold Heat Control Solvent
SG	Steering Gear Grease

*All manual transmissions except A745, use SAE50 engine oil (MS) above 32°F. (Multi-purpose Gear Oil, SAE 90, SAE 140 for extreme high temperatures, optional). Use SAE 30 engine oil (MS) below 32°F. (Multi-purpose Gear Oil, SAE 80, optional). A745 manual transmissions use Automatic Transmission Fluid AQ-ATF, Suffix "A" (Multi-Purpose Gear Oil SAE 90, optional in warm climates).

FREQUENCY SYMBOLS

(2)	Every 2,000 Miles
(3)	3 Months or 4,000 Miles
(4)	4,000 Miles
(6)	6 Months
(10)	10,000 Miles
(12)	12 Months or 12,000 Miles
(20)	20,000 Miles
(24)	24 Months or 24,000 Miles
(32)	32,000 Miles
(S)	As specified

TIRE PRESSURES
Shown on decal on body pillar, left side.

Fig. 60 Lubrication interval and location chart for 1968–71 100 thru 300 models

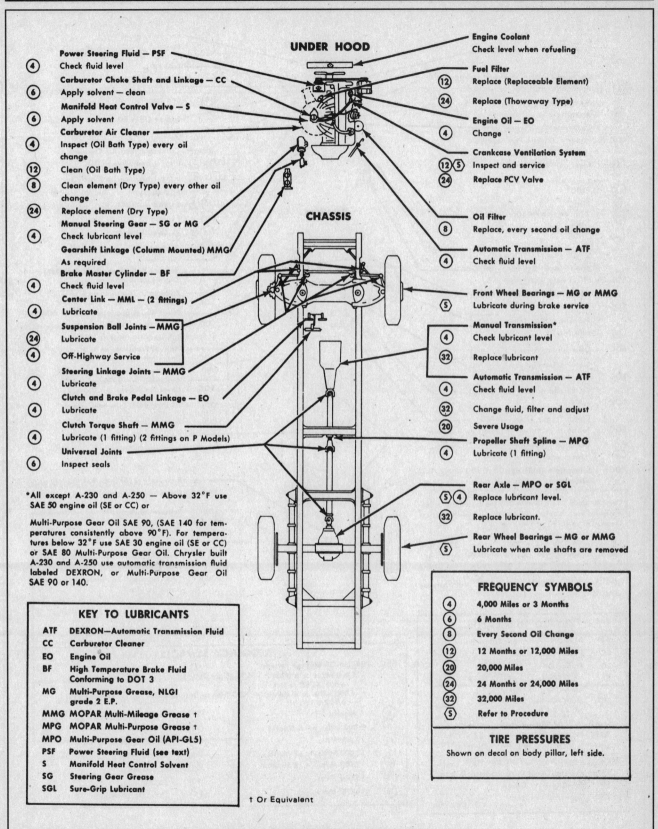

UNDER HOOD

Engine Coolant
Check level when refueling

④ Power Steering Fluid — PSF
Check fluid level

⑥ Carburetor Choke Shaft and Linkage — CC
Apply solvent — clean

⑥ Manifold Heat Control Valve — S
Apply solvent

Carburetor Air Cleaner

④ Inspect (Oil Bath Type) every oil change

⑫ Clean (Oil Bath Type)

⑧ Clean element (Dry Type) every other oil change

㉔ Replace element (Dry Type)

Manual Steering Gear — SG or MG
④ Check lubricant level

Gearshift Linkage (Column Mounted) MMG
As required

Brake Master Cylinder — BF
④ Check fluid level

Center Link — MML — (2 fittings)
④ Lubricate

Suspension Ball Joints — MMG
㉔ Lubricate
④ Off-Highway Service

Steering Linkage Joints — MMG
④ Lubricate

Clutch and Brake Pedal Linkage — EO
④ Lubricate

Clutch Torque Shaft — MMG
④ Lubricate (1 fitting) (2 fittings on P Models)

Universal Joints
⑥ Inspect seals

⑫ Fuel Filter
Replace (Replaceable Element)

㉔ Replace (Thowaway Type)

④ Engine Oil — EO
Change

Crankcase Ventilation System
⑫⑤ Inspect and service
㉔ Replace PCV Valve

Oil Filter
⑧ Replace, every second oil change

Automatic Transmission — ATF
④ Check fluid level

Front Wheel Bearings — MG or MMG
⑤ Lubricate during brake service

Manual Transmission*
④ Check lubricant level
㉜ Replace lubricant

Automatic Transmission — ATF
④ Check fluid level
㉜ Change fluid, filter and adjust
⑳ Severe Usage

Propeller Shaft Spline — MPG
④ Lubricate (1 fitting)

Rear Axle — MPO or SGL
⑤④ Replace lubricant level.
㉜ Replace lubricant.

Rear Wheel Bearings — MG or MMG
⑤ Lubricate when axle shafts are removed

CHASSIS

*All except A-230 and A-250 — Above 32°F use SAE 50 engine oil (SE or CC) or

Multi-Purpose Gear Oil SAE 90, (SAE 140 for temperatures consistently above 90°F). For temperatures below 32°F use SAE 30 engine oil (SE or CC) or SAE 80 Multi-Purpose Gear Oil. Chrysler built A-230 and A-250 use automatic transmission fluid labeled DEXRON, or Multi-Purpose Gear Oil SAE 90 or 140.

KEY TO LUBRICANTS

ATF	DEXRON—Automatic Transmission Fluid
CC	Carburetor Cleaner
EO	Engine Oil
BF	High Temperature Brake Fluid Conforming to DOT 3
MG	Multi-Purpose Grease, NLGI grade 2 E.P.
MMG	MOPAR Multi-Mileage Grease †
MPG	MOPAR Multi-Purpose Grease †
MPO	Multi-Purpose Gear Oil (API-GL5)
PSF	Power Steering Fluid (see text)
S	Manifold Heat Control Solvent
SG	Steering Gear Grease
SGL	Sure-Grip Lubricant

FREQUENCY SYMBOLS

④	4,000 Miles or 3 Months
⑥	6 Months
⑧	Every Second Oil Change
⑫	12 Months or 12,000 Miles
⑳	20,000 Miles
㉔	24 Months or 24,000 Miles
㉜	32,000 Miles
⑤	Refer to Procedure

TIRE PRESSURES

Shown on decal on body pillar, left side.

† Or Equivalent

Fig. 61 Lubrication interval and location chart for 1972-74 100 thru 300 models

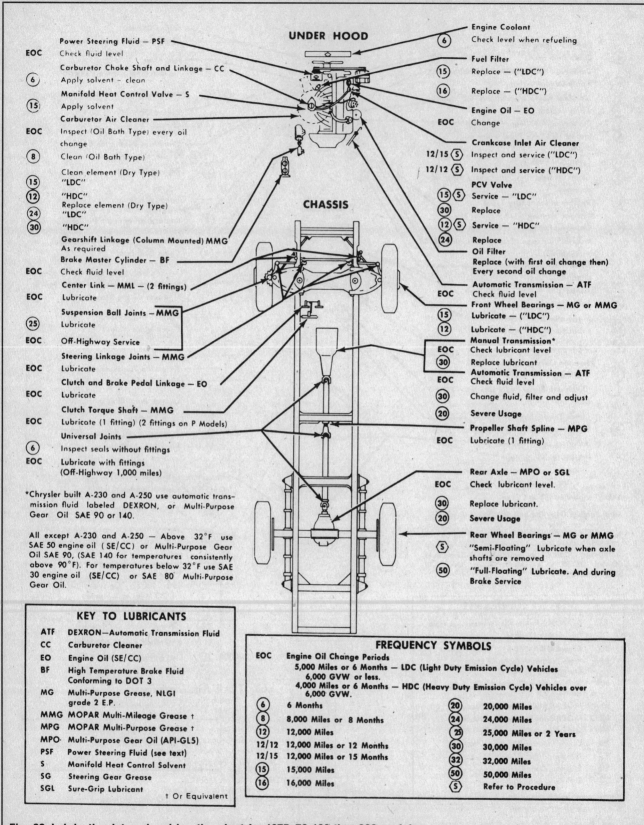

UNDER HOOD

Power Steering Fluid — PSF
EOC   Check fluid level

Carburetor Choke Shaft and Linkage — CC
(6)   Apply solvent – clean

Manifold Heat Control Valve — S
(15)   Apply solvent

Carburetor Air Cleaner
EOC   Inspect (Oil Bath Type) every oil change
(8)   Clean (Oil Bath Type)

       Clean element (Dry Type)
(15)   "LDC"
(12)   "HDC"
       Replace element (Dry Type)
(24)   "LDC"
(30)   "HDC"

       Gearshift Linkage (Column Mounted) MMG
       As required

       Brake Master Cylinder — BF
EOC   Check fluid level

       Center Link — MML — (2 fittings)
EOC   Lubricate

       Suspension Ball Joints — MMG
(25)   Lubricate
EOC   Off-Highway Service

       Steering Linkage Joints — MMG
EOC   Lubricate

       Clutch and Brake Pedal Linkage — EO
EOC   Lubricate

       Clutch Torque Shaft — MMG
EOC   Lubricate (1 fitting) (2 fittings on P Models)

       Universal Joints
(6)   Inspect seals without fittings
EOC   Lubricate with fittings
       (Off-Highway 1,000 miles)

*Chrysler built A-230 and A-250 use automatic transmission fluid labeled DEXRON, or Multi-Purpose Gear Oil SAE 90 or 140.

All except A-230 and A-250 — Above 32°F use SAE 50 engine oil (SE/CC) or Multi-Purpose Gear Oil SAE 90, (SAE 140 for temperatures consistently above 90°F). For temperatures below 32°F use SAE 30 engine oil (SE/CC) or SAE 80 Multi-Purpose Gear Oil.

CHASSIS

Engine Coolant
(6)   Check level when refueling

Fuel Filter
(15)   Replace — ("LDC")
(16)   Replace — ("HDC")

Engine Oil — EO
EOC   Change

Crankcase Inlet Air Cleaner
12/15 (S)   Inspect and service ("LDC")
12/12 (S)   Inspect and service ("HDC")

PCV Valve
(15)(S)   Service — "LDC"
(30)   Replace
(12)(S)   Service — "HDC"
(24)   Replace

Oil Filter
       Replace (with first oil change then)
       Every second oil change

Automatic Transmission — ATF
EOC   Check fluid level

Front Wheel Bearings — MG or MMG
(15)   Lubricate — ("LDC")
(12)   Lubricate — ("HDC")

Manual Transmission*
EOC   Check lubricant level
(30)   Replace lubricant

Automatic Transmission — ATF
EOC   Check fluid level
(30)   Change fluid, filter and adjust
(20)   Severe Usage

Propeller Shaft Spline — MPG
EOC   Lubricate (1 fitting)

Rear Axle — MPO or SGL
EOC   Check lubricant level.
(30)   Replace lubricant.
(20)   Severe Usage

Rear Wheel Bearings — MG or MMG
(S)   "Semi-Floating" Lubricate when axle shafts are removed
(50)   "Full-Floating" Lubricate. And during Brake Service

KEY TO LUBRICANTS

ATF   DEXRON—Automatic Transmission Fluid
CC   Carburetor Cleaner
EO   Engine Oil (SE/CC)
BF   High Temperature Brake Fluid Conforming to DOT 3
MG   Multi-Purpose Grease, NLGI grade 2 E.P.
MMG   MOPAR Multi-Mileage Grease †
MPG   MOPAR Multi-Purpose Grease †
MPO   Multi-Purpose Gear Oil (API-GL5)
PSF   Power Steering Fluid (see text)
S   Manifold Heat Control Solvent
SG   Steering Gear Grease
SGL   Sure-Grip Lubricant
                        † Or Equivalent

FREQUENCY SYMBOLS

EOC   Engine Oil Change Periods
       5,000 Miles or 6 Months — LDC (Light Duty Emission Cycle) Vehicles 6,000 GVW or less.
       4,000 Miles or 6 Months — HDC (Heavy Duty Emission Cycle) Vehicles over 6,000 GVW.

(6) 6 Months	(20)	20,000 Miles
(8) 8,000 Miles or 8 Months	(24)	24,000 Miles
(12) 12,000 Miles	(25)	25,000 Miles or 2 Years
12/12 12,000 Miles or 12 Months	(30)	30,000 Miles
12/15 12,000 Miles or 15 Months	(32)	32,000 Miles
(15) 15,000 Miles	(50)	50,000 Miles
(16) 16,000 Miles	(S)	Refer to Procedure

Fig. 62 Lubrication interval and location chart for 1975–76 100 thru 300 models

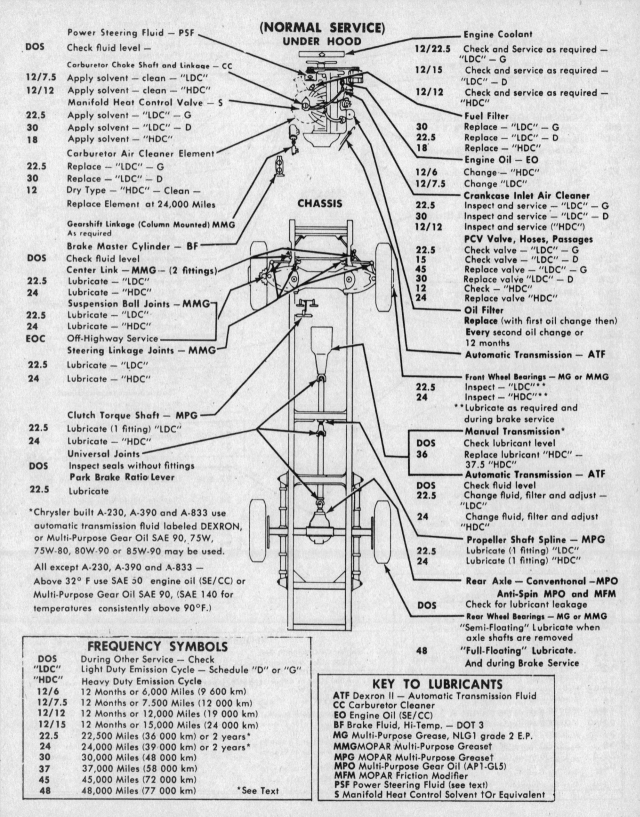

Power Steering Fluid — PSF
DOS   Check fluid level —

Carburetor Choke Shaft and Linkage — CC
12/7.5   Apply solvent – clean – "LDC"
12/12   Apply solvent – clean – "HDC"
Manifold Heat Control Valve — S
22.5   Apply solvent – "LDC" – G
30   Apply solvent – "LDC" – D
18   Apply solvent – "HDC"

Carburetor Air Cleaner Element
22.5   Replace – "LDC" – G
30   Replace – "LDC" – D
12   Dry Type – "HDC" – Clean –
Replace Element at 24,000 Miles

Gearshift Linkage (Column Mounted) MMG
As required
Brake Master Cylinder — BF
DOS   Check fluid level
Center Link — MMG — (2 fittings)
22.5   Lubricate – "LDC"
24   Lubricate – "HDC"
Suspension Ball Joints — MMG
22.5   Lubricate – "LDC"
24   Lubricate – "HDC"
EOC   Off-Highway Service
Steering Linkage Joints — MMG
22.5   Lubricate – "LDC"
24   Lubricate – "HDC"

Clutch Torque Shaft — MPG
22.5   Lubricate (1 fitting) "LDC"
24   Lubricate – "HDC"
Universal Joints
DOS   Inspect seals without fittings
Park Brake Ratio Lever
22.5   Lubricate

*Chrysler built A-230, A-390 and A-833 use
automatic transmission fluid labeled DEXRON,
or Multi-Purpose Gear Oil SAE 90, 75W,
75W-80, 80W-90 or 85W-90 may be used.

All except A-230, A-390 and A-833 —
Above 32° F use SAE 50 engine oil (SE/CC) or
Multi-Purpose Gear Oil SAE 90, (SAE 140 for
temperatures consistently above 90°F.)

(NORMAL SERVICE)
UNDER HOOD

CHASSIS

Engine Coolant
12/22.5   Check and Service as required – "LDC" – G
12/15   Check and service as required – "LDC" – D
12/12   Check and service as required – "HDC"
Fuel Filter
30   Replace – "LDC" – G
22.5   Replace – "LDC" – D
18   Replace – "HDC"
Engine Oil — EO
12/6   Change – "HDC"
12/7.5   Change "LDC"
Crankcase Inlet Air Cleaner
22.5   Inspect and service – "LDC" – G
30   Inspect and service – "LDC" – D
12/12   Inspect and service ("HDC")
PCV Valve, Hoses, Passages
22.5   Check valve – "LDC" – G
15   Check valve – "LDC" – D
45   Replace valve – "LDC" – G
30   Replace valve "LDC" – D
12   Check – "HDC"
24   Replace valve "HDC"
Oil Filter
Replace (with first oil change then)
Every second oil change or
12 months
Automatic Transmission — ATF

Front Wheel Bearings — MG or MMG
22.5   Inspect – "LDC"**
24   Inspect – "HDC"**
**Lubricate as required and
during brake service
Manual Transmission*
DOS   Check lubricant level
36   Replace lubricant "HDC" – 37.5 "HDC"
Automatic Transmission — ATF
DOS   Check fluid level
22.5   Change fluid, filter and adjust – "LDC"
24   Change fluid, filter and adjust "HDC"
Propeller Shaft Spline — MPG
22.5   Lubricate (1 fitting) "LDC"
24   Lubricate (1 fitting) "HDC"

Rear Axle — Conventional —MPO
       Anti-Spin MPO and MFM
DOS   Check for lubricant leakage
Rear Wheel Bearings — MG or MMG
"Semi-Floating" Lubricate when
axle shafts are removed
48   "Full-Floating" Lubricate.
And during Brake Service

FREQUENCY SYMBOLS	
DOS	During Other Service — Check
"LDC"	Light Duty Emission Cycle — Schedule "D" or "G"
"HDC"	Heavy Duty Emission Cycle
12/6	12 Months or 6,000 Miles (9 600 km)
12/7.5	12 Months or 7.500 Miles (12 000 km)
12/12	12 Months or 12,000 Miles (19 000 km)
12/15	12 Months or 15,000 Miles (24 000 km)
22.5	22,500 Miles (36 000 km) or 2 years*
24	24,000 Miles (39 000 km) or 2 years*
30	30,000 Miles (48 000 km)
37	37,000 Miles (58 000 km)
45	45,000 Miles (72 000 km)
48	48,000 Miles (77 000 km) *See Text

KEY TO LUBRICANTS
ATF Dexron II — Automatic Transmission Fluid
CC Carburetor Cleaner
EO Engine Oil (SE/CC)
BF Brake Fluid, Hi-Temp. — DOT 3
MG Multi-Purpose Grease, NLG1 grade 2 E.P.
MMG MOPAR Multi-Purpose Grease†
MPG MOPAR Multi-Purpose Grease†
MPO Multi-Purpose Gear Oil (AP1-GL5)
MFM MOPAR Friction Modifier
PSF Power Steering Fluid (see text)
S Manifold Heat Control Solvent †Or Equivalent

Fig. 63 Lubrication interval and location chart for 1977–79 100 thru 300 models

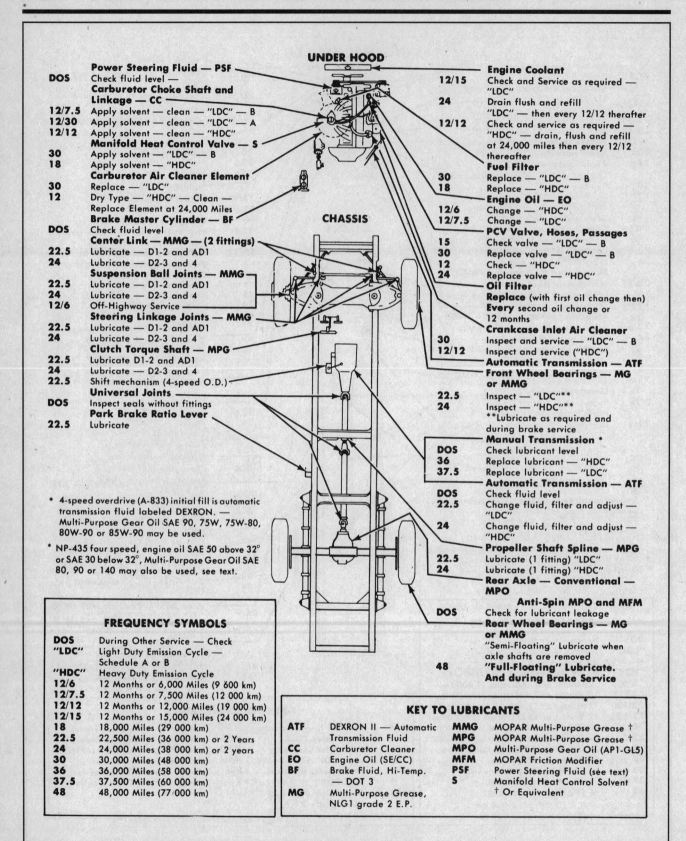

UNDER HOOD

DOS	**Power Steering Fluid — PSF** Check fluid level —
	Carburetor Choke Shaft and Linkage — CC
12/7.5	Apply solvent — clean — "LDC" — B
12/30	Apply solvent — clean — "LDC" — A
12/12	Apply solvent — clean — "HDC"
	Manifold Heat Control Valve — S
30	Apply solvent — "LDC" — B
18	Apply solvent — "HDC"
	Carburetor Air Cleaner Element
30	Replace — "LDC"
12	Dry Type — "HDC" — Clean — Replace Element at 24,000 Miles
	Brake Master Cylinder — BF
DOS	Check fluid level
	Center Link — MMG — (2 fittings)
22.5	Lubricate — D1-2 and AD1
24	Lubricate — D2-3 and 4
	Suspension Ball Joints — MMG
22.5	Lubricate — D1-2 and AD1
24	Lubricate — D2-3 and 4
12/6	Off-Highway Service
	Steering Linkage Joints — MMG
22.5	Lubricate — D1-2 and AD1
24	Lubricate — D2-3 and 4
	Clutch Torque Shaft — MPG
22.5	Lubricate D1-2 and AD1
24	Lubricate — D2-3 and 4
22.5	Shift mechanism (4-speed O.D.)
	Universal Joints
DOS	Inspect seals without fittings
	Park Brake Ratio Lever
22.5	Lubricate

CHASSIS

12/15	**Engine Coolant** Check and Service as required — "LDC"
24	Drain flush and refill "LDC" — then every 12/12 therafter
12/12	Check and service as required — "HDC" — drain, flush and refill at 24,000 miles then every 12/12 thereafter
	Fuel Filter
30	Replace — "LDC" — B
18	Replace — "HDC"
	Engine Oil — EO
12/6	Change — "HDC"
12/7.5	Change — "LDC"
	PCV Valve, Hoses, Passages
15	Check valve — "LDC" — B
30	Replace valve — "LDC" — B
12	Check — "HDC"
24	Replace valve — "HDC"
	Oil Filter
	Replace (with first oil change then) **Every** second oil change or 12 months
	Crankcase Inlet Air Cleaner
30	Inspect and service — "LDC" — B
12/12	Inspect and service ("HDC")
	Automatic Transmission — ATF
	Front Wheel Bearings — MG or MMG
22.5	Inspect — "LDC"**
24	Inspect — "HDC"**
	**Lubricate as required and during brake service
	Manual Transmission *
DOS	Check lubricant level
36	Replace lubricant — "HDC"
37.5	Replace lubricant — "LDC"
	Automatic Transmission — ATF
DOS	Check fluid level
22.5	Change fluid, filter and adjust — "LDC"
24	Change fluid, filter and adjust — "HDC"
	Propeller Shaft Spline — MPG
22.5	Lubricate (1 fitting) "LDC"
24	Lubricate (1 fitting) "HDC"
	Rear Axle — Conventional — MPO
	Anti-Spin MPO and MFM
DOS	Check for lubricant leakage
	Rear Wheel Bearings — MG or MMG
	"Semi-Floating" Lubricate when axle shafts are removed
48	**"Full-Floating" Lubricate. And during Brake Service**

* 4-speed overdrive (A-833) initial fill is automatic transmission fluid labeled DEXRON. — Multi-Purpose Gear Oil SAE 90, 75W, 75W-80, 80W-90 or 85W-90 may be used.

* NP-435 four speed, engine oil SAE 50 above 32° or SAE 30 below 32°, Multi-Purpose Gear Oil SAE 80, 90 or 140 may also be used, see text.

FREQUENCY SYMBOLS

DOS	During Other Service — Check
"LDC"	Light Duty Emission Cycle — Schedule A or B
"HDC"	Heavy Duty Emission Cycle
12/6	12 Months or 6,000 Miles (9 600 km)
12/7.5	12 Months or 7,500 Miles (12 000 km)
12/12	12 Months or 12,000 Miles (19 000 km)
12/15	12 Months or 15,000 Miles (24 000 km)
18	18,000 Miles (29 000 km)
22.5	22,500 Miles (36 000 km) or 2 Years
24	24,000 Miles (38 000 km) or 2 years
30	30,000 Miles (48 000 km)
36	36,000 Miles (58 000 km)
37.5	37,500 Miles (60 000 km)
48	48,000 Miles (77 000 km)

KEY TO LUBRICANTS

ATF	DEXRON II — Automatic Transmission Fluid	MMG	MOPAR Multi-Purpose Grease †
CC	Carburetor Cleaner	MPG	MOPAR Multi-Purpose Grease †
EO	Engine Oil (SE/CC)	MPO	Multi-Purpose Gear Oil (AP1-GL5)
BF	Brake Fluid, Hi-Temp. — DOT 3	MFM	MOPAR Friction Modifier
MG	Multi-Purpose Grease, NLG1 grade 2 E.P.	PSF	Power Steering Fluid (see text)
		S	Manifold Heat Control Solvent
		†	Or Equivalent

Fig. 64 Lubrication interval and location chart for 1980 100 thru 300 models

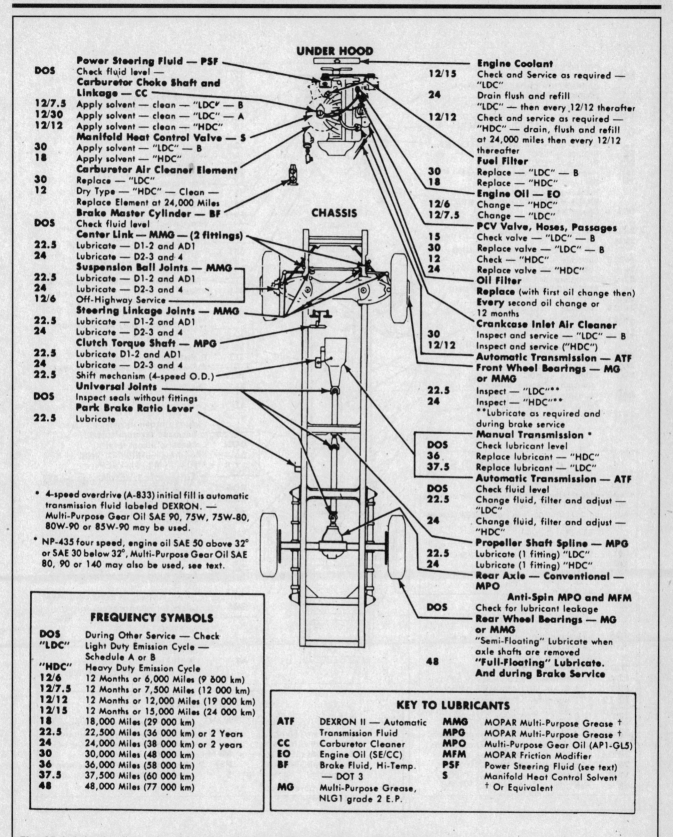

UNDER HOOD

	Power Steering Fluid — PSF
DOS	Check fluid level —
	Carburetor Choke Shaft and
	Linkage — CC
12/7.5	Apply solvent — clean — "LDC" — B
12/30	Apply solvent — clean — "LDC" — A
12/12	Apply solvent — clean — "HDC"
	Manifold Heat Control Valve — S
30	Apply solvent — "LDC" — B
18	Apply solvent — "HDC"
	Carburetor Air Cleaner Element
30	Replace — "LDC"
12	Dry Type — "HDC" — Clean —
	Replace Element at 24,000 Miles
	Brake Master Cylinder — BF
DOS	Check fluid level
	Center Link — MMG — (2 fittings)
22.5	Lubricate — D1-2 and AD1
24	Lubricate — D2-3 and 4
	Suspension Ball Joints — MMG
22.5	Lubricate — D1-2 and AD1
24	Lubricate — D2-3 and 4
12/6	Off-Highway Service
	Steering Linkage Joints — MMG
22.5	Lubricate — D1-2 and AD1
24	Lubricate — D2-3 and 4
	Clutch Torque Shaft — MPG
22.5	Lubricate D1-2 and AD1
24	Lubricate — D2-3 and 4
22.5	Shift mechanism (4-speed O.D.)
	Universal Joints
DOS	Inspect seals without fittings
	Park Brake Ratio Lever
22.5	Lubricate

CHASSIS

	Engine Coolant
12/15	Check and Service as required —
	"LDC"
24	Drain flush and refill
	"LDC" — then every 12/12 therafter
12/12	Check and service as required —
	"HDC" — drain, flush and refill
	at 24,000 miles then every 12/12
	thereafter
	Fuel Filter
30	Replace — "LDC" — B
18	Replace — "HDC"
	Engine Oil — EO
12/6	Change — "HDC"
12/7.5	Change — "LDC"
	PCV Valve, Hoses, Passages
15	Check valve — "LDC" — B
30	Replace valve — "LDC" — B
12	Check — "HDC"
24	Replace valve — "HDC"
	Oil Filter
	Replace (with first oil change then)
	Every second oil change or
	12 months
	Crankcase Inlet Air Cleaner
30	Inspect and service — "LDC" — B
12/12	Inspect and service ("HDC")
	Automatic Transmission — ATF
	Front Wheel Bearings — MG
	or MMG
22.5	Inspect — "LDC"**
24	Inspect — "HDC"**
	**Lubricate as required and
	during brake service
	Manual Transmission *
DOS	Check lubricant level
36	Replace lubricant — "HDC"
37.5	Replace lubricant — "LDC"
	Automatic Transmission — ATF
DOS	Check fluid level
22.5	Change fluid, filter and adjust —
	"LDC"
24	Change fluid, filter and adjust —
	"HDC"
	Propeller Shaft Spline — MPG
22.5	Lubricate (1 fitting) "LDC"
24	Lubricate (1 fitting) "HDC"
	Rear Axle — Conventional —
	MPO
	Anti-Spin MPO and MFM
DOS	Check for lubricant leakage
	Rear Wheel Bearings — MG
	or MMG
	"Semi-Floating" Lubricate when
	axle shafts are removed
48	"Full-Floating" Lubricate.
	And during Brake Service

* 4-speed overdrive (A-833) initial fill is automatic
transmission fluid labeled DEXRON. —
Multi-Purpose Gear Oil SAE 90, 75W, 75W-80,
80W-90 or 85W-90 may be used.

* NP-435 four speed, engine oil SAE 50 above 32°
or SAE 30 below 32°, Multi-Purpose Gear Oil SAE
80, 90 or 140 may also be used, see text.

FREQUENCY SYMBOLS

DOS	During Other Service — Check
"LDC"	Light Duty Emission Cycle —
	Schedule A or B
"HDC"	Heavy Duty Emission Cycle
12/6	12 Months or 6,000 Miles (9 600 km)
12/7.5	12 Months or 7,500 Miles (12 000 km)
12/12	12 Months or 12,000 Miles (19 000 km)
12/15	12 Months or 15,000 Miles (24 000 km)
18	18,000 Miles (29 000 km)
22.5	22,500 Miles (36 000 km) or 2 Years
24	24,000 Miles (38 000 km) or 2 years
30	30,000 Miles (48 000 km)
36	36,000 Miles (58 000 km)
37.5	37,500 Miles (60 000 km)
48	48,000 Miles (77 000 km)

KEY TO LUBRICANTS

ATF	DEXRON II — Automatic	MMG	MOPAR Multi-Purpose Grease †
	Transmission Fluid	MPG	MOPAR Multi-Purpose Grease †
CC	Carburetor Cleaner	MPO	Multi-Purpose Gear Oil (AP1-GL5)
EO	Engine Oil (SE/CC)	MFM	MOPAR Friction Modifier
BF	Brake Fluid, Hi-Temp.	PSF	Power Steering Fluid (see text)
	— DOT 3	S	Manifold Heat Control Solvent
MG	Multi-Purpose Grease,		† Or Equivalent
	NLG1 grade 2 E.P.		

Fig. 65 Lubrication interval and location chart for 1981–82 100 thru 350 models

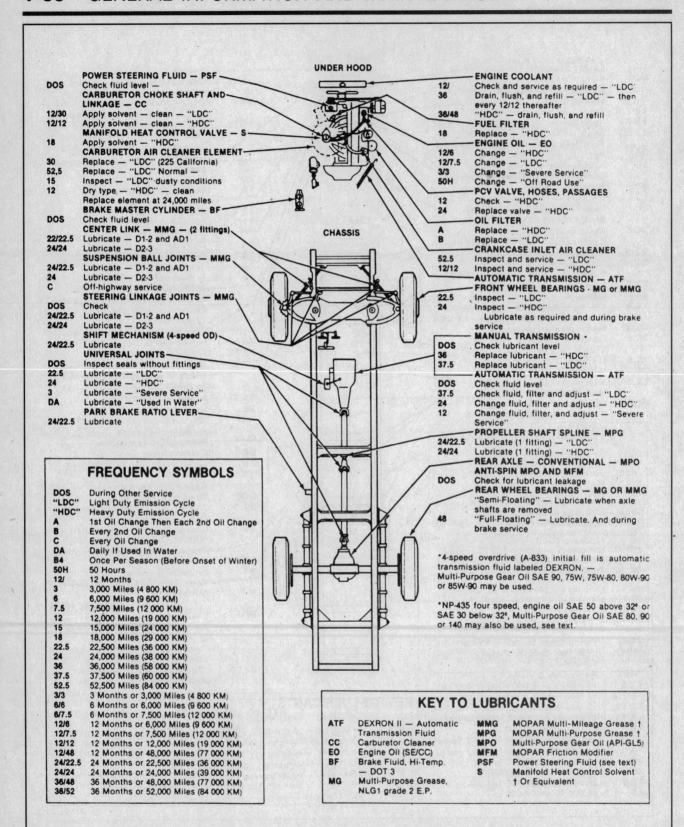

UNDER HOOD

POWER STEERING FLUID — PSF
DOS   Check fluid level —
CARBURETOR CHOKE SHAFT AND LINKAGE — CC
12/30 Apply solvent — clean — "LDC"
12/12 Apply solvent — clean — "HDC"
MANIFOLD HEAT CONTROL VALVE — S
18   Apply solvent — "HDC"
CARBURETOR AIR CLEANER ELEMENT
30   Replace — "LDC" (225 California)
52.5   Replace — "LDC" Normal —
15   Inspect — "LDC" dusty conditions
12   Dry type — "HDC" — clean
        Replace element at 24,000 miles
BRAKE MASTER CYLINDER — BF
DOS   Check fluid level
CENTER LINK — MMG — (2 fittings)
22/22.5 Lubricate — D1-2 and AD1
24/24 Lubricate — D2-3
SUSPENSION BALL JOINTS — MMG
24/22.5 Lubricate — D1-2 and AD1
24   Lubricate — D2-3
C   Off-highway service
STEERING LINKAGE JOINTS — MMG
DOS   Check
24/22.5 Lubricate — D1-2 and AD1
24/24 Lubricate — D2-3
SHIFT MECHANISM (4-speed OD)
24/22.5 Lubricate
UNIVERSAL JOINTS
DOS   Inspect seals without fittings
22.5   Lubricate — "LDC"
24   Lubricate — "HDC"
3   Lubricate — "Severe Service"
DA   Lubricate — "Used In Water"
PARK BRAKE RATIO LEVER
24/22.5 Lubricate

CHASSIS

ENGINE COOLANT
12/   Check and service as required — "LDC"
36   Drain, flush, and refill — "LDC" — then every 12/12 thereafter
36/48 "HDC" — drain, flush, and refill
FUEL FILTER
18   Replace — "HDC"
ENGINE OIL — EO
12/6   Change — "HDC"
12/7.5 Change — "LDC"
3/3   Change — "Severe Service"
50H   Change — "Off Road Use"
PCV VALVE, HOSES, PASSAGES
12   Check — "HDC"
24   Replace valve — "HDC"
OIL FILTER
A   Replace — "HDC"
B   Replace — "LDC"
CRANKCASE INLET AIR CLEANER
52.5   Inspect and service — "LDC"
12/12 Inspect and service — "HDC"
AUTOMATIC TRANSMISSION — ATF
FRONT WHEEL BEARINGS · MG or MMG
22.5   Inspect — "LDC"
24   Inspect — "HDC"
        Lubricate as required and during brake service
MANUAL TRANSMISSION ·
DOS   Check lubricant level
36   Replace lubricant — "HDC"
37.5   Replace lubricant — "LDC"
AUTOMATIC TRANSMISSION — ATF
DOS   Check fluid level
37.5   Check fluid, filter and adjust — "LDC"
24   Change fluid, filter and adjust — "HDC"
12   Change fluid, filter, and adjust — "Severe Service"
PROPELLER SHAFT SPLINE — MPG
24/22.5 Lubricate (1 fitting) — "LDC"
24/24 Lubricate (1 fitting) — "HDC"
REAR AXLE — CONVENTIONAL — MPO ANTI-SPIN MPO AND MFM
DOS   Check for lubricant leakage
REAR WHEEL BEARINGS — MG OR MMG
        "Semi-Floating" — Lubricate when axle shafts are removed
48   "Full-Floating" — Lubricate. And during brake service

*4-speed overdrive (A-833) initial fill is automatic transmission fluid labeled DEXRON. — Multi-Purpose Gear Oil SAE 90, 75W, 75W-80, 80W-90 or 85W-90 may be used.

*NP-435 four speed, engine oil SAE 50 above 32° or SAE 30 below 32°, Multi-Purpose Gear Oil SAE 80, 90 or 140 may also be used, see text.

FREQUENCY SYMBOLS

DOS	During Other Service
"LDC"	Light Duty Emission Cycle
"HDC"	Heavy Duty Emission Cycle
A	1st Oil Change Then Each 2nd Oil Change
B	Every 2nd Oil Change
C	Every Oil Change
DA	Daily If Used In Water
B4	Once Per Season (Before Onset of Winter)
50H	50 Hours
12/	12 Months
3	3,000 Miles (4 800 KM)
6	6,000 Miles (9 600 KM)
7.5	7,500 Miles (12 000 KM)
12	12,000 Miles (19 000 KM)
15	15,000 Miles (24 000 KM)
18	18,000 Miles (29 000 KM)
22.5	22,500 Miles (36 000 KM)
24	24,000 Miles (38 000 KM)
36	36,000 Miles (58 000 KM)
37.5	37,500 Miles (60 000 KM)
52.5	52,500 Miles (84 000 KM)
3/3	3 Months or 3,000 Miles (4 800 KM)
6/6	6 Months or 6,000 Miles (9 600 KM)
6/7.5	6 Months or 7,500 Miles (12 000 KM)
12/6	12 Months or 6,000 Miles (9 600 KM)
12/7.5	12 Months or 7,500 Miles (12 000 KM)
12/12	12 Months or 12,000 Miles (19 000 KM)
12/48	12 Months or 48,000 Miles (77 000 KM)
24/22.5	24 Months or 22,500 Miles (36 000 KM)
24/24	24 Months or 24,000 Miles (39 000 KM)
36/48	36 Months or 48,000 Miles (77 000 KM)
36/52	36 Months or 52,000 Miles (84 000 KM)

KEY TO LUBRICANTS

ATF	DEXRON II — Automatic Transmission Fluid	MMG	MOPAR Multi-Mileage Grease †
		MPG	MOPAR Multi-Purpose Grease †
CC	Carburetor Cleaner	MPO	Multi-Purpose Gear Oil (API-GL5)
EO	Engine Oil (SE/CC)	MFM	MOPAR Friction Modifier
BF	Brake Fluid, Hi-Temp. — DOT 3	PSF	Power Steering Fluid (see text)
		S	Manifold Heat Control Solvent
MG	Multi-Purpose Grease, NLG1 grade 2 E.P.		† Or Equivalent

Fig. 66 Lubrication interval and location chart for 1983–84 100 thru 350 models

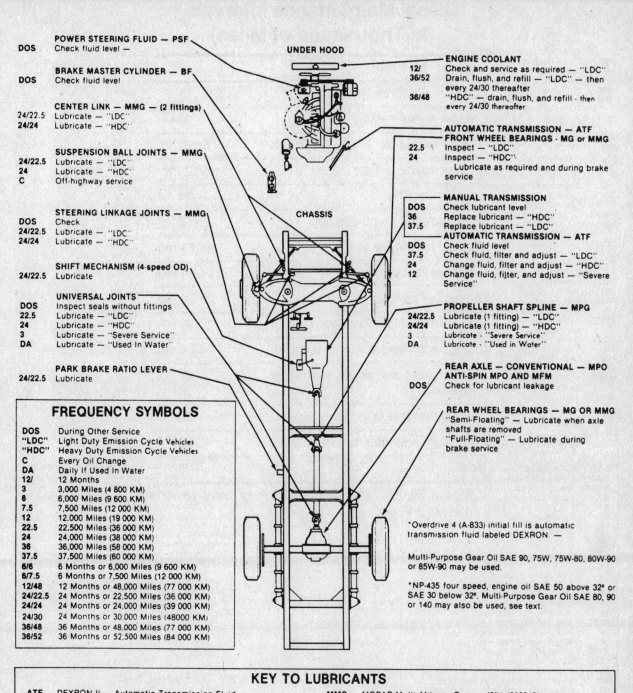

DOS	**POWER STEERING FLUID — PSF** Check fluid level —
DOS	**BRAKE MASTER CYLINDER — BF** Check fluid level
24/22.5 24/24	**CENTER LINK — MMG — (2 fittings)** Lubricate — "LDC" Lubricate — "HDC"
24/22.5 24 C	**SUSPENSION BALL JOINTS — MMG** Lubricate — "LDC" Lubricate — "HDC" Off-highway service
DOS 24/22.5 24/24	**STEERING LINKAGE JOINTS — MMG** Check Lubricate — "LDC" Lubricate — "HDC"
24/22.5	**SHIFT MECHANISM (4-speed OD)** Lubricate
DOS 22.5 24 3 DA	**UNIVERSAL JOINTS** Inspect seals without fittings Lubricate — "LDC" Lubricate — "HDC" Lubricate — "Severe Service" Lubricate — "Used In Water"
24/22.5	**PARK BRAKE RATIO LEVER** Lubricate

UNDER HOOD

CHASSIS

12/ 36/52 36/48	**ENGINE COOLANT** Check and service as required — "LDC" Drain, flush, and refill — "LDC" — then every 24/30 thereafter "HDC" — drain, flush, and refill - then every 24/30 thereafter
22.5 24	**AUTOMATIC TRANSMISSION — ATF** **FRONT WHEEL BEARINGS · MG or MMG** Inspect — "LDC" Inspect — "HDC" Lubricate as required and during brake service
DOS 36 37.5	**MANUAL TRANSMISSION** Check lubricant level Replace lubricant — "HDC" Replace lubricant — "LDC"
DOS 37.5 24 12	**AUTOMATIC TRANSMISSION — ATF** Check fluid level Check fluid, filter and adjust — "LDC" Change fluid, filter and adjust — "HDC" Change fluid, filter, and adjust — "Severe Service"
24/22.5 24/24 3 DA	**PROPELLER SHAFT SPLINE — MPG** Lubricate (1 fitting) — "LDC" Lubricate (1 fitting) — "HDC" Lubricate - "Severe Service" Lubricate - "Used in Water"
DOS	**REAR AXLE — CONVENTIONAL — MPO** **ANTI-SPIN MPO AND MFM** Check for lubricant leakage
	REAR WHEEL BEARINGS — MG OR MMG "Semi-Floating" — Lubricate when axle shafts are removed "Full-Floating" — Lubricate during brake service

FREQUENCY SYMBOLS

DOS	During Other Service
"LDC"	Light Duty Emission Cycle Vehicles
"HDC"	Heavy Duty Emission Cycle Vehicles
C	Every Oil Change
DA	Daily If Used In Water
12/	12 Months
3	3,000 Miles (4 800 KM)
6	6,000 Miles (9 600 KM)
7.5	7,500 Miles (12 000 KM)
12	12,000 Miles (19 000 KM)
22.5	22,500 Miles (36 000 KM)
24	24,000 Miles (38 000 KM)
36	36,000 Miles (58 000 KM)
37.5	37,500 Miles (60 000 KM)
6/6	6 Months or 6,000 Miles (9 600 KM)
6/7.5	6 Months or 7,500 Miles (12 000 KM)
12/48	12 Months or 48,000 Miles (77 000 KM)
24/22.5	24 Months or 22,500 Miles (36 000 KM)
24/24	24 Months or 24,000 Miles (39 000 KM)
24/30	24 Months or 30,000 Miles (48000 KM)
36/48	36 Months or 48,000 Miles (77 000 KM)
36/52	36 Months or 52,500 Miles (84 000 KM)

*Overdrive 4 (A-833) initial fill is automatic
transmission fluid labeled DEXRON. —

Multi-Purpose Gear Oil SAE 90, 75W, 75W-80, 80W-90
or 85W-90 may be used.

*NP-435 four speed, engine oil SAE 50 above 32°
SAE 30 below 32°. Multi-Purpose Gear Oil SAE 80, 90
or 140 may also be used, see text.

KEY TO LUBRICANTS

ATF	DEXRON II — Automatic Transmission Fluid 1 qt (0.95 L), P/N 4271243 55 gal (208L), P/N 4271245
CC	Carburetor Cleaner
EO	Engine Oil (SF/CC)
BF	Brake Fluid, Hi-Temp. — DOT 3
MG	Multi-Purpose Grease, NLG1 grade 2 E.P. (P/N 4318063)

MMG	MOPAR Multi-Mileage Grease (P/N 4318062)
MPO	Multi-Purpose Gear Oil MOPAR Hypoid Lubricant 1 qt (0.95 L), P/N 4318058 16 gal (60.6 L), P/N 4318059
MFM	MOPAR Friction Modifier
PSF	Power Steering Fluid (see text)
S	Manifold Heat Control Valve Solvent Or Equivalent

Fig. 67 Lubrication interval and location chart for 1985–88 100 thru 350 models

Diesel Maintenance Intervals
(in Thousands of Miles)

Clean air clean filter	6
Replace air cleaner filter	18
Change engine coolant	①
Change engine oil	6/12 mo
Change engine oil filter	6/12 mo
Replace fuel filter	24
Clean fuel feed pump strainer	12
Grease steering linkage	24/24 mo
Grease U-joints	24/24 mo
Grease ball joints	24/24 mo
Change manual transmission fluid	36
Change automatic transmission fluid	24/24 mo
Check, grease and adjust front wheel bearings	24
Change rear axle fluid	36
Check axle and transmission fluids	6
Rotate tires	6

① First at 36,000 miles or 2 years, then every 18,000 miles or 1 year.

Capacities Chart

Years	Engine cu. in.	Crank-case Incl. Filter (qt)	Transmission (pt.) 3-sp	4-sp	5-sp	Auto	Drive Axle (pt.)	Fuel Tank (gal.)	Cooling System (qt) w/AC	wo/AC
1967–69	6-170	5.0	①	—	—	18.0	4.0	21.0	12.5	11.5
	6-225	5.0	①	—	—	18.0	4.0	21.0	14.5	13.5
	8-318	5.0	①	—	—	18.0	4.0	21.0	19.0	18.0
1970	6-198	5.0	4.0	—	—	19.0	②	25.0	14.0	13.0
	6-225	5.0	4.0	—	—	19.0	②	25.0	14.0	13.0
	8-318	5.0	4.25	—	—	19.0	②	25.0	19.0	18.0
1971–72	6-225	6.0	4.0	—	—	19.0	②	26.0	14.0	13.0
	8-318	6.0	4.25	—	—	19.0	②	26.0	18.0	17.0
	8-360	6.0	4.25	—	—	19.0	②	26.0	18.0	17.0
1973–75	6-225	6.0	4.0	—	—	19.0	③	26.0	14.0	13.0
	8-318	6.0	4.25	—	—	19.0	③	26.0	18.0	17.0
	8-360	6.0	4.25	—	—	19.0	③	26.0	16.5	15.5
1976–77	6-225	6.0	④	7.0	—	⑤	③	⑥	14.0	13.0
	8-318	6.0	④	7.0	—	⑤	③	⑥	18.0	17.0
	8-360	6.0	④	7.0	—	⑤	③	⑥	17.0	16.0
	8-400	6.0	④	7.0	—	⑤	③	⑥	17.5	15.5
	8-440	6.0	④	7.0	—	⑤	③	⑥	17.5	15.5
1978–79	6-225	6.0	④	7.0	—	⑤	③	⑥	14.0	13.0
	6-243	8.0	④	7.0	—	⑤	③	⑦	14.0	13.0
	8-318	6.0	④	7.0	—	⑤	③	⑥	18.0	17.0
	8-360	6.0	④	7.0	—	⑤	③	⑥	17.0	16.0
	8-400	6.0	④	7.0	—	⑤	③	⑥	16.5	14.5
	8-440	6.0	④	7.0	—	⑤	③	⑥	16.5	14.5
1980–86	6-225	6.0	④	7.0	—	16.6	③	⑥	14.0	12.0
	8-318	6.0	④	7.0	—	16.6	③	⑥	18.0	16.0
	8-360	6.0	④	7.0	—	16.6	③	⑥	16.5	14.5
1987	6-225	6.0	—	7.5	—	13.0	③	⑥	14.5	13.5
	8-318	6.0	—	7.5	—	13.0	③	⑥	17.5	16.5
	8-360	6.0	—	7.5	—	13.0	③	⑥	16.0	15.0
1988	6-238	4.0	—	4.0	4.0	13.0	③	⑥	15.6	14.6
	8-318	5.0	—	4.0	4.0	13.0	③	⑥	17.5	16.5
	8-360	5.0	—	4.0	4.0	13.0	③	35.0	16.0	15.0

① A903: 6.0
   A745: 3.25
② Chrysler axle: 4.25
   Dana axle: 6.0
③ Chrysler 8⅜: 4.4
   Chrysler 8¾: 4.4
   Chrysler 9¼: 4.5
   Dana 60: 6.0
   Dana 70: 7.0
④ A230: 4.25
   A390: 3.5

⑤ 1976: 19.0
   1977: 16.66
⑥ Standard: 22.0
   Optional: 36.0
⑦ Standard: 18.0
   Optional: 20.0

ENGLISH TO METRIC CONVERSION: MASS (WEIGHT)

Current mass measurement is expressed in pounds and ounces (lbs. & ozs.). The metric unit of mass (or weight) is the kilogram (kg). Even although this table does not show conversion of masses (weights) larger than 15 lbs, it is easy to calculate larger units by following the data immediately below.

To convert ounces (oz.) to grams (g): multiply th number of ozs. by 28
To convert grams (g) to ounces (oz.): multiply the number of grams by .035

To convert pounds (lbs.) to kilograms (kg): multiply the number of lbs. by .45
To convert kilograms (kg) to pounds (lbs.): multiply the number of kilograms by 2.2

lbs	kg	lbs	kg	oz	kg	oz	kg
0.1	0.04	0.9	0.41	0.1	0.003	0.9	0.024
0.2	0.09	1	0.4	0.2	0.005	1	0.03
0.3	0.14	2	0.9	0.3	0.008	2	0.06
0.4	0.18	3	1.4	0.4	0.011	3	0.08
0.5	0.23	4	1.8	0.5	0.014	4	0.11
0.6	0.27	5	2.3	0.6	0.017	5	0.14
0.7	0.32	10	4.5	0.7	0.020	10	0.28
0.8	0.36	15	6.8	0.8	0.023	15	0.42

ENGLISH TO METRIC CONVERSION: TEMPERATURE

To convert Fahrenheit (F) to Celsius (°C): take number of °F and subtract 32; multiply result by 5; divide result by 9

To convert Celsius (°C) to Fahrenheit (°F): take number of °C and multiply by 9; divide result by 5; add 32 to total

Fahrenheit (F)		Celsius (C)		Fahrenheit (F)		Celsius (C)		Fahrenheit (F)		Celsius (C)	
°F	°C	°C	°F	°F	°C	°C	°F	°F	°C	°C	°F
−40	−40	−38	−36.4	80	26.7	18	64.4	215	101.7	80	176
−35	−37.2	−36	−32.8	85	29.4	20	68	220	104.4	85	185
−30	−34.4	−34	−29.2	90	32.2	22	71.6	225	107.2	90	194
−25	−31.7	−32	−25.6	95	35.0	24	75.2	230	110.0	95	202
−20	−28.9	−30	−22	100	37.8	26	78.8	235	112.8	100	212
−15	−26.1	−28	−18.4	105	40.6	28	82.4	240	115.6	105	221
−10	−23.3	−26	−14.8	110	43.3	30	86	245	118.3	110	230
−5	−20.6	−24	−11.2	115	46.1	32	89.6	250	121.1	115	239
0	−17.8	−22	−7.6	120	48.9	34	93.2	255	123.9	120	248
1	−17.2	−20	−4	125	51.7	36	96.8	260	126.6	125	257
2	−16.7	−18	−0.4	130	54.4	38	100.4	265	129.4	130	266
3	−16.1	−16	3.2	135	57.2	40	104	270	132.2	135	275
4	−15.6	−14	6.8	140	60.0	42	107.6	275	135.0	140	284
5	−15.0	−12	10.4	145	62.8	44	112.2	280	137.8	145	293
10	−12.2	−10	14	150	65.6	46	114.8	285	140.6	150	302
15	−9.4	−8	17.6	155	68.3	48	118.4	290	143.3	155	311
20	−6.7	−6	21.2	160	71.1	50	122	295	146.1	160	320
25	−3.9	−4	24.8	165	73.9	52	125.6	300	148.9	165	329
30	−1.1	−2	28.4	170	76.7	54	129.2	305	151.7	170	338
35	1.7	0	32	175	79.4	56	132.8	310	154.4	175	347
40	4.4	2	35.6	180	82.2	58	136.4	315	157.2	180	356
45	7.2	4	39.2	185	85.0	60	140	320	160.0	185	365
50	10.0	6	42.8	190	87.8	62	143.6	325	162.8	190	374
55	12.8	8	46.4	195	90.6	64	147.2	330	165.6	195	383
60	15.6	10	50	200	93.3	66	150.8	335	168.3	200	392
65	18.3	12	53.6	205	96.1	68	154.4	340	171.1	205	401
70	21.1	14	57.2	210	98.9	70	158	345	173.9	210	410
75	23.9	16	60.8	212	100.0	75	167	350	176.7	215	414

ENGLISH TO METRIC CONVERSION: LENGTH

To convert inches (ins.) to millimeters (mm): multiply number of inches by 25.4

To convert millimeters (mm) to inches (ins.): multiply number of millimeters by .04

Inches		Decimals	Milli-meters	Inches to millimeters		Inches		Decimals	Milli-meters	Inches to millimeters	
				inches	mm					inches	mm
	1/64	0.051625	0.3969	0.0001	0.00254		33/64	0.515625	13.0969	0.6	15.24
	1/32	0.03125	0.7937	0.0002	0.00508	17/32		0.53125	13.4937	0.7	17.78
	3/64	0.046875	1.1906	0.0003	0.00762		35/64	0.546875	13.8906	0.8	20.32
1/16		0.0625	1.5875	0.0004	0.01016	9/16		0.5625	14.2875	0.9	22.86
	5/64	0.078125	1.9844	0.0005	0.01270		37/64	0.578125	14.6844	1	25.4
	3/32	0.09375	2.3812	0.0006	0.01524	19/32		0.59375	15.0812	2	50.8
	7/64	0.109375	2.7781	0.0007	0.01778		39/64	0.609375	15.4781	3	76.2
1/8		0.125	3.1750	0.0008	0.02032	5/8		0.625	15.8750	4	101.6
	9/64	0.140625	3.5719	0.0009	0.02286		41/64	0.640625	16.2719	5	127.0
	5/32	0.15625	3.9687	0.001	0.0254	21/32		0.65625	16.6687	6	152.4
	11/64	0.171875	4.3656	0.002	0.0508		43/64	0.671875	17.0656	7	177.8
3/16		0.1875	4.7625	0.003	0.0762	11/16		0.6875	17.4625	8	203.2
	13/64	0.203125	5.1594	0.004	0.1016		45/64	0.703125	17.8594	9	228.6
	7/32	0.21875	5.5562	0.005	0.1270	23/32		0.71875	18.2562	10	254.0
	15/64	0.234375	5.9531	0.006	0.1524		47/64	0.734375	18.6531	11	279.4
1/4		0.25	6.3500	0.007	0.1778	3/4		0.75	19.0500	12	304.8
	17/64	0.265625	6.7469	0.008	0.2032		49/64	0.765625	19.4469	13	330.2
	9/32	0.28125	7.1437	0.009	0.2286	25/32		0.78125	19.8437	14	355.6
	19/64	0.296875	7.5406	0.01	0.254		51/64	0.796875	20.2406	15	381.0
5/16		0.3125	7.9375	0.02	0.508	13/16		0.8125	20.6375	16	406.4
	21/64	0.328125	8.3344	0.03	0.762		53/64	0.828125	21.0344	17	431.8
	11/32	0.34375	8.7312	0.04	1.016	27/32		0.84375	21.4312	18	457.2
	23/64	0.359375	9.1281	0.05	1.270		55/64	0.859375	21.8281	19	482.6
3/8		0.375	9.5250	0.06	1.524	7/8		0.875	22.2250	20	508.0
	25/64	0.390625	9.9219	0.07	1.778		57/64	0.890625	22.6219	21	533.4
	13/32	0.40625	10.3187	0.08	2.032	29/32		0.90625	23.0187	22	558.8
	27/64	0.421875	10.7156	0.09	2.286		59/64	0.921875	23.4156	23	584.2
7/16		0.4375	11.1125	0.1	2.54	15/16		0.9375	23.8125	24	609.6
	29/64	0.453125	11.5094	0.2	5.08		61/64	0.953125	24.2094	25	635.0
	15/32	0.46875	11.9062	0.3	7.62	31/32		0.96875	24.6062	26	660.4
	31/64	0.484375	12.3031	0.4	10.16		63/64	0.984375	25.0031	27	690.6
1/2		0.5	12.7000	0.5	12.70						

ENGLISH TO METRIC CONVERSION: TORQUE

To convert foot-pounds (ft. lbs.) to Newton-meters: multiply the number of ft. lbs. by 1.3

To convert inch-pounds (in. lbs.) to Newton-meters: multiply the number of in. lbs. by .11

in lbs	N-m	in lbs	N-m	in lbs	N-m	in lbs	N-m	in lbs	N-m
0.1	0.01	1	0.11	10	1.13	19	2.15	28	3.16
0.2	0.02	2	0.23	11	1.24	20	2.26	29	3.28
0.3	0.03	3	0.34	12	1.36	21	2.37	30	3.39
0.4	0.04	4	0.45	13	1.47	22	2.49	31	3.50
0.5	0.06	5	0.56	14	1.58	23	2.60	32	3.62
0.6	0.07	6	0.68	15	1.70	24	2.71	33	3.73
0.7	0.08	7	0.78	16	1.81	25	2.82	34	3.84
0.8	0.09	8	0.90	17	1.92	26	2.94	35	3.95
0.9	0.10	9	1.02	18	2.03	27	3.05	36	4.0

ENGLISH TO METRIC CONVERSION: TORQUE

Torque is now expressed as either foot-pounds (ft./lbs.) or inch-pounds (in./lbs.). The metric measurement unit for torque is the Newton-meter (Nm). This unit—the Nm—will be used for all SI metric torque references, both the present ft./lbs. and in./lbs.

ft lbs	N-m	ft lbs	N-m	ft lbs	N-m	ft lbs	N-m
0.1	0.1	33	44.7	74	100.3	115	155.9
0.2	0.3	34	46.1	75	101.7	116	157.3
0.3	0.4	35	47.4	76	103.0	117	158.6
0.4	0.5	36	48.8	77	104.4	118	160.0
0.5	0.7	37	50.7	78	105.8	119	161.3
0.6	0.8	38	51.5	79	107.1	120	162.7
0.7	1.0	39	52.9	80	108.5	121	164.0
0.8	1.1	40	54.2	81	109.8	122	165.4
0.9	1.2	41	55.6	82	111.2	123	166.8
1	1.3	42	56.9	83	112.5	124	168.1
2	2.7	43	58.3	84	113.9	125	169.5
3	4.1	44	59.7	85	115.2	126	170.8
4	5.4	45	61.0	86	116.6	127	172.2
5	6.8	46	62.4	87	118.0	128	173.5
6	8.1	47	63.7	88	119.3	129	174.9
7	9.5	48	65.1	89	120.7	130	176.2
8	10.8	49	66.4	90	122.0	131	177.6
9	12.2	50	67.8	91	123.4	132	179.0
10	13.6	51	69.2	92	124.7	133	180.3
11	14.9	52	70.5	93	126.1	134	181.7
12	16.3	53	71.9	94	127.4	135	183.0
13	17.6	54	73.2	95	128.8	136	184.4
14	18.9	55	74.6	96	130.2	137	185.7
15	20.3	56	75.9	97	131.5	138	187.1
16	21.7	57	77.3	98	132.9	139	188.5
17	23.0	58	78.6	99	134.2	140	189.8
18	24.4	59	80.0	100	135.6	141	191.2
19	25.8	60	81.4	101	136.9	142	192.5
20	27.1	61	82.7	102	138.3	143	193.9
21	28.5	62	84.1	103	139.6	144	195.2
22	29.8	63	85.4	104	141.0	145	196.6
23	31.2	64	86.8	105	142.4	146	198.0
24	32.5	65	88.1	106	143.7	147	199.3
25	33.9	66	89.5	107	145.1	148	200.7
26	35.2	67	90.8	108	146.4	149	202.0
27	36.6	68	92.2	109	147.8	150	203.4
28	38.0	69	93.6	110	149.1	151	204.7
29	39.3	70	94.9	111	150.5	152	206.1
30	40.7	71	96.3	112	151.8	153	207.4
31	42.0	72	97.6	113	153.2	154	208.8
32	43.4	73	99.0	114	154.6	155	210.2

ENGLISH TO METRIC CONVERSION: FORCE

Force is presently measured in pounds (lbs.). This type of measurement is used to measure spring pressure, specifically how many pounds it takes to compress a spring. Our present force unit (the pound) will be replaced in SI metric measurements by the Newton (N). This term will eventually see use in specifications for electric motor brush spring pressures, valve spring pressures, etc.

To convert pounds (lbs.) to Newton (N): multiply the number of lbs. by 4.45

lbs	N	lbs	N	lbs	N	oz	N
0.01	0.04	21	93.4	59	262.4	1	0.3
0.02	0.09	22	97.9	60	266.9	2	0.6
0.03	0.13	23	102.3	61	271.3	3	0.8
0.04	0.18	24	106.8	62	275.8	4	1.1
0.05	0.22	25	111.2	63	280.2	5	1.4
0.06	0.27	26	115.6	64	284.6	6	1.7
0.07	0.31	27	120.1	65	289.1	7	2.0
0.08	0.36	28	124.6	66	293.6	8	2.2
0.09	0.40	29	129.0	67	298.0	9	2.5
0.1	0.4	30	133.4	68	302.5	10	2.8
0.2	0.9	31	137.9	69	306.9	11	3.1
0.3	1.3	32	142.3	70	311.4	12	3.3
0.4	1.8	33	146.8	71	315.8	13	3.6
0.5	2.2	34	151.2	72	320.3	14	3.9
0.6	2.7	35	155.7	73	324.7	15	4.2
0.7	3.1	36	160.1	74	329.2	16	4.4
0.8	3.6	37	164.6	75	333.6	17	4.7
0.9	4.0	38	169.0	76	338.1	18	5.0
1	4.4	39	173.5	77	342.5	19	5.3
2	8.9	40	177.9	78	347.0	20	5.6
3	13.4	41	182.4	79	351.4	21	5.8
4	17.8	42	186.8	80	355.9	22	6.1
5	22.2	43	191.3	81	360.3	23	6.4
6	26.7	44	195.7	82	364.8	24	6.7
7	31.1	45	200.2	83	369.2	25	7.0
8	35.6	46	204.6	84	373.6	26	7.2
9	40.0	47	209.1	85	378.1	27	7.5
10	44.5	48	213.5	86	382.6	28	7.8
11	48.9	49	218.0	87	387.0	29	8.1
12	53.4	50	224.4	88	391.4	30	8.3
13	57.8	51	226.9	89	395.9	31	8.6
14	62.3	52	231.3	90	400.3	32	8.9
15	66.7	53	235.8	91	404.8	33	9.2
16	71.2	54	240.2	92	409.2	34	9.4
17	75.6	55	244.6	93	413.7	35	9.7
18	80.1	56	249.1	94	418.1	36	10.0
19	84.5	57	253.6	95	422.6	37	10.3
20	89.0	58	258.0	96	427.0	38	10.6

ENGLISH TO METRIC CONVERSION: LIQUID CAPACITY

Liquid or fluid capacity is presently expressed as pints, quarts or gallons, or a combination of all of these. In the metric system the liter (l) will become the basic unit. Fractions of a liter would be expressed as deciliters, centiliters, or most frequently (and commonly) as milliliters.

To convert pints (pts.) to liters (l): multiply the number of pints by .47
To convert liters (l) to pints (pts.): multiply the number of liters by 2.1
To convert quarts (qts.) to liters (l): multiply the number of quarts by .95

To convert liters (l) to quarts (qts.): multiply the number of liters by 1.06
To convert gallons (gals.) to liters (l): multiply the number of gallons by 3.8
To convert liters (l) to gallons (gals.): multiply the number of liters by .26

gals	liters	qts	liters	pts	liters
0.1	0.38	0.1	0.10	0.1	0.05
0.2	0.76	0.2	0.19	0.2	0.10
0.3	1.1	0.3	0.28	0.3	0.14
0.4	1.5	0.4	0.38	0.4	0.19
0.5	1.9	0.5	0.47	0.5	0.24
0.6	2.3	0.6	0.57	0.6	0.28
0.7	2.6	0.7	0.66	0.7	0.33
0.8	3.0	0.8	0.76	0.8	0.38
0.9	3.4	0.9	0.85	0.9	0.43
1	3.8	1	1.0	1	0.5
2	7.6	2	1.9	2	1.0
3	11.4	3	2.8	3	1.4
4	15.1	4	3.8	4	1.9
5	18.9	5	4.7	5	2.4
6	22.7	6	5.7	6	2.8
7	26.5	7	6.6	7	3.3
8	30.3	8	7.6	8	3.8
9	34.1	9	8.5	9	4.3
10	37.8	10	9.5	10	4.7
11	41.6	11	10.4	11	5.2
12	45.4	12	11.4	12	5.7
13	49.2	13	12.3	13	6.2
14	53.0	14	13.2	14	6.6
15	56.8	15	14.2	15	7.1
16	60.6	16	15.1	16	7.6
17	64.3	17	16.1	17	8.0
18	68.1	18	17.0	18	8.5
19	71.9	19	18.0	19	9.0
20	75.7	20	18.9	20	9.5
21	79.5	21	19.9	21	9.9
22	83.2	22	20.8	22	10.4
23	87.0	23	21.8	23	10.9
24	90.8	24	22.7	24	11.4
25	94.6	25	23.6	25	11.8
26	98.4	26	24.6	26	12.3
27	102.2	27	25.5	27	12.8
28	106.0	28	26.5	28	13.2
29	110.0	29	27.4	29	13.7
30	113.5	30	28.4	30	14.2

ENGLISH TO METRIC CONVERSION: PRESSURE

The basic unit of pressure measurement used today is expressed as pounds per square inch (psi). The metric unit for psi will be the kilopascal (kPa). This will apply to either fluid pressure or air pressure, and will be frequently seen in tire pressure readings, oil pressure specifications, fuel pump pressure, etc.

To convert pounds per square inch (psi) to kilopascals (kPa): multiply the number of psi by 6.89

Psi	kPa	Psi	kPa	Psi	kPa	Psi	kPa
0.1	0.7	37	255.1	82	565.4	127	875.6
0.2	1.4	38	262.0	83	572.3	128	882.5
0.3	2.1	39	268.9	84	579.2	129	889.4
0.4	2.8	40	275.8	85	586.0	130	896.3
0.5	3.4	41	282.7	86	592.9	131	903.2
0.6	4.1	42	289.6	87	599.8	132	910.1
0.7	4.8	43	296.5	88	606.7	133	917.0
0.8	5.5	44	303.4	89	613.6	134	923.9
0.9	6.2	45	310.3	90	620.5	135	930.8
1	6.9	46	317.2	91	627.4	136	937.7
2	13.8	47	324.0	92	634.3	137	944.6
3	20.7	48	331.0	93	641.2	138	951.5
4	27.6	49	337.8	94	648.1	139	958.4
5	34.5	50	344.7	95	655.0	140	965.2
6	41.4	51	351.6	96	661.9	141	972.2
7	48.3	52	358.5	97	668.8	142	979.0
8	55.2	53	365.4	98	675.7	143	985.9
9	62.1	54	372.3	99	682.6	144	992.8
10	69.0	55	379.2	100	689.5	145	999.7
11	75.8	56	386.1	101	696.4	146	1006.6
12	82.7	57	393.0	102	703.3	147	1013.5
13	89.6	58	399.9	103	710.2	148	1020.4
14	96.5	59	406.8	104	717.0	149	1027.3
15	103.4	60	413.7	105	723.9	150	1034.2
16	110.3	61	420.6	106	730.8	151	1041.1
17	117.2	62	427.5	107	737.7	152	1048.0
18	124.1	63	434.4	108	744.6	153	1054.9
19	131.0	64	441.3	109	751.5	154	1061.8
20	137.9	65	448.2	110	758.4	155	1068.7
21	144.8	66	455.0	111	765.3	156	1075.6
22	151.7	67	461.9	112	772.2	157	1082.5
23	158.6	68	468.8	113	779.1	158	1089.4
24	165.5	69	475.7	114	786.0	159	1096.3
25	172.4	70	482.6	115	792.9	160	1103.2
26	179.3	71	489.5	116	799.8	161	1110.0
27	186.2	72	496.4	117	806.7	162	1116.9
28	193.0	73	503.3	118	813.6	163	1123.8
29	200.0	74	510.2	119	820.5	164	1130.7
30	206.8	75	517.1	120	827.4	165	1137.6
31	213.7	76	524.0	121	834.3	166	1144.5
32	220.6	77	530.9	122	841.2	167	1151.4
33	227.5	78	537.8	123	848.0	168	1158.3
34	234.4	79	544.7	124	854.9	169	1165.2
35	241.3	80	551.6	125	861.8	170	1172.1
36	248.2	81	558.5	126	868.7	171	1179.0

ENGLISH TO METRIC CONVERSION: PRESSURE

The basic unit of pressure measurement used today is expressed as pounds per square inch (psi). The metric unit for psi will be the kilopascal (kPa). This will apply to either fluid pressure or air pressure, and will be frequently seen in tire pressure readings, oil pressure specifications, fuel pump pressure, etc.

To convert pounds per square inch (psi) to kilopascals (kPa): multiply the number of psi by 6.89

Psi	kPa	Psi	kPa	Psi	kPa	Psi	kPa
172	1185.9	216	1489.3	260	1792.6	304	2096.0
173	1192.8	217	1496.2	261	1799.5	305	2102.9
174	1199.7	218	1503.1	262	1806.4	306	2109.8
175	1206.6	219	1510.0	263	1813.3	307	2116.7
176	1213.5	220	1516.8	264	1820.2	308	2123.6
177	1220.4	221	1523.7	265	1827.1	309	2130.5
178	1227.3	222	1530.6	266	1834.0	310	2137.4
179	1234.2	223	1537.5	267	1840.9	311	2144.3
180	1241.0	224	1544.4	268	1847.8	312	2151.2
181	1247.9	225	1551.3	269	1854.7	313	2158.1
182	1254.8	226	1558.2	270	1861.6	314	2164.9
183	1261.7	227	1565.1	271	1868.5	315	2171.8
184	1268.6	228	1572.0	272	1875.4	316	2178.7
185	1275.5	229	1578.9	273	1882.3	317	2185.6
186	1282.4	230	1585.8	274	1889.2	318	2192.5
187	1289.3	231	1592.7	275	1896.1	319	2199.4
188	1296.2	232	1599.6	276	1903.0	320	2206.3
189	1303.1	233	1606.5	277	1909.8	321	2213.2
190	1310.0	234	1613.4	278	1916.7	322	2220.1
191	1316.9	235	1620.3	279	1923.6	323	2227.0
192	1323.8	236	1627.2	280	1930.5	324	2233.9
193	1330.7	237	1634.1	281	1937.4	325	2240.8
194	1337.6	238	1641.0	282	1944.3	326	2247.7
195	1344.5	239	1647.8	283	1951.2	327	2254.6
196	1351.4	240	1654.7	284	1958.1	328	2261.5
197	1358.3	241	1661.6	285	1965.0	329	2268.4
198	1365.2	242	1668.5	286	1971.9	330	2275.3
199	1372.0	243	1675.4	287	1978.8	331	2282.2
200	1378.9	244	1682.3	288	1985.7	332	2289.1
201	1385.8	245	1689.2	289	1992.6	333	2295.9
202	1392.7	246	1696.1	290	1999.5	334	2302.8
203	1399.6	247	1703.0	291	2006.4	335	2309.7
204	1406.5	248	1709.9	292	2013.3	336	2316.6
205	1413.4	249	1716.8	293	2020.2	337	2323.5
206	1420.3	250	1723.7	294	2027.1	338	2330.4
207	1427.2	251	1730.6	295	2034.0	339	2337.3
208	1434.1	252	1737.5	296	2040.8	240	2344.2
209	1441.0	253	1744.4	297	2047.7	341	2351.1
210	1447.9	254	1751.3	298	2054.6	342	2358.0
211	1454.8	255	1758.2	299	2061.5	343	2364.9
212	1461.7	256	1765.1	300	2068.4	344	2371.8
213	1468.7	257	1772.0	301	2075.3	345	2378.7
214	1475.5	258	1778.8	302	2082.2	346	2385.6
215	1482.4	259	1785.7	303	2089.1	347	2392.5

2
ENGINE PERFORMANCE AND TUNE-UP

SPARK PLUGS AND WIRES

In order to extract the full measure of performance and economy from your engine it is essential that it be properly tuned at regular intervals. A regular tune-up will keep your vehicle's engine running smoothly and will prevent the annoying minor breakdowns and poor performance associated with an untuned engine.

A complete tune-up should be performed every 12,000 miles or twelve months, whichever comes first. This interval should be halved if the vehicle is operated under severe conditions, such as trailer towing, prolonged idling, continual stop and start driving,

or if starting or running problems are noticed. It is assumed that the routine maintenance described in Section 1 has been kept up, as this will have a decided effect on the results of a tune-up. All of the applicable steps of a tune-up should be followed in order, as the result is a cumulative one.

If the specifications on the tune-up sticker in the engine compartment disagree with the Tune-Up Specifications chart in this chapter, the figures on the sticker must be used. The sticker often reflects changes made during the production run.

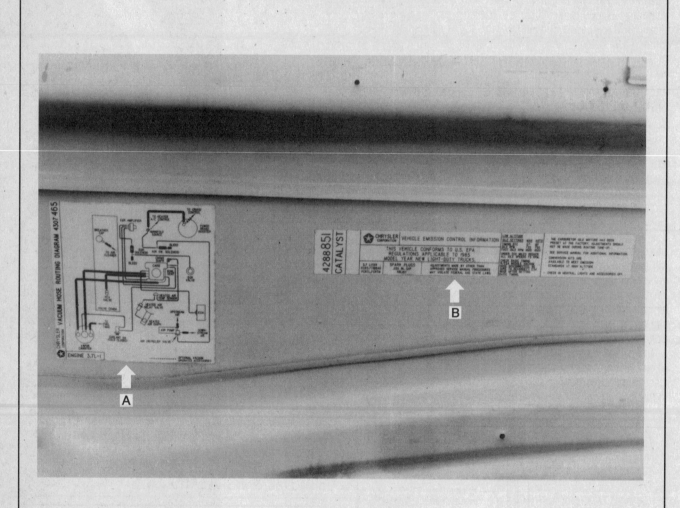

A. Vacuum hose routing label
B. Emissions control label

Tune-up information can also be found on the emission label on the underside of the hood

Spark Plugs

A typical spark plug consists of a metal shell surrounding a ceramic insulator. A metal electrode extends downward through the center of the insulator and protrudes a small distance. Located at the end of the plug and attached to the side of the outer metal shell is the side electrode. The side electrode bends in at a 90° angle so that its tip is just past and parallel to the tip of the center electrode. The distance between these two electrodes (measured in thousandths of an inch or hundredths of a millimeter) is called the spark plug gap.

The spark plug does not produce a spark but instead provides a gap across which the current can arc. The coil produces anywhere from 20,000 to 50,000 volts (depending on the type and application) which travels through the wires to the spark plugs. The current passes along the center electrode and jumps the gap to the side electrode, and in doing so, ignites the air/fuel mixture in the combustion chamber.

SPARK PLUG HEAT RANGE

Spark plug heat range is the ability of the plug to dissipate heat. The longer the insulator (or the farther it extends into the engine), the hotter the plug will operate; the shorter the insulator (the closer the electrode is to the block's cooling passages) the cooler it will operate. A plug that absorbs little heat and remains too cool will quickly accumulate deposits of oil and carbon since it is not hot enough to burn them off. This leads to plug fouling and consequently to misfiring. A plug that absorbs too much heat will have no deposits but, due to the excessive heat, the electrodes will burn away quickly and might possibly lead to preignition or other ignition problems. Preignition takes place when plug tips get so hot that they glow sufficiently to ignite the air/fuel mixture before the actual spark occurs. This early ignition will usually cause a pinging during low speeds and heavy loads.

The general rule of thumb for choosing the correct heat range when picking a spark plug is: if most of your driving is long distance, high speed travel, use a colder plug; if most of your driving is stop and go, use a hotter plug. Original equipment plugs

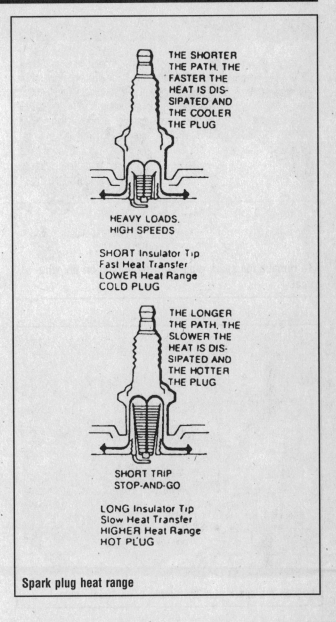

Spark plug heat range

are generally a good compromise between the 2 styles and most people never have the need to change their plugs from the factory-recommended heat range.

REMOVAL & INSTALLATION

A set of spark plugs usually requires replacement after about 20,000–30,000 miles (32,000–48,000 km), depending on your style of driving. In normal operation plug gap increases about 0.001 in. (0.025mm) for every 2500 miles (4000 km). As the gap increases, the plug's voltage requirement also increases. It requires a greater voltage to jump the wider gap and about two to three times as much voltage to fire the plug at high speeds than at idle. The improved air/fuel ratio control of modern fuel injection combined with the higher voltage output of modern ignition systems will often allow an engine to run significantly longer on a set of standard spark plugs, but keep in mind that efficiency will drop as the gap widdens (along with fuel economy and power).

When you're removing spark plugs, work on one at a time.

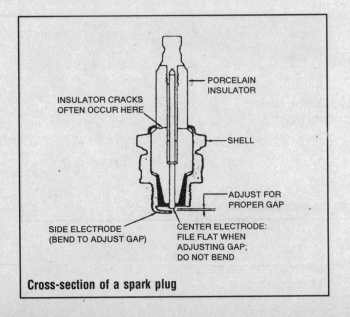

Cross-section of a spark plug

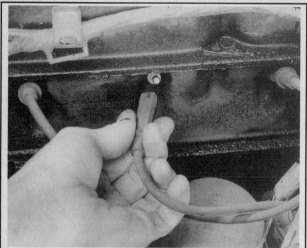

To remove the spark plug, start by pulling on the wire boot

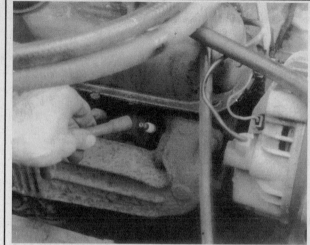

On a V8 engine, the spark plugs are close to the exhaust manifolds, which can be quite HOT

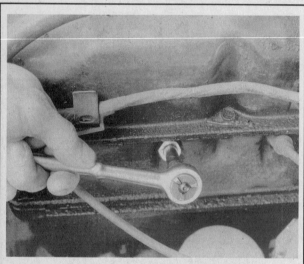

Loosen the spark plug by turning counterclockwise . . .

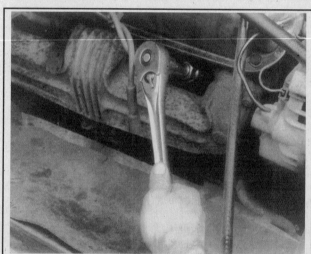

Allow the engine to cool down before removing the spark plugs

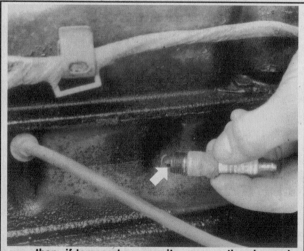

. . . then, if temperature permits, remove the plug and inspect the electrodes (arrow)

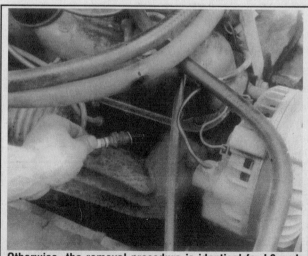

Otherwise, the removal procedure is identical for L6 and V8 engines

Don't start by removing the plug wires all at once, because, unless you number them, they may become mixed up. Take a minute before you begin and number the wires with tape.

1. Disconnect the negative battery cable, and if the vehicle has been run recently, allow the engine to thoroughly cool.

2. Carefully twist the spark plug wire boot to loosen it, then pull upward and remove the boot from the plug. Be sure to pull on the boot and not on the wire, otherwise the connector located inside the boot may become separated.

3. Using compressed air, blow any water or debris from the spark plug well to assure that no harmful contaminants are allowed to enter the combustion chamber when the spark plug is removed. If compressed air is not available, use a rag or a brush to clean the area.

➡**Remove the spark plugs when the engine is cold, if possible, to prevent damage to the threads. If removal of the plugs is difficult, apply a few drops of penetrating oil or silicone spray to the area around the base of the plug, and allow it a few minutes to work.**

4. Using a spark plug socket that is equipped with a rubber insert to properly hold the plug, turn the spark plug counterclockwise to loosen and remove the spark plug from the bore.

✳✳ WARNING

Be sure not to use a flexible extension on the socket. Use of a flexible extension may allow a shear force to be applied to the plug. A shear force could break the plug off in the cylinder head, leading to costly and frustrating repairs.

To install:

5. Inspect the spark plug boot for tears or damage. If a damaged boot is found, the spark plug wire must be replaced.

6. Using a wire feeler gauge, check and adjust the spark plug gap. When using a gauge, the proper size should pass between the electrodes with a slight drag. The next larger size should not be able to pass while the next smaller size should pass freely.

7. Carefully thread the plug into the bore by hand. If resistance is felt before the plug is almost completely threaded, back the plug out and begin threading again. In small, hard to reach areas, an old spark plug wire and boot could be used as a threading tool. The boot will hold the plug while you twist the end of the wire and the wire is supple enough to twist before it would allow the plug to crossthread.

✳✳ WARNING

Do not use the spark plug socket to thread the plugs. Always carefully thread the plug by hand or using an old plug wire to prevent the possibility of crossthreading and damaging the cylinder head bore.

8. Carefully tighten the spark plug. If the plug you are installing is equipped with a crush washer, seat the plug, then tighten about 1/4 turn to crush the washer. If you are installing a tapered seat plug, tighten the plug to specifications provided by the vehicle or plug manufacturer.

9. Apply a small amount of silicone dielectric compound to the end of the spark plug lead or inside the spark plug boot to prevent sticking, then install the boot to the spark plug and push un-

til it clicks into place. The click may be felt or heard, then gently pull back on the boot to assure proper contact.

INSPECTION & GAPPING

Check the plugs for deposits and wear. If they are not going to be replaced, clean the plugs thoroughly. Remember that any kind of deposit will decrease the efficiency of the plug. Plugs can be cleaned on a spark plug cleaning machine, which can sometimes be found in service stations, or you can do an acceptable job of cleaning with a stiff brush. If the plugs are cleaned, the electrodes must be filed flat. Use an ignition points file, not an emery board or the like, which will leave deposits. The electrodes must be filed perfectly flat with sharp edges; rounded edges reduce the spark plug voltage by as much as 50%.

Check spark plug gap before installation. The ground electrode (the L-shaped one connected to the body of the plug) must be parallel to the center electrode and the specified size wire gauge (please refer to the Tune-Up Specifications chart for details) must pass between the electrodes with a slight drag.

A normally worn spark plug should have light tan or gray deposits on the firing tip

A carbon fouled plug, identified by soft, sooty, black deposits, may indicate an improperly tuned vehicle. Check the air cleaner, ignition components and engine control system

A physically damaged spark plug may be evidence of severe detonation in that cylinder. Watch that cylinder carefully between services, as a continued detonation will not only damage the plug, but could also damage the engine

A variety of tools and gauges are needed for spark plug service

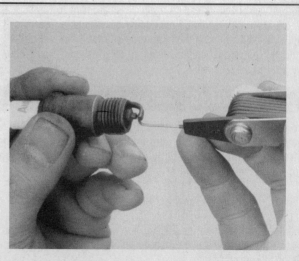

Checking the spark plug gap with a feeler gauge

An oil fouled spark plug indicates an engine with worn piston rings and/or bad valve seals allowing excessive oil to enter the chamber

This spark plug has been left in the engine too long, as evidenced by the extreme gap—Plugs with such an extreme gap can cause misfiring and stumbling accompanied by a noticeable lack of power

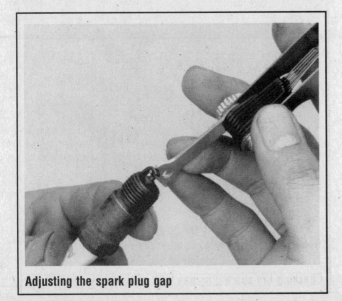

Adjusting the spark plug gap

If the standard plug is in good condition, the electrode may be filed flat—CAUTION: do not file platinum plugs

A bridged or almost bridged spark plug, identified by a build-up between the electrodes caused by excessive carbon or oil build-up on the plug

→**NEVER** adjust the gap on a used platinum type spark plug.

Always check the gap on new plugs as they are not always set correctly at the factory. Do not use a flat feeler gauge when measuring the gap on a used plug, because the reading may be inaccurate. A round-wire type gapping tool is the best way to check the gap. The correct gauge should pass through the electrode gap with a slight drag. If you're in doubt, try one size smaller and one larger. The smaller gauge should go through easily, while the larger one shouldn't go through at all. Wire gapping tools usually have a bending tool attached. Use that to adjust the side electrode until the proper distance is obtained. Absolutely never attempt to bend the center electrode. Also, be careful not to bend the side electrode too far or too often as it may weaken and break off within the engine, requiring removal of the cylinder head to retrieve it.

Spark Plug Wires

CHECKING & REPLACING SPARK PLUG CABLES

Visually inspect the spark plug cables for burns, cuts, or breaks in the insulation. Check the spark plug boots and the nipples on the distributor cap and coil. Replace any damaged wiring. If no physical damage is obvious, the wires can be checked with an ohmmeter for excessive resistance.

When installing a new set of spark plug cables, replace the cables on at a time so there will be no mixup. Start by replacing the longest cable first. Install the boot firmly over the spark plug. Route the wire exactly the same as the original. Insert the nipple firmly into the tower on the distributor cap. Repeat the process for each cable.

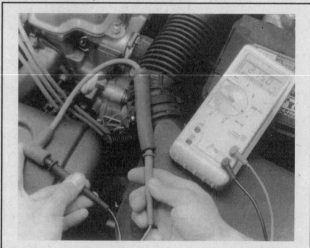

Checking individual plug wire resistance with a digital ohmmeter

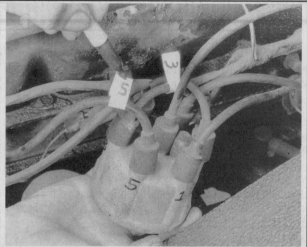

Before removing any wires from the distributor cap, label them to avoid mixing up the firing order

After removing the distributor cap, the rotor easily pulls off of the shaft

FIRING ORDERS

♦ See Figures 1, 2, 3 and 4

➡To avoid confusion, remove and tag the spark plug wires one at a time, for replacement.

If a distributor is not keyed for installation with only one orientation, it could have been removed previously and rewired. The resultant wiring would hold the correct firing order, but could change the relative placement of the plug towers in relation to the engine. For this reason it is imperative that you label all wires before disconnecting any of them. Also, before removal, compare the current wiring with the accompanying illustrations. If the current wiring does not match, make notes in your book to reflect how your engine is wired.

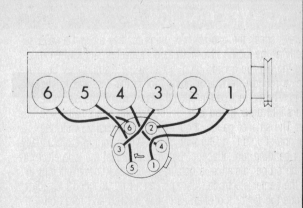

Fig. 1 Engine: 170, 198 and 225 cu. in.
Engine Firing Order: 1-5-3-6-2-4
Distributor Rotation: Clockwise

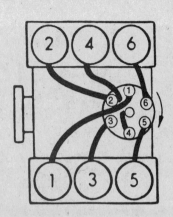

Fig. 2 Engine: 238 cu. in.
Engine Firing Order: 1–6–5–4–3–2
Distributor Rotation: Clockwise

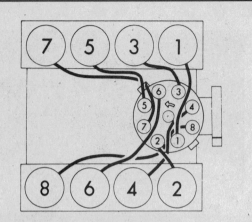

Fig. 4 Engine: 400 and 440 cu. in.
Engine Firing Order: 1–8–4–3–6–5–7–2
Distributor Rotation: Clockwise

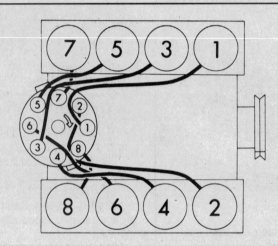

Fig. 3 Engine: 318 and 360 cu. in.
Engine Firing Order: 1–8–4–3–6–5–7–2
Distributor Rotation: Clockwise

POINT TYPE IGNITION

All 1967–73 vans use breaker point type ignition systems.

Breaker Points and Condenser

▶ **See Figures 5 and 6**

The points function as a circuit breaker for the primary circuit of the ignition system. The ignition coil must boost the 12 volts of electrical pressure supplied by the battery to as much as 25,000 volts in order to fire the plugs. To do this, the coil depends on the points and the condenser to make a clean break in the primary circuit.

The coil has both primary and secondary circuits. When the ignition is turned on, the battery supplies voltage through the coil to the points. The points are connected to ground, completing the primary circuit. As the current passes through the coil, a magnetic field is created in the iron center core of the oil. As the cam in

the distributor turns, the points open and the primary circuit collapses. The magnetic field in the primary circuit of the coil cuts through the secondary circuit winding around the iron core. Because of the scientific phenomenon called electromagnetic induction, the battery voltage is increased to a level sufficient to fire the spark plugs.

When the points open, the electrical charge in the primary circuit jumps the gap created between the two open contacts of the points. If this electrical charge were not transferred elsewhere, the metal contacts of the points would melt and the gap between the points would start to change rapidly. If this gap is not maintained, the points will not break the primary circuit. If the primary circuit is not broken, the secondary circuit will not have enough voltage to fire the spark plugs.

The function of the condenser is to absorb excessive voltage from the points when they open and thus prevent the points from becoming pitted or burned.

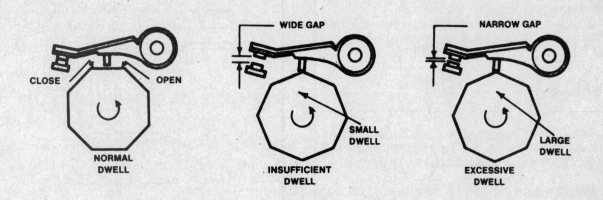

Fig. 5 Dwell is a function of point gap. Decreasing the dwell will increase the gap; increasing the dwell will decrease the gap

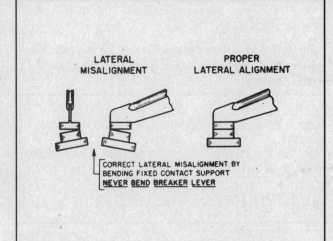

Fig. 6 Insuring proper breaker point alignment will increase their service life

It is interesting to note that the above cycle must be completed by the ignition system every time spark fires. In a V8 engine, all of the spark plugs fire once for every two revolutions of the crankshaft. That means that in one revolution, four spark plugs fire. So when the engine is at an idle speed of 800 rpm, the points are opening and closing 3,200 times a minute.

There are two ways to check the breaker point gap: it can be done with a feeler gauge or a dwell meter. Either way you set the points, you are basically adjusting the amount of time that the points remain open. The time is measured in degrees of distributor rotation. When you measure the gap between the breaker points with a feeler gauge, you are setting the maximum amount the points will open when the rubbing block on the points is on a high point of the distributor cam. When you adjust the points with a dwell mete, you are adjusting the number of degrees that the points will remain closed before they start to open as a high point of the distributor cam approaches the rubbing block of the points.

When you replace a set of points, always replace the condenser at the same time.

When you change the point gap or dwell, you will also have the ignition timing. So, if the point gap or dwell is changed, the ignition timing must be adjusted also.

INSPECTION

▶ **See Figure 7**

1. Disconnect the high tension wire from the top of the distributor and the coil.
2. Remove the distributor cap by prying off the spring clips on the sides of the cap.
3. Remove the rotor from the distributor shaft by pulling it straight up. Examine the condition of the rotor. If it is cracked or the metal tip is excessively worn or burned it should be replaced.

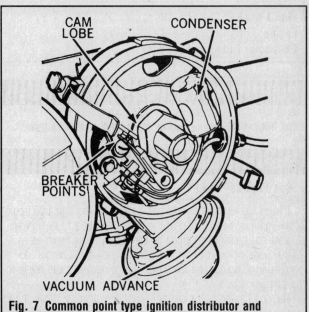

Fig. 7 Common point type ignition distributor and component location

4. Pry open the contacts of the points with a screwdriver and check the condition of the contacts. If they are excessively worn, burned or pitted, they should be replaced.

5. If the points are in good condition, adjust them, and replace the rotor and the distributor cap. If the points need to be replaced, follow the replacement procedure given below.

REPLACEMENT

1. Remove the coil high tension wire from the top of the distributor cap. Remove the distributor cap from the distributor and place it out of the way. Remove the rotor from the distributor shaft.

2. Loosen the screw that holds the condenser lead to the body of the breaker points and remove the condenser lead from the points.

3. Remove the screw that holds and grounds the condenser to the distributor body. Remove the condenser from the distributor and discard it.

4. Remove the points assembly attaching screws and adjustment lockscrews. A screwdriver with a holding mechanism will come in handy here so you don't drop a screw into the distributor and have to remove the entire distributor to retrieve it.

5. Remove the points. Wipe off the cam and apply new cam lubricant. Discard the old set of points.

6. Position the new set of points with the locating peg in the hole on the breaker plate, and install the screws that hold the assembly onto the plate. Do not tighten them all the way.

7. Attach the new condenser to the plate to the ground screw.

8. Attach the condenser lead to the points at the proper place.

9. Apply a small amount of cam lubricant to the shaft where the rubbing block of the points touches.

ADJUSTMENT WITH A FEELER GAUGE

▶ **See Figure 8**

1. If the contact points of the assembly are not parallel, bent the stationary contact so they make contact across across the entire surface of the contacts. Bend only the stationary bracket part of the point assembly, not the movable contact.

2. Turn the engine until the rubbing block of the points is on one of the high points of the distributor cam. You can do this by either turning the ignition switch to the start position and releasing it quickly (bumping the engine) or by using a wrench on the bolt that holds the crankshaft pulley to the crankshaft. Be sure to remove the wrench before starting the engine!

3. Place the correct size feeler gauge between the contacts. Make sure it is parallel with the contact surfaces.

4. With your free hand, insert a screw driver into the notch provided for adjustment or into the eccentric adjusting screw, then twist the screw driver to either increase or decrease the gap to the proper setting.

5. Tighten the adjustment lockscrew and recheck the contact gap to make sure that it didn't change when the lockscrew was tightened.

6. Replace the rotor and distributor cap, and the high tension wire that connects the top of the distributor and the coil. Make sure that the rotor is firmly seated all the way onto the distributor shaft. Align the tab in the base of the distributor cap with the

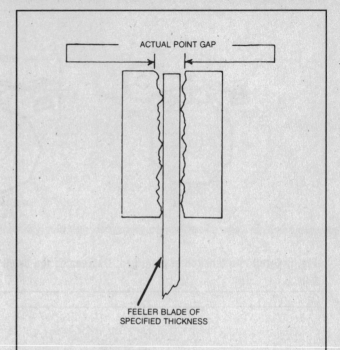

Fig. 8 Due to surface irregularities on the contacts, the feeler blade method is less accurate than the dwell meter method

notch in the distributor body. Make sure that the cap is firmly seated on the distributor and that the retainer springs are in place. Make sure that the end of the high tension wire is firmly placed in the top of the distributor and the coil.

ADJUSTMENT WITH A DWELL METER

1. Adjust the points with a feeler gauge as described above.

2. Connect the dwell meter to ignition circuit according to the manufacturer's instructions. One lead of the meter is connected to a ground an the other lead is to be connected to the distributor post on the coil. An adapter is usually provided for this purpose.

3. If the dwell meter has a set line on it, adjust the meter to zero the indicator.

4. Start the engine.

➡**Be careful when working on any vehicle while the engine is running. Make sure that the transmission is in Neutral and that the parking brake is applied. Keep hands, clothing, tools, and the wires of the test instruments clear of the rotating fan blades.**

5. Observe the reading on the dwell meter. If the reading is within the specified range, turn off the engine and remove the dwell meter.

6. If the reading is above the specified range, the breaker point gap is too small. If the reading gets below the specified range, the gap is too large. In either case, the engine must be stopped and the gap adjusted in the manner previously covered. After making the adjustment, start the engine and check the reading on the dwell meter. When the correct reading is obtained, disconnect the dwell meter.

7. Check the adjustment of the ignition timing.

TROUBLESHOOTING BASIC POINT-TYPE IGNITION SYSTEM PROBLEMS

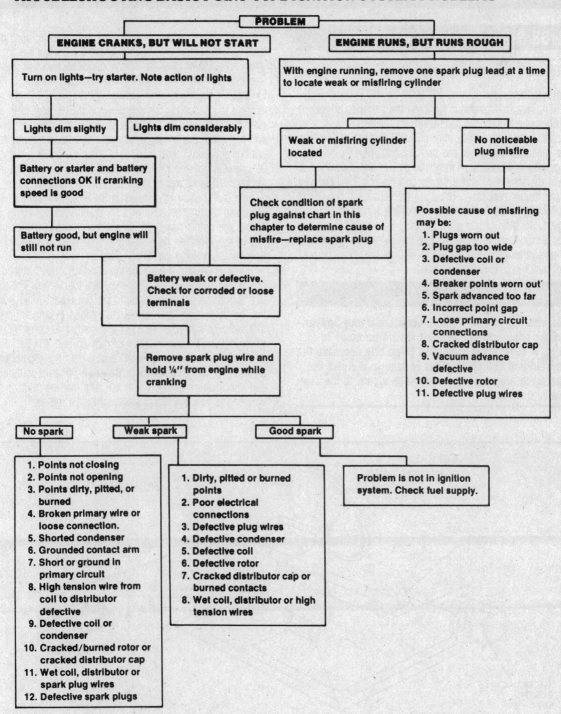

PROBLEM

ENGINE CRANKS, BUT WILL NOT START

Turn on lights—try starter. Note action of lights

Lights dim slightly

Lights dim considerably

Battery or starter and battery connections OK if cranking speed is good

Battery good, but engine will still not run

Battery weak or defective. Check for corroded or loose terminals

Remove spark plug wire and hold ¼" from engine while cranking

No spark
1. Points not closing
2. Points not opening
3. Points dirty, pitted, or burned
4. Broken primary wire or loose connection.
5. Shorted condenser
6. Grounded contact arm
7. Short or ground in primary circuit
8. High tension wire from coil to distributor defective
9. Defective coil or condenser
10. Cracked/burned rotor or cracked distributor cap
11. Wet coil, distributor or spark plug wires
12. Defective spark plugs

Weak spark
1. Dirty, pitted or burned points
2. Poor electrical connections
3. Defective plug wires
4. Defective condenser
5. Defective coil
6. Defective rotor
7. Cracked distributor cap or burned contacts
8. Wet coil, distributor or high tension wires

Good spark
Problem is not in ignition system. Check fuel supply.

ENGINE RUNS, BUT RUNS ROUGH

With engine running, remove one spark plug lead at a time to locate weak or misfiring cylinder

Weak or misfiring cylinder located

No noticeable plug misfire

Check condition of spark plug against chart in this chapter to determine cause of misfire—replace spark plug

Possible cause of misfiring may be:
1. Plugs worn out
2. Plug gap too wide
3. Defective coil or condenser
4. Breaker points worn out
5. Spark advanced too far
6. Incorrect point gap
7. Loose primary circuit connections
8. Cracked distributor cap
9. Vacuum advance defective
10. Defective rotor
11. Defective plug wires

VACUUM ADVANCE ELECTRONIC IGNITION

1972–83 Single Pick-Up Distributors

▶ **See Figures 9, 9a, 10 and 11**

Electronic ignition was optional in 1972–73 and became standard in 1974. This unit functions basically the same as a breaker point distributor, although the parts used are different.

The distributor housing, cap, rotor and advance are the same on the conventional distributor and both systems use the same spark plugs and ignition coil. A magnetic pickup and a control (reluctor) have replaced the breaker points and the rotor. A condenser is no longer necessary. The only maintenance required on electronic ignition units is the inspection of the wiring and the cleaning and changing of the spark plugs.

Also, as a result of the elimination of the contact points, the dwell on electronic ignition units is non-adjustable. It can be read on a dwell meter but cannot be adjusted.

✳✳ CAUTION

Don't fool with the reluctor. The reluctor teeth may appear ragged at the edges, but no attempt should be made to clean them. A sharp edge is needed to quickly decrease the magnetic field and induce negative voltage in the pick-up coil. If the teeth are rounded, the voltage signal to the control unit may be erratic.

The magnetic pick-up and control unit have replaced the functions of the contact points and, unlike the contact points, normally show no sings of wear. Therefore, periodic checks of dwell are unnecessary, and the dwell cannot be altered anyway.

There is however, an adjusting slot on the distributor plate that is used to change the air gap between the reluctor teeth and the pole piece of the coil. Unlike breaker points, reducing the air gap will not retard the timing and since dwell is determined by the control unit and is independent of the pick-up unit, changing the air gap will not affect timing or dwell. The gap between the pick-up and the reluctor should be properly set however.

One of the main advantages of the electronic ignition system is improved starting because with no points, the possibility of arcing across the points has been eliminated. However, a pick-up gap that is too wide can cause starting problems. A "no-start" condition can exist if the gap is too wide.

If you encounter a hard staring condition, don't immediately blame the pick-up gap and change the adjustment. The entire system should be left alone except as a last resort. Make sure that the fuel system and the rest of the ignition system are performing satisfactorily. Although setting the pick-up gap correctly is a must when installing a new reluctor or pick-up unit, the gap does not change in service (due to wear) and should not require periodic checking or adjustment. The main reason that the minimum air gap specification exists is to make sure that the reluctor does not contact the pole piece as the vacuum plate moves.

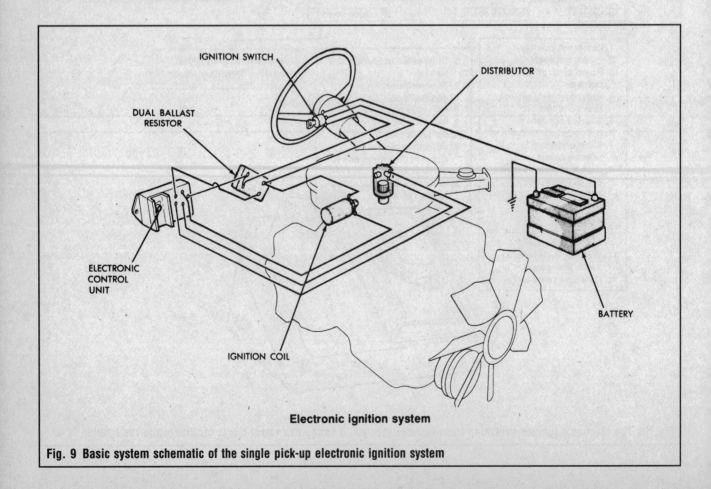

Electronic ignition system

Fig. 9 Basic system schematic of the single pick-up electronic ignition system

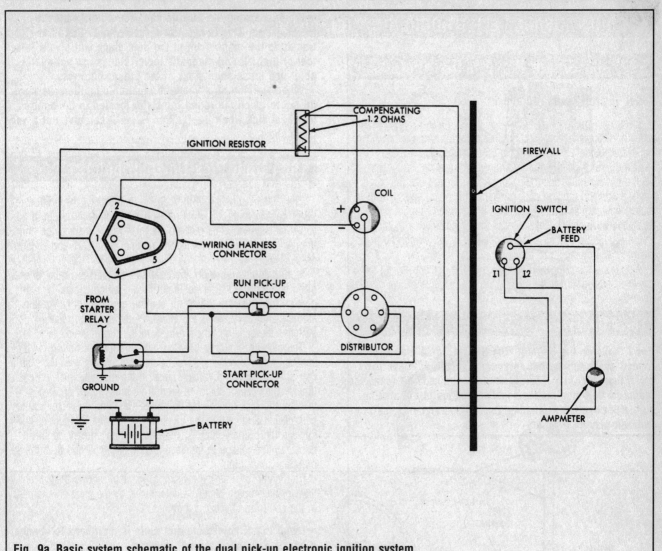

Fig. 9a Basic system schematic of the dual pick-up electronic ignition system

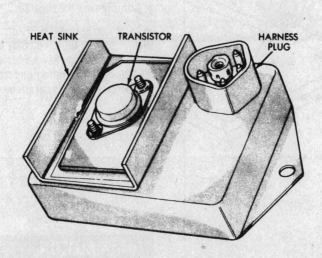

Fig. 10 The electronic ignition switching transistor can give you a dangerous shock if it is touched while the ignition is on

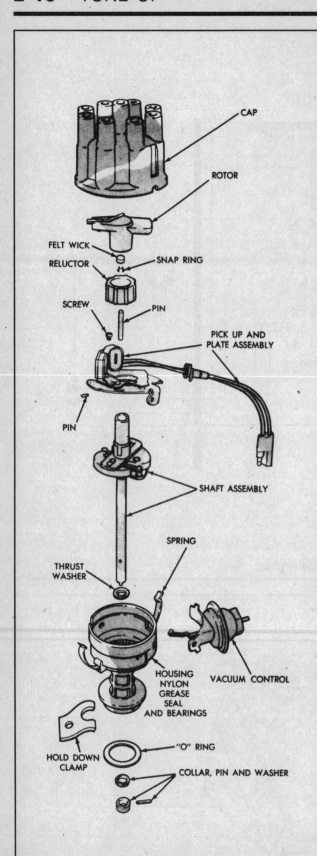

Fig. 11 Exploded view of a single pick-up distributor with vacuum advance—dual pick-up is similar except with an additional pick-up assembly

➡When checking the pick-up gap, use a non-magnetic feeler gauge. This is because a feeler blade that is attracted to the magnetism of the pole piece will give a false feel or drag. If non-magnetic feeler blades are not available, use brass shim stock of the proper thickness.

When working on a van with electronic ignition, be careful not to touch the round transistor located in the control unit heat sink when the ignition is on. It can give out a very large shock.

1984 Dual Pick-Up Distributors

The system consists of the battery, ignition switch, ignition resistor control unit, coil, dual pick-up distributor with vacuum advance mechanism, dual pick-up start/run relay, spark plugs and the necessary components for the routing of primary and secondary current.

During engine cranking, the dual pick-up start-run relay is energized through the starter solenoid circuit, which allows the start pick-up to adjust the timing for starting purposes only. As soon as the starter solenoid is de-energized, the start-run relay switches the sensing function back to the run pick-up.

The pick-up circuit is used to sense the proper timing for the control unit switch transistor. The reluctor rotating with the distributor shaft produces a voltage pulse in the magnetic pick-up each time a spark plug should be fired. This pulse is transmitted through the pick-up coil to the power switching transistor in the control unit and causes the transistor to interupt the current flow through the primary circuit. This break in the primary circuit induces a high voltage in the secondary coil circuit and fires the appropriate spark plug.

The length of time the switching transistor allows the current to flow in the primary circuit is determined by the electronic circuitry in the control unit. This determines "DWELL".

➡Dwell is not adjustable and there is no means to change it because changes are not required.

Diagnosis and Testing

◆ See Figures 12 thru 20

➡To properly test the Electronic Ignition System, special testers should be used. But, in the event they are not available, the system may be tested using a voltmeter with a 20,000 ohm/volt rating and an ohmmeter which uses a 9 volt battery for its operation. Both meters should be in calibration.

PRELIMINARY TESTS

1. Visually inspect all secondary cables at the coil, distributor and spark plugs for cracks and tightness.
2. Check the primary wire at the coil and ballast resistor for tightness.

✳✳ CAUTION

Whenever removing or installing the wiring harness connector to the control unit, the ignition switch must be in the OFF position.

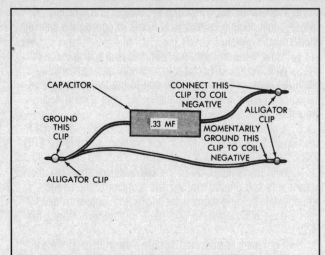

Fig. 12 Special jumper wire used to ground the coil negative terminal on 1972–87 systems

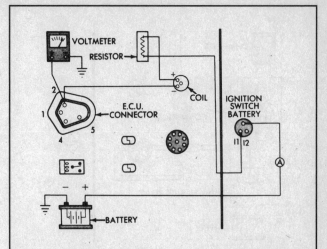

Fig. 15 Testing for voltage at cavity no. 2 of the ECU connector—should be within one volt of battery voltage

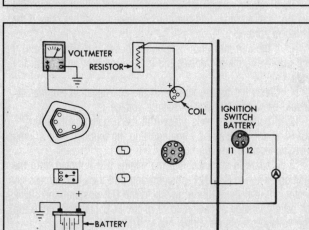

Fig. 13 Test for battery voltage at the coil positive terminal. If no voltage is found, check the wires and ballast resistor

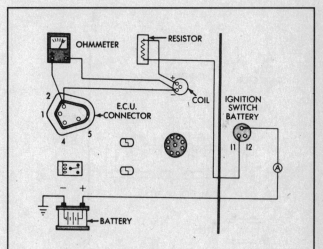

Fig. 16 Checking for continuity between cavity no. 2 and the ignition coil negative terminal

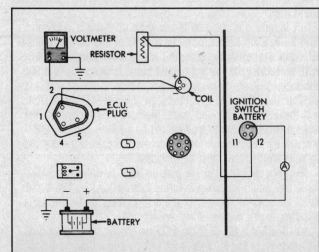

Fig. 14 Test for battery voltage at the coil negative terminal—should be within one volt of battery voltage

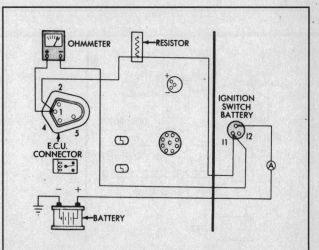

Fig. 17 Checking for continuity between cavity no. 1 and the ignition switch

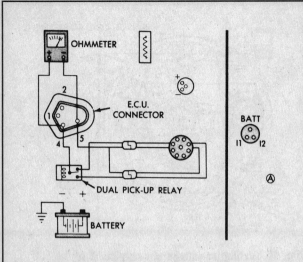

Fig. 18 Checking resistance between cavity nos. 4 and 5

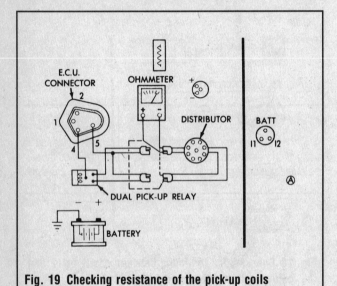

Fig. 19 Checking resistance of the pick-up coils

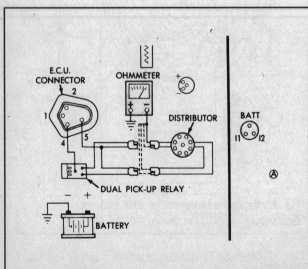

Fig. 20 Testing for a short at each pick-up coil terminal

3. With a voltmeter, measure the voltage at the battery and to ascertain that enough current is available to operate the cranking and ignition systems.

4. Remove the coil secondary wire from the distributor cap.

5. With the key **ON,** use a jumper wire and momentarily touch the negative terminal of the coil to ground while holding the coil secondary wire approximately ¼" from a good engine ground. A spark should be observed.

6. If no spark is obtained, turn the ignition key to the **OFF** position and disconnect the four wire harness going to the ECU control unit.

7. With the ignition key in the **ON** position, again use the jumper wire and ground the negative terminal of the coil to ground while holding the coil secondary wire approximately ¼" from a good engine ground. If a spark is observed, replace the ECU.

8. If no spark is observed, measure the voltage at the coil positive terminal. The voltage should be within one volt of battery voltage.

9. If battery voltage is not present, check wiring between battery positive terminal and the coil. Replace the starter relay if the wiring is correct.

10. If the current is not continuous between the battery and the coil positive terminal, replace the ignition resistor and repeat the test.

11. Check the battery voltage at the coil negative terminal. It should be within one volt of battery voltage.

12. If battery voltage is present at the negative coil terminal, but no spark is obtained when shorting the terminal with a jumper wire, replace the ignition coil.

13. If spark is obtained, but the engine will not start, turn the ignition switch to the **OFF** position and pull the ECU harness connector off, turn the ignition switch to the **ON** position and check for battery voltage at cavity No. 2 of the ECU harness connector. The voltage should be within one volt of battery voltage.

14. If no battery voltage is present, turn the ignition switch to the **OFF** position and check for continuity between cavity No. 2 and the coil negative terminal. If no continity is obtained, find the wiring fault, repair it and retest.

15. Check for continity between cavity No. 1 of the ECU connector and the ignition switch. If none exists, find the fault, repair it and retest.

16. If voltage is obtained at cavity No. 2 of the ECU connector, Turn the ignition switch to the **OFF** position and with an ohmmeter, check the resistance between cavities No. 4 and No. 5 of the ECU connector. The reading should range between 150 and 900 ohms.

17. If the resistance is not between 150 and 900 ohms, Disconnect the distributor pick-up leads. Measure the resistance at the pick-up leads. The resistance should be between 150 and 900 ohms. If the resistance is not within the accepted range, the pick-up coils are bad and must be replaced.

18. If the resistance at the pick-up leads is within specifications, thei would indicate the wiring between cavities No. 4 and No. 5 are open or shorted, or the dual pick-up start/run relay is defective. Repair and retest as required.

19. Check pin No. 5 of the ECU for ground. If no ground is obtained, check the ECU for poor or dirty connections and tight mounting screws.

20. Reinstall all connections and check for spark. If no spark occurs, replace the ECU.

DUAL PICK-UP START/RUN RELAY TEST

1. Remove the two way connector from pins No. 4 and No. 5 of the dual pick-up start/run relay.
2. Using an ohmmeter, touch pins No. 4 and No. 5. The meter should read 20–30 ohms. If not, replace the relay.

CENTRIFUGAL ADVANCE

Test

1. With a timing light connected, operate the engine at idle and remove the vacuum hose from the vacuum controller.
2. Slowly accelerate the engine to check for advance.
3. Excessive advance indicates a damaged governor spring (a broken spring will result in abrupt advance).
4. Insufficient advance is usually caused by a broken governor weight or a malfunction in cam operation. Correct as needed.

VACUUM ADVANCE

Test

1. Connect a timing light and adjust the engine speed to 2500 rpm.
2. Check for advance by disconnecting and then reconnecting the vacuum hose at the distributor and watching the advance or retard at the crankshaft indicator.
3. For a more accurate determination of whether the vacuum advance mechanism is operating properly, remove the vacuum hose from the distributor and connect a hand vacuum pump.
4. Run the engine at idle and slowly apply vacuum pressure to check for advance.
5. If excessive advance is noted, look for a deteriorated vacuum controller spring.
6. If insufficient advance or no advance is noted, this could be caused by linkages problems or a ruptured vacuum diaphragm. Correct as necessary.

Air Gap Adjustment

SINGLE PICKUP DISTRIBUTOR

▶ **See Figure 21**

1. Raise the hood or engine compartment lid.
2. Remove the distributor cap.
3. Align one reluctor tooth with the pole piece pick-up coil. If the van is equipped with an automatic transmission, bump the starter motor using the key. If it is equipped with a manual transmission, place the van in 3rd or 4th gear and roll the van until the tooth is aligned.
4. Loosen the pick-up adjusting screw and insert a 0.008″ (0.006 for 1977 and later) in feeler gauge. The gauge should not fit into the gap. Do not try to force it in.
5. Apply vacuum to the vacuum unit and crank the engine. The pick-up pole should not hit the reluctor teeth. If it does hit, read-

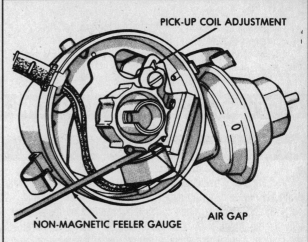

Fig. 21 Air gap adjustment on single pick-up distributors—8-cylinder shown, others similar

just the gap. If it only hits on one side, the distributor shaft is probably bent and must be replaced.
6. Install the distributor cap.

DUAL PICKUP DISTRIBUTOR

▶ **See Figure 22**

In the dual pick-up distributor, the start pickup is identified by a two prong male connector. The run pickup is identified by a male and a female plug.

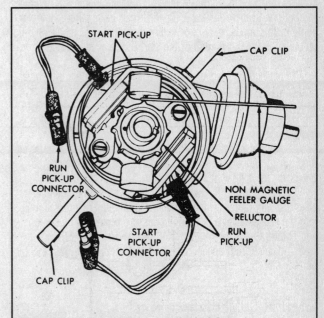

Fig. 22 Air gap adjustment on dual pick-up distributors—8-cylinder shown, others similar

Start Pickup

To adjust the air gap on the start pickup follow the procedure above for single pickup distributors.

Run Pickup

1. Align one reluctor tooth with the pickup coil tooth.
2. Loosen the pickup coil hold-down screw.
3. Insert a non-magnetic feeler gauge (0.012) between the reluctor tooth and the pickup coil tooth.

4. Adjust the air gap so that the contact is made between the reluctor tooth, feeler gauge and pickup coil tooth.
5. Tighten the hold-down screw.

COMPUTER CONTROLLED ELECTRONIC IGNITION

Description and Operation

The computer provides the engine with Ignition Spark Control during starting and during engine operation, providing an infinitely variable spark advance curve. Input data is fed instantaneously to the computer by a series of sensors located in the engine compartment which monitor timing, water temperature, air temperature, idle/off-idle operation and intake manifold vacuum. The program schedule module of the Spark Control Computer receives the information from the sensors, processes it and then directs the ignition control module to advance or retard the timing as necessary. This whole process is going on continuously as the engine is running, taking only milliseconds to complete a circuit from sensor to distributor. The main components of the system are a modified carburetor and Spark Control Computer, which is responsible for translating input data and which transmits data to the distributor to advance or retard the timing.

There are two functional modes of the computer, start and run. The start mode will only function during engine cranking and starting. The run mode only functions after the engine start and during engine operation. The two will never operate together.

Should a failure of the run mode of the computer occur, the system will go into a limp-in mode. This will enable the operator to continue to drive the vehicle until it can be repaired. However, while in this mode, very poor engine operation will result. Should failure of the pick-up coils or the start mode of the computer occur, the engine will not start.

The pick-up coil signal is a reference signal. When the signal is received by the computer the maximum amount of timing advance is made available. Based on the data from all the sensors, the computer determines how much of this maximum advance is needed at that instant.

The amount of spark advance is determined by two factors, engine speed and engine vacuum. However, when it happens depends on the following conditions:

1. Advance from the vacuum will be given by the computer when the carburetor switch is open. The amount is programmed into the computer and is proportional to the amount of vacuum and engine rpm.
2. Advance from speed is given by the computer when the carburetor switch is open and is programmed to engine rpm.

IGNITION COMPUTER

The computer consists of one electronic printed circuit board which simultaneously receives signals from all the sensors and within milliseconds, analyzes them to determine how the engine is operating and then advances or retards the ignition timing by signaling the ignition coil to produce the electrical impulses to fire the spark plugs at the exact instant when ignition is required.

MICROPROCESSOR ELECTRONIC SPARK CONTROL

The microprocessor is an electronic module located within the computer that processes the signals from the engine sensor for accurate engine spark timing. Its digital electronic circuitry offers more operating precision and programming flexibility than the voltage dependent analog system used previously.

MAGNETIC PICK-UP ASSEMBLIES

The start and the run pick-up sensors are located inside the distributor, suppling a signal to the computer to provide a fixed timing point that is used for starting (start pick-up) and the second for normal engine operation (run pick-up). The start pick-up also has a back-up function of taking over engine timing in case the run pick-up fails. Since the timing in this pick-up is fixed at one point, the car will be able to run, but not very well. The run pick-up sensor also monitors engine speed and helps the computer decide when the piston is reaching the top of its compression stroke.

➡**The two systems will not operate at the same time.**

COOLANT SENSOR

The coolant temperature sensor, located in the intake manifold, informs the computer when the coolant temperature reaches a predetermined operating level. This information is required when the engine is equipped with a feedback carburetor, to prevent changing of the air/fuel ratio with the engine in a non-operating temperature mode. Its signals to the computer also help to control the amount of spark advance with a cold engine.

CARBURETOR SWITCH

The carburetor switch sensor is located on the end of the idle stop solenoid and tells the computer when the engine is at idle or off-idle. With the carburetor switch grounding out at idle, the computer cancels the spark advance and the idle control of the air/fuel ratio at the carburetor.

VACUUM TRANSDUCER

The vacuum transducer, located on the computer, monitors the amount of intake manifold vacuum present in the engine. The engine vacuum is one of the factors that will determine how the computer will advance/retard the ignition timing and with a feedback carburetor, change the air/fuel ratio.

DETONATION SENSOR

The detonation sensor is mounted in the number two branch of the intake manifold and is tuned to the frequency characteristic of engine knocking. When detonation (knocking) occurs, the sensor sends a low voltage signal to the computer, which retards ignition timing in proportion to the strength and frequency of the signal. The maximum amount of retard is 11° for 1984 models and 20° for 1985 and later models. When the detonation has ceased, the computer advances timing to the original value.

OXYGEN SENSOR

The oxygen sensor is used when the engine is equipped with a feedback carburetor. The sensor is located in the exhaust manifold and through the use of a self-produced electrical current, signals the computer as to the oxygen content within the exhaust gases flowing past it. Since the electrical output of the oxygen sensor reflects the amount of oxygen in the exhaust, the results are proportional to the rich and lean mixture of the air/fuel ratio. The computer then adjusts the air/fuel ratio to a level that maintains the operating efficiency of the three-way catalytic converter and the engine.

CHARGE TEMPERATURE SWITCH

The charge temperature switch is located in the No. 8 runner of the intake manifold. When the intake air temperature is below approximately 60°F., the CTS will be closed, allowing no EGR timer function or valve operation. The air injection air is switched to the exhaust manifold (upstream). The CTS opens when the intake air temperature is above approximately 60°F., thus allowing the EGR

timer to time out, the EGR valve to operate and switches the air injection air to the catalytic converter (downstream).

Diagnosis and Testing

▶ **See Figures 23 thru 30**

➡**The electronic ignition system can be tested with either special ignition testers or a voltmeter with a 20,000 ohm/volt rating and an ohmmeter using a 9 volt battery as a power source. Since the special ignition system testers have manufacturer's instructions accompanying the units, the technician can refer to the procedural steps necessary to operate them. The following outline will cover the ohm/volt meter unit.**

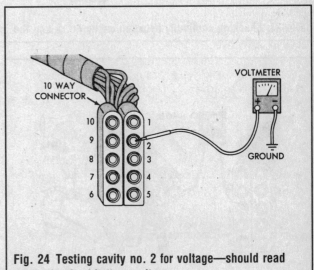

Fig. 24 Testing cavity no. 2 for voltage—should read within 1 volt of battery voltage

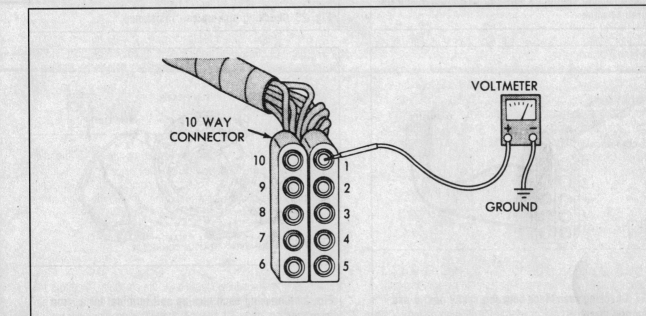

Fig. 23 Checking voltage from cavity no. 1 to ground on the 10 way connector

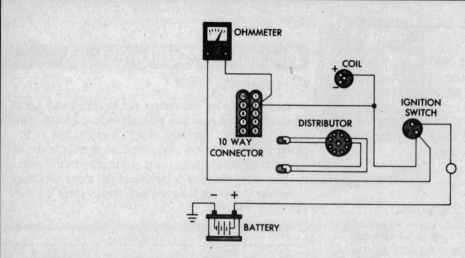

Fig. 25 Checking continuity between cavity no. 2 and the ignition switch

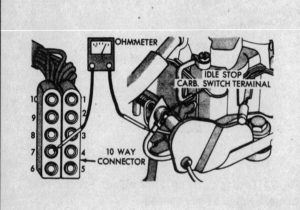

Fig. 26 Checking continuity between cavity no. 7 and the carburetor switch

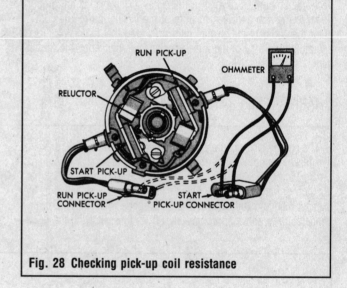

Fig. 28 Checking pick-up coil resistance

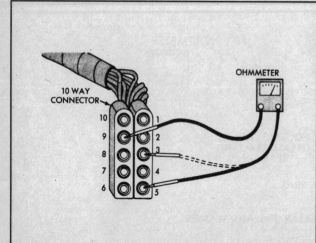

Fig. 27 Checking resistance between cavity nos. 5 and 9; then nos. 3 and 9

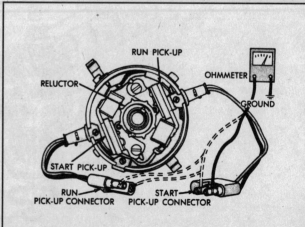

Fig. 29 Checking each pick-up coil terminal for a short to ground

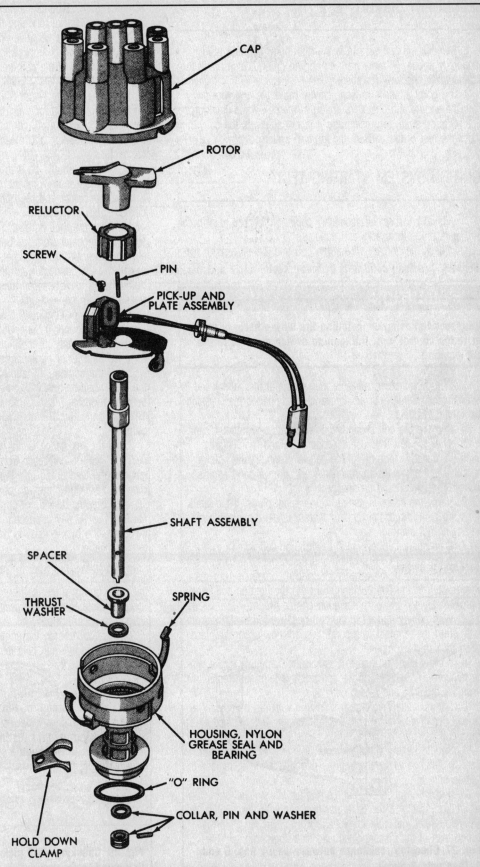

Fig. 30 Exploded view of the computer controlled single pick-up distributor—dual pick-up similar except with an additional pick-up assembly

SECONDARY CIRCUIT TEST

1. Remove the coil wire from the distributor cap and hold it cautiously about ¼" away from an engine ground, then crank the engine while checking for spark.

2. If a good spark is present, slowly move the coil wire away from the engine and check for arcing at the coil while cranking.

3. If good spark is present and it is not arcing at the coil, check the rest of the parts of the ignition system.

IGNITION SYSTEM STARTING TEST

1. Visually inspect all secondary cables at the coil, distributor and spark plugs for cracks and tightness.

2. Check the primary wire at the coil and ballast resistor for tightness.

✳✳ CAUTION

Whenever removing or installing the wiring harness connector to the control unit, the ignition switch must be in the OFF position.

3. With a voltmeter, measure the voltage at the battery and to ascertain that enough current is available to operate the cranking and ignition systems.

4. Remove the coil secondary wire from the distributor cap.

5. With the key **ON,** use a jumper wire and momentarily touch the negative terminal of the coil to ground while holding the coil secondary wire approximately ¼" from a good engine ground. A spark should be observed.

6. Verify the spark is getting to the spark plugs. If the spark plugs are being fired, the ignition system is not responsible for the engine not starting.

7. If no spark is observed at the ignition coil wire, turn the ignition switch to the **OFF** position and disconnect the 10 way connector from the bottom of the spark control computer. Turn the ignition switch to the **ON** position and hold the ignition coil wire approximately ¼" away from a good engine ground.

8. With battery current to the coil negative terminal, intermittantly short the terminal to ground. If spark now occurs, replace the spark control computer.

9. If the voltage is incorrect, check the continuity of the wiring between the battery and the coil positive terminal. Repair the wiring as required and retest.

10. Should battery voltage (within one volt) not be present at the coil negative terminal with the ignition key **ON,** replace the ignition coil.

11. Should battery voltage (within one volt) be present, but no spark is obtained when shorting the negative terminal, replace the ignition coil.

12. If spark is obtained, but the engine will still not start, turn the ignition switch to the **RUN** position and with the positive lead of the voltmeter, measure the voltage from cavity No. 1 to the ground lead of the disconnected lead from the computer. The voltage should be within 1 volt of the battery voltage noted earlier.

13. If battery voltage is not present, check the wire for an open circuit and repair. Retest as required.

14. Place a thin insulator between the curb idle adjusting screw and the carburetor switch or, make sure the curb idle adjusting screw is not touching the carburetor switch.

15. Connect the negative voltmeter lead to a good engine ground. Turn the ignition switch to the **RUN** position and measure the voltage at the carburetor switch terminal. The voltage should be approximately 5 volts.

16. If the voltage is not 5 volts, turn the ignition switch to the **OFF** position and disconnect the 10 way connector from the bottom of the spark control computer. Turn the ignition switch back to the **RUN** position and measure the voltage at terminal 2 of the connector.

17. Voltage should be within 1 volt of battery voltage. If the correct voltage is not present, check the wiring between terminal 2 of the connector and the ignition switch for open or shorted circuits or poor connections.

18. Turn the ignition switch to the **OFF** position and disconnect the connector from the bottom of the spark computer, if not already done. With an ohmmeter, check the continuity between terminal 7 of the connector and the carburetor switch terminal. Continuity should exist between these two points. If not, check for opens or poor connections.

19. Check for continuity between terminal 10 of the connector and engine ground. If continuity exists, replace the Spark Control Computer assembly. If continuity does not exist, check the wiring for open circuits or poor connections. Repeat Step 18.

20. If the engine still fails to start, turn the ignition switch to the **OFF** position and with an ohmmeter, measure the resistance between terminal 5 and terminal 9 for the start pick-up coil of the 10 way connector. The resistance should be between 150–900 ohms.

21. If the resistance is not within the specified range, disconnect the Pick-up coil leads from the distributor. Measure the resistance at the lead going into the distributor. If the reading is now between 150–900 ohms, an open circuit or faulty connections exists between the distributor connector and terminals 5 and terminal 9 of the 10 way connector. If the resistance is not within specifications, the pick-up coil is bad. Replace it and set the air gap to specifications.

22. Connect one lead of the ohmmeter to the engine ground and with the other lead, check for continuity at each terminal of the leads going to the distributor. There should be no continuity.

23. If there is continuity, replace the pick-up coils. Adjust the air gap to specifications.

24. Attempt to start the engine. If it fails to start, repeat the tests. If the engine still fails to start, replace the Spark Control Computer.

➡**Should the engine still fail to start with the replaced Spark Control Computer, Chrysler Corp. suggests reinstalling the original Spark Control Computer and repeating the tests. However, proper testing of the circuits and pick-up should result in the engine starting, unless unrelated problems exist in the systems.**

TESTING FOR POOR PERFORMANCE

Basic Timing

Correct basic timing is essential for optimum engine performance. Before any testing and service is begun on a poor performance complaint, the basic timing must be checked and adjusted as required. Refer to the underhood specifications label for timing adjustment specifications.

Spark Computer Advance of Spark Control Computer Testing

Incorporated within the digital microprocessor electronics are programmed spark advance schedules which occur during cold engine operation. These programmed advance schedules have been added to reduce engine emissions and improve driveability. Because they will be changing at different engine operating temperatures during warm-up, all spark advance testing should be done with the engine at normal operating temperature and a temperature sensor that is connected and operating correctly.

1. With an attached timing light, be sure basic timing is correctly adjusted.
2. Place an insulator between the curb idle adjusting screw and the carburetor switch, or be sure the screw is not touching the switch.
3. Remove tand plug the vacuum line at vacuum transducer.
4. Connect an auxiliary vacuum source to the vacuum transducer and set the vacuum at 16 in.Hg (318 CID engines).
5. Increase the engine speed to 2,000 rpm. Wait for approximately one minute or specified accumulator clock-up time and check the specifications. On certain systems with an accumulator, the specified time must be reached with the carburetor switch ungrounded before checking the specified spark advance schedule. This would be noted on the information specification label.

➡**Advance specifications are in addition to basic timing.**

6. Should the computer fail to obtain specified specifications, the Spark Control Computer should be replaced. Perform the same test on the replacement computer.

Carburetor Switch Testing

➡**Grounding the carburetor switch eliminates all spark advance on mosts systems.**

1. With the ignition key in the **OFF** position, disconnect the 10 way connector from the Spark Control Computer.
2. With the throttle completely closed, check the continuity between pin 7 of the disconnected 10 way connector and a good engine ground.
3. If no continuity exists, check the wires and the carburetor switch. Recheck the basic timing.
4. With the throttle open, check the continuity between pin 7 of the disconnected 10 way connector harness connector and a good engine ground. There should be no continuity.

Engine Temperature Sensor Testing

ENGINE TEMPERATURE SWITCH (CHARGE TEMPERATURE AND COOLANT)

1. Turn the ignition switch to the **OFF** position and disconnect the wire from the temperature switch.
2. Connect one lead of an ohmmeter to a good ground on the engine, or in the case of the charge temperature switch, to its ground terminal.
3. Connect the other lead of the ohmmeter to the center terminal of the coolant switch.
4. Check for continuity using the following ohmmeter readings:
   a. Cold engine-The continuity should be present with a resistance less than 100 ohms. If not, replace the switch. The

charge temperature switch must be cooler than 60°F in order to achieve this reading.
   b. Hot engine at normal operating temperature-The terminal reading should show no continuity. If it does, replace the coolant switch or the charge temperature switch.

COOLANT SENSOR

1. Connect the leads of an ohmmeter to the terminals of the sensor.
2. With the engine cold and the ambient temperature less than 90°F., the resistance should be between 500–1100 ohms.
3. With the engine at normal operating temperature, the resistance should be greater than 1300 ohms.
4. If the resistance is not within the specified range, replace the sensor. The sensor will continually change its resistance with a change in engine operating temperature.

Detonation Sensor Testing

1. Connect an adjustable timing light to the engine.
2. Start the engine and run it on the second highest step of the fast idle cam (at least 1200 rpm).
3. Connect an auxiliary vacuum supply to the vacuum transducer and set on 16 in.Hg.
4. Tap lightly on the intake manifold near the sensor with a small metal object.
5. Using the timing light, look for a decrease in the spark advance. The amount of decrease in the timing is directly proportional to the strength and frequency of the tapping. The most decrease in timing will be 11° for 1984 models and 20° for 1985 and later models.
6. Turn the ignition switch to the **OFF** position. With the engine stopped, disconnect the timing light.

Electronic Exhaust Gas Recirculation System Testing

➡**The Electronic EGR control is located within the electronic circuitry of the Spark Control Computer and its testing procedure is outlined.**

1. All the engine temperature sensors must be operating properly before the tests can be done.
2. With the engine temperature cold and the ignition switch turned to the **OFF** position, connect one voltmeter lead to the gray wire on the EGR solenoid and the second to a good engine ground.
3. Start the engine. The voltage should be less than one volt. It will remain at this level until the engine has reached its normal operating temperature range and the electronic EGR schedule has timed out. The solenoid will then de-energize and the voltmeter will read charging system voltage.
4. If the charging system voltage is not obtained, replace the solenoid and repeat the test.
5. If the voltmeter indicates charging system voltage before the EGR schedule is complete, replace the computer or the externally mounted timer.

➡**The 318-2 Federal engines have no thermal delay below 60°F ambient temperature. It will follow the EGR time delay schedule only.**

6. If an engine is started with the temperature hot, the EGR solenoid will be energized for the length of the time delay schedule only. It will then de-energize.

Electronic Throttle Control System Testing

Incorporated within the Spark Control Computer is the electronic throttle system. A carburetor mounted solenoid is energized when the air conditioner, electric back light or the electric timers are activated. The two timers which are incorporated in the ignition electronics, operate when the throttle is closed, plus a time delay (2 seconds), or after an engine start condition.

1. Connect a tachometer to the engine.
2. Start the engine and run it until normal operating temperature is reached.
3. Depress the accelerator and release it. A higher than curb idle speed should be seen on the tachometer for the length of the EGR schedule.
4. On vehicles equipped with/and turning on the air conditioning or the back light, depressing the accelerator for a moment should give a higher than curb idle speed. Turning the air conditioning and Back light off will produce the normal idle speed.

➡**With the air conditioning system on, the air conditioning clutch will cycle on and off. This should not be mistaken as a part of the electronic control system.**

5. If the speed increases do not occur, disconnect the three way connector at the carburetor.
6. Check the solenoid with an ohmmeter by measuring the resistance from the terminal that contains the black wire to ground. The resistance should be between 15–35 ohms. If not within specifications, replace the solenoid.
7. Start the engine and before the delay has timed out, measure the voltage of the black wire of the three way connector. The voltmeter should read charging system voltage. If it does not, replace the computer.
8. Turning the air conditioning or the back light on should also produce charging system voltage after the time delay has timed out. If not, check the wiring back to the instrument panel for open circuits.

Dual Pick-Up Start/Run Relay Test

1. Remove the two way connector from pins No. 4 and No. 5 of the dual pick-up start/run relay.

2. Using an ohmmeter, touch pins No. 4 and No. 5. The meter should read 20–30 ohms. If not, replace the relay.

Adjustments

PICK-UP COIL AIR GAP ADJUSTMENT

▶ **See Figure 31**

In the dual pick-up distributor, the start pick-up is identified by a two prong male connector and the run pick-up is identified by a male and female plug.

Start Pick-Up

1. Align one reluctor tooth with the pick-up coil tooth.
2. Loosen the pick-up coil hold-down screw.
3. Insert a 0.006″ non-magnetic feeler gauge between the reluctor tooth and the pick-up coil tooth.
4. Adjust the air gap so that contact is made between the reluctor tooth, the feeler gauge and the pick-up tooth.
5. Carefully tighten the hold-down screw.
6. Remove the feeler gauge. There should be no force needed to remove the gauge.
7. Check the air gap with a NO-GO 0.008″ feeler gauge. Do not force the gauge in the air gap.

Run Pick-Up

1. Align on reluctor tooth with the pick-up coil tooth.
2. Loosen the pick-up coil hold-down screw.
3. Insert a 0.012″ non-magnetic feeler gauge between the reluctor tooth and the pick-up tooth.
4. Adjust the air gap so that contact is made between the reluctor tooth, feeler gauge and the pick-up tooth.
5. Carefully tighten the hold-down screw.
6. Remove the feeler gauge. There should be no force required to remove it.
7. Check the air gap with a NO-GO 0.014″ feeler gauge. Do not force the gauge in the air gap.

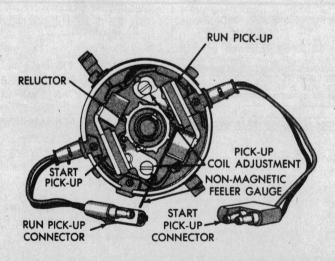

Fig. 31 Checking the dual pick-up air gaps on 84 and later vehicles

ELECTRONIC IGNITION SYSTEM DIAGNOSIS

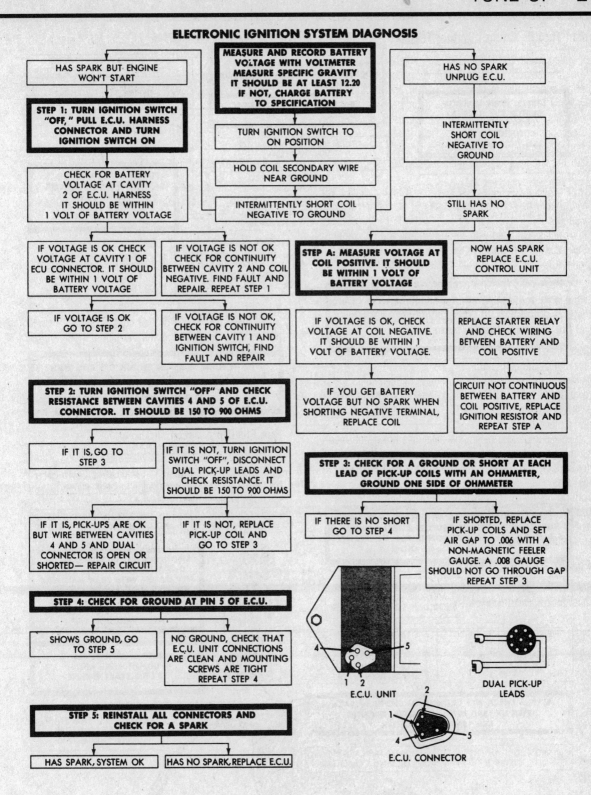

HAS SPARK BUT ENGINE WON'T START

STEP 1: TURN IGNITION SWITCH "OFF," PULL E.C.U. HARNESS CONNECTOR AND TURN IGNITION SWITCH ON

CHECK FOR BATTERY VOLTAGE AT CAVITY 2 OF E.C.U. HARNESS IT SHOULD BE WITHIN 1 VOLT OF BATTERY VOLTAGE

IF VOLTAGE IS OK CHECK VOLTAGE AT CAVITY 1 OF ECU CONNECTOR. IT SHOULD BE WITHIN 1 VOLT OF BATTERY VOLTAGE

IF VOLTAGE IS NOT OK CHECK FOR CONTINUITY BETWEEN CAVITY 2 AND COIL NEGATIVE. FIND FAULT AND REPAIR. REPEAT STEP 1

IF VOLTAGE IS OK GO TO STEP 2

IF VOLTAGE IS NOT OK, CHECK FOR CONTINUITY BETWEEN CAVITY 1 AND IGNITION SWITCH, FIND FAULT AND REPAIR

STEP 2: TURN IGNITION SWITCH "OFF" AND CHECK RESISTANCE BETWEEN CAVITIES 4 AND 5 OF E.C.U. CONNECTOR. IT SHOULD BE 150 TO 900 OHMS

IF IT IS, GO TO STEP 3

IF IT IS NOT, TURN IGNITION SWITCH "OFF", DISCONNECT DUAL PICK-UP LEADS AND CHECK RESISTANCE. IT SHOULD BE 150 TO 900 OHMS

IF IT IS, PICK-UPS ARE OK BUT WIRE BETWEEN CAVITIES 4 AND 5 AND DUAL CONNECTOR IS OPEN OR SHORTED— REPAIR CIRCUIT

IF IT IS NOT, REPLACE PICK-UP COIL AND GO TO STEP 3

STEP 4: CHECK FOR GROUND AT PIN 5 OF E.C.U.

SHOWS GROUND, GO TO STEP 5

NO GROUND, CHECK THAT E.C.U. UNIT CONNECTIONS ARE CLEAN AND MOUNTING SCREWS ARE TIGHT REPEAT STEP 4

STEP 5: REINSTALL ALL CONNECTORS AND CHECK FOR A SPARK

HAS SPARK, SYSTEM OK

HAS NO SPARK, REPLACE E.C.U.

MEASURE AND RECORD BATTERY VOLTAGE WITH VOLTMETER MEASURE SPECIFIC GRAVITY IT SHOULD BE AT LEAST 12.20 IF NOT, CHARGE BATTERY TO SPECIFICATION

TURN IGNITION SWITCH TO ON POSITION

HOLD COIL SECONDARY WIRE NEAR GROUND

INTERMITTENTLY SHORT COIL NEGATIVE TO GROUND

STEP A: MEASURE VOLTAGE AT COIL POSITIVE. IT SHOULD BE WITHIN 1 VOLT OF BATTERY VOLTAGE

IF VOLTAGE IS OK, CHECK VOLTAGE AT COIL NEGATIVE. IT SHOULD BE WITHIN 1 VOLT OF BATTERY VOLTAGE.

IF YOU GET BATTERY VOLTAGE BUT NO SPARK WHEN SHORTING NEGATIVE TERMINAL, REPLACE COIL

STEP 3: CHECK FOR A GROUND OR SHORT AT EACH LEAD OF PICK-UP COILS WITH AN OHMMETER, GROUND ONE SIDE OF OHMMETER

IF THERE IS NO SHORT GO TO STEP 4

IF SHORTED, REPLACE PICK-UP COILS AND SET AIR GAP TO .006 WITH A NON-MAGNETIC FEELER GAUGE. A .008 GAUGE SHOULD NOT GO THROUGH GAP REPEAT STEP 3

HAS NO SPARK UNPLUG E.C.U.

INTERMITTENTLY SHORT COIL NEGATIVE TO GROUND

STILL HAS NO SPARK

NOW HAS SPARK REPLACE E.C.U. CONTROL UNIT

REPLACE STARTER RELAY AND CHECK WIRING BETWEEN BATTERY AND COIL POSITIVE

CIRCUIT NOT CONTINUOUS BETWEEN BATTERY AND COIL POSITIVE, REPLACE IGNITION RESISTOR AND REPEAT STEP A

E.C.U. UNIT

DUAL PICK-UP LEADS

E.C.U. CONNECTOR

ELECTRONIC SPARK CONTROL SYSTEM DIAGNOSIS

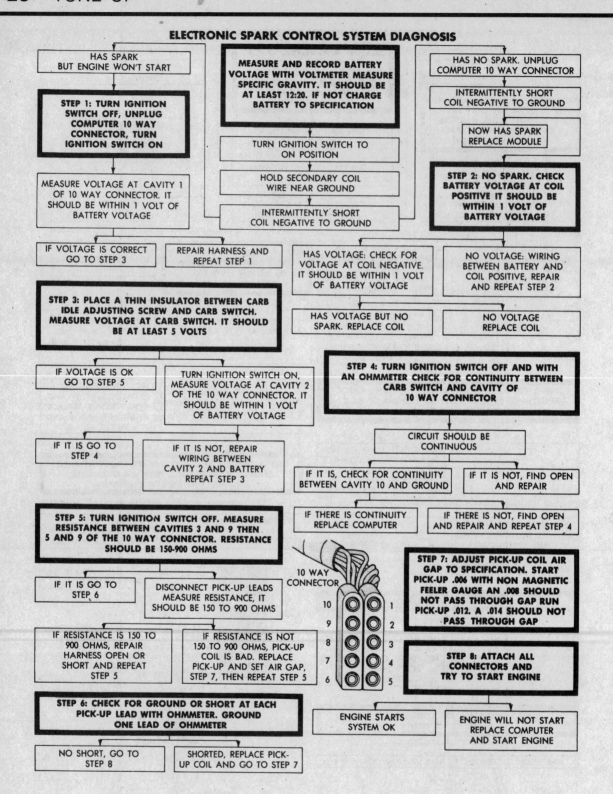

HAS SPARK BUT ENGINE WON'T START

STEP 1: TURN IGNITION SWITCH OFF, UNPLUG COMPUTER 10 WAY CONNECTOR, TURN IGNITION SWITCH ON

MEASURE VOLTAGE AT CAVITY 1 OF 10 WAY CONNECTOR. IT SHOULD BE WITHIN 1 VOLT OF BATTERY VOLTAGE

IF VOLTAGE IS CORRECT GO TO STEP 3

REPAIR HARNESS AND REPEAT STEP 1

STEP 3: PLACE A THIN INSULATOR BETWEEN CARB IDLE ADJUSTING SCREW AND CARB SWITCH. MEASURE VOLTAGE AT CARB SWITCH. IT SHOULD BE AT LEAST 5 VOLTS

IF VOLTAGE IS OK GO TO STEP 5

TURN IGNITION SWITCH ON, MEASURE VOLTAGE AT CAVITY 2 OF THE 10 WAY CONNECTOR. IT SHOULD BE WITHIN 1 VOLT OF BATTERY VOLTAGE

IF IT IS GO TO STEP 4

IF IT IS NOT, REPAIR WIRING BETWEEN CAVITY 2 AND BATTERY REPEAT STEP 3

STEP 5: TURN IGNITION SWITCH OFF. MEASURE RESISTANCE BETWEEN CAVITIES 3 AND 9 THEN 5 AND 9 OF THE 10 WAY CONNECTOR. RESISTANCE SHOULD BE 150-900 OHMS

IF IT IS GO TO STEP 6

DISCONNECT PICK-UP LEADS MEASURE RESISTANCE, IT SHOULD BE 150 TO 900 OHMS

IF RESISTANCE IS 150 TO 900 OHMS, REPAIR HARNESS OPEN OR SHORT AND REPEAT STEP 5

IF RESISTANCE IS NOT 150 TO 900 OHMS, PICK-UP COIL IS BAD. REPLACE PICK-UP AND SET AIR GAP, STEP 7, THEN REPEAT STEP 5

STEP 6: CHECK FOR GROUND OR SHORT AT EACH PICK-UP LEAD WITH OHMMETER. GROUND ONE LEAD OF OHMMETER

NO SHORT, GO TO STEP 8

SHORTED, REPLACE PICK-UP COIL AND GO TO STEP 7

MEASURE AND RECORD BATTERY VOLTAGE WITH VOLTMETER MEASURE SPECIFIC GRAVITY. IT SHOULD BE AT LEAST 12:20. IF NOT CHARGE BATTERY TO SPECIFICATION

TURN IGNITION SWITCH TO ON POSITION

HOLD SECONDARY COIL WIRE NEAR GROUND

INTERMITTENTLY SHORT COIL NEGATIVE TO GROUND

HAS VOLTAGE: CHECK FOR VOLTAGE AT COIL NEGATIVE. IT SHOULD BE WITHIN 1 VOLT OF BATTERY VOLTAGE

HAS VOLTAGE BUT NO SPARK. REPLACE COIL

HAS NO SPARK. UNPLUG COMPUTER 10 WAY CONNECTOR

INTERMITTENTLY SHORT COIL NEGATIVE TO GROUND

NOW HAS SPARK REPLACE MODULE

STEP 2: NO SPARK. CHECK BATTERY VOLTAGE AT COIL POSITIVE IT SHOULD BE WITHIN 1 VOLT OF BATTERY VOLTAGE

NO VOLTAGE: WIRING BETWEEN BATTERY AND COIL POSITIVE, REPAIR AND REPEAT STEP 2

NO VOLTAGE REPLACE COIL

STEP 4: TURN IGNITION SWITCH OFF AND WITH AN OHMMETER CHECK FOR CONTINUITY BETWEEN CARB SWITCH AND CAVITY OF 10 WAY CONNECTOR

CIRCUIT SHOULD BE CONTINUOUS

IF IT IS, CHECK FOR CONTINUITY BETWEEN CAVITY 10 AND GROUND

IF IT IS NOT, FIND OPEN AND REPAIR

IF THERE IS CONTINUITY REPLACE COMPUTER

IF THERE IS NOT, FIND OPEN AND REPAIR AND REPEAT STEP 4

STEP 7: ADJUST PICK-UP COIL AIR GAP TO SPECIFICATION. START PICK-UP .006 WITH NON MAGNETIC FEELER GAUGE AN .008 SHOULD NOT PASS THROUGH GAP RUN PICK-UP .012. A .014 SHOULD NOT PASS THROUGH GAP

STEP 8: ATTACH ALL CONNECTORS AND TRY TO START ENGINE

10 WAY CONNECTOR

10 1
9   2
8   3
7   4
6   5

ENGINE STARTS SYSTEM OK

ENGINE WILL NOT START REPLACE COMPUTER AND START ENGINE

IGNITION TIMING

General Information

♦ **See Figures 32, 33 and 34**

Ignition timing is the measurement, in degrees of crankshaft rotation, of the point at which the spark plugs fire in each of the cylinders. It is measured in degrees before or after Top Dead Center (TDC) of the compression stroke.

Ideally, the air/fuel mixture in the cylinder will be ignited by the spark plug just as the piston passes TDC of the compression stroke. If this happens, the piston will be beginning the power stroke just as the compressed and ignited air/fuel mixture starts to expand. The expansion of the air/fuel mixture then forces the piston down on the power stroke and turns the crankshaft.

Because it takes a fraction of a second for the spark plug to ignite the mixture in the cylinder, the spark plug must fire a little before the piston reaches TDC. Otherwise, the mixture will not be completely ignited as the piston passes TDC and the full power of the explosion will not be used by the engine.

The timing measurement is given in degrees of crankshaft rotation before the piston reaches TDC (BTDC, or Before Top Dead Center). If the setting for the ignition timing is 5°BTDC, each

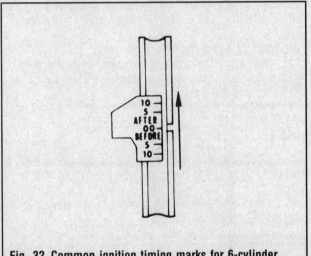

Fig. 32 Common ignition timing marks for 6-cylinder engines

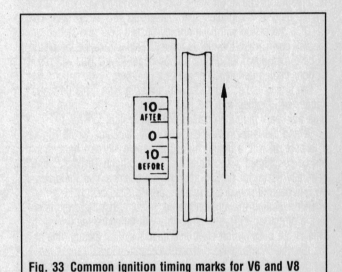

Fig. 33 Common ignition timing marks for V6 and V8 engines

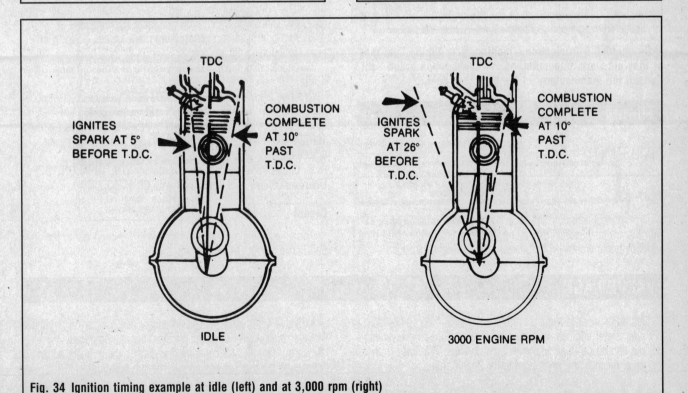

Fig. 34 Ignition timing example at idle (left) and at 3,000 rpm (right)

spark plug must fire 5° before each piston reaches TDC. This only holds true, however, when the engine is at idle speed.

As the engine speed increases, the piston go faster. The spark plugs have to ignite the fuel even sooner if it is to be completely ignited when the piston reaches TDC.

With both the Point Type and electronic ignition systems, the distributor has a means to advance the timing of the spark as the engine speed increases. This is accomplished by centrifugal weights within the distributor and a vacuum diaphragm mounted on the side of the distributor. It is necessary to disconnect the vacuum lines from the diaphragm when the ignition timing is being set.

If the ignition is set too far advanced (BTDC), the ignition and expansion of the fuel in the cylinder will occur too soon and tend to force the piston down while it is still traveling up. This causes engine ping. If the ignition spark is set too far retarded after TDC (ATDC), the piston will have already passed TDC and started on its way down when the fuel is ignited. This will cause the piston to be forced down for only a portion of its travel. This will result in poor engine performance and lack of power.

The timing is best checked with a timing light. This device is connected in series with the No. 1 spark plug. The current that fires the spark plug also causes the timing light to flash.

Setting the ignition timing is basically the same for all engines. It is best set with a timing light. The simple 12v test light should not be considered a substitute for a timing light. Test lights are generally useful for finding approximate settings after the distributor has been removed and ignition timing disturbed.

Before setting the ignition timing, be sure that the dwell is set to the proper specification since this will influence the timing. This is not possible on electronic ignitions. The vacuum line at the distributor should be disconnected and plugged (a golf tee is handy for doing this) and the timing set at the idle speed.

It is a good idea to paint the timing mark with day-glow or white paint to make it quickly and easily visible. Be sure that all wires, hands and arms are out of the way of the fan. Do not wear any loose clothing when reaching anywhere near the fan.

➡**On engines with electronic ignition, your timing light may or may not work, depending on the construction of the light. Consult the manufacturer of the light if in doubt.**

Timing

ADJUSTMENT

1967–83

1. Connect a timing light and a tachometer in accordance with the manufacturers instructions. Never puncture the spark plug wires or boots with a probe. Always use the proper adapters.

2. Start the engine and allow it to reach normal operating temperature.

3. Set the idle speed.

4. Put the transmission in Neutral.

5. On models through 1980, disconnect and plug the vacuum advance line at the distributor. A golf tee or pencil usually works well for this.

6. On 1981–83 and later models, disconnect and plug the vacuum hoses to the EGR valve and the distributor.

7. Loosen the distributor hold-down screw just enough to permit the distributor to be turned.

8. Aim the timing light at the timing marks on the case cover. As the light flashes, you will be able to see the timing scale. Slowly turn the distributor to align the marks at the proper setting.

9. Turn the engine **OFF** and tighten the distributor hold-down bolt. Be careful not to move the distributor while you are tightening.

10. Start the engine and recheck the timing.

11. When the timing is correct, reconnect the vacuum lines.

12. If the engine idle speed has changed, readjust the carburetor. Do not reset the timing.

13. Remove the timing light from the engine.

1984–88

1. Connect a power timing light to the number one cylinder, or a magnetic timing unit to the engine. Use a 10° offset when required.

2. Connect a tachometer to the engine and turn selector to the proper cylinder position.

3. Start engine and run until operating temperature is reached.

4. On 1984–86 models, disconnect and reconnect the coolant temperature sensor connector on the thermostat housing. The loss of power lamp on the dash must come on and stay on. On 1987–88 models, disconnect coolant temperature sensor connector. Engine rpm should be within emission label specifications.

5. Aim power timing light at timing hole in bell housing or read the magnetic timing unit.

6. Loosen distributor and adjust timing to emission label specifications if necessary.

7. Shut the engine **OFF.** On 1987–88 models, reconnect coolant temperature sensor. Disconnect and reconnect positive battery quick disconnect (or erase the fault codes with sensor test #10 on 1987½–88 models), then start the vehicle. The loss of power (check engine) lamp should be off.

8. Shut engine **OFF,** then turn ignition **ON, OFF, ON, OFF, ON.** Fault codes should be clear with 88-51-55 shown.

Diesel

The only timing adjustment possible is injection pump timing. See Section 5 for the procedures.

VALVE LASH

This adjustment is required only on the 170, 198, 1967–80 225 and diesel engines. It doesn't have to be done at every tune-up, but should be done whenever there is excessive noise from the valve mechanism, or at least every 20,000 miles.

No valve lash adjustment is necessary or possible on any other Chrysler built engine. Hydraulic valve lifters automatically maintain zero clearance. After engine reassembly, these lifters adjust themselves as soon as engine oil pressure builds up.

Do not set the valve lash closer than specified in an attempt to quiet the valve mechanism. This will result in burned valves.

Gasoline Engines

ADJUSTMENT

♦ See Figure 35

Inline 6-Cylinder Engines

The valves are adjusted with the engine at normal operating temperature (hot). The valve cover and rocker arms will also be hot, and they could burn you if you're not careful.

1. Start the engine and allow it to warm to normal operating temperature. Make sure that the engine idles down to normal curb idle speed.
2. Turn the engine **OFF.** Remove the valve cover.
3. Using a socket and a breaker bar on the crankshaft bolt, turn the engine in the normal direction of rotation. Locate the #1 cylinder intake rocker arm and watch it's movement as you rotate the engine (the number one cylinder is the front most cylinder). Refer to the illustration for valve identification.
4. As the engine rotates, the #1 intake valve will open (compress the valve spring) and then close (uncompress the valve spring). Once the valve has closed, align the mark on the crankshaft pulley to the 0 degree mark on the timing scale. The #1 piston is now at TDC (Top Dead Center).
5. The lash is measured between the rocker arm and the tip of the valve. To check the lash, insert the proper size feeler gauge

between the rocker arm and the valve tip. A slight drag should be felt. The valve clearances should be:

1967–76 engines
* Intake: 0.012"
* Exhaust: 0.024"
1977–80 engines
* Intake: 0.010"
* Exhaust: 0.020"

6. If there is no drag, or the feeler gauge won't fit, adjust the clearance by tightening or loosening the adjusting screw on the end of the rocker arm. Once both intake and exhaust valves have been adjusted, rotate the engine ⅓ of a revolution (or 120 degrees) and adjust the valves on the next cylinder in the firing order. The firing order is: 1–5–3–6–2–4.
7. Repeat step 6 until you have gone through the firing order. Once all the valves have been adjusted, install the valve cover, using a new gasket coated with sealer. Run the engine and check for oil leaks.

Diesel Engine

ADJUSTMENT

♦ See Figures 36 and 37

Valve adjustment is required on the diesel engine every 36,000 miles.

Do not set the valve lash closer than specified in an attempt to quiet the lifters. This will only result in burned valves.

1. The engine must be cold for this adjustment. Mark the crankshaft pulley into three equal 120° sections, starting at TDC or **0** mark.
2. Remove the valve cover.
3. Disconnect the fuel line from the injector on cylinder #1. Be very careful not to kink the line.

Inline 6-cylinder: 170, 198 and 225 cu. in.
Firing order: 1-5-3-6-2-4

E = Exhaust valve   I = Intake valve

Fig. 35 Valve location for gasoline inline 6-cylinder engines

Inline 6-cylinder diesel engine

E = Exhaust valve   I = Intake valve

Fig. 36 Valve location for diesel engines

Fig. 37 Measuring the valve clearance on the diesel engine

4. Using a socket and a breaker bar on the crankshaft bolt, turn the engine in the same direction as it normally runs until the **0** mark on the crankshaft damper rear face is aligned with the pointer on the bottom of the timing gear case. As you are turning,

keep an eye on the fuel line that was disconnected. Fuel will squirt out of the line a few degrees before you reach the **0** mark. If it doesn't squirt out, you've got the wrong cylinder at TDC. Turn the engine another 360° (one revolution) and you will have #1 at TDC.

5. The cylinders are numbered from front to rear. Refer to the illustration for valve identification.

6. The lash is measured between the rocker arm and the end of the valve. To check the lash, insert a 0.012″ feeler gauge between the rocker arm and the valve as illustrated. Adjust the proper clearance by loosening the locknut on the rocker arm and turning the adjusting screw. After the adjustment is made, tighten the locknut and recheck the clearance to be sure it did not change as the locknut was being tightened.

7. After both valves for the No. 1 cylinder are adjusted, turn the engine so that the pulley turns 120° in the normal direction of rotation (clockwise). The distributor rotor will turn 60° since it turns at half engine speed.

8. Check that the rocker arms are free and adjust the valves for the next cylinder in the firing order, 5. The firing order is 1-5-3-6-2-4.

9. Turn the engine 120° to adjust each of the remaining cylinders in the firing order. When you are done the crankshaft will have made two complete revolutions (720°).

10. Replace the rocker cover with a new gasket. Attach the fuel line to the injector. Start the engine and check for leaks.

IDLE SPEED AND MIXTURE

General Information

The only adjustments covered here are the idle speed and mixture adjustments. These are performed in the course of a normal tune-up. Other carburetor adjustments are covered are covered in Section 5.

Attempting to reset the mixture on your van can be difficult and expensive. It is generally not recommended except on 1967 models without the Cleaner Air Package. No special equipment is required for these models. On all other models, CO meters and pro-

pane enrichment systems must be used. These are not only difficult to obtain, but can be very expensive.

Mixture is preset at the factory when the engine is manufactured and tampering with the mixture screws will usually produce very little change. When performing a tune-up, it is best to simply adjust the idle speed screw or solenoid screw, and leave the mixture alone.

Before suspecting the carburetor as the cause of poor performance or rough idle, check the ignition system thoroughly, including the distributor, timing, spark plugs and wires. Also be sure to check the air cleaner, evaporative emission system, PCV system, EGR valve and engine compression. Check the intake manifold, vacuum hoses and other connections for leaks and cracks.

Non-Feedback Carburetors

ADJUSTMENTS

1967 Carburetors Without Cleaner Air Package

➡1967 CAP carburetors can be identified by a green tag on the air horn.

1. Remove the air cleaner.
2. Run the engine at fast idle to stabilize the engine temperature.
3. Make sure that the choke plate is fully released.
4. Connect a tachometer to the engine following the manufacturer's instructions.
5. On models with 6 cylinder engines, turn the high beams on. If equipped with air conditioning, turn the air conditioner on. The transmission should be in Neutral, Park for automatic.
6. Adjust the carburetor idle speed screw to obtain the specified idle speed.
7. Turn the idle mixture screws in or out to obtain the highest possible rpm. After obtaining the highest rpm, turn each mixture screw clockwise until the rpm's start to drop. Then turn the screws counterclockwise just enough to regain the lost rpm.
8. If the idle mixture adjustment has changed the idle speed, readjust the idle speed.
9. Remove the tachometer and install the air cleaner.
10. Remember to turn the lights off when you're finished.

Except 1967 Carburetors Without Cleaner Air Package

The CAS replaced the CAP in the 1968 model year. CAP carburetors are identified by a green tag attached to the carburetor air horn.

To adjust the idle speed and mixture on these carburetors, particularly on later models, it is best to use an exhaust gas analyzer. This will insure that the proper level of emissions is maintained. However, if you do not have an exhaust gas analyzer, use the following procedure and eliminate those steps which pertain to the exhaust gas analyzer. When you have adjusted the carburetor it would be wise to have it checked with an exhaust gas analyzer.

1. Leave the air cleaner installed.
2. Run the engine at fast idle speed to stabilize the engine temperature.
3. Make sure the choke plate is fully released.
4. Connect a tachometer to the engine, following the manufacturer's instructions.
5. Connect an exhaust gas analyzer and insert the probe as far into the tailpipe as possible. On vehicles with dual exhaust, insert the probe into the left side pipe, since this is the side with the heat riser.
6. Check the ignition timing and set it to specification if necessary.
7. If equipped with air conditioning, turn the air conditioner off. On 6-cylinder engines, turn the high beam lights on.
8. Put the transmission in Neutral, Park for automatic. Make sure the hot idle compensator valve is fully seated.

9. If equipped with a distributor vacuum control valve, place a clamp on the line between the valve and the intake manifold.
10. Turn the engine idle speed adjusting screw in or out to adjust the idle speed to specification. If the carburetor is equipped with an electric solenoid throttle positioner, turn the solenoid adjusting screw in or out to obtain the specified rpm.
11. Adjust the curb idle speed screw until it just touches the stop on the carburetor body. Back the curb idle speed screw out 1 full turn.
12. Turn each idle mixture adjustment screw 1/16 turn richer (counterclockwise). Wait 10 seconds and observe the reading on the exhaust gas analyzer. Continue this procedure until the meter indicates a definite increase in richness of the mixture.

➡This step is very important when using an exhaust gas analyzer. A carburetor that is set too lean will cause a false reading from the analyzer, indicating a rich mixture. Because of this, the carburetor must first be known to have a rich mixture to verify the reading on the analyzer.

13. After verifying the reading on the meter, adjust the mixture screws to obtain an air/fuel ratio of 14.2:1. Turn the mixture screws clockwise (leaner) to raise the meter reading or counterclockwise (richer) to lower the meter reading.

➡On 1975–77 models, adjust to get the air/fuel ratio and percentage of CO indicated on the engine compartment sticker.

14. If the idle speed changes as the mixture screws are adjusted, adjust the speed to specification (see Step 10) and readjust the mixture so that the specified air/fuel ratio is maintained at the specified idle speed.
If the idle is rough, the screws may be adjusted independently provided that the 14.2:1 air/fuel ratio is maintained.
15. Remove the analyzer, the tachometer and the clamp on the vacuum line.

Feedback Carburetors

ADJUSTMENTS

Holley 6145

▶ See Figures 38 and 39

IDLE SET RPM

1. Disconnect and plug vacuum hose at the EGR valve and ground the carburetor switch with a jumper wire.
2. Disconnect and plug the 3/16" diameter hose at the canister.
3. Remove the PCV valve from the valve cover and allow it to draw underhood air.
4. Connect a tachometer to the engine, start engine and let speed stabilize for two minutes.
5. Remove and plug the vacuum hose from the computer. Connect an auxiliary vacuum supply to the computer and apply 16 in.Hg.
6. Disconnect the engine harness connector from the O_2 sensor and ground the engine harness lead with a jumper wire.

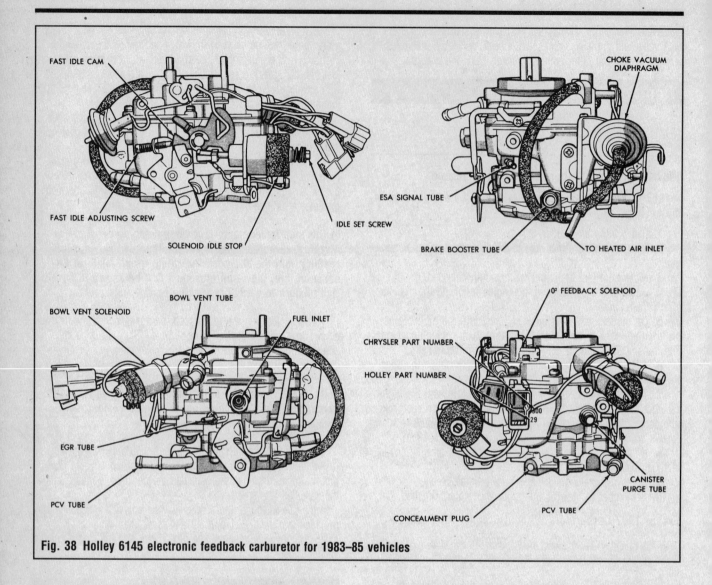

Fig. 38 Holley 6145 electronic feedback carburetor for 1983–85 vehicles

➡**Care should be exercised so that no pulling force is put on the wire attached to the O₂ sensor. The bullet connector to be disconnected is approximately 4″ from the sensor. Use care in working around the sensor as the exhaust manifold is extremely hot.**

7. Let the engine to run for 4 minutes to allow the effect of disconnecting the O_2 sensor to take place.

8. Turn the screw on the solenoid and adjust to specified idle rpm as shown on the Emission Label.

9. Reconnect O_2 sensor wire, hose to computer, PCV valve and canister hose.

10. Remove ground wire from carburetor switch and reconnect hose to EGR valve.

➡**The idle speed with the engine in normal operating condition (everything connected) may vary from set speeds. DO NOT READJUST.**

11. Turn off engine and remove tachometer.

SOLENOID IDLE STOP (SIS) RPM

1. Disconnect and plug vacuum hose at the EGR valve.
2. Ground the carburetor switch with a jumper wire.

3. Disconnect and plug the ³⁄₁₆″ diameter hose at the canister and remove the PCV valve from the valve cover and allow it to draw underhood air.

4. Connect a tachometer to the engine, start engine and let stabilize for two minutes.

5. Energize the solenoid by one of the following methods:

a. Without air conditioning: Connect one end of a jumper wire to the solenoid wire and the other end to the battery positive post.

➡**Use care in jumping to the correct wire on the solenoid. Applying battery voltage to the wrong wire will damage the wiring harness.**

b. With air conditioning: Press the air conditioning button on, set blower speed to low and disconnect the air conditioning compressor clutch wire.

6. Open throttle slightly to allow the solenoid plunger to extend.

7. Remove the adjusting screw and spring from the solenoid. Insert a ⅛″ allen wrench into the solenoid and turn to adjust to specified S.I.S. rpm.

8. Reinstall solenoid screw and spring and de-energize solenoid.

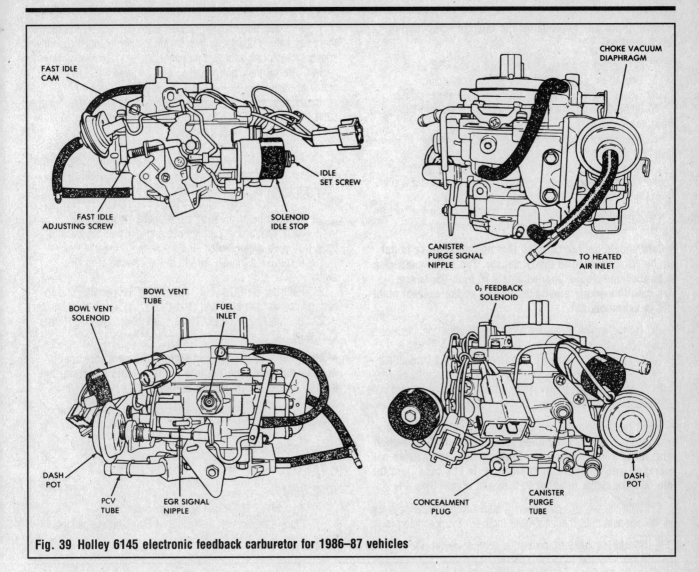

Fig. 39 Holley 6145 electronic feedback carburetor for 1986–87 vehicles

9. Remove and plug the vacuum hose from the computer. Connect an auxiliary vacuum supply to the computer and apply 16 in.Hg.

10. Disconnect the engine harness connector from the O_2 sensor and ground the engine harness lead with a jumper wire.

➡️**Care should be exercised so that no pulling force is put on the wire attached to the O_2 sensor. The bullet connector to be disconnected is approximately 4″ from the sensor. Use care in working around the sensor as the exhaust manifold is extremely hot.**

11. Let the engine to run for 4 minutes to allow the effect of disconnecting the O_2 sensor to take place.

12. Turn the screw on the solenoid and adjust to specified idle rpm as shown on the Emission Label.

13. Reconnect the O_2 sensor wire, hose the computer, PCV valve and canister hose.

14. Remove ground wire from carburetor switch and reconnect hose to EGR valve.

➡️**The idle rpm with the engine in normal operating condition (everything connected) may vary from set speeds. DO NOT READJUST.**

15. Turn engine off and remove tachometer.

PROPANE ASSISTED IDLE MIXTURE

➡️**This procedure should only be used if an idle defect still exists after normal diagnosis has revealed no other faulty condition, such as, incorrect idle speed, incorrect basic timing, faulty hose or wire connections, etc. It is also important to make sure the combustion computer systems are operating properly. Adjustment of the air-fuel mixture should also be performed after a major carburetor overhaul.**

1. If the concealment plugs have already been removed, skip to step 2, otherwise:
   a. Remove air cleaner.
   b. Disconnect all hoses from front of carburetor base.
   c. Center punch at a point ¼″ from end of mixture screw housing. The center punch mark should be indexed at about the 2 o'clock position.
   d. Drill through outer housing at punch mark with a ³⁄₁₆″ drill bit.
   e. If the concealment plug does not pop out when the drill bit enters the plug cavity, use a small drift, punch or allen wrench to pry out plug. Save concealment plug for reinstallation.

➡**Never place any tool against the mixture screw during this operation.**

2. Disconnect and plug vacuum hose at the EGR valve.

3. Ground the carburetor switch with a jumper wire.

4. Disconnect and plug ³⁄₁₆″ diameter hose at the canister.

5. Remove the PCV valve from the valve cover and allow it to draw underhood air.

6. Connect a tachometer to the engine, start engine and let speed stabilize for two minutes.

7. Remove and plug the vacuum hose from the computer. Connect an auxiliary vacuum supply to the computer and apply 16 in.Hg.

8. Disconnect the engine harness connector from the O_2 sensor and ground the engine harness lead with a jumper wire.

➡**Care should be exercised so that no pulling force is put on the wire attached to the O_2 sensor. The bullet connector to be disconnected is approximately 4″ from the sensor. Use care in working around the sensor as the exhaust manifold is extremely hot.**

9. Let the engine to run for 4 minutes to allow the effect of disconnecting the O_2 sensor to take place.

10. Disconnect the vacuum hose from the heated air door sensor at the carburetor and install the propane supply in its place.

11. Open the propane main valve. Slowly open the propane metering valve until maximum engine rpm is reached.

➡**When too much propane is added, engine speed will decrease. Fine tune the metering valve for the highest engine rpm. Also, if idle mixture is extremely rich, engine rpm will decrease with any amount of propane. In this case, turn the idle mixture screw in about ½ turn and repeat Step 11.**

12. With the propane still flowing, adjust the idle speeds screw on the solenoid until the tachometer indicates the specified propane rpm.

13. Fine tune the metering valve for the highest engine rpm. If there has been a change in the maximum rpm, readjust the idle speed screw to the specified propane rpm.

14. Turn off the main propane valve and allow the engine speed to stabilize.

15. Slowly adjust the mixture screw until the tachometer indicates the specified idle rpm. Pause between adjustments to allow the engine speed to stabilize.

16. Turn on the propane valve.

17. Fine turn the metering valve to get the highest engine rpm. If the maximum speed is more than 25 rpm different than the specified propane rpm, repeat Steps 11–16. If okay, proceed to Step 18.

18. Turn off both valves on the propane bottle.

19. Remove propane supply hose and reinstall the vacuum hose that goes to the heated air door sensor.

20. Remove the jumper wire from the carburetor ground switch.

21. Reinstall the PCV valve, remove the jumper wire and reconnect radiator fan plug and reconnect O_2 system test connector.

22. Unplug and reconnect the vacuum hose connector to the EGR valve.

➡**After Steps 18–22 are completed, the curb idle speed may be different than the idle set rpm. This is normal and engine speed should not be readjusted.**

23. Turn engine off and remove tachometer. Reinstall the concealment plug.

Holley 2280/6280

◆ **See Figures 40 thru 45**

IDLE RPM

1. Turn off all lights and accessories.

2. Place transmission in Neutral or Park and set parking brake.

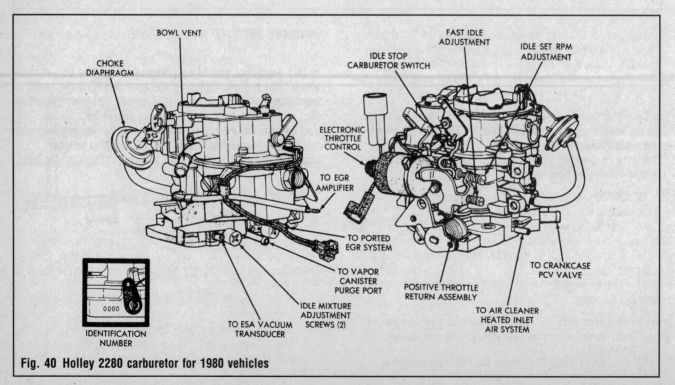

Fig. 40 Holley 2280 carburetor for 1980 vehicles

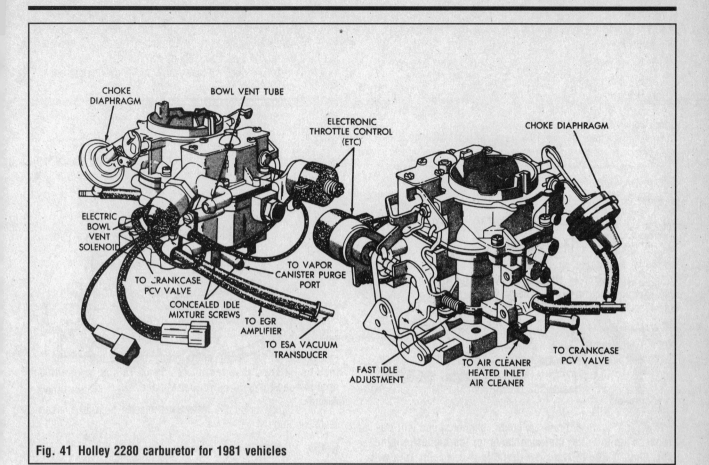

Fig. 41 Holley 2280 carburetor for 1981 vehicles

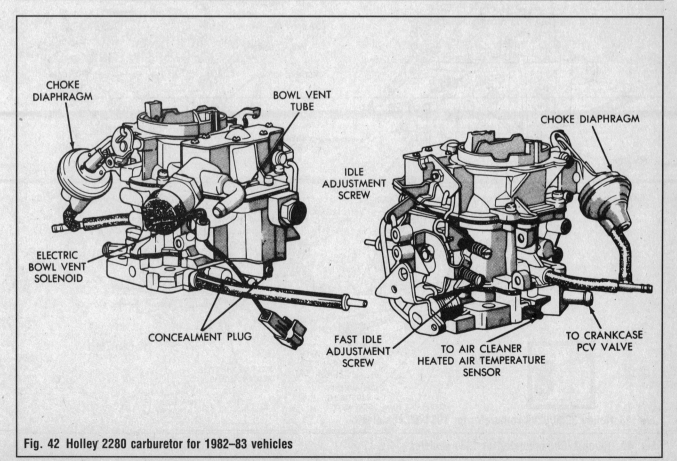

Fig. 42 Holley 2280 carburetor for 1982–83 vehicles

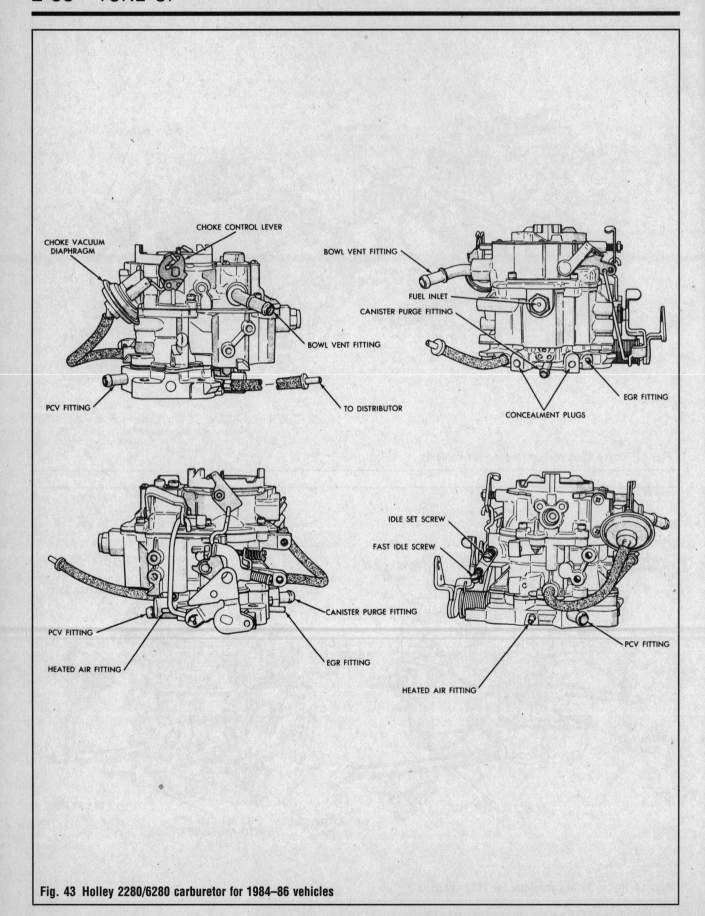

Fig. 43 Holley 2280/6280 carburetor for 1984–86 vehicles

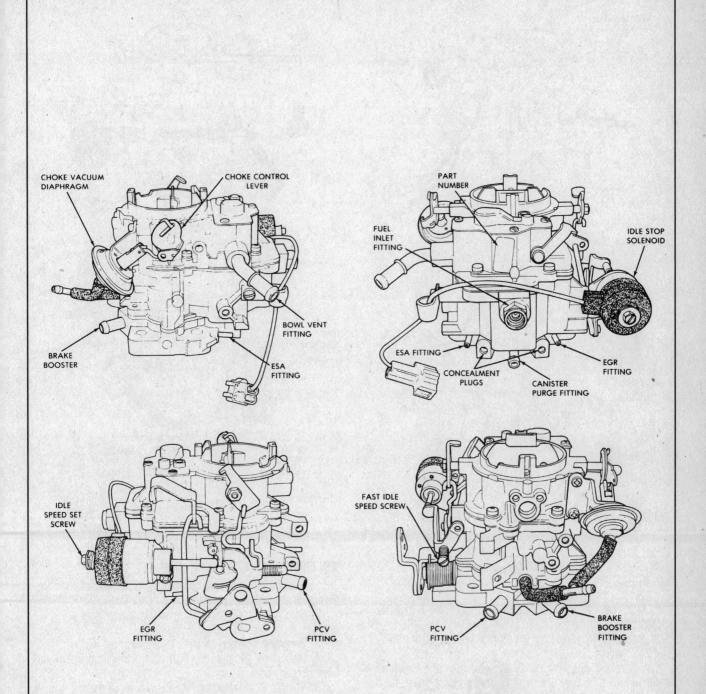

Fig. 44 Holley 2280 Carburetor for 1987 vehicles

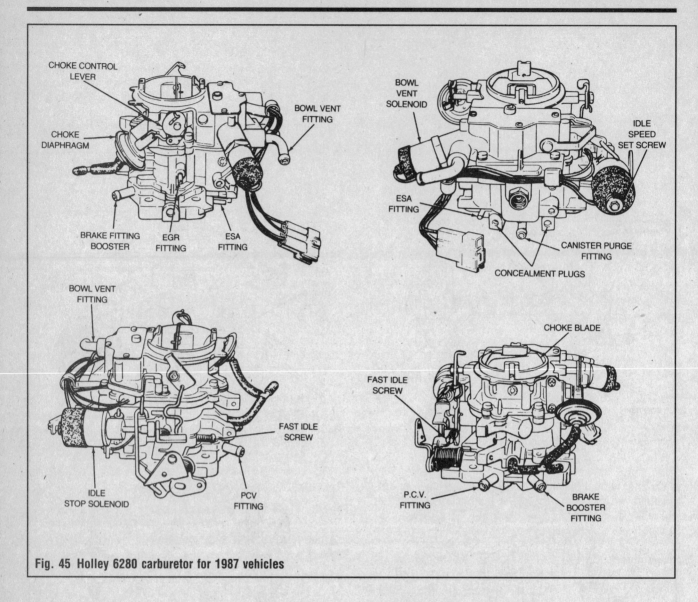

Fig. 45 Holley 6280 carburetor for 1987 vehicles

3. Start engine and run until operating temperature is reached.

4. Ground the carburetor switch with a jumper wire.

5. Disconnect and plug computer, EGR valve and 3/16" diameter canister vacuum hoses.

6. Remove PCV valve from the valve cover and allow it to draw underhood air.

7. Disconnect wire from the O_2 sensor and ground it with a jumper wire. Let the engine run for 4 minutes before proceeding.

8. Connect a tachometer to engine.

9. Turn the screw on the solenoid and adjust engine speed to specified rpm as shown on the emission label.

10. Remove jumper wire from O_2 sensor harness connector and reconnect to O_2 sensor.

11. Reinstall PCV into valve cover.

12. Reconnect all vacuum hoses.

13. Remove jumper wire from carburetor switch.

➡**The idle speed with the engine in normal operating condition (everything connected) may vary from set speeds. DO NOT READJUST.**

14. Turn off engine and remove tachometer.

SOLENOID IDLE STOP (SIS) RPM

1. Turn off all lights and accessories, place transmission in Neutral or Park and set parking brake.

2. Start and run engine until operating temperature is reached.

3. Ground the carburetor switch with a jumper wire.

4. Disconnect and plug the EGR valve and 3/16" diameter canister vacuum hoses.

5. Remove PCV valve from the valve cover and allow to draw underhood air.

6. Connect a tachometer to engine.

7. Energize the solenoid by one of the following methods:

a. Without air conditioning: Connect one end of a jumper wire to the solenoid wire and the other end to the battery positive post.

➡**Use care in jumping to the correct wire on the solenoid. Applying battery voltage to the wrong wire will damage the wiring harness.**

b. With air conditioning: Press the air conditioning button on, set blower speed to low and disconnect the air conditioning compressor clutch wire.

8. Open throttle slightly to allow the solenoid plunger to extend.

9. Remove the adjusting screw and spring from the solenoid. Insert a ⅛" allen wrench into the solenoid and turn to adjust to specified SIS rpm.

10. Reinstall solenoid screw and spring until it lightly bottoms out and de-energize solenoid.

11. Remove and plug the vacuum hose from the computer.

12. Disconnect the engine harness connector from the O₂ sensor and ground the engine harness lead with a jumper wire.

➡ Care should be exercised so that no pulling force is put on the wire attached to the O₂ sensor. The bullet connector to be disconnected is approximately 4" from the sensor. Use care in working around the sensor as the exhaust manifold is extremely hot.

13. Let the engine to run for 4 minutes to allow the effect of disconnecting the O₂ sensor to take place.

14. Turn the screw on the solenoid and adjust to specified idle rpm as shown on the Emission Label.

15. Reconnect the O₂ sensor wire, hose the computer, PCV valve and canister hose.

16. Remove ground wire from carburetor switch and reconnect hose to EGR valve. The idle rpm with the engine in normal operating condition (everything connected) may vary from set speeds. DO NOT READJUST.

17. Turn engine off and remove tachometer.

PROPANE ASSISTED IDLE MIXTURE

➡ This procedure should only be used if an idle defect still exists after normal diagnosis has revealed no other faulty condition, such as, incorrect idle speed, incorrect basic timing, faulty hose or wire connections, etc. It is also important to make sure the combustion computer systems are operating properly. Adjustment of the air-fuel mixture should also be performed after a major carburetor overhaul.

1. If the concealment plugs have already been removed, skip to step 2, otherwise:

   a. Remove air cleaner and disconnect all hoses from front of carburetor base.

   b. Center punch at a point ¼" from end of mixture screw housing.

   c. Drill through at punch mark with ³⁄₁₆" drill bit.

   d. Repeat operation on opposite side.

   e. Pry out plugs and save for reuse.

2. Turn off all lights and accessories.

3. Place transmission in Neutral or Park and set parking brake.

4. Start engine and run until operating temperature is reached.

5. Ground the carburetor switch with a jumper wire.

6. Disconnect and plug computer, EGR valve and ³⁄₁₆" diameter canister vacuum hoses.

7. Remove PCV valve from the valve cover and allow it to draw underhood air.

8. Disconnect wire from the O₂ sensor and ground it with a jumper wire. Let the engine run for 4 minutes before proceeding.

9. Connect a tachometer to engine.

10. Tee in propane supply hose in the vacuum line to the choke vacuum kick diaphrapm.

11. Open the propane main valve. Slowly open the propane metering valve until maximum engine rpm is reached.

➡ When too much propane is added, engine speed will decrease. Fine tune the metering valve for the highest engine rpm. Also, if idle mixture is extremely rich, engine rpm will decrease with any amount of propane. In this case, turn the idle mixture screw in about ½ turn and repeat Step 11.

12. With the propane still flowing, adjust the idle speeds screw on the solenoid until the tachometer indicates the specified propane rpm.

13. Fine tune the metering valve for the highest engine rpm. If there has been a change in the maximum rpm, readjust the idle speed screw to the specified propane rpm.

14. Turn off the main propane valve and allow the engine speed to stabilize.

15. Slowly adjust the mixture screw(s) until the tachometer indicates the specified idle rpm. Pause between adjustments to allow the engine speed to stabilize.

16. Turn on the propane valve.

17. Fine tune the metering valve to get the highest engine rpm. If the maximum speed is more than 25 rpm different than the specified propane rpm, repeat Steps 11–16. If okay, proceed to Step 18.

18. Turn off both valves on the propane bottle.

19. Remove propane supply hose.

20. Remove the jumper wire from the carburetor ground switch.

21. Reinstall the PCV valve, remove the jumper wire from O₂ sensor harness connector and reconnect O₂ sensor connector.

22. Unplug and reconnect the vacuum hose connector to the computer, canister and EGR valve.

➡ After Steps 18–22 are completed, the curb idle speed may be different than the idle set rpm. This is normal and engine speed should not be readjusted.

23. Turn engine off and remove tachometer. Reinstall the concealment plug.

Carter BBD

▶ See Figures 46 thru 51

IDLE RPM

1. Disconnect and plug vacuum hose at the EGR valve and ground the carburetor switch with a jumper wire.

2. Disconnect and plug the ³⁄₁₆" diameter hose at the canister.

3. Remove the PCV valve from the valve cover and allow it to draw underhood air.

4. Connect a tachometer to the engine, start engine and let speed stabilize for two minutes.

5. Remove and plug the vacuum hose from the computer. Connect an auxiliary vacuum supply to the computer and apply 16 in.Hg.

6. Disconnect the engine harness connector from the O₂ sensor and ground the engine harness lead with a jumper wire.

➡ Care should be exercised so that no pulling force is put on the wire attached to the O₂ sensor. The bullet connector to be disconnected is approximately 4" from the sensor. Use care in working around the sensor as the exhaust manifold is extremely hot.

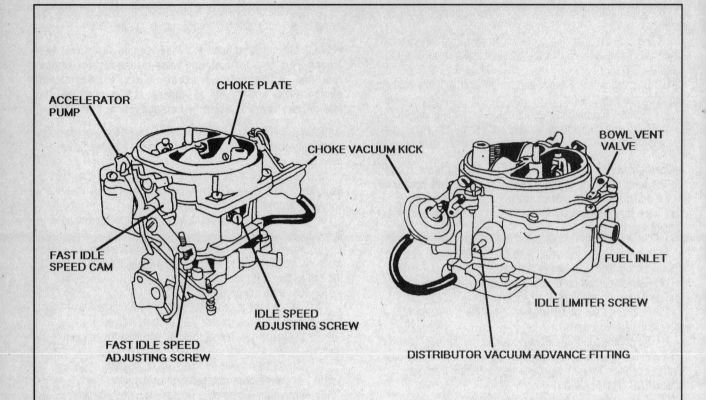

Fig. 46 Carter BBD carburetor for 1967–72 vehicles

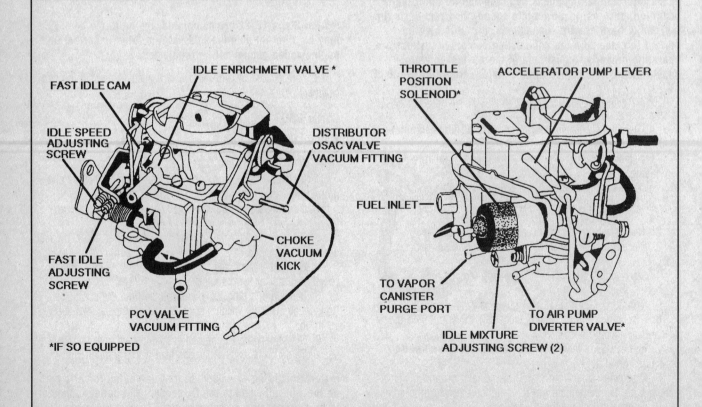

Fig. 47 Carter BBD carburetor for 1973–79 vehicles

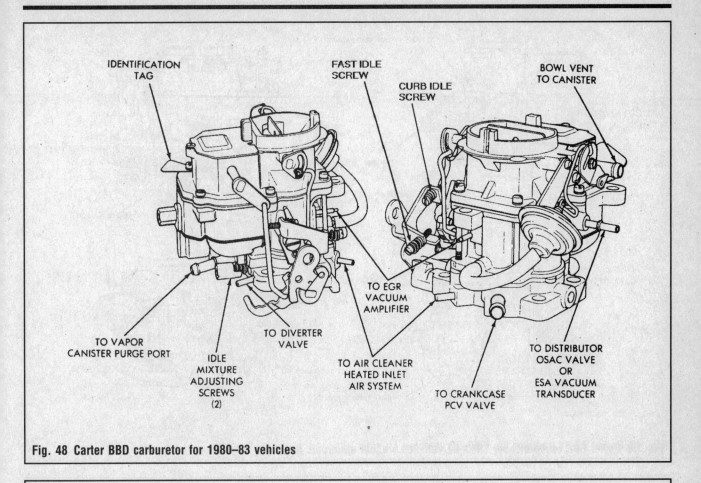

IDENTIFICATION TAG

FAST IDLE SCREW

CURB IDLE SCREW

BOWL VENT TO CANISTER

TO EGR VACUUM AMPLIFIER

TO VAPOR CANISTER PURGE PORT

IDLE MIXTURE ADJUSTING SCREWS (2)

TO DIVERTER VALVE

TO AIR CLEANER HEATED INLET AIR SYSTEM

TO CRANKCASE PCV VALVE

TO DISTRIBUTOR OSAC VALVE OR ESA VACUUM TRANSDUCER

Fig. 48 Carter BBD carburetor for 1980–83 vehicles

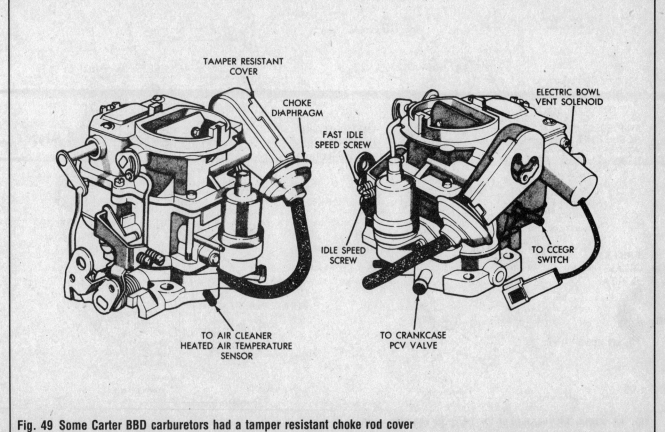

TAMPER RESISTANT COVER

CHOKE DIAPHRAGM

ELECTRIC BOWL VENT SOLENOID

FAST IDLE SPEED SCREW

IDLE SPEED SCREW

TO AIR CLEANER HEATED AIR TEMPERATURE SENSOR

TO CRANKCASE PCV VALVE

TO CCEGR SWITCH

Fig. 49 Some Carter BBD carburetors had a tamper resistant choke rod cover

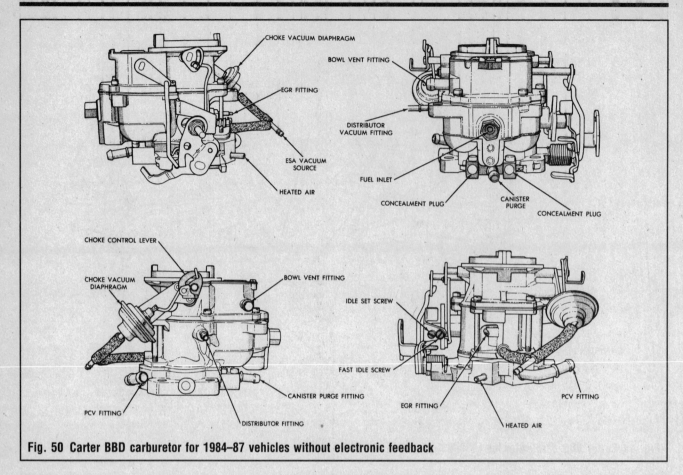

Fig. 50 Carter BBD carburetor for 1984–87 vehicles without electronic feedback

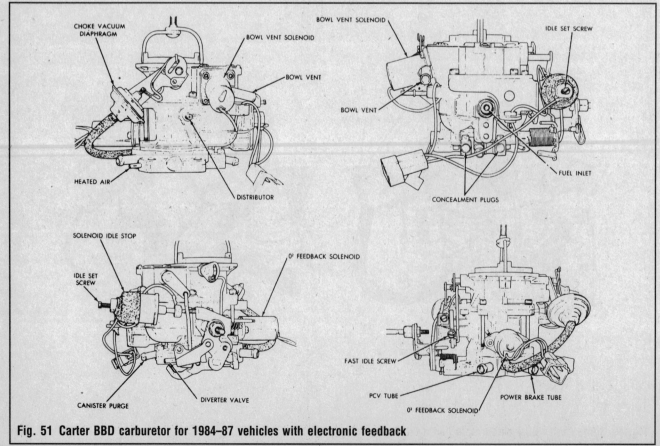

Fig. 51 Carter BBD carburetor for 1984–87 vehicles with electronic feedback

7. Let the engine to run for 4 minutes to allow the effect of disconnecting the O$_2$ sensor to take place.

8. Turn the screw on the solenoid and adjust to specified idle rpm as shown on the Emission Label.

9. Reconnect O$_2$ sensor wire, hose to computer, PCV valve and canister hose.

10. Remove ground wire from carburetor switch and reconnect hose to EGR valve.

11. The idle speed with the engine in normal operating condition (everything connected) may vary from set speeds. DO NOT READJUST. Turn off engine and remove tachometer.

SOLENOID IDLE STOP (SIS) RPM

1. Disconnect and plug vacuum hose at the EGR valve.

2. Ground the carburetor switch with a jumper wire.

3. Disconnect and plug the ³/₁₆" diameter hose at the canister and remove the PCV valve from the valve cover and allow it to draw underhood air.

4. Connect a tachometer to the engine, start engine and let stabilize for two minutes.

5. Energize the solenoid by one of the following methods:

a. Without air conditioning: Connect one end of a jumper wire to the solenoid wire and the other end to the battery positive post.

➡**Use care in jumping to the correct wire on the solenoid. Applying battery voltage to the wrong wire will damage the wiring harness.**

b. With air conditioning: Press the air conditioning button ON, set blower speed to low and disconnect the air conditioning compressor clutch wire.

6. Open throttle slightly to allow the solenoid plunger to extend.

7. Turn the screw on the throttle lever to adjust to specified SIS rpm.

8. De-energize solenoid.

9. Remove and plug the vacuum hose from the computer. Connect an auxiliary vacuum supply to the computer and apply 16 in.Hg.

10. Disconnect the engine harness connector from the O$_2$ sensor and ground the engine harness lead with a jumper wire.

➡**Care should be exercised so that no pulling force is put on the wire attached to the O$_2$ sensor. The bullet connector to be disconnected is approximately 4" from the sensor. Use care in working around the sensor as the exhaust manifold is extremely hot.**

11. Let the engine to run for 4 minutes to allow the effect of disconnecting the O$_2$ sensor to take place.

12. Turn the screw on the solenoid and adjust to specified idle rpm as shown on the Emission Label.

13. Reconnect the O$_2$ sensor wire, hose the computer, PCV valve and canister hose.

14. Remove ground wire from carburetor switch and reconnect hose to EGR valve.

15. The idle rpm with the engine in normal operating condition (everything connected) may vary from set speeds. DO NOT READJUST. Turn engine off and remove tachometer.

PROPANE ASSISTED IDLE MIXTURE

➡**This procedure should only be used if an idle defect still exists after normal diagnosis has revealed no other faulty**
condition, such as, incorrect idle speed, incorrect basic timing, faulty hose or wire connections, etc. It is also important to make sure the combustion computer systems are operating properly. Adjustment of the air-fuel mixture should also be performed after a major carburetor overhaul.

1. If the concealment plugs have already been removed, skip to step 2, otherwise:

a. Remove air cleaner assembly, vacuum hoses, throttle linkage, etc.

b. Locate and center punch on the side surface of the mixture screw housing ⁵/₁₆" from the front end of the housing in the center of both mixture screw housings.

c. Using a ³/₁₆" drill bit, drill at a right angle (90°) to the mixture screw housing through the outer surface of the housing.

d. Use a small drift, punch or allen wrench to pry out plug. Retain plug for reinstallation.

➡**Never place any tool against the mixture screw during this operation.**

2. Disconnect and plug vacuum hose at the EGR valve.

3. Ground the carburetor switch with a jumper wire.

4. Disconnect and plug ³/₁₆" diameter hose at the canister.

5. Remove the PCV valve from the valve cover and allow it to draw underhood air.

6. Connect a tachometer to the engine, start engine and let speed stabilize for two minutes.

7. Remove and plug the vacuum hose from the computer. Connect an auxiliary vacuum supply to the computer and apply 16 in.Hg.

8. Disconnect the engine harness connector from the O$_2$ sensor and ground the engine harness lead with a jumper wire.

➡**Care should be exercised so that no pulling force is put on the wire attached to the O$_2$ sensor. The bullet connector to be disconnected is approximately 4" from the sensor. Use care in working around the sensor as the exhaust manifold is extremely hot.**

9. Let the engine to run for 4 minutes to allow the effect of disconnecting the O$_2$ sensor to take place.

10. Disconnect the vacuum hose from the heated air door sensor at the carburetor and install the propane supply in its place.

11. Open the propane main valve. Slowly open the propane metering valve until maximum engine rpm is reached.

➡**When too much propane is added, engine speed will decrease. Fine tune the metering valve for the highest engine rpm. Also, if idle mixture is extremely rich, engine rpm will decrease with any amount of propane. In this case, turn the idle mixture screw in about ½ turn and repeat Step 11.**

12. With the propane still flowing, adjust the idle speeds screw on the solenoid until the tachometer indicates the specified propane rpm.

13. Fine tune the metering valve for the highest engine rpm. If there has been a change in the maximum rpm, readjust the idle speed screw to the specified propane rpm.

14. Turn off the main propane valve and allow the engine speed to stabilize.

15. Slowly adjust the mixture screw until the tachometer indicates the specified idle rpm. Pause between adjustments to allow the engine speed to stabilize.

16. Turn on the propane valve.

17. Fine tune the metering valve to get the highest engine rpm. If the maximum speed is more than 25 rpm different than the specified propane rpm, repeat Steps 11–16. If okay, proceed to Step 18.

18. Turn off both valves on the propane bottle.

19. Remove propane supply hose and reinstall the vacuum hose that goes to the heated air door sensor.

20. Remove the jumper wire from the carburetor ground switch.

21. Reinstall the PCV valve, remove the jumper wire and reconnect radiator fan plug and reconnect O_2 system test connector.

22. Unplug and reconnect the vacuum hose connector to the EGR valve.

23. After Steps 18–22 are completed, the curb idle speed may be different than the idle set rpm. This is normal and engine speed should not be readjusted. Turn engine off and remove tachometer. Reinstall the concealment plug.

Carter Thermo-Quad®

▶ **See Figures 52, 53, 54, 55 and 56**

IDLE RPM

1. Disconnect and plug vacuum hose at the EGR valve and ground the carburetor switch with a jumper wire.

2. Disconnect and plug the $3/16''$ diameter hose at the canister.

3. Remove the PCV valve from the valve cover and allow it to draw underhood air.

4. Connect a tachometer to the engine, start engine and let speed stabilize for two minutes.

5. Remove and plug the vacuum hose from the computer. Connect an auxiliary vacuum supply to the computer and apply 16 in.Hg.

6. Disconnect the engine harness connector from the O_2 sensor and ground the engine harness lead with a jumper wire.

➡**Care should be exercised so that no pulling force is put on the wire attached to the O_2 sensor. The bullet connector to be disconnected is approximately 4″ from the sensor. Use care in working around the sensor as the exhaust manifold is extremely hot.**

7. Let the engine to run for 4 minutes to allow the effect of disconnecting the O_2 sensor to take place.

8. Turn the screw on the solenoid and adjust to specified idle rpm as shown on the Emission Label.

9. Reconnect O_2 sensor wire, hose to computer, PCV valve and canister hose.

10. Remove ground wire from carburetor switch and reconnect hose to EGR valve.

11. The idle speed with the engine in normal operating condition (everything connected) may vary from set speeds. DO NOT READJUST. Turn off engine and remove tachometer.

SOLENOID IDLE STOP (SIS) RPM

1. Disconnect and plug vacuum hose at the EGR valve.

2. Ground the carburetor switch with a jumper wire.

3. Disconnect and plug the $3/16''$ diameter hose at the canister and remove the PCV valve from the valve cover and allow it to draw underhood air.

4. Connect a tachometer to the engine, start engine and let stabilize for two minutes.

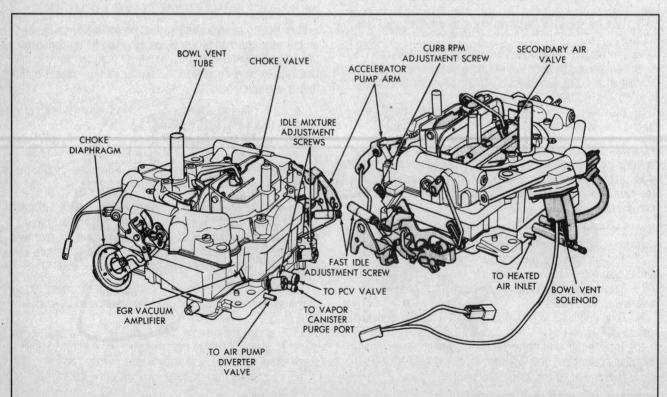

Fig. 52 Carter Thermo-Quad carburetor for 1979 vehicles—the 1975–78 Thermo-Quad carburetor is similar except without the bowl vent solenoid

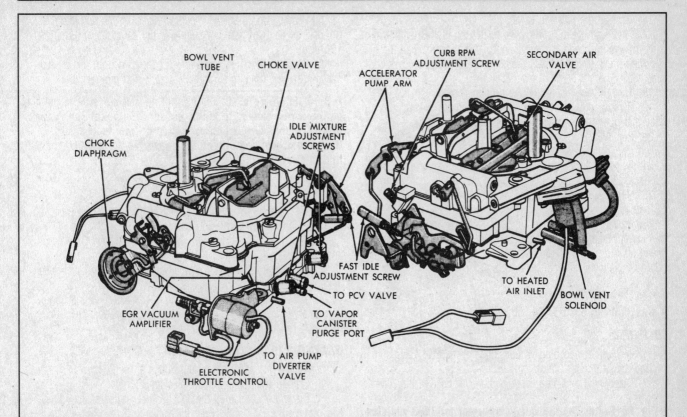

Fig. 53 Carter Thermo-Quad carburetor for 1980–81 vehicles—the 1973–74 Thermo-Quad is similar except without the bowl vent solenoid

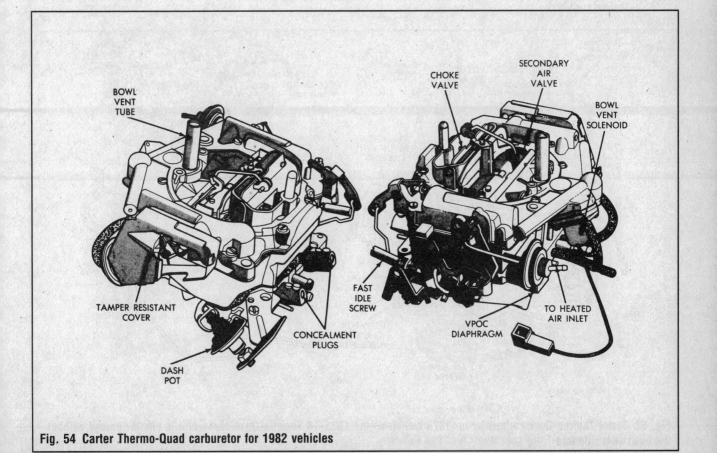

Fig. 54 Carter Thermo-Quad carburetor for 1982 vehicles

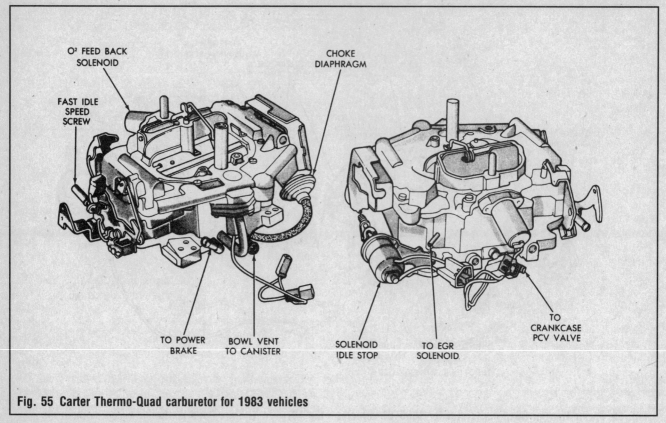

Fig. 55 Carter Thermo-Quad carburetor for 1983 vehicles

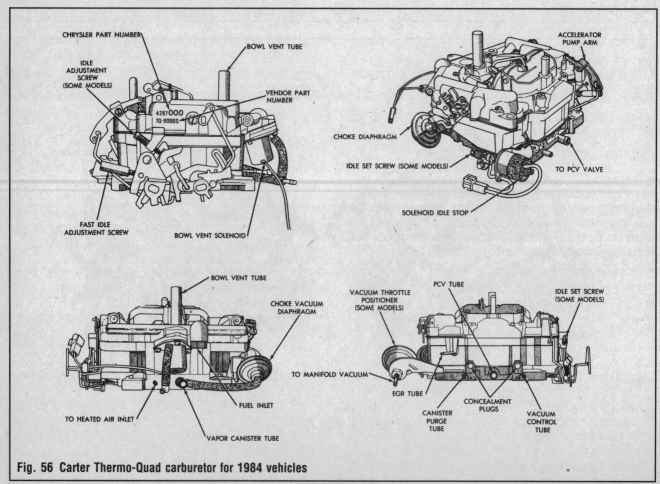

Fig. 56 Carter Thermo-Quad carburetor for 1984 vehicles

5. Energize the solenoid by one of the following methods:

a. Without air conditioning: Connect one end of a jumper wire to the solenoid wire and the other end to the battery positive post.

➡**Use care in jumping to the correct wire on the solenoid. Applying battery voltage to the wrong wire will damage the wiring harness.**

b. With air conditioning: Press the air conditioning button on, set blower speed to low and disconnect the air conditioning compressor clutch wire.

6. Open throttle slightly to allow the solenoid plunger to extend.

7. Turn the screw on the throttle lever to adjust to specified SIS rpm.

8. De-energize solenoid.

9. Remove and plug the vacuum hose from the computer. Connect an auxiliary vacuum supply to the computer and apply 16 in.Hg.

10. Disconnect the engine harness connector from the O_2 sensor and ground the engine harness lead with a jumper wire.

➡**Care should be exercised so that no pulling force is put on the wire attached to the O_2 sensor. The bullet connector to be disconnected is approximately 4″ from the sensor. Use care in working around the sensor as the exhaust manifold is extremely hot.**

11. Let the engine to run for 4 minutes to allow the effect of disconnecting the O_2 sensor to take place.

12. Turn the screw on the solenoid and adjust to specified idle rpm as shown on the Emission Label.

13. Reconnect the O_2 sensor wire, hose to the computer, PCV valve and canister hose.

14. Remove ground wire from carburetor switch and reconnect hose to EGR valve.

15. The idle rpm with the engine in normal operating condition (everything connected) may vary from set speeds. DO NOT READJUST. Turn engine off and remove tachometer.

PROPANE ASSISTED IDLE MIXTURE

➡**This procedure should only be used if an idle defect still exists after normal diagnosis has revealed no other faulty condition, such as, incorrect idle speed, incorrect basic timing, faulty hose or wire connections, etc. It is also important to make sure the combustion computer systems are operating properly. Adjustment of the air-fuel mixture should also be performed after a major carburetor overhaul.**

1. If the concealment plugs have already been removed, skip to step 2, otherwise:

a. Remove air cleaner.

b. Disconnect all hoses from front of carburetor base.

c. Center punch at a point ¼″ from end of mixture screw housing. Use a 10 o'clock indexing on the right bank and 2 o'clock indexing on the left bank.

d. Drill through outer housing at a (90°) angle at punch mark and a ³⁄₁₆″ drill bit.

e. Use a small drift, punch or allen wrench to pry out plug. Save concealment plug for reinstallation. Never place any tool against the mixture screw during this operation.

2. Disconnect and plug vacuum hose at the EGR valve.

3. Ground the carburetor switch with a jumper wire.

4. Disconnect and plug ³⁄₁₆″ diameter hose at the canister.

5. Remove the PCV valve from the valve cover and allow it to draw underhood air.

6. Connect a tachometer to the engine, start engine and let speed stabilize for two minutes.

7. Remove and plug the vacuum hose from the computer. Connect an auxiliary vacuum supply to the computer and apply 16 in.Hg.

8. Disconnect the engine harness connector from the O_2 sensor and ground the engine harness lead with a jumper wire.

➡**Care should be exercised so that no pulling force is put on the wire attached to the O_2 sensor. The bullet connector to be disconnected is approximately 4″ from the sensor. Use care in working around the sensor as the exhaust manifold is extremely hot.**

9. Let the engine to run for 4 minutes to allow the effect of disconnecting the O_2 sensor to take place.

10. Disconnect the vacuum hose from the heated air door sensor at the carburetor and install the propane supply in its place.

11. Open the propane main valve. Slowly open the propane metering valve until maximum engine rpm is reached.

➡**When too much propane is added, engine speed will decrease. Fine tune the metering valve for the highest engine rpm. Also, if idle mixture is extremely rich, engine rpm will decrease with any amount of propane. In this case, turn the idle mixture screw in about ½ turn and repeat Step 11.**

12. With the propane still flowing, adjust the idle speeds screw on the solenoid until the tachometer indicates the specified propane rpm.

13. Fine tune the metering valve for the highest engine rpm. If there has been a change in the maximum rpm, readjust the idle speed screw to the specified propane rpm.

14. Turn off the main propane valve and allow the engine speed to stabilize.

15. Slowly adjust the mixture screw until the tachometer indicates the specified idle rpm. Pause between adjustments to allow the engine speed to stabilize.

16. Turn on the propane valve.

17. Fine tune the metering valve to get the highest engine rpm. If the maximum speed is more than 25 rpm different than the specified propane rpm, repeat Steps 11–16. If okay, proceed to Step 18.

18. Turn off both valves on the propane bottle.

19. Remove propane supply hose and reinstall the vacuum hose that goes to the heated air door sensor.

20. Remove the jumper wire from the carburetor ground switch.

21. Reinstall the PCV valve, remove the jumper wire and reconnect radiator fan plug and reconnect O_2 system test connector.

22. Unplug and reconnect the vacuum hose connector to the EGR valve.

23. After Steps 18–22 are completed, the curb idle speed may be different than the idle set rpm. This is normal and engine speed should not be readjusted. Turn engine off and remove tachometer. Reinstall the concealment plug.

Rochester Quadrajet®

▶ **See Figure 57**

IDLE RPM

1. Disconnect and plug vacuum hose at the EGR valve.
2. Ground the carburetor switch with a jumper wire.
3. Disconnect and plug the ³⁄₁₆" diameter hose at the canister.
4. Remove the PCV valve from the valve cover and allow it to draw underhood air.
5. Connect a tachometer to the engine.
6. Start engine and let speed stabilize for two minutes.
7. Disconnect the engine harness connector from the O_2 sensor and ground the engine harness lead with a jumper wire.

➡**Care should be exercised so that no pulling force is put on the wire attached to the O_2 sensor. The bullet connector to be disconnected is approximately 4" from the sensor. Use care in working around the sensor as the exhaust manifold is extremely hot.**

8. Let the engine to run for four minutes to allow the effect of disconnecting the O_2 sensor to take place.
9. Turn the screw on the solenoid and adjust to the specified idle rpm as shown on the Emission Label.
10. Reconnect O_2 sensor wire.
11. Reinstall PCV valve.
12. Reconnect canister hose.
13. Remove ground wire from carburetor switch.
14. Reconnect hose to EGR valve.
15. The idle speed with the engine in normal operating condition (everything connected) may vary from set speeds. DO NOT READJUST. Turn engine off and remove tachometer.

SOLENOID IDLE STOP (SIS) RPM

1. Disconnect and plug vacuum hose at the EGR valve.
2. Ground the carburetor switch with a jumper wire.
3. Disconnect and plug the ³⁄₁₆" diameter hose at the canister.

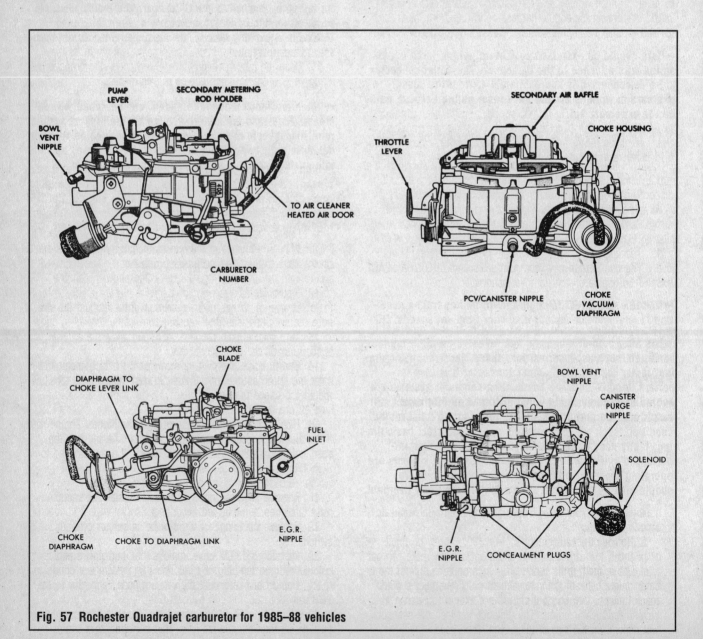

Fig. 57 Rochester Quadrajet carburetor for 1985–88 vehicles

4. Remove the PCV valve from the valve cover and allow it to draw underhood air.

5. Connect a tachometer to the engine.

6. Start the engine and let speed stabilize for two minutes.

7. Energize the solenoid by one of the following methods:

a. Without air conditioning: Connect one end of a jumper wire to the solenoid wire and the other end to the battery positive post.

➠**Use care in jumping to the correct wire on the solenoid. Applying battery voltage to the wrong wire will damage the wiring harness.**

b. With air conditioning: Press the air conditioning button on, set blower speed to low and disconnect the air conditioning compressor clutch wire.

8. Open throttle slightly to allow the solenoid plunger to extend.

9. Remove the adjusting screw and spring from the solenoid. Insert a 1/8" allen wrench into the solenoid and turn to adjust to specified SIS rpm.

10. Reinstall solenoid screw and spring until it lightly bottoms out. De-energize solenoid.

11. Disconnect the engine harness connector from the O_2 sensor and ground the engine harness lead with a jumper wire.

➠**Care should be exercised so that no pulling force is put on the wire attached to the O_2 sensor. The bullet connector to be disconnected is approximately 4" from the sensor. Use care in working around the sensor as the exhaust manifold is extremely hot.**

12. Let the engine to run for 4 minutes to allow the effect of disconnecting the O_2 sensor to take place.

13. Turn the screw on the solenoid and adjust to specified idle rpm as shown on the Emission Label.

14. Reconnect the O_2 sensor wire, hose to the computer, PCV valve and canister hose.

15. Remove ground wire from carburetor switch and reconnect hose to EGR valve.

➠**The idle rpm with the engine in normal operating condition (everything connected) may vary from set speeds. DO NOT READJUST.**

16. Turn engine off and remove tachometer.

PROPANE IDLE MIXTURE

➠**This procedure should only be used if an idle defect still exists after normal diagnosis has revealed no other faulty condition, such as, incorrect idle speed, incorrect basic timing, faulty hose or wire connections, etc. It is also important to make sure the combustion computer systems are operating properly. Adjustment of the air/fuel mixture should also be performed after a major carburetor overhaul.**

1. If the concealment plugs have already been removed, skip to step 2, otherwise:

a. Remove the carburetor.

b. Invert the carburetor and use a hacksaw to make two parallel cuts in the throttle body. Make cuts on each side of the locator points beneath the concealment plug. The cuts should reach down to the plug but should not extend more than 1/8" beyond the locator points. The distance between the saw cuts will depend on the size of the punch to be used.

c. Place a flat punch at a point near the ends of the saw marks in the throttle body. Hold the punch at a 45° angle and drive it into the throttle body until the casting breaks away, exposing the steel plug.

d. Repeat the procedure for the other concealment plug.

e. Reinstall the carburetor.

f. Use Tool C-4895 (BT-7610B) or equivalent, to adjust the idle mixture screws.

2. Disconnect and plug vacuum hose at the EGR valve.

3. Ground the carburetor switch with a jumper wire.

4. Disconnect and plug 3/16" diameter hose at the canister.

5. Remove the PCV valve from the valve cover and allow it to draw underhood air.

6. Connect a tachometer to the engine, start engine and let speed stabilize for two minutes.

7. Disconnect the engine harness connector from the O_2 sensor and ground the engine harness lead with a jumper wire.

➠**Care should be exercised so that no pulling force is put on the wire attached to the O_2 sensor. The bullet connector to be disconnected is approximately 4" from the sensor. Use care in working around the sensor as the exhaust manifold is extremely hot.**

8. Let the engine to run for 4 minutes to allow the effect of disconnecting the O_2 sensor to take place.

9. Disconnect the vacuum hose from the heated air door sensor at the carburetor and install the propane supply in its place.

10. Open the propane main valve. Slowly open the propane metering valve until maximum engine rpm is reached.

➠**When too much propane is added, engine speed will decrease. Fine tune the metering valve for the highest engine rpm. Also, if idle mixture is extremely rich, engine rpm will decrease with any amount of propane. In this case, turn the idle mixture screw in about 1/2 turn and repeat Step 10.**

11. With the propane still flowing, adjust the idle speeds screw on the solenoid until the tachometer indicates the specified propane rpm.

12. Fine tune the metering valve for the highest engine rpm. If there has been a change in the maximum rpm, readjust the idle speed screw to the specified propane rpm.

13. Turn off the main propane valve and allow the engine speed to stabilize.

14. Slowly adjust the mixture screw until the tachometer indicates the specified idle rpm. Pause between adjustments to allow the engine speed to stabilize.

15. Turn on the propane valve.

16. Fine tune the metering valve to get the highest engine rpm. If the maximum speed is more than 25 rpm different than the specified propane rpm, repeat Steps 10–15. If okay, proceed to Step 17.

17. Turn off both valves on the propane bottle.

18. Remove propane supply hose and reinstall the vacuum hose that goes to the heated air door sensor.

19. Remove the jumper wire from the carburetor ground switch.

20. Reinstall the PCV valve, remove the jumper wire and reconnect radiator fan plug and reconnect O_2 system test connector.

21. Unplug and reconnect the vacuum hose connector to the EGR valve.

22. After Steps 17–21 are completed, the curb idle speed may be different than the idle set rpm. This is normal and engine

speed should not be readjusted. Turn engine off and remove tachometer. Reinstall the concealment plug.

Holley 2210

▶ See Figure 58

IDLE RPM

1. Check and adjust the timing.
2. Disconnect the vacuum hose at the EGR valve.
3. Disconnect and plug the 3/16" hose at the canister.
4. Remove the PCV valve from the valve cover.
5. Connect a tachometer.
6. Start the engine and run it to normal operating temperature.
7. Turn the idle speed control screw to adjust the engine rpm.

PROPANE IDLE MIXTURE

➡This procedure should only be used if an idle defect still exists after normal diagnosis has revealed no other faulty condition, such as, incorrect idle speed, incorrect basic timing, faulty hose or wire connections, etc. It is also important to make sure the combustion computer systems are operating properly. Adjustment of the air/fuel mixture should also be performed after a major carburetor overhaul.

1. If the concealment plugs have already been removed, skip to step 2, otherwise:
    a. Remove the carburetor.
    b. Invert the carburetor and use a hacksaw to make two parallel cuts in the throttle body. Make cuts on each side of the locator points beneath the concealment plug. The cuts should reach down to the plug but should not extend more than 1/8" beyond the locator points. The distance between the saw cuts will depend on the size of the punch to be used.
    c. Place a flat punch at a point near the ends of the saw marks in the throttle body. Hold the punch at a 45° angle and drive it into the throttle body until the casting breaks away, exposing the steel plug.
    d. Repeat the procedure for the other concealment plug.
    e. Reinstall the carburetor.
    f. Use Tool C-4895 (BT-7610B) or equivalent, to adjust the idle mixture screws.
2. Disconnect and plug vacuum hose at the EGR valve.
3. Ground the carburetor switch with a jumper wire.
4. Disconnect and plug 3/16" diameter hose at the canister.
5. Remove the PCV valve from the valve cover and allow it to draw underhood air.
6. Connect a tachometer to the engine, start engine and let speed stabilize for two minutes.
7. Disconnect the engine harness connector from the O_2 sensor and ground the engine harness lead with a jumper wire.

➡Care should be exercised so that no pulling force is put on the wire attached to the O_2 sensor. The bullet connector to be disconnected is approximately 4" from the sensor. Use care in working around the sensor as the exhaust manifold is extremely hot.

8. Let the engine to run for 4 minutes to allow the effect of disconnecting the O_2 sensor to take place.
9. Disconnect the vacuum hose from the heated air door sensor at the carburetor and install the propane supply in its place.
10. Open the propane main valve. Slowly open the propane metering valve until maximum engine rpm is reached.

➡When too much propane is added, engine speed will decrease. Fine tune the metering valve for the highest engine rpm. Also, if idle mixture is extremely rich, engine rpm will decrease with any amount of propane. In this case, turn the idle mixture screw in about 1/2 turn and repeat Step 10.

11. With the propane still flowing, adjust the idle speeds screw on the solenoid until the tachometer indicates the specified propane rpm.
12. Fine tune the metering valve for the highest engine rpm. If there has been a change in the maximum rpm, readjust the idle speed screw to the specified propane rpm.
13. Turn off the main propane valve and allow the engine speed to stabilize.
14. Slowly adjust the mixture screw until the tachometer indicates the specified idle rpm. Pause between adjustments to allow the engine speed to stabilize.
15. Turn on the propane valve.
16. Fine tune the metering valve to get the highest engine rpm. If the maximum speed is more than 25 rpm different than the specified propane rpm, repeat Steps 10–15. If okay, proceed to Step 17.
17. Turn off both valves on the propane bottle.
18. Remove propane supply hose and reinstall the vacuum hose that goes to the heated air door sensor.
19. Remove the jumper wire from the carburetor ground switch.
20. Reinstall the PCV valve, remove the jumper wire and reconnect radiator fan plug and reconnect O_2 system test connector.
21. Unplug and reconnect the vacuum hose connector to the EGR valve.
22. After Steps 17–21 are completed, the curb idle speed may be different than the idle set rpm. This is normal and engine speed should not be readjusted. Turn engine off and remove tachometer. Reinstall the concealment plug.

Holley 2245

▶ See Figure 58

IDLE RPM ADJUSTMENT

1. Check and adjust the timing.
2. Disconnect the vacuum hose at the EGR valve.
3. Disconnect and plug the 3/16" hose at the canister.
4. Remove the PCV valve from the valve cover.
5. Connect a tachometer.
6. Start the engine and run it to normal operating temperature.
7. Turn the idle speed control screw to adjust the engine rpm.

PROPANE IDLE MIXTURE

➡This procedure should only be used if an idle defect still exists after normal diagnosis has revealed no other faulty condition, such as, incorrect idle speed, incorrect basic timing, faulty hose or wire connections, etc. It is also important to make sure the combustion computer systems are operating properly. Adjustment of the air/fuel mixture should also be performed after a major carburetor overhaul.

1. If the concealment plugs have already been removed, skip to step 2, othersie:
    a. Remove the carburetor.
    b. Invert the carburetor and use a hacksaw to make two parallel cuts in the throttle body. Make cuts on each side of the locator points beneath the concealment plug. The cuts should

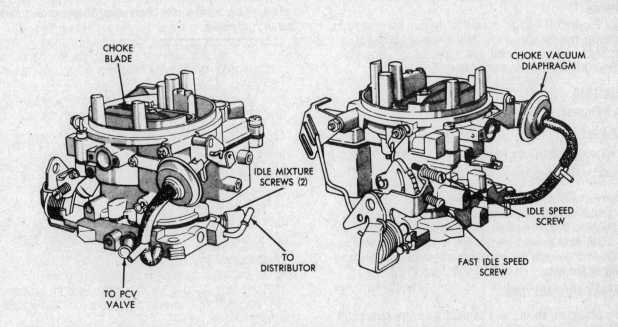

Fig. 58 Holley 2245 carburetor for 1982–84 vehicles—earlier 2245 and 2210 carburetors are similar

reach down to the plug but should not extend more than ⅛" beyond the locator points. The distance between the saw cuts will depend on the size of the punch to be used.

c. Place a flat punch at a point near the ends of the saw marks in the throttle body. Hold the punch at a 45° angle and drive it into the throttle body until the casting breaks away, exposing the steel plug.

d. Repeat the procedure for the other concealment plug.

e. Reinstall the carburetor.

f. Use Tool C-4895 (BT-7610B) or equivalent, to adjust the idle mixture screws.

2. Disconnect and plug vacuum hose at the EGR valve.

3. Ground the carburetor switch with a jumper wire.

4. Disconnect and plug ³⁄₁₆" diameter hose at the canister.

5. Remove the PCV valve from the valve cover and allow it to draw underhood air.

6. Connect a tachometer to the engine, start engine and let speed stabilize for two minutes.

7. Disconnect the engine harness connector from the O_2 sensor and ground the engine harness lead with a jumper wire.

➥**Care should be exercised so that no pulling force is put on the wire attached to the O_2 sensor. The bullet connector to be disconnected is approximately 4" from the sensor. Use care in working around the sensor as the exhaust manifold is extremely hot.**

8. Let the engine to run for 4 minutes to allow the effect of disconnecting the O_2 sensor to take place.

9. Disconnect the vacuum hose from the heated air door sensor at the carburetor and install the propane supply in its place.

10. Open the propane main valve. Slowly open the propane metering valve until maximum engine rpm is reached.

➥**When too much propane is added, engine speed will decrease. Fine tune the metering valve for the highest engine rpm. Also, if idle mixture is extremely rich, engine rpm will decrease with any amount of propane. In this case, turn the idle mixture screw in about ½ turn and repeat Step 10.**

11. With the propane still flowing, adjust the idle speeds screw on the solenoid until the tachometer indicates the specified propane rpm.

12. Fine tune the metering valve for the highest engine rpm. If there has been a change in the maximum rpm, readjust the idle speed screw to the specified propane rpm.

13. Turn off the main propane valve and allow the engine speed to stabilize.

14. Slowly adjust the mixture screw until the tachometer indicates the specified idle rpm. Pause between adjustments to allow the engine speed to stabilize.

15. Turn on the propane valve.

16. Fine tune the metering valve to get the highest engine rpm. If the maximum speed is more than 25 rpm different than the specified propane rpm, repeat Steps 10–15. If okay, proceed to Step 17.

17. Turn off both valves on the propane bottle.

18. Remove propane supply hose and reinstall the vacuum hose that goes to the heated air door sensor.

19. Remove the jumper wire from the carburetor ground switch.

20. Reinstall the PCV valve, remove the jumper wire and reconnect radiator fan plug and reconnect O_2 system test connector.

21. Unplug and reconnect the vacuum hose connector to the EGR valve.

22. After Steps 17–21 are completed, the curb idle speed may be different than the idle set rpm. This is normal and engine speed should not be readjusted. Turn engine off and remove tachometer. Reinstall the concealment plug.

Holley 1945

▶ See Figures 59, 60, 61, 62 and 63

IDLE RPM

1. Check and adjust the timing.
2. Disconnect the vacuum hose at the EGR valve.
3. Disconnect and plug the 3/16" hose at the canister.
4. Remove the PCV valve from the valve cover.
5. Ground the carburetor switch with a jumper wire.
6. Connect a tachometer.
7. Start the engine and run it to normal operating temperature.
8. Turn the idle speed control screw on the idle solenoid to adjust the engine rpm.

PROPANE IDLE MIXTURE

➡This procedure should only be used if an idle defect still exists after normal diagnosis has revealed no other faulty condition, such as, incorrect idle speed, incorrect basic timing, faulty hose or wire connections, etc. It is also important to make sure the combustion computer systems are operating properly. Adjustment of the air/fuel mixture should also be performed after a major carburetor overhaul.

1. If the concealment plugs have already been removed, skip to step 2, otherwise:
    a. Remove the carburetor.
    b. Invert the carburetor and use a hacksaw to make two parallel cuts in the throttle body. Make cuts on each side of the locator points beneath the concealment plug. The cuts should reach down to the plug but should not extend more than 1/8" beyond the locator points. The distance between the saw cuts will depend on the size of the punch to be used.
    c. Place a flat punch at a point near the ends of the saw marks in the throttle body. Hold the punch at a 45° angle and drive it into the throttle body until the casting breaks away, exposing the steel plug.
    d. Repeat the procedure for the other concealment plug.
    e. Reinstall the carburetor.
    f. Use Tool C-4895 (BT-7610B) or equivalent, to adjust the idle mixture screws.
2. Disconnect and plug vacuum hose at the EGR valve.
3. Ground the carburetor switch with a jumper wire.
4. Disconnect and plug 3/16" diameter hose at the canister.
5. Remove the PCV valve from the valve cover and allow it to draw underhood air.
6. Connect a tachometer to the engine, start engine and let speed stabilize for two minutes.
7. Disconnect the engine harness connector from the O_2 sensor and ground the engine harness lead with a jumper wire.

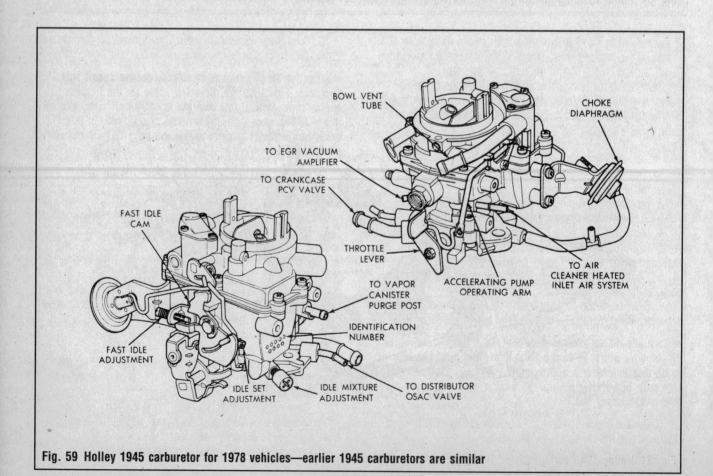

Fig. 59 Holley 1945 carburetor for 1978 vehicles—earlier 1945 carburetors are similar

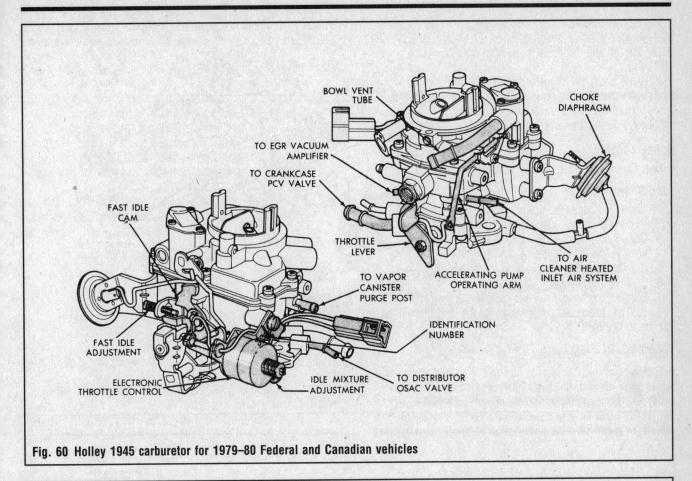

Fig. 60 Holley 1945 carburetor for 1979–80 Federal and Canadian vehicles

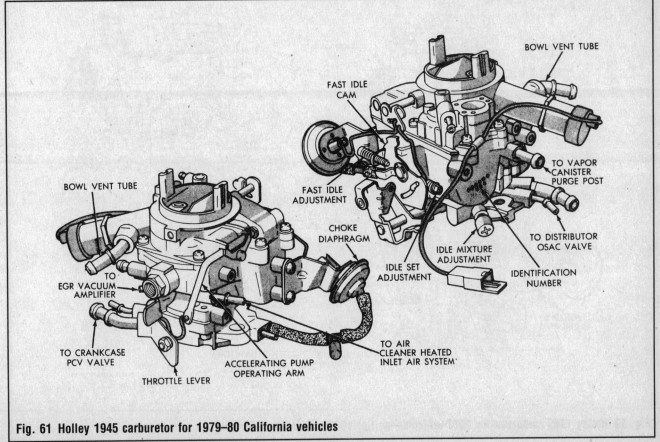

Fig. 61 Holley 1945 carburetor for 1979–80 California vehicles

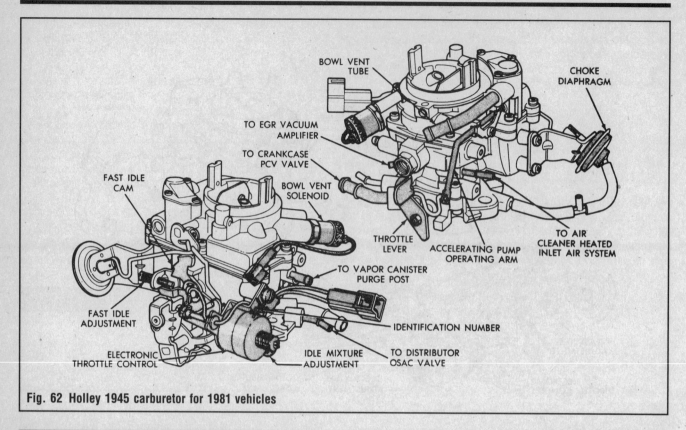

Fig. 62 Holley 1945 carburetor for 1981 vehicles

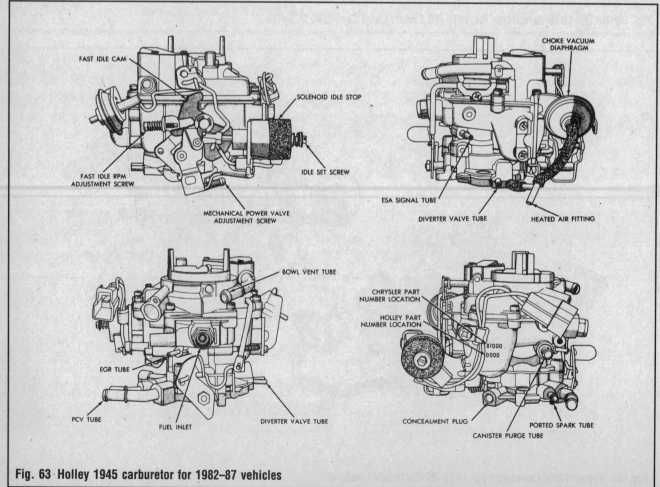

Fig. 63 Holley 1945 carburetor for 1982–87 vehicles

➡ Care should be exercised so that no pulling force is put on the wire attached to the O₂ sensor. The bullet connector to be disconnected is approximately 4″ from the sensor. Use care in working around the sensor as the exhaust manifold is extremely hot.

8. Let the engine to run for 4 minutes to allow the effect of disconnecting the O₂ sensor to take place.

9. Disconnect the vacuum hose from the heated air door sensor at the carburetor and install the propane supply in its place.

10. Open the propane main valve. Slowly open the propane metering valve until maximum engine rpm is reached.

➡ When too much propane is added, engine speed will decrease. Fine tune the metering valve for the highest engine rpm. Also, if idle mixture is extremely rich, engine rpm will decrease with any amount of propane. In this case, turn the idle mixture screw in about ½ turn and repeat Step 10.

11. With the propane still flowing, adjust the idle speeds screw on the solenoid until the tachometer indicates the specified propane rpm.

12. Fine tune the metering valve for the highest engine rpm. If there has been a change in the maximum rpm, readjust the idle speed screw to the specified propane rpm.

13. Turn off the main propane valve and allow the engine speed to stabilize.

14. Slowly adjust the mixture screw until the tachometer indicates the specified idle rpm. Pause between adjustments to allow the engine speed to stabilize.

15. Turn on the propane valve.

16. Fine tune the metering valve to get the highest engine rpm. If the maximum speed is more than 25 rpm different than the specified propane rpm, repeat Steps 10–15. If okay, proceed to Step 17.

17. Turn off both valves on the propane bottle.

18. Remove propane supply hose and reinstall the vacuum hose that goes to the heated air door sensor.

19. Remove the jumper wire from the carburetor ground switch.

20. Reinstall the PCV valve, remove the jumper wire and reconnect radiator fan plug and reconnect O₂ system test connector.

21. Unplug and reconnect the vacuum hose connector to the EGR valve.

22. After Steps 17–21 are completed, the curb idle speed may be different than the idle set rpm. This is normal and engine speed should not be readjusted. Turn engine off and remove tachometer. Reinstall the concealment plug.

Fuel Injected Engines

➤ See Figures 64 and 65

MINIMUM IDLE SPEED ADJUSTMENT

➡ Normal idle speed is controlled by the logic module or SMEC. This adjustment is the minimum idle speed with the Automatic Idle Speed (AIS) closed.

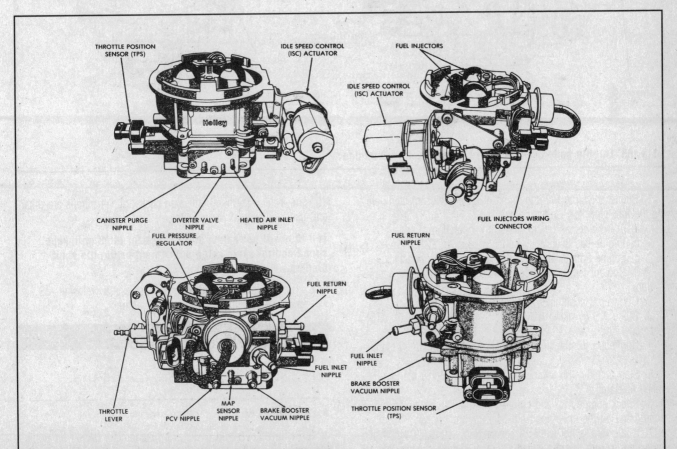

Fig. 64 Throttle body used on the 1988 238 cu. in. V6 engine

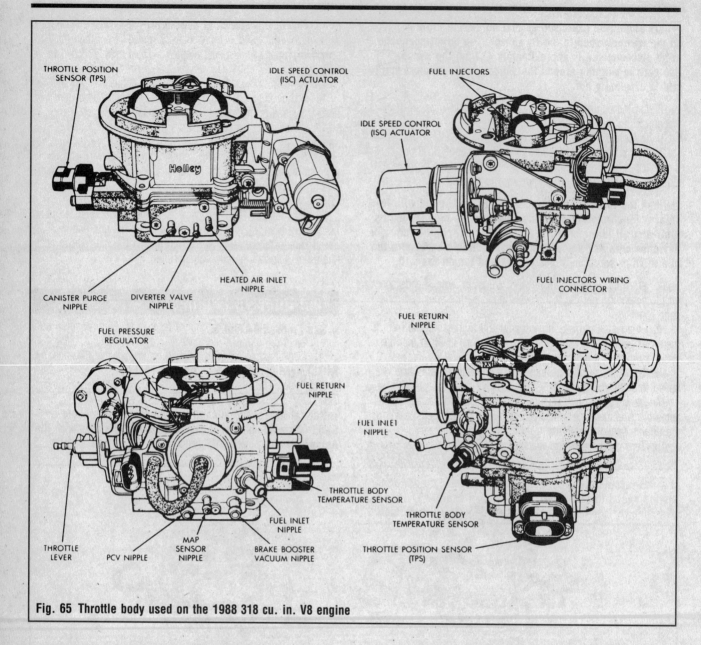

Fig. 65 Throttle body used on the 1988 318 cu. in. V8 engine

1. Before adjusting the idle on an electronic fuel injected vehicle the following items must be checked.

    a. AIS motor has been checked for operation.

    b. Engine has been checked for vacuum or EGR leaks.

    c. Engine timing has been checked and set to specifications.

    d. Coolant temperature sensor has been checked for operation.

2. Connect a tachometer and timing light to engine.

3. Close AIS by using ATM tester C-4805 or equivalent, ATM test code #03.

4. Connect a jumper to radiator fan so that it will run continuously.

5. Start and run the engine for 3 minutes to allow the idle speed to stabilize.

6. Check engine rpm and compare the result with the specifications listed on the underhood emission control sticker.

7. If idle rpm is not within specifications, use tool C-4804 or equivalent to turn the idle speed adjusting screw to obtain 800 ± 10 rpm. If the underhood emission sticker specifications are different, use those values for adjustment.

➡️**If idle will not adjust down check for binding linkage, speed control servo cable adjustment or throttle shaft binding.**

8. Turn off the engine, disconnect tachometer, reinstall AIS wire and remove jumper wire from fan motor.

Diesel Engines

IDLE SPEED ADJUSTMENT

◆ **See Figure 66**

1. Remove cover and basket from tachometer takeoff on right side of engine in front of oil filter assembly. Install mechanical ta-

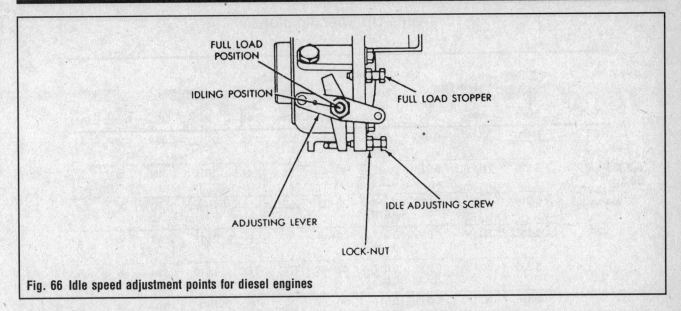

Fig. 66 Idle speed adjustment points for diesel engines

chometer adapter and attach mechanical tachometer and drive cable.

2. Turn hand throttle counterclockwise and pull all the way out. Depress accelerator to floor and crank engine. Hold accelerator to floor after engine starts. Allow engine to warm up until some speed is attained (1,250–1,500 rpm). Release accelerator slowly until engine runs smoothly. When engine begins to warm, turn hand throttle clockwise to reduce engine speed to idle.

✳✳ CAUTION

If a new accelerator pump has been installed, do not allow engine speed to rise about 1,300 rpm. If engine overspeeds, it may run away and damage or destroy itself.

3. Be sure that governor control lever is at idling position before attempting to adjust idle speed.

4. Check tachometer. If idle speed is not between 600 and 700 rpm, adjust idle speed.

5. Loosen idle adjusting screw locknut. Adjust screw as necessary to set idle to specifications. Turn adjusting screw IN to increase idle speed: OUT to decrease idle speed.

6. When idle speed is as specified, tighten idle adjusting screw locknut. Recheck idle speed to be sure it has not shifted.

Tune-Up Specifications
Gasoline Engines

Years	Engine	Spark Plugs Type	Gap (in.)	Distributor Point Gap (in.)	Dwell (deg.)	Ignition Timing (deg.) Man. Trans.	Auto. Trans.	Valve Clearance In.	Exh.	Idle Speed Man. Trans.	Auto. Trans.
1967	6-170	N11Y	0.035	0.017–0.023	40–45	[31]	[31]	0.012	0.024	[36]	[37]
	6-225	N11Y	0.035	0.017–0.023	40–45	[31]	[31]	0.012	0.024	[36]	[37]
	8-318	[32]	0.035	0.014–0.019	28–32	5B	[33]	Hyd.	Hyd.	[38]	[39]
1968	6-198	N11Y	0.035	0.017–0.023	42–47	[31]	—	0.012	0.024	[36]	—
	6-225	N11Y	0.035	0.017–0.023	42–47	TDC	TDC	0.012	0.024	[36]	[37]
	8-318	N11Y	0.035	0.014–0.019	30–35	[92]	[92]	Hyd.	Hyd.	[38]	[39]
1969–72	6-225	N11Y	0.035	0.017–0.023	42–47	TDC	TDC	0.012	0.024	[21]	[21]
	8-318	N11Y	0.035	0.014–0.019	30–35	5B	5B	Hyd.	Hyd.	[22]	[22]
1973–74	6-225	N11Y	0.035	Electronic		[85]	[85]	0.012	0.024	800	[86]
	8-318	N11Y	0.035	Electronic		[87]	[87]	Hyd.	Hyd.	750	750
	8-360	N12Y	0.035	Electronic		TDC	[88]	Hyd.	Hyd.	750	750
	8-400	[89]	0.035	Electronic		[90]	[90]	Hyd.	Hyd.	750	750
	8-440	J11Y	0.035	Electronic		7.5B	[91]	Hyd.	Hyd.	700	700
1975–76	6-225	BL11Y	0.035	Electronic		TDC	TDC	0.012	0.024	800	750
	8-318	N11Y	0.035	Electronic		[49]	[49]	Hyd.	Hyd.	[50]	[51]
	8-360	N12Y	0.035	Electronic		[52]	[52]	Hyd.	Hyd.	[53]	[53]
	8-440	J11Y	0.035	Electronic		8B	8B	Hyd.	Hyd.	700	700
1977–78	6-225	RBL11Y	0.035	Electronic		[93]	[93]	0.010	0.020	[94]	[94]
	8-318	RN11Y	0.035	Electronic		[95]	[96]	Hyd.	Hyd.	[99]	[99]
	8-360	RN12Y	0.035	Electronic		TDC	[97]	Hyd.	Hyd.	750	[98]
	8-400	RJ11Y	0.035	Electronic		2B	2B	Hyd.	Hyd.	700	700
	8-440	RJ11Y	0.035	Electronic		—	8B	Hyd.	Hyd.	—	700
1979	6-225	RBL15Y	0.035	Electronic		[61]	[61]	0.010	0.020	[62]	[62]
	8-318	N12YC	0.035	Electronic		[63]	[64]	Hyd.	Hyd.	[65]	[66]
	8-360	N12YC	0.035	Electronic		[67]	[68]	Hyd.	Hyd.	[69]	[69]
1980	6-225	RBL16Y	0.035	Electronic		12B	12B	0.010	0.020	[70]	[70]
	8-318	RN12YC	0.035	Electronic		[71]	[72]	Hyd.	Hyd.	[73]	[74]
	8-360	RN12YC	0.035	Electronic		[75]	[76]	Hyd.	Hyd.	[77]	[78]
1981	6-225	RBL16Y	0.035	Electronic		12B	16B	Hyd.	Hyd.	[40]	[41]
	8-318	RN12YC	0.035	Electronic		[42]	[43]	Hyd.	Hyd.	[44]	[45]
	8-360	RN12YC	0.035	Electronic		12B	[46]	Hyd.	Hyd.	[47]	[48]
1982	6-225	RBL16Y	0.035	Electronic		12B	16B	Hyd.	Hyd.	[79]	[80]
	8-318	RN12YC	0.035	Electronic		[81]	[82]	Hyd.	Hyd.	750	750

Tune-Up Specifications (cont.)
Gasoline Engines

Years	Engine	Spark Plugs		Distributor		Ignition Timing (deg.)		Valve * Clearance		Idle Speed	
		Type	Gap (in.)	Point Gap (in.)	Dwell (deg.)	Man. Trans.	Auto. Trans.	In.	Exh.	Man. Trans.	Auto. Trans.
1982	8-360	RN12YC	0.035	Electronic		83	83	Hyd.	Hyd.	84	84
1983	6-225	RBL16Y	0.035	Electronic		12B	16B	Hyd.	Hyd.	725	750
	8-318	RN12YC	0.035	Electronic		①	②	Hyd.	Hyd.	⑨	⑩
	8-360	RN12YC	0.035	Electronic		⑪	⑫	Hyd.	Hyd.	⑬	⑭
1984	6-225	RBL16Y	0.035	Electronic		12B	16B	Hyd.	Hyd.	54	55
	8-318	RN12YC	0.035	Electronic		56	56	Hyd.	Hyd.	57	58
	8-360	RN12YC	0.035	Electronic		—	59	Hyd.	Hyd.	—	60
1985	6-225	RBL16Y	0.035	Electronic		12B	16B	Hyd.	Hyd.	725	⑮
	8-318	RN12YC	0.035	Electronic		⑯	⑯	Hyd.	Hyd.	⑰	⑱
	8-360	RN12YC	0.035	Electronic		6B	⑲	Hyd.	Hyd.	800	⑳
1986	6-225	RBL16Y	0.035	Electronic		12B	16B	Hyd.	Hyd.	725	750
	8-318	RN12YC	0.035	Electronic		①	②	Hyd.	Hyd.	③	④
	8-360	RN12YC	0.035	Electronic		⑤	⑥	Hyd.	Hyd.	⑦	⑧
1987	6-225	RBL16Y	0.035	Electronic		12B	16B	Hyd.	Hyd.	23	24
	8-318	RN12YC	0.035	Electronic		25	25	Hyd.	Hyd.	26	26
	8-360	RN12YC	0.035	Electronic		13B	27	Hyd.	Hyd.	800	28
1988	6-238	RN12YC	0.035	Electronic		10B	10B	Hyd.	Hyd.	750	750
	8-318	RN12YC	0.035	Electronic		10B	10B	Hyd.	Hyd.	700	700
	8-360	RN12YC	0.035	Electronic		29	30	Hyd.	Hyd.	800	28

*Valves are adjusted HOT

① Exc. high altitude: 12B
  High altitude: 8B
② Exc. high altitude, Calif. and heavy duty Canada: 12B
  High altitude, Calif. and heavy duty Canada: 8B
③ Exc. high altitude: 700
  High altitude: 650
④ Exc. high altitude, Calif. and heavy duty Canada: 700
  High altitude, and Calif.: 650
  Heavy duty Canada: 750
⑤ Light duty: 12B
  Heavy duty: 10B
⑥ Light duty: 16B
  Heavy duty: 10B
⑦ US, exc. high altitude and heavy duty: 800
  High altitude: 750
  Heavy duty: 710
  Canada light duty: 750
  Canada heavy duty: 800
⑧ Exc. high altitude: 800
  High altitude: 710
⑨ 49 states and Canada: 700
  High altitude and California: 650
⑩ High altitude and Calif.: 650
  49 states and light duty Canada: 700
  Heavy duty Canada: 750
⑪ Light duty: 12B
  Heavy duty: 10B
⑫ Light duty: 16B
  Heavy duty: 10B

⑬ 49 states and Canada: 800
  High altitude: 750
  49 states heavy duty: 750
  Calif. and Canada heavy duty: 800
⑭ 49 states and Canada: 800
  High altitude: 710
  49 states and Canada heavy duty: 750
  California heavy duty: 800
⑮ Exc. Calif.: 750
  Calif.: 775
⑯ High altitude and Calif.: 8B
  49 states and Canada: 12B
  Heavy duty Canada: 8B
⑰ High altitude: 650
  Calif.: 725
  49 states and Canada: 700
  Heavy duty Canada: 750
⑱ High altitude and Calif.: 650
  49 states: 700
  Canada: 750
⑲ Light duty: 16B
  Heavy duty: 6B
⑳ Esc. high altitude: 800
  High altitude: 750
㉑ w/o Clean Air System: 550
  w/Clean Air System: 650
㉒ w/o Clean Air System: 500
  w/Clean Air System:
  Carb. #WW3-300—650
  Carb. #WW3-302—650

Tune-Up Specifications (cont.)
Gasoline Engines

Carb. #WW3-303—500
Carb. #WW3-304—500
Carb. #WW3-299—600
Carb. #WW3-301—600
㉓ Exc. Calif.: 725
  Calif.: 775
㉔ Exc. Calif.: 750
  Calif.: 775
㉕ Exc. heavy duty Canada: 8B
  Heavy duty Canada: 6B
㉖ Exc. heavy duty Canada: 650
  Heavy duty Canada: 750
㉗ Exc. heavy duty: 12B
  Heavy duty, exc. distributor #4145399: 10B
  Heavy duty, w/distributor #4145399: 13B
㉘ High altitude: 750
  Canada light duty: 750
  49 states light duty: 710
  All others: 800
㉙ 49 states: 710
  All others: 800
㉚ All light duty: 12B
  Heavy duty w/distributor #4111950: 10B
  All other heavy duty: 13B
㉛ Without Clean Air Package: 5B
  With Clean Air Package: TDC
㉜ With distributor #2444258: J14Y
  All others: N11Y
㉝ With distributor #2642718: 10B
  All others: 5B
㊱ Without Clean Air Package: 550
  With Clean Air Package: 650
㊲ Without Clean Air Package: 550
  With Clean Air Package: 600
㊳ Without Clean Air Package: 500
  With Clean Air Package: 650
㊴ Without Clean Air Package: 500
  With Clean Air Package: 600
㊵ 49 States: 600
  Calif.: 800
  Canada: 725
㊶ 49 States: 600
  Calif.: 800
  Canada: 750
㊷ Light Duty 2-bbl 49 states and Canada: 10B
  Heavy Duty Canada: 2A
  Calif. light duty 4-bbl: 12B
  Heavy duty 4-bbl: 12B
㊸ Light duty 2-bbl 49 states: 16B
  Heavy duty 2-bbl Canada: 2A
  Light duty 4-bbl US: 16B
  Light duty 4-bbl Canada: 10B
  Heavy duty 4-bbl: 12B
㊹ Light duty 2-bbl 49 states: 650
  Light duty 2-bbl Canada: 750
  Light duty 4-bbl Calif.: 750
  Heavy duty 4-bbl: 750
㊺ Light duty 2-bbl 49 states: 650
  Heavy duty 2-bbl Canada: 750
  Light duty 4-bbl: 750
  Heavy duty 4-bbl: 750
㊻ Heavy duty 2-bbl Canada: 4B
  Light duty 4-bbl US: 16B
  Heavy duty 4-bbl: 4B
㊼ Light duty 4-bbl 49 states: 600
  Light duty 4-bbl Calif.: 750

㊽ Light duty 2-bbl Canada: 750
  Light duty 4-bbl 49 states: 625
  Light duty 4-bbl Calif.: 750
  Heavy duty 4-bbl: 700
㊾ Light duty 49 states and Canada: 2B
  Light duty Calif.: TDC
  Heavy duty 49 states and Canada: 2A
  Heavy duty Calif.: TDC
㊿ Light duty US: 750
  Light duty Canada: 800
  Heavy duty 49 states and Canada: 750
  Heavy duty Calif.: 700
51 Light duty: 750
  Heavy duty 49 states and Canada: 2A
  Heavy duty Calif.: TDC
52 49 states and Canada: TDC
  Calif.: 4B
53 49 states and Canada: 750
  Calif.: 700
54 US: 700
  Canada: 725
55 US: 725
  Canada: 750
56 With ESA spark system: 16B
  With ECU spark system: 12B
  Heavy duty Canada with ECU spark system: 2A
57 49 states with ESA spark system: 800
  Calif. with ESA spark system: 740
  With ECU spark system: 760
  Heavy duty Canada with ECU spark system: 750
58 49 states with ESA spark system: 800
  Calif. with ESA spark system: 700
  49 states with ECU spark system: 760
  Canada with ECU spark system: 750
  Heavy duty Canada with ECU spark system: 750
59 Light duty: 14B
  Heavy duty without catalyst: 4B
  Heavy duty with catalyst: 10B
60 Light duty with catalyst: 760
  Light duty without catalyst: 725
  Heavy duty: 700
61 Except Calif.: 12B
  Calif.: 8B
62 Except Calif.: 675
  Calif.: 800
63 49 states and Canada 2-bbl: 12B
  Heavy duty 2-bbl Canada: 2A
  Light duty Calif. 4-bbl: 6B
  Medium duty Calif. 4-bbl: 6B
64 49 states and Canada 2-bbl: 12B
  Heavy duty Canada 2-bbl: 2A
  Light duty Canada 4-bbl: 8B
  Light duty Calif. 4-bbl: 8B
  Medium duty Calif. 4-bbl: 6B
65 49 states and Canada 2-bbl: 680
  Heavy duty Canada 2-bbl: 750
  Calif. 4-bbl: 6B
66 49 states and Canada 2-bbl: 680
  All others: 750
67 Light duty 49 states 2-bbl: 10B
  Heavy duty Canada 2-bbl: 4B
  Calif. 4-bbl: 10B
  40 states and Canada 4-bbl: 4B
68 49 states 2-bbl: 10B
  Heavy duty Canada: 4B
  49 states 4-bbl: 4B

Tune-Up Specifications (cont.)
Gasoline Engines

Calif. medium duty 4-bbl: 10B
Canada 4-bbl: 4B
Calif. heavy duty 4-bbl: 4B
⑥⑨ All 2-bbl and Calif. medium duty 4-bbl: 750
Canada heavy duty 4-bbl: 750
All other heavy duty 4-bbl: 700
⑦⓪ 49 states: 600
Calif.: 800
Canada: 675
⑦① 49 states and Canada 2-bbl: 12B
Heavy duty Canada 2-bbl: 2A
Heavy duty US 4-bbl: 8B
⑦② 49 states and Canada 2-bbl: 12B
Heavy duty Canada 2-bbl: 2A
Canada light duty 4-bbl: 10B
Calif. medium duty 4-bbl: 10B
Heavy duty US 4-bbl: 8B
⑦③ 49 states and Canada 2-bbl: 600
Heavy duty Canada 2-bbl: 750
US 4-bbl: 750
⑦④ 49 states and Canada 2-bbl: 600
Heavy duty Canada 2-bbl: 750
Canada 4-bbl: 750
Calif. medium duty 4-bbl: 750
Heavy duty US 4-bbl: 750
⑦⑤ Calif. medium duty 4-bbl: 10B
49 states and Canada light duty 4-bbl: 12B
Heavy duty Calif. 4-bbl: 10B
49 states and Canada heavy duty 4-bbl: 4 bbl
⑦⑥ 2-bbl heavy duty Canada: 4B
Calif. medium duty 4-bbl: 10B
49 states and Canada light duty 4-bbl with air pump: 12B
Heavy duty Calif. 4-bbl: 10B
49 states and Canada heavy duty 4-bbl: 4 bbl
49 states and Canada heavy duty with aspirator: 10B
⑦⑦ Calif. medium duty 4-bbl: 750
49 states and Canada light duty 4-bbl: 650
Calif. heavy duty 4-bbl: 750
49 states and Canada heavy duty 4-bbl: 700
⑦⑧ Heavy duty Canada 2-bbl: 750
Calif. medium duty 4-bbl: 750
49 states and Canada light duty 4-bbl with air pump: 650
Calif. heavy duty 4-bbl: 750
49 states and Canada heavy duty 4-bbl: 700
49 states and Canada light duty with aspirator: 750
⑦⑨ 49 states 1-bbl: 600
Calif. 1-bbl: 800
Canada 1-bbl: 725
49 states and Canada 2-bbl: 700
⑧⓪ 49 states 1-bbl: 600
Calif. 1-bbl: 800
Canada 1-bbl: 725

⑧① 49 states and Canada 2-bbl: 12B
Heavy duty Canada 2-bbl: 2A
US light duty 4-bbl: 12B
US heavy duty 4-bbl: 8B
⑧② 49 states and Canada 2-bbl: 12B
Heavy duty Canada 2-bbl: 2A
US light duty 4-bbl: 16B
US heavy duty 4-bbl: 8B
⑧③ 2-bbl Canada: 4B
4-bbl US and Canada: 4B
4-bbl Calif. 10B
⑧④ 2-bbl Canada: 750
4-bbl US and Canada: 700
4-bbl Calif. 750
⑧⑤ Light duty: TDC
Heavy duty: 2.5A
⑧⑥ Holley 1945: 750
Carter BBS: 800
⑧⑦ Light duty: TDC
Heavy duty: 2.5A
⑧⑧ Light duty: 2.5B
Heavy duty: TDC
⑧⑨ Light duty: J13Y
Heavy duty: J11Y
⑨⓪ Light duty: 7.5B
Heavy duty: 2.5B
⑨① 49 states: 10B
Calif. light duty: 5B
Calif. heavy duty: 7.5B
⑨② With Clean Air System: 5A
Without Clean Air System: 5B
⑨③ 49 states 1-bbl: 2B
Canada 1-bbl: 2A
49 states and Canada 2-bbl: TDC
Calif. manual trans.: TDC
Calif. automatic trans.: 2A
⑨④ 49 states and Canada 1-bbl: 750
49 states and Canada 2-bbl: 700
Calif.: 750
⑨⑤ Light duty: 2B
Heavy duty: 2A
⑨⑥ Light duty: 2B
Heavy duty: 2A
High altitude: 6B
⑨⑦ Light duty: 6B
Heavy duty: TDC
Calif.: TDC
⑨⑧ Light duty: 700
Heavy duty: 750
Calif.: 700
⑨⑨ Heavy duty Calif.: 700
All others: 750

Tune-Up Specifications
Diesel Engines

Years	Engine	Inject. Timing	Nozzle Opening Pressure (psi)	Curb Idle Speed (rpm)	Maximum Speed (rpm)	Valve Clearance Cold (in.)		Maximum Compress Pressure (psi)
						Int.	Exh.	
1978–79	6-243	18B	1706–1848	600–700	3950–4050	0.012	0.012	426

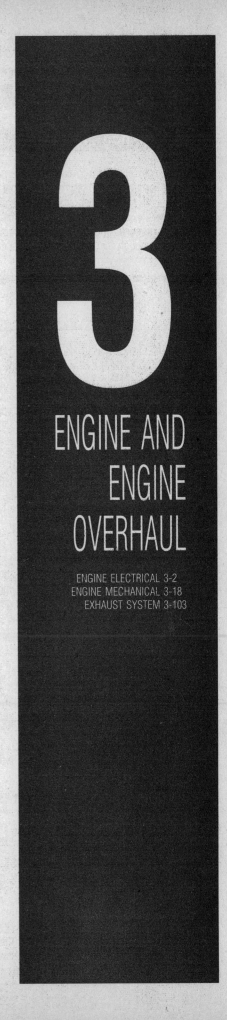

3

ENGINE AND ENGINE OVERHAUL

ENGINE ELECTRICAL

Understanding Electricity

For any electrical system to operate, there must be a complete circuit. This simply means that the power flow from the battery must make a full circle. When an electrical component is operating, power flows from the battery to the components, passes through the component (load) causing it to function, and returns to the battery through the ground path of the circuit. This ground may be either another wire or a metal part of the vehicle (depending upon how the component is designed).

BASIC CIRCUITS

Perhaps the easiest way to visualize a circuit is to think of connecting a light bulb (with two wires attached to it) to the battery. If one of the two wires was attached to the negative post (−) of the battery and the other wire to the positive post (+), the circuit would be complete and the light bulb would illuminate. Electricity could follow a path from the battery to the bulb and back to the battery. It's not hard to see that with longer wires on our light bulb, it could be mounted anywhere on the vehicle. Further, one wire could be fitted with a switch so that the light could be turned on and off. Various other items could be added to our primitive circuit to make the light flash, become brighter or dimmer under certain conditions, or advise the user that it's burned out.

Ground

Some automotive components are grounded through their mounting points. The electrical current runs through the chassis of the vehicle and returns to the battery through the ground (−) cable; if you look, you'll see that the battery ground cable connects between the battery and the body of the vehicle.

Load

Every complete circuit must include a "load" (something to use the electricity coming from the source). If you were to connect a wire between the two terminals of the battery (DON'T do this, but take our word for it) without the light bulb, the battery would attempt to deliver its entire power supply from one pole to another almost instantly. This is a short circuit. The electricity is taking a short cut to get to ground and is not being used by any load in the circuit. This sudden and uncontrolled electrical flow can cause great damage to other components in the circuit and can develop a tremendous amount of heat. A short in an automotive wiring harness can develop sufficient heat to melt the insulation on all the surrounding wires and reduce a multiple wire cable to one sad lump of plastic and copper. Two common causes of shorts are broken insulation (thereby exposing the wire to contact with surrounding metal surfaces or other wires) or a failed switch (the pins inside the switch come out of place and touch each other).

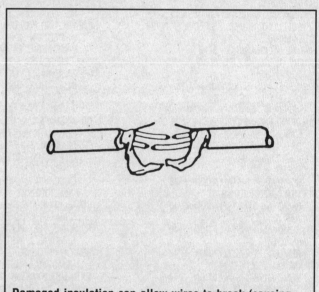

Damaged insulation can allow wires to break (causing an open circuit) or touch (causing a short circuit)

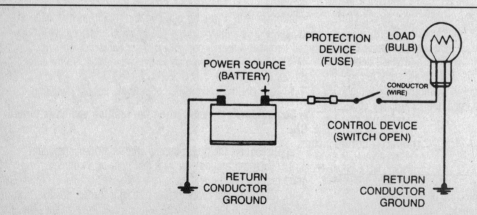

Here is an example of a simple automotive circuit. When the switch is closed, power from the positive battery terminal flows through the fuse, the switch and then the load (light bulb). The light illuminates and the circuit is completed through the return conductor and the vehicle ground. If the light did not work, the tests could be made with a voltmeter or test light at the battery, fuse, switch or bulb socket

Switches and Relays

Some electrical components which require a large amount of current to operate also have a relay in their circuit. Since these circuits carry a large amount of current (amperage or amps), the thickness of the wire in the circuit (wire gauge) is also greater. If this large wire were connected from the load to the control switch on the dash, the switch would have to carry the high amperage load and the dash would be twice as large to accommodate wiring harnesses as thick as your wrist. To prevent these problems, a relay is used. The large wires in the circuit are connected from the battery to one side of the relay and from the opposite side of the relay to the load. The relay is normally open, preventing current from passing through the circuit. An additional, smaller wire is connected from the relay to the control switch for the circuit. When the control switch is turned on, it grounds the smaller wire to the relay and completes its circuit. The main switch inside the relay closes, sending power to the component without routing the main power through the inside of the vehicle. Some common circuits which may use relays are the horn, headlights, starter and rear window defogger systems.

Protective Devices

It is possible for larger surges of current to pass through the electrical system of your vehicle. If this surge of current were to reach the load in the circuit, it could burn it out or severely damage it. To prevent this, fuses, circuit breakers and/or fusible links are connected into the supply wires of the electrical system. These items are nothing more than a built-in weak spot in the system. It's much easier to go to a known location (the fusebox) to see why a circuit is inoperative than to dissect 15 feet of wiring under the dashboard, looking for what happened.

When an electrical current of excessive power passes through the fuse, the fuse blows (the conductor melts) and breaks the circuit, preventing the passage of current and protecting the components.

A circuit breaker is basically a self repairing fuse. It will open the circuit in the same fashion as a fuse, but when either the short is removed or the surge subsides, the circuit breaker resets itself and does not need replacement.

A fuse link (fusible link or main link) is a wire that acts as a fuse. One of these is normally connected between the starter relay and the main wiring harness under the hood. Since the starter is usually the highest electrical draw on the vehicle, an internal short during starting could direct about 130 amps into the wrong places. Consider the damage potential of introducing this current into a system whose wiring is rated at 15 amps and you'll understand the need for protection. Since this link is very early in the electrical path, it's the first place to look if nothing on the vehicle works, but the battery seems to be charged and is properly connected.

TROUBLESHOOTING

Electrical problems generally fall into one of three areas:
• The component that is not functioning is not receiving current.
• The component is receiving power but is not using it or is using it incorrectly (component failure).
• The component is improperly grounded.
The circuit can be can be checked with a test light and a

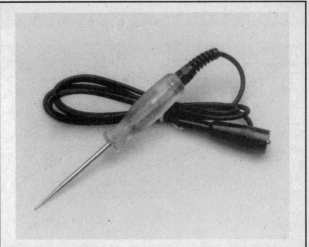

A 12 volt test light is useful when checking parts of a circuit for power

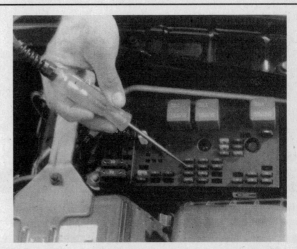

Here, someone is checking a circuit by making sure there is power to the component's fuse

jumper wire. The test light is a device that looks like a pointed screwdriver with a wire on one end and a bulb in its handle. A jumper wire is simply a piece of wire with alligator clips or special terminals on each end. If a component is not working, you must follow a systematic plan to determine which of the three causes is the villain.

1. Turn ON the switch that controls the item not working.

➡**Some items only work when the ignition switch is turned ON.**

2. Disconnect the power supply wire from the component.
3. Attach the ground wire of a test light or a voltmeter to a good metal ground.
4. Touch the end probe of the test light (or the positive lead of the voltmeter) to the power wire; if there is current in the wire, the light in the test light will come on (or the voltmeter will indicate the amount of voltage). You have now established that current is getting to the component.
5. Turn the ignition or dash switch **OFF** and reconnect the wire to the component.

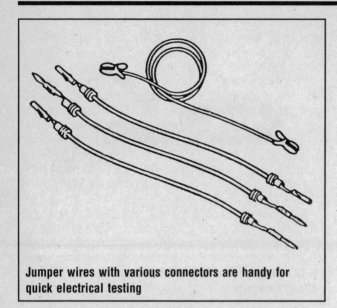

Jumper wires with various connectors are handy for quick electrical testing

If there was no power, then the problem is between the battery and the component. This includes all the switches, fuses, relays and the battery itself. The next place to look is the fusebox; check carefully either by eye or by using the test light across the fuse clips. The easiest way to check is to simply replace the fuse. If the fuse is blown, and upon replacement, immediately blows again, there is a short between the fuse and the component. This is generally (not always) a sign of an internal short in the component. Disconnect the power wire at the component again and replace the fuse; if the fuse holds, the component is the problem.

✳✳ WARNING

DO NOT test a component by running a jumper wire from the battery UNLESS you are certain that it operates on 12 volts. Many electronic components are designed to operate with less voltage and connecting them to 12 volts could destroy them. Jumper wires are best used to bypass a portion of the circuit (such as a stretch of wire or a switch) that DOES NOT contain a resistor and is suspected to be bad.

If all the fuses are good and the component is not receiving power, find the switch for the circuit. Bypass the switch with the jumper wire. This is done by connecting one end of the jumper to the power wire coming into the switch and the other end to the wire leaving the switch. If the component comes to life, the switch has failed.

✳✳ WARNING

Never substitute the jumper for the component. The circuit needs the electrical load of the component. If you bypass it, you will cause a short circuit.

Checking the ground for any circuit can mean tracing wires to the body, cleaning connections or tightening mounting bolts for the component itself. If the jumper wire can be connected to the case of the component or the ground connector, you can ground the other end to a piece of clean, solid metal on the vehicle. Again, if the component starts working, you've found the problem.

A systematic search through the fuse, connectors, switches and

the component itself will almost always yield an answer. Loose and/or corroded connectors, particularly in ground circuits, are becoming a larger problem in modern vehicles. The computers and on-board electronic (solid state) systems are highly sensitive to improper grounds and will change their function drastically if one occurs.

Remember that for any electrical circuit to work, ALL the connections must be clean and tight.

➡**For more information on Understanding and Troubleshooting Electrical Systems, please refer to Section 6 of this manual.**

Battery, Starting and Charging Systems

BASIC OPERATING PRINCIPLES

Battery

The battery is the first link in the chain of mechanisms which work together to provide cranking of the automobile engine. In most modern vehicles, the battery is a lead/acid electrochemical device consisting of six 2v subsections (cells) connected in series so the unit is capable of producing approximately 12v of electrical pressure. Each subsection consists of a series of positive and negative plates held a short distance apart in a solution of sulfuric acid and water.

The two types of plates are of dissimilar metals. This sets-up a chemical reaction, and it is this reaction which produces current flow from the battery when its positive and negative terminals are connected to an electrical accessory such as a lamp or motor. The continued transfer of electrons would eventually convert the sulfuric acid to water, and make the two plates identical in chemical composition. As electrical energy is removed from the battery, its voltage output tends to drop. Thus, measuring battery voltage and battery electrolyte composition are two ways of checking the ability of the unit to supply power. During engine cranking, electrical energy is removed from the battery. However, if the charging circuit is in good condition and the operating conditions are normal, the power removed from the battery will be replaced by the alternator which will force electrons back through the battery, reversing the normal flow, and restoring the battery to its original chemical state.

Starting System

The battery and starting motor are linked by very heavy electrical cables designed to minimize resistance to the flow of current. Generally, the major power supply cable that leaves the battery goes directly to the starter, while other electrical system needs are supplied by a smaller cable. During starter operation, power flows from the battery to the starter and is grounded through the vehicle's frame/body or engine and the battery's negative ground strap.

The starter is a specially designed, direct current electric motor capable of producing a great amount of power for its size. One thing that allows the motor to produce a great deal of power is its tremendous rotating speed. It drives the engine through a tiny pinion gear (attached to the starter's armature), which drives the very large flywheel ring gear at a greatly reduced speed. Another factor allowing it to produce so much power is that only intermittent operation is required of it. Thus, little allowance for air circulation is necessary, and the windings can be built into a very small space.

The starter solenoid is a magnetic device which employs the small current supplied by the start circuit of the ignition switch. This magnetic action moves a plunger which mechanically engages the starter and closes the heavy switch connecting it to the battery. The starting switch circuit usually consists of the starting switch contained within the ignition switch, a neutral safety switch or clutch pedal switch, and the wiring necessary to connect these in series with the starter solenoid or relay.

The pinion, a small gear, is mounted to a one way drive clutch. This clutch is splined to the starter armature shaft. When the ignition switch is moved to the **START** position, the solenoid plunger slides the pinion toward the flywheel ring gear via a collar and spring. If the teeth on the pinion and flywheel match properly, the pinion will engage the flywheel immediately. If the gear teeth butt one another, the spring will be compressed and will force the gears to mesh as soon as the starter turns far enough to allow them to do so. As the solenoid plunger reaches the end of its travel, it closes the contacts that connect the battery and starter, then the engine is cranked.

As soon as the engine starts, the flywheel ring gear begins turning fast enough to drive the pinion at an extremely high rate of speed. At this point, the one-way clutch begins allowing the pinion to spin faster than the starter shaft so that the starter will not operate at excessive speed. When the ignition switch is released from the starter position, the solenoid is de-energized, and a spring pulls the gear out of mesh interrupting the current flow to the starter.

Some starters employ a separate relay, mounted away from the starter, to switch the motor and solenoid current on and off. The relay replaces the solenoid electrical switch, but does not eliminate the need for a solenoid mounted on the starter used to mechanically engage the starter drive gears. The relay is used to reduce the amount of current the starting switch must carry.

Charging System

The automobile charging system provides electrical power for operation of the vehicle's ignition system, starting system and all electrical accessories. The battery serves as an electrical surge or storage tank, storing (in chemical form) the energy originally produced by the engine driven generator. The system also provides a means of regulating output to protect the battery from being overcharged and to avoid excessive voltage to the accessories.

The storage battery is a chemical device incorporating parallel lead plates in a tank containing a sulfuric acid/water solution. Adjacent plates are slightly dissimilar, and the chemical reaction of the two dissimilar plates produces electrical energy when the battery is connected to a load such as the starter motor. The chemical reaction is reversible, so that when the generator is producing a voltage (electrical pressure) greater than that produced by the battery, electricity is forced into the battery, and the battery is returned to its fully charged state.

Newer automobiles use alternating current generators or alternators, because they are more efficient, can be rotated at higher speeds, and have fewer brush problems. In an alternator, the field usually rotates while all the current produced passes only through the stator winding. The brushes bear against continuous slip rings. This causes the current produced to periodically reverse the direction of its flow. Diodes (electrical one way valves) block the flow of current from traveling in the wrong direction. A series of diodes is wired together to permit the alternating flow of the stator to be rectified back to 12 volts DC for use by the vehicle's electrical system.

The voltage regulating function is performed by a regulator. The regulator is often built in to the alternator; this system is termed an integrated or internal regulator.

Ignition Coil

REMOVAL & INSTALLATION

▶ See Figure 1

1. Disconnect the battery ground.
2. Disconnect the two small and one large wires from the coil.
3. Disconnect the condenser connector from the coil, if equipped.
4. Unbolt and remove the coil.
5. Installation is the reverse of removal.

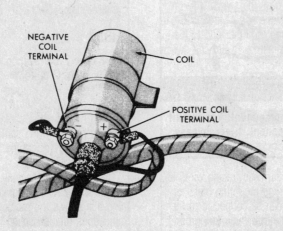

NEGATIVE COIL TERMINAL

COIL

POSITIVE COIL TERMINAL

Fig. 1 View of the coil connections

Electronic Ignition Control Unit

REMOVAL & INSTALLATION

Carbureted Engines

▶ See Figure 2

Simply unplug the control unit connector and remove the mounting screws.

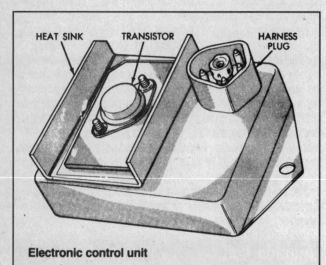

Electronic control unit

Fig. 2 View of the electronic ignition control unit

Fuel Injected Engines

▶ See Figure 3

This unit is called a, Single Module Engine Controller (SMEC).

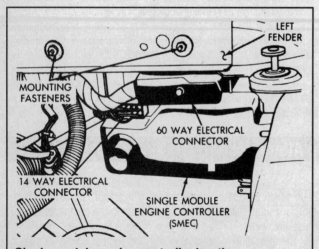

Single module engine controller location

Fig. 3 View of the Single Module Engine Controller (SMEC) used on feedback carbureted and fuel injected engines

✳✳ WARNING

Don't remove the grease from the 14-way connector or the connector cavity in the computer. The grease is used to prevent corrosion of the terminals. There should be at least a 1/8" coating of grease on the bottom of the connector cavities. If not, apply a liberal coating of Mopar Multi-purpose grease, part number 2932524, or equivalent over the entire end of the connector plug.

1. Remove the air cleaner duct from the SMEC.
2. Remove the 3 module retaining screws.
3. Remove the 14-way and 60-way connectors from the SMEC.
4. Installation is the reverse of removal.

Distributor

REMOVAL

1. Remove the splash shield (if equipped). Disconnect the vacuum line(s) at the distributor.
2. Disconnect the pickup lead wire connector or connectors from the wiring harness.
3. Unfasten the clips or screws that retain the distributor cap and lift off the cap.
4. Bump the engine around until the rotor is pointing at no. 1 cylinder firing position and the timing marks on the front case and crank pulley are aligned. Disconnect the negative battery cable from the battery.
5. Mark the distributor body and the engine block to indicate the position of the distributor in the block. Mark the distributor body to indicate the rotor position. These marks are used as guides when installing the distributor.
6. Remove the distributor hold-down bolt and bracket. Carefully lift the distributor from the engine. The shaft may rotate slightly as the distributor is removed. Make a note of where the movement stops. That point is where the rotor must point when the distributor is reinstalled into the block.

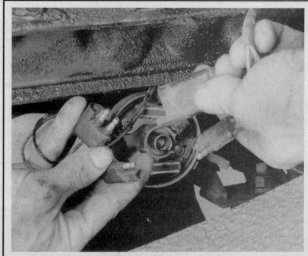

To remove the distributor, first remove the cap and rotor, then disconnect the pickup lead wire(s)

Loosen the distributor hold-down bolt . . .

. . . and remove the hold-down

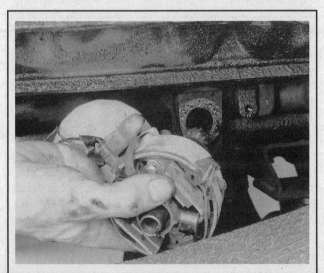

Pull the distributor out of the engine

INSTALLATION

Engine Not Disturbed

1. If the crankshaft has not been rotated while the distributor was removed from the engine, use the reference marks made before removal to correctly position the distributor in the block. The shaft may have to be rotated slightly to engage the came gear (inline 6-cylinder) or intermediate shaft gear (V6 and V8).

2. If the crankshaft was rotated or otherwise distributed (e.g. during engine rebuilding) after the distributor was removed, proceed as follows:

Engine Disturbed

170, 198 AND 225 ENGINES

1. Remove no. 1 spark plug and, with your thumb plugging the hole, rotate the engine until no 1 piston is up on the compression at top dead center. You'll feel the pressure of the compression stroke with your thumb and the **O** mark on the crankshaft pulley hub will be aligned with the timing pointer.

2. Turn the rotor to a position just ahead of the no. 1 distributor cap terminal.

3. Lower the distributor into the opening engaging the distributor gear with the drive gear on camshaft. With the distributor fully seated in the engine, the rotor should be under the cap no. 1 tower.

4. Install the cap, tighten the hold-down bracket bolt. Connect the wiring and the vacuum hose. Check the timing with a timing light. Adjust if necessary.

V6 AND V8 ENGINES

1. Rotate the crankshaft until no. 1 cylinder is at top dead center (TDC) of the compression stroke. To do this, remove the spark plug from cylinder no. 1 and place your thumb over the hole. Slowly turn the engine by hand in the normal direction of rotation until compression is felt at the hole. The **O** mark on the crankshaft pulley should be aligned with the pointer on the timing case cover.

2. Hold the distributor over the mounting pad on the cylinder block so that the distributor body flange coincides with the mounting pad and the rotor points to the no. 1 cylinder firing position.

3. Install the distributor while holding the rotor in position, allowing it to move only enough to engage the slot in the drive gear.

4. Install the cap, tighten the hold-down bracket bolt. Connect the wiring and vacuum hose. Check the timing with a timing light. Adjust if necessary.

Alternator

The alternator charging system is a negative ($-$) ground system which consists of an alternator, a regulator, a charge indicator, a storage battery and wiring connecting the components, and fuse link wire.

The alternator is belt-driven from the engine. Energy is supplied from the alternator/regulator system to the rotating field through two brushes to two slip-rings. The slip-rings are mounted on the rotor shaft and are connected to the field coil. This energy supplied to the rotating field from the battery is called excitation current and is used to initially energize the field to begin the generation of electricity. Once the alternator starts to generate electricity, the excitation current comes from its own output rather than the battery.

The alternator produces power in the form of alternating current. The alternating current is rectified by 6 diodes into direct current. The direct current is used to charge the battery and power the rest of the electrical system.

When the ignition key is turned on, current flows from the battery, through the charging system indicator light on the instrument panel, to the voltage regulator, and to the alternator. Since the alternator is not producing any current, the alternator warning light comes on. When the engine is started, the alternator begins to produce current and turns the alternator light off. As the alternator turns and produces current, the current is divided in two ways: part to the battery to charge the battery and power the electrical components of the vehicle, and part is returned to the alternator to enable it to increase its output. In this situation, the alternator is receiving current from the battery and from itself. A voltage regulator is wired into the current supply to the alternator to prevent it from receiving too much current which would cause it to put out too much current. Conversely, if the voltage regulator does not allow the alternator to receive enough current, the battery will not be fully charged and will eventually go dead.

The battery is connected to the alternator at all times, whether the ignition key is turned on or not. If the battery were shorted to ground, the alternator would also be shorted. This would damage the alternator. To prevent this, a fuse link is installed in the wiring between the battery and the alternator. If the battery is shorted, the fuse link is melted, protecting the alternator.

PRECAUTIONS

To prevent damage to the alternator and regulator, the following precautions should be taken when working with the electrical system.

1. Never reverse the battery connections.

2. Booster batteries for starting must be connected properly: positive-to-positive and negative-to-ground.

3. Disconnect the battery cables before using a fast charger; the charger has a tendency to force current through the diodes in the opposite direction for which they were designed. This burns out the diodes.

4. Never use a fast charger as a booster for starting the vehicle.

5. Never disconnect the voltage regulator while the engine is running.

6. Avoid long soldering times when replacing diodes or transistors. Prolonged heat is damaging to AC generators.

7. Do not use test lamps of more than 12 volts (V) for checking diode continuity.

8. Do not short across or ground any of the terminals on the AC generator.

9. The polarity of the battery, generator, and regulator must be matched and considered before making any electrical connections within the system.

10. Never operate the alternator on an open circuit. Make sure that all connections within the circuit are clean and tight.

11. Disconnect the battery terminals when performing any service on the electrical system. This will eliminate the possibility of accidental reversal of polarity.

12. Disconnect the battery ground cable if arc welding is to be done on any part of the car.

CHARGING SYSTEM TROUBLESHOOTING

There are many possible ways in which the charging system can malfunction. Often the source of a problem is difficult to diagnose, requiring special equipment and a good deal of experience. This is usually not the case, however, where the charging system fails completely and causes the dash board warning light to come on or the battery to become dead. To troubleshoot a complete system failure only two pieces of equipment are needed: a test light, to determine that current is reaching a certain point; and a current indicator (ammeter), to determine the direction of the current flow and its measurement in amps.

This test works under three assumptions:

1. The battery is known to be good and fully charged.

2. The alternator belt is in good condition and adjusted to the proper tension.

3. All connections in the system are clean and tight.

➡**In order for the current indicator to give a valid reading, the car must be equipped with battery cables which are of the same gauge size and quality as original equipment battery cables.**

1. Turn off all electrical components on the car. Make sure the doors of the car are closed. If the car is equipped with a clock, disconnect the clock by removing the lead wire from the rear of the clock. Disconnect the positive battery cable from the battery and connect the ground wire on a test light to the disconnected positive battery cable. Touch the probe end of the test light to the positive battery post. The test light should not light. If the test light does light, there is a short or open circuit on the car.

2. Disconnect the voltage regulator wiring harness connector at the voltage regulator. Turn on the ignition key. Connect the wire on a test light to a good ground (engine bolt). Touch the probe end of a test light to the ignition wire connector into the voltage regulator wiring connector. This wire corresponds to the / terminal on the regulator. If the test light goes on, the charging system warning light circuit is complete. If the test light does not come on and the warning light on the instrument panel is on, either the resistor wire, which is parallel with the warning light, or the wiring to the voltage regulator, is defective. If the test light does not come on and the warning light is not on, either the bulb is defective or the power supply wire form the battery through the ignition switch to the bulb has an open circuit. Connect the wiring harness to the regulator.

3. Examine the fuse link wire in the wiring harness from the starter relay to the alternator. If the insulation on the wire is cracked or split, the fuse link may be melted. Connect a test light to the fuse link by attaching the ground wire on the test light to an engine bolt and touching the probe end of the light to the bottom of the fuse link wire where it splices into the alternator output wire. If the bulb in the test light does not light, the fuse link is melted.

4. Start the engine and place a current indicator on the positive battery cable. Turn off all electrical accessories and make sure the doors are closed. If the charging system is working properly, the gauge will show a draw of less than 5 amps. If the system is not working properly, the gauge will show a draw of more

than 5 amps. A charge moves the needle toward the battery, a draw moves the needle away from the battery. Turn the engine off.

5. Disconnect the wiring harness from the voltage regulator at the regulator at the regulator connector. Connect a male spade terminal (solderless connector) to each end of a jumper wire. Insert one end of the wire into the wiring harness connector which corresponds to the **A** terminal on the regulator. Insert the other end of the wire into the wiring harness connector which corresponds to the **F** terminal on the regulator. Position the connector with the jumper wire installed so that it cannot contact any metal surface under the hood. Position a current indicator gauge on the positive battery cable. Have an assistant start the engine. Observe the reading on the current indicator. Have your assistant slowly raise the speed of the engine to about 2,000 rpm or until the current indicator needle stops moving, whichever comes first. Do not run the engine for more than a short period of time in this condition. If the wiring harness connector or jumper wire becomes excessively hot during this test, turn off the engine and check for a grounded wire in the regulator wiring harness. If the current indicator shows a charge of about three amps less than the output of the alternator, the alternator is working properly. If the previous tests showed a draw, the voltage regulator is defective. If the gauge does not show the proper charging rate, the alternator is defective.

REMOVAL & INSTALLATION

While internal alternator repairs are possible, they require specialized tools and training. Therefore, it is advisable to replace a defective alternator, or have it repaired by a qualified shop.

1. Disconnect the battery ground cable at the battery.

2. Disconnect and label the alternator output (BATT) and field (FLD) leads and disconnect the ground wire.

3. Loosen the alternator adjusting bolt and swing the alternator in toward the engine. Disengage the alternator drive belt.

4. Remove the alternator mounting bolts and remove the alternator from the vehicle.

5. Installation is the reverse of removal. Be sure to connect all ground wires and leads securely.

6. Adjust the belt tension.

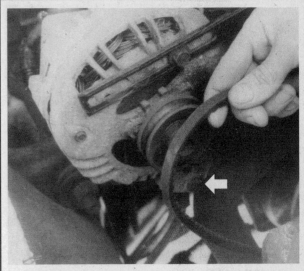

. . . and the pivot bolt (arrow), then remove the alternator belt

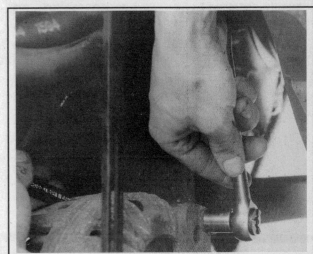

Remove the mounting bolts, then lift the alternator up to gain access to the wires

To remove the alternator on inline 6-cylinder engines, loosen the adjusting bolt . . .

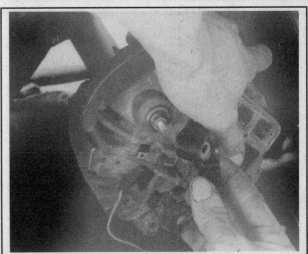

Disconnect the push-on field wires, and unbolt the battery wire. Remove the alternator

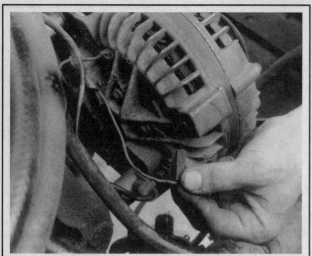

To remove the alternator on V8 engines, label and disconnect the field (FLD) leads

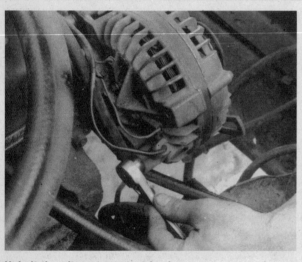

Unbolt the alternator output lead . . .

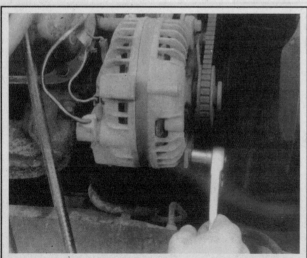

. . . then loosen the adjusting bolt and remove the alternator belt

Remove the mounting bolts and lift the alternator out of the engine compartment

BELT TENSION ADJUSTMENT

➡**On some models it may be necessary to remove the lower splash shield to gain clearance when installing a new drive belt.**

Belt tension should be checked with a gauge made for the purpose. If a gauge is not available, tension can be checked with moderate thumb pressure applied to the belt at its longest span midway between pulleys. If the belt has a free span less than 12″, it should deflect approximately ¼″. If the span is longer than 12″, deflection can range between ¼″ and ⅜″.

1. Loosen the driven accessory's pivot and mounting bolts.
2. Move the accessory toward or away from the engine until the tension is correct. You can use a wood hammer handle or broomstick as a lever, but do not use anything metallic.
3. Tighten the bolts and re-check the tension. If new belts have been installed, run the engine for a few minutes, then re-check and re-adjust as necessary.

➡**If the driven component has two drive belts, the belts should be replaced in pairs to maintain proper tension.**

It is better to have belts too loose than too tight, because overtight belts will lead to bearing failure, particularly in the water pump and alternator. However, loose belts place an extremely high impact load on the driven components due to the whipping action of the belt.

Regulator

REMOVAL & INSTALLATION

1967–69 with a Mechanical Regulator

1. Disconnect the battery ground cable at the battery negative terminal.
2. Disconnect the alternator output (BAT) and field (FLD) leads, then disconnect the alternator ground wire.

3. Remove the alternator mounting bracket bolts and remove the alternator.

4. Installation is the reverse of the above. Adjust the alternator drive belt tension. Check the alternator and regulator circuits and perform any necessary adjustment.

1970–88 with an Electronic Regulator

▶ **See Figure 4**

1. Release the spring clips and pull off the regulator wiring plug.

2. Unbolt and remove the regulator.

3. Installation is he reverse of removal. Be sure that the spring clips engage the wiring plug.

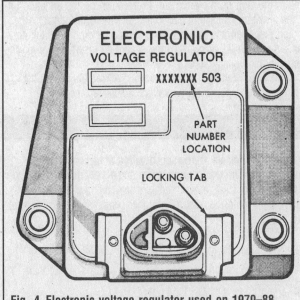

Fig. 4 Electronic voltage regulator used on 1970–88 vehicles

ADJUSTMENTS

1967–69 Mechanical Regulator Only

Normally, when the voltage regulator is suspected of being the cause of a vehicle charging system problem, the procedure is to remove the old unit and replace it with a new or reconditioned regulator. However, since these regulators are adjustable, it is advisable to perform the adjustments before removing the old unit. If the problem cannot be corrected easily by adjusting the voltage regulator, and no other possible causes of the problem can be found, the old regulator should then be replaced. In addition, adjustment procedures can be used when installing a new regulator to check to be sure that the voltage setting is correct.

➡**Do not remove the regulator or regulator cover to make the voltage adjustment. The stop in the regulator cover will limit the voltage adjustment range and the voltage adjusting screw should not be forced beyond this point.**

1. Adjust the lower contact voltage setting as necessary by turning the adjustment screw clockwise to increase the voltage or counter-clockwise to decrease the voltage.

If Step 1 does not bring the voltage regulator to within specifications, proceed to Step 2.

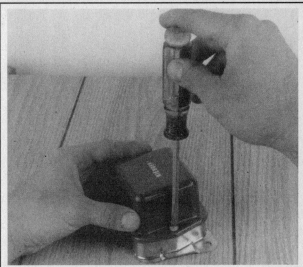

If cover removal is necessary for adjustment, remove the retaining screws

Lift the cover off for access to the internal components

Use a wire gauge to measure the gap(s) . . .

. . . and, if necessary, bend the contact to adjust the gap(s)

Always double check the gap(s) after an adjustment has been made

When installing the cover, make sure the rubber gasket is in position to avoid any water damage

2. Remove the regulator cover and measure the upper contact point gap with a wire gauge. The point gap should be 0.014″ ± 0.004″. Adjust the upper contact gap as necessary by bending the armature upper contact bracket, making sure the contacts are in alignment. If the upper contact gap is correct and a difference of 0.02–0.7 volts exists between the upper and lower points, adjust the air gap as follows:

3. If the difference is above 0.7 volts, reduce the air gapy by bending down the fixed contact bracket; if the difference is below 0.2 volts, increase the air gap by bending the fixed contact bracket up.

4. Connect a small dry cell test lamp in series with a IGN and FLD terminals of the voltage regulator. Insert a 0.032″ wire gauge between the regulator armature and the core of the voltage coil next to the stop on the armature. Press down on the armature until the armature contacts the wire gauge. The lower contacts should just open and the test lamp should be dim. With the air gap adjusted, a 0.042″ wire gauge cannot be inserted between the armature and voltage core.

5. Before installing the cover screws, make sure the rubber grommet is engaged over the voltage adjustment screw.

Starter

Almost all models are equipped with a reduction gear type starter motor. The only exception are some 1967 models with the 318 engine. In 1967, a few models came equipped with a direct drive starter motor because of a higher compression ratio in some 318 engines.

The diesel uses a reduction gear starter but it differs slightly from the regular unit, having a 3.75:1 ratio rather than the 3.5:1 ration.

REMOVAL & INSTALLATION

Gasoline Engines

1. Disconnect the ground cable at the battery.
2. Remove the cable from the starter.

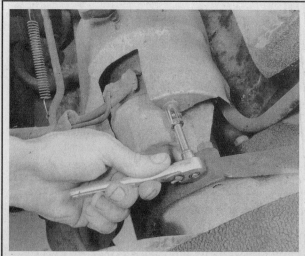

Disconnect the negative battery wire. If equipped, remove the starter heat shield

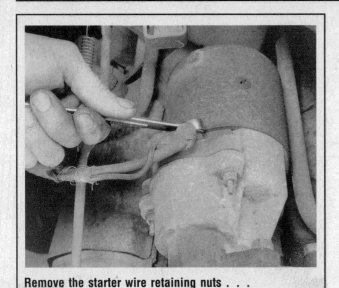

Remove the starter wire retaining nuts . . .

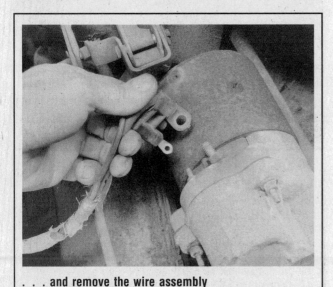

. . . and remove the wire assembly

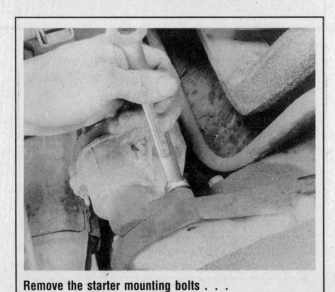

Remove the starter mounting bolts . . .

. . . then slide the starter back and remove it from the vehicle

3. Disconnect the solenoid leads at their solenoid terminals.

4. Remove the starter attachment bolts and withdraw the starter from the engine flywheel housing. On some models with automatic transmissions, the oil cooler tube bracket will interfere with the starter removal. In this case, remove the starter attachment bolts, slide the cooler tube bracket off the stud, and then withdraw the starter.

5. Installation is the reverse of the above. Be sure that the starter and flywheel housing mating surfaces are free of dirt and oil to make a good electrical contact.

➡When tightening the mounting bolt and nut on the starter, hold the starter away from the engine for the correct alignment.

Diesel Engine

1. Disconnect the negative battery cable.
2. Raise the truck and support it safely on jackstands.
3. Disconnect and label the wires at the starter motor.
4. Remove the attaching bolt, nut and washer and lift the starter and solenoid assembly from the engine.
5. Before installing the starter motor, be sure the mounting surface on the drive end housing and the flywheel housing are clean, to ensure good electrical contact. When tightening the attaching bolt and nut, hold the starter away from the engine to ensure the proper alignment.
6. Attach the wiring at the starter.
7. Attach the negative battery cable.

SOLENOID AND BRUSH SERVICE

Reduction Gear Starter

1. Remove the starter from the car and support the starter gear housing in a vise fitted with soft jaws. Do not clamp.
2. Remove the two through-bolts and the starter end assembly.
3. Carefully pull the armature up and out of the gear housing and the starter frame field assembly.

4. Carefully pull the frame and field assembly up just enough to expose the terminal screw (which connects the series field coils to one pair of motor brushes) and support it with two blocks.

5. Support the terminal by placing a finger behind the terminal and remove the terminal screw.

6. Unwrap the shunt field coil lead from the other starter brush terminal. Unwrap the solenoid lead wire from the brush terminal.

7. Remove the steel and fiber thrust washer.

8. Remove the nut, steel washer, and insulating washer from the solenoid terminal.

9. Straighten the solenoid wire and remove the brush holder plate with the brushes and solenoid as an assembly.

✷✷ WARNING

Do not break the shunt field wire units when removing and installing the brushes.

10. Inspect the starter brushes. Brushes that are worn more than one-hold the length of the new brushes, or are oil-soaked, should be replaced.

➡ **When resoldering the shunt field and solenoid leads, make a strong, low-resistance connection using a high-temperature solder and resin flux.**

11. Install the brush holder plate with the brushes and solenoid as an assembly.

12. Install the nut, steel washer, and insulating washer on the solenoid terminal.

13. Install the steel and fiber thrust washer.

14. Wrap the shunt field coil lead around the other starter brush terminal. Wrap the solenoid lead wire around the brush terminal.

15. Install the terminal screw which connects the series field coils to one pair of motor brushes.

16. Carefully push the armature down and into the gear housing and the starter frame field assembly.

17. Install the starter end assembly and the two through-bolts.

18. Install the starter.

Direct Drive Starter

♦ **See Figure 5**

1. Remove the starter from the van and support it in a vise fitted with soft jaws. Do not clamp.

2. Remove the through-bolts and tap the commutator and head from the field frame.

3. Remove the thrust washers from the armature shaft.

4. Lift the brush holder springs and remove the brushes from the brush holders. Remove the brush plate.

5. Disconnect the field coil leads at the solenoid connector.

6. Inspect the starter brushes. Brushes that are worn more than one-half the length of new brushes, or are oil-soaked, should be replaced. To replace the brushes, continue this procedure as follows:

7. Remove the ground brush terminal screw and carefully remove the ground brush set to prevent breaking the shunt field lead. Remove the shunt field lead from the old brush set to ensure as much length as possible.

8. Remove the field terminal plastic covering and remove the

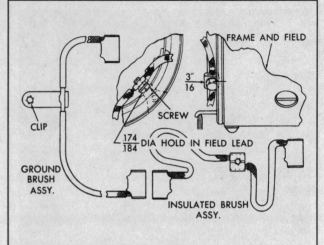

Fig. 5 Brush replacement on the 1967 direct drive starter

old brushes. Use side cutters to break the weld by rolling the stranded wire off the terminal.

9. Drill a 0.174–0.184" hole in the series coil terminal ³⁄₁₆" from the top of the terminal to the centerline of the hole (use a number 16 drill).

✷✷ WARNING

Do not damage the field coil during the drilling operation.

10. Attach the insulated brush set to the series field terminal with a flat washer and a number 8 self-tapping screw. Attach the shunt field lead to the new ground brush set by making a loop around the terminal and soldering the lead to the terminal with resin core solder.

11. Attach the ground brush terminal to the field frame with the attachment screw. Fold the extra shunt field lead back along the brush lead and secure it with electrical tape.

12. Connect the field coil leads at the solenoid connector.

13. Install the brush plate. Install the brushes in the brush holders.

14. Install the thrust washers on the armature shaft.

15. Install the armature.

16. Install the field frame and through-bolts.

17. Install the starter.

OVERHAUL

Chrysler Direct Drive Starter

1967 MODELS

1. Remove the through-bolts and tap the commutator end frame from the field frame.

2. Remove the thrust washers from the armature shaft.

3. Lift the brush holder springs and remove the brushes.

4. Remove the brush plate.

5. Disconnect the field coil leads at the solenoid connector.

6. Remove the solenoid attaching screws and remove the solenoid and boot.

7. Drive out the overrunning clutch shift fork pivot pin.

8. Remove the drive end pinion housing and spacer washer.

➡**If the rubber seal is damaged, the pinion housing will have to be replaced.**

9. Note the position of the shifter fork on the starter drive and remove the fork.

10. Slide the overrunning clutch pinion gear towards the commutator end of the armature.

11. Slide the drive stop retainer toward the clutch pinion gear to expose the snapring and remove the snapring.

12. Slide the overrunning clutch drive from the armature shaft.

13. If it is necessary to replace the field coils, remove the ground brushes terminal attaching screw and raise the brushes with the terminal and shunt wire up and out of the way. Remove the pole shoe screws with an impact screwdriver.

14. When assembling the starter, lubricate the armature shaft and splines with 10W-30 engine oil.

15. Install the starter drive, stop-collar, lock ring and spacer.

16. Install the shifter fork over the starter drive spring retainer washer with the narrow leg of the fork towards the commutator. THIS IS IMPORTANT!. If the fork is not properly positioned, the starter gear travel will be restricted causing a lockup in the drive mechanism.

17. Install the drive end pinion hosuign, inexing the shifting fork with the slot in the drive end housing.

18. Install the shifter fork pivot pin.

19. Slide the armature into the field frame until the pinion housing indexes with the slot in the field frame.

20. Install the solenoid and boot and torque the bolts to 60–70 in.lb.

21. Connect the field coil leads at the solenoid connector. **Make sure that the terminals do not touch the field frame!**

22. Install the brush holder ring, indexing the tang on the ring with the hole in the field frame.

23. Position the brushes in the holders. Make sure that the field coil lead wires are properly positioned behind the brush holder plate to avoid interference with the brush operation.

24. Install the thrust washers on the commutator to establish an end-play of 0.010″ minimum.

25. Install the comutator end head.

26. Install the through-bolts and torque them to 40–50 in.lb.

Chrysler Reduction Gear Starter

1967–87 MODELS

◗ **See Figures 6 and 7**

1. Support the assembly in a vise equipped with soft jaws; do not clamp. Care must be used not to distort or damage the die cast aluminum.

2. Remove the through-bolts and the end housing.

3. Carefully pull the armature up and out of the gear housing, then the starter frame and the field assembly. Remove the steel and the fiber thrust washer.

➡**On V8 engines the starting motors have the wire of the shunt field coil soldered to the brush terminal. The 6 cylinder engines have the four coils in series and do not have a wire soldered to the brush terminal. One pair of brushes is connected to this terminal, while the other pair is attached to the series field coils by means of a terminal screw. Carefully pull the frame and the field assembly up enough to expose the terminal screw and the solder connection of the shunt field at the brush terminal. Place two wooden blocks between the starter frame and gear housing to facilitate re-**

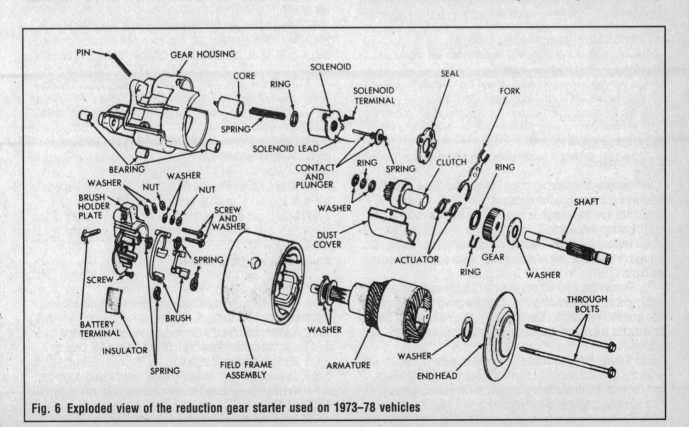

Fig. 6 Exploded view of the reduction gear starter used on 1973–78 vehicles

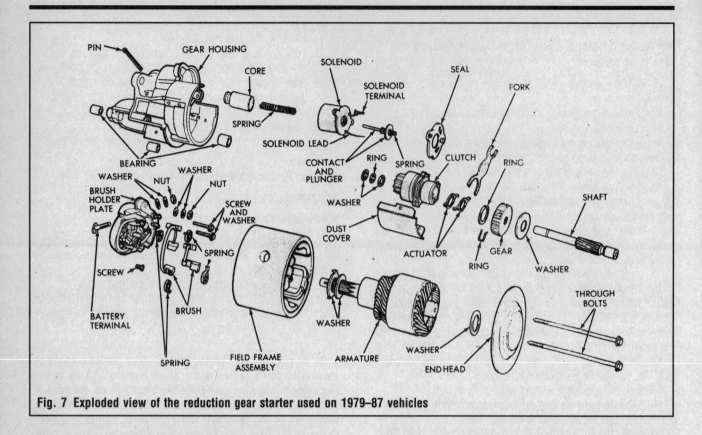

Fig. 7 Exploded view of the reduction gear starter used on 1979–87 vehicles

moval of the terminal screw and unsoldering of the shunt field wire at the brush terminal.

4. Support the brush terminal with a finger behind the terminal and remove the screw.

5. On the V8 engine starters, unsolder the shunt field coil lead from the brush terminal and the housing.

6. The brush holder plate with the terminal, the contact and the brushes is serviced as an assembly.

7. Clean the old sealant from around the plate and the housing, then remove the brush holder attaching screw.

8. On the shunt type, unsolder the solenoid winding from the brush terminal, then remove the 11/32" nut, the washer and the insulator from solenoid terminal.

9. Remove the brush holder plate with the brushes as an assembly.

10. Remove gear housing ground screw, then the solenoid assembly from the well. Remove the nut, the washer and the seal from starter (battery) terminal, then the terminal from plate.

11. Remove the solenoid contact and the plunger from solenoid, then the coil sleeve. Remove the solenoid return spring, the coil retaining washer, the retainer and the dust cover from the gear housing.

12. Release the snapring which locates the driven gear pinion shaft, then the front retaining ring. Push the pinion shaft rearward, then remove the snapring, the thrust washers, the clutch and the pinion, then the two shift fork nylon actuators.

13. Remove the driven gear and the friction washer. Pull the shifting fork forward and remove the moving core.

14. Remove the fork retainer pin and the shifting fork assembly. The gear housing with bushings is serviced as an assembly.

15. The brushes that are worn more than 1/2 the length of new brushes or are oil soaked, should be replaced.

16. When resoldering the shunt field and the solenoid lead, make a strong low resistance connection using a high temperature solder and a resin flux. Do not use acid or acid core solder. Do not break the shunt field wire units when removing and installing the brushes.

17. Do not immerse the starter clutch unit in a cleaning solvent. The outside of the clutch and the pinion must be cleaned with a cloth so as not to wash the lubricant from the inside of the clutch.

18. Rotate the pinion, the pinion gear should rotate smoothly and in one direction only. If the starter clutch unit does not function properly or if the pinion is worn, chipped or burred, replace the starter clutch unit.

19. Inspect the commutator and the brush contact surface when the starter is assembled, for flat spots, out of roundness or excessive wear.

20. Reface the commutator (if necessary), by removing only a sufficient amount of metal to provide a smooth, even surface.

21. Using light pressure, clean the grooves of the face of the commutator with a pointed tool, neither remove any metal nor widen the grooves.

22. Install the fork retainer pin and the shifting fork assembly.

23. Pull the shifting fork forward and install the moving core. Install the driven gear and the friction washer.

24. Push the pinion shaft rearward, then install the snapring, the thrust washers, the clutch and the pinion, then the two shift fork nylon actuators. Install the snapring which locates the driven gear pinion shaft, then the front retaining ring.

25. Install the solenoid return spring, the coil retaining washer, the retainer and the dust cover from the gear housing. Install the coil sleeve then the solenoid contact and the plunger on the solenoid.

26. Install the solenoid assembly then the gear housing

ground screw, in the well. Install the nut, the washer and the seal on the starter (battery) terminal, then the terminal on the plate.

27. After lubricating the plates with a small amount of SAE 10 engine oil, they should have about 1/16" side movement to insure proper pinion gear engagement.

28. Install the brush holder plate with the brushes as an assembly.

29. On the shunt type, solder the solenoid winding from the brush terminal, then install the 11/32" nut, the washer and the insulator on solenoid terminal.

30. Install the brush holder attaching screw.

31. Install the brush holder plate with the terminal, the contact and the brushes as an assembly.

32. On the V8 engine starters, solder the shunt field coil lead from the brush terminal and the housing.

33. Support the brush terminal with a finger behind the terminal and install the screw.

➡On V8 engines the starting motors have the wire of the shunt field coil soldered to the brush terminal. The 6-cylinder engines have the four coils in series and do not have a wire soldered to the brush terminal. One pair of brushes is connected to this terminal, while the other pair is attached to the series field coils by means of a terminal screw. Carefully pull the frame and the field assembly up enough to expose the terminal screw and the solder connection of the shunt field at the brush terminal. Place two wooden blocks between the starter frame and gear housing to facilitate installation of the terminal screw and soldering of the shunt field wire at the brush terminal.

34. Install the steel and the fiber thrust washer. Carefully push the armature down and into the gear housing, then the starter frame and the field assembly.

35. Install the end housing and the through-bolts.

36. Install the starter.

Nippondenso Starter

1988 MODELS

▶ See Figure 8

1. Position the assembly in a suitable holding fixture. Remove the rubber boot from the field coil terminal. Remove the nut from the field coil terminal stud. Remove the field coil terminal from the stud.

2. Remove the through bolts. Remove the splash shield. Remove the end shield screws from the brush plate. Remove the starter end shield.

3. Slide the brushes from there holders. As pry the retaining springs back for access. Remove the brush plate.

4. Slide the armature out of the starter housing. Remove the starter housing from the gear housing. Remove the solenoid terminal cover.

5. Remove the solenoid terminal nut and washer. Remove the battery terminal nut and washer. Remove the solenoid terminal assembly from the terminal posts.

6. Remove the solenoid terminal from the insulator. Remove the battery terminal from the insulator.

7. Remove the solenoid cover screws from the solenoid assembly. Remove the solenoid cover. Remove the seal. Remove the solenoid plunger from the housing. Remove the plunger spring.

8. Remove the gear housing to solenoid retaining screws. Separate the gear housing from the solenoid housing.

9. Remove the reduction gear and clutch assembly from the gear housing.

10. Remove the reduction gear, pinion gear, retainer and roller assembly from the gear housing.

11. Inspect and clean all parts, as required. Repair or replace defective parts as required. Brushes that are worn more than one half the length of new brushes, or are oil soaked should be replaced.

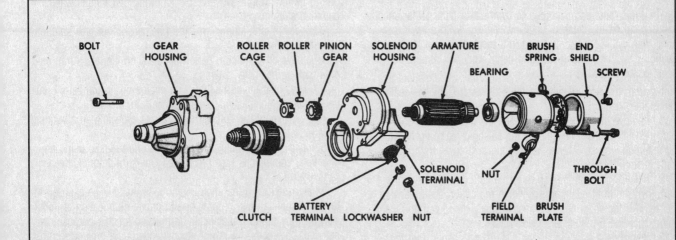

Fig. 8 Exploded view of the Nippondenso starter used on 1988 vehicles

12. Install the reduction gear, pinion gear, retainer and roller assembly in the gear housing.

13. Install the reduction gear and clutch assembly in the gear housing.

14. Join the gear housing to the solenoid housing. Install the gear housing to solenoid retaining screws.

15. Install the plunger spring.

16. Install the solenoid plunger in the housing.

17. Install the seal.

18. Install the solenoid cover.

19. Install the solenoid terminal on the insulator.

20. Install the battery terminal on the insulator.

21. Install the solenoid terminal nut and washer.

22. Install the battery terminal nut and washer.

23. Install the solenoid terminal assembly on the terminal posts.

24. Install the solenoid terminal cover.

25. Install the starter housing from the gear housing.

26. Slide the armature into the starter housing.

27. Install the brush plate. Slide the brushes into their holders.

28. Install the starter end shield. Install the end shield screws from the brush plate. Install the splash shield. Install the through bolts.

29. Install the field coil terminal from the stud.

30. Install the nut from the field coil terminal stud.

31. Install the rubber boot from the field coil terminal.

ENGINE MECHANICAL

Engine Overhaul Tips

Most engine overhaul procedures are fairly standard. In addition to specific parts replacement procedures and specifications for your individual engine, this section is also a guide to acceptable rebuilding procedures. Examples of standard rebuilding practice are given and should be used along with specific details concerning your particular engine.

Competent and accurate machine shop services will ensure maximum performance, reliability and engine life. In most instances it is more profitable for the do-it-yourself mechanic to remove, clean and inspect the component, buy the necessary parts and deliver these to a shop for actual machine work.

On the other hand, much of the rebuilding work (crankshaft, block, bearings, piston rods, and other components) is well within the scope of the do-it-yourself mechanic's tools and abilities. You will have to decide for yourself the depth of involvement you desire in an engine repair or rebuild.

TOOLS

The tools required for an engine overhaul or parts replacement will depend on the depth of your involvement. With a few exceptions, they will be the tools found in a mechanic's tool kit (see Section 1 of this manual). More in-depth work will require some or all of the following:

• A dial indicator (reading in thousandths) mounted on a universal base
• Micrometers and telescope gauges
• Jaw and screw-type pullers
• Scraper
• Valve spring compressor
• Ring groove cleaner
• Piston ring expander and compressor
• Ridge reamer
• Cylinder hone or glaze breaker
• Plastigage®
• Engine stand

The use of most of these tools is illustrated in this chapter. Many can be rented for a one-time use from a local parts jobber or tool supply house specializing in automotive work.

Occasionally, the use of special tools is called for. See the information on Special Tools and the Safety Notice in the front of this book before substituting another tool.

INSPECTION TECHNIQUES

Procedures and specifications are given in this chapter for inspecting, cleaning and assessing the wear limits of most major components. Other procedures such as Magnaflux® and Zyglo® can be used to locate material flaws and stress cracks. Magnaflux® is a magnetic process applicable only to ferrous materials. The Zyglo® process coats the material with a fluorescent dye penetrant and can be used on any material.

Checking for suspected surface cracks can be more readily made using spot check dye. The dye is sprayed onto the suspected area, wiped off and the area sprayed with a developer. Cracks will show up brightly.

OVERHAUL TIPS

Aluminum has become extremely popular for use in engines, due to its low weight. Observe the following precautions when handling aluminum parts:

• Never hot tank aluminum parts (the caustic hot tank solution will eat the aluminum.
• Remove all aluminum parts (identification tag, etc.) from engine parts prior to the tanking.
• Always coat threads lightly with engine oil or anti-seize compounds before installation, to prevent seizure.
• Never overtorque bolts or spark plugs especially in aluminum threads.

Stripped threads in any component can be repaired using any of several commercial repair kits (Heli-Coil®, Microdot®, Keenserts®, etc.).

When assembling the engine, any parts that will be exposed to frictional contact must be prelubed to provide lubrication at initial start-up. Any product specifically formulated for this purpose can be used, but engine oil is not recommended as a prelube in most cases.

When semi-permanent (locked, but removable) installation of bolts or nuts is desired, threads should be cleaned and coated with Loctite® or another similar, commercial non-hardening sealant.

REPAIRING DAMAGED THREADS

Several methods of repairing damaged threads are available. Heli-Coil® (shown here), Keenserts® and Microdot® are among the most widely used. All involve basically the same principle—drilling out stripped threads, tapping the hole and installing a pre-wound insert—making welding, plugging and oversize fasteners unnecessary.

Two types of thread repair inserts are usually supplied: a standard type for most inch coarse, inch fine, metric course and metric fine thread sizes and a spark lug type to fit most spark plug port sizes. Consult the individual tool manufacturer's catalog to determine exact applications. Typical thread repair kits will contain a selection of prewound threaded inserts, a tap (corresponding to the outside diameter threads of the insert) and an installation tool. Spark plug inserts usually differ because they require a tap equipped with pilot threads and a combined reamer/tap section. Most manufacturers also supply blister-packed thread repair inserts separately in addition to a master kit containing a variety of taps and inserts plus installation tools.

Before attempting to repair a threaded hole, remove any snapped, broken or damaged bolts or studs. Penetrating oil can be used to free frozen threads. The offending item can usually be removed with locking pliers or using a screw/stud extractor. After the hole is clear, the thread can be repaired, as shown in the series of accompanying illustrations and in the kit manufacturer's instructions.

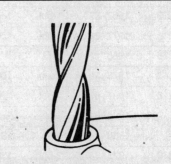

Drill out the damaged threads with the specified size bit. Be sure to drill completely through the hole or to the bottom of a blind hole

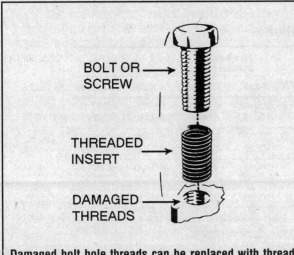

Damaged bolt hole threads can be replaced with thread repair inserts

BOLT OR SCREW

THREADED INSERT

DAMAGED THREADS

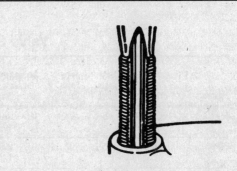

Using the kit, tap the hole in order to receive the thread insert. Keep the tap well oiled and back it out frequently to avoid clogging the threads

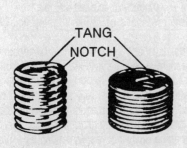

TANG
NOTCH

Standard thread repair insert (left), and spark plug thread insert

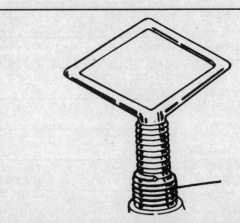

Screw the insert onto the installer tool until the tang engages the slot. Thread the insert into the hole until it is ¼–½ turn below the top surface, then remove the tool and break off the tang using a punch

General Engine Specifications

Engine	Years	Fuel System Type	SAE net Horsepower @ rpm	SAE net Torque ft. lb. @ rpm	Bore x Stroke (in.)	Comp. Ratio	Oil Press. (psi.) @ 2000 rpm
6-170	1967–69	1-bbl	115 @ 3900	170 @ 1600	3.400 x 3.120	8.50:1	30–70
6-198	1968	1-bbl	125 @ 3900	190 @ 1600	3.400 x 3.640	8.40:1	30–70
6-225	1967–87	1-bbl	140 @ 3900	215 @ 1600	3.400 x 4.125	8.40:1	30–70
	1977–82	2-bbl	150 @ 3700	225 @ 1800	3.400 x 4.125	8.40:1	30–70
6-238	1988	EFI	N.A.	N.A.	3.910 x 3.310	9.0:1	30–80
6-243	1978–79	Diesel	100 @ 3700	163 @ 2200	3.620 x 3.940	20.0:1	40–45
8-318	1967–87	2-bbl	120 @ 4200	250 @ 1600	3.910 x 3.310	8.6:1	30–80
	1979–84	4-bbl	150 @ 3900	245 @ 1800	3.910 x 3.310	8.5:1	30–80
	1988	EFI	135 @ 4000	240 @ 1800	3.910 x 3.310	9.0:1	30–80
8-360	1972–84	2-bbl	130 @ 3200	255 @ 2000	4.000 x 3.580	8.5:1	30–80
	1972–88	4-bbl	170 @ 3300	275 @ 2000	4.000 x 3.580	8.5:1	30–80
8-400	1972–78	2-bbl	180 @ 3600	315 @ 2400	4.340 x 3.380	8.2:1	45–65
8-440	1974–78	4-bbl	225 @ 4400	360 @ 3200	4.320 x 3.750	8.2:1	30–80

Valve Specifications

Engines	Years	Seat Angle (deg)	Face Angle (deg)	Spring Test Pressure (lbs. @ In.)	Spring Installed Height (in.)	Stem-to-Guide Clearance (in.) Intake	Exhaust	Stem Diameter (in.) Intake	Exhaust
6-170	1967–69	45	①	137–150 @ 1.3125	1.6875	0.0010–0.0030	0.0020–0.0040	0.3720–0.3730	0.3710–0.3720
6-198	1968	45	①	137–150 @ 1.3125	1.6875	0.0010–0.0030	0.0020–0.0040	0.3720–0.3730	0.3710–0.3720
6-225	1967–87	45	①	137–150 @ 1.3125	1.6875	0.0010–0.0030	0.0020–0.0040	0.3720–0.3730	0.3710–0.3720
6-238	1988	45	45	⑩	⑪	0.0010–0.0030	0.0020–0.0040	0.3720–0.3730	0.3710–0.3720
6-243	1978–79	45	45	⑮	⑯	0.0020–0.0030	0.0030–0.0040	0.3150	0.3150
8-318	1967–68	45	④	170–184 @ 1.3125	1.6875	0.0010–0.0030	0.0020–0.0040	0.3720–0.3730	0.3710–0.3720
	1969–74	45	⑧	170–184 @ 1.3125	1.6875	0.0010–0.0030	0.0020–0.0040	0.3720–0.3730	0.3710–0.3720
	1975–76	45	45	⑭	1.65625	0.0010–0.0030	0.0020–0.0040	0.3720–0.3730	0.3710–0.3720
	1979	45	①	⑩	⑫	0.0010–0.0030	0.0020–0.0040	0.3720–0.3730	0.3710–0.3720
	1980–88	45	45	⑩	⑫	0.0010–0.0030	0.0020–0.0040	0.3720–0.3730	0.3710–0.3720
8-360	1972–76	45	①	170–184 @ 1.3125	1.6875	0.0010–0.0030	0.0020–0.0040	0.3720–0.3730	0.3710–0.3720
	1979	45	①	⑩	⑫	0.0010–0.0030	0.0020–0.0040	0.3720–0.3730	0.3710–0.3720
	1980–88	45	45	⑬	⑫	0.0010–0.0030	0.0020–0.0040	0.3720–0.3730	0.3710–0.3720

Camshaft Specifications

(All specifications in inches)

| Engine | Journal Diameter | | | | | Bearing Clearance | Lobe Lift | | End Play |
	1	2	3	4	5		Int.	Exh.	
6-170	2.0015	1.9845	1.9695	1.9535	—	0.0010–0.0030	0.397	0.392	0
6-198	2.0015	1.9845	1.9695	1.9535	—	0.0010–0.0030	0.397	0.392	0
6-225	1.9980–1.9990	1.9820–1.9830	1.9670–1.9680	1.9510–1.9520	—	0.0010–0.0030	②	②	0
6-238	1.9980–1.9990	1.9670–1.9680	1.9510–1.9520	1.5605–1.5615	—	0.0010–0.0030	0.373	0.400	0.006
6-243	2.1450–2.1460	2.1450–2.1460	2.1250–2.1260	2.0864–2.0865	—	0.0016–0.0035	0.419	0.419	0
8-318	⑤	⑤	⑤	⑤	⑤	0.0010–0.0030	①	①	③
8-360	1.9980–1.9990	1.9820–1.9830	1.9670–1.9680	1.9510–1.9520	1.5605–1.5615	0.0010–0.0030	0.410	⑥	③
8-400	1.9980–1.9990	1.9820–1.9830	1.9670–1.9680	1.9510–1.9520	1.7480–1.7500	0.0010–0.0030	0.434	0.430	0.004
8-440	1.9980–1.9990	1.9820–1.9830	1.9670–1.9680	1.9510–1.9520	1.7480–1.7500	0.0010–0.0030	④	④	0.004

① 1967–68:
   Intake—0.390
   Exhaust—0.391
1969–88:
   Intake—0.372
   Exhaust—0.400
② 1967–73:
   Intake—0.397
   Exhaust—0.392
1974–80:
   Intake—0.406
   Exhaust—0.414
1981–87:
   Intake: 0.378
   Exhaust: 0.378
③ 1967–74: 0.004
1975–88: 0.006

④ 1972–74:
   Intake—0.464
   Exhaust—0.464
1975–76:
   Intake—0.425
   Exhaust—0.435
1977:
   Intake—0.434
   Exhaust—0.430
⑤ 1967–76:
   No. 1—1.9980–1.9990
   No. 2—1.9820–1.9830
   No. 3—1.9670–1.9680
   No. 4—1.9510–1.9520
   No. 5—1.5605–1.5615

1977–80:
   No. 1—1.9970–1.9990
   No. 2—1.9830–1.9910
   No. 3—1.9680–1.9960
   No. 4—1.9500–1.9520
   No. 5—1.5595–1.5615
1981–88:
   No. 1—1.9980–1.9990
   No. 2—1.9820–1.9830
   No. 3—1.9670–1.9680
   No. 4—1.9510–1.9520
   No. 5—1.5605–1.5615
⑥ 1972–76: 0.400
1977–88: 0.410

Crankshaft and Connecting Rod Specifications

(All specifications in inches)

Engines	Years	Crankshaft				Connecting Rod		
		Main Bearing Journal Dia.	Main Bearing Oil Clearance	Shaft End Play	Thrust on No.	Journal Dia.	Oil Clearance	Side Clearance
6-170	1968	2.7495–2.7505	0.0005–0.0015	0.0035–0.0085	3	2.1865–2.1875	0.0005–0.0015	0.006–0.012
6-198	1968	2.7495–2.7505	0.0005–0.0015	0.0035–0.0085	3	2.1865–2.1875	0.0005–0.0015	0.006–0.012
6-225	1967–76	2.7495–2.7505	0.0005–0.0015	③	3	2.1865–2.1875	0.0005–0.0015	0.006–0.012
	1977–78	2.7495–2.7505	0.0005–0.0020	0.0020–0.0090	3	2.1865–2.1875	0.0005–0.0025	0.006–0.025
	1979–80	2.7495–2.7505	0.0002–0.0022	0.0020–0.0090	3	2.1865–2.1875	0.0002–0.0022	0.006–0.025
	1981–87	2.7495–2.7505	0.0010–0.0025	0.0035–0.0090	3	2.1865–2.1875	0.0010–0.0022	0.007–0.013
6-238	1988	2.4995–2.5005	②	0.0020–0.0070	3	2.1240–2.1250	0.0005–0.0022	0.006–0.014
6-243	1978–79	2.7539–2.7547	0.0012–0.0035	0.0039–0.0098	7	2.2813–2.2821	0.0015–0.0044	0.005–0.018
8-318	1967–72	2.4995–2.5005	0.0005–0.0015	0.0020–0.0070	3	2.1240–2.1250	0.0005–0.0015	0.006–0.014
	1973–74	2.4995–2.5005	0.0005–0.0020	0.0020–0.0090	3	2.1240–2.1250	0.0005–0.0015	0.006–0.014
	1975–76	2.4995–2.5005	0.0005–0.0015	0.0020–0.0090	3	2.1240–2.1250	0.0002–0.0022	0.006–0.014
	1977–79	2.4995–2.5005	0.0005–0.0020	④	3	2.1240–2.1250	0.0005–0.0025	0.006–0.014
	1980–88	2.4995–2.5005	①	0.0020–0.0070	3	2.1240–2.1250	0.0005–0.0022	0.006–0.014

Crankshaft and Connecting Rod Specifications (cont.)

(All specifications in inches)

		Crankshaft				Connecting Rod		
Engines	Years	Main Bearing Journal Dia.	Main Bearing Oil Clearance	Shaft End Play	Thrust on No.	Journal Dia.	Oil Clearance	Side Clearance
8-360	1972–74	2.8095–2.8105	0.0005–0.0020	0.0020–0.0090	3	2.1240–2.1250	0.0005–0.0020	0.006–0.014
	1975–79	2.8095–2.8105	0.0005–0.0020	0.0020–0.0090	3	2.1240–2.1250	0.0005–0.0025	0.006–0.014
	1980–88	2.8095–2.8105	①	0.0020–0.0090	3	2.1240–2.1250	0.0005–0.0022	0.006–0.014
8-400	1974–78	2.6245–2.6255	0.0005–0.0020	⑥	3	2.3750–2.3760	⑤	0.009–0.017
8-440	1974	2.7495–2.7505	0.0005–0.0020	0.0020–0.0070	3	2.3740–2.3750	0.0010–0.0025	0.009–0.017
	1975–76	2.7495–2.7505	0.0002–0.0022	0.0020–0.0070	3	2.3740–2.3750	0.0005–0.0015	0.009–0.017
	1977–78	2.7495–2.7505	0.0005–0.0020	0.0020–0.0090	3	2.3750–2.3760	0.0005–0.0030	0.009–0.017

① No. 1: 0.0005–0.0015
   Nos. 2, 3, 4, 5: 0.0005–0.0020
② No. 1: 0.0005–0.0015
   Nos. 2, 3, 4: 0.0005–0.0020

③ 1967–74: 0.0035–0.0085
   1975–76: 0.0020–0.0090
④ 1977–78: 0.0020–0.0090
   1979: 0.0020–0.0070

⑤ 2-bbl: 0.0005–0.0025
   4-bbl: 0.0005–0.0030
⑥ 1974: 0.0020–0.0070
   1975–78: 0.0020–0.0090

Piston and Ring Specifications

(All specifications in inches)

		Ring Gap			Ring Side Clearance			Piston-to-Bore * Clearance
Engines	Years	#1 Compr.	#2 Compr.	Oil Control	#1 Compr.	#2 Compr.	Oil Control	
6-170	1967–69	0.010–0.020	0.010–0.020	0.010–0.020	0.0015–0.0030	0.0015–0.0030	0.0015–0.0030	0.0005–0.0015
6-198	1968	0.010–0.020	0.010–0.020	0.015–0.025	0.0015–0.0030	0.0015–0.0030	0.0010–0.0030	0.0005–0.0015
6-225	1967–72	0.010–0.020	0.010–0.020	0.015–0.025	0.0015–0.0030	0.0015–0.0030	0.0010–0.0030	0.0005–0.0015
	1973–76	0.010–0.020	0.010–0.020	0.015–0.055	0.0015–0.0030	0.0015–0.0030	0.0010–0.0030	0.0005–0.0015
	1977–87	0.010–0.020	0.010–0.020	0.015–0.055	0.0015–0.0030	0.0015–0.0030	0.0002–0.0050	0.0005–0.0015
6-238	1988	0.010–0.020	0.010–0.020	0.015–0.055	0.0015–0.0030	0.0015–0.0030	0.0002–0.0050	0.0005–0.0015
6-243	1978–79	0.012–0.020	0.012–0.020	0.012–0.020	0.0010–0.0020	0.0010–0.0020	0.0010–0.0020	0.0060–0.0080
8-318	1967–72	0.010–0.020	0.010–0.020	0.010–0.020	0.0015–0.0030	0.0015–0.0030	0.0010–0.0050	0.0005–0.0015
	1973–74	0.010–0.020	0.010–0.020	0.015–0.055	0.0015–0.0030	0.0015–0.0030	0.0020–0.0050	0.0005–0.0015
	1975–76	0.010–0.020	0.010–0.020	0.015–0.055	0.0015–0.0030	0.0015–0.0030	0.0005–0.0050	0.0005–0.0015
	1977–88	0.010–0.020	0.010–0.020	0.015–0.055	0.0015–0.0030	0.0015–0.0030	0.0002–0.0050	0.0005–0.0015

Piston and Ring Specifications *(cont.)*

(All specifications in inches)

Engines	Years	Ring Gap			Ring Side Clearance			Piston-to-Bore * Clearance
		#1 Compr.	#2 Compr.	Oil Control	#1 Compr.	#2 Compr.	Oil Control	
8-360	1972–74	0.010–0.020	0.010–0.020	0.015–0.055	0.0015–0.0030	0.0015–0.0030	0.0020–0.0050	0.0005–0.0015
	1975–76	0.010–0.020	0.010–0.020	0.015–0.055	0.0015–0.0030	0.0015–0.0030	0.0005–0.0050	0.0005–0.0015
	1977–88	0.010–0.020	0.010–0.020	0.015–0.055	0.0015–0.0030	0.0015–0.0030	0.0002–0.0050	0.0005–0.0015
8-400	1972–76	0.010–0.020	0.010–0.020	0.015–0.055	0.0015–0.0030	0.0015–0.0030	0.0020–0.0050	0.0003–0.0013
	1977–78	0.013–0.023	0.013–0.023	0.015–0.055	0.0015–0.0030	0.0015–0.0030	0.0002–0.0050	0.0003–0.0013
8-440	1972–74	0.010–0.020	0.010–0.020	0.015–0.055	0.0015–0.0040	0.0015–0.0040	0.0020–0.0050	0.0003–0.0013
	1975–76	0.010–0.020	0.010–0.020	0.015–0.055	0.0015–0.0030	0.0015–0.0030	0.0010–0.0030	0.0003–0.0013
	1977–78	0.013–0.023	0.013–0.023	0.015–0.055	0.0015–0.0030	0.0015–0.0030	0.0002–0.0050	0.0003–0.0013

* Measured at the top of the skirt

Torque Specifications
(All specifications in ft. lb.)

Engines	Years	Cyl. Head	Conn. Rod	Main Bearing	Crankshaft Damper	Flywheel	Manifold	
							Intake	Exhaust
6-170	1967–69	65	45	85	—	55	15	10
6-198	1968	65	45	85	—	55	20	10
6-225	1975–87	70	45	85	—	55	②	10
	1967–74	65	45	85	—	55	③	10
6-238	1988	105	45	85	135	55	45	①
6-243	1978–79	90	58	80	289	65	—	—
8-318	1986–88	105	45	85	100	55	45	①
	1985	105	45	85	100	55	40	①
	1981–84	95	45	85	100	55	40	①
	1978–80	105	45	85	100	55	40	①
	1977	95	45	85	100	55	45	①
	1972–76	95	45	85	100	55	35	20
	1967–71	85	45	85	135	55	35	25
8-360	1986–88	105	45	85	100	55	45	①
	1984–85	105	45	85	100	55	40	①
	1981–83	95	45	85	100	55	40	①
	1978–80	105	45	85	100	55	40	①
	1977	95	45	85	100	55	45	①
	1972–76	95	45	85	100	55	35	20

Torque Specifications (cont.)
(All specifications in ft. lb.)

Engines	Years	Cyl. Head	Conn. Rod	Main Bearing	Crankshaft Damper	Flywheel	Manifold	
							Intake	Exhaust
8-400	1975–78	70	45	85	135	55	45	30
	1973–74	70	45	85	135	55	40	30
8-440	1975–78	70	45	85	135	55	45	30
	1973–74	70	45	85	135	55	40	30

① Screw: 20
   Nut: 15
② 1978–87:
   Intake-to-exhaust manifold stud: 25
   Intake-to-exhaust manifold bolt: 22
  1975–77:
   Intake-to-exhaust manifold stud: 20
   Intake-to-exhaust manifold bolt: 16

③ 1967–74:
   Intake-to-exhaust manifold nut: 30
   Intake-to-exhaust manifold screw: 20

Checking Engine Compression

A noticeable lack of engine power, excessive oil consumption and/or poor fuel mileage measured over an extended period are all indicators of internal engine war. Worn piston rings, scored or worn cylinder bores, blown head gaskets, sticking or burnt valves and worn valve seats are all possible culprits here. A check of each cylinder's compression will help you locate the problems.

As mentioned earlier, a screw-in type compression gauge is more accurate than the type you simply hold against the spark plug hole, although it takes slightly longer to use. It's worth it to obtain a more accurate reading. Follow the procedures below.

GASOLINE ENGINES

1. Warm up the engine to normal operating temperature.
2. Remove all the spark plugs.
3. Disconnect the high tension lead from the ignition coil.
4. Fully open the throttle either by operating the carburetor throttle linkage by hand or by having an assistant floor the accelerator pedal.
5. Screw the compression gauge into the no.1 spark plug hole until the fitting is snug.

✳✳ WARNING

Be careful not to crossthread the plug hole. On aluminum cylinder heads use extra care, as the threads in these heads are easily ruined.

6. Ask an assistant to depress the accelerator pedal fully on both carbureted and fuel injected vehicles. Then, while you read the compression gauge, ask the assistant to crank the engine two or three times in short bursts using the ignition switch.
7. Read the compression gauge at the end of each series of

A screw-in type compression gauge is more accurate and easier to use without an assistant

cranks, and record the highest of these readings. Repeat this procedure for each of the engine's cylinders. A cylinder's compression pressure is usually acceptable if it is not less than 80% of maximum. The difference between any two cylinders should be no more than 12–14 pounds.

8. If a cylinder is unusually low, pour a tablespoon of clean engine oil into the cylinder through the spark plug hole and repeat the compression test. If the compression comes up after adding the oil, it appears that the cylinder's piston rings or bore are damaged or worn. If the pressure remains low, the valves may not be seating properly (a valve job is needed), or the head gasket may be blown near that cylinder. If compression in any two adjacent cylinders is low, and if the addition of oil doesn't help the compression, there is leakage past the head gasket. Oil and coolant water in the combustion chamber can result from this problem. There may be evidence of water droplets on the engine dipstick when a head gasket has blown.

DIESEL ENGINES

▶ **See Figure 9**

Checking cylinder compression on diesel engines is basically the same procedure as on gasoline engines except for the following:

1. A special compression gauge adaptor suitable for diesel engines (because these engines have much greater compression pressures) must be used.

2. Remove the injector tubes and remove the injectors from each cylinder.

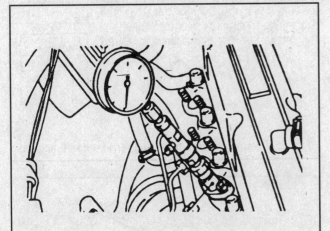

Fig. 9 Diesel engines require a special compression gauge adaptor

✳✳ WARNING

Don't forget to remove the washer underneath each injector. Otherwise, it may get lost when the engine is cranked.

3. When fitting the compression gauge adaptor to the cylinder head, make sure the bleeder of the gauge (if equipped) is closed.

4. When reinstalling the injector assemblies, install new washers underneath each injector.

Engine Design

▶ **See Figure 10**

The 170, 198 and 225 Slant-Six engines are inclined toward the right at an angle of 30° from the vertical. The engine uses in-line overhead valves and wedge shaped combustion chambers with adjustable mechanical tappets through 1980. 1981 and later engines employ hydraulic lifters. The lubrication system consists of an externally mounted rotor type oil pump on the lower right-hand side of the block. The semi-series flow cooling system contains an aluminum water pump body with a pressed-in ball bearing and seal assembly.

The diesel engine is a Mitsubishi built, inline 6-cylinder with overhead valves. The diesel engine is entirely metric, therefore requiring the use of metric tools.

All V6 and V8 engines used are valve-in head type engines with wedge shaped combustion chambers. All are equipped with hydraulic tappets. The 318 and 360 lubrication system is a rotor type oil pump mounted on the rear main bearing cap and a full-flow, throwaway element filter located on the lower right-hand side of the block. The 400 and 440 oil pump and filter are on the outside of the block at the front of the engine.

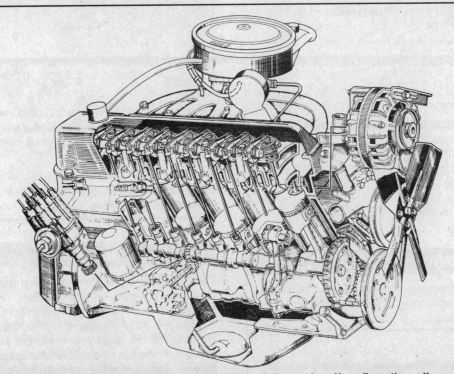

Fig. 10 Cutaway view of the 225 Slant Six engine—whether it's an inline or in a V configuration, all over head valve push rod engines have a similar internal component relationship

Engine

REMOVAL & INSTALLATION

◆ **See Figures 11, 12 and 13**

1967–69 Inline 6-Cylinder Engines

1. Drain the cooling system.

✳ CAUTION

When draining the coolant, keep in mind that cats and dogs are attracted by the ethylene glycol antifreeze, and are quite likely to drink any that is left in an uncovered container or in puddles on the ground. This will prove fatal in sufficient quantity. Always drain the coolant into a sealable container. Coolant should be reused unless it is contaminated or several years old.

2. Disconnect the battery.
3. Disconnect the upper and lower radiator hoses.
4. Disconnect the heater hoses.
5. Disconnect the:
   • throttle linkage
   • alternator wiring
   • distributor wiring
   • starter wiring
   • engine-to-body ground strap
   • temperature sending unit
   • oil pressure sending unit
6. Remove the alternator.
7. Raise and support the van on jackstands.
8. Drain the engine oil.

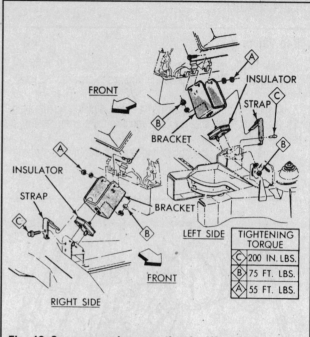

Fig. 12 Common engine mounting for V6 and V8 engines

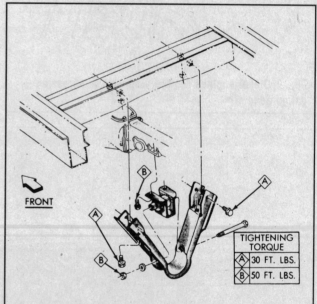

Fig. 13 Common engine rear mount, or transmission mount, for all vehicles

✳ CAUTION

The EPA warns that prolonged contact with used engine oil may cause a number of skin disorders, including cancer! You should make every effort to minimize your exposure to used engine oil. Protective gloves should be worn when changing the oil. Wash your hands and any other exposed skin areas as soon as possible after exposure to used engine oil. Soap and water, or waterless hand cleaner should be used.

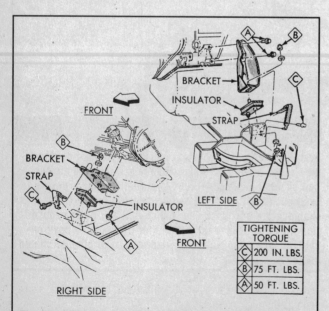

Fig. 11 Common engine mounting for inline 6-cylinder engines

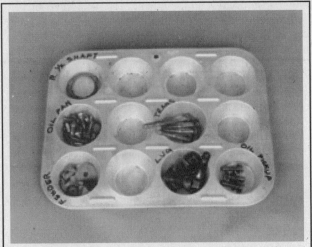

When removing nuts, bolts and other parts, place them in a tray or other container

9. Drain the transmission. On automatic transmissions, also drain the torque converter.

10. Disconnect the shift linkage at the transmission.

11. Disconnect the anti-rattle block from the sill.

12. Disconnect the speedometer cable at the transmission.

13. Remove the clutch torque shaft, transmission shift control rod, parking lock cable, neutral start switch wiring and oil cooler lines.

14. Disconnect the exhaust pipe at the manifold.

15. Matchmark and remove the driveshaft.

16. Disconnect the fuel line at the pump.

17. Support the engine and transmission as an assembly, with a floor jack and safety chain.

18. Remove the engine cover.

19. Open the side doors and hook an engine crane to the engine.

20. Remove the engine rear support bolt and the front engine mount loer stud nuts.

21. Remove the right engine support bracket from the body sill.

22. Lower the transmission and engine assembly, separate them and place the engine on a work stand.

To install:

23. Join the transmission and engine and raise into the van.

24. Install the right engine support bracket. Torque the bolts to 65 ft. lbs.

25. Install the engine rear support bolt and the front engine mount lower stud nuts. Torque the bolt to 35 ft. lbs.; the nuts to 45 ft. lbs.

26. Remove the engine crane.

27. Install the engine cover.

28. Connect the fuel line at the pump.

29. Install the driveshaft.

30. Connect the exhaust pipe at the manifold.

31. Install the clutch torque shaft, transmission shift control rod, parking lock cable, neutral start switch wiring and oil cooler lines.

32. Connect the speedometer cable at the transmission.

33. Connect the anti-rattle block at the sill.

34. Connect the shift linkage at the transmission.

35. Fill the transmission.

36. Fill the crankcase.

37. Install the alternator.

38. Connect the:
- throttle linkage
- alternator wiring
- distributor wiring
- starter wiring
- engine-to-body ground strap
- temperature sending unit
- oil pressure sending unit

39. Connect the heater hoses.

40. Connect the upper and lower radiator hoses.

41. Connect the battery.

42. Fill the cooling system.

1967–69 318 Engine

1. Drain the cooling system.

✳✳ CAUTION

When draining the coolant, keep in mind that cats and dogs are attracted by the ethylene glycol antifreeze, and are quite likely to drink any that is left in an uncovered container or in puddles on the ground. This will prove fatal in sufficient quantity. Always drain the coolant into a sealable container. Coolant should be reused unless it is contaminated or several years old.

2. Disconnect the battery.

3. Disconnect the upper and lower radiator hoses.

4. Disconnect the heater hoses.

5. Disconnect the:
- throttle linkage
- alternator wiring
- starter wiring
- engine-to-body ground strap
- temperature sending unit
- oil pressure sending unit

6. Remove the right inner valve cover nuts and remove the distributor cap and rotor.

7. Remove the alternator.

8. Raise and support the van on jackstands.

9. Drain the engine oil.

✳✳ CAUTION

The EPA warns that prolonged contact with used engine oil may cause a number of skin disorders, including cancer! You should make every effort to minimize your exposure to used engine oil. Protective gloves should be worn when changing the oil. Wash your hands and any other exposed skin areas as soon as possible after exposure to used engine oil. Soap and water, or waterless hand cleaner should be used.

10. Drain the transmission. On automatic transmissions, also drain the torque converter.

11. Disconnect the shift linkage at the transmission.

12. Disconnect the anti-rattle block from the sill.

13. Disconnect the speedometer cable at the transmission.

14. Remove the clutch torque shaft, transmission shift control rod, parking lock cable, neutral start switch wiring and oil cooler lines.

15. Disconnect the exhaust pipe at the manifold.

16. Matchmark and remove the driveshaft.

17. Disconnect the fuel line at the pump.

18. Support the engine and transmission as an assembly, with a floor jack and safety chain.

19. Remove the engine cover.

20. Open the side doors and hook an engine crane to the engine.

21. Remove the engine rear support bolt and the front engine mount loer stud nuts.

22. Remove the right engine support bracket from the body sill.

23. Lower the transmission and engine assembly, separate them and place the engine on a work stand.

To install:

24. Join the transmission and engine and raise into the van.

25. Install the right engine support bracket. Torque the bolts to 65 ft. lbs.

26. Install the engine rear support bolt and the front engine mount lower stud nuts. Torque the bolt to 35 ft. lbs.; the nuts to 45 ft. lbs.

27. Remove the engine crane.

28. Install the engine cover.

29. Connect the fuel line at the pump.

30. Install the driveshaft.

31. Connect the exhaust pipe at the manifold.

32. Install the clutch torque shaft, transmission shift control rod, parking lock cable, neutral start switch wiring and oil cooler lines.

33. Connect the speedometer cable at the transmission.

34. Connect the anti-rattle block at the sill.

35. Connect the shift linkage at the transmission.

36. Fill the transmission.

37. Fill the crankcase.

38. Install the alternator.

39. Install the distributor cap and rotor and the valve cover nuts.

40. Connect the:
- throttle linkage
- alternator wiring
- distributor wiring
- starter wiring
- engine-to-body ground strap
- temperature sending unit
- oil pressure sending unit

41. Connect the heater hoses.

42. Connect the upper and lower radiator hoses.

43. Connect the battery.

44. Fill the cooling system.

1970–72 Inline 6-Cylinder Engines

1. Drain the cooling system.

✳✳ CAUTION

When draining the coolant, keep in mind that cats and dogs are attracted by the ethylene glycol antifreeze, and are quite likely to drink any that is left in an uncovered con-tainer or in puddles on the ground. This will prove fatal in sufficient quantity. Always drain the coolant into a sealable container. Coolant should be reused unless it is contaminated or several years old.

2. Disconnect the battery.

3. Remove the engine cover.

4. Remove the air cleaner.

5. Remove the starter.

6. If so equipped, discharge the air conditioning system. See Section 1.

7. Disconnect the refrigerant lines at the condenser. Cap all openings at once.

8. Remove the front bumper.

9. Remove the grille and support brace.

10. Disconnect the upper radiator hose.

11. Disconnect the lower radiator hose.

12. Remove the radiator and condenser as an assembly.

13. Remove the air conditioning compressor.

14. Remove the power steering pump from its bracket and position it out of the way, WITHOUT DISCONNECTING THE HOSES!

15. Disconnect the heater hoses.

16. Tag and disconnect all vacuum lines at the engine.

17. Disconnect the:
- coil
- alternator
- temperature sending unit
- oil pressure sending unit
- engine-to-body ground strap

18. Disconnect the throttle linkage and remove the operating lever from the accelerator bellcrank.

19. Remove the alternator.

20. Remove the fan, pulley and drive belts.

21. Disconnect the fuel line at the pump.

22. Remove the oil dipstick and tube.

23. Remove the intake manifold with the carburetor attached.

24. Remove the exhaust manifolds.

25. Raise and support the van on jackstands.

26. Remove the entire exhaust system.

27. Matchmark and remove the driveshaft.

28. Disconnect the shift rods.

29. Remove the clutch torque shaft, or the shifter torque shaft and oil cooler lines.

30. Disconnect the speedometer cable at the transmission.

31. Disconnect any electrical connections at the transmission.

32. Remove the inspection plate or converter cover plate from the bellhousing.

33. Support the transmission on a transmission jack.

34. Remove the rear engine support.

35. Position a ¾″ thick piece of wood between the oil pan and crossmember.

36. Remove the transmission-to-bellhousing bolts, or the converter housing-to-engine bolts.

37. Roll the transmission back until it is clear of the engine or clutch, then lower it and move it away.

38. Lower the van to the ground.

39. Install an engine lifting fixture to the number 3, 4, and 5 lower exhaust manifold studs.

40. Attach a shop crane to the lifting fixture. Take up the weight of the engine.

41. Remove the front engine mounts.

42. Raise the engine and maneuver it through the front of the van. It may be necessary to raise the van slightly to keep the crane arm horizontal.

To install:

43. Lower the engine into the van.
44. Install the front engine mounts. Don't tighten them yet!
45. Position a ¾″ thick piece of wood between the oil pan and crossmember.
46. Remove the shop crane.
47. Install the transmission.
48. Install the transmission-to-bellhousing bolts, or the converter housing-to-engine bolts.
49. Install the rear engine support.
50. Remove the holding fixture.
51. Install the inspection plate or converter cover plate.
52. Connect the electrical connections at the transmission.
53. Connect the speedometer cable at the transmission.
54. Install the clutch torque shaft, or the shifter torque shaft and oil cooler lines.
55. Connect the shift rods.
56. Matchmark and install the driveshaft.
57. Install the exhaust system.
58. Install the exhaust manifolds.
59. Install the intake manifold with the carburetor attached.
60. Install the oil dipstick and tube.
61. Connect the fuel line at the pump.
62. Tighten the front engine mounts. Tighten the nuts to 45 ft. lbs.
63. Install the fan, pulley and drive belts.
64. Install the alternator.
65. Connect the throttle linkage and install the operating lever on the accelerator bellcrank.
66. Connect the:
  • coil
  • alternator
  • temperature sending unit
  • oil pressure sending unit
  • engine-to-body ground strap
67. Connect all vacuum lines at the engine.
68. Connect the heater hoses.
69. Install the power steering pump.
70. Install the air conditioning compressor.
71. Install the radiator and condenser as an assembly.
72. Connect the lower radiator hose.
73. Connect the upper radiator hose.
74. Install the grille and support brace.
75. Install the front bumper.
76. Connect the refrigerant lines at the condenser.
77. Evacuate, charge and leak test the air conditioning system. See Section 1.
78. Install the starter.
79. Install the air cleaner.
80. Install the engine cover.
81. Connect the battery.
82. Fill the cooling system.

1970–72 V8 Engines

1. Drain the cooling system.
2. Disconnect the battery.

✳✳ CAUTION

When draining the coolant, keep in mind that cats and dogs are attracted by the ethylene glycol antifreeze, and are quite likely to drink any that is left in an uncovered container or in puddles on the ground. This will prove fatal in sufficient quantity. Always drain the coolant into a sealable container. Coolant should be reused unless it is contaminated or several years old.

2. Disconnect the battery.
3. Remove the engine cover.
4. Remove the air cleaner.
5. Remove the starter.
6. If so equipped, discharge the air conditioning system. See Section 1.
7. Disconnect the regrigerant lines at the condenser. Cap all openings at once.
8. Remove the front bumper.
9. Remove the grille and support brace.
10. Remove the fan shroud.
11. Disconnect the upper radiator hose.
12. Disconnect the lower radiator hose.
13. Remove the radiator and condenser as an assembly.
14. Remove the air conditioning compressor.
15. Remove the heater blower motor.
16. Remove the power steering pump with its bracket and position it out of the way, WITHOUT DISCONNECTING THE HOSES!
17. Disconnect the heater hoses.
18. Tag and disconnect all vacuum lines at the engine.
19. Disconnect the:
  • coil
  • alternator
  • temperature sending unit
  • oil pressure sending unit
  • engine-to-body ground strap
20. Disconnect the throttle linkage and remove the operating lever from the accelerator bellcrank.
21. Remove the alternator.
22. Remove the fan, pulley and drive belts.
23. Disconnect the fuel line at the pump.
24. Remove the oil dipstick and tube.
25. Remove the intake manifold with the carburetor attached.
26. Remove the exhaust manifolds.
27. Raise and support the van on jackstands.
28. Remove the entire exhaust system.
29. Matchmark and remove the driveshaft.
30. Disconnect the shift rods.
31. Remove the clutch torque shaft, or the shifter torque shaft and oil cooler lines.
32. Disconnect the speedometer cable at the transmission.
33. Disconnect any electrical connections at the transmission.
34. Remove the inspection plate or converter cover plate from the bellhousing.
35. Support the transmission on a transmission jack.
36. Remove the rear engine support throughbolt.
37. Install an engine lifting fixture to the heads.
38. Attach a shop crane and take up the weight of the engine.

39. Remove the front engine mount insulator top stud nuts and washers.

40. Remove the transmission-to-bellhousing bolts, or the converter housing-to-engine bolts.

41. Roll the transmission back until it is clear of the engine or clutch, then lower it and move it away.

42. Lower the van to the ground.

43. Raise the engine and maneuver it through the front of the van. It may be necessary to raise the van slightly to keep the crane arm horizontal.

To install:

44. Lower the engine into the front of the van.

45. Install the transmission.

46. Install the transmission-to-bellhousing bolts, or the converter housing-to-engine bolts.

47. Install the front engine mount insulator top stud nuts and washers. Torque them to 65 ft. lbs.

48. Install the rear engine support throughbolt. Torque to 65 ft. lbs.

49. Remove the shop crane.

50. Install the inspection plate or converter cover plate on the bellhousing.

51. Connect any electrical connections at the transmission.

52. Connect the speedometer cable at the transmission.

53. Install the clutch torque shaft, or the shifter torque shaft and oil cooler lines.

54. Connect the shift rods.

55. Matchmark and install the driveshaft.

56. Install the exhaust system.

57. Install the exhaust manifolds.

58. Install the intake manifold with the carburetor attached.

59. Install the oil dipstick and tube.

60. Connect the fuel line at the pump.

61. Install the fan, pulley and drive belts.

62. Install the alternator.

63. Connect the throttle linkage and install the operating lever on the accelerator bellcrank.

64. Connect the:
   • coil
   • alternator
   • temperature sending unit
   • oil pressure sending unit
   • engine-to-body ground strap

65. Connect all vacuum lines at the engine.

66. Connect the heater hoses.

67. Install the power steering pump.

68. Install the heater blower motor.

69. Install the air conditioning compressor.

70. Install the radiator and condenser as an assembly.

71. Connect the lower radiator hose.

72. Connect the upper radiator hose.

73. Install the fan shroud.

74. Install the grille and support brace.

75. Install the front bumper.

76. Connect the refrigerant lines at the condenser.

77. Evacuate, charge and leak test the air conditioning system. See Section 1.

78. Install the starter.

79. Install the air cleaner.

80. Install the engine cover.

81. Connect the battery.

82. Fill the cooling system.

1973–79 Inline 6-Cylinder Engines

1. Drain the cooling system.

✳✳ CAUTION

When draining the coolant, keep in mind that cats and dogs are attracted by the ethylene glycol antifreeze, and are quite likely to drink any that is left in an uncovered container or in puddles on the ground. This will prove fatal in sufficient quantity. Always drain the coolant into a sealable container. Coolant should be reused unless it is contaminated or several years old.

2. Disconnect the battery.

3. Remove the engine cover.

4. Remove the air cleaner.

5. Drain the engine oil.

✳✳ CAUTION

The EPA warns that prolonged contact with used engine oil may cause a number of skin disorders, including cancer! You should make every effort to minimize your exposure to used engine oil. Protective gloves should be worn when changing the oil. Wash your hands and any other exposed skin areas as soon as possible after exposure to used engine oil. Soap and water, or waterless hand cleaner should be used.

6. Remove the starter.

7. Remove the distributor.

8. If so equipped, discharge the air conditioning system. See Section 1.

9. Disconnect the refrigerant lines at the condenser. Cap all openings at once.

10. Remove the front bumper.

11. Remove the grille and support brace.

12. Disconnect the upper radiator hose.

13. Disconnect the lower radiator hose.

14. Remove the radiator and condenser as an assembly.

15. Remove the air conditioning compressor.

16. Remove the power steering pump from its bracket and position it out of the way, WITHOUT DISCONNECTING THE HOSES!

17. Disconnect the heater hoses.

18. Remove the heater blower motor.

19. Tag and disconnect all vacuum lines at the engine.

20. Disconnect the:
   • coil
   • alternator
   • temperature sending unit
   • oil pressure sending unit
   • engine-to-body ground strap

21. Disconnect the throttle linkage and remove the operating lever from the accelerator bellcrank.

22. Remove the alternator.

23. Remove the fan, pulley and drive belts.

24. Disconnect the fuel line at the pump.

25. Remove the oil dipstick and tube.

26. Remove the intake manifold with the carburetor attached.

27. Remove the exhaust manifolds.

28. Raise the engine slightly and support it in this position with a holding fixture fabricated from 1½" ID galvanized pipe

straddling the engine compartment opening, or with a shop crane through the side doors.

29. Raise and support the van on jackstands.
30. Remove the engine oil pan.
31. Remove the entire exhaust system.
32. Matchmark and remove the driveshaft.
33. Disconnect the shift rods.
34. Remove the clutch torque shaft, or the shifter torque shaft and oil cooler lines.
35. Disconnect the speedometer cable at the transmission.
36. Disconnect any electrical connections at the transmission.
37. Remove the inspection plate or converter cover plate from the bellhousing.
38. Support the transmission on a transmission jack.
39. Remove the rear engine support.
40. Remove the transmission-to-bellhousing bolts, or the converter housing-to-engine bolts.
41. Roll the transmission back until it is clear of the engine or clutch, then lower it and move it away.
42. On vans with manual transmission, remove the clutch and flywheel.
43. On vans with automatic transmission, remove the flex plate.
44. Lower the van to the ground.
45. Install an engine lifting fixture to the number 3, 4, and 5 lower exhaust manifold studs.
46. Attach a shop crane to the lifting fixture. Take up the weight of the engine.
47. Remove the front engine mounts.
48. Raise the engine and maneuver it through the front of the van. It may be necessary to raise the van slightly to keep the crane arm horizontal.

To install:

49. Lower the engine into the van.
50. Installt he front engine mounts. Torque the bolts to 50 ft. lbs.
51. Remove the shop crane.
52. Remove the engine lifting fixture.
53. Raise and support the front end on jackstands.
54. On vans with automatic transmission, install the flex plate. Torque the bolts to 55 ft. lbs.
55. On vans with manual transmission, install the clutch and flywheel. Torque the flywheel bolts to 55 ft. lbs.
56. Roll the transmission into position.
57. On vans with manual transmission, install the transmission-to-bellhousing bolts. Torque the 3/8-16 bolts to 30 ft. lbs.; the 7/16-14 bolts to 50 ft. lbs.
58. On vans with automatic transmission, install the converter housing-to-engine bolts. Torque the 3/8-16 bolts to 30 ft. lbs.; the 7/16-14 bolts to 50 ft. lbs.
59. Install the rear engine support. Torque the bolts to 50 ft. lbs.
60. On vans with manual transmission, install the inspection plate.
61. On vans with automatic transmission, install the converter cover plate.
62. Connect any electrical connections at the transmission.
63. Connect the speedometer cable at the transmission.
64. Install the clutch torque shaft, or the shifter torque shaft and oil cooler lines.
65. Connect the shift rods.
66. Install the driveshaft.

67. Install the exhaust system.
68. Install the engine oil pan. Torque the bolts to 15 ft. lbs.
69. Lower the van.
70. Remove the holding fixture.
71. Install the exhaust manifolds.
72. Install the intake manifold with the carburetor attached.
73. Install the oil dipstick and tube.
74. Connect the fuel line at the pump.
75. Install the fan, pulley and drive belts. Torque the fan bolts to 15 ft. lbs.
76. Install the alternator.
77. Connect the throttle linkage and install the operating lever on the accelerator bellcrank.
78. Connect the coil.
79. Connect the alternator.
80. Connect the temperature sending unit.
81. Connect the oil pressure sending unit.
82. Connect the engine-to-body ground strap.
83. Connect all vacuum lines at the engine.
84. Install the heater blower motor.
85. Connect the heater hoses.
86. Install the power steering pump on its bracket.
87. Install the air conditioning compressor.
88. Install the radiator and condenser as an assembly.
89. Connect the lower radiator hose.
90. Connect the upper radiator hose.
91. Install the grille and support brace.
92. Install the front bumper.
93. Connect the refrigerant lines at the condenser.
94. Evacuate, charge and leak test the air conditioning system.
95. Install the distributor.
96. Install the crankcase.
97. Fill the crankcase.
98. Install the air cleaner.
99. Installt engine cover.
100. Connect the battery.
101. Fill the cooling system.

1978–79 Diesel Engine

1. Disconnect the battery cables and remove the battery.
2. Remove the air cleaner.
3. Scribe matchmarks on the hood hinges and remove the hood.
4. Drain the cooling system.

✳✳ CAUTION

When draining the coolant, keep in mind that cats and dogs are attracted by the ethylene glycol antifreeze, and are quite likely to drink any that is left in an uncovered container or in puddles on the ground. This will prove fatal in sufficient quantity. Always drain the coolant into a sealable container. Coolant should be reused unless it is contaminated or several years old.

5. Remove the upper and lower radiator hoses.
6. Remove the coolant reserve tank.
7. If so equipped, discharge the air conditioning system. See Section 1.
8. Disconnect the refrigerant lines at the condenser. Cap all openings at once.

9. Remove the front bumper.
10. Remove the grille and support brace.
11. Remove the air conditioning compressor.
12. Raise the truck and safely support on jackstands. Disconnect and remove the transmission oil cooler lines from the radiator. Remove the lower radiator and fan shroud mounting screws.
13. Lower the truck and remove the upper radiator and fan shroud mounting screws and remove the radiator, condenser and fan shroud.
14. Remove the heater blower motor.
15. Disconnect the heater hoses from the engine and push them aside.
16. Disconnect the speedometer cable housing from the engine.
17. Disconnect the electrical connections at the alternator, temperature sending unit, starter relay-to-solenoid wires, the oil gauge sending unit and the injection pump control motor. Set the wiring harness aside.
18. Disconnect the plug and fuel line at the transfer pump inlet. Disconnect and cap return line at the injector lines bleed-back connection.
19. Disconnect and remove the injection pump linkage. Disconnect and remove the accelerator and throttle cable linkage.
20. Disconnect the starter motor wire from the solenoid. Remove the starter motor.
21. Remove the battery ground cable from the engine block.
22. Disconnect and plug the power steering hoses at the power steering gear.
23. Raise the truck and disconnect the exhaust pipe from the exhaust manifold.
24. Drain the engine oil and remove the dipstick tube from the oil pan. Remove the transmission cooler line and road draft tube bracket from the oil pan.

✳✳ CAUTION

The EPA warns that prolonged contact with used engine oil may cause a number of skin disorders, including cancer! You should make every effort to minimize your exposure to used engine oil. Protective gloves should be worn when changing the oil. Wash your hands and any other exposed skin areas as soon as possible after exposure to used engine oil. Soap and water, or waterless hand cleaner should be used.

25. Remove the oil pan bolts from the oil pan.
26. Remove the transmission inspection plate. Remove the oil pan to gain clearance if necessary. Use a new gasket on installation.
27. Remove the four flex plate-to-torque converter bolts.
28. Remvoe the exhaust pipe bracket and the lower housing bolts.
29. Remove any other brackets that can interfere with removal.
30. Support the transmission with a floor jack.
31. Remove the cylinder head (valve) cover and the gasket.
32. Attach a boom hoist to the engine, wrapping the chain as tight and close as possible.
33. Remove the four bolts and six nuts from the engine mounts.
34. Remove the two upper bell housing bolts.
35. Roll the boom hoist back, removing the engine from the van.

To install:
36. Lower the engine into the van.
37. Install the two upper bell housing bolts.
38. Install the bolts and nuts in the engine mounts.
39. Remove the shop crane.
40. Install the cylinder head (valve) cover.
41. Remove the floor jack.
42. Install any brackets which were removed.
43. Install the exhaust pipe bracket and the lower housing bolts.
44. Install the flex plate-to-torque converter bolts.
45. Install the transmission inspection plate.
46. Install the oil pan.
47. Install the dipstick tube.
48. Install the transmission cooler line and road draft tube bracket.
49. Connect the exhaust pipe at the exhaust manifold.
50. Connect the power steering hoses at the power steering gear.
51. Install the battery ground cable.
52. Install the starter motor.
53. Connect the starter motor wire at the solenoid.
54. Install the injection pump linkage.
55. Install the accelerator and throttle cable linkage.
56. Connect the fuel line at the transfer pump inlet.
57. Connect the return line at the injector lines bleed-back connection.
58. Connect the electrical connections at the alternator, temperature sending unit, starter relay-to-solenoid wires, the oil gauge sending unit and the injection pump control motor.
59. Connect the speedometer cable housing.
60. Connect the heater hoses.
61. Install the heater blower motor.
62. Install the radiator, condenser and fan shroud.
63. Connect the transmission oil cooler lines at the radiator.
64. Install the air conditioning compressor.
65. Install the grille and support brace.
66. Install the front bumper.
67. Connect the refrigerant lines at the condenser.
68. Evacuate, charge and leak test the air conditioning system.
69. Install the coolant reserve tank.
70. Install the upper and lower radiator hoses.
71. Fill the crankcase.
72. Fill the cooling system.
73. Install the air cleaner.
74. Install the hood.
75. Install the battery.

1973–79 V8 Engines

1. Drain the cooling system.

✳✳ CAUTION

When draining the coolant, keep in mind that cats and dogs are attracted by the ethylene glycol antifreeze, and are quite likely to drink any that is left in an uncovered container or in puddles on the ground. This will prove fatal in sufficient quantity. Always drain the coolant into a sealable container. Coolant should be reused unless it is contaminated or several years old.

2. Disconnect the battery.

3. Drain the engine oil.

✳✳ CAUTION

The EPA warns that prolonged contact with used engine oil may cause a number of skin disorders, including cancer! You should make every effort to minimize your exposure to used engine oil. Protective gloves should be worn when changing the oil. Wash your hands and any other exposed skin areas as soon as possible after exposure to used engine oil. Soap and water, or waterless hand cleaner should be used.

4. Remove the oil filter.

5. Remove the engine cover.

6. Remove the air cleaner.

7. Remove the starter.

8. If so equipped, discharge the air conditioning system. See Section 1.

9. Disconnect the refrigerant lines at the condenser. Cap all openings at once.

10. Remove the front bumper.

11. Remove the grille and support brace.

12. Remove the fan shroud.

13. Disconnect the upper radiator hose.

14. Disconnect the lower radiator hose.

15. Remove the radiator and condenser as an assembly.

16. Remove the air conditioning compressor.

17. Remove the heater blower motor.

18. Remove the power steering pump from its bracket and position it out of the way, WITHOUT DISCONNECTING THE HOSES!

19. Disconnect the heater hoses.

20. Tag and disconnect all vacuum lines at the engine.

21. Disconnect the coil.

22. Disconnect the alternator and air pump.

23. Disconnect the temperature sending unit.

24. Disconnect the oil pressure sending unit.

25. Disconnect the engine-to-body ground strap.

26. Disconnect the throttle linkage and remove the operating lever from the accelerator bellcrank.

27. Remove the alternator.

28. Remove the fan, pulley and drive belts.

29. Disconnect the fuel line at the pump.

30. Remove the oil dipstick and tube.

31. Remove the heater blower motor.

32. Remove the intake manifold with the carburetor attached.

33. On the 8-318 and 8-360, remove the left exhaust manifold.

34. On the 8-318 and 8-360 with air conditioning, remove the right valve cover.

35. Raise the engine slightly and support it in this position with a holding fixture fabricated from 1½" ID galvanized pipe straddling the engine compartment opening, or with a shop crane through the side doors.

36. Raise and support the van on jackstands.

37. Remove the entire exhaust system.

38. Matchmark and remove the driveshaft.

39. Disconnect the shift rods.

40. Remove the clutch torque shaft, or the shifter torque shaft and oil cooler lines.

41. Disconnect the speedometer cable at the transmission.

42. Disconnect any electrical connections at the transmission.

43. Remove the inspection plate or converter cover plate from the bellhousing.

44. Support the transmission on a transmission jack.

45. Remove the rear engine support.

46. Install an engine lifting fixture to the heads.

47. Attach a shop crane and take up the weight of the engine.

48. Remove the front engine mount insulator top stud nuts and washers.

49. Remove the transmission-to-bellhousing bolts, or the converter housing-to engine bolts.

50. Roll the transmission back until it is clear of the engine or clutch, then lower it and move it away.

51. On vans with manual transmission, remove the clutch.

52. Remove the flywheel or flex plate.

53. Raise the rear of the engine about 2".

54. On the 8-318 and 8-360, turn the crankshaft until the cutout portion of the crankshaft flange is at the 3 o'clock position.

55. On the 8-318 and 8-360, remove the oil pan bolts, lower the pan just enough to reach the oil pick-up tube and turn the tube and strainer slightly to the right side to clear the pan. Remove the pan.

56. Lower the van to the ground.

57. Raise the engine and maneuver it through the front of the van. It may be necessary to raise the van slightly to keep the crane arm horizontal.

To install:

58. Lower the engine into the van.

59. Raise and support the front end on jackstands.

60. Install the oil pan. Torque the bolts to 15 ft. lbs.

61. Install the flywheel or flex plate. Torque the bolts to 55 ft. lbs.

62. On vans with manual transmission, install the clutch.

63. Position the transmission.

64. Install the transmission-to-bellhousing bolts, or the converter housing-to-engine bolts. Torque the ⅜-16 bolts to 30 ft. lbs.; the ⁷⁄₁₆-14 bolts to 50 ft. lbs.

65. Install the front engine mount insulator top stud nuts and washers. Torque the nuts to 75 ft. lbs.

66. Remove the shop crane.

67. Remove the engine lifting fixture.

68. Install the rear engine support. Torque the bolts to 50 ft. lbs.

69. Remove the transmission jack.

70. Install the inspection plate or converter cover plate on the bellhousing.

71. Connect any electrical connections at the transmission.

72. Connect the speedometer cable at the transmission.

73. Install the clutch torque shaft, or the shifter torque shaft and oil cooler lines.

74. Connect the shift rods.

75. Matchmark and install the driveshaft.

76. Install the exhaust system.

77. Lower the van.

78. Remove the holding fixture.

79. If equipped with air conditioning, install the right valve cover.

80. Install the left exhaust manifold.

81. Install the intake manifold with the carburetor attached.

82. Install the heater blower motor.

83. Install the oil dipstick and tube.

84. Connect the fuel line at the pump.

85. Install the fan, pulley and drive belts.
86. Install the alternator.
87. Connect the throttle linkage and install the operating lever from the accelerator bellcrank.
88. Connect the engine-to-body ground strap.
89. Connect the oil pressure sending unit.
90. Connect the temperature sending unit.
91. Connect the alternator.
92. Connect the coil.
93. Connect all vacuum lines at the engine.
94. Connect the heater hoses.
95. Install the power steering pump.
96. Install the heater blower motor.
97. Install the air conditioning compressor.
98. Install the radiator and condenser as an assembly.
99. Connect the lower radiator hose.
100. Connect the upper radiator hose.
101. Install the fan shroud.
102. Install the grille and support brace.
103. Install the front bumper.
104. Connect the refrigerant lines at the condenser.
105. Evacuate, charge and leak test the system.
106. Install the starter.
107. Install the air cleaner.
108. Install the engine cover.
109. Install the oil filter.
110. Fill the crankcase.
111. Connect the battery.
112. Fill the cooling system.

1980-87 Inline 6-Cylinder Engine

1. Drain the cooling system.

> ❊❊ **CAUTION**
>
> When draining the coolant, keep in mind that cats and dogs are attracted by the ethylene glycol antifreeze, and are quite likely to drink any that is left in an uncovered container or in puddles on the ground. This will prove fatal in sufficient quantity. Always drain the coolant into a sealable container. Coolant should be reused unless it is contaminated or several years old.

2. Disconnect the battery.
3. Remove the engine cover.
4. Remove the air cleaner.
5. Drain the engine oil.

> ❊❊ **CAUTION**
>
> The EPA warns that prolonged contact with used engine oil may cause a number of skin disorders, including cancer! You should make every effort to minimize your exposure to used engine oil. Protective gloves should be worn when changing the oil. Wash your hands and any other exposed skin areas as soon as possible after exposure to used engine oil. Soap and water, or waterless hand cleaner should be used.

6. Remove the engine-to-transmission strut.
7. Remove the engine oil pan.
8. Remove the entire exhaust system.
9. Remove the inspection cover on vans with automatic transmission, and remove the torque converter-to-flex plate bolts.
10. Remove the lower bellhousing bolts.
11. Remove the starter.
12. Remove the lower right engine mount insulator nut.
13. Remove the distributor.
14. If so equipped, discharge the air conditioning system. See Section 1.
15. Disconnect the refrigerant lines at the condenser. Cap all openings at once.
16. Remove the front bumper.
17. Remove the coolant overflow bottle.
18. Remove the windshield washer reservoir.
19. Remove the grille and support brace.
20. Disconnect the upper radiator hose.
21. Disconnect the lower radiator hose.
22. Remove the radiator and condenser as an assembly.
23. Remove the air conditioning compressor.
24. Remove the power steering pump from its bracket and position it out of the way, WITHOUT DISCONNECTING THE HOSES!
25. Disconnect the heater hoses.
26. Remove the heater blower motor.
27. Tag and disconnect all vacuum lines at the engine.
28. Disconnect the:
    - coil
    - alternator
    - temperature sending unit
    - oil pressure sending unit
    - engine-to-body ground strap.
29. Disconnect the throttle linkage and remove the operating lever from the accelerator bellcrank.
30. Remove the alternator.
31. Remove the fan, pulley and drive belts.
32. Disconnect the fuel line at the pump.
33. Remove the oil dipstick and tube.
34. Remove the intake manifold with the carburetor attached.
35. Remove the exhaust manifolds.
36. Raise and support the van on jackstands.
37. Matchmark and remove the driveshaft.
38. Disconnect the shift rods.
39. Remove the clutch torque shaft, or the shifter torque shaft and oil cooler lines.
40. Disconnect the speedometer cable at the transmission.
41. Disconnect any electrical connections at the transmission.
42. Support the transmission on a transmission jack.
43. Attach a shop crane to the lifting fixture. Take up the weight of the engine.
44. Remove the upper left engine mount insulator nut.
45. Remove the rear engine support.
46. Remove the remaining transmission-to-bellhousing bolts, or the converter housing-to-engine bolts.
47. Roll the transmission back until it is clear of the engine or clutch, then lower it and move it away.
48. On vans with manual transmission, remove the clutch and flywheel.
49. On vans with automatic transmission, remove the flex plate.
50. Lower the van to the ground.
51. Install an engine lifting fixture to the number 3, 4, and 5 lower exhaust manifold studs.

52. Raise the engine and maneuver it through the front of the van. It may be necessary to raise the van slightly to keep the crane arm horizontal.

To install:

53. Lower the engine into the van.
54. On vans with manual transmission, install the flex plate.
55. On vans with manual transmission, install the clutch and flywheel.
56. Roll the transmission into position.
57. Install the transmission-to-bellhousing bolts, or the converter housing-to-engine bolts.
58. Install the rear engine support.
59. Install the upper left engine mount insulator nut.
60. Remove the shop crane.
61. Install any electrical connections at the transmission.
62. Install the speedometer cable at the transmission.
63. Install the clutch torque shaft, or the shifter torque shaft and oil cooler lines.
64. Connect the shift rods.
65. Install the driveshaft.
66. Install the exhaust manifold.
67. Install the intake manifold with the carburetor attached.
68. Install the oil dipstick and tube.
69. Connect the fuel line at the pump.
70. Install the fan, pulley and drive belts.
71. Install the alternator.
72. Connect the throttle linkage.
73. Connect the coil.
74. Connect the alternator.
75. Connect the temperature sending unit.
76. Connect the oil pressure sending unit.
77. Connect the engine-to-body ground strap.
78. Connect all vacuum lines at the engine.
79. Install the heater blower motor.
80. Connect the heater hoses.
81. Install the power steering pump.
82. Install the air conditioning compressor.
83. Install the radiator and condenser as an assembly.
84. Connect the lower radiator hose.
85. Connect the upper radiator hose.
86. Install the grille and support brace.
87. Install the windshield washer reservoir.
88. Install the coolant overflow bottle.
89. Install the front bumper.
90. Connect the refrigerant lines at the condenser.
91. Evacuate, charge and leak test the air conditioning system. See Section 1.
92. Install the distributor.
93. Install the lower right engine mount insulator nut.
94. Install the starter.
95. Install the lower bellhousing bolts.
96. Install the torque converter-to-flex plate bolts. Install the inspection cover.
97. Install the exhaust system.
98. Install the engine oil pan.
99. Install the engine-to-transmission strut.
100. Fill the crankcase.
101. Install the air cleaner.
102. Install the engine cover.
103. Connect the battery.
104. Fill the cooling systme.

1980–88 V8 Engines

1. Drain the cooling system.

❊❊ CAUTION

When draining the coolant, keep in mind that cats and dogs are attracted by the ethylene glycol antifreeze, and are quite likely to drink any that is left in an uncovered container or in puddles on the ground. This will prove fatal in sufficient quantity. Always drain the coolant into a sealable container. Coolant should be reused unless it is contaminated or several years old.

2. Disconnect the battery.
3. Drain the engine oil.

❊❊ CAUTION

The EPA warns that prolonged contact with used engine oil may cause a number of skin disorders, including cancer! You should make every effort to minimize your exposure to used engine oil. Protective gloves should be worn when changing the oil. Wash your hands and any other exposed skin areas as soon as possible after exposure to used engine oil. Soap and water, or waterless hand cleaner should be used.

4. Remove the oil filter and oil dipstick.
5. Remove the engine-to-transmission strut.
6. Remove the engine cover.
7. Remove the air cleaner, and, on 1988 models, the throttle body.
8. Remove the starter.
9. If so equipped, discharge the air conditioning system. See Section 1.
10. Disconnect the refrigerant lines at the condenser. Cap all openings at once.
11. Remove the front bumper.
12. Remove the grille and support brace.
13. Remove the fan shroud.
14. Disconnect the upper radiator hose.
15. Disconnect the lower radiator hose.
16. Remove the radiator and condenser as an assembly.
17. Remove the air conditioning compressor.
18. Remove the heater blower motor.
19. Remove the power steering pump from its bracket and position it out of the way, WITHOUT DISCONNECTING THE HOSES!
20. Disconnect the heater hoses.
21. Tag and disconnect all vacuum lines at the engine.
22. Disconnect the coil.
23. Disconnect the alternator and air pump.
24. Disconnect the temperature sending unit.
25. Disconnect the oil pressure sending unit.
26. Disconnect the engine-to-body ground strap.
27. Disconnect the throttle linkage and remove the operating lever from the accelerator bellcrank.
28. Remove the alternator.
29. Remove the fan, pulley and drive belts.
30. Disconnect the fuel line at the pump.
31. Remove the oil dipstick and tube.
32. Remove the heater blower motor.

33. Remove the intake manifold, and, on models through 1987, the carburetor.
34. Remove the left exhaust manifold.
35. Raise and support the van on jackstands.
36. Remove the entire exhaust system.
37. Matchmark and remove the driveshaft.
38. Disconnect the shift rods.
39. Remove the clutch torque shaft, or the shifter torque shaft and oil cooler lines.
40. Disconnect the speedometer cable at the transmission.
41. Disconnect the electrical connections at the transmission.
42. Remove the inspection plate or converter cover plate from the bellhousing.
43. Support the transmission on a transmission jack.
44. Remove the rear engine support.
45. Install an engine lifting fixture to the heads.
46. Attach a shop crane and take up the weight of the engine.
47. Remove the front engine mount insulator top stud nuts and washers.
48. Remove the transmission-to-bellhousing bolts, or the converter housing-to-engine bolts.
49. Roll the transmission back until it is clear of the engine or clutch, then lower it and move it away.
50. On vans with manual transmission, remove the clutch.
51. Remove the flywheel or flex plate.
52. Raise the rear of the engine about 2″.
53. Turn the crankshaft until the cutout portion of the crankshaft flange is at the 3 o'clock position.
54. Remove the oil pan bolts, lower the pan just enough to reach the oil pick-up tube and turn the tube and strainer slightly to the right side to clear the pan. Remove the pan.
55. Lower the van to the ground.
56. Raise the engine and maneuver it through the front of the van. It may be necessary to raise the van slightly to keep the crane arm horizontal.

To install:
58. Lower the engine into the van.
59. Raise and support the front end on jackstands.
60. Install the oil pan. Torque the bolts to 15 ft. lbs.
61. Install the flywheel or flex plate. Torque the bolts to 55 ft. lbs.
62. On vans with manual transmission, install the clutch.
63. Position the transmission.
64. Install the transmission-to-bellhousing bolts, or the converter housing-to-engine bolts. Torque the ⅜-16 bolts to 30 ft. lbs.; the ⁷⁄₁₆-14 bolts to 50 ft. lbs.
65. Install the front engine mount insulator top stud nuts and washers. Torque the nuts to 75 ft. lbs.
66. Remove the shop crane.
67. Remove the engine lifting fixture.
68. Install the rear engine support. Torque the bolts to 50 ft. lbs.
69. Remove the transmission jack.
70. Install the inspection place or converter cover plate on the bellhousing.
71. Connect the electrical connections at the transmission.
72. Connect the speedometer cable at the transmission.
73. Install the clutch torque shaft, or the shifter torque shaft and oil cooler lines.
74. Connect the shift rods.
75. Install the transmission-to-engine strut.
76. Install the driveshaft.

77. Install the exhaust system.
78. Lower the van.
79. Remove the holding fixture.
80. If equipped with air conditioning, install the right valve cover.
81. Install the left exhaust manifold.
82. Install the intake manifold with the carburetor attached.
83. Install the heater blower motor.
84. Install the oil dipstick and tube.
85. Connect the fuel line at the pump.
86. Install the fan, pulley and drive belts.
87. Install the alternator.
88. Connect the throttle linkage and install the operating lever from the accelerator bellcrank.
89. Connect the engine-to-body ground strap.
90. Connect the oil pressure sending unit.
91. Connect the temperature sending unit.
92. Connect the alternator.
93. Connect the coil.
94. Connect all vacuum lines at the engine.
95. Connect the heater hoses.
96. Install the power steering pump.
97. Install the heater blower motor.
98. Install the air conditioning compressor.
99. Install the radiator and condenser as an assembly.
100. Connect the lower radiator hose.
101. Connect the upper radiator hose.
102. Install the fan shroud.
103. Install the grille and support brace.
104. Install the front bumper.
105. Connect the refrigerant lines at the condenser.
106. Evacuate, charge and leak test the system.
107. Install the starter.
108. On 1988 models, install the throttle body.
109. Install the air cleaner.
110. Install the engine cover.
111. Install the oil filter.
112. Fill the crankcase.
113. Connect the battery.
114. Fill the cooling system.

1988 V6 Engine

1. Drain the cooling system.

✳✳ CAUTION

When draining the coolant, keep in mind that cats and dogs are attracted by the ethylene glycol and antifreeze, and are quite likely to drink any that is left in an uncovered container or in puddles on the ground. This will prove fatal in sufficient quantity. Always drain the coolant into a sealable container. Coolant should be reused unless it is contaminated or several years old.

2. Disconnect the battery.
3. Drain the engine oil.

✳✳ CAUTION

The EPA warns that prolonged contact with used engine oil may cause a number of skin disorders, including cancer! You should make every effort to minimize your exposure to used engine oil. Protective gloves should be worn when changing the oil. Wash your hands and any other exposed skin areas as soon as possible after exposure to used engine oil. Soap and water, or waterless hand cleaner should be used.

4. Remove oil filter and oil dipstick.
5. Remove the engine-to-transmission strut.
6. Remove the engine cover.
7. Remove the air cleaner.
8. Remove the throttle body.
9. Remove the starter.
10. If so equipped, discharge the air conditioning system. See Section 1.
11. Disconnect the refrigerant lines at the condenser. Cap all openings at once.
12. Remove the front bumper.
13. Remove the grille and support brace.
14. Remove the fan shroud.
15. Disconnect the upper radiator hose.
16. Disconnect the lower radiator hose.
17. Remove the radiator and condenser as an assembly.
18. Remove the air conditioning compressor.
19. Remove the power steering pump from its bracket and position it out of the way, WITHOUT DISCONNECTING THE HOSES!
20. Disconnect the heater hoses.
21. Tag and disconnect all vacuum lines at the engine.
22. Disconnect the coil.
23. Disconnect the alternator and air pump.
24. Disconnect the temperature sending unit.
25. Disconnect the oil pressure sending unit.
26. Disconnect the engine-to-body ground strap.
27. Disconnect the throttle linkage.
28. Remove the alternator.
29. Remove the fan, pulley and drive belts.
30. Disconnect the fuel line at the pump.
31. Remove the oil dipstick and tube.
32. Remove the heater blower motor.
33. Remove the intake manifold.
34. Remove the left exhaust manifold.
35. Raise and support the van on jackstands.
36. Remove the entire exhaust system.
37. Matchmark and remove the driveshaft.
38. Disconnect the shift rods.
39. Remove the clutch torque shaft, or the shifter torque shaft and oil cooler lines.
40. Disconnect the speedometer cable at the transmission.
41. Disconnect any electrical connections at the transmission.
42. Remove the inspection plate or converter cover plate from the bellhousing.
43. Support the transmission on a transmission jack.
44. Remove the rear engine support.
45. Install an engine lifting fixture to the heads.
46. Attach a shop crane and take up the weight of the engine.
47. Remove the front engine mount insulator top stud nuts and washers.
48. Remove the transmission-to-bellhousing bolts, or the converter housing-to-engine bolts.
49. Roll the transmission back until it is clear of the engine or clutch, then lower it and more it away.
50. On vans with manual transmission, remove the clutch.

51. Remove the flywheel or flex plate.
52. Raise the rear of the engine about 2″.
53. Turn the crankshaft until the cutout portion of the crankshaft flange is at the 3 o'clock position.
54. Remove the oil pan bolts, lower the pan just enough to reach the oil pick-up tube and turn the tube and strainer slightly to the right side to clear the pan. Remove the pan.
55. Lower the van to the ground.
56. Raise the engine and maneuver it through the front of the an. It may be necessary to raise the van slightly to keep the crane arm horizontal.

To install:
58. Lower the engine into the van.
59. Raise and support the front end on jackstands.
60. Install the oil pan. Torque the bolts to 15 ft. lbs.
61. Install the flywheel or flex plate. Torque the bolts to 55 ft. lbs.
62. On vans with manual transmission, install the clutch.
63. Position the transmission.
64. Install the transmission-to-bellhousing bolts, or the converter housing-to-engine bolts. Torque the 3/8-16 bolts to 30 ft. lbs.; the 7/16-14 bolts to 50 ft. lbs.
65. Install the front engine mount insulator top stud nuts and washers. Torque the nuts to 75 ft. lbs.
66. Remove the shop crane.
67. Remove the engine lifting fixture.
68. Install the rear engine support. Torque the bolts to 50 ft. lbs.
69. Remove the transmission jack.
70. Install the inspection plate or converter cover plate on the bellhousing.
71. Connect any electrical connections at the transmission.
72. Connect the speedometer cable at the transmission.
73. Install the clutch torque shaft, or the shifter torque shaft and oil cooler lines.
74. Connect the shift rods.
75. Install the transmission-to-engine strut.
76. Install the driveshaft.
77. Install the exhaust system.
78. Lower the van.
79. Remove the holding fixture.
80. If equipped with air conditioning, install the right valve cover.
81. Install the left exhaust manifold.
82. Install the intake manifold.
83. Install the heater blower motor.
84. Install the oil dipstick and tube.
85. Connect the fuel line at the pump.
86. Install the fan, pulley and drive belts.
87. Install the alternator.
88. Connect the throttle linkage and install the operating lever from the accelerator bellcrank.
89. Connect the engine-to-body ground strap.
90. Connect the oil pressure sending unit.
91. Connect the temperature sending unit.
92. Connect the alternator.
93. Connect the coil.
94. Connect all vacuum lines at the engine.
95. Connect the heater hoses.
96. Install the power steering pump.
97. Install the air conditioning compressor.
98. Install the throttle body.

99. Install the radiator and condenser as an assembly.
100. Connect the lower radiator hose.
101. Connect the upper radiator hose.
102. Install the fan shroud.
103. Install the grille and support brace.
104. Install the front bumper.
105. Connect the refrigerant lines at the condenser.
106. Evacuate, charge and leak test the system.
107. Install the starter.
108. Install the air cleaner.
109. Install the engine cover.
110. Install the oil filter.
111. Fill the crankcase.
112. Connect the battery.
113. Fill the cooling system.

Rocker Arm Cover

REMOVAL & INSTALLATION

1. Disconnect all wires, cable and hoses crossing the rocker cover.
2. Remove the rocker cover bolts.
3. Using a soft mallet, tap loose the rocker cover.

✳✳ WARNING

Never pry the cover loose. You may damage the cover or head surface!

4. Lift the cover off the engine.
5. Thoroughly clean all gasket material from the mating surfaces of the head and cover. On models which use RTV silicone sealant instead of a gasket, make sure that all material is removed.
6. On models using a gasket, place a new gasket on the head, coated with sealer. Coat the rocker cover mating surface with

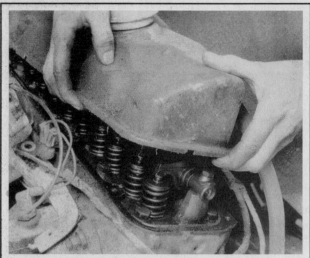
If necessary, tap the cover loose with a soft mallet. Lift the rocker arm cover off of the engine

sealer and install the cover. Tighten the bolts to 40 in. lbs. on models with a gasket.

On models with RTV silicone material, torque the nuts to 80 in. lbs.; the studs to 115 in. lbs.

Rocker Shafts

REMOVAL & INSTALLATION

Inline 6-Cylinder Engines

♦ See Figure 14

The rocker arm shaft has 12 straight steel rocker arms arranged on it with hardened steel spacers fitted between each pair of rocker arms. The shaft is secured by bolts and steel retainers which are attached to the 7 cylinder head brackets. To remove the rocker arm and shaft:

To remove the rocker arm cover, loosen and remove the hold-down bolts.

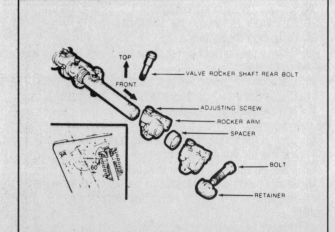
Fig. 14 Inline 6-cylinder adjustable style rocker arm and shaft components

After removing the rocker arm cover on L6 engines, remove the rocker shaft retaining bolts . . .

. . . then lift the rocker shaft assembly from the cylinder head

Before installing the rocker arm shaft and cover, scrape the old gasket off of the cylinder head

1. Remove the closed ventilation system.
2. Remove the evaporative control system (if so equipped).
3. Remove the valve cover and its gasket.
4. Remove the rocker shaft bolts and retainers.
5. Remove the rocker arm and shaft assembly.
6. Reverse the above for installation. The oil hole on the end of the shaft must be on top and point toward the front of the engine to provide proper lubrication to the rocker arms. The special bolt goes to the rear. 6-238, 8-318, 8-360, 8-400, 8-4407. Torque all bolts to 25 ft. lbs.
7. Temporarily set the intake valve tappet at 0.015″ and the exhaust valve at 0.025″.
8. Run the engine at 550 rpm until it is fully warmed up and adjust the valves.

V6 and V8 Engines

▶ See Figures 15 and 16

The stamped steel rocker arms are arranged on one rocker arm shaft per cylinder head. Because the angle of the pushrods tend to force the rocker arm pairs toward each other, oilite spacers are

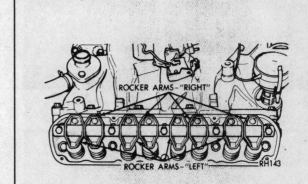

Fig. 15 Proper rocker arm locations on the shaft for V8 engines—the rocker arms are either stamped with an R or an L

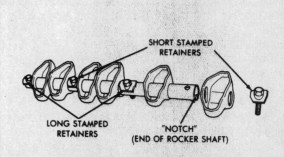

Fig. 16 The V6 rocker shaft is similar to the V8 one except it has two less rockers and one less attaching bolt

After removing the valve cover on V8 engines, remove the rocker arm shaft retaining bolts . . .

. . . then lift the rocker shaft assembly from the cylinder head as one unit

fitted to absorb the side thrust at each rocker arm. The shaft is secured by bolts and steel retainers attached to the brackets on the cylinder head. To remove the arm and shaft from each cylinder head:

1. Disconnect the spark plug wires.
2. Disconnect the closed ventilation system and evaporative control system (if so equipped) from the valve cover.
3. Remove each valve cover and gasket.
4. Remove the rocker shaft bolts and retainer.
5. Remove each rocker arm and shaft assembly. Keep everything in order for installation in the original position.
6. Reverse the above for installation. The notch on the end of both 318 and 360 rocker shafts should point to the engine centerline and toward the front of the engine on the left cylinder head and toward the rear on the right side. On the 400 and 440, the rocker arm lubrication holes must point down and toward the valves. Torque the rocker shaft bolts to 17 ft. lbs. on the 318 and 360, and 25 ft. lbs. on the others.

Diesel Engine

▶ **See Figure 17**

1. Remove the valve cover and gasket.
2. Remove the nozzle holders and the glow plug.
3. Remove the rocker shaft retaining bolts.
4. Remove the rocker arm and shaft assembly. Keep everything in order so the rocker assembly can be installed in the original position.
5. To install, position the rocker arm and shaft assembly so the bracket with the oil hole is at the front of the engine.
6. Install the rocker shaft retaining bolts and tighten them to 90 ft. lbs.
7. Install the nozzle holders and the glow plugs.
8. Install and tighten the injection lines. Tighten the nozzle holder retaining nuts to between 36 ft. lbs.
9. Adjust the valves.

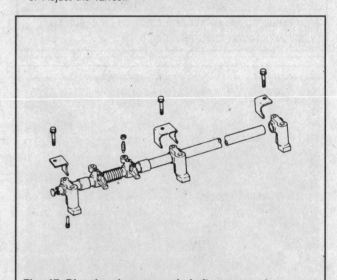

Fig. 17 Diesel rocker arm and shaft components

Thermostat

REMOVAL & INSTALLATION

▶ **See Figure 18**

1. Drain the cooling system to below the level of the thermostat.

✳✳ CAUTION

When draining the coolant, keep in mind that cats and dogs are attracted by the ethylene glycol antifreeze, and are quite likely to drink any that is left in an uncovered container or in puddles on the ground. This will prove fatal in sufficient quantity. Always drain the coolant into a sealable container. Coolant should be reused unless it is contaminated or several years old.

2. Remove the upper radiator hose from the thermostat housing. Note the positioning of the thermostat. It is important that the thermostat is correctly installed.

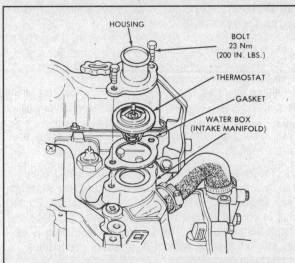

Fig. 18 Thermostat mounting details for the V6 engine— similar to the V8 engines

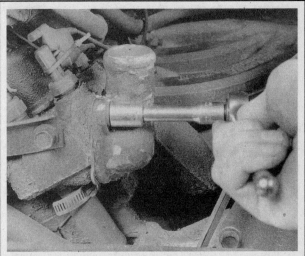

Loosen and remove the thermostat housing retaining bolts

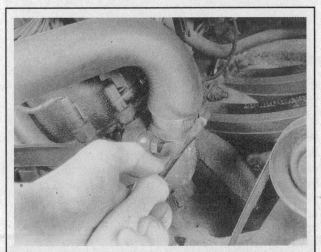

To remove the thermostat on L6 engines, loosen the upper radiator hose clamp . . .

Pull the housing off of the engine . . .

. . . and remove the upper radiator hose

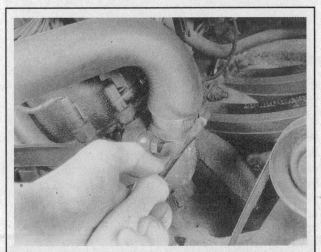

. . . then, noting its position, remove the thermostat from the engine

For thermostat removal on V8 engines, unbolt the water outlet housing . . .

. . . then, lift the housing and remove the thermostat

3. Withdraw the housing bolts and remove the housing and the thermostat.

4. Check to make sure that the thermostat valve closes tightly. If the valve does not close completely due to foreign material, carefully clean the sealing edge of the valve while being careful not to damage the sealing edge. If the valve does not close tightly after it has been cleaned, a new thermostat must be installed.

5. Immerse the thermostat in a container of warm water so that its pellet is completely covered and does not touch the bottom or sides of the container.

6. Heat the water and, while stirring the water continuously (to ensure uniform temperature), check the water temperature with a thermometer at the point when a 0.001″ feeler gauge can be inserted in the valve opening at a water temperature with ±5° of the standard thermostat temperature. If the thermostat does not open within the temperature range, replace it with a new thermostat.

7. Continue heating the water to a temperature of approximately 20° higher than the standard thermostat opening tempera-

ture. At this point, the thermostat should be fully open. If it is not, install a new thermostat.

8. To install, use a new gasket and position the thermostat so that its pellet end (the part with the spring) is toward the engine block. On the six, the vent hole must be up. Refit the thermostat housing and tighten its securing bolts to 25–30 ft. lbs..

9. Connect the upper radiator hose.

10. Fill the cooling system to 1.25″ below the filler neck with the correct water and antifreeze mixture. Warm the engine and inspect the upper radiator hose and the thermostat housing for leaks.

➡Poor heater output and slow engine warm-ups is often caused by a thermostat stuck in the open position; occasionally one sticks shut causing immediate overheating. Do not attempt to correct an overheating condition by permanently removing the thermostat. Thermostat flow restriction is designed into the system; without it, localized overheating due to turbulence may occur.

Intake Manifold

REMOVAL & INSTALLATION

V6 and V8 Engines

▶ See Figures 19 thru 24

1. Drain the cooling system and disconnect the battery.

✳✳ CAUTION

When draining the coolant, keep in mind that cats and dogs are attracted by the ethylene glycol antifreeze, and are quite likely to drink any that is left in an uncovered container or in puddles on the ground. This will prove fatal in sufficient quantity. Always drain the coolant into a sealable container. Coolant should be reused unless it is contaminated or several years old.

2. Remove alternator, carburetor air cleaner and fuel line.
3. Disconnect accelerator linkage.

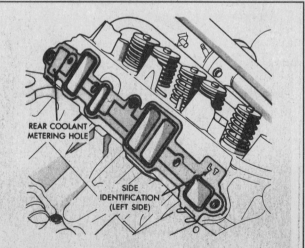

Fig. 19 Intake manifold side gasket for the 238 engine—left side shown

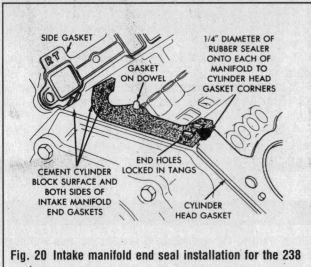

Fig. 20 Intake manifold end seal installation for the 238 engine

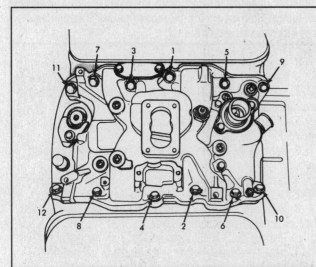

Fig. 21 Intake manifold torque sequence for the 238 engine

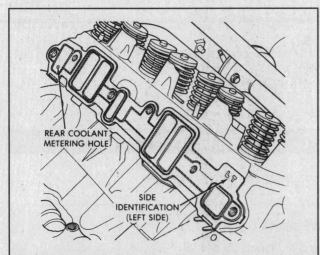

Fig. 22 Intake manifold side gasket for the 318 and 360 engines—left side shown

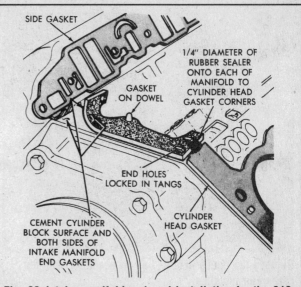

Fig. 23 Intake manifold end seal installation for the 318 and 360 engines

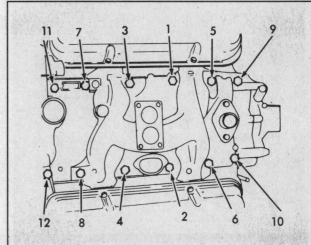

Fig. 24 Intake manifold torque sequence for the V8 engine

For intake removal on V8 engines, label and remove all hoses, wires, and attaching bolts

Remove the intake manifold as an assembly with the carburetor installed

Remove the old intake gasket side seals . . .

. . . and the end seals then, clean all gasket mating surfaces

4. Remove vacuum hose between carburetor and distributor.

5. Remove the distributor cap and wires.

6. Disconnect coil wires, temperature sending unit wire, heater hoses and bypass hose.

7. Remove intake manifold, ignition coil and carburetor as an assembly.

8. Installation is the reverse of the above procedure. Tighten the intake manifold to head bolts in the sequence illustrated, from center alternating out.

9. Tighten the exhaust manifold mounting nuts to the required torque which is listed in the specifications chart of this section.

Diesel Engine

1. Drain the cooling system.

✳✳ CAUTION

When draining the coolant, keep in mind that cats and dogs are attracted by the ethylene glycol antifreeze, and are quite likely to drink any that is left in an uncovered container or in puddles on the ground. This will prove fatal in sufficient quantity. Always drain the coolant into a sealable container. Coolant should be reused unless it is contaminated or several years old.

2. Disconnect the battery ground cable.

3. Remove the air cleaner.

4. Disconnect the fuel lines at the fuel filter, transfer pump and injection pump. See Section 5.

5. Drain the fuel filter and remove it from the back of the manifold. See Section 1.

6. Remove the manifold and air cleaner mounting bracket bolts.

7. Disconnect the injection lines at the injection pump and remove the nozzle holder from the cylinder head. See Section 5.

8. Remove the fuel line clamps from the manifold and push the fuel lines up and out of the way.

9. Remove the manifold and gaskets from the head.

10. Install the manifold and new gaskets on the head.

11. Install the fuel lines and clamps on the manifold.

12. Connect the injection lines at the injection pump.

13. Install the nozzle holder on the cylinder head. See Chapter 5.

14. Install the manifold and air cleaner mounting bracket bolts.

15. Install the fuel filter on the back of the manifold. See Chapter 1.

16. Connect the fuel lines at the fuel filter, transfer pump and injection pump. See Section 5.

17. Install the air cleaner.

18. Connect the battery ground cable.

19. Fill the cooling system.

Exhaust Manifold

REMOVAL & INSTALLATION

V6 and V8 Engines

⬥ **See Figures 25 and 26**

1. Disconnect the exhaust manifold at the flange where it mates to the exhaust pipe.

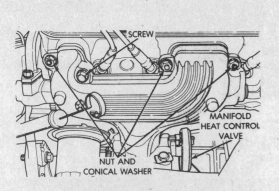

Fig. 25 Exhaust manifold installation details for the 238 engine

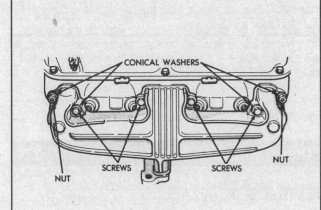

Fig. 26 Exhaust manifold installation details for the 318 and 360 engines

2. If the vehicle is equipped with air injection and/or a carburetor-heated air stove, remove them.

3. Remove the exhaust manifold by removing the securing bolts and washers. To reach these bolts, it may be necessary to jack the engine slightly off its front mounts. When the exhaust manifold is removed, sometimes the securing studs will screw out with the nuts. If this occurs, the studs must be replaced with the aid of sealing compound on the coarse thread ends. If this is not done, water leaks may develop at the studs.

4. To install, reverse the removal procedures. On the center branch of 318 and the 360 exhaust manifold, no conical washers are used.

Diesel Engine

1. Disconnect the battery ground cable.
2. Remove the air cleaner.
3. Remove the exhaust manifold heat shield.
4. Disconnect the exhaust pipe from the manifold.
5. Remove the exhaust manifold bridges and manifold hold-down bolts.

6. Remove the manifold and gaskets.
7. Inspect the manifold for cracks and heat damage. The gasket surfaces must be flat within 0.008″.
8. Installation is the reverse of removal. Check for leaks.

Combination Manifold

REMOVAL & INSTALLATION

Inline 6-Cylinder Engines

◗ **See Figure 27**

1. Remove the air cleaner, lines and tubes to the carburetor.
2. Disconnect all the linkages to the carburetor and remove the carburetor from the manifold.
3. Disconnect the exhaust pipe from the manifold, remove the manifold attaching washers and retaining nuts, and remove the manifold from the cylinder head.

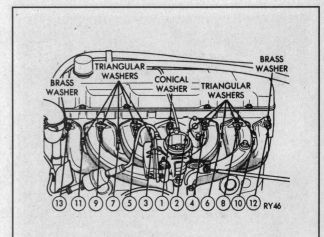

Fig. 27 Inline 6-cylinder combination manifold torque sequence

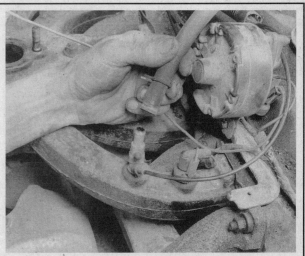

To remove the combination manifold, first remove the carburetor and all connections to the manifold

Disconnect the exhaust pipe and remove all of the manifold retaining nuts and washers

Remove any old gaskets, and clean the mating surfaces for a new gasket

5. Position the manifold on the cylinder head using a new gasket, and install the conical and triangular washers, the retaining nuts, and torque the retaining nuts and the three securing bolts to the specified torque in a spiral sequence from the center to the ends.

6. Attach the exhaust pipe to the exhaust manifold flange.

7. Install the carburetor and attach all the lines, tubes, and linkages. Install the air cleaner assembly.

Diesel Injection Pump

REMOVAL & INSTALLATION

For injection pump removal and installation please refer to Section 5.

Radiator

REMOVAL & INSTALLATION

▶ See Figure 28

1. Drain the cooling system.

✳✳ CAUTION

When draining the coolant, keep in mind that cats and dogs are attracted by the ethylene glycol antifreeze, and are quite likely to drink any that is left in an uncovered container or in puddles on the ground. This will prove fatal in sufficient quantity. Always drain the coolant into a sealable container. Coolant should be reused unless it is contaminated or several years old.

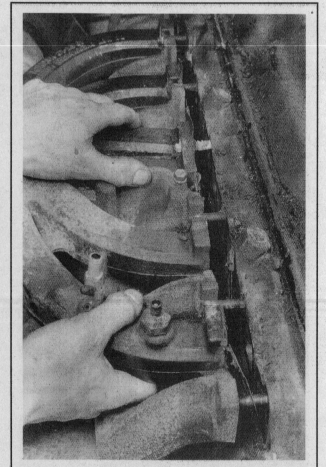

Pull the manifold away from the cylinder head

4. Separate the exhaust manifold from the intake manifold, if necessary, and install a new gasket between the two upon re-assembly.

➡Do not tighten the three securing bolts until the manifold assembly has been installed on the cylinder head.

2. Disconnect the battery ground cable.

3. Detach the upper hose from the radiator. If necessary, remove the overflow tank.

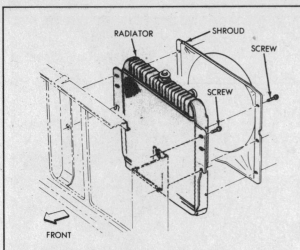

Fig. 28 Exploded view of a common radiator mounting for all vehicles covered in this manual

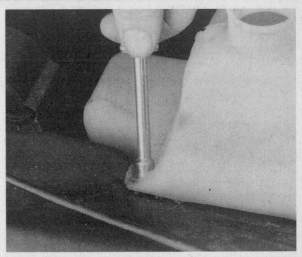

Remove the reservoir retaining bolts . . .

Some vehicles may require the radiator reservoir to be removed. Loosen the clamp. . .

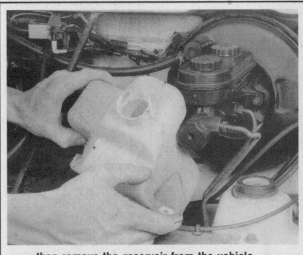

. . . then remove the reservoir from the vehicle

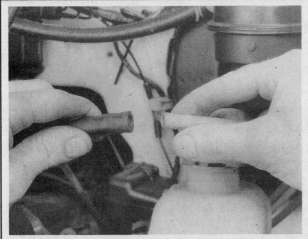

. . . that retains the overflow hose to the reservoir and disconnect the hose

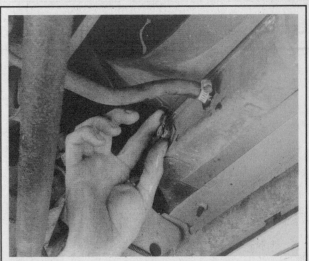

To remove the radiator, first open the radiator petcock to drain the cooling system

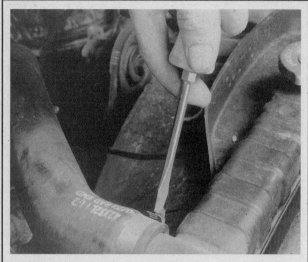

Loosen the upper radiator hose clamp . . .

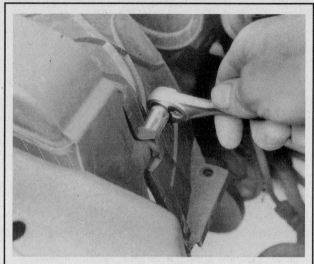

Remove the all of the fan shroud-to-radiator bolts

. . . and disconnect the hose from the radiator. Position the hose out of the way

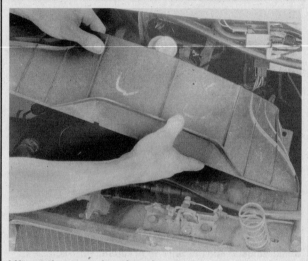

Lift out the upper fan shroud . . .

Remove the upper fan shroud-to-lower fan shroud attaching bolts

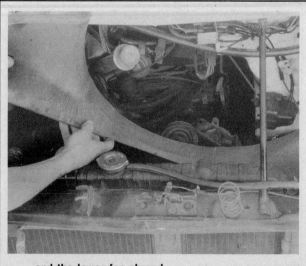

. . . and the lower fan shroud

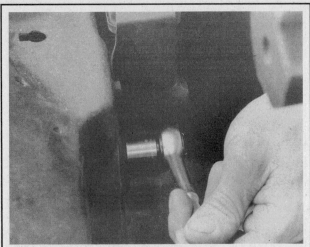

Remove the upper radiator retaining bolts, and loosen the lower retaining bolts

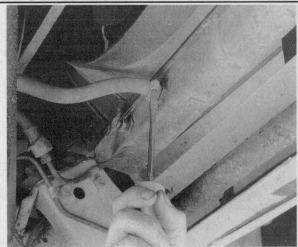

If equipped, loosen the automatic transmission cooler lines at the radiator . . .

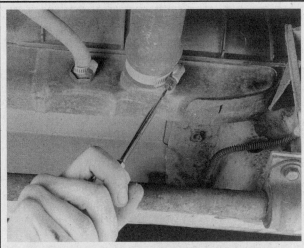

From underneath, loosen the lower radiator hose clamp . . .

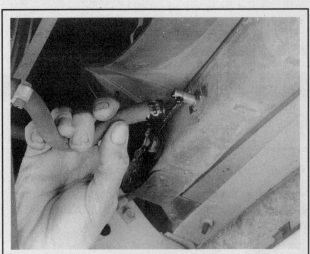

. . . and disconnect them from the radiator. Plug the line and cap the radiator fitting

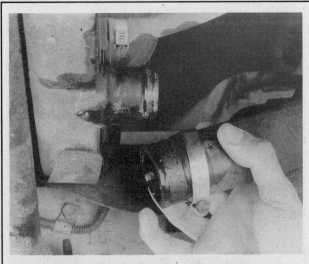

. . . and disconnect the hose from the radiator

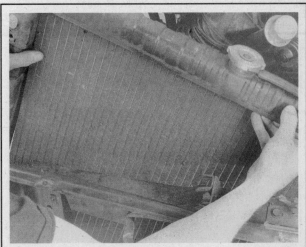

Remove the lower mounting bolts, then carefully lift the radiator out of the vehicle

4. Remove the shroud mounting nuts and position it out of the way.

5. Remove the radiator top mounting screws. If equipped with air conditioning, remove the condenser attaching screws, accessible through the grille. Do not disconnect any air conditioning lines.

6. Raise the vehicle and support it. Disconnect and plug the automatic transmission cooler lines and cap the openings in the cooler.

7. Hold the radiator in place and remove the lower mounting screws. Carefully lift it up and out of the truck.

To install:

8. Hold the radiator in place and install the lower mounting screws.

9. Connect the automatic transmission cooler lines.

10. Install the radiator top mounting screws. If equipped with air conditioning, install the condenser attaching screws, accessible through the grille.

11. Install the shroud mounting nuts.

12. Connect the upper hose from the radiator.

13. Connect the battery ground cable.

14. Fill the cooling system.

15. Check all fluid levels and run the engine, making sure there are no leaks.

Water Pump

REMOVAL & INSTALLATION

170, 198 and 225 Engines

➡This job can sometimes be done without removing the radiator on models without air conditioning, if there is enough room to get at the water pump bolts.

1. Remove the radiator.
2. Remove the tension from the drive belts.
3. Remove the fan, spacer, pulley, and bolts as an assembly.
4. If equipped with an air pump, remove the pump brackets with the hoses attached and tie it out of the way.

. . . and remove the fan, spacer and water pump pulley

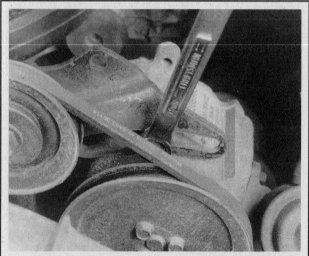

If equipped, remove the air pump mounting bolts and remove the belt

To replace the water pump on L6 engines, remove the cooling fan attaching bolts . . .

Position the air pump out of the way

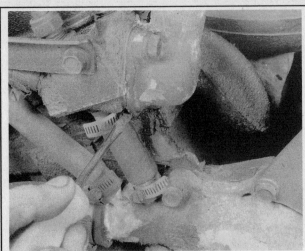

Loosen the clamps on the hoses connected to the water pump

Disconnect the hoses from the water pump as you pull it off of the engine

5. Disconnect the heater hose and all other hoses from the pump.

6. Remove the pump from the block.

7. Installation is the reverse of removal. Use a new gasket coated with sealer. Torque the bolts to 30 ft. lbs. Fill the cooling system and adjust the tension of the drive belts.

238, 318 and 360 Engines

1. Remove the radiator.

2. Loosen all accessories that are belt driven and remove all the drive belts.

3. On engines without air conditioning, remove the alternator bracket attaching bolts and tie the alternator and bracket out of the way.

4. On engines with air conditioning, remove the idler pulley assembly, alternator, and adjusting bracket.

5. Remove the fan blade, spacer (or fluid unit), pulley, and bolts as an assembly.

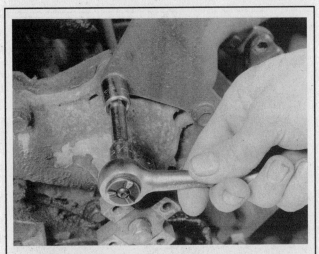

Unbolt the air pump mounting bracket from the water pump . . .

. . . and remove the bracket. Remove the remaining water pump bolts

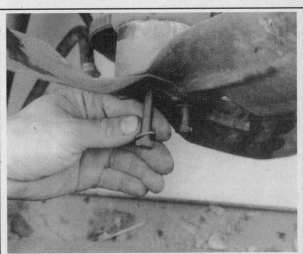

To remove the water pump on V8 engines, remove the four cooling fan bolts . . .

. . . then remove the fan, spacer, and pulley from the water pump

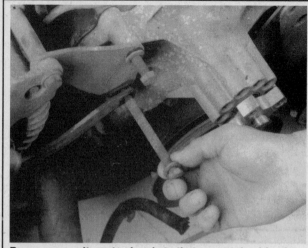

Remove any alternator brackets that are retained by the water pump bolts. Remove the water pump

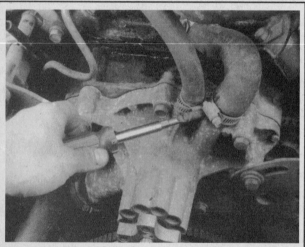

Loosen the clamps and disconnect the hoses from the water pump

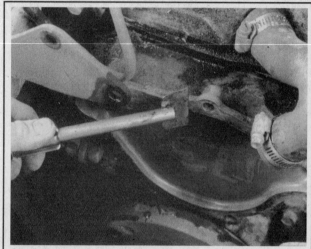

Clean the water pump mounting are well to prevent leaks when you install the pump

Loosen and remove the power steering pump bracket, and bolt

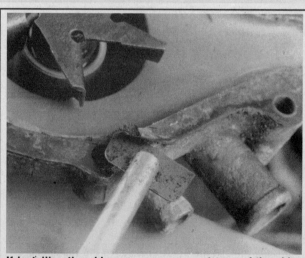

If installing the old pump, remove any traces of the old gasket with a scraper

➡**To prevent silicone fluid from draining into the drive bearing and ruining the lubricant, do not place the thermostatic fan drive unit with the shaft pointing downward.**

6. Disconnect all hoses from the water pump.

7. Remove the air conditioning compressor front mounting bolts.

8. Remove the water pump-to-compressor front bracket bolts and the bracket.

➡**Do not disconnect any refrigerant lines from the compressor.**

9. Remove the water pump.

10. Installation is the reverse of removal. Use a new gasket coated with sealer. Torque the bolts to 30 ft. lbs. Fill the cooling system and adjust the tension of the drive belts.

400 and 440 Engines

1. Disconnect the negative battery cable and drain the cooling system.

✳✳ CAUTION

When draining the coolant, keep in mind that cats and dogs are attracted by the ethylene glycol antifreeze, and are quite likely to drink any that is left in an uncovered container or in puddles on the ground. This will prove fatal in sufficient quantity. Always drain the coolant into a sealable container. Coolant should be reused unless it is contaminated or several years old.

2. Loosen all of the drive belts.

3. Remove the lower crankshaft pulley.

4. Remove the fan shroud screws and set the shroud back out of the way.

5. Remove the fluid fan drive bolts and set the fluid fan and the fan assembly aside.

6. Remove the water pump and the gasket.

7. Installation is the reverse of removal. Use a new gasket coated with sealer. Torque the bolts to 30 ft. lbs. Fill the cooling system and adjust the tension of the drive belts.

Diesel Engine

1. Drain the cooling system and remove the heater hoses and the bypass hose.

✳✳ CAUTION

When draining the coolant, keep in mind that cats and dogs are attracted by the ethylene glycol antifreeze, and are quite likely to drink any that is left in an uncovered container or in puddles on the ground. This will prove fatal in sufficient quantity. Always drain the coolant into a sealable container. Coolant should be reused unless it is contaminated or several years old.

2. Loosen the alternator mounting bolts and remove the belt.

3. Remove the cooling fan, the spacer and the drive pulley.

4. Remove the water pump mounting bolts and remove the pump.

5. Installation is the reverse of removal. Use a new gasket coated with sealer. Torque the bolts to 30 ft. lbs. Fill the cooling system and adjust the tension of the drive belts.

Cylinder Head

REMOVAL & INSTALLATION

Inline 6-Cylinder Engines

▶ **See Figures 29 and 30**

1. Drain the cooling system and disconnect the battery.

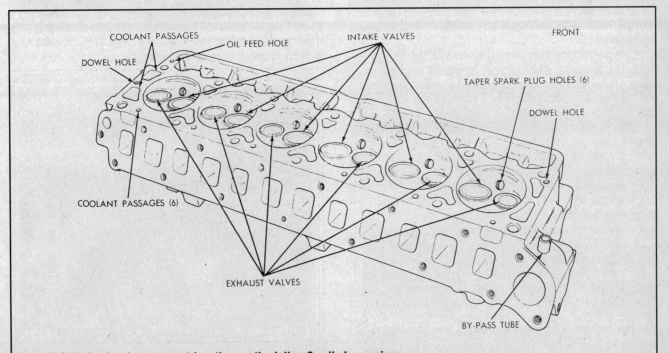

Fig. 29 Cylinder head component location on the inline 6-cylinder engines

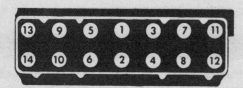

Fig. 30 Inline 6-cylinder head bolt torque sequence

✳✳ CAUTION

When draining the coolant, keep in mind that cats and dogs are attracted by the ethylene glycol antifreeze, and are quite likely to drink any that is left in an uncovered container or in puddles on the ground. This will prove fatal in sufficient quantity. Always drain the coolant into a sealable container. Coolant should be reused unless it is contaminated or several years old.

2. Remove the air cleaner and the fuel line from the carburetor.

3. Disconnect the accelerator linkage.

4. Remove the vacuum advance line from between the carburetor and the distributor.

5. Disconnect the cables from the spark plugs.

6. Disconnect the heater hose and the clamp which secures the by-pass hose.

7. Disconnect the water temperature sending unit.

8. Disconnect the exhaust pipe at the exhaust manifold flange. Disconnect the diverter valve line (if equipped) from the intake manifold and remove the air tube assembly from the cylinder head.

9. Remove the intake and exhaust manifolds and the carburetor as an assembly.

10. Remove the closed ventilation systems, the evaporative control system (if so equipped), and the valve cover.

11. Remove the rocker arm and shaft assembly.

12. Remove the pushrods and keep them in order to ensure installation in their original locations.

13. Remove the head bolts and remove the cylinder head.

14. Clean all of the gasket surfaces of the engine block and the cylinder head, an install the spark plugs.

15. Inspect all surfaces with a straightedge. If warpage is indicated, measure the amount. This amount must not exceed 0.00075 times the span length in any direction. For example, if a 12″ span is 0.004″ warped, the maximum allowable is $12 \times 0.00075″ = 0.009″$. In this case, the head is within limits. If warpage exceeds the specified limits, either replace the head or lightly machine the head gasket surface.

For cylinder head removal on L6 engines, remove the combination manifold (A) and air pipe (B)

Remove the rocker arm cover and shaft then, keeping them in order, remove the pushrods

Using a breaker bar, remove the cylinder head bolts . . .

. . . then lift the cylinder head off of the engine

When installing, follow the torque specification and tightening sequence given

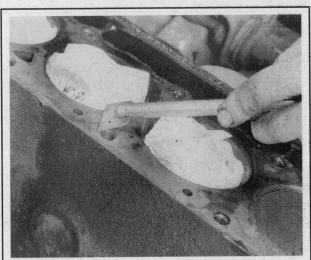

Stuff the bores with rags, then remove any traces of the old cylinder head gasket

To install:

16. Coat a new cylinder head gasket with sealer, install the gasket and install the cylinder head.

17. Install the cylinder had bolts. Torque the cylinder head bolts to 50 ft. lbs. in the sequence indicated in the illustration. Repeat this sequence to retorque all the head bolts to specifications.

18. Install the pushrods in their original locations.

19. Install the rocker arm and shaft assembly.

20. Install valve cover, the closed ventilation systems, and the evaporative control system.

21. Install the intake and exhaust manifolds and the carburetor as an assembly.

➡When installing the intake and exhaust manifold assembly, loosen the 3 bolts which secure the intake manifold to the exhaust manifold to maintain proper alignment. After installation, torque the 3 bolts in this sequence: inner bolts, then outer bolts. Refer to the manifold section, later in this chapter, for the proper tightening sequence. Check the valve adjustment.

22. Connect the exhaust pipe at the exhaust manifold flange. Connect the diverter valve line (if equipped) at the intake manifold and install the air tube assembly from the cylinder head.

23. Connect the water temperature sending unit.

24. Connect the heater hose and the clamp which secures the by-pass hose.

25. Connect the cables at the spark plugs.

26. Install the vacuum advance line between the carburetor and the distributor.

27. Connect the accelerator linkage.

28. Install the air cleaner and the fuel line at the carburetor.

29. Fill the cooling system and connect the battery.

V6 and V8 Engines

▶ See Figures 31, 32 and 33

1. Drain the cooling system and disconnect the battery ground cable.

❊❊ CAUTION

When draining the coolant, keep in mind that cats and dogs are attracted by the ethylene glycol antifreeze, and are quite likely to drink any that is left in an uncovered container or in puddles on the ground. This will prove fatal in sufficient quantity. Always drain the coolant into a sealable container. Coolant should be reused unless it is contaminated or several years old.

2. Remove the alternator, air cleaner, and fuel line.

3. Disconnect the accelerator linkage.

4. Remove the vacuum advance line from between the carburetor and the distributor. On trucks with the 360 cu. in. engine, remove the battery.

5. Remove the distributor cap and wires as an assembly.

6. Disconnect the coil wires, water temperature sending unit, heater hoses, and bypass hose. On the 360 engine remove the distributor and governor.

7. Remove the closed ventilation system, the evaporative control system (if so equipped), and the valve covers.

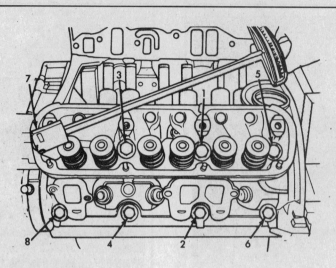

Fig. 31 V6 cylinder head bolt torque sequence

For cylinder head removal on V8 engines, remove the valve covers, rocker shafts and pushrods

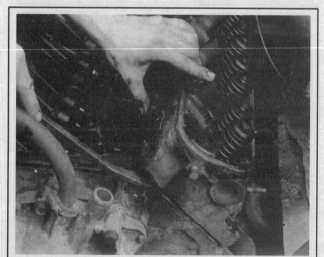

After removing the cylinder head attaching bolts, pry the head up to break it free of the engine

Keep the pushrods in order. Remove the intake and exhaust manifolds

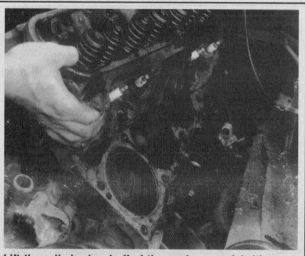

Lift the cylinder head off of the engine; careful, it's heavy

Remove and discard the old cylinder head gasket . . .

. . . and scrape the cylinder block of any remaining gasket material

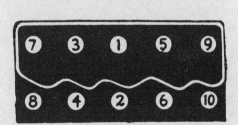

Fig. 32 Cylinder head bolt torque sequence for the 318 and 360 engines

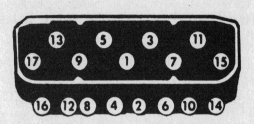

Fig. 33 Cylinder head bolt torque sequence for the 400 and 440 engines

8. Remove the intake manifold, ignition coil, and carburetor as an assembly.

9. Remove the exhaust manifolds. On 360 engines tag the center bolts.

10. Remove the tappet chamber cover. Remove the rocker and shaft assemblies.

11. Remove the pushrods and keep them in order to ensure installation in their original locations. On the 360 engines remove the water pump-to-heads bolts.

12. Remove the head bolts from each cylinder head and remove the cylinder heads.

13. Clean all the gasket surfaces of the engine block and the cylinder heads. Install the spark plugs.

14. Inspect all surfaces with a straight edge. If warpage is indicated, measure the amount. This amount must not exceed 0.00075 times the span length in any direction. For example, if a 12″ span is 0.004″ warped, the maximum allowable difference is $12 \times 0.00075 = 0.009″$. In this case, the head is within limits. If the warpage exceeds the specified limits, either replace the head or lightly machine the head gasket surface.

To install:

15. Coat new cylinder head gaskets with sealer, install the gaskets and install the cylinder heads.

➡**The number and size of the cooling passages in the 318 heads were changed during the 1976 model year. The new type gasket can be used with the old heads, but the old type gasket can't be used with the new heads.**

16. Install the cylinder head bolts. Torque the cylinder head bolts to 50 ft. lbs. in the sequence indicated. Repeat this sequence to re-torque all the cylinder head bolts to specifications.

17. Install the pushrods.

18. On the 8-360 install the water pump-to-heads bolts.

19. Install the rocker and shaft assemblies. Install the tappet chamber cover.

20. Install the exhaust manifolds.

21. Install the intake manifold, ignition coil, and carburetor as an assembly.

22. Install the closed ventilation system, the evaporative control system (if so equipped), and the valve covers.

23. Connect the coil wires, water temperature sending unit, heater hoses, and bypass hose. On the 360 engines, install the distributor and governor.

24. Install the distributor cap and wires as an assembly.

25. Install the vacuum advance line between the carburetor and the distributor. On trucks with the 360 engine, install the battery.

26. Connect the accelerator linkage.

27. Install the alternator, air cleaner, and fuel line.

28. Fill the cooling system and connect the battery ground cable.

Diesel Engine

▶ **See Figures 34 and 35**

1. Drain the cooling system.

✳✳ CAUTION

When draining the coolant, keep in mind that cats and dogs are attracted by the ethylene glycol antifreeze, and are quite likely to drink any that is left in an uncovered container or in puddles on the ground. This will prove fatal in sufficient quantity. Always drain the coolant into a sealable container. Coolant should be reused unless it is contaminated or several years old.

2. Disconnect the negative battery cable.

3. Remove the air cleaner.

4. Disconnect the hoses from the fuel filter at the transfer pump and the injection pump. Drain the filter and remove it from the manifold.

5. Remove the manifold nuts and air cleaner mounting bracket attaching nuts.

6. Disconnect the injection lines for cylinders 3 and 6 from the injection pump.

7. Remove the intake manifold and gaskets from the head.

8. Push the exhaust manifold shield to one side.

9. Remove the heater hose and the bypass hose.

10. Remove the thermostat housing and the upper radiator hose from the water manifold. Remove the spray gasket.

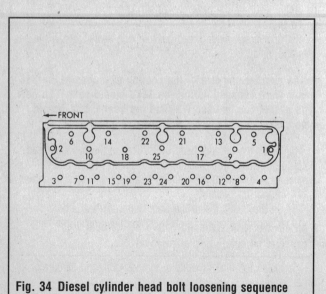

Fig. 34 Diesel cylinder head bolt loosening sequence

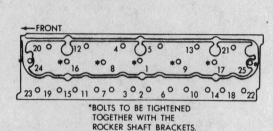

Fig. 35 Diesel cylinder head bolt tightening sequence

11. Disconnect the temperature sending unit wire.

12. Disconnect the fuel line mounting brackets from the cylinder head and push the fuel lines aside.

13. Remove the three exhaust manifold bridges.

14. Remove the water manifold and gasket from the cylinder head.

15. Raise the truck and support with jackstands.

16. Disconnect the exhaust pipe from the exhaust manifold.

17. Lower the truck. Remove the exhaust manifold, heat shield and gasket.

18. Disconnect and remove the wire from the glow plug buss bar.

19. Remove the injection lines from the injection pump.

20. Disconnect the fuel injection line from the head. Remove the bracket and the ground strap.

21. Disconnect the alternator bracket and the engine lifting fixture. Push them aside.

22. Remove the cylinder head cover and the gasket.

23. Loosen and remove the cylinder head bolts in the sequence illustrated.

24. Lift out the rocker arm and shaft assembly.

25. Remove the pushrods, keeping them in order. The pushrods MUST be installed in their original location.

26. Remove the injector tubes, injector holds and the injectors.

27. Disconnect and remove the glow plug buss bar.

28. Remove the six glow plugs from the cylinder head.

29. Remove the cylinder head. Check the head for cracks, damage or evidence of water leaks. Clean all the oil, grease, scale, sealant and carbon from the head. Thoroughly clean the gasket surfaces. Also check each combustion chamber jet for cracks or melting. If a jet is cracked or melted, remove it with a pushrod inserted through a glow plug bore.

30. Inspect all cylinder head surfaces with a straightedge. Out-of-flatness must not exceed 0.010″. If it does, a surface grinder must be used to bring the head to an out-of-flatness of less than 0.006″.

To install:

31. Install the glow plugs in the head. Tighten them firmly.

32. Install the injectors, injector tubes and the injector holders in the head. Tighten the nozzle holder attaching nuts to 37 ft. lbs.

33. Coat the new gasket lightly with sealer. Place the gasket on the block and place the cylinder head over the dowels.

34. Install the cylinder head bolts and tighten them in the sequence illustrated to 90,4 ft. lbs. Do not install the head bolts which retain the rocker shaft assembly.

35. Install the pushrods in their original locations.

36. Install the rocker arm and shaft assembly. Tighten the mounting bolts, the same as the cylinder head bolts, to 90.4 ft. lbs.

37. Adjust the valve clearance to 0.012″ at top dead center of each compression stroke.

38. Install the cylinder head cover and gasket.

39. Install the alternator bracket and the engine lifting fixture.

40. Connect the fuel lines to the injection pump (except nos. 3 and 6). Install the bracket and the group strap.

41. Install the fuel line to the transfer pump.

42. Install the exhaust manifold and the heat shield assembly, using a new gasket.

43. Raise the trunk and support it safely. Attach the exhaust pipe to the exhaust manifold.

44. Lower the truck and install the water manifold on the head using a new gasket.

45. Install the three exhaust manifold bridges.

46. Install the fuel lines in the bracket.

47. Connect the temperature sending unit wire.

48. Using a new gasket, install the thermostat housing. Attach the upper radiator hose to the thermostat housing.

49. Install the bypass and heater hoses.

50. Install the exhaust manifold heat shield and the exhaust manifold.

51. Using a new gasket and spray shield, install the air intake manifold.

52. Connect the injection lines from cylinders 3 and 6 to the injection pump.

53. Install the fuel filter to the back of the manifold.

54. Connect the fuel hoses.

55. Install the air cleaner bracket and install the air cleaner.

56. Fill the cooling system and connect the battery cables.

CLEANING AND INSPECTION

1. With the valves installed to protect the valve seats, remove deposits from the combustion chambers and valve heads with a scraper and a wire brush. Be careful not to damage the cylinder head gasket surface. After the valves are removed, clean the valve guide bores with a valve guide cleaning tool. Using cleaning solvent to remove dirt, grease and other deposits, clean all bolts holes; be sure the oil passage is clean (V8 engines).

2. Remove all deposits from the valves with a fine wire brush or buffing wheel.

3. Inspect the cylinder heads for cracks or excessively burned areas in the exhaust outlet ports.

4. Check the cylinder head for cracks and inspect the gasket surface for burrs and nicks. Replace the head if it is cracked.

5. On cylinder heads that incorporate valve seat inserts, check the inserts for excessive wear, cracks, or looseness.

RESURFACING

Cylinder Head Flatness

▶ See Figure 36

When the cylinder head is removed, check the flatness of the cylinder head gasket surfaces.

1. Place a straightedge across the gasket surface of the cylinder head. Using feeler gauges, determine the clearance at the center of the straightedge.

2. If warpage exceeds 0.003″ in a 6″ span, or 0.006″ (0.008″ for the diesel) over the total length, the cylinder head must be resurfaced.

3. If necessary to refinish the cylinder head gasket surface, do not plane or grind off more than 0.010″ (0.002″ for the diesel) from the original gasket surface.

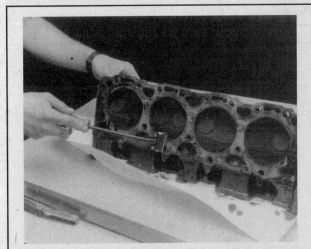

Use a gasket scraper to remove the bulk of the old head gasket from the mating surface

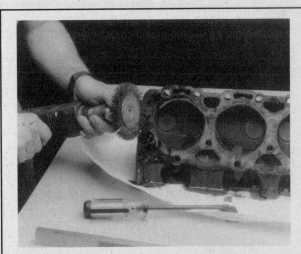

An electric drill equipped with a wire wheel will expedite complete gasket removal

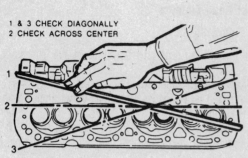

Fig. 36 Check the cylinder head for warpage along these lines

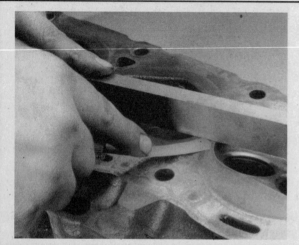

Check the cylinder head for flatness across the head surface

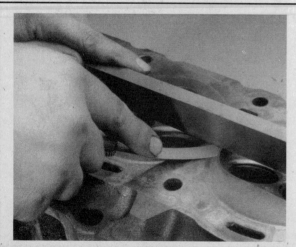

Checks should be made both straight across the cylinder head and at both diagonals

➡When milling the cylinder heads of V6 and V8 engines, the intake manifold mounting position is altered, and must be corrected by milling the manifold flange a proportionate amount. Consult an experienced machinist about this.

Valves and Springs

REMOVAL & INSTALLATION

◆ **See Figures 37 thru 44**

➡The diesel has inner and outer springs.

1. Block the head on its side, or install a pair of head-holding brackets made especially for valve removal.
2. Use a socket slightly larger than the valve stem and keepers, place the socket over the valve stem and gently hit the socket with a plastic hammer to break loose any varnish buildup.

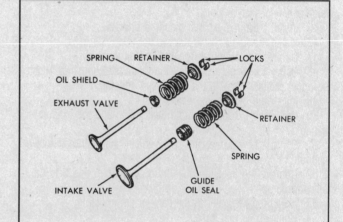

Fig. 37 Exploded view of the inline 6-cylinder valve and spring components

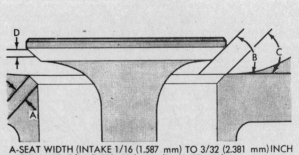

A-SEAT WIDTH (INTAKE 1/16 (1.587 mm) TO 3/32 (2.381 mm) INCH
  EXHAUST: 3/64 (1.190 mm) TO 1/16 (1.587 mm)
B-FACE ANGLE (INTAKE: 44½°-45° EXHAUST: 42½°-43°
C-SEAT ANGLE (INTAKE: 45°-45½° EXHAUST: 45°-45½°
D-CONTACT SURFACE

Fig. 38 Inline 6-cylinder valve face and seat angles

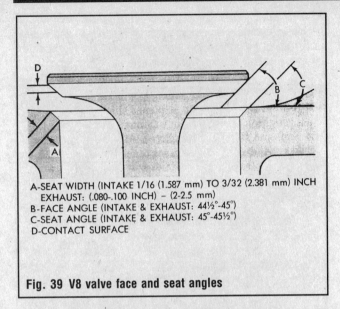

A—SEAT WIDTH (INTAKE 1/16 (1.587 mm) TO 3/32 (2.381 mm) INCH
  EXHAUST: (.080-.100 INCH) – (2-2.5 mm)
B—FACE ANGLE (INTAKE & EXHAUST: 44½°-45°)
C—SEAT ANGLE (INTAKE & EXHAUST: 45°-45½°)
D—CONTACT SURFACE

Fig. 39 V8 valve face and seat angles

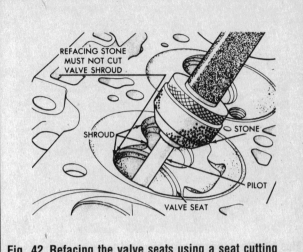

Fig. 42 Refacing the valve seats using a seat cutting stone

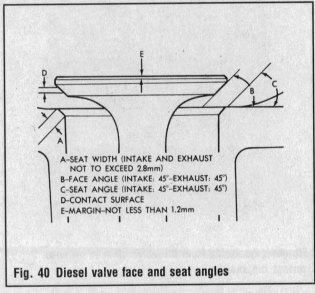

A—SEAT WIDTH (INTAKE AND EXHAUST
  NOT TO EXCEED 2.8mm)
B—FACE ANGLE (INTAKE: 45°—EXHAUST: 45°)
C—SEAT ANGLE (INTAKE: 45°—EXHAUST: 45°)
D—CONTACT SURFACE
E—MARGIN—NOT LESS THAN 1.2mm

Fig. 40 Diesel valve face and seat angles

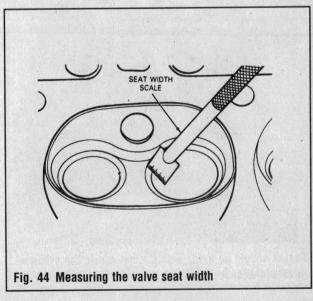

Fig. 43 Lapping the valves by hand

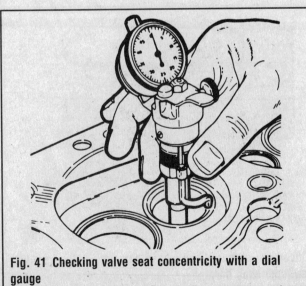

Fig. 41 Checking valve seat concentricity with a dial gauge

Fig. 44 Measuring the valve seat width

Use a valve spring compressor tool to relieve spring tension from the valve caps

Remove the spring from the valve stem in order to access the seal

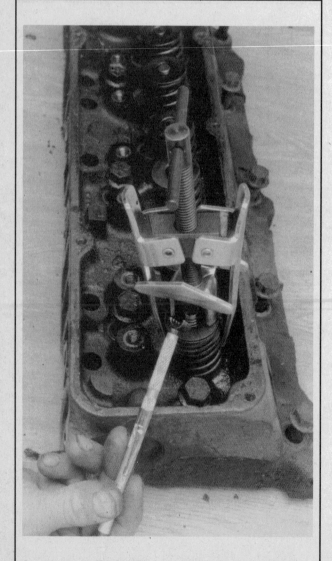

A magnet may be helpful in removing the valve keepers

Invert the cylinder head and withdraw the valve from the cylinder head bore

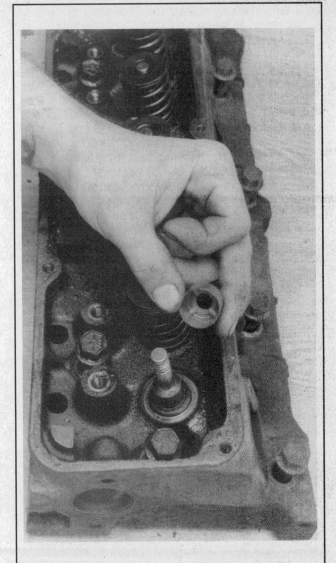

Remove the valve stem seal from the cylinder head

A dial gauge may be used to check valve stem-to-guide clearance

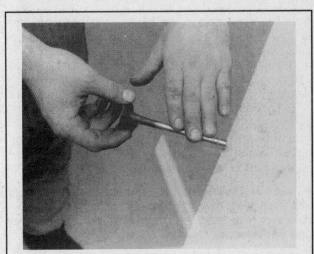

Valve stems may be rolled on a flat surface to check for bends

A wire wheel may be used to clean the combustion chambers of carbon deposits

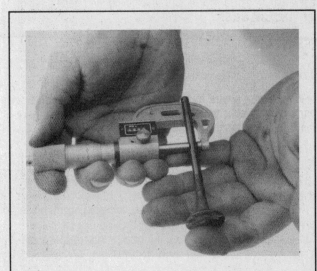

Use a micrometer to check the valve stem diameter

With the valve spring out of the way, the valve stem seals may now be replaced

3. Remove the valve keepers, retainer, spring shield and valve spring using a valve spring compressor (the locking C-clamp type is the easiest kind to use).

4. Put the parts in a separate container numbered for the cylinder being worked on; do not mix them with other parts removed.

5. Remove and discard the valve stem oil seals. A new seal will be used at assembly time.

6. Remove the valves from the cylinder head and place them, in order, through numbered holes punched in a stiff piece of cardboard or wood valve holding stick.

➡**The exhaust valve stems, on some engines, are equipped with small metal caps. Take care not to lose the caps. Make sure to re-install them at assembly time. Replace any caps that are worn.**

7. Use an electric drill and rotary wire brush to clean the intake and exhaust valve ports, combustion chamber and valve seats. In some cases, the carbon will need to be chipped away. Use a blunt pointed drift for carbon chipping. Be careful around the valve seat areas.

8. Use a wire valve guide cleaning brush and safe solvent to clean the valve guides.

9. Clean the valves with a revolving wires brush. Heavy carbon deposits may be removed with the blunt drift.

➡**When using a wire brush to clean carbon on the valve ports, valves etc., be sure that the deposits are actually removed, rather than burnished.**

10. Wash and clean all valve springs, keepers, retaining caps etc., in safe solvent.

11. Clean the head with a brush and some safe solvent and wipe dry.

12. Check the head for cracks. Cracks in the cylinder head usually start around an exhaust valve seat because it is the hottest part of the combustion chamber. If a crack is suspected but cannot be detected visually have the area checked with dye penetrant or other method by the machine shop.

13. After all cylinder head parts are reasonably clean, check the valve stem-to-guide clearance. If a dial indicator is not on hand, a visual inspection can give you a fairly good idea if the guide, valve stem or both are worn.

14. Insert the valve into the guide until slight away from the valve seat. Wiggle the valve sideways. A small amount of wobble is normal, excessive wobble means a worn guide or valve stem. If a dial indicator is on hand, mount the indicator so that the stem of the valve is at 90° to the valve stem, as close to the valve guide as possible. Move the valve off the seat, and measure the valve guide-to-stem clearance by rocking the stem back and forth to actuate the dial indicator. Measure the valve stem using a micrometer and compare to specifications to determine whether stem or guide wear is causing excessive clearance.

15. The valve guide, if worn, must be repaired before the valve seats can be resurfaced. Chrysler supplies valves with oversize stems to fit valve guides that are reamed to oversize for repair. The machine shop will be able to handle the guide reaming for you. In some cases, if the guide is not too badly worn, knurling may be all that is required.

16. Reface, or have the valve seats refaced. The valve seats should be a true 45° angle. Remove only enough material to clean up any pits or grooves. Be sure the valve seat is not too wide or narrow. Use a 60° grinding wheel to remove material from the bottom of the seat for raising and a 30° grinding wheel to remove material from the top of the seat to narrow.

17. Valves should be refaced to a true angle of 45°. Remove only enough metal to clean up the valve face or to correct runout. If the edge of a valve head, after machining, is 1/32″ (0.8mm) or less replace the valve. The tip of the valve stem should also be dressed on the valve grinding machine, however, do not remove more than 0.010″ (0.254mm).

18. Refer to the valve lapping procedure in this section.

19. After all valve and valve seats have been machined, check the remaining valve train parts (springs, retainers, keepers, etc.) for wear. Check the valve springs for straightness and tension.

20. Install the valves in the cylinder head and metal caps.

21. Install new valve stem oil seals.

22. Install the valve keepers, retainer, spring shield and valve spring using a valve spring compressor (the locking C-clamp type is the easiest kind to use).

23. Check the valve spring installed height, shim or replace as necessary.

VALVE LAPPING

After machine work has been performed on the valves, it may be necessary to lap the valve to assure proper contact. For this, you should first contact your machine shop to determine if lapping is necessary. Some machine shops will perform this for you as part of the service, but the precision machining which is available today often makes lapping unnecessary. Additionally, the hardened valves/seats used in modern automobiles may make lapping difficult or impossible. If your machine shop recommends that you lap the valves, proceed as follows:

1. Set the cylinder head on the workbench, combustion chamber side up. Rest the head on wooden blocks on either end, so there are two or three inches between the tops of the valve guides and the bench.

2. Lightly lube the valve stem with clean engine oil. Coat the valve seat completely with valve grinding compound. Use just enough compound that the full width and circumference of the seat are covered.

3. Install the valve in its proper location in the head. Attach the suction cup end of the valve lapping tool to the valve head. It usually helps to put a small amount of saliva into the suction cup to aid it sticking to the valve.

4. Rotate the tool between the palms, changing position and lifting the tool often to prevent grooving. Lap the valve in until a smooth, evenly polished seat and valve face are evident.

5. Remove the valve from the head. Wipe away all traces of grinding compound from the valve face and seat. Wipe out the port with a solvent soaked rag, and swab out the valve guide with a piece of solvent soaked rag to make sure there are no traces of compound grit inside the guide. This cleaning is important.

6. Proceed through the remaining valves, one at a time. Make sure the valve faces, seats, cylinder ports and valve guides are clean before reassembling the valve train.

CHECKING VALVE SPRINGS

▶ **See Figure 45**

Place the valve spring on a flat surface next to a carpenter's square. Measure the height of the spring, and rotate the spring against the edge of the square to measure distortion. If the spring height varies (by comparison) by more than 1/16″ (1.6mm) or if the distortion exceeds 1/16″ (1.6mm), replace the spring.

Have the valve springs tested for spring pressure at the installed and compressed (installed height minus valve lift) height using a valve spring tester. Springs should be within one pound, plus or minus each other. Replace springs as necessary.

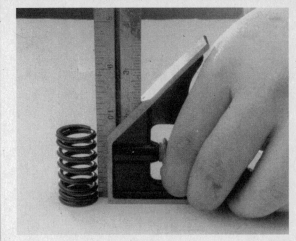

Check the valve spring for squareness on a flat service; a carpenter's square can be used

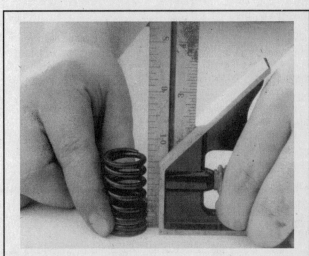

The valve spring should be straight up and down when placed like this

VALVE SPRING INSTALLED HEIGHT

▶ **See Figure 46**

After installing the valve spring, measure the distance between the spring mounting pad and the lower edge of the spring retainer. Compare the measurement to specifications. If the installed height is incorrect, add shim washers between the spring mounting pad and the spring. Use only washers designed for valve springs, available at most parts houses.

VALVE SEATS

Except Diesel Engines

If the valve seat is damaged or burnt and cannot be serviced by refacing, it may be possible to have the seat machined and an insert installed. Consult an automotive machine shop for their advice.

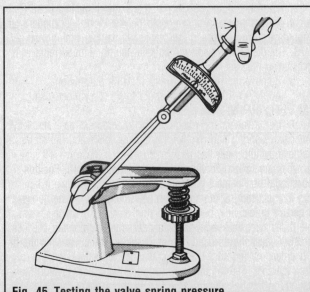

Fig. 45 Testing the valve spring pressure

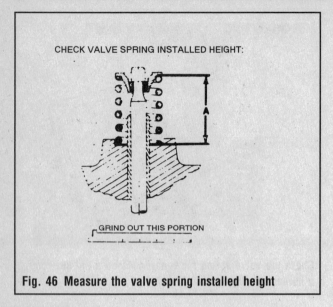

CHECK VALVE SPRING INSTALLED HEIGHT:

GRIND OUT THIS PORTION

Fig. 46 Measure the valve spring installed height

Diesel Engines

Valve seats are replaceable. Special tools are required to remove and install the seats. Considerable care must be exercised when installing the seat inserts. The inserts are installed with a 0.002–0.004″ press fit and must be started in place, true with the counterbore in the block. To install the inserts:

1. Place the inserts in a container of dry ice for at least 10 minutes.
2. Make certain that the block and counterbore are absolutely clean.
3. Place the chilled inserts in the counterbore and, using a seat driver, drive the insert in until it bottoms.

➡**If the standard insert is too loose, 0.010″ oversizes are available.**

4. Counterbore the block 0.0035″ smaller than the insert to be installed. Run the boring tool down until it bottoms.

VALVE GUIDES

Except Diesel Engines

Worn valve guides can, in most cases, be reamed to accept a valve with an oversized stem. Valve guides that are not excessively worn or distorted may, in some cases, be knurled rather than reamed. However, if the valve stem is worn reaming for an oversized valve stem is the answer since a new valve would be required.

Knurling is a process in which metal is displaced and raised, thereby reducing clearance. Knurling also produces excellent oil control. The possibility of knurling instead of reaming the valve guides should be discussed with a machinist.

Diesel Engine

♦ **See Figure 47**

These guides are replaceable.
1. Press out the old guide using tool 31691-10500.
2. Press the new guide into the head using tool 31691-00800. Installed height, above the head, should be 17.7–18.3mm.

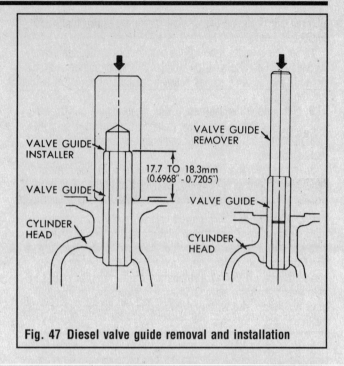

VALVE GUIDE INSTALLER

VALVE GUIDE

CYLINDER HEAD

17.7 TO 18.3mm (0.6968″ - 0.7205″)

VALVE GUIDE REMOVER

VALVE GUIDE

CYLINDER HEAD

Fig. 47 Diesel valve guide removal and installation

Valve Stem Oil Seal

REMOVAL & INSTALLATION

Gasoline Engines

➡**This procedure is done with the cylinder head installed.**

If valve stem oil seals are found to be the cause of excessive oil consumption, they may be replaced without removing the cylinder block.

1. Remove the air cleaner.
2. Remove rocker arm covers and spark plugs.
3. Detach the coil wire from the distributor.
4. Turn the engine so that no. 1 cylinder is at Top Dead Center on the compression stroke. Both valves for no. 1 cylinder should be fully closed and the crankshaft damper timing mark at TDC. The distributor rotor will point at the no. 1 spark plug wire location in the cap.
5. Remove the rocker shaft and install a dummy shaft.
6. Apply 90–100 psi air pressure to no. 1 cylinder, using a spark plug hole air hose adaptor.
7. Use a valve spring compressor to compress each no. 1 cylinder valve spring and remove the retainer locks and the spring. Remove the old seals.
8. Install a cup shield on the exhaust valve stem. Position it down against the valve guide.
9. Push the intake valve stem seal firmly and squarely over the valve guide.
10. Compress the valve spring only enough to install the lock.
11. Repeat the operation on each successive cylinder in the firing order, making sure that the crankshaft is exactly on TDC for each cylinder. See the Firing Order and Distributor Rotation illustrations in the Specifications section of this chapter for cylinder numbering.
12. Replace the rocker arms, covers, spark plugs and coil wire.

Oil Pan

REMOVAL & INSTALLATION

170, 198 and 225 Engines

▶ See Figures 48 and 49

1. Drain the oil.

✳✳ CAUTION

The EPA warns that prolonged contact with used engine oil may cause a number of skin disorders, including cancer! You should make every effort to minimize your exposure to used engine oil. Protective gloves should be worn when changing the oil. Wash your hands and any other exposed skin areas as soon as possible after exposure to used engine oil. Soap and water, or waterless hand cleaner should be used.

2. Remove the dipstick.
3. On models with automatic transmission, remove the torque converter inspection cover.
4. Raise and support the front end on jackstands placed under the frame. This will drop the driving axle far enough to clear the pan.
5. Remove the crossmember if it interferes, and the left bell-housing brace.
6. Remove the pan bolts and, if necessary, tap the pan loose with a soft mallet. Never pry the pan loose!
7. Thoroughly clean all gasket material from the pan and block. On engines using RTV silicone sealer in place of a gasket, remove all traces of the material.

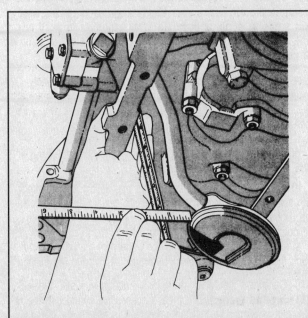

Fig. 48 Positioning the oil pick-up tube and screen—you want about 3/8 to 1/2 inch between the pick-up and the bottom of the oil pan

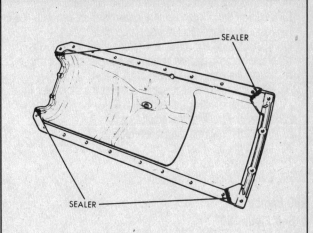

Fig. 49 Apply a 1/8 in. bead of RTV sealer at the points indicated on the inline 6-cylinder

8. When installing the pan, coat the block and pan mating surfaces with sealer and place a new gasket on the pan. Place new rubber end seals in the pan. Put a ⅛″ drop of silicone sealer at the 4 points where the seals and gaskets meet.

On models using RTV silicone material instead of a gasket, apply a ⅛″ diameter bead of seal on the pan, around the bolt holes.

On models with a gasket, position the pan and install the bolts. Tighten the bolts to 75 in. lbs., then, retighten the bolts to 200 in. lbs.

On models with RTV silicone sealant in place of a gasket, torque the bolts to 200 in. lbs.

Diesel Engine

1. Disconnect the battery ground.
2. Remove the oil dipstick.
3. Raise and support the front end on jackstands.
4. Drain the oil.

✳✳ CAUTION

The EPA warns that prolonged contact with used engine oil may cause a number of skin disorders, including cancer! You should make every effort to minimize your exposure to used engine oil. Protective gloves should be worn when changing the oil. Wash your hands and any other exposed skin areas as soon as possible after exposure to used engine oil. Soap and water, or waterless hand cleaner should be used.

5. Remove the dipstick tube from the pan.
6. With automatic transmission, disconnect the oil cooler lines.
7. Remove the road draft tube.
8. Remove the oil pan bolts and lower the truck to the ground.
9. Remove the nuts from the engine mounts.
10. Raise and support the front end on jackstands.
11. Install a jackstand under the compressor bracket.
12. Remove the transmission inspection plate.
13. Remove the oil pan and discard the gasket.

14. Thoroughly clean the gasket mating surfaces.
15. Position the oil pan using a new gasket coated with sealer.
16. Install the transmission inspection plate.
17. Install the oil pan bolts and torque them to 15 ft. lbs.
18. Remove the jackstand under the compressor bracket.
19. Install the road draft tube.
20. With automatic transmission, connect the oil cooler lines.
21. Install the dipstick tube on the pan.
22. Lower the truck to the ground.
23. Install the nuts on the engine mounts.
24. Install the oil dipstick.
25. Fill the crankcase.
26. Connect the battery ground.

238 Engine
▶ See Figure 50

1. Disconnect the battery ground cable.
2. Remove the oil dipstick.
3. Raise and support the front end on jackstands.
4. Drain the oil.

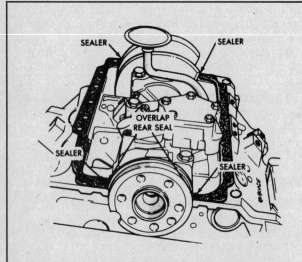

Fig. 50 Oil pan gasket installation on the 238 engine

✱✱ CAUTION

The EPA warns that prolonged contact with used engine oil may cause a number of skin disorders, including cancer! You should make every effort to minimize your exposure to used engine oil. Protective gloves should be worn when changing the oil. Wash your hands and any other exposed skin areas as soon as possible after exposure to used engine oil. Soap and water, or waterless hand cleaner should be used.

5. Remove the exhaust cross-over pipe.
6. Remove the left engine-to-transmission strut.
7. Remove the bolts and lower the oil pan.
8. Thoroughly clean the gasket mating surfaces.
9. When installing the pan, always use new gaskets coated with sealer. Apply a drop of RTV silicone sealer where the cork and rubber gaskets meet. Torque the oil pan bolts to 15 ft. lbs. Tighten the cross-over pipe to 24 ft. lbs.

318 and 360 Engines
▶ See Figure 51

1. Disconnect the battery ground cable.
2. Remove the oil dipstick.
3. Raise and support the front end on jackstands.
4. Drain the oil.

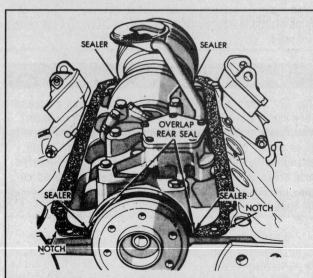

Fig. 51 Oil pan gasket installation on the 318 and 360 engines

✱✱ CAUTION

The EPA warns that prolonged contact with used engine oil may cause a number of skin disorders, including cancer! You should make every effort to minimize your exposure to used engine oil. Protective gloves should be worn when changing the oil. Wash your hands and any other exposed skin areas as soon as possible after exposure to used engine oil. Soap and water, or waterless hand cleaner should be used.

5. Remove the exhaust cross-over pipe.
6. On 1979 and later trucks, remove the left engine-to-transmission strut.
7. If equipped with an automatic transmission, remove torque converter inspection cover.
8. Remove the bolts and lower the oil pan.
9. Thoroughly clean the gasket mating surfaces.
10. When installing the pan, always use new gaskets coated with sealer. Apply a drop of RTV silicone sealer where the cork and rubber gaskets meet. On the 360 engine, make sure the gasket notches are positioned as shown. On trucks through 1977, the oil strainer must be parallel with the bottom of the pan and must touch the pan with a $1/16$–$1/8$" interference fit. Torque the oil pan bolts to 15 ft. lbs. Tighten the cross-over pipe to 24 ft. lbs.

400 and 440 Engines

1. Disconnect the battery ground cable.
2. Remove the oil dipstick.
3. Raise and support the front end on jackstands.
4. Drain the oil.

5. Remove the bolts and lower the oil pan.
6. Thoroughly clean the gasket mating surfaces.
7. When installing the pan, always use new gaskets coated with sealer. Apply a drop of RTV silicone sealer where the cork and rubber gaskets meet. The oil strainer must be parallel with the bottom of the pan and must touch the pan with a ¹⁄₁₆–⅛″ interference fit. Torque the oil pan bolts to 15 ft. lbs. Tighten the cross-over pipe to 24 ft. lbs.

Oil Pump

REMOVAL & INSTALLATION

170, 198 and 225 Engines

▶ See Figure 52

The rotor type of pump is externally mounted on the rear right-hand (camshaft) side of the engine and is gear driven (helical) from the camshaft. The oil filter screws into the pump body.

1. Remove the outer cover and catch the rotor, as it will fall. Remove oil pump mounting bolts and remove pump and filter assembly from engine.
2. Disassemble the oil pump (drive gear must be pressed off) and inspect the following clearances: maximum cover wear is 0.0015″; outer rotor to body maximum clearance is 0.014″; maximum clearance between rotors is 0.010″. Inspect the pressure relief valve for scoring and free operation. Relief valve spring should have a free length of 2¼″.

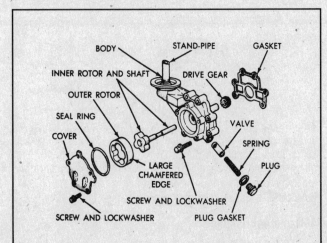

Fig. 52 Exploded view of the inline 6-cylinder engine oil pump

3. Install oil pump to engine block using a new gasket and tightening mounting bolts to 200 in. lbs.
4. Install new oil seal rings between cover and body, tightening cover attaching bolts to 95 in. lbs.

Diesel Engine

1. Remove the oil pan.
2. Remove the oil pickup tube, strainer and all old gaskets.
3. Remove the oil pump joint bolt.
4. Remove the filter assembly-to-oil pump tube.
5. Remove the joint bolt and remove the oil pump and gasket.
6. Clean all gasket surfaces. Discard all old gaskets.
7. Remove the oil pump cover.
8. Remove the inner rotor and shaft assembly and lift out the outer rotor.
9. Clean all parts thoroughly. Mating surfaces of the pump should be smooth. Replace the cover if it is scratched or grooved.
10. Install the outer rotor into the pump body. Install the inner rotor onto the outer rotor and seat it into the pump body. Place a straight edge across the pump face. Insert a feeler gauge between the straight edge and the rotors. Clearance should be 0.035–0.095mm. If clearance exceeds 0.15mm replace both the inner and outer rotors. Check the clearance between the inner and outer rotor. Clearance should be 0.17mm or less. If clearance exceeds 0.25mm replace both the inner and outer rotors. Measure the clearance between the outer rotor and the pump body. Clearance should be 0.2–0.3mm. If clearance exceeds 0.5mm replace the outer rotor. Measure the rotor shaft OD and the pump body ID. The clearance between the shaft and the body should be 0.032–0.074mm. If clearance exceeds 0.15mm replace the inner rotor and shaft and/or the pump body.
11. Replace all parts that show signs of wear.
12. Assemble the pump.
13. Use all new gaskets.
14. Install the oil pump and gasket.
15. Install the filter assembly-to-oil pump tube.
16. Install the oil pump joint bolt. Torque the bolt to 39 ft. lbs.
17. Install the oil pickup tube and strainer.
18. Install the oil pan.

238, 318 and 360 Engines

▶ See Figures 53 thru 59

➡ It is necessary to remove the oil pan, and to remove the oil pump from the rear main bearing cap to service the oil pump.

1. Drain the engine oil and remove the oil pan.

2. Remove the oil pump mounting bolts and remove the oil pump from the rear main bearing cap.

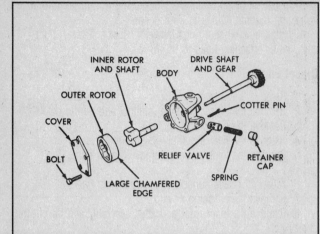

Fig. 53 Exploded view of the 238, 318 and 360 engines oil pump

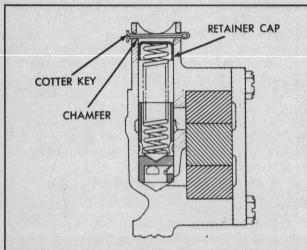

Fig. 54 Pressure relief valve, spring and retainer cup installation on the V6 and V8 engines

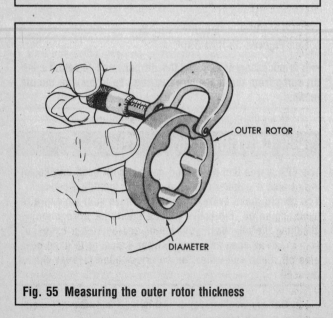

Fig. 55 Measuring the outer rotor thickness

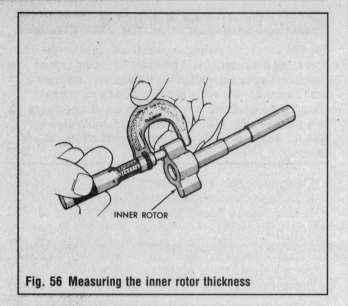

Fig. 56 Measuring the inner rotor thickness

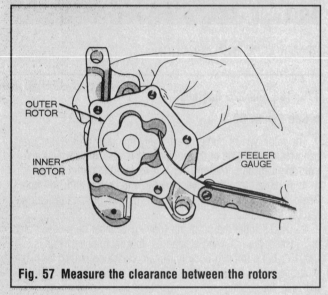

Fig. 57 Measure the clearance between the rotors

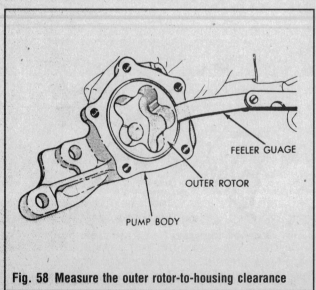

Fig. 58 Measure the outer rotor-to-housing clearance

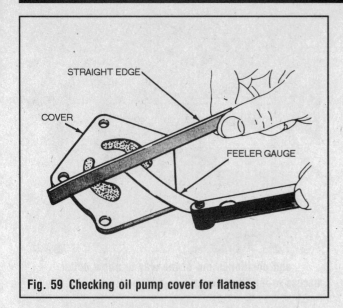

Fig. 59 Checking oil pump cover for flatness

3. To remove the relief valve, drill a ⅛" hole into the relief valve retainer cap and insert a self-threading sheet metal screw into the cap. Clamp the screw into a vise and while supporting the oil pump, remove the cap by tapping the pump body using a soft hammer. Discard the retainer cap and remove the spring and the relief valve.

4. Remove the oil pump cover and lockwashers, and lift off the cover. Discard the oil ring seal. Remove the pump rotor and shaft, and lift out the outer rotor.

➡ Wash all parts in solvent and inspect for damage or wear. The mating surfaces of the oil pump cover should be smooth. Replace the pump assembly if this is not the case.

5. Lay a straight edge across the pump cover surface and if a 0.0015" feeler gauge can be inserted between the cover and the straight edge, the pump assembly should be replaced. Measure the thickness and the diameter of the outer rotor. If the outer rotor thickness measures 0.825" or less, (0.943" or less on 360 cu.in. engines 1977–88) or if the diameter is 2.469" or less, replace the outer rotor. If the inner rotor measures 0.825" or less, (0.943" or less on 360 cu.in. engines 1977–88) then the inner rotor and shaft assembly must be replaced.

6. Slide the outer rotor into the pump body, do this by pressing it to one side with your fingers and measure the clearance between the rotor and the pump body. If the measurement is 0.014" or more, replace the oil pump assembly. Install the inner rotor and shaft into the pump body. If the clearance between the inner and outer rotors is 0.010" or more, replace the shaft and both rotors.

7. Place a straightedge across the face of the pump, between the bolt holes. If a feeler gauge of 0.004" or more can be inserted between the rotors and the straight edge, replace the pump assembly.

8. Inspect the oil pressure relief valve plunger for scoring and free operation in its bore. Small marks may be removed with 400-grit wet or dry sandpaper.

9. The relief valve spring has a free length of 2¹⁄₃₂–2³⁄₆₄" and should test between 16.2 and 17.2 lbs. when compressed to 1¹¹⁄₃₂". Replace the spring if it fails to meet this specification.

10. To install, assemble the oil pump, using new parts as required. Tighten the cover bolts to 95 in. lbs.

11. Prime the oil pump before installation by filling the rotor cavity with engine oil. Install the oil pump on the engine and tighten attaching bolts to 30 ft. lbs.

12. Install the oil pan.

13. Fill the engine with the proper grade motor oil. Start the engine and check for leaks.

400 and 440 Engines
▸ See Figure 60

The rotor type oil pump is externally mounted and gear driven from the camshaft. The oil filters screws into the pump body.

1. Drain engine oil.

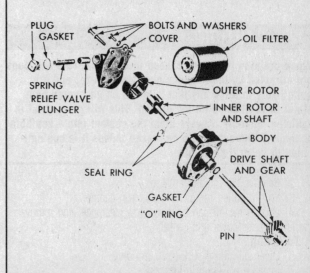

Fig. 60 Exploded view of the 400 and 440 engine oil pump

✳✳ CAUTION

The EPA warns that prolonged contact with used engine oil may cause a number of skin disorders, including cancer! You should make every effort to minimize your exposure to used engine oil. Protective gloves should be worn when changing the oil. Wash your hands and any other exposed skin areas as soon as possible after exposure to used engine oil. Soap and water, or waterless hand cleaner should be used.

2. Remove oil pump and filter assembly.

3. Disassemble and inspect pump components for wear. Of 0.0015" feeler gauge can be inserted between cover and straight edge, replace cover. Install outer rotor in pump body and holding against one side of body measure clearance between rotor and body. If clearance is greater than 0.014", replace oil pump body. Install inner rotor into pump body and place straight edge across pump body between bolt holes. If feeler gauge is greater than 0.004" can be inserted between rotors and body, replace oil pump body. Measure clearance between tips of inner and outer rotor where they are opposed. If clearance exceeds 0.010", replace inner and outer rotors. Use new oil seal rings between filter base and body. Tighten bolts to 10 ft. lbs. Use a new O-ring seal on pilot of oil pump before attaching pump to engine block.

4. Install oil pump on engine using new gasket and tightening bolts to 30 ft. lbs. The distributor drive gear slot should parallel the crankshaft with no.1 cylinder on TDC.

5. Install oil filter and fill crankcase with oil.

Front Cover

REMOVAL & INSTALLATION

Inline 6-Cylinder Engines

1. Drain the cooling system and disconnect the battery.

✳✳ CAUTION

When draining the coolant, keep in mind that cats and dogs are attracted by the ethylene glycol antifreeze, and are quite likely to drink any that is left in an uncovered container or in puddles on the ground. This will prove fatal in sufficient quantity. Always drain the coolant into a sealable container. Coolant should be reused unless it is contaminated or several years old.

2. Remove the radiator and fan.
3. With a puller, remove the vibration damper.
4. Loosen the oil pan bolts to allow clearance, and remove the timing case cover and gasket.

To install:

5. Clean all gasket surfaces thoroughly.
6. Install a new seal in the case.
7. Install the timing case cover with a new gasket and torque the bolts to 17 ft. lbs. Retighten the engine oil pan to 17 ft. lbs. Always use a centering tool to ensure that the seal will not be damaged and that it is properly aligned.
8. Press the vibration damper back on.
9. Replace the radiator and hoses.
10. Refill the cooling system.

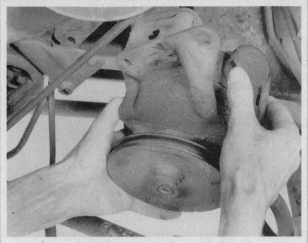

. . . and positioned out of the way to allow better access to the front cover

Remove all of the accessory belts. If equipped, remove the three pulley attaching bolts . . .

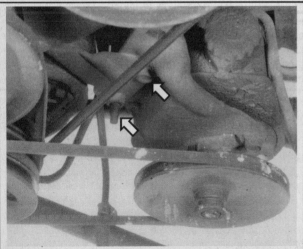

Although it is not necessary, the power steering pump can be unbolted (arrows) . . .

. . . and remove the pulley

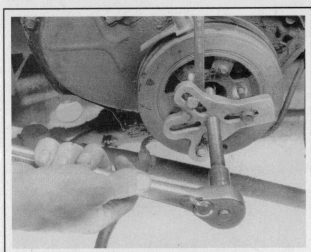

Attach a puller onto the crankshaft dampener. Use a pry bar to prevent the engine from turning

. . . and the front cover-to-engine block retaining bolts

Once loosened, remove the dampener from the crankshaft

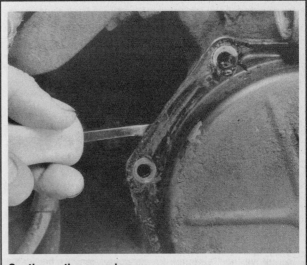

Gently pry the cover loose . . .

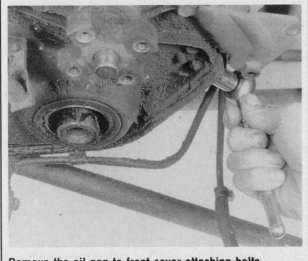

Remove the oil pan-to-front cover attaching bolts . . .

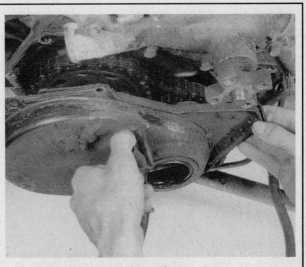

. . . and pull it free of the engine

V6 and V8 Engines

1. Disconnect the battery and drain the cooling system. Remove the radiator.

✳✳ CAUTION

When draining the coolant, keep in mind that cats and dogs are attracted by the ethylene glycol antifreeze, and are quite likely to drink any that is left in an uncovered container or in puddles on the ground. This will prove fatal in sufficient quantity. Always drain the coolant into a sealable container. Coolant should be reused unless it is contaminated or several years old.

2. Remove the water pump.
3. Remove the power steering pump.
4. Remove the crankshaft pulley.
5. Remove the vibration damper with a puller. On 318 and 360 engines, remove the fuel lines and fuel pump, then loosen the oil pan bolts and remove the front bolt on each side.

Loosen and remove the crankshaft balancer retaining bolt

To remove the V8 engine timing cover, remove the water pump, then unbolt the crankshaft pulley

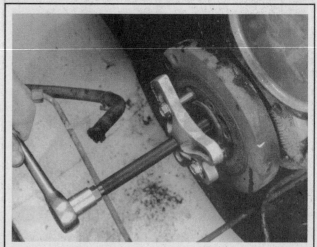

Use a threaded puller to remove the balancer from the crankshaft

To ease assembly, align the TDC mark on the pulley to the 0° mark on the cover

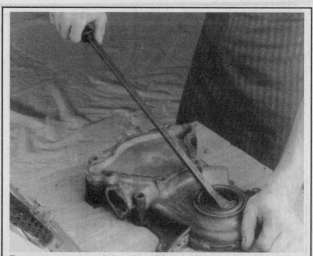

Remove any remaining attaching bolts and remove the cover

6. Remove the timing gear cover and the crankshaft oil slinger.

To install:

7. Clean all gasket surfaces thoroughly.

8. Install a new seal in the case.

9. Install the timing case cover with a new gasket. A ⅛″ bead of RTV sealer is recommended on the oil pan gasket. Torque the cover bolts to 30 ft. lbs. Retighten the engine oil pan to 17 ft. lbs. Always use a centering tool to ensure that the seal will not be damaged and that it is properly aligned.

Position a new gasket onto the timing cover and coat with a bead of sealer

Also, use a bead of sealer on the oil pan gasket mating surfaces

10. Lubricate the seal lip with lithium white grease and slide the damper back into position. Using tool C-3688, press the damper onto the shaft. Torque the bolt to 135 ft. lbs.

11. Install the fuel pump and lines.

12. Install the water pump.

13. Install the power steering pump.

14. Replace the radiator and hoses.

15. Tighten all drive belts.

Diesel Engine

1. Disconnect the battery ground cable.

2. Drain the cooling system.

✳✳ CAUTION

When draining the coolant, keep in mind that cats and dogs are attracted by the ethylene glycol antifreeze, and are quite likely to drink any that is left in an uncovered container or in puddles on the ground. This will prove fatal in sufficient quantity. Always drain the coolant into a sealable container. Coolant should be reused unless it is contaminated or several years old.

3. Remove the upper and lower hoses.

4. Disconnect the overflow tank.

5. Remove the automatic transmission oil cooler lines and bracket.

6. Loosen the radiator mount bolts.

7. Remove the fan.

8. Remove the rubber shield from between the radiator and grille.

9. Remove the radiator and fan shroud.

10. Remove all drive belts.

11. Remove the crankshaft pulley nut.

12. Turn the crankshaft until the keyway is at the 12 o'clock position.

13. Remove the crankshaft pulley and damper assembly with tool MH-061101.

14. Remove the timing gear case and gasket.

15. Remove the front oil seal from the case.

To install:

16. Coat a new timing case gasket with sealer and position it over the dowels on the block.

17. Install the timing gear case. Torque the bolts to 84 in. lb. (7 ft. lbs.).

18. Install the crankshaft pulley and damper assembly. Be careful to avoid damage to the seal.

19. Install the the crankshaft pulley cone and nut. Torque the nut to 290 ft. lbs.

20. Install all drive belts.

21. Install the radiator and fan shroud. Tighten the lower radiator mounting nuts finger-tight.

22. Install the rubber shield between the radiator and grille.

23. Install the fan.

24. Align the radiator and tighten the radiator mount bolts.

25. Install the automatic transmission oil cooler lines and bracket.

26. Connect the overflow tank.

27. Install the upper and lower hoses.

28. Fill the cooling system.

29. Connect the battery ground cable.

Front Cover Seal

REMOVAL & INSTALLATION

◆ See Figures 61 and 62

➡A seal remover and installer tool is required to prevent seal damage.

1. Using a seal puller, separate the seal from the retainer.
2. Pull the seal from the case.

To install:

3. To install the seal place it face down in the case with the seal lips downward.
4. Seat the seal tightly against the cover face. There should be a maximum clearance of 0.0014″ between the seal and the cover. Be careful not to over-compress the seal.

Timing Chain

REMOVAL & INSTALLATION

Inline 6-Cylinder Engines

◆ See Figure 63

1. Remove the front cover.
2. Slide the crankshaft oil slinger off the front of the crankshaft.
3. Remove the camshaft sprocket bolt.
4. Remove the timing chain with the camshaft sprocket.

To install:

5. Turn the crankshaft to line up the timing mark on the crankshaft sprocket with the centerline of the camshaft (without the chain).

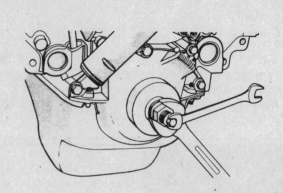

Fig. 62 Installing a new front seal on the 238, 318 and 360 engines—cover installed

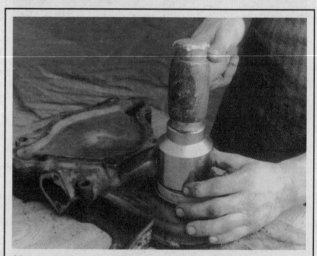

After removing the old seal, use a large socket and a hammer to install the new seal

6. Install the camshaft sprocket and chain. Align the timing marks.
7. Torque the camshaft sprocket bolt to 35 ft. lbs.
8. Replace the oil slinger.
9. Install the timing case cover.

V6 and V8 Engines

◆ See Figure 64

1. Remove the front cover.
2. On 318 and 360 engines, remove the cam shaft sprocket lockbolt, securing cup washer, and fuel pump eccentric. Remove the timing chain with both sprockets. On 400 and 440 engines, remove the camshaft sprocket lockbolt and remove the timing chain with the camshaft and crankshaft sprockets.
3. To begin the installation procedure, place the camshaft and crankshaft sprockets on a flat surface with the timing indicators on an imaginary centerline through both sprocket boxes. Place the timing chain around both sprockets. Be sure that the timing marks are in alignment.

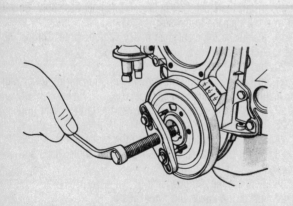

Fig. 61 Removing the front seal on the 238, 318 and 360 engines—cover installed

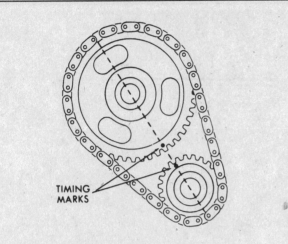

Fig. 63 Timing mark alignment on inline 6-cylinder engines

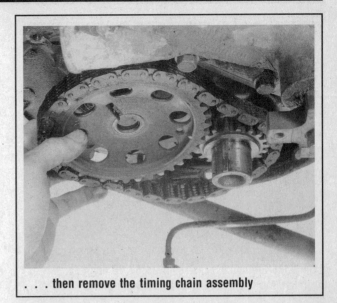

. . . then remove the timing chain assembly

✳✳ CAUTION

When installing the timing chain, have an assistant support the camshaft with a suitable tool to prevent it from contacting the plug in the rear of the engine block. Remove the distributor and the oil pump/distributor drive gear. Position the suitable tool against the rear side of the cam gear and be careful not to damage the cam lobes.

4. Turn the crankshaft and camshaft to align them with the keyway location in the crankshaft sprocket and the keyway or dowel hole in the camshaft sprocket.

5. Lift the sprockets and timing chain while keeping the sprockets tight against the chain in the correct position. Slide both sprockets evenly onto their respective shafts.

6. Use a straightedge to measure the alignment of the sprocket timing marks. They must be perfectly aligned.

7. On 318 and 360 engines, install the fuel pump eccentric, cup washer, and camshaft sprocket lockbolt and torque to 35 ft.

Before removing the timing chain assembly, align the timing marks on the gears (arrows)

Loosen and remove the camshaft sprocket bolt . . .

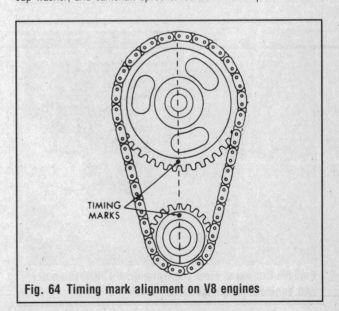

Fig. 64 Timing mark alignment on V8 engines

Once the timing cover is removed on V8 engines, remove the upper timing gear retaining bolt . . .

When removing and installing the chain, make sure the timing marks are in alignment

. . . and the fuel pump eccentric

Always double check timing mark alignment before installing the cover

Remove the chain assembly by hand; DO NOT use a pry tool as you can damage the assembly

lbs. If camshaft end-play exceeds 0.010″, install a new thrust plate. It should be 0.002–0.006″ with the new plate.

On 400 and 440 engines, install the washer and camshaft sprocket lockbolt(s) and then torque the lockbolt to 35–40 ft. lbs. Check to make sure that the rear face of the camshaft sprocket is flush with the camshaft end.

CHECKING TIMING CHAIN SLACK

▶ **See Figures 65 and 66**

1. Position a scale (ruler or straightedge) next to the timing chain to detect any movement in the chain.
2. Place a torque wrench and socket on the camshaft sprocket attaching bolt. Apply either 30 ft. lbs. (if the cylinder heads are installed on the engine) or 15 ft. lbs. (cylinder heads removed) of force to the bolt and rotate the bolt in the direction of crankshaft rotation in order to remove all slack from the chain.

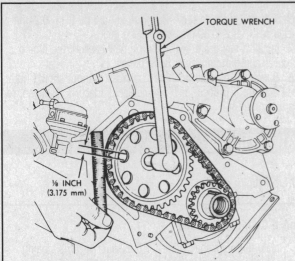

Fig. 65 Measuring the timing chain slack on inline 6-cylinder engines

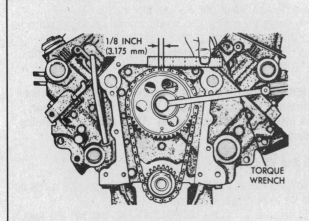

Fig. 66 Measuring the timing chain slack on V6 and V8 engines

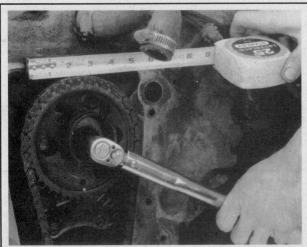

Measure the timing chain wear on V6 and V8 engines—if wear exceeds 1/8 in. replace the chain

3. While applying torque to the camshaft sprocket bolt, the crankshaft should not be allowed to rotate. It may be necessary to block the crankshaft to prevent rotation.

4. Position the scale over the edge of a timing chain link and apply an equal amount of torque in the opposite direction. If the movement of the chain exceeds 1/8", replace the chain.

Timing Gears

REMOVAL & INSTALLATION

Diesel Engine

▶ **See Figures 67 and 68**

1. Remove the timing gear cover, the gasket and the front seal.
2. Remove the idler pulley bracket.
3. Align the timing marks.
4. Using a puller, remove the camshaft drive gear.
5. Turn the injection pump to allow the notch in the drive gear to pass by the idler gear teeth.
6. Loosen the idler gear mounting bolt. Remove the thrust plate and remove the idler gear.
7. Disconnect the injection lines at the pump.
8. Disconnect the fuel line at the transfer pump and cap all openings.
9. Disconnect the transfer pump-to-filter hose.
10. Disconnect the filter-to-injection pump hose.
11. Loosen the stay bolt on the back of the injection pump. Remove the pump and automatic timing gear, and the flange, by pulling toward the back of the engine.
12. Inspect all parts for wear or damage. Replace any suspect parts.

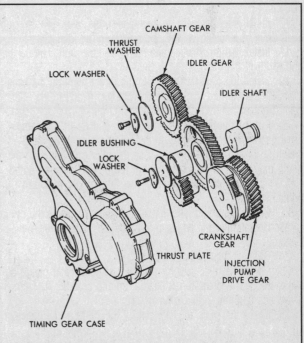

Fig. 67 Diesel engine timing gear cover and gear system

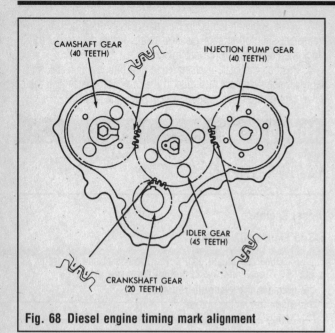

CAMSHAFT GEAR
(40 TEETH)

INJECTION PUMP GEAR
(40 TEETH)

IDLER GEAR
(45 TEETH)

CRANKSHAFT GEAR
(20 TEETH)

Fig. 68 Diesel engine timing mark alignment

13. Put the camshaft gear back on the shaft and check for shaft end-play with a dial indicator. End-play should be 0.05–0.22mm. If end-play exceeds the limit of 0.30mm, replace the thrust plate.

14. Check the idler gear and shaft to make sure that the oil passage is open.

15. Measure the inside diameter of the idler bushing and the outside diameter of the idler shaft. ID should be 40.000–40.025mm. OD should be 39.950–39.975mm. Idler shaft-to-bushing clearance should be 0.025–0.075mm. If the clearance exceeds 0.100mm, replace the bushing. Use bushing replacer tool MH-061228.

16. Be sure that the crankshaft is set with no.1 cylinder at TDC.

17. Install the idler gear on the shaft so the marks on the camshaft drive gear match up with the marks on the idler gear.

18. Install the thrust plate and the hold-down bolt. Torque the bolt to 25 ft. lbs.

19. Install the camshaft gear and the thrust plate on the camshaft. Be sure all the marks line up with the marks on the idler gear. Tighten the hold-down bolt to 12 ft. lbs.

20. Put the injection pump in position and mesh the pump drive gear with the idler gear so the marks on the drive gear match up properly with the marks on the idler gear. Be sure the pump mounting flange scale is set at the proper injection point.

21. Install the mounting nuts on the timing gear case and tighten them.

22. Connect the fuel feed line and the filter hoses to the pump.

23. Operate the primer pump to bleed the air from the fuel system.

24. Connect the injector pipes.

25. Check the idler gear for end-play using a feeler gauge between the gear and the thrust plate. It should be 0.05–0.15mm. If it exceeds 0.35mm, replace the thrust plate.

26. Check the gears for backlash by mounting a dial indicator so that lash is measured from the gear tooth profile at right angles to the gear shaft. When checking lash between the idler

gear and injection pump drive gear, be sure that the stay bolt at the back of the pump is tight. Backlash should be 0.11–0.24mm. If backlash exceeds 0.30mm, replace the gear.

27. Install a new front seal (using a new gasket), the timing gear cover and the crankshaft drive pulley.

28. Check the oil seal and cone surfaces. Runout should not exceed 0.5mm. If it does, or if any contact surface is damaged, replace the pulley.

Valve Timing

CHECKING

Inline 6-Cylinder Engines

1. Rotate the crankshaft until no. 6 exhaust valve is closing and no. 6 intake valve is opening.

2. Install a dial indicator so that the indicator pointer contact the valve spring retainer on the no. 1 intake valve parallel to the axis of the valve stem.

3. Turn no. 1 intake adjusting screw in one complete turn to remove the lash. Adjust the dial indicator to zero.

4. Rotate the crankshaft clockwise normal running direction until the valve has lifted 0.029″.

5. The timing of the crankshaft pulley should now read from 12° BTDC to DC. Re-adjust lash.

➡**If the reading is not within specified limits, inspect the sprocket index marks, inspect the timing chain for wear, and inspect the accuracy of the "TDC" mark on the timing indicator.**

V6 and V8 Engines

1. Turn the crankshaft until the No. 6 exhaust valve is closing and the intake valve is opening.

2. Insert a ¼″ spacer between the rocker arm pad and stem tip of No. 1 intake valve. Allow the spring load to bleed the tappet down.

3. Install a dial indicator so that the plunger contacts the valve spring retainer and nearly perpendicular as possible. Zero the indicator.

4. Rotate the crankshaft clockwise until the valve has lifted 0.010″ on the 318; 034″ on the 360; 0.025″ on the 400 and 440.

Diesel Engine

Valve timing is accomplished by simply aligning all gear timing marks as illustrated.

❋❋ WARNING

Do not rotate the crankshaft any further, as serious damage will result!

5. The ignition timing marks should now read anywhere from 10°BTDC to 2°ATDC.

6. If the reading is not within specifications, check for timing amrk alignment, timing chain wear and the accuracy of the ignition timing indicator.

Idler Shaft

REMOVAL & INSTALLATION

Diesel Engine

1. Remove the timing gear cover, the gasket and the front seal. Remove the idler pulley bracket.

2. Align the timing marks.

3. Using a puller, remove the camshaft drive gear.

4. Turn the injection pump to allow the notch in the drive gear to pass by the idler gear teeth.

5. Loosen the idler gear mounting bolt. Remove the thrust plate and remove the idler gear.

6. Using puller MH-061077, remove the idler shaft from the block.

7. The idler gear is installed with a brass drift and soft hammer.

8. Install the idler gear on the shaft so that the timing marks are aligned.

9. Install the thrust plate and torque the bolt to 25 ft. lbs.

10. Check the idler gear end-play at the thrust plate. End-play can be measured with a flat feeler gauge. End-play should be 0.05–0.15mm. If the end-play exceeds 0.35mm, you must replace the thrust plate.

11. Check the idler gear backlash at the injection pump gear. Backlash should be 0.11–0.24mm. If the backlash exceeds 0.30mm, replace the idler gear.

Camshaft and Bearings

REMOVAL & INSTALLATION

Gasoline Engines

INLINE 6-CYLINDER ENGINE

▶ **See Figures 69 and 70**

1. Remove the cylinder head, timing gear cover, camshaft sprocket, and timing chain.

2. Remove the valve tappets, keeping them in order to ensure installation in their original locations.

3. Remove the camshaft sprocket.

4. Remove the distributor and oil pump.

5. Remove the fuel pump.

6. Install a long bolt into the front of the camshaft to facilitate its removal.

7. Remove the camshaft, being careful not to damage the cam bearings with the cam lobes.

8. Prior to installation, lubricate the camshaft lobes and bearing journals. It is recommended that 1 pt. of crankcase conditioner be added to the initial crankcase oil fill.

9. Install the camshaft in the engine block. From this point, reverse the removal procedure.

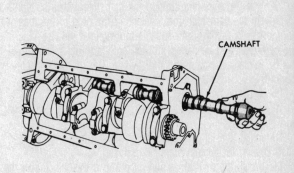

Fig. 69 Removing the camshaft from the inline 6-cylinder engine—engine removed

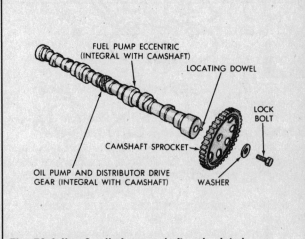

Fig. 70 Inline 6-cylinder camshaft and related components

V6 AND V8 ENGINES

▶ **See Figures 71, 72 73, 74 and 75**

1. Remove the intake manifold, cylinder head covers, rocker arm assemblies, pushrods, and valve tappets, keeping them in order to insure the installation in their original locations.

2. Remove the timing gear cover, the camshaft and the crankshaft sprockets, and the timing chain.

3. Remove the distributor and lift out the oil pump and distributor driveshaft. On 400 and 440 cu.in. engines, remove the fuel pump to allow the pushrod to drop away from the cam eccentric.

4. Remove the camshaft thrust plate (on 318 and 360).

5. Install a long bolt into the front of the camshaft and remove the camshaft, being careful not to damage the cam bearings with the cam lobes.

6. Prior to installation, lubricate the camshaft lobes and bearings journals. It is recommended that 1 pt. of Crankcase Condi-

tioner be added to the initial crankcase oil fill. Insert the camshaft into the engine block within 2″ of its final position in the block.

7. Have an assistant support the camshaft with a suitable tool to prevent the camshaft from contacting the plug in the rear of the engine block. Position the suitable tool against the rear side of the cam gear and be careful not to damage the cam lobes.

8. Replace the camshaft thrust plate. If camshaft end-play exceeds 0.010″, install a new thrust plate. It should be 0.002–0.006″ with the new plate.

9. Install the timing chain and sprockets, timing gear cover, and pulley.

10. Install the tappets, pushrods, rocker arms, and cylinder head covers. Install fuel pump, if removed.

11. Install the distributor and oil pump driveshaft, Install the distributor.

12. After starting the engine, adjust the ignition timing.

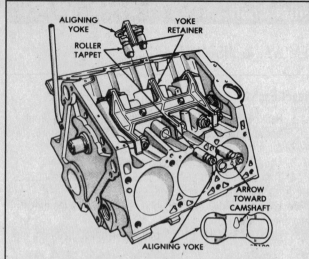

Fig. 73 Roller valve tappet installation on the 238 engine—V8 engines are similar

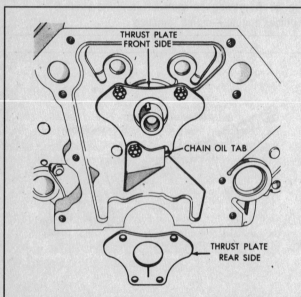

Fig. 71 Camshaft thrust plate on the V6 and V8 engines—note the position of the timing chain oil tab for installation

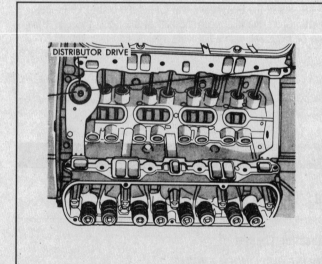

Fig. 74 Distributor drive gear positioning

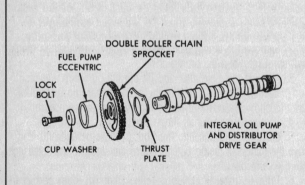

Fig. 72 Camshaft and related components for the 238 engine—V8 engines are similar

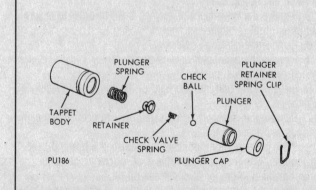

Fig. 75 Exploded view of the hydraulic flat valve tappet used in most engines

Diesel Engine

1. Remove the timing gear cover, the gasket and the front seal.
2. Remove the idler pulley bracket.
3. Align the timing marks.
4. Using a puller, remove the camshaft drive gear.
5. Remove the camshaft thrust plate.
6. Remove the cylinder head.
7. Using a magnet, remove the tappets, keeping them in order.
8. Drain the cooling system and remove the radiator.

✳✳ CAUTION

When draining the coolant, keep in mind that cats and dogs are attracted by the ethylene glycol antifreeze, and are quite likely to drink any that is left in an uncovered container or in puddles on the ground. This will prove fatal in sufficient quantity. Always drain the coolant into a sealable container. Coolant should be reused unless it is contaminated or several years old.

9. If equipped with air conditioning, remove the condenser. See Chapter 1.
10. Carefully slide the camshaft from the block.
11. Be sure that the crankshaft is set with no. 1 cylinder at TDC. Torque the bolt to 25 ft. lbs.
12. Coat the camshaft with engine oil and carefully slide it into place. Don't damage the bearings.
13. Install the tappets and assemble the cylinder head.
14. Install the camshaft gear and the thrust plate on the camshaft. Be sure all the marks line up with the marks on the idler gear. Tighten the hold-down bolt to 12 ft. lbs.
15. Put the injection pump in position and mesh the pump drive gear with the idler gear so the marks on the drive gear match up properly with the marks on the idler gear. Be sure the pump mounting flange scale is set at the proper injection point.
16. Install the mounting nuts on the timing gear case and tighten them.
17. Connect the fuel feed line and the filter hoses to the pump.
18. Operate the primer pump to bleed the air from the fuel system.
19. Connect the injector pipes.
20. Check the idler gear for end-play using a feeler gauge between the gear and the thrust plate. It should be 0.05–0.15mm. If it exceeds 0.35mm, replace the thrust plate.
21. Check the gears for backlash by mounting a dial indicator so that lash is measured from the gear tooth profile at right angles to the gear shaft. When checking lash between the idler gear and injection pump drive gear, be sure that the stay bolt at the back of the pump is tight. Backlash should be 0.11–0.24mm. If backlash exceeds 0.30mm, replace the gear.
22. Install a new front seal (using a new gasket), the timing gear cover and the crankshaft drive pulley.
23. Check the oil seal and cone surfaces. Runout should not exceed 0.5mm. If it does, or if any contact surface is damaged, replace the pulley.
24. Install the radiator and condenser.
25. Fill the cooling system and crankcase.

INSPECTION

Gasoline Engines

CAMSHAFT LOBE LIFT

Check the lift of each lobe in consecutive order and make a note of the reading.

1. Remove the fresh air inlet tube and the air cleaner. Remove the heater hose and crankcase ventilation hoses. Remove valve rocker arm cover(s).
2. Remove the rocker arm stud nut or fulcrum bolts, fulcrum seat and rocker arm.
3. Make sure the pushrod is in the valve tappet socket. Install a dial indicator so that the actuating point of the indicator is in the pushrod socket (or the indicator ball socket adaptor is on the end of the pushrod) and in the same plane as the pushrod movement.
4. Disconnect the I terminal and the S terminal at the starter relay. Install an auxiliary starter switch between the battery and S terminals of the start relay. Crank the engine with the ignition switch off. Turn the crankshaft over until the tappet is on the base circle of the camshaft lobe. At this position, the pushrod will be in its lowest position.
5. Zero the dial indicator. Continue to rotate the crankshaft slowly until the pushrod is in the fully raised position.
6. Compare the total lift recorded on the dial indicator with the specification shown on the Camshaft Specification chart.

To check the accuracy of the original indicator reading, continue to rotate the crankshaft until the indicator reads zero. If the left on any lobe is below specified wear limits listed, the camshaft and the valve tappet operating on the worn lobe(s) must be replaced.

7. Install the dial indicator and auxiliary starter switch.
8. Install the rocker arm, fulcrum seat and stud nut or fulcrum bolts. Check the valve clearance. Adjust if required (refer to procedure in this chapter).
9. Install the valve rocker arm cover(s) and the air cleaner.

CAMSHAFT END-PLAY

➥**On all gasoline V8 engines, prying against the aluminum-nylon camshaft sprocket, with the valve train load on the camshaft, can break or damage the sprocket. Therefore, the rocker arm adjusting nuts must be backed off, or the rocker arm and shaft assembly must be loosened sufficiently to free the camshaft. After checking the camshaft end-play, check the valve clearance. Adjust if required (refer to procedure in this chapter).**

1. Push the camshaft toward the rear of the engine. Install a dial indicator so that the indicator point is on the camshaft sprocket attaching screw.
2. Zero the dial indicator. Position a prybar between the camshaft gear and the block. Pull the camshaft forward and release it. Compare the dial indicator reading with the specifications.
3. If the end-play is excessive, check the spacer for correct installation before it is removed. If the spacer is correctly installed, replace the thrust plate.
4. Remove the dial indicator.

Diesel Engines

1. Check the runout with a dial indicator. Support journals 1 and 4 on V-blocks and set the dial indicator on 2 and 3. Runout should be less than 0.02mm. If runout exceeds 0.05mm, replace the camshaft.

2. Check the cam profile by measuring the cam long and short diameters with a micrometer. Inspect the cam profile for wear or damage. The long diameter should measure 46.615mm; the short diameter should measure 39.426mm. If the cam profile is worn or damaged, or the diameters differ from standard by 0.5mm or more, replace the camshaft.

3. Check the camshaft journals for damage and wear. If excessively worn or damaged, the camshaft must be replaced.

4. Check the journal ODs as given in the chart. Check the bearing IDs and figure the clearances. Clearances are given in the charts.

CAMSHAFT BEARING REPLACEMENT

◆ **See Figures 76, 77, 78 and 79**

1. Remove the engine following the procedures in this chapter and install it on a work stand.

2. Remove the camshaft, flywheel and crankshaft, following the appropriate procedures. Push the pistons to the top of the cylinder.

3. Remove the camshaft rear bearing bore plug. Remove the camshaft bearings with a bearing removal tool.

➡**Diesel engines use tool MH-061070 for cam bearing removal and installation.**

4. Select the proper size expanding collet and back-up nut and assemble on the mandrel. With the expanding collet collapsed, install the collet assembly in the camshaft bearing and tighten the back-up nut on the expanding mandrel until the collet fits the camshaft bearing.

5. Assemble the puller screw and extension (if necessary) and install on the expanding mandrel. Wrap a cloth around the threads of the puller screw to protect the front bearing or journal. Tighten the pulling nut against the thrust bearing and pulling plate to re-

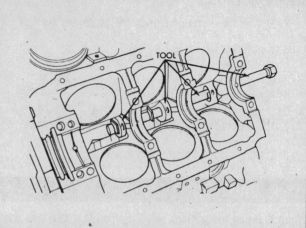

Fig. 77 Removal and installation of the camshaft bearings on the V6 engine

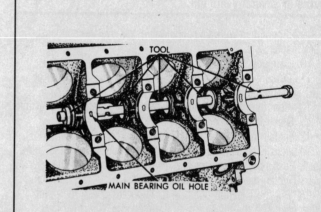

Fig. 78 Camshaft bearing removal and installation on the V8 engines

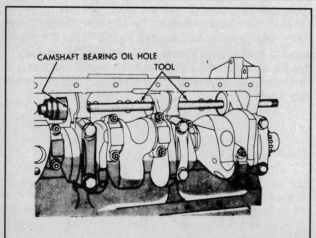

Fig. 76 Removing and installing the camshaft bearings on the inline 6-cylinder engines

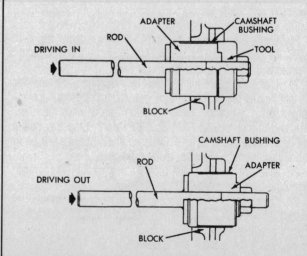

Fig. 79 Diesel engine camshaft bearing removal and installation

move the camshaft bearing. Be sure to hold a wrench on the end of the puller screw to prevent it from turning.

6. To remove the front bearing, install the puller from the rear of the cylinder block.

7. Position the new bearings at the bearing bores, and press them in place. Be sure to center the pulling plate and puller screw to avoid damage to the bearing. Failure to use the correct expanding collet can cause severe bearing damage. Align the oil holes in the bearings with the oil holes in the cylinder block before pressing bearings into place.

8. Install the camshaft rear bearing bore plug.

9. Install the camshaft, crankshaft, flywheel and related parts, following the appropriate procedures.

10. Install the engine in the truck, following procedures described earlier in this chapter.

Pistons and Connecting Rods

♦ See Figures 80 and 81

The notch on the top of each piston must face the front of the engine.

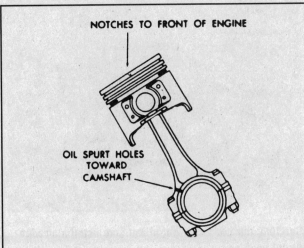

Fig. 80 Relationship of the piston and connecting rod on inline 6-cylinder engines

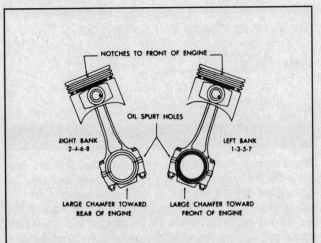

Fig. 81 Relationship of the piston and connecting rod on V8 engines

To position the connecting rod correctly, the oil squirt hole should point to the right side on all six-cylinder engines. On all V8 engines, the larger chamfer of the lower connecting rod bore must face to the rear on the right bank and to the front on the left bank.

REMOVAL

♦ See Figures 82, 83 and 84

All Gasoline Engines

1. Remove the cylinder head.
2. Remove the timing chain/gears.
3. Remove the oil pan.
4. Pistons should be removed following the firing order of the

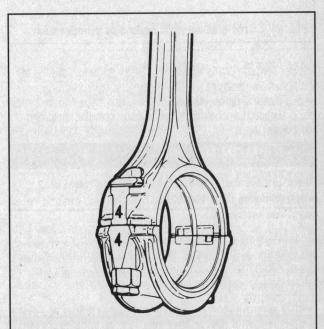

Fig. 82 Number each connecting rod and cap with its cylinder number for correct assembly

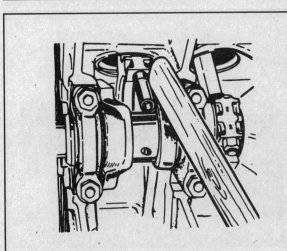

Fig. 83 Push the piston assembly out of the engine block with a hammer handle

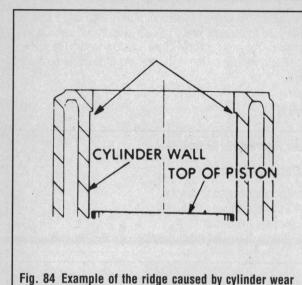

Fig. 84 Example of the ridge caused by cylinder wear

engine. Turn the crankshaft until the piston to be removed is at the bottom of its stroke.

5. Place a cloth on the head of the piston to be removed and, using a ridge reamer, remove the deposits from the upper end of the cylinder bore.

✳✳ WARNING

Never remove more than 1/32" from the ring travel area when removing the ridges!

6. Mark all connecting rod bearing caps so that they may be returned to their original locations in the engine. The connecting rod caps are usually marked. The marks must be matched when re-assembling the engine. Mark all pistons so they can be returned to their original cylinders.

➡ **After removing the connecting rod cap and bearing, place a short length of rubber hose over the rod bolts to prevent cylinder wall and crank journal scoring when removing or installing the piston and rod assembly.**

Place rubber hose over the connecting rod studs to protect the crank and bores from damage

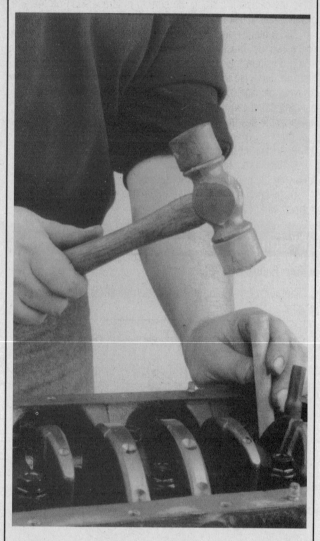

Carefully tap the piston out of the bore using a wooden dowel

7. Carefully tap the piston out of the bore using a wooden dowel. Once the piston rings have cleared the top edge of the bore, remove the piston assembly from the engine.

Diesel Engine

1. Disconnect the battery ground.
2. Drain the cooling system.

✳✳ CAUTION

When draining the coolant, keep in mind that cats and dogs are attracted by the ethylene glycol antifreeze, and are quite likely to drink any that is left in an uncovered container or in puddles on the ground. This will prove fatal in sufficient quantity. Always drain the coolant into a sealable container. Coolant should be reused unless it is contaminated or several years old.

3. Drain the oil.

4. Remove the dipstick and tube.

5. Remove the road draft tube.

6. Remove the automatic transmission cooling lines and bracket.

7. Remove the oil pan.

8. Remove the oil pick-up tube and gasket.

9. Turn the crankshaft until the connecting rod journal of the piston to be removed is at bottom center. Remove the connecting rod cap nuts. Install short pieces of hose on the studs to prevent journal damage. Mark the rod cap to ensure proper identification. Remove the cap and bearing inserts.

10. Remove the cylinder head.

11. Remove the ridge from the top of the sleeve with a ridge reamer.

12. Using a hardwood block, drive the piston up and out of the block.

PISTON RING & WRIST PIN REMOVAL

All of the gasoline engines covered in this guide utilize pressed-in wrist pins, which can only be removed by an arbor press. The diesel piston pins are removed in the same way, only the pistons are heated before the wrist pins are pressed out.

A piston ring expander is necessary for removing the piston rings without damaging them; any other method (screwdriver blades, pliers, etc.) usually results in the rings being bent, scratched or distorted, or the piston itself being damaged. When the rings are removed, clean the ring grooves using an appro-

Clean the piston grooves using a ring groove cleaner

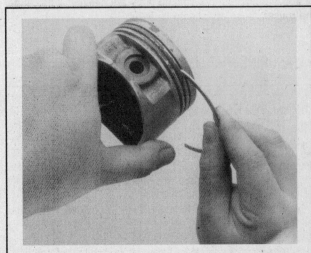

You can use a piece of an old ring to clean the piston grooves, BUT be careful, the ring is sharp

priate ring groove cleaning tool, using care not to cut too deeply. Thoroughly clean all carbon and varnish from the piston with solvent.

✳✳ WARNING

Do not use a wire brush or caustic solvent (acids, etc.) on pistons.

Inspect the pistons for scuffing, scoring, cracks, pitting, or excessive ring groove wear. If these are evident, the piston must be replaced.

The piston should also be checked in relation to the cylinder diameter. Using a telescoping gauge and micrometer, or a dial gauge, measure the cylinder bore diameter perpendicular (90%) to the piston pin, 2½″ (64mm) below the cylinder block deck (surface where the block mates with the heads). Then, with the micrometer, measure the piston, perpendicular to its wrist pin on the skirt. the difference between the two measurements is the piston clearance. If the clearance is within specifications or slightly be-

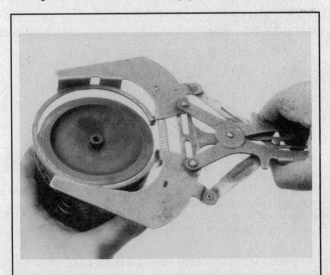

Use a ring expander tool to remove the piston rings

low (after the cylinders have been bored or hones), finish honing is all that is necessary. If the clearance is excessive, try to obtain a slightly larger piston to bring clearance to within specifications. If this is not possible, obtain the first oversize piston and hone (or if necessary, bore) the cylinder to size. Generally, if the cylinder bore is tapered 0.005″ (0.127mm) or more or is out-of-round 0.003″ (0.076mm) or more, it is advisable to rebore for the smallest possible oversize piston and rings.

After measuring, mark pistons with a felt tip pen for reference and for assembly.

➡**Cylinder honing and/or boring should be performed by a reputable, professional mechanic with the proper equipment. In some cases, clean-up honing can be done with the cylinder block in the car, but most excessive honing and all cylinder boring must be done with the block stripped and removed from the car.**

Before honing the diesel cylinders, the piston oil cooling jets must be removed. This procedure should be handled by a diesel specialist, as special tools are needed. Jets cannot be reused; new jets should be fitted.

MEASURING THE OLD PISTONS

Check used piston-to-cylinder bore clearance as follows:

1. Measure the cylinder bore diameter with a telescope gauge.
2. Measure the piston diameter. When measuring the pistons for size or taper, measurements must be made with the piston pin removed.
3. Subtract the piston diameter from the cylinder bore diameter to determine piston-to-bore clearance.
4. Compare the piston-to-bore clearances obtained with those clearances recommended. Determine if the piston-to-bore clearance is in the acceptable range.
5. When measuring taper, the largest reading must be at the bottom of the skirt.

Measure the piston's outer diameter using a micrometer

SELECTING NEW PISTONS

1. If the used piston is not acceptable, check the service piston size and determine if a new piston can be selected. (Service pistons are available in standard, high limit and standard oversize.
2. If the cylinder bore must be reconditioned, measure the new piston diameter, then hone the cylinder bore to obtain the preferred clearance.
3. Select a new piston and mark the piston to identify the cylinder for which it was fitted. (On some vehicles, oversize pistons may be found. These pistons will be 0.254mm [0.010″] oversize).

CYLINDER HONING

1. When cylinders are being honed, follow the manufacturer's recommendations for the use of the hone.

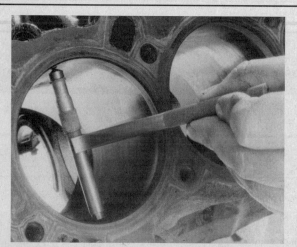

A telescoping gauge may be used to measure the cylinder bore diameter

Removing cylinder glazing using a flexible hone

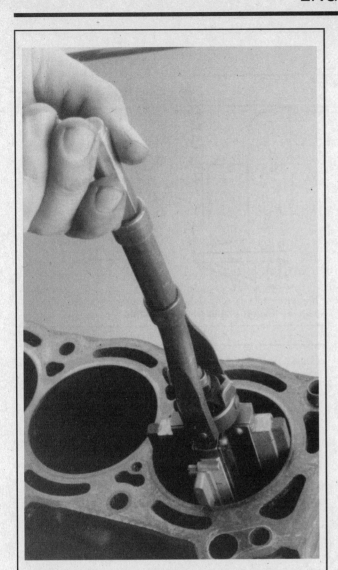

A solid hone can also be used to cross-hatch the cylinder bore

As with a ball hone, work the hone carefully up and down the bore to achieve the desired results

A properly cross-hatched cylinder bore

2. Occasionally, during the honing operation, the cylinder bore should be thoroughly cleaned and the selected piston checked for correct fit.

3. When finish-honing a cylinder bore, the hone should be moved up and down at a sufficient speed to obtain a very fine uniform surface finish in a cross-hatch pattern of approximately 45–65° included angle. The finish marks should be clean but not sharp, free from imbedded particles and torn or folded metal.

4. Permanently mark the piston for the cylinder to which it has been fitted and proceed to hone the remaining cylinders.

✳✳ WARNING

Handle the pistons with care. Do not attempt to force the pistons through the cylinders until the cylinders have been honed to the correct size. Pistons can be distorted through careless handling.

5. Thoroughly clean the bores with hot water and detergent. Scrub well with a stiff bristle brush and rinse thoroughly with hot water. It is extremely essential that a good cleaning operation be performed. If any of the abrasive material is allowed to remain in the cylinder bores, it will rapidly wear the new rings and cylinder bores. The bores should be swabbed several times with light engine oil and a clean cloth and then wiped with a clean dry cloth. CYLINDERS SHOULD NOT BE CLEANED WITH KEROSENE OR GASOLINE! Clean the remainder of the cylinder block to remove the excess material spread during the honing operation.

PISTON RING INSTALLATION

End-gap

▶ **See Figure 85**

Piston ring end-gap should be checked while the rings are removed from the pistons. Incorrect end-gap indicates that the wrong size rings are being used; ring breakage could occur.

Compress the piston rings to be used in a cylinder, one at a time, into that cylinder. Squirt clean oil into the cylinder, so that

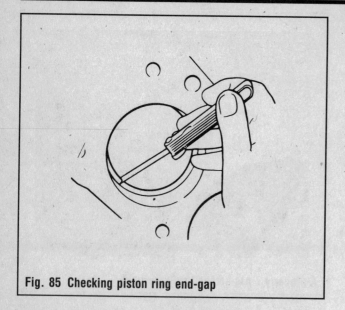

Fig. 85 Checking piston ring end-gap

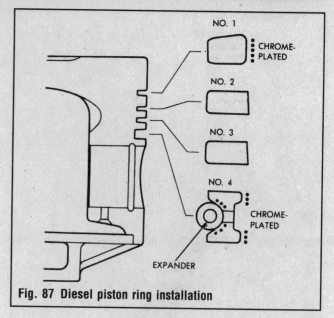

Fig. 87 Diesel piston ring installation

the rings and the top 2″ (51mm) of cylinder wall are coated. Using an inverted piston, press the rings approximately 1″ (25mm) below the deck of the block (on diesels, measure ring gap clearance with the ring positioned at the bottom of ring travel in the bore). Measure the ring end-gap with the feeler gauge, and compare to the Ring Gap chart in this chapter. Carefully pull the ring out of the cylinder and file the ends squarely with a fine file to obtain the proper clearance.

Side Clearance Check

▶ See Figures 86, 87 and 88

Check the pistons to see that the ring grooves and oil return holes have been properly cleaned. Slide a piston ring into its groove, and check the side clearance with a feeler gauge. On gasoline engines, make sure you insert the gauge between the ring and its lower land (lower edge of the groove), because any wear that occurs forms a step at the inner portion of the lower land. On diesels, insert the gauge between the ring and the upper land. If the piston grooves have worn to the extend that relatively high steps exist on the lower land, the piston grooves have worn to the

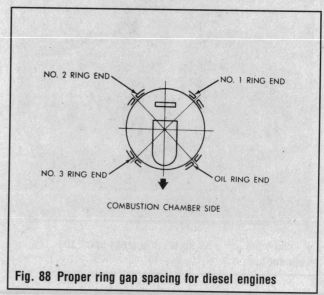

Fig. 88 Proper ring gap spacing for diesel engines

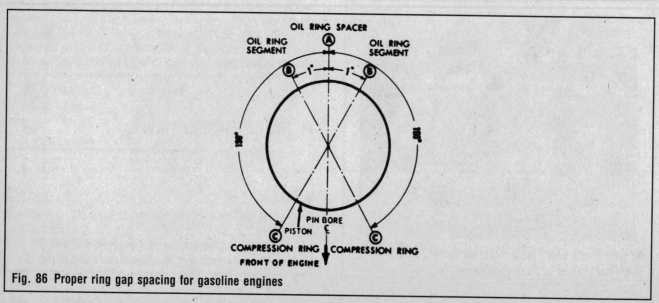

Fig. 86 Proper ring gap spacing for gasoline engines

extent that relatively high steps exist on the lower land, the piston should be replaced, because these will interfere with the operation of the new rings and ring clearance will be excessive. Piston rings are not furnished in oversize widths to compensate for ring groove wear.

Install the rings on the piston, lowest ring first, using a piston ring expander. There is a high risk of breaking or distorting the rings, or scratching the piston, if the rings are installed by hand or other means.

Position the rings on the piston as illustrated; spacing of the various piston ring gaps is crucial to proper oil retention and even cylinder wear. When installing new rings, refer to the installation diagram furnished with the new parts.

INSTALLATION

Install the connecting rod to the piston making sure piston installation notches and any marks on the rod are in proper relation to one another. Lubricate the wrist pin with clean engine oil and install the pin into the rod and piston assembly by using an arbor press as required. Install the wrist pin snaprings if equipped, and rotate them in their grooves to make sure they are seated. To install the piston and rod assemblies:

1. Make sure the connecting rod big bearings (including end cap) are of the correct size and properly installed.

2. Fit rubber hoses over the connecting rod bolt to protect the crankshaft journals, as in the Piston Removal procedure. Coat the rod bearings with clean oil.

3. Using the proper ring compressor, insert the piston assembly into the cylinder so that the notch in the top of the piston faces the front of the engine (this assumes that the dimple(s) or other markings on the connecting rods are in correct relation to the piston notch(s)).

4. From beneath the engine, coat each crank journal with clean oil. Pull the connecting rod, with the bearing shell in place, into position against the crank journal.

5. Remove the rubber hoses. Install the bearing cap and cap nuts and torque to specification.

Checking the ring-to-ring groove clearance

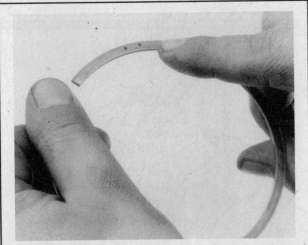

Most rings are marked to show which side should face upward

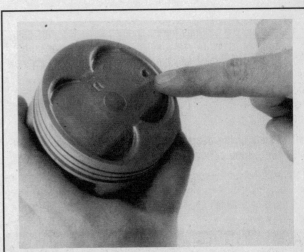

Most pistons are marked to indicate positioning in the engine (usually a mark means the side facing front)

Installing the piston into the block using a ring compressor and the handle of a hammer

The notch on the the side of the bearing cap matches the groove on the bearing insert

➡️**When more than one rod and piston assembly is being installed, the connecting rod cap attaching nuts should only be tightened enough to keep each rod in position until all have been installed. This will ease the installation of the remaining piston assemblies.**

6. Check the clearance between the sides of the connecting rods and the crankshaft using a feeler gauge. Spread the rods slightly with a screwdriver to insert the gauge. If clearance is below the minimum tolerance, the rod may be machined to provide adequate clearance. If clearance is excessive, substitute an unworn rod, and recheck. If clearance is still outside specifications, the crankshaft must be welded and reground, or replaced.

7. Replace the oil pump if removed, and the oil pan.
8. Install the cylinder head(s) and intake manifold.

Connecting Rod Bearings

INSPECTION

Connecting rod bearings for the engines covered in this guide consist of two halves or shells which are interchangeable in the rod and cap. when the shells are placed in position, the ends extend slightly beyond the rod and cap surfaces so that when the rod bolts are torqued the shells will be clamped tightly in place to insure positive seating and to prevent turning. A tang holds the shells in place.

➡️**The ends of the bearing shells must never be filed flush with the mating surfaces of the rod and cap.**

If a rod bearing becomes noisy or is worn so that its clearance on the crank journal is sloppy, a new bearing of the correct undersize must be selected and installed since there is a provision for adjustment.

✳️✳️ WARNING

Under no circumstances should the rod end or cap be filed to adjust the bearing clearance, nor should shims of any kind be used.

Inspect the rod bearings while the rod assemblies are out of the engine. If the shells are scored or show flaking, they should be replaced. If they are in good shape, check for proper clearance on the crank journal. Any scoring or ridges on the crank journal means the crankshaft must be reground and fitted with undersized bearings, or replaced.

CHECKING CLEARANCE & REPLACING BEARINGS

▶ **See Figure 89**

➡️**Make sure connecting rods and their caps are kept together, and that the caps are installed in the proper direction.**

Fig. 89 Checking rod side clearance with a flat feeler gauge. Use a small prybar to spread the rods

Replacement bearings are available in standard size, and in undersizes for reground crankshaft. Connecting rod-to-crankshaft bearing clearance is checked using Plastigage® at either the top or bottom of each crank journal. the Plastigage® has a range of 0 to 0.003″ (0.076mm).

1. Remove the rod cap with the bearing shell. Completely clean the bearing shell and the crank journal, and blow any oil from the oil hole in the crankshaft.

➡ **The journal surfaces and bearing shells must be completely free of oil, because Plastigage® is soluble in oil.**

2. Place a strip of Plastigage® lengthwise along the bottom center of the lower bearing shell, then install the cap with shell and torque the bolt or nuts to specification. DO NOT TURN the crankshaft with the Plastigage® installed in the bearing.

3. Remove the the bearing cap with the shell. The flattened Plastigage® will be found sticking to either the bearing shell or crank journal. Do not remove it yet.

4. Use the printed scale on the Plastigage® envelope to measure the flattened material at its widest point. The number within the scale which most closely corresponds to the width of the Plastigage® indicated bearing clearance in thousandths of an inch.

5. Check the specifications chart in this chapter for the desired clearance. It is advisable to install a new bearing if clearance exceeds 0.003″ (0.076mm); however, if the bearing is in good condition and is not being checked because of bearing noise, bearing replacement is not necessary.

6. If you are installing new bearings, try a standard size, then each undersize in order until one is found that is within the specified limits when checked for clearance with Plastigage®. Each under size has its size stamped on it.

7. When the proper size shell is found, clean off the Plastigage® material from the shell, oil the bearing thoroughly, reinstall the cap with its shell and torque the rod bolt nuts to specification.

➡ **With the proper bearing selected and the nuts torqued, it should be possible to move the connecting rod back and forth freely on the crank journal as allowed by the specified connecting rod end clearance. If the rod cannot be moved, either the rod bearing is too far undersize or the rod is misaligned.**

Diesel Engine Cylinder Sleeves

INSPECTION

1. Check the front plate mounting surface and flywheel housing for distortion.

2. Using a straightedge, check cylinder block mating surface. The mating surface must be flat within 0.07mm. If distortion exceeds 0.2mm, the block surface may be reground.

3. Measure the ID of the sleeve at 3 points: top, middle and bottom. Measurements should be both parallel to and at right angles with the crankshaft centerline at each point.

4. The sleeve ID should be 92mm + 0.035mm/−0mm. Allowable out-of-round should be 0.075mm or less. Allowable taper is 0.05mm or less. If the ID deviates more than the standard diameter by +1.20mm or more, the sleeve must be replaced. If ID deviation is between +0.25mm and +1.20mm the sleeve may be

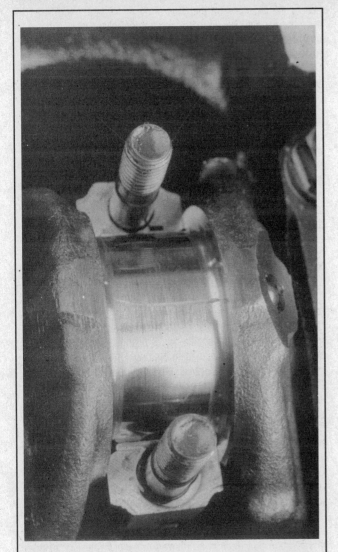

Apply a strip of gauging material to the bearing journal, then install and torque the cap

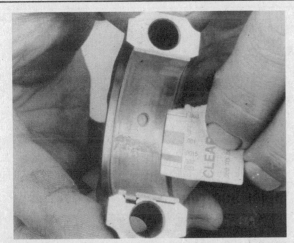

After the cap is removed again, use the scale supplied with the gauge material to check clearances

overbored to oversizes from +0.25mm to +1.00mm in increments of 0.25mm. Rebored sleeves must be hond to within −0 and 0.035mm. Oversized pistons and rings must be used. If the ID deviates from the standard dimension by less than +0.25mm, hone out the sleeve and replace the rings. If the sleeve wear is uneven, the amount of oversize is determined by maximum wear. If maximum uneven wear is 0.4mm, the sleeve must be rebored to +1.00mm to ensure compliance with taper and out-of-round.

➡ If one sleeve is rebored to a given oversize, all other sleeves must be rebored to the same oversize.

REMOVAL

1. Mount a portable boring bar on the top of the block.
2. Align a boring bar with the center of the sleeve at the bottom where the eccentric wear is minimum.
3. Bore the sleeve wall out to a thickness of 0.5mm.
4. Pull the sleeve with a puller.

✳✳ WARNING

Take great pains to avoid damage to the block!

5. Check the bottom hole condition after the sleeve has been pulled. If damage or any defect is noted, the bottom hole must be rebored.

INSTALLATION

Bottom Hole Not Rebored

1. Measure the inside diameter of the bottom hole and the outside diamtere of the sleeve. Sleeve-to-bottom hole interference must be 0.08–0.145mm after installation.
2. Press the sleeve into the block with a hydraulic press and sleeve installer. The sleeve is pressed in flush with the block surface.
3. After installation, bore the sleeve and finish it to an ID of 92.000–92.035mm by honing.

Bottom Hole Rebored

1. The standard bottom hole dimension is 94.955–94.990mm. Select an oversize sleeve with an OD 0.5mm larger.
2. Bore the bottom hole to 95.455–95.490mm. This will ensure an interference fit of 0.08–0.145mm.
3. Press the sleeve in as described above.
4. After the sleeves are installed, bore the sleeves and finish hone to an ID of 92.000–92.035mm.

Crankshaft and Main Bearings

PRECAUTIONS

Inline 6-Cylinder Engines

The maximum allowable bearing clearance is 0.001″ no. 1, no. 2 and no. 4 lower inserts are interchangeable no. 1 upper insert has a chamfer on the tab side for timing chain oiling and is identi-

fied by the red mark on the edge of the no. 3 upper and lower inserts are flanged. Bearing caps are not interchangeable and are numbered for correct installation. Maximum end-play is 0.0085″. Replace no. 3 (thrust) bearing if end-play exceeds that amount.

V6 and V8 Engines

A Maltese Cross stamped on the engine (except on the 318 and 360) numbering pad indicates that the engine is equipped with a crankshaft which has one or more connecting rods and/or main bearing journal finished 0.001″ undersize. The position of the underside journal(s) is stamped on a machine surface of the no. 3 counterweight. The letter R or M signifies whether the undersize journal is a rod or main, and the number following the letter indicates which one it is. A Maltese Cross with an X indicates that all those journals are 0.010″ undersize. On the 318 and 360 engines, 0.001″ undersize journals are indicated by marks on the no. 8 crankshaft counterweight. If the R or M is followed by an X, all those journals are 0.010″ undersize.

Upper and lower bearing inserts are not interchangeable on any of the V8 engines due to oil hole and V-groove in the uppers. On the 318 and 360 cu.in. engine lower bearing halves no. 1, no. 2 and no. 4 are interchangeable; no. 1, no. 2 and no. 4 upper bearing halves are interchangeable. no. 3 bearing is the thrust bearing and no. 5 is the wider rear main bearing. On 400 and 440 cu.in. engines the no. 1, no. 2, no. 4 and no. 5 lower bearing halves are interchangeable; no. 2, no. 4 and no. 5 upper bearing halves are interchangeable no. 1 upper insert has a chamfer on the tab side for timing chain oiling and is identified by the red marking on the edge no. 3 bearing is a thrust bearing and should be replaced if end-play exceeds 0.007″.

Remove main bearing caps one at a time and check clearance. Check number of cap for proper location.

On the 400 and 440 cu.in. engines, the rear main bearing lower seal is held in place by a seal retainer. On the 318 and 360 cu.in. engine, the rear main bearing lower seal is held in place by the rear main bearing cap. Note that the oil pump is mounted on this cap and that there is a hollow dowel which must be in place when the cap is installed.

REMOVAL & INSTALLATION

Engine Removed

GASOLINE ENGINES

1. With the engine removed from the vehicle and placed in a work stand, disconnect the spark plug wires from the spark plugs and remove the wires and bracket assembly from the attaching stud on the valve rocker arm cover(s) if so equipped. Disconnect the coil to distributor high tension lead at the coil. Remove the distributor cap and spark plug wires as an assembly. Remove the spark plugs to allow easy rotation of the crankshaft.
2. Remove the fuel pump and oil filter. Slide the water pump by-pass hose clamp (if so equipped) toward the water pump. Remove the alternator and mounting brackets.
3. Remove the crankshaft pulley from the crankshaft vibration damper. Remove the capscrew and washer from the end of the crankshaft. Install a universal puller on the crankshaft vibration damper and remove the damper.
4. Remove the cylinder front cover and crankshaft gear, refer to Cylinder Front Cover and Timing Chain in this chapter.

5. Invert the engine on the work stand. Remove the clutch pressure plate and disc (manual shift transmission). Remove the flywheel and engine rear cover plate. Remove the oil pan and gasket. Remove the oil pump.

6. Make sure all bearing caps (main and connecting rod) are marked so that they can be installed in their original locations. Turn the crankshaft until the connecting rod from which the cap is being removed is down, and remove the bearing cap. Push the connecting rod and piston assembly up into the cylinder. Repeat this procedure until all the connecting rod bearing caps are removed.

7. Remove the main bearing caps.

8. Carefully lift the crankshaft out of the block so that the thrust bearing surfaces are not damaged. Handle the crankshaft with care to avoid possible fracture to the finished surfaces.

9. Remove the rear journal seal from the block and rear main bearing cap.

10. Remove the main bearing inserts from the block and bearing caps.

11. Remove the connecting rod bearing inserts from the connecting rods and caps.

12. If the crankshaft main bearing journals have been refinished to a definite undersize, install the correct undersize bearings. Be sure the bearing inserts and bearing bores are clean. Foreign material under the inserts will distort the bearing and cause a failure.

13. Place the upper main bearing inserts in position in the bores with the tang fitting in the slot. Be sure the oil holes in the bearing inserts are aligned with the oil holes in the cylinder block.

14. Install the lower main bearing inserts in the bearing caps.

15. Clean the rear journal oil seal groove and the mating surfaces of the block and rear main bearing cap.

16. Dip the lip-type seal halves in clean engine oil. Install the seals in the bearing cap and block with the undercut side of the seal toward the front of the engine.

➡**This procedure applies only to engines with two piece rear main bearing oil seals. those having one piece seals will be installed after the crankshaft is in place.**

17. Carefully lower the crankshaft into place. Be careful not to damage the bearing surfaces.

➡**Refer to Rear Main Oil Seal removal and installation, for special instructions in applying RTV sealer to rear main bearing cup.**

18. Install all the bearing caps except the thrust bearing cap. Be sure the main bearing caps are installed in their original locations. Tighten the bearing cap bolts to specifications.

19. Install the thrust bearing cap with the bolts finger-tight.

20. Pry the crankshaft forward against the thrust surface of the upper half of the bearing.

21. Hold the crankshaft forward and pry the thrust bearing cap to the rear. This will align the thrust surfaces of both halves of the bearing.

22. Retain the forward pressure on the crankshaft. Tighten the cap bolts to specifications.

23. On engines with one piece rear main bearing oil seal, coat a new crankshaft rear oil seal with oil and install using a seal driver. Inspect the seal to be sure it was not damaged during installation.

24. Install new bearing inserts in the connecting rods and caps. Check the clearance of each bearing, following the procedure.

25. After the connecting rod bearings have been fitted, apply a light coat of engine oil to the journals and bearings.

26. Turn the crankshaft throw to the bottom of its stroke. Push the piston all the way down until the rod bearing seats on the crankshaft journal.

27. Install the connecting rod cap. Tighten the nuts to specification.

28. After the piston and connecting rod assemblies have been installed, check the side clearance with a feeler gauge between the connecting rods on each connecting rod crankshaft journal. Refer to Crankshaft and Connecting Rod specifications chart in this chapter.

29. Install the timing chain and sprockets or gears, cylinder front cover and crankshaft pulley and adapter, following steps under Cylinder Front Cover and Timing Chain Installation in this chapter.

DIESEL ENGINES

1. With the engine on a workstand, remove the front cover and timing gears. Remove the piston and rod assemblies. Identify each one for assembly.

2. Remove the main bearing caps from Nos. 1 and 7 bearings using puller C-3752-D and adapters. Remove the lower bearing inserts.

3. Remove the caps from Nos. 2 through 6 main bearings using the puller and adapters. Remove the lower bearing inserts.

4. Lift out the crankshaft.

5. Remove the upper bearing inserts.

6. Remove the thrust plates from No. 7 insert.

➡**Refer to Rear Main Oil Seal removal and installation, for special instructions in applying RTV sealer to rear main bearing cup.**

7. Install all the bearing caps except the thrust bearing cap. Be sure the main bearing caps are installed in their original locations. Tighten the bearing cap bolts to specifications.

8. Install the thrust bearing cap with the bolts finger-tight.

9. Pry the crankshaft forward against the thrust surface of the upper half of the bearing.

10. Hold the crankshaft forward and pry the thrust bearing cap to the rear. This will align the thrust surfaces of both halves of the bearing.

11. Retain the forward pressure on the crankshaft. Tighten the cap bolts to specifications.

12. On engines with one piece rear main bearing oil seal, coat a new crankshaft rear oil seal with oil and install using a seal driver. Inspect the seal to be sure it was not damaged during installation.

13. Install new bearing inserts in the connecting rods and caps. Check the clearance of each bearing, following the procedure.

14. After the connecting rod bearings have been fitted, apply a light coat of engine oil to the journals and bearings.

15. Turn the crankshaft throw to the bottom of its stroke. Push the piston all the way down until the rod bearing seats on the crankshaft journal.

16. Install the connecting rod cap. Tighten the nuts to specification.

17. After the piston and connecting rod assemblies have been

installed, check the side clearance with a feeler gauge between the connecting rods on each connecting rod crankshaft journal. Refer to Crankshaft and Connecting Rod specifications chart in this chapter.

18. Install the timing chain and sprockets or gears, cylinder front cover and crankshaft pulley and adapter, following steps under Cylinder Front Cover and Timing Chain Installation in this chapter.

Engine Installed

➡**This won't be possible on all engines or vehicles.**

1. With the oil pan, oil pump and spark plugs removed, remove the cap from the main bearing needing replacement and remove the bearing from the cap.

2. Make a bearing roll-out pin, using a bent cotter pin as shown in the illustration. Install the end of the pin in the oil hole in the crankshaft journal.

3. Rotate the crankshaft clockwise as viewed from the front of the engine. This will roll the upper bearing out of the block.

4. Lube the new upper bearing with clean engine oil and insert the plain (unnotch) end between the crankshaft and the indented or notched side of the block. Roll the bearing into place, making sure that the oil holes are aligned. Remove the roll pin from the oil hole.

5. Lube the new lower bearing and install it in the main bearing cap. Install the main bearing cap onto the block, making sure it is positioned in proper direction with the matchmarks in alignment.

6. Torque the main bearing cap to specification.

➡**See Crankshaft Installation for thrust bearing alignment.**

CRANKSHAFT CLEANING AND INSPECTION

➡**Handle the crankshaft carefully to avoid damage to the finish surfaces.**

1. Clean the crankshaft with solvent, and blow out all oil passages with compressed air.

2. Use crocus cloth to remove any sharp edges, burrs or other imperfections which might damage the oil seal during installation or cause premature seal wear.

➡**Do not use crocus cloth to polish the seal surfaces. A finely polished surface may produce poor sealing or cause premature seal wear.**

3. Inspect the main and connecting rod journals for cracks, scratches, grooves or scores.

4. Measure the diameter of each journal at least four places to determine out-of-round, taper or undersize condition.

5. On an engine with a manual transmission, check the fit of the clutch pilot bearing in the bore of the crankshaft. A needle roller bearing and adapter assembly is used as a clutch pilot bearing. It is inserted directly into the engine crank shaft. The bearing and adapter assembly cannot be serviced separately. A new bearing must be installed whenever a bearing is removed.

6. Inspect the pilot bearing, when used, for roughness, evidence of overheating or loss of lubricant. Replace if any of these conditions are found.

Main Bearings

1. Clean the bearing inserts and caps thoroughly in solvent, and dry them with compressed air.

➡**Do not scrape varnish or gum deposits from the bearing shells.**

2. Inspect each bearing carefully. Bearings that have a scored, chipped, or worn surface should be replaced.

3. The copper-lead bearing base may be visible through the bearing overlay in small localized areas. This may not mean that the bearing is excessively worn. It is not necessary to replace the bearing if the bearing clearance is within recommended specifications.

4. Check the clearance of bearings that appear to be satisfactory with Plastigage® or its equivalent. Fit the new bearings following the procedure below. They should be reground to size for the next undersize bearing.

5. Regrind the journals to give the proper clearance with the next undersize bearing. If the journal will not clean up to maximum undersize bearing available, replace the crankshaft.

6. Always reproduce the same journal shoulder radius that existed originally. Too small a radius will result in fatigue failure of the crankshaft. Too large a radius will result in bearing failure due to radius ride of the bearing.

7. After regrinding the journals, chamfer the oil holes, then polish the journals with a #320 grit polishing cloth and engine oil. Crocus cloth may also be used as a polishing agent.

CHECKING MAINBEARING CLEARANCES

Bearing Clearance

1. Check the clearance of each main bearing by using the following procedure:

   a. Place a piece of Plastigage® or its equivalent, on bearing surface across full width of bearing cap and about 1/4" (6mm) off center.

   b. Install cap and tighten bolts to specifications. Do not turn crankshaft while Plastigage® is in place.

   c. Remove the cap. Using Plastigage® scale, check width of Plastigage® at widest point to get the minimum clearance. Check at narrowest point to get maximum clearance. Difference between readings is taper of journal.

   d. If clearance exceeds specified limits, try a 0.001" (0.0254mm) or 0.002" (0.051mm) undersize bearing in combination with the standard bearing. Bearing clearance must be within specified limits. If standard and 0.002" (0.051mm) undersize bearing does not bring clearance within desired limits, refinish crankshaft journal, then install undersize bearings.

End-Play

1. Check the crankshaft end-play using the following procedures:

   a. Force the crankshaft toward the rear of the engine.

   b. Install a dial indicator so that the contact point rests against the crankshaft flange and the indicator axis is parallel to the crankshaft axis.

   c. Zero the dial indicator. Push the crankshaft forward and note the reading on the dial.

A dial gauge may be used to check crankshaft end-play

Turn the crankshaft slowly by hand while checking the gauge

Carefully pry the shaft back and forth while reading the dial gauge for play

A dial gauge may also be used to check crankshaft run-out

Mounting a dial gauge to read crankshaft run-out

d. If the end-play exceeds the wear limit listed in the Crankshaft and Connecting Rod Specifications chart, replace the thrust bearing. If the end-play is less than the minimum limit, inspect the thrust bearing faces for scratches, burrs, nicks, or dirt. If the thrust faces are not damaged or dirty, then they probably were not aligned properly. Lubricate and install the new thrust bearing and align the faces following procedures 21 through 24.

Completing the Rebuilding Process

Fill the oil pump with oil, to prevent cavitating (sucking air) on initial engine start up. Install the oil pump and the pickup tube on the engine. Coat the oil pan gasket as necessary, and install the gasket and the oil pan. Mount the flywheel and the crankshaft vibration damper or pulley on the crankshaft.

➡**Always use new bolts when installing the flywheel. Inspect the clutch shaft pilot bushing in the crankshaft. If the bushing is excessively worn, remove it with an expanding puller and a slide hammer, and tap a new bushing into place.**

Position the engine, cylinder head side up. Lubricate the lifters, and install them into their bores. Install the cylinder head, and torque it as specified. Insert the pushrods (where applicable), and install the rocker shaft(s) (if so equipped) or position the rocker.

Install the intake and exhaust manifolds, the carburetor(s), the distributor and spark plugs. Mount all accessories and install the engine in the car. Fill the radiator with coolant, and the crankcase with high quality engine oil.

BREAK-IN PROCEDURE

Start the engine, and allow it to run at low speed for a few minutes, while checking for leaks. Stop the engine, check the oil level, and fill as necessary. Restart the engine, and fill the cooling system to capacity. Check and adjust the ignition timing. Run the engine at low to medium speed (800–2,500 rpm) for approximately ½ hour, and retorque the cylinder head bolts. Road test the car, and check again for leaks.

➡**Some gasket manufacturers recommend not retorquing the cylinder head(s) due to the composition of the head gasket. Follow the directions in the gasket set.**

Flywheel/Flex Plate and Ring Gear

➡**Flex plate is the term for a flywheel mated with an automatic transmission.**

REMOVAL & INSTALLATION

➡**The ring gear is replaceable only on engines mated with a manual transmission. Engines with automatic transmissions have ring gears which are welded to the flex plate.**

1. Remove the transmission and transfer case.
2. Remove the clutch, if equipped, or torque converter from the flywheel. The flywheel bolts should be loosened a little at a time

If necessary, lock the flywheel in place and remove the retaining bolts . . .

. . . then remove the flywheel from the crankshaft in order replace it or have it machined

Upon installation, it is usually a good idea to apply a thread-locking compound to the flywheel bolts

in a cross pattern to avoid warping the flywheel. On cars with manual transmissions, replace the pilot bearing in the end of the crankshaft if removing the flywheel.

3. The flywheel should be checked for cracks and glazing. It can be resurfaced by a machine shop.

4. If the ring gear is to be replaced, drill a hole in the gear between two teeth, being careful not to contact the flywheel surface. Using a cold chisel at this point, crack the ring gear and remove it.

5. Polish the inner surface of the new ring gear and heat it in an oven to about 600°F (316° C). Quickly place the ring gear on the flywheel and tap it into place, making sure that it is fully seated.

✳✳ WARNING

Never heat the ring gear past 800°F (426° C), or the tempering will be destroyed.

6. Position the flywheel on the end of the crankshaft. Torque the bolts a little at a time, in a cross pattern, to the torque figure shown in the Torque Specifications Chart.

7. Install the clutch or torque converter.

8. Install the transmission and transfer case.

Rear Main Oil Seal

REMOVAL & INSTALLATION

Two Piece Seal

▶ **See Figures 90 thru 98**

1. Remove the oil pan and the oil pump (if required).

2. Loosen all the main bearing cap bolts, thereby lowering the crankshaft slightly but not to exceed 1/32″ (0.8mm).

3. Remove the rear main bearing cap, and remove the oil seal from the bearing cap and cylinder block. On the block half of the seal use a seal removal tool, or install a small metal screw in one

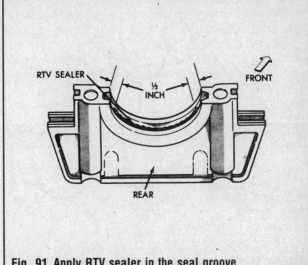

Fig. 91 Apply RTV sealer in the seal groove

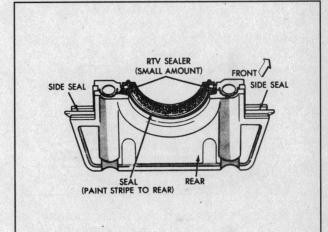

Fig. 92 Apply RTV sealer around the bolt holes on the rear main seal plate

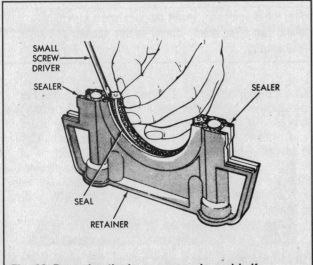

Fig. 90 Removing the lower rear main seal half

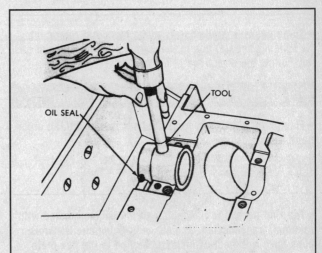

Fig. 93 Installing a rope seal using a special seating tool

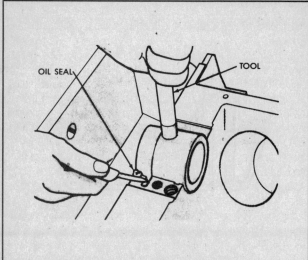

Fig. 94 Trim the seal ends after seating the rope seal

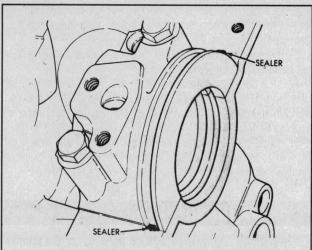

Fig. 97 Apply RTV sealer to the outer corners of the rear cap

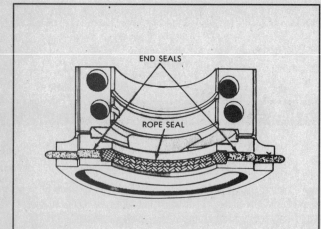

Fig. 95 View of a properly installed rear main seal—318 engine shown, others similar

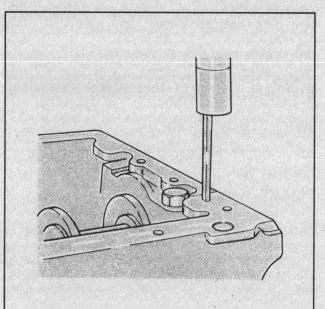

Fig. 98 If equipped, insert the side seals carefully to avoid damaging them—diesel engine shown, 400 and 440 similar

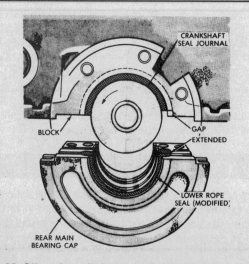

Fig. 96 Offset the split between the seal halves so that they do not match the mating surfaces

end of the seal, and pull on the screw to remove the seal. Exercise caution to prevent scratching or damaging the crankshaft seal surfaces.

4. Remove the oil seal retaining pin from the bearing cap if so equipped. The pin is not used with the split-lip seal.

5. Carefully clean the seal groove in the cap and block with a brush and solvent such as lacquer thinner, spot remover, or equivalent, or trichlorethylene. Also, clean the area thoroughly, so that no solvent touches the seal.

6. Dip the split lip-type seal halves in clean engine oil.

7. Carefully install the upper seal (cylinder block) into its groove with undercut side of the seal toward the FRONT of the engine, by rotating it on the seal journal of the crankshaft until approximately ⅜" (9.5mm) protrudes below the parting surface.

Be sure no rubber has been shaved from the outside diameter

of the seal by the bottom edge of the groove. Do not allow oil to get on the sealer area.

8. Tighten the remaining bearing cap bolts to the specifications listed in the Torque chart at the beginning of this chapter.

9. Install the lower seal in the rear main bearing cap under undercut side of seal toward the FRONT of the engine, allow the seal to protrude approximately 3/8″ (9.5mm) above the parting surface to mate with the upper seal when the cap is installed.

10. Apply an even 1/16″ (1.6mm) bead of RTV silicone-rubber sealer, to the areas shown, following the procedure given in the illustration.

→This sealer sets up in 15 minutes.

11. Install the rear main bearing cap. Tighten the cap bolts to specifications.

12. Install the oil pump and oil pan. Fill the crankcase with the proper amount and type of oil.

13. Operate the engine and check for oil leaks.

One Piece Seal

1. Remove the transmission, clutch assembly or converter and flywheel.

2. (See Step 7 for diesel engines). Lower the oil pan if necessary for working room.

3. On gasoline engines, use an awl to punch two small holes on opposite sides of the seal just above the split between the main bearing cap and engine block. Install a sheet metal screw in each hole. Use two small prybars and pry evenly on both screws using two small blocks of wood as a fulcrum point for the prybars. Use caution throughout to avoid scratching or damage to the oil seal mounting surfaces.

4. When the seal has been removed, clean the mounting recess.

5. Coat the seal and block mounting surfaces with oil. Apply white lube to the contact surface of the seal and crankshaft. Start the seal into the mounting recess and install with a seal driver.

6. Install the remaining components in the reverse of removal.

EXHAUST SYSTEM

General Information

→Safety glasses should be worn at all times when working on or near the exhaust system. Older exhaust systems will almost always be covered with loose rust particles which will shower you when disturbed. These particles are more than a nuisance and could injure your eye.

Whenever working on the exhaust system always keep the following in mind:
• Check the complete exhaust system for open seams, holes, loose connections, or other deterioration which could permit exhaust fumes to seep into the passenger compartment.
• The exhaust system is usually supported by free-hanging rubber mountings which permit some movement of the exhaust system, but does not permit transfer of noise and vibration into the passenger compartment. Do not replace the rubber mounts with solid ones.
• Before removing any component of the exhaust system, ALWAYS squirt a liquid rust dissolving agent onto the fasteners for ease of removal. A lot of knuckle skin will be saved by following this rule. It may even be wise to spray the fasteners and allow them to sit overnight.

✸✸ CAUTION

Because many rust dissolving liquids are flammable, never use them on a hot exhaust system, or near an open flame.

• Annoying rattles and noise vibrations in the exhaust system are usually caused by misalignment of the parts. When aligning the system, leave all bolts and nuts loose until all parts are properly aligned, then tighten, working from front to rear.
• When installing exhaust system parts, make sure there is enough clearance between the hot exhaust parts and pipes and hoses that would be adversely affected by excessive heat. Also make sure there is adequate clearance from the floor pan to avoid possible overheating of the floor.

Safety Precautions

For a number of reasons, exhaust system work can be among the most dangerous type of work you can do on your car. Always observe the following precautions:
• Support the vehicle extra securely. Not only will you often be working directly under it, but you'll frequently be using a lot of force, say, heavy hammer blows, to dislodge rusted parts. This can cause a vehicle that's improperly supported to shift and possibly fall.
• Wear goggles. Exhaust system parts are always rusty. Metal chips can be dislodged, even when you're only turning rusted bolts. Attempting to pry pipes apart with a chisel makes the chips fly even more frequently.
• If you're using a cutting torch, keep it a great distance from either the fuel tank or lines. Stop what you're doing and feel the temperature of the fuel bearing pipes on the tank frequently. Even slight heat can expand and/or vaporize fuel, resulting in accumulated vapor, or even a liquid leak, near your torch.
• Watch where your hammer blows fall and make sure you hit squarely. You could easily tap a brake or fuel line when you hit an exhaust system part with a glancing blow. Inspect all lines and hoses in the area where you've been working.

✸✸ CAUTION

Be very careful when working on or near the catalytic converter. External temperatures can reach 1,500°F (816°C) and more, causing severe burns. Removal or installation should be performed only on a cold exhaust system.

A number of special exhaust system tools can be rented from auto supply houses or local stores that rent special equipment. A common one is a tail pipe expander, designed to enable you to join pipes of identical diameter.

It may also be quite helpful to use solvents designed to loosen rusted bolts or flanges. Soaking rusted parts the night before you do the job can speed the work of freeing rusted parts considerably. Remember that these solvents are often flammable. Apply only to parts after they are cool!

COMPONENT REPLACEMENT

◆ **See Figures 99 and 100**

System components may be welded or clamped together. The system consists of a head pipe, catalytic converter, intermediate pipe, muffler and tail pipe, in that order from the engine to the back of the vehicle.

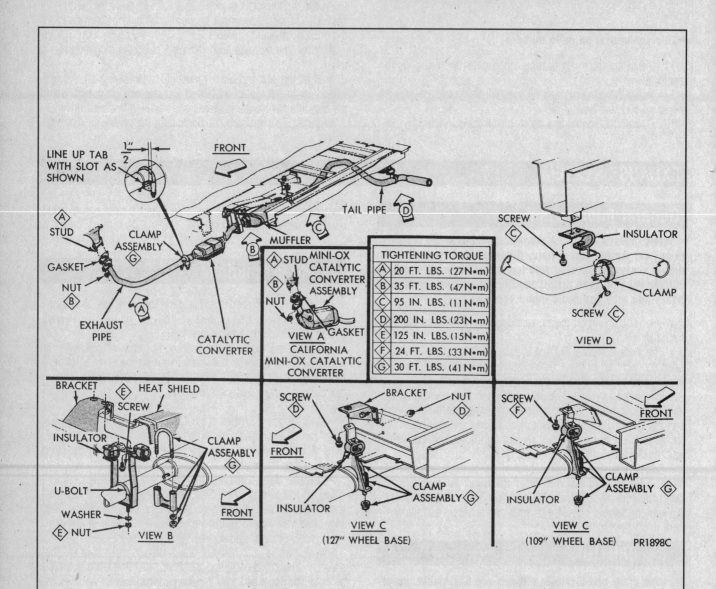

TIGHTENING TORQUE	
Ⓐ	20 FT. LBS. (27 N•m)
Ⓑ	35 FT. LBS. (47 N•m)
Ⓒ	95 IN. LBS. (11 N•m)
Ⓓ	200 IN. LBS. (23 N•m)
Ⓔ	125 IN. LBS. (15 N•m)
Ⓕ	24 FT. LBS. (33 N•m)
Ⓖ	30 FT. LBS. (41 N•m)

Fig. 99 Typical exhaust system routing and components for inline 6-cylinder engine equipped vehicles

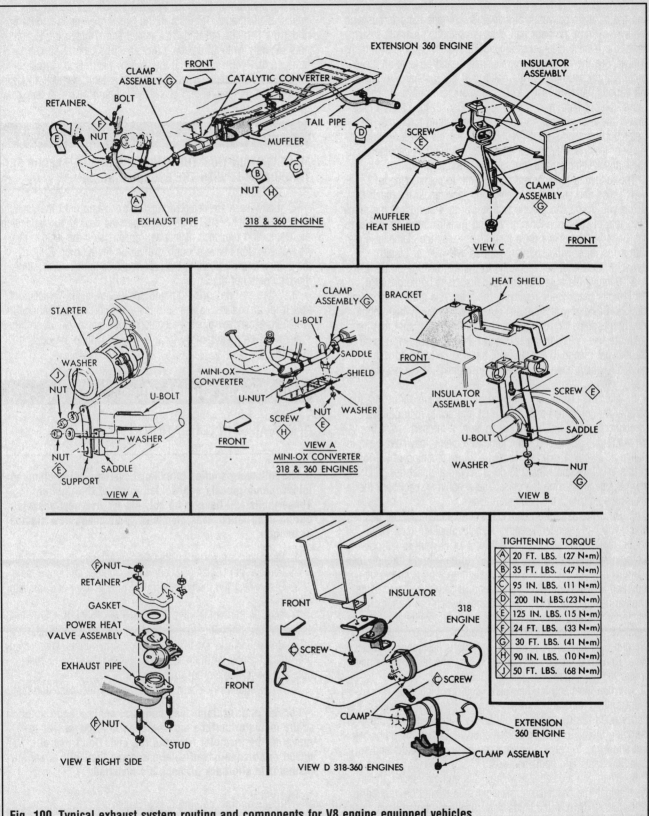

Fig. 100 Typical exhaust system routing and components for V8 engine equipped vehicles

The head pipe is bolted to the exhaust manifold, on one end, and the catalytic converter on the other. Various hangers suspend the system from the floor pan. When assembling exhaust system parts, the relative clearances around all system parts is extremely critical. See the accompanying illustration and observe all clearances during assembly. In the event that the system is welded, the various parts will have to be cut apart for removal. In these cases, the cut parts may not be reused. To cut the parts, a hacksaw is the best choice. An oxy-acetylene cutting torch may be faster but the sparks are DANGEROUS near the fuel tank, and, at the very least, accidents could happen, resulting in damage to other under-vehicle parts, not to mention yourself!

The following replacement steps relate to clamped parts:

1. Raise and support the vehicle on jackstands. It's much easier on you if you can get the vehicle up on 4 stands. Some pipes need lots of clearance for removal and installation. If the system has been in the vehicle for a long time, spray the clamped joints with a rust dissolving solution such as WD-40® or Liquid Wrench®, and let it set according to the instructions on the can.

2. Remove the nuts from the U-bolts; don't be surprised if the U-bolts break while removing the nuts. Age and rust account for this. Besides, you shouldn't reuse old U-bolts. When unbolting the headpipe from the exhaust manifold, make sure that the bolts are free before trying to remove them. If you snap a stud in the exhaust manifold, the stud will have to be removed with a bolt extractor, which often necessitates the removal of the manifold itself.

3. After the clamps are removed from the joints, first twist the parts at the joints to break loose rust and scale, then pull the components apart with a twisting motion. If the parts twist freely but won't pull apart, check the joint. The clamp may have been installed so tightly that it has caused a slight crushing of the joint. In this event, the best thing to do is secure a chisel designed for the purpose and, using the chisel and a hammer, peel back the female pipe end until the parts are freed.

4. Once the parts are freed, check the condition of the pipes which you had intended keeping. If their condition is at all in doubt, replace them too. You went to a lot of work to get one or more components out. You don't want to have to go through that again in the near future. If you are retaining a pipe, check the pipe end. If it was crushed by a clamp, it can be restored to its original diameter using a pipe expander, which can be rented at many good auto parts stores. Check, also, the condition of the exhaust system hangers. If ANY deterioration is noted, replace them. Oh, and one note about parts: use only parts designed for your vehicle. Don't use fits-all parts or flex pipes. The fits-all parts never fit and the flex pipes don't last very long.

5. When installing the new parts, coat the pipe ends with exhaust system lubricant. It makes fitting the parts much easier. It's also a good idea to assemble all the parts in position before clamping them. This will ensure a good fit, detect any problems and allow you to check all clearances between the parts and surrounding frame and floor members.

6. When you are satisfied with all fits and clearances, install the clamps. The headpipe-to-manifold nuts should be torqued to 20 ft. lbs. (27Nm). If the studs were rusty, wire-brush them clean and spray them with WD-40® or Liquid Wrench®. This will ensure a proper torque reading. Position the clamps on the slip points as illustrated. The slits in the female pipe ends should be under the U-bolts, not under the clamp end. Tighten the U-bolt nuts securely, without crushing the pipe. The pipe fit should be tight, so that you can't swivel the pipe by hand. Don't forget: always use new clamps. When the system is tight, recheck all clearances. Start the engine and check the joints for leaks. A leak can be felt by hand.

✳✳ CAUTION

MAKE CERTAIN THAT THE VEHICLE IS SECURE BEFORE GETTING UNDER IT WITH THE ENGINE RUNNING!!

7. If any leaks are detected, tighten the clamp until the leak stops. If the pipe starts to deform before the leak stops, reposition the clamp and tighten it. If that still doesn't stop the leak, it may be that you don't have enough overlap on the pipe fit. Shut off the engine and try pushing the pipe together further. Be careful; the pipe gets hot quickly.

8. When everything is tight and secure, lower the vehicle and take it for a road test. Make sure there are no unusual sounds or vibration. Most new pipes are coated with a preservative, so the system will be pretty smelly for a day or two while the coating burns off.

Muffler and Outlet Pipes

REMOVAL & INSTALLATION

➡The following applies to exhaust systems using clamped joints. Some models use welded joints at the muffler. These joints will have to be cut. Always use new gaskets during installation. It is also wise to purchase new clamps or hangers.

1. Raise and support the vehicle on jackstands.
2. Remove the U-clamps securing the muffler and outlet pipe.
3. Disconnect the muffler and outlet pipe bracket and insulator assemblies.
4. Remove the muffler and outlet pipe assembly. It may be necessary to heat the joints to get the parts to come off. Special tools are available to aid in breaking loose the joints. Discard any old exhaust pipes, or mufflers, along with any clamps or rusty nuts and bolts that are not usable again.
5. On extended wheelbase models, remove the extension pipe.

➡For rod and insulator type hangers, apply a soap solution to the insulator surface and rod ends to allow easier removal of the insulator from the rod end. Don't use oil-based or silicone-based solutions since they will allow the insulator to slip back off once it's installed.

To install:
6. Assemble the muffler and rear exhaust pipes together, along with supports and clamps before installing.

7. Install the components making sure that all the components in the system are properly aligned before tightening any fasteners. Make sure all tabs are indexed and all parts are clear of surrounding body panels.

Front Header Pipes, Catalytic Converter and Inlet Pipes

REMOVAL & INSTALLATION

➡**The following applies to exhaust systems using clamped joints. Some models use welded joints at the muffler. These joints will have to be cut. Always use new gaskets during installation. It is also wise to purchase new clamps or hangers.**

1. Raise and support the vehicle on jackstands.
2. Disconnect the front exhaust pipe flange or flanges for V engines, nuts and bolts connected to the exhaust manifold.
3. Loosen and remove any bolts to the catalytic converter (if equipped), or the flange prior to the muffler. If your system has no flanges all the way to the end of the exhaust, you will either have to cut the exhaust where you are replacing the piece, or replace the unit as an assembly.
4. Most aftermarket parts suppliers have your exhaust in cut sections (unlike your original exhaust). It is wise to look at your exhaust before cutting any pipe if you are not purchasing your exhaust parts from the dealer.
5. Remove the pipe assembly. It may be necessary to heat the joints to separate the parts. Special tools are available to aid in breaking loose the joint. Discard any old pipes, and any clamps or rusty nuts and bolts.

➡**For rod and insulator type hangers, apply a soap solution to the insulator surface and rod ends to allow easier removal of the insulator from the rod end. Don't use oil-based or silicone-based solutions since they will allow the insulator to slip back off once it's installed.**

To install:
6. Install the front header pipe with new exhaust nuts and gaskets. Attach the catalytic converter (if equipped) at the flange of the header pipe and tighten. Install any rear exhaust pipes together, along with supports and clamps.
7. Make sure that all the system components are properly aligned before tightening fasteners. Make sure all tabs are indexed and all parts are clear of surrounding body panels.

USING A VACUUM GAUGE

White needle = steady needle   *Dark needle = drifting needle*

The vacuum gauge is one of the most useful and easy-to-use diagnostic tools. It is inexpensive, easy to hook up, and provides valuable information about the condition of your engine.

Indication: Normal engine in good condition

Gauge reading: Steady, from 17 – 22 in./Hg.

Indication: Sticking valve or ignition miss

Gauge reading: Needle fluctuates from 15 – 20 in./Hg. at idle

Indication: Late ignition or valve timing, low compression, stuck throttle valve, leaking carburetor or manifold gasket.

Gauge reading: Low (15 – 20 in./Hg.) but steady

Indication: Improper carburetor adjustment, or minor intake leak at carburetor or manifold

NOTE: Bad fuel injector O-rings may also cause this reading.

Gauge reading: Drifting needle

Indication: Weak valve springs, worn valve stem guides, or leaky cylinder head gasket (vibrating excessively at all speeds).

NOTE: A plugged catalytic converter may also cause this reading.

Gauge reading: Needle fluctuates as engine speed increases

Indication: Burnt valve or improper valve clearance. The needle will drop when the defective valve operates.

Gauge reading: Steady needle, but drops regularly

Indication: Choked muffler or obstruction in system. Speed up the engine. Choked muffler will exhibit a slow drop of vacuum to zero.

Gauge reading: Gradual drop in reading at idle

Indication: Worn valve guides

Gauge reading: Needle vibrates excessively at idle, but steadies as engine speed increases

Troubleshooting Engine Mechanical Problems

Problem	Cause	Solution
External oil leaks	· Cylinder head cover RTV sealant broken or improperly seated	· Replace sealant; inspect cylinder head cover sealant flange and cylinder head sealant surface for distortion and cracks
	· Oil filler cap leaking or missing	· Replace cap
	· Oil filter gasket broken or improperly seated	· Replace oil filter
	· Oil pan side gasket broken, improperly seated or opening in RTV sealant	· Replace gasket or repair opening in sealant; inspect oil pan gasket flange for distortion
	· Oil pan front oil seal broken or improperly seated	· Replace seal; inspect timing case cover and oil pan seal flange for distortion
	· Oil pan rear oil seal broken or improperly seated	· Replace seal; inspect oil pan rear oil seal flange; inspect rear main bearing cap for cracks, plugged oil return channels, or distortion in seal groove
	· Timing case cover oil seal broken or improperly seated	· Replace seal
	· Excess oil pressure because of restricted PCV valve	· Replace PCV valve
	· Oil pan drain plug loose or has stripped threads	· Repair as necessary and tighten
	· Rear oil gallery plug loose	· Use appropriate sealant on gallery plug and tighten
	· Rear camshaft plug loose or improperly seated	· Seat camshaft plug or replace and seal, as necessary
Excessive oil consumption	· Oil level too high	· Drain oil to specified level
	· Oil with wrong viscosity being used	· Replace with specified oil
	· PCV valve stuck closed	· Replace PCV valve
	· Valve stem oil deflectors (or seals) are damaged, missing, or incorrect type	· Replace valve stem oil deflectors
	· Valve stems or valve guides worn	· Measure stem-to-guide clearance and repair as necessary
	· Poorly fitted or missing valve cover baffles	· Replace valve cover
	· Piston rings broken or missing	· Replace broken or missing rings
	· Scuffed piston	· Replace piston
	· Incorrect piston ring gap	· Measure ring gap, repair as necessary
	· Piston rings sticking or excessively loose in grooves	· Measure ring side clearance, repair as necessary
	· Compression rings installed upside down	· Repair as necessary
	· Cylinder walls worn, scored, or glazed	· Repair as necessary

Troubleshooting Engine Mechanical Problems

Problem	Cause	Solution
Excessive oil consumption (cont.)	• Piston ring gaps not properly staggered • Excessive main or connecting rod bearing clearance	• Repair as necessary • Measure bearing clearance, repair as necessary
No oil pressure	• Low oil level • Oil pressure gauge, warning lamp or sending unit inaccurate • Oil pump malfunction • Oil pressure relief valve sticking • Oil passages on pressure side of pump obstructed • Oil pickup screen or tube obstructed • Loose oil inlet tube	• Add oil to correct level • Replace oil pressure gauge or warning lamp • Replace oil pump • Remove and inspect oil pressure relief valve assembly • Inspect oil passages for obstruction • Inspect oil pickup for obstruction • Tighten or seal inlet tube
Low oil pressure	• Low oil level • Inaccurate gauge, warning lamp or sending unit • Oil excessively thin because of dilution, poor quality, or improper grade • Excessive oil temperature • Oil pressure relief spring weak or sticking • Oil inlet tube and screen assembly has restriction or air leak • Excessive oil pump clearance • Excessive main, rod, or camshaft bearing clearance	• Add oil to correct level • Replace oil pressure gauge or warning lamp • Drain and refill crankcase with recommended oil • Correct cause of overheating engine • Remove and inspect oil pressure relief valve assembly • Remove and inspect oil inlet tube and screen assembly. (Fill inlet tube with lacquer thinner to locate leaks.) • Measure clearances • Measure bearing clearances, repair as necessary
High oil pressure	• Improper oil viscosity • Oil pressure gauge or sending unit inaccurate • Oil pressure relief valve sticking closed	• Drain and refill crankcase with correct viscosity oil • Replace oil pressure gauge • Remove and inspect oil pressure relief valve assembly
Main bearing noise	• Insufficient oil supply • Main bearing clearance excessive • Bearing insert missing • Crankshaft end-play excessive • Improperly tightened main bearing cap bolts • Loose flywheel or drive plate • Loose or damaged vibration damper	• Inspect for low oil level and low oil pressure • Measure main bearing clearance, repair as necessary • Replace missing insert • Measure end-play, repair as necessary • Tighten bolts with specified torque • Tighten flywheel or drive plate attaching bolts • Repair as necessary

Troubleshooting Engine Mechanical Problems

Problem	Cause	Solution
Connecting rod bearing noise	• Insufficient oil supply	• Inspect for low oil level and low oil pressure
	• Carbon build-up on piston	• Remove carbon from piston crown
	• Bearing clearance excessive or bearing missing	• Measure clearance, repair as necessary
	• Crankshaft connecting rod journal out-of-round	• Measure journal dimensions, repair or replace as necessary
	• Misaligned connecting rod or cap	• Repair as necessary
	• Connecting rod bolts tightened improperly	• Tighten bolts with specified torque
Piston noise	• Piston-to-cylinder wall clearance excessive (scuffed piston)	• Measure clearance and examine piston
	• Cylinder walls excessively tapered or out-of-round	• Measure cylinder wall dimensions, rebore cylinder
	• Piston ring broken	• Replace all rings on piston
	• Loose or seized piston pin	• Measure piston-to-pin clearance, repair as necessary
	• Connecting rods misaligned	• Measure rod alignment, straighten or replace
	• Piston ring side clearance excessively loose or tight	• Measure ring side clearance, repair as necessary
	• Carbon build-up on piston is excessive	• Remove carbon from piston
Valve actuating component noise	• Insufficient oil supply	• Check for: (a) Low oil level (b) Low oil pressure (c) Wrong hydraulic tappets (d) Restricted oil gallery (e) Excessive tappet to bore clearance
	• Rocker arms or pivots worn	• Replace worn rocker arms or pivots
	• Foreign objects or chips in hydraulic tappets	• Clean tappets
	• Excessive tappet leak-down	• Replace valve tappet
	• Tappet face worn	• Replace tappet; inspect corresponding cam lobe for wear
	• Broken or cocked valve springs	• Properly seat cocked springs; replace broken springs
	• Stem-to-guide clearance excessive	• Measure stem-to-guide clearance, repair as required
	• Valve bent	• Replace valve
	• Loose rocker arms	• Check and repair as necessary
	• Valve seat runout excessive	• Regrind valve seat/valves
	• Missing valve lock	• Install valve lock
	• Excessive engine oil	• Correct oil level

Troubleshooting Engine Performance

Problem	Cause	Solution
Hard starting (engine cranks normally)	• Faulty engine control system component	• Repair or replace as necessary
	• Faulty fuel pump	• Replace fuel pump
	• Faulty fuel system component	• Repair or replace as necessary
	• Faulty ignition coil	• Test and replace as necessary
	• Improper spark plug gap	• Adjust gap
	• Incorrect ignition timing	• Adjust timing
	• Incorrect valve timing	• Check valve timing; repair as necessary
Rough idle or stalling	• Incorrect curb or fast idle speed	• Adjust curb or fast idle speed (If possible)
	• Incorrect ignition timing	• Adjust timing to specification
	• Improper feedback system operation	• Refer to Chapter 4
	• Faulty EGR valve operation	• Test EGR system and replace as necessary
	• Faulty PCV valve air flow	• Test PCV valve and replace as necessary
	• Faulty TAC vacuum motor or valve	• Repair as necessary
	• Air leak into manifold vacuum	• Inspect manifold vacuum connections and repair as necessary
	• Faulty distributor rotor or cap	• Replace rotor or cap (Distributor systems only)
	• Improperly seated valves	• Test cylinder compression, repair as necessary
	• Incorrect ignition wiring	• Inspect wiring and correct as necessary
	• Faulty ignition coil	• Test coil and replace as necessary
	• Restricted air vent or idle passages	• Clean passages
	• Restricted air cleaner	• Clean or replace air cleaner filter element
Faulty low-speed operation	• Restricted idle air vents and passages	• Clean air vents and passages
	• Restricted air cleaner	• Clean or replace air cleaner filter element
	• Faulty spark plugs	• Clean or replace spark plugs
	• Dirty, corroded, or loose ignition secondary circuit wire connections	• Clean or tighten secondary circuit wire connections
	• Improper feedback system operation	• Refer to Chapter 4
	• Faulty ignition coil high voltage wire	• Replace ignition coil high voltage wire (Distributor systems only)
	• Faulty distributor cap	• Replace cap (Distributor systems only)
Faulty acceleration	• Incorrect ignition timing	• Adjust timing
	• Faulty fuel system component	• Repair or replace as necessary
	• Faulty spark plug(s)	• Clean or replace spark plug(s)
	• Improperly seated valves	• Test cylinder compression, repair as necessary
	• Faulty ignition coil	• Test coil and replace as necessary

Troubleshooting Engine Performance

Problem	Cause	Solution
Faulty acceleration (cont.)	• Improper feedback system operation	• Refer to Chapter 4
Faulty high speed operation	• Incorrect ignition timing	• Adjust timing (if possible)
	• Faulty advance mechanism	• Check advance mechanism and repair as necessary (Distributor systems only)
	• Low fuel pump volume	• Replace fuel pump
	• Wrong spark plug air gap or wrong plug	• Adjust air gap or install correct plug
	• Partially restricted exhaust manifold, exhaust pipe, catalytic converter, muffler, or tailpipe	• Eliminate restriction
	• Restricted vacuum passages	• Clean passages
	• Restricted air cleaner	• Cleaner or replace filter element as necessary
	• Faulty distributor rotor or cap	• Replace rotor or cap (Distributor systems only)
	• Faulty ignition coil	• Test coil and replace as necessary
	• Improperly seated valve(s)	• Test cylinder compression, repair as necessary
	• Faulty valve spring(s)	• Inspect and test valve spring tension, replace as necessary
	• Incorrect valve timing	• Check valve timing and repair as necessary
	• Intake manifold restricted	• Remove restriction or replace manifold
	• Worn distributor shaft	• Replace shaft (Distributor systems only)
	• Improper feedback system operation	• Refer to Chapter 4
Misfire at all speeds	• Faulty spark plug(s)	• Clean or relace spark plug(s)
	• Faulty spark plug wire(s)	• Replace as necessary
	• Faulty distributor cap or rotor	• Replace cap or rotor (Distributor systems only)
	• Faulty ignition coil	• Test coil and replace as necessary
	• Primary ignition circuit shorted or open intermittently	• Troubleshoot primary circuit and repair as necessary
	• Improperly seated valve(s)	• Test cylinder compression, repair as necessary
	• Faulty hydraulic tappet(s)	• Clean or replace tappet(s)
	• Improper feedback system operation	• Refer to Chapter 4
	• Faulty valve spring(s)	• Inspect and test valve spring tension, repair as necessary
	• Worn camshaft lobes	• Replace camshaft
	• Air leak into manifold	• Check manifold vacuum and repair as necessary
	• Fuel pump volume or pressure low	• Replace fuel pump
	• Blown cylinder head gasket	• Replace gasket
	• Intake or exhaust manifold passage(s) restricted	• Pass chain through passage(s) and repair as necessary
Power not up to normal	• Incorrect ignition timing	• Adjust timing
	• Faulty distributor rotor	• Replace rotor (Distributor systems only)

Troubleshooting Engine Performance

Problem	Cause	Solution
Power not up to normal (cont.)	• Incorrect spark plug gap	• Adjust gap
	• Faulty fuel pump	• Replace fuel pump
	• Faulty fuel pump	• Replace fuel pump
	• Incorrect valve timing	• Check valve timing and repair as necessary
	• Faulty ignition coil	• Test coil and replace as necessary
	• Faulty ignition wires	• Test wires and replace as necessary
	• Improperly seated valves	• Test cylinder compression and repair as necessary
	• Blown cylinder head gasket	• Replace gasket
	• Leaking piston rings	• Test compression and repair as necessary
	• Improper feedback system operation	• Refer to Chapter 4
Intake backfire	• Improper ignition timing	• Adjust timing
	• Defective EGR component	• Repair as necessary
	• Defective TAC vacuum motor or valve	• Repair as necessary
Exhaust backfire	• Air leak into manifold vacuum	• Check manifold vacuum and repair as necessary
	• Faulty air injection diverter valve	• Test diverter valve and replace as necessary
	• Exhaust leak	• Locate and eliminate leak
Ping or spark knock	• Incorrect ignition timing	• Adjust timing
	• Distributor advance malfunction	• Inspect advance mechanism and repair as necessary (Distributor systems only)
	• Excessive combustion chamber deposits	• Remove with combustion chamber cleaner
	• Air leak into manifold vacuum	• Check manifold vacuum and repair as necessary
	• Excessively high compression	• Test compression and repair as necessary
	• Fuel octane rating excessively low	• Try alternate fuel source
	• Sharp edges in combustion chamber	• Grind smooth
	• EGR valve not functioning properly	• Test EGR system and replace as necessary
Surging (at cruising to top speeds)	• Low fuel pump pressure or volume	• Replace fuel pump
	• Improper PCV valve air flow	• Test PCV valve and replace as necessary
	• Air leak into manifold vacuum	• Check manifold vacuum and repair as necessary
	• Incorrect spark advance	• Test and replace as necessary
	• Restricted fuel filter	• Replace fuel filter
	• Restricted air cleaner	• Clean or replace air cleaner filter element
	• EGR valve not functioning properly	• Test EGR system and replace as necessary
	• Improper feedback system operation	• Refer to Chapter 4

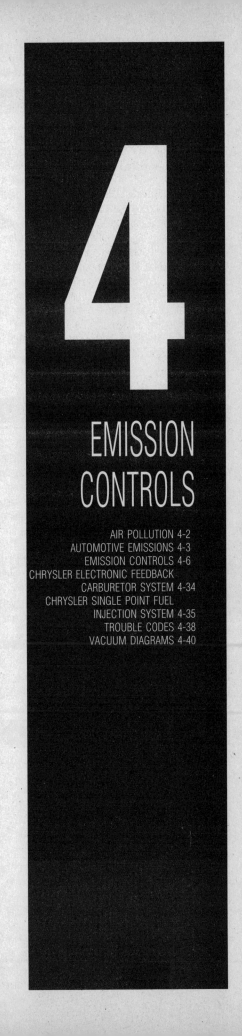

4

EMISSION CONTROLS

AIR POLLUTION

The earth's atmosphere, at or near sea level, consists approximately of 78 percent nitrogen, 21 percent oxygen and 1 percent other gases. If it were possible to remain in this state, 100 percent clean air would result. However, many varied sources allow other gases and particulates to mix with the clean air, causing our atmosphere to become unclean or polluted.

Some of these pollutants are visible while others are invisible, with each having the capability of causing distress to the eyes, ears, throat, skin and respiratory system. Should these pollutants become concentrated in a specific area and under certain conditions, death could result due to the displacement or chemical change of the oxygen content in the air. These pollutants can also cause great damage to the environment and to the many man made objects that are exposed to the elements.

To better understand the causes of air pollution, the pollutants can be categorized into 3 separate types, natural, industrial and automotive.

Natural Pollutants

Natural pollution has been present on earth since before man appeared and continues to be a factor when discussing air pollution, although it causes only a small percentage of the overall pollution problem. It is the direct result of decaying organic matter, wind born smoke and particulates from such natural events as plain and forest fires (ignited by heat or lightning), volcanic ash, sand and dust which can spread over a large area of the countryside.

Such a phenomenon of natural pollution has been seen in the form of volcanic eruptions, with the resulting plume of smoke, steam and volcanic ash blotting out the sun's rays as it spreads and rises higher into the atmosphere. As it travels into the atmosphere the upper air currents catch and carry the smoke and ash, while condensing the steam back into water vapor. As the water vapor, smoke and ash travel on their journey, the smoke dissipates into the atmosphere while the ash and moisture settle back to earth in a trail hundreds of miles long. In some cases, lives are lost and millions of dollars of property damage result.

Industrial Pollutants

Industrial pollution is caused primarily by industrial processes, the burning of coal, oil and natural gas, which in turn produce smoke and fumes. Because the burning fuels contain large amounts of sulfur, the principal ingredients of smoke and fumes are sulfur dioxide and particulate matter. This type of pollutant occurs most severely during still, damp and cool weather, such as at night. Even in its less severe form, this pollutant is not confined to just cities. Because of air movements, the pollutants move for miles over the surrounding countryside, leaving in its path a barren and unhealthy environment for all living things.

Working with Federal, State and Local mandated regulations and by carefully monitoring emissions, big business has greatly reduced the amount of pollutant introduced from its industrial sources, striving to obtain an acceptable level. Because of the mandated indistrial emission clean up, many land areas and streams in and around the cities that were formerly barren of vege-

tation and life, have now begun to move back in the direction of nature's intended balance.

Automotive Pollutants

The third major source of air pollution is automotive emissions. The emissions from the internal combustion engines were not an appreciable problem years ago because of the small number of registered vehicles and the nation's small highway system. However, during the early 1950's, the trend of the American people was to move from the cities to the surrounding suburbs. This caused an immediate problem in transportation because the majority of suburbs were not afforded mass transit conveniences. This lack of transportation created an attractive market for the automobile manufacturers, which resulted in a dramatic increase in the number of vehicles produced and sold, along with a marked increase in highway construction between cities and the suburbs. Multi-vehicle families emerged with a growing emphasis placed on an individual vehicle per family member. As the increase in vehicle ownership and usage occurred, so did pollutant levels in and around the cities, as suburbanites drove daily to their businesses and employment, returning at the end of the day to their homes in the suburbs.

It was noted that a smoke and fog type haze was being formed and at times, remained in suspension over the cities, taking time to dissipate. At first this "smog," derived from the words "smoke" and "fog," was thought to result from industrial pollution but it was determined that automobile emissions shared the blame. It was discovered that when normal automobile emissions were exposed to sunlight for a period of time, complex chemical reactions would take place.

It is now known that smog is a photo chemical layer which develops when certain oxides of nitrogen (NOx) and unburned hydrocarbons (HC) from automobile emissions are exposed to sunlight. Pollution was more severe when smog would become stagnant over an area in which a warm layer of air settled over the top of the cooler air mass, trapping and holding the cooler mass at ground level. The trapped cooler air would keep the emissions from being dispersed and diluted through normal air flows. This type of air stagnation was given the name "Temperature Inversion."

TEMPERATURE INVERSION

In normal weather situations, surface air is warmed by heat radiating from the earth's surface and the sun's rays. This causes it to rise upward, into the atmosphere. Upon rising it will cool through a convection type heat exchange with the cooler upper air. As warm air rises, the surface pollutants are carried upward and dissipated into the atmosphere.

When a temperature inversion occurs, we find the higher air is no longer cooler, but is warmer than the surface air, causing the cooler surface air to become trapped. This warm air blanket can extend from above ground level to a few hundred or even a few thousand feet into the air. As the surface air is trapped, so are the pollutants, causing a severe smog condition. Should this stagnant air mass extend to a few thousand feet high, enough air movement with the inversion takes place to allow the smog layer to rise above ground level but the pollutants still cannot dissipate. This inversion can remain for days over an area, with the smog level only rising or lowering from ground level to a few hundred feet high. Meanwhile, the pollutant levels increase, causing eye irritation, respiratory problems, reduced visibility, plant damage and in some cases, even disease.

This inversion phenomenon was first noted in the Los Angeles, California area. The city lies in terrain resembling a basin and with certain weather conditions, a cold air mass is held in the basin while a warmer air mass covers it like a lid.

Because this type of condition was first documented as prevalent in the Los Angeles area, this type of trapped pollution was named Los Angeles Smog, although it occurs in other areas where a large concentration of automobiles are used and the air remains stagnant for any length of time.

HEAT TRANSFER

Consider the internal combustion engine as a machine in which raw materials must be placed so a finished product comes out. As in any machine operation, a certain amount of wasted material is formed. When we relate this to the internal combustion engine, we find that through the input of air and fuel, we obtain power during the combustion process to drive the vehicle. The by-product or waste of this power is, in part, heat and exhaust gases with which we must dispose.

The heat from the combustion process can rise to over 4000°F (2204°C). The dissipation of this heat is controlled by a ram air effect, the use of cooling fans to cause air flow and a liquid coolant solution surrounding the combustion area to transfer the heat of combustion through the cylinder walls and into the coolant. The coolant is then directed to a thin-finned, multi-tubed radiator, from which the excess heat is transferred to the atmosphere by 1 of the 3 heat transfer methods, conduction, convection or radiation.

The cooling of the combustion area is an important part in the control of exhaust emissions. To understand the behavior of the combustion and transfer of its heat, consider the air/fuel charge. It is ignited and the flame front burns progressively across the combustion chamber until the burning charge reaches the cylinder walls. Some of the fuel in contact with the walls is not hot enough to burn, thereby snuffing out or quenching the combustion process. This leaves unburned fuel in the combustion chamber. This unburned fuel is then forced out of the cylinder and into the exhaust system, along with the exhaust gases.

Many attempts have been made to minimize the amount of unburned fuel in the combustion chambers due to quenching, by increasing the coolant temperature and lessening the contact area of the coolant around the combustion area. However, design limitations within the combustion chambers prevent the complete burning of the air/fuel charge, so a certain amount of the unburned fuel is still expelled into the exhaust system, regardless of modifications to the engine.

AUTOMOTIVE EMISSIONS

Before emission controls were mandated on internal combustion engines, other sources of engine pollutants were discovered along with the exhaust emissions. It was determined that engine combustion exhaust produced approximately 60 percent of the total emission pollutants, fuel evaporation from the fuel tank and carburetor vents produced 20 percent, with the final 20 percent being produced through the crankcase as a by-product of the combustion process.

cess would be the only process to take place, the exhaust emissions would be harmless. However, during the combustion process, other compounds are formed which are considered dangerous. These pollutants are hydrocarbons (HC), carbon monoxide (CO), oxides of nitrogen (NOx) oxides of sulfur (SOx) and engine particulates.

Exhaust Gases

The exhaust gases emitted into the atmosphere are a combination of burned and unburned fuel. To understand the exhaust emission and its composition, we must review some basic chemistry.

When the air/fuel mixture is introduced into the engine, we are mixing air, composed of nitrogen (78 percent), oxygen (21 percent) and other gases (1 percent) with the fuel, which is 100 percent hydrocarbons (HC), in a semi-controlled ratio. As the combustion process is accomplished, power is produced to move the vehicle while the heat of combustion is transferred to the cooling system. The exhaust gases are then composed of nitrogen, a diatomic gas (N_2), the same as was introduced in the engine, carbon dioxide (CO_2), the same gas that is used in beverage carbonation, and water vapor (H_2O). The nitrogen (N_2), for the most part, passes through the engine unchanged, while the oxygen (O_2) reacts (burns) with the hydrocarbons (HC) and produces the carbon dioxide (CO_2) and the water vapors (H_2O). If this chemical pro-

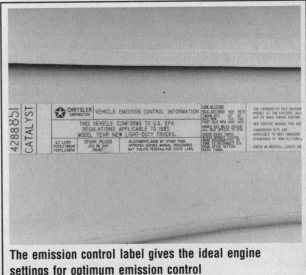

The emission control label gives the ideal engine settings for optimum emission control

HYDROCARBONS

Hydrocarbons (HC) are essentially fuel which was not burned during the combustion process or which has escaped into the atmosphere through fuel evaporation. The main sources of incomplete combustion are rich air/fuel mixtures, low engine temperatures and improper spark timing. The main sources of hydrocarbon emission through fuel evaporation on most vehicles used to be the vehicle's fuel tank and carburetor float bowl.

To reduce combustion hydrocarbon emission, engine modifications were made to minimize dead space and surface area in the combustion chamber. In addition, the air/fuel mixture was made more lean through the improved control which feedback carburetion and fuel injection offers and by the addition of external controls to aid in further combustion of the hydrocarbons outside the engine. Two such methods were the addition of air injection systems, to inject fresh air into the exhaust manifolds and the installation of catalytic converters, units that are able to burn traces of hydrocarbons without affecting the internal combustion process or fuel economy.

To control hydrocarbon emissions through fuel evaporation, modifications were made to the fuel tank to allow storage of the fuel vapors during periods of engine shut-down. Modifications were also made to the air intake system so that at specific times during engine operation, these vapors may be purged and burned by blending them with the air/fuel mixture.

CARBON MONOXIDE

Carbon monoxide is formed when not enough oxygen is present during the combustion process to convert carbon (C) to carbon dioxide (CO_2). An increase in the carbon monoxide (CO) emission is normally accompanied by an increase in the hydrocarbon (HC) emission because of the lack of oxygen to completely burn all of the fuel mixture.

Carbon monoxide (CO) also increases the rate at which the photo chemical smog is formed by speeding up the conversion of nitric oxide (NO) to nitrogen dioxide (NO_2). To accomplish this, carbon monoxide (CO) combines with oxygen (O_2) and nitric oxide (NO) to produce carbon dioxide (CO_2) and nitrogen dioxide (NO_2). $(CO + O_2 + NO \rightarrow CO_2 + NO_2)$.

The dangers of carbon monoxide, which is an odorless and colorless toxic gas are many. When carbon monoxide is inhaled into the lungs and passed into the blood stream, oxygen is replaced by the carbon monoxide in the red blood cells, causing a reduction in the amount of oxygen supplied to the many parts of the body. This lack of oxygen causes headaches, lack of coordination, reduced mental alertness and, should the carbon monoxide concentration be high enough, death could result.

NITROGEN

Normally, nitrogen is an inert gas. When heated to approximately 2500°F (1371°C) through the combustion process, this gas becomes active and causes an increase in the nitric oxide (NO) emission.

Oxides of nitrogen (NOx) are composed of approximately 97-98 percent nitric oxide (NO). Nitric oxide is a colorless gas but when it is passed into the atmosphere, it combines with oxygen and forms nitrogen dioxide (NO_2). The nitrogen dioxide then combines with chemically active hydrocarbons (HC) and when in the presence of sunlight, causes the formation of photo-chemical smog.

Ozone

To further complicate matters, some of the nitrogen dioxide (NO_2) is broken apart by the sunlight to form nitric oxide and oxygen. $(NO_2 + sunlight \rightarrow NO + O)$. This single atom of oxygen then combines with diatomic (meaning 2 atoms) oxygen (O_2) to form ozone (O_3). Ozone is one of the smells associated with smog. It has a pungent and offensive odor, irritates the eyes and lung tissues, affects the growth of plant life and causes rapid deterioration of rubber products. Ozone can be formed by sunlight as well as electrical discharge into the air.

The most common discharge area on the automobile engine is the secondary ignition electrical system, especially when inferior quality spark plug cables are used. As the surge of high voltage is routed through the secondary cable, the circuit builds up an electrical field around the wire, which acts upon the oxygen in the surrounding air to form the ozone. The faint glow along the cable with the engine running that may be visible on a dark night, is called the "corona discharge." It is the result of the electrical field passing from a high along the cable, to a low in the surrounding air, which forms the ozone gas. The combination of corona and ozone has been a major cause of cable deterioration. Recently, different and better quality insulating materials have lengthened the life of the electrical cables.

Although ozone at ground level can be harmful, ozone is beneficial to the earth's inhabitants. By having a concentrated ozone layer called the "ozonosphere," between 10 and 20 miles (16–32 km) up in the atmosphere, much of the ultra violet radiation from the sun's rays are absorbed and screened. If this ozone layer were not present, much of the earth's surface would be burned, dried and unfit for human life.

OXIDES OF SULFUR

Oxides of sulfur (SOx) were initially ignored in the exhaust system emissions, since the sulfur content of gasoline as a fuel is less than 1/10 of 1 percent. Because of this small amount, it was felt that it contributed very little to the overall pollution problem. However, because of the difficulty in solving the sulfur emissions in industrial pollutions and the introduction of catalytic converter to the automobile exhaust systems, a change was mandated. The automobile exhaust system, when equipped with a catalytic converter, changes the sulfur dioxide (SO_2) into sulfur trioxide (SO_3).

When this combines with water vapors (H_2O), a sulfuric acid mist (H_2SO_4) is formed and is a very difficult pollutant to handle since it is extremely corrosive. This sulfuric acid mist that is formed, is the same mist that rises from the vents of an automobile battery when an active chemical reaction takes place within the battery cells.

When a large concentration of vehicles equipped with catalytic converters are operating in an area, this acid mist may rise and be distributed over a large ground area causing land, plant, crop, paint and building damage.

PARTICULATE MATTER

A certain amount of particulate matter is present in the burning of any fuel, with carbon constituting the largest percentage of the particulates. In gasoline, the remaining particulates are the burned remains of the various other compounds used in its manufacture. When a gasoline engine is in good internal condition, the particulate emissions are low but as the engine wears internally, the particulate emissions increase. By visually inspecting the tail pipe emissions, a determination can be made as to where an engine defect may exist. An engine with light gray or blue smoke emitting from the tail pipe normally indicates an increase in the oil consumption through burning due to internal engine wear. Black smoke would indicate a defective fuel delivery system, causing the engine to operate in a rich mode. Regardless of the color of the smoke, the internal part of the engine or the fuel delivery system should be repaired to prevent excess particulate emissions.

Diesel and turbine engines emit a darkened plume of smoke from the exhaust system because of the type of fuel used. Emission control regulations are mandated for this type of emission and more stringent measures are being used to prevent excess emission of the particulate matter. Electronic components are being introduced to control the injection of the fuel at precisely the proper time of piston travel, to achieve the optimum in fuel ignition and fuel usage. Other particulate after-burning components are being tested to achieve a cleaner emission.

Good grades of engine lubricating oils should be used, which meet the manufacturers specification. Cut-rate oils can contribute to the particulate emission problem because of their low flash or ignition temperature point. Such oils burn prematurely during the combustion process causing emission of particulate matter.

The cooling system is an important factor in the reduction of particulate matter. The optimum combustion will occur, with the cooling system operating at a temperature specified by the manufacturer. The cooling system must be maintained in the same manner as the engine oiling system, as each system is required to perform properly in order for the engine to operate efficiently for a long time.

Crankcase Emissions

Crankcase emissions are made up of water, acids, unburned fuel, oil fumes and particulates. These emissions are classified as hydrocarbons (HC) and are formed by the small amount of unburned, compressed air/fuel mixture entering the crankcase from the combustion area (between the cylinder walls and piston rings) during the compression and power strokes. The head of the compression and combustion help to form the remaining crankcase emissions.

Since the first engines, crankcase emissions were allowed into the atmosphere through a road draft tube, mounted on the lower side of the engine block. Fresh air came in through an open oil filler cap or breather. The air passed through the crankcase mixing with blow-by gases. The motion of the vehicle and the air blowing past the open end of the road draft tube caused a low pressure area (vacuum) at the end of the tube. Crankcase emissions were simply drawn out of the road draft tube into the air.

To control the crankcase emission, the road draft tube was deleted. A hose and/or tubing was routed from the crankcase to the intake manifold so the blow-by emission could be burned with the air/fuel mixture. However, it was found that intake manifold vacuum, used to draw the crankcase emissions into the manifold, would vary in strength at the wrong time and not allow the proper emission flow. A regulating valve was needed to control the flow of air through the crankcase.

Testing, showed the removal of the blow-by gases from the crankcase as quickly as possible, was most important to the longevity of the engine. Should large accumulations of blow-by gases remain and condense, dilution of the engine oil would occur to form water, soots, resins, acids and lead salts, resulting in the formation of sludge and varnishes. This condensation of the blow-by gases occurs more frequently on vehicles used in numerous starting and stopping conditions, excessive idling and when the engine is not allowed to attain normal operating temperature through short runs.

Evaporative Emissions

Gasoline fuel is a major source of pollution, before and after it is burned in the automobile engine. From the time the fuel is refined, stored, pumped and transported, again stored until it is pumped into the fuel tank of the vehicle, the gasoline gives off unburned hydrocarbons (HC) into the atmosphere. Through the redesign of storage areas and venting systems, the pollution factor was diminished, but not eliminated, from the refinery standpoint. However, the automobile still remained the primary source of vaporized, unburned hydrocarbon (HC) emissions.

Fuel pumped from an underground storage tank is cool but when exposed to a warmer ambient temperature, will expand. Before controls were mandated, an owner might fill the fuel tank with fuel from an underground storage tank and park the vehicle for some time in warm area, such as a parking lot. As the fuel would warm, it would expand and should no provisions or area be provided for the expansion, the fuel would spill out of the filler neck and onto the ground, causing hydrocarbon (HC) pollution and creating a severe fire hazard. To correct this condition, the vehicle manufacturers added overflow plumbing and/or gasoline tanks with built in expansion areas or domes.

However, this did not control the fuel vapor emission from the fuel tank. It was determined that most of the fuel evaporation occurred when the vehicle was stationary and the engine not operating. Most vehicles carry 5–25 gallons (19–95 liters) of gasoline. Should a large concentration of vehicles be parked in one area, such as a large parking lot, excessive fuel vapor emissions would take place, increasing as the temperature increases.

To prevent the vapor emission from escaping into the atmosphere, the fuel systems were designed to trap the vapors while the vehicle is stationary, by sealing the system from the atmosphere. A storage system is used to collect and hold the fuel vapors from the carburetor (if equipped) and the fuel tank when the engine is not operating. When the engine is started, the storage system is then purged of the fuel vapors, which are drawn into the engine and burned with the air/fuel mixture.

EMISSION CONTROLS

Positive Crankcase Ventilation System

OPERATION

♦ **See Figures 1 and 2**

The crankcase emission control equipment consists of a positive crankcase ventilation (PCV) valve, a closed oil filler cap and the hoses that connect this equipment.

When the engine is running, a small portion of the gases which are formed in the combustion chamber leak by the piston rings and enter the crankcase. Since these gases are under pressure they tend to escape from the crankcase and enter into the atmosphere. If these gases are allowed to remain in the crankcase for any length of time, they would contaminate the engine oil and cause sludge to build up. If the gases are allowed to escape into

the atmosphere, they would pollute the air, as they contain unburned hydrocarbons. The crankcase emission control equipment recycles these gases back into the engine combustion chamber, where they are burned.

Crankcase gases are recycled in the following manner. While the engine is running, clean filtered air is drawn into the crankcase through the intake air filter and then through a hose leading to the oil filler cap. As the air passes through the crankcase it picks up the combustion gases and carries them out of the crankcase, up through the PCV valve and into the intake manifold. After they enter the intake manifold they are drawn into the combustion chamber and are burned.

The most critical component of the system is the PCV valve. This vacuum-controlled valve regulates the amount of gases which are recycled into the combustion chamber. At low engine speeds the valve is partially closed, limiting the flow of gases into the intake manifold. As engine speed increases, the valve opens to admit greater quantities of the gases into the intake manifold. If the valve should become blocked or plugged, the gases will be prevented from escaping the crankcase by the normal route. Since these gases are under pressure, they will find their own way out of the crankcase. This alternate route is usually a weak oil seal or gasket in the engine. As the gas escapes by the gasket, it also creates an oil leak. Besides causing oil leaks, a clogged PCV valve also allows these gases to remain in the crankcase for an extended period of time, promoting the formation of sludge in the engine.

The above explanation and the troubleshooting procedure which follows applies to all of the gasoline engines installed in these trucks, since all are equipped with PCV systems.

TROUBLESHOOTING

♦ **See Figure 3**

With the engine running, pull the PCV valve and hose from the valve rocker cover rubber grommet.

A hissing noise should be heard as air passes through the

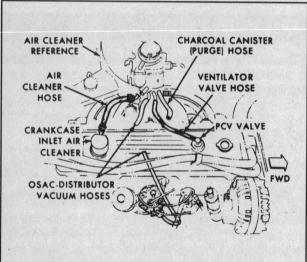

Fig. 1 Common inline 6-cylinder engine PCV system

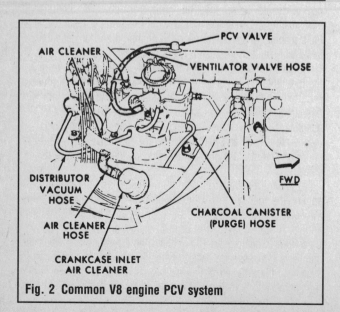

Fig. 2 Common V8 engine PCV system

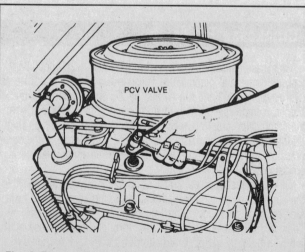

Fig. 3 Place your finger over the valve to check for vacuum

valve and a strong vacuum should be felt when you place a finger over the valve inlet if the valve is working properly. While you have your finger over the PCV valve inlet, check for vacuum leaks in the hose and at the connections.

When the PCV valve is removed from the engine, a metallic clicking noise should be heard when it is shaken. This indicates that the metal check ball inside the valve is still free and is not gummed up.

REMOVAL & INSTALLATION

1. Pull the PCV valve and hose from the rubber grommet in the rocker cover.
2. Remove the PCV valve from the hose. Inspect the inside of the PCV valve. If it is dirty, disconnect it from the intake manifold and clean it in a suitable, safe solvent.

To install:

1. If the PCV valve hose was removed, connect it to the intake manifold.
2. Connect the PCV valve to its hose.

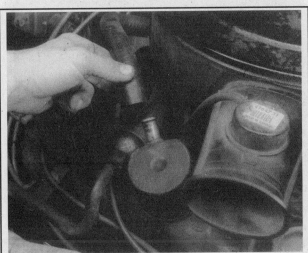

To change the crankcase inlet air filter, remove the air cleaner housing-to-filter hose . . .

. . . then pull the filter from the retaining grommet in the rocker cover

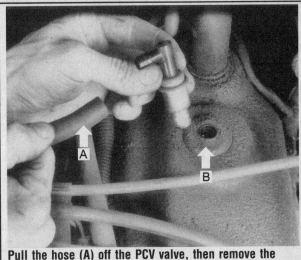

Pull the hose (A) off the PCV valve, then remove the valve from the rocker arm grommet (B)

3. Install the PCV valve into the rubber grommet in the valve rocker cover.

Evaporative Emission Controls

OPERATION

▶ **See Figures 4, 5 and 6**

Changes in atmospheric temperature cause fuel tanks to breathe; that is, the air within the tank expands and contracts with outside temperature changes. As the temperature rises, air escapes through the tank vent tube or the vent in the tank cap. The air which escapes contains gasoline vapors. In a similar manner on carbureted engines, the gasoline which fills the carburetor float bowl expands when the engine is stopped. Engine heat causes this expansion. The vapors escape through the air cleaner.

The Evaporative Emission Control System provides a sealed fuel system with the capability to store and condense fuel vapors. The system has three parts: a fill control vent system; a vapor vent and storage system; and a pressure and vacuum relief system (special fill cap).

The fill control vent system is a modification to the fuel tank. It uses a dome air space within the tank which is 10–12% of the tank's volume. The air space is sufficient to provide for the thermal expansion of the fuel. The space also serves as part of the in-tank vapor vent system.

The in-tank vent system consists of the domed air space previously described and a vapor separator assembly. The separator assembly is mounted to the top of the fuel tank and is secured by a cam-lockring, similar to the one which secures the fuel sending unit. Foam material fills the vapor separator assembly. The foam material separates raw fuel and vapors, thus retarding the entrance of fuel into the vapor line.

The vapor separator is an orifice valve located in the dome of the tank. The restricted size of the orifice, 0.050" (1.27mm) tends to allow only vapor to pass out of the tank. The orifice valve is connected to the vent line which runs forward to the carbon filled canister in the engine compartment.

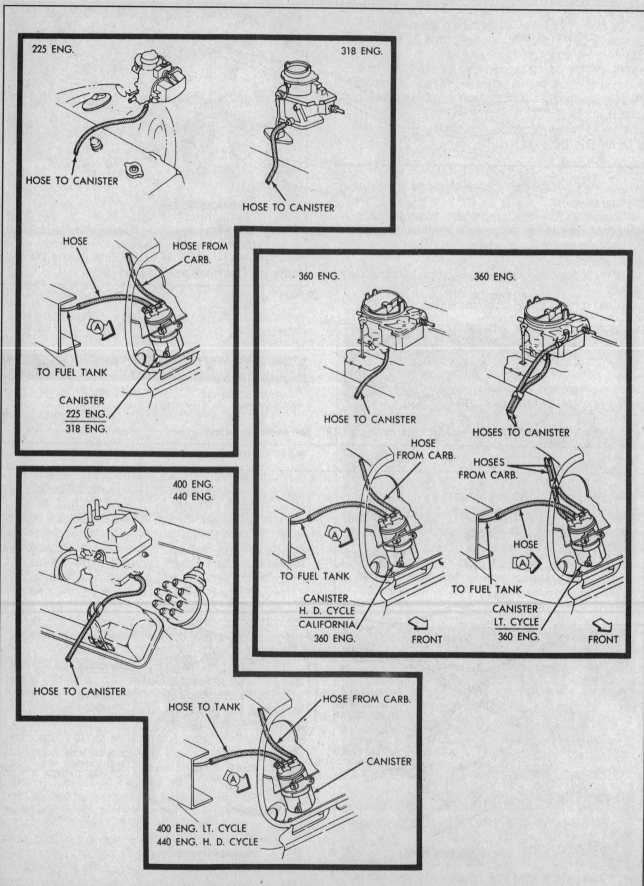

Fig. 4 Common ECS vapor hose routing for 1978 and earlier vehicles—Federal and California shown

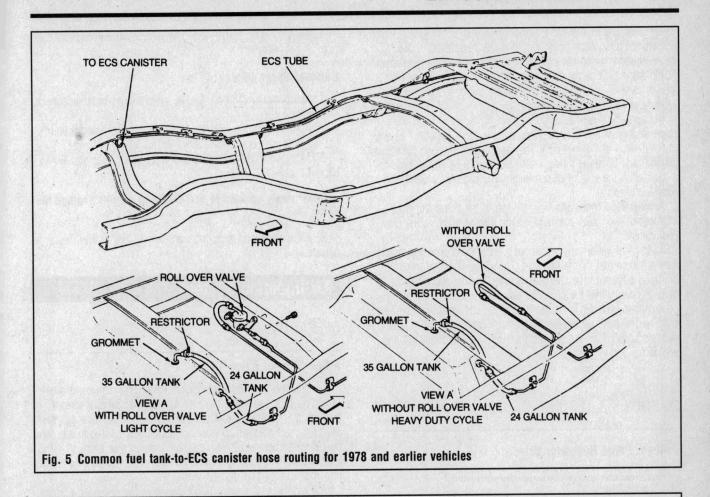

Fig. 5 Common fuel tank-to-ECS canister hose routing for 1978 and earlier vehicles

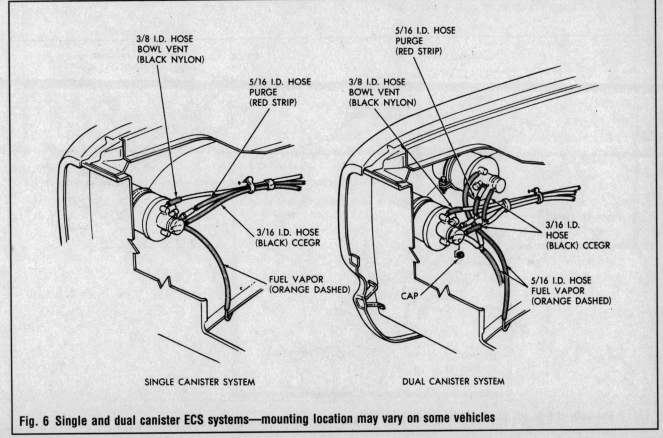

Fig. 6 Single and dual canister ECS systems—mounting location may vary on some vehicles

The sealed filler cap has a pressure-vacuum relief valve. Under normal operating conditions, the filler cap operates as a check valve, allowing air to enter the tank to replace the fuel consumed. At the same time, it prevents vapors from escaping through the cap. In case of excessive pressure within the tank, the filler cap valve opens to relieve the pressure.

Because the filler cap is sealed, fuel vapors have only one place through which they may escape: the vapor separator assembly at the top of the fuel tank. The vapors pass through the foam material and continue through a single vapor line which leads to a canister in the engine compartment. The canister is filled with activated charcoal.

Another vapor line runs from the top of the carburetor float chamber or the intake manifold, or the throttle body, to the charcoal canister.

As the fuel vapors (hydrocarbons), enter the charcoal canister, they are absorbed by the charcoal. The air is dispelled through the open bottom of the charcoal canister, leaving the hydrocarbons trapped within the charcoal. When the engine is started, vacuum causes fresh air to be drawn into the canister from its open bottom. The fresh air passes through the charcoal picking up the hydrocarbons which are trapped there and feeding them into the engine for burning with the fuel mixture.

DIAGNOSIS & TESTING

Canister Purge Regulator Valve

1. Disconnect the hoses at the purge regulator valve. Disconnect the electrical lead.
2. Connect a vacuum pump to the vacuum source port.

3. Apply 5 in.Hg to the port. The valve should hold the vacuum. If not, replace it.

Canister Purge Valve

1. Apply vacuum to port **A**. The valve should hold vacuum. If not, replace it.
2. Apply vacuum to port **B**. All valves should hold vacuum. If the valve doesn't operate properly, replace it.
3. Apply 16 in.Hg to port **A** and apply vacuum to port **B**. Air should pass.

➡**Never apply vacuum to port C. Doing so will damage the valve.**

4. If the valve fails to perform properly in any of these tests, replace it.

Air Injection System

OPERATION

▶ **See Figures 7 thru 13**

The air injection emission control system makes use of a belt driven air pump to inject fresh air into the hot exhaust stream through the engine exhaust ports. The result is the extended burning of those fumes which were not completely ignited in the combustion chamber, and the subsequent reduction of some of the hydrocarbon and carbon monoxide content of the exhaust emissions into harmless carbon dioxide and water.

The air injection system is composed of the following components:

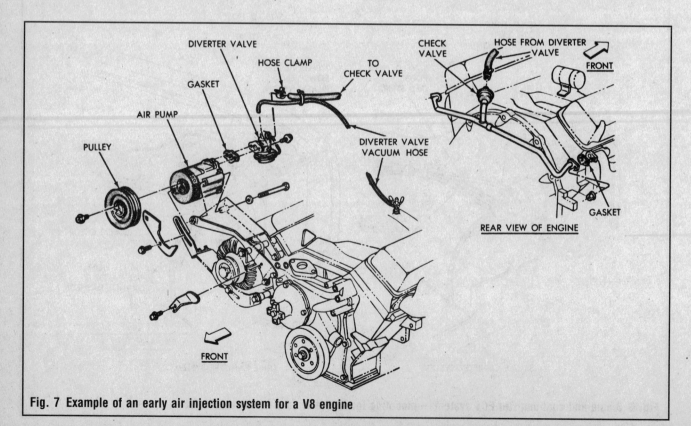

Fig. 7 Example of an early air injection system for a V8 engine

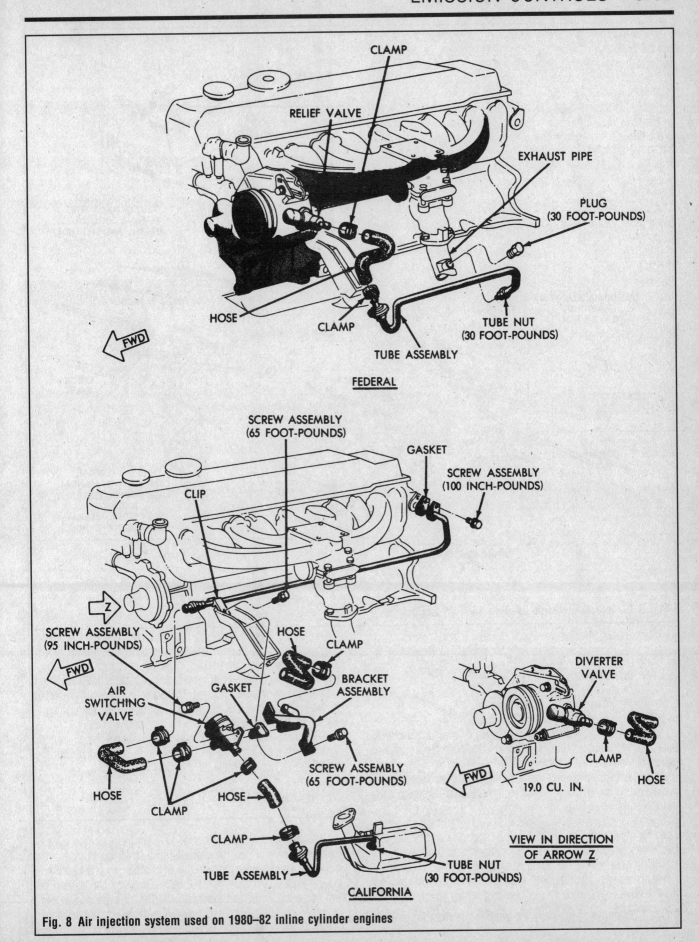

Fig. 8 Air injection system used on 1980–82 inline cylinder engines

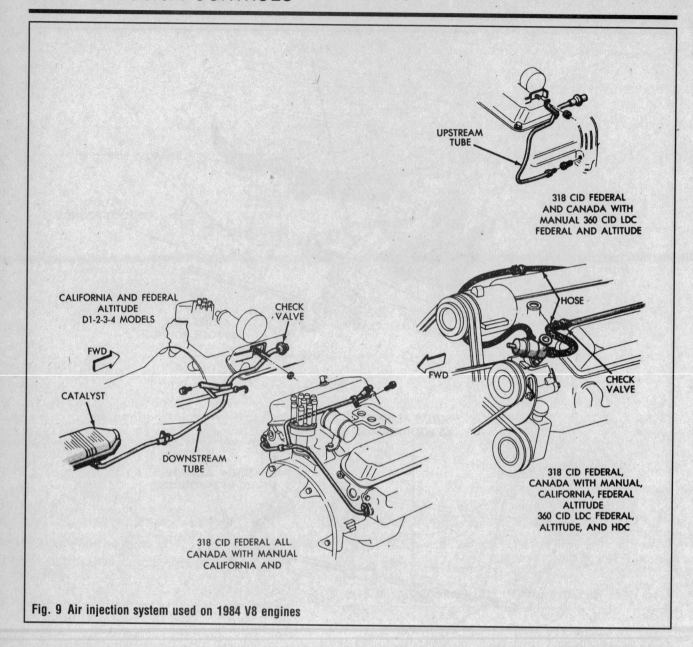

UPSTREAM TUBE

318 CID FEDERAL AND CANADA WITH MANUAL 360 CID LDC FEDERAL AND ALTITUDE

CALIFORNIA AND FEDERAL ALTITUDE D1-2-3-4 MODELS

CHECK VALVE

FWD

HOSE

FWD

CHECK VALVE

CATALYST

DOWNSTREAM TUBE

318 CID FEDERAL ALL. CANADA WITH MANUAL CALIFORNIA AND

318 CID FEDERAL, CANADA WITH MANUAL, CALIFORNIA, FEDERAL ALTITUDE 360 CID LDC FEDERAL, ALTITUDE, AND HDC

Fig. 9 Air injection system used on 1984 V8 engines

1. Air supply pump (belt driven)
2. Air by-pass valve.
3. Check valves
4. Air manifolds (internal or external)
5. Air supply tubes (on external manifolds only).

Air for the air injection system is cleaned by means of a centrifugal filter fan mounted on the air pump driveshaft. The air filter does not require a replaceable element.

To prevent excessive pressure, the air pump is equipped with a pressure relief valve which uses a replaceable plastic plug to control the pressure setting.

The air injection air pump has sealed bearings which are lubricated for the life of the unit, and preset rotor vane and bearing clearances, which do not require any periodic adjustments.

The air supply from the pump is controlled by the air by-pass valve, sometimes called a dump valve. During deceleration, the air bypass valve opens, momentarily diverting the air supply through a silencer and into the atmosphere, thus preventing backfires within the exhaust system.

A check valve is incorporated in the air inlet side of the air manifolds. Its purpose is to prevent exhaust gases from backing up into the air injection system. This valve is especially important in the event of drive belt failure, and during deceleration, when the air by-pass valve is dumping the air supply.

The air manifolds and air supply tubes channel the air from the air injection air pump into the exhaust ports of each cylinder, thus completing the cycle of the air injection system

DIAGNOSIS & TESTING

The air injection system is used to inject fresh air into the exhaust manifolds or catalytic converters via an air control valve. Under some operating conditions, the air can be dumped back into the atmosphere via an air bypass valve. On some applications the two valves are combined into one unit. The air bypass valve can be either the normally closed type, when the valves are separate, or the normally open type, when the valves are combined.

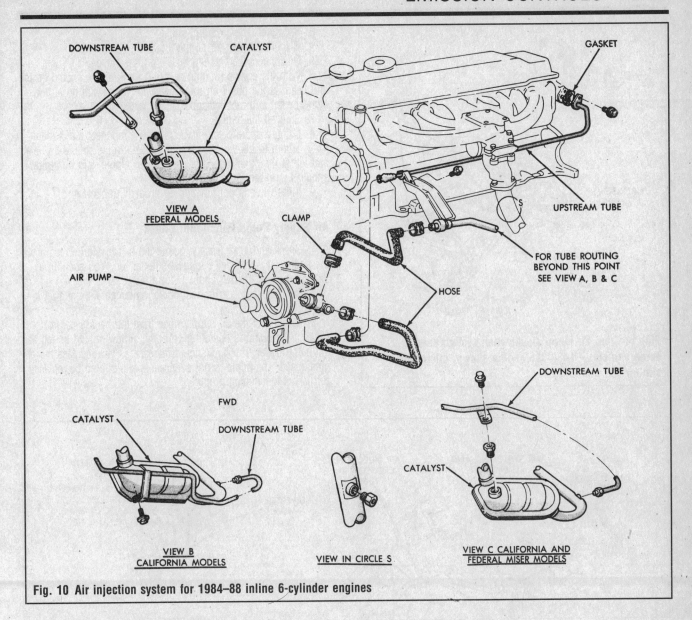

Fig. 10 Air injection system for 1984–88 inline 6-cylinder engines

Normally Closed Air Bypass Valve Functional Test

1. Disconnect the air supply hose at the valve.
2. Run the engine to normal operating temperature.
3. Disconnect the vacuum line and make sure vacuum is present. If no vacuum is present, remove or bypass any restrictors or delay valves in the vacuum line.
4. Run the engine at 1,500 rpm with the vacuum line connected. Air pump supply air should be heard and felt at the valve outlet.
5. With the engine still at 1,500 rpm, disconnect the vacuum line. Air at the outlet should shut off or dramatically decrease. Air pump supply air should now be felt or heard at the silencer ports.
6. If the valve doesn't pass each of these tests, replace it.

Normally Open Air Bypass Valve Functional Test

1. Disconnect the air supply hose at the valve.
2. Run the engine to normal operating temperature.
3. Disconnect the vacuum lines from the valve.
4. Run the engine at 1,500 rpm with the vacuum lines discon-

nected. Air pump supply air should be heard and felt at the valve outlet.
5. Shut off the engine. Using a spare length of vacuum hose, connect the vacuum nipple of the valve to direct manifold vacuum.
6. Run the engine at 1,500 rpm. Air at the outlet should shut off or dramatically decrease. Air pump supply air should now be felt or heard at the silencer ports.
7. With the engine still in this mode, cap the vacuum vent. Accelerate the engine to 2,000 rpm and suddenly release the throttle. A momentary interruption of air pump supply air should be felt at the valve outlet.
8. If the valve doesn't pass each of these tests, replace it. Reconnect all lines.

Air Control Valve Functional Test

1. Run the engine to normal operating temperature, then increase the speed to 1,500 rpm.
2. Disconnect the air supply hose at the valve inlet and verify that there is airflow present.

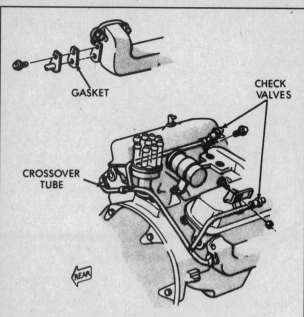

Fig. 11 Dual air pump air injection system used on some vehicles—1986 318 engine shown, others are similar

3. Reconnect the air supply hose.

4. Disconnect both air supply hoses.

5. Disconnect the vacuum hose from the valve.

6. With the engine running at 1,500 rpm, airflow should be felt and heard at the outlet on the side of the valve, with no airflow heard or felt at the outlet opposite the vacuum nipple.

7. Shut off the engine.

8. Using a spare piece of vacuum hose, connect direct manifold vacuum to the valve's vacuum fitting. Airflow should be heard and felt at the outlet opposite the vacuum nipple, and no airflow should be present at the other outlet.

9. If the valve is not functioning properly, replace it.

Air Supply Pump Functional Check

1. Check and, if necessary, adjust the belt tension. Press at the mid-point of the belt's longest straight run. You should be able to depress the belt about ½" at most.

2. Run the engine to normal operating temperature and let it idle.

3. Disconnect the air supply hose from the bypass control valve. If the pump is operating properly, airflow should be felt at the pump outlet. The flow should increase as you increase the engine speed. The pump is not serviceable and should be replaced if it is not functioning properly.

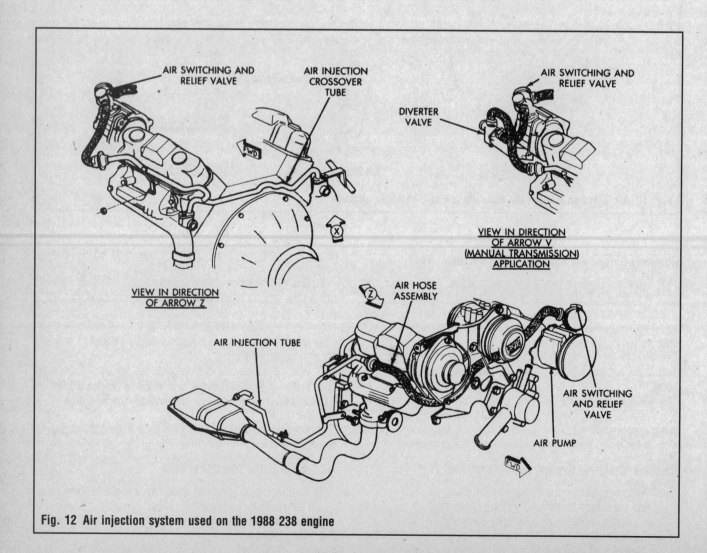

Fig. 12 Air injection system used on the 1988 238 engine

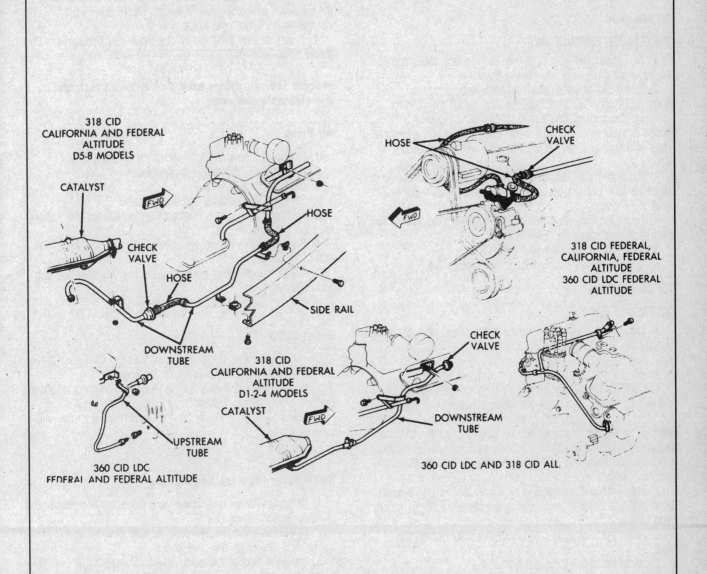

Fig. 13 Air injection system used on 1988 318 and 360 engines

REMOVAL & INSTALLATION

Air By-Pass Valve

1. Disconnect the air and vacuum hoses at the air by-pass valve body.

2. Position the air by-pass valve and connect the respective hoses.

Check Valve

1. Disconnect the air supply hose at the valve. Use a 1¼" crowfoot wrench. The valve has a standard, right-hand pipe thread.

2. Clean the threads on the air manifold adapter (air supply tube on the V8 engines) with a wire brush. Do not blow compressed air through the check valve in either direction.

3. Install the check valve and tighten.

4. Connect the air supply hose.

Air Manifold

6-CYLINDER ENGINES ONLY

1. Disconnect the air supply hose at the check valve, position the hose out of the way and remove the valve.

2. Loosen all of the air manifold-to-cylinder head tube coupling nuts (compression fittings). Inspect the air manifold for damaged threads and fittings and for leaking connections. Repair or replace as required. Clean the manifold and associated parts with kerosene. Do not dry the parts with compressed air.

3. Position the air manifold on the cylinder head. Be sure that all of the tube coupling nuts are aligned with the cylinder head.

4. Screw each coupling nut into the cylinder head, one or two threads. Tighten the tube coupling nuts.

5. Install the check valve and tighten it.

6. Connect the air supply hose to the check valve.

Air Supply Tube

V8 ENGINE ONLY

1. Disconnect the air supply hose at the check valve and position the hose out of the way.

2. Remove the check valve.

3. Remove the air supply tube bolt and seal washer.

4. Carefully remove the air supply tube and seal washer from the cylinder head. Inspect the air supply tube for evidence of leaking threads or seal surfaces. Examine the attaching bolt head, seal washers, and supply tube surface for leaks. Inspect the attaching bolt and cylinder head threads for damage. Clean the air supply tube, seal washers, and bolt with kerosene. Do not dry the parts with compressed air.

5. Install the seal washer and air supply tube on the cylinder head. Be sure that it is positioned in the same manner as before removal.

6. Install the seal washer and mounting bolt. Tighten the bolt.

7. Install the check valve and tighten it.

8. Connect the air supply hose to the check valve.

Air Nozzle

6-CYLINDER ENGINES ONLY

Normally, air nozzles should be replaced during cylinder head reconditioning. A nozzle may be replaced, however, without removing the cylinder head, by removing the air manifold and using a hooked tool.

Clean the nozzle with kerosene and a stiff brush. Inspect the air nozzles for eroded tips.

Air Pump and Filter Fan

1. Loosen the air pump attaching bolts.

2. Remove the drive pulley attaching bolts and pull the pulley off the air pump shaft.

3. Pry the outer disc loose, then remove the centrifugal filter fan. Care must be used to prevent foreign matter from entering the air intake hole, especially if the fan breaks during removal. Do not attempt to remove the metal drive hub.

4. Install the new filter fan by drawing it into position with the pulley bolts.

➡**Some 1967 air pumps have air filters with replaceable, non-cleanable elements.**

Air Pump

1. Disconnect the air outlet hose at the air pump.

2. Loosen the pump belt tension adjuster.

3. Disengage the drive belt.

4. Remove the mounting bolt and air pump.

5. Position the air pump on the mounting bracket and install the mounting bolt.

6. Place the drive belt in the pulley and attach the adjusting arm to the air pump.

7. Adjust the drive belt tension and tighten the adjusting arm and mounting bolts.

8. Connect the air outlet hose to the air pump.

Relief Valve

Do not disassemble the air pump on the truck to replace the relief valve, but remove the pump from the engine.

1. Remove the relief valve on the pump housing and hold it in position with a block of wood.

2. Use a hammer to lightly tap the wood block until the relief valve is seated.

Relief Valve Pressure Setting Plug

1. Compress the locking tabs inward (together) and remove the plastic pressure setting plug.

2. Before installing the new plug, be sure that the plug is the correct one. The plugs are color coded.

3. Insert the plug in the relief valve hole and push in until it snaps into place.

Aspirator Air System

OPERATION

◆ **See Figure 14**

This system utilizes exhaust pressure pulsation to draw clean air from the inside of the air cleaner, into the exhaust system. The system's function is to reduce hydrocarbon (HC) emissions.

The only service possible is replacement of the aspirator or check valve. See the air injection check valve procedures in this section.

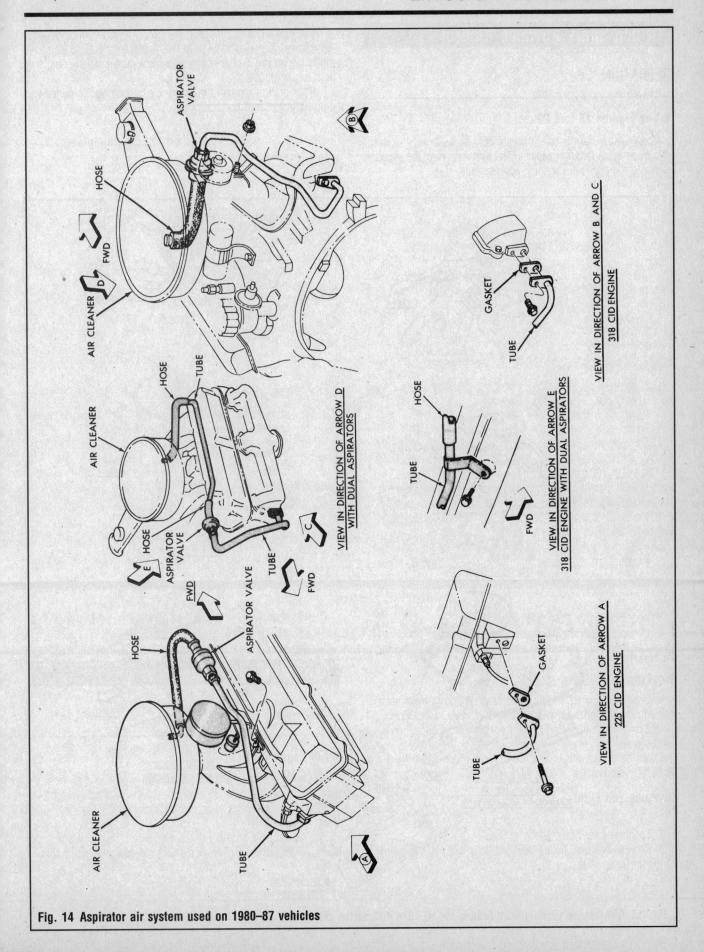

Fig. 14 Aspirator air system used on 1980–87 vehicles

Orifice Spark Advance Control

OPERATION

◆ **See Figures 15 thru 20**

The OSAC system is used on light duty trucks to aid in control of nitrous oxide (NOx) emissions. The system control the vacuum signal to the distributor vacuum advance unit.

A tiny orifice is incorporated in the OSAC valve which delays the change in ported vacuum to the distributor by 17 to 27 seconds, depending on the engine and truck model, when going from idle to part throttle.

When going from part throttle to idle, the change in ported vacuum is instantaneous.

Fig. 15 OSAC valve vacuum hose routing for all 1974 100 series vehicles

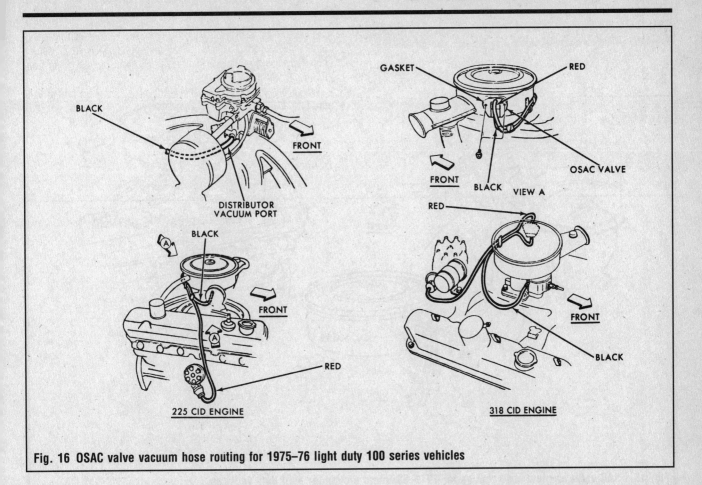

Fig. 16 OSAC valve vacuum hose routing for 1975–76 light duty 100 series vehicles

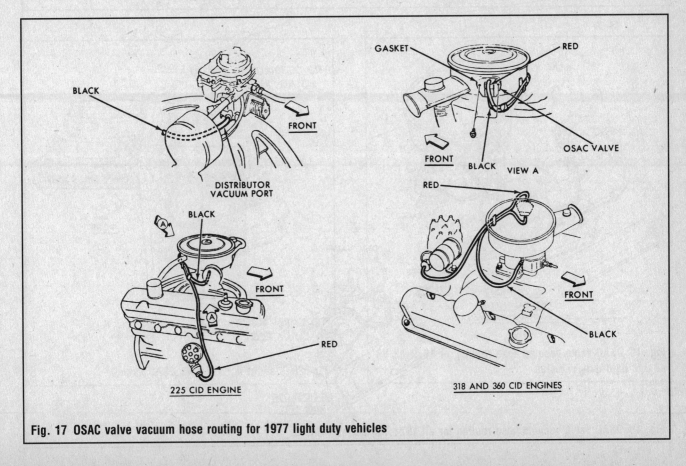

Fig. 17 OSAC valve vacuum hose routing for 1977 light duty vehicles

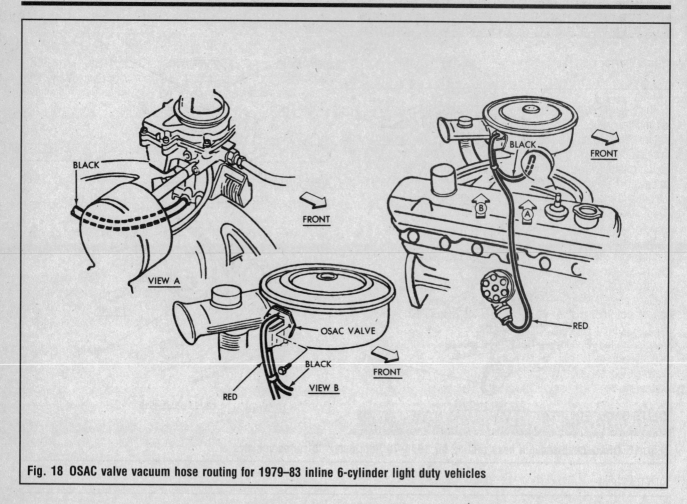

Fig. 18 OSAC valve vacuum hose routing for 1979–83 inline 6-cylinder light duty vehicles

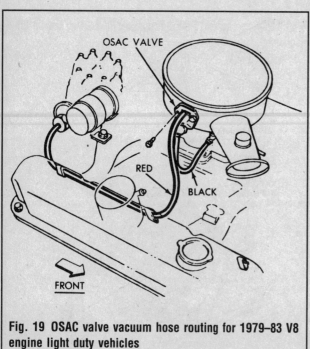

Fig. 19 OSAC valve vacuum hose routing for 1979–83 V8 engine light duty vehicles

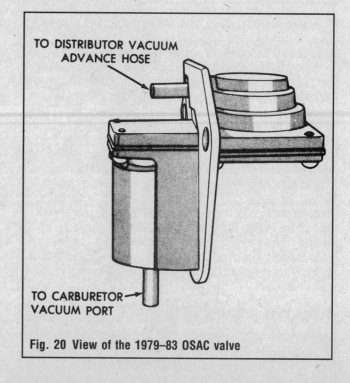

Fig. 20 View of the 1979–83 OSAC valve

Catalytic Converter

OPERATION

The catalytic converter, mounted in the trucks exhaust system is a muffler-shaped device containing a ceramic honeycomb shaped material coated with alumina and impregnated with catalytically active precious metals such as platinum, palladium and rhodium.

The catalyst's job is to reduce air pollutants by oxidizing hydrocarbons (HC) and carbon monoxide (CO). Catalysts containing palladium and rhodium also oxidize nitrous oxides (NOx).

On some trucks, the catalyst is also fed by the secondary air system, via a small supply tube in the side of the catalyst.

No maintenance is possible on the converter, other than keeping the heat shield clear of flammable debris, such as leaves and twigs.

Other than external damage, the only significant damage possible to a converter is through the use of leaded gasoline, or by way of a too rich fuel/air mixture. Both of these problems will ruin the converter through contamination of the catalyst and will eventually plug the converter causing loss of power and engine performance.

When this occurs, the catalyst must be replaced. For catalyst replacement, see the Exhaust System section in Section 3.

Exhaust Gas Recirculation

▶ **See Figures 21 thru 43**

OPERATION

Oxides of nitrogen (NOx) in engine exhausts are reduced by lowering the combustion temperature inside the cylinders. This is accomplished by allowing a predetermined amount of exhaust gas to recirculate into and dilute the incoming air/fuel mixture. However, a problem arises with this system. When an engine is cold, the combustion temperature is not high enough to create NOx emissions, and if you recirculate exhaust gasses into a cold engine, it usually causes the engine to stumble or stall. So additional systems were designed to correct this problem. The first addition was a simple vacuum delay valve, which stopped the opening of the EGR valve for several seconds, usually enough time to raise the engine rpm high enough to not be affected by the exhaust gasses now being introduced into the air/fuel mixture. Next, temperature controlled vacuum switches were used, which shut off the vacuum until a certain engine temperature was reached. Then, through advancements in electronics, control devices appeared first as electrical switches, and eventually became computer controlled, which can precisely control the timing of the EGR valve.

Venturi Vacuum Control System

The venturi vacuum control system utilizes a vacuum tap at the throat of the carburetor venturi to provide a control signal. However, this is a very weak vacuum source which requires the use of a vacuum amplifier to increase the vacuum to a level required to properly operate the EGR valve. The vacuum amplifier is not serviceable, and must be replaced if found to be defective.

Ported Vacuum EGR

The ported EGR valve is operated by engine vacuum. A vacuum signal from the carburetor or throttle bodyactivates the EGR valve diaphragm. As the vacuum signal increase it gradually opens the valve pintle allowing exhaust gases to flow. The amount of flow is directly proportional to the pintle position.

COMPONENT TESTING

EGR System

1. The engine should be warmed up, at normal operating temperature, with the parking brake set.
2. Allow the engine to idle in Neutral with the throttle closed, then quickly accelerate to approximately 2,000 rpm, watching the groove carefully on the EGR valve stem.
3. You should notice movement of the valve stem during the acceleration period, and there should be a change in the location of the groove on the stem. If movement is noticed this means that the control system is functioning properly and the EGR flow test can be performed.
4. If no movement is noticed, you may have to replace the valve or another component in the system.

EGR Gas Flow

1. Connect a tachometer to the engine.
2. Remove the vacuum hose from the EGR valve and connect a hand vacuum pump to the valve vacuum motor nipple.
3. Start the engine and slowly apply vacuum to the motor.
4. The engine rpm should drop as the vacuum reaches 3–5 in. Hg (10–17 kPa), and continue to drop as more vacuum is applied. Your engine may even stall out during this test (meaning that EGR gases are flowing through the system).
5. If this and system tests are good, your EGR system is fully functioning.
6. If the rpm does not drop, the valve may be plugged or defective. If so, remove the valve and inspect it, along with the intake manifold passages for any deposits. Clean if necessary.

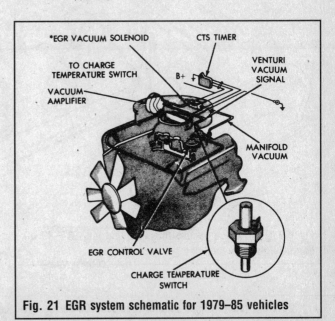

Fig. 21 EGR system schematic for 1979–85 vehicles

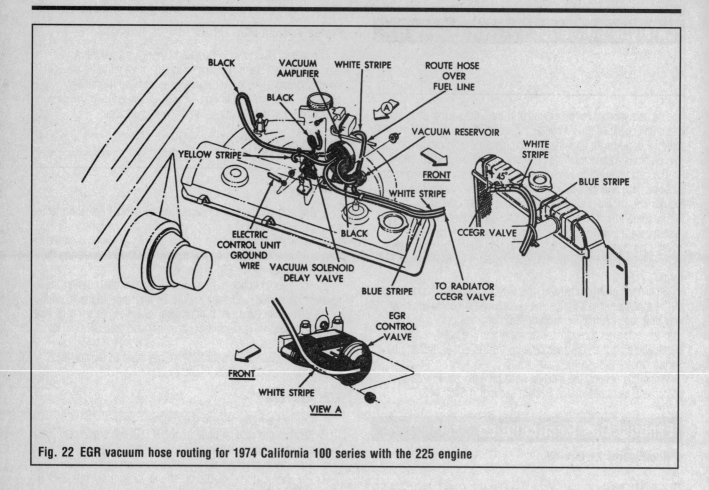

Fig. 22 EGR vacuum hose routing for 1974 California 100 series with the 225 engine

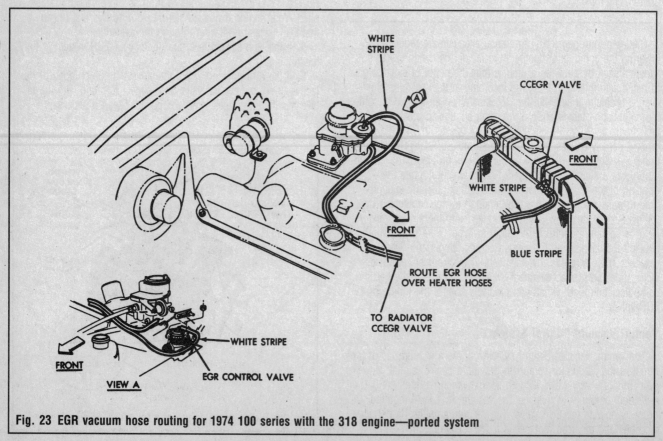

Fig. 23 EGR vacuum hose routing for 1974 100 series with the 318 engine—ported system

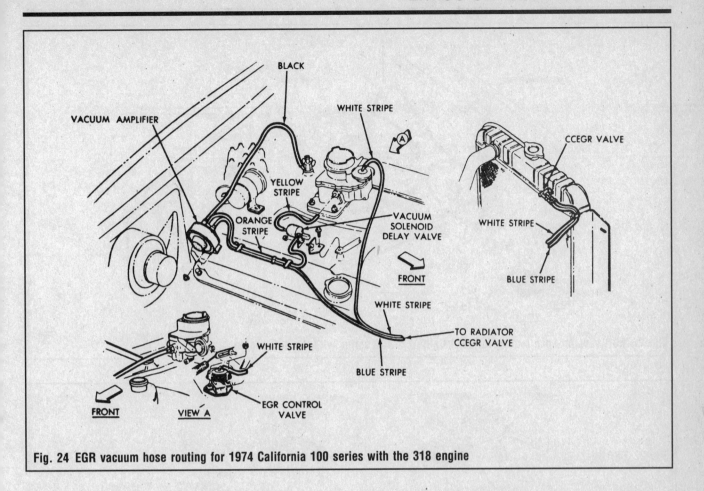

Fig. 24 EGR vacuum hose routing for 1974 California 100 series with the 318 engine

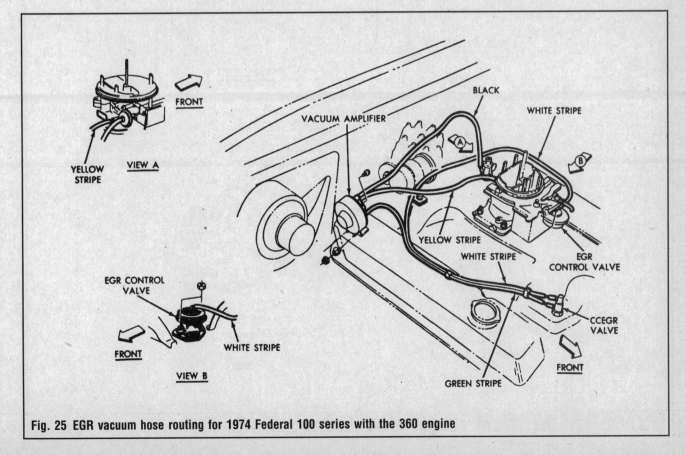

Fig. 25 EGR vacuum hose routing for 1974 Federal 100 series with the 360 engine

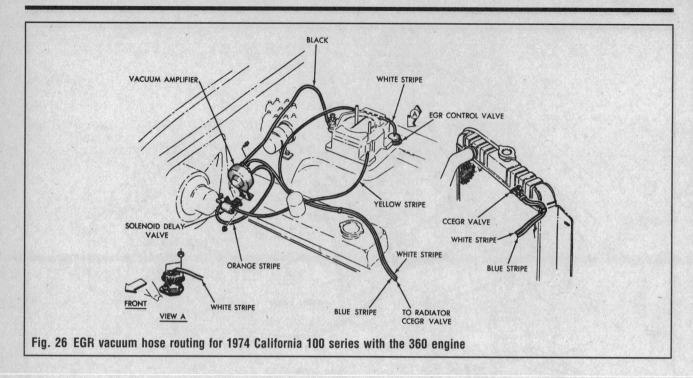

Fig. 26 EGR vacuum hose routing for 1974 California 100 series with the 360 engine

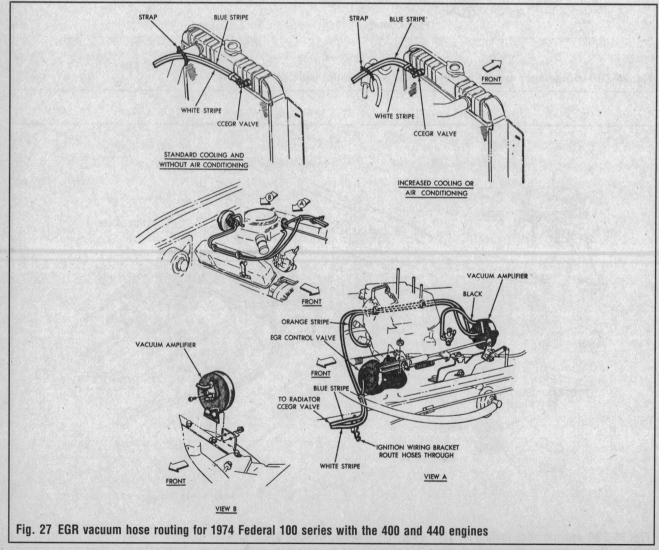

Fig. 27 EGR vacuum hose routing for 1974 Federal 100 series with the 400 and 440 engines

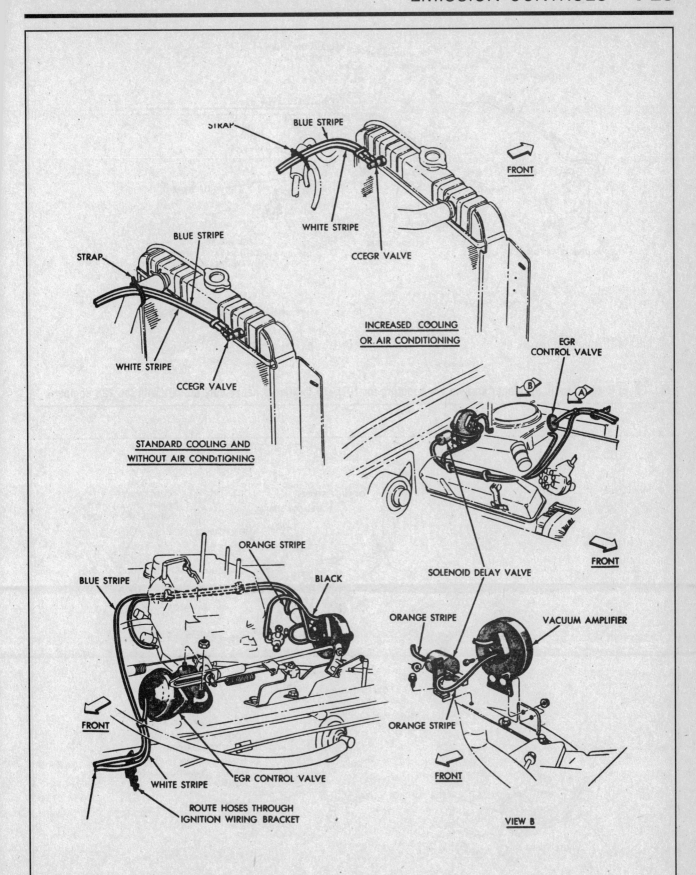

Fig. 28 EGR vacuum hose routing for 1974 California 100 series with the 400 and 440 engines

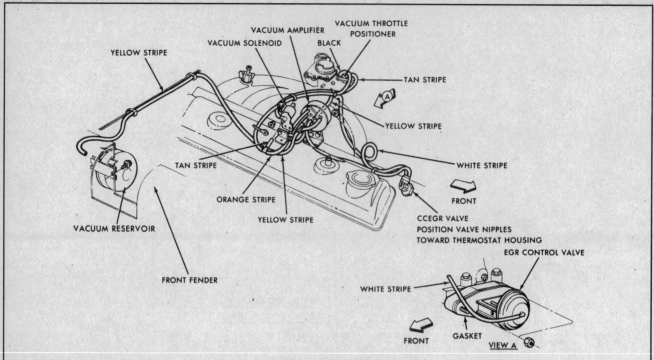

Fig. 29 EGR and throttle positioner vacuum hose routing for 1975–76 California heavy duty models with the 225 engine

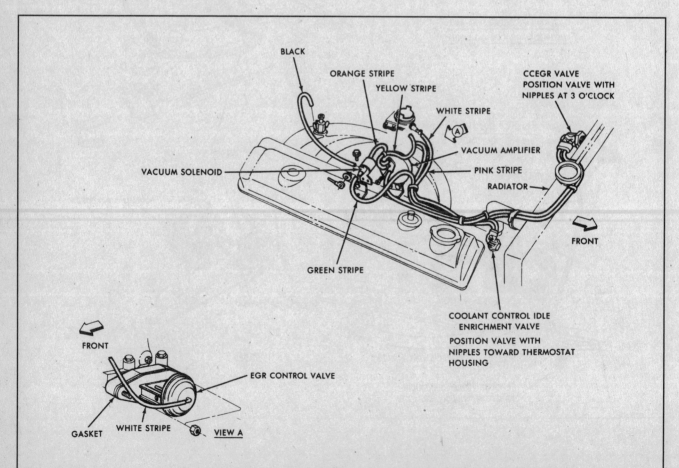

Fig. 30 EGR and idle enrichment vacuum hose routing for 1975–76 Federal 100 series with the 225 engine and automatic transmission

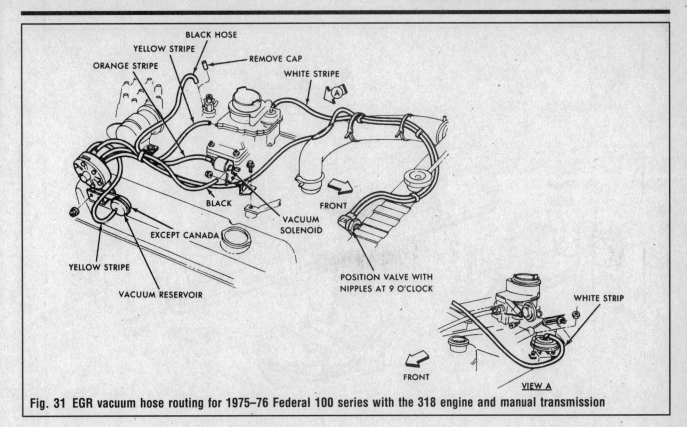

Fig. 31 EGR vacuum hose routing for 1975–76 Federal 100 series with the 318 engine and manual transmission

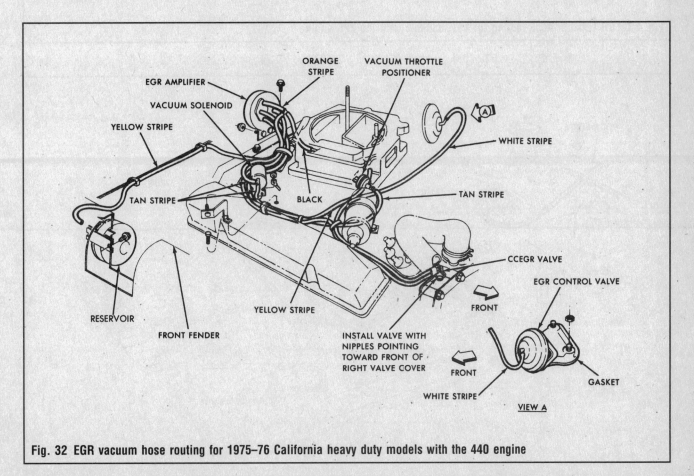

Fig. 32 EGR vacuum hose routing for 1975–76 California heavy duty models with the 440 engine

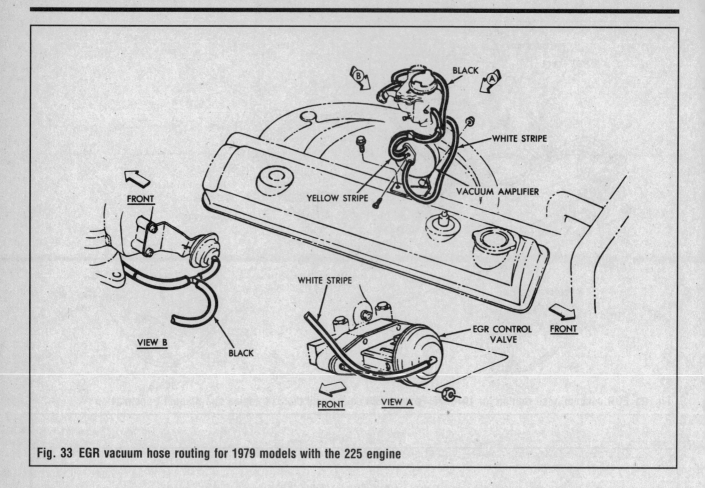

Fig. 33 EGR vacuum hose routing for 1979 models with the 225 engine

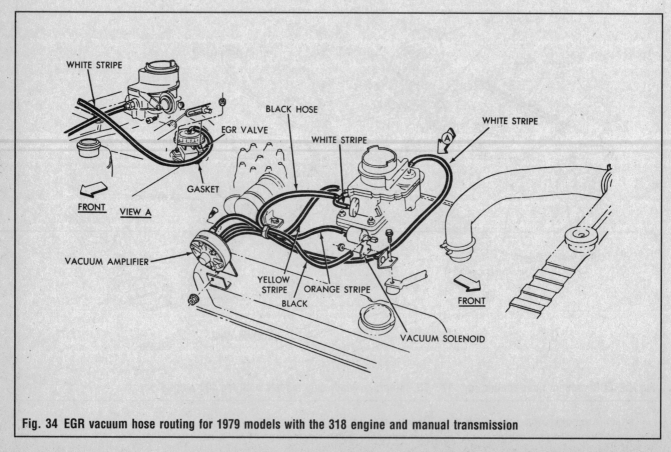

Fig. 34 EGR vacuum hose routing for 1979 models with the 318 engine and manual transmission

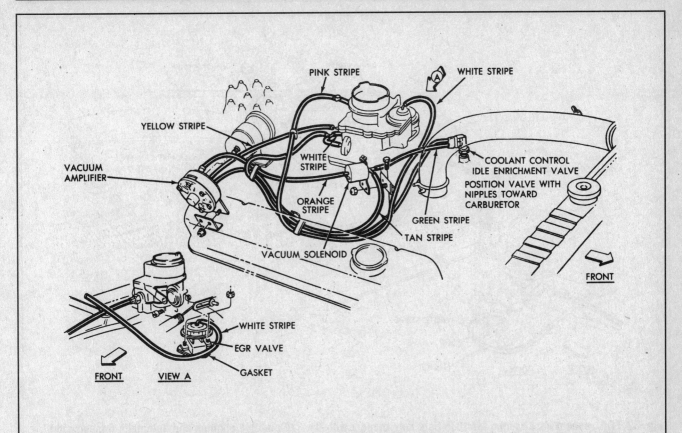

Fig. 35 EGR vacuum hose routing for 1979 light duty models with the 318 and 360 engines and automatic transmission

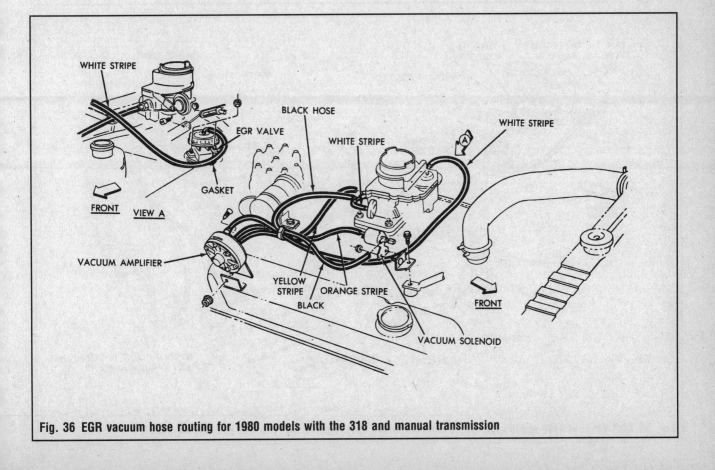

Fig. 36 EGR vacuum hose routing for 1980 models with the 318 and manual transmission

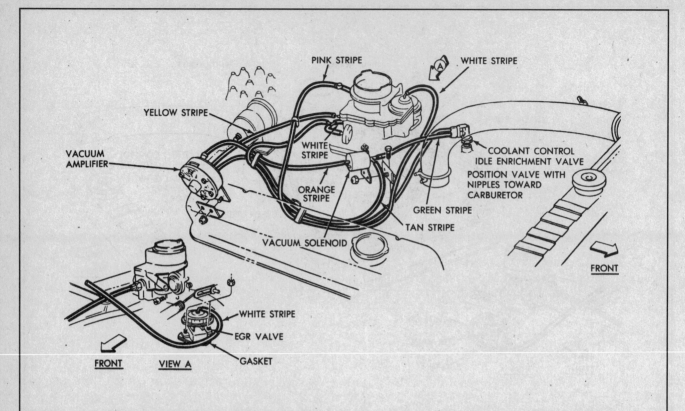

Fig. 37 EGR vacuum hose routing for 1980 light duty models with the 318 and 360 engines and automatic transmission

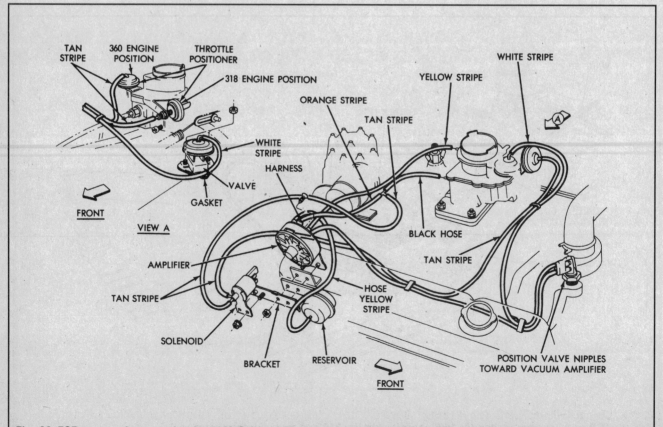

Fig. 38 EGR vacuum hose routing for 1980 California heavy duty models with the 318 and 360 engines

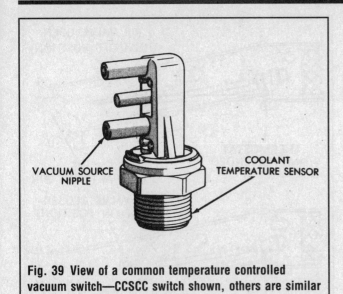

Fig. 39 View of a common temperature controlled vacuum switch—CCSCC switch shown, others are similar

VACUUM SOURCE NIPPLE

COOLANT TEMPERATURE SENSOR

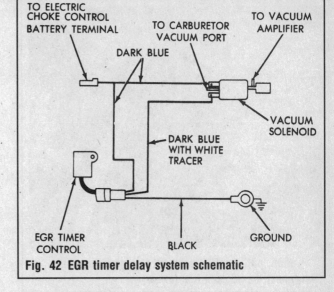

TO ELECTRIC CHOKE CONTROL BATTERY TERMINAL

TO CARBURETOR VACUUM PORT

TO VACUUM AMPLIFIER

DARK BLUE

VACUUM SOLENOID

DARK BLUE WITH WHITE TRACER

EGR TIMER CONTROL

BLACK

GROUND

Fig. 42 EGR timer delay system schematic

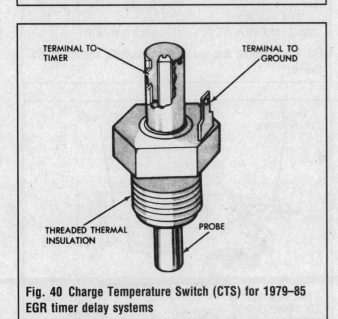

TERMINAL TO TIMER

TERMINAL TO GROUND

THREADED THERMAL INSULATION

PROBE

Fig. 40 Charge Temperature Switch (CTS) for 1979–85 EGR timer delay systems

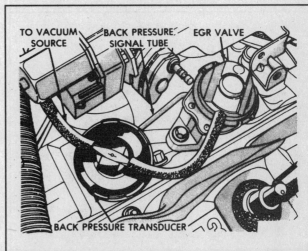

TO VACUUM SOURCE

BACK PRESSURE SIGNAL TUBE

EGR VALVE

BACK PRESSURE TRANSDUCER

Fig. 43 EGR transducer mounting for 1988 V6 and V8 engines

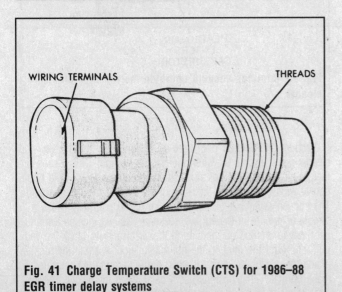

WIRING TERMINALS

THREADS

Fig. 41 Charge Temperature Switch (CTS) for 1986–88 EGR timer delay systems

To remove the EGR valve on the inline 6-cylinder engine, remove the retaining nuts . . .

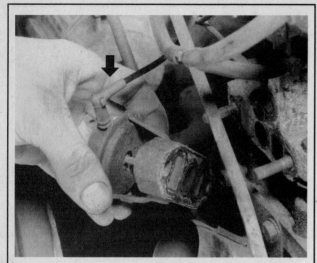

. . . then, pull the EGR valve off the mounting studs. Disconnect the vacuum line (arrow)

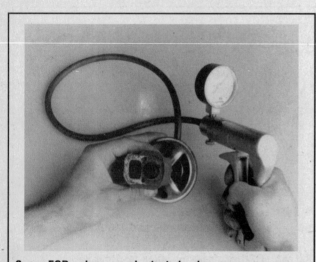

Some EGR valves may be tested using a vacuum pump by watching for diaphragm movement

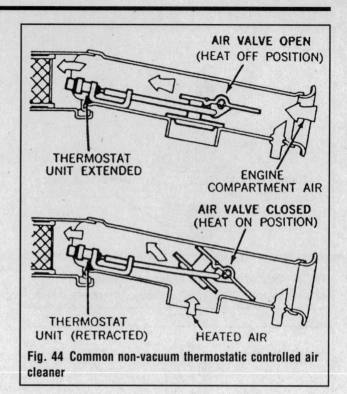

Fig. 44 Common non-vacuum thermostatic controlled air cleaner

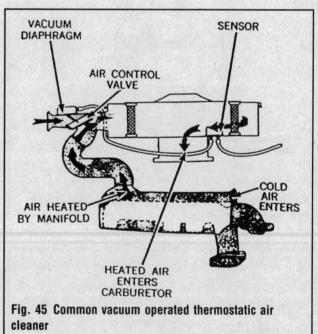

Fig. 45 Common vacuum operated thermostatic air cleaner

Heated Air Intake System

OPERATION

▶ See Figures 44, 45 and 46

Fresh air supplied to the air cleaner comes either from the normal snorkel, or from a tube connected to an exhaust manifold stove. A door in the snorkel regulates the source of incoming air so that a warm engine always takes in warm air, approximately 100°F. The door may be controlled by a thermostatic spring or expansion bulb, or it may be vacuum operated. The vacuum operated designs use a thermostatic bimetal switch inside the air cleaner that bleeds off vacuum as the engine warms up, and regulates the position of the air door. On all late models, the snorkel is connected to a long tube so it takes in cooler air from outside the engine compartment. In hot climates the cool air tube is necessary because underhood air can easily reach 200°F.

Vacuum operated air doors are all designed so that the air cleaner takes in cold air when there is no vacuum. This means that an air door in the hot air position will switch to the cold position at wide open throttle because of the loss of manifold vacuum. The sudden switching of the door from hot to cold may cause a tumble or misfire in the engine, so some designs include a modulator valve mounted on the side of the air cleaner to block the vacuum and hold the door in the hot air position. A small thermostat inside the modulator opens it when the underhood temperatures reach normal. Other designs use a delay valve that allows the air door to move to the cold position slowly, to prevent stumble.

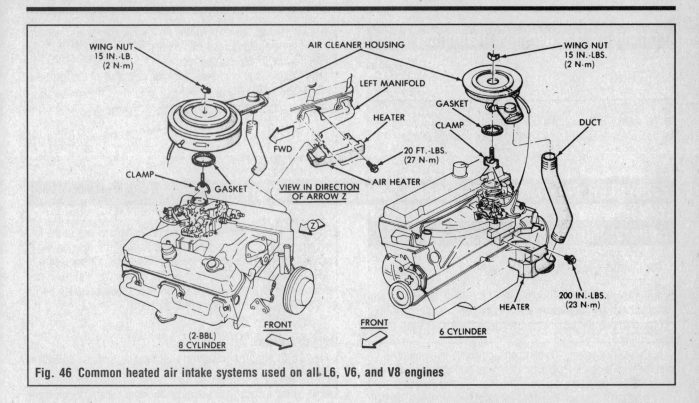

Fig. 46 Common heated air intake systems used on all L6, V6, and V8 engines

TESTING

Non-Vacuum Type

To test the non-vacuum type of heated air cleaner, start with an engine that is cold enough to have the air door in the hot air position. Remove the top of the air cleaner and put a thermometer inside the cleaner, then replace the cover without the nuts. Start the engine and watch the air door through the end of the air cleaner. You may have to remove some air ducting to be able to see the air door. As soon as the air door starts to move from the hot air position, lift the top off the air cleaner and read the temperature. If the temperature is between 130 and 150°F., the thermostat is working correctly. If not, replace the thermostat.

✳✳ CAUTION

Do not replace the thermostat if the temperature is off by only a few degrees. It must be considerably out of specification, or perhaps not opening at all, to affect the running of the vehicle.

Vacuum Type

To test the vacuum type of heated air cleaner, inspect the air door with the engine off. It should be in the cold air position. Start the engine. If the engine is cold, the air door should move to the hot air position. As the engine warms up, the air door should move to a mid position, depending on the outside air temperature.

If the outside air is extremely cold, the air door may stay in the hot air position indefinitely. On a warm day, after the engine warms up the air door should move to the cold air position. If it doesn't, the temperature sensor inside the air cleaner might be faulty, or the air door itself might be hanging up. Check the air door by running a hose from manifold vacuum to the vacuum motor. Connect and disconnect the hose to see if the air door moves freely. If the air door is free, check out the hoses for leaks or blockage. If the hoses are okay, the trouble must be in the temperature sensor, and it should be replaced.

Modulators are used in the air cleaner vacuum line on some engines. The modulator mounts on the side of the air cleaner and has two hose connections, one to the air cleaner temperature sensor, and the other to the vacuum motor. Below 50–80°F. the modulator is a one-way check valve, which allows vacuum to move the air door to the hot air position, but traps the vacuum so the door will not jump back to the cold air position during acceleration. This prevents a stumble.

After the modulator warms up, the check valve unseats so that the vacuum can pass freely in either direction, and the air door then operates normally. The connections for the modulator are important. The connection in the center goes to the vacuum motor, and the connection on the edge goes to the vacuum source, which is the temperature sensor.

To test the modulator on a cold engine, apply enough vacuum to the edge port to move the air door to the hot position. Then remove the hose from the port, and the air door should stay in the hot position. Make the same test when the engine is warmed up, and the air door should move to the cold position when you pull off the hose.

Emissions Maintenance Reminder Light

RESETTING

The system is based on a time measuring module which uses ignition on-time as a basis to calculate maintenance intervals.

When the interval has elapsed, the light will come on and remain on until the module is reset by inserting a small rod into the hole in the module to depress the reset switch.

The module is located behind the far right side of the instrument panel, next to the glove box.

CHRYSLER ELECTRONIC FEEDBACK CARBURETOR SYSTEM

General Information

The Chrysler Electronic Feedback Carburetor (EFC) system incorporates an oxygen sensor, a three-way catalytic converter, an oxidizing catalytic converter, a feedback carburetor, a solenoid-operated vacuum regulator valve, and a Combustion Computer. Also incorporated into the system are Chrysler's Electronic Spark Control.

In Chrysler's system, "Combustion Computer" is a collective term for the Feedback Carburetor Controller and the Electronic Spark Control computer, which are housed together in a case located on the air cleaner. The feedback carburetor controller is the information processing component of the system, monitoring oxygen sensor voltage (low voltage/lean mixture, high voltage/rich mixture), engine coolant temperature, manifold vacuum, engine speed, and engine operating mode (starting or running). The controller examines the incoming information and then sends a signal to the solenoid-operated vacuum regulator valve (also located in the Combustion Computer housing), which then sends the proper rich or lean signal to the carburetor.

COMPONENTS & OPERATION

Electronic Feedback Control (EFC) System

The EFC system is essentially an emissions control system which utilizes an electronic signal, generated by an exhaust gas oxygen sensor to precisely control the air/fuel mixture ratio in the carburetor. This in turn allows the engine to produce exhaust gases of the proper composition to permit the use of a three-way catalyst. The three-way catalyst is designed to convert the three pollutant (1) hydrocarbons (HC), (2) carbon monoxide (CO), and (3) oxides of Nitrogen (NOx) into harmless substances.

There are two operating modes in the EFC system:

1. Open Loop—air/fuel ratio is controlled by information programmed into the computer at manufacture.

2. Closed Loop—air/fuel ratio is varied by the computer based on information supplied by the oxygen sensor.

When the engine is cold, the system will be operating in the open loop mode. During that time, the air/fuel ratio will be fixed at a richer level. This will allow proper engine warm up. Also, during this period, air injection (from the air injection pump) will be injected upstream in the exhaust manifold.

Both closed loop and open loop operation are possible in the EFC system. Open loop operation occurs under any one of the following conditions: coolant temperature under 150°F; oxygen sensor temperature under 660°F; low manifold vacuum (less than 4.5 in. Hg. engine cold, or less than 3.0 in. Hg. engine hot); oxygen sensor failure; or hot engine starting. Closed loop operation begins when engine temperature reaches 150°F.

Oxygen Sensor

The oxygen sensor is a device which produces electrical voltage. The sensor is mounted in the exhaust manifold and must be heated by the exhaust gas before producing a voltage. When there is a large amount of oxygen present (lean mixture) the sensor produces a low voltage. When there is a lesser amount present, it produces a higher voltage. By monitoring the oxygen content and converting it to electrical voltage, the sensor acts as a rich/lean switch. The voltage is transmitted to the Spark Control Computer. The computer sends a signal to the Oxygen Feedback Solenoid mounted on the carburetor to change the air/fuel ratio back to stoichiometric.

Electric Choke Assembly

An electric heater and switch assembly is sealed within the choke housing. Electrical current is supplied through the oil pressure switch. A minimum of 4 psi (2.7 kPa) oil pressure is necessary to close the contacts in the oil pressure switch and feed current to the automatic choke system. Electricity must be present when the engine is running to open the choke and keep it open.

The heater can be tested with a direct B+ connection. The choke valve should reach the open position within five minutes.

✲✲ WARNING

Operation of any type, including idling should be avoided if there is any loss of choke power. Under this condition, any loss of power to the choke will cause the choke to remain fully on during the operation of the vehicle. This will cause a very rich mixture to burn and result in abnormally high exhaust system temperatures, which may cause damage to the catalyst or to the underbody parts of the car. It is advised that the electric choke power not be disconnected to troubleshoot cold start problems.

CHRYSLER SINGLE POINT FUEL INJECTION SYSTEM

General Information

The Electronic Fuel Injection System is a computer regulated single point fuel injection system that provides precise air/fuel ratio for all driving conditions. At the center of this system is a Single Module Engine Controller (SMEC) that regulates ignition timing, air/fuel ratio, emission control devices, idle speed and cooling fan and charging system. This component has the ability to update and revise its programming to meet changing operating conditions.

Various sensors provide the input necessary for the SMEC to correctly regulate the fuel flow at the fuel injector. These include the manifold absolute pressure, throttle position, oxygen sensor, coolant temperature, charge temperature, vehicle speed (distance) sensors and throttle body temperature. In addition to the sensors, various switches also provide important information. These include the neutral-safety, heated rear window, air conditioning, air conditioning clutch switches, and an electronic idle switch.

All inputs to the SMEC are converted into signals sent to the power module. These signals cause the power module to change either the fuel flow at the injector or ignition timing or both.

The SMEC tests many of its own input and output circuits. If a fault is found in a major system this information is stored in the SMEC. Information on this fault can be displayed to a technician by means of the instrument panel power loss (check engine) lamp or by connecting a diagnostic read out and reading a numbered display code which directly relates to a specific fault.

Inexpensive scan tools, such as this Auto X-ray®, are available to interface with your Chrysler

COMPONENTS & OPERATION

Power Module

The power module contains the circuits necessary to power the ignition coil and the fuel injector. These are high current devices and their power supply has been isolated to minimize any "electrical noise" reaching the SMEC. The power module also energizes the Automatic Shut Down (ASD) relay which activates the fuel pump, ignition coil, and the power module itself. The module also receives a signal from the distributor and sends this signal to the logic module. In the event of no distributor signal, the ASD relay is not activated and power is shut off from the fuel pump and ignition coil. The power module contains a voltage converter which reduces battery voltage to a regulated 8.0 volt output. This 8.0 volt output powers the distributor and also powers the SMEC.

Single Module Engine Controller (SMEC)

The SMEC contains the circuits necessary to drive the ignition coil, fuel injector, and the alternator field. These are high current devices and have been isolated to minimize any electrical noise in the passenger compartment.

The Automatic Shut Down (ASD) relay is mounted externally, but is turned on and off by the SMEC. Distributor pick-up signal goes to the SMEC. In the event of no distributor signal, the ASD relay is not activated and power is shut off from the fuel injector and ignition coil. The SMEC contains a voltage convertor which converts battery voltage to a regulated 8.0 volt output. This 8.0 volt output powers the distributor pick-up. The internal 5 volt supply which, in turn, powers the MAP sensor and TPS.

The SMEC is a digital computer containing a microprocessor. The module receives input signals from various switches and sensors. It then computes the fuel injector pulse width, spark advance, ignition coil dwell, idle speed, purge and cooling fan turn on and alternator charge rate.

The SMEC tests many of its own input and output circuits. If a fault is found in a major system, this information is stored in the SMEC. Information on this fault can be displayed to a technician by means of the instrument panel check engine lamp or by connecting the diagnostic read out tool C-4805 and reading a numbered display code which directly relates to a general fault.

Manifold Absolute Pressure (MAP) Sensor

The Manifold Absolute Pressure (MAP) sensor is a device which monitors manifold vacuum. It is connected to a vacuum nipple on the throttle body and electrically to the logic module or SMEC. The sensor transmits information on manifold vacuum conditions and barometric pressure to the logic module or SMEC. The MAP sensor data on engine load is used with data from other sensors to determine the correct air/fuel mixture.

Oxygen Sensor (O_2 Sensor)
▶ See Figures 47, 48, 49 and 50

The oxygen sensor (O_2 sensor) is a device which produces an electrical voltage when exposed to the oxygen present in the exhaust gases. The sensor is mounted in the exhaust manifold. The oxygen sensor is electrically heated internally for faster switching when the engine is running. When there is a large amount of oxygen present (lean mixture), the sensor produces a low voltage. When there is a lesser amount present (rich mixture) it produces a higher voltage. By monitoring the oxygen content and converting it to electrical voltage, the sensor acts as a rich-lean switch. The voltage is transmitted to the SMEC. The SMEC signals the power module to trigger the fuel injector. The injector changes the mixture.

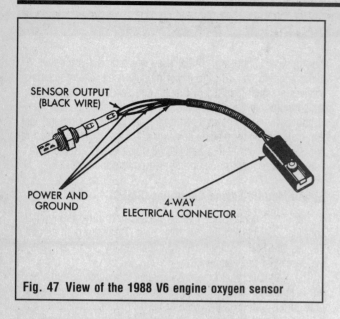

Fig. 47 View of the 1988 V6 engine oxygen sensor

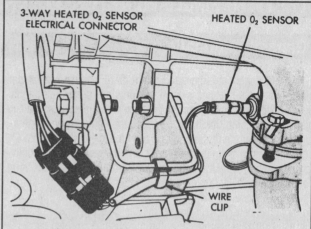

Fig. 50 Oxygen sensor location on the 1988 V8 engine—earlier models are similar in appearance and location, including inline 6-cylinder engines

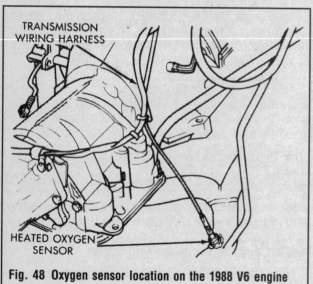

Fig. 48 Oxygen sensor location on the 1988 V6 engine

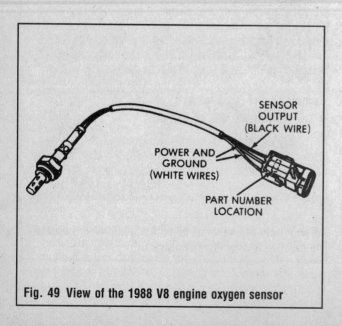

Fig. 49 View of the 1988 V8 engine oxygen sensor

Coolant Temperature Sensor

The coolant temperature sensor is a device that monitors coolant temperature (which is the same as engine operating temperature). It is mounted in the thermostat housing. This sensor provides data on engine operating temperature to the SMEC. This allows the SMEC to demand slightly richer air/fuel mixtures and higher idle speeds until normal operating temperatures are reached. This sensor is also used for cooling fan control.

TESTING

1. With the key in the **OFF** position, detach the wire connector from the coolant sensor.
2. Connect one lead of an ohmmeter to one terminal on the sensor, and the other lead to the sensor's remaining connector. The ohmmeter should read 700–1,000 ohms at 200°F (93°C), and 7,000–13,000 ohms at 70°F (21°C).

Switch Input

Various switches provide information to the SMEC. These include the neutral safety, electric rear window heater, air conditioning, air conditioning clutch, and brake light switches. If one or more of these switches is sensed as being in the **ON** position, the SMEC signals the automatic idle speed motor to increase idle speed to a scheduled rpm.

With the air conditioning on and the throttle blade above a specific angle, the wide open throttle cut-out relay prevents the air conditioning clutch from engaging until the throttle blade is below this angle.

Power Loss/Limited (Check Engine) Lamp

The power loss (check engine) lamp comes on each time the ignition key is turned on and stays on for a few seconds as a bulb test. If the SMEC receives an incorrect signal or no signal from either the coolant temperature sensor, manifold absolute pressure sensor, or the throttle position sensor, the lamp on the instrument panel is illuminated. This is a warning that the SMEC has gone into limp-in mode in an attempt to keep the system operational.

The lamp can also be used to display fault codes. Cycle the ignition switch on, off, on, off, on, within five seconds and any fault code stored in the memory will be displayed.

Exhaust Gas Recirculation Solenoid

The EGR solenoid is operated by the SMEC. When engine temperature is below 70°F (21°C), the module energizes the solenoid by grounding it. This closes the solenoid and prevents ported vacuum from reaching the EGR valve. When the prescribed temperature is reached, the module will turn off the ground for the solenoid de-energizing it. Once the solenoid is de-energized, ported vacuum from the throttle body will pass through to the EGR valve. At idle and wide open throttle the solenoid is energized which prevents EGR operation.

Purge Solenoid

The purge solenoid is controlled by the SMEC. When engine temperature is below 145°F (61°C) the module grounds the purge solenoid, energizing it. This prevents vacuum from reaching the charcoal canister valve. When this temperature is reached, the module de-energizes the solenoid by turning the ground off. Once this occurs, vacuum will flow to the canister purge valve and purge fuel vapors through the throttle body.

Air Conditioning Cutout Relay

The air conditioning cutout relay is connected, in series, electrically with the A/C damped pressure switch, the A/C switch and, on some models, the A/C fan relay. This relay is in the energized, closed (on), position during engine operation. When the module senses low idle speeds and wide open throttle through the throttle position sensor, it will de-energize the relay, open its contacts and prevent air conditioning clutch engagement.

Throttle Body

The throttle body assembly replaces a conventional carburetor and is mounted on top of the intake manifold. The throttle body houses the fuel injector, pressure regulator, throttle position sensor, automatic idle speed motor and throttle body temperature sensor. Air flow through the throttle body is controlled by a cable operated throttle blade located in the base of the throttle body. The throttle body itself provides the chamber for metering atomizing and distributing fuel throughout the air entering the engine.

Fuel Injector

The fuel injector is an electric solenoid driven by the power module, but controlled by the SMEC. The SMEC, based on ambient, mechanical, and sensor input, determines when and how long the power module should operate the injector. When an electric current is supplied to the injector, a spring loaded ball is lifted from its seat. This allows fuel to flow through six spray orifices and deflects off the sharp edge of the injector nozzle. This action causes the fuel to form a 45° cone shaped spray pattern before entering the air stream in the throttle body.

Fuel Pressure Regulator

The pressure regulator is a mechanical device located downstream of the fuel injector on the throttle body. Its function is to

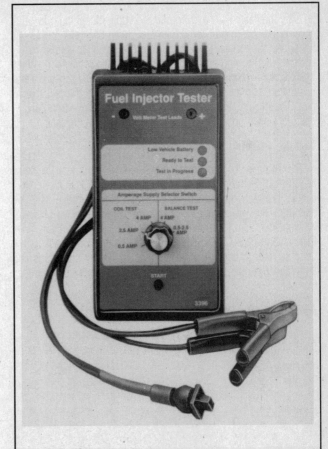

Fuel injector testers can be purchased or sometimes rented

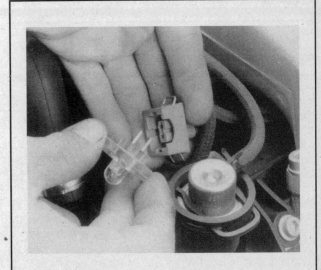

A noid light can be attached to the fuel injector harness in order to test for injector pulse

maintain a constant 14.5 psi (100 kPa) across the fuel injector tip. The regulator uses a spring loaded rubber diaphragm to uncover a fuel return port. When the fuel pump becomes operational, fuel flows past the injector into the regulator, and is restricted from flowing any further by the blocked return port. When fuel pressure reaches the predetermined setting, it pushes on the diaphragm, compressing the spring, and uncovers the fuel return port. The diaphragm and spring will constantly move from an open to closed position to keep the fuel pressure constant.

Throttle Position Sensor (TPS)

The Throttle Position Sensor (TPS) is an electric resistor which is activated by the movement of the throttle shaft. It is mounted on the throttle body and senses the angle of the throttle blade opening. The voltage that the sensor produces increases or decreases according to the throttle blade opening. This voltage is transmitted to the SMEC, where it is used along with data from other sensors to adjust the air/fuel ratio to varying conditions and during acceleration, deceleration, idle, and wide open throttle operations.

Automatic Idle Speed (AIS) Motor

The Automatic Idle Speed (AIS) motor is operated by the SMEC. Data from the throttle position sensor, speed sensor, coolant temperature sensor, and various switch operations, (heated rear window, air conditioning, safety/neutral, brake) are used by the module to adjust engine idle to an optimum during all idle conditions. The AIS adjusts the air portion of the air/fuel mixture through an air bypass on the back of the throttle body. Basic (no load) idle is determined by the minimum air flow through the throttle body. The AIS opens or closes off the air bypass as an increase or decrease is needed due to engine loads or ambient conditions. The module senses an air/fuel change and increases or decreases fuel proportionally to change engine idle. Deceleration die out is also prevented by increasing engine idle when the throttle is closed quickly after a driving (speed) condition.

Throttle Body Temperature Sensor

The throttle body temperature sensor is a device that monitors throttle body temperature which is the same as fuel temperature. It is mounted in the throttle body. This sensor provides information on fuel temperature which allows the SMEC to provide the correct air fuel mixture for a hot restart condition.

TROUBLE CODES

General Information

FEEDBACK CARBURETORS

The Electronic Spark Advance computer/Electronic Fuel Control computer (ESA/EFC) has been programmed to monitor various component systems. If a problem is detected, with a monitored circuit often enough to indicate a problem, its fault code will be stored in the computer. If the problem is repaired or corrects itself the computer will destroy the fault code after thirty ignition key on/off cycles. In order to read the computer and find the fault code diagnostic readout tool C–4805 or equivalent will be needed. If a fault code appears on the readout tool perform a careful visual check of all vacuum lines and electrical connections before doing any repairs to the system. The diagnostic readout tool can be used to check out three different problem modes. They are diagnostic test mode, circuit actuation test mode, and switch test mode. The diagnostic test mode is used to retrieve fault codes that are stored in the computer. The circuit actuation test mode is used to analyze various systems. The switch test mode is used to test various switch circuits.

A scan tool combines many standard testers into a single tool for quick and accurate diagnosis

FUEL INJECTION

The logic module has been programmed to monitor several different circuits of the fuel injection system. The monitoring is called On Board Diagnosis. If a problem is sensed with a monitored circuit, often enough to indicate an actual problem, its Fault Code is stored in the Logic Module for eventual display to the service technician. If the problem is repaired or ceases to exist, the logic module cancels the Fault Code after 20 to 40 vehicle starts.

Reading Codes

FEEDBACK CARBURETORS

➡The following information requires the use of the Chrysler Diagnostic Readout Tool number C–4805 or equivalent.

Diagnostic Mode Testing

1. Install the tool to the wiring connector which is located on the left shock tower.
2. Position the read/hold switch on the tool to the read position.
3. Open the carburetor switch by placing the fast idle screw on the highest step of the fast idle cam.
4. Position the ignition switch in the run position and wait for fault code 00 to appear on the tool display screen.
5. Move the read/switch to the hold position.
6. Record all fault codes that may appear. The display fault codes may be stopped by switching the tool to the read position. Fault codes will continue when the tool is switched back to the hold position.

➡Fault codes indicate the result of a failure, but do not always identify the failed component.

Code 00 indicates that the diagnostic readout tool is functioning and receiving power.

Code 11 indicates that a problem exists in the oxygen solenoid control circuit.

Code 13 indicates that a problem exists in the canister purge solenoid circuit.

Code 16 indicates that there is a problem in the radiator fan control circuit. If vehicle is equipped with air condition disregard this fault code.

Code 17 indicates that a problem exists in the electronic throttle control vacuum solenoid system.

Code 18 indicates a problem in the vacuum operated secondary control solenoid system.

Code 21 indicates a problem in the distributor pick up system.

Code 22 indicates that the oxygen system is stuck in either the full rich position or full lean position.

Code 24 indicates a problem in the computer.

Inexpensive scan tools, such as this Auto X-ray®, are available to interface with your Chrysler

Code 25 indicates a problem in the radiator fan coolant sensor portion of the engine temperature dual sensor system.

Code 26 indicates a problem in the engine temperature portion of the engine temperature dual sensor system.

Code 28 indicates a problem in the distance sensor system on vehicles equipped with manual transmission.

Code 31 indicates that the engine has not been cranked since the battery was disconnected.

Code 32 indicates a problem in the computer.

Code 33 indicates a problem in the computer.

Code 55 indicates the end of a message.

Code 88 indicates the end of a message.

FUEL INJECTION

1. Connect Diagnostic Readout Box tool C–4805 or equivalent, to the diagnostic connector located in the engine compartment near the passenger side strut tower.

2. Start the engine if possible, cycle the transmission selector and the A/C switch if applicable. Shut off the engine. Turn the ignition switch On, Off, On, Off within five seconds.

3. Record all the diagnostic codes shown on the Diagnostic Readout Box Tool C–4805 or equivalent, observe the power loss lamp on the instrument panel; the lamp should light for three seconds then go out (bulb check).

When a fault code appears, either by flashes of the power loss/limited lamp or by watching the diagnostic readout—tool C–4805, it indicates that the Logic Module has recognized an abnormal signal in the system. Fault codes indicate the results of a failure but never identify the failed component directly. The following is a list of fault codes.

Code 88—Start of the test.

Code 11—Engine not cranked since the battery was disconnected.

Code 12—Memory Standby power lost.

Code 13—MAP sensor pneumatic circuit (Power loss/limited lamp on).

Code 14—MAP sensor electrical circuit (Power loss/limited lamp on).

Code 15—Vehicle speed/distance sensor.

Code 16—Loss of battery voltage sense (Power loss/limifed lamp on).

Code 17—Engine running too cool (trouble in the cooling system).

Code 21—Oxygen sensor circuit.

Code 22—Coolant temperature sensor circuit (Power loss/limited lamp on).

Code 23—Throttle body temperature sensor circuit.

Code 24—Throttle position sensor.

Code 25—AIS motor driven circuit.

Code 26—Peak injection current has not been reached.

Code 27—Internal problem in logic module fuel circuit.

Code 31—Purge solenoid circuit.

Code 33—A/C cutout relay circuit.

Code 35—Fan control relay circuit.

Code 37—Shift indicator light circuit.

Code 41—Charging system excess or no field circuit.

Code 42—Auto shutdown relay driver.

Code 43—Spark interface circuit.

Code 44—Battery temperature is out of range.

Code 46—Battery voltage is too high (Power loss/limited lamp on).

Code 47—Battery voltage is too low.

Code 51—Oxygen feedback system stuck in the lean position.

Code 52—Oxygen feedback system stuck in the rich position.

Code 53—Internal logic module problem.

Code 55—End of message.

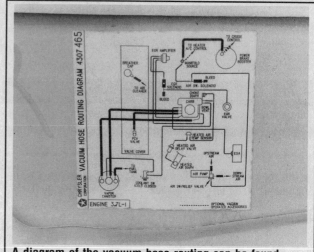

A diagram of the vacuum hose routing can be found under the hood

VACUUM DIAGRAMS

Following are vacuum diagrams for most of the engine and emissions package combinations covered by this manual. Because vacuum circuits will vary based on various engine and vehicle options, always refer first to the vehicle emission control information label, if present. Should the label be missing, or should vehicle be equipped with a different engine from the vehicle's original equipment, refer to the diagrams below for the same or similar configuration.

If you wish to obtain a replacement emissions label, most manufacturers make the labels available for purchase. The labels can usually be ordered from a local dealer.

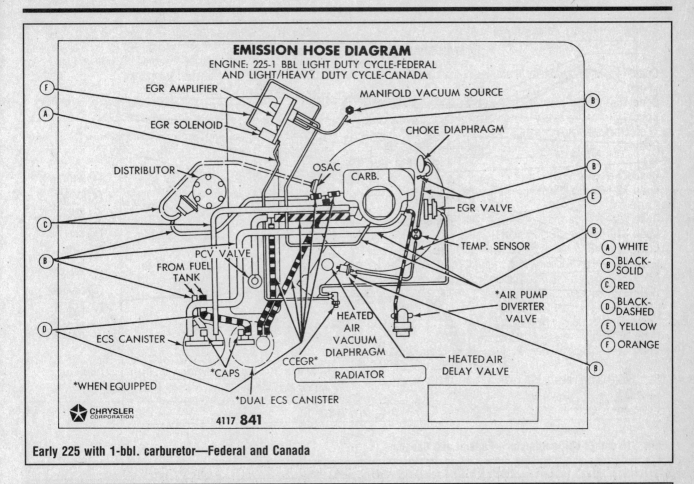

Early 225 with 1-bbl. carburetor—Federal and Canada

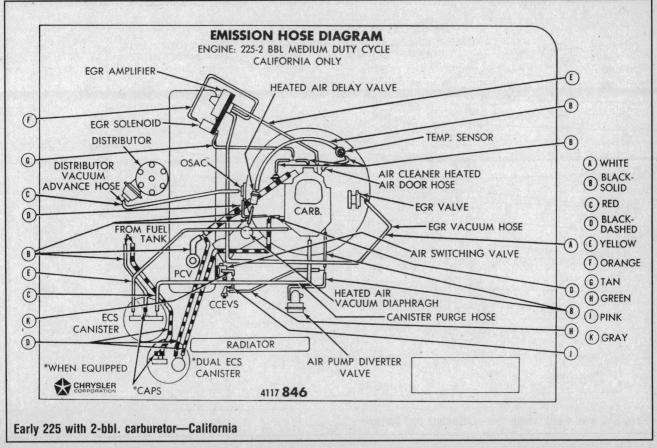

Early 225 with 2-bbl. carburetor—California

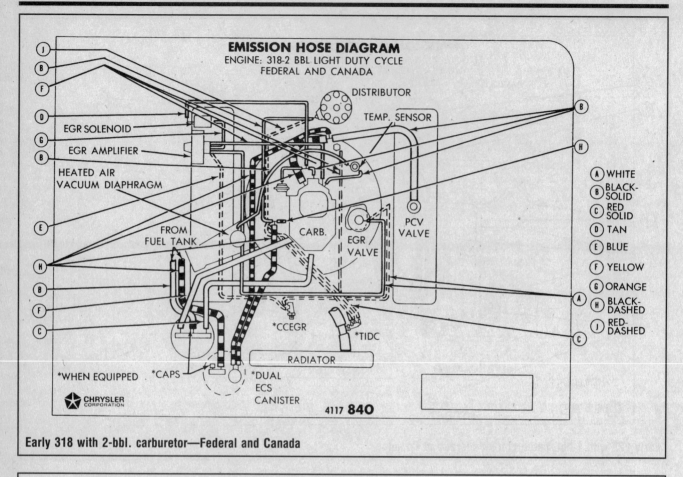

EMISSION HOSE DIAGRAM
ENGINE: 318-2 BBL LIGHT DUTY CYCLE
FEDERAL AND CANADA

DISTRIBUTOR

TEMP. SENSOR

EGR SOLENOID

EGR AMPLIFIER

HEATED AIR
VACUUM DIAPHRAGM

FROM
FUEL TANK

CARB.

EGR
VALVE

PCV
VALVE

*CCEGR

*TIDC

RADIATOR

*WHEN EQUIPPED   *CAPS   *DUAL
ECS
CANISTER

CHRYSLER
CORPORATION

4117 **840**

A) WHITE
B) BLACK-SOLID
C) RED SOLID
D) TAN
E) BLUE
F) YELLOW
G) ORANGE
H) BLACK-DASHED
J) RED-DASHED

Early 318 with 2-bbl. carburetor—Federal and Canada

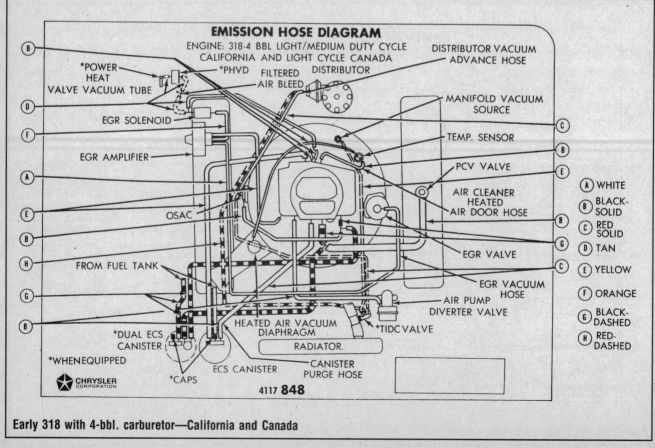

EMISSION HOSE DIAGRAM
ENGINE: 318-4 BBL LIGHT/MEDIUM DUTY CYCLE
CALIFORNIA AND LIGHT CYCLE CANADA

DISTRIBUTOR VACUUM
ADVANCE HOSE

*POWER
HEAT
VALVE VACUUM TUBE

*PHVD   FILTERED
AIR BLEED
DISTRIBUTOR

MANIFOLD VACUUM
SOURCE

EGR SOLENOID

TEMP. SENSOR

EGR AMPLIFIER

PCV VALVE

AIR CLEANER
HEATED
AIR DOOR HOSE

OSAC

EGR VALVE

FROM FUEL TANK

EGR VACUUM
HOSE

AIR PUMP
DIVERTER VALVE

HEATED AIR VACUUM
DIAPHRAGM

*TIDC VALVE

*DUAL ECS
CANISTER

RADIATOR.

*WHEN EQUIPPED

ECS CANISTER

CANISTER
PURGE HOSE

*CAPS

CHRYSLER
CORPORATION

4117 **848**

A) WHITE
B) BLACK-SOLID
C) RED SOLID
D) TAN
E) YELLOW
F) ORANGE
G) BLACK-DASHED
H) RED-DASHED

Early 318 with 4-bbl. carburetor—California and Canada

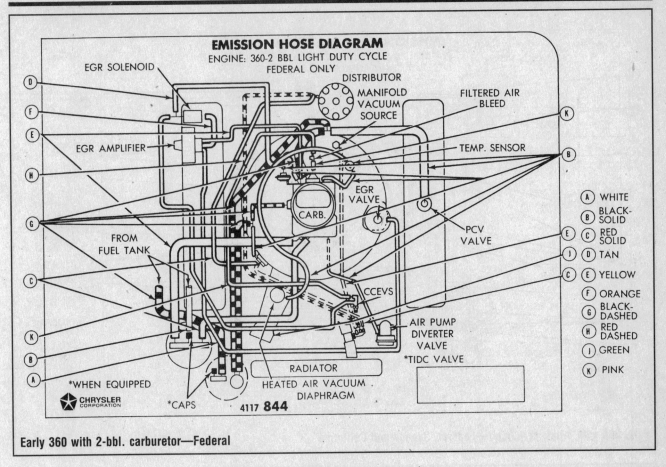

Early 360 with 2-bbl. carburetor—Federal

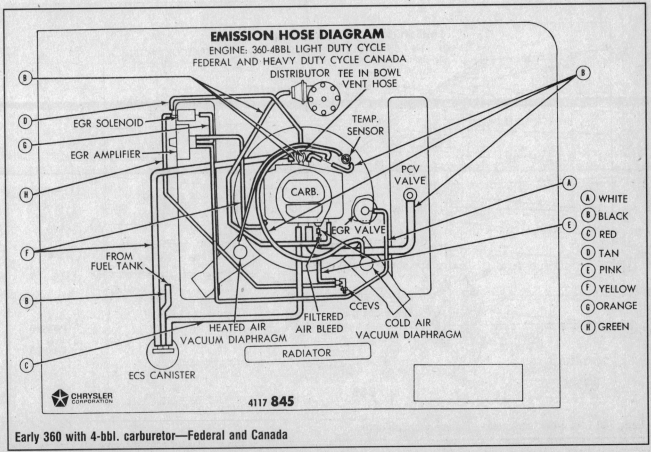

Early 360 with 4-bbl. carburetor—Federal and Canada

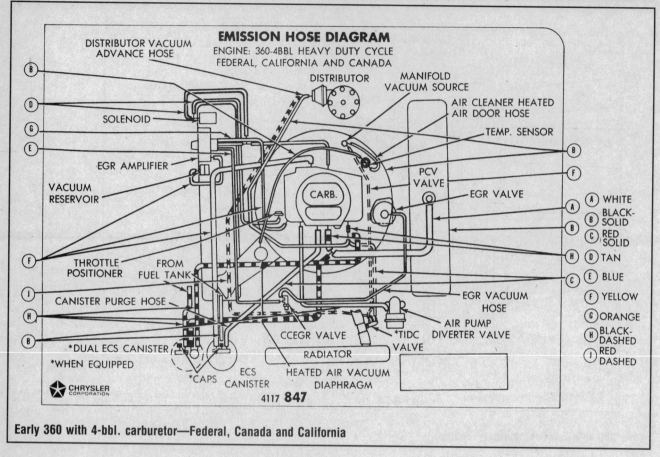

Early 360 with 4-bbl. carburetor—Federal, Canada and California

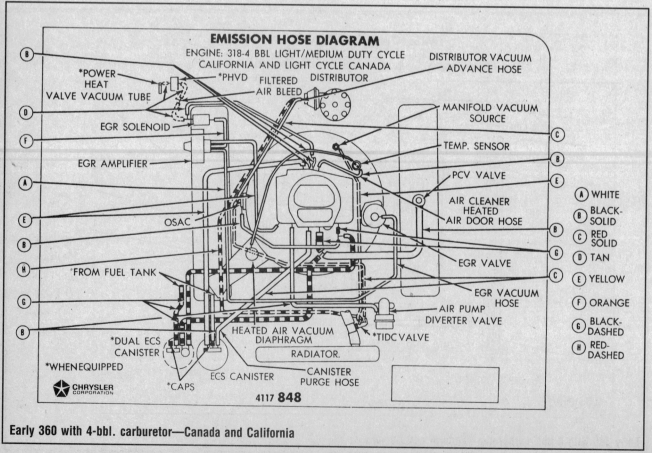

Early 360 with 4-bbl. carburetor—Canada and California

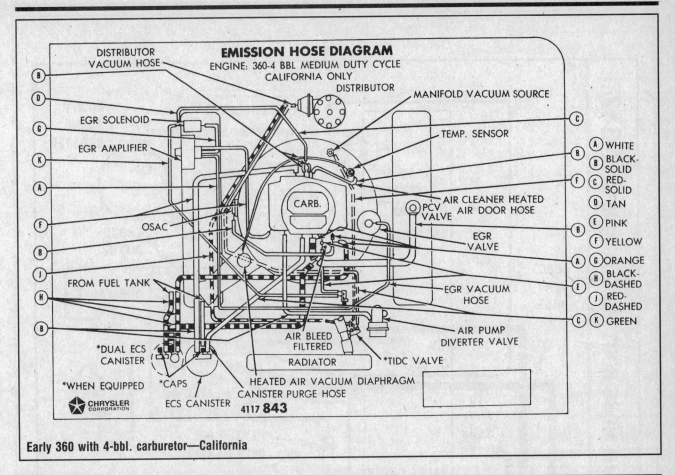

EMISSION HOSE DIAGRAM
ENGINE: 360-4 BBL MEDIUM DUTY CYCLE
CALIFORNIA ONLY

DISTRIBUTOR VACUUM HOSE
DISTRIBUTOR
MANIFOLD VACUUM SOURCE
TEMP. SENSOR
EGR SOLENOID
EGR AMPLIFIER
CARB.
AIR CLEANER HEATED AIR DOOR HOSE
PCV VALVE
EGR VALVE
OSAC
EGR VACUUM HOSE
FROM FUEL TANK
AIR PUMP DIVERTER VALVE
AIR BLEED FILTERED
*DUAL ECS CANISTER
RADIATOR
*TIDC VALVE
*WHEN EQUIPPED   *CAPS
HEATED AIR VACUUM DIAPHRAGM
CANISTER PURGE HOSE
ECS CANISTER
4117 **843**

B
D
G
K
A
F
B
J
H
B

C
B
F
B
A
E
C

(A) WHITE
(B) BLACK-SOLID
(C) RED-SOLID
(D) TAN
(E) PINK
(F) YELLOW
(G) ORANGE
(H) BLACK-DASHED
(J) RED-DASHED
(K) GREEN

Early 360 with 4-bbl. carburetor—California

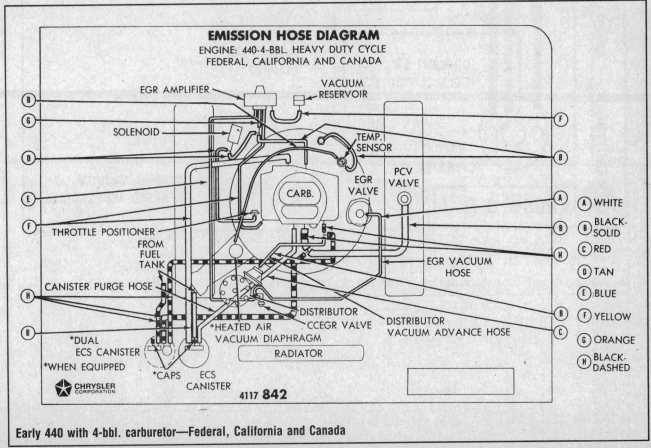

EMISSION HOSE DIAGRAM
ENGINE: 440-4-BBL. HEAVY DUTY CYCLE
FEDERAL, CALIFORNIA AND CANADA

EGR AMPLIFIER
VACUUM RESERVOIR
SOLENOID
TEMP. SENSOR
CARB.
EGR VALVE
PCV VALVE
THROTTLE POSITIONER
FROM FUEL TANK
EGR VACUUM HOSE
CANISTER PURGE HOSE
DISTRIBUTOR
*DUAL ECS CANISTER
*HEATED AIR VACUUM DIAPHRAGM
CCEGR VALVE
DISTRIBUTOR VACUUM ADVANCE HOSE
*WHEN EQUIPPED
*CAPS   ECS CANISTER
RADIATOR
4117 **842**

B
G
D
E
F
H
B

F
B
A
B
H
B
C

(A) WHITE
(B) BLACK-SOLID
(C) RED
(D) TAN
(E) BLUE
(F) YELLOW
(G) ORANGE
(H) BLACK-DASHED

Early 440 with 4-bbl. carburetor—Federal, California and Canada

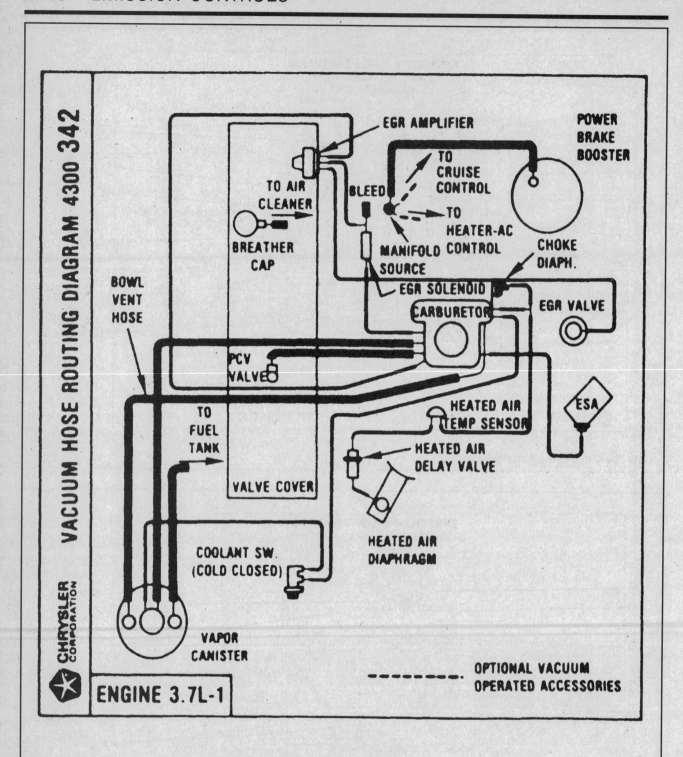

VACUUM HOSE ROUTING DIAGRAM 4300 342

EGR AMPLIFIER

POWER
BRAKE
BOOSTER

TO AIR
CLEANER

BLEED

TO
CRUISE
CONTROL

TO
HEATER-AC
CONTROL

CHOKE
DIAPH.

BREATHER
CAP

MANIFOLD
SOURCE

EGR SOLENOID

CHRYSLER CORPORATION

BOWL
VENT
HOSE

CARBURETOR

EGR VALVE

PCV
VALVE

HEATED AIR
TEMP SENSOR

ESA

TO
FUEL
TANK

HEATED AIR
DELAY VALVE

VALVE COVER

HEATED AIR
DIAPHRAGM

COOLANT SW.
(COLD CLOSED)

VAPOR
CANISTER

OPTIONAL VACUUM
OPERATED ACCESSORIES

ENGINE 3.7L-1

1984 225 engine with automatic transmission, ESA and catalyst—Federal

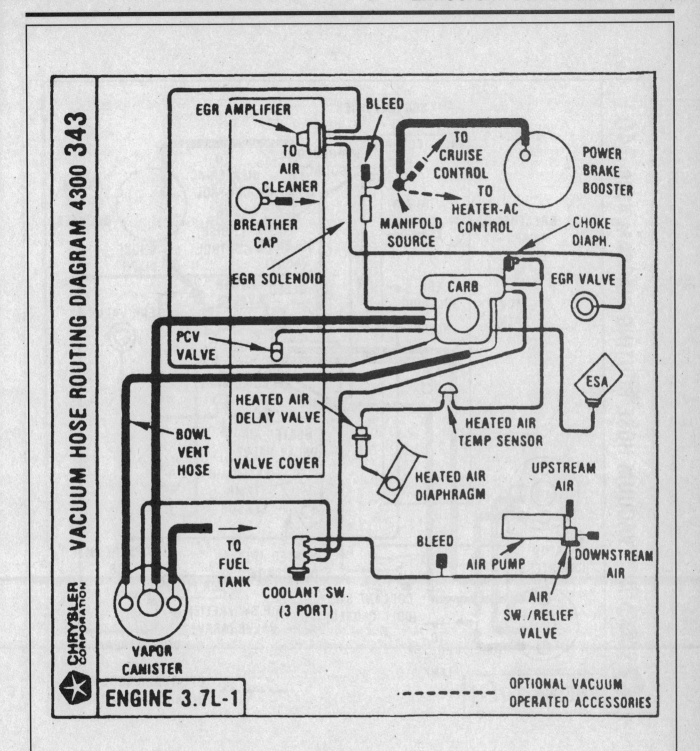

VACUUM HOSE ROUTING DIAGRAM 4300 343

EGR AMPLIFIER

BLEED

TO CRUISE CONTROL

TO HEATER-AC CONTROL

POWER BRAKE BOOSTER

TO AIR CLEANER

BREATHER CAP

MANIFOLD SOURCE

CHOKE DIAPH.

EGR SOLENOID

CARB

EGR VALVE

PCV VALVE

ESA

HEATED AIR DELAY VALVE

BOWL VENT HOSE

HEATED AIR TEMP SENSOR

VALVE COVER

HEATED AIR DIAPHRAGM

UPSTREAM AIR

TO FUEL TANK

BLEED

AIR PUMP

DOWNSTREAM AIR

COOLANT SW. (3 PORT)

AIR SW./RELIEF VALVE

VAPOR CANISTER

CHRYSLER CORPORATION

ENGINE 3.7L-1

OPTIONAL VACUUM OPERATED ACCESSORIES

1984 225 engine with manual transmission, ESA and catalyst—Federal

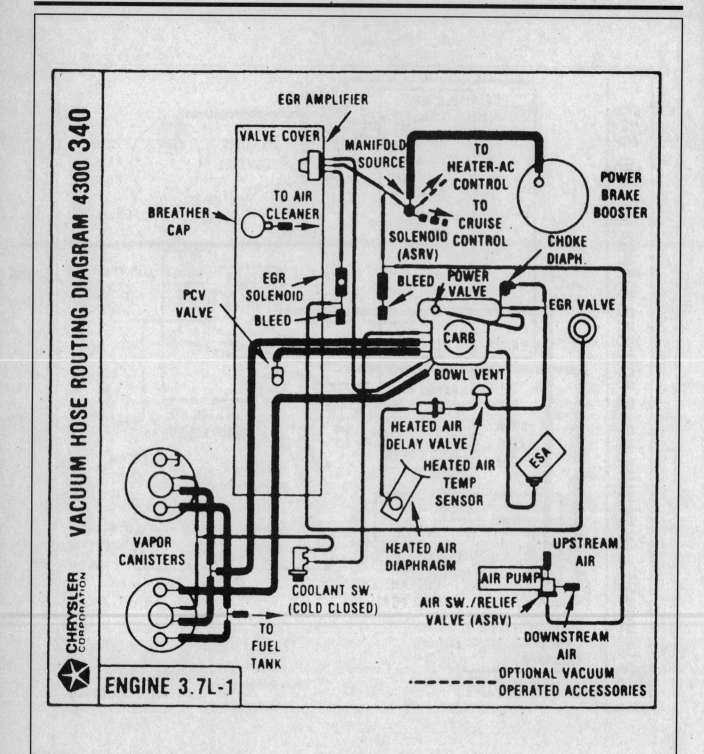

VACUUM HOSE ROUTING DIAGRAM 4300 340

CHRYSLER CORPORATION

EGR AMPLIFIER

VALVE COVER

MANIFOLD SOURCE

TO HEATER-AC CONTROL

TO CRUISE CONTROL

POWER BRAKE BOOSTER

BREATHER CAP

TO AIR CLEANER

SOLENOID (ASRV)

CHOKE DIAPH.

PCV VALVE

EGR SOLENOID

BLEED

POWER VALVE

EGR VALVE

BLEED

BLEED

CARB

BOWL VENT

HEATED AIR DELAY VALVE

HEATED AIR TEMP SENSOR

ESA

VAPOR CANISTERS

HEATED AIR DIAPHRAGM

UPSTREAM AIR

AIR PUMP

COOLANT SW. (COLD CLOSED)

AIR SW./RELIEF VALVE (ASRV)

DOWNSTREAM AIR

TO FUEL TANK

ENGINE 3.7L-1

OPTIONAL VACUUM OPERATED ACCESSORIES

1984 225 engine, all models—California

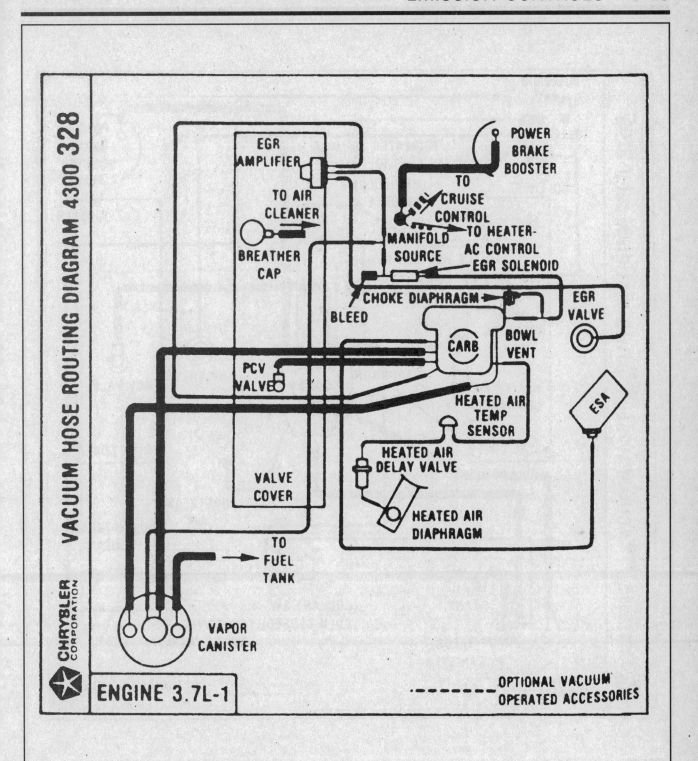

VACUUM HOSE ROUTING DIAGRAM 4300 328

EGR AMPLIFIER

POWER BRAKE BOOSTER

TO AIR CLEANER

TO CRUISE CONTROL

BREATHER CAP

MANIFOLD SOURCE

TO HEATER-AC CONTROL

EGR SOLENOID

BLEED

CHOKE DIAPHRAGM

EGR VALVE

CARB

BOWL VENT

PCV VALVE

HEATED AIR TEMP SENSOR

ESA

HEATED AIR DELAY VALVE

VALVE COVER

HEATED AIR DIAPHRAGM

TO FUEL TANK

VAPOR CANISTER

CHRYSLER CORPORATION

ENGINE 3.7L-1

OPTIONAL VACUUM OPERATED ACCESSORIES

1984 225 engine with ESA and catalyst—Canada

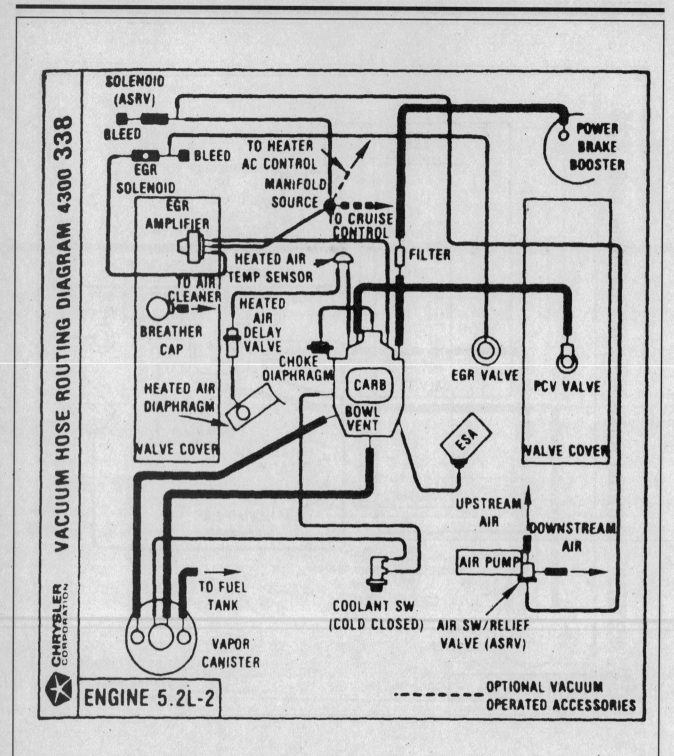

VACUUM HOSE ROUTING DIAGRAM 4300 338

CHRYSLER CORPORATION

SOLENOID (ASRV)

BLEED

EGR SOLENOID

BLEED

TO HEATER AC CONTROL

MANIFOLD SOURCE

TO CRUISE CONTROL

POWER BRAKE BOOSTER

EGR AMPLIFIER

HEATED AIR TEMP SENSOR

FILTER

TO AIR CLEANER

HEATED AIR DELAY VALVE

BREATHER CAP

CHOKE DIAPHRAGM

HEATED AIR DIAPHRAGM

CARB BOWL VENT

EGR VALVE

PCV VALVE

VALVE COVER

ESA

VALVE COVER

UPSTREAM AIR

DOWNSTREAM AIR

AIR PUMP

TO FUEL TANK

COOLANT SW. (COLD CLOSED)

AIR SW/RELIEF VALVE (ASRV)

VAPOR CANISTER

ENGINE 5.2L-2

OPTIONAL VACUUM OPERATED ACCESSORIES

1984 318 engine with ESA and catalyst high altitude—California

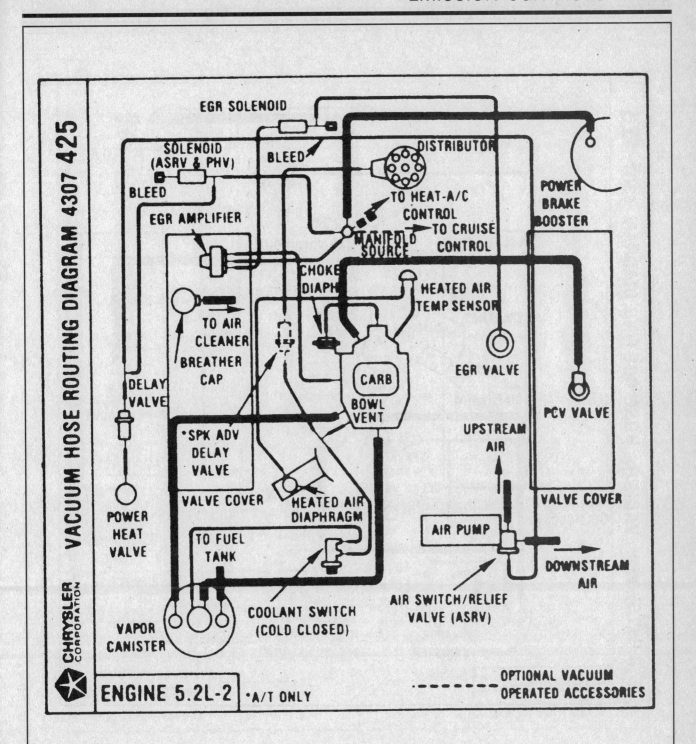

VACUUM HOSE ROUTING DIAGRAM 4307 425

EGR SOLENOID

SOLENOID
(ASRV & PHV)

BLEED

BLEED

DISTRIBUTOR

POWER
BRAKE
BOOSTER

EGR AMPLIFIER

TO HEAT-A/C
CONTROL
TO CRUISE
CONTROL

MANIFOLD
SOURCE

CHOKE
DIAPH

HEATED AIR
TEMP SENSOR

TO AIR
CLEANER
BREATHER
CAP

DELAY
VALVE

CARB
BOWL
VENT

EGR VALVE

·SPK ADV
DELAY
VALVE

POWER
HEAT
VALVE

VALVE COVER

HEATED AIR
DIAPHRAGM

PCV VALVE

UPSTREAM
AIR

VALVE COVER

TO FUEL
TANK

AIR PUMP

DOWNSTREAM
AIR

VAPOR
CANISTER

COOLANT SWITCH
(COLD CLOSED)

AIR SWITCH/RELIEF
VALVE (ASRV)

CHRYSLER CORPORATION

ENGINE 5.2L-2 ·A/T ONLY

OPTIONAL VACUUM
OPERATED ACCESSORIES

1984 318 engine with manual transmission and catalyst—Federal and Canada

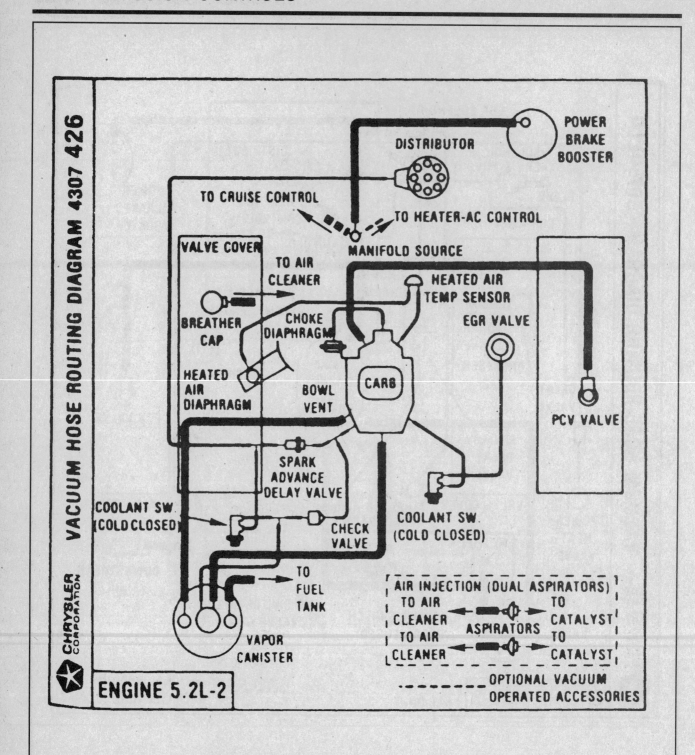

VACUUM HOSE ROUTING DIAGRAM 4307 426

CHRYSLER CORPORATION

POWER BRAKE BOOSTER

DISTRIBUTOR

TO CRUISE CONTROL

TO HEATER-AC CONTROL

MANIFOLD SOURCE

VALVE COVER

TO AIR CLEANER

HEATED AIR TEMP SENSOR

BREATHER CAP

CHOKE DIAPHRAGM

EGR VALVE

HEATED AIR DIAPHRAGM

BOWL VENT

CARB

SPARK ADVANCE DELAY VALVE

PCV VALVE

COOLANT SW. (COLD CLOSED)

CHECK VALVE

COOLANT SW. (COLD CLOSED)

TO FUEL TANK

VAPOR CANISTER

AIR INJECTION (DUAL ASPIRATORS)
TO AIR CLEANER — TO CATALYST
ASPIRATORS
TO AIR CLEANER — TO CATALYST

OPTIONAL VACUUM OPERATED ACCESSORIES

ENGINE 5.2L-2

1984 318 engine with automatic transmission and catalyst—Canada

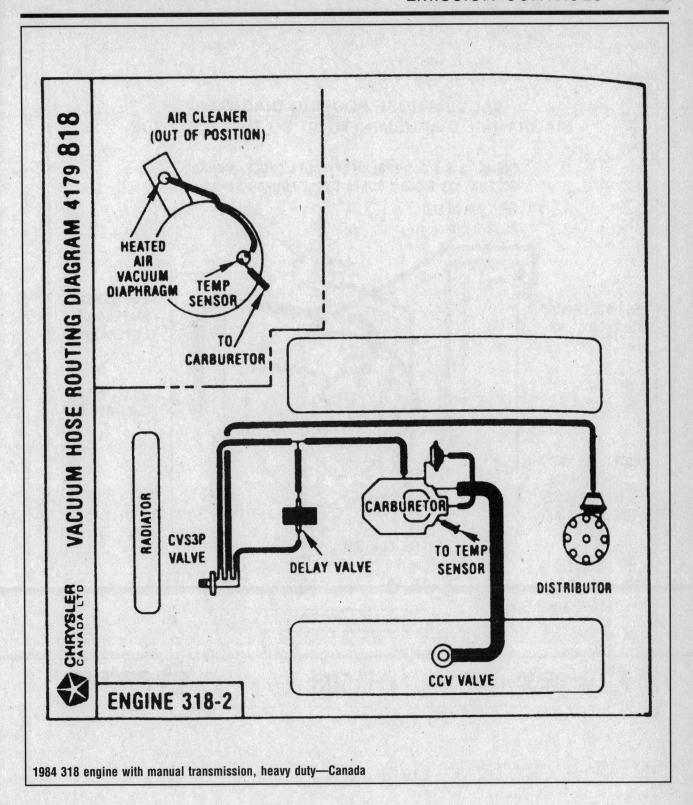

VACUUM HOSE ROUTING DIAGRAM 4179 **818**

AIR CLEANER
(OUT OF POSITION)

HEATED
AIR
VACUUM
DIAPHRAGM

TEMP
SENSOR

TO
CARBURETOR

RADIATOR

CVS3P
VALVE

DELAY VALVE

CARBURETOR

TO TEMP
SENSOR

CCV VALVE

DISTRIBUTOR

CHRYSLER CANADA LTD

ENGINE 318-2

1984 318 engine with manual transmission, heavy duty—Canada

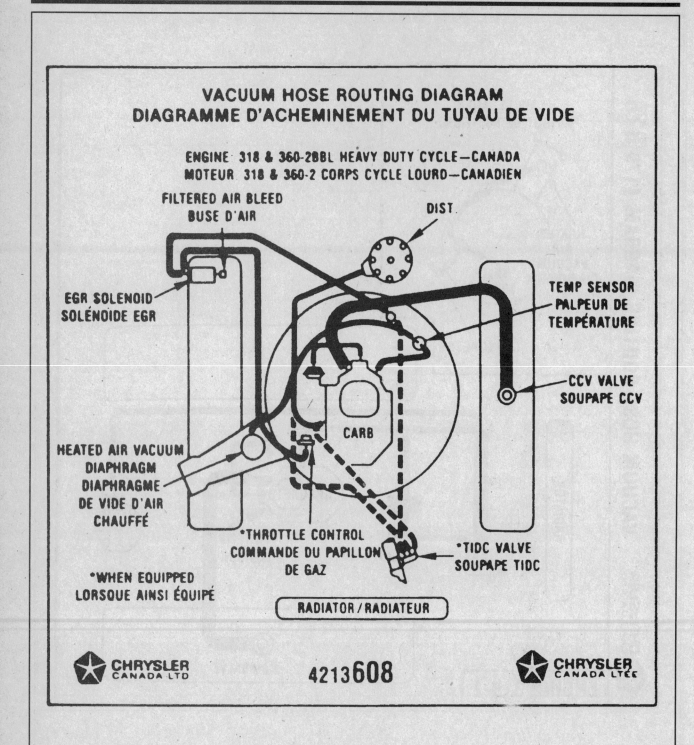

VACUUM HOSE ROUTING DIAGRAM
DIAGRAMME D'ACHEMINEMENT DU TUYAU DE VIDE

ENGINE 318 & 360-2BBL HEAVY DUTY CYCLE—CANADA
MOTEUR 318 & 360-2 CORPS CYCLE LOURD—CANADIEN

FILTERED AIR BLEED
BUSE D'AIR

DIST.

EGR SOLENOID
SOLÉNOIDE EGR

TEMP SENSOR
PALPEUR DE
TEMPÉRATURE

CCV VALVE
SOUPAPE CCV

CARB

HEATED AIR VACUUM
DIAPHRAGM
DIAPHRAGME
DE VIDE D'AIR
CHAUFFÉ

*THROTTLE CONTROL
COMMANDE DU PAPILLON
DE GAZ

*TIDC VALVE
SOUPAPE TIDC

*WHEN EQUIPPED
LORSQUE AINSI ÉQUIPÉ

RADIATOR / RADIATEUR

CHRYSLER CANADA LTD

4213608

CHRYSLER CANADA LTÉE

1984 318 engine with automatic transmission, heavy duty—Canada

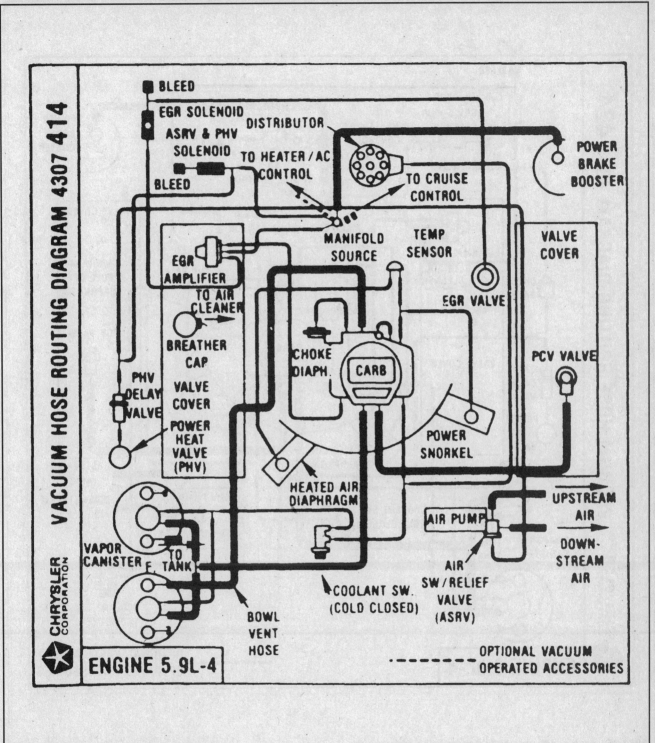

VACUUM HOSE ROUTING DIAGRAM 4307 414

CHRYSLER CORPORATION

BLEED

EGR SOLENOID

ASRV & PHV SOLENOID

BLEED

DISTRIBUTOR

TO HEATER/AC CONTROL

TO CRUISE CONTROL

POWER BRAKE BOOSTER

MANIFOLD SOURCE

TEMP SENSOR

VALVE COVER

EGR AMPLIFIER

TO AIR CLEANER

EGR VALVE

BREATHER CAP

VALVE COVER

CHOKE DIAPH.

CARB

PCV VALVE

PHV DELAY VALVE

POWER HEAT VALVE (PHV)

POWER SNORKEL

HEATED AIR DIAPHRAGM

UPSTREAM AIR

AIR PUMP

DOWN-STREAM AIR

VAPOR CANISTER

TO TANK

COOLANT SW. (COLD CLOSED)

AIR SW/RELIEF VALVE (ASRV)

BOWL VENT HOSE

ENGINE 5.9L-4

-------- OPTIONAL VACUUM OPERATED ACCESSORIES

1984 360 engine with catalyst—Federal

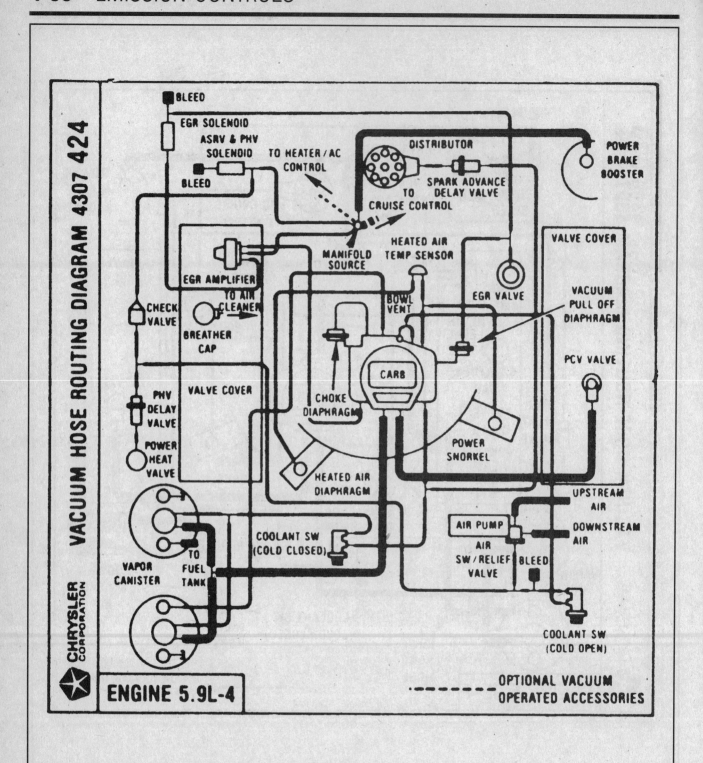

1984 360 engine with automatic transmission and catalyst—Federal

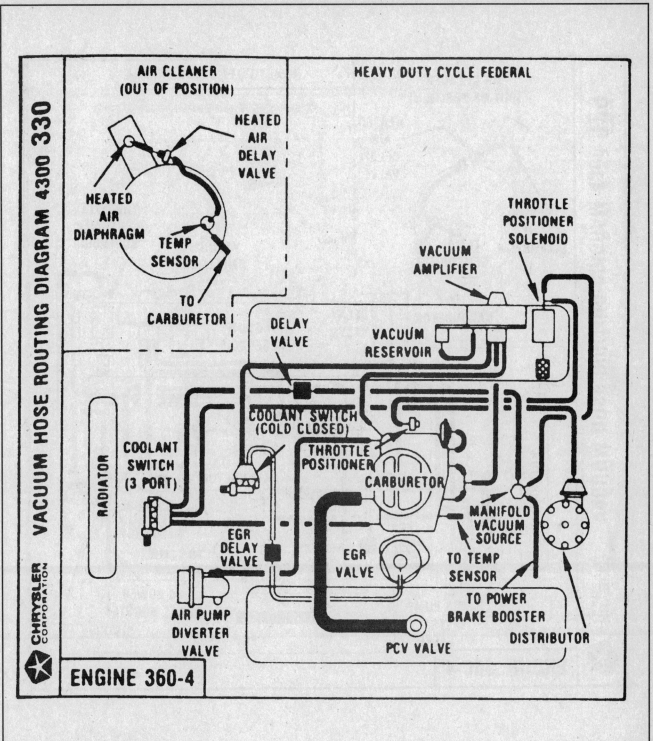

VACUUM HOSE ROUTING DIAGRAM 4300 330

CHRYSLER CORPORATION

ENGINE 360-4

AIR CLEANER (OUT OF POSITION)

HEATED AIR DELAY VALVE

HEATED AIR DIAPHRAGM

TEMP SENSOR

TO CARBURETOR

HEAVY DUTY CYCLE FEDERAL

THROTTLE POSITIONER SOLENOID

VACUUM AMPLIFIER

DELAY VALVE

VACUUM RESERVOIR

COOLANT SWITCH (COLD CLOSED)

THROTTLE POSITIONER

CARBURETOR

RADIATOR

COOLANT SWITCH (3 PORT)

EGR DELAY VALVE

MANIFOLD VACUUM SOURCE

TO TEMP SENSOR

EGR VALVE

TO POWER BRAKE BOOSTER

DISTRIBUTOR

AIR PUMP DIVERTER VALVE

PCV VALVE

1984 360 engine, heavy duty—Federal

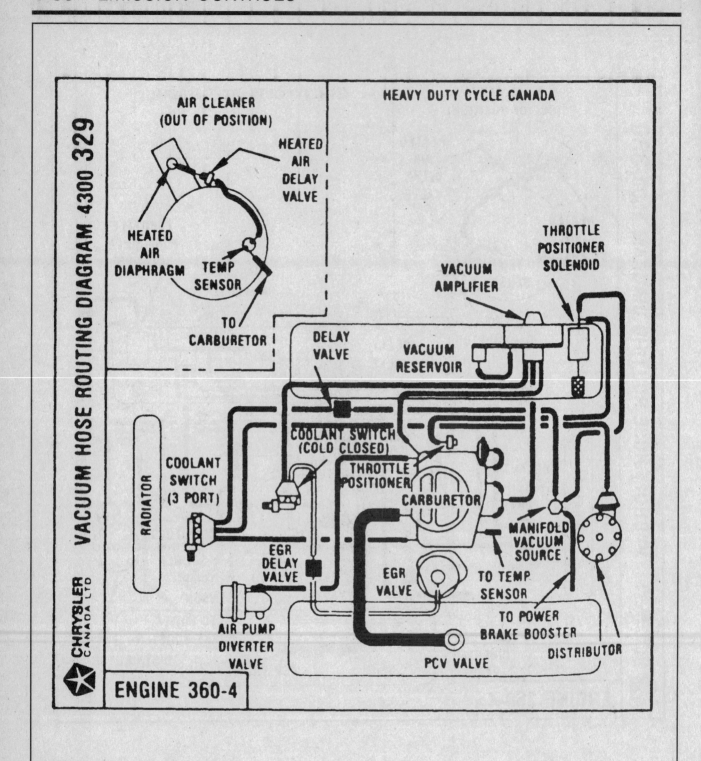

VACUUM HOSE ROUTING DIAGRAM 4300 329

CHRYSLER CANADA LTD

ENGINE 360-4

AIR CLEANER
(OUT OF POSITION)

HEATED
AIR
DELAY
VALVE

HEATED
AIR
DIAPHRAGM

TEMP
SENSOR

TO
CARBURETOR

HEAVY DUTY CYCLE CANADA

THROTTLE
POSITIONER
SOLENOID

VACUUM
AMPLIFIER

DELAY
VALVE

VACUUM
RESERVOIR

RADIATOR

COOLANT
SWITCH
(3 PORT)

COOLANT SWITCH
(COLD CLOSED)

THROTTLE
POSITIONER

CARBURETOR

MANIFOLD
VACUUM
SOURCE

EGR
DELAY
VALVE

EGR
VALVE

TO TEMP
SENSOR

TO POWER
BRAKE BOOSTER

DISTRIBUTOR

AIR PUMP
DIVERTER
VALVE

PCV VALVE

1984 360 engine, heavy duty—Canada

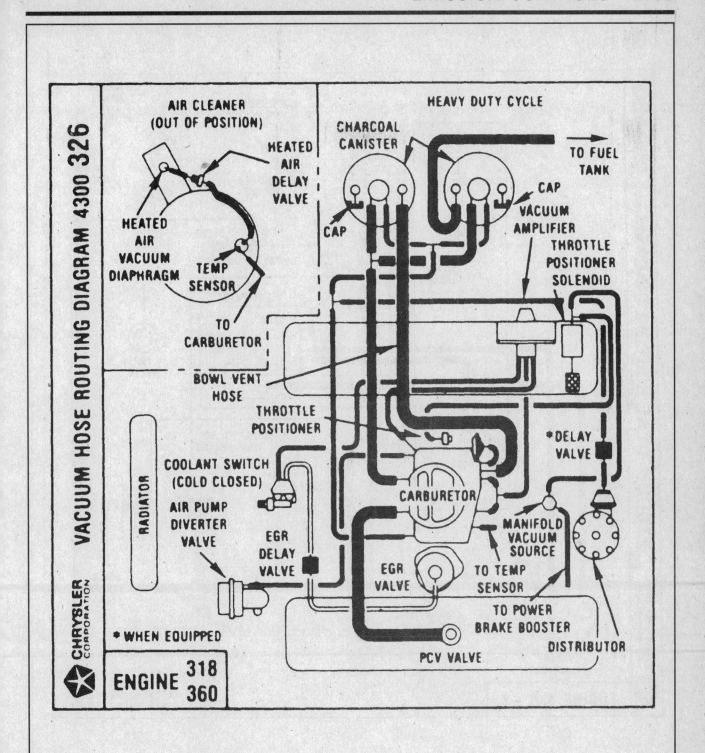

VACUUM HOSE ROUTING DIAGRAM 4300 326

AIR CLEANER (OUT OF POSITION)

HEATED AIR DELAY VALVE

HEATED AIR VACUUM DIAPHRAGM

TEMP SENSOR

TO CARBURETOR

HEAVY DUTY CYCLE

CHARCOAL CANISTER

TO FUEL TANK

CAP

CAP

VACUUM AMPLIFIER

THROTTLE POSITIONER SOLENOID

BOWL VENT HOSE

THROTTLE POSITIONER

RADIATOR

COOLANT SWITCH (COLD CLOSED)

AIR PUMP DIVERTER VALVE

EGR DELAY VALVE

*DELAY VALVE

CARBURETOR

MANIFOLD VACUUM SOURCE

EGR VALVE

TO TEMP SENSOR

TO POWER BRAKE BOOSTER

DISTRIBUTOR

PCV VALVE

*WHEN EQUIPPED

CHRYSLER CORPORATION

ENGINE 318 360

1984 360 engine, heavy duty—California

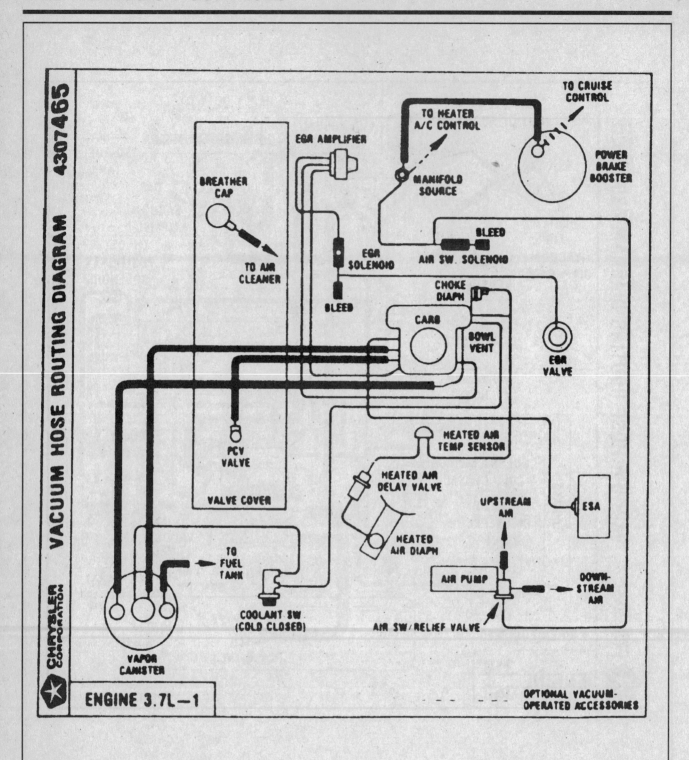

VACUUM HOSE ROUTING DIAGRAM   4307465

CHRYSLER CORPORATION

ENGINE 3.7L—1

BREATHER CAP

TO AIR CLEANER

EGA AMPLIFIER

BLEED

EGR SOLENOID

BLEED

TO HEATER A/C CONTROL

MANIFOLD SOURCE

AIR SW. SOLENOID

BLEED

TO CRUISE CONTROL

POWER BRAKE BOOSTER

CHOKE DIAPH

CARB

BOWL VENT

EGR VALVE

PCV VALVE

VALVE COVER

HEATED AIR TEMP SENSOR

HEATED AIR DELAY VALVE

HEATED AIR DIAPH

UPSTREAM AIR

ESA

TO FUEL TANK

COOLANT SW (COLD CLOSED)

AIR PUMP

AIR SW/RELIEF VALVE

DOWN-STREAM AIR

VAPOR CANISTER

OPTIONAL VACUUM-OPERATED ACCESSORIES

1985 225 engine with ESA—Federal

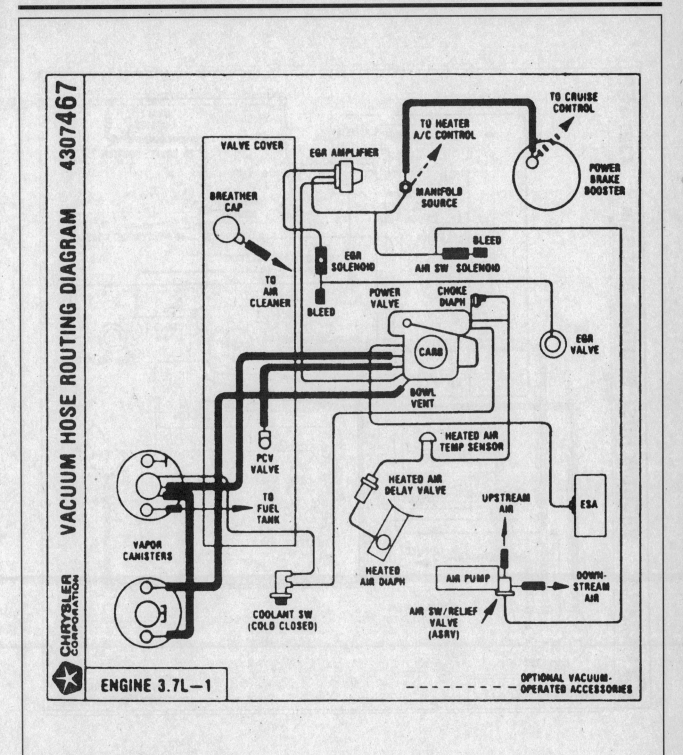

VACUUM HOSE ROUTING DIAGRAM 4307467

CHRYSLER CORPORATION

ENGINE 3.7L—1

VALVE COVER

BREATHER CAP

TO AIR CLEANER

EGR AMPLIFIER

TO HEATER A/C CONTROL

TO CRUISE CONTROL

MANIFOLD SOURCE

POWER BRAKE BOOSTER

EGR SOLENOID

BLEED

BLEED

AIR SW SOLENOID

POWER VALVE

CHOKE DIAPH

EGR VALVE

CARB

BOWL VENT

PCV VALVE

TO FUEL TANK

VAPOR CANISTERS

HEATED AIR TEMP SENSOR

HEATED AIR DELAY VALVE

HEATED AIR DIAPH

COOLANT SW (COLD CLOSED)

UPSTREAM AIR

ESA

AIR PUMP

DOWN-STREAM AIR

AIR SW/RELIEF VALVE (ASRV)

OPTIONAL VACUUM-OPERATED ACCESSORIES

1985 225 engine with ESA—California

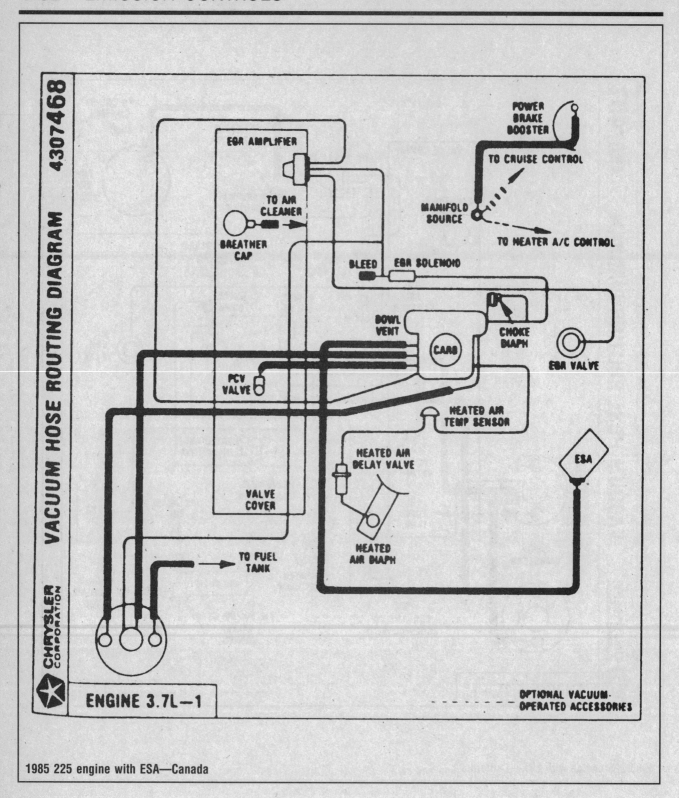

4307468

VACUUM HOSE ROUTING DIAGRAM

CHRYSLER CORPORATION

ENGINE 3.7L—1

POWER BRAKE BOOSTER

TO CRUISE CONTROL

MANIFOLD SOURCE

TO HEATER A/C CONTROL

EGR AMPLIFIER

TO AIR CLEANER

BREATHER CAP

BLEED

EGR SOLENOID

BOWL VENT

CARB

CHOKE DIAPH

EGR VALVE

PCV VALVE

HEATED AIR TEMP SENSOR

HEATED AIR DELAY VALVE

ESA

VALVE COVER

HEATED AIR DIAPH

TO FUEL TANK

OPTIONAL VACUUM-OPERATED ACCESSORIES

1985 225 engine with ESA—Canada

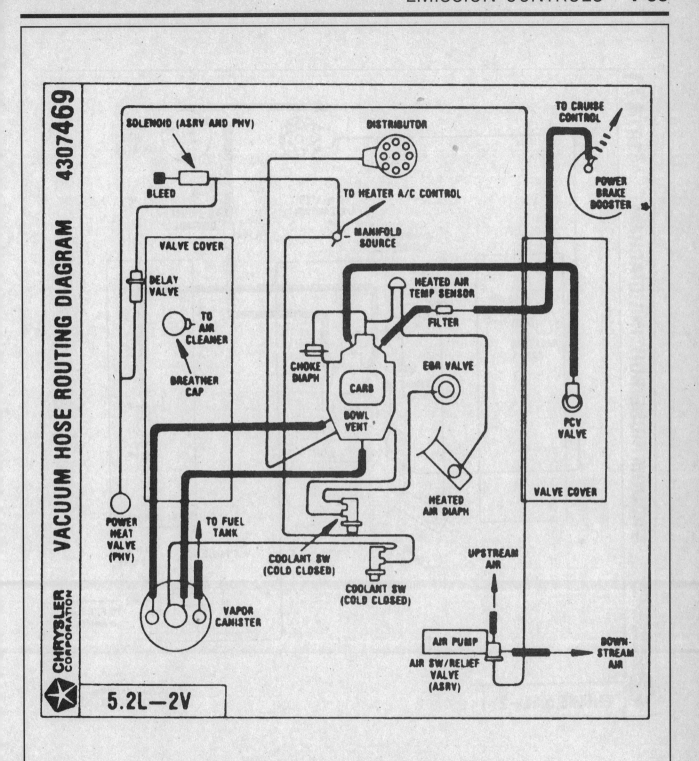

VACUUM HOSE ROUTING DIAGRAM 4307469

CHRYSLER CORPORATION

5.2L—2V

1985 318 engine with manual transmission and catalyst—Federal and Canada

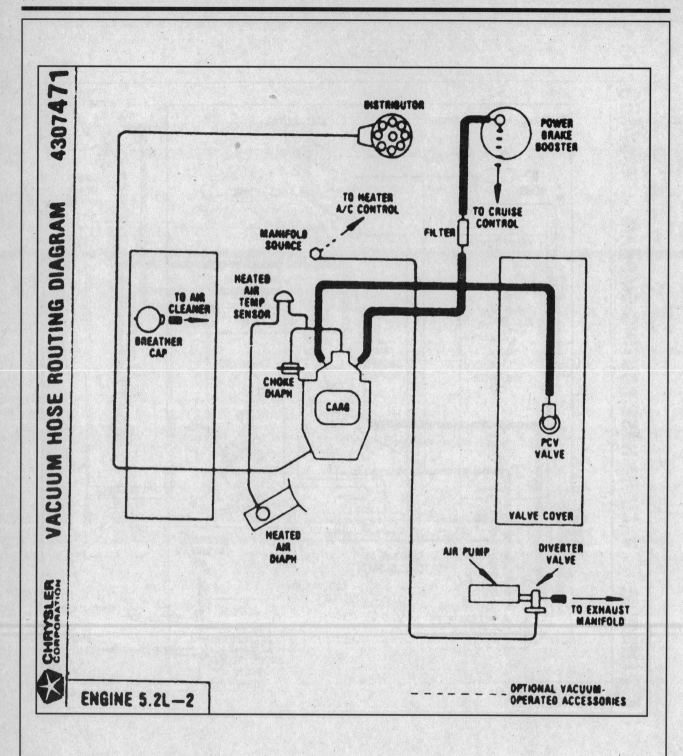

VACUUM HOSE ROUTING DIAGRAM 4307471

DISTRIBUTOR

POWER
BRAKE
BOOSTER

TO HEATER
A/C CONTROL

MANIFOLD
SOURCE

TO CRUISE
CONTROL

FILTER

TO AIR
CLEANER

HEATED
AIR
TEMP
SENSOR

BREATHER
CAP

CHOKE
DIAPH

CARB

PCV
VALVE

HEATED
AIR
DIAPH

VALVE COVER

AIR PUMP

DIVERTER
VALVE

TO EXHAUST
MANIFOLD

CHRYSLER
CORPORATION

ENGINE 5.2L—2

OPTIONAL VACUUM-
OPERATED ACCESSORIES

1985 318 engine, heavy duty—Canada

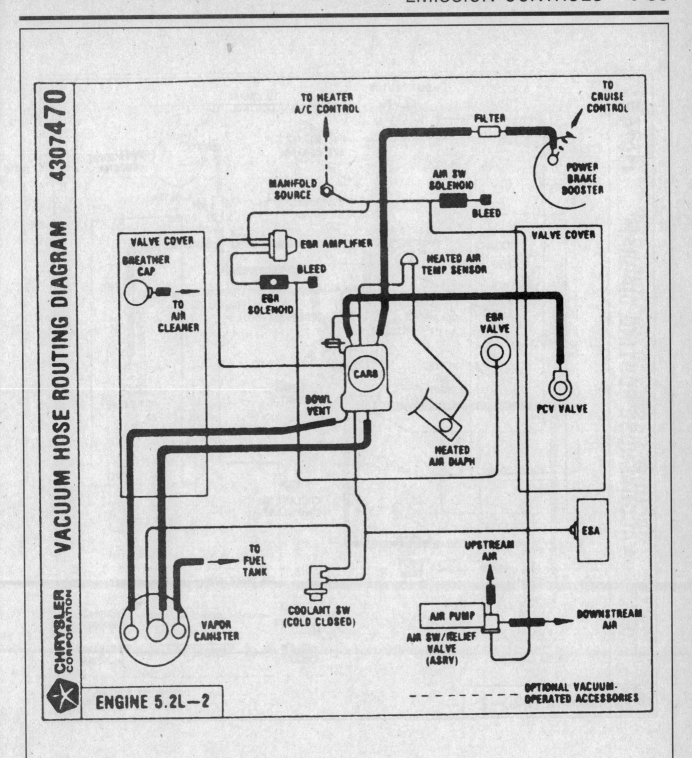

TO HEATER A/C CONTROL

TO CRUISE CONTROL

FILTER

MANIFOLD SOURCE

AIR SW SOLENOID

BLEED

POWER BRAKE BOOSTER

VALVE COVER

BREATHER CAP

TO AIR CLEANER

EGR AMPLIFIER

BLEED

HEATED AIR TEMP SENSOR

VALVE COVER

EGR SOLENOID

EGR VALVE

CARB

PCV VALVE

BOWL VENT

HEATED AIR DIAPH

TO FUEL TANK

E&A

UPSTREAM AIR

VAPOR CANISTER

COOLANT SW (COLD CLOSED)

AIR PUMP

DOWNSTREAM AIR

AIR SW/RELIEF VALVE (ASRV)

OPTIONAL VACUUM-OPERATED ACCESSORIES

VACUUM HOSE ROUTING DIAGRAM   4307470

CHRYSLER CORPORATION

ENGINE 5.2L—2

1985 318 engine, high altitude—California

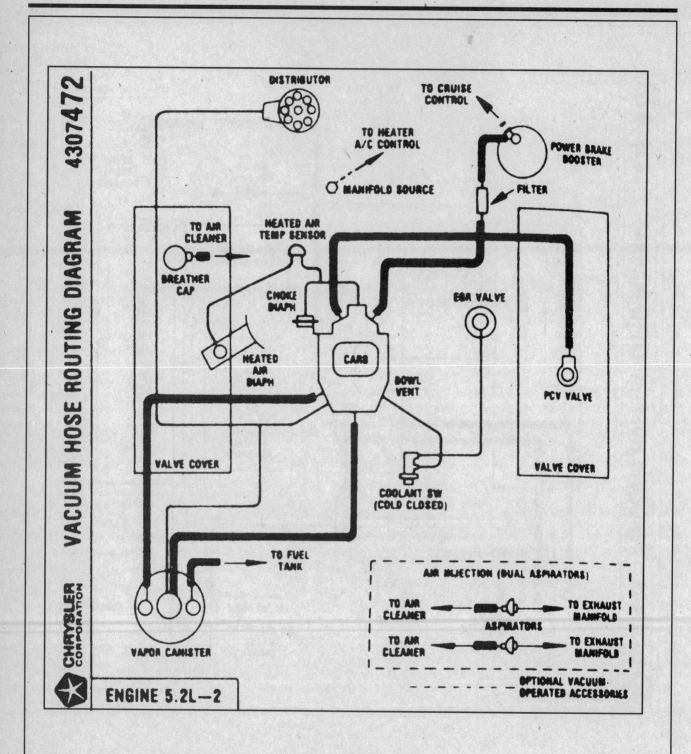

1985 318 engine with automatic transmission, aspirator and catalyst—Canada

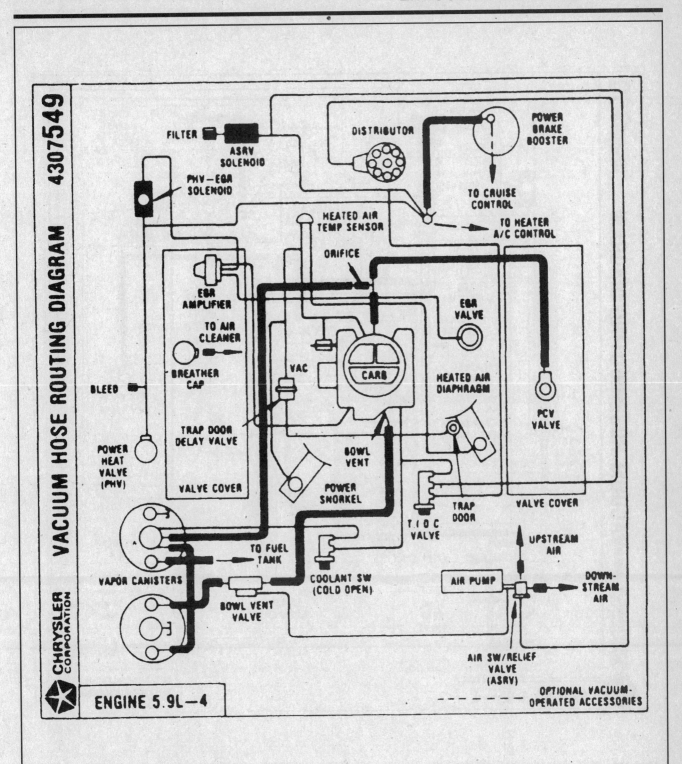

VACUUM HOSE ROUTING DIAGRAM 4307549

CHRYSLER CORPORATION

ENGINE 5.9L—4

1985 360 engine, high altitude—Federal

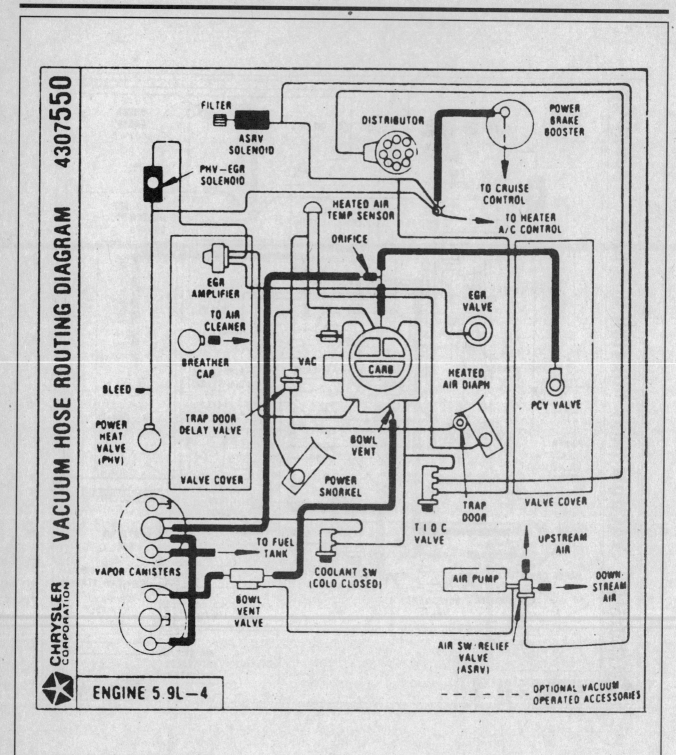

VACUUM HOSE ROUTING DIAGRAM 4307550

FILTER

ASRV SOLENOID

PMV—EGR SOLENOID

DISTRIBUTOR

POWER BRAKE BOOSTER

TO CRUISE CONTROL

HEATED AIR TEMP SENSOR

ORIFICE

TO HEATER A/C CONTROL

EGR AMPLIFIER

EGR VALVE

TO AIR CLEANER

BREATHER CAP

VAC

CARB

HEATED AIR DIAPH

PCV VALVE

BLEED

POWER HEAT VALVE (PHV)

TRAP DOOR DELAY VALVE

BOWL VENT

VALVE COVER

POWER SNORKEL

TRAP DOOR

VALVE COVER

TO FUEL TANK

T10C VALVE

UPSTREAM AIR

VAPOR CANISTERS

BOWL VENT VALVE

COOLANT SW (COLD CLOSED)

AIR PUMP

DOWN-STREAM AIR

AIR SW RELIEF VALVE (ASRV)

CHRYSLER CORPORATION

ENGINE 5.9L—4

OPTIONAL VACUUM OPERATED ACCESSORIES

1985 360 engine with catalyst—Federal

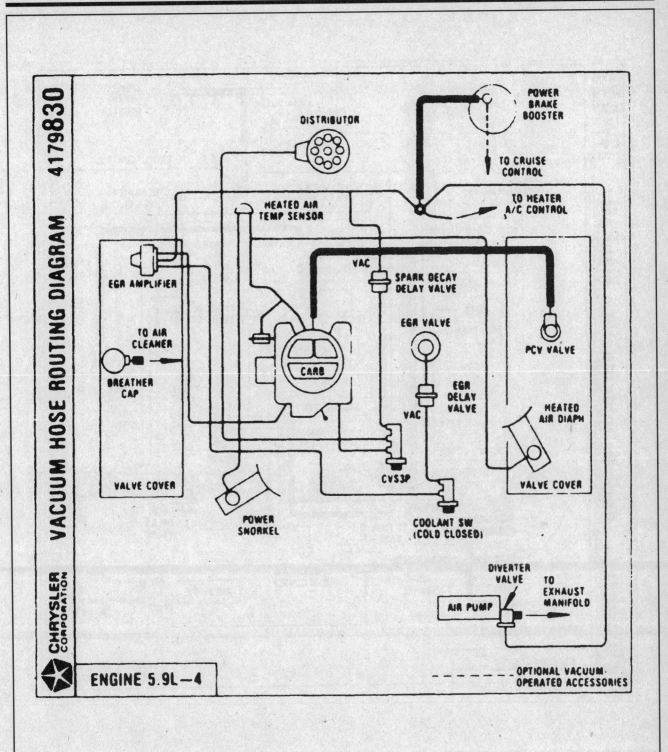

VACUUM HOSE ROUTING DIAGRAM 4179830

CHRYSLER CORPORATION

ENGINE 5.9L—4

DISTRIBUTOR

POWER BRAKE BOOSTER

TO CRUISE CONTROL

TO HEATER A/C CONTROL

HEATED AIR TEMP SENSOR

VAC

SPARK DECAY DELAY VALVE

EGR VALVE

PCV VALVE

EGR AMPLIFIER

TO AIR CLEANER

BREATHER CAP

CARB

VAC

EGR DELAY VALVE

HEATED AIR DIAPH

VALVE COVER

VALVE COVER

POWER SNORKEL

CVS3P

COOLANT SW (COLD CLOSED)

DIVERTER VALVE

TO EXHAUST MANIFOLD

AIR PUMP

OPTIONAL VACUUM OPERATED ACCESSORIES

1985 360 engine, heavy duty—Federal and Canada

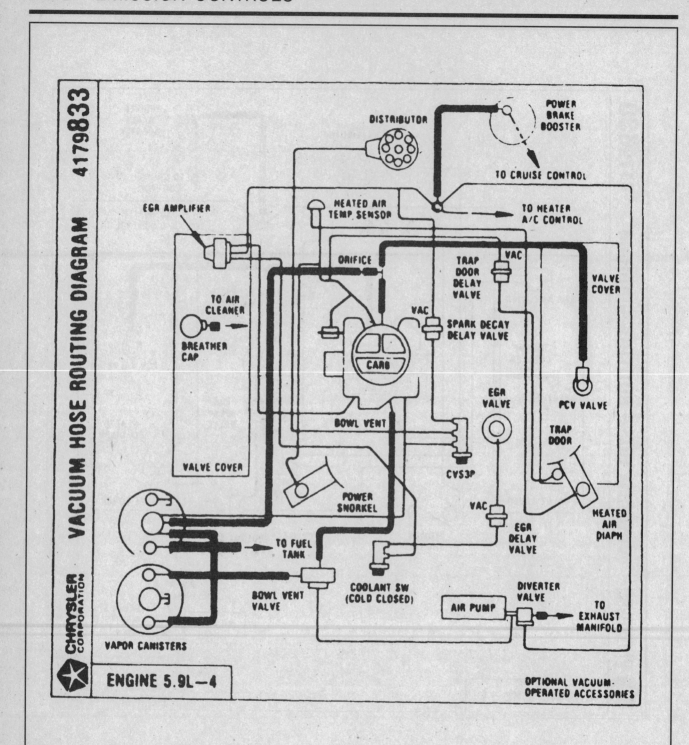

VACUUM HOSE ROUTING DIAGRAM 4179833

DISTRIBUTOR

POWER BRAKE BOOSTER

TO CRUISE CONTROL

EGR AMPLIFIER

HEATED AIR TEMP SENSOR

TO HEATER A/C CONTROL

ORIFICE

TRAP DOOR DELAY VALVE

VAC

VALVE COVER

TO AIR CLEANER

VAC

SPARK DECAY DELAY VALVE

BREATHER CAP

CARB

EGR VALVE

PCV VALVE

VALVE COVER

BOWL VENT

TRAP DOOR

CVS3P

POWER SNORKEL

VAC

EGR DELAY VALVE

HEATED AIR DIAPH

TO FUEL TANK

BOWL VENT VALVE

COOLANT SW (COLD CLOSED)

DIVERTER VALVE

AIR PUMP

TO EXHAUST MANIFOLD

VAPOR CANISTERS

CHRYSLER CORPORATION

ENGINE 5.9L—4

OPTIONAL VACUUM-OPERATED ACCESSORIES

1985 360 engine, heavy duty—California

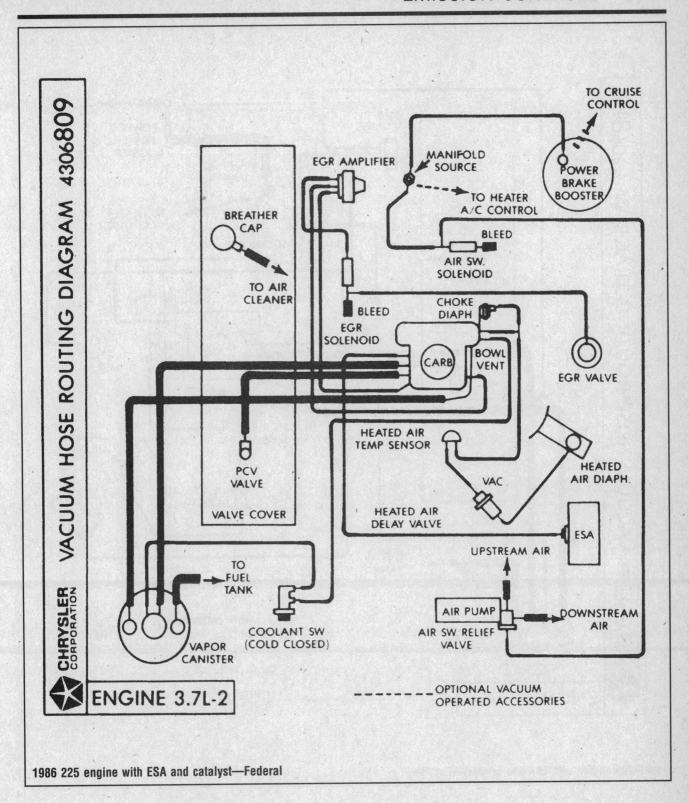

VACUUM HOSE ROUTING DIAGRAM 4306809

CHRYSLER CORPORATION

ENGINE 3.7L-2

1986 225 engine with ESA and catalyst—Federal

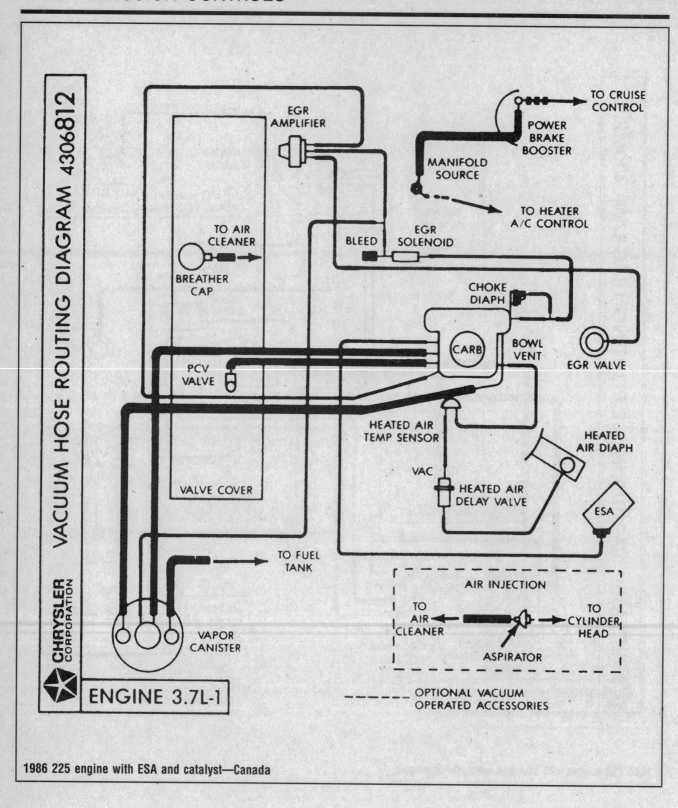

VACUUM HOSE ROUTING DIAGRAM 4306812

CHRYSLER CORPORATION

ENGINE 3.7L-1

EGR AMPLIFIER

TO AIR CLEANER

BREATHER CAP

TO CRUISE CONTROL

POWER BRAKE BOOSTER

MANIFOLD SOURCE

TO HEATER A/C CONTROL

BLEED

EGR SOLENOID

CHOKE DIAPH

CARB

BOWL VENT

EGR VALVE

PCV VALVE

HEATED AIR TEMP SENSOR

VALVE COVER

VAC

HEATED AIR DELAY VALVE

HEATED AIR DIAPH

ESA

TO FUEL TANK

VAPOR CANISTER

AIR INJECTION

TO AIR CLEANER

TO CYLINDER HEAD

ASPIRATOR

OPTIONAL VACUUM OPERATED ACCESSORIES

1986 225 engine with ESA and catalyst—Canada

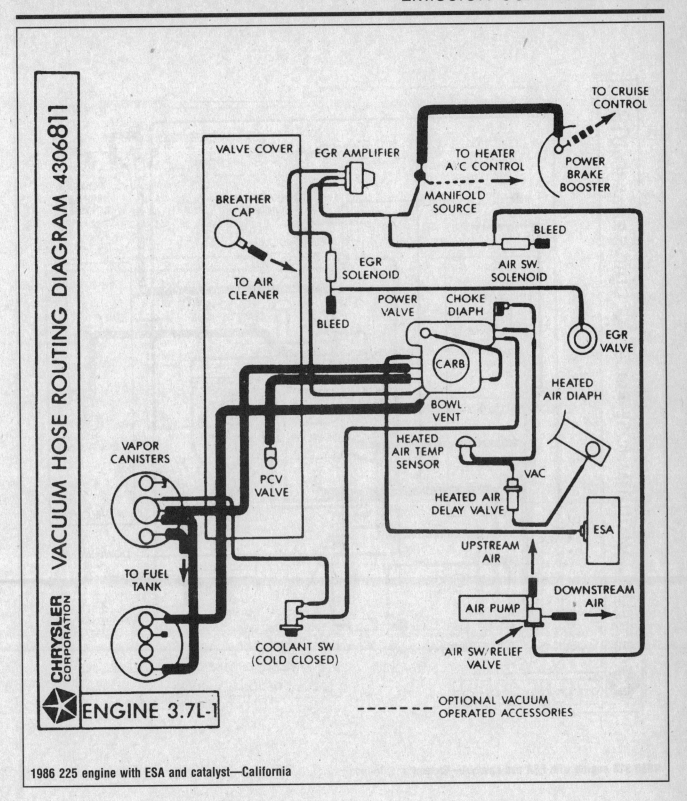

VACUUM HOSE ROUTING DIAGRAM 4306811

VALVE COVER

BREATHER CAP

TO AIR CLEANER

EGR AMPLIFIER

EGR SOLENOID

BLEED

TO HEATER A/C CONTROL

MANIFOLD SOURCE

POWER BRAKE BOOSTER

TO CRUISE CONTROL

BLEED

AIR SW. SOLENOID

POWER VALVE

CHOKE DIAPH

CARB

BOWL VENT

EGR VALVE

HEATED AIR DIAPH

VAPOR CANISTERS

PCV VALVE

HEATED AIR TEMP SENSOR

VAC

HEATED AIR DELAY VALVE

ESA

TO FUEL TANK

UPSTREAM AIR

DOWNSTREAM AIR

AIR PUMP

AIR SW/RELIEF VALVE

COOLANT SW (COLD CLOSED)

OPTIONAL VACUUM OPERATED ACCESSORIES

CHRYSLER CORPORATION

ENGINE 3.7L-1

1986 225 engine with ESA and catalyst—California

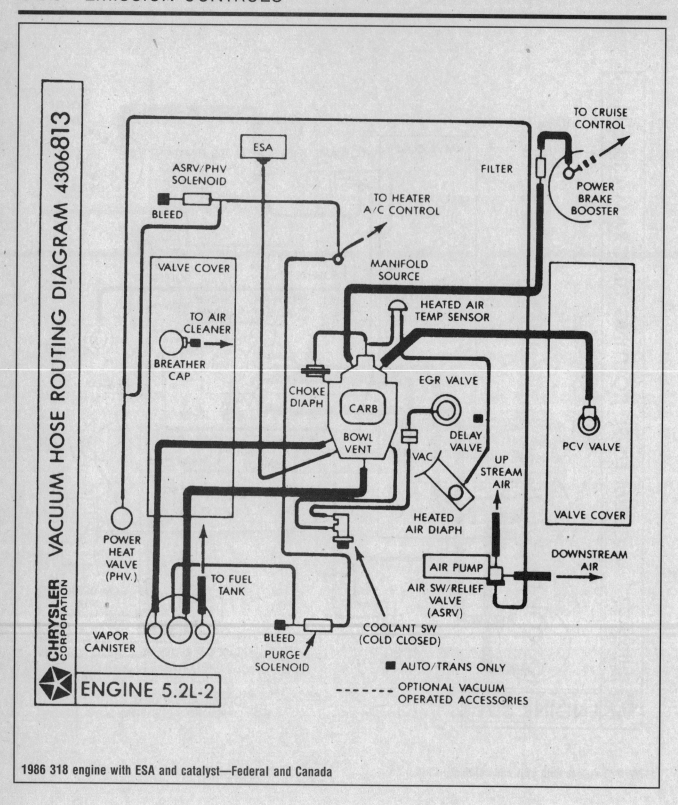

VACUUM HOSE ROUTING DIAGRAM 4306813

CHRYSLER CORPORATION

ENGINE 5.2L-2

ESA

ASRV/PHV SOLENOID

BLEED

VALVE COVER

TO AIR CLEANER

BREATHER CAP

TO HEATER A/C CONTROL

FILTER

TO CRUISE CONTROL

POWER BRAKE BOOSTER

MANIFOLD SOURCE

HEATED AIR TEMP SENSOR

CHOKE DIAPH

CARB

BOWL VENT

EGR VALVE

DELAY VALVE

VAC

PCV VALVE

VALVE COVER

UP STREAM AIR

HEATED AIR DIAPH

POWER HEAT VALVE (PHV.)

TO FUEL TANK

VAPOR CANISTER

BLEED PURGE SOLENOID

COOLANT SW (COLD CLOSED)

AIR PUMP

AIR SW/RELIEF VALVE (ASRV)

DOWNSTREAM AIR

■ AUTO/TRANS ONLY

------- OPTIONAL VACUUM OPERATED ACCESSORIES

1986 318 engine with ESA and catalyst—Federal and Canada

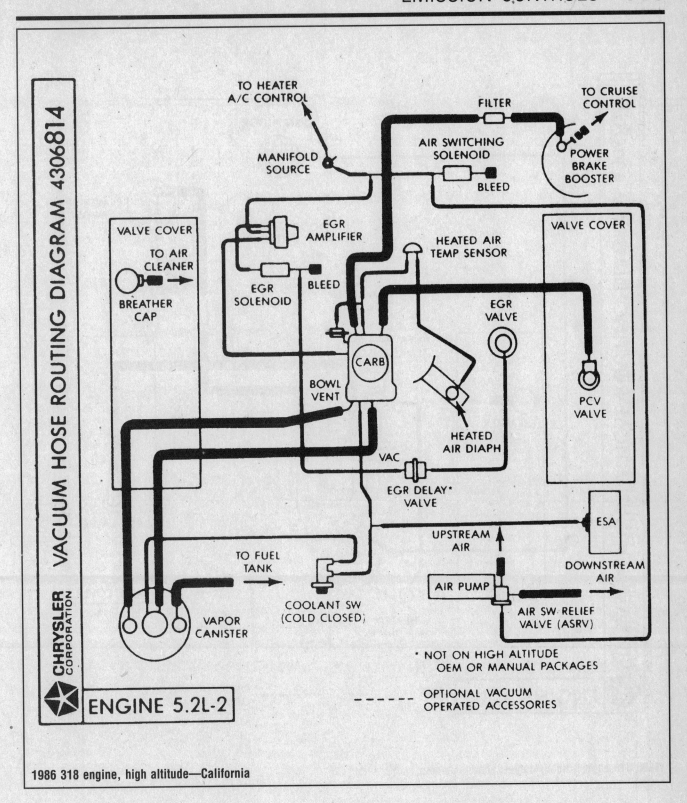

VACUUM HOSE ROUTING DIAGRAM 4306814

TO HEATER
A/C CONTROL

FILTER

TO CRUISE
CONTROL

MANIFOLD
SOURCE

AIR SWITCHING
SOLENOID

POWER
BRAKE
BOOSTER

BLEED

VALVE COVER

TO AIR
CLEANER

EGR
AMPLIFIER

HEATED AIR
TEMP SENSOR

VALVE COVER

BREATHER
CAP

EGR
SOLENOID

BLEED

EGR
VALVE

CARB

PCV
VALVE

BOWL
VENT

HEATED
AIR DIAPH

VAC

TO FUEL
TANK

EGR DELAY
VALVE

UPSTREAM
AIR

ESA

DOWNSTREAM
AIR

VAPOR
CANISTER

COOLANT SW
(COLD CLOSED)

AIR PUMP

AIR SW. RELIEF
VALVE (ASRV)

• NOT ON HIGH ALTITUDE
OEM OR MANUAL PACKAGES

------- OPTIONAL VACUUM
OPERATED ACCESSORIES

CHRYSLER CORPORATION

ENGINE 5.2L-2

1986 318 engine, high altitude—California

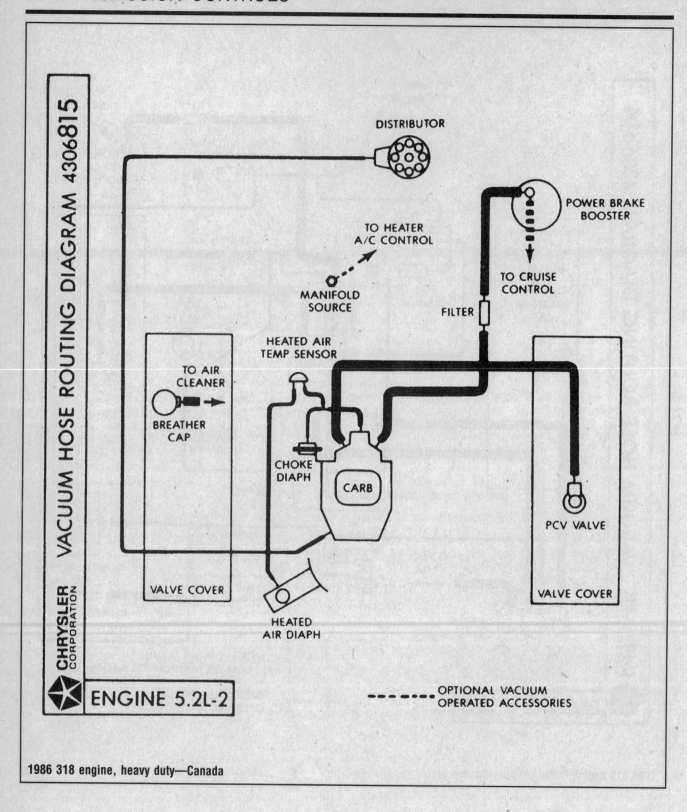

VACUUM HOSE ROUTING DIAGRAM 4306815

CHRYSLER CORPORATION

ENGINE 5.2L-2

DISTRIBUTOR

POWER BRAKE BOOSTER

TO HEATER A/C CONTROL

TO CRUISE CONTROL

MANIFOLD SOURCE

FILTER

HEATED AIR TEMP SENSOR

TO AIR CLEANER

BREATHER CAP

CHOKE DIAPH

CARB

PCV VALVE

VALVE COVER

VALVE COVER

HEATED AIR DIAPH

- - - - - OPTIONAL VACUUM OPERATED ACCESSORIES

1986 318 engine, heavy duty—Canada

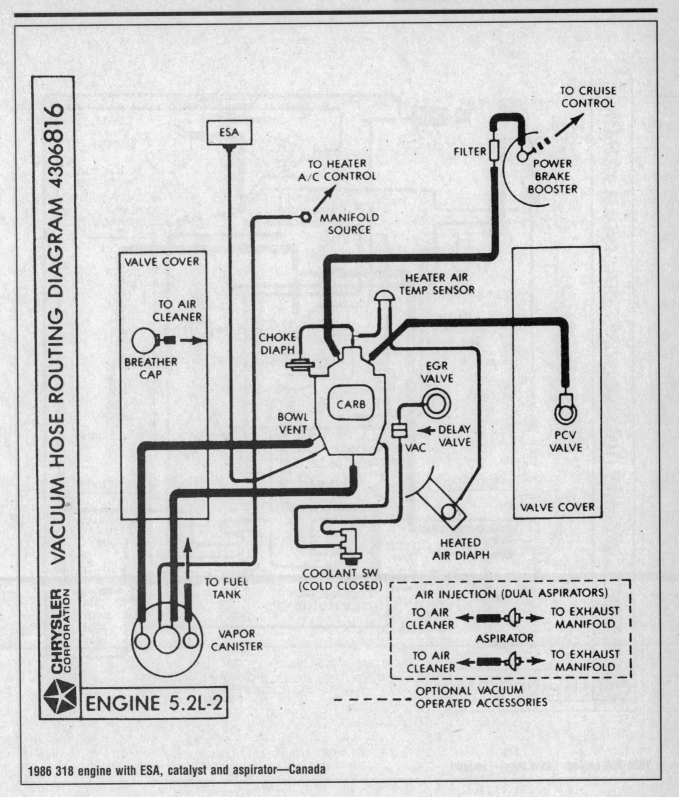

VACUUM HOSE ROUTING DIAGRAM 4306816

CHRYSLER CORPORATION

ENGINE 5.2L-2

ESA

TO HEATER A/C CONTROL

MANIFOLD SOURCE

TO CRUISE CONTROL

FILTER

POWER BRAKE BOOSTER

VALVE COVER

TO AIR CLEANER

BREATHER CAP

HEATER AIR TEMP SENSOR

CHOKE DIAPH

CARB

EGR VALVE

VAC

DELAY VALVE

PCV VALVE

VALVE COVER

BOWL VENT

HEATED AIR DIAPH

COOLANT SW (COLD CLOSED)

TO FUEL TANK

VAPOR CANISTER

AIR INJECTION (DUAL ASPIRATORS)

TO AIR CLEANER — ASPIRATOR — TO EXHAUST MANIFOLD

TO AIR CLEANER — TO EXHAUST MANIFOLD

OPTIONAL VACUUM OPERATED ACCESSORIES

1986 318 engine with ESA, catalyst and aspirator—Canada

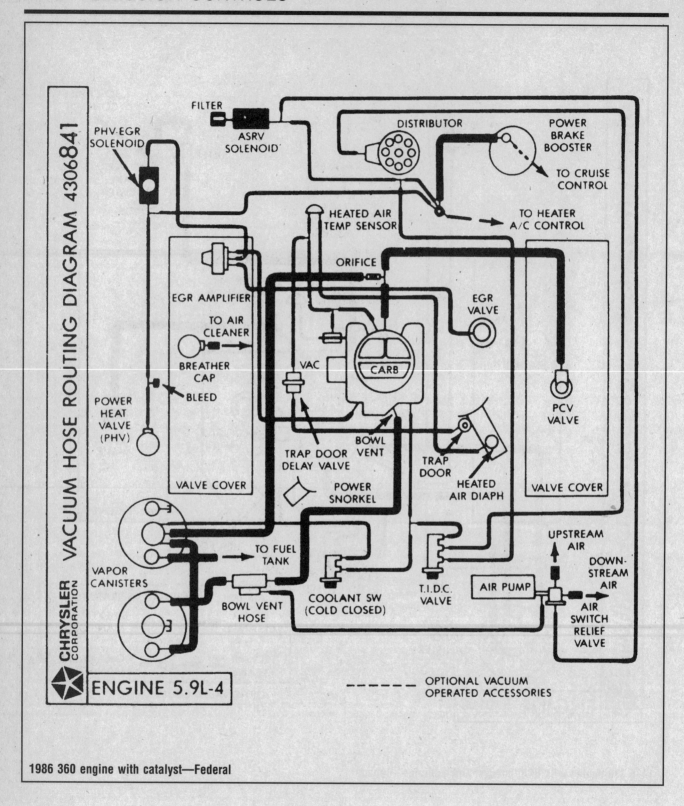

VACUUM HOSE ROUTING DIAGRAM 4306841

PHV-EGR SOLENOID

FILTER

ASRV SOLENOID

DISTRIBUTOR

POWER BRAKE BOOSTER

TO CRUISE CONTROL

TO HEATER A/C CONTROL

HEATED AIR TEMP SENSOR

ORIFICE

EGR VALVE

EGR AMPLIFIER

TO AIR CLEANER

BREATHER CAP

BLEED

POWER HEAT VALVE (PHV)

VAC

CARB

PCV VALVE

TRAP DOOR DELAY VALVE

BOWL VENT

TRAP DOOR

HEATED AIR DIAPH

VALVE COVER

POWER SNORKEL

VALVE COVER

UPSTREAM AIR

DOWN-STREAM AIR

VAPOR CANISTERS

TO FUEL TANK

BOWL VENT HOSE

COOLANT SW (COLD CLOSED)

T.I.D.C. VALVE

AIR PUMP

AIR SWITCH RELIEF VALVE

CHRYSLER CORPORATION

ENGINE 5.9L-4

– – – – – – OPTIONAL VACUUM OPERATED ACCESSORIES

1986 360 engine with catalyst—Federal

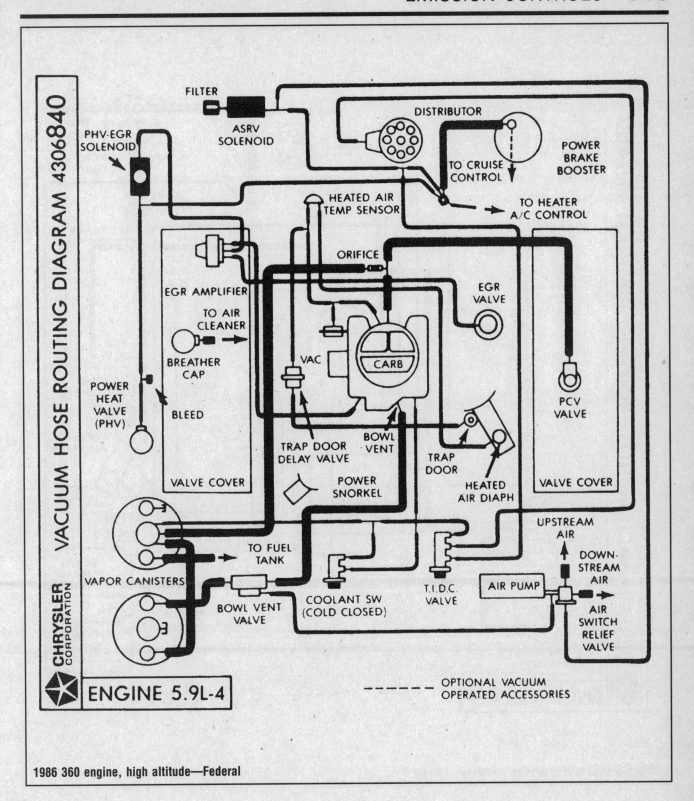

VACUUM HOSE ROUTING DIAGRAM 4306840

FILTER

PHV-EGR SOLENOID

ASRV SOLENOID

DISTRIBUTOR

TO CRUISE CONTROL

POWER BRAKE BOOSTER

TO HEATER A/C CONTROL

HEATED AIR TEMP SENSOR

ORIFICE

EGR VALVE

EGR AMPLIFIER

TO AIR CLEANER

BREATHER CAP

VAC

CARB

BLEED

POWER HEAT VALVE (PHV)

TRAP DOOR DELAY VALVE

BOWL VENT

TRAP DOOR

HEATED AIR DIAPH

PCV VALVE

VALVE COVER

POWER SNORKEL

VALVE COVER

UPSTREAM AIR

DOWN-STREAM AIR

VAPOR CANISTERS

TO FUEL TANK

BOWL VENT VALVE

COOLANT SW (COLD CLOSED)

T.I.D.C. VALVE

AIR PUMP

AIR SWITCH RELIEF VALVE

CHRYSLER CORPORATION

ENGINE 5.9L-4

— — — — OPTIONAL VACUUM OPERATED ACCESSORIES

1986 360 engine, high altitude—Federal

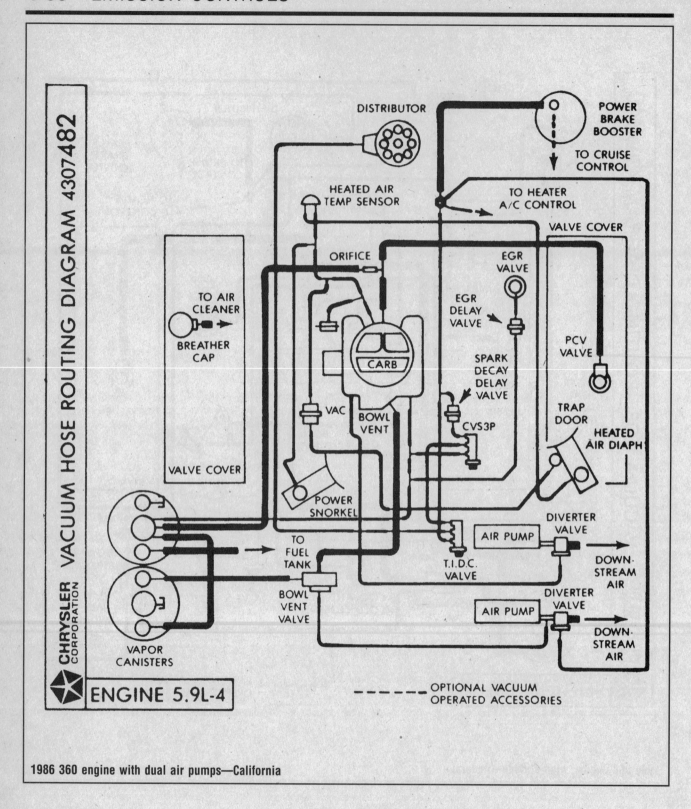

1986 360 engine with dual air pumps—California

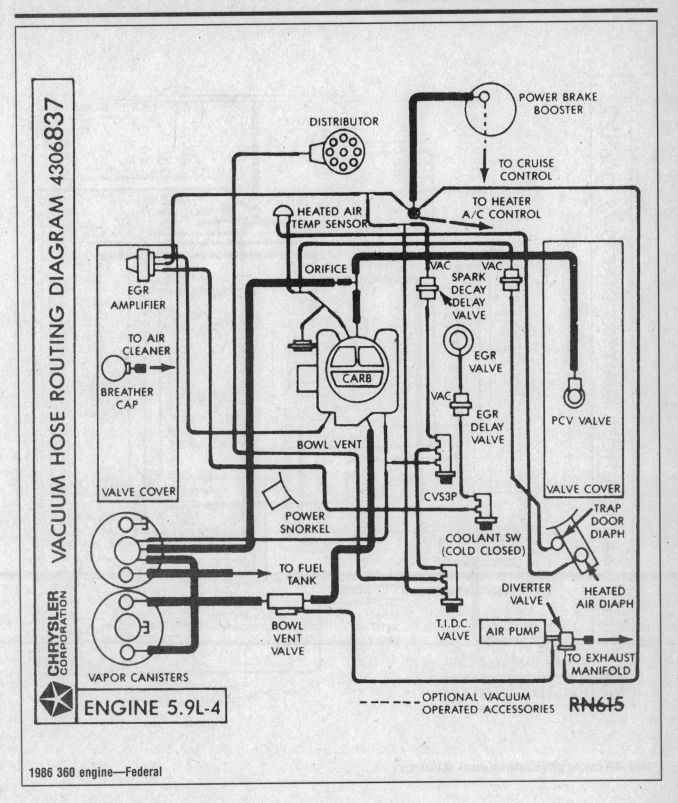

VACUUM HOSE ROUTING DIAGRAM 4306837

CHRYSLER CORPORATION

ENGINE 5.9L-4

POWER BRAKE BOOSTER

DISTRIBUTOR

TO CRUISE CONTROL

TO HEATER A/C CONTROL

HEATED AIR TEMP SENSOR

ORIFICE

EGR AMPLIFIER

TO AIR CLEANER

BREATHER CAP

VALVE COVER

VAC

VAC SPARK DECAY DELAY VALVE

EGR VALVE

VAC EGR DELAY VALVE

PCV VALVE

VALVE COVER

CARB

BOWL VENT

CVS3P

POWER SNORKEL

COOLANT SW (COLD CLOSED)

TRAP DOOR DIAPH

DIVERTER VALVE

HEATED AIR DIAPH

TO FUEL TANK

BOWL VENT VALVE

T.I.D.C. VALVE

AIR PUMP

TO EXHAUST MANIFOLD

VAPOR CANISTERS

------- OPTIONAL VACUUM OPERATED ACCESSORIES

RN615

1986 360 engine—Federal

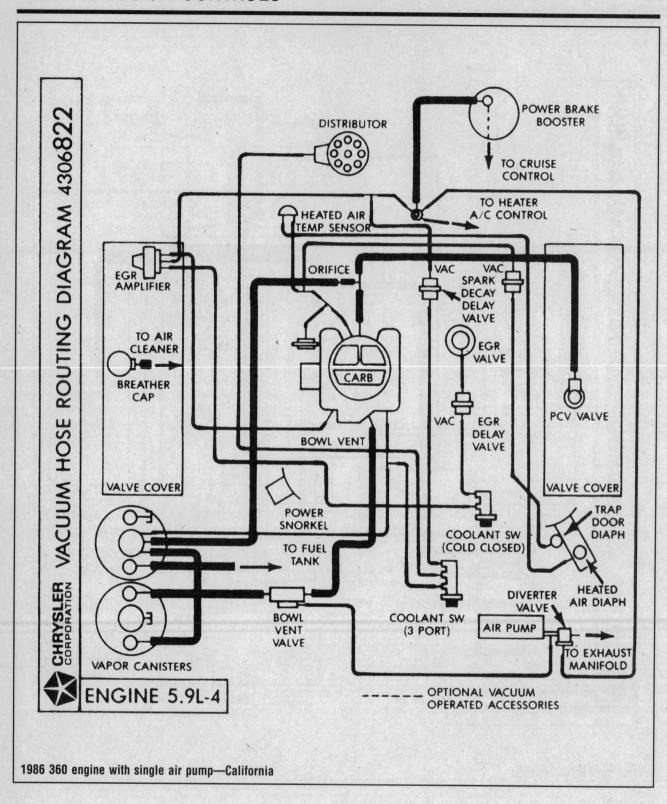

CHRYSLER CORPORATION

VACUUM HOSE ROUTING DIAGRAM 4306822

ENGINE 5.9L-4

DISTRIBUTOR

POWER BRAKE BOOSTER

TO CRUISE CONTROL

TO HEATER A/C CONTROL

HEATED AIR TEMP SENSOR

EGR AMPLIFIER

TO AIR CLEANER

BREATHER CAP

ORIFICE

VAC

VAC SPARK DECAY DELAY VALVE

EGR VALVE

VAC

EGR DELAY VALVE

PCV VALVE

CARB

BOWL VENT

VALVE COVER

VALVE COVER

POWER SNORKEL

TO FUEL TANK

COOLANT SW (COLD CLOSED)

TRAP DOOR DIAPH

HEATED AIR DIAPH

VAPOR CANISTERS

BOWL VENT VALVE

COOLANT SW (3 PORT)

DIVERTER VALVE

AIR PUMP

TO EXHAUST MANIFOLD

------- OPTIONAL VACUUM OPERATED ACCESSORIES

1986 360 engine with single air pump—California

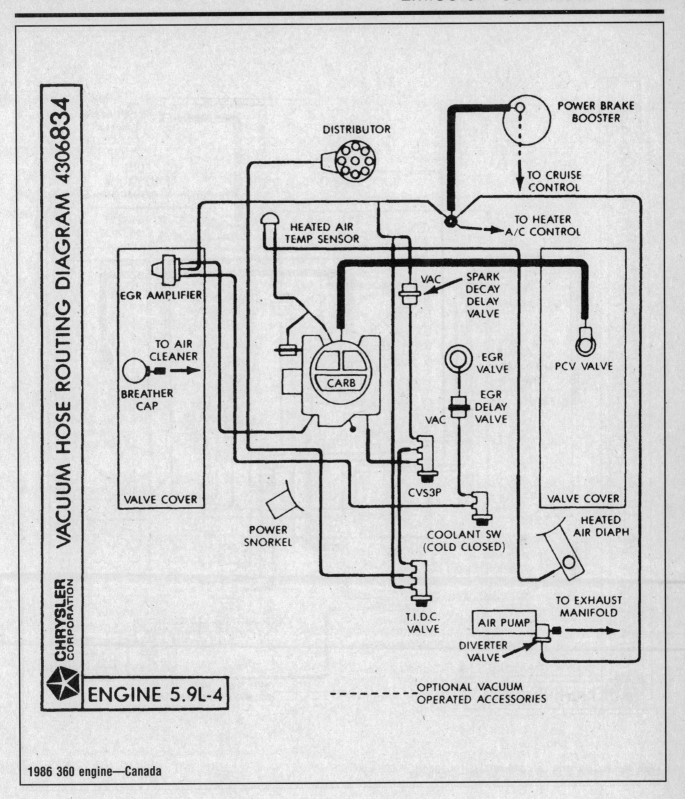

VACUUM HOSE ROUTING DIAGRAM 4306834

CHRYSLER CORPORATION

ENGINE 5.9L-4

DISTRIBUTOR

POWER BRAKE BOOSTER

TO CRUISE CONTROL

TO HEATER A/C CONTROL

HEATED AIR TEMP SENSOR

EGR AMPLIFIER

TO AIR CLEANER

BREATHER CAP

VALVE COVER

POWER SNORKEL

CARB

VAC SPARK DECAY DELAY VALVE

EGR VALVE

EGR DELAY VALVE

VAC

CVS3P

COOLANT SW (COLD CLOSED)

PCV VALVE

VALVE COVER

HEATED AIR DIAPH

T.I.D.C. VALVE

AIR PUMP

TO EXHAUST MANIFOLD

DIVERTER VALVE

OPTIONAL VACUUM OPERATED ACCESSORIES

1986 360 engine—Canada

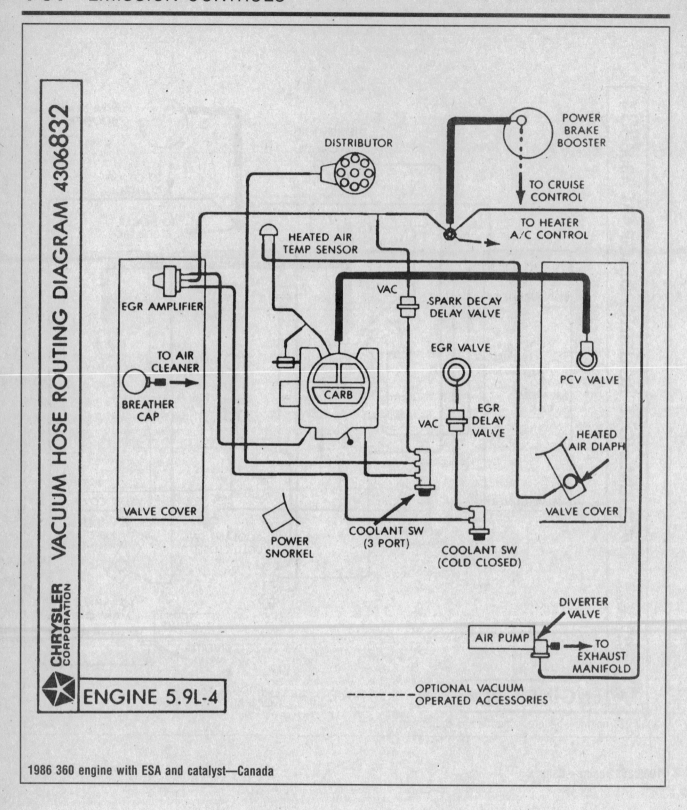

VACUUM HOSE ROUTING DIAGRAM 4306832

CHRYSLER CORPORATION

ENGINE 5.9L-4

DISTRIBUTOR

POWER BRAKE BOOSTER

TO CRUISE CONTROL

TO HEATER A/C CONTROL

HEATED AIR TEMP SENSOR

EGR AMPLIFIER

TO AIR CLEANER

BREATHER CAP

VALVE COVER

VAC

SPARK DECAY DELAY VALVE

EGR VALVE

PCV VALVE

CARB

VAC

EGR DELAY VALVE

HEATED AIR DIAPH

VALVE COVER

POWER SNORKEL

COOLANT SW (3 PORT)

COOLANT SW (COLD CLOSED)

DIVERTER VALVE

AIR PUMP

TO EXHAUST MANIFOLD

OPTIONAL VACUUM OPERATED ACCESSORIES

1986 360 engine with ESA and catalyst—Canada

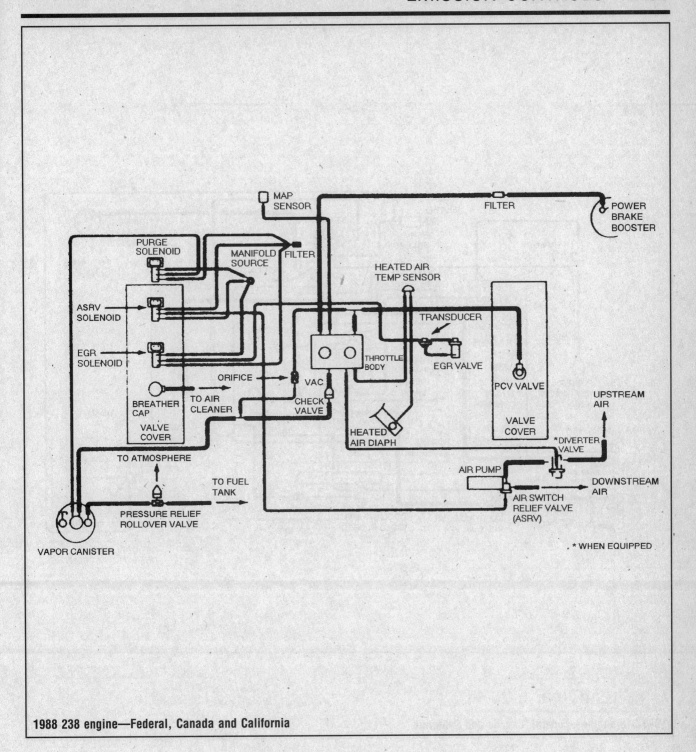

1988 238 engine—Federal, Canada and California

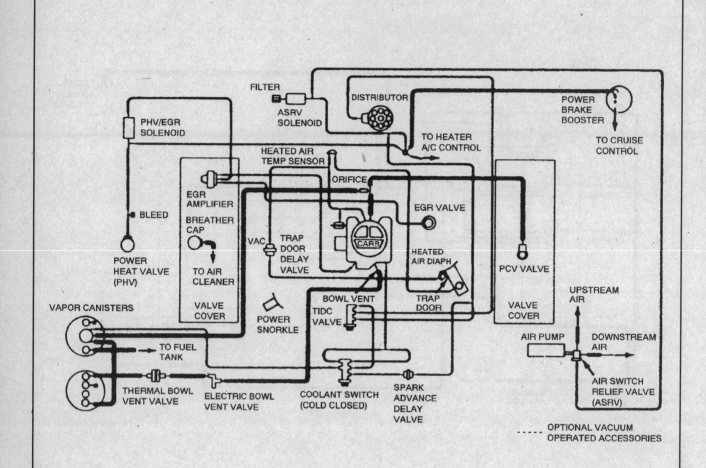

1988 318 engine—Federal, Canada and California

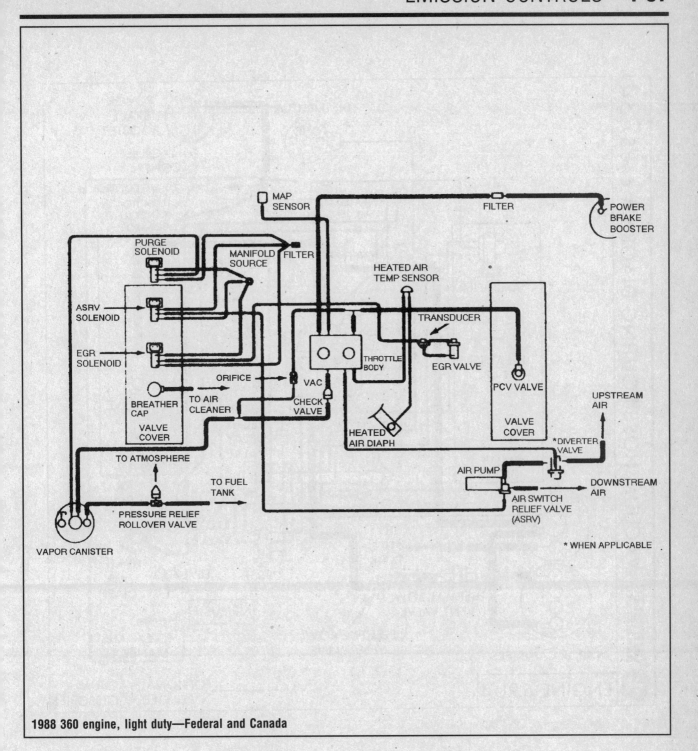

1988 360 engine, light duty—Federal and Canada

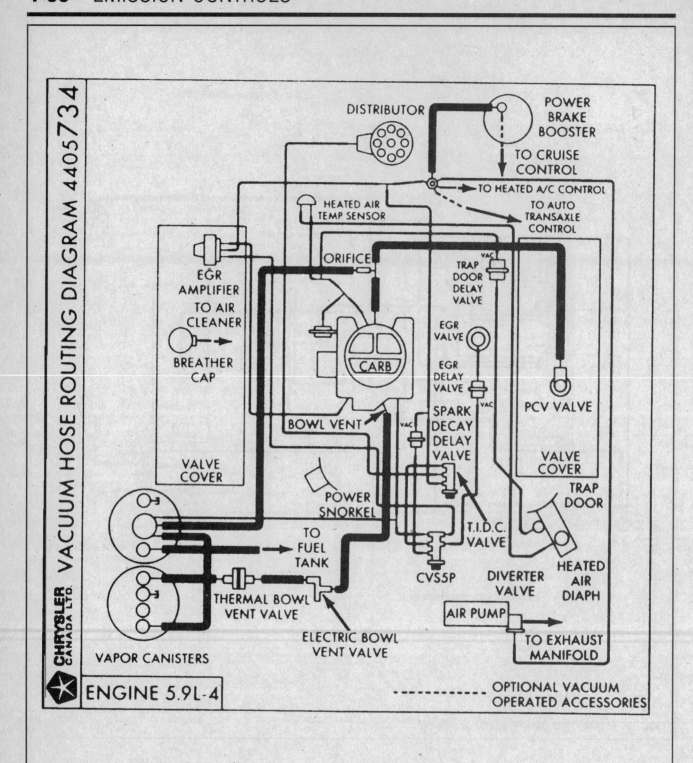

VACUUM HOSE ROUTING DIAGRAM 4405734

DISTRIBUTOR

POWER BRAKE BOOSTER

TO CRUISE CONTROL

TO HEATED A/C CONTROL

TO AUTO TRANSAXLE CONTROL

HEATED AIR TEMP SENSOR

EGR AMPLIFIER

TO AIR CLEANER

BREATHER CAP

ORIFICE

CARB

BOWL VENT

VALVE COVER

POWER SNORKEL

TO FUEL TANK

THERMAL BOWL VENT VALVE

ELECTRIC BOWL VENT VALVE

VAPOR CANISTERS

TRAP DOOR DELAY VALVE

EGR VALVE

EGR DELAY VALVE

SPARK DECAY DELAY VALVE

CVS5P

T.I.D.C. VALVE

DIVERTER VALVE

AIR PUMP

TO EXHAUST MANIFOLD

PCV VALVE

VALVE COVER

TRAP DOOR

HEATED AIR DIAPH

CHRYSLER CANADA LTD.

ENGINE 5.9L-4

------------ OPTIONAL VACUUM OPERATED ACCESSORIES

1988 360 engine—California

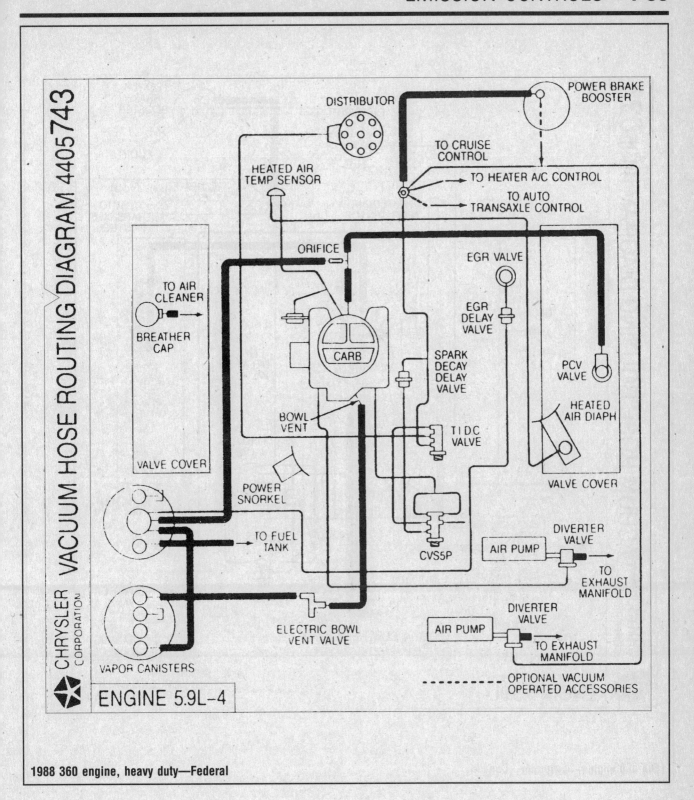

VACUUM HOSE ROUTING DIAGRAM 4405743

CHRYSLER CORPORATION

ENGINE 5.9L-4

1988 360 engine, heavy duty—Federal

DISTRIBUTOR

POWER BRAKE BOOSTER

TO CRUISE CONTROL

TO HEATER A/C CONTROL

TO AUTO TRANSAXLE CONTROL

HEATED AIR TEMP SENSOR

ORIFICE

EGR VALVE

EGR DELAY VALVE

PCV VALVE

TO AIR CLEANER

BREATHER CAP

CARB

SPARK DECAY DELAY VALVE

HEATED AIR DIAPH

VALVE COVER

BOWL VENT

TIDC VALVE

VALVE COVER

POWER SNORKEL

TO FUEL TANK

CVS5P

DIVERTER VALVE

AIR PUMP

TO EXHAUST MANIFOLD

ELECTRIC BOWL VENT VALVE

DIVERTER VALVE

AIR PUMP

TO EXHAUST MANIFOLD

VAPOR CANISTERS

OPTIONAL VACUUM OPERATED ACCESSORIES

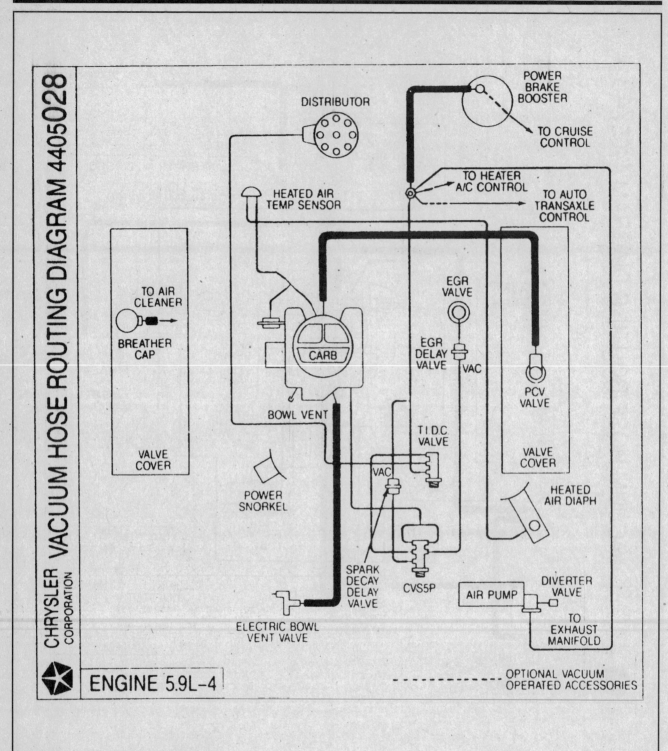

CHRYSLER VACUUM HOSE ROUTING DIAGRAM 4405028
CORPORATION

ENGINE 5.9L-4

DISTRIBUTOR

POWER
BRAKE
BOOSTER

TO CRUISE
CONTROL

TO HEATER
A/C CONTROL

TO AUTO
TRANSAXLE
CONTROL

HEATED AIR
TEMP SENSOR

TO AIR
CLEANER

BREATHER
CAP

VALVE
COVER

CARB

EGR
VALVE

EGR
DELAY
VALVE   VAC

PCV
VALVE

VALVE
COVER

BOWL VENT

POWER
SNORKEL

T.I.D.C.
VALVE

VAC

HEATED
AIR DIAPH

SPARK
DECAY
DELAY
VALVE

CVS5P

DIVERTER
VALVE

AIR PUMP

TO
EXHAUST
MANIFOLD

ELECTRIC BOWL
VENT VALVE

OPTIONAL VACUUM
OPERATED ACCESSORIES

1988 360 engine, heavy duty—Canada

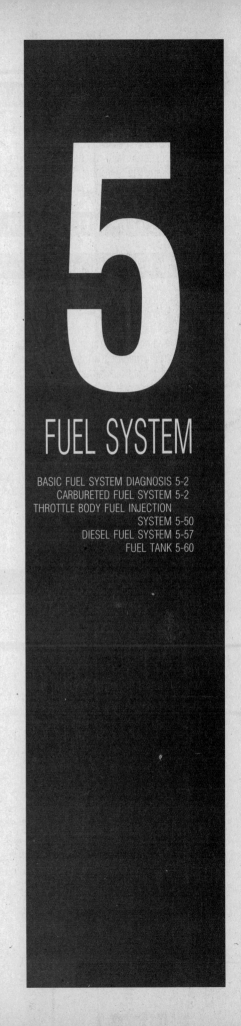

5

FUEL SYSTEM

BASIC FUEL SYSTEM DIAGNOSIS

When there is a problem starting or driving a vehicle, two of the most important checks involve the ignition and the fuel systems. The questions most mechanics attempt to answer first, "is there spark?" and "is there fuel?" will often lead to solving most basic problems. For ignition system diagnosis and testing, please refer to the information on engine electrical components and ignition systems found earlier in this manual. If the ignition system checks out (there is spark), then you must determine if the fuel system is operating properly (is there fuel?).

CARBURETED FUEL SYSTEM

General Information

The carbureted fuel system uses a mechanical fuel pump to draw gasoline from the fuel tank and deliver it to the carburetor. The carburetor then carefully meters the fuel based on air flow through it. As air flows through the carburetor, it creates vacuum signals in varying degrees within the carburetor, thereby drawing the fuel out of the carburetor and mixing with the air stream. The more air that is allowed to pass through the carburetor (i.e. the farther you press the accelerator pedal down), will pull that much more fuel out of the carburetor. This air/fuel mixture then enters the engine to be burned in the combustion chamber. The system has remained relatively unchanged until mid 1984. In 1984, the Electronic Feedback Carburetor system was introduced. This system functions the same as the old carbureted system except that it incorporated some electronic devices to accurately maintain a constant air/fuel mixture. All 1984 vehicles, without a vacuum advance on the distributor, and all 1985–88 vehicles are equipped with this system. See Section 4 to read a more detailed description of the system and its components.

Carburetor Applications

1967

Holley 1920 1-bbl:
- 170 and 225 Engines

Stromberg WW3 2-bbl:
- 318 Engines with manual transmission (manual choke) and automatic transmission (automatic choke)

1968–69

Carter BBD 2-bbl:
- 318 Engines (manual and automatic choke)

Holley 1920 1-bbl:
- 170 and 225 Engines

1970–71

Carter BBD 2-bbl:
- 318 Engines

Holley 1920 1-bbl:
- 198 and 225 Engines

1972–73

Carter BBS 1-bbl:
- 225 Engine on 15 passenger van

Carter BBD 2-bbl:
- 318 Engines

Holley 1920 1-bbl:
- 225 Engines exc. 15 passenger van

Holley 2210 2-bbl:
- 360 Engines

1974–77

Holley 1945 1-bbl:
- 225 Engines

Carter BBD 2-bbl:
- 318 Engines

Holley 2210 2-bbl:
- 360 and 400 Engines

Holley 2245 2-bbl:
- 360 Engines

Carter Thermo-Quad 4-bbl:
- 440 Engines

1978

Carter BBD 2-bbl:
- 225 Engines (California)
- 318 Engines (49S)

Carter Thermo-Quad 4-bbl:
- 318 Engines (Calif. and Canada)
- 360 Engines (Calif.)
- 440 Engines

Holley 2210:
- 400 Engines

Holley 2245:
- 360 Engines

1979

Holley 1945:
- 225 Engines (49S and Canada)

Carter BBD:
- 225 Engines (Calif.)
- 318 Engines (49S)

Holley 2245:
- 360 Engines (49S)

Carter Thermo-Quad:
- 318 Engines (Calif. and Canada)
- 360 Engines (US and Canada)
- 440 Engines (US and Canada)

1980–81

Holley 1945 1-bbl:
- 225 Engines (US and Canada)

Holley 2280 2-bbl:
- 318 Engines (49S and Canada)

Carter BBD 2-bbl:
- 318 Engines (Canada)

Holley 2245 2-bbl:
- 360 Engines (Canada)

Carter Thermo-Quad 4-bbl:
- 318 Engines (US and Canada)
- 360 Engines (US and Canada)

1982

Holley 1945 1-bbl:
- 225 Engines (US and Canada)

Holley 2280 2-bbl:
- 318 Engines (US and Canada)

Carter BBD 2-bbl:
- 225 Engines (US)
- 318 Engines (US and Canada)

Holley 2245 2-bbl:
- 360 Engines (Canada)

Carter Thermo-Quad 4-bbl:
- 318 Engines (US and Canada)
- 360 Engines (California)

1983

Holley 1945 1-bbl:
- 225 Engines (US and Canada)

Holley 6145 1-bbl:
- 225 Engines (California)

Holley 2280 2-bbl:
- 318 Engines (US)

Holley 2245 2-bbl:
- 360 Engines (Canada)

Carter BBD 2-bbl:
- 225 Engines (US)
- 318 Engines (US and Canada)

Carter Thermo-Quad 4-bbl:
- 318 Engines (US)
- 360 Engines (US and Canada)

1984

Holley 1945 1-bbl:
- 225 Engines (49S and Canada)

Holley 6145 1-bbl:
- 225 Engines (California)

Holley 2280 2-bbl:
- 318 Engines (US and Canada)

Carter BBD 2-bbl:
- 318 Engines (US and Canada)

Carter Thermo-Quad 4-bbl:
- 360 Engines (US and Canada)

1985–87

Holley 1945 1-bbl:
- 225 Engines ((49S and Canada)

Holley 6145 1-bbl:
- 225 Engines (California)

Holley 2280 2-bbl:
- 318 Engines (49S and Canada)

Holley 6280 2-bbl:
- 318 Engines (US)

Rochester Quadrajet 4-bbl:
- 360 Engines (US and Canada)

1988

Rochester Quadrajet 4-bbl:
- 360 Engines (US and Canada)

Fuel Pump

REMOVAL & INSTALLATION

◆ See Figures 1, 2 and 3

✲✲ CAUTION

Never smoke when working around gasoline! Avoid all sources of sparks or ignition. Gasoline vapors are EXTREMELY volatile!

1. Disconnect the fuel lines from the inlet and output sides of the fuel pump.
2. Plug these lines to prevent gasoline from leaking out.
3. Unbolt the retaining bolts from the fuel pump and remove the fuel pump from the engine.
4. Remove the old gasket from the engine and/or fuel pump.
5. Clean all mounting surfaces.
6. Using a new gasket, install the fuel pump. Installation is the reverse of removal.

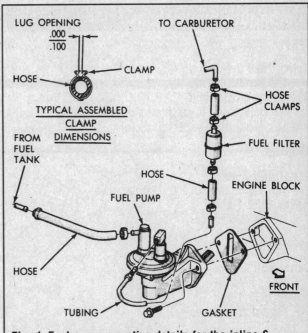

Fig. 1 Fuel pump mounting details for the inline 6-cylinder engines

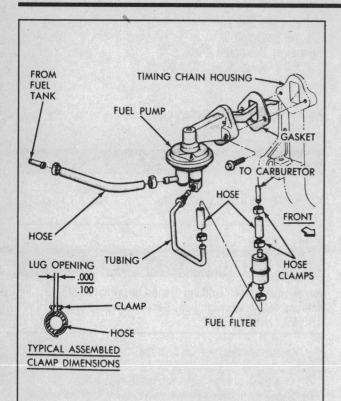

FROM FUEL TANK

TIMING CHAIN HOUSING

FUEL PUMP

GASKET

TO CARBURETOR

HOSE

FRONT

HOSE

HOSE

TUBING

HOSE CLAMPS

LUG OPENING
.000
.100

CLAMP

HOSE

FUEL FILTER

CLAMP

HOSE

TYPICAL ASSEMBLED CLAMP DIMENSIONS

Fig. 2 Fuel pump mounting details for the 318 and 360 engines

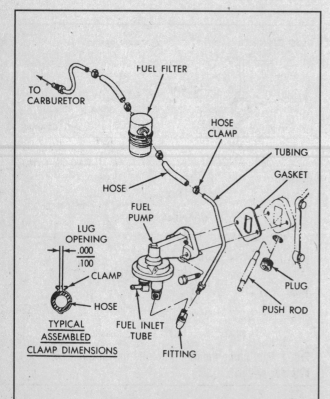

TO CARBURETOR

FUEL FILTER

HOSE CLAMP

TUBING

GASKET

HOSE

FUEL PUMP

LUG OPENING
.000
.100

CLAMP

HOSE

PLUG

PUSH ROD

TYPICAL ASSEMBLED CLAMP DIMENSIONS

FUEL INLET TUBE

FITTING

Fig. 3 Fuel pump mounting details for the 400 and 440 engines

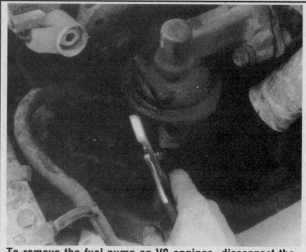

To remove the fuel pump on V8 engines, disconnect the fuel lines at the pump

After you have loosened the mounting bolts, remove the pump from the engine

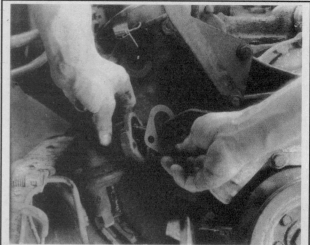

Before installation, clean all traces of the old gasket, then position a new one on the pump

TESTING

♦ See Figure 4

Pressure Test

1. If leakage is not apparent, the following pressure test should be performed.

2. Insert a "Tee" fitting into the fuel line at the carburetor.

3. Connect a 6 in. piece of hose between the "Tee" fitting and a pressure gauge.

4. Vent the pump for a few seconds to allow the pump to operate at maximum capacity.

5. Connect a tachometer and start the engine. Allow the engine to run at idle speed. The fuel pump pressure should be 3.5–5.0 (6-cylinder) or 5.0–7.0 psi (V8s). When the engine is stopped, the pressure should return to zero very slowly. If it rapidly or instantly drops to zero, a leaky outlet valve is indicated.

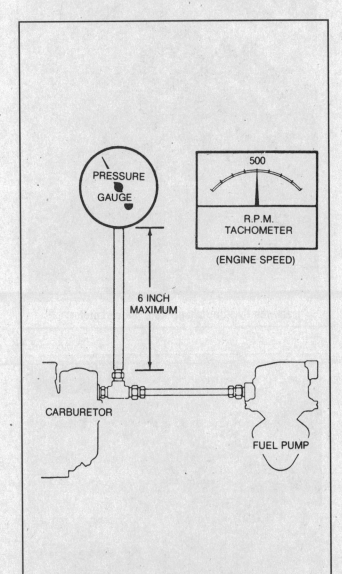

Fig. 4 Testing the fuel pump for the correct output pressure

Volume Test

1. Disconnect the fuel line from the carburetor. Place the end of the line in a container holding at least 1 quart.

2. The fuel pump should pump our 1 quart in 1 minute or less at 500 rpm.

Carburetors

REMOVAL & INSTALLATION

The following is general removal procedure for all carburetors.

1. Disconnect the battery ground cable.

2. Remove the air cleaner.

3. Remove the fuel tank filler cap. The tank could be under a small amount of pressure.

4. Disconnect and plug the fuel lines. Use two wrenches to

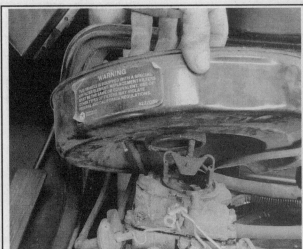

Remove the air cleaner housing on L6 engines to gain access to the carburetor

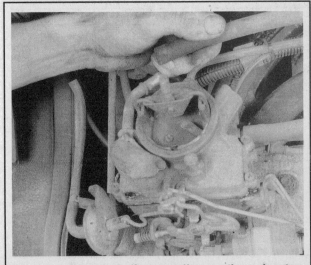

Label and disconnect all vacuum lines on the carburetor

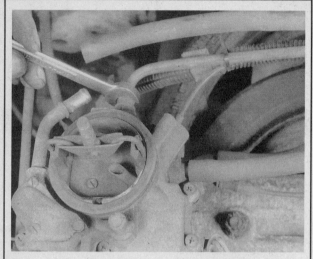

Disconnect the fuel inlet line to the carburetor

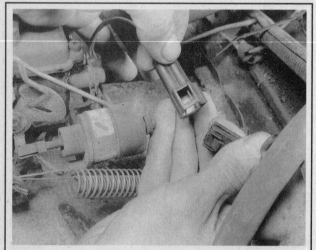

Unplug any electrical connections. Label them if there's more than one

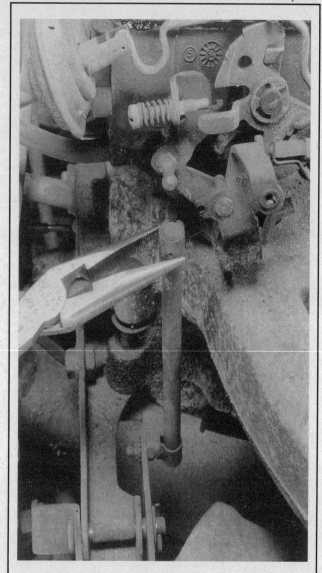

. . . and the throttle linkage from the carburetor

Remove the throttle return springs (A) from the throttle lever (B) . . .

Also disconnect the choke linkage

Remove the carburetor retaining nuts, NOT the intake-to-exhaust manifold nuts (arrow) . . .

Note the positions and routing of all carburetor linkages

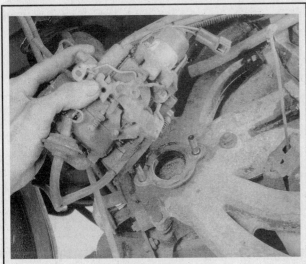

. . . then lift the carburetor off of the engine

Tag all vacuum lines before disconnecting them from the carburetor

Remove the air cleaner on V8 engines to gain access to the carburetor

As you disconnect each vacuum line, inspect them for holes or deterioration

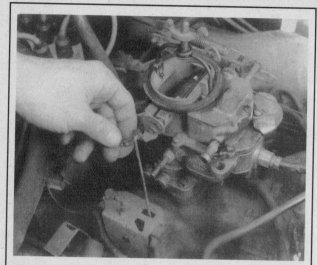

Unhook the choke rod from the carburetor

Remove the four retaining nuts and lift the carburetor from the engine

Using two wrenches, disconnect the fuel line inlet to the carburetor

Remove the carburetor insulator/gasket assembly—clean all mounting surfaces

Remove the return springs and the accelerator linkage connected to the carburetor

avoid twisting the fuel line. A container is also useful to catch any fuel which spills from the lines.

5. Disconnect the throttle and choke linkage.

6. Label and disconnect any vacuum lines.

7. Remove the mounting bolts.

8. Carefully remove the carburetor from the engine and carry it in a level position to a clean work place.

9. Installation is the reverse of removal.

CARBURETOR TROUBLESHOOTING

The best way to diagnose a bad carburetor is to eliminate all other possible sources of the problem. If the carburetor is suspected to be the problem, first perform all of the adjustments given in this section. If this doesn't correct the difficulty, then check the following. Check the ignition system to make sure that the spark plugs, breaker points, and condenser are in good condition and adjusted to the proper specifications. Examine the emission control equipment to make sure that all the vacuum lines are connected and none are blocked or clogged (See Section 4). Check the ignition timing adjustment. Check all of the vacuum lines on the engine for loose connections, slips or breaks. Torque the carburetor and intake manifold attaching bolts to the proper specifications. If, after performing all of these checks and adjustments, the problem is still not solved, then you can safely assume that the carburetor is the source of the problem.

OVERHAUL

Efficient carburetion depends greatly on careful cleaning and inspection during overhaul since dirt, gum, water or varnish in or on the carburetor parts are often responsible for poor performance.

Overhaul the carburetor in a clean, dust free area. Carefully disassembly the carburetor, referring often to the exploded views. Keep all similar and look-alike parts segregated during disassembly and cleaning to avoid accidental interchange during assembly. Make a note of all jet sizes.

When the carburetor is disassembled, wash all parts (except diaphragms, electric choke units, pump plunger and any other plastic, leather, fiber, or rubber parts) in clean carburetor solvent. Do not leave the parts in the solvent any longer than is necessary to sufficiently loosen the dirt and deposits. Excessive cleaning may remove the special finish from the float bowl and choke valve bodies, leaving these parts unfit for service. Rinse all parts in clean solvent and blow them dry with compressed air or allow them to air dry, while resting on clean, lintless paper. Wipe clean all cork, plastic, leather and fiber parts with clean, lint free cloth.

Blow out all passages and jets with compressed air and be sure that there are no restrictions or blockages. Never use wire or similar tools to clean jets, fuel passages or air bleeds. Clean all jets and valves separately to avoid accidental interchange.

Examine all parts for wear or damage. If wear or damage is found, replace the defective parts. Especially, inspect the following:

1. Check the float needle and seat for wear. If wear is found, replace the complete assembly.

2. Check the float hinge pin for wear and the float(s) for dents or distortion, replace the float if fuel has leaked into it.

3. Check the throttle and choke shaft bores for wear or an out-of-round condition. Damage or wear to the throttle arm, shaft or shaft bore will often require replacement of the throttle body. These parts require a close tolerance of fit; wear may allow air leakage, which could affect starting and idling.

➡ **Throttle shaft and bushings are not normally included in overhaul kits. They can be purchased separately.**

4. Inspect the idle mixture adjusting needles for burrs and grooves. Any such condition requires replacement of the needle, since you will not be able to obtain a satisfactory idle.

5. Test the accelerator pump check valves. They should pass air one way, but not the other. Test for proper seating by blowing and sucking on the valve. Replace the valve as necessary. If the valve is satisfactory, wash the valve again to remove moisture.

6. Check the bowl cover for warped surfaces with a straightedge.

7. Closely inspect the valves and seats for wear and damage, replacing as necessary.

8. After the carburetor is assembled, check the choke valve for freedom of operation.

Carburetor overhaul kits are recommended for each overhaul. These kits contain all gaskets and new parts to replace those which deteriorate most rapidly. Failure to replace all of the parts supplied with the kit (especially gaskets) can result in poor performance later.

Most carburetor manufacturers supply overhaul kits of three basic types: minor repair; major repair; and gasket kits. Basically, they contain the following:

Minor Repair Kits:
- All gaskets
- Float needle valve
- All diagrams
- Spring for the pump diaphragm

Major Repair Kits:
- All jets and gaskets
- All diaphragms
- Float needle valve
- Pump ball valve
- Float
- Complete intermediate rod
- Intermediate pump lever
- Some cover hold-down screws and washers

Gasket kits:
- All gaskets

After cleaning and checking all components, reassemble the carburetor, using new parts and referring to the exploded view. When reassembling, make sure that all screws and jets are right in their seat, but do not overtighten, as the tip will be distorted. Tighten all screws gradually, in rotation. Do not tighten needle valves into their seats; uneven jetting will result. Always use new gaskets. Be sure to adjust the float level.

➡ **Most carburetor rebuilding kits contain a sheet of specific instructions pertaining to the carburetor the kit is for.**

Carter BBS

ADJUSTMENTS

Accelerator Pump and Bowl Vent

1. Back off the idle speed screw and open the choke valve so that when the throttle valves are closed the fast idle adjustment screw does not contact the fast idle cam.

2. Be sure that the pump operating rod is in the medium stroke hole (long hole for the BBS-4340S and BBS-4341S) in the throttle lever and that the bowl vent clip on the pump stem is in the center notch (lower notch on the BBS-4340S and BBS-4341S).

3. Close the throttle valves tightly. It should just be possible to insert a 1/16″ drill bit between the bowl vent and the air horn (27/32″ on the BBS-3277S pump plunger travel).

4. If an adjustment is necessary, bend the pump operating rod at the lower angle.

Fast Idle Cam Position

AUTOMATIC CHOKE ONLY

1. Adjust the fast idle speed as described later.

2. Place the fast idle screw on the second highest step of the fast idle cam.

3. Move the choke valve towards the closed position with light pressure on the choke shaft lever.

4. Insert a #48 drill bit between the choke valve and the wall of the air horn. If an adjustment is necessary, bend the fast idle rod at the upper angle.

Vacuum Kick

1. If the adjustment is to be made on the engine (with the engine running at curb idle), back off the fast idle screw until the choke can be closed to the kick position. Note the number of screw turns required so that the fast idle can be returned to the original adjustment.

2. If the adjustment is to be made off the engine, open the throttle valve and move the choke to its closed position. Release the throttle first and then release the choke. Disconnect the vacuum hose from the carburetor body and apply a vacuum of at least 10 in.Hg (15 in.Hg for 1976 and later models).

3. Insert a #35 drill bit between the choke valve and the wall of the air horn.

4. Apply sufficient closing pressure to the choke lever to provide a minimum valve opening without distorting the diaphragm link (which connects the choke lever to the vacuum diaphragm). Note that the cylindrical stem of the diaphragm will extend as its internal spring is compressed. This spring must be fully compressed for the proper measurement of the vacuum kick adjustment.

5. Remove the drill bit. If a slight drag is not felt as the drill bit is removed, an adjustment of the diaphragm link is necessary to obtain the proper clearance. Shorten or lengthen the diaphragm link by carefully closing or opening the U-bend in the link until the correct adjustment is obtained.

✳✳ WARNING

When adjusting the link, be careful not to bend or twist the diaphragm.

6. Refit the vacuum hose to the carburetor body (if it had been removed) and return the fast idle screw to its original location.

7. With no vacuum applied to the diaphragm, the choke valve should move freely between its open and closed positions. If it does not move freely, examine the linkage for misalignment or interference which may have been caused by the bending operation. If necessary, repeat the adjustment to provide the proper link operation.

Choke Unloader

The choke unloader adjustment is a mechanical device that partially opens the choke valve at wide open throttle. It should be adjusted as follows:

1. Hold the throttle valve in the wide open position.

2. Insert a ³⁄₁₆″ drill bit between the upper edge of the choke valve and the wall of the air horn.

3. With a finger pressing lightly against the choke plate, a slight drag should be felt as the drill is being withdrawn.

4. If adjustment is necessary, bend the unloader tang on the throttle lever until the correct opening is obtained.

Fast Idle Speed

1. Warm the engine by driving at least five miles.

2. With the engine off and the transmission in Park or Neutral, open the throttle slightly.

3. On models without the Clean Air Package, close the choke plate about 20°, then allow the throttle plates to close. The fast idle screw should now rest on the slowest speed step of the cam.

On models with the Clean Air Package, close the choke plate until the fast idle screw can be positioned on the second highest speed step of the cam.

4. Start the engine.

5. Turn the fast idle speed screw in or out until the specified speed is obtained.

6. Stopping the engine between adjustments is not necessary. However, be sure to position the fast idle speed screw on the cam after each speed adjustment.

Spring Staged Choke

1. Push on the choke hub lever with your finger, at the closed position. A small opening should exist between the shaft and hub levers.

2. Using a drill bit, measure the opening. The opening should be 0.010–0.040″.

3. If not, bend the hub lever tang until the correct opening is reached.

Dashpot

1. With the idle speed and mixture properly set and a tachometer installed, position the throttle lever so that the actuating tab on the lever contacts the stem of the dashpot but does not depress it.

2. The engine speed should be 1,00 rpm. To adjust the setting, if necessary, loosen the locknut and screw the dashpot in or out as required. When the correct setting has been obtained, tighten the locknut against the bracket.

Float

This procedure can be performed without removing the carburetor from the engine.

1. Remove the accelerator pump operating rod.

2. Remove 2 of the long air horn screws and 2 of the short screws. Install the 2 short screws in place of the 2 long screws. This will hold the main body to the throttle body. Tighten the screws securely.

3. Remove the remaining air horn screws.

4. Tilt the air horn far enough to disengage the fast idle cam link from the fast idle cam. Remove the air horn and gasket.

5. Seat the float fulcrum pin by pressing on the fulcrum pin retainer. There should be enough fuel in the bowl to raise the float so that the lip bears firmly against the needle. Additional fuel may be entered by slightly depressing the float. If there is not enough pressure in the line to enter more fuel, you'll have to add some from a clean container.

✳✳ CAUTION

Never smoke when working around gasoline! Avoid all sources of sparks or ignition. Gasoline vapors are EXTREMELY volatile!

6. With the fuel level holding the tip of the float against the inlet needle, check the gap between the gasket surface of the bowl (gasket removed) and the center crown of the floats. The gap should be ¼″ on BBS models 4177S, 4342S and 4341S; ⁷⁄₃₂″ on models 4340S and 3277S.

7. If adjustment is necessary, hold the float on the bottom of the bowl and bend the float tip toward or away from the needle as required. Recheck the gap.

➡**Do not allow the float lip to depress the needle, as this will give you a false reading. When correctly set, the float lip should be perpendicular to the needle ±10°.**

8. Assemble the air horn.
9. Check the idle speed.

Carter BBD

ADJUSTMENTS

Accelerator Pump

1967–72 MODELS

1. Back off the idle speed screw.
2. Make sure that the pump connector rod is in the center hole of the throttle lever.
3. Close the throttle valves tightly. It should just be possible to insert a 1/64″ drill bit between the top of the air horn and the end of the plunger shaft.
4. If an adjustment is necessary, bend the pump operating rod at the lower angle.
5. Reset the idle.

1973–84 MODELS

♦ **See Figure 5**

1. Back off the idle speed screw to completely close the throttle plate.
2. Open the choke plate so that the fast idle cam allows the throttle plates to seat in their bores.
3. Make sure that the accelerator pump S-link is in the outer hole of the pump arm.
4. Turn the curb idle adjusting screw clockwise until it just contacts the stop, then, turn it 2 full turns more.
5. Measure the distance between the surface of the air horn and the top of the accelerator pump shaft. The gap should be ½″.

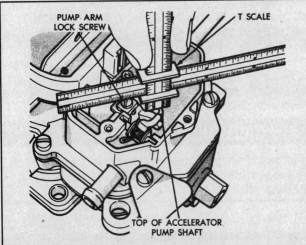

Fig. 5 Checking the 1973–84 BBD accelerator pump stroke

6. To adjust the pump travel, loosen the pump arm adjusting lockscrew and rotate the sleeve until the proper gap is reached.

Fast Idle Cam

AUTOMATIC CHOKE ONLY

♦ **See Figure 6**

1. Adjust the fast idle speed as described later.
2. Place the fast idle screw on the second highest step of the fast idle cam.
3. Move the choke valve towards the closed position with light pressure on the choke shaft lever.
4. Insert a #48 drill bit between the choke valve and the wall of the air horn on models through 1972. On 1973–84 models use a 0.110″ drill bit on carb. models 8147S; an 0.070″ drill bit on all other models. If an adjustment is necessary, bend the fast idle rod at the upper angle.

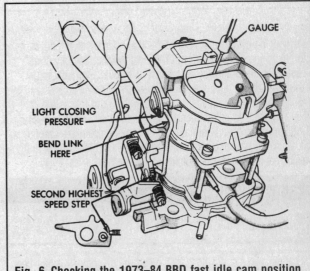

Fig. 6 Checking the 1973–84 BBD fast idle cam position

Vacuum Kick

♦ **See Figure 7**

1. If the adjustment is to be made on the engine (with the engine running at curb idle), back off the fast idle screw until the choke can be closed to the kick position. Note the number of screw turns required so that the fast idle can be returned to the original adjustment.
2. If the adjustment is to be made off the engine, open the throttle valve and move the choke to its closed position. Release the throttle first and then release the choke. Disconnect the vacuum hose from the carburetor body and apply a vacuum of at least 10 in.Hg (15 in.Hg for 1976 and later models).
3. Insert a #35 drill bit between the choke valve and the wall of the air horn on models through 1972. On models through 1979, use a 0.110″ drill bit. On models through 1981, use a 0.070″ drill bit on models 8146S or 0.150″ on models 8147S. On models through 1984 use a 0.070″ drill bit on model 8146S, 0.150″ drill bit on model 8147S, and 0.130″ on all others.
4. Apply sufficient closing pressure to the choke lever to provide a minimum valve opening without distorting the diaphragm link (which connects the choke lever to the vacuum diaphragm).

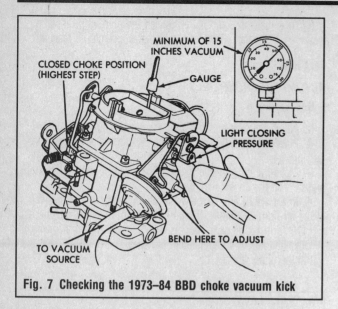

Fig. 7 Checking the 1973–84 BBD choke vacuum kick

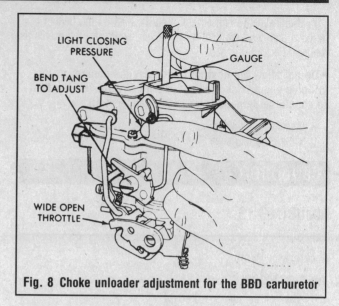

Fig. 8 Choke unloader adjustment for the BBD carburetor

Note that the cylindrical stem of the diaphragm will extend as its internal spring is compressed. This spring must be fully compressed for the proper measurement of the vacuum kick adjustment.

5. Remove the drill bit. If a slight drag is not felt as the drill bit is removed, an adjustment of the diaphragm link is necessary to obtain the proper clearance. Shorten or lengthen the diaphragm link by carefully closing or opening the U-bend in the link until the correct adjustment is obtained.

✳✶ WARNING

When adjusting the link, be careful not to bend or twist the diaphragm.

6. Refit the vacuum hose to the carburetor body (if it had been removed) and return the fast idle screw to its original location.

7. With no vacuum applied to the diaphragm, the choke valve should move freely between its open and closed positions. If it does not move freely, examine the linkage for misalignment or interference which may have been caused by the bending operation. If necessary, repeat the adjustment to provide the proper link operation.

Choke Unloader
▶ See Figure 8

The choke unloader adjustment is a mechanical device that partially opens the choke valve at wide open throttle. It should be adjusted as follows:

1. Hold the throttle valve in the wide open position.
2. Insert a ³⁄₁₆″ drill bit between the upper edge of the choke valve and the wall of the air horn on models through 1972. On 1973–79 models, use a 0.280″ drill bit. On 1980–81 models, use a 0.310″ drill bit. On 1982–84 models use a 0.310″ drill bit for carb.# 8146S and 8147S, and 0.280″ for all others.
3. With a finger pressing lightly against the choke plate, a slight drag should be felt as the drill is being withdrawn.
4. If adjustment is necessary, bend the unloader tang on the throttle lever until the correct opening is obtained.

Bowl Vent Valve
▶ See Figure 9

1. Hold the throttle plates closed. It should be possible to insert a 0.060″ drill bit between the bowl vent valve and the air horn on models through 1979; 0.080″ on 1980–84 models.
2. If adjustment is necessary, bend the short tang on the vent operating lever until the proper clearance is reached.

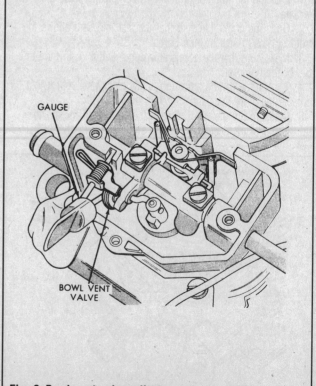

Fig. 9 Bowl vent valve adjustment for the BBD carburetor

Float

♦ See Figure 10

This procedure is performed with the carburetor on the engine.

1. Remove the clips and disengage the accelerator pump operating rod from the throttle lever and the pump rocker arm.

2. Remove the air horn attachment screws and lift the air horn straight up, and away from the main body. Remove the gasket.

3. Seat the float fulcrum pin by pressing on the fulcrum pin retainer. There should be enough fuel in the bowl to raise the float so that the lip bears firmly against the needle. Additional fuel may be entered by slightly depressing the float. If there is not enough pressure in the line to enter more fuel, you'll have to add some from a clean container.

✳✳ CAUTION

Never smoke when working around gasoline! Avoid all sources of sparks or ignition. Gasoline vapors are EXTREMELY volatile!

4. With the fuel level holding the tip of the float against the inlet needle, check the gap between the gasket surface of the bowl (gasket removed) and the center crown of the floats. On models through 1972, the gap should be $15/64''$ on models with a manual choke; $5/16''$ on models with an automatic choke. On later models, the gap should be $1/4''$.

5. If adjustment is necessary, hold the float on the bottom of the bowl and bend the float tip toward or away from the needle as required. Recheck the gap.

➡**Do not allow the float lip to depress the needle, as this will give you a false reading. When correctly set, the float lip should be perpendicular to the needle ±10°.**

6. Assemble the air horn.
7. Check the idle speed.

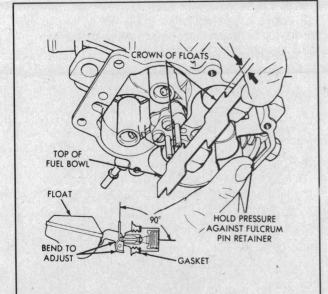

Fig. 10 Float level adjustment on the 1973–84 BBD carburetor

Fast Idle Speed

♦ See Figure 11

1. Warm the engine by driving at least five miles.

2. With the engine off and the transmission in Park or Neutral, open the throttle slightly.

3. On models without the Clean Air Package, close the choke plate about 20°, then allow the throttle plates to close. The fast idle screw should now rest on the slowest speed step of the cam.

On models with the Clean Air Package, close the choke plate until the fast idle screw can be positioned on the second highest speed step of the cam.

4. Start the engine.

5. On trucks through 1972, turn the fast idle speed screw in or out until 1,700 rpm is obtained for carb. model 6536S; 1,500 rpm for all other models.

On 1973–84 models, check your underhood sticker for the proper speed.

6. Stopping the engine between adjustments is not necessary. However, be sure to position the fast idle speed screw on the cam after each speed adjustment.

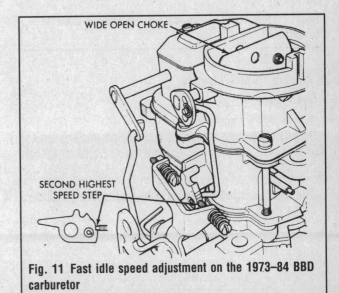

Fig. 11 Fast idle speed adjustment on the 1973–84 BBD carburetor

Carter Thermo-Quad

ADJUSTMENTS

Float Setting

♦ See Figure 12

1. Remove the bowl cover and invert it.

2. Place the gasket on the cover and, with the floats resting on the needle check the distance from the gasket surface to the float bottom (now upside) on each float. The distance should be $27/32''$.

3. If not, bend the float lever arm.

➡**Never allow the float lever to depress the needle when measuring or adjusting!**

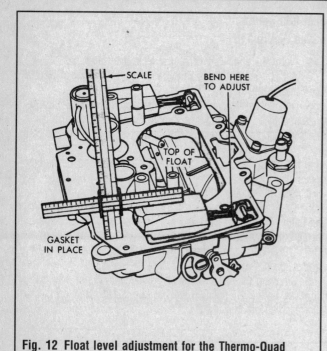

Fig. 12 Float level adjustment for the Thermo-Quad carburetor

Secondary Throttle Linkage
◆ **See Figure 13**

1. Remove the carburetor.
2. Hold the fast idle lever in the curb idle position and invert the carburetor.
3. Slowly open the primary throttle plates. The primary and secondary levers should both contact the stops at the same time.
4. If an adjustment is necessary, bend the secondary throttle operating rod at the angle.

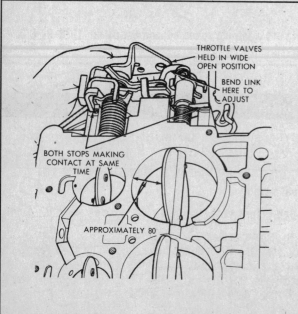

Fig. 13 Secondary throttle linkage adjustment for the Thermo-Quad carburetor

Secondary Air Valve Opening
◆ **See Figure 14**

1. With the air valve in the wide open, the gap between the air valve at the short side and the air horn should be ½".
2. If not, the corner of the air valve is notched for adjustment. Bend the corner with a needle-nosed pliers for proper adjustment.

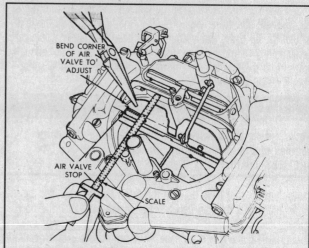

Fig. 14 Secondary air valve opening adjustment on the Thermo-Quad carburetor

Secondary Air Valve Spring Tension
◆ **See Figure 15**

➡**Hold the air valve adjustment plug with a screwdriver while loosening the lock plug to avoid the spring's snapping out of position. If the spring snaps out, you'll have to disassemble the carburetor!**

1. Loosen the air valve lock plug and allow the air valve to position itself in the wide open position.
2. Using a long screwdriver and tool C-4152 on the plug, turn the plug counterclockwise until the air valve contacts its stop lightly, then give it 1¼ turns more.

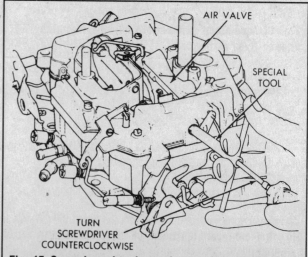

Fig. 15 Secondary air valve spring tension adjustment on the Thermo-Quad

3. Hold the adjustment plug securely and tighten the lock plug with tool C-4152.

Accelerator Pump Stroke
▶ See Figure 16

FIRST STAGE

1. Be sure that the throttle connector rod is in the center hole of the pump arm, or, on 2-hole arms, the inner hole.

2. Measure the height of the accelerator pump plunger link at curb idle. On trucks with a solenoid idle stop, the ignition switch should be in the **ON** position.

3. The height should be ½″. If not, bend the throttle connector rod at the second angle from the top.

SECOND STAGE

1. Open the choke, then open the throttle until the secondary lockout latch is *just* applied. Downward travel of the plunger stops at this point.

2. Measure the height of the pump plunger link. The height should be ⁵⁄₁₆″. If not, bend the tang at the bottom of the throttle lever.

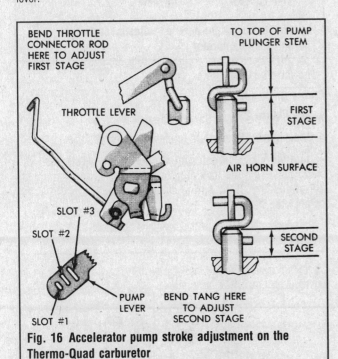

Fig. 16 Accelerator pump stroke adjustment on the Thermo-Quad carburetor

Choke Control Lever
▶ See Figure 17

1. Remove the carburetor.

2. Place the carburetor on a clean, flat surface with the surface flush with the bottom of the flange and extending out under the choke control lever.

3. Close the choke by pushing the lever with the throttle partially open.

4. Measure the vertical distance from the top of the rod hole in the control lever, down to the flat surface on which the carburetor is resting. The distance should be 3⅜″.

5. If not, bend the link connecting the two choke shafts at the upper angle.

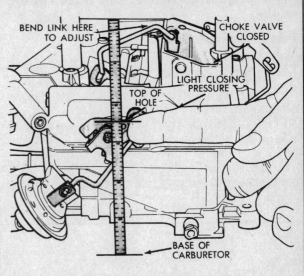

Fig. 17 Choke control lever adjustment on the Thermo-Quad

➡If you change this adjustment, you'll have to reset the vacuum kick, fast idle cam and choke unloader adjustments.

Choke Diaphragm Connector Rod
▶ See Figure 18

1. Using a vacuum source, or by hand, fully depress the diaphragm stem.

2. With light opening pressure on the air valve connector rod, check the gap between the air valve and its stop. The gap should be 0.040″.

3. If not, bend the diaphragm control rod at its angle.

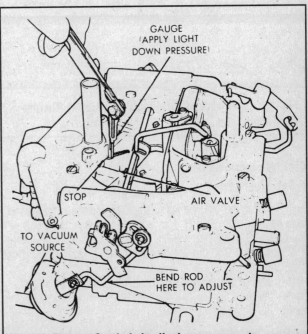

Fig. 18 Thermo-Quad choke diaphragm connector adjustment

➡️If you change this setting, you'll have to adjust the vacuum kick.

Choke Vacuum Kick

◆ See Figure 19

1. Remove the carburetor.

2. Using a vacuum source, or by hand, fully depress the vacuum diaphragm plunger.

3. Using a 0.160″ drill bit for 49 states and Canada, or 0.100″ for California, measure between the lower edge of the choke plate and the air horn wall at a point close to the outboard end.

4. Adjustment will be necessary if a slight drag is not felt. Bend the tang on the diaphragm rod operating lever to adjust the gap.

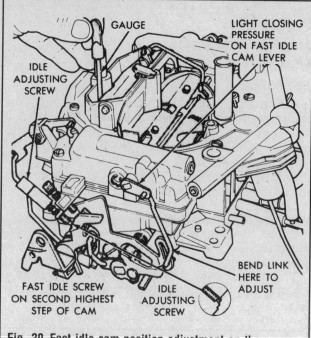

Fig. 20 Fast idle cam position adjustment on the Thermo-Quad carburetor

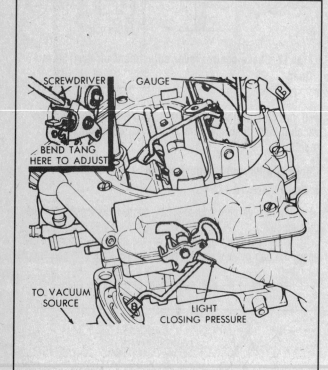

Fig. 19 Choke vacuum kick adjustment on the Thermo-Quad carburetor

Fast Idle Cam Position

◆ See Figure 20

1. Position the fast idle speed adjusting screw so that it contacts the second highest step of the cam. Move the choke valve toward the closed position with light pressure on the choke linkage.

2. Insert a 0.100″ drill bit between the lower edge of the choke plate and the wall of the air horn.

3. If adjustment is necessary, bend the fast idle link at the angle until the specified drill fits between the choke plate and the wall of the air horn.

➡️When this adjustment is made, the choke unloader adjustment and secondary throttle lockout adjustment must be reset.

Choke Unloader

◆ See Figure 21

1. Hold the throttle valves in the wide open position.

2. Insert a 0.310″ drill bit between the lower edge of the choke valve and the wall of the air horn.

3. With a finger pressing lightly against the choke plate, a slight drag should be felt as the drill is being withdrawn.

4. If adjustment is necessary, bend the unloader tang on the throttle lever until the correct opening is obtained.

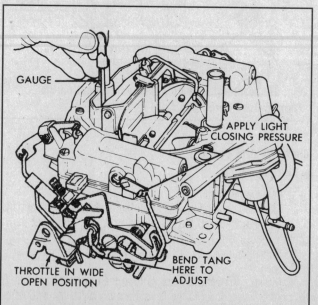

Fig. 21 Choke unloader adjustment on the Thermo-Quad carburetor

Secondary Throttle Lockout

▶ **See Figure 22**

1. Move the fast idle control lever to the open choke position.
2. Measure the clearance between the lockout lever and the stop. The gap should be 0.060–0.090".
3. If not, bend the tang on the fast idle control lever.

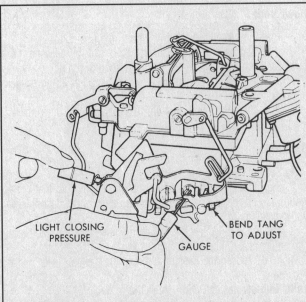

LIGHT CLOSING
PRESSURE

BEND TANG
TO ADJUST

GAUGE

Fig. 22 Secondary throttle lockout adjustment on the Thermo-Quad carburetor

Fast Idle Speed

▶ **See Figure 23**

1. Run the engine to normal operating temperature.
2. With the engine off and the transmission in Park or Neutral, open the throttle slightly. Remove the air cleaner and disconnect the vacuum lines to the heated air control and the OSAC (Orifice Spark Advance Control) valve. If there is no OSAC valve, discon-

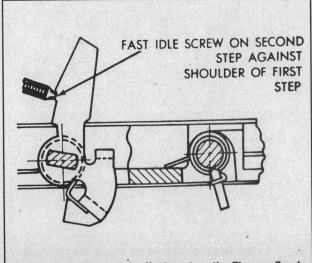

FAST IDLE SCREW ON SECOND
STEP AGAINST
SHOULDER OF FIRST
STEP

Fig. 23 Fast idle speed adjustment on the Thermo-Quad

nect the distributor vacuum advance line. Disconnect the EGR hose. Cap all carburetor vacuum fittings.

3. Close the throttle plates until the fast idle screw can be positioned on the second highest speed step of the cam.
4. Start the engine. Adjust the idle speed and mixture, if necessary.
5. Turn the fast idle speed screw in or out until 1,700 rpm is obtained.
6. Stopping the engine between adjustments is not necessary. However, be sure to position the fast idle speed screw on the cam after each speed adjustment.

Vacuum Throttle Positioner

1. Run the engine to normal operating temperature.
2. With the transmission in Neutral and the brakes applied, accelerate the engine to above 2,000 rpm. Note that the vacuum positioner unit operates and can withstand a hand-applied load in the operating position. If not, replace the positioner.
3. Accelerate the engine, by hand-moving the linkage, to 2,500 rpm.
4. Loosen the positioner adjustment locknut and rotate the positioner assembly until the positioner just contacts the throttle lever.
5. Release the throttle lever and slowly adjust the positioner to decrease the engine speed until a sudden drop in engine speed occurs, above 1,000 rpm. At this point, continue turning the positioner, in the decreasing direction, an additional ¼ turn. Hold the positioner and tighten the locknut.
6. Accelerate the engine, by hand, to 2,500 rpm and release the throttle. The engine should return to normal idle.

Holley 1920

ADJUSTMENT

Float Setting

1. Remove the carburetor.
2. Remove the float bowl cover.
3. Place a ²⁷/₃₂" feeler gauge between the float arm and inlet needle and invert the carburetor.
4. Tighten the seat screw to set the fuel level.
5. Remove the feeler gauge.
6. With the carburetor inverted, place an ¹¹/₆₄" gauge between the top of the float and the inside surface of the float chamber. The gauge should pass lightly between the float and the chamber. If not, bend the tab on the float arm to adjust it.
7. Upright the carburetor. Slide a ³/₁₆" gauge between the bottom of the float and float chamber. The gauge should pass lightly between the float and chamber. If not, adjust the float by bending the upright tang on the float lever.
8. Install the float bowl cover using a new gasket.
9. Install the carburetor using a new mounting gasket.
10. Run the engine and check for leaks.

Fast Idle Cam Position

1. Position the fast idle speed adjusting screw so that it contacts the second highest step of the cam. Move the choke valve toward the closed position with light pressure on the choke linkage.
2. Insert a #52 drill bit between the upper edge of the choke plate and the wall of the air horn.

3. If adjustment is necessary, bend the fast idle link at the angle until the specified drill fits between the choke plate and the wall of the air horn.

Fast Idle Speed

1. Warm the engine by driving at least five miles.

2. With the engine off and the transmission in Park or Neutral, open the throttle slightly.

3. On models without the Clean Air Package, close the choke plate about 20°, then allow the throttle plates to close. The fast idle screw should now rest on the slowest speed step of the cam.

On models with the Clean Air Package, close the choke plate until the fast idle screw can be positioned on the second highest speed step of the cam.

4. Start the engine.

5. Turn the fast idle speed screw in or out until 700 rpm is obtained.

6. Stopping the engine between adjustments is not necessary. However, be sure to position the fast idle speed screw on the cam after each speed adjustment.

Choke Vacuum Kick

1. If the adjustment is to be made on the engine (with the engine running at curb idle), back off the fast idle screw until the choke can be closed to the kick position. Note the number of screw turns required so that the fast idle can be returned to the original adjustment.

2. If the adjustment is to be made off the engine, open the throttle valve and move the choke to its closed position. Release the throttle first and then release the choke. Disconnect the vacuum hose from the carburetor body and apply a vacuum of at least 15 in.Hg.

3. On models 1967 without the Clean Air Package but with manual transmission, insert a #30 drill bit between the choke valve and the wall of the air horn.

On 1967 models without the CAP but with automatic transmission, use a #38 drill bit.

On 1967 models with CAP, use a #28 drill bit.

On 1968–69 models, use a #30 drill bit.

On 1970–71 models, use a #39 drill bit on all carburetors except model #R-4641A. On that model use a #59 drill bit.

On 1972–73 models, except California, use a #58 drill bit.

On 1972–73 California models use a #62 drill bit with manual transmission; a #61 drill bit with automatic transmission.

4. Apply sufficient closing pressure to the choke lever to provide a minimum valve opening without distorting the diaphragm link (which connects the choke lever to the vacuum diaphragm). Note that the cylindrical stem of the diaphragm will extend as its internal spring is compressed. This spring must be fully compressed for the proper measurement of the vacuum kick adjustment.

5. Remove the drill bit. If a slight drag is not felt as the drill or gauge is removed, an adjustment of the diaphragm link is necessary to obtain the proper clearance. Shorten or lengthen the diaphragm link by carefully closing or opening the U-bend in the link until the correct adjustment is obtained.

✳✳ WARNING

When adjusting the link, be careful not to bend or twist the diaphragm.

6. Refit the vacuum hose to the carburetor body (if it had been removed) and return the fast idle screw to its original location.

7. With no vacuum applied to the diaphragm, the choke valve should move freely between its open and closed positions. If it does not move freely, examine the linkage for misalignment or interference which may have been caused by the bending operation. If necessary, repeat the adjustment to provide the proper link operation.

Bowl Vent

1. Place the throttle plate in the curb idle position.

2. It should be possible to insert a 3/32″ drill bit between the bowl vent and the seat. A 5/32″ drill but should *not* fit.

3. To make an adjustment, bend the vent rod at its horizontal portion.

4. After the adjustment, be sure that the vent rod does not bind in the guide.

Dashpot

1. Set the curb idle and mixture.

2. Start the engine and position the throttle lever so that the actuating tab on the lever is contacting the stem of the dashpot *without depressing it!*

3. Allow about 30 seconds for the engine speed to stabilize. The engine speed should be 2,500 rpm.

4. If not, loosen the locknut and turn the dashpot in or out as necessary.

5. Hold the dashpot and tighten the locknut.

Holley 1945

ADJUSTMENTS

Float Setting

◆ **See Figure 24**

1. Remove the carburetor.

2. Remove the float bowl cover and invert the bowl. Hold the retaining spring in place.

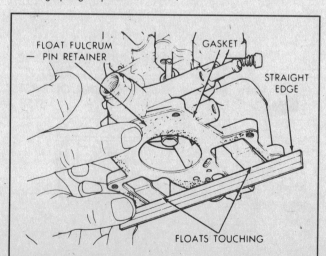

Fig. 24 Float level adjustment for the Holley 1945 and 6145 carburetors

3. Place the gasket on the float bowl.

4. Place a straightedge across the surface of the bowl. It should just touch the floats ± 1/32".

5. If adjustment is necessary, bend the float tang to obtain the correct adjustment.

Accelerator Pump Piston Stroke

▶ **See Figure 25**

1. Place the throttle linkage in the curb idle position.

2. Place the pump operating link in the middle slot on model R-7847-A, or in the left slot on all others.

3. With a T-scale, measure the length of the pump operating link. On models through 1972, the link should be 2⁷/₃₂" on R-7847-A models; 2²¹/₆₄" on all other models. On 1973–79 models, the link should be 2⁷/₃₂" for trucks with manual transmission, or 2¹¹/₃₂" for trucks with automatic transmission. On 1980 and later trucks, the link should be 1⁵/₈". Bend the link at the angle, to adjust.

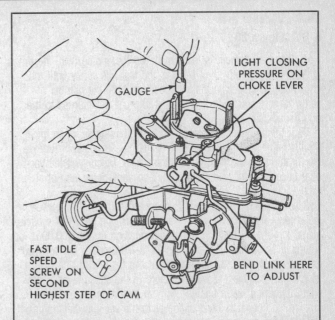

Fig. 26 Fast idle cam position adjustment on the Holley 1945 carburetor

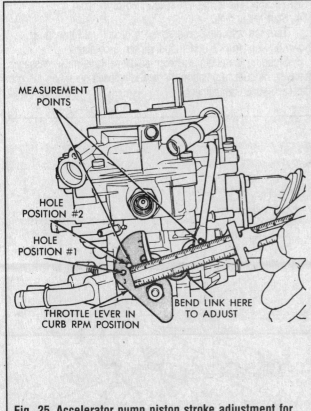

Fig. 25 Accelerator pump piston stroke adjustment for the Holley 1945 carburetor

Fast Idle Cam Position

▶ **See Figure 26**

1. Position the fast idle speed adjusting screw so that it contacts the second highest step of the cam. Move the choke valve toward the closed position with light pressure on the choke linkage.

2. Insert a 0.080" drill bit between the upper edge of the choke plate and the wall of the air horn.

3. If adjustment is necessary, bend the fast idle link at the angle until the specified drill fits between the choke plate and the wall of the air horn.

Choke Unloader

▶ **See Figure 27**

1. Hold the throttle valve in the wide open position.

2. Insert a 1/4" drill bit between the upper edge of the choke valve and the wall of the air horn.

3. With a finger pressing lightly against the choke plate, a slight drag should be felt as the drill is being withdrawn.

4. If adjustment is necessary, bend the unloader tang on the throttle lever until the correct opening is obtained.

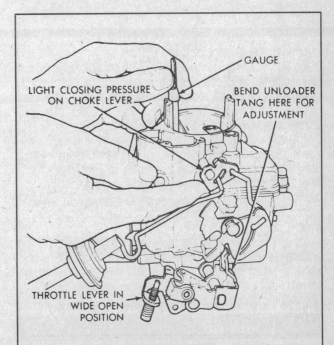

Fig. 27 Choke unloader adjustment for the Holley 1945 carburetor

Choke Vacuum Kick

▶ **See Figure 28**

1. If the adjustment is to be made on the engine (with the engine running at curb idle), back off the fast idle screw until the choke can be closed to the kick position. Note the number of screw turns required so that the fast idle can be returned to the original adjustment.

2. If the adjustment is to be made off the engine, open the throttle valve and move the choke to its closed position. Release the throttle first and then release the choke. Disconnect the vacuum hose from the carburetor body and apply a vacuum of at least 15 in.Hg.

3. On models through 1972, insert a 0.110″ drill bit between the choke valve and the wall of the air horn. On 1973–77 models, use a 0.140″ drill bit for manual transmission trucks or 0.090″ for automatic transmission trucks. On 1978–79 models, use a 0.100″ drill bit. On 1980 and later models, use a 0.130″ drill bit.

4. Apply sufficient closing pressure to the choke lever to provide a minimum valve opening without distorting the diaphragm link (which connects the choke lever to the vacuum diaphragm). Note that the cylindrical stem of the diaphragm will extend as its internal spring is compressed. This spring must be fully compressed for the proper measurement of the vacuum kick adjustment.

5. Remove the drill bit. If a slight drag is not felt as the drill or gauge is removed, an adjustment of the diaphragm link is necessary to obtain the proper clearance. Shorten or lengthen the diaphragm link by carefully closing or opening the U-bend in the link until the correct adjustment is obtained.

✳✳ WARNING

When adjusting the link, be careful not to bend or twist the diaphragm.

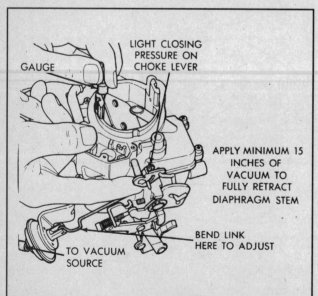

Fig. 28 Choke vacuum kick adjustment for the Holley 1945 carburetor

6. Refit the vacuum hose to the carburetor body (if it had been removed) and return the fast idle screw to its original location.

7. With no vacuum applied to the diaphragm, the choke valve should move freely between its open and closed positions. If it does not move freely, examine the linkage for misalignment or interference which may have been caused by the bending operation. If necessary, repeat the adjustment to provide the proper link operation.

Fast Idle Speed

▶ **See Figure 29**

1. Run the engine to normal operating temperature.

2. With the engine off and the transmission in Park or Neutral, open the throttle slightly. Remove the air cleaner and disconnect the vacuum lines to the heated air control and the OSAC (Orifice Spark Advance Control) valve. If there is no OSAC valve, disconnect the distributor vacuum advance line. Disconnect the EGR hose. Cap all carburetor vacuum fittings.

3. Close the choke plate until the fast idle screw can be positioned on the second highest speed step of the cam.

4. Start the engine.

5. Turn the fast idle speed screw in or out until the speed shown on your truck's underhood sticker is obtained.

6. Stopping the engine between adjustments is not necessary. However, be sure to position the fast idle speed screw on the cam after each speed adjustment.

Fig. 29 Fast idle speed adjustment for the Holley 1945 and 6145 carburetors

Dashpot

▶ **See Figure 30**

1. Set the curb idle and mixture.
2. Start the engine and position the throttle lever so that the actuating tab on the lever is contacting the stem of the dashpot *without depressing it!*
3. Allow about 30 seconds for the engine speed to stabilize. The engine speed should be 2,500 rpm.
4. If not, loosen the locknut and turn the dashpot in or out as necessary.
5. Hold the dashpot and tighten the locknut.

Holley 2210

ADJUSTMENTS

Fast Idle Cam Position

1. Position the fast idle speed adjusting screw so that it contacts the second highest step of the cam. Move the choke valve toward the closed position with 000031 pressure on the choke linkage.
2. Insert a 0.110″ drill bit between the upper edge of the choke plate and the wall of the air horn.
3. If adjustment is necessary, bend the fast idle link at the angle until the specified drill fits between the choke plate and the wall of the air horn.

Vacuum Kick

• 1. If the adjustment is to be made on the engine (with the engine running at curb idle), back off the fast idle screw until the choke can be closed to the kick position. Note the number of screw turns required so that the fast idle can be returned to the original adjustment.
2. If the adjustment is to be made off the engine, open the throttle valve and move the choke to its closed position. Release

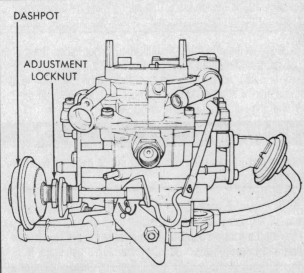

DASHPOT

ADJUSTMENT LOCKNUT

Fig. 30 Dashpot adjustment for the Holley 1945 carburetor

the throttle first and then release the choke. Disconnect the vacuum hose from the carburetor body and apply a vacuum of at least 15 in.Hg.
3. Insert a 0.150″ drill bit between the choke valve and the wall of the air horn.
4. Apply sufficient closing pressure to the choke lever to provide a minimum valve opening without distorting the diaphragm link (which connects the choke lever to the vacuum diaphragm). Note that the cylindrical stem of the diaphragm will extend as its internal spring is compressed. This spring must be fully compressed for the proper measurement of the vacuum kick adjustment.
5. Remove the drill bit. If a slight drag is not felt as the drill or gauge is removed, an adjustment of the diaphragm link is necessary to obtain the proper clearance. Shorten or lengthen the diaphragm link by carefully closing or opening the U-bend in the link until the correct adjustment is obtained.

✳✳ WARNING

When adjusting the link, be careful not to bend or twist the diaphragm.

6. Refit the vacuum hose to the carburetor body (if it had been removed) and return the fast idle screw to its original location.
7. With no vacuum applied to the diaphragm, the choke valve should move freely between its open and closed positions. If it does not move freely, examine the linkage for misalignment or interference which may have been caused by the bending operation. If necessary, repeat the adjustment to provide the proper link operation.

Choke Unloader

1. Hold the throttle valve in the wide open position.
2. Insert a 0.170″ drill bit between the upper edge of the choke valve and the wall of the air horn.
3. With a finger pressing lightly against the choke plate, a slight drag should be felt as the drill is being withdrawn.
4. If adjustment is necessary, bend the unloader tang on the throttle lever until the correct opening is obtained.

Accelerator Pump Stroke

1. Make sure that the pump connector rod is in the first slot (next to the retaining nut) of the pump arm.
2. Measure the travel (drop) of the accelerator pump plunger between curb idle, or closed throttle, and wide open throttle. Travel should be 0.260″ for curb idle-to-wide open throttle, or 0.310″ for closed throttle-to-wide open throttle.
3. If not, bend the pump operating rod at the angle to adjust.

Fast Idle Speed

1. Warm the engine by driving at least five miles.
2. With the engine off and the transmission in Park or Neutral, open the throttle slightly. Remove the air cleaner and disconnect the vacuum lines to the heated air control and the OSAC (Orifice Spark Advance Control) valve. If there is no OSAC valve, disconnect the distributor vacuum advance line. Disconnect the EGR hose. Cap all carburetor vacuum fittings.
3. Close the choke plate until the fast idle screw can be positioned on the second highest speed step of the cam.
4. Start the engine.

5. Turn the fast idle speed screw in or out until the speed of 1,700 rpm for manual transmission or 1,800 rpm is reached.

6. Stopping the engine between adjustments is not necessary. However, be sure to position the fast idle speed screw on the cam after each speed adjustment.

Vacuum Throttle Positioner

1. Run the engine to normal operating temperature.

2. With the transmission in Neutral and the brakes applied, accelerate the engine to above 2,000 rpm. Note that the vacuum positioner unit operates and can withstand a hand-applied load in the operating position. If not, replace the positioner.

3. Accelerate the engine, by hand-moving the linkage, to 2,500 rpm.

4. Loosen the positioner adjustment locknut and rotate the positioner assembly until the positioner just contacts the throttle lever.

5. Release the throttle lever and slowly adjust the positioner to decrease the engine speed until a sudden drop in engine speed occurs, above 1,000 rpm. At this point, continue turning the positioner, in the decreasing direction, an additional 1/4 turn. Hold the positioner and tighten the locknut.

6. Accelerate the engine, by hand, to 2,500 rpm and release the throttle. The engine should return to normal idle.

Float Setting

1. Invert the air horn so that the weight of the float alone is forcing the needle against the seat.

2. Measure the clearance between the top of the float and the float stop. The clearance should be 0.080".

3. If an adjustment is necessary, bend the flat tab toward or away from the needle using a narrow blade screwdriver.

4. Check the float drop by holding the air horn in an upright position. The bottom edge of the float should be even with and parallel to the underside surface of the air horn. If necessary, bend the tang on the float arm to make an adjustment.

Holley 2245

ADJUSTMENTS

Fast Idle Cam Position

1. Position the fast idle speed adjusting screw so that it contacts the second highest step of the cam. Move the choke valve toward the closed position with light pressure on the choke linkage.

2. Insert a 0.110" drill bit between the upper edge of the choke plate and the wall of the air horn.

3. If adjustment is necessary, bend the fast idle link at the angle until the specified drill fits between the choke plate and the wall of the air horn.

Vacuum Kick
♦ See Figure 31

1. If the adjustment is to be made on the engine (with the engine running at curb idle), back off the fast idle screw until the choke can be closed to the kick position. Note the number of screw turns required so that the fast idle can be returned to the original adjustment.

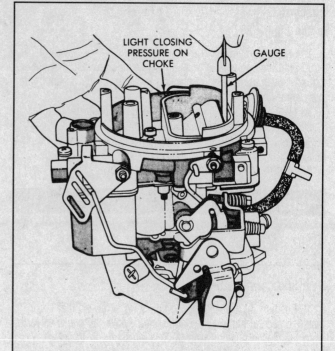

Fig. 31 Choke vacuum kick adjustment for the Holley 2245 carburetor

2. If the adjustment is to be made off the engine, open the throttle valve and move the choke to its closed position. Release the throttle first and then release the choke. Disconnect the vacuum hose from the carburetor body and apply a vacuum of at least 15 in.Hg.

3. For models through 1977, insert a 0.150" drill bit between the choke valve and the wall of the air horn. On 1978 and later models, use a 0.110" drill bit.

4. Apply sufficient closing pressure to the choke lever to provide a minimum valve opening without distorting the diaphragm link (which connects the choke lever to the vacuum diaphragm). Note that the cylindrical stem of the diaphragm will extend as its internal spring is compressed. This spring must be fully compressed for the proper measurement of the vacuum kick adjustment.

5. Remove the drill bit. If a slight drag is not felt as the drill or gauge is removed, an adjustment of the diaphragm link is necessary to obtain the proper clearance. Shorten or lengthen the diaphragm link by carefully closing or opening the U-bend in the link until the correct adjustment is obtained.

✳✳ WARNING

When adjusting the link, be careful not to bend or twist the diaphragm.

6. Refit the vacuum hose to the carburetor body (if it had been removed) and return the fast idle screw to its original location.

7. With no vacuum applied to the diaphragm, the choke valve should move freely between its open and closed positions. If it does not move freely, examine the linkage for misalignment or interference which may have been caused by the bending operation. If necessary, repeat the adjustment to provide the proper link operation.

Choke Unloader
▶ See Figure 32

1. Hold the throttle valve in the wide open position.
2. Insert a 0.170" drill bit between the upper edge of the choke valve and the wall of the air horn.
3. With a finger pressing lightly against the choke plate, a slight drag should be felt as the drill is being withdrawn.
4. If adjustment is necessary, bend the unloader tang on the throttle lever until the correct opening is obtained.

Accelerator Pump Stroke

1. Make sure that the pump connector rod is in the first slot (next to the retaining nut) of the pump arm.
2. Measure the travel (drop) of the accelerator pump plunger between curb idle, or closed throttle, and wide open throttle. Travel should be 0.260" for curb idle-to-wide open throttle, or 0.310" for closed throttle-to-wide open throttle.
3. If not, bend the pump operating rod at the angle to adjust.

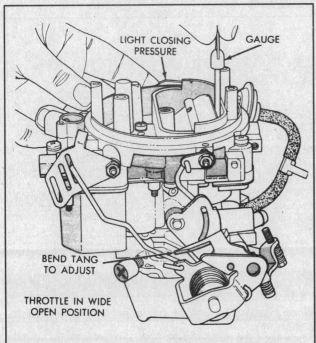

Fig. 32 Choke unloader adjustment for the Holley 2245 carburetor

Fast Idle Speed
▶ See Figure 33

1. Warm the engine by driving at least five miles.
2. With the engine off and the transmission in Park or Neutral, open the throttle slightly. Remove the air cleaner and disconnect the vacuum lines to the heated air control and the OSAC (Orifice Spark Advance Control) valve. If there is no OSAC valve, disconnect the distributor vacuum advance line. Disconnect the EGR hose. Cap all carburetor vacuum fittings.
3. Close the choke plate until the fast idle screw can be positioned on the second highest speed step of the cam.
4. Start the engine.
5. Turn the fast idle speed screw in or out until the speed of

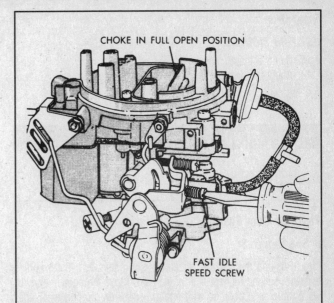

Fig. 33 Fast idle speed adjustment for the Holley 2245 carburetor

1,700 rpm for manual transmission or 1,800 rpm is reached on models through 1977; 1,600 rpm on 1978 and later models.
6. Stopping the engine between adjustments is not necessary. However, be sure to position the fast idle speed screw on the cam after each speed adjustment.

Vacuum Throttle Positioner

1. Run the engine to normal operating temperature.
2. With the transmission in Neutral and the brakes applied, accelerate the engine to above 2,000 rpm. Note that the vacuum positioner unit operates and can withstand a hand-applied load in the operating position. If not, replace the positioner.
3. Accelerate the engine, by hand-moving the linkage, to 2,500 rpm.
4. Loosen the positioner adjustment locknut and rotate the positioner assembly until the positioner just contacts the throttle lever.
5. Release the throttle lever and slowly adjust the positioner to decrease the engine speed until a sudden drop in engine speed occurs, above 1,000 rpm. At this point, continue turning the positioner, in the decreasing direction, an additional ¼ turn. Hold the positioner and tighten the locknut.
6. Accelerate the engine, by hand, to 2,500 rpm and release the throttle. The engine should return to normal idle.

Float Setting

1. Invert the air horn so that the weight of the float alone is forcing the needle against the seat.
2. Measure the clearance between the top of the float and the float stop. The clearance should be 0.080" on models through 1977; 0.200" on 1978 and later models.
3. If an adjustment is necessary, bend the flat tab toward or away from the needle using a narrow blade screwdriver.
4. Check the float drop by holding the air horn in an upright position. The bottom edge of the float should be even with and parallel to the underside surface of the air horn. If necessary, bend the tang on the float arm to make an adjustment.

Float Drop

1978–83 MODELS

1. Remove the air horn.
2. Allow the float to hang. The bottom of the float should be parallel with the air horn gasket surface.
3. Bend the tang on the float arm to correct the float drop.

Holley 2280

ADJUSTMENTS

Fast Idle Cam Position

◆ **See Figure 34**

1. Position the fast idle speed adjusting screw so that it contacts the second highest step of the cam. Move the choke valve toward the closed position with light pressure on the choke linkage.
2. Insert a 0.070″ drill bit between the upper edge of the choke plate and the wall of the air horn. On carb. #40172-A, use a 0.052″ drill bit.
3. If adjustment is necessary, bend the fast idle link at the angle until the specified drill fits between the choke plate and the wall of the air horn.

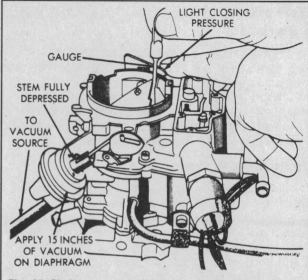

Fig. 35 Choke vacuum kick adjustment for the Holley 2280 carburetor

Fig. 34 Fast idle cam position adjustment for the Holley 2280 carburetor

Vacuum Kick

◆ **See Figure 35**

1. If the adjustment is to be made on the engine (with the engine running at curb idle), back off the fast idle screw until the choke can be closed to the kick position. Note the number of screw turns required so that the fast idle can be returned to the original adjustment.
2. If the adjustment is to be made off the engine, open the throttle valve and move the choke to its closed position. Release the throttle first and then release the choke. Disconnect the vacuum hose from the carburetor body and apply a vacuum of at least 15 in.Hg.

3. For models R-8999A and R-9000A, insert a 0.130″ drill bit between the choke valve and the wall of the air horn. On all other models, use a 0.150″ drill bit.
4. Apply sufficient closing pressure to the choke lever to provide a minimum valve opening without distorting the diaphragm link (which connects the choke lever to the vacuum diaphragm). Note that the cylindrical stem of the diaphragm will extend as its internal spring is compressed. This spring must be fully compressed for the proper measurement of the vacuum kick adjustment.
5. Remove the drill bit. If a slight drag is not felt as the drill or gauge is removed, an adjustment of the diaphragm link is necessary to obtain the proper clearance. Shorten or lengthen the diaphragm link by carefully closing or opening the U-bend in the link until the correct adjustment is obtained.

✳✳ WARNING

When adjusting the link, be careful not to bend or twist the diaphragm.

6. Refit the vacuum hose to the carburetor body (if it had been removed) and return the fast idle screw to its original location.
7. With no vacuum applied to the diaphragm, the choke valve should move freely between its open and closed positions. If it does not move freely, examine the linkage for misalignment or interference which may have been caused by the bending operation. If necessary, repeat the adjustment to provide the proper link operation.

Choke Unloader

◆ **See Figure 36**

1. Hold the throttle valve in the wide open position.
2. On 1980–81 trucks, insert a 0.310″ drill bit between the upper edge of the choke valve and the wall of the air horn. On 1982–84 models, use a 0.200″ drill bit. On 1985–87 models the drill bit is 0.150″ for all except carb. #40172-A; that carb. is 0.200″.

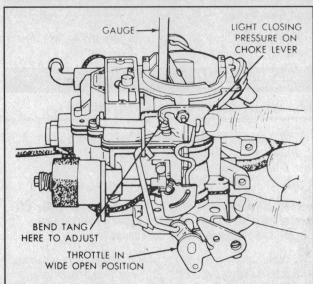

Fig. 36 Choke unloader adjustment for the Holley 2280 carburetor

3. With a finger pressing lightly against the choke plate, a slight drag should be felt as the drill is being withdrawn.

4. If adjustment is necessary, bend the unloader tang on the throttle lever until the correct opening is obtained.

Mechanical Power Valve

♦ **See Figure 37**

1. Remove the bowl vent cover plate, vent valve lever spring and retainer. Remove the vent valve lever and pivot pin.

2. Hold the throttle in the wide open position.

3. Insert a 5/64" Allen wrench in the power valve adjustment screw.

4. Push the screw down and release it to determine if clearance exists. Turn the screw clockwise until clearance is zero.

5. Turn the screw 1 turn counterclockwise.

6. Install the removed parts.

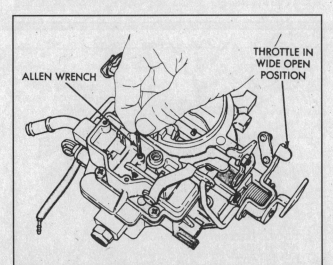

Fig. 37 Mechanical power valve adjustment for the Holley 2280 carburetor

Accelerator Pump Stroke

♦ **See Figure 38**

1. Remove the bowl vent cover plate and vent valve lever spring. Be careful not to dislodge or lose the vent valve retainer.

2. Make sure that the pump connector rod is in the inner slot of the pump arm.

3. Position the throttle at curb idle.

4. Place a straightedge on the bowl vent cover surface of the air horn over the accelerator pump connector rod in the center of the bowl.

5. Bend the accelerator pump connector rod until the lever surface is flush with the air horn surface on models through 1985. On 1986–87 models, set the float for a 0.050" gap.

6. Install the vent valve lever spring and bowl vent cover plate.

➡**If this adjustment is changed, both the bowl vent and the mechanical power valve adjustment must be reset.**

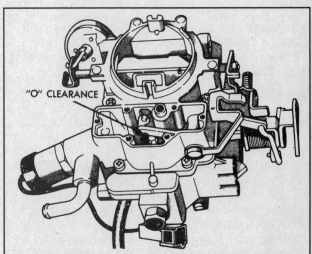

Fig. 38 Accelerator pump stroke adjustment, at idle, for the Holley 2280

Fast Idle Speed

♦ **See Figure 39**

1. Run the engine to normal operating temperature.

2. Remove the air cleaner and disconnect and plug the EGR vacuum line and distributor advance vacuum line. If the engine has Electronic Spark Control, remove only the top of the air cleaner housing and lift the air cleaner to access the carburetor. Do not disconnect the vacuum line to the spark control computer. Instead, use a jumper wire to ground the idle stop switch.

3. Set the parking brake and place the transmission in Neutral. With the engine off, open the throttle, close the choke and close the throttle.

4. Rotate the fast idle cam until the fast idle screw can be positioned on the second highest speed step of the cam.

5. Start the engine. Let the engine speed stabilize. If the engine speed continues to rise, the idle switch has not been properly grounded.

6. Turn the fast idle speed screw in or out until the engine speed listed on your truck's underhood sticker is reached.

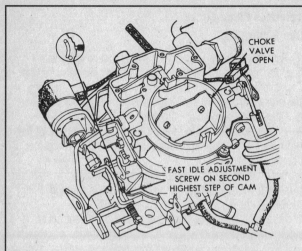

Fig. 39 Fast idle speed adjustment for the Holley 2280 carburetor

7. Reposition the screw on the cam after each adjustment to provide the correct closing torque.

8. Remove the jumper wire, reconnect the vacuum hoses and install the air cleaner.

Float Setting

▶ **See Figure 40**

1. Remove the carburetor.
2. Remove the air horn.
3. Invert the carburetor body. THE PUMP INTAKE CHECK BALL WILL DROP OUT. BE SURE TO CATCH IT!
4. Allow the weight of the floats to rest on the needle valve. Hold your finger against the hinge pin retainer to fully seat it in the float pin cradle.
5. Using a straightedge, measure the gap between surface of the float bowl to the toe of each float. The gap should be $9/32''$ ± $1/32''$.
6. If adjustment is necessary, bend the float tang. Bend either float arm to equalize the individual float positions.

Bowl Vent Valve

1. Remove the bowl vent valve cover plate and the vent lever spring.

✳✳ WARNING

Don't dislodge the vent valve lever retainer/pivot pin.

2. With the throttle in the curb idle position, press down firmly on the vent valve lever where the spring seats. Simultaneously, press down on the vent valve tang until the vent valve is lightly seated.

➡**If this adjustment is being performed off-engine, the carburetor must be on a raised flat surface so that the curb idle throttle plate position is not changed.**

3. While holding these things down, measure the gap between the contact surfaces of the vent valve lever and the vent valve tang. The gap should be 0.030″.
4. If not, adjust by bending the end of the vent valve lever.
5. Install the lever spring and cover.

➡**If this adjustment is changed, the accelerator pump adjustment must be reset.**

Holley 6145

ADJUSTMENTS

Fast Idle Cam

▶ **See Figure 41**

1. Position the fast idle speed adjusting screw so that it contacts the second highest step of the cam. Move the choke valve toward the closed position with light pressure on the choke linkage.
2. Insert a 0.070″ drill bit between the upper edge of the choke plate and the wall of the air horn on trucks with automatic transmission; 0.060″ on trucks with manual transmission.

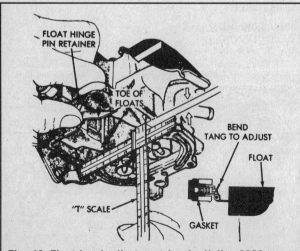

Fig. 40 Float level adjustment for the Holley 2280 carburetor

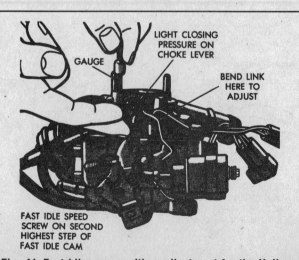

Fig. 41 Fast idle cam position adjustment for the Holley 6145 carburetor

3. If adjustment is necessary, bend the fast idle link at the angle until the specified drill fits between the choke plate and the wall of the air horn.

Vacuum Kick
♦ See Figure 42

1. If the adjustment is to be made on the engine (with the engine running at curb idle), back off the fast idle screw until the choke can be closed to the kick position. Note the number of screw turns required so that the fast idle can be returned to the original adjustment.

2. If the adjustment is to be made off the engine, open the throttle valve and move the choke to its closed position. Release the throttle first and then release the choke. Disconnect the vacuum hose from the carburetor body and apply a vacuum of at least 15 in.Hg.

3. Apply sufficient closing pressure to the choke lever to provide a minimum valve opening without distorting the diaphragm link (which connects the choke lever to the vacuum diaphragm). Note that the cylindrical stem of the diaphragm will extend as its internal spring is compressed. This spring must be fully compressed for the proper measurement of the vacuum kick adjustment.

4. Using a 5/64" Allen wrench in the diaphragm adjuster, adjust the clearance so that a 0.150" drill bit can fit between the choke valve and the wall of the air horn.

5. Remove the drill bit.

6. Refit the vacuum hose to the carburetor body (if it had been removed) and return the fast idle screw to its original location.

7. With no vacuum applied to the diaphragm, the choke valve should move freely between its open and closed positions. If it does not move freely, examine the linkage for misalignment or interference which may have been caused by the bending operation. If necessary, repeat the adjustment to provide the proper link operation.

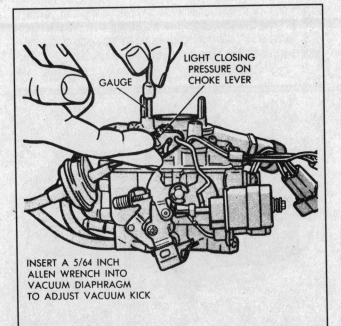

INSERT A 5/64 INCH ALLEN WRENCH INTO VACUUM DIAPHRAGM TO ADJUST VACUUM KICK

GAUGE

LIGHT CLOSING PRESSURE ON CHOKE LEVER

Fig. 42 Choke vacuum kick adjustment for the Holley 6145 carburetor

Choke Unloader
♦ See Figure 43

1. Hold the throttle valve in the wide open position.

2. Insert a 1/4" drill bit between the upper edge of the choke valve and the wall of the air horn.

3. With a finger pressing lightly against the choke plate, a slight drag should be felt as the drill is being withdrawn.

4. If adjustment is necessary, bend the unloader tang on the throttle lever until the correct opening is obtained.

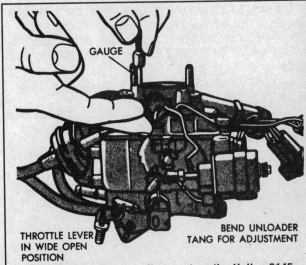

GAUGE

THROTTLE LEVER IN WIDE OPEN POSITION

BEND UNLOADER TANG FOR ADJUSTMENT

Fig. 43 Choke unloader adjustment on the Holley 6145 carburetor

Accelerator Pump Stroke
♦ See Figure 44

1. Place the throttle in the curb idle position.

2. Make sure that the pump operating link is in the #2 (upper) hole in the throttle lever.

3. Measure the length of the operating link. The length should

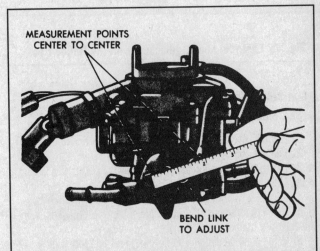

MEASUREMENT POINTS CENTER TO CENTER

BEND LINK TO ADJUST

Fig. 44 Accelerator pump piston stroke adjustment on the Holley 6145

be 1.61" on 1983–84 models; 1.75" on 1985–87 models. If not, bend it at the U-bend.

Fast Idle Speed

▶ See Figure 45

1. Run the engine to normal operating temperature.

2. Remove the air cleaner and disconnect and plug the EGR vacuum line. Disconnect the vacuum hose at the heated air temperature sensor. Plug the hose. Remove the air cleaner and disconnect and plug the ³⁄₁₆" hose at the canister. Remove the PCV valve from the rocker cover and allow it to draw fresh air.

3. Disconnect and plug the vacuum advance hose at the distributor. Disconnect the engine harness lead at the oxygen sensor. Ground the harness lead. Don't put any stress on this lead! Allow the engine to run for at least 2 minutes after disconnecting the O_2 sensor.

4. Open the throttle slightly and place the fast idle screw on the second highest speed step of the cam.

5. With the choke fully open, turn the fast idle speed screw in or out until the engine speed listed on your truck's underhood sticker is reached.

6. Reposition the screw on the cam after each adjustment to provide the correct closing torque.

7. Remove the jumper wire, reconnect the vacuum hoses and install the air cleaner.

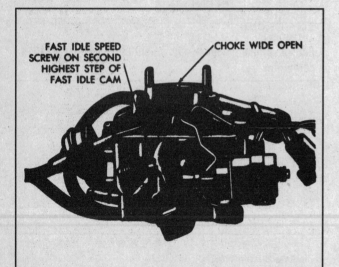

Fig. 45 Fast idle speed adjustment on the Holley 6145

Float Setting

▶ See Figure 46

1. Remove the carburetor.

2. Remove the air horn.

3. Invert the carburetor body. THE PUMP INTAKE CHECK BALL WILL DROP OUT. BE SURE TO CATCH IT!

4. Allow the weight of the floats to rest on the needle valve. Hold your finger against the hinge pin retainer to fully seat it in the float pin cradle.

5. Using a straightedge, the floats should just touch the straightedge at the point on the floats farthest from the fuel inlet.

6. If adjustment is necessary, bend the float tang. Bend either float arm to equalize the individual float positions.

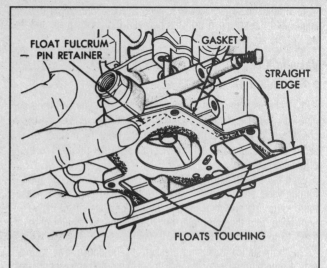

Fig. 46 Float setting adjustment for the Holley 6145

Solenoid Idle Stop

▶ See Figure 47

1. Run the engine to normal operating temperature.

2. Disconnect and plug the EGR vacuum line. Connect a jumper wire between the carburetor switch and a good ground. Disconnect and plug the ³⁄₁₆" hose at the canister. The air cleaner cannot be removed, but should be propped up to gain access to the carburetor. Remove the PCV valve from the rocker cover and allow it to draw fresh air.

3. Turn on the air conditioning and set the blower to **LOW**.

4. Disconnect the compressor clutch wire.

5. On models without air conditioning, connect a jumper wire between the battery positive pole and the solenoid idle stop lead wire.

6. Open the throttle slightly and allow the plunger to extend.

7. Remove the adjusting screw and spring from the solenoid.

8. Insert a ¹⁄₈" Allen wrench into the solenoid and adjust the engine speed to 850 rpm.

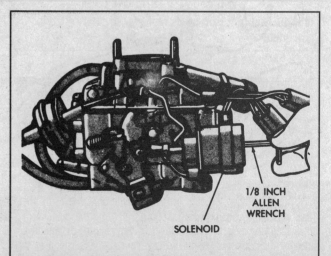

Fig. 47 Solenoid idle stop adjustment for the Holley 6145 carburetor

9. Turn off the air conditioning and reconnect all wires and hoses.

Holley 6280

ADJUSTMENTS

Fast Idle Cam Position

▸ **See Figure 48**

1. Position the fast idle speed adjusting screw so that it contacts the second highest step of the cam. Move the choke valve toward the closed position with light pressure on the choke linkage.

2. Insert a 0.070" drill bit between the upper edge of the choke plate and the wall.

3. If adjustment is necessary, bend the fast idle link at the angle until the specified drill fits between the choke plate and the wall of the air horn.

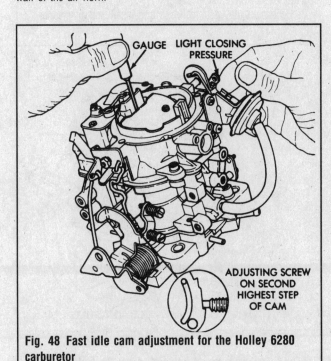

Fig. 48 Fast idle cam adjustment for the Holley 6280 carburetor

Vacuum Kick

▸ **See Figure 49**

1. If the adjustment is to be made off the engine, open the throttle valve and move the choke to its closed position. Release the throttle first and then release the choke. Disconnect the vacuum hose from the carburetor body and apply a vacuum of at least 15 in.Hg.

2. Apply sufficient closing pressure to the choke lever to provide a minimum valve opening without distorting the diaphragm link (which connects the choke lever to the vacuum diaphragm). Note that the cylindrical stem of the diaphragm will extend as its internal spring is compressed. This spring must be fully compressed for the proper measurement of the vacuum kick adjustment.

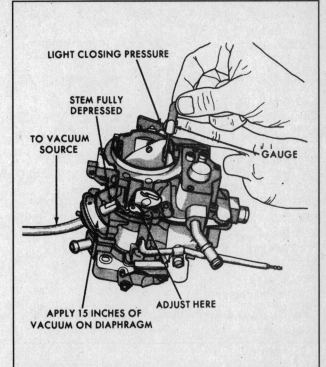

Fig. 49 Choke vacuum kick adjustment for the Holley 6280 carburetor

3. Insert a 0.130" drill bit between the choke valve and the wall of the air horn.

4. Remove the drill bit. If a slight drag is not felt as the drill or gauge is removed, an adjustment of the diaphragm link is necessary to obtain the proper clearance. Shorten or lengthen the diaphragm link by carefully closing or opening the U-bend in the link until the correct adjustment is obtained.

✳✳ WARNING

When adjusting the link, be careful not to bend or twist the diaphragm.

5. Refit the vacuum hose to the carburetor body (if it had been removed) and return the fast idle screw to its original location.

6. With no vacuum applied to the diaphragm, the choke valve should move freely between its open and closed positions. If it does not move freely, examine the linkage for misalignment or interference which may have been caused by the bending operation. If necessary, repeat the adjustment to provide the proper link operation.

Choke Unloader

▸ **See Figure 50**

1. Hold the throttle valve in the wide open position.

2. Insert a 0.250" drill bit between the upper edge of the choke valve and the wall of the air horn for model R-40132; 0.150" for all other carburetors.

3. With a finger pressing lightly against the choke plate, a slight drag should be felt as the drill is being withdrawn.

4. If adjustment is necessary, bend the unloader tang on the throttle lever until the correct opening is obtained.

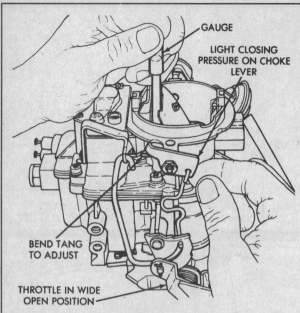

Fig. 50 Choke unloader adjustment on the Holley 6280 carburetor

Accelerator Pump Stroke
▶ **See Figure 51**

1. Remove the bowl vent cover plate and vent valve lever spring. Be careful not to dislodge or lose the vent valve retainer.
2. Make sure that the pump connector rod is in the inner slot of the pump arm.
3. Position the throttle at curb idle.
4. Place a straightedge on the bowl vent cover surface of the air horn over the accelerator pump connector rod in the center of the bowl.
5. Bend the accelerator pump connector rod until the lever surface is flush with the air horn surface on 1985 models; 0.135" above the casting on 1986–87 models.
6. Install the vent valve lever spring and bowl vent cover plate.

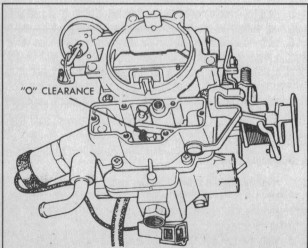

Fig. 51 Accelerator pump piston stroke adjustment on the Holley 6280

➡ **If this adjustment is changed, both the bowl vent and the mechanical power valve adjustment must be reset.**

Fast Idle Speed
▶ **See Figure 52**

1. Run the engine to normal operating temperature.
2. Disconnect and plug the EGR vacuum line and distributor advance vacuum line. Disconnect and plug the vacuum advance line at the distributor. Disconnect and plug the carburetor vacuum line at the heated air temperature sensor. Remove the air cleaner and plug the 3/16" vacuum line at the canister. Remove the PCV valve from the rocker cover and allow it to draw fresh air.
3. Set the parking brake and place the transmission in Neutral.
4. With the engine off, open the throttle and place the fast idle adjusting screw on the second highest speed step of the cam.
5. Start the engine. Let the engine speed stabilize.
6. Turn the fast idle speed screw in or out until the engine speed listed on the underhood sticker is reached.
7. Reposition the screw on the cam after each adjustment to provide the correct closing torque.
8. Reconnect the vacuum hoses and install the air cleaner.

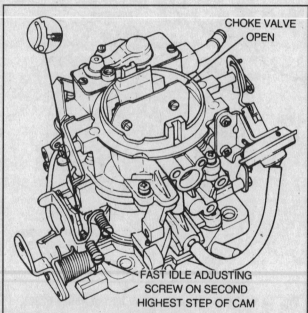

Fig. 52 Fast idle speed adjustment on the Holley 6280 carburetor

Float Setting
▶ **See Figure 53**

1. Remove the carburetor.
2. Remove the air horn.
3. Invert the carburetor body. THE PUMP INTAKE CHECK BALL WILL DROP OUT. BE SURE TO CATCH IT!
4. Allow the weight of the floats to rest on the needle valve. Hold your finger against the hinge pin retainer to fully seat it in the float pin cradle.
5. Using a straightedge, measure the gap between surface of the float bowl to the toe of each float. The gap should be 9/32" ± 1/32".

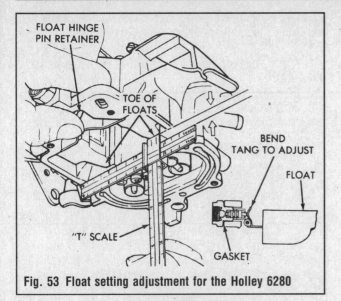

Fig. 53 Float setting adjustment for the Holley 6280

6. If adjustment is necessary, bend the float tang. Bend either float arm to equalize the individual float positions.

Rochester Quadrajet

ADJUSTMENTS

Float Level

EXTERNAL CHECK
▶ **See Figure 54**

1. With the engine idling at normal operating temperature and the choke wide open, insert float gauge C-4900 in the vent hole and allow the gauge to float freely. DO NOT PRESS DOWN ON THE GAUGE, AS THIS WILL RESULT IN FLOODING AND/OR FLOAT DAMAGE!

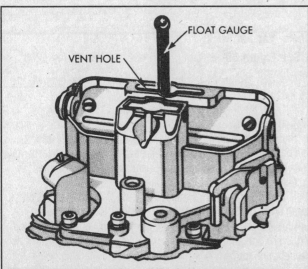

Fig. 54 Float level external check for the Rochester Quadrajet

2. Look at the mark on the gauge that lines up with the top of the casting. The reading should be $13/32'' \pm 1/16''$.

3. If not, remove the air horn and set the float as described immediately following.

Setting
▶ **See Figure 55**

1. Remove the air horn, gasket and power piston, and plastic float bowl insert.
2. Hold the float bowl retainer firmly in place.
3. Push the float down *lightly* against the needle.
4. Measure the float height from the top of the casting to the top of the float at a point $3/16''$ from the end of the float. The height should be $13/32''$.
5. If the float level is too high, hold the retainer in place and push down on the center of the float pontoon to get the correct setting.
6. If the float level is too low, bend the float upward to get the correct setting.
7. Recheck the float level.
8. Install the bowl insert, power piston and gasket, and air horn.

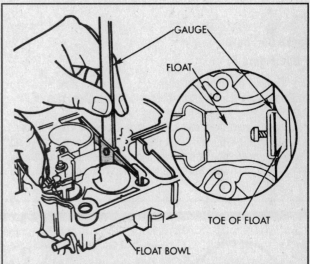

Fig. 55 Float level adjustment for the Quadrajet carburetor

Air Valve Spring
▶ **See Figure 56**

1. Using a $3/32''$ wrench, loosen the air valve spring lockscrew.
2. Turn the tension adjusting screw counterclockwise until the air valve opens part way.
3. Turn the screw clockwise the following number of turns:
- 17085408—$1/2$ turn
- 17085409—$5/8$ turn
- 17085415—$1/2$ turn
- 17085417—$3/4$ turn
- 17086425—$1/2$ turn
- 17087245—$5/8$ turn
- 17087176—$3/4$ turn
- 17087175—$3/4$ turn
- 17087177—1 turn

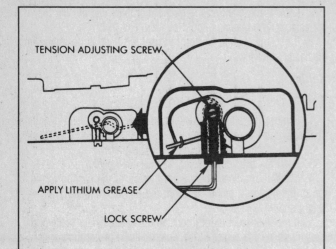

Fig. 56 Air valve spring adjustment for the Quadrajet carburetor

- 17085431—½ turn
5. Hold the adjusting screw and tighten the locknut.
6. Apply a light film of lithium based grease to the contact area.

Choke Coil Lever

▶ **See Figure 57**

1. Remove the choke cover.
2. Place the fast idle cam follower on the highest step of the cam.
3. Push up on the choke coil lever to close the choke plate.
4. Insert a 0.120" drill bit in the hole just below the choke coil lever. The lower edge of the lever should *just* contact the drill bit.
5. If not, bend the choke rod at the upper angle.

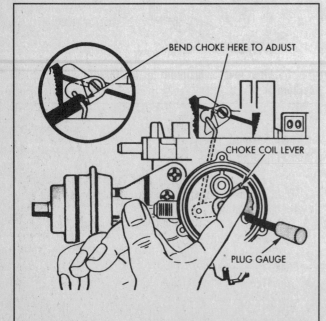

Fig. 57 Choke coil lever adjustment for the Quadrajet carburetor

Fast Idle Cam

▶ **See Figure 58**

1. Attach a rubber band to the green tang of the intermediate choke shaft.
2. Open the throttle to allow the choke valve to close.
3. Place the cam follower on the second step of the cam. If the cam follower won't touch the cam, turn the fast idle speed screw in until it does.
4. Apply a slight opening pressure on the choke plate and insert a 0.143 drill bit between the top of the choke plate and the air horn wall. A slight drag should be felt on the drill bit.
5. If adjustment is needed, bend the tang of the fast idle cam.

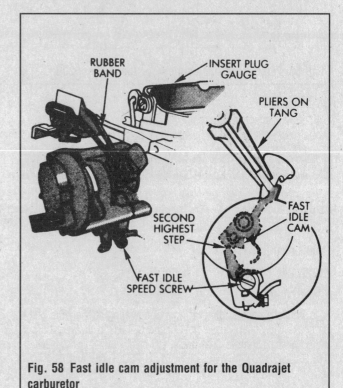

Fig. 58 Fast idle cam adjustment for the Quadrajet carburetor

Choke Vacuum Kick

▶ **See Figure 59**

1. Attach a rubber band to the green tang of the intermediate choke shaft.
2. Open the throttle to allow the choke valve to close.
3. Using a vacuum pump, apply at least 18 in.Hg to the nipple on the choke diaphragm. The air valve rod must not restrict the plunger from fully retracting. If necessary, bend the rod to permit full plunger travel. The final rod clearance must be set after the vacuum kick setting has been made.
4. With the vacuum still applied, apply a slight opening pressure on the choke plate and insert a 0.214" drill bit between the top of the choke plate and the air horn casting on all 1985 models; 0.170" on all 1986 models; on 1987–88 models, the drill bit should be 0.150" for 49s models, 0.170 for high altitude models, or 0.140" for California and Canada models. A slight drag should be felt.
5. If adjustment is necessary, bend the link at the upper angle.

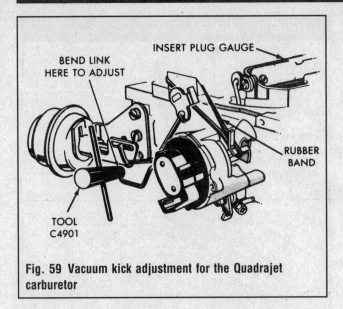

Fig. 59 Vacuum kick adjustment for the Quadrajet carburetor

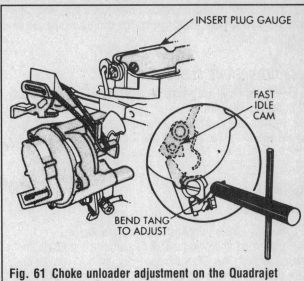

Fig. 61 Choke unloader adjustment on the Quadrajet carburetor

Air Valve Rod

◆ See Figure 60

1. Using a vacuum pump, apply at least 18 in.Hg to the vacuum nipple on the choke vacuum diaphragm.
2. Close the air valve.
3. Insert a 0.025″ drill bit between the rod and the end of the slot. The drill bit should *just* fit.
4. To adjust, bend the rod at the lower left angle.

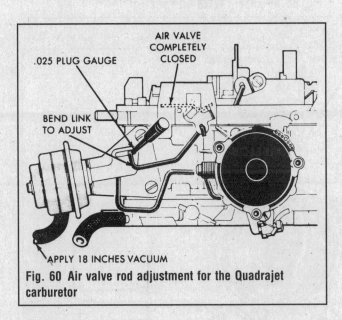

Fig. 60 Air valve rod adjustment for the Quadrajet carburetor

Choke Unloader

◆ See Figure 61

1. Attach a rubber band to the green tang of the intermediate choke shaft.
2. Open the throttle to allow the choke plate to close.
3. Hold the secondary lockout lever away from the pin.
4. Hold the throttle lever in the wide open position.

5. Apply a slight opening pressure on the choke plate and insert a 0.345″ drill bit between the top of the choke plate and the air horn wall for all 1985 models; 0.260″ for all 1986 models; for 1987–88 models use a 0.200″ drill bit for 49 states models, 0.220″ for high altitude models; 0.209″ for California and Canada models. A slight drag should be felt.
6. If adjustment is required, bend the tang of the fast idle lever.

Secondary Lockout

◆ See Figure 62

LOCKOUT LEVER

1. Close the choke plate.
2. Close the throttle plates.

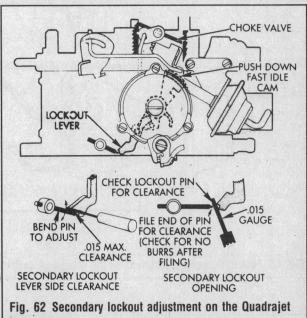

Fig. 62 Secondary lockout adjustment on the Quadrajet carburetor

3. Insert a 0.015″ drill bit between the lockout lever and the secondary throttle plate actuating pin. The drill bit should *just* fit. If not, bend the pin.

LOCKOUT OPENING CLEARANCE

1. Hold the choke plate wide open by pushing down on the tail of the fast idle cam.
2. Insert a 0.015″ drill bit between the end of the lockout lever and the end of the secondary throttle actuating pin. The drill bit should *just* fit. If not, file the end of the pin.

Fast Idle Speed

▶ **See Figure 63**

1. Run the engine to normal operating temperature.
2. Disconnect and plug the EGR vacuum line and distributor advance vacuum line. Disconnect and plug the ³⁄₁₆″ vacuum hose at the canister. Remove the PCV valve from the rocker cover and allow it to draw fresh air.
3. Set the parking brake and place the transmission in Neutral.
4. With the engine off, open the throttle and place the fast idle adjusting screw on the second highest speed step of the cam.
5. Start the engine. Let the engine speed stabilize.
6. Turn the fast idle speed screw in or out until the engine speed listed on the underhood sticker is reached.
7. Reposition the screw on the cam after each adjustment to provide the correct closing torque.
8. Reconnect the vacuum hoses and install the air cleaner.

Stromberg WW3

ADJUSTMENTS

Float Height

▶ **See Figure 64**

1. Remove the carburetor.
2. Remove the air horn.

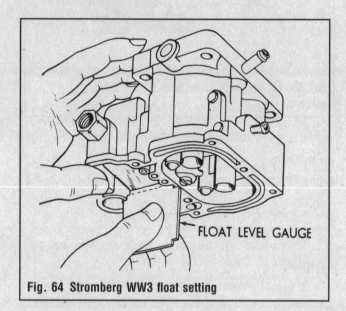

FLOAT LEVEL GAUGE

Fig. 64 Stromberg WW3 float setting

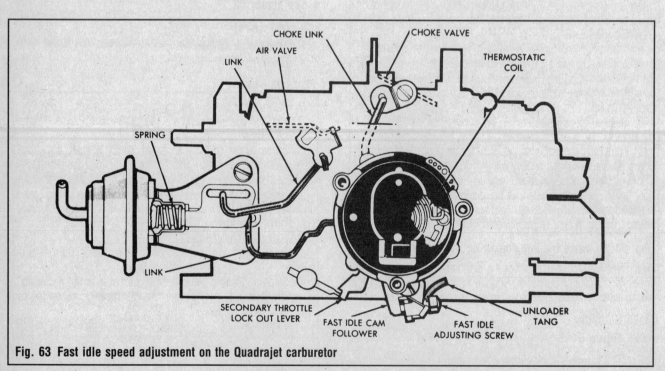

Fig. 63 Fast idle speed adjustment on the Quadrajet carburetor

3. Invert the main body and let the weight of the float rest on the needle and seat.

4. Using a T-scale, check the distance between the gasket surface of the fuel bowl (gasket removed) and the top of the float at the center. The gap should be $7/32''$.

5. If adjustment is necessary, hold the float against the bottom of the float bowl and bend the lip towards or away from the needle.

➡ **When bending, don't allow the float lip to push against the needle. The tip of the needle will compress and give a false reading.**

6. Recheck your adjustment a couple of times. It is *very* important that the float lip be perpendicular to the needle $\pm 10°$ after the adjustment!

7. Assemble the carburetor.

Fast Idle Cam

1. Position the fast idle speed adjusting screw so that it contacts the second highest step of the cam. Move the choke valve toward the closed position with light pressure on the choke linkage.

2. Insert a #44 drill bit between the upper edge of the choke plate and the wall of the air horn on all engines except the 8-318 with the Clean Air Package. On these engines, use a #20 drill bit. A slight drag should be felt.

3. If adjustment is necessary, bend the fast idle link at the upper angle until the specified drill bit fits between the choke plate and the wall of the air horn.

Vacuum Kick

1. If the adjustment is to be made on the engine (with the engine running at curb idle), back off the fast idle screw until the choke can be closed to the kick position. Note the number of screw turns required so that the fast idle can be returned to the original adjustment.

2. If the adjustment is to be made off the engine, open the throttle valve and move the choke to its closed position. Release the throttle first and then release the choke. Disconnect the vacuum hose from the carburetor body and apply a vacuum of at least 10 in.Hg.

3. Insert a #4 drill bit between the choke valve and the wall of the air horn.

4. Apply sufficient closing pressure to the choke lever to provide a minimum valve opening without distorting the diaphragm link (which connects the choke lever to the vacuum diaphragm). Note that the cylindrical stem of the diaphragm will extend as its internal spring is compressed. This spring must be fully compressed for the proper measurement of the vacuum kick adjustment.

5. Remove the drill bit. If a slight drag is not felt as the drill bit is removed, an adjustment of the diaphragm link is necessary to obtain the proper clearance. Shorten or lengthen the diaphragm link by carefully closing or opening the U-bend in the link until the correct adjustment is obtained.

✳ WARNING

When adjusting the link, be careful not to bend or twist the diaphragm.

6. Refit the vacuum hose to the carburetor body (if it had been removed) and return the fast idle screw to its original location.

7. With no vacuum applied to the diaphragm, the choke valve should move freely between its open and closed positions. If it does not move freely, examine the linkage for misalignment or interference which may have been caused by the bending operation. If necessary, repeat the adjustment to provide the proper link operation.

Choke Unloader

1. Hold the throttle valve in the wide open position.

2. Insert a $5/16''$ drill bit between the upper edge of the choke valve and the wall of the air horn.

3. With a finger pressing lightly against the choke plate, a slight drag should be felt as the drill bit is being withdrawn.

4. If adjustment is necessary, bend the unloader tang on the throttle lever until the correct opening is obtained.

Accelerator Pump and Bowl Vent

1. Back off the idle speed adjusting screw.

2. Open the choke plate so that, with the throttle plates closed, the fast idle adjusting screw will not contact the fast idle cam.

3. Make sure that the pump rod is in the medium stroke hole in the throttle lever and the bowl vent clip on the pump stem is in the center notch.

4. Close the throttle plates tightly. It should be *just* possible to insert a 0.060″ drill bit (0.050″ with Clean Air Package) between the bowl vent and the vent seal.

5. If adjustment is necessary, bend the pump rod at the lower angle with a needle-nosed pliers.

Fast Idle Speed

1. Warm the engine by driving at least five miles.

2. With the engine off and the transmission in Park or Neutral, open the throttle slightly.

3. On models without the Clean Air Package, close the choke plate about 20°, then allow the throttle plates to close. The fast idle screw should now rest on the slowest speed step of the cam.

On models with the Clean Air Package, close the choke plate until the fast idle screw can be positioned on the second highest speed step of the cam.

4. Start the engine.

5. Turn the fast idle speed screw in or out until 700 rpm is obtained.

6. Stopping the engine between adjustments is not necessary. However, be sure to position the fast idle speed screw on the cam after each speed adjustment.

CARTER THERMO-QUAD CARBURETORS

	TQ-9208S	TQ-9209S	TQ-9210S	TQ-9211S	TQ-9212S	TQ-9247S	TQ-9248S
Carter Model Number							
Requirement	Cal.	Fed./Can.	Cal.	Fed./Can.	Cal.	Fed./Can.	Cal.
Engine Displacement (Cu. In.)	360-1	360-3	360-3	440-1,3	440-1,3	440-1,3	440-1,3
Transmission	Man.	Auto.	Auto.	Auto.	Auto.	Auto.	Auto.
Bore							
Primary	1-3/8"	1-3/8"	1-3/8"	1-1/2"	1-1/2"	1-1/2"	1-1/2"
Secondary	2-1/4"	2-1/4"	2-1/4"	2-1/4"	2-1/4"	2-1/4"	2-1/4"
Main Venturi							
Primary	1-1/16"	1-1/16"	1-1/16"	1-3/16"	1-3/16"	1-3/16"	1-3/16"
Secondary	2-1/4"	2-1/4"	2-1/4"	2-1/4"	2-1/4"	2-1/4"	2-1/4"
Adjustments							
Float Setting (± 1/32")	29/32"	29/32"	29/32"	29/32"	29/32"	29/32"	29/32"
Secondary Throttle Linkage	Adjust Links so that Primary and Secondary Stops both contact at the same time.						
Secondary Air Valve Opening	7/16"	7/16"	7/16"	1/2"	1/2"	7/16"	7/16"
Secondary Air Valve Spring Tension (From Contact)	2 Turns	2 Turns	2 Turns	1-1/2 Turns	1-1/2 Turns	1-1/2 Turns	1-1/2 Turns
Accelerator Pump Stroke (Top of pump plunger stem to top of bowl cover @ curb idle) (Stage 1)	31/64"	31/64"	31/64"	31/64"	31/64"	31/64"	31/64"
At Secondary Pick Up (Stage 2)	23/64"	23/64"	23/64"	23/64"	23/64"	23/64"	23/64"
Choke Control Lever Adjustment Off Vehicle	3.30"	3.30"	3.30"	3.30"	3.30"	3.30"	3.30"
Choke Diaphragm Connector Rod (Clearance between Air Valve and Stop)	.040"	.040"	.040"	.040"	.040"	.040"	.040"
Vacuum Kick**	.150"	.150"	.150"	.100"	.100"	.100"	.100"
Fast Idle Cam Position**	.100"	.100"	.100"	.100"	.100"	.100"	.100"
Choke Unloader (Wide Open Kick)**	.310"	.310"	.310"	.500"	.500"	.500"	.500"
Secondary Throttle Lockout	.060"-.090"	.060"-.090"	.060"-.090"	.060"-.090"	.060"-.090"	.060"-.090"	.060"-.090"
Timing	4°BTDC	4°BTDC	4°BTDC	8°BTDC	8°BTDC	8°BTDC	8°BTDC
Propane rpm	800	820	820	790	790	790	790
Idle set rpm	700	700	700	700	700	700	700
Fast idle rpm	1600	1600	1600	1400	1400	1400	1400
Carbon monoxide (co)	*	-	*	-	*	-	*

*Refer To Emissions Label.

**Thermo-Quad Choke Adjustments are measured at the lowest edge of the choke plate.

HOLLEY MODEL 2245 DUAL VENTURI CARBURETORS

	R-8597A	R-8598A	R-8925A
Holley Model Number			
Requirement	Fed.	Fed.	Fed.
Engine Displacement (Cu. In.)	360-1	360-1	360-1
Transmission	Man.	Auto.	Auto.
Bore	1-9/16″	1-9/16″	1-9/16″
Venturi	1-5/16″	1-5/16″	1-5/16″
Main Metering Jet	632	641	651
Adjustments			
Accelerator Pump Setting (From Curb Idle)	.290″	.290″	.290″
Accelerator Pump Setting (From Closed Throttle)	#1 Slot .290″	#1 Slot .290″	#1 Slot .290″
*Dry Float Setting Between Toe of Float and Float Stop (± 1/32″)	.200″	.200″	.200″
Bowl Vent	.025″	.025″	.025″
Vacuum Kick	.110″	.110″	.110″
Fast Idle Cam Position	.110″	.110″	.110″
Choke Unloader	.170″	.170″	.170″
Timing	10°BTDC	10°BTDC	10°BTDC
Propane rpm	1000	975	975
Idle set rpm	750	750	750
Fast idle rpm	1600	1600	1600

CARTER THERMO-QUAD CARBURETORS

	TQ-9228S	TQ-9229S	TQ-9223S	TQ-9227S	TQ-9224S	TQ-9225S	TQ-9207S
Carter Model Number							
Requirement	Cal.	Cal.	Cal.	Can.	Cal.	Cal.	Fed./Can.
Engine Displacement (Cu. In.)	318-1	318-1	318-1	318-1	360-1	360-1	360-1
Transmission	Man.	Auto.	Auto.	Auto.	Man.	Auto.	Man.
Bore							
Primary	1-3/8″	1-3/8″	1-3/8″	1-3/8″	1-3/8″	1-3/8″	1-3/8″
Secondary	2-1/4″	2-1/4″	2-1/4″	2-1/4″	2-1/4″	2-1/4″	2-1/4″
Main Venturi							
Primary	1-1/16″	1-1/16″	1-1/16″	1-1/16″	1-1/16″	1-1/16″	1-1/16″
Secondary	2-1/4″	2-1/4″	2-1/4″	2-1/4″	2-1/4″	2-1/4″	2-1/4″
Adjustments							
Float Setting (±1/32″)	29/32″	29/32″	29/32″	29/32″	29/32″	29/32″	29/32″
Secondary Throttle Linkage	Adjust Links so that Primary and Secondary Stops both contact at the same time.						
Secondary Air Valve Opening	1/2″	1/2″	1/2″	1/2″	1/2″	1/2″	7/16″
Secondary Air Valve Spring Tension (From Contact)	3 Turns	3 Turns	3 Turns	3 Turns	3 Turns	3 Turns	2 Turns
Accelerator Pump Stroke (Top of pump plunger stem to top of bowl cover @ curb idle) (Stage 1)	11/32″	11/32″	11/32″	11/32″	5/16″	5/16″	31/64″
At Secondary Pick Up (Stage 2)	3/16″	3/16″	9/64″	9/64″	3/16″	3/16″	23/64″
Choke Control Lever Adjustment Off Vehicle	3.30″	3.30″	3.30″	3.30″	3.30″	3.30″	3.30″
Choke Diaphragm Connector Rod (Clearance between Air Valve and Stop)	.040″	.040″	.040″	.040″	.040″	.040″	.040″
Vacuum Kick**	.100″	.100″	.100″	.100″	.100″	.100″	.150″
Fast Idle Cam Position**	.100″	.100″	.100″	.100″	.100″	.100″	.100″
Choke Unloader (Wide Open Kick)**	.500″	.500″	.500″	.500″	.500″	.500″	.310″
Secondary Throttle Lockout	.060″-.090″	.060″-.090″	.060″-.090″	.060″-.090″	.060″-.090″	.060″-.090″	.060″-.090″
Timing	6°BTDC	6°BTDC	6°BTDC	8°BTDC	6°BTDC	10°BTDC	4°BTDC
Propane rpm	865	860	860	880	980	960	800
Idle set rpm	750	750	750	750	750	750	700
Fast idle rpm	1600	1600	1600	1600	1600	1600	1600
Carbon monoxide (co)	*	*	*	-	*	*	-

*Refer To Emissions Label.
**Thermo-Quad Choke Adjustments are measured at the lowest edge of the choke plate.

HOLLEY MODEL 1945 SINGLE VENTURI CARBURETORS

Holley Carburetor Number	R-8593A	R-8594A	R-8799A	R-8800A
Requirement	Federal	Federal	Canada	Canada
Engine (Cubic Inch)	225	225	225	225
Transmission	Manual	Automatic	Manual	Automatic
Bore	1-9/16″	1-9/16″	1-9/16″	1-9/16″
Venturi	1-5/16″	1-5/16″	1-5/16″	1-5/16″
Adjustments				
Accelerator Pump	2-7/32″	2-21/64″	2-7/32″	2-21/64″
	Position-1	Position-2	Position-1	Position-2
Dry Float Setting ± (1/32)	FLUSH WITH TOP OF BOWL COVER GASKET			
Bowl Vent	1/16″	1/16″	1/16″	1/16″
Vacuum Kick	.100″	.100″	.100″	.100″
Fast Idle Cam Position	.080″	.080″	.080″	.080″
Choke Unloader	.250″	.250″	.250″	.250″
Timing	12°BTDC	12°BTDC	12°BTDC	12°BTDC
Propane rpm	875	875	875	875
Idle set rpm	675	675	675	675
Fast idle rpm	1600	1600	1600	1600

CARTER MODEL BBD CARBURETOR

Carter Model Number	BBD-8214S	BBD-8215S	BBD-8249S	BBD-8232S	BBD-8210S	BBD-8211S
Requirement	Calif.	Calif.	Fed.	Fed.	Fed.	Fed.
Engine Displacement (Cu. In.)	225-1	225-1	318-1	318-1	318-1	318-1
Transmission	Man.	Auto.	Man.	Auto.	Man.	Auto.
Bore	1-7/16″	1-7/16″	1-7/16″	1-7/16″	1-7/16″	1-7/16″
Venturi	1-1/16″	1-1/16″	1-1/16″	1-1/16″	1-3/16″	1-1/16″
Main Metering Jets						
Standard	.086″	.086″	.086″	.086″	.086″	.086″
Metering Rods (Standard)	75-2264	75-2264	75-2216	75-2231	75-2229	75-2229
Adjustments						
Float Setting (At Center of Floats ± 1/32″)	1/4″	1/4″	1/4″	1/4″	1/4″	1/4″
Accelerator Pump Setting (At Curb Idle)	.500″	.500″	.500″	.500″	.500″	.500″
Choke Unloader	.280″	.280″	.280″	.280″	.280″	.280″
Vacuum Kick	.110″	.110″	.110″	.110″	.110″	.110″
Fast Idle Cam Position	.070″	.070″	.070″	.070″	.070″	.070″
Timing	8° BTDC	8° BTDC	12° BTDC	12° BTDC	12° BTDC	12° BTDC
Propane rpm	975	975	820	820	820	820
Idle set rpm	800	800	680	680	680	680
Fast idle rpm	1400	1600	1400	1500	1400	1500
Carbon monoxide (co)	*	*	-	-	-	-

* Refer To Emissions Label For Carbon Monoxide Percentage.

CARTER THERMO-QUAD CARBURETORS

Chrysler Number	4287013	4241752	4287016	4241753
Carter Model Number	TQ-9342S	TQ-9375S	TQ-9379S	TQ-9376S
Requirement	Fed./Cal.	Fed./Cal.	Fed./CAN.	Cal.
Engine Displacement (Cu. In.)	318/5.2	318/5.2	360/5.9	360/5.9
Transmission	Both	Auto	Both	Both
Bore				
Primary	1-3/8"	1-3/8"	1-3/8"	1-3/8"
Secondary	2-1/4"	2-1/4"	2-1/4"	2-1/4"
Main Venturi				
Primary	1-1/16"	1-1/16"	1-1/16"	1-1/16"
Secondary		AIR VALVE		
Adjustments				
Float Setting (± 1/32")	29/32"	29/32"	29/32"	29/32"
Secondary Throttle Linkage	Adjust links so that primary and secondary stops both contact at the same time			
Secondary Air Valve Opening	27/64"	27/64"	27/64"	27/64"
Secondary Air Valve Spring				
Tension (From Contact)	2-1/2 Turns	2 Turns	2 Turns	2 Turns
Accelerator Pump Stroke				
(Top of pump plunger stem to top of bowl cover @ curb idle) (Stage 1)	.340"	.340"	.340"	.340"
At Secondary Pick Up (Stage 2)	.190"	.190"	None	.190"
Choke Diaphragm Connector Rod (Clearance between Air Valve and Stop)	.040"	.040"	.040"	.040"
Vacuum Kick**	.130"	.130"	.130"	.130"
Fast Idle Cam Position**	.100"	.130"	.130"	.130"
Choke Unloader (Wide Open Kick)**	.310"	.310"	.310"	.310"
Secondary Throttle Lockout	.060"-.090"	.060"-.090"	.060"-.090"	.060"-.090"
Timing	8°BTDC	16°BTDC	4°BTDC	10°BTDC
Propane rpm	840	810	800	800
Idle set rpm	750	750	700	750
Fast idle rpm	1600	1800	1500	1700

*Refer To Emissions Label.
**Thermo-Quad Choke Adjustments are measured at the lowest edge of the choke plate.

CARTER MODEL BBD CARBURETORS

Chrysler Number	4041580	4041583	4041756	4287010
Carter Model Number	BBD-8146S	BBD-8147S	BBD-8352S	BBD-8348S
Requirement	Can.	Can.	Fed.	Fed.
Engine Displacement (Cu. In.)	318/5.2	318/5.2	225/3.7	318/5.2
Transmission	Auto.	Man.	Man.	Auto.
Bore	1-7/16"	1-7/16"	1-7/16"	1-7/16"
Venturi	1-1/16"	1-1/16"	1-1/16"	1-1/16"
Main Metering Jets				
Standard	.086"	.086"	.086"	.086"
Metering Rods (Standard)	75-2288	75-2092	75-2374	75-2216
Adjustments				
Float Setting (At Center of Floats ± 1/32")	1/4"	1/4"	1/4"	1/4"
Accelerator Pump Setting (At Curb Idle)	.500"	.500"	.500"	.500"
Choke Unloader	.31"	.31"	.31"	.31"
Vacuum Kick	.070"	.150"	.130"	.130"
Fast Idle Cam Position	.070"	.110"	.070"	.070"
Timing	2°ATDC	2°ATDC	12°BTDC	12°BTDC
Propane rpm	800	800	750	830
Idle set rpm	750	750	700	750
Fast idle rpm	1500	1500	1600	1600
Carbon monoxide (co)	*	*		

* Refer To Emissions Label For Carbon Monoxide Percentage.

HOLLEY MODEL 2245 DUAL VENTURI CARBURETORS

Chrysler Number	4241755
Holley Model Number	R-9816A
Requirement	Can.
Engine Displacement (Cu. In.)	360/5.9
Transmission	Automatic
Bore	1-9/16"
Venturi	1-5/16"
Main Metering Jet	632
Adjustments	
Accelerator Pump Setting (From Closed Throttle)	#1 Slot—17/64"
*Dry Float Setting Between Toe of Float and Float Stop (± 1/32")	3/16"
Vacuum Kick	.150"
Fast Idle Cam Position	.110"
Choke Unloader	.170"
Timing	4°BTDC
Propane rpm	810
Idle set rpm	750
Fast idle rpm	1700

HOLLEY MODEL 1945 SINGLE VENTURI CARBURETORS

Chrysler Number	4287014	4287015	4213712	4213711	4213722	4213771
Holley Carburetor Number	R-9765A	R-9762A	R-9153A	R-9132A	R-9399A	R-9134A
Requirement	Fed.	Fed.	Cal.	Cal.	Can.	Can.
Engine (Cubic Inch)	225	225	225	225	225	225
Transmission	Man	Auto	Man	Auto	Man	Auto
Bore	1-11/16"	1-11/16"	1-11/16"	1-11/16"	1-11/16"	1-11/16"
Venturi	1-9/32"	1-9/32"	1-9/32"	1-9/32"	1-9/32"	1-9/32"
Adjustments						
Accelerator Pump	1.70"	1.61"	1.70"	1.61"	1.70"	1.61"
Dry Float Setting ± (1/32)	FLUSH WITH TOP OF BOWL COVER GASKET					
Vacuum Kick	.130"	.130"	.130"	.130"	.130"	.130"
Fast Idle Cam Position	.080"	.090"	.080"	.090"	.080"	.090"
Choke Unloader	.250"	.250"	.250"	.250"	.250"	.250"
Timing	12°BTDC	16°BTDC	12°BTDC	16°BTDC	12°BTDC	16°BTDC
Propane rpm	675	675	825	850	900	900
Idle set rpm	600	600	800	800	725	750
ETC rpm	800	800	—	—	—	—
Fast idle rpm	1800	1600	1800	1600	1800	1600

HOLLEY MODEL 2280 CARBURETORS

Chrysler Number	4241719	4287011	4241721
Holley Carburetor Number	R-9493A	R-9491A	R-9572A
Requirement	Fed.	Fed.-Asp.	Can.
Engine (Cu. In.)	318	318	318
Transmission	Man/Auto	Man/Auto	Man/Auto
Bore	1-7/16"	1-7/16"	1-7/16"
Venturi	1-1/16"	1-1/16"	1-1/16"
Adjustments			
Dry Float Setting (At End of Floats Furthest From Pivot (± 1/32")	9/32"	9/32"	9/32"
Accelerator Pump Setting At Idle)	Flush With Top of Bowl Vent Casting		
Bowl Vent	Non/Adj.	Non/Adj.	
Vacuum Kick	.140"	.140"	.140"
Fast Idle Cam Position	.052"	.052"	.052"
Choke Unloader	.200"	.200"	.200"
Timing	12°BTDC	12°BTDC	12°BTDC
Propane RPM	850	880	850
Idle Set RPM	750	750	750
Fast Idle Speed	1500	1500	1500

HOLLEY MODEL 2280 CARBURETORS

Chrysler Number	4287026	4287028
Holley Carburetor Number	R-9949A	R-9951A
Requirement	Fed.	Fed.-Asp.
Engine (Cu. In.)	318	318
Transmission	Auto	Man/Auto
Bore	1-7/16"	1-7/16"
Venturi	1-1/16"	1-1/16"
Adjustments		
Dry Float Setting (At End of Floats Furthest From Pivot (± 1/32")	9/32"	9/32"
Accelerator Pump Setting At Idle)	Flush With Top of Bowl Vent Casting	
Bowl Vent	Non/Adj.	Non/Adj.
Vacuum Kick	.140"	.140"
Fast Idle Cam Position	.052"	.052"
Choke Unloader	.200"	.200"
Propane RPM	880	850
Idle Set RPM	750	750
Fast Idle Speed	1500	1500

HOLLEY MODEL 2245 DUAL VENTURI CARBURETORS

Chrysler Number	4241755
Holley Model Number	R-9816A
Requirement	Can.
Engine Displacement (Cu. In.)	360/5.9
Transmission	Automatic
Bore	1-9/16"
Venturi	1-5/16"
Main Metering Jet	632
Adjustments	
Accelerator Pump Setting (From Closed Throttle)	#1 Slot—17/64"
Dry Float Setting Between Toe of Float and Float Stop (± 1/32")	3/16"
Vacuum Kick	.150"
Fast Idle Cam Position	.110"
Choke Unloader	.170"
Propane rpm	810
Idle set rpm	750
Fast idle rpm	1700

HOLLEY MODEL 1945 SINGLE VENTURI CARBURETORS

Chrysler Number	4287032	4287033	4287049	4287048
Holley Carburetor Number	R-40055A	R-40056A	R-9399-1A	R-9134-1A
Requirement	Fed.	Fed.	Can.	Can.
Engine (Cubic Inch)	225	225	225	225
Transmission	Man	Auto	Man	Auto
Bore	1-11/16"	1-11/16"	1-11/16"	1-11/16"
Venturi	1-9/32"	1-9/32"	1-9/32"	1-9/32"
Adjustments				
Accelerator Pump	1.70"	1.61"	1.70"	1.61"
Dry Float.Setting ± (1/32) ...	FLUSH WITH TOP OF BOWL COVER GASKET			
Vacuum Kick	.130"	.130"	.130"	.130"
Fast Idle Cam Position	.080"	.090"	.080"	.090"
Choke Unloader	.250"	.250"	.250"	.250"
Propane rpm	675	725	825	850
Idle set rpm	600	650	725	750
ETC rpm	800	800	—	—
Fast idle rpm	1600	1600	1800	1600

HOLLEY MODEL 6145 SINGLE VENTURI CARBURETORS

Chrysler Number	4287019	4287020
Holley Carburetor Number	R-40029A	R-40030A
Requirement	Cal.	Cal.
Engine (Cu. In.)	225	225
Transmission	Man.	Auto
Bore	1-11/16"	1-11/16"
Venturi	1-9/32"	1-9/32"
Adjustments		
Accelerator Pump	1.70"	1.61"
Dry Float Setting	Flush with top of main body casting to .050" above	
Vacuum Kick	.150"	.150"
Fast Idle Cam Position	.090"	.090"
Choke Unloader	.250"	.250"
Propane rpm	850	850
Idle Set RPM	750	750
Solenoid Idle Stop	850	850
Fast Idle Speed	1600	1600

CARTER MODEL BBD CARBURETORS

Chrysler Number	4041580	4041583	4287129	4287055	4287018	4287017
Carter Model Number	BBD-8146S	BBD-8147S	BBD-8371S	BBD-8374S	BBD-8359S	BBD-8358S
Requirement	Can.	Can.	Fed.	Fed.-Hi-Alt.	Cal.	Cal.
Engine Displacement (Cu. In.)	318/5.2	318/5.2	225/3.7	318/5.2	318/5.2	318/5.2
Transmission	Auto.	Man.	Man.	Man./Auto	Auto.	Man.
Bore	1-7/16"	1-7/16"	1-7/16"	1-7/16"	1-7/16"	1-7/16"
Venturi	1-1/16"	1-1/16"	1-1/16"	1-1/16"	1-1/16"	1-1/16"
Adjustments						
Float Setting (At Center of Floats ± (1/32"))	1/4"	1/4"	1/4"	1/4"	1/4"	1/4"
Accelerator Pump Setting (At Curb Idle)	.470"	.470"	.470"	.470"	.470"	.470"
Choke Unloader	.31"	.31"	.28"	.28"	.28"	.28"
Vacuum Kick	.70"	.150"	.130"	.130"	.130"	.130"
Fast Idle Cam Position	.070"	.110"	.070"	.070"	.070"	.070"
Propane rpm	820	800	750	800	760	825
Idle set rpm	750	750	700	800	700	740
Fast idle rpm	1500	1500	1600	1400	1400	1400
Solenoid Idle Stop	—	—	—	850	850	850

CARTER THERMO-QUAD CARBURETORS

Chrysler Number	4287013	4241752	4287016	4241753
Carter Model Number	TQ-9342S	TQ-9375S	TQ-9379S	TQ-9376S
Requirement	Fed.	Fed./Cal.	Fed./Can.	Cal.
Engine Displacement (Cu. In.)	318/5.2	318/5.2	360/5.9	360/5.9
Transmission	Both	Both	Both	Both
Bore				
Primary	1-3/8"	1-3/8"	1-3/8"	1-1/2"
Secondary	2-1/4"	2-1/4"	2-1/4"	2-1/4"
Main Venturi				
Primary	1-1/16"	1-1/16"	1-1/16"	1-3/8"
Secondary		AIR VALVE		
Adjustments				
Float Setting (± 1/32")	29/32"	29/32"	29/32"	29/32"
Secondary Throttle Linkage	Adjust links so that primary and secondary stops both contact at the same time			
Secondary Air Valve Opening	27/64"	3/8"	7/16"	3/8"
Secondary Air Valve Spring Tension (From Contact)	2-1/2 Turns	2-1/2 Turns	2 Turns	2 Turns
Accelerator Pump Stroke (Top of pump plunger stem to top of bowl cover @ curb idle) (Stage 1)	.340"	.340"	.340"	.340"
At Secondary Pick Up (Stage 2)	.190"	.190"	None	.190"
Choke Diaphragm Connector Rod (Clearance between Air Valve and Stop)	.040"	.040"	.040"	.040"
Vaccum Kick**	.130"	.130"	.130"	.180"
Fast Idle Cam Position**	.100"	.130"	.130"	.100"
Choke Unloader (Wide Open Kick)**	.310"	.310"	.310"	.310"
Secondary Throttle Lockout	.060"-.090"	.060"-.090"	.060"-.090"	.060"-.090"
Propane rpm	840	810	800	800
Idle set rpm	750	750	700	750
Fast idle rpm	1600	1800	1500	1700

*Refer To Emissions Label.
**Thermo-Quad Choke Adjustments are measured at the lowest edge of the choke plate.

ROCHESTER QUADRAJET CARBURETORS

	4306417	4306408	4306409	4306431
Chrysler Number	4306417	4306408	4306409	4306431
Vendor Number	17085417	17085408	17085409	17085431
Requirement	Fed.	Fed.	Fed./Alt.	Cal./Can.
Engine	360/5.9L	360/5.9L	360/5.9L	360/5.9L
Transmission	Manual	Automatic	Automatic	Both
Adjustments				
Float		13/32 ± 2/32		
Air Valve Springs	3/4 Turn	1/2 Turn	5/8 Turn	1/2 Turn
Choke Coil Lever	.120"	.120"	.120"	.120"
Choke Rod Fast Idle Cam				
Angle Gauge Method	20°	20°	20°	20°
Plug Gauge Method	.125"	.125"	.125"	.125"
Choke Vacuum Kick				
Angle Gauge Method	27°	27°	27°	27°
Plug Gauge Method	.170"	.170"	.170"	.170"
Air Valve Rod	.025"	.025"	.025"	.025"
Choke Unloader				
Angle Gauge Method	38°	38°	38°	38°
Plug Gauge Method	.260"	.260"	.260"	.260"
Secondary Lockout	.015"	.015"	.015"	.015"
Solenoid Idle rpm		900	850	
Idle rpm				
Fast Idle rpm		Refer to VECI Label		
Propane rpm				

	4306425	4306434
Chrysler Number	4306425	4306434
Vendor Number	17085425	17085434
Requirement	Fed.	Fed.
Engine	360/5.9L	360/5.9L
Transmission	Both	Both
Adjustments		
Float	13/32 ± 2/32	
Air Valve Springs	1/2 Turn	1/2 Turn
Choke Coil Lever	.120"	.120"
Choke Rod Fast Idle Cam		
Angle Gauge Method	20°	20°
Plug Gauge Method	.125"	.125"
Choke Vacuum Kick		
Angle Gauge Method	23°	24°
Plug Gauge Method	.140	.150
Air Valve Rod	.025"	.025"
Choke Unloader		
Angle Gauge Method	38°	38°
Plug Gauge Method	.260"	.260"
Secondary Lockout	.015"	.015"
Solenoid Idle rpm	800	950
Idle rpm		
Fast Idle rpm	Refer to VECI Label	
Propane rpm		

HOLLEY MODEL 1945 SINGLE VENTURI CARBURETORS

Chrysler Number	4306459	4306460	4287076	4300046
Holley Carburetor Number	R-40159	R-40160	R-40102A	R-40244A
Requirement	Fed.	Fed.	Can.	Can.
Engine (Cubic Inch) Liters	225/3.7L	225/3.7L	225/3.7L	225/3.7L
Transmission	Manual	Automatic	Manual	Automatic
Bore	1-11/16"	1-11/16"	1-11/16"	1-11/16"
Venturi	1-9/32"	1-9/32"	1-9/32"	1-9/32"
Adjustments				
Accelerator Pump and Position	1.61" (2)	1.61" (2)	1.70" (1)	1.61" (2)
Dry Float Setting ± (1/32)	FLUSH WITH TOP OF BOWL COVER GASKET			
Vacuum Kick	.130"	.150"	.130"	.130"
Fast Idle Cam Position	.080"	.080"	.080"	.090"
Choke Unloader	.250"	.250"	.250"	.250"
Propane rpm				
Idle rpm	Refer to VECI Label			
Fast Idle rpm				
Solenoid Idle Stop rpm	825	850	—	850

HOLLEY MODEL 6145 SINGLE VENTURI CARBURETORS

Chrysler Number	4306461	4306462
Holley Carburetor Number	R-40161	R-40162
Requirement	Cal.	Cal.
Engine (Cu. In.) Liters	225/3.7L	225/3.7L
Transmission	Manual	Automatic
Bore	1-11/16"	1-11/16"
Venturi	1-9/32"	1-9/32"
Adjustments		
Accelerator Pump and Position	1.75" (2)	1.75" (2)
Dry Float Setting	FLUSH WITH TOP OF BOWL COVER GASKET	
Vacuum Kick	.150"	.150"
Fast Idle Cam Position	.060"	.070"
Choke Unloader	.250"	.250"
Propane rpm		
Idle Set rpm	Refer to VECI Label	
Fast Idle rpm		
Solenoid Idle Stop rpm	850	850

HOLLEY MODEL 2280 CARBURETORS

Chrysler Number	4324629	4324631
Holley Carburetor Number	R-40214A	R-40216A
Requirement	Fed./Can.	Canada
Engine (Cu. In.) Liters	318/5.2L	318/5.2L
Transmission	Both	Automatic
Bore	1-7/16"	1-7/16"
Venturi	1-1/16"	1-1/16"
Adjustments		
Dry Float Setting (At End of Floats Furthest From Pivot (± 1/32")	9/32"	9/32"
Accelerator Pump Setting (At Idle)	.210"	.210"
Vacuum Kick	.140"	.140"
Fast Idle Cam Position	.070"	.070"
Choke Unloader	.250"	.250"
Bowl Vent	.035"	.035"
Propane rpm		
Idle rpm .... }	Refer to VECI Label	
Fast Idle rpm		
Solenoid rpm	875	875

HOLLEY MODEL 6280 CARBURETORS

Chrysler Number	4324632	4324633
Holley Carburetor Number	R-40221A	R-40222A
Requirement	Federal, Altitude	California
Engine (Cu. In.) Liters	318/5.2L	318/5.2L
Transmission	Both	Both
Bore	1-7/16"	1-7/16"
Venturi	1-1/16"	1-1/16"
Adjustments		
Dry Float Setting (At End of Floats Furthest From Pivot (±1/32")	9/32"	9/32"
Accelerator Pump Setting (At Idle)	.210"	.210"
Vacuum Kick	.130"	.130"
Fast Idle Cam Position	.070"	.070"
Choke Unloader	.150"	.150"
Propane rpm		
Idle rpm .... }	Refer to VECI Label	
Fast Idle rpm		
Solenoid rpm	780	850* 800

* Manual Transmission

CARTER MODEL BBD CARBURETOR

Carter Model Number	BBD-8085S	BBD-8115S	BBD-8081S	BBD-8082S	BBD-8108S	BBD-8146S
Requirement	**Fed/Can**	**Fed/Can**	**Fed/Can/Calif**	**Calif**	**Fed/Calif**	**Fed/Can**
Engine Displacement (Cu. In.)	318-1	318-1	318-1	318-1	318-1	318-1
Transmission	Man	Man/4 Sp.	Auto	Man	Auto	Man
Bore	1-7/16″	1-7/16″	1-7/16″	1-7/16″	1-7/16″	1-7/16″
Venturi	1-3/16″	1-3/16″	1-3/16″	1-3/16″	1-3/16″	1-3/16″
Main Metering Jets						
Standard	120-392	120-389	120-392	120-392	120-392	120-386
Metering Rods (Standard)	2105	2170	2158	2104	2158	2092
Adjustments						
Step-Up Piston Gap	.035	.035	.035	.035	.035	.035
Float Setting (At Center of Floats (± 1/32″)	.250	.250	.250	.250	.250	.250
Accelerator Pump Setting (At Idle)	.500	.500	.500	.500	.500	.500
Choke Unloader	.280	.280	.280	.280	.310	.280
Idle Speed RPM (Curb Idle)	750	750	750	750	750	750
Vacuum Kick	.130	.130	.150	.130	.150	.070
Fast Idle Cam Position	.070	.070	.070	.070	.070	.070
Fast Idle Speed (RPM after 500 Miles)	1500	1500	1500	1500	1500	1600
Ignition Timing	2B	2B	2B(TDC-Calif.)	2BTDC	Cal. TDC	2 ATC
*Carbon Monoxide (enriched or speed rise)	.5%-(850)	.3%-(850)	.5%-(920)	.3%	.3%	800

Carter Model Number	BBD-8147S BBD-8121S	BBD-8113S	BBD-8112S	BBD-6585S	BBD-8110S	BBD-6586S
Requirement	**Fed/Can**	**Calif**	**Fed. Altitude**	**Fed/Can**	**Fed/Can**	**Fed/Can**
Engine Displacement (Cu. In.)	318-1	318-1	318-1	318-3	225	318-3
Transmission	Auto	Man/Auto	Auto	Man	Man/Auto	Auto
Bore	1-7/16″	1-7/16″	1-7/16″	1-7/16″	1-7/16″	1-7/16″
Venturi	1-3/16″	1-3/16″	1-3/16″	1-3/16″	1-3/16″	1-3/16″
Main Metering Jets						
Standard	120-386	120-392	120-392	120-392	120-392	120-392
Metering Rods (Standard)	2092	2083	2112	2023	2203	2023
Adjustments						
Step-Up Piston Gap	.035″	.035″	.035″	.035″	.035″	.035″
Float Setting (At Center of Floats (± 1/32″)	1/4″	1/4″	1/4″	1/4″	1/4″	1/4″
Accelerator Pump Setting (At Idle)	.500″	.500″	.500″	.500″	.500″	.500″
Choke Unloader	.310	.310	.310	—	.380	—
Idle Speed RPM (Curb Idle)	750	700	750	700	700	700
Vacuum Kick	.070	.130	.110	—	.095	—
Fast Idle Cam Position	.070	.070	.070	—	.070	—
Fast Idle Speed (RPM after 500 Miles)	1500	1500	1500	1900	1500	1900
Ignition Timing	2 ATC	TDC	6BTDC	TDC	TDC	TDC
*Carbon Monoxide (enriched or speed rise)	820	.5%T	885	750	750-M 770-Auto.	770

*P = @ Front of Catalyst   T = @ Tailpipe

HOLLEY MODEL 1945 SINGLE VENTURI CARBURETOR

Holley Carburetor Number	R-7849A	R-7815A	R-7816A	R-7847A	R-7848A
Requirement	**Fed/Can**	**Calif**	**Calif**	**Fed/Can**	**Fed/Can**
Engine Displacement (Cu. In.)	225-1	225-1	225-1	225-1	225-1
Transmission	4 Sp/OD	Man	Auto	Man	Auto
Bore	1-11/16″	1-11/16″	1-11/16″	1-11/16″	1-11/16″
Venturi	1-9/32″	1-9/32″	1-9/32″	1-9/32″	1-9/32″
Main Metering Jet	#623	#631	#623	#623	#623
Adjustments					
Accelerator Pump	2-21/64″	2-7/32″	2-21/64″	2-7/32″	2-21/64″
Dry Float Setting (± 1/32″)	3/64″	3/64″	3/64″	3/64″	3/64″
Vacuum Kick	.110	.110	.110	.110	.110
Fast Idle Cam Position	.080	.080	.080	.080	.080
Choke Unloader	.250	.250	.250	.250	.250
Curb Idle Speed (RPM)	750	800	750	750	750
Fast Idle Speed (RPM after 500 miles)	1600	1600	1700	1600	1700
Ignition Timing	2BTDC	TDC	2ATDC	2BTDC	2BTDC
*Carbon Monoxide (CO) (enriched or speed rise)	825	.3%P	.3%P	825	825

*P = @ Front of Catalyst
T = @ Tailpipe

ROCHESTER QUADRAJET CARBURETORS

Chrysler Number	4306420	4306419	4306424	4306431
Vendor Number	17087176	17087175	17087177	17085431
Requirement	Fed.	Fed.	Fed./Alt.	Can./Can.
Engine	360/5.9L	360/5.9L	360/5.9L	360/5.9L
Transmission	Manual	Automatic	Manual	Both
Adjustments				
Float		13/32±2/32		
Air Valve Springs	3/4 Turn	3/4 Turn	1 Turn	1/2 Turn
Chock Coil Lever	.120"	.120"	.120"	.120"
Choke Rod Fast Idle Cam				
Angle Gauge Method	20°	20°	20°	20°
Plug Gauge Method	.125"	.125"	.125"	.125"
Choke Vacuum Kick				
Angle Gauge Method	.26°	.26°	.27°	.23°
Plug Gauge Method	.150"	.150"	.170"	.140"
Air Valve Rod	.025"	.025"	.025"	.025"
Choke Unloader				
Angle Gauge Method	30°	30°	33°	32°
Plug Gauge Method	.200"	.200"	.220"	.209"
Secondary Lockout	.015"	.015"	.015"	.015"
Solenoid Idle rpm	800	850	850	
Idle rpm				
Fast Idle rpm		Refer to EAR Label		
Propane rpm				

Chrysler Number	4306425		4306437
Vendor Number	17086425		17087245
Requirement	Can/Fed.		Can/Fed.
Engine	360/5.9L		360/5.9L
Transmission	Both		Both
Adjustments			
Float		13/32±2/32	
Air Valve Springs	1/2 Turn		5/8 Turn
Choke Coil Lever	.120"		.120"
Choke Rod Fast Idle Cam			
Angle Gauge Method	20°		20°
Plug Gauge Method	.125"		.125"
Choke Vacuum Kick			
Angle Gauge Method	.23°		.23°
Plug Gauge Method	.140		.140
Air Valve Rod	.025"		.025"
Choke Unloader			
Angle Gauge Method	38°		32°
Plug Gauge Method	.260"		.209"
Secondary Lockout	.015"		.015"
Solenoid Idle rpm	950		950
Idle rpm			
Fast Idle rpm		Refer to EAR Label	
Propane rpm			

THROTTLE BODY FUEL INJECTION SYSTEM

Description

▶ **See Figure 65**

The TBI system is used on 1988 238 and 318 engines. The system is controlled by a pre-programmed digital computer known as the Single Module Engine Controller. The SMEC controls ignition timing, air/fuel ratio, emission control devices, charging system and idle speed. The SMEC constantly varies all settings to meet changing operating conditions.

Various sensors provide the input necessary for the logic module or SMEC to correctly regulate the fuel flow at the fuel injector. These include the manifold absolute pressure, throttle position, oxygen sensor, coolant temperature, charge temperature, vehicle speed (distance) sensors and throttle body temperature. In addition to the sensors, various switches also provide important information. These include the neutral-safety, heated backlite, air conditioning, air conditioning clutch switches, and an electronic idle switch.

All inputs to the logic module or SMEC are converted into signals sent to the power module. These signals cause the power module to change either the fuel flow at the injector or ignition timing or both.

The SMEC tests many of its own input and output circuits. If a fault is found in a major system this information is stored in the logic module or SMEC. Information on this fault can be displayed to a technician by means of the instrument panel power loss (check engine) lamp or by connecting a diagnostic read out and reading a numbered display code which directly relates to a specific fault.

COMPONENTS

Throttle Body

The throttle body assembly replaces a conventional carburetor and is mounted on top of the intake manifold. The throttle body houses the fuel injector, pressure regulator, throttle position sensor, automatic idle speed motor and throttle body temperature sensor. Air flow through the throttle body is controlled by a cable operated throttle blade located in the base of the throttle body. The throttle body itself provides the chamber for metering atomizing and distributing fuel throughout the air entering the engine.

Fuel Injector

The fuel injector is an electric solenoid driven by the power module, but controlled by the SMEC. The SMEC, based on ambient, mechanical, and sensor input, determines when and how long the power module should operate the injector. When an electric current is supplied to the injector, a spring loaded ball is lifted from its seat. This allows fuel to flow through six spray orifices

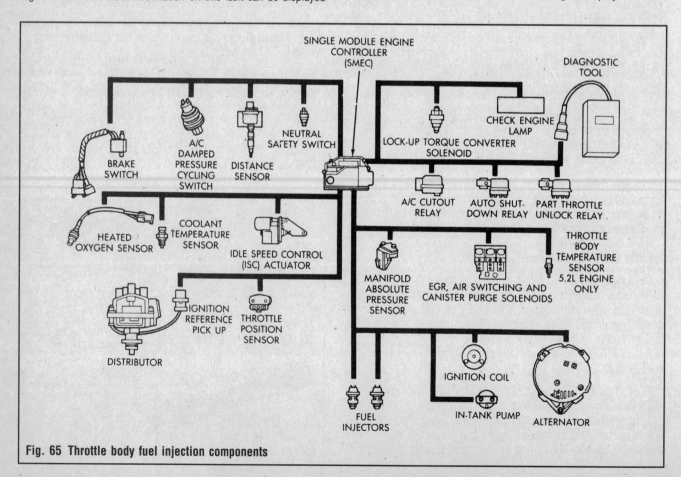

Fig. 65 Throttle body fuel injection components

and deflects off the sharp edge of the injector nozzle. This action causes the fuel to form a 45° cone shaped spray pattern before entering the air stream in the throttle body.

Fuel Pressure Regulator

The pressure regulator is a mechanical device located downstream of the fuel injector on the throttle body. Its function is to maintain a constant 14.5 psi across the fuel injector tip. The regulator uses a spring loaded rubber diaphragm to uncover a fuel return port. When the fuel pump becomes operational, fuel flows past the injector into the regulator, and is restricted from flowing any further by the blocked return port. When fuel pressure reaches the predetermined setting, it pushes on the diaphragm, compressing the spring, and uncovers the fuel return port. The diaphragm and spring will constantly move from an open to closed position to keep the fuel pressure constant.

Throttle Position Sensor (TPS)

The Throttle Position Sensor (TPS) is an electric resistor which is activated by the movement of the throttle shaft. It is mounted on the throttle body and senses the angle of the throttle blade opening. The voltage that the sensor produces increases or decreases according to the throttle blade opening. This voltage is transmitted to the SMEC, where it is used along with data from other sensors to adjust the air/fuel ratio to varying conditions and during acceleration, deceleration, idle, and wide open throttle operations.

Automatic Idle Speed (AIS) Motor

The Automatic Idle Speed (AIS) motor is operated by the SMEC. Data from the throttle position sensor, speed sensor, coolant temperature sensor, and various switch operations, (electric backlite, air conditioning, safety/neutral, brake) are used by the module to adjust engine idle to an optimum during all idle conditions. The AIS adjusts the air portion of the air/fuel mixture through an air bypass on the back of the throttle body. Basic (no load) idle is determined by the minimum air flow through the throttle body. The AIS opens or closes off the air bypass as an increase or decrease is needed due to engine loads or ambient conditions. The module senses an air/fuel change and increases or decreases fuel proportionally to change engine idle. Deceleration die out is also prevented by increasing engine idle when the throttle is closed quickly after a driving (speed) condition.

Throttle Body Temperature Sensor

The throttle body temperature sensor is a device that monitors throttle body temperature which is the same as fuel temperature. It is mounted in the throttle body. This sensor provides information on fuel temperature which allows the SMEC to provide the correct air fuel mixture for a hot restart condition.

Fuel Pump

The fuel pump used in this system is a positive displacement, roller vane immersible pump with a permanent magnet electric motor. The fuel is drawn in through a filter sock and pushed through the electric motor to the outlet. The pump contains two check valves. One valve is used to relieve internal fuel pump pressure and regulate maximum pump output. The other check valve, located near the pump outlet, restricts fuel movement in either direc-

tion when the pump is not operational. Voltage to operate the pump is supplied through the auto shutdown relay (ASD).

Service Precautions

1. When working around any part of the fuel system, take precautionary steps to prevent possible fire and/or explosion:
    a. Disconnect the negative battery terminal, except when testing with battery voltage is required.
    b. Whenever possible, use a flashlight instead of a drop light to inspect fuel system components or connections.
    c. Keep all open flames and smoking material out of the area and make sure there is adequate ventilation to remove fuel vapors.
    d. Use a clean shop cloth to catch fuel when opening a fuel system. Dispose of gasoline-soaked rags properly.
    e. Relieve the fuel system pressure before any service procedures are attempted that require disconnecting a fuel line.
    f. Use eye protection.
    g. Always keep a dry chemical (class B) fire extinguisher near the area.

➡**Many procedures may require new seals or gaskets for assembly. Read through the procedure first to ensure that you have all of the necessary components.**

Minimum Idle Speed Adjustment

◗ **See Figure 66**

➡**Normal idle speed is controlled by the SMEC. This adjustment is the minimum idle speed with the Automatic Idle Speed (AIS) motor closed.**

1. Before adjusting the idle on an electronic fuel injected vehicle the following items must be checked.
    a. AIS motor has been checked for operation.
    b. Engine has been checked for vacuum or EGR leaks.
    c. Engine timing has been checked and set to specifications.
    d. Coolant temperature sensor has been checked for operation.
2. Connect a tachometer and timing light to engine.

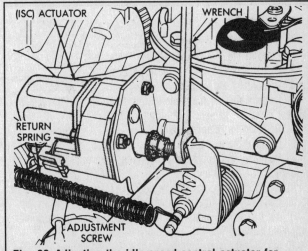

Fig. 66 Adjusting the idle speed control actuator for minimum idle speed

3. Close AIS by using ATM tester C-4805 or equivalent, ATM test code #03.

4. Connect a jumper to radiator fan so that it will run continuously.

5. Start and run the engine for 3 minutes to allow the idle speed to stabilize.

6. Check engine rpm and compare the result with the specifications listed on the underhood emission control sticker.

7. If idle rpm is not within specifications, use tool C-4804 or equivalent to turn the idle speed adjusting screw to obtain 800 ± 10 rpm. If the underhood emission sticker specifications are different, use those values for adjustment.

➡ **If idle will not adjust down check for binding linkage, speed control servo cable adjustment or throttle shaft binding.**

8. Turn off the engine, disconnect tachometer, reinstall AIS wire and remove jumper wire from fan motor.

✳✳ CAUTION

The fuel injection system is under a constant pressure of approximately 14.5 psi. Before servicing any part of the fuel injection system, the system pressure must be released. Use a clean shop towel to catch any fuel spray and take precautions to avoid the risk of fire.

Fuel System Pressure Release

1. Loosen the gas cap to release tank pressure.
2. Remove the wiring harness connector from the injector.
3. Ground one terminal of the injector.
4. Connect a jumper wire to the second terminal and touch the battery positive post for no longer than ten seconds. This releases system pressure.
5. Remove the jumper wire and continue fuel system service.

Throttle Body

REMOVAL & INSTALLATION

▸ **See Figure 67**

1. Remove the air cleaner.
2. Perform the fuel system pressure release.
3. Disconnect the negative battery cable.
4. Disconnect the vacuum hoses and electrical connectors.
5. Remove the throttle cable and, if so equipped, speed control and kickdown cables.
6. Remove the return spring.
7. Remove the fuel intake and return hoses.
8. Remove the throttle body mounting screws and lift the throttle body from the engine.
9. When installing the throttle body, use a new gasket. Install the throttle body and torque the mounting screws to 175 in. lbs.
10. Install the fuel intake and return hoses using new original equipment type clamps.
11. Install the return spring.
12. Install the throttle cable and, if so equipped, install the kickdown and speed control cables.

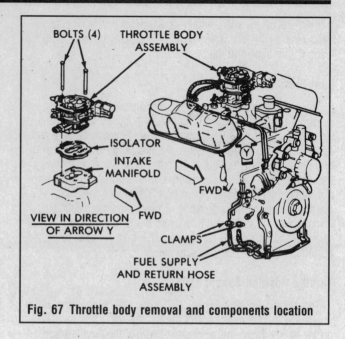

Fig. 67 Throttle body removal and components location

13. Install the wiring connectors and vacuum hoses.
14. Install the air cleaner.
15. Reconnect the negative battery cable.

Fuel Fittings

REMOVAL & INSTALLATION

▸ **See Figure 68**

1. Remove the air cleaner assembly.
2. Perform the fuel system pressure release.
3. Disconnect the negative battery cable.
4. Loosen the fuel intake and return hose clamps. Wrap a shop towel around each hose, twist and pull off each hose.
5. Remove each fitting and note the inlet diameter. Remove the copper washers.

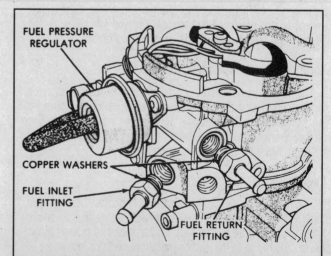

Fig. 68 Mounting details of the fuel inlet and return fittings on the injector throttle body

To install:

6. Replace the copper washers with new washers.

7. Install the fuel fittings in the proper ports and torque to 175 inch lbs.

8. Using new original equipment type hose clamps, install the fuel return and supply hoses.

9. Reconnect the negative battery cable.

10. Test for leaks using ATM tester C-4805 or equivalent. With the ignition in the **RUN** position depress the ATM button. This will activate the pump and pressurize the system. Check for leaks.

11. Reinstall the air cleaner assembly.

Fuel Pressure Regulator

REMOVAL & INSTALLATION

▶ **See Figure 69**

1. Remove the air cleaner assembly.

2. Perform the fuel system pressure release.

3. Disconnect the negative battery cable.

4. Remove the three screws attaching the pressure regulator to the throttle body. Place a shop towel around the inlet chamber to contain any fuel remaining in the system.

5. Pull the pressure regulator from the throttle body.

6. Carefully remove the O-ring from the pressure regulator and remove the gasket.

7. To install, place a new gasket on the pressure regulator and carefully install a new O-ring.

8. Position the pressure regulator on the throttle body press it into place.

9. Install the three screws and torque them to 40 in. lbs.

10. Connect the negative battery cable.

11. Test for leaks using ATM tester C-4805 or equivalent. With the ignition in the **RUN** position depress ATM button. This will activate the pump and pressurize the system. Check for leaks.

12. Reinstall the air cleaner assembly.

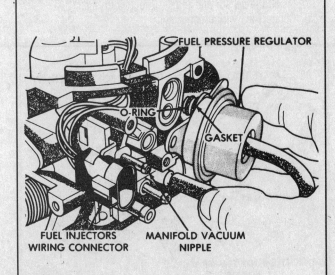

Fig. 69 Fuel pressure regulator mounting for fuel injected vehicles

Fuel Injector

REMOVAL & INSTALLATION

▶ **See Figures 70, 71 and 72**

1. Remove the air cleaner assembly.

2. Perform the fuel system pressure release.

3. Disconnect the negative battery cable.

4. Remove the fuel pressure regulator.

5. Remove the Torx® screw holding down the injector cap.

6. With two small screwdrivers, lift the cap off the injector using the slots provided.

7. Using a small screwdriver placed in the hole in the front of the electrical connector, gently pry the injector from pod.

8. Make sure the injector lower O-ring has been removed from the pod.

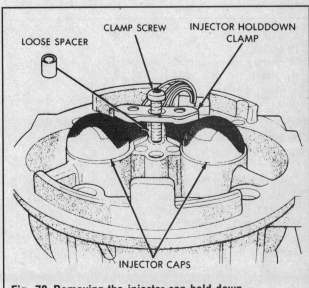

Fig. 70 Removing the injector cap hold-down

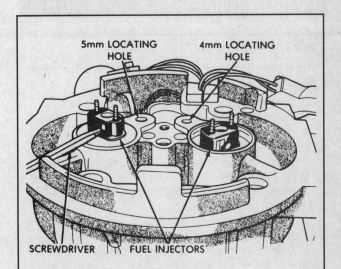

Fig. 71 Remove the fuel injector from the throttle body by gently prying it up

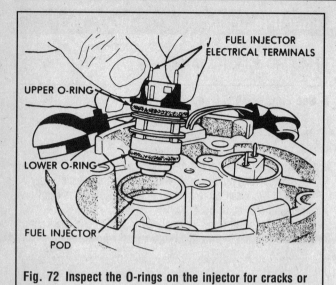

Fig. 72 Inspect the O-rings on the injector for cracks or splits

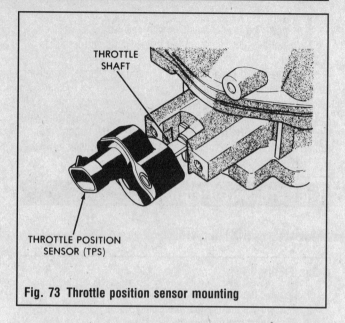

Fig. 73 Throttle position sensor mounting

To install:

9. Place a new lower O-ring on the injector and a new O-ring on the injector cap. The injector will have the upper O-ring already installed.

10. Put the injector cap on injector. (Injector and cap are keyed). The cap should sit on the injector without interference. Apply a light coating of castor oil or petroleum jelly on the O-rings. Place the assembly in the pod.

11. Rotate the cap and injector to line up the attachment hole.

12. Push down on the cap until it contacts the injector pod.

13. Install the Torx® screw and torque it to 35–45 in. lbs.

14. Install the fuel pressure regulator.

15. Connect the negative battery cable.

16. Test for leaks using ATM tester C-4805 or equivalent. With the ignition in the **RUN** position depress the ATM button. This will activate the pump and pressurize the system. Check for leaks.

17. Reinstall the air cleaner assembly.

Throttle Position Sensor

REMOVAL & INSTALLATION

▶ **See Figure 73**

1. Disconnect the negative battery cable.
2. Remove the air cleaner.
3. Disconnect the three way connector at the throttle position sensor.
4. Remove the two screws mounting the throttle position sensor to the throttle body.
5. Lift the throttle position sensor off the throttle shaft.

To install:

6. Install the throttle position sensor on the throttle body. Position the connector toward the rear of vehicle.
7. Connect the three way connector at the throttle position sensor.
8. Install the air cleaner.
9. Connect the negative battery cable.
10. Check operation with sensor read test #5.

Throttle Body Temperature Sensor

REMOVAL & INSTALLATION

▶ **See Figure 74**

1. Remove the air cleaner.
2. Disconnect the throttle cables from the throttle body linkage.
3. Remove the two screws from the throttle cable bracket and lay the bracket aside.
4. Disconnect the wiring connector.
5. Unscrew the sensor.

To install:

6. Apply heat transfer compound to the tip portion of the new sensor.
7. Install the sensor and torque it to 100 in. lbs.
8. Connect the wiring connector.

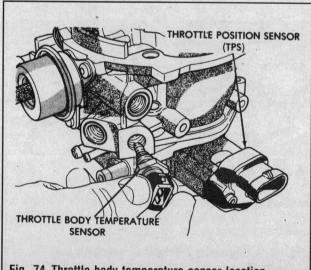

Fig. 74 Throttle body temperature sensor location

9. Install the throttle cable bracket with two screws.

10. Connect the throttle cables to the throttle body linkage and install the clips.

11. Install the air cleaner.

Automatic Idle Speed (AIS) Motor Assembly

REMOVAL & INSTALLATION

1. Remove the air cleaner.
2. Disconnect the negative battery cable.
3. Disconnect the four pin connector on the AIS.
4. Remove the temperature sensor from the throttle body housing.
5. Remove the two Torx® head screws.
6. Remove the AIS from the throttle body housing, making sure that the O-ring is with the AIS.

To install:

7. Be sure that the pintle is in the retracted position. If the pintle measures more than 1", it must be retracted by using ATM test code #03.

➡**The battery must be connected for this operation.**

8. Install new a O-ring on the AIS.
9. Install the AIS into the housing making sure the O-ring is in place.
10. Install the two Torx® head screws.
11. Connect the four pin connector to the AIS.
12. Install the temperature sending unit into the throttle body housing.
13. Connect the negative battery cable.

Fuel Pump

The TBI system uses an electric fuel pump mounted in the fuel tank.

TESTING

1. Remove the fuel intake hose from the throttle body and connect fuel system pressure testers C-3292, and C-4749, or equivalent, between the fuel filter hose and the throttle body.

2. Start the engine and read the gauge. Pressure should be 14.5 psi.

➡**ATM tester C-4805 or equivalent can be used. With the ignition in RUN, depress the ATM button. This activates the fuel pump and pressurizes the system.**

3. If the fuel pressure is below specifications:

   a. Install the tester between the fuel filter hose and the fuel line.

b. Start the engine. If the pressure is now correct, replace the fuel filter. If no change is observed, gently squeeze the return hose. If the pressure increases, replace the pressure regulator. If no change is observed, the problem is either a plugged pump filter sock or a defective fuel pump.

4. If the pressure is above specifications:

   a. Remove the fuel return hose from the throttle body. Connect a substitute hose and place the other end of the hose in a clean container.

   b. Start the engine. If the pressure is now correct, check for a restricted fuel return line. If no change is observed, replace the fuel regulator.

REMOVAL & INSTALLATION

▶ **See Figures 75, 76, 77 and 78**

✳✳ CAUTION

Perform the fuel pressure release procedure.

1. Remove the fuel tank from the truck.
2. Remove the locking ring and lift out the fuel pump module.
3. Remove the sending unit attaching screws from the mounting bracket located on the drain tube.
4. Disconnect the wires from the sending unit and remove the sending unit.
5. Remove the drain tube from the mounting lug at the bottom of the reservoir.
6. Remove the lower-most coil of the drain tube from the mounting lugs on top of the reservoir. Be careful to avoid unsnapping the return line check valve cover from the bottom of the reservoir.
7. Release the pump mounting bracket from the reservoir. Press the bracket with both thumbs toward the center of the reservoir.
8. Remove the pump mounting bracket and rubber collar from the hose. Cut the hose clamp on the supply line and discard the clamp. Remove the pump/filter assembly. Pry the filter from the pump.

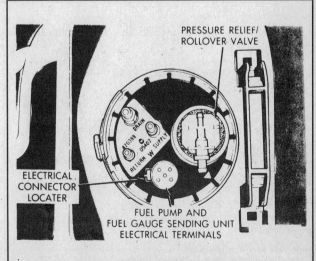

Fig. 75 Top view of the fuel pump module

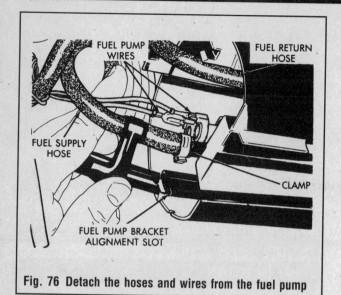

Fig. 76 Detach the hoses and wires from the fuel pump

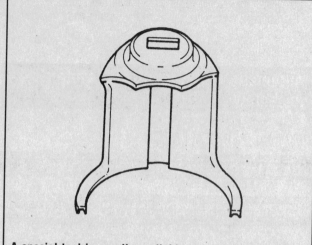

A special tool is usually available to remove or install the fuel pump locking cam

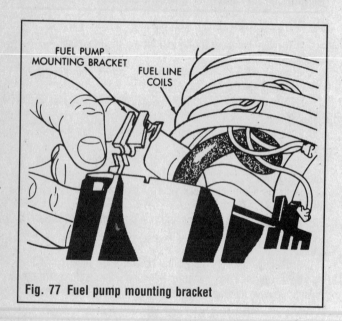

Fig. 77 Fuel pump mounting bracket

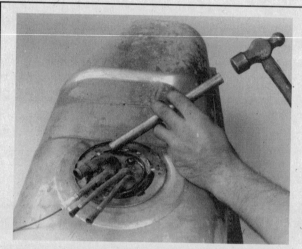

A brass drift and a hammer can be used to loosen the fuel pump locking cam

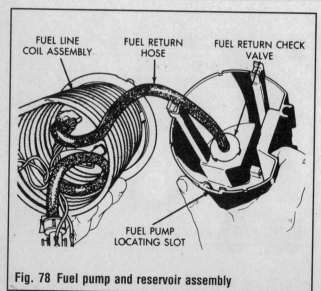

Fig. 78 Fuel pump and reservoir assembly

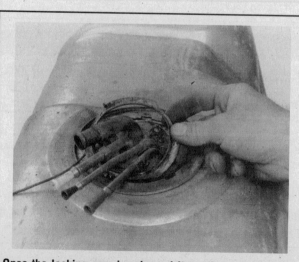

Once the locking cam is released it can be removed to free the fuel pump

To install:

9. Press a new filter onto the pump.

10. Using a new clamp, attach the supply hose.

11. Position the pump mounting bracket and rubber collar on the supply hose between the bulge in the hose and the pump.

12. Position the pump in the reservoir so that the filter aligns with the cavity in the reservoir.

13. Snap the pump bracket into the reservoir.

14. Position the coil tube on the reservoir so that the drain tube aligns with the mounting lugs on the reservoir.

15. Snap the lower-most coil into the mounting lugs on top of the reservoir.

16. Snap the drain tube into the lugs on the bottom of the reservoir.

17. Connect the wires to the new sending unit.

18. Align the index tab on the level unit with the index hole in the mounting bracket.

19. Install the level unit screws.

20. Install the assembly in the tank.

DIESEL FUEL SYSTEM

General Information

▶ **See Figure 79**

The diesel engine fuel system consists of the fuel tank, fuel line, feed pump, fuel filter, injection pump, injector lines, nozzle holders and nozzles, leak-off lines, and the fuel return line.

※※ CAUTION

Observe caution when working with any diesel fuel system. At specified pressure, fuel can be sprayed through the flesh of a hand or an arm. Diesel fuel injected in this way can enter the blood stream!

The feed pump draws fuel from the tank through the fuel line. It passes through the fuel filter mounted at the back of the intake manifold and enters the injection pump. At the proper intervals, the injection pump forces fuel at high pressure into the injector lines. High-pressure fuel is sprayed into the combustion chambers through the nozzles. Fuel not used during operation is drawn off the leakoff lines and returned to the fuel tank by the fuel return line.

Bleeding the Fuel System

▶ **See Figure 80**

Air entrapped in the fuel system can cause inadequate fuel injection, poor operation, and hard starting. Whenever the fuel system is serviced, it should be bled of entrapped air in the proper sequence.

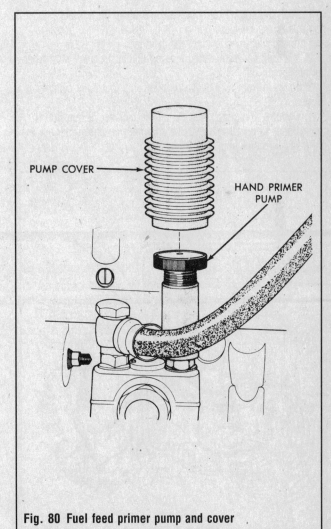

Fig. 80 Fuel feed primer pump and cover

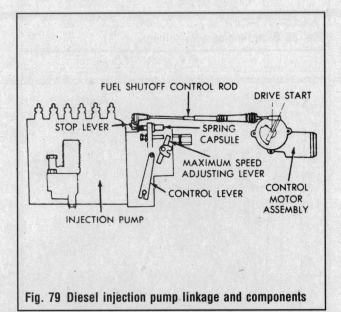

Fig. 79 Diesel injection pump linkage and components

PROCEDURE

1. Loosen the fuel filter petcock or valve and operate the priming pump on the feed pump. If the filter is filled with fuel, fuel containing air bubbles will be discharged from the petcock or valve. Continue pumping until the discharge fuel contains no more air bubbles. Then tighten the fuel valve or petcock securely.

2. Loosen the air bleeder screw at the top of the injection pump and operate the priming pump. Continue pumping until all air is bled from the fuel in the pump reservoir. Then close the air bleeder screw securely.

Injection Pump

♦ **See Figure 81**

TESTING

➡**This procedure is performed with the injection pump installed.**

1. With the engine running, loosen the cap on the fuel injection line at the injection pump outlet. This will relieve pressure and prevent fuel injection into the cylinder.

2. If a cylinder is misfiring, uneven combustion will stop when the fuel is cut off.

3. Proceed from cylinder to cylinder until the faulty cylinder is located.

4. Perform a compression test on the cylinder in question. If the cylinder in question meets the compression specifications, replace the injection pump.

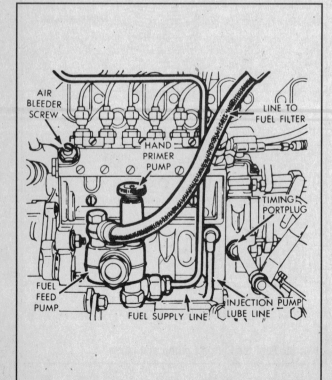

Fig. 81 Diesel injection pump components

REMOVAL & INSTALLATION

♦ **See Figures 82 and 83**

1. Disconnect the batteries.

2. Disconnect the fuel shutoff rod at the stop lever.

3. Remove the power steering pump and the mounting bracket from the engine and set it aside.

4. Thoroughly clean the area around the hose fittings and the injection pipes.

5. Drain the engine oil and remove the dipstick and the dipstick tube.

6. Disconnect the throttle cable and the linkage from the injection pump control lever.

7. Remove the throttle control bracket assembly from the crankcase, injection pump and the control bracket and set it aside.

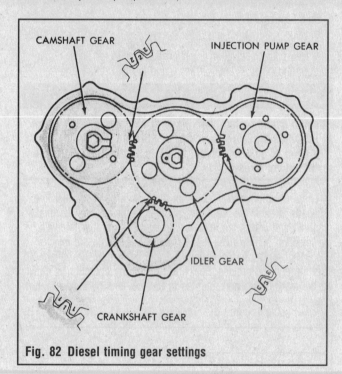

Fig. 82 Diesel timing gear settings

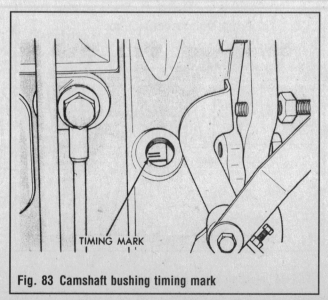

Fig. 83 Camshaft bushing timing mark

8. Disconnect the fuel supply line to the fuel feed pump and set it aside, loosening the anchoring clamps as necessary.

9. Disconnect the fuel hoses leading to the filter from the feed pump and the injection pump. Replace the screws and seals to prevent dirt from getting into the pump.

10. Rotate the engine so piston no. 1 is approximately 7° before top dead center on the compression stroke.

11. Disconnect the injection pipes from the delivery valves and set them aside. Cap the ends of the valves to prevent the entry of dirt.

12. Disconnect the injection pump lube lines.

13. Remove the five screws and one bolt attaching the pump.

14. Pull the pump to the rear and disengage it from the front plate and timing gear case. Rotate the pump toward the crankcase and continue pulling it to the rear until the automatic timer is freed.

To install:

15. Loosen the four nuts attaching the pump to the mounting flange plate and align the center timing mark on the pump flange with the pointer on the plate. Tighten the four nuts.

16. Be sure that the O-ring is in place on the forward face of the pump mounting flange.

17. Remove the threaded timing port plug on the governor housing behind the control lever to expose the camshaft bushing timing mark. Rotate the pump drive gear to align the timing mark on the camshaft bushing with the pointer on the governor. The guide plate notch will be approximately the 8 o'clock position as viewed from the front. Be sure the engine is positioned as described in step 10 of the removal procedure.

18. Insert the automatic timer into the timing gear case and with the injection pump rotated against the crankshaft, rotate the pump driver gear to mesh the drive and idler gears. Do not force the pump into position.

19. Push the pump forward into the case. Rotate it away from the crankcase to align the attachment holes.

20. Attach the pump to the timing gear case.

21. Rotate the engine crankshaft in the opposite direction of normal operation until the crankshaft reaches the 18° before TDC mark on the crankshaft pulley. The governor pointer and the injec-

tion pump camshaft bushing timing marks should now be aligned. If they are not aligned, the pump has been installed incorrectly and must be removed and reinstalled.

22. Install the governor housing timing port plug and proceed with the pump installation by reversing the remainder of the removal procedure. Do not connect the no. 1 injecting pipe, fuel control rod or the batteries.

23. Bleed the air from the fuel filter and the injection pump by removing the air bleeder screws.

24. Time the injection pump.

INJECTION PUMP TIMING

▶ **See Figure 84**

1. Disconnect the batteries and the fuel shut off rod at the stop lever.

2. Rotate the crankshaft in the direction of normal operation until no. 1 cylinder reaches top dead center of the compression stroke. This is done by aligning the lines on the crankshaft pulley rear face with the pointer on the bottom of the case.

3. Remove the forward oil filler cap on the rocker cover and check the no. 1 cylinder valves for looseness. If they are loose, you are at TDC.

4. Rotate the crankshaft in the normal direction of engine operation 1¾ turns.

5. Disconnect no. 1 injection pipe from the delivery valve holder.

6. Turn the crankshaft in the normal direction of engine operation in small steps. Stop when fuel begins to flow from the delivery valve holder. Injection begins at this point. The control lever must be in the idle position.

7. Read the injection timing point from the scale on the back of the crankshaft damper. If the timing is correct, the timing mark should be at the value shown on the Vehicle Emission Control Information label on the rocker cover ± 2 degrees.

8. If the timing point determined differs from the standard value, minus 2 degrees, loosen the four pump-to-flange plate nuts and rotate the pump (toward the crankcase to advance the timing,

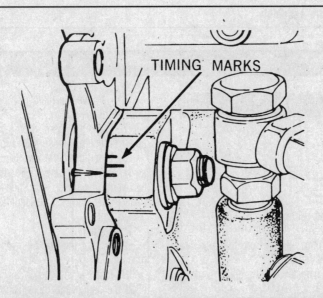

Fig. 84 Injection pump timing marks

away from the crankcase to retard it) to correct the difference. Each mark on the injection pump timing scale represents 6 degrees. Tighten the flange plate nuts and repeat the timing procedure to be sure the timing is correct.

Nozzle Holder and Tip

REMOVAL & INSTALLATION

▶ See Figure 85

1. Remove the injection line at the nozzle holder.
2. Unscrew the nozzle holder.

3. Place the nozzle holder in a vise bearing on the nut.
4. Remove the nozzle body from the nut. Lift the pressure adjusting shim, spring, retaining pin, spacer and nozzle tip from the nozzle holder body.
5. Clean all parts in clean fuel oil. Replace any part which shows signs of wear or damage.
6. Assemble all parts and install the assembly in the engine. Torque the assembly to 45–55 ft. lbs. Connect the injection line.

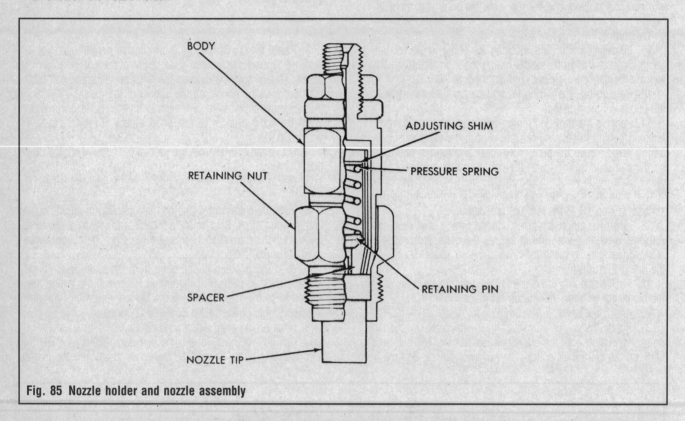

BODY

ADJUSTING SHIM

PRESSURE SPRING

RETAINING NUT

SPACER

RETAINING PIN

NOZZLE TIP

Fig. 85 Nozzle holder and nozzle assembly

FUEL TANK

Tank Assembly

REMOVAL & INSTALLATION

▶ See Figures 86, 87 and 88

1. Disconnect the battery ground cable.
2. Remove the fuel tank filler cap.
3. Raise the vehicle on a lift. Pump all fuel from the tank into an approved holding tank, and raise the vehicle.
4. Disconnect the fuel line and wire lead to the gauge unit. Remove the ground strap.
5. Remove the vent hose shield and the hose clamps from the hoses running to the vapor vent tube.

6. Remove the filler tube hose clamps and disconnect the hose from the tank.
7. Place a transmission jack under the center of the tank and apply sufficient pressure to support the tank.
8. Disconnect the two J-bolts and remove the retaining straps at the rear of the tank. Lower the tank from the vehicle. Feed the two vent tube hoses and filler tube vent hose through the grommets in the frame as the tank is being lowered. Remove the tank gauge unit.
To install:
9. Inspect the fuel filter, and if it is clogged or damaged, replace it.
10. Insert a new gasket in the recess of the fuel gauge and slide the gauge into the tank. Align the positioning tangs on the gauge with those on the tank. Install the lock ring and tighten securely.

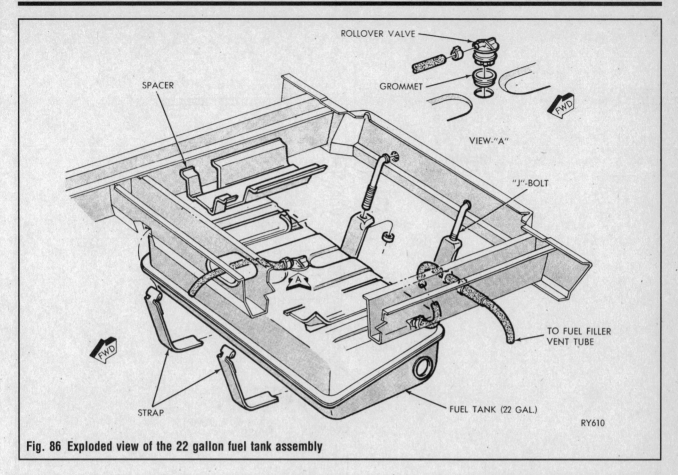

Fig. 86 Exploded view of the 22 gallon fuel tank assembly

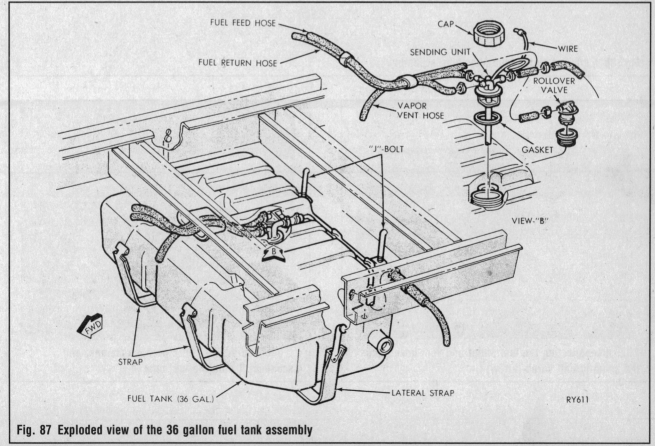

Fig. 87 Exploded view of the 36 gallon fuel tank assembly

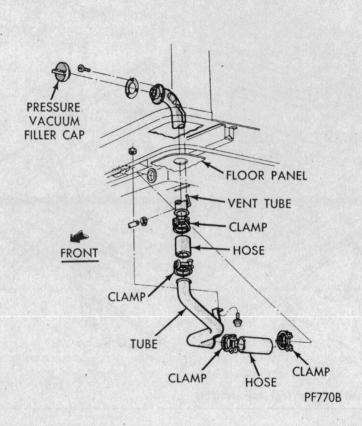

PRESSURE VACUUM FILLER CAP

FLOOR PANEL

VENT TUBE

CLAMP

HOSE

FRONT

CLAMP

TUBE

CLAMP

HOSE

CLAMP

PF770B

Fig. 88 Exploded view of the filler tube assembly

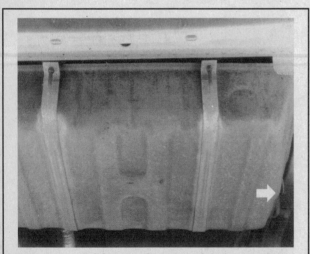

After disconnecting the fuel outlet and vent hoses and the sending unit wires (arrow) . . .

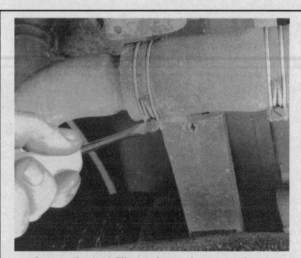

. . . loosen the fuel fill pipe hose clamps, and disconnect it from the fuel tank

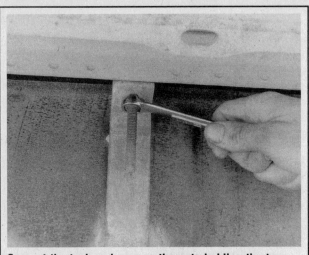

Support the tank and remove the nuts holding the two restraining straps then slowly lower the tank

11. Position the tank on a transmission jack and hoist it into place, feeding the vent hoses through the grommets on the way up.

12. Connect the J-bolts and retaining straps, and tighten to 40 in. lbs. Remove the jack.

13. Connect the filler tube and all vent hoses.

14. Connect the fuel supply line, ground strap, and gauge unit wire lead.

15. Refill the tank and inspect it for leaks. Connect the battery ground cable.

Sending Unit

REMOVAL & INSTALLATION

Carbureted Models

▶ **See Figure 89**

1. Disconnect the negative battery cable.
2. Raise and support the vehicle.

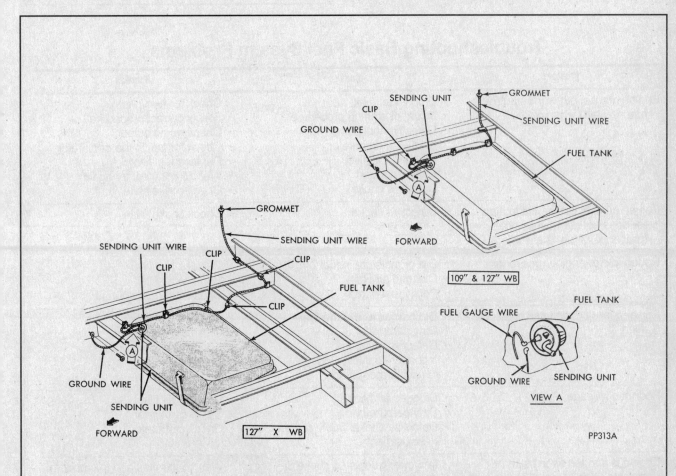

Fig. 89 Fuel gauge sending unit location—22 gallon tank shown

3. Remove the fuel tank from the vehicle.

4. Unfasten the sending unit with the proper tool (either spanner wrench or screwdriver), then remove.

To install:

5. Insert a new gasket in the recess of the fuel sending unit and slide the sending unit into the tank. Align the positioning tangs on the sender with those on the tank. Install the lockring or screws and tighten securely.

6. Install the fuel tank on the vehicle.

7. Lower the vehicle, then connect the negative battery cable.

Fuel Injected Models

▶ **See Figure 90**

To remove the sending unit on a fuel injected vehicle, refer to the fuel pump procedure earlier in this section.

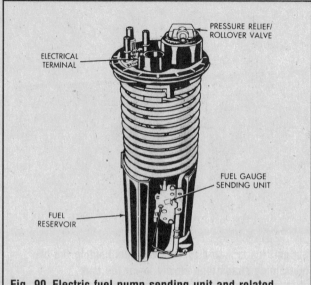

Fig. 90 Electric fuel pump sending unit and related components

Troubleshooting Basic Fuel System Problems

Problem	Cause	Solution
Engine cranks, but won't start (or is hard to start) when cold	• Empty fuel tank • Incorrect starting procedure • Defective fuel pump • No fuel in carburetor • Clogged fuel filter • Engine flooded • Defective choke	• Check for fuel in tank • Follow correct procedure • Check pump output • Check for fuel in the carburetor • Replace fuel filter • Wait 15 minutes; try again • Check choke plate
Engine cranks, but is hard to start (or does not start) when hot— (presence of fuel is assumed)	• Defective choke	• Check choke plate
Rough idle or engine runs rough	• Dirt or moisture in fuel • Clogged air filter • Faulty fuel pump	• Replace fuel filter • Replace air filter • Check fuel pump output
Engine stalls or hesitates on acceleration	• Dirt or moisture in the fuel • Dirty carburetor • Defective fuel pump • Incorrect float level, defective accelerator pump	• Replace fuel filter • Clean the carburetor • Check fuel pump output • Check carburetor
Poor gas mileage	• Clogged air filter • Dirty carburetor • Defective choke, faulty carburetor adjustment	• Replace air filter • Clean carburetor • Check carburetor
Engine is flooded (won't start accompanied by smell of raw fuel)	• Improperly adjusted choke or carburetor	• Wait 15 minutes and try again, without pumping gas pedal • If it won't start, check carburetor

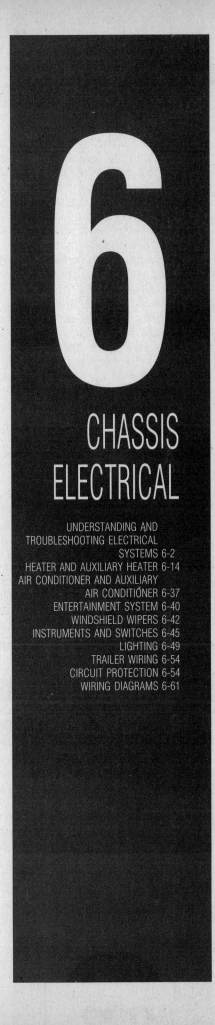

6

CHASSIS ELECTRICAL

UNDERSTANDING AND TROUBLESHOOTING ELECTRICAL SYSTEMS

Over the years import and domestic manufacturers have incorporated electronic control systems into their production lines. In fact, electronic control systems are so prevalent that all new cars and trucks built today are equipped with at least one on-board computer. These electronic components (with no moving parts) should theoretically last the life of the vehicle, provided that nothing external happens to damage the circuits or memory chips.

While it is true that electronic components should never wear out, in the real world malfunctions do occur. It is also true that any computer-based system is extremely sensitive to electrical voltages and cannot tolerate careless or haphazard testing/service procedures. An inexperienced individual can literally cause major damage looking for a minor problem by using the wrong kind of test equipment or connecting test leads/connectors with the ignition switch **ON**. When selecting test equipment, make sure the manufacturer's instructions state that the tester is compatible with whatever type of system is being serviced. Read all instructions carefully and double check all test points before installing probes or making any test connections.

The following section outlines basic diagnosis techniques for dealing with automotive electrical systems. Along with a general explanation of the various types of test equipment available to aid in servicing modern automotive systems, basic repair techniques for wiring harnesses and connectors are also given. Read the basic information before attempting any repairs or testing. This will provide the background of information necessary to avoid the most common and obvious mistakes that can cost both time and money. Although the replacement and testing procedures are simple in themselves, the systems are not, and unless one has a thorough understanding of all components and their function within a particular system, the logical test sequence these systems demand cannot be followed. Minor malfunctions can make a big difference, so it is important to know how each component affects the operation of the overall system in order to find the ultimate cause of a problem without replacing good components unnecessarily. It is not enough to use the correct test equipment; the test equipment must be used correctly.

Safety Precautions

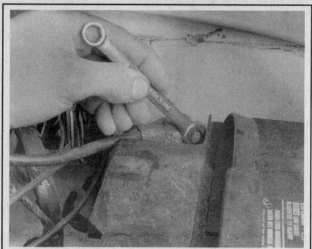

It's always a good idea to disconnect the negative battery cable before doing any electrical work

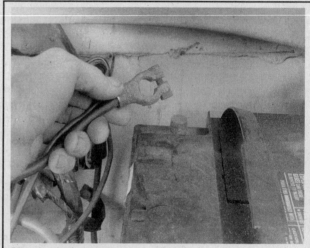

After loosening the battery clamp bolt, pull the cable end off of the battery

❊❊ CAUTION

Whenever working on or around any electrical or electronic systems, always observe these general precautions to prevent the possibility of personal injury or damage to electronic components.

• Never install or remove battery cables with the key **ON** or the engine running. Jumper cables should be connected with the key **OFF** to avoid power surges that can damage electronic control units. Engines equipped with computer controlled systems should avoid both giving and getting jump starts due to the possibility of serious damage to components from arcing in the engine compartment if connections are made with the ignition **ON**.

• Always remove the battery cables before charging the battery. Never use a high output charger on an installed battery or attempt to use any type of "hot shot" (24 volt) starting aid.

• Exercise care when inserting test probes into connectors to insure good contact without damaging the connector or spreading the pins. Always probe connectors from the rear (wire) side, NOT the pin side, to avoid accidental shorting of terminals during test procedures.

• Never remove or attach wiring harness connectors with the ignition switch **ON**, especially to an electronic control unit.

• Do not drop any components during service procedures and never apply 12 volts directly to any component (like a solenoid or relay) unless instructed specifically to do so. Some component electrical windings are designed to safely handle only 4 or 5 volts and can be destroyed in seconds if 12 volts are applied directly to the connector.

• Remove the electronic control unit if the vehicle is to be placed in an environment where temperatures exceed approximately 176°F (80°C), such as a paint spray booth or when arc/gas welding near the control unit location.

Understanding Basic Electricity

Understanding the basic theory of electricity makes electrical troubleshooting much easier. Several gauges are used in electrical troubleshooting to see inside the circuit being tested. Without a basic understanding, it will be difficult to understand testing procedures.

THE WATER ANALOGY

Electricity is the flow of electrons—hypothetical particles thought to constitute the basic stuff of electricity. Many people have been taught electrical theory using an analogy with water. In a comparison with water flowing in a pipe, the electrons would be the water. As the flow of water can be measured, the flow of electricity can be measured. The unit of measurement is amperes, frequently abbreviated amps. An ammeter will measure the actual amount of current flowing in the circuit.

Just as the water pressure is measured in units such as pounds per square inch, electrical pressure is measured in volts. When a voltmeter's two probes are placed on two live portions of an electrical circuit with different electrical pressures, current will flow through the voltmeter and produce a reading which indicates the difference in electrical pressure between the two parts of the circuit.

While increasing the voltage in a circuit will increase the flow of current, the actual flow depends not only on voltage, but on the resistance of the circuit. The standard unit for measuring circuit resistance is an ohm, measured by an ohmmeter. The ohmmeter is somewhat similar to an ammeter, but incorporates its own source of power so that a standard voltage is always present.

CIRCUITS

An actual electric circuit consists of four basic parts. These are: the power source, such as a generator or battery; a hot wire, which conducts the electricity under a relatively high voltage to the component supplied by the circuit; the load, such as a lamp, motor, resistor or relay coil; and the ground wire, which carries the current back to the source under very low voltage. In such a circuit the bulk of the resistance exists between the point where the hot wire is connected to the load, and the point where the load is grounded. In an automobile, the vehicle's frame or body, which is made of steel, is used as a part of the ground circuit for many of the electrical devices.

Remember that, in electrical testing, the voltmeter is connected in parallel with the circuit being tested (without disconnecting any wires) and measures the difference in voltage between the locations of the two probes; that the ammeter is connected in series with the load (the circuit is separated at one point and the ammeter inserted so it becomes a part of the circuit); and the ohmmeter is self-powered, so that all the power in the circuit should be off and the portion of the circuit to be measured contacted at either end by one of the probes of the meter.

For any electrical system to operate, it must make a complete circuit. This simply means that the power flow from the battery must make a complete circle. When an electrical component is operating, power flows from the battery to the component, passes through the component causing it to perform it to function (such as lighting a light bulb) and then returns to the battery through the ground of the circuit. This ground is usually (but not always) the metal part of the vehicle on which the electrical component is mounted.

Perhaps the easiest way to visualize this is to think of connecting a light bulb with two wires attached to it to your vehicle's battery. The battery in your vehicle has two posts (negative and positive). If one of the two wires attached to the light bulb was attached to the negative post of the battery and the other wire was attached to the positive post of the battery, you would have a complete circuit. Current from the battery would flow out one post, through the wire attached to it and then to the light bulb, where it would pass through causing it to light. It would then leave the light bulb, travel through the other wire, and return to the other post of the battery.

AUTOMOTIVE CIRCUITS

The normal automotive circuit differs from this simple example in two ways. First, instead of having a return wire from the bulb to the battery, the light bulb return the current to the battery through the chassis of the vehicle. Since the negative battery cable is attached to the chassis and the chassis is made of electrically conductive metal, the chassis of the vehicle can serve as a ground wire to complete the circuit. Secondly, most automotive circuits contain switches to turn components on and off.

Some electrical components which require a large amount of current to operate also have a relay in their circuit. Since these circuits carry a large amount of current, the thickness of the wire in the circuit (gauge size) is also greater. If this large wire were connected from the component to the control switch on the instrument panel, and then back to the component, a voltage drop would occur in the circuit. To prevent this potential drop in voltage, an electromagnetic switch (relay) is used. The large wires in the circuit are connected from the vehicle battery to one side of the relay, and from the opposite side of the relay to the component. The relay is normally open, preventing current from passing through the circuit. An additional, smaller wire is connected from the relay to the control switch for the circuit. When the control switch is turned on, it grounds the smaller wire from the relay and completes the circuit.

SHORT CIRCUITS

If you were to disconnect the light bulb (from the previous example of a light-bulb being connected to the battery by two wires) from the wires and touch the two wires together (please take our word for this; don't try it), the result will be a shower of sparks. A similar thing happens (on a smaller scale) when the power supply wire to a component or the electrical component itself becomes grounded before the normal ground connection for the circuit. To prevent damage to the system, the fuse for the circuit blows to interrupt the circuit—protecting the components from damage. Because grounding a wire from a power source makes a complete circuit—less the required component to use the power—the phenomenon is called a short circuit. The most common causes of short circuits are: the rubber insulation on a wire breaking or rubbing through to expose the current carrying core of the wire to a metal part of the car, or a shorted switch.

Some electrical systems on the vehicle are protected by a circuit breaker which is, basically, a self-repairing fuse. When either of the described events takes place in a system which is protected by a circuit breaker, the circuit breaker opens the circuit the same way a fuse does. However, when either the short is removed from the circuit or the surge subsides, the circuit breaker resets itself and does not have to be replaced as a fuse does.

Troubleshooting

When diagnosing a specific problem, organized troubleshooting is a must. The complexity of a modern automobile demands that you approach any problem in a logical, organized manner. There are certain troubleshooting techniques that are standard:

1. Establish when the problem occurs. Does the problem appear only under certain conditions? Were there any noises, odors, or other unusual symptoms?

2. Isolate the problem area. To do this, make some simple tests and observations; then eliminate the systems that are working properly. Check for obvious problems such as broken wires, dirty connections or split/disconnected vacuum hoses. Always check the obvious before assuming something complicated is the cause.

3. Test for problems systematically to determine the cause once the problem area is isolated. Are all the components functioning properly? Is there power going to electrical switches and motors? Is there vacuum at vacuum switches and/or actuators? Is there a mechanical problem such as bent linkage or loose mounting screws? Performing careful, systematic checks will often turn up most causes on the first inspection without wasting time checking components that have little or no relationship to the problem.

4. Test all repairs after the work is done to make sure that the problem is fixed. Some causes can be traced to more than one component, so a careful verification of repair work is important in order to pick up additional malfunctions that may cause a problem to reappear or a different problem to arise. A blown fuse, for example, is a simple problem that may require more than another fuse to repair. If you don't look for a problem that caused a fuse to blow, a shorted wire (for example) may go undetected.

Experience has shown that most problems tend to be the result of a fairly simple and obvious cause, such as loose or corroded connectors or air leaks in the intake system. This makes careful inspection of components during testing essential to quick and accurate troubleshooting.

BASIC TROUBLESHOOTING THEORY

Electrical problems generally fall into one of three areas:
• The component that is not functioning is not receiving current.
• The component itself is not functioning.
• The component is not properly grounded.

Problems that fall into the first category are by far the most complicated. It is the current supply system to the component which contains all the switches, relay, fuses, etc.

The electrical system can be checked with a test light and a jumper wire. A test light is a device that looks like a pointed screwdriver with a wire attached to it. It has a light bulb in its handle. A jumper wire is a piece of insulated wire with an alligator clip attached to each end.

If a light bulb is not working, you must follow a systematic plan to determine which of the three causes is the villain.

1. Turn on the switch that controls the inoperable bulb.
2. Disconnect the power supply wire from the bulb.
3. Attach the ground wire to the test light to a good metal ground.
4. Touch the probe end of the test light to the end of the power supply wire that was disconnected from the bulb. If the bulb is receiving current, the test light will go on.

➡**If the bulb is one which works only when the ignition key is turned on (turn signal), make sure the key is turned on.**

If the test light does not go on, then the problem is in the circuit between the battery and the bulb. As mentioned before, this includes all the switches, fuses, and relays in the system. Turn to a wiring diagram and find the bulb on the diagram. Follow the wire that runs back to the battery. The problem is an open circuit between the battery and the bulb. If the fuse is blown and, when replaced, immediately blows again, there is a short circuit in the system which must be located and repaired. If there is a switch in the system, bypass it with a jumper wire. This is done by connecting one end of the jumper wire to the power supply wire into the switch and the other end of the jumper wire to the wire coming out of the switch. If the test light illuminates with the jumper wire installed, the switch or whatever was bypassed is defective.

➡**Never substitute the jumper wire for the bulb, as the bulb is the component required to use the power from the power source.**

5. If the bulb in the test light goes on, then the current is getting to the bulb that is not working in the car. This eliminates the first of the three possible causes. Connect the power supply wire and connect a jumper wire from the bulb to a good metal ground. Do this with the switch which controls the bulb works with jumper wire installed, then it has a bad ground. This is usually caused by the metal area on which the bulb mounts to the vehicle being coated with some type of foreign matter.

6. If neither test located the source of the trouble, then the light bulb itself is defective.

The above test procedure can be applied to any of the components of the chassis electrical system by substituting the component that is not working for the light bulb. Remember that for any electrical system to work, all connections must be clean and tight.

TEST EQUIPMENT

➡**Pinpointing the exact cause of trouble in an electrical system can sometimes only be accomplished by the use of special test equipment. The following describes different types of commonly used test equipment and explains how to use them in diagnosis. In addition to the information covered below, the tool manufacturer's instructions booklet (provided with the tester) should be read and clearly understood before attempting any test procedures.**

Jumper Wires

Jumper wires are simple, yet extremely valuable, pieces of test equipment. They are basically test wires which are used to bypass sections of a circuit. The simplest type of jumper wire is a length of multi-strand wire with an alligator clip at each end. Jumper wires are usually fabricated from lengths of standard automotive wire and whatever type of connector (alligator clip, spade connector or pin connector) that is required for the particular vehicle being tested. The well equipped tool box will have several different styles of jumper wires in several different lengths. Some jumper wires are made with three or more terminals coming from a common splice for special purpose testing. In cramped, hard-to-reach areas it is advisable to have insulated boots over the jumper wire terminals in order to prevent accidental grounding, sparks, and possible fire, especially when testing fuel system components.

Jumper wires are used primarily to locate open electrical circuits, on either the ground (−) side of the circuit or on the hot (+) side. If an electrical component fails to operate, connect the jumper wire between the component and a good ground. If the component operates only with the jumper installed, the ground circuit is open. If the ground circuit is good, but the component does not operate, the circuit between the power feed and component may be open. By moving the jumper wire successively back from the lamp toward the power source, you can isolate the area of the circuit where the open is located. When the component

stops functioning, or the power is cut off, the open is in the segment of wire between the jumper and the point previously tested.

You can sometimes connect the jumper wire directly from the battery to the hot terminal of the component, but first make sure the component uses 12 volts in operation. Some electrical components, such as fuel injectors, are designed to operate on about 4 volts and running 12 volts directly to the injector terminals can cause damage.

By inserting an in-line fuse holder between a set of test leads, a fused jumper wire can be used for bypassing open circuits. Use a 5 amp fuse to provide protection against voltage spikes. When in doubt, use a voltmeter to check the voltage input to the component and measure how much voltage is normally being applied.

✳✳ CAUTION

Never use jumpers made from wire that is of lighter gauge than that which is used in the circuit under test. If the jumper wire is of too small a gauge, it may overheat and possibly melt. Never use jumpers to bypass high resistance loads in a circuit. Bypassing resistances, in effect, creates a short circuit. This may, in turn, cause damage and fire. Jumper wires should only be used to bypass lengths of wire.

Unpowered Test Lights

The 12 volt test light is used to check circuits and components while electrical current is flowing through them. It is used for voltage and ground tests. Twelve volt test lights come in different styles but all have three main parts; a ground clip, a probe, and a light. The most commonly used 12 volt test lights have pick-type probes. To use a 12 volt test light, connect the ground clip to a good ground and probe wherever necessary with the pick. The pick should be sharp so that it can be probed into tight spaces.

✳✳ CAUTION

Do not use a test light to probe electronic ignition spark plug or coil wires. Never use a pick-type test light to probe wiring on computer controlled systems unless specifically instructed to do so. Any wire insulation that is pierced by the test light probe should be taped and sealed with silicone after testing.

Like the jumper wire, the 12 volt test light is used to isolate opens in circuits. But, whereas the jumper wire is used to bypass the open to operate the load, the 12 volt test light is used to locate the presence of voltage in a circuit. If the test light glows, you know that there is power up to that point; if the 12 volt test light does not glow when its probe is inserted into the wire or connector, you know that there is an open circuit (no power). Move the test light in successive steps back toward the power source until the light in the handle does glow. When it glows, the open is between the probe and point which was probed previously.

➡The test light does not detect that 12 volts (or any particular amount of voltage) is present; it only detects that some voltage is present. It is advisable before using the test light to touch its terminals across the battery posts to make sure the light is operating properly.

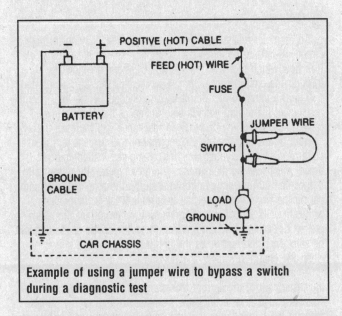

Example of using a jumper wire to bypass a switch during a diagnostic test

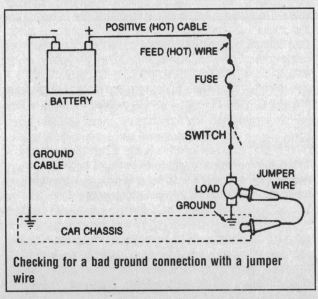

Checking for a bad ground connection with a jumper wire

Self-Powered Test Lights

The self-powered test light usually contains a 1.5 volt penlight battery. One type of self-powered test light is similar in design to the 12 volt unit. This type has both the battery and the light in the handle, along with a pick-type probe tip. The second type has the light toward the open tip, so that the light illuminates the contact point. The self-powered test light is a dual purpose piece of test equipment. It can be used to test for either open or short circuits when power is isolated from the circuit (continuity test). A powered test light should not be used on any computer controlled system or component unless specifically instructed to do so. Many engine sensors can be destroyed by even this small amount of voltage applied directly to the terminals.

Voltmeters

A voltmeter is used to measure voltage at any point in a circuit, or to measure the voltage drop across any part of a circuit. It can also be used to check continuity in a wire or circuit by indicating current flow from one end to the other. Analog voltmeters usually have various scales on the meter dial and a selector switch to allow the selection of different voltages. The voltmeter has a positive and a negative lead. To avoid damage to the meter, always connect the negative lead to the negative (−) side of the circuit (to ground or nearest the ground side of the circuit) and connect the positive lead to the positive (+) side of the circuit (to the power source or the nearest power source). Note that the negative voltmeter lead will always be black and that the positive voltmeter will always be some color other than black (usually red).

Depending on how the voltmeter is connected into the circuit, it has several uses. A voltmeter can be connected either in parallel or in series with a circuit and it has a very high resistance to current flow. When connected in parallel, only a small amount of current will flow through the voltmeter current path; the rest will flow through the normal circuit current path and the circuit will work normally. When the voltmeter is connected in series with a circuit, only a small amount of current can flow through the circuit. The circuit will not work properly, but the voltmeter reading will show if the circuit is complete or not.

Ohmmeters

The ohmmeter is designed to read resistance (which is measured in ohms or Ω) in a circuit or component. Although there are several different styles of ohmmeters, all analog meters will usually have a selector switch which permits the measurement of different ranges of resistance (usually the selector switch allows the multiplication of the meter reading by 10, 100, 1000, and 10,000). A calibration knob allows the meter to be set at zero for accurate measurement. Since all ohmmeters are powered by an internal battery, the ohmmeter can be used as a self-powered test light. When the ohmmeter is connected, current from the ohmmeter flows through the circuit or component being tested. Since the ohmmeter's internal resistance and voltage are known values, the amount of current flow through the meter depends on the resistance of the circuit or component being tested.

The ohmmeter can be used to perform a continuity test for opens or shorts (either by observation of the meter needle or as a self-powered test light), and to read actual resistance in a circuit. It should be noted that the ohmmeter is used to check the resistance of a component or wire while there is no voltage applied to the circuit. Current flow from an outside voltage source (such as

the vehicle battery) can damage the ohmmeter, so the circuit or component should be isolated from the vehicle electrical system before any testing is done. Since the ohmmeter uses its own voltage source, either lead can be connected to any test point.

➡ **When checking diodes or other solid state components, the ohmmeter leads can only be connected one way in order to measure current flow in a single direction. Make sure the positive (+) and negative (−) terminal connections are as described in the test procedures to verify the one-way diode operation.**

In using the meter for making continuity checks, do not be concerned with the actual resistance readings. Zero resistance, or any ohm reading, indicates continuity in the circuit. Infinite resistance indicates an open in the circuit. A high resistance reading where there should be none indicates a problem in the circuit. Checks for short circuits are made in the same manner as checks for open circuits except that the circuit must be isolated from both power and normal ground. Infinite resistance indicates no continuity to ground, while zero resistance indicates a dead short to ground.

Ammeters

An ammeter measures the amount of current flowing through a circuit in units called amperes or amps. Amperes are units of electron flow which indicate how fast the electrons are flowing through the circuit. Since Ohms Law dictates that current flow in a circuit is equal to the circuit voltage divided by the total circuit resistance, increasing voltage also increases the current level (amps). Likewise, any decrease in resistance will increase the amount of amps in a circuit. At normal operating voltage, most circuits have a characteristic amount of amperes, called "current draw" which can be measured using an ammeter. By referring to a specified current draw rating, measuring the amperes, and comparing the two values, one can determine what is happening within the circuit to aid in diagnosis. An open circuit, for example, will not allow any current to flow so the ammeter reading will be zero. More current flows through a heavily loaded circuit or when the charging system is operating.

An ammeter is always connected in series with the circuit being tested. All of the current that normally flows through the circuit must also flow through the ammeter; if there is any other path for the current to follow, the ammeter reading will not be accurate. The ammeter itself has very little resistance to current flow and therefore will not affect the circuit, but it will measure current draw only when the circuit is closed and electricity is flowing. Excessive current draw can blow fuses and drain the battery, while a reduced current draw can cause motors to run slowly, lights to dim and other components to not operate properly. The ammeter can help diagnose these conditions by locating the cause of the high or low reading.

Multimeters

Different combinations of test meters can be built into a single unit designed for specific tests. Some of the more common combination test devices are known as Volt/Amp testers, Tach/Dwell meters, or Digital Multimeters. The Volt/Amp tester is used for charging system, starting system or battery tests and consists of a voltmeter, an ammeter and a variable resistance carbon pile. The voltmeter will usually have at least two ranges for use with 6, 12 and/or 24 volt systems. The ammeter also has more than one range for testing various levels of battery loads and starter current draw. The carbon pile can be adjusted to offer different amounts of resistance. The Volt/Amp tester has heavy leads to carry large amounts of current and many later models have an inductive ammeter pickup that clamps around the wire to simplify test connections. On some models, the ammeter also has a zero-center scale to allow testing of charging and starting systems without switching leads or polarity. A digital multimeter is a voltmeter, ammeter and ohmmeter combined in an instrument which gives a digital readout. These are often used when testing solid state circuits because of their high input impedance (usually 10 megohms or more).

The tach/dwell meter that combines a tachometer and a dwell (cam angle) meter is a specialized kind of voltmeter. The tachometer scale is marked to show engine speed in rpm and the dwell scale is marked to show degrees of distributor shaft rotation. In most electronic ignition systems, dwell is determined by the control unit, but the dwell meter can also be used to check the duty cycle (operation) of some electronic engine control systems. Some tach/dwell meters are powered by an internal battery, while others take their power from the vehicle battery in use. The battery powered testers usually require calibration (much like an ohmmeter) before testing.

TESTING

Open Circuits

To use the self-powered test light or a multimeter to check for open circuits, first isolate the circuit from the vehicle's 12 volt power source by disconnecting the battery or wiring harness connector. Connect the test light or ohmmeter ground clip to a good ground and probe sections of the circuit sequentially with the test light. (start from either end of the circuit). If the light is out/or there is infinite resistance, the open is between the probe and the circuit ground. If the light is on/or the meter shows continuity, the open is between the probe and end of the circuit toward the power source.

Short Circuits

By isolating the circuit both from power and from ground, and using a self-powered test light or multimeter, you can check for shorts to ground in the circuit. Isolate the circuit from power and ground. Connect the test light or ohmmeter ground clip to a good ground and probe any easy-to-reach test point in the circuit. If the light comes on or there is continuity, there is a short somewhere in the circuit. To isolate the short, probe a test point at either end of the isolated circuit (the light should be on/there should be continuity). Leave the test light probe engaged and open connectors, switches, remove parts, etc., sequentially, until the light goes out/continuity is broken. When the light goes out, the short is between the last circuit component opened and the previous circuit opened.

➡The battery in the test light and does not provide much current. A weak battery may not provide enough power to illuminate the test light even when a complete circuit is made (especially if there are high resistances in the circuit). Always make sure that the test battery is strong. To check the battery, briefly touch the ground clip to the probe; if the light glows brightly the battery is strong enough for testing. Never use a self-powered test light to perform checks for opens or shorts when power is applied to the electrical system under test. The 12 volt vehicle power will quickly burn out the light bulb in the test light.

Available Voltage Measurement

Set the voltmeter selector switch to the 20V position and connect the meter negative lead to the negative post of the battery. Connect the positive meter lead to the positive post of the battery and turn the ignition switch **ON** to provide a load. Read the voltage on the meter or digital display. A well charged battery should register over 12 volts. If the meter reads below 11.5 volts, the battery power may be insufficient to operate the electrical system properly. This test determines voltage available from the battery and should be the first step in any electrical trouble diagnosis procedure. Many electrical problems, especially on computer controlled systems, can be caused by a low state of charge in the battery. Excessive corrosion at the battery cable terminals can cause a poor contact that will prevent proper charging and full battery current flow.

Normal battery voltage is 12 volts when fully charged. When the battery is supplying current to one or more circuits it is said to be "under load." When everything is off the electrical system is under a "no-load" condition. A fully charged battery may show about 12.5 volts at no load; will drop to 12 volts under medium load; and will drop even lower under heavy load. If the battery is partially discharged the voltage decrease under heavy load may be excessive, even though the battery shows 12 volts or more at no load. When allowed to discharge further, the battery's available voltage under load will decrease more severely. For this reason, it is important that the battery be fully charged during all testing procedures to avoid errors in diagnosis and incorrect test results.

Voltage Drop

When current flows through a resistance, the voltage beyond the resistance is reduced (the larger the current, the greater the reduction in voltage). When no current is flowing, there is no voltage drop because there is no current flow. All points in the circuit which are connected to the power source are at the same voltage as the power source. The total voltage drop always equals the total source voltage. In a long circuit with many connectors, a series of small, unwanted voltage drops due to corrosion at the connectors can add up to a total loss of voltage which impairs the operation of the normal loads in the circuit. The maximum allowable voltage drop under load is critical, especially if there is more than one high resistance problem in a circuit because all voltage drops are cumulative. A small drop is normal due to the resistance of the conductors.

INDIRECT COMPUTATION OF VOLTAGE DROPS

1. Set the voltmeter selector switch to the 20 volt position.
2. Connect the meter negative lead to a good ground.
3. While operating the circuit, probe all loads in the circuit with the positive meter lead and observe the voltage readings. A drop should be noticed after the first load. But, there should be little or no voltage drop before the first load.

DIRECT MEASUREMENT OF VOLTAGE DROPS

1. Set the voltmeter switch to the 20 volt position.
2. Connect the voltmeter negative lead to the ground side of the load to be measured.

3. Connect the positive lead to the positive side of the resistance or load to be measured.

4. Read the voltage drop directly on the 20 volt scale.

Too high a voltage indicates too high a resistance. If, for example, a blower motor runs too slowly, you can determine if perhaps there is too high a resistance in the resistor pack. By taking voltage drop readings in all parts of the circuit, you can isolate the problem. Too low a voltage drop indicates too low a resistance. Take the blower motor for example again. If a blower motor runs too fast in the MED and/or LOW position, the problem might be isolated in the resistor pack by taking voltage drop readings in all parts of the circuit to locate a possibly shorted resistor.

HIGH RESISTANCE TESTING

1. Set the voltmeter selector switch to the 4 volt position.
2. Connect the voltmeter positive lead to the positive post of the battery.
3. Turn on the headlights and heater blower to provide a load.
4. Probe various points in the circuit with the negative voltmeter lead.
5. Read the voltage drop on the 4 volt scale. Some average maximum allowable voltage drops are:
   - FUSE PANEL: 0.7 volts
   - IGNITION SWITCH: 0.5 volts
   - HEADLIGHT SWITCH: 0.7 volts
   - IGNITION COIL (+): 0.5 volts
   - ANY OTHER LOAD: 1.3 volts

➡**Voltage drops are all measured while a load is operating; without current flow, there will be no voltage drop.**

Resistance Measurement

The batteries in an ohmmeter will weaken with age and temperature, so the ohmmeter must be calibrated or "zeroed" before taking measurements. To zero the meter, place the selector switch in its lowest range and touch the two ohmmeter leads together. Turn the calibration knob until the meter needle is exactly on zero.

➡**All analog (needle) type ohmmeters must be zeroed before use, but some digital ohmmeter models are automatically calibrated when the switch is turned on. Self-calibrating digital ohmmeters do not have an adjusting knob, but its a good idea to check for a zero readout before use by touching the leads together. All computer controlled systems require the use of a digital ohmmeter with at least 10 megohms impedance for testing. Before any test procedures are attempted, make sure the ohmmeter used is compatible with the electrical system or damage to the on-board computer could result.**

To measure resistance, first isolate the circuit from the vehicle power source by disconnecting the battery cables or the harness connector. Make sure the key is **OFF** when disconnecting any components or the battery. Where necessary, also isolate at least one side of the circuit to be checked in order to avoid reading parallel resistances. Parallel circuit resistances will always give a lower reading than the actual resistance of either of the branches. When measuring the resistance of parallel circuits, the total resistance will always be lower than the smallest resistance in the cir-

cuit. Connect the meter leads to both sides of the circuit (wire or component) and read the actual measured ohms on the meter scale. Make sure the selector switch is set to the proper ohm scale for the circuit being tested to avoid misreading the ohmmeter test value.

✳✳ WARNING

Never use an ohmmeter with power applied to the circuit. Like the self-powered test light, the ohmmeter is designed to operate on its own power supply. The normal 12 volt automotive electrical system current could damage the meter!

Wiring Harnesses

The average automobile contains about ½ mile of wiring, with hundreds of individual connections. To protect the many wires from damage and to keep them from becoming a confusing tangle, they are organized into bundles, enclosed in plastic or taped together and called wiring harnesses. Different harnesses serve different parts of the vehicle. Individual wires are color coded to help trace them through a harness where sections are hidden from view.

Automotive wiring or circuit conductors can be in any one of three forms:
1. Single strand wire
2. Multi-strand wire
3. Printed circuitry

Single strand wire has a solid metal core and is usually used inside such components as alternators, motors, relays and other devices. Multi-strand wire has a core made of many small strands of wire twisted together into a single conductor. Most of the wiring in an automotive electrical system is made up of multi-strand wire, either as a single conductor or grouped together in a harness. All wiring is color coded on the insulator, either as a solid color or as a colored wire with an identification stripe. A printed circuit is a thin film of copper or other conductor that is printed on an insulator backing. Occasionally, a printed circuit is sandwiched between two sheets of plastic for more protection and flexibility. A complete printed circuit, consisting of conductors, insulating material and connectors for lamps or other components is called a printed circuit board. Printed circuitry is used in place of individual wires or harnesses in places where space is limited, such as behind instrument panels.

Since automotive electrical systems are very sensitive to changes in resistance, the selection of properly sized wires is critical when systems are repaired. A loose or corroded connection or a replacement wire that is too small for the circuit will add extra resistance and an additional voltage drop to the circuit. A ten percent voltage drop can result in slow or erratic motor operation, for example, even though the circuit is complete. The wire gauge number is an expression of the cross-section area of the conductor. The most common system for expressing wire size is the American Wire Gauge (AWG) system.

Gauge numbers are assigned to conductors of various cross-section areas. As gauge number increases, area decreases and the conductor becomes smaller. A 5 gauge conductor is smaller than a 1 gauge conductor and a 10 gauge is smaller than a 5 gauge. As the cross-section area of a conductor decreases, resistance increases and so does the gauge number. A conductor with a higher gauge number will carry less current than a conductor with a lower gauge number.

➡**Gauge wire size refers to the size of the conductor, not the size of the complete wire. It is possible to have two wires of the same gauge with different diameters because one may have thicker insulation than the other.**

12 volt automotive electrical systems generally use 10, 12, 14, 16 and 18 gauge wire. Main power distribution circuits and larger accessories usually use 10 and 12 gauge wire. Battery cables are usually 4 or 6 gauge, although 1 and 2 gauge wires are occasionally used. Wire length must also be considered when making repairs to a circuit. As conductor length increases, so does resistance. An 18 gauge wire, for example, can carry a 10 amp load for 10 feet without excessive voltage drop; however if a 15 foot wire is required for the same 10 amp load, it must be a 16 gauge wire.

An electrical schematic shows the electrical current paths when a circuit is operating properly. It is essential to understand how a circuit works before trying to figure out why it doesn't. Schematics break the entire electrical system down into individual circuits and show only one particular circuit. In a schematic, no attempt is made to represent wiring and components as they physically appear on the vehicle; switches and other components are shown as simply as possible. Face views of harness connectors show the cavity or terminal locations in all multi-pin connectors to help locate test points.

If you need to backprobe a connector while it is on the component, the order of the terminals must be mentally reversed. The wire color code can help in this situation, as well as a keyway, lock tab or other reference mark.

WIRING REPAIR

Soldering is a quick, efficient method of joining metals permanently. Everyone who has the occasion to make wiring repairs should know how to solder. Electrical connections that are soldered are far less likely to come apart and will conduct electricity much better than connections that are only "pig-tailed" together. The most popular (and preferred) method of soldering is with an electrical soldering gun. Soldering irons are available in many sizes and wattage ratings. Irons with higher wattage ratings deliver higher temperatures and recover lost heat faster. A small soldering iron rated for no more than 50 watts is recommended, especially on electrical systems where excess heat can damage the components being soldered.

There are three ingredients necessary for successful soldering; proper flux, good solder and sufficient heat. A soldering flux is necessary to clean the metal of tarnish, prepare it for soldering and to enable the solder to spread into tiny crevices. When soldering, always use a rosin core solder which is non-corrosive and will not attract moisture once the job is finished. Other types of flux (acid core) will leave a residue that will attract moisture and

cause the wires to corrode. Tin is a unique metal with a low melting point. In a molten state, it dissolves and alloys easily with many metals. Solder is made by mixing tin with lead. The most common proportions are 40/60, 50/50 and 60/40, with the percentage of tin listed first. Low priced solders usually contain less tin, making them very difficult for a beginner to use because more heat is required to melt the solder. A common solder is 40/60 which is well suited for all-around general use, but 60/40 melts easier and is preferred for electrical work.

Soldering Techniques

Successful soldering requires that the metals to be joined be heated to a temperature that will melt the solder, usually 360–460°F (182–238°C). Contrary to popular belief, the purpose of the soldering iron is not to melt the solder itself, but to heat the parts being soldered to a temperature high enough to melt the solder when it is touched to the work. Melting flux-cored solder on the soldering iron will usually destroy the effectiveness of the flux.

➡**Soldering tips are made of copper for good heat conductivity, but must be "tinned" regularly for quick transference of heat to the project and to prevent the solder from sticking to the iron. To "tin" the iron, simply heat it and touch the flux-cored solder to the tip; the solder will flow over the hot tip. Wipe the excess off with a clean rag, but be careful as the iron will be hot.**

After some use, the tip may become pitted. If so, simply dress the tip smooth with a smooth file and "tin" the tip again. Flux-cored solder will remove oxides but rust, bits of insulation and oil or grease must be removed with a wire brush or emery cloth. For maximum strength in soldered parts, the joint must start off clean and tight. Weak joints will result in gaps too wide for the solder to bridge.

If a separate soldering flux is used, it should be brushed or swabbed on only those areas that are to be soldered. Most solders contain a core of flux and separate fluxing is unnecessary. Hold the work to be soldered firmly. It is best to solder on a wooden board, because a metal vise will only rob the piece to be soldered of heat and make it difficult to melt the solder. Hold the soldering tip with the broadest face against the work to be soldered. Apply solder under the tip close to the work, using enough solder to give a heavy film between the iron and the piece being soldered, while moving slowly and making sure the solder melts properly. Keep the work level or the solder will run to the lowest part and favor the thicker parts, because these require more heat to melt the solder. If the soldering tip overheats (the solder coating on the face of the tip burns up), it should be retinned. Once the soldering is completed, let the soldered joint stand until cool. Tape and seal all soldered wire splices after the repair has cooled.

Wire Harness Connectors

Most connectors in the engine compartment or that are otherwise exposed to the elements are protected against moisture and dirt which could create oxidation and deposits on the terminals.

These special connectors are weather-proof. All repairs require the use of a special terminal and the tool required to service it. This tool is used to remove the pin and sleeve terminals. If removal is attempted with an ordinary pick, there is a good chance that the terminal will be bent or deformed. Unlike standard blade type terminals, these weather-proof terminals cannot be straightened once they are bent. Make certain that the connectors are properly seated and all of the sealing rings are in place when connecting leads. On some models, a hinge-type flap provides a backup or secondary locking feature for the terminals. Most secondary locks are used to improve connector reliability by retaining the terminals if the small terminal lock tangs are not positioned properly.

Molded-on connectors require complete replacement of the connection. This means splicing a new connector assembly into the harness. All splices should be soldered to insure proper contact. Use care when probing the connections or replacing terminals in them as it is possible to short between opposite terminals. If this happens to the wrong terminal pair, it is possible to damage certain components. Always use jumper wires between connectors for circuit checking and never probe through weatherproof seals.

Open circuits are often difficult to locate by sight because corrosion or terminal misalignment are hidden by the connectors. Merely wiggling a connector on a sensor or in the wiring harness may correct the open circuit condition. This should always be considered when an open circuit or a failed sensor is indicated. Intermittent problems may also be caused by oxidized or loose connections. When using a circuit tester for diagnosis, always probe connections from the wire side. Be careful not to damage sealed connectors with test probes.

All wiring harnesses should be replaced with identical parts, using the same gauge wire and connectors. When signal wires are spliced into a harness, use wire with high temperature insulation only. It is seldom necessary to replace a complete harness. If replacement is necessary, pay close attention to insure proper harness routing. Secure the harness with suitable plastic wire clamps to prevent vibrations from causing the harness to wear in spots or contact any hot components.

➡**Weatherproof connectors cannot be replaced with standard connectors. Instructions are provided with replacement connector and terminal packages. Some wire harnesses have mounting indicators (usually pieces of colored tape) to mark where the harness is to be secured.**

In making wiring repairs, its important that you always replace damaged wires with wiring of the same gauge as the wire being replaced. The heavier the wire, the smaller the gauge number. Wires are color-coded to aid in identification and whenever possible the same color coded wire should be used for replacement. A wire stripping and crimping tool is necessary to install solderless terminal connectors. Test all crimps by pulling on the wires; it should not be possible to pull the wires out of a good crimp.

Wires which are open, exposed or otherwise damaged are repaired by simple splicing. Where possible, if the wiring harness is accessible and the damaged place in the wire can be located, it is best to open the harness and check for all possible damage. In an inaccessible harness, the wire must be bypassed with a new insert, usually taped to the outside of the old harness.

When replacing fusible links, be sure to use fusible link wire, NOT ordinary automotive wire. Make sure the fusible segment is of the same gauge and construction as the one being replaced and double the stripped end when crimping the terminal connector for a good contact. The melted (open) fusible link segment of the wiring harness should be cut off as close to the harness as

possible, then a new segment spliced in as described. In the case of a damaged fusible link that feeds two harness wires, the harness connections should be replaced with two fusible link wires so that each circuit will have its own separate protection.

➡**Most of the problems caused in the wiring harness are due to bad ground connections. Always check all vehicle ground connections for corrosion or looseness before performing any power feed checks to eliminate the chance of a bad ground affecting the circuit.**

Hard-Shell Connectors

Unlike molded connectors, the terminal contacts in hard-shell connectors can be replaced. Weatherproof hard-shell connectors with the leads molded into the shell have non-replaceable terminal ends. Replacement usually involves the use of a special terminal removal tool that depresses the locking tangs (barbs) on the connector terminal and allows the connector to be removed from the rear of the shell. The connector shell should be replaced if it shows any evidence of burning, melting, cracks, or breaks. Replace individual terminals that are burnt, corroded, distorted or loose.

➡**The insulation crimp must be tight to prevent the insulation from sliding back on the wire when the wire is pulled. The insulation must be visibly compressed under the crimp tabs, and the ends of the crimp should be turned in for a firm grip on the insulation.**

The wire crimp must be made with all wire strands inside the crimp. The terminal must be fully compressed on the wire strands with the ends of the crimp tabs turned in to make a firm grip on the wire. Check all connections with an ohmmeter to insure a good contact. There should be no measurable resistance between the wire and the terminal when connected.

Fusible Links

The fuse link is a short length of special, Hypalon (high temperature) insulated wire, integral with the engine compartment wiring harness and should not be confused with standard wire. It is several wire gauges smaller than the circuit which it protects. Under no circumstances should a fuse link replacement repair be made using a length of standard wire cut from bulk stock or from another wiring harness.

To repair any blown fuse link use the following procedure:

1. Determine which circuit is damaged, its location and the cause of the open fuse link. If the damaged fuse link is one of three fed by a common No. 10 or 12 gauge feed wire, determine the specific affected circuit.

2. Disconnect the negative battery cable.

3. Cut the damaged fuse link from the wiring harness and discard it. If the fuse link is one of three circuits fed by a single feed wire, cut it out of the harness at each splice end and discard it.

4. Identify and procure the proper fuse link with butt connectors for attaching the fuse link to the harness.

➡**Heat shrink tubing must be slipped over the wire before crimping and soldering the connection.**

5. To repair any fuse link in a 3-link group with one feed:

a. After cutting the open link out of the harness, cut each of the remaining undamaged fuse links close to the feed wire weld.

REMOVE EXISTING VINYL TUBE SHIELDING
REINSTALL OVER FUSE LINK BEFORE CRIMPING
FUSE LINK TO WIRE ENDS

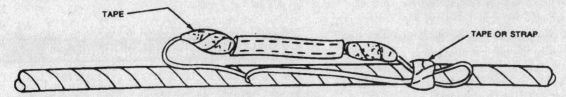

TAPE

TAPE OR STRAP

TYPICAL REPAIR USING THE SPECIAL #17 GA. (9.00" LONG-YELLOW) FUSE LINK REQUIRED FOR THE AIR/COND.
CIRCUITS (2) #687E and #261A LOCATED IN THE ENGINE COMPARTMENT

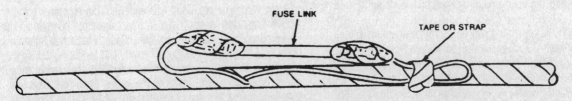

FUSE LINK

TAPE OR STRAP

TYPICAL REPAIR FOR ANY IN-LINE FUSE LINK USING THE SPECIFIED GAUGE FUSE LINK FOR THE SPECIFIC CIRCUIT

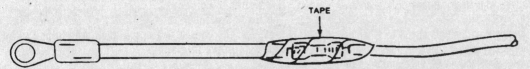

TAPE

TYPICAL REPAIR USING THE EYELET TERMINAL FUSE LINK OF THE SPECIFIED GAUGE FOR ATTACHMENT TO A CIRCUIT WIRE END

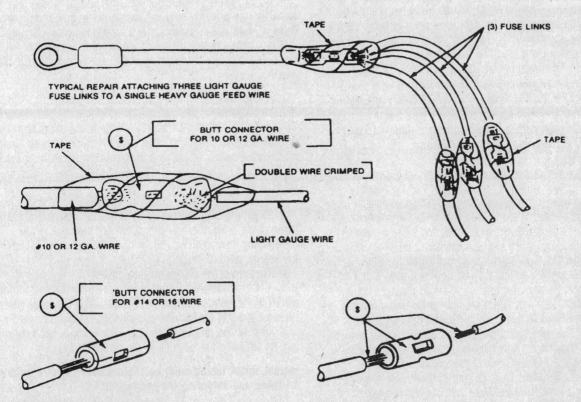

TAPE

(3) FUSE LINKS

TYPICAL REPAIR ATTACHING THREE LIGHT GAUGE
FUSE LINKS TO A SINGLE HEAVY GAUGE FEED WIRE

TAPE

BUTT CONNECTOR
FOR 10 OR 12 GA. WIRE

DOUBLED WIRE CRIMPED

S

TAPE

#10 OR 12 GA. WIRE

LIGHT GAUGE WIRE

S

BUTT CONNECTOR
FOR #14 OR 16 WIRE

S

FUSIBLE LINK REPAIR PROCEDURE

General fusible link repair—never replace a fusible link with regular wire or a fusible link rated at a higher amperage than the one being replaced

b. Strip approximately ½ in. (13mm) of insulation from the detached ends of the two good fuse links. Insert two wire ends into one end of a butt connector, then carefully push one stripped end of the replacement fuse link into the same end of the butt connector and crimp all three firmly together.

➡**Care must be taken when fitting the three fuse links into the butt connector as the internal diameter is a snug fit for three wires. Make sure to use a proper crimping tool. Pliers, side cutters, etc. will not apply the proper crimp to retain the wires and withstand a pull test.**

c. After crimping the butt connector to the three fuse links, cut the weld portion from the feed wire and strip approximately ½ in. (13mm) of insulation from the cut end. Insert the stripped end into the open end of the butt connector and crimp very firmly.

d. To attach the remaining end of the replacement fuse link, strip approximately ½ in. (13mm) of insulation from the wire end of the circuit from which the blown fuse link was removed, and firmly crimp a butt connector or equivalent to the stripped wire. Then, insert the end of the replacement link into the other end of the butt connector and crimp firmly.

e. Using rosin core solder with a consistency of 60 percent tin and 40 percent lead, solder the connectors and the wires at the repairs then insulate with electrical tape or heat shrink tubing.

6. To replace any fuse link on a single circuit in a harness, cut out the damaged portion, strip approximately ½ in. (13mm) of insulation from the two wire ends and attach the appropriate replacement fuse link to the stripped wire ends with two proper size butt connectors. Solder the connectors and wires, then insulate.

7. To repair any fuse link which has an eyelet terminal on one end such as the charging circuit, cut off the open fuse link behind the weld, strip approximately ½ in. (13mm) of insulation from the cut end and attach the appropriate new eyelet fuse link to the cut stripped wire with an appropriate size butt connector. Solder the connectors and wires at the repair, then insulate.

8. Connect the negative battery cable to the battery and test the system for proper operation.

➡**Do not mistake a resistor wire for a fuse link. The resistor wire is generally longer and has print stating, "Resistor-don't cut or splice."**

When attaching a single No. 16, 17, 18 or 20 gauge fuse link to a heavy gauge wire, always double the stripped wire end of the fuse link before inserting and crimping it into the butt connector for positive wire retention.

Add-On Electrical Equipment

The electrical system in your vehicle is designed to perform under reasonable operating conditions without interference between components. Before any additional electrical equipment is installed, it is recommended that you consult your dealer or a reputable repair facility that is familiar with the vehicle and its systems.

If the vehicle is equipped with mobile radio equipment and/or mobile telephone, it may have an effect upon the operation of any on-board computer control modules. Radio Frequency Interference (RFI) from the communications system can be picked up by the vehicle's wiring harnesses and conducted into the control module, giving it the wrong messages at the wrong time. Although well shielded against RFI, the computer should be further protected by taking the following measures:

• Install the antenna as far as possible from the control module. For instance, if the module is located behind the center console area, then the antenna should be mounted at the rear of the vehicle.

• Keep the antenna wiring a minimum of eight inches away from any wiring running to control modules and from the module itself. NEVER wind the antenna wire around any other wiring.

• Mount the equipment as far from the control module as possible. Be very careful during installation not to drill through any wires or short a wire harness with a mounting screw.

• Insure that the electrical feed wire(s) to the equipment are properly and tightly connected. Loose connectors can cause interference.

• Make certain that the equipment is properly grounded to the vehicle. Poor grounding can damage expensive equipment.

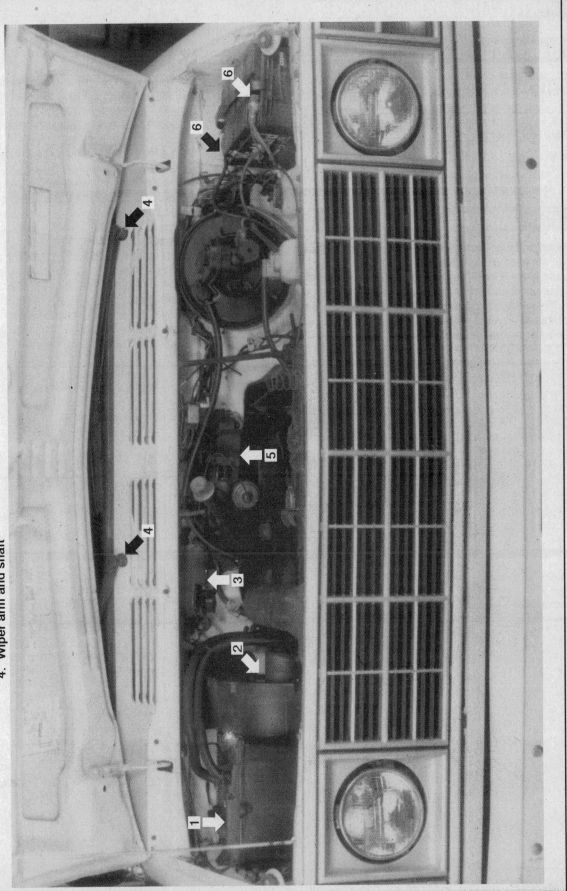

TYPICAL UNDERHOOD ELECTRICAL COMPONENT LOCATIONS

1. Heater box
2. Heater blower motor
3. Wiper motor
4. Wiper arm and shaft
5. Electronic Spark Advance (ESA) computer
6. Battery terminals

HEATER AND AUXILIARY HEATER

Heater Core

REMOVAL & INSTALLATION

1967–69 Models

♦ **See Figures 1 and 2**

1. Disconnect the battery ground cable.
2. Drain the cooling system.

✳✳ CAUTION

When draining the coolant, keep in mind that cats and dogs are attracted by the ethylene glycol antifreeze, and are quite likely to drink any that is left in an uncovered container or in puddles on the ground. This will prove fatal in sufficient quantity. Always drain the coolant into a sealable container. Coolant should be reused unless it is contaminated or several years old.

3. Working through the grille, disconnect the heater hoses from the core tubes.
4. Remove the 2 screws that attach the heater control assembly to the instrument panel and allow the bezel to drop.
5. Disconnect the heater control switch wire at the fuse panel.
6. Remove the 7 screws that attach the fresh air inlet to the dash panel.
7. Remove the 2 screws from the small heater mounting bracket at the top right corner of the heater.
8. Remove the 2 screws that mount the heater support bracket to the floor pan. Loosen the 2 adjusting screws on the heater support bracket.
9. Remove the 2 nuts that attach the heater assembly to the dash panel mounting studs.
10. Pull the heater assembly off the mounting studs, lower the heater assembly and disconnect the defroster hoses.
11. Remove the 7 screws that attach the cover to the heater and pry off the cover.
12. Disconnect the inlet hose coupling at the core.
13. Remove the core.
14. Replace any damaged sealing material.

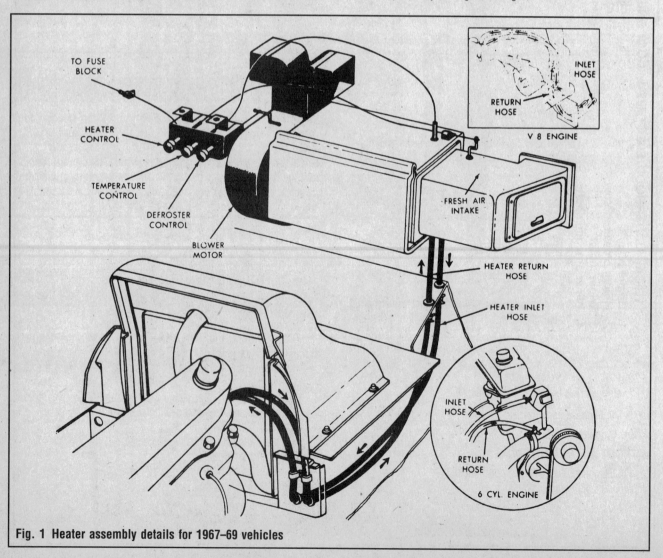

Fig. 1 Heater assembly details for 1967–69 vehicles

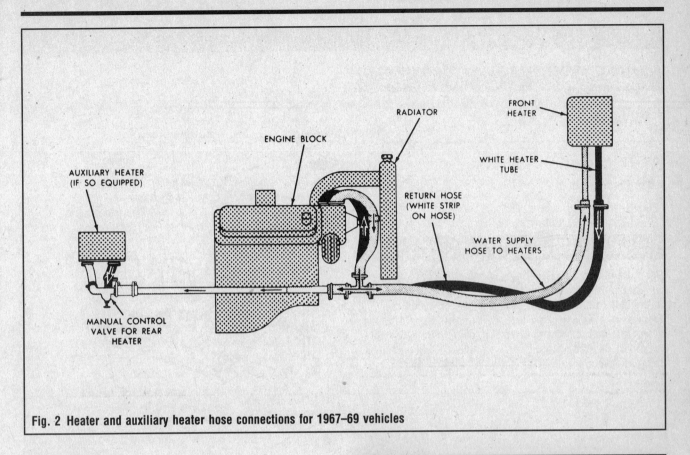

Fig. 2 Heater and auxiliary heater hose connections for 1967–69 vehicles

To install:

15. Install the core.
16. Connect the inlet hose coupling at the core.
17. Install the cover on the heater.
18. Connect the defroster hoses. Position the heater assembly on the mounting studs.
19. Install the 2 nuts that attach the heater assembly to the dash panel mounting studs.
20. Install the 2 screws that mount the heater support bracket to the floor pan. Tighten the 2 adjusting screws on the heater support bracket.
21. Install the 2 screws in the small heater mounting bracket at the top right corner of the heater.
22. Install the 7 screws that attach the fresh air inlet to the dash panel.
23. Connect the heater control switch wire at the fuse panel.
24. Install the 2 screws that attach the heater control assembly to the instrument panel.
25. Working through the grille, connect the heater hoses to the core tubes.
26. Fill the cooling system.
27. Connect the battery ground cable.

1970–77 Models

▶ See Figures 3 and 4

WITHOUT AIR CONDITIONING

1. Disconnect the battery ground cable.
2. Drain the cooling system.

✳✳ CAUTION

When draining the coolant, keep in mind that cats and dogs are attracted by the ethylene glycol antifreeze, and are quite likely to drink any that is left in an uncovered container or in puddles on the ground. This will prove fatal in sufficient quantity. Always drain the coolant into a sealable container. Coolant should be reused unless it is contaminated or several years old.

3. Cover the alternator with a plastic bag.
4. Disconnect the wiring at the blower.
5. Disconnect the hoses at the core tubes.
6. Disconnect the control cables at the case.
7. Unbolt the water valve and move it aside without disconnecting the hoses.
8. Remove the blower motor cooling tube.
9. Remove the 3 housing retaining nuts and tip the unit out through the hood opening.
10. Remove the 3 nuts and lift the blower motor from the case.
11. Remove the 4 cover nuts and lift the cover off.
12. Remove the 4 core retaining screws and lift out the core.
13. Replace any damaged sealing material.
14. Install the core in the case.
15. Install the 4 core retaining screws.
16. Install the cover.
17. Install the blower motor in the case.
18. Install the housing.

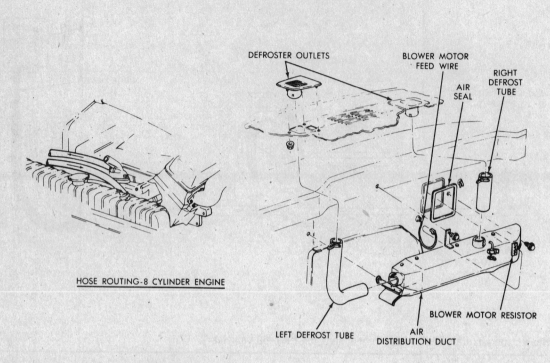

HOSE ROUTING-8 CYLINDER ENGINE

DEFROSTER OUTLETS

BLOWER MOTOR FEED WIRE

AIR SEAL

RIGHT DEFROST TUBE

LEFT DEFROST TUBE

AIR DISTRIBUTION DUCT

BLOWER MOTOR RESISTOR

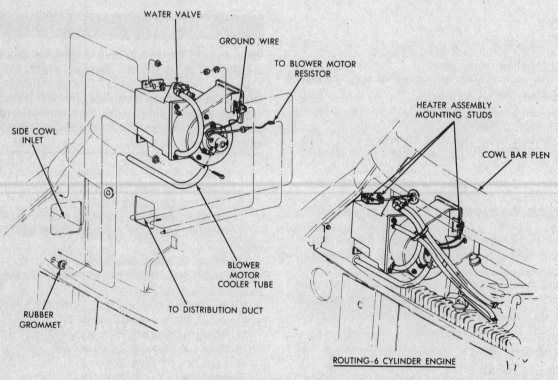

WATER VALVE

GROUND WIRE

TO BLOWER MOTOR RESISTOR

SIDE COWL INLET

RUBBER GROMMET

TO DISTRIBUTION DUCT

BLOWER MOTOR COOLER TUBE

HEATER ASSEMBLY MOUNTING STUDS

COWL BAR PLEN

ROUTING-6 CYLINDER ENGINE

Fig. 3 Heater assembly details for 1970–77 vehicles

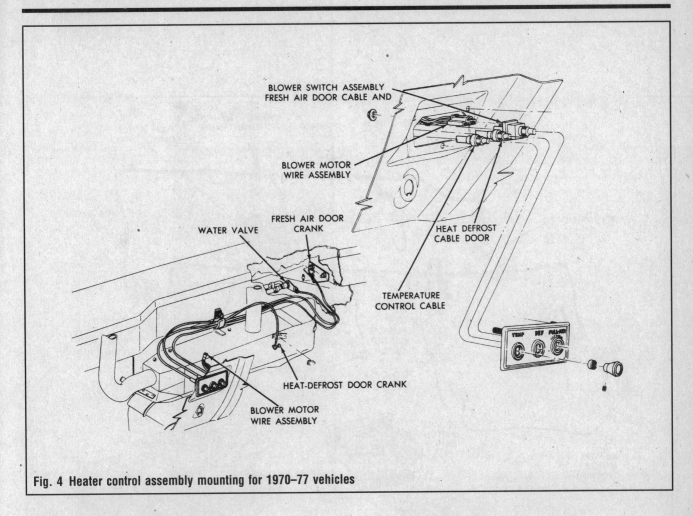

Fig. 4 Heater control assembly mounting for 1970–77 vehicles

19. Install the blower motor cooling tube.
20. Install the water valve.
21. Connect the control cables at the case.
22. Connect the hoses at the core tubes.
23. Connect the wiring at the blower.
24. Uncover the alternator.
25. Fill the cooling system.
26. Connect the battery ground cable.

WITH AIR CONDITIONING
▶ See Figures 5, 6, 7 and 8

1. Discharge the system. Refer to Section 1.
2. Disconnect the battery ground.
3. Drain the cooling system.

✳✳ CAUTION

When draining the coolant, keep in mind that cats and dogs are attracted by the ethylene glycol antifreeze, and are quite likely to drink any that is left in an uncovered container or in puddles on the ground. This will prove fatal in sufficient quantity. Always drain the coolant into a sealable container. Coolant should be reused unless it is contaminated or several years old.

4. Remove the grille.
5. Remove the condenser. Refer to the applicable procedure in this section.

6. Remove the radiator. Refer to Section 3.
7. Cover the alternator with a plastic bag.
8. Disconnect the heater hoses at the core tubes.
9. Using a back-up wrench on the fittings, disconnect the refrigerant lines at the case. Cap all openings at once!
10. Remove the glove box.
11. Remove the spot cooler bezel and appearance shield.
12. Working through the glove box, remove the evaporator housing-to-dash panel attaching screws and nuts.
13. Remove the windshield wiper motor.
14. Tag and disconnect all wiring and hoses at the evaporator case.
15. Disconnect the blower motor cooler hose and drain hoses.
16. Remove the two 2¼" bolts from the crossbar and the four screws from the sealplate on the front of the housing.
17. Separate the evaporator housing from the blower motor housing and carefully remove it from the van.
18. Remove the receiver-drier and cap all openings at once!
19. Carefully pry the heater core from the housing. Don't remove the air seal from the front of the core unless it is damaged.
To install:
20. Carefully install the heater core in the housing. Replace the air seal if it is damaged.
21. Install the receiver-drier. Use a back-up wrench on the fittings.
22. Install the evaporator housing on the blower motor housing.
23. Install the two 2¼" bolts in the crossbar and the four screws in the sealplate on the front of the housing.

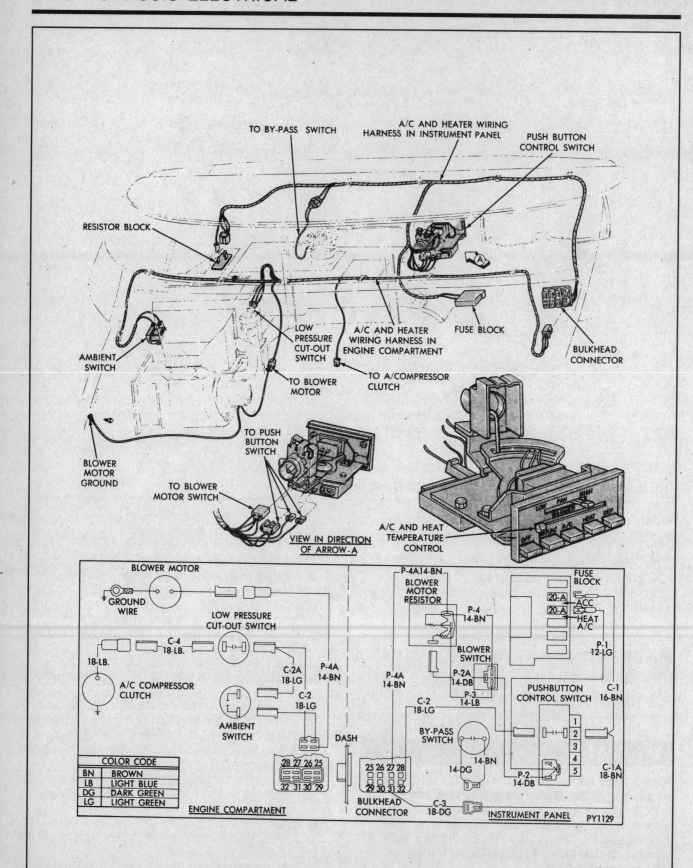

Fig. 5 Heating/air conditioning control unit and schematic for 1970–75 vehicles

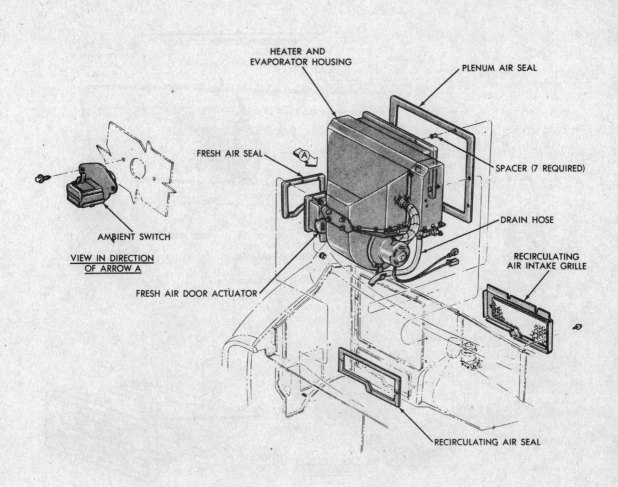

HEATER AND
EVAPORATOR HOUSING

PLENUM AIR SEAL

FRESH AIR SEAL

SPACER (7 REQUIRED)

DRAIN HOSE

AMBIENT SWITCH

RECIRCULATING
AIR INTAKE GRILLE

**VIEW IN DIRECTION
OF ARROW A**

FRESH AIR DOOR ACTUATOR

RECIRCULATING AIR SEAL

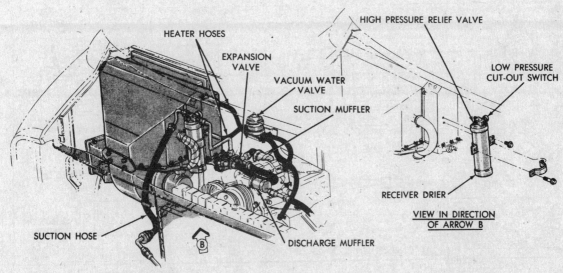

HEATER HOSES

HIGH PRESSURE RELIEF VALVE

EXPANSION
VALVE

LOW PRESSURE
CUT-OUT SWITCH

VACUUM WATER
VALVE

SUCTION MUFFLER

SUCTION HOSE

RECEIVER DRIER

**VIEW IN DIRECTION
OF ARROW B**

DISCHARGE MUFFLER

Fig. 6 Heating/air conditioning assembly mounting for 1970–75 vehicles

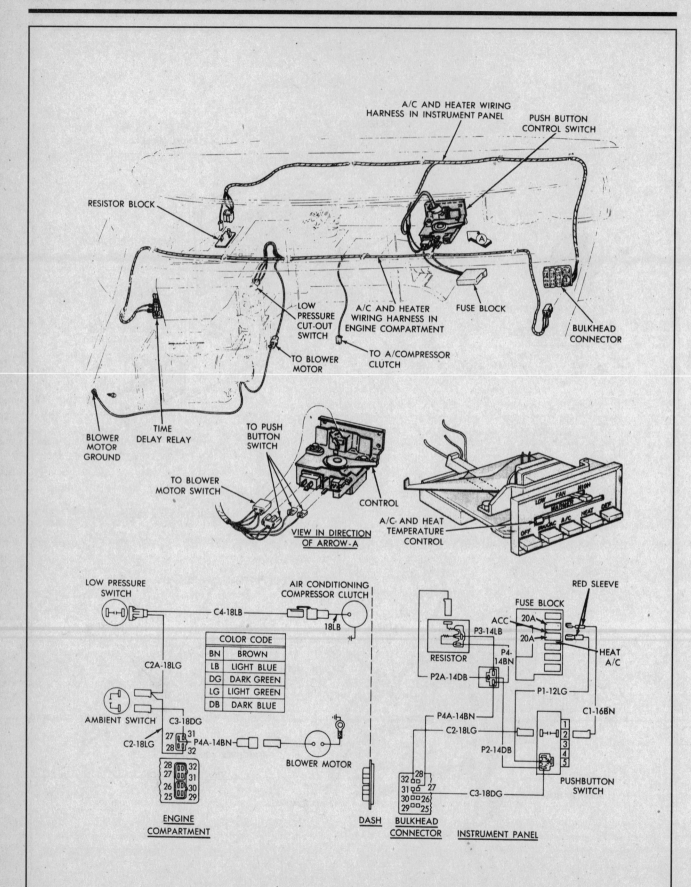

Fig. 7 Heating/air conditioning control unit and schematic for 1976–77 vehicles

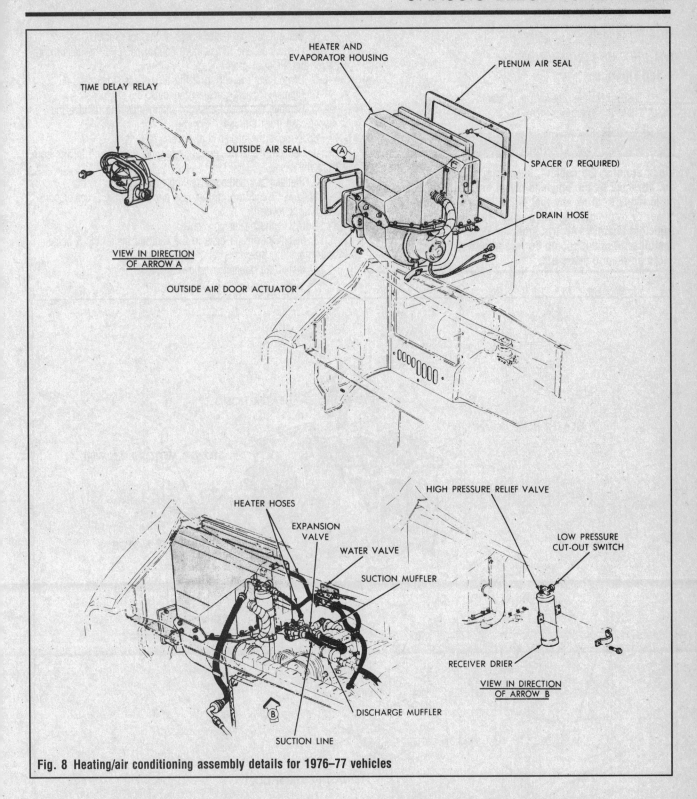

Fig. 8 Heating/air conditioning assembly details for 1976–77 vehicles

24. Connect the blower motor cooler hose and drain hoses.
25. Connect all wiring and hoses at the evaporator case.
26. Install the windshield wiper motor.
27. Working through the glove box, install the evaporator housing-to-dash panel attaching screws and nuts.
28. Install the spot cooler bezel and appearance shield.
29. Install the glove box.
30. Using a back-up wrench on the fittings, connect the refrigerant lines at the case.

31. Connect the heater hoses at the core tubes.
32. Uncover the alternator.
33. Install the radiator. Refer to Section 3.
34. Install the condenser. Refer to the applicable procedure in this section.
35. Install the grille.
36. Fill the cooling system.
37. Connect the battery ground.
38. Evacuate, charge and leak test the system. Refer to Section 1.

1978–79 Models

WITHOUT AIR CONDITIONING

♦ **See Figure 9**

1. Disconnect the battery ground cable.
2. Drain the cooling system.

✳✳ CAUTION

When draining the coolant, keep in mind that cats and dogs are attracted by the ethylene glycol antifreeze, and are quite likely to drink any that is left in an uncovered container or in puddles on the ground. This will prove fatal in sufficient quantity. Always drain the coolant into a sealable container. Coolant should be reused unless it is contaminated or several years old.

3. Disconnect the heater hoses at the core tubes.
4. Disconnect the temperature control cable at the heater core cover and air door crank.
5. Disconnect the wiring at the blower resistor.
6. Remove the coolant overflow tank.
7. Remove the heater case mounting nuts and remove the heater case from the van.
8. Remove the heater core cover.
9. Remove the 2 heater core retaining screws and lift the core from the case.
10. Replace any damaged sealing material.
11. Lower the core into the case and install the 2 heater core retaining screws.
12. Install the heater core cover.
13. Install the heater case in the van and install the 5 heater case mounting nuts.
14. Install the coolant overflow tank.

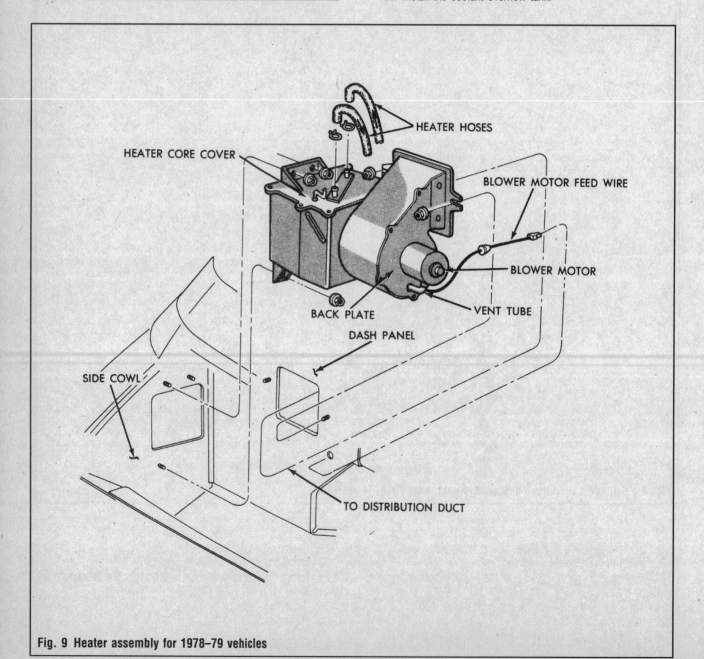

Fig. 9 Heater assembly for 1978–79 vehicles

15. Connect the wiring at the blower resistor.
16. Connect the temperature control cable at the heater core cover and air door crank.
17. Connect the heater hoses at the core tubes.
18. Fill the cooling system.
19. Connect the battery ground cable.

WITH AIR CONDITIONING

▸ **See Figures 10 and 11**

1. Discharge the system. Refer to Section 1.
2. Disconnect the battery ground.
3. Drain the cooling system.

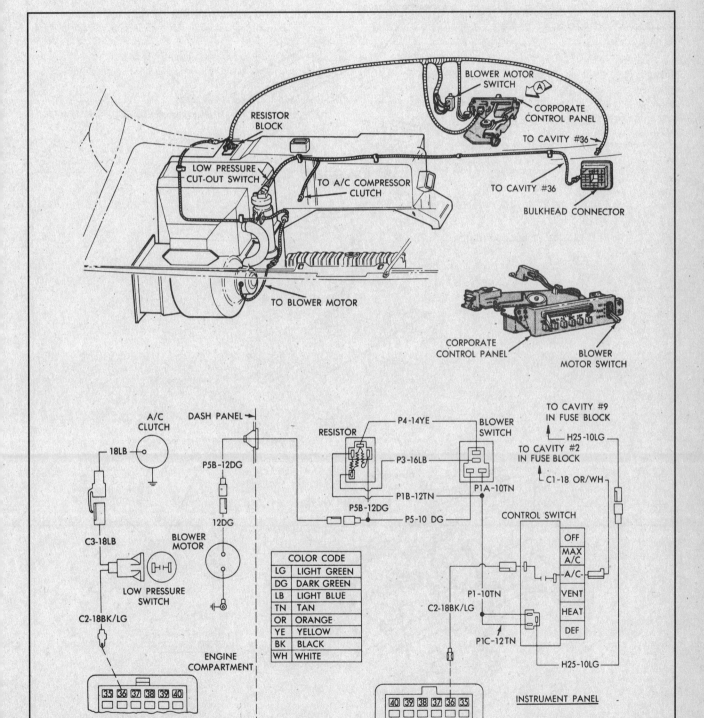

Fig. 10 Heating/air conditioning control unit and schematic for 1978–79 vehicles

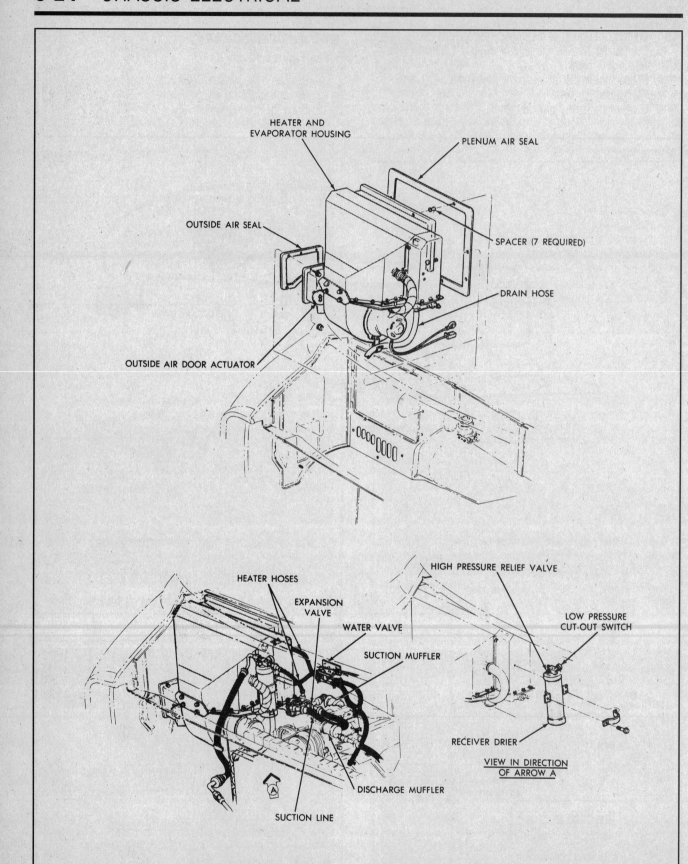

Fig. 11 Heating/air conditioning assembly for 1978–79 vehicles

✳✳ CAUTION

When draining the coolant, keep in mind that cats and dogs are attracted by the ethylene glycol antifreeze, and are quite likely to drink any that is left in an uncovered container or in puddles on the ground. This will prove fatal in sufficient quantity. Always drain the coolant into a sealable container. Coolant should be reused unless it is contaminated or several years old.

4. Remove the grille.
5. Remove the condenser. Refer to the applicable procedure in this section.
6. Remove the radiator. Refer to Section 3.
7. Cover the alternator with a plastic bag.
8. Disconnect the heater hoses at the core tubes.
9. Using a back-up wrench on the fittings, disconnect the refrigerant lines at the case. Cap all openings at once!
10. Remove the glove box.

Disconnect the temperature control cable from the air door crank . . .

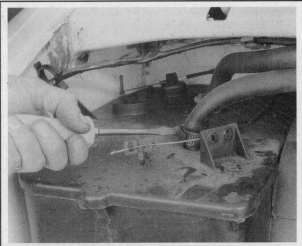

To remove the heater core, drain the cooling system and loosen the heater hose clamps . . .

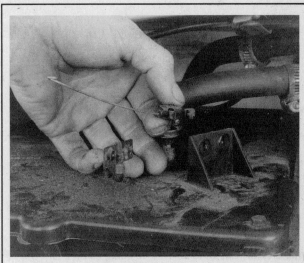

. . . and unsnap the cable housing from the heater box

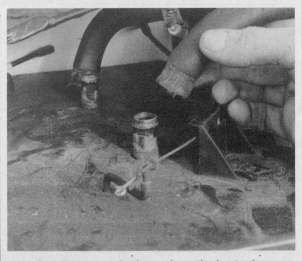

. . . then disconnect the hoses from the heater box

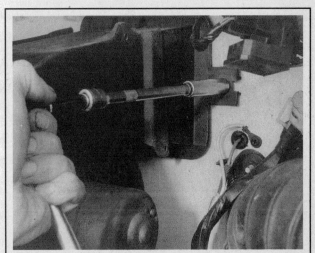

Unplug any electrical connections to the heater box, then remove the box retaining nuts

Pull the heater box assembly out of the vehicle

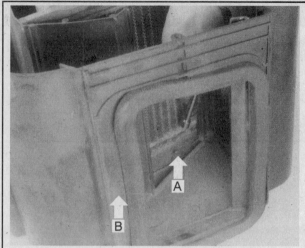

Remove the two heater core retaining screws (A & B; A is visible, B is behind the box opening) . . .

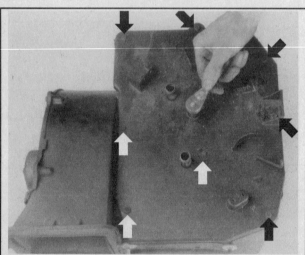

Remove the heater box cover retaining screws (arrows) . . .

. . . and lift the heater core out of the box

. . . and remove the cover from the heater box

11. Remove the spot cooler bezel and appearance shield.

12. Working through the glove box, remove the evaporator housing-to-dash panel attaching screws and nuts.

13. Remove the windshield wiper motor.

14. Tag and disconnect all wiring and hoses at the evaporator case.

15. Disconnect the blower motor cooler hose and drain hoses.

16. Remove the two 2¼" bolts from the crossbar and the four screws from the sealplate on the front of the housing.

17. Separate the evaporator housing from the blower motor housing and carefully remove it from the van.

18. Remove the receiver-drier and cap all openings at once!

19. Carefully pry the heater core from the housing. Don't remove the air seal from the front of the core unless it is damaged.

To install:

20. Carefully install the heater core in the housing. Replace the air seal if it is damaged.

21. Install the receiver-drier. Use a back-up wrench on the fittings.

22. Install the evaporator housing on the blower motor housing.

23. Install the two 2¼" bolts in the crossbar and the four screws in the sealplate on the front of the housing.

24. Connect the blower motor cooler hose and drain hoses.

25. Connect all wiring and hoses at the evaporator case.

26. Install the windshield wiper motor.

27. Working through the glove box, install the evaporator housing-to-dash panel attaching screws and nuts.

28. Install the spot cooler bezel and appearance shield.

29. Install the glove box.

30. Using a back-up wrench on the fittings, connect the refrigerant lines at the case.

31. Connect the heater hoses at the core tubes.

32. Uncover the alternator.

33. Install the radiator. Refer to Section 3.

34. Install the condenser. Refer to the applicable procedure in this section.

35. Install the grille.

36. Fill the cooling system.

37. Connect the battery ground.

38. Evacuate, charge and leak test the system. Refer to Section 1.

1980–88 Models

WITHOUT AIR CONDITIONING

▶ **See Figure 12**

1. Disconnect the battery ground cable.

2. Drain the cooling system.

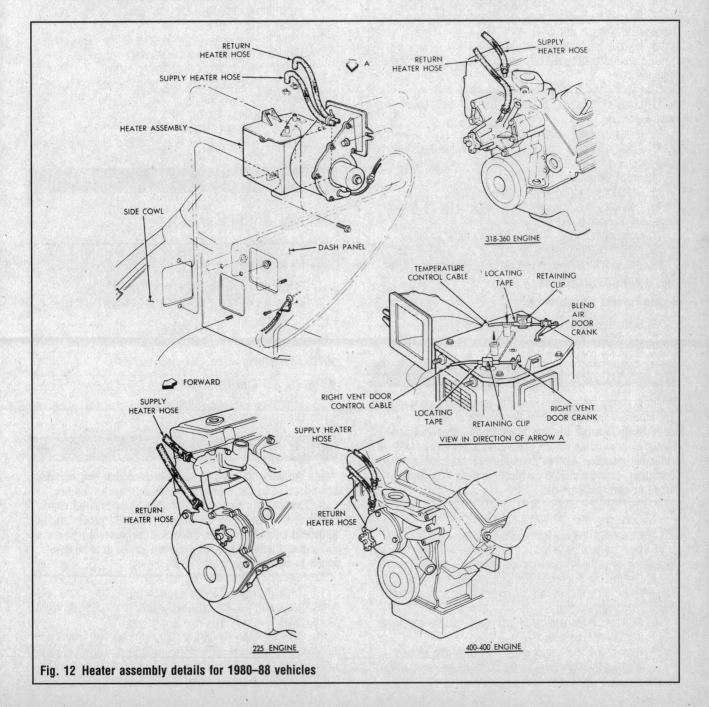

Fig. 12 Heater assembly details for 1980–88 vehicles

❋ CAUTION

When draining the coolant, keep in mind that cats and dogs are attracted by the ethylene glycol antifreeze, and are quite likely to drink any that is left in an uncovered container or in puddles on the ground. This will prove fatal in sufficient quantity. Always drain the coolant into a sealable container. Coolant should be reused unless it is contaminated or several years old.

3. Disconnect the heater hoses at the core tubes.
4. Disconnect the temperature control cable at the heater core cover and air door crank.
5. Disconnect the wiring at the blower resistor.
6. Remove the coolant overflow tank.
7. Remove the 5 heater case mounting nuts and remove the heater case from the van.
8. Remove the heater core cover.
9. Remove the 2 heater core retaining screws and lift the core from the case.
10. Replace any damaged sealing material.
11. Lower the core into the case and install the 2 heater core retaining screws.
12. Install the heater core cover.
13. Install the heater case in the van and install the 5 heater case mounting nuts.
14. Install the coolant overflow tank.
15. Connect the wiring at the blower resistor.
16. Connect the temperature control cable at the heater core cover and air door crank.
17. Connect the heater hoses at the core tubes.
18. Fill the cooling system.
19. Connect the battery ground cable.

WITH AIR CONDITIONING

▶ **See Figures 13 and 14**

1. Discharge the system. Refer to Section 1.
2. Disconnect the battery ground.
3. Drain the cooling system.

❋ CAUTION

When draining the coolant, keep in mind that cats and dogs are attracted by the ethylene glycol antifreeze, and are quite likely to drink any that is left in an uncovered container or in puddles on the ground. This will prove fatal in sufficient quantity. Always drain the coolant into a sealable container. Coolant should be reused unless it is contaminated or several years old.

4. Cover the alternator with a plastic bag.
5. Disconnect the heater hoses at the core tubes.
6. Using a back-up wrench on the fittings, disconnect the refrigerant lines at the H-valve. Cap all openings at once!
7. Remove the 2 screws from the filter-drier bracket and swing the piping out of the way, towards the center of the van. Cap all openings at once!
8. Remove the temperature control cable from the case cover.
9. Remove the glove box.
10. Remove the spot cooler bezel and appearance shield.
11. Working through the glove box, remove the evaporator housing-to-dash panel attaching screws and nuts.

12. Remove the 2 screws from the flange connection at the blower housing. Separate the evaporator housing from the blower motor housing and carefully remove it from the van.
13. Remove the cover from the housing.
14. Remove 1 screw from the strap on the heater core tubes and pull the core from the housing.

To install:

15. Put the core in the housing. Install 1 screw in the strap on the heater core tubes.
16. Install the cover on the housing.
17. Join the evaporator housing to the blower motor housing. Install the 2 screws in the flange connection at the blower housing.
18. Working through the glove box, install the evaporator housing-to-dash panel attaching screws and nuts.
19. Install the spot cooler bezel and appearance shield.
20. Install the glove box.
21. Install the temperature control cable on the case cover.
22. Install the 2 screws from the filter-drier bracket.
23. Connect the refrigerant lines at the H-valve.
24. Connect the heater hoses at the core tubes.
25. Uncover the alternator.
26. Fill the cooling system.
27. Connect the battery ground.
28. Evacuate, charge and leak test the system. Refer to Section 1.

Blower Motor

REMOVAL & INSTALLATION

1967–69 Models

1. Disconnect the wiring at the blower motor.
2. Remove the 6 blower motor mounting screws and lift out the blower motor.
3. Installation is the reverse of removal.

1970–77 Models

WITHOUT AIR CONDITIONING

1. Disconnect the battery ground cable.
2. Drain the cooling system.

❋ CAUTION

When draining the coolant, keep in mind that cats and dogs are attracted by the ethylene glycol antifreeze, and are quite likely to drink any that is left in an uncovered container or in puddles on the ground. This will prove fatal in sufficient quantity. Always drain the coolant into a sealable container. Coolant should be reused unless it is contaminated or several years old.

3. Cover the alternator with a plastic bag.
4. Disconnect the wiring at the blower.
5. Disconnect the hoses at the core tubes.
6. Disconnect the control cables at the case.
7. Unbolt the water valve and move it aside without disconnecting the hoses.
8. Remove the blower motor cooling tube.

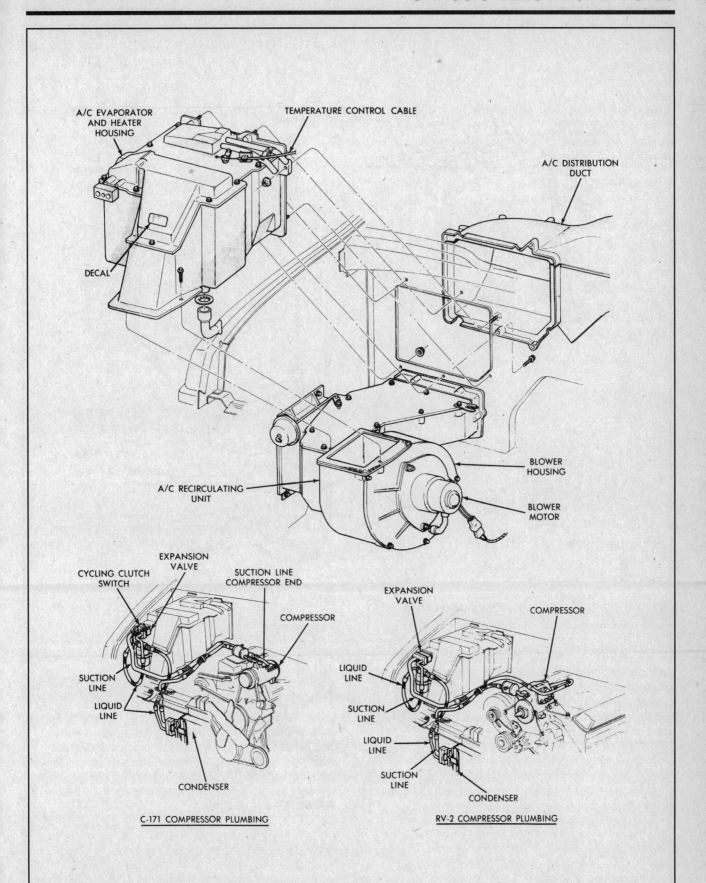

A/C EVAPORATOR AND HEATER HOUSING

TEMPERATURE CONTROL CABLE

A/C DISTRIBUTION DUCT

DECAL

BLOWER HOUSING

A/C RECIRCULATING UNIT

BLOWER MOTOR

CYCLING CLUTCH SWITCH

EXPANSION VALVE

SUCTION LINE COMPRESSOR END

COMPRESSOR

SUCTION LINE

LIQUID LINE

CONDENSER

C-171 COMPRESSOR PLUMBING

EXPANSION VALVE

COMPRESSOR

LIQUID LINE

SUCTION LINE

LIQUID LINE

SUCTION LINE

CONDENSER

RV-2 COMPRESSOR PLUMBING

Fig. 13 Heating/air conditioning assembly for 1980–82 vehicles

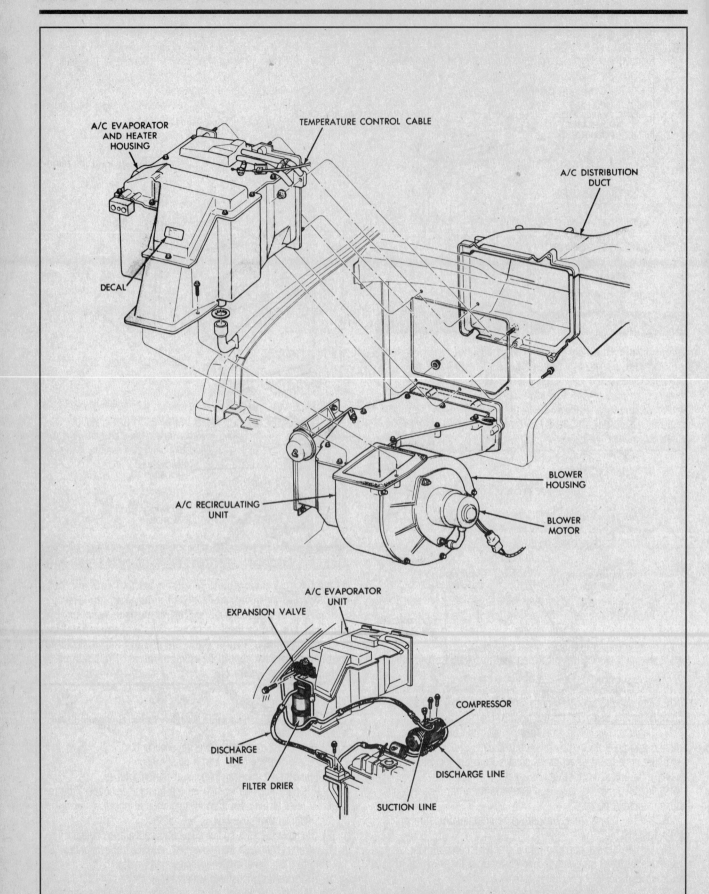

Fig. 14 Heating/air conditioning assembly for 1983–88 vehicles

9. Remove the 3 housing retaining nuts and tip the unit out through the hood opening.

10. Remove the 3 nuts and lift the blower motor from the case.

11. Replace any damaged sealing material.

12. Install the blower motor in the case.

13. Install the housing.

14. Install the blower motor cooling tube.

15. Install the water valve.

16. Connect the control cables at the case.

17. Connect the hoses at the core tubes.

18. Connect the wiring at the blower.

19. Uncover the alternator.

20. Fill the cooling system.

21. Connect the battery ground cable.

WITH AIR CONDITIONING

1. Discharge the system. Refer to Section 1.

2. Disconnect the battery ground.

3. Drain the cooling system.

✳✳ CAUTION

When draining the coolant, keep in mind that cats and dogs are attracted by the ethylene glycol antifreeze, and are quite likely to drink any that is left in an uncovered container or in puddles on the ground. This will prove fatal in sufficient quantity. Always drain the coolant into a sealable container. Coolant should be reused unless it is contaminated or several years old.

4. Remove the grille.

5. Remove the condenser. Refer to the applicable procedure in this section.

6. Remove the radiator. Refer to Section 3.

7. Cover the alternator with a plastic bag.

8. Disconnect the heater hoses at the core tubes.

9. Using a back-up wrench on the fittings, disconnect the refrigerant lines at the case. Cap all openings at once!

10. Remove the glove box.

11. Remove the spot cooler bezel and appearance shield.

12. Working through the glove box, remove the evaporator housing-to-dash panel attaching screws and nuts.

13. Remove the windshield wiper motor.

14. Tag and disconnect all wiring and hoses at the evaporator case.

15. Disconnect the blower motor cooler hose and drain hoses.

16. Remove the two 2¼" bolts from the crossbar and the four screws from the sealplate on the front of the housing.

17. Separate the evaporator housing from the blower motor housing and carefully remove it from the van.

18. Remove the 4 sheet metal screws from the recirculating air intake grille under the instrument panel.

19. Remove the 3 screws and one stud nut from the fresh air housing-to-cowl panel.

20. Lift the blower housing out of the engine compartment.

To install:

21. Lift the blower housing into the engine compartment.

22. Install the 3 screws and one stud nut in the fresh air housing-to-cowl panel.

23. Install the 4 sheet metal screws in the recirculating air intake grille under the instrument panel.

24. Install the evaporator housing on the blower motor housing.

25. Install the two 2¼" bolts in the crossbar and the four screws in the sealplate on the front of the housing.

26. Connect the blower motor cooler hose and drain hoses.

27. Connect all wiring and hoses at the evaporator case.

28. Install the windshield wiper motor.

29. Working through the glove box, install the evaporator housing-to-dash panel attaching screws and nuts.

30. Install the spot cooler bezel and appearance shield.

31. Install the glove box.

32. Using a back-up wrench on the fittings, connect the refrigerant lines at the case.

33. Connect the heater hoses at the core tubes.

34. Uncover the alternator.

35. Install the radiator. Refer to Section 3.

36. Install the condenser. Refer to the applicable procedure in this section.

37. Install the grille.

38. Fill the cooling system.

39. Connect the battery ground.

40. Evacuate, charge and leak test the system. Refer to Section 1.

1978 Models

▶ See Figure 15

WITHOUT AIR CONDITIONING

1. Disconnect the battery ground cable.

2. Disconnect the blower motor wire at the resitor block.

3. Remove the blower backing plate-to-cowl panel nut.

4. Remove the 7 backing plate-to-heater housing screws and remove the blower motor. Replace any damaged sealing material.

5. Installation is the reverse of removal.

WITH AIR CONDITIONING

1. Discharge the system. Refer to Section 1.

2. Disconnect the battery ground.

3. Drain the cooling system.

✳✳ CAUTION

When draining the coolant, keep in mind that cats and dogs are attracted by the ethylene glycol antifreeze, and are quite likely to drink any that is left in an uncovered container or in puddles on the ground. This will prove fatal in sufficient quantity. Always drain the coolant into a sealable container. Coolant should be reused unless it is contaminated or several years old.

4. Remove the grille.

5. Remove the condenser. See Refer to the applicable procedure in this section.

6. Remove the radiator. Refer to Section 3.

7. Cover the alternator with a plastic bag.

8. Disconnect the heater hoses at the core tubes.

9. Using a back-up wrench on the fittings, disconnect the refrigerant lines at the case. Cap all openings at once!

10. Remove the glove box.

11. Remove the spot cooler bezel and appearance shield.

12. Working through the glove box, remove the evaporator housing-to-dash panel attaching screws and nuts.

13. Remove the windshield wiper motor.

14. Tag and disconnect all wiring and hoses at the evaporator case.

15. Disconnect the blower motor cooler hose and drain hoses.

16. Remove the two 2¼" bolts from the crossbar and the four screws from the sealplate on the front of the housing.

17. Separate the evaporator housing from the blower motor housing and carefully remove it from the van.

18. Remove the 4 sheet metal screws from the recirculating air intake grille under the instrument panel.

19. Remove the 3 screws and one stud nut from the fresh air housing-to-cowl panel.

20. Lift the blower housing out of the engine compartment.

To install:

21. Lift the blower housing into the engine compartment.

22. Install the 3 screws and one stud nut in the fresh air housing-to-cowl panel.

23. Install the 4 sheet metal screws in the recirculating air intake grille under the instrument panel.

24. Install the evaporator housing on the blower motor housing.

25. Install the two 2¼" bolts in the crossbar and the four screws in the sealplate on the front of the housing.

26. Connect the blower motor cooler hose and drain hoses.

27. Connect all wiring and hoses at the evaporator case.

28. Install the windshield wiper motor.

29. Working through the glove box, install the evaporator housing-to-dash panel attaching screws and nuts.

30. Install the spot cooler bezel and appearance shield.

31. Install the glove box.

32. Using a back-up wrench on the fittings, connect the refrigerant lines at the case.

33. Connect the heater hoses at the core tubes.

34. Uncover the alternator.

35. Install the radiator. Refer to Section 3.

36. Install the condenser. Refer to the applicable procedure in this section.

37. Install the grille.

38. Fill the cooling system.

39. Connect the battery ground.

40. Evacuate, charge and leak test the system. Refer to Section 1.

1979 Models

▶ See Figure 15

WITHOUT AIR CONDITIONING

1. Disconnect the battery ground cable.
2. Disconnect the blower motor wire at the resitor block.
3. Remove the blower backing plate-to-cowl panel nut.
4. Remove the 7 backing plate-to-heater housing screws and remove the blower motor. Replace any damaged sealing material.
5. Installation is the reverse of removal.

WITH AIR CONDITIONING

1. Disconnect the battery ground cable.
2. Raise and support the front end on jackstands.
3. Remove the blower motor cooler tube from the blower.
4. Disconnect the wiring at the blower.
5. Remove the 3 mounting plate screws and remove the blower motor from the housing.

1980–88 Models

▶ See Figure 15

WITHOUT AIR CONDITIONING

1. Disconnect the battery ground cable.
2. Disconnect the blower motor wire at the resitor block.

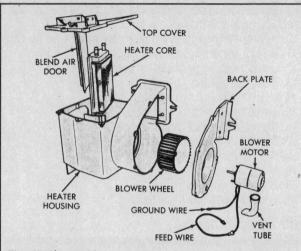

Fig. 15 Heater blower motor and related components on 1978–88 vehicles

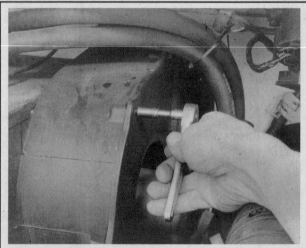

To remove the blower motor, disconnect the wires and remove the motor plate screws . . .

. . . then remove the assembly from the vehicle

3. Remove the blower backing plate-to-cowl panel nut.

4. Remove the 7 backing plate-to-heater housing screws and remove the blower motor. Replace any damaged sealing material.

5. Installation is the reverse of removal.

WITH AIR CONDITIONING

1. Remove the top half of the shroud by removing the 4 screws: 2 from the radiator support and the 2 holding the shroud halves together.

➡ On 6-cylinder engines, the upper right screw is hidden behind the discharge line muffler.

2. Remove the blower motor cooler tube from the blower.

3. Disconnect the wiring at the blower.

4. Remove the 3 mounting plate screws.

5. While holding the suction and discharge lines inboard and upward, pull the blower motor from the housing.

6. Installation is the reverse of removal. Replace any damaged sealing material.

Auxiliary Heater Core

REMOVAL & INSTALLATION

1967–77 Models

▶ See Figure 16

1. Drain the cooling system.

❄ CAUTION

When draining the coolant, keep in mind that cats and dogs are attracted by the ethylene glycol antifreeze, and are quite likely to drink any that is left in an uncovered container or in puddles on the ground. This will prove fatal in sufficient quantity. Always drain the coolant into a sealable container. Coolant should be reused unless it is contaminated or several years old.

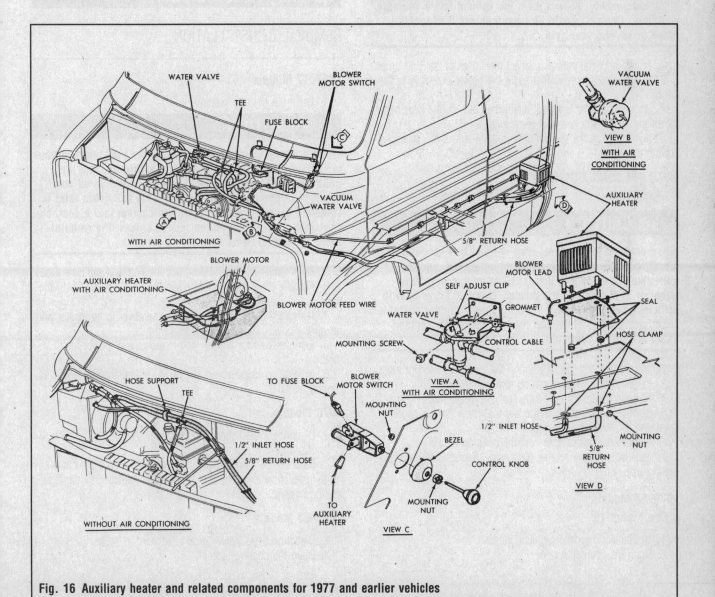

Fig. 16 Auxiliary heater and related components for 1977 and earlier vehicles

2. From under the van, disconnect the hoses at the core tubes.

3. Remove the 4 screws that retain the heater assembly to the floor.

4. Remove the 4 screws that retain the cover to the heater and lift off the cover. The core will come with it.

5. Installation is the reverse of removal. Replace any damaged sealing material.

1978 Models

♦ See Figure 17

WITHOUT AUXILIARY AIR CONDITIONING

1. Drain the cooling system.

> ❊❊ **CAUTION**
>
> **When draining the coolant, keep in mind that cats and dogs are attracted by the ethylene glycol antifreeze, and are quite likely to drink any that is left in an uncovered container or in puddles on the ground. This will prove fatal in sufficient quantity. Always drain the coolant into a sealable container. Coolant should be reused unless it is contaminated or several years old.**

2. From under the van, disconnect the hoses at the core tubes.

3. Remove the 4 screws that retain the heater assembly to the floor.

4. Remove the 4 screws that retain the cover to the heater and lift off the cover. The core will come with it.

5. Installation is the reverse of removal. Replace any damaged sealing material.

WITH AIR CONDITIONING

1. Drain the cooling system.

> ❊❊ **CAUTION**
>
> **When draining the coolant, keep in mind that cats and dogs are attracted by the ethylene glycol antifreeze, and are quite likely to drink any that is left in an uncovered container or in puddles on the ground. This will prove fatal in sufficient quantity. Always drain the coolant into a sealable container. Coolant should be reused unless it is contaminated or several years old.**

2. From under the van, disconnect the hoses at the core tubes.

3. Remove the auxiliary housing lower cover screws.

4. Remove the heater core tube seal and cover plate.

5. Remove the 2 screws that retain the heater core support bracket and remove the bracket.

6. Remove the heater core from the housing.

7. Installation is the reverse of removal. Replace any damaged sealing material.

1979–88 Models

♦ See Figure 18

1. Disconnect the battery ground cable.

2. Drain the cooling system.

> ❊❊ **CAUTION**
>
> **When draining the coolant, keep in mind that cats and dogs are attracted by the ethylene glycol antifreeze, and are quite likely to drink any that is left in an uncovered container or in puddles on the ground. This will prove fatal in sufficient quantity. Always drain the coolant into a sealable container. Coolant should be reused unless it is contaminated or several years old.**

3. Disconnect the hoses at the core.

4. Remove the nuts that mount the heater to the floor pan.

5. Disconnect the blower wiring at the blower and remove the heater assembly from inside the van.

6. Remove the cover screws and lift off the cover. The core is attached to the cover.

7. Installation is the reverse of removal. Replace any sealing material.

Auxiliary Heater Blower

REMOVAL & INSTALLATION

1967–77 Models

1. Drain the cooling system.

> ❊❊ **CAUTION**
>
> **When draining the coolant, keep in mind that cats and dogs are attracted by the ethylene glycol antifreeze, and are quite likely to drink any that is left in an uncovered container or in puddles on the ground. This will prove fatal in sufficient quantity. Always drain the coolant into a sealable container. Coolant should be reused unless it is contaminated or several years old.**

2. From under the van, disconnect the hoses at the core tubes.

3. Remove the 4 screws that retain the heater assembly to the floor.

4. Remove the 4 screws that retain the cover to the heater and lift off the cover. The core will come with it.

5. Remove the four blower motor screws and lift out the motor.

6. Installation is the reverse of removal. Replace any damaged sealing material.

1978 Models

1. Disconnect the battery ground cable.

2. Disconnect the blower wires.

3. Remove the blower-to-floor screws and lift out the blower.

4. Installation is the reverse of removal. Replace any damaged sealing material.

1979–88 Models

1. Disconnect the battery ground cable.

2. Drain the cooling system.

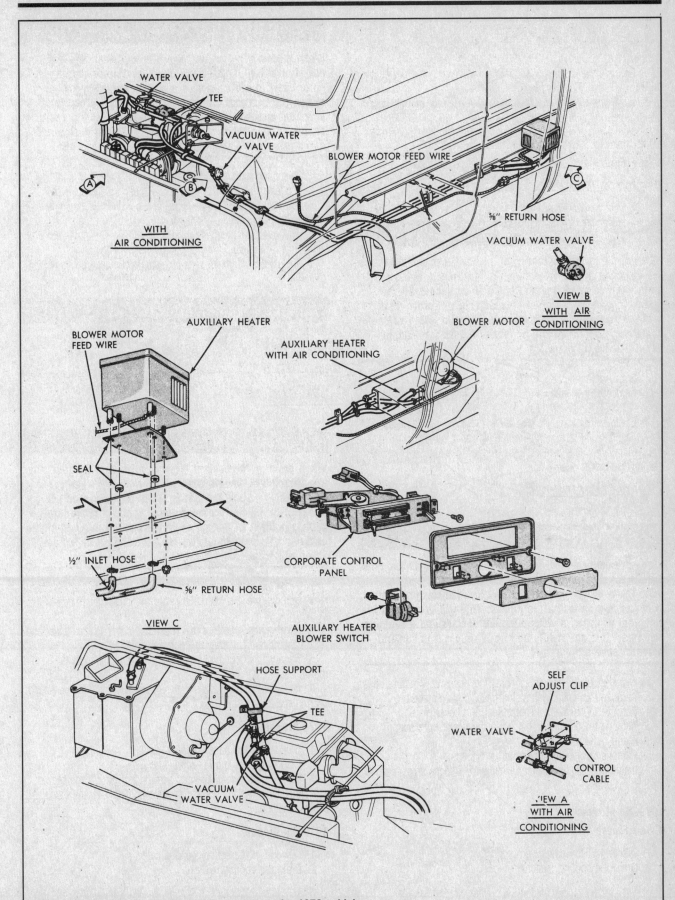

Fig. 17 Auxiliary heater and related components for 1978 vehicles

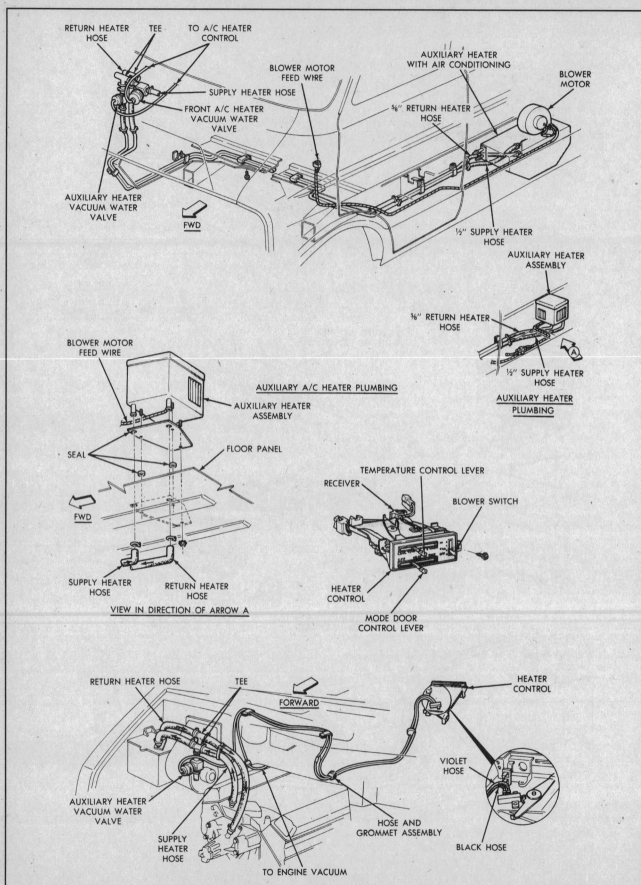

Fig. 18 Auxiliary heater and related components for 1979—88 vehicles

✳✳ CAUTION

When draining the coolant, keep in mind that cats and dogs are attracted by the ethylene glycol antifreeze, and are quite likely to drink any that is left in an uncovered container or in puddles on the ground. This will prove fatal in sufficient quantity. Always drain the coolant into a sealable container. Coolant should be reused unless it is contaminated or several years old.

3. Disconnect the hoses at the core.
4. Remove the nuts that mount the heater to the floor pan.

AIR CONDITIONER AND AUXILIARY AIR CONDITIONER

Air Conditioning Compressor

REMOVAL & INSTALLATION

RV-2 Compressor

1. Discharge the refrigerant system. See ROUTINE MAINTENANCE for the proper procedure.
2. Disconnect the two refrigerant lines from the compressor. Cap the openings immediately!
3. Remove tension from the drive belt. Remove the belt.
4. Disconnect the clutch wire at the connector.
5. Remove the compressor-to-bracket bolts. It may be necessary to loosen the bracket-to-engine bolts.
6. Remove the compressor.
7. Installation is the reverse of removal. Use new O-rings coated with clean refrigerant oil at all fittings. New, replacement compressors contain 10 oz. of refrigerant oil. Prior to installation, pour off 4 oz. of oil. This will maintain the oil charge in the system. Evacuate, charge and leak test the system.

✳✳ WARNING

When replacing the compressor, the compressor crankshaft should be rotated several times by hand to clear oil accumulation from the compressor head before the clutch is energized, to avoid damaging the compressor reed valves.

C-171 Compressor

1. Discharge the refrigerant system. See ROUTINE MAINTENANCE for the proper procedure.
2. Disconnect the two refrigerant lines from the compressor. Cap the openings immediately!
3. Remove tension from the drive belt. Remove the belt.
4. Disconnect the clutch wire at the connector.
5. Remove the compressor-to-bracket bolts. It may be necessary to loosen the bracket-to-engine bolts.
6. Remove the compressor.
7. Installation is the reverse of removal. Use new O-rings coated with clean refrigerant oil at all fittings. New, replacement compressors contain 10 oz. of refrigerant oil. Prior to installation, pour off 4 oz. of oil. This will maintain the oil charge in the system. Evacuate, charge and leak test the system.

5. Disconnect the blower wiring at the blower and remove the heater assembly from inside the van.
6. Remove the cover screws and lift off the cover. The core is attached to the cover.
7. Remove the attaching screws and lift out the blower motor.
8. Installation is the reverse of removal. Replace any sealing material.

Air Conditioning Condenser

REMOVAL & INSTALLATION

1. Discharge the refrigerant system. See Section 1.
2. Disconnect the refrigerant lines from the condenser. Cap all openings immediately!
3. Drain the cooling system.

✳✳ CAUTION

When draining the coolant, keep in mind that cats and dogs are attracted by the ethylene glycol antifreeze, and are quite likely to drink any that is left in an uncovered container or in puddles on the ground. This will prove fatal in sufficient quantity. Always drain the coolant into a sealable container. Coolant should be reused unless it is contaminated or several years old.

4. Disconnect the upper radiator hose.
5. Remove the bolts retaining the ends of the radiator upper support to the side supports.
6. Carefully pull the top edge of the radiator rearward and remove the condenser upper support.
7. Lift out the condenser.
8. If a new condenser is being installed, add 1 fl.oz. of new refrigerant oil to the new condenser. Installation is the reverse of removal. Always use new O-rings coated with clean refrigerant oil on the line fittings. Evacuate, charge and leak test the system.

Evaporator Core

REMOVAL & INSTALLATION

1970–79 Models

1. Discharge the system. Refer to Section 1.
2. Disconnect the battery ground.
3. Drain the cooling system.

✳✳ CAUTION

When draining the coolant, keep in mind that cats and dogs are attracted by the ethylene glycol antifreeze, and are quite likely to drink any that is left in an uncovered container or in puddles on the ground. This will prove fatal in sufficient quantity. Always drain the coolant into a sealable container. Coolant should be reused unless it is contaminated or several years old.

4. Remove the grille.
5. Remove the condenser.
6. Remove the radiator. Refer to Section 3.
7. Cover the alternator with a plastic bag.
8. Disconnect the heater hoses at the core tubes.
9. Using a back-up wrench on the fittings, disconnect the refrigerant lines at the case. Cap all openings at once!
10. Remove the glove box.
11. Remove the spot cooler bezel and appearance shield.
12. Working through the glove box, remove the evaporator housing-to-dash panel attaching screws and nuts.
13. Remove the windshield wiper motor.
14. Tag and disconnect all wiring and hoses at the evaporator case.
15. Disconnect the blower motor cooler hose and drain hoses.
16. Remove the two 2¼″ bolts from the crossbar and the four screws from the sealplate on the front of the housing.
17. Separate the evaporator housing from the blower motor housing and carefully remove it from the van.
18. Remove the receiver-drier, using a back-up wrench on the fittings, and cap all openings at once!
19. Carefully pry the heater core from the housing. Don't remove the seal unless it is damaged and is being replaced.
20. Remove the 6 evaporator core mounting screws from the housing; 3 on each side.
21. Remove the 19 sheet metal screws joining the top and bottom of the housing.
22. Lift the evaporator core from the housing.
To install:
23. Install the evaporator in the housing.
24. Install the 19 sheet metal screws joining the top and bottom of the housing.
25. Install the 6 evaporator core mounting screws in the housing.
26. Install the evaporator housing on the blower motor housing.
27. Install the two 2¼″ bolts in the crossbar and the four screws in the sealplate on the front of the housing.
28. Connect the blower motor cooler hose and drain hoses.
29. Connect all wiring and hoses at the evaporator case.
30. Install the windshield wiper motor.
31. Working through the glove box, install the evaporator housing-to-dash panel attaching screws and nuts.
32. Install the spot cooler bezel and appearance shield.
33. Install the glove box.
34. Using a back-up wrench on the fittings, connect the refrigerant lines at the case.
35. Connect the heater hoses at the core tubes.
36. Uncover the alternator.
37. Install the radiator. Refer to Section 3.
38. Install the condenser.

39. Install the grille.
40. Fill the cooling system.
41. Connect the battery ground.
42. Evacuate, charge and leak test the system. Refer to Section 1.

1980–88 Models

1. Discharge the system. Refer to Section 1.
2. Disconnect the battery ground.
3. Drain the cooling system.

✳✳ CAUTION

When draining the coolant, keep in mind that cats and dogs are attracted by the ethylene glycol antifreeze, and are quite likely to drink any that is left in an uncovered container or in puddles on the ground. This will prove fatal in sufficient quantity. Always drain the coolant into a sealable container. Coolant should be reused unless it is contaminated or several years old.

4. Cover the alternator with a plastic bag.
5. Disconnect the heater hoses at the core tubes.
6. Using a back-up wrench on the fittings, disconnect the refrigerant lines at the H-valve. Cap all openings at once!
7. Remove the 2 screws from the filter-drier bracket and swing the piping out of the way, towards the center of the van. Cap all openings at once!
8. Remove the temperature control cable from the case cover.
9. Remove the glove box.
10. Remove the spot cooler bezel and appearance shield.
11. Working through the glove box, remove the evaporator housing-to-dash panel attaching screws and nuts.
12. Remove the 2 screws from the flange connection at the blower housing. Separate the evaporator housing from the blower motor housing and carefully remove it from the van.
13. Remove the cover from the housing.
14. Remove 1 screw from the strap on the heater core tubes and pull the core from the housing.
15. Remove the attaching screw from under the plumbing attachment plate and pull the evaporator core from the housing.
To install:
16. Put the evaporator core in the housing. Install the attaching screw under the plumbing attachment plate.
17. Put the heater core in the housing. Install 1 screw in the strap on the heater core tubes.
18. Install the cover on the housing.
19. Join the evaporator housing to the blower motor housing. Install the 2 screws in the flange connection at the blower housing.
20. Working through the glove box, install the evaporator housing-to-dash panel attaching screws and nuts.
21. Install the spot cooler bezel and appearance shield.
22. Install the glove box.
23. Install the temperature control cable on the case cover.
24. Install the 2 screws from the filter-drier bracket.
25. Connect the refrigerant lines at the H-valve.
26. Connect the heater hoses at the core tubes.
27. Uncover the alternator.
28. Fill the cooling system.
29. Connect the battery ground.
30. Evacuate, charge and leak test the system. Refer to Section 1.

Auxiliary Evaporator Core

REMOVAL & INSTALLATION

1974–88 Models

1. Discharge the refrigerant system. Refer to Section 1.
2. From under the van, using a back-up wrench on the fittings, disconnect the refrigerant lines from the core tubes. Cover all openings at once!
3. Remove the auxiliary unit lower cover.
4. Remove the seal and cover plate.
5. Remove the core.
6. Installation is the reverse of removal. Evacuate, charge and leak test the system. Refer to Section 1.

Auxiliary Evaporator Blower Motor

▶ **See Figure 19**

REMOVAL & INSTALLATION

1974–88 Models

1. Disconnect the battery ground cable.
2. Disconnect the wiring at the blower.

3. Remove the blower motor-to-floor screws and lift out the blower motor.
4. Installation is the reverse of removal.

Control Unit

REMOVAL & INSTALLATION

1967–69 Models

1. Disconnect the wiring at the control.
2. Disconnect the cables at the heater.
3. Remove the 2 screws and remove the control unit.
4. Installation is the reverse of removal. Adjust the cables.

1970–73 Models

1. Disconnect the battery ground cable.
2. Disconnect the cables at the heater.
3. Remove the setscrews and pull the knobs off the controls.
4. Reach behind the control panel and disconnect the wiring plug. Remove the mounting nuts.
5. Pull the control panel out.
6. Installation is the reverse of removal.

1974–77 Models

1. Remove the instrument cluster.
2. Disconnect the wiring and hoses.

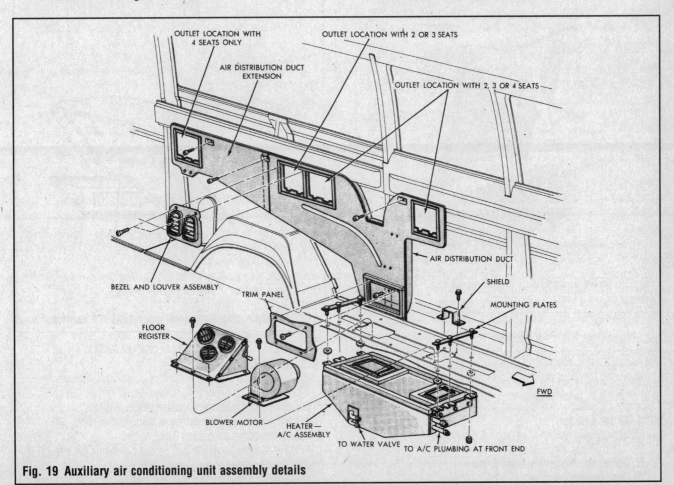

Fig. 19 Auxiliary air conditioning unit assembly details

3. Remove the switch mounting screws.
4. Remove the switch.
5. Installation is the reverse of removal.

1978–88 Models

1. Disconnect the battery ground cable.
2. Remove the control unit bezel.

ENTERTAINMENT SYSTEM

Radio

REMOVAL & INSTALLATION

1967–69 Models

▶ See Figure 20

1. Disconnect the battery ground cable.
2. Remove the glove box.
3. Working through the glove box opening, disconnect the speaker wires, radio wiring and antenna cable.
4. Remove the control knobs, bezel screws, bezel and radio mounting nuts.
5. Working through the glove box opening again, loosen the radio support bracket retaining nut on the bottom of the radio.

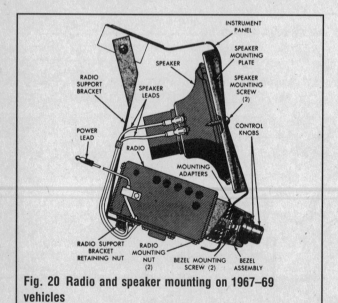

Fig. 20 Radio and speaker mounting on 1967–69 vehicles

6. Remove the 2 speaker mounting screws and remove the speaker and mounting plate through the glove box opening.
7. Working through the glove box opening, pull the radio support bracket away from the radio and pull the radio out.
8. Installation is the reverse of removal.

1970–77 Models

▶ See Figure 21

1. Disconnect the battery ground cable.
2. Remove the glove box.

3. Remove the control unit screws.
4. Pull the control unit out just far enough to disconnect the wiring and hoses and then remove the unit.
5. Installation is the reverse of removal.

3. On vans with air conditioning, remove the defroster duct.
4. Remove the radio bezel.
5. Unplug the antenna from the radio.
6. Remove the front mounting screws.
7. Working through the glove box, remove the rear radio mounting screws.
8. Push in on the radio to clear the lugs, tilt the front upwards and towards you to clear the rear mount bolt.
9. Turn the radio towards the glove box opening and disconnect the wiring.
10. On vans without air conditioning, remove the radio through the glove box opening.
On vans with air conditioning, remove the radio through the front mount opening.
11. Installation is the reverse of removal.

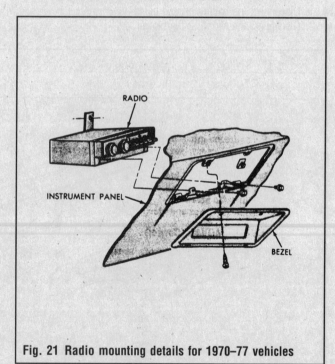

Fig. 21 Radio mounting details for 1970–77 vehicles

1978–88 Models

▶ See Figure 22 and 23

1. Remove the instrument cluster bezel.
2. Remove the radio mounting screws.
3. Remove the radio ground strap screw.
4. Pull the radio from the instrument panel just far enough to disconnect the wiring and antenna lead.
5. Installation is the reverse of removal.

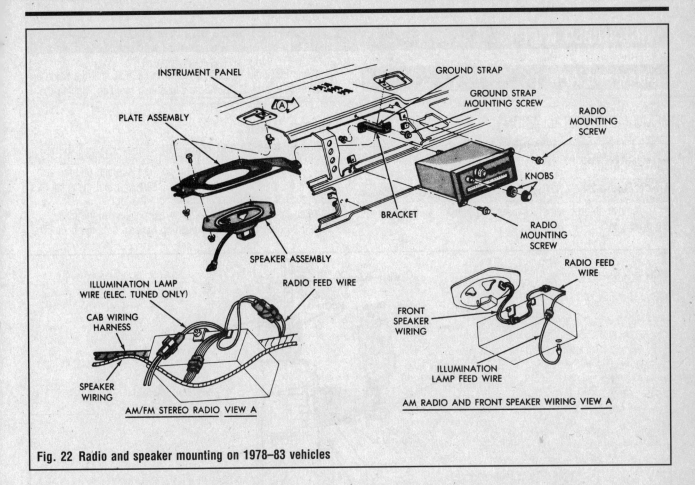

Fig. 22 Radio and speaker mounting on 1978–83 vehicles

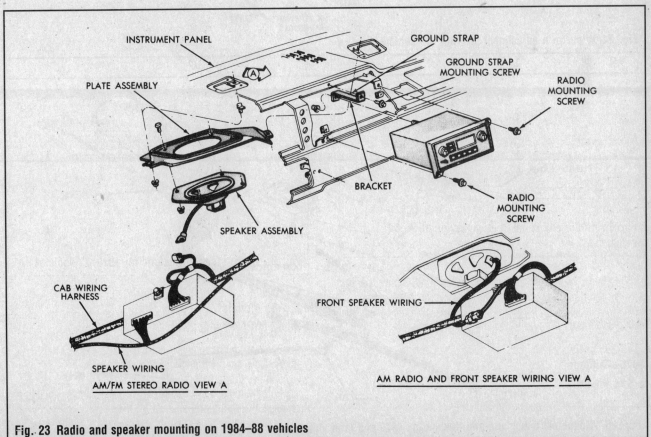

Fig. 23 Radio and speaker mounting on 1984–88 vehicles

WINDSHIELD WIPERS

Blade and Arm

REMOVAL & INSTALLATION

1967–69 Models

♦ **See Figure 24**

To remove an arm, remove the nut and pull the arm straight off the drive pivot.

When installing the arm, position the arm so that the blade is parallel with, and 1″ above the windshield molding. Tighten the nut to 85 in. lbs.

1970–73 Models

♦ **See Figures 25 and 26**

To remove a wiper arm, lift up on the blade and pull the arm straight off the splines on the pivot. There is a tool made for this purpose, but it's not hard to do without the tool.

When installing the arms, the at-rest position of the blades should be determined before pushing the arm onto the pivot. The

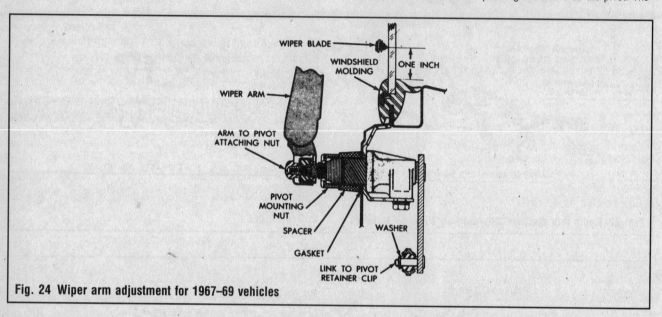

Fig. 24 Wiper arm adjustment for 1967–69 vehicles

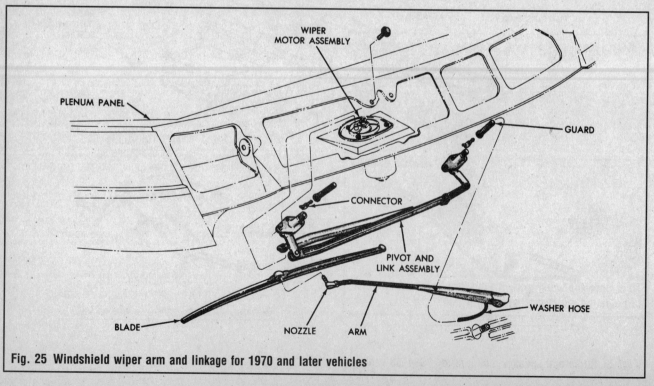

Fig. 25 Windshield wiper arm and linkage for 1970 and later vehicles

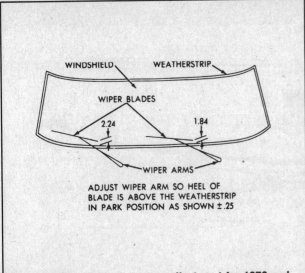

Fig. 26 Windshield wiper arm adjustment for 1970 and later vehicles

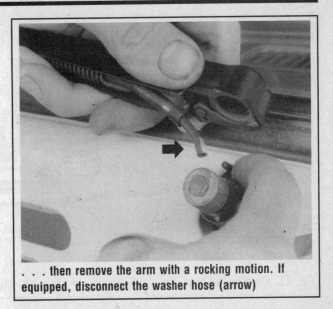

. . . then remove the arm with a rocking motion. If equipped, disconnect the washer hose (arrow)

driver's side blade should be 1.84″ above the windshield weatherstripping at the heel of the blade; the passenger's side blade should be 2.24″ above the weatherstripping.

1974–88 Models

▶ See Figures 25 and 26

To remove the arm from the pivot, lift the arm to permit the latch to be pulled out to the holding position and remove the arm from the pivot with a rocking motion.

When installing the arms, the at-rest position of the blades should be determined before pushing the arm onto the pivot. The driver's side blade should be 1.84″ above the windshield weatherstripping at the heel of the blade; the passenger's side blade should be 2.24″ above the weatherstripping.

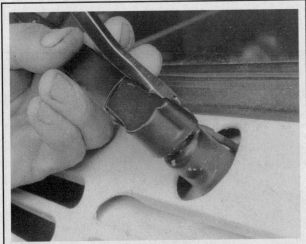

To remove the wiper arm, lift the arm to permit the latch to be pulled out to the holding position . . .

Windshield Wiper Motor

REMOVAL & INSTALLATION

1967–69 Models

▶ See Figure 27

1. Disconnect the battery ground cable.
2. Remove the glove box and ashtray.
3. Remove the instrument cluster.
4. Disconnect the wiper switch wiring.
5. Remove the wiper linkage-to-pivots retaining clips and disconnect the linkage from the pivots.
6. Remove the 4 wiper motor mounting plate nuts and lift the motor and mounting plate off the studs and out from under the dash panel through the glove box opening.
7. Installation is the reverse of removal.

1970–78 Models

1. Raise the hood.
2. Unplug the wiring at the motor.
3. Remove the 3 wiper motor mounting flange bolts.
4. Lower the motor to gain access to the spring clip that retains the wiper linkage. Release the spring clip and remove the motor.
5. Installation is the reverse of removal.

1979–88 Models

1. Raise the hood.
2. Unplug the wiring at the motor.
3. Remove the wiper motor mounting bolts.
4. Lower the motor to gain access to the crank arm-to-drive link bushing.

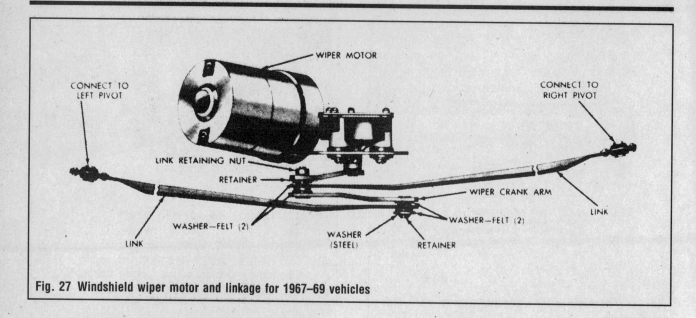

Fig. 27 Windshield wiper motor and linkage for 1967–69 vehicles

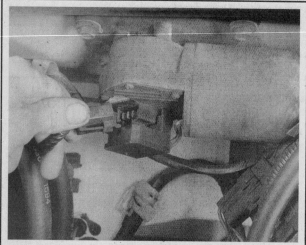

To remove the wiper motor, unplug the wiring connector at the motor . . .

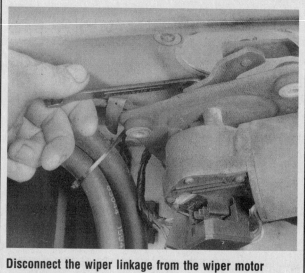

Disconnect the wiper linkage from the wiper motor

. . . and remove the wiper motor mounting bolts

Remove the wiper motor assembly from the vehicle

5. Disconnect the crank arm from the drive link by prying the bushing off.

6. Remove the motor.

7. Installation is the reverse of removal.

Wiper Linkage

REMOVAL & INSTALLATION

1967–69 Models

LEFT LINK

1. Remove the motor and linkage as described above.
2. Remove the left link-to-crank arm retainer.
3. Installation is the reverse of removal.

RIGHT LINK

1. Remove the motor and linkage as described above.
2. Remove the link retaining nut from the crank arm.
3. Installation is the reverse of removal.

1970–72 Models

1. Remove the cowl grille.
2. Disconnect the washer hoses.
3. Release the linkage-to-motor clip.
4. Remove the 2 mount bolts on each pivot.
5. Push the pivots into the plenum chamber and remove the pivots and linkage through the cowl grille opening.

1973 Models

DRIVE LINK

1. Remove the cowl grille.
2. Remove the retainer, metal washer and rubber washer attaching the drive link to the connecting link.

3. Remove the retainer and wave washer attaching the drive link to the wiper motor arm.
4. Remove the drive link from the plenum chamber.
5. Installation is the reverse of removal.

CONNECTING LINK

1. Remove the cowl grille.
2. Remove the retainer, metal washer and rubber washer attaching the connecting link to the drive link.
3. Remove the retainers, metal washers and rubber washers attaching the connecting link to the pivots.
4. Remove the connecting link from the plenum chamber.
5. Installation is the reverse of removal.

1974–88 Models

DRIVE LINK

1. Remove the wiper arms and washer hoses.
2. Remove the cowl grille.
3. Reach through the access hole, remove the drive link from the crank arm and connecting links by prying the retainer bushings apart with a screwdriver.
4. Remove the drive link through the access hole.

CONNECTING LINK

1. Remove the cowl grille.
2. Reach through the access hole, remove the connecting link from the drive link by prying the retainer bushings apart with a screwdriver.
3. Remove the connecting link through the access hole.

INSTRUMENTS AND SWITCHES

Instrument Cluster

REMOVAL & INSTALLATION

▶ **See Figures 28, 29 and 30**

1967–69 Models

1. Disconnect the battery ground cable.
2. Disconnect the speedometer cable at the back of the speedometer.
3. Remove the 4 screws and carefully remove the mounting plate and glass.
4. Pull the cluster out of the panel just far enough to disconnect the wiring. If the cluster is equipped with a mechanical oil pressure gauge, disconnect and plug the tube.
5. Installation is the reverse of removal.

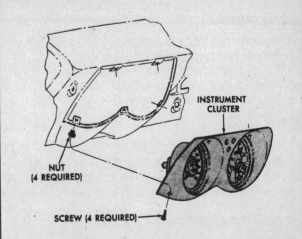

Fig. 28 Instrument cluster mounting details for 1977 and earlier vehicles

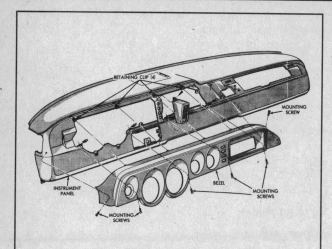

Fig. 29 Instrument cluster hood and bezel mounting on 1978–88 vehicles

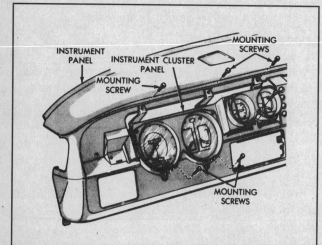

Fig. 30 Instrument cluster mounting details for 1978–88 vehicles

1970–73 Models

1. Disconnect the battery ground cable.
2. Remove the 4 cluster mounting screws.
3. Pull the cluster out of the panel just far enough to disconnect the wiring. Disconnect the speedometer cable.
4. Installation is the reverse of removal.

1974–77 Models

1. Disconnect the battery ground cable.
2. Remove the cluster mounting screws.
3. Pull the cluster out just far enough to disconnect the speedometer cable, printed circuit board multiple connector and gauge wires.
4. Installation is the reverse of removal.

1978–88 Models

1. Disconnect the battery ground cable.
2. Remove the screws securing the instrument panel hood and bezel. Pull the bezel off of the upper retaining clips.

3. Remove the cluster mounting screws.
4. Pull the cluster out just far enough to disconnect the speedometer cable.
5. Unplug the wiring connectors at the back of the cluster.
6. Installation is the reverse of removal.

Dash-Mounted Ignition Switch

REMOVAL & INSTALLATION

➡**For column-mounted switches, refer to Section 8.**

1. Remove the instrument cluster.
2. Through the cluster opening, disconnect the wiring connector at the switch.
3. Remove the switch retaining nut from the front of the switch.
4. Remove the lamp and bracket assembly from the switch.
5. Remove the switch.

Windshield Wiper Switch

REMOVAL & INSTALLATION

▶ **See Figures 31 and 32**

1967–72 Models

1. Disconnect the battery ground cable.
2. Pull the knob from the switch.
3. Remove the switch retaining nut.
4. Lower the switch and disconnect the wiring.
5. Installation is the reverse of removal.

1973–77 Models

1. Remove the cluster screws and pull the cluster out far enough to access the wiper switch.
2. Loosen the setscrew on the switch knob and pull off the knob.

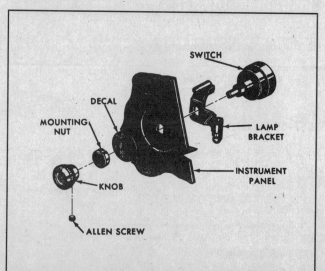

Fig. 31 Early model windshield wiper/washer switch

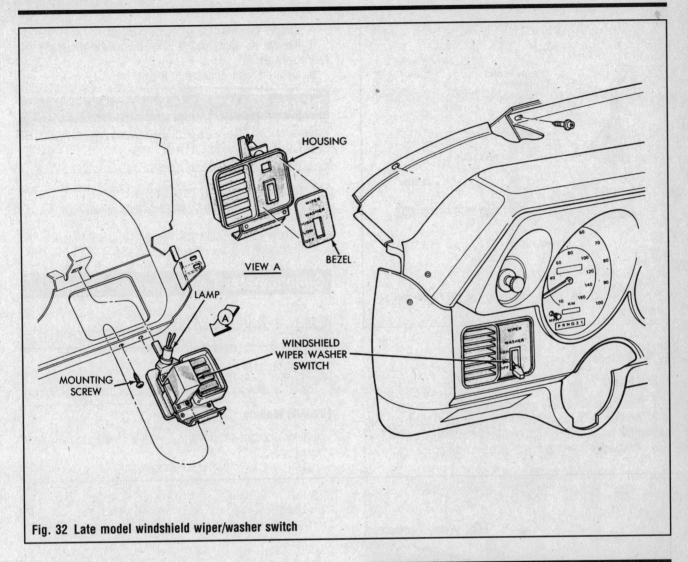

Fig. 32 Late model windshield wiper/washer switch

3. Unplug the wiring harness from the switch.
4. Remove the retaining nut and clip from the switch.
5. Remove the switch.

1978–84 Models

1. Remove the 2 mounting screws from under the instrument panel.
2. Unplug the wiring from the switch.
3. Disconnect the switch lamp.
4. Pull the switch out from under the panel.
5. Installation is the reverse of removal.

1985–86 Models

1. Remove the steering column cover.
2. Remove the 2 mounting screws from under the instrument panel.
3. Unplug the wiring from the switch.
4. Disconnect the switch lamp.
5. Pull the switch out from under the panel.
6. Installation is the reverse of removal.

1987–88 Models

The wiper switch is incorporated into the turn signal switch stalk. For switch removal and installation, see Chapter 8.

Headlight Switch

REMOVAL & INSTALLATION

1967–72 Models

◆ See Figure 33

1. Disconnect the battery ground cable.
2. Pull the knob from the switch.
3. Remove the switch retaining nut.
4. Lower the switch and disconnect the wiring.
5. Installation is the reverse of removal.

1973–77 Models

◆ See Figure 33

1. Remove the cluster screws and pull the cluster out far enough to access the wiper switch.
2. Unplug the wiring harness from the switch.
3. Depress the locking button on the bottom of the switch and pull the knob and shaft from the switch.
4. Remove the retaining nut from the switch.
5. Remove the switch.

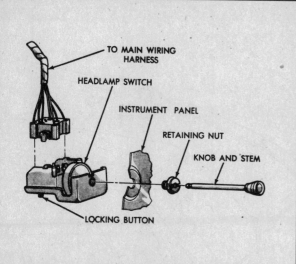

Fig. 33 Headlight switch mounting for 1977 and earlier vehicles

1978–88 Models

▶ **See Figure 34**

1. Disconnect the battery ground cable.
2. Working under the instrument panel, depress the locking button on the switch and pull the knob and stem from the switch.
3. Remove the instrument panel hood and bezel.

4. Remove the switch bezel mounting screws.
5. Remove the switch mounting nut, remove the switch and disconnect the wiring.
6. Installation is the reverse of removal.

Clock

REMOVAL & INSTALLATION

1. Disconnect the battery ground cable.
2. Reach under the instrument panel and unplug the wiring from the clock.
3. Remove the 2 mounting screws and remove the clock.
4. Installation is the reverse of removal.

Speedometer Cable

REMOVAL & INSTALLATION

1967–69 Models

The cable housing screws onto the back of the speedometer.

1970–88 Models

A quick-disconnect clip retains the cable housing to the speedometer head.

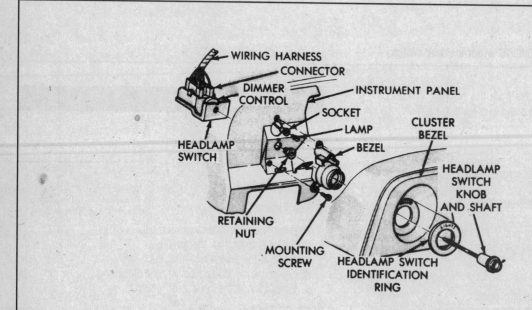

Fig. 34 Headlight switch mounting for 1978 and later vehicles

LIGHTING

Headlights

REMOVAL & INSTALLATION

1. Remove the headlight bezel.
2. Remove the headlight mounting ring screws.

➡**Don't mistake the headlight aiming screws for the headlight mounting screws!**

3. Pull out the headlight slowly and disconnect the wiring.
4. Installation is the reverse of removal.

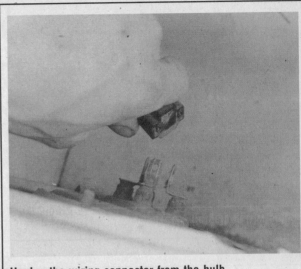

Unplug the wiring connector from the bulb

For headlight replacement, remove the mounting ring screws . . .

Rear License Plate Light

REMOVAL & INSTALLATION

1. Remove the lens screws.
2. Pull off the lens, turn the bulb and pull it out of its socket.
3. Installation is the reverse of removal.

. . . then remove the mounting ring and slowly pull the headlight outward

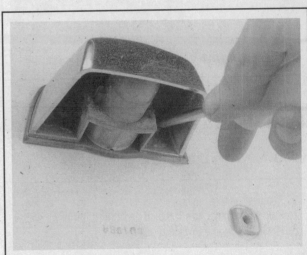

For license plate light replacement, remove the two lens and directional hood retaining screws

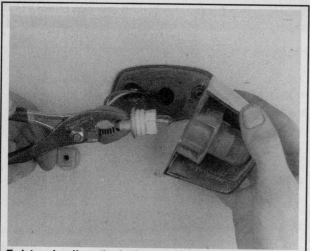

Twist and pull on the bulb socket to remove it from the lens

For front signal and marker lights, remove the lens mounting screws . . .

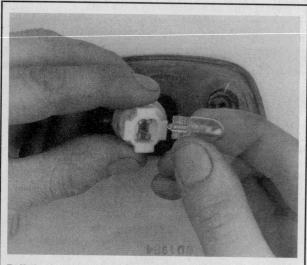

Pull the bulb out of the socket

. . . and remove the lens

Front Turn Signal and Parking Lights

REMOVAL & INSTALLATION

1. Remove the lens screws.
2. Pull off the lens, turn the bulb and pull it out of its socket.
3. Installation is the reverse of removal.

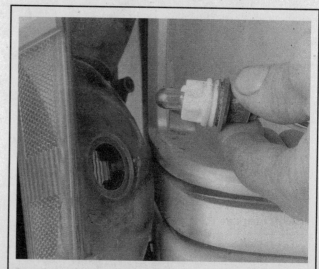

For marker lights, twist and pull on the bulb socket . . .

. . . then pull the bulb out of the socket

For signal lights, twist and pull on the bulb socket . . .

. . . then push in and turn the bulb to remove it from the socket

Side Marker Lights

REMOVAL & INSTALLATION

1. Remove the lens screws.
2. Pull off the lens, turn the bulb housing and pull the bulb out of its socket.
3. Installation is the reverse of removal.

For bulb replacement on side marker lights, remove the lens mounting screws . . .

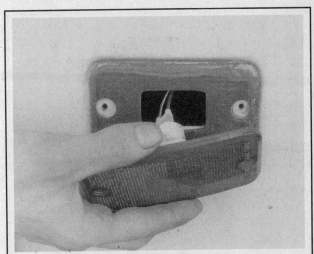

. . . then pull out of the body. Bulb removal is the same as front marker lights

Rear Turn Signal, Brake and Parking Lights

REMOVAL & INSTALLATION

1. Remove the lens screws.
2. Pull off the lens, turn the bulb and pull it out of its socket.
3. Installation is the reverse of removal.

Push in and turn the bulb to remove it from the housing

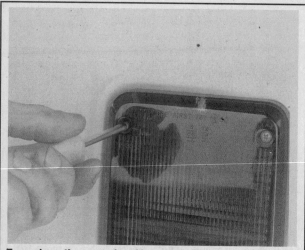

To replace the rear signal/marker bulbs, remove the lens retaining screws . . .

Dome Lights

REMOVAL & INSTALLATION

1. Remove the dome light lens.
2. Pull the bulb out of the light housing.
3. Installation is the reverse of removal.

. . . then remove the lens

Gently pry the dome light lens down . . .

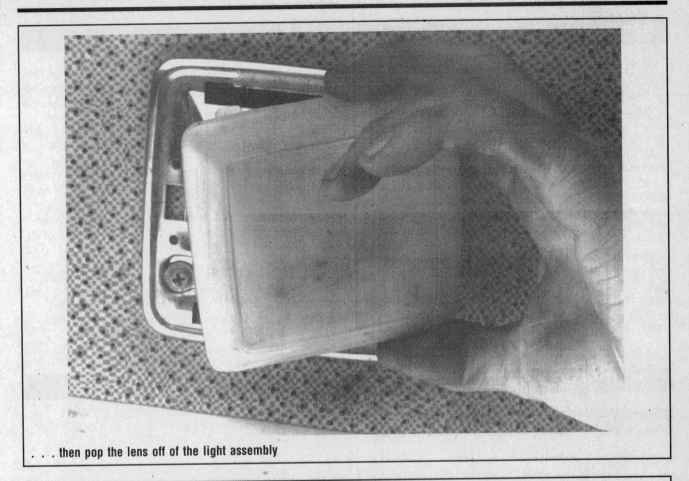

. . . then pop the lens off of the light assembly

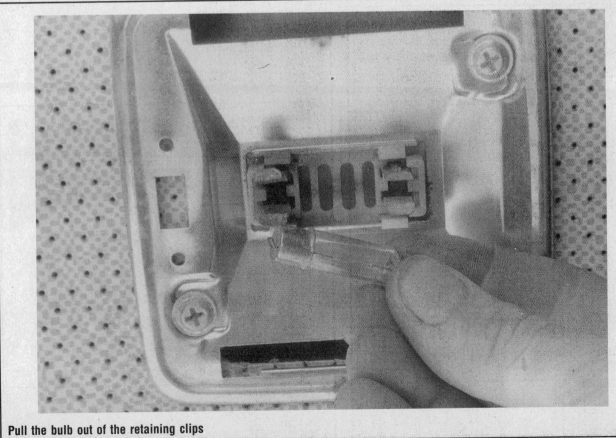

Pull the bulb out of the retaining clips

TRAILER WIRING

Wiring the vehicle for towing is fairly easy. There are a number of good wiring kits available and these should be used, rather than trying to design your own.

All trailers will need brake lights and turn signals as well as tail lights and side marker lights. Most areas require extra marker lights for overwide trailers. Also, most areas have recently required back-up lights for trailers, and most trailer manufacturers have been building trailers with back-up lights for several years.

Additionally, some Class I, most Class II and just about all Class III trailers will have electric brakes. Add to this number an accessories wire, to operate trailer internal equipment or to charge the trailer's battery, and you can have as many as seven wires in the harness.

Determine the equipment on your trailer and buy the wiring kit necessary. The kit will contain all the wires needed, plus a plug adapter set which includes the female plug, mounted on the bumper or hitch, and the male plug, wired into, or plugged into the trailer harness.

When installing the kit, follow the manufacturer's instructions.

The color coding of the wires is usually standard throughout the industry. One point to note: some domestic vehicles, and most imported vehicles, have separate turn signals. On most domestic vehicles, the brake lights and rear turn signals operate with the same bulb. For those vehicles with separate turn signals, you can purchase an isolation unit so that the brake lights won't blink whenever the turn signals are operated, or, you can go to your local electronics supply house and buy four diodes to wire in series with the brake and turn signal bulbs. Diodes will isolate the brake and turn signals. The choice is yours. The isolation units are simple and quick to install, but far more expensive than the diodes. The diodes, however, require more work to install properly, since they require the cutting of each bulb's wire and soldering in place of the diode.

One, final point, the best kits are those with a spring loaded cover on the vehicle mounted socket. This cover prevents dirt and moisture from corroding the terminals. Never let the vehicle socket hang loosely; always mount it securely to the bumper or hitch.

CIRCUIT PROTECTION

Fuses

REPLACEMENT

The fuse panel may be located in one of two spots, depending on the vehicle year or configuration: under the driver's side of the instrument panel on the firewall, or under the left side of the glove box cover.

To change or check a fuse, locate the fuse box cover which is under the glove box lid . . .

. . . and unfasten it to gain access to the fuses

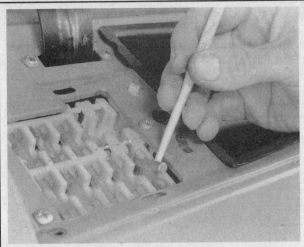

Gently pry up one end of the fuse with a non-metallic tool to ease removal

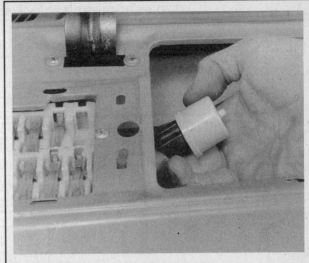

Pull the flasher out of its mounting clip . . . .

Flashers

REPLACEMENT

On the firewall-mounted fuse panel, the flashers are plugged into the fuse panel. To replace them, pull them straight out of the fuse panel. On the glove box-mounted fuse panel, you must remove the glove box liner to gain access to the flashers, which are mounted next to the fuse panel, behind the dash board. To replace them, pull the flashers from their mounting clip, then unplug the wiring harness connectors from the flashers.

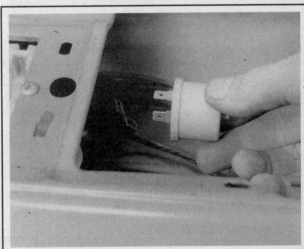

. . . and unplug the wiring harness connector from the flasher

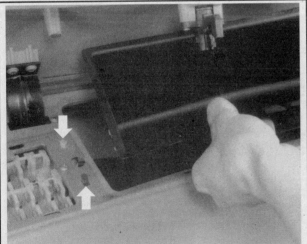

To gain access to the flashers, remove the glove box liner (flashers located under arrows)

Troubleshooting Basic Turn Signal and Flasher Problems

Most problems in the turn signals or flasher system, can be reduced to defective flashers or bulbs, which are easily replaced. Occasionally, problems in the turn signals are traced to the switch in the steering column, which will require professional service.

F = Front   R = Rear   ● = Lights off   o = Lights on

Problem		Solution
Turn signals light, but do not flash		· Replace the flasher
No turn signals light on either side		· Check the fuse. Replace if defective. · Check the flasher by substitution · Check for open circuit, short circuit or poor ground
Both turn signals on one side don't work		· Check for bad bulbs · Check for bad ground in both housings
One turn signal light on one side doesn't work		· Check and/or replace bulb · Check for corrosion in socket. Clean contacts. · Check for poor ground at socket
Turn signal flashes too fast or too slow		· Check any bulb on the side flashing too fast. A heavy-duty bulb is probably installed in place of a regular bulb. · Check the bulb flashing too slow. A standard bulb was probably installed in place of a heavy-duty bulb. · Check for loose connections or corrosion at the bulb socket
Indicator lights don't work in either direction		· Check if the turn signals are working. · Check the dash indicator lights · Check the flasher by substitution
One indicator light doesn't light		· On systems with 1 dash indicator: See if the lights work on the same side. Often the filaments have been reversed in systems combining stoplights with taillights and turn signals. Check the flasher by substitution · On systems with 2 indicators: Check the bulbs on the same side. Check the indicator light bulb. Check the flasher by substitution

Troubleshooting Basic Turn Signal and Flasher Problems (cont.)

Most problems in the turn signals or flasher system can be reduced to defective flashers or bulbs, which are easily replaced. Occasionally, problems in the turn signals are traced to the switch in the steering column, which will require professional service.

F = Front   R = Rear   ● = Lights off   ○ = Lights on

Problem		Solution
Turn signal flashes too fast or too slow	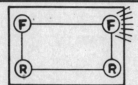	• Check any bulb on the side flashing too fast. A heavy-duty bulb is probably installed in place of a regular bulb. • Check the bulb flashing too slow. A standard bulb was probably installed in place of a heavy-duty bulb. • Check for loose connections or corrosion at the bulb socket
Indicator lights don't work in either direction		• Check if the turn signals are working • Check the dash indicator lights • Check the flasher by substitution

One indicator light doesn't light		• On systems with 1 dash indicator: See if the lights work on the same side. Often the filaments have been reversed in systems combining stoplights with taillights and turn signals.
		   Check the flasher by substitution
		• On systems with 2 indicators: Check the bulbs on the same side
		   Check the indicator light bulb
		   Check the flasher by substitution

Troubleshooting the Heater

Problem	Cause	Solution
Blower motor will not turn at any speed	• Blown fuse • Loose connection • Defective ground • Faulty switch • Faulty motor • Faulty resistor	• Replace fuse • Inspect and tighten • Clean and tighten • Replace switch • Replace motor • Replace resistor
Blower motor turns at one speed only	• Faulty switch • Faulty resistor	• Replace switch • Replace resistor
Blower motor turns but does not circulate air	• Intake blocked • Fan not secured to the motor shaft	• Clean intake • Tighten security
Heater will not heat	• Coolant does not reach proper temperature • Heater core blocked internally • Heater core air-bound • Blend-air door not in proper position	• Check and replace thermostat if necessary • Flush or replace core if necessary • Purge air from core • Adjust cable
Heater will not defrost	• Control cable adjustment incorrect • Defroster hose damaged	• Adjust control cable • Replace defroster hose

Troubleshooting Basic Dash Gauge Problems

Problem	Cause	Solution
Coolant Temperature Gauge		
Gauge reads erratically or not at all	• Loose or dirty connections • Defective sending unit • Defective gauge	• Clean/tighten connections • Bi-metal gauge: remove the wire from the sending unit. Ground the wire for an instant. If the gauge registers, replace the sending unit. • Magnetic gauge: disconnect the wire at the sending unit. With ignition ON gauge should register COLD. Ground the wire; gauge should register HOT.
Ammeter Gauge—Turn Headlights ON (do not start engine). Note reaction		
Ammeter shows charge Ammeter shows discharge Ammeter does not move	• Connections reversed on gauge • Ammeter is OK • Loose connections or faulty wiring • Defective gauge	• Reinstall connections • Nothing • Check/correct wiring • Replace gauge
Oil Pressure Gauge		
Gauge does not register or is inaccurate	• On mechanical gauge, Bourdon tube may be bent or kinked • Low oil pressure • Defective gauge • Defective wiring • Defective sending unit	• Check tube for kinks or bends preventing oil from reaching the gauge • Remove sending unit. Idle the engine briefly. If no oil flows from sending unit hole, problem is in engine. • Remove the wire from the sending unit and ground it for an instant with the ignition ON. A good gauge will go to the top of the scale. • Check the wiring to the gauge. If it's OK and the gauge doesn't register when grounded, replace the gauge. • If the wiring is OK and the gauge functions when grounded, replace the sending unit
All Gauges		
All gauges do not operate	• Blown fuse • Defective instrument regulator	• Replace fuse • Replace instrument voltage regulator
All gauges read low or erratically	• Defective or dirty instrument voltage regulator	• Clean contacts or replace
All gauges pegged	• Loss of ground between instrument voltage regulator and car • Defective instrument regulator	• Check ground • Replace regulator
Warning Lights		
Light(s) do not come on when ignition is ON, but engine is not started	• Defective bulb • Defective wire • Defective sending unit	• Replace bulb • Check wire from light to sending unit • Disconnect the wire from the sending unit and ground it. Replace the sending unit if the light comes on with the ignition ON.
Light comes on with engine running	• Problem in individual system • Defective sending unit	• Check system • Check sending unit (see above)

Troubleshooting Basic Lighting Problems

Problem	Cause	Solution
Lights		
One or more lights don't work, but others do	• Defective bulb(s) • Blown fuse(s) • Dirty fuse clips or light sockets • Poor ground circuit	• Replace bulb(s) • Replace fuse(s) • Clean connections • Run ground wire from light socket housing to car frame
Lights burn out quickly	• Incorrect voltage regulator setting or defective regulator • Poor battery/alternator connections	• Replace voltage regulator • Check battery/alternator connections
Lights go dim	• Low/discharged battery • Alternator not charging • Corroded sockets or connections • Low voltage output	• Check battery • Check drive belt tension; repair or replace alternator • Clean bulb and socket contacts and connections • Replace voltage regulator
Lights flicker	• Loose connection • Poor ground • Circuit breaker operating (short circuit)	• Tighten all connections • Run ground wire from light housing to car frame • Check connections and look for bare wires
Lights "flare"—Some flare is normal on acceleration—if excessive, see "Lights Burn Out Quickly"	• High voltage setting	• Replace voltage regulator
Lights glare—approaching drivers are blinded	• Lights adjusted too high • Rear springs or shocks sagging • Rear tires soft	• Have headlights aimed • Check rear springs/shocks • Check/correct rear tire pressure
Turn Signals		
Turn signals don't work in either direction	• Blown fuse • Defective flasher • Loose connection	• Replace fuse • Replace flasher • Check/tighten all connections
Right (or left) turn signal only won't work	• Bulb burned out • Right (or left) indicator bulb burned out • Short circuit	• Replace bulb • Check/replace indicator bulb • Check/repair wiring
Flasher rate too slow or too fast	• Incorrect wattage bulb • Incorrect flasher	• Flasher bulb • Replace flasher (use a variable load flasher if you pull a trailer)
Indicator lights do not flash (burn steadily)	• Burned out bulb • Defective flasher	• Replace bulb • Replace flasher
Indicator lights do not light at all	• Burned out indicator bulb • Defective flasher	• Replace indicator bulb • Replace flasher

Troubleshooting Basic Windshield Wiper Problems

Problem	Cause	Solution
Electric Wipers		
Wipers do not operate— Wiper motor heats up or hums	• Internal motor defect • Bent or damaged linkage • Arms improperly installed on link- ing pivots	• Replace motor • Repair or replace linkage • Position linkage in park and rein- stall wiper arms

Troubleshooting Basic Windshield Wiper Problems

Problem	Cause	Solution
Electric Wipers		
Wipers do not operate— No current to motor	• Fuse or circuit breaker blown • Loose, open or broken wiring • Defective switch • Defective or corroded terminals • No ground circuit for motor or switch	• Replace fuse or circuit breaker • Repair wiring and connections • Replace switch • Replace or clean terminals • Repair ground circuits
Wipers do not operate— Motor runs	• Linkage disconnected or broken	• Connect wiper linkage or replace broken linkage
Vacuum Wipers		
Wipers do not operate	• Control switch or cable inoperative • Loss of engine vacuum to wiper motor (broken hoses, low engine vacuum, defective vacuum/fuel pump) • Linkage broken or disconnected • Defective wiper motor	• Repair or replace switch or cable • Check vacuum lines, engine vacuum and fuel pump • Repair linkage • Replace wiper motor
Wipers stop on engine acceleration	• Leaking vacuum hoses • Dry windshield • Oversize wiper blades • Defective vacuum/fuel pump	• Repair or replace hoses • Wet windshield with washers • Replace with proper size wiper blades • Replace pump

WIRING DIAGRAMS

IGNITION SWITCH

COMPONENT NAME

FUSIBLE LINK

RED

YEL

DK BLU

STARTER RELAY

BLK

RED

RED

BRN/YEL

BRN/YEL

TO A/C SYSTEM

BATTERY

BLK

RED

BLK

AMMETER

RED

BRN

M/T   A/T

NEUTRAL START SWICTH

BLK

WIRE COLOR CHART

BLACK	BLK	LIGHT GREEN	LT GRN
BROWN	BRN	ORANGE	ORG
BLUE	BLU	PINK	PNK
DARK BLUE	DK BLU	PURPLE	PPL
DARK GREEN	DK GRN	RED	RED
GREEN	GRN	TAN	TAN
GRAY	GRY	WHITE	WHT
LIGHT BLUE	LT BLU	YELLOW	YEL

STARTER MOTOR

DK BLU

DK BLU

WIRE COLOR

DK BLU

OIL PRESSURE SWITCH

BLK

DK GRN

DK GRN

DK BLU

SPLICE OR CONNECTOR

CONDITIONS WHEN POWER IS APPLIED

ALTERNATOR

VOLTAGE REGULATOR

DK BLU

TAN

OXYGEN SENSOR SOLENOID

LT BLU

BLK

DK BLU

HOT IN START OR RUN

DK GRN

FUSE 10 10A

SPARK PLUGS

RED

IGNITION CONTROL UNIT

IGNITION COIL

GRN

OXYGEN VACUUM DELAY SWITCH

ELECTRIC CHOKE

BULB

CHECK ENGINE INDICATOR

SPARK PLUGS

BLK/LT BLU

PNK

BLK/LT BLU

ORG

GRY

BLK/YEL

DK BLU

DK GRN

GRN

TERMINAL NUMBER

| 20 | 9 | 3 | 5 | | 1 | 2 | 15 | 11 |

ENGINE CONTROL MODULE

| 14 | | 10 | | 13 | | 7 |

OTHER SYSTEM REFERENCE

BLK/RED

BLK

BLK

VIO

TO A/C SYSTEM

DK BLU

OXYGEN SENSOR

DK BLU/RED

BLK/RED

BLK/LT BLU

BLK/RED

CASE GROUND

W/ A/C   W/O A/C

MODEL OPTIONS BRACKET

SOLENOID

COOLANT SWITCH

GROUND

BLK/RED

IDLE STOP SWITCH AND SOLENOID

Sample diagram—how to read and interpret wiring

WIRING DIAGRAM SYMBOLS

BATTERY	CONNECTOR OR SPLICE	CIRCUIT BREAKER	CAPACITOR	COIL	DIODE	FUSE	FUSIBLE LINK	GROUND	LED

RESISTOR	SINGLE FILAMENT BULB	DUAL FILAMENT BULB	HEATING ELEMENT	SOLENOID OR COIL	VARIABLE RESISTOR	CRYSTAL	POTENTIOMETER	HORN OR SPEAKER

ALTERNATOR	DISTRIBUTOR ASSEMBLY	IGNITION COIL	SPARK PLUG	STEPPER MOTOR	HEAT ACTIVATED SWITCH	RELAY

NORMALLY OPEN SWITCH	NORMALLY CLOSED SWITCH	GANGED SWITCH	3-POSITION SWITCH	REED SWITCH	MOTOR OR ACTUATOR	SPEED SENSOR	JUNCTION BLOCK	MODEL OPTIONS BRACKET

Common wiring diagram symbols

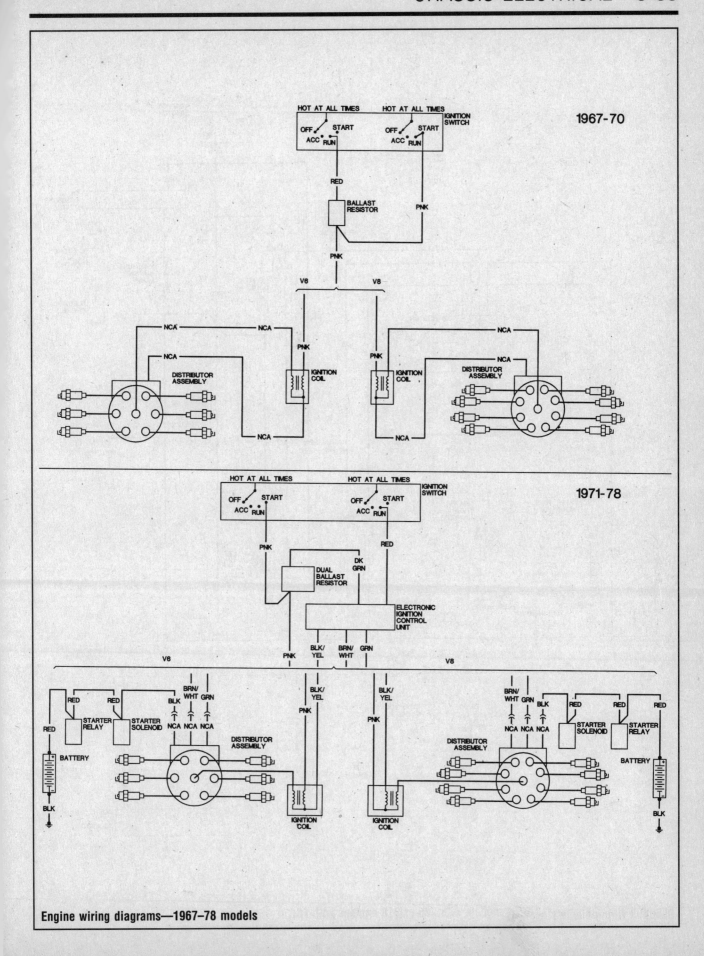

Engine wiring diagrams—1967–78 models

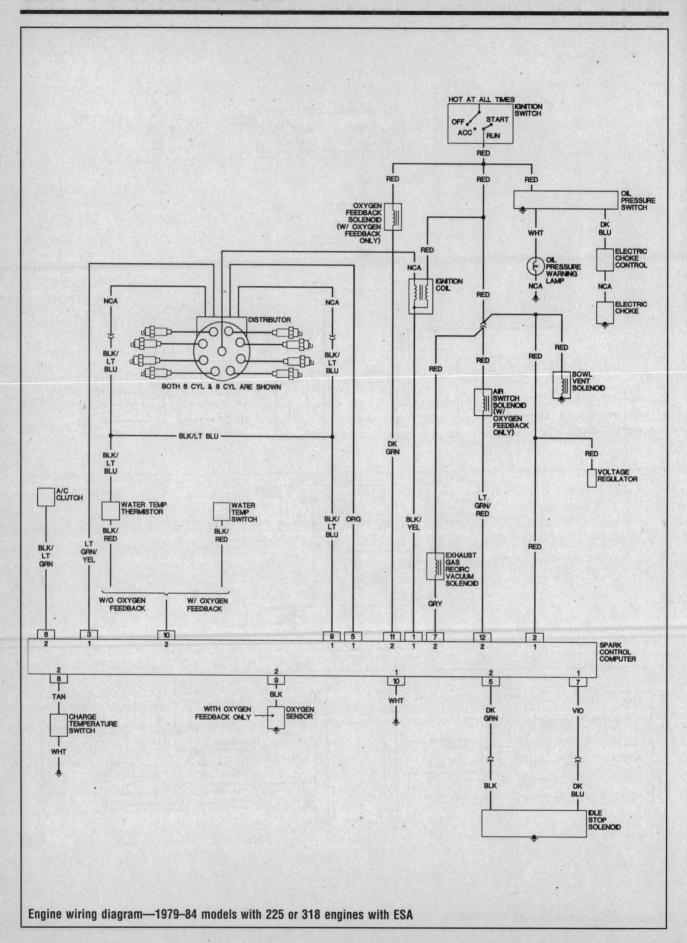

Engine wiring diagram—1979-84 models with 225 or 318 engines with ESA

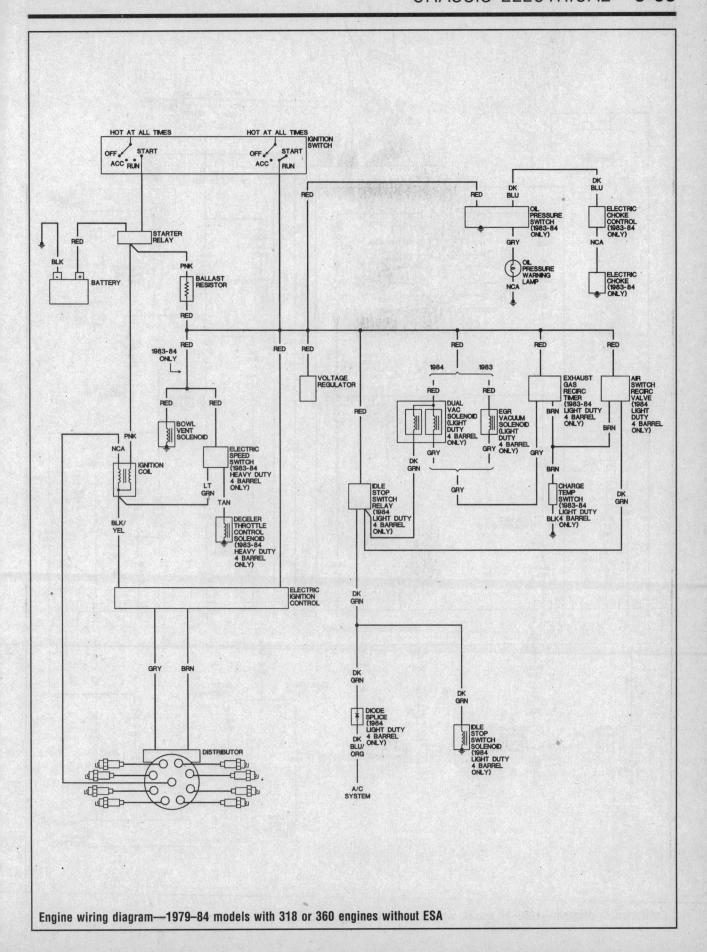

Engine wiring diagram—1979–84 models with 318 or 360 engines without ESA

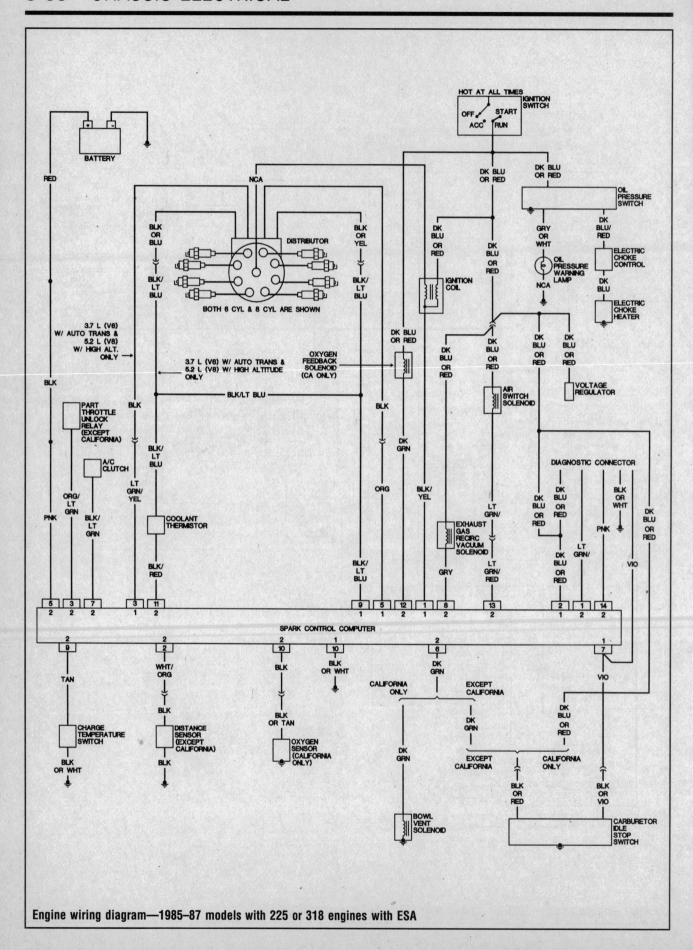

Engine wiring diagram—1985–87 models with 225 or 318 engines with ESA

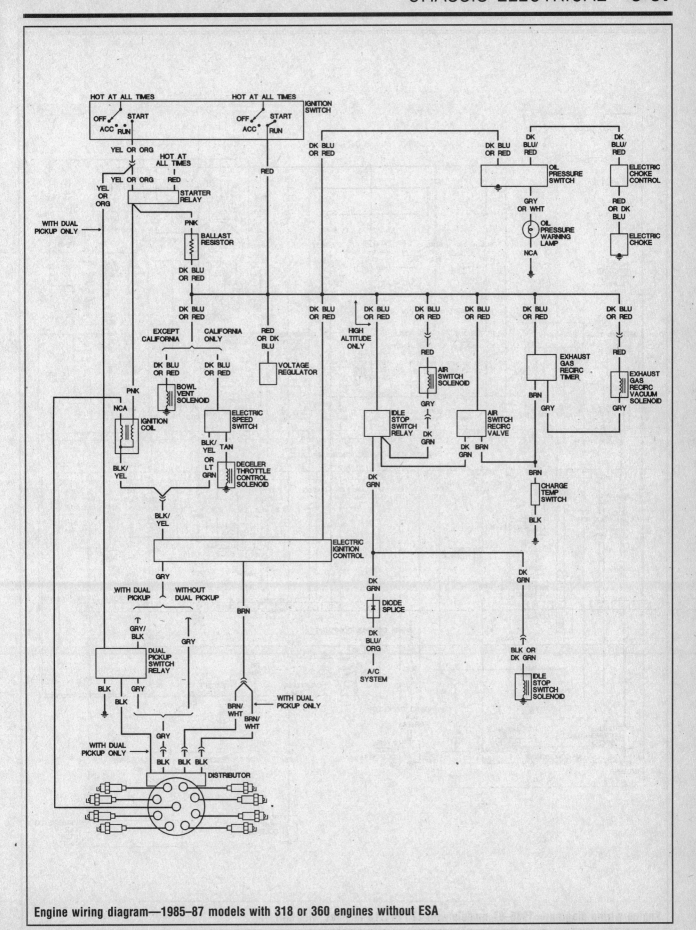

Engine wiring diagram—1985–87 models with 318 or 360 engines without ESA

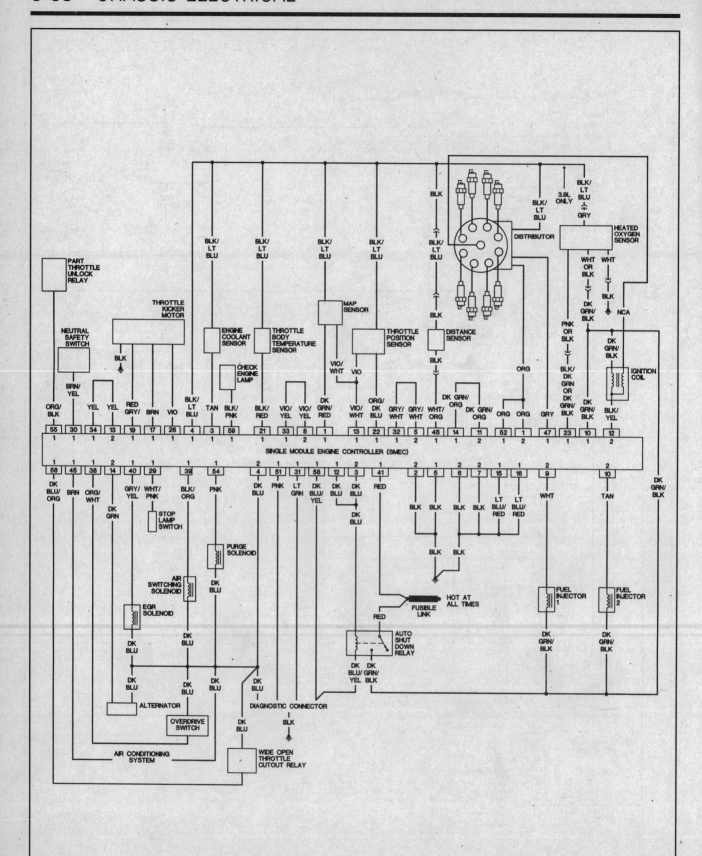

Engine wiring diagram—1988 models with 238 or 318 engines and fuel injection

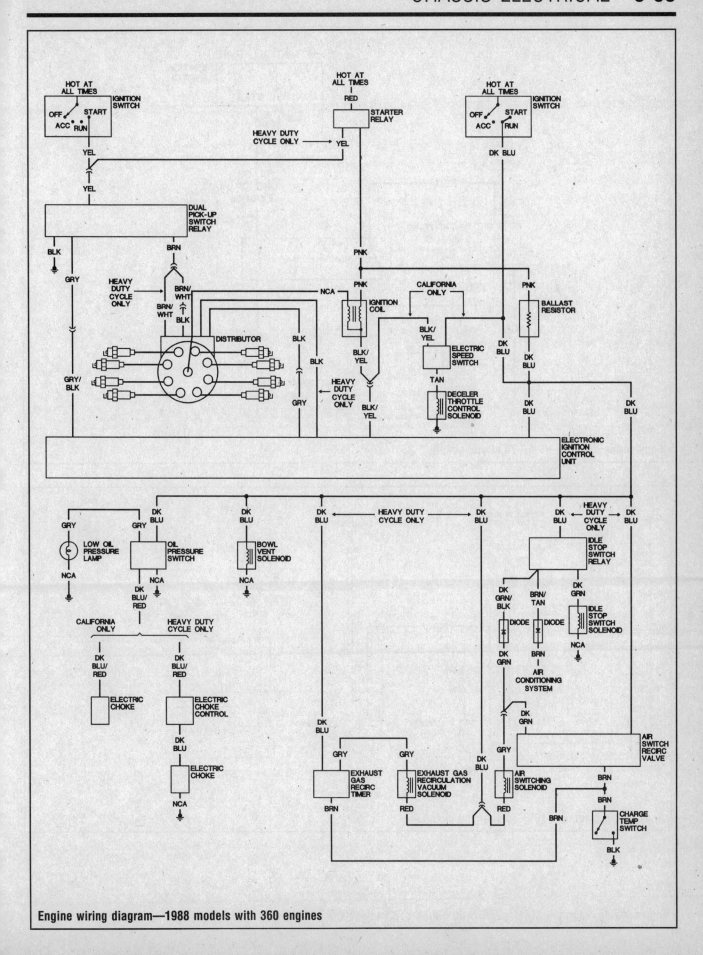

Engine wiring diagram—1988 models with 360 engines

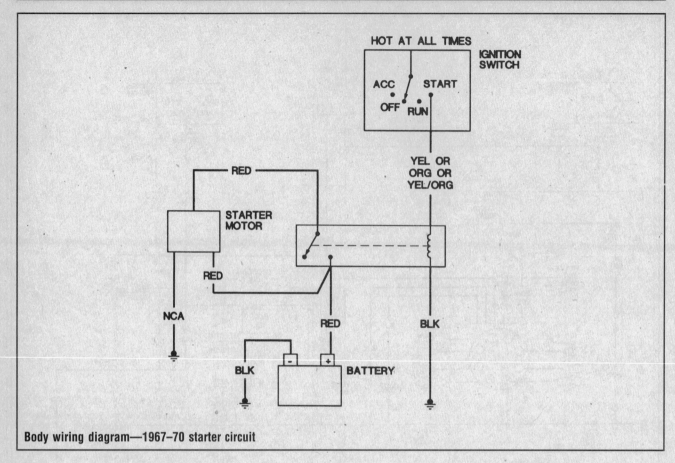

Body wiring diagram—1967–70 starter circuit

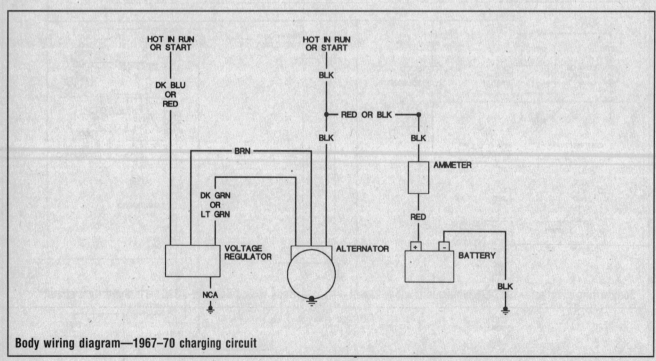

Body wiring diagram—1967–70 charging circuit

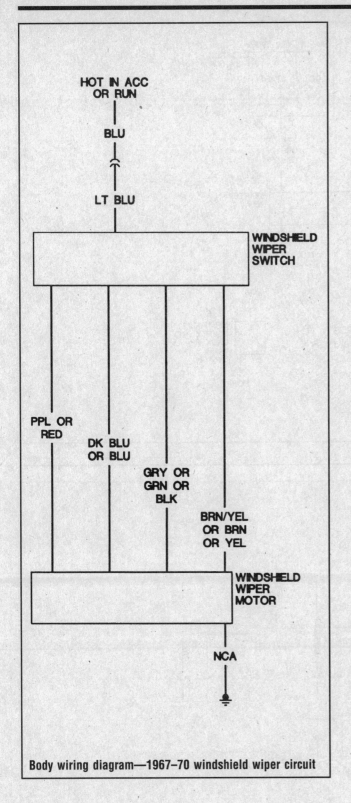

Body wiring diagram—1967–70 windshield wiper circuit

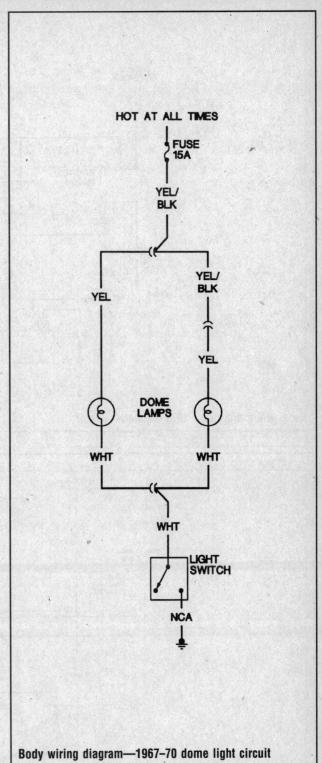

Body wiring diagram—1967–70 dome light circuit

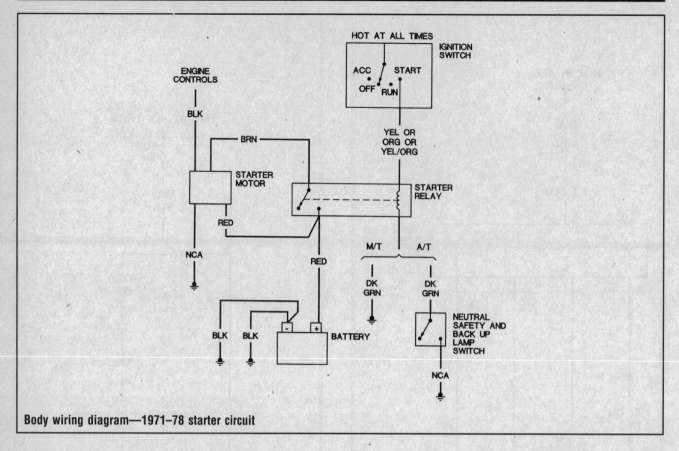

Body wiring diagram—1971–78 starter circuit

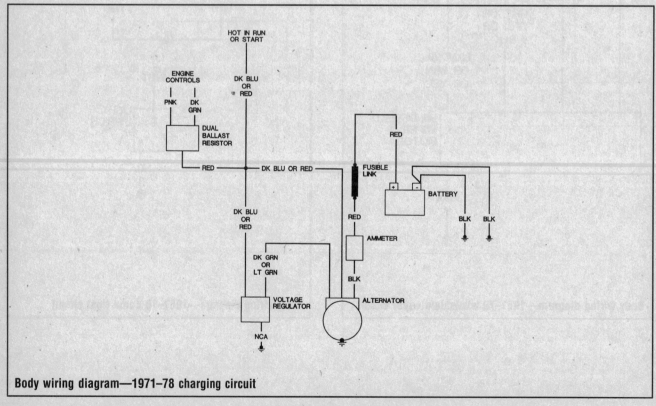

Body wiring diagram—1971–78 charging circuit

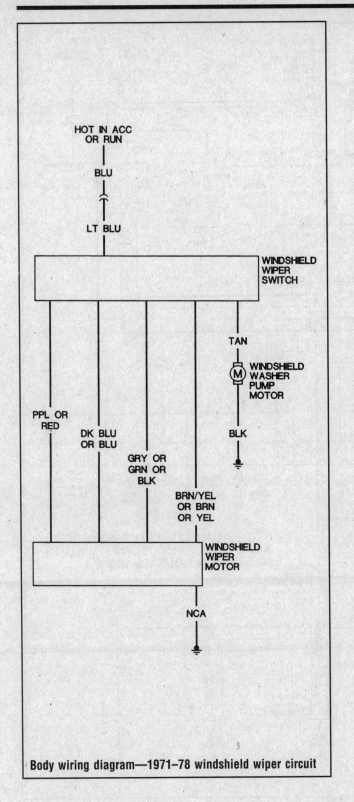

Body wiring diagram—1971-78 windshield wiper circuit

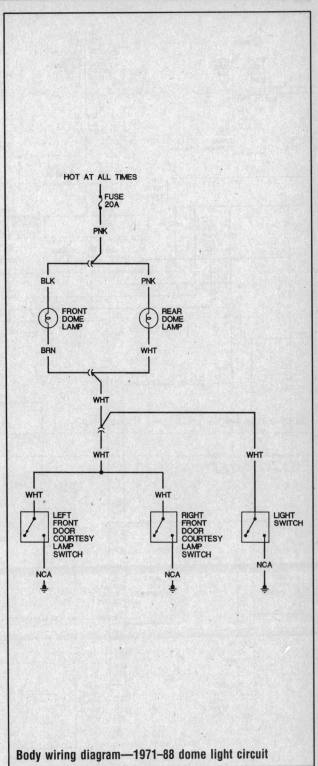

Body wiring diagram—1971-88 dome light circuit

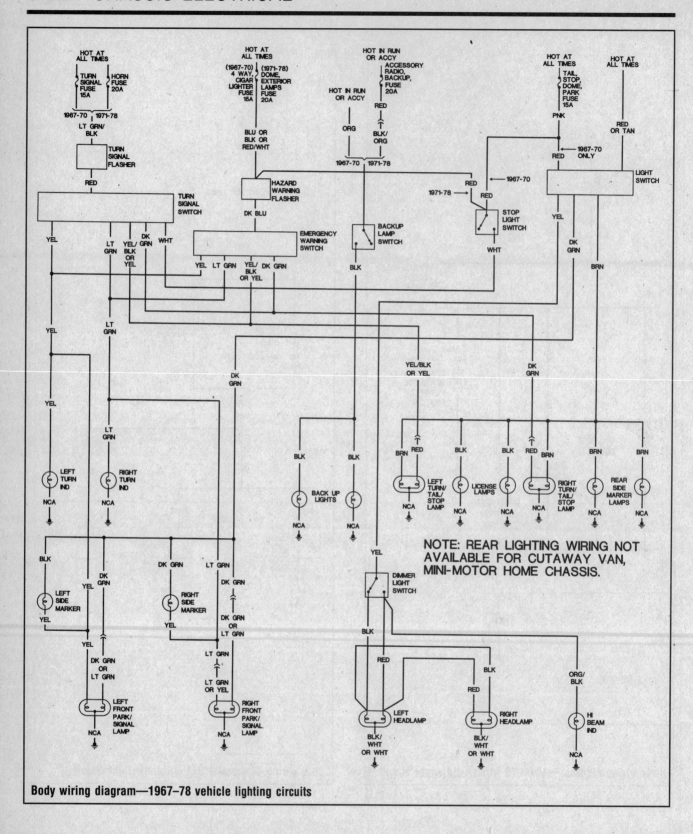

Body wiring diagram—1967-78 vehicle lighting circuits

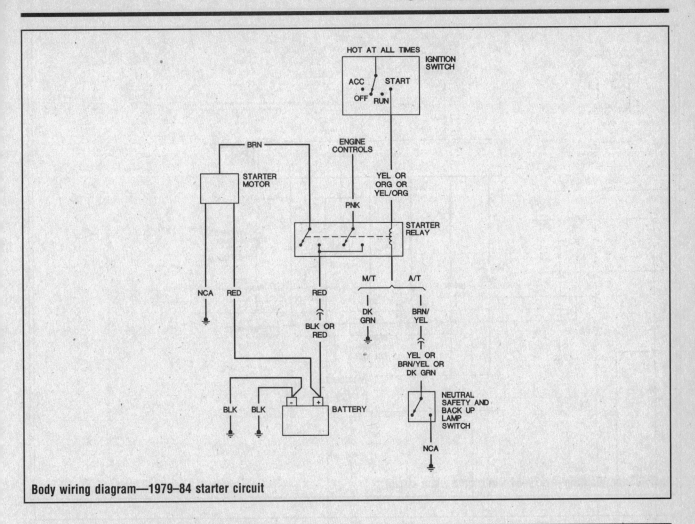

Body wiring diagram—1979–84 starter circuit

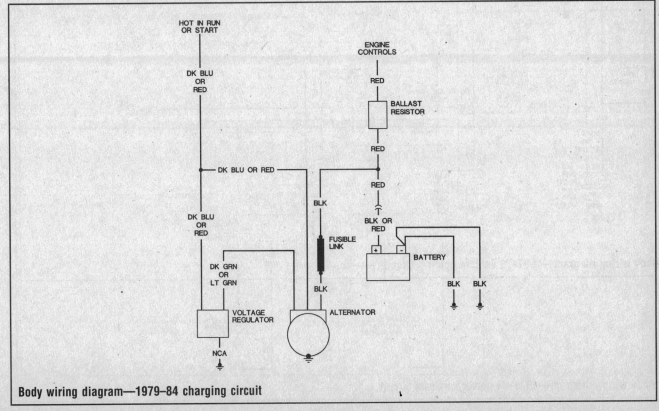

Body wiring diagram—1979–84 charging circuit

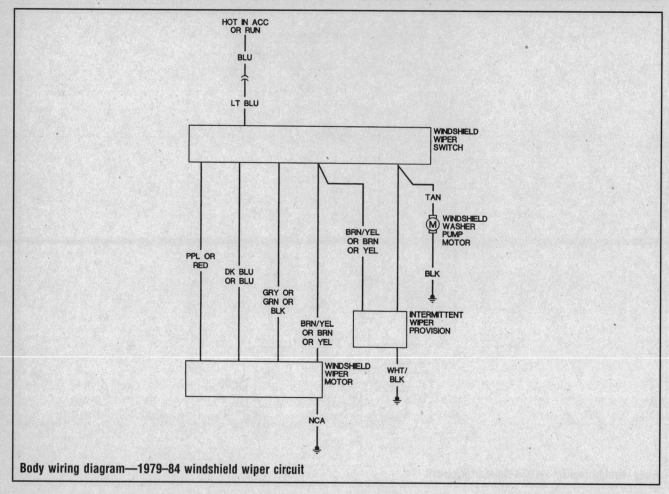

Body wiring diagram—1979–84 windshield wiper circuit

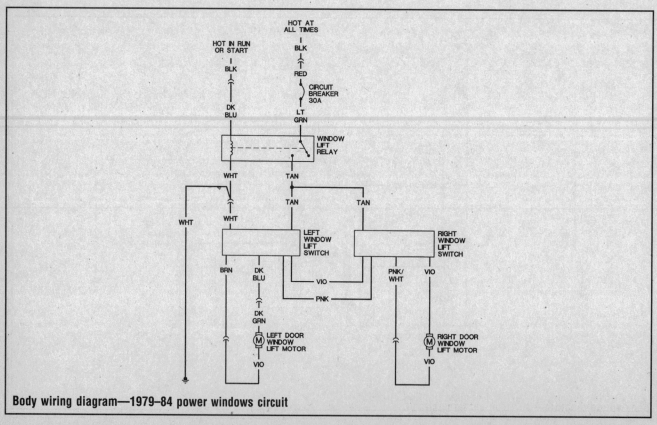

Body wiring diagram—1979–84 power windows circuit

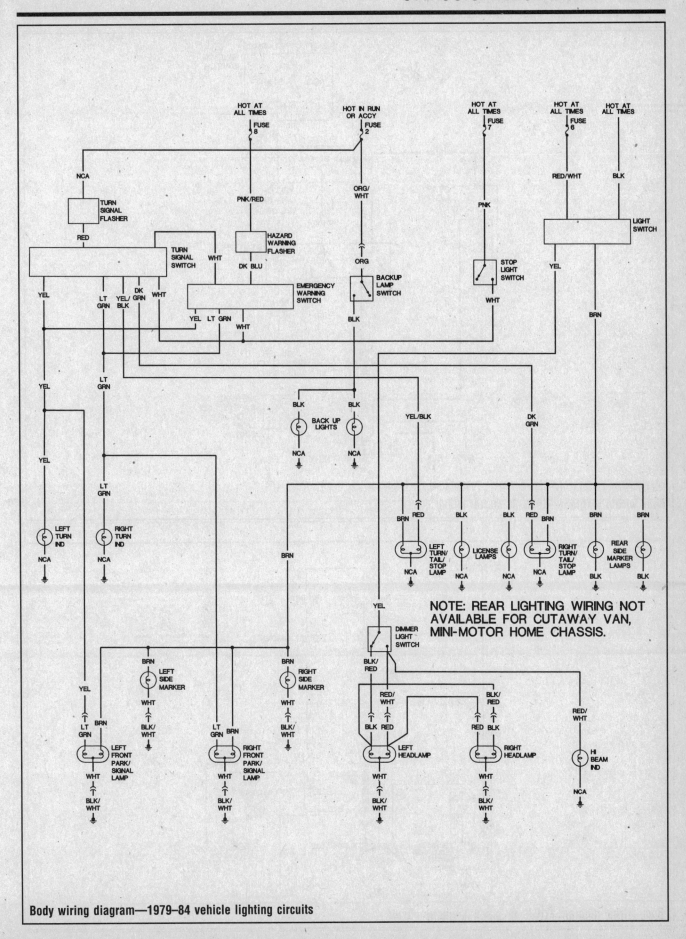

Body wiring diagram—1979–84 vehicle lighting circuits

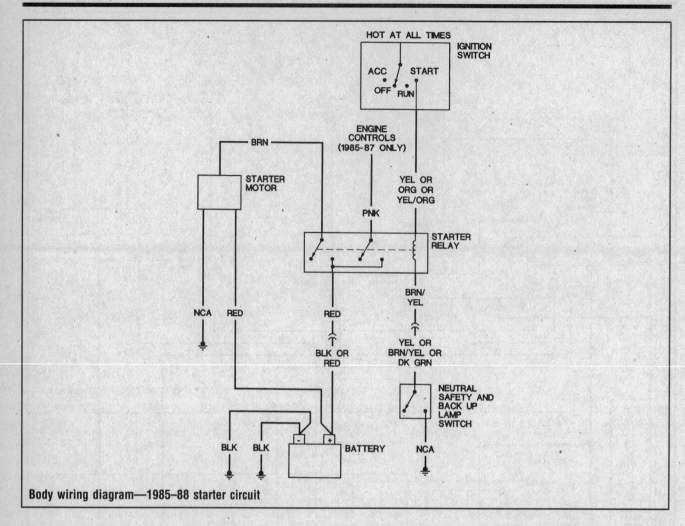

Body wiring diagram—1985–88 starter circuit

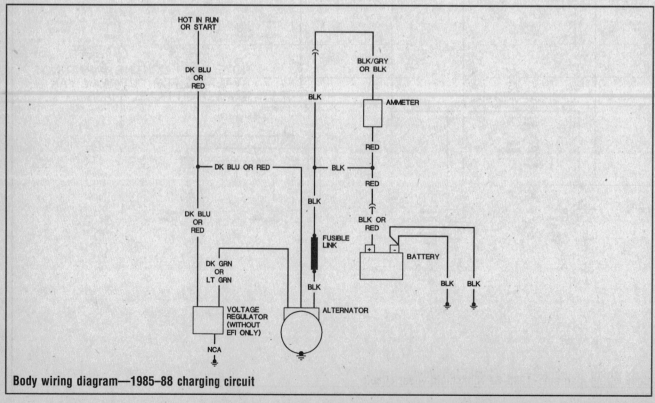

Body wiring diagram—1985–88 charging circuit

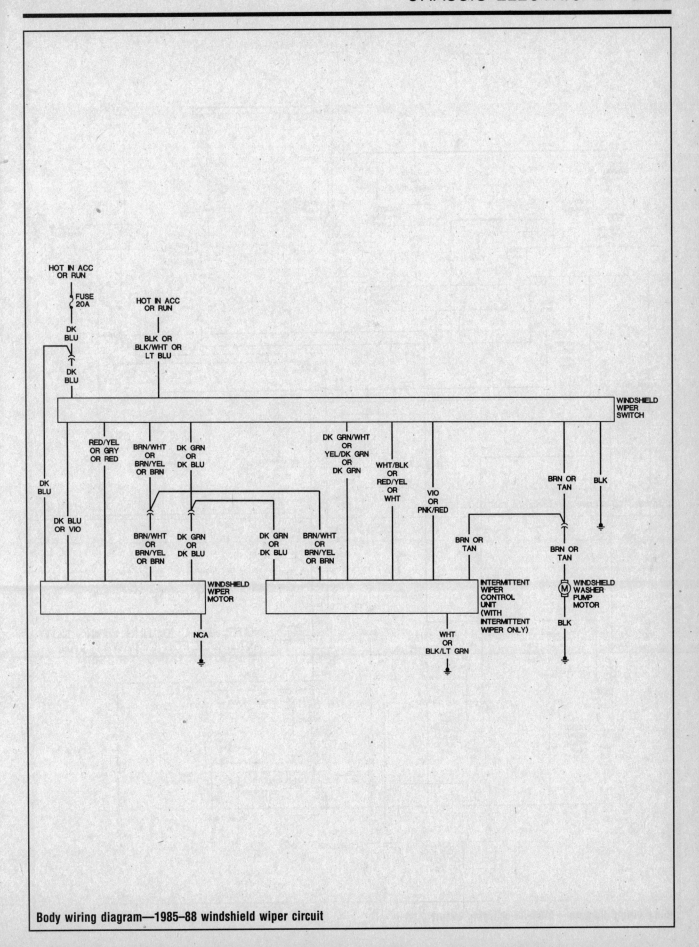

Body wiring diagram—1985–88 windshield wiper circuit

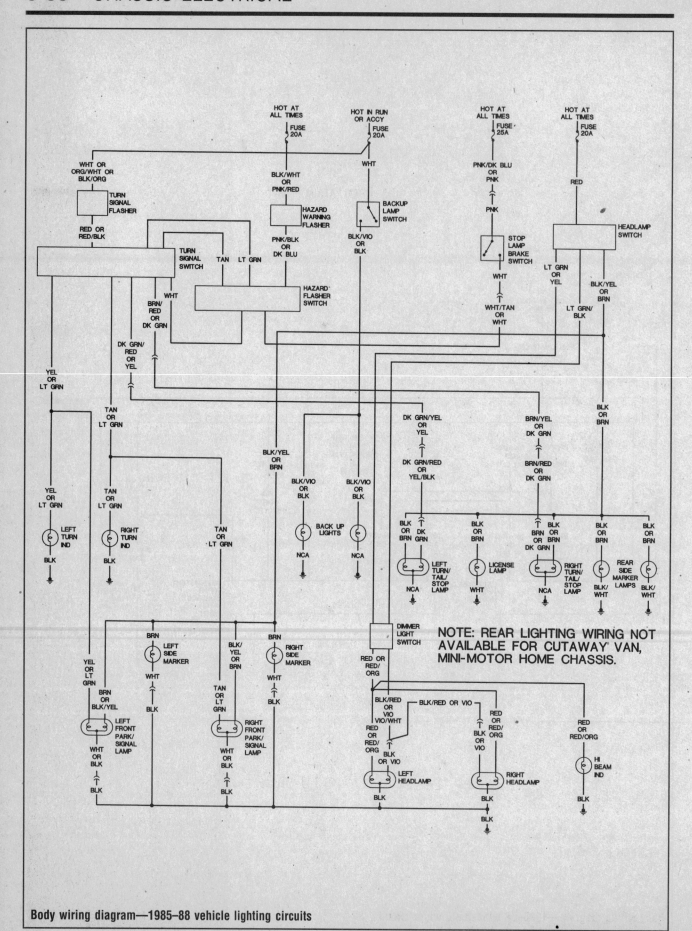

Body wiring diagram—1985-88 vehicle lighting circuits

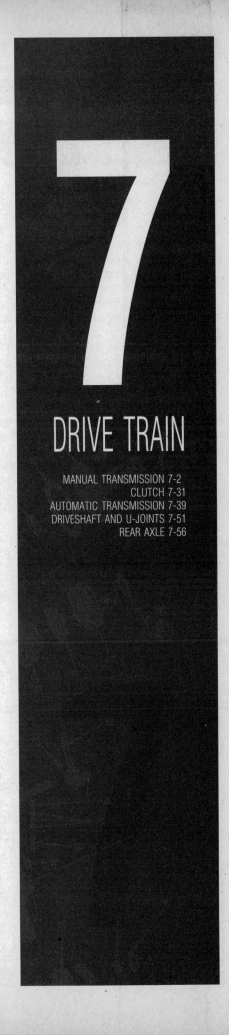

7

DRIVE TRAIN

MANUAL TRANSMISSION

Understanding the Manual Transmission

Because of the way an internal combustion engine breathes, it can produce torque (or twisting force) only within a narrow speed range. Most overhead valve pushrod engines must turn at about 2500 rpm to produce their peak torque. Often by 4500 rpm, they are producing so little torque that continued increases in engine speed produce no power increases.

The torque peak on overhead camshaft engines is, generally, much higher, but much narrower.

The manual transmission and clutch are employed to vary the relationship between engine RPM and the speed of the wheels so that adequate power can be produced under all circumstances. The clutch allows engine torque to be applied to the transmission input shaft gradually, due to mechanical slippage. The vehicle can, consequently, be started smoothly from a full stop.

The transmission changes the ratio between the rotating speeds of the engine and the wheels by the use of gears. 4-speed or 5-speed transmissions are most common. The lower gears allow full engine power to be applied to the rear wheels during acceleration at low speeds.

The clutch driveplate is a thin disc, the center of which is splined to the transmission input shaft. Both sides of the disc are covered with a layer of material which is similar to brake lining and which is capable of allowing slippage without roughness or excessive noise.

The clutch cover is bolted to the engine flywheel and incorporates a diaphragm spring which provides the pressure to engage the clutch. The cover also houses the pressure plate. When the clutch pedal is released, the driven disc is sandwiched between the pressure plate and the smooth surface of the flywheel, thus

forcing the disc to turn at the same speed as the engine crankshaft.

The transmission contains a mainshaft which passes all the way through the transmission, from the clutch to the driveshaft. This shaft is separated at one point, so that front and rear portions can turn at different speeds.

Power is transmitted by a countershaft in the lower gears and reverse. The gears of the countershaft mesh with gears on the mainshaft, allowing power to be carried from one to the other. Countershaft gears are often integral with that shaft, while several of the mainshaft gears can either rotate independently of the shaft or be locked to it. Shifting from one gear to the next causes one of the gears to be freed from rotating with the shaft and locks another to it. Gears are locked and unlocked by internal dog clutches which slide between the center of the gear and the shaft. The forward gears usually employ synchronizers; friction members which smoothly bring gear and shaft to the same speed before the toothed dog clutches are engaged.

Shift Linkage

ADJUSTMENTS

A-230, A-250

♦ **See Figures 1 and 2**

1. Adjust the length of the 2nd-3rd shift rod so the position of the shift lever on the steering column will be correct.
2. Loosen the swivel clamp bolts on each shift rod.
3. Move the 2nd-3rd shift lever into 3rd position (this means

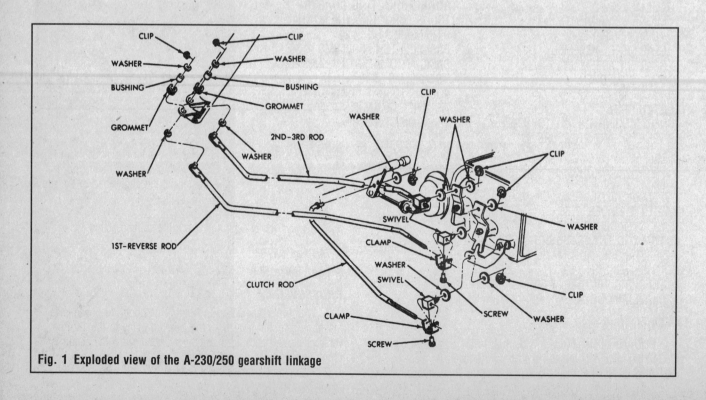

Fig. 1 Exploded view of the A-230/250 gearshift linkage

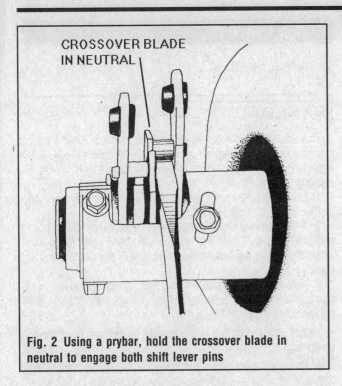

Fig. 2 Using a prybar, hold the crossover blade in neutral to engage both shift lever pins

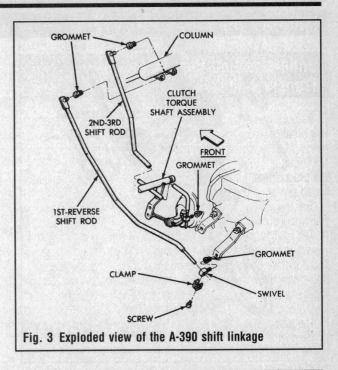

Fig. 3 Exploded view of the A-390 shift linkage

moving forward lever forward). Move the steering column lever until it is about 5° above the horizontal. Tighten the shift rod swivel clamp bolt to 125 in. lbs.

4. Shift the transmission to neutral. Place a small prybar between the crossover blade and the 2nd-3rd lever at the steering column so that both lever pins are engaged by the crossover blade.

5. Set the 1st-Reverse lever in neutral. Tighten the swivel clamp bolt to 125 in. lbs.

6. Remove the tool from the crossover blade, and check all shifts for smoothness.

A-390
◆ See Figure 3

1. Loosen both shift rod swivels. Make sure that the transmission shift levers are in the neutral position (middle detent).

2. Move the shift lever to line up the locating slots in the bottom of the steering column shift housing and bearing housing. Install a suitable tool in the slot.

3. Place a suitable tool between the crossover blade and the 2nd-3rd lever at the steering column so that both lever pins are engaged by the crossover blade.

4. Tighten both rod swivel bolts. Remove the gearshift housing locating tool.

5. Remove the tool from the crossover blade at the steering column and shift the transmission through all gears to check adjustment and crossover smoothness.

6. Check for proper operation of the steering column lock in reverse. With the proper linkage adjustment, the ignition should lock in reverse only, with hands off the gearshift lever.

Overdrive-4
◆ See Figure 4

1. Place the floorshift lever in Neutral. Insert a ¼" drill bit through the bottom of the shifter to hold the levers in place.

2. Detach the shift rods. Make sure that the three transmission

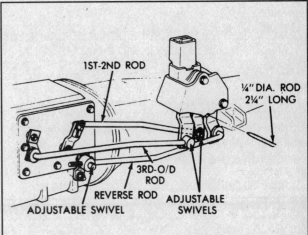

Fig. 4 Linkage adjustment point for the Overdrive-4 (A-833) transmission

levers are in their Neutral detents.

3. Adjust the shift rods to make the length exactly right to fit into the transmission levers. Start with the 1st-2nd shift rod. It may be necessary to remove the clip at the shifter end of the rod to rotate this rod.

4. Replace the washers and the clips.

5. Remove the drill bit and check the shifting action.

A-745 and A-903
◆ See Figure 5

CROSSOVER

1. With the transmission in Neutral, it should be possible to move the gearshift lever from the 2nd-3rd plane to the 1st-Reverse plane and back again, smoothly. If not, or if the action is rough, proceed with the adjustment.

2. Place the transmission in Neutral.

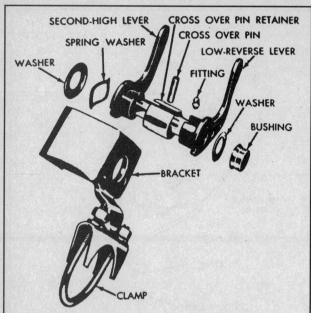

SECOND-HIGH LEVER · CROSS OVER PIN RETAINER · SPRING WASHER · CROSS OVER PIN · WASHER · LOW-REVERSE LEVER · FITTING · WASHER · BUSHING · BRACKET · CLAMP

Fig. 5 Shift linkage selector components for the A-745/ 903 transmissions—located on the steering column

3. Loosen the 2nd-3rd control rod adjuster at the transmission.

4. Move the lever as necessary to align the notches in both shift levers.

5. Tighten the adjuster nut.

CROSSOVER INTERFERENCE

1. Have an assistant place the gearshift lever in Neutral and hold it there in an upwards position.

2. Check the clearance between the pin and the 1st-Reverse shift lever slot.

3. Move the gearshift lever down and check the clearance between the pin and 2nd-3rd shift lever slot. The two clearances should be equal. If not, hard shifting will be the result. To correct or equalize the clearances:

4. Loosen the tube support clamp and move the lever support bracket up or down as required.

5. Make sure that the floor mat does not interfere with the shift tube, that there is no damage to the control rods or linkage, and that there is no misalignment between the steering column and shift lever tube.

CONTROL ROD

1. Place the transmission in Neutral.

2. Loosen and back off both adjusting nuts on the 1st-Reverse and 2nd-3rd control rods.

3. Move the crossover pin into engagement with the 2nd-3rd lever slot.

4. Without moving the 2nd-3rd lever, adjust and tighten the 2nd-3rd shift rod adjusting nut to 70 in. lbs.

5. Move the gearshift lever across the Neutral position to align the slots in the lever hubs. Without moving the 1st-Reverse shift rod, adjust and tighten the 1st-Reverse shift rod adjusting nut to 70 in. lbs.

6. Road test the van. If the shifts are rough, re-adjust the 1st-Reverse shift rod adjuster.

Clutch Interlock

ADJUSTMENT

A-250 3-Speed

This adjustment is required only on the A-250 3-Speed transmission. This is a top cover unit used only as base equipment on light duty six cylinder models. It has synchromesh only on second and third gears.

1. Disconnect the clutch rod swivel from the interlock pawl. Adjust the clutch pedal free-play.

2. Shift the transmission to neutral. Loosen swivel clamp bolt and slide the swivel onto the rod until the pawl is positioned fully within the slot in the first-reverse lever. Install the washers and clips.

3. Hold the interlock pawl forward and tighten the swivel clamp bolt. The clutch pedal must be in full returned position during the adjustment.

➡**Do not pull the clutch rod rearward to engage the swivel in the panel.**

4. Shift the transmission into first and reverse and release the clutch pedal while in either gear to check for normal clutch action. Then, shift halfway between neutral and either gear and release clutch. The interlock should hold it to within one or two inches of the floor.

Back-Up Light Switch

REMOVAL & INSTALLATION

NP-2500

▶ See Figure 6

The switch is located on the left side of the transmission just below and behind the shifter. It screws into place. Tighten it to 15 ft. lbs.

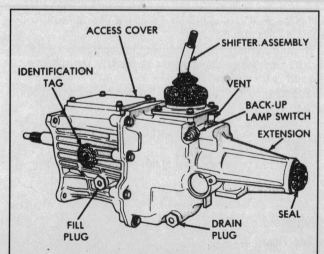

ACCESS COVER · SHIFTER ASSEMBLY · IDENTIFICATION TAG · VENT · BACK-UP LAMP SWITCH · EXTENSION · SEAL · FILL PLUG · DRAIN PLUG

Fig. 6 Back-up light switch location and related components on the NP-2500 transmission

Overdrive-4

▶ See Figure 7

The switch is located on the left side of the case, just behind the shift linkage housing. It screws into place. Tighten it to 15 ft. lbs.

A-230, A-250

The switch is located in the left case, just below the shifters. It screws into place. Tighten it to 15 ft. lbs.

A-390

The switch is located on the left side of the extension housing at the case end. It screws into place. Tighten it to 15 ft. lbs.

A-745, A-903

The switch is located on the left side of the case, just behind the shift linkage housing. It screws into place. Tighten it to 15 ft. lbs.

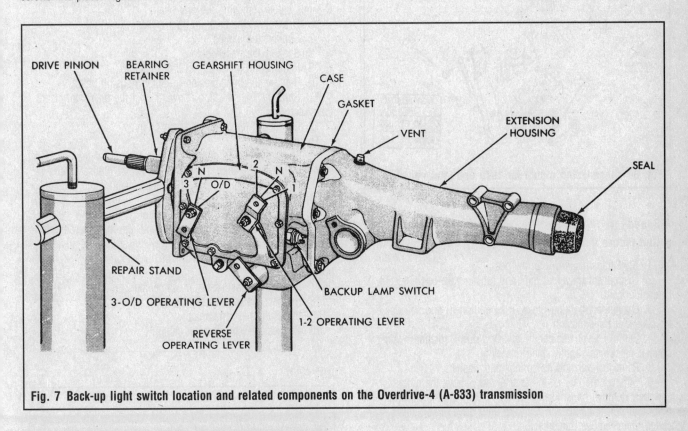

Fig. 7 Back-up light switch location and related components on the Overdrive-4 (A-833) transmission

Transmission Assembly

REMOVAL & INSTALLATION

▶ See Figure 8

3-Speed

1. Drain lubricant.
2. Disconnect and match-mark the driveshaft. On the sliding spline type, disconnect driveshaft at the rear universal joint, then carefully pull the shaft yoke out of the transmission extension housing. Do not nick or scratch splines.
3. Disconnect gearshift control rods and speedometer cable.
4. Remove backup light switch if so equipped.
5. Support engine.
6. Remove crossmember and rubber insulator on 1975 and later models with A-390 transmission. On all other models, unbolt the insulator or mount from the crossmember. Support the transmission with a jack.
7. Remove transmission to clutch housing bolts.

8. Slide transmission rearward until pinion shaft clears clutch completely, then lower transmission from vehicle.
   To install:
9. Before inserting transmission drive shaft into clutch, make sure clutch housing bore, disc and face are aligned.
10. Slide transmission forward until the pinion shaft enters the clutch completely, then push the transmission forward all the way.
11. Install transmission to clutch housing bolts. Tighten the bolts to 50 ft. lbs. torque.
12. Install crossmember and rubber insulator on 1975 and later models with A-390 transmission. On all other models, bolt the insulator or mount to the crossmember.
13. Install backup light switch if so equipped.
14. Connect gearshift control rods and speedometer cable.
15. Connect the driveshaft. On the sliding spline type, carefully slide the shaft yoke into the transmission extension housing. Do not nick or scratch splines. Connect the driveshaft at the rear universal joint.
16. Fill with lubricant.
17. Adjust shift linkage.
18. Road test.

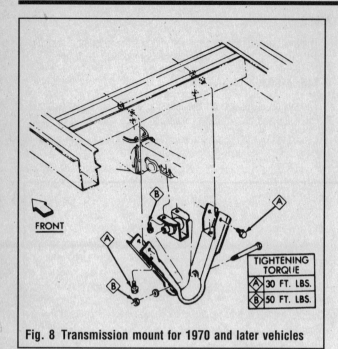

Fig. 8 Transmission mount for 1970 and later vehicles

TIGHTENING TORQUE	
A	30 FT. LBS.
B	50 FT. LBS.

4-Speed

▶ **See Figure 9**

1. Shift transmission into any gear.

2. Disconnect universal joint and loosen yoke retaining nut. Drain lubricant.

3. Disconnect parking brake (if so equipped) and speedometer cables at transmission.

4. Remove lever retainer by pressing down, rotating retainer counter-clockwise slightly, then releasing.

5. Remove lever and its springs and washers.

6. Support the rear of the engine and remove the cross-member. Remove transmission to clutch bell housing retaining bolts and pull transmission rearward until drive pinion clears clutch, then remove transmission.

To install:

7. Place ½ teaspoon of short fibre grease in pinion shaft pilot bushing, taking care not to get any grease on flywheel face.

8. Align clutch disc and backing plate with a spare drive pinion shaft or clutch aligning tool, then carefully install transmission.

9. Install transmission to bell housing bolts, tightening to 50 ft. lbs. torque. Replace the crossmember.

10. Install gear shift lever, shift into any gear and tighten yoke nut to 95–105 ft. lbs. torque.

11. Install universal joint, speedometer cable and brake cable.

12. Adjust clutch.

13. Install transmission drain plug and fill transmission with lubricant.

14. Road test.

5-Speed Models

1. Raise and support the truck.

2. Remove the skid plate, if any. Drain lubricant from the transmission.

3. Disconnect the speedometer cable.

4. Disconnect and matchmark the front and rear driveshafts. Suspend each shaft from a convenient place; do not allow them to hang free.

5. Remove the driveshaft. Matchmark the driveshaft and rear U-joints before removing the driveshaft.

6. Disconnect the back-up light switch.

7. Support the engine.

8. Support the transmission.

9. Remove the transmission crossmember.

10. Remove the transmission-to-clutch housing bolts.

11. Slide the transmission rearward until the mainshaft clears the clutch disc.

12. Lower and remove the transmission.

To install:

13. The transmission pilot bushing in the end of the crankshaft requires high-temperature grease. Multipurpose grease should be used. Do not lubricate the end of the mainshaft, clutch splines, or clutch release levers.

14. Raise and position the transmission.

15. Slide the transmission forward until the mainshaft enters the clutch disc, then push it all the way forward.

16. Install the transmission-to-clutch housing bolts. Torque the bolts to 50 ft. lbs.

17. Install the transmission crossmember.

18. Connect the back-up light switch.

19. Install the rear driveshaft.

20. Connect the speedometer cable.

21. Lower the truck.

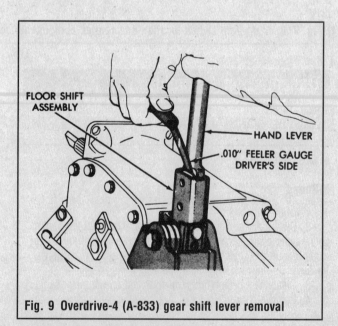

Fig. 9 Overdrive-4 (A-833) gear shift lever removal

Overdrive-4 Overhaul

▶ **See Figures 10 and 11**

The Overdrive-4 Speed transmission is a four speed unit with all forward gears synchronized. Third gear is direct, while the fourth gear is the overdrive ratio. Lubricant capacity is 7 pints.

DISASSEMBLY

Gearshift Housing and Mechanism

1. If available, mount transmission in a repair stand.
2. Disconnect gearshift control rods from the shift control levers and the transmission operating levers.
3. Remove the two gearshift control housing mounting bolts.
4. Remove gearshift control housing from the transmission extension housing or mounting bracket (if so equipped).
5. Remove the gearshift control housing mounting bracket bolts, then remove the bracket (if so equipped).
6. Remove back-up light switch (if so equipped).
7. Remove output companion flange nut and washer, if used, then pull the flange from the mainshaft (output shaft).
8. Remove gearshift housing-to-transmission case attaching bolts.
9. With all levers in the neutral detent position, pull housing out and away from the case.

➡**If first and second, or third and fourth shift forks remain in engagement with the synchronizer sleeves, move the sleeves and remove forks from the case.**

10. Remove nuts, lock washers and flat washers that hold first/second, and third/fourth speed shift operating levers to the shafts.
11. Disengage shift levers from the flats on the shafts and remove levers. Remove the E-ring on the overdrive four speed.

Extension Housing, Mainshaft & Main Drive Pinion

▶ **See Figures 12 and 13**

1. Remove the bolt and retainer holding the speedometer pinion adapter in the extension housing, then remove the pinion adapter.
2. Remove the bolts attaching the extension housing to the transmission case.
3. Rotate the extension housing on the output shaft to expose the rear of the countershaft. Install one bolt to hold the extension in place.
4. Drill a hole in the countershaft extension plug at the front of the case.
5. Reaching through this hole, push the countershaft to the rear to expose the Woodruff key; when exposed, remove it. Push the countershaft forward against the expansion plug, and using a brass drift, tap the countershaft forward until the expansion plug is removed.
6. Using a countershaft arbor, push the countershaft out the rear of the case, but don't let the countershaft washers fall out of position. Lower the cluster gear to the bottom of the transmission case.
7. Remove the bolt and rotate the extension back to the normal position.
8. Remove the drive pinion attaching bolts and slide the re-

tainer and gasket from the pinion shaft, then pry the pinion or seal from the retainer. When installing the new seal, don't nick or scratch the seal bore in the retainer or the surface on which the seal bottoms.

9. Using a brass drift, tap the pinion and bearing assembly forward and remove through the front of the case.
10. Slide the third and overdrive synchronizer sleeve slightly forward, slide the reverse idler gear to the center of its shaft, and tap the extension housing rearward. Slide the housing and mainshaft assembly out and away from the case.
11. Remove the snapring holding the third and overdrive synchronizer clutch gear and sleeve assembly to the mainshaft, then remove the synchronizer assembly.
12. Slide the overdrive gear and stop ring off the mainshaft. Using pair of long nose pliers, compress the snapring holding the mainshaft bearing in the extension housing. With it compressed, pull the mainshaft assembly and bearing out of the extension housing.
13. Remove the snapring holding the mainshaft on the shaft. The bearing is removed by inserting steel plates on the front side of the first speed gear, then pressing the mainshaft through the bearing being careful not to damage the gear teeth.
14. Remove the bearing, retainer ring, first speed gear and stop ring from the shaft.
15. Remove the snapring. Remove the first and second clutch gear and sleeve assembly from the mainshaft.
16. Remove the drive pinion bearing inner snapring, then using an arbor press, remove the bearing. Remove the snapring and bearing rollers from the cavity in the drive pinion.
17. Remove the countershaft gear from the bottom of the case, then remove the arbor, needle bearings, thrust washers and spacers from the center of the countershaft gear.
18. Remove the reverse gearshift lever detent spring retainer, gasket, plug, and detent ball spring from the rear of the case.
19. The reverse idler gear shaft is a tight fit in the case and will have to be pressed out.
20. If there is oil leakage visible around the reverse gearshift lever shaft, push the lever shaft in and remove it from the case. Remove the detent ball from the bottom of the transmission case and remove the shift fork from the shaft and detent plate.

ASSEMBLY

Reverse Shaft

Follow the first four steps only if you removed the reverse shaft in the disassembly procedure.

1. Install a new oil seal O-ring on the lever shaft and coat the shaft with grease; insert it into its bore and install the reverse fork in the lever.
2. Install the reverse detent spring and gasket; insert the ball and spring and install the plug and gasket.
3. Place the reverse idler gear shaft in position in the end of the case and drive it in far enough to position the reverse idler gear on the protruding end of the shaft with the fork slot toward the rear. While doing this, engage the slot with the reverse shift fork.
4. With the reverse idler gear correctly positioned, drive the reverse gear shaft into the case far enough to install the Woodruff key. Drive the shaft in flush with the end of the transmission case. Install the back-up light switch and gasket.

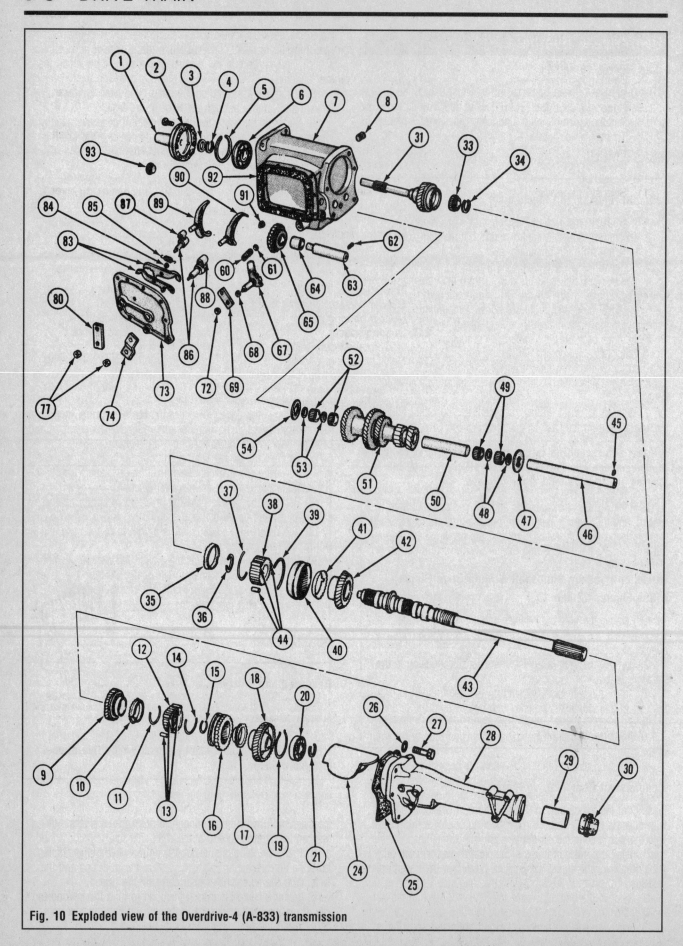

Fig. 10 Exploded view of the Overdrive-4 (A-833) transmission

1. Bearing retainer
2. Bearing retainer gsket
3. Bearing retainer oil seal
4. Snap ring, bearing (inner)
5. Snap ring, bearing (outer)
6. Pinion bearing
7. Transmission case
8. Filler plug
9. Gear, 2nd speed
10. Snap ring
11. Shift strut springs
12. Clutch gear
13. Shift struts (3)
14. Shift strut spring
15. Snap ring
16. 1st and 2nd clutch sleeve gear
17. Stop ring
18. 1st speed gear
19. Snap ring
20. Rear bearing
21. Snap ring
24. Baffle
25. Gasket, case to extension housing
26. Lockwasher
27. Bolt
28. Extension housing
29. Mainsahft yoke bushing
30. Oil seal
31. Main Drive pinion
33. Needle bearing rollers
34. Snap ring
35. Stop ring
36. Snap ring
37. Shift strut spring
38. Clutch gear
39. Shift strut spring
40. Clutch sleeve
41. Stop ring
42. OD gear
43. Mainshaft (output)
44. Shift struts (3)
45. Woodruff key
46. Countershaft
47. Thrustwasher, gear (1)
48. Spacer ring needle roller bearing
49. Needle bearing rollers
50. Bearing spacer
51. Countershaft gear (cluster)
52. Needle bearing rollers
53. Spacer ring needle roller bearing
54. Thrustwasher, gear (1)
60. Spring, reverse detent ball
61. Ball, reverse detent
62. Woodruff key
63. Reverse idler gear shaft
64. Bushing, reverse idler gear
65. Gear, reverse idler
67. Reverse lever
68. Oil seal, reverse lever shaft
69. Reverse operating lever
72. Nut, lever
73. Gearshift control housing
74. 1st and 2nd operating lever
77. Nut, lever
80. 3rd and O/D operating lever
83. Interlock lever (2)
84. E-clip
85. Spring
86. Oil seal (2)
87. 3rd and O/D lever
88. 1st and 2nd lever
89. 3rd and O/D speed fork
90. 1st and 2nd speed fork
91. Drain plug
92. Gasket, shift control housing
93. Expansion plug

Fig. 11 Component list of the Overdrive-4 (A-833) transmission exploded view

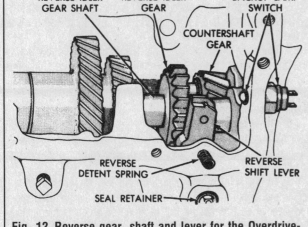

Fig. 12 Reverse gear, shaft and lever for the Overdrive-4 (A-833) transmission

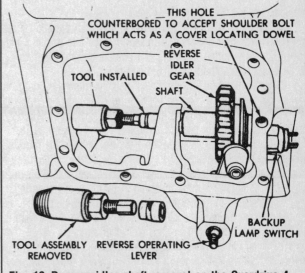

Fig. 13 Reverse idler shaft removal on the Overdrive-4 (A-833) transmission

Countershaft Gear & Drive Pinion

1. Coat the inside bore of the countershaft gear with a thin film of grease and install the roller bearing spacer with an arbor, into the gear; center the spacer and arbor.

2. Install the roller bearings and a spacer ring on each end.

3. Replace worn thrust washers; coat the new ones with grease and install them over the arbor with the tang side toward the case boss.

4. Install the countershaft assembly into the case and allow the gear assembly to sit on the bottom of the case so that the thrust washers won't come out of position.

5. Press the drive pinion bearing on the pinion shaft. Make sure the outer snapring groove is toward the front end and the bearing is seated against the shoulder on the gear.

6. Install a new snapring on the shaft to hold the bearing in place; make sure the snapring is seated and that there is mini-

mum end-play. There are several snapring thicknesses available for adjustment.

7. Place the pinion shaft in a soft-jawed vise and install the roller bearings in the cavity of the shaft. Coat them with grease and install the bearing retaining snapring.

8. Install a new oil seal in the bore.

Extension Housing Bushing

1. Remove the yoke seal from the extension housing.

2. Drive out the old bushing and drive in a new one, aligning the oil hole in the bushing with the slot in the housing.

3. Place a new seal in the opening of the extension housing and then drive it into place.

Mainshaft

1. Place a stop ring flat on a bench followed by the clutch gear and sleeve; drop the struts in their slots and snap in a strut spring placing the tang inside one strut. Install the second strut spring tang in a different strut after turning the assembly over.

2. Slide the second speed gear over the mainshaft with the synchronizer cone toward the rear and down against the shoulder on the shaft.

3. Slide the first and second gear synchronizer assembly including stop rings with lugs indexed in the hub slots, over the mainshaft down against the second gear cone and hold it there with a new snapring. Slide the next snapring over the shaft and index the lugs into the clutch hub slots.

4. Slide the first speed gear with the synchronizer cone toward the clutch sleeve just installed over the mainshaft and into position against the clutch sleeve gear.

5. Install the mainshaft bearing retaining ring followed by the mainshaft rear bearing; press the bearing down into position and install a new snapring to secure it. There are several snapring thicknesses available for minimum end-play.

6. Install the partially assembled mainshaft into the extension housing far enough to engage the bearing retaining ring in the slot in the extension housing. Compress the ring with pliers so that the mainshaft ball bearing can move in and bottom against its thrust shoulder in the extension housing. Release the ring and make sure that it is seated.

7. Slide the overdrive gear over the mainshaft with the synchronizer cone toward the front followed by the gear's snapring.

8. Install the third-overdrive gear synchronizer clutch gear assembly on the mainshaft against the overdrive gear. Make sure to index the rear stop ring with the clutch gear struts.

9. Install the snapring and position the front stop ring over the clutch gear again lining up the ring lugs with the struts; coat a new extension gasket with grease and place it in position.

10. Slide the reverse idler gear to the center of its shaft and move the third/overdrive synchronizer as far forward as possible without losing the struts.

11. Insert the mainshaft assembly in the case tilting it as necessary. Place the third/overdrive sleeve in the neutral detent.

12. Rotate the extension on the mainshaft to expose the rear of the countershaft and install one bolt to hold it in position.

13. Install the drive pinion and bearing assembly through the front of the case and position it in the front bore. Install the outer snapring in the bearing groove and tap lightly into place. If it

doesn't bottom easily, check to see if a strut, pinion roller or stop ring is out of position.

14. Turn the transmission upside down while holding the countershaft gear to prevent damage. Then lower the countershaft gear assembly into position making sure that the teeth mesh with the drive pinion gear.

15. Start the countershaft into the bore at the rear of the case and push until it is in about halfway; then install the Woodruff key and push it in until it is flush with the rear of the case.

16. Rotate the extension back to normal position and install the bolts; turn the transmission upright and install the drive pinion bearing retainer and gasket. Coat the threads with sealing compound and tighten the attaching bolts to 30 ft. lbs.

17. Install a new expansion plug in its bore.

Gearshift Housing & Mechanism

1. Install the interlock levers on the pivot pin and secure with the E-ring. Install the spring with a pair of pliers.

2. Grease and install new O-ring seals on both shift shafts; grease the housing bores and push the shafts through.

3. Install the operating levers and tighten the retaining nuts to 18 ft. lbs.; make sure the third-overdrive lever points down.

4. Rotate each shift shaft fork bore straight up and install the third/overdrive shift fork in its bore and under both interlock levers.

5. Position both synchronizer sleeves in neutral and place the first and second gear shift fork in the groove of the first and second gear synchronizer sleeve. Slide the reverse idler gear to neutral. Turn the transmission on its right side and place the gearshift housing gasket in place holding it there with grease. Install the reverse detent ball and spring into the case bore.

6. As the shift housing is lowered in place, guide the third-overdrive shift fork into its synchronizer groove then lead the shaft of the first and second shift lever.

7. Raise the interlock lever with a screwdriver to allow the first and second shift fork to slip under the levers. The shift housing will now seat against the case.

8. Install the bolts lightly and shift through all the gears to check for proper operation.

9. The reverse shift lever and the first and second gear shift lever have cam surfaces which mate in reverse position to lock the first and second lever, the fork and synchronizer in the neutral position.

10. To check for proper operation, put the transmission in reverse, and, while turning the input shaft, move the first and second lever in each direction. If it locks up or becomes harder to turn, select a new shift lever size with more or less clearance. If there is too little cam clearance, it will be difficult or impossible to shift into reverse.

11. Grease the reverse shaft, install the operating lever and nut, and install the speedometer drive pinion gear and adapter, making sure the range number is in the straight down position.

New Process A-230 3-Speed Overhaul

The A-230 is a three-speed transmission equipped with two synchronizer units to assist in the engagement of all forward gears. Lubricant capacity is 5 pints.

DISASSEMBLY

♦ **See Figure 14**

Shift Housing and Mechanism

1. Shift to second gear.
2. Remove side cover. If shaft O-ring seals need replacement: Pull shift-forks out of shafts. Remove nuts and operating levers from shafts. Deburr shafts. Remove shafts.

Drive Pinion Retainer & Extension Housing

1. Remove pinion bearing retainer from front of transmission case. Pry off retainer oil seal.
2. For clearance: With a brass drift, tap drive pinion as far forward as possible. Rotate cut away part of second gear next to countershaft gear. Shift second/third synchronizer sleeve forward.
3. Remove speedometer pinion adapter retainer. Work adapter and pinion out of extension housing.
4. Unbolt extension housing. Break housing loose with plastic hammer and carefully remove.

Idler Gear & Mainshaft

1. Insert dummy shaft in case to push reverse idler shaft and key out of case.

2. Remove dummy shaft and idler rollers.
3. Remove both tanged idler gear thrust washers.
4. Remove mainshaft assembly through rear of case.

Countershaft Gear & Drive Pinion

1. Using a mallet and dummy shaft, tap the countershaft rearward enough to remove key. Drive countershaft out of case, being careful not to drop the washers.
2. Lower countershaft gear to bottom of case.
3. Remove snapring from pinion bearing outer race (outside front of case).
4. Drive pinion shaft into case with plastic hammer. Remove assembly through rear of case.
5. If bearing is to be replaced, remove snapring and press off bearing.
6. Lift counter shaft gear and dummy shaft out through rear of case.

Mainshaft

1. Remove snapring from front end of mainshaft along with second gear stop ring and second gear.
2. Spread snapring in mainshaft bearing retainer. Slide retainer back off the bearing race.
3. Remove snapring at rear of mainshaft. Support front side of reverse gear. Press bearing off mainshaft.

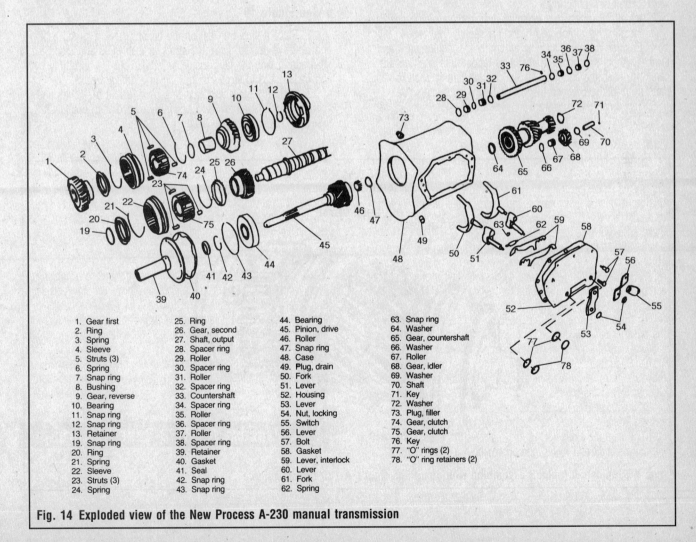

1. Gear first	25. Ring	44. Bearing	63. Snap ring
2. Ring	26. Gear, second	45. Pinion, drive	64. Washer
3. Spring	27. Shaft, output	46. Roller	65. Gear, countershaft
4. Sleeve	28. Spacer ring	47. Snap ring	66. Washer
5. Struts (3)	29. Roller	48. Case	67. Roller
6. Spring	30. Spacer ring	49. Plug, drain	68. Gear, idler
7. Snap ring	31. Roller	50. Fork	69. Washer
8. Bushing	32. Spacer ring	51. Lever	70. Shaft
9. Gear, reverse	33. Countershaft	52. Housing	71. Key
10. Bearing	34. Spacer ring	53. Lever	72. Washer
11. Snap ring	35. Roller	54. Nut, locking	73. Plug, filler
12. Snap ring	36. Spacer ring	55. Switch	74. Gear, clutch
13. Retainer	37. Roller	56. Lever	75. Gear, clutch
19. Snap ring	38. Spacer ring	57. Bolt	76. Key
20. Ring	39. Retainer	58. Gasket	77. "O" rings (2)
21. Spring	40. Gasket	59. Lever, interlock	78. "O" ring retainers (2)
22. Sleeve	41. Seal	60. Lever	
23. Struts (3)	42. Snap ring	61. Fork	
24. Spring	43. Snap ring	62. Spring	

Fig. 14 Exploded view of the New Process A-230 manual transmission

4. Remove from press. Remove mainshaft bearing and reverse gear from shaft.

5. Remove snapring and first-reverse synchronizer assembly from shaft. Remove stop ring and first gear rearward.

ASSEMBLY

Countershaft Gear

1. Slide dummy shaft into countershaft gear.
2. Slide one roller thrust washer over dummy shaft and into gear, followed by 22 greased rollers.
3. Repeat Step 2, adding one roller thrust washer on end.
4. Repeat Steps 2 and 3 at other end of countershaft gear. There is a total of 88 rollers and 6 thrust washers.
5. Place greased front thrust washer on dummy shaft against gear with tangs forward.
6. Grease rear thrust washer and stick it in place in the case, with tangs rearward. Place countershaft gear assembly in bottom of transmission case until drive pinion is installed.

Pinion Gear

◗ **See Figure 15**

1. Press new bearing on pinion shaft with snapring groove forward. Install new snapring.
2. Install 15 rollers and retaining ring in drive pinion gear.
3. Install drive pinion and bearing assembly into case.
4. Position countershaft gear assembly by positioning it and thrust washers so countershaft can be tapped into position. Be careful to keep the countershaft against the dummy shaft to keep parts from falling between them. Install key in countershaft.
5. Tap drive pinion forward for clearance.

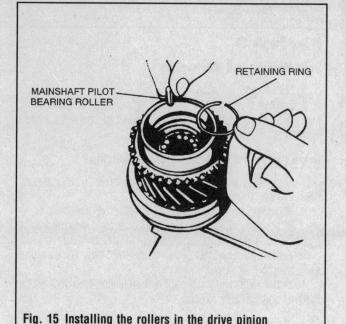

Fig. 15 Installing the rollers in the drive pinion

Mainshaft

◗ **See Figure 16**

1. Place a stop ring flat on the bench. Place a clutch gear and a sleeve on top. Drop the struts in their slots and insert a strut spring with the tang inside on strut. Turn the assembly over and install second strut spring, tang in a different strut.
2. Slide first gear and stop ring over rear of mainshaft and against thrust flange between assembly over rear of mainshaft, first and second gears on shaft.

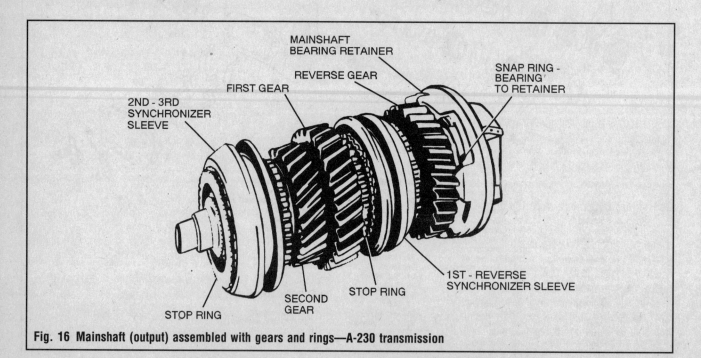

Fig. 16 Mainshaft (output) assembled with gears and rings—A-230 transmission

3. Slide first/reverse synchronizer indexing hub slots to first gear stop ring lugs.

4. Install first/reverse synchronizer clutch gear snapring on mainshaft.

5. Slide reverse gear and mainshaft bearing on shaft, supporting inner race of bearing. Be sure snapring groove on outer race is forward.

6. Install bearing retaining snapring on mainshaft. Slide snapring over the bearing and seat it in groove.

7. Place second gear over front of mainshaft with thrust surface against flange.

8. Install stop ring and second/third synchronizer assembly against second gear. Install second/third synchronizer clutch gear snapring on shaft.

9. Move second/third synchronizer sleeve forward as far as possible. Install front stop ring inside sleeve with lugs indexed to struts.

10. Rotate cut out on second gear toward countershaft gear for clearance.

11. Insert mainshaft assembly into case. Tilt assembly to clear cluster gears and insert pilot rollers in drive pinion gear. If assembly is correct, the bearing retainer will bottom to the case without force. If not, check for a misplaced strut, pinion roller, or stop ring.

Reverse Idler Gear

1. Place dummy shaft into idler gear. Insert 22 greased rollers.
2. Position reverse idler thrust washers in case with grease.
3. Position idler gear and dummy shaft in case. Install idler shaft and key.

Extension Housing

1. Remove extension housing yoke seal. Drive bushing out from inside housing.

2. Align oil hole in bushing with oil slot in housing. Drive bushing into place. Drive new seal into housing.

3. Install extension housing and gasket to hold mainshaft and bearing retainer in place.

Drive Pinion Bearing Retainer

1. Install outer snapring on drive pinion bearing. Tap assembly back until snapring contacts case.

2. Using seal installer tool or equivalent, install a new seal in retainer bore.

3. Position main drive pinion bearing retainer and gasket on front of case. Coat threads with sealing compound, install bolts, torque to 30 ft. lbs.

Gearshaft Mechanism and Housing

1. If removed, place two interlock levers in pivot pin with spring hangers offset toward each other, so that spring installs in a straight line. Place E-clip on pivot pin.

2. Grease and install new O-ring seals on both shift shafts. Grease housing bores and insert shafts.

3. Install spring on interlock lever hangers.

4. Rotate each shift shaft fork bore to straight up position. Install shift forks through bores and under both interlock levers.

5. Position second/third synchronizer sleeve to rear, in second gear position. Position first/reverse synchronizer sleeve to middle of travel, in neutral position. Place shift forks in the same positions.

6. Install gasket and gearshift mechanism. The bolt with the extra long shoulder must be installed at the center rear of the case. Torque bolts to 15 ft. lbs.

7. Install speedometer drive pinion gear and adapter. Range number on adapter, which represents the number of teeth on the gear, should be in 6 o'clock position.

New Process A-250 3-Speed Overhaul

The A-250 is a three speed transmission equipped with a synchronizer between second and third gears. Lubricant capacity is 4½ pints.

DISASSEMBLY

▶ **See Figure 17**

1. Remove case cover and gasket.

2. Measure the synchronizer "float" with a pair of feeler gauges. Measurement is made between the synchronizer outer ring pin and the opposite synchronizer outer ring. This measurement must be made on two pins 180 degrees apart with equal gap on both ends for "float" determination. The measurement should be between 0.060–0.117″. A snug fit should be maintained between feeler gauge and pins.

3. Remove the bolt and retainer holding the speedometer pinion adapter in the extension housing. Carefully work the adapter and pinion out of the extension housing.

4. Remove extension housing bolts and extension housing.

5. Remove the bolts that attach the drive pinion bearing retainer to case, then slide the retainer off the pinion. Pry the seal out of retainer using a screwdriver. Be cautious not to nick or scratch the bore.

6. Rotate the drive pinion so that the blank clutch tooth area is opposite the countershaft for removal clearance.

7. Slide drive pinion assembly slightly out of case. Move the synchronizer front inner stop ring from the short splines on the pinion shaft. Slowly remove drive pinion assembly.

8. Remove snapring that holds bearing on pinion shaft. Remove pinion bearing washer. Using an arbor press, press pinion shaft out of bearing. Remove oil slinger.

9. Remove snapring and bearing rollers from the end of the drive pinion.

10. Remove clutch gear retaining snapring from the mainshaft.

11. Remove the mainshaft bearing securing snapring from case.

12. Slide mainshaft and bearing rearward out of case while holding the gears as they drop free.

13. Remove the snapring from mainshaft and press the bearing off of mainshaft.

14. Remove the synchronizer components, second gear, first/reverse gear and shift forks from case.

➡**Steps 15 thru 18 need only be performed if gear shift lever seals are leaking.**

15. Remove the shift levers from the shift shafts.

16. Drive out the tapered retaining pin from the first/reverse shift shaft. Remove the shift shaft from inside the case. As the detent balls are spring loaded, when the shafts are removed the balls will drop to the bottom of the transmission case.

17. Remove the interlock sleeve, spring and both detent balls

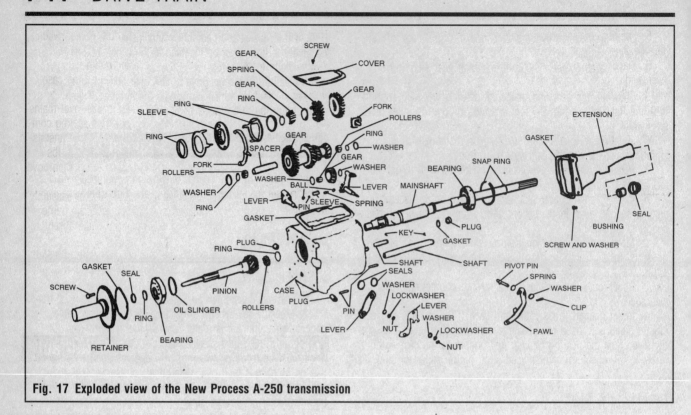

Fig. 17 Exploded view of the New Process A-250 transmission

from case. Drive tapered retaining pin out of second/third shaft and remove shaft from case.

18. Drive shift shaft seals out of case with a suitable drift.

19. Check end-play of countershaft gear with a feeler gauge. The end-play should be between 0.005–0.022". This measurement is used to determine if a new thrust washer is necessary during reassembly.

20. Using a countershaft bearing arbor, drive the countershaft towards the rear of the case until the small key can be removed from the countershaft.

21. Drive the countershaft the rest of the way out of the case, keeping the arbor tight against the end of the countershaft. This will prevent loss of roller bearings.

22. Remove the countershaft gear, front thrust washer and rear thrust washer from the case.

23. Remove the bearing rollers, spacer ring and center spacer from the countershaft gear.

24. Drive the reverse idler gear shaft out of the transmission case using a suitable drift. Remove the Woodruff key from the end of the reverse idler shaft.

25. Remove the reverse idler gear and thrust washers out of the case. Remove the bearing rollers from the gear.

ASSEMBLY

◆ **See Figure 18**

1. Slide the countershaft gear bearing roller spacer over arbor tool. Coat the bore of gear with lubricant and slide tool and spacer into gear bore.

2. Lubricate the bearing rollers with heavy grease and install two rows of 22 rollers each in both ends of gear in area around arbor. Cover with heavy grease and install bearing spacer rings in each end of gear and between roller rows.

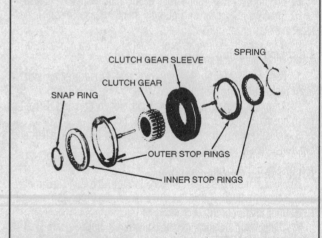

Fig. 18 Exploded view of the synchronizer assembly on the A-250 transmission

3. If countershaft gear end-play was found to be excessive during disassembly, install new thrust washers. Cover with heavy grease and install thrust washer and thrust needle bearing and cap at each end of countershaft gear and over arbor. Install gear and arbor in the case, and make sure that tabs on rear thrust washer slide into grooves in the case.

4. Drive the arbor forward out of the countershaft gear and through the bore in the front of the case using the countershaft and a soft faced hammer. When the countershaft is almost in place, make certain the keyway in the countershaft is aligned with the key slot in the rear of the case. Insert the shaft key and continue to drive the countershaft into the case until the key is bottomed in the slot.

5. Position special arbor tool in the reverse idler gear and install the 22 roller bearings using a heavy grease.

6. Place the front and rear thrust washers at each end of the reverse idler gear. Position the assembly in the transmission case with the chamfered end of the gear teeth towards the front. Make sure that the thrust washer tabs engage the slots in case.

7. Insert reverse idler shaft into the bore at rear of case with keyway to the rear, pushing the arbor towards the front of the case.

8. When the keyway is aligned with the slot in the case, insert the key in the keyway. Drive the shaft forward until the key is seated in the recess.

➡ **Steps 9 through 14 need only be performed if the shift levers have been disassembled.**

9. Place new shift shaft seals in the case and drive it into position with suitable drift.

10. Carefully slide the first/reverse shift shaft into the case and lock into place with a tapered retaining pin. Position the lever so that the center detent is aligned with the interlock bore.

11. Install the interlock sleeve into the bore followed by a detent ball, spring and pin.

12. Install remaining detent ball and hold in place with detent ball holding tool.

13. Depress the detent ball and carefully install the second/third shift shaft. Align center detent with detent ball and secure lever with tapered retaining pin.

14. Install shift levers and tighten retaining nuts to 18 ft. lbs.

15. Press the bearing on the mainshaft and select and install snapring that gives minimum end-play.

16. Move shift lever to reverse position, and then place the first/reverse gear and shift fork in the case.

➡ **Both shift forks are offset toward the rear of the transmission case.**

17. Assemble the synchronizer parts with shift fork and second gear.

18. Place the second gear assembly in the transmission case and insert the shift fork into its lever.

19. Install the mainshaft carefully through the gear assembly until it bottoms in rear of case.

20. Install synchronizer clutch gear snapring on mainshaft.

21. Select and install mainshaft bearing snapring in case.

22. If "float" measurement was found to be above or below 0.117", install or remove shims to place "float" within range.

23. Install oil slinger on drive pinion shaft and slide against the gear.

24. Slide the bearing over the pinion shaft with snapring groove away from gear, then seat bearing on shaft using an arbor press.

25. Install keyed washer between bearing and retaining snapring groove.

26. Secure bearing and washer with selected thickness snapring. If large snapring around bearing was removed, install it at this time.

27. Place drive pinion shaft in a vise with soft faced jaws and install the 14 roller bearings in the shaft cavity. Coat the roller bearings with a heavy grease and install retaining ring in groove.

28. Rotate the drive pinion so that the blank clutch tooth area is next to the countershaft. Guide the drive pinion through the front of case and engage the inner stop ring with the clutch teeth.

Then seat pinion bearing. The pinion shaft is fully seated when the snapring is in full contact with the case.

29. Install a new seal in the pinion bearing retainer.

30. Position retainer assembly and new gasket on the case. Use sealing compound on bolts and tighten to 30 ft. lbs.

31. Slide the extension housing and a new gasket over mainshaft. Guide shaft through bushing and oil seal. Use sealing compound on the bolt used in the hole tapped through the transmission case. Install remaining bolts and tighten all to 50 ft. lbs.

32. Install the transmission cover and gasket and tighten cover bolts to 12 ft. lbs.

33. Rotate the speedometer pinion gear and adapter assembly so that the number on the adapter corresponding to the number of teeth on the gear is in the 6 o'clock position as the assembly is installed.

34. Fill the transmission with the proper lubricant and install the drain plug and tighten to 25 ft. lbs. Install the back-up light switch and tighten to 15 ft. lbs.

35. Rotate the drive pinion shaft and check operation of transmission by running the transmission through all gear ranges.

New Process A-390 3-Speed Overhaul

The A-390 is a three speed synchromesh transmission. Lubricant capacity is 4½ pints.

DISASSEMBLY

◆ **See Figures 19 and 20**

1. Remove the bolts that attach the cover to the case. Remove the cover and gasket.

2. Remove the long spring that retains the detent plug in the case. Remove the detent plug with a small magnet.

3. Remove the bolt and retainer securing the speedometer pinion adapter to the transmission case. Carefully work the adapter and pinion out of the extension housing.

4. Remove the bolts that attach the extension housing to the transmission case. Slide the extension housing off the output shaft.

5. Remove the bolts that attach the input shaft bearing retainer to the case. Slide the retainer off the shaft. Using a suitable tool, pry the seal out of the retainer. Be careful not to nick or scratch the bore in which the seal is pressed or the surface on which the seal is bottomed.

6. Remove the lubricant fill plug from the right side of the case. Working through the fill plug opening, drive the roll pin out of the countershaft with a ¼" punch.

7. Working with the countershaft bearing arbor and a soft faced hammer, tap the countershaft toward the front of the case with the arbor tool to remove the expansion plug from the countershaft bore at the front of the case. The countershaft is a loose fit in the case and will slide easily.

8. Insert the arbor tool through the front of the case and push the countershaft out of the rear of the case so the roll pin hole in the countershaft does not travel through the roller bearings. The countershaft gear will drop to the bottom of the case. Remove the countershaft from the rear of the case.

9. Place both shift levers in neutral (center) position.

10. Remove the input shaft assembly and stop ring from the front of the case.

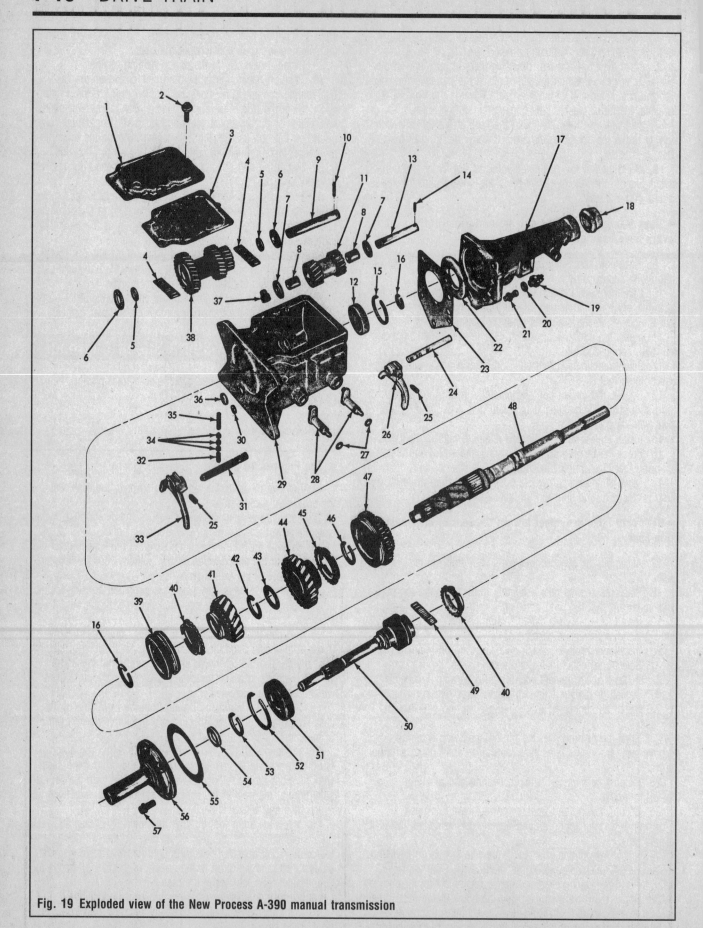

Fig. 19 Exploded view of the New Process A-390 manual transmission

1. Cover, case
2. Screw, case cover
3. Gasket, case cover
4. Roller, countershaft brg.
5. Washer, countershaft brg.
6. Washer, countershaft thrust
7. Washer, reverse idler thrust
8. Bushing, reverse idler
9. Countershaft
10. Pin, countershaft roll
11. Gear, reverse idler
12. Bearing, output shaft
13. Shaft, reverse idler
14. Pin, reverse idler stop
15. Snap ring, output shaft brg., outer
16. Snap ring, output shaft, inner
17. Extension
18. Seal, extension
19. Switch, back-up lamp
20. Gasket, back-up lamp switch
21. Screw, extension
     lockwasher, extension screw
22. Retainer, output shaft brg.
23. Gasket, extension
24. Rail, gearshift first and reverse
25. Screw, fork set
26. Fork, gearshift first and reverse
27. Seal, gearshift lever shaft oil
28. Lever, gearshift
29. Case
30. Plug
31. Rail, gearshift second and third
32. Spring, gearshift detent pin
33. Fork, gearshift second and third
34. Pin, gearshift detent
35. Spring, gearshift detent pin
36. Plug
37. Plug, case filler
38. Gear, countershaft
39. Synchronizer assy., second and third
40. Ring, synchronizer second and third stop
41. Gear, second speed
42. Snap ring, low speed gear thrust washer
43. Washer, low speed gear thrust
44. Gear, low speed
45. Ring, synchronizer low stop
46. Snap ring, synchronizer low and reverse clutch gear
47. Synchronizer assy., low and reverse
48. Shaft, output
49. Roller, output shaft pilot
50. Shaft, input
51. Bearing, input shaft
52. Snap ring, bearing, outer
53. Snap ring, bearing inner
54. Seal, bearing retainer oil
55. Gasket, bearing retainer
56. Retainer, bearing
57. Screw, bearing retainer

Fig. 20 Component list of the New Process A-390 manual transmission exploded view

11. Remove the set screw that secures the first/reverse shift fork to the shift rail. Slide the first/reverse shift rail out through the rear of the case.

12. Move the second/third shift fork rearward for access to the set screw. Remove the set screw from the fork. Using a suitable tool, rotate the shift rail one quarter (1/4) turn.

13. Lift the interlock plug from the case with a magnet.

14. Tap on the inner end of the second/third shift rail to remove the expansion plug from the front of the case. Remove the shift rail through the front of the case.

15. Remove the second/third shift rail detent plug and spring from the detent bore with a magnet.

16. Tap the output shaft assembly rearward until the output shaft bearing clears the case. Remove both shift forks. Remove the snapring that retains the output shaft bearing to the output shaft.

17. Assemble the output shaft bearing removal tool over the output shaft and bearing. Remove the output shaft bearing.

18. Remove the output shaft assembly through top of the case.

19. Using a suitable drift, drive the reverse idler gear shaft toward the rear, and out of the transmission case.

20. Lift the reverse idler gear and thrust washer out of the case.

21. Remove the countershaft gear, arbor assembly, and thrust washers from the bottom of the case.

22. Remove the countershaft roll pin from the bottom of the case.

23. Remove the snapring that retains the second/third synchronizer clutch gear and sleeve assembly on the output shaft. Slide the second/third synchronizer assembly off the end of the output shaft.

➡ **Do not separate the second-third synchronizer clutch gear, sleeve, struts, or spring unless inspection reveals that a replacement is necessary.**

24. Slide the second gear and stop ring off the output shaft.

25. Remove the snapring and thrust washer retaining the first gear. Slide the first gear and stop ring off the output shaft.

26. Remove the snapring that retains the first/reverse synchronizer hub on the output shaft. The first/reverse synchronizer hub is a press fit on the output shaft. To avoid damage to the synchronizer, remove the synchronizer hub using an arbor press. Do not attempt to remove or install the hub by hammering or prying.

Shift Levers and Seals

1. Remove the operating levers from their respective shafts. Remove any burrs from the shafts to avoid damage to the case.

2. Push the shift levers out of the transmission case. Remove and discard the O-ring seal from each shaft.

3. Lubricate the new seals with transmission oil and install them on the shafts.

4. Install the shift levers in the case.

5. Install the operating levers and tighten the retaining nuts to 18 ft. lbs.

Input Shaft Bearing and Rollers

1. Remove the snapring securing the bearing on the input shaft. Carefully press the input shaft out of the bearing with an arbor press.

2. Remove the fifteen bearing rollers from the cavity in the end of the input shaft.

3. Install the 15 bearing rollers in the cavity of the input shaft. Coat the rollers with a thin film of grease to retain them during installation.

4. Slide the input shaft bearing over the input shaft, snapring groove away from the gear end. Seat the bearing assembly on the input shaft with an arbor press.

5. Secure the bearing with the snapring. Be sure the snapring is properly seated. If a large snapring around the bearing was removed, be sure to install it at this time.

Synchronizers

➡**If either synchronizer is to be disassembled, mark all parts so that they will be reassembled in the same position. Do not mix parts from the two synchronizers.**

1. Push the synchronizer hub off each synchronizer sleeve.
2. Separate the struts and springs from the hubs.
3. Install the spring on the front side of the first/reverse synchronizer hub, making sure that all three strut slots are fully covered. Hang the three struts on the spring and in the slots with the wide end of the strut inside the hub.
4. With the alignment marks on the hub and sleeve aligned, push the sleeve down on the hub until the struts are in the neutral detent. Place the stop ring on top of the synchronizer assembly.
5. With the alignment marks on the second/third synchronizer sleeve and hub aligned, slide the sleeve on the hub. Drop in the three struts in the strut slots. Install the spring with the hump in the center, into the hollow of the strut. Turn the assembly over and install the other spring so that the hump in the center of the spring is inserted in the same strut. Place the stop ring on each end of the synchronizer assembly.

Countershaft Gear and Bearings

1. Remove the countershaft bearing arbor, the roller bearings and the two bearing retainers from the countershaft gear.
2. Coat the bore in each end of the countershaft gear with grease.
3. Insert the countershaft arbor and install twenty five roller bearings and the retainer washer in each end of the countershaft gear.
4. Position the countershaft gear and arbor assembly in the transmission case. Align the gear bore and the thrust washers with the bores in the case and install the countershaft.
5. Using a feeler gauge, check the countershaft gear end-play. The end-play should be within 0.004–0.018″. If the clearance is not within limits, replace the thrust washers.
6. After establishing the correct end-play, install the arbor tool in the countershaft gear and lower the gear and tool out of the bottom of the transmission case.

ASSEMBLY

1. Coat the countershaft gear thrust surfaces in the case with a thin film of grease and position the two thrust washers in place. Place the countershaft gear and arbor assembly in the proper position in the bottom of the transmission case. The countershaft gear will remain in the bottom of the case until the output and input shafts are installed.

2. Coat the reverse idler gear thrust surfaces in the case with a thin film of grease and position the two thrust washers in place. Install the reverse idler gear in the case and align the gear bore with the thrust washers in the case bore. Install the reverse idler shaft.

3. Measure the reverse idler gear end-play with a feeler gauge. End-play should be 0.004–0.018″. If the clearance is not within limits, replace the thrust washers. If the end-play is correct, leave the reverse idler gear in place.

4. Lubricate the output shaft splines and the machined surfaces with transmission oil.

5. Slide the first reverse synchronizer onto the output shaft with the fork groove toward the front. The first/reverse synchronizer hub is a press fit on the output shaft. To eliminate the possibility of damage to the hub, install the hub using an arbor press.

➡**Do not attempt to install the hub by hammering or driving.**

6. Secure the hub on the output shaft with the snapring. Slide the first gear and stop ring onto the output shaft, aligning the slots in the stop ring with the struts. Install the thrust washer and snapring.

7. Slide the second gear and stop ring on the output shaft.

8. Install the second/third synchronizer assembly on the output shaft. Rotate the second gear to index the struts with the slots in the stop ring. Secure the synchronizer with a snapring.

9. Position the output shaft assembly in the transmission case. Place the transmission in a vertical position with the front of the case flat on the work bench. Place a 1¼″ block of wood under the end of the output shaft. The block of wood will hold the output shaft assembly up during installation of the output shaft bearing.

10. Install the large snapring on the output shaft bearing. Place the bearing on the output shaft with the large snapring up. Drive the bearing on the shaft until it is seated on the shaft. Secure the bearing on the output shaft with the snapring. Return the transmission to a horizontal position.

11. Insert both shift forks in the case and in their proper sleeves. Push the output shaft assembly into position and tap it forward until the output shaft bearing is seated in the transmission case.

12. Install the shortest detent spring followed by a detent plug into the case. Place the second/third synchronizer assembly in the second gear position.

13. Align the second/third shift fork and install the second/third shift rail. The second/third shift rail is the shortest of the two shift rails. It will be necessary to depress the detent plug to enter the shift rail in the bore. Move the rail inward until the detent plug engages the forward notch (second gear position).

14. Secure the fork to the rail with the set screw. Move the synchronizer to the neutral position.

15. Install a new expansion plug in the transmission case.

16. Install the interlock plug in the transmission case with a magnet. If the second/third shift rail is in the neutral position, the top of the interlock plug will be slightly lower than the surface of the first/reverse shift rail bore.

17. Align the first/reverse fork and install the first/reverse shift rail. Move the rail inward until the center notch (neutral) is aligned with the detent bore. Secure the fork to the rail with the set screw.

18. Using a suitable tool, install a new oil seal in the input shaft bearing retainer bore.

19. Coat the bore of the input shaft gear with a thin film of grease.

➡**A thick, heavy grease will plug the lubricant holes and prevent lubrication of the roller bearings.**

20. Install the fifteen roller bearings in the bore. Place the stop ring, slots aligned with the struts, into the second/third synchronizer. Tap the input shaft assembly into place in the case while holding the output shaft to prevent the roller bearings from dropping.

21. Roll the transmission over so that it rests on both the top edge and the shift levers. The countershaft gear will drop into place. Using a screwdriver, align the countershaft gear and thrust washers with the bore in the transmission case.

22. Working from the rear of the case, slide the countershaft into position being careful to keep the countershaft in contact with the arbor to avoid dropping parts out of position. Be sure that the roll pin hole in the countershaft aligns with the roll pin hole in the case.

23. Install the roll pin. Install a new expansion plug in the countershaft bore at the front of the case. Install the plug flush or below the face of the case to prevent interference with the clutch housing.

24. Slide the extension housing, with a new gasket, over the output shaft and against the case. Coat the attaching bolt threads with a sealing compound. Install and tighten the attaching bolts to 50 ft. lbs.

25. Install the input shaft bearing retainer and a new gasket. Make sure that the oil return slot is at the bottom. Coat the threads with a sealing compound, install the attaching bolts and tighten to 30 ft. lbs.

26. Install the remaining detent plug into the case followed by the detent spring.

27. Install the filler plug and the back-up light switch. Pour lubricant over the entire gear train while rotating the input shaft and the output shaft.

28. Place the cover and a new gasket on the transmission. Coat the attaching screw threads with a sealing compound. Install and tighten the attaching screws to 22 ft. lbs.

New Process A-903 3-Speed Overhaul

The A-903 is a 3-speed unit with helical type gears. It is fully synchronized in all gears. Lubricant capacity is 6 pints.

DISASSEMBLY

1. Remove output shaft yoke.
2. Remove case cover. Measure synchronizer float with a feeler gauge between the end of a synchronizer pin and the opposite synchronizer outer ring. A measurement from 0.050–0.090" is acceptable for 1967 models. The measurement should be 0.060–0.117" for 1968 and later models.
3. Remove the extension housing from the case.
4. Remove the main drive pinion bearing retainer.

➡**Be careful to avoid binding the inner synchronizer ring on the drive pinion clutch teeth.**

5. When removing the drive pinion and bearing assembly from the pinion shaft. Remove the bearing washer, press the shaft out of the bearing and remove the oil slinger.

6. Remove the mainshaft pilot bearing snapring from the cavity of the pinion gear.

7. Remove the 14 pilot roller bearings.

8. Place the transmission in reverse. Remove the outer center bearing snapring, then, partially remove the mainshaft.

9. Remove clutch gear retaining snapring and clutch gear from the mainshaft.

10. Slide the 2nd gear, stop ring and synchronizer spring off the mainshaft.

11. Remove the low and reverse sliding gear and shift fork as the mainshaft is completely withdrawn from the case.

12. Measure cluster gear end-play. End-play should be 0.005–0.22". This will determine what thrust washers are used at re-assembly.

13. Remove the countershaft key and the countershaft.

14. Lift the cluster gear and thrust washers from the case. Remove the 22 needle bearings from each end. Remove the spacer from the cluster.

15. Remove the reverse idler shaft from the case. Remove the key.

16. Remove the reverse idler gear, thrust washers and 22 needle bearings out of the case.

17. Remove the gearshift operating levers.

18. Drive out the tapered retaining pin from either of the two lever shafts and withdraw the shaft from the case. The detent balls are springloaded, so, as the shaft is being withdrawn, the balls will fall to the bottom of the case.

19. Remove the interlock sleeve, spring pin and detent balls. Drive out the remaining tapered pin, then slide the lever shaft out of the transmission.

20. Remove both lever shaft seals and discard same.

ASSEMBLY

1. Install two new shift lever seals in the case.
2. Carefully insert the low and reverse lever shaft into the rear of the case, through the seal, and into position. Insert a tapered pin to lock it. Turn the lever until the center detent is in line with the interlock bore.
3. Install the interlock sleeve in its bore in the case, an interlock ball, spring and pin.
4. Place the remaining interlock ball on top of the interlock spring.
5. Depress the interlock ball and, simultaneously, install the 2nd-3rd lever shaft into the fully seated position, with the center detent aligned with the detent ball. Secure the shaft with the remaining tapered pin.
6. Install the operating levers and secure them to the shafts with nuts torqued to 18 ft. lbs.
7. Slide the dummy shaft and tubular spacer into the bore of the countergear.
8. Grease and install 22 bearing rollers into each end of the countergear bore in the area around the arbor. Install the bearing retaining rings at each end of the gear, covering the bearings.
9. Install a thrust washer at each end of the countergear and over the arbor. Install the countergear assembly into the case, making sure that the tabs on the thrust washers slide into the

grooves in the case. Correct cluster gear end-play is determined by the thrust washer thickness.

10. Grease the reverse idler gear and slide the dummy shaft into the bore. Install 22 rollers in the bore and around the dummy shaft.

11. Install a new thrust washer at each end of the gear and over the arbor.

12. With the beveled end of the teeth forward, slide the gear into position in the case. Install the reverse idler shaft in its bore in the rear of the case. Install the key and align it with the keyway in the case.

13. Drive the shaft into the case and the idler gear until the key seats in the recess.

14. Install the rear bearing on the mainshaft and install the selective fit snapring.

15. Hold the 1st-Reverse sliding gear into position with the shift fork. Insert the mainshaft with rear bearing retainer through the rear of the case and into the sliding gear.

16. Place the synchronizer spreader ring, and then the rear stop ring, on the synchronizer splines of the 2nd speed gear.

17. Install the 2nd speed gear on the mainshaft, with shims, if required. Shims should be used to correct excessive synchronizer float. If synchronizer float is below minimum, as determined during disassembly, shorten all synchronizer pins.

18. Install the synchronizer clutch gear and snapring on the mainshaft.

19. Install the 2nd and 3rd fork in the lever shaft with the offset towards the rear of the transmission. Hold the synchronizer clutch gear sleeve and two outer rings together, with the pins in the holes in the clutch gear sleeve. Engage the 2nd-3rd fork with the clutch gear sleeve.

20. While holding the synchronizer parts and fork in position, slide the mainshaft forward, starting the synchronizer clutch gear into the clutch gear sleeve and the mainshaft rear bearing into the case bore. The synchronizer parts must be correctly positioned before the mainshaft is positioned.

21. While holding the synchronizer parts in position, tap the mainshaft forward until the rear bearing bottoms in the case bore.

22. Install the mainshaft rear bearing selective fit snapring into the case bore groove.

23. Slide the oil slinger over the pinion shaft against the gear.

24. Slide the bearing over the pinion shaft with snapring groove away from gear, then seat bearing on shaft using an arbor press.

25. Install the keyed washer and snapring. Four thicknesses of snapring are available to eliminate end-play. Install the large snapring onto the race of the ball bearing.

26. Install the 14 greased bearing rollers into the bore of the pinion shaft gear. Install the bearing roller retaining ring in the pinion gear bore.

27. Install the 3rd gear outer stop ring and 3rd gear inner stop ring onto the mainshaft. Guide the drive pinion through the front of the case and engage the inner stop ring with the clutch teeth, then, seat the bearing so the large snapring is flush against the case.

28. Install a new bearing retainer seal and gasket.

29. Install the retainer and torque it to 30 ft. lbs.

30. Install a new rear mainshaft bushing and a new oil seal.

31. Protect the oil seal with a thimble-type seal protector and, with the gasket attached, slide the extension housing against the case. Torque the bolts to 50 ft. lbs.

32. Install the flange assembly and install a new washer and nut. Torque the nut to 140 ft. lbs.

33. Grease the cover gasket and install the gasket on the cover. Install the cover and torque the bolts to 12 ft. lbs.

34. Install the drain plug and back-up light switch.

Observe the following torques:
- Back-up light switch—15 ft. lbs.
- Drain plug—20 ft. lbs.
- Filler plug—30 ft. lbs.
- Case-to-clutch housing—50 ft. lbs.
- Drive pinion bearing retainer—15 ft. lbs.
- Extension hosuing—30 ft. lbs.
- Gearshift fork lockbolt—30 ft. lbs.
- Gearshift housing lower bolt—15 ft. lbs.
- Gerrshift housing upper bolt—20 ft. lbs.
- Gearshift operating lever nut—35 ft. lbs.
- Gearshift rod and swivel nuts—70 in. lbs.
- Gearshift selector ball spring bolt—25 ft. lbs.
- Gearshift selector lever washer nut—20 ft. lbs.
- Mainshaft flange nut—175 ft. lbs.
- Gearshift lever shaft bolt—10 ft. lbs.
- Operating lever nuts—18 ft. lbs.
- Pinion bearing retainer bolt—30 ft. lbs.

New Process A-745 3-Speed Overhaul

The Dodge A-745 is a three-speed synchromesh transmission having helical type gears. Lubricant capacity is 3¼ pints.

DISASSEMBLY

▶ **See Figure 21**

1. Remove output flange nut, then the drum and flange assembly, if so equipped. Remove parking brake assembly, if so equipped.

2. Remove case cover. Measure synchronizer float with a feeler gauge between the end of a synchronizer pin and the opposite synchronizer outer ring. A measurement from 0.050–0.090″ is acceptable for 1964–67 models. The measurement should be 0.060–0.117″ for 1968 and up models.

3. Remove the extension housing from the case.

4. Remove the mainshaft rear bearing, if it did not come off with the extension housing.

5. Remove transmission case cover and gasket.

6. Remove the drive pinion bearing retainer.

7. When removing the drive pinion and bearing assembly from the transmission case, slide the front inner stop ring from the short splines on the pinion as the assembly is being removed from the case.

8. Remove the main drive pinion bearing snapring.

9. Press bearing off pinion shaft and remove oil slinger.

10. Remove the mainshaft pilot bearing snapring from the cavity of the pinion gear.

11. Remove the 15 pilot roller bearings.

12. Remove seal from pinion retainer.

13. Remove mainshaft rear bearing snapring from groove in mainshaft rear bearing bore in the case.

14. Remove the rear bearing snapring from groove in mainshaft rear bearing bore in the case.

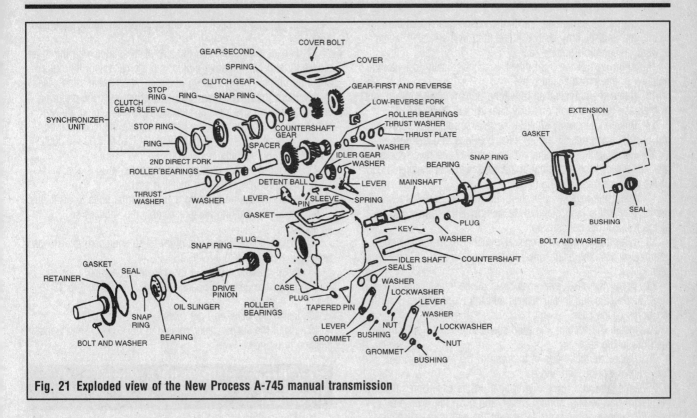

Fig. 21 Exploded view of the New Process A-745 manual transmission

15. Remove synchronizer assembly from the case.

16. Remove second and third-speed shift fork.

17. Remove synchronizer clutch gear, snapring, clutch gear, second-speed gear, and first and reverse sliding gear from the mainshaft.

18. Withdraw mainshaft and bearing out through rear of case.

19. Remove the synchronizer clutch gear, second-speed gear, low and reverse sliding gear, and low and reverse shift fork from the case.

20. With a dummy shaft, drive the countershaft toward the rear of the case until the small key can be removed from the countershaft.

21. Remove the countershaft from the case.

22. Lift the cluster gear, the thrust washers and the dummy shaft assembly out of the case.

23. Dismantle the cluster gear, (88 rollers, four spacer rings and the center spacer from the cluster).

24. With a blunt drift, drive the reverse idler shaft toward the rear of the case far enough to remove the key from the shaft.

25. Completely remove the shaft from the case, then remove the idler gear.

26. Remove the thrust washers and 22 rollers.

27. With a small punch, remove low and reverse gear lever shaft tapered lock pin by driving it toward the top of the transmission case.

28. Remove the second and third gear lever shaft in the same manner.

29. Remove the lever shafts from the transmission case being careful not to lose the spring-loaded detent balls.

30. Remove the interlock sleeve, spring pin and detent balls.

31. Remove both lever shaft seals and discard same.

ASSEMBLY

1. Place oil slinger on the main drive pinion with the offset outer portion next to the drive pinion teeth.

2. Place the main drive pinion bearing on the pinion shaft with the outer snapring away from the pinion gear.

3. Press the bearing into position so it is seated firmly against the oil slinger and pinion gear.

4. Install the bearing retaining snapring in its groove on the pinion shaft.

5. Heavily grease the 15 pilot bearing rollers and install them in the cavity at the rear of the main pilot drive.

6. Install the snapring.

7. Place the bearing spacer in the center of the bore in the cluster gear and use the dummy shaft to assist in assembling the roller bearings.

8. Install a row of 22 rollers next to one end of the spacer, using heavy grease to hold them.

9. Place one of the four bearing spacer rings next to the row of the rollers, and install another row of 22 rollers next to the spacer ring.

10. Install another spacer ring at the outside end of the second row of bearing rollers.

11. At the opposite end of the cluster gear bore, install the remaining spacer rings and bearing rollers in the same sequence as listed in Steps 8, 9, and 10.

12. With a small amount of grease, install the front thrust washer on the dummy shaft at the front end of the cluster gear, with the tabs outward.

13. Install the tabbed rear thrust washer onto the dummy shaft against the rear of the cluster gear with the tabs inserted in the cluster gear grooves.

14. Install the remaining rear thrust washer plate onto the rear of the gear and dummy shaft with the step in the washer facing upward, as viewed from the rear.

15. Align tabs of the front thrust washer vertically to index the notches in the transmission case.

16. Using the countershaft, drive the dummy shaft forward, out of the case. Countershaft end-play should be 0.0045–0.028".

17. Position a dummy shaft in the reverse idler gear and, using heavy grease, install the 22 roller bearings into the gear.

18. Place the thrust washers at each end of the reverse idler gear, then place the assembly in the case with the chamfered end of the gear teeth toward the front.

19. Insert the reverse idler shaft into the rear case bore with the keyway to the rear, pushing the dummy shaft toward and out of the front of the transmission.

20. With the keyway in proper alignment, insert the key and continue driving the shaft forward until the key seats in the recess.

21. Install two new lever shaft seals in the transmission case.

22. Lubricate and install second and third-speed lever shaft in the bores of the case.

23. Install the second and third speed lever shaft lock pin in the hole in the case.

24. Place interlock parts in the case in the following order: ball, sleeve, spring, pin and ball.

25. Enter low and reverse lever shaft in the case bore, depress the detent ball against spring tension and push the lever shaft firmly into position, in order to prevent the ball from escaping.

26. Install low and reverse lever shaft lock pin in the case.

27. Place low and reverse fork in the lever shaft, with the offset facing the rear.

28. While holding the low and reverse sliding gear in position in the fork, with the hub extension to the rear, insert the mainshaft with the rear bearing through the rear of the case and into the sliding gear.

29. Place synchronizer stop ring spring, then the rear stop ring, on the synchronizer splines of the second-speed gear. Install the second-speed gear onto the mainshaft. Synchronizer shims must be added if synchronizer float is more than the maximum in Step 2, disassembly. If float was less than minimum, the six pins must be shortened.

30. Install the synchronizer clutch to shoulder to the front.

31. Select the thickest synchronizer clutch gear snapring that can be used, and install it in the mainshaft groove.

32. Check to see that clearance between clutch gear and second-speed gear is 0.004–0.014".

33. Hold the synchronizer clutch gear sleeve and two outer rings together with pins properly entered into the holes in the clutch gear sleeve and with the clutch gear sleeve engaged in the groove of the second- and third-speed shift fork, position the fork in the second- and third-speed lever shaft.

34. While holding the synchronizer parts and fork in position, slide the mainshaft forward, entering the synchronizer clutch gear into the clutch gear sleeve and simultaneously entering the mainshaft rear bearing in the case bore.

35. While still holding the synchronizer parts in position, tap the mainshaft forward until the rear bearing bottoms in the case bore.

36. Install the mainshaft rear bearing snapring into place in the case bore.

37. Install a new drive pinion retainer seal.

38. Place the synchronizer front inner ring in position in the front outer ring, and enter the main drive pinion through the case bore.

39. Engage the splines on the rear of the pinion with the inner stop ring, and tap the drive pinion into the case until the outer snapring on the pinion bearing is against the transmission case.

40. Place the drive pinion bearing retainer over the pinion shaft and against the transmission case. While holding the retainer against the transmission case, measure the clearance between the retainer and case and choose a gasket 0.003–0.005" thicker than this reading.

41. Torque the front bearing retainer bolts to 30 ft. lbs.

42. Install a new extension housing seal.

43. Install extension housing and torque the bolts to 50 ft. lbs.

44. Install the parking brake assembly, on vehicles so equipped.

45. Install the parking brake drum (if so equipped) and flange assembly and torque to 175 ft. lbs.

46. Install the drain plug in the transmission case.

47. Install the gearshift operating levers, and torque to 12 ft. lbs.

48. Install the back-up light switch.

49. Install the speedometer cable and drive gear. Bring transmission to lubricant level.

New Process NP-2500 5-Speed Overhaul

MAJOR COMPONENT DISASSEMBLY

▶ **See Figures 22 thru 31**

1. Remove the transmission from the truck.

2. Remove the shifter assembly bolts.

3. The shifter assembly is sealed with a bead of RTV sealant so it must be pried loose before removal. Clean all RTV sealant from both mating surfaces.

4. Remove the access cover bolts.

5. The access cover is sealed with a bead of RTV sealant so

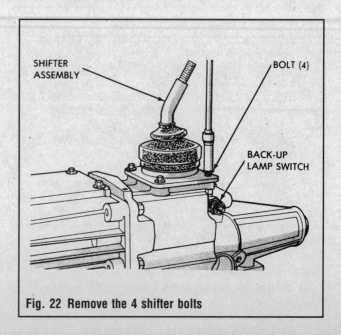

Fig. 22 Remove the 4 shifter bolts

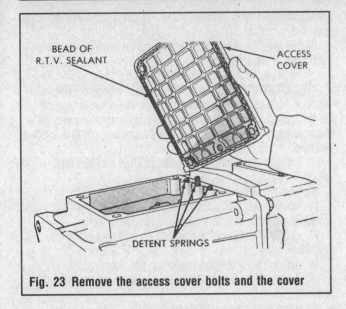

Fig. 23 Remove the access cover bolts and the cover

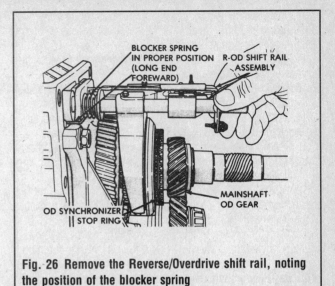

Fig. 26 Remove the Reverse/Overdrive shift rail, noting the position of the blocker spring

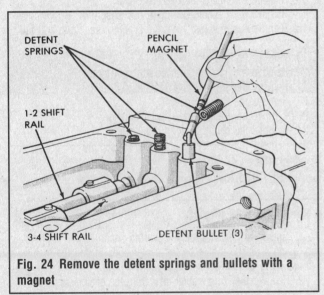

Fig. 24 Remove the detent springs and bullets with a magnet

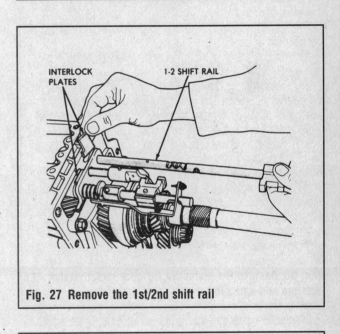

Fig. 27 Remove the 1st/2nd shift rail

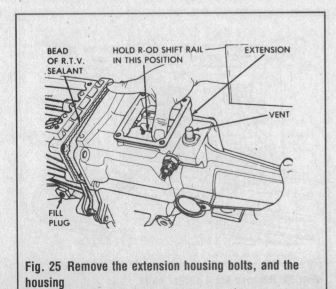

Fig. 25 Remove the extension housing bolts, and the housing

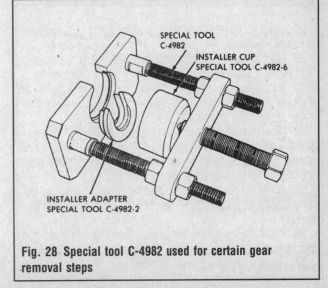

Fig. 28 Special tool C-4982 used for certain gear removal steps

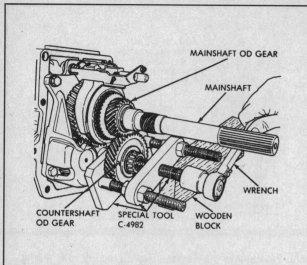

Fig. 29 Countershaft Overdrive (OD) gear removal

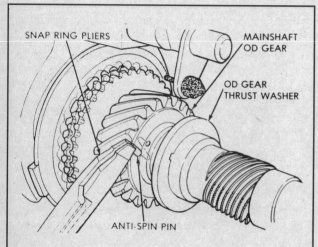

Fig. 30 Remove the mainshaft OD gear thrust washer and the anti-spin pin

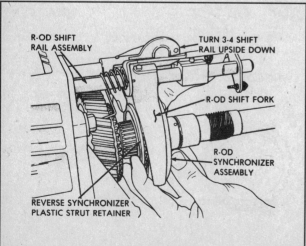

Fig. 31 Remove the R/OD synchronizer, fork, and shift rail assembly

it must be pried loose before removal. Clean all RTV sealant from both mating surfaces.

6. Remove the detent springs and bullets with a magnet. Keep track of which is which.

7. Remove the extension housing-to-case bolts.

8. The extension housing is sealed with a bead of RTV sealant so it must be pried loose before removal. When pulling off the housing, hold the Reverse/Overdrive shift rail as shown in the accompanying illustration. Clean all RTV sealant from both mating surfaces.

9. Remove the Reverse/Overdrive shift rail and blocker spring.

10. Remove the tapered pins from the shift forks.

11. Remove the 1st/2nd shift rail.

12. Remove the countershaft overdrive gear snapring.

13. Remove the countershaft overdrive gear using tool C-4982.

14. Remove the mainshaft overdrive gear snapring.

15. Remove the mainshaft overdrive gear thrust washer and anti-spin pin.

16. Remove the mainshaft overdrive gear.

17. Remove the Reverse/Overdrive hub snapring.

18. Remove the Reverse/Overdrive synchronizer, fork, and rail assembly.

19. Remove the 3rd/4th shift rail.

20. Remove the 1st/2nd and 3rd/4th shift forks.

21. Remove the 1st/2nd and 3rd/4th shift rails.

22. Remove the Reverse gear.

23. Remove the Reverse gear thrust washer.

24. Remove the center support plate bolts.

25. Remove the gear set/support plate assembly.

GEAR SET DISASSEMBLY

◆ **See Figures 32 thru 43**

1. Open the mainshaft center bearing snapring with a pliers and, using a plastic mallet on the center support, tap the mainshaft assembly out of the center support.

2. Remove the countershaft gear from the center support.

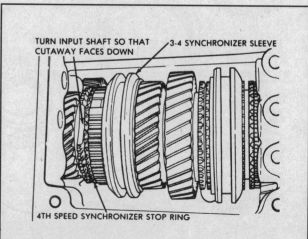

Fig. 32 Drive pinion gear cutaway area, facing the countershaft

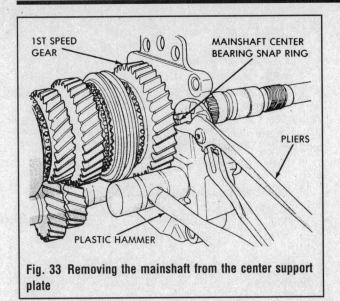

Fig. 33 **Removing the mainshaft from the center support plate**

1ST SPEED GEAR

MAINSHAFT CENTER BEARING SNAP RING

PLIERS

PLASTIC HAMMER

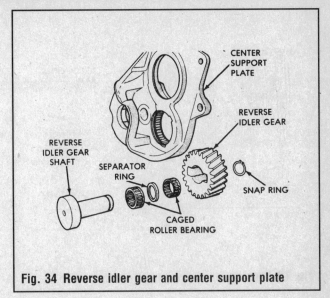

Fig. 34 **Reverse idler gear and center support plate**

CENTER SUPPORT PLATE

REVERSE IDLER GEAR

REVERSE IDLER GEAR SHAFT

SEPARATOR RING

SNAP RING

CAGED ROLLER BEARING

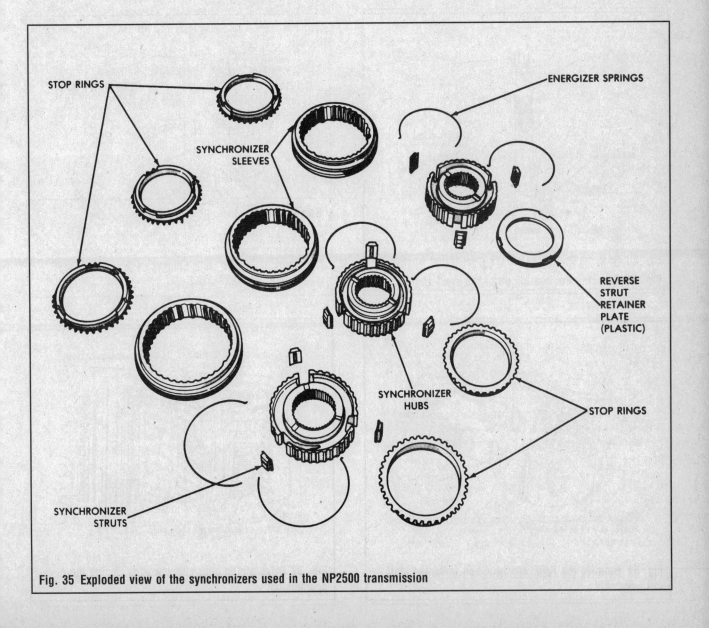

STOP RINGS

SYNCHRONIZER SLEEVES

ENERGIZER SPRINGS

REVERSE STRUT RETAINER PLATE (PLASTIC)

SYNCHRONIZER HUBS

STOP RINGS

SYNCHRONIZER STRUTS

Fig. 35 **Exploded view of the synchronizers used in the NP2500 transmission**

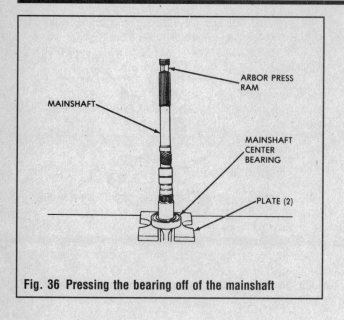

Fig. 36 Pressing the bearing off of the mainshaft

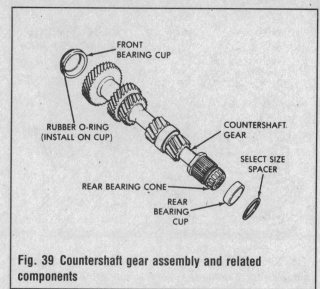

Fig. 39 Countershaft gear assembly and related components

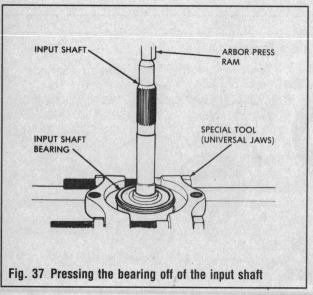

Fig. 37 Pressing the bearing off of the input shaft

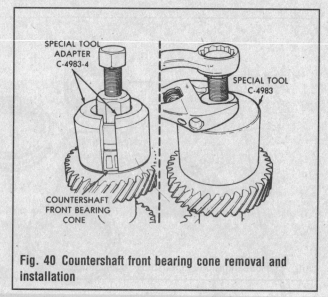

Fig. 40 Countershaft front bearing cone removal and installation

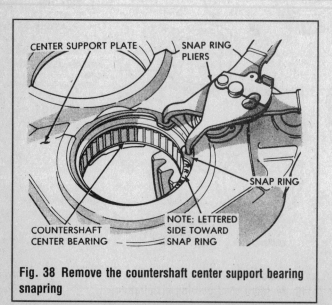

Fig. 38 Remove the countershaft center support bearing snapring

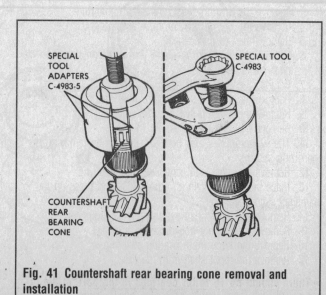

Fig. 41 Countershaft rear bearing cone removal and installation

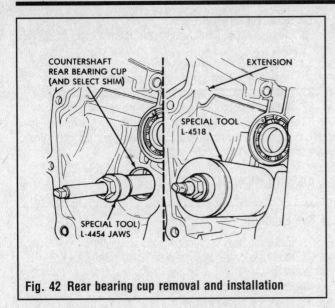

Fig. 42 Rear bearing cup removal and installation

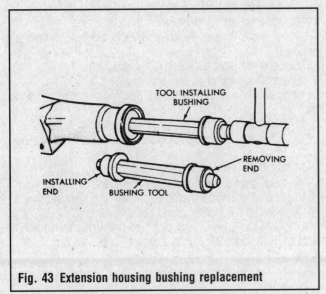

Fig. 43 Extension housing bushing replacement

3. Remove the 3rd/4th synchronizer hub snapring.
4. Remove the 3rd/4th synchronizer assembly.
5. Remove the 3rd speed gear.
6. Remove the split thrust washer and retaining ring from the mainshaft.
7. Remove the 2nd speed gear.
8. Remove the 1st/2nd synchronizer hub snapring.
9. Remove the 1st/2nd synchronizer assembly.
10. Remove the 1st speed gear.
11. The synchronizers may be disassembled by removing the energizing springs.
12. Remove the mainshaft center bearing snapring.
13. Place the mainshaft in an arbor press and press off the mainshaft center bearing.
14. Remove the input shaft bearing retainer bolts.
15. Remove the retainer and discard the gasket.
16. Remove the large input bearing snapring.
17. Remove the input shaft from the case.

➡**There should be 16 roller bearings in the bore of the input shaft.**

18. Remove the small input shaft bearing retaining snapring.
19. Using an arbor press, remove the input bearing.
20. Remove the reverse idler shaft snapring from the center support plate.
21. Remove the reverse idler gear and shaft.
22. Remove the countershaft center bearing snapring.
23. Using an arbor press, remove the countershaft center bearing.
24. Using tool C-4983-4 and adapter, remove the front bearing cone from the countershaft.
25. Using an arbor press remove the front bearing cup from the case.
26. Using tool C-4983-5 and adapter, remove the rear bearing cone from the countershaft.
27. Using tools L-4454 and L-4518, remove the countershaft rear bearing cup from the extension housing.
28. Remove the snapring and remove the extension housing ball bearing.
29. Remove the extension housing yoke seal.
30. Drive out the extension housing bushing.

GEAR SET ASSEMBLY

▶ **See Figures 44 and 45**

1. Drive in a new extension housing bushing.
2. Install a new extension housing yoke seal.
3. Install the extension housing ball bearing and snapring.
4. Using an arbor press and tools C-4171 and C-4973, install the countershaft rear bearing cup in the extension housing.
5. Using an arbor press and tool C-4966, install the rear bearing cone on the countershaft.
6. Using an arbor press and tool C-4171, install the front bearing cup in the case.
7. Using an arbor press and tool C-4967, install the front bearing cone on the countershaft.
8. Using an arbor press and tool C-4171, install the countershaft center bearing.
9. Install the countershaft center bearing snapring.
10. Using a dial indicator, check the countershaft gear end-play with the assembly positioned in the case. End-play should be

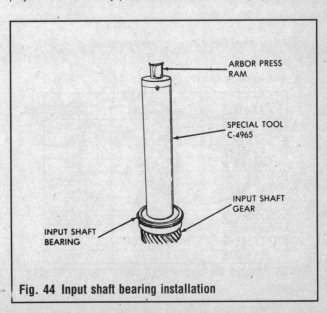

Fig. 44 Input shaft bearing installation

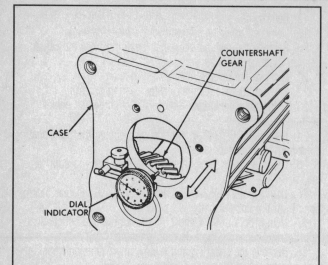

Fig. 45 Checking the countershaft gear end-play

0.03–0.13mm. Select-fit shims are available in 0.02mm increments in sizes from 1.37mm to 2.29mm.

11. Assemble and install the reverse idler gear and shaft.

12. Install the reverse idler shaft snapring on the center support plate.

13. Install a new input shaft retainer oil seal.

14. Using an arbor press and tool C-4965, install the input bearing.

15. Install the small input shaft bearing retaining snapring.

16. Install the input shaft in the case.

17. Install the large input bearing snapring.

18. Install the retainer and new gasket. Torque the bolts to 21 ft. lbs.

19. Assemble the 16 roller bearings in the bore of the input shaft. Hold them in place by coating them with heavy grease.

20. Place the mainshaft in an arbor press and press on the mainshaft center bearing.

21. Install the mainshaft center bearing snapring.

22. Assemble the synchronizers.

23. Install the needle bearings and snapring with the chamfered side of the snapring facing 1st gear.

24. Install the 1st speed gear.

25. Install the 1st/2nd synchronizer assembly.

26. Install the 1st/2nd synchronizer hub snapring.

27. Install the 2nd speed gear.

28. Install the split thrust washer and retaining ring on the mainshaft.

29. Install the 3rd speed gear.

30. Install the 3rd/4th synchronizer assembly.

31. Install the 3rd/4th synchronizer hub snapring.

32. Install the countershaft gear from the center support.

33. Open the mainshaft center bearing snapring with a pliers and, using a plastic mallet on the center support, tap the mainshaft assembly onto the center support.

MAIN COMPONENT ASSEMBLY

▶ **See Figure 46**

1. Install the gear set/support plate assembly.

2. Install the center support plate bolts. Torque the bolts to 40 ft. lbs.

3. Install the Reverse gear thrust washer.

4. Install the Reverse gear.

5. Install the 1st/2nd and 3rd/4th shift forks.

6. Install the 3rd/4th shift rail.

7. Install the Reverse/Overdrive synchronizer, fork, and rail assembly.

8. Install the Reverse/Overdrive hub snapring.

9. Install the mainshaft overdrive gear.

10. Install the mainshaft overdrive gear thrust washer and anti-spin pin.

11. Install the mainshaft overdrive gear snapring.

12. Install the countershaft overdrive gear using tool C-4982.

13. Install the countershaft overdrive gear snapring.

14. Install the 1st/2nd shift rail.

15. Install the tapered pins on the shift forks.

16. Install the Reverse/Overdrive shift rail and blocker spring. The long end of the blocker spring faces forward.

17. Install the extension housing. The housing is sealed with a bead of RTV sealant rather than a gasket. Torque the bolts to 40 ft. lbs.

Select Shim Chart

| Part No. | Thickness | |
	Millimeters	Inches
4338275	1.37-1.39	.0539
4338276	1.46-1.48	.0579
4338277	1.55-1.57	.0614
4338278	1.64-1.66	.0650
4338279	1.73-1.75	.0685
4338280	1.82-1.84	.0720
4338281	1.91-1.93	.0756
4338282	2.00-2.02	.0791
4338283	2.09-2.11	.0827
4338284	2.18-2.20	.0862
4338285	2.27-2.29	.0898

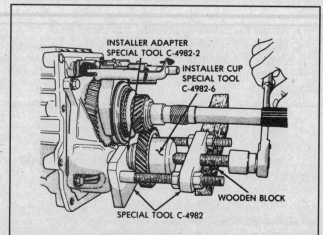

Fig. 46 Installing the countershaft OD gear using tool C-4982

18. Install the detent springs and bullets.

19. Install the access cover. The access cover is sealed with a bead of RTV sealant rather than a gasket.

20. Install the access cover bolts. Torque the bolts to 21 ft. lbs.

21. Install the shifter assembly. The shifter assembly is sealed with a bead of RTV sealant rather than a gasket.

22. Install the shifter assembly bolts. Torque the bolts to 21 ft. lbs.

23. Install the transmission.

Troubleshooting the Manual Transmission

Problem	Cause	Solution
Transmission shifts hard	• Clutch adjustment incorrect • Clutch linkage or cable binding • Shift rail binding	• Adjust clutch • Lubricate or repair as necessary • Check for mispositioned selector arm roll pin, loose cover bolts, worn shift rail bores, worn shift rail, distorted oil seal, or extension housing not aligned with case. Repair as necessary.
	• Internal bind in transmission caused by shift forks, selector plates, or synchronizer assemblies • Clutch housing misalignment • Incorrect lubricant • Block rings and/or cone seats worn	• Remove, dissemble and inspect transmission. Replace worn or damaged components as necessary. • Check runout at rear face of clutch housing • Drain and refill transmission • Blocking ring to gear clutch tooth face clearance must be 0.030 inch or greater. If clearance is correct it may still be necessary to inspect blocking rings and cone seats for excessive wear. Repair as necessary.
Gear clash when shifting from one gear to another	• Clutch adjustment incorrect • Clutch linkage or cable binding • Clutch housing misalignment • Lubricant level low or incorrect lubricant • Gearshift components, or synchronizer assemblies worn or damaged	• Adjust clutch • Lubricate or repair as necessary • Check runout at rear of clutch housing • Drain and refill transmission and check for lubricant leaks if level was low. Repair as necessary. • Remove, disassemble and inspect transmission. Replace worn or damaged components as necessary.
Transmission noisy	• Lubricant level low or incorrect lubricant • Clutch housing-to-engine, or transmission-to-clutch housing bolts loose • Dirt, chips, foreign material in transmission • Gearshift mechanism, transmission gears, or bearing components worn or damaged • Clutch housing misalignment	• Drain and refill transmission. If lubricant level was low, check for leaks and repair as necessary. • Check and correct bolt torque as necessary • Drain, flush, and refill transmission • Remove, disassemble and inspect transmission. Replace worn or damaged components as necessary. • Check runout at rear face of clutch housing
Jumps out of gear	• Clutch housing misalignment • Gearshift lever loose • Offset lever nylon insert worn or lever attaching nut loose • Gearshift mechanism, shift forks, selector plates, interlock plate, selector arm, shift rail, detent plugs, springs or shift cover worn or damaged • Clutch shaft or roller bearings worn or damaged	• Check runout at rear face of clutch housing • Check lever for worn fork. Tighten loose attaching bolts. • Remove gearshift lever and check for loose offset lever nut or worn insert. Repair or replace as necessary. • Remove, disassemble and inspect transmission cover assembly. Replace worn or damaged components as necessary. • Replace clutch shaft or roller bearings as necessary

Troubleshooting the Manual Transmission *(cont.)*

Problem	Cause	Solution
Jumps out of gear (cont.)	• Gear teeth worn or tapered, synchronizer assemblies worn or damaged, excessive end play caused by worn thrust washers or output shaft gears	• Remove, disassemble, and inspect transmission. Replace worn or damaged components as necessary.
	• Pilot bushing worn	• Replace pilot bushing
Will not shift into one gear	• Gearshift selector plates, interlock plate, or selector arm, worn, damaged, or incorrectly assembled	• Remove, disassemble, and inspect transmission cover assembly. Repair or replace components as necessary.
	• Shift rail detent plunger worn, spring broken, or plug loose	• Tighten plug or replace worn or damaged components as necessary
	• Gearshift lever worn or damaged	• Replace gearshift lever
	• Synchronizer sleeves or hubs, damaged or worn	• Remove, disassemble and inspect transmission. Replace worn or damaged components.
Locked in one gear—cannot be shifted out	• Shift rail(s) worn or broken, shifter fork bent, setscrew loose, center detent plug missing or worn	• Inspect and replace worn or damaged parts
	• Broken gear teeth on countershaft gear, clutch shaft, or reverse idler gear	• Inspect and replace damaged part
	Gearshift lever broken or worn, shift mechanism in cover incorrectly assembled or broken, worn damaged gear train components	• Disassemble transmission. Replace damaged parts or assemble correctly.
Transfer case difficult to shift or will not shift into desired range	• Vehicle speed too great to permit shifting	• Stop vehicle and shift into desired range. Or reduce speed to 3–4 km/h (2–3 mph) before attempting to shift.
	• If vehicle was operated for extended period in 4H mode on dry paved surface, driveline torque load may cause difficult shifting	• Stop vehicle, shift transmission to neutral, shift transfer case to 2H mode and operate vehicle in 2H on dry paved surfaces
	• Transfer case external shift linkage binding	• Lubricate or repair or replace linkage, or tighten loose components as necessary
	• Insufficient or incorrect lubricant	• Drain and refill to edge of fill hole with SAE 85W-90 gear lubricant only
	• Internal components binding, worn, or damaged	• Disassemble unit and replace worn or damaged components as necessary
Transfer case noisy in all drive modes	• Insufficient or incorrect lubricant	• Drain and refill to edge of fill hole with SAE 85W-90 gear lubricant only. Check for leaks and repair if necessary. Note: If unit is still noisy after drain and refill, disassembly and inspection may be required to locate source of noise.
Noisy in—or jumps out of four wheel drive low range	• Transfer case not completely engaged in 4L position	• Stop vehicle, shift transfer case in Neutral, then shift back into 4L position
	• Shift linkage loose or binding	• Tighten, lubricate, or repair linkage as necessary
	• Shift fork cracked, inserts worn, or fork is binding on shift rail	• Disassemble unit and repair as necessary
Lubricant leaking from output shaft seals or from vent	• Transfer case overfilled	• Drain to correct level
	• Vent closed or restricted	• Clear or replace vent if necessary

Troubleshooting the Manual Transmission *(cont.)*

Problem	Cause	Solution
Lubricant leaking from output shaft seals or from vent (cont.)	• Output shaft seals damaged or installed incorrectly	• Replace seals. Be sure seal lip faces interior of case when installed. Also be sure yoke seal surfaces are not scored or nicked. Remove scores, nicks with fine sandpaper or replace yoke(s) if necessary.
Abnormal tire wear	• Extended operation on dry hard surface (paved) roads in 4H range	• Operate in 2H on hard surface (paved) roads

CLUTCH

Understanding the Clutch

▶ **See Figure 47**

The purpose of the clutch is to disconnect and connect engine power at the transmission. A vehicle at rest requires a lot of engine torque to get all that weight moving. An internal combustion engine does not develop a high starting torque (unlike steam engines) so it must be allowed to operate without any load until it builds up enough torque to move the vehicle. To a point, torque increases with engine rpm. The clutch allows the engine to build up torque by physically disconnecting the engine from the transmission, relieving the engine of any load or re sistance.

The transfer of engine power to the transmission (the load) must be smooth and gradual; if it weren't, drive line components would wear out or break quickly. This gradual power transfer is made possible by gradually releasing the clutch pedal. The clutch disc and pressure plate are the connecting link between the engine and transmission. When the clutch pedal is released, the disc and plate contact each other (the clutch is engaged) physically joining the engine and transmission. When the pedal is pushed in, the disc and plate separate (the clutch is disengaged) disconnecting the engine from the transmission.

Most clutch assemblies consists of the flywheel, the clutch disc, the clutch pressure plate, the throw out bearing and fork, the actuating linkage and the pedal. The flywheel and clutch pressure plate (driving members) are connected to the engine crankshaft and rotate with it. The clutch disc is located between the flywheel and pressure plate, and is splined to the transmission shaft. A driving member is one that is attached to the engine and transfers engine power to a driven member (clutch disc) on the transmission shaft. A driving member (pressure plate) rotates (drives) a driven member (clutch disc) on contact and, in so doing, turns the transmission shaft.

There is a circular diaphragm spring within the pressure plate cover (transmission side). In a relaxed state (when the clutch pedal is fully released) this spring is convex; that is, it is dished outward toward the transmission. Pushing in the clutch pedal actuates the attached linkage. Connected to the other end of this is the throw out fork, which hold the throw out bearing. When the clutch pedal is depressed, the clutch linkage pushes the fork and bearing forward to contact the diaphragm spring of the pressure plate. The outer edges of the spring are secured to the pressure plate and are pivoted on rings so that when the center of the spring is compressed by the throw out bearing, the outer edges bow outward and, by so doing, pull the pressure plate in the same direction away from the clutch disc. This action separates the disc from the plate, disengaging the clutch and allowing the transmission to be shifted into another gear. A coil type clutch return spring attached to the clutch pedal arm permits full release of the pedal. Releasing the pedal pulls the throw out bearing away from the diaphragm spring resulting in a reversal of spring position. As bearing pressure is gradually released from the spring center, the outer edges of the spring bow outward, pushing the pressure plate into closer contact with the clutch disc. As the disc and plate move closer together, friction between the two increases and slippage is reduced until, when full spring pressure is applied (by fully releasing the pedal) the speed of the disc and plate are the same. This stops all slipping, creating a direct connection between the plate and disc which results in the transfer of power from the engine to the transmission. The clutch disc is now rotating with the pressure plate at engine speed and, because it is splined to the transmission shaft, the shaft now turns at the same engine speed.

The clutch is operating properly if:

1. It will stall the engine when released with the vehicle held stationary.

2. The shift lever can be moved freely between 1st and reverse gears when the vehicle is stationary and the clutch disengaged.

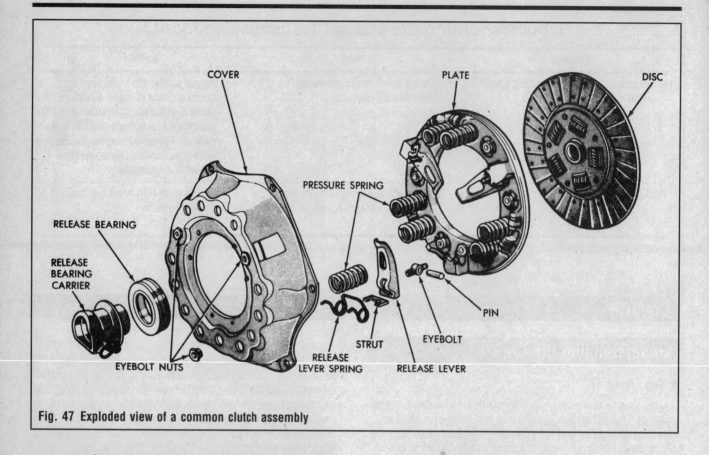

Fig. 47 Exploded view of a common clutch assembly

Driven Disc and Pressure Plate

REMOVAL AND INSTALLATION

▶ See Figures 48, 49, 50 and 51

With Mechanical Linkage

1. Support the engine on a suitable jack.
2. Remove crossmember.
3. Remove transmission.
4. Remove clutch housing pan if so equipped.
5. Remove clutch fork, clutch bearing and sleeve assembly if not removed with transmission.
6. Mark clutch cover and flywheel, with a suitable tool to assure correct reassembly.
7. Remove clutch cover retaining bolts, loosening them evenly so clutch cover will not be distorted.
8. Pull pressure plate assembly clear of flywheel and, while supporting pressure plate, slide clutch disc from between flywheel and pressure plate.

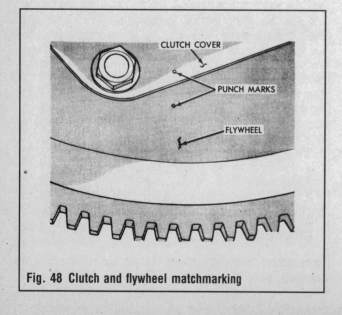

Fig. 48 Clutch and flywheel matchmarking

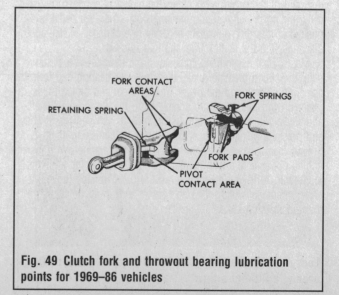

Fig. 49 Clutch fork and throwout bearing lubrication points for 1969-86 vehicles

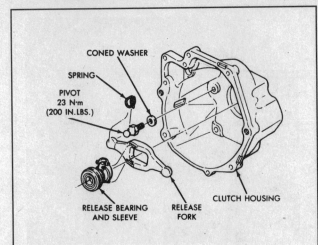

Fig. 50 Release fork, bearing and carrier for 1987–88 vehicles

. . . then carefully remove the clutch and pressure plate assembly from the flywheel

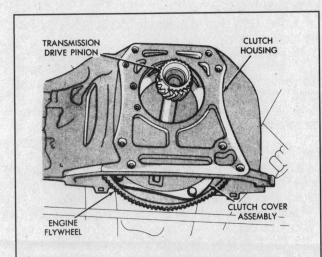

Fig. 51 Clutch disc-to-pilot bushing alignment using an old drive pinion from a transmission

Check across the flywheel surface, it should be flat

Loosen and remove the clutch and pressure plate bolts evenly, a little at a time . . .

If necessary, lock the flywheel in place and remove the retaining bolts . . .

. . . then remove the flywheel from the crankshaft in order replace it or have it machined

Be sure that the flywheel surface is clean, before installing the clutch

Upon installation, it is usually a good idea to apply a thread-locking compound to the flywheel bolts

To install:

9. Thoroughly clean all working surfaces of the flywheel and the pressure plate.

10. Grease radius at back of bushing.

11. Rotate clutch cover and pressure plate assembly for maximum clearance between flywheel and frame crossmember if crossmember was not removed during clutch removal.

12. Tilt top edge of clutch cover and pressure plate assembly back and move it up into the clutch housing. Support clutch cover and pressure plate assembly and slide clutch disc into position.

13. Position clutch disc and plate against flywheel and insert spare transmission main drive gear shaft or clutch installing tool through clutch disc hub and into main drive pilot bearing.

14. Rotate clutch cover until the punch marks on cover and flywheel line up.

15. Bolt cover loosely to flywheel. Tighten cover bolts a few turns at a time, in progression, until tight. Then tighten bolts to 20 ft. lbs. torque.

16. Install transmission.

17. Install frame crossmembers and insulator, tighten all bolts.

Check the pressure plate for excessive wear

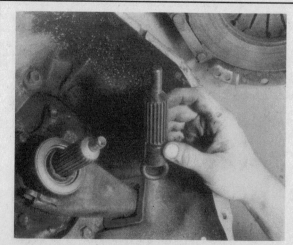

Typical clutch alignment tool, note how the splines match the transmission's input shaft

Install a clutch alignment arbor, to align the clutch assembly during installation

Pressure plate-to-flywheel bolt holes should align

Clutch plate installed with the arbor in place

You may want to use a thread locking compound on the clutch assembly bolts

Clutch plate and pressure plate installed with the alignment arbor in place

Install the clutch assembly bolts and tighten in steps, using an X pattern

Be sure to use a torque wrench to tighten all bolts

With Hydraulic Clutch

1. Remove transmission.
2. Remove clutch housing.
3. Remove clutch fork and release bearing assembly.
4. Mark clutch cover and flywheel, with a suitable tool to assure correct reassembly.
5. Remove the pressure plate retaining bolts, loosening them evenly so the clutch cover will not be distorted.
6. Pull pressure plate assembly clear of flywheel and, while supporting pressure plate, slide clutch disc from between flywheel and pressure plate.

To install:

7. Thoroughly clean all working surfaces of the flywheel and the pressure plate.
8. Grease radius at back of bushing.
9. Rotate clutch cover and pressure plate assembly for maximum clearance between flywheel and frame crossmember if crossmember was not removed during clutch removal.
10. Tilt top edge of clutch cover and pressure plate assembly back and move it up into the clutch housing. Support clutch cover and pressure plate assembly and slide clutch disc into position.
11. Position clutch disc and plate against flywheel and insert spare transmission main drive gear shaft or clutch installing tool through clutch disc hub and into main drive pilot bearing.
12. Rotate clutch cover until the punch marks on cover and flywheel line up.
13. Bolt the pressure plate loosely to flywheel. Tighten the bolts a few turns at a time, in progression, until tight. Then tighten bolts to:
- $5/16''$ bolts: 20 ft. lbs.
- $3/8''$ bolts: 30 ft. lbs.
16. Install transmission.
17. Install frame crossmembers and insulator, tighten all bolts.

MECHANICAL LINKAGE ADJUSTMENT

▶ **See Figures 52, 53, 54 and 55**

The only adjustment required is pedal free-play. Adjust the clutch actuating fork rod by turning the self-locking adjusting nut to provide $1/8''$ free movement at the end of the fork. This will provide the recommended $1\frac{1}{2}''$ free-play at the pedal.

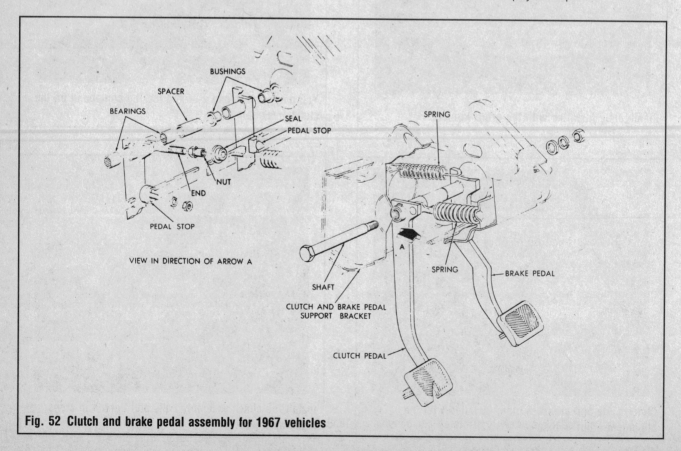

Fig. 52 Clutch and brake pedal assembly for 1967 vehicles

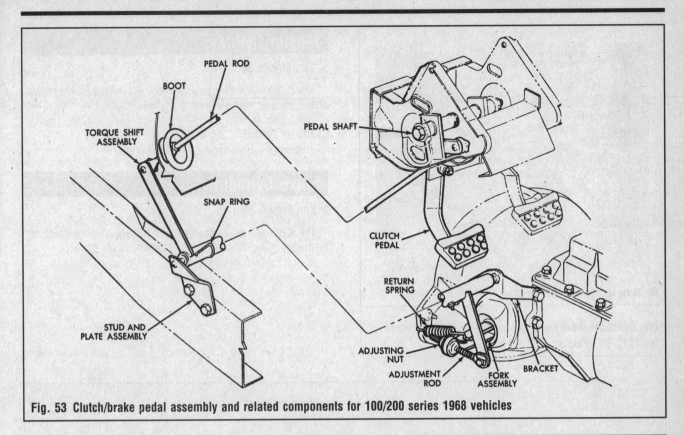

Fig. 53 Clutch/brake pedal assembly and related components for 100/200 series 1968 vehicles

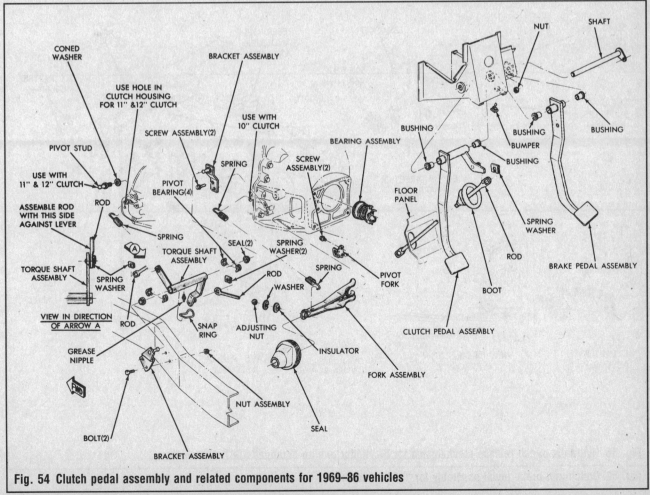

Fig. 54 Clutch pedal assembly and related components for 1969–86 vehicles

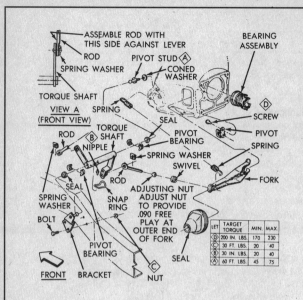

Fig. 55 Exploded view of the torque shaft and linkage for 1977–86 vehicles

Master Cylinder

▶ See Figure 56

The hydraulic clutch master cylinder is mounted on the firewall and is fed fluid via gravity from a remote reservoir.

The master cylinder mounting nuts are inside the cab. The torque for the nuts is 200 in. lbs.

Torque the the reservoir nuts is 95 in. lbs.

Slave Cylinder

▶ See Figure 56

The slave cylinder is mounted on a bracket on the left side of the transmission. Mounting nut torque is 200 in. lbs.

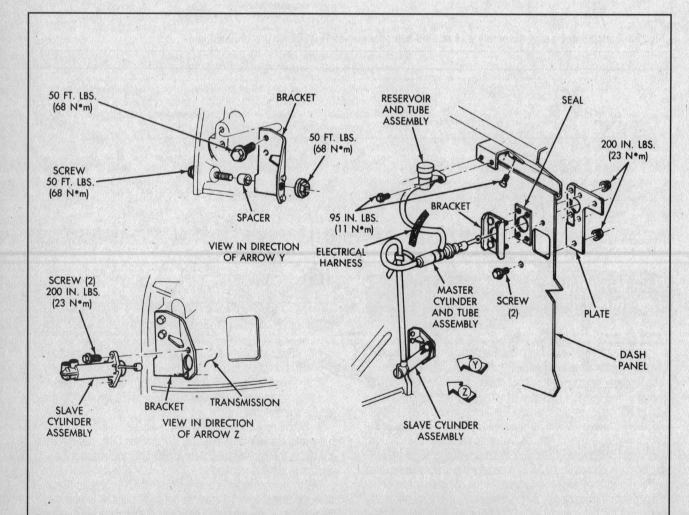

Fig. 56 Hydraulic clutch release mechanisms for 6-cylinder engine equipped 1987–88 vehicles

Troubleshooting Basic Clutch Problems

Problem	Cause
Excessive clutch noise	Throwout bearing noises are more audible at the lower end of pedal travel. The usual causes are: • Riding the clutch • Too little pedal free-play • Lack of bearing lubrication A bad clutch shaft pilot bearing will make a high pitched squeal, when the clutch is disengaged and the transmission is in gear or within the first 2″ of pedal travel. The bearing must be replaced. Noise from the clutch linkage is a clicking or snapping that can be heard or felt as the pedal is moved completely up or down. This usually requires lubrication. Transmitted engine noises are amplified by the clutch housing and heard in the passenger compartment. They are usually the result of insufficient pedal free-play and can be changed by manipulating the clutch pedal.
Clutch slips (the car does not move as it should when the clutch is engaged)	This is usually most noticeable when pulling away from a standing start. A severe test is to start the engine, apply the brakes, shift into high gear and SLOWLY release the clutch pedal. A healthy clutch will stall the engine. If it slips it may be due to: • A worn pressure plate or clutch plate • Oil soaked clutch plate • Insufficient pedal free-play
Clutch drags or fails to release	The clutch disc and some transmission gears spin briefly after clutch disengagement. Under normal conditions in average temperatures, 3 seconds is maximum spin-time. Failure to release properly can be caused by: • Too light transmission lubricant or low lubricant level • Improperly adjusted clutch linkage
Low clutch life	Low clutch life is usually a result of poor driving habits or heavy duty use. Riding the clutch, pulling heavy loads, holding the car on a grade with the clutch instead of the brakes and rapid clutch engagement all contribute to low clutch life.

AUTOMATIC TRANSMISSION

Understanding Automatic Transmissions

The automatic transmission allows engine torque and power to be transmitted to the rear wheels within a narrow range of engine operating speeds. It will allow the engine to turn fast enough to produce plenty of power and torque at very low speeds, while keeping it at a sensible rpm at high vehicle speeds (and it does this job without driver assistance). The transmission uses a light fluid as the medium for the transmission of power. This fluid also works in the operation of various hydraulic control circuits and as a lubricant. Because the transmission fluid performs all of these functions, trouble within the unit can easily travel from one part to another. For this reason, and because of the complexity and unusual operating principles of the transmission, a very sound understanding of the basic principles of operation will simplify troubleshooting.

TORQUE CONVERTER

The torque converter replaces the conventional clutch. It has three functions:

1. It allows the engine to idle with the vehicle at a standstill, even with the transmission in gear.

2. It allows the transmission to shift from range-to-range smoothly, without requiring that the driver close the throttle during the shift.

3. It multiplies engine torque to an increasing extent as vehicle speed drops and throttle opening is increased. This has the effect of making the transmission more responsive and reduces the amount of shifting required.

The torque converter is a metal case which is shaped like a sphere that has been flattened on opposite sides. It is bolted to the rear end of the engine's crankshaft. Generally, the entire metal case rotates at engine speed and serves as the engine's flywheel.

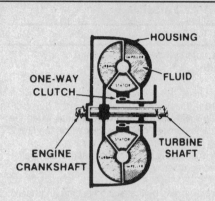

The torque converter housing is rotated by the engine's crankshaft, and turns the impeller—The impeller then spins the turbine, which gives motion to the turbine shaft, driving the gears

The case contains three sets of blades. One set is attached directly to the case. This set forms the torus or pump. Another set is directly connected to the output shaft, and forms the turbine. The third set is mounted on a hub which, in turn, is mounted on a stationary shaft through a one-way clutch. This third set is known as the stator.

A pump, which is driven by the converter hub at engine speed, keeps the torque converter full of transmission fluid at all times. Fluid flows continuously through the unit to provide cooling.

Under low speed acceleration, the torque converter functions as follows:

The torus is turning faster than the turbine. It picks up fluid at the center of the converter and, through centrifugal force, slings it outward. Since the outer edge of the converter moves faster than the portions at the center, the fluid picks up speed.

The fluid then enters the outer edge of the turbine blades. It then travels back toward the center of the converter case along the turbine blades. In impinging upon the turbine blades, the fluid loses the energy picked up in the torus.

If the fluid was now returned directly into the torus, both halves of the converter would have to turn at approximately the same speed at all times, and torque input and output would both be the same.

In flowing through the torus and turbine, the fluid picks up two types of flow, or flow in two separate directions. It flows through the turbine blades, and it spins with the engine. The stator, whose blades are stationary when the vehicle is being accelerated at low speeds, converts one type of flow into another. Instead of allowing the fluid to flow straight back into the torus, the stator's curved blades turn the fluid almost 90° toward the direction of rotation of the engine. Thus the fluid does not flow as fast toward the torus, but is already spinning when the torus picks it up. This has the effect of allowing the torus to turn much faster than the turbine. This difference in speed may be compared to the difference in speed between the smaller and larger gears in any gear train. The result is that engine power output is higher, and engine torque is multiplied.

As the speed of the turbine increases, the fluid spins faster and faster in the direction of engine rotation. As a result, the ability of

the stator to redirect the fluid flow is reduced. Under cruising conditions, the stator is eventually forced to rotate on its one-way clutch in the direction of engine rotation. Under these conditions, the torque converter begins to behave almost like a solid shaft, with the torus and turbine speeds being almost equal.

PLANETARY GEARBOX

The ability of the torque converter to multiply engine torque is limited. Also, the unit tends to be more efficient when the turbine is rotating at relatively high speeds. Therefore, a planetary gearbox is used to carry the power output of the turbine to the driveshaft.

Planetary gears function very similarly to conventional transmission gears. However, their construction is different in that three elements make up one gear system, and, in that all three elements are different from one another. The three elements are: an outer gear that is shaped like a hoop, with teeth cut into the inner surface; a sun gear, mounted on a shaft and located at the very center of the outer gear; and a set of three planet gears, held by pins in a ring-like planet carrier, meshing with both the sun gear and the outer gear. Either the outer gear or the sun gear may be held stationary, providing more than one possible torque multiplication factor for each set of gears. Also, if all three gears are forced to rotate at the same speed, the gearset forms, in effect, a solid shaft.

Most automatics use the planetary gears to provide various reductions ratios. Bands and clutches are used to hold various portions of the gearsets to the transmission case or to the shaft on which they are mounted. Shifting is accomplished, then, by changing the portion of each planetary gearset which is held to the transmission case or to the shaft.

SERVOS AND ACCUMULATORS

The servos are hydraulic pistons and cylinders. They resemble the hydraulic actuators used on many other machines, such as

Planetary gears work in a similar fashion to manual transmission gears, but are composed of three parts

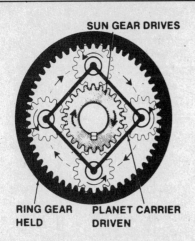

Planetary gears in the maxium reduction (low) range. The ring gear is held and a lower gear ratio is obtained

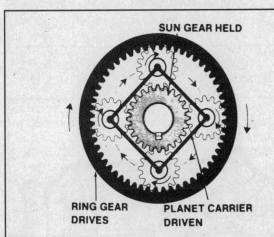

Planetary gears in the minimum reduction (drive) range. The ring gear is allowed to revolve, providing a higher gear ratio

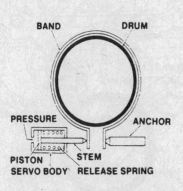

Servos, operated by pressure, are used to apply or release the bands, to either hold the ring gear or allow it to rotate

bulldozers. Hydraulic fluid enters the cylinder, under pressure, and forces the piston to move to engage the band or clutches.

The accumulators are used to cushion the engagement of the servos. The transmission fluid must pass through the accumulator on the way to the servo. The accumulator housing contains a thin piston which is sprung away from the discharge passage of the accumulator. When fluid passes through the accumulator on the way to the servo, it must move the piston against spring pressure, and this action smooths out the action of the servo.

HYDRAULIC CONTROL SYSTEM

The hydraulic pressure used to operate the servos comes from the main transmission oil pump. This fluid is channeled to the various servos through the shift valves. There is generally a manual shift valve which is operated by the transmission selector lever and an automatic shift valve for each automatic upshift the transmission provides.

➡**Many new transmissions are electronically controlled. On these models, electrical solenoids are used to better control the hydraulic fluid. Usually, the solenoids are regulated by an electronic control module.**

There are two pressures which affect the operation of these valves. One is the governor pressure which is effected by vehicle speed. The other is the modulator pressure which is effected by intake manifold vacuum or throttle position. Governor pressure rises with an increase in vehicle speed, and modulator pressure rises as the throttle is opened wider. By responding to these two pressures, the shift valves cause the upshift points to be delayed with increased throttle opening to make the best use of the engine's power output.

Most transmissions also make use of an auxiliary circuit for downshifting. This circuit may be actuated by the throttle linkage the vacuum line which actuates the modulator, by a cable or by a solenoid. It applies pressure to a special downshift surface on the shift valve or valves.

The transmission modulator also governs the line pressure, used to actuate the servos. In this way, the clutches and bands will be actuated with a force matching the torque output of the engine.

Pan and Filter Service

➡**Refer to Section 1 for the procedures for pan removal and filter service.**

Kickdown Band

ADJUSTMENTS

◆ **See Figure 57**

The kickdown band adjusting screw is located on the left-hand side of the transmission case near the throttle lever shaft.

1. Loosen the locknut and back it off about five turns. Be sure that the adjusting screw turns freely in the case.
2. Torque the adjusting screw to 72 in. lbs.

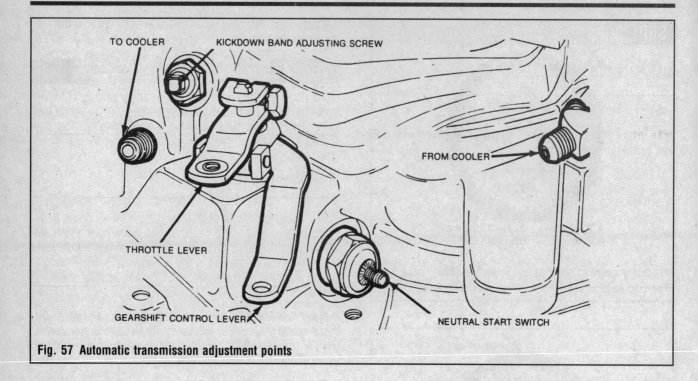

Fig. 57 Automatic transmission adjustment points

3. Back off the adjusting screw as follows:
- 1967–72: 2 turns
- 1973–88 V8: 2½ turns
- 1973–84 6-cyl.: 2 turns
- 1985–88 6-cyl.: 2½ turns
- Diesel—2 turns

Tighten the Locknut as follows:
- 1967–72: 29 ft. lb.
- 1973–75: 35 ft. lb.
- 1976–88: 30 ft. lb.

Low and Reverse Band

ADJUSTMENT

◆ **See Figure 58**

The pan must be removed from the transmission to gain access to the low and reverse band adjusting screw.

1. Remove the skid plate, if any. Drain the transmission fluid and remove the pan.

2. Loosen the band adjusting screw locknut and back it off about five turns. Be sure that the adjusting screw turns freely in the lever.

3. Torque the adjusting screw to 72 in. lbs.

4. Back off the adjusting screw as follows:
- A-727: 2 turns
- A-904T and A-999: 4 turns

Keep the adjusting screw from turning, tighten and torque the locknut to 30 ft. lbs.

5. Use a new gasket and install the transmission pan. Torque the pan bolts to 150 in. lbs. Refill the transmission with Dexron® II fluid.

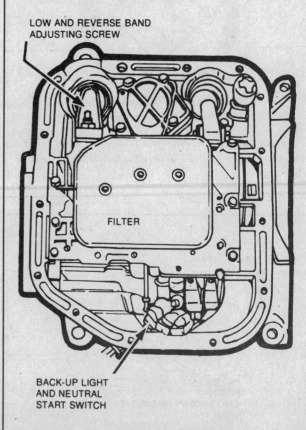

Fig. 58 Low and Reverse band adjusting screw locations—transmission pan must be removed for access

Shift Linkage

ADJUSTMENT

▶ **See Figures 59, 60 and 61**

➡ **To insure proper adjustment, it is suggested that new linkage grommets be installed.**

1. Place the gearshift lever in Park position.
2. Move the shift control lever on the transmission all the way to the rear (in the Park detent).
3. Set the adjustable rod to the proper length and install it with no load in either direction. Tighten the swivel bolt.
4. The shift linkage must be free of binding and be positive in all positions. Make sure that the engine can start only when the gearshift lever is in the Park or Neutral position. Be sure that the gearshift lever will not jump into an unwanted gear.

Throttle Kickdown Rod

ADJUSTMENT

1967–69 Models

▶ **See Figures 62 and 63**

1. Warm the engine to operating temperature and adjust the idle speed to 550 rpm (6-cyl.) or 500 rpm (V8s).
2. Disconnect the transmission throttle rod at the bellcrank on the carburetor. Hold the transmission throttle rod forward so that the lever at the transmission is against its stop. Adjust the rod

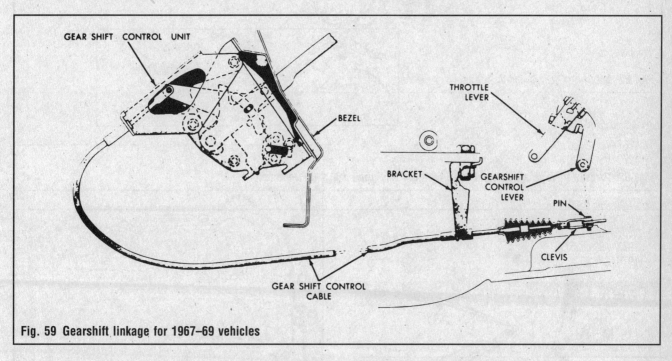

Fig. 59 Gearshift linkage for 1967–69 vehicles

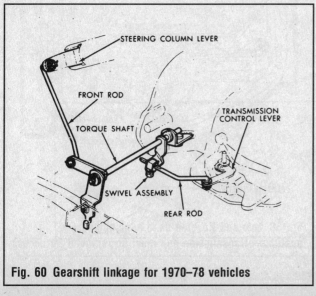

Fig. 60 Gearshift linkage for 1970–78 vehicles

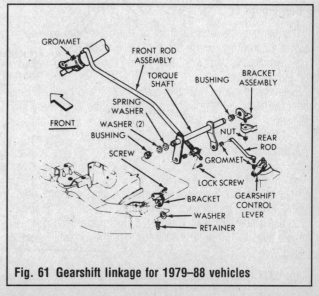

Fig. 61 Gearshift linkage for 1979–88 vehicles

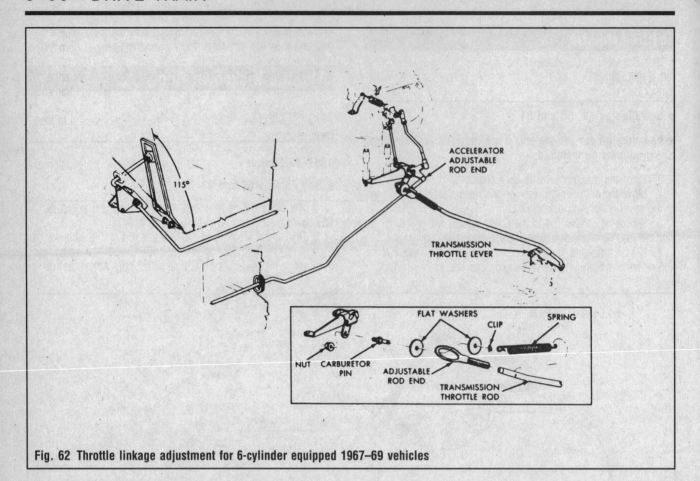

Fig. 62 Throttle linkage adjustment for 6-cylinder equipped 1967–69 vehicles

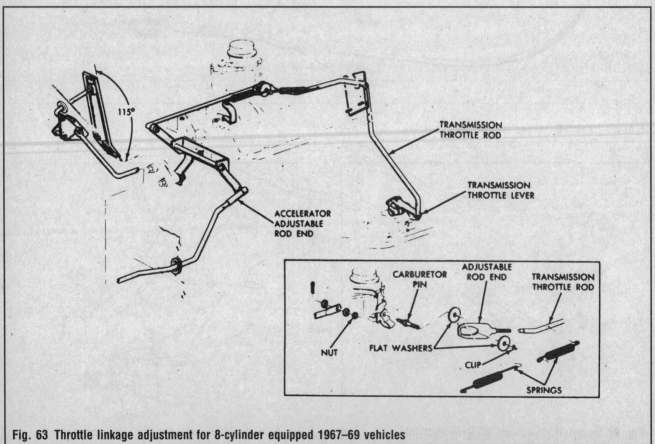

Fig. 63 Throttle linkage adjustment for 8-cylinder equipped 1967–69 vehicles

length so that the ball socket aligns with the bellcrank ball end and engage the ball and socket.

3. Disconnect the throttle rod at the other bellcrank. Adjust the rod length to produce a pedal angle of 115° and re-engage the bellcrank ball and socket.

1970–78 Models

▶ **See Figures 64 and 65**

1. Warm the engine to operating temperature.
2. Block the choke plate fully open.

3. Remove the throttle return spring from the carburetor.
4. Remove the clip, washer and slotted throttle rod from the carburetor pin.
5. Rotate the threaded end of the rod so that the rear edge of the slot in the rod contacts the carburetor pin when the transmission throttle lever is held forward against its stop.
6. Install the washer and clip to retain the throttle rod to the carburetor.
7. Install the throttle rod return spring.
8. Check the transmission linkage for freedom of operation and unblock the choke plate.

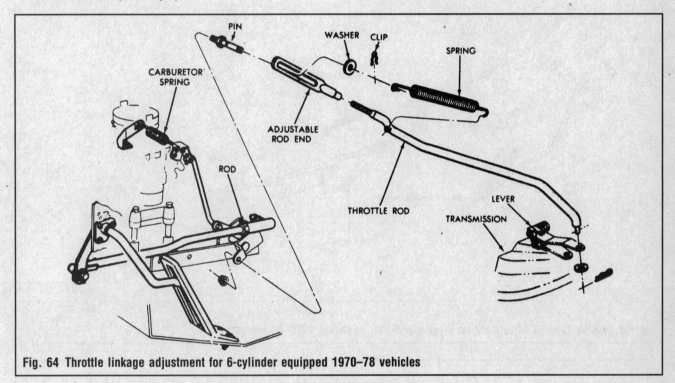

Fig. 64 Throttle linkage adjustment for 6-cylinder equipped 1970–78 vehicles

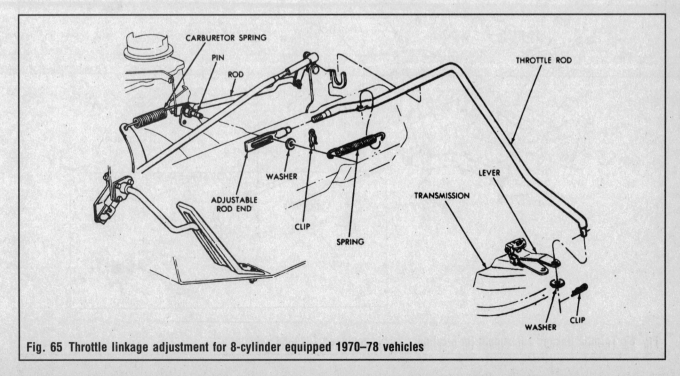

Fig. 65 Throttle linkage adjustment for 8-cylinder equipped 1970–78 vehicles

1979–88 Models

▶ **See Figures 66, 67 and 68**

1. Warm the engine up to normal operating temperature. Turn the engine Off.
2. Block the choke plate fully open.
3. Raise the truck on a hoist.

4. Loosen the adjusting swivel lock screw.
5. To insure the proper alignment, the swivel must be free to slide along the flat end of the throttle rod so the preload spring action is not restricted. Clean the parts if necessary.
6. Hold the transmission lever firmly forward against the internal stop and tighten the swivel lock screw to 100 in. lbs. Linkage backlash will automatically be taken up by the preload spring.

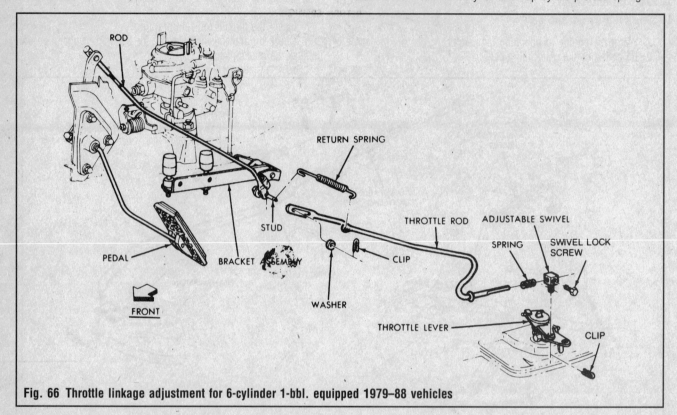

Fig. 66 Throttle linkage adjustment for 6-cylinder 1-bbl. equipped 1979–88 vehicles

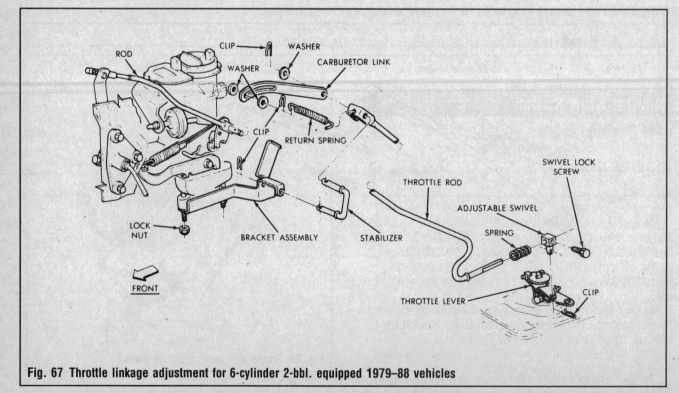

Fig. 67 Throttle linkage adjustment for 6-cylinder 2-bbl. equipped 1979–88 vehicles

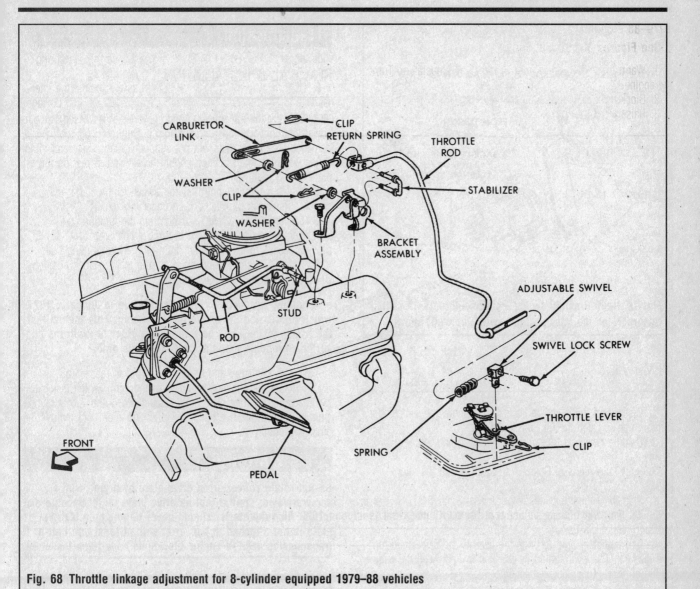

Fig. 68 Throttle linkage adjustment for 8-cylinder equipped 1979–88 vehicles

Neutral Start Switch

▶ See Figures 69 and 70

ADJUSTMENT

The neutral safety switch is thread mounted into the transmission case. When the gearshift lever is placed in either the Park or Neutral position, a cam, which is attached to the transmission throttle lever inside the transmission, contact the neutral safety switch and provides a ground to complete the starter solenoid circuit.

The back-up light switch is incorporated into the neutral safety switch. The center terminal is for the neutral safety switch and the two outer terminals are for the back-up lamps.

There is no adjustment for the switch. If a malfunction occurs, the switch must be removed and replaced.

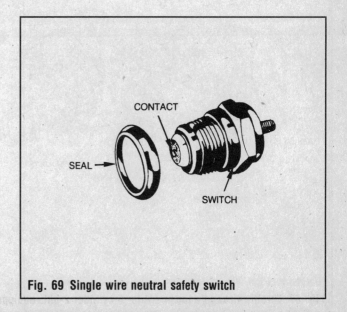

Fig. 69 Single wire neutral safety switch

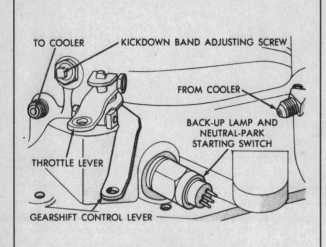

Fig. 70 Neutral safety switch location—three wire switch (incorporates the back-up light switch as well) shown

REMOVAL & INSTALLATION

1. Disconnect the electrical leads and unscrew the switch. Use a drain pan to catch the transmission fluid.

2. Using a new seal, install the new switch and torque it to 24 ft. lbs.

3. Pour four quarts of Dexron® II fluid through the filler tube.

4. Start the engine and idle it for at least 2 minutes.

5. Set the parking brake and move the selector through each position, ending in Park.

6. Add sufficient fluid to bring the level to the FULL mark on the dipstick. The level should be checked in Park, with the engine idling at normal operating temperature.

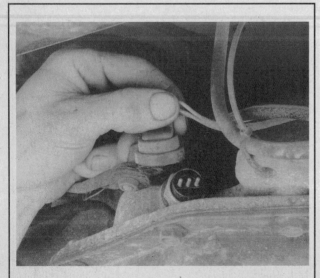

Disconnect the wire harness from the back-up light/ neutral safety switch before removal

Transmission

REMOVAL & INSTALLATION

1. Remove the transmission and converter as an assembly; otherwise the converter drive plate pump bushing and oil seal will be damaged. The drive plate will not support a load. Therefore, none of the weight of transmission should be allowed to rest on the plate during removal.

2. Attach a remote control starter switch to the starter solenoid so the engine can be rotated from under the vehicle.

3. Disconnect high tension cable from the ignition coil.

4. Remove cover plate from in front of converter assembly to provide access to the converter drain plug and mounting bolts.

5. Rotate engine to bring drain plug to the 6 o'clock position. Drain the converter and transmission.

➥**A running production change was made in January, 1977 which eliminated the converter drain plug. This means that the transmission must be removed in order to drain the converter on models manufactured after this date.**

6. Mark converter and drive plate to aid in reassembly.

7. Rotate the engine with the remote control switch to locate two converter to drive plate bolts located and 5 and 7 o'clock positions. Remove the two bolts, rotate engine again and remove the other two bolts.

✳✳ WARNING

Do not rotate converter on drive plate by prying with a screwdriver or similar tool as drive plate might become distorted. Also the starter should never be engaged if drive plate is not attached to converter with at least one bolt or if transmission case to engine blockbolts have been loosened.

8. Disconnect battery ground cable. Remove engine to transmission struts, if necessary. You may have to drop the exhaust system on some models.

9. Remove the starter.

10. Remove wire from the neutral starting switch.

11. Remove gearshift cable or rod from the transmission and the lever.

12. Disconnect the throttle rod from left side of transmission.

13. Disconnect the oil cooler lines at transmission and remove the oil filler tube. Disconnect the speedometer cable.

14. Disconnect the driveshaft.

15. Install engine support fixture to hold up the rear of the engine.

16. Raise transmission slightly with jack to relieve load and remove support bracket or crossmember. Remove all bell housing bolts and carefully work transmission and converter rearward off engine dowels and disengage converter hub from end of crankshaft.

✳✳ WARNING

Attach a small C-clamp to edge of bell housing to hold converter in place during transmission removal; otherwise the front pump bushing might be damaged.

To install:

➡ **Install transmission and converter as an assembly. The drive plate will not support a load. Do not allow weight of transmission to rest on the plate during installation.**

17. Rotate pump rotors until the rotor lugs are vertical.
18. Carefully slide converter assembly over input shaft and reaction shaft. Make sure converter impeller shaft slots are also vertical and fully engage front pump inner rotor lugs.
19. Use a C-clamp on edge of converter housing to hold converter in place during transmission installation.
20. Converter drive plate should be free of distortion and drive plate to crankshaft bolts tightened to 55 ft. lbs. torque.
21. Using a jack, position transmission and converter assembly in alignment with engine.
22. Rotate converter so mark on converter (made during removal) will align with the mark on the drive plate. The offset holes in plate are located next to the ⅛" hole in inner circle of the plate. A stamped **V** mark identifies the offset hole in converter front cover. Carefully work transmissio assembly forward over engine block dowels with converter hub entering the crankshaft opening.
23. Install converter housing to engine bolts and tighten to 28 ft. lbs.

24. Install the two lower drive plate to converter bolts and tighten to 270 in. lbs. torque.
25. Install engine to transmission struts, if required. Install starting motor and connect battery ground cable.
26. Rotate engine and install two remaining drive plate to converter bolts.
27. Install crossmember and tighten attaching bolts to 90 ft. lbs. torque. Lower transmission so that extension housing is aligned and rests on the rear mount. Install bolts and tighten to 40 ft. lbs. torque.
28. Remove transmission jack and engine support fixture; then install tie-bars under the transmission.
29. Replace the driveshaft.
30. Connect oil cooler lines, install oil filler tube and connect the speedometer cable.
31. Connect gearshift cable or rod and torque shaft assembly to the transmission case and to the lever.
32. Connect throttle rod to the lever at left side of transmission bell housing.
33. Connect wire to back-up and neutral starting switch.
34. Install cover plate in front of the converter assembly.
35. Refill transmission with fluid.
36. Adjust throttle and shift linkage.

Troubleshooting Basic Automatic Transmission Problems

Problem	Cause	Solution
Fluid leakage	• Defective pan gasket	• Replace gasket or tighten pan bolts
	• Loose filler tube	• Tighten tube nut
	• Loose extension housing to transmission case	• Tighten bolts
	• Converter housing area leakage	• Have transmission checked professionally
Fluid flows out the oil filler tube	• High fluid level	• Check and correct fluid level
	• Breather vent clogged	• Open breather vent
	• Clogged oil filter or screen	• Replace filter or clean screen (change fluid also)
	• Internal fluid leakage	• Have transmission checked professionally
Transmission overheats (this is usually accompanied by a strong burned odor to the fluid)	• Low fluid level	• Check and correct fluid level
	• Fluid cooler lines clogged	• Drain and refill transmission. If this doesn't cure the problem, have cooler lines cleared or replaced.
	• Heavy pulling or hauling with insufficient cooling	• Install a transmission oil cooler
	• Faulty oil pump, internal slippage	• Have transmission checked professionally
Buzzing or whining noise	• Low fluid level	• Check and correct fluid level
	• Defective torque converter, scored gears	• Have transmission checked professionally
No forward or reverse gears or slippage in one or more gears	• Low fluid level	• Check and correct fluid level
	• Defective vacuum or linkage controls, internal clutch or band failure	• Have unit checked professionally
Delayed or erratic shift	• Low fluid level	• Check and correct fluid level
	• Broken vacuum lines	• Repair or replace lines
	• Internal malfunction	• Have transmission checked professionally

Lockup Torque Converter Service Diagnosis

Problem	Cause	Solution

No lockup	• Faulty oil pump
	• Sticking governor valve
	• Valve body malfunction
	   (a) Stuck switch valve
	   (b) Stuck lockup valve
	   (c) Stuck fail-safe valve
	• Failed locking clutch
	• Leaking turbine hub seal
	• Faulty input shaft or seal ring
		• Replace oil pump
		• Repair or replace as necessary
		• Repair or replace valve body or its internal components as necessary
		
		• Replace torque converter
		• Replace torque converter
		• Repair or replace as necessary

Will not unlock	• Sticking governor valve
	• Valve body malfunction
	   (a) Stuck switch valve
	   (b) Stuck lockup valve
	   (c) Stuck fail-safe valve
		• Repair or replace as necessary
		• Repair or replace valve body or its internal components as necessary

Stays locked up at too low a speed in direct	• Sticking governor valve
	• Valve body malfunction
	   (a) Stuck switch valve
	   (b) Stuck lockup valve
	   (c) Stuck fail-safe valve
		• Repair or replace as necessary
		• Repair or replace valve body or its internal components as necessary

Locks up or drags in low or second	• Faulty oil pump
	• Valve body malfunction
	   (a) Stuck switch valve
	   (b) Stuck fail-safe valve
		• Replace oil pump
		• Repair or replace valve body or its internal components as necessary

Sluggish or stalls in reverse	• Faulty oil pump
	• Plugged cooler, cooler lines or fittings
	• Valve body malfunction
	   (a) Stuck switch valve
	   (b) Faulty input shaft or seal ring
		• Replace oil pump as necessary
		• Flush or replace cooler and flush lines and fittings
		• Repair or replace valve body or its internal components as necessary

Loud chatter during lockup engagement (cold)	• Faulty torque converter • Failed locking clutch • Leaking turbine hub seal	• Replace torque converter • Replace torque converter • Replace torque converter
Vibration or shudder during lockup engagement	• Faulty oil pump • Valve body malfunction • Faulty torque converter • Engine needs tune-up	• Repair or replace oil pump as necessary • Repair or replace valve body or its internal components as necessary • Replace torque converter • Tune engine
Vibration after lockup engagement	• Faulty torque converter • Exhaust system strikes underbody • Engine needs tune-up • Throttle linkage misadjusted	• Replace torque converter • Align exhaust system • Tune engine • Adjust throttle linkage
Vibration when revved in neutral Overheating: oil blows out of dip stick tube or pump seal	• Torque converter out of balance • Plugged cooler, cooler lines or fittings • Stuck switch valve	• Replace torque converter • Flush or replace cooler and flush lines and fittings • Repair switch valve in valve body or replace valve body
Shudder after lockup engagement	• Faulty oil pump • Plugged cooler, cooler lines or fittings • Valve body malfunction • Faulty torque converter • Fail locking clutch • Exhaust system strikes underbody • Engine needs tune-up • Throttle linkage misadjusted	• Replace oil pump • Flush or replace cooler and flush lines and fittings • Repair or replace valve body or its internal components as necessary • Replace torque converter • Replace torque converter • Align exhaust system • Tune engine • Adjust throttle linkage

Transmission Fluid Indications

The appearance and odor of the transmission fluid can give valuable clues to the overall condition of the transmission. Always note the appearance of the fluid when you check the fluid level or change the fluid. Rub a small amount of fluid between your fingers to feel for grit and smell the fluid on the dipstick.

If the fluid appears:	It indicates:
Clear and red colored	• Normal operation
Discolored (extremely dark red or brownish) or smells burned	• Band or clutch pack failure, usually caused by an overheated transmission. Hauling very heavy loads with insufficient power or failure to change the fluid, often result in overheating. Do not confuse this appearance with newer fluids that have a darker red color and a strong odor (though not a burned odor).
Foamy or aerated (light in color and full of bubbles)	• The level is too high (gear train is churning oil) • An internal air leak (air is mixing with the fluid). Have the transmission checked professionally.
Solid residue in the fluid	• Defective bands, clutch pack or bearings. Bits of band material or metal abrasives are clinging to the dipstick. Have the transmission checked professionally.
Varnish coating on the dipstick	• The transmission fluid is overheating

DRIVESHAFT AND U-JOINTS

Driveshaft

REMOVAL & INSTALLATION

Ball and Trunnion Type

1. Raise the vehicle and support it on jackstands.
2. Matchmark the U-joint and pinion flange to ensure proper installation. Remove both rear U-joint roller and bearing assembly clamps from the pinion yoke. Do not disturb the retaining clamp used to hold the roller assemblies in place.
3. Disconnect the front U-joint from the transmission flange and remove the shaft from the vehicle.
4. Installation is the reverse of removal.

Cross and Roller Type

1967–69 MODELS

1. Raise and support the vehicle. Matchmark the U-joints and sliding yokes.
2. Remove the U-joint at the rear axle by removing the two strap bolts and straps.
3. Remove the two bushing and roller assemblies.
4. Remove the front U-joint in the same manner by removing the strap bolts and straps.
5. Remove the driveshaft from the vehicle.
6. Installation is the reverse of removal. Coat the bushing rollers with short fiber grease and tap the bushings into the yoke on the cross bearing journals.

1970–88 MODELS WITH A ONE PIECE SHAFT

1. Raise and support the truck.
2. Matchmark the shaft and pinion flange to assure proper balance at installation.
3. Remove both rear U-joint roller and bushing clamps from the rear axle pinion flange. Do not disturb the retaining strap that holds the bushing assemblies on the U-Joint cross.

➡ **Do not allow the driveshaft to hang during removal. Suspend it from the frame with a piece of wire. Before removing the driveshaft, lower the front end to prevent loss of fluid.**

4. Slide the driveshaft from the truck.
5. Installation is the reverse of removal. Align the matchmarks made during removal.

1970–88 MODELS WITH A TWO-SECTION TYPE

This driveshaft has a universal joint at either end, with a third universal joint and a support bearing at the center.
1. Matchmark the shaft and the rear axle pinion hub yoke. Matchmark the center bearing spline and slip yoke.

➡ **Do not allow the driveshaft to hang down during removal. Suspend it from the frame. Raise the rear of the truck to prevent loss of transmission fluid.**

2. Remove both rear U-joint roller and bushing assembly clamps from the rear axle pinion yoke. Do not disturb the retaining strap used to hold the bushing assemblies on the U-joint cross.

3. Slide the rear half of the shaft off the front shaft splines at the center bearing. Remove the rear half.

4. At the transmission end of the front half, remove the bushing retaining bolts and clamps, after matchmarking. If there is a driveshaft brake, there will be flange nuts.

5. Unbolt the center bearing mounting nuts and bolts and remove the front half of the shaft.

6. On installation, align the matchmarks at the transmission and start all the bolts and nuts at the front U-joint and the center support bearing.

7. Tighten ¼" clamp bolts to 170 in. lbs. and ⁵⁄₁₆" bolts to 300 in. lbs. Tighten driveshaft brake flange nuts to 35 ft. lbs. Leave the center bearing bolts just snug.

8. Align the rear shaft matchmarks and slide the yoke onto the front shaft splines.

9. Align the rear U-joint matchmarks and install the bushing clamps and bolts. Tighten the bolts to the torque given in step 7. Grease the joints and splines.

10. Jack up the rear wheels and let the engine drive the shaft. The center support bearing will align itself.

11. Tighten the center bearing bolts to 50 ft. lbs.

U-JOINT OVERHAUL

Ball and Trunnion Type

1. Remove the driveshaft.
2. Straighten the tabs on the grease cover and remove the grease cover and gasket.
3. Push the body back and remove the components from both ends of the trunnion pin.

4. Remove the clamps and loosen the dust cover. Remove and save the breather located between the driveshaft and rear end of the cover.

5. Clean and examine the trunnion pin for wear. If wear in the body is noticeable, it should be replaced. A press is necessary to remove the pin.

6. Clean all parts in kerosene or a similar solvent.

7. When the trunnion pin and body have not been replaced, a new boot can be installed after coating all parts with U-joint grease. Stretch the boot over the pin and work it through the body into position on the shaft.

8. The trunnion pin must be pressed into the driveshaft with a hydraulic press.

9. Install a thrust washer, rollers, ball, button spring, and thrust button on each end of the trunnion pin and position the body over the pin.

10. Install the boot on the driveshaft with the breather parallel to the shaft. Install the clamp.

11. Position the boot on the U-joint body and install the retaining clamp.

12. Lubricate the U-joint with 2 oz. of U-joint grease applied evenly in both races.

13. Install the gasket on the cover and install the cover on the body. Bend the tabs to retain the cover.

14. Install the driveshaft and U-joint assembly.

Lock Ring and Snapring Types
▶ **See Figure 71**

1. Hammer the bushings (roller caps) slightly inward to relieve pressure on the retainers. Remove the retainers.

2. Place the yoke in a vice with a socket bigger than the bush-

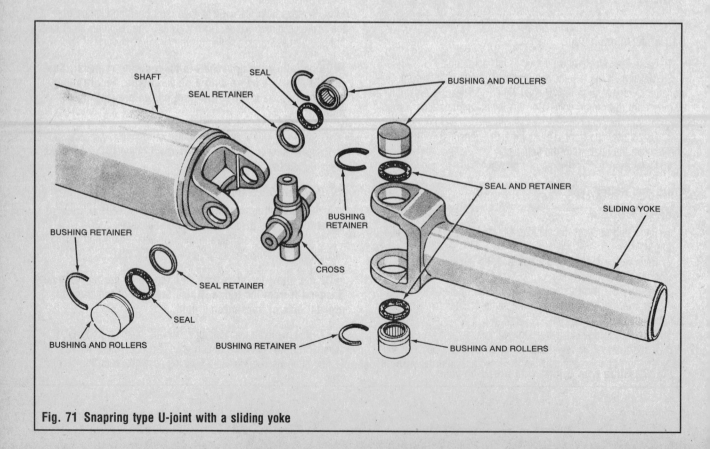

Fig. 71 Snapring type U-joint with a sliding yoke

ing on one side and one smaller than the bushing on the other side.

3. Apply pressure, forcing one bushing out into the larger socket.

4. Reverse the vise and socket arrangement to remove the other bushing and the cross.

5. On installation, press the new bushings in just far enough to install the retainers.

Strap Clamp Type (Rear Axle Yoke)

♦ See Figure 72

Unbolt strap bolts and remove straps, bushings, seals and washer retainers. Install new components as required. When assembling, grease bearings. Install with grease fitting parallel to other fittings in drive train. Tighten strap bolts to 20 ft. lbs. torque.

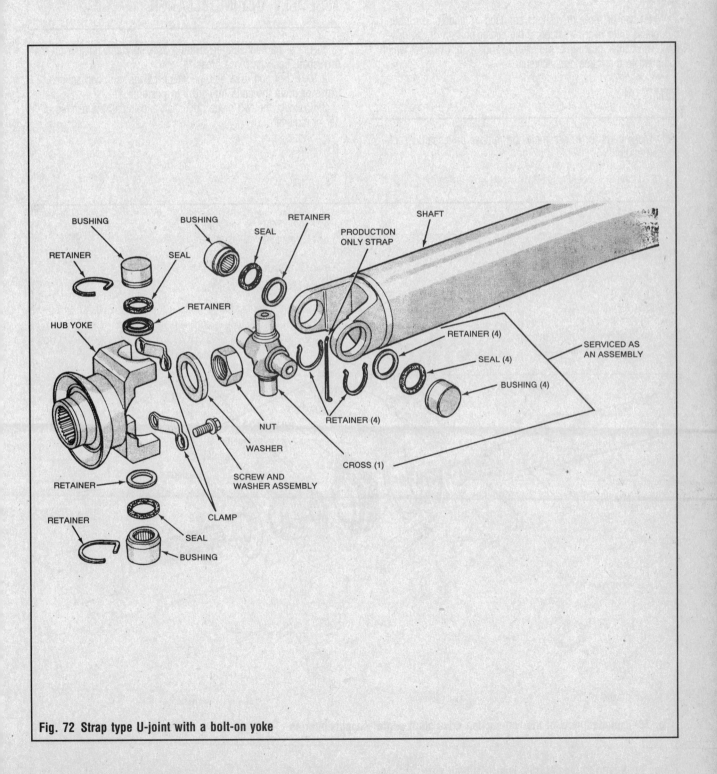

Fig. 72 Strap type U-joint with a bolt-on yoke

Slip Joints

When re-assembling slip joints, make sure that arrows stamped on each side are matched. This will assure proper universal joint alignment.

Center Bearing

▶ **See Figure 73**

When two or more driveshafts are used in tandem, a rubber-mounted center bearing supports the center portion of the drive line. The center bearing is mounted in rubber in a bracket which is bolted to the frame crossmember.

REMOVAL

1. Make parts for re-assembly and remove driveshafts as described earlier.

2. Place the front shaft in a vise and pull the bearing support and insulator away from the bearing.

3. Bend the slinger away from the bearing with a hammer to obtain clearance to install a bearing puller.

4. Remove the bearing with a puller. Remove the slinger. Discard all parts. A replacement kit contains all necessary repair parts.

ASSEMBLY AND INSTALLATION

1. Place the new slinger, bearing assembly and retainer on the driveshaft. Each part is a press fit.

2. Use a strong tube or pipe which cleans the shaft spline. Press or drive the parts forward into position.

3. Connect the two piece driveshaft and install the reverse order of removal.

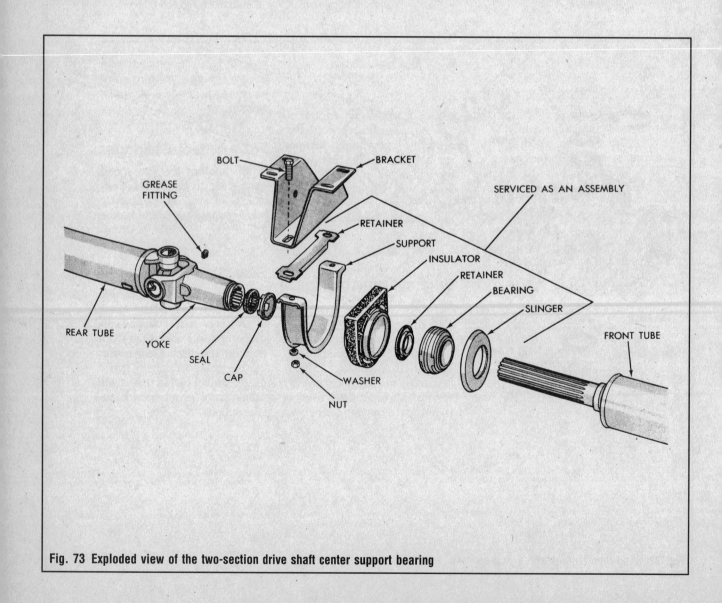

Fig. 73 Exploded view of the two-section drive shaft center support bearing

Troubleshooting Basic Driveshaft and Rear Axle Problems

When abnormal vibrations or noises are detected in the driveshaft area, this chart can be used to help diagnose possible causes. Remember that other components such as wheels, tires, rear axle and suspension can also produce similar conditions.

BASIC DRIVESHAFT PROBLEMS

Problem	Cause	Solution
Shudder as car accelerates from stop or low speed	• Loose U-joint • Defective center bearing	• Replace U-joint • Replace center bearing
Loud clunk in driveshaft when shifting gears	• Worn U-joints	• Replace U-joints
Roughness or vibration at any speed	• Out-of-balance, bent or dented driveshaft • Worn U-joints • U-joint clamp bolts loose	• Balance or replace driveshaft • Replace U-joints • Tighten U-joint clamp bolts
Squeaking noise at low speeds	• Lack of U-joint lubrication	• Lubricate U-joint; if problem persists, replace U-joint
Knock or clicking noise	• U-joint or driveshaft hitting frame tunnel • Worn CV joint	• Correct overloaded condition • Replace CV joint

BASIC REAR AXLE PROBLEMS

First, determine when the noise is most noticeable.

Drive Noise: Produced under vehicle acceleration.

Coast Noise: Produced while the car coasts with a closed throttle.

Float Noise: Occurs while maintaining constant car speed (just enough to keep speed constant) on a level road.

Road Noise

Brick or rough surfaced concrete roads produce noises that seem to come from the rear axle. Road noise is usually identical in Drive or Coast and driving on a different type of road will tell whether the road is the problem.

Tire Noise

Tire noises are often mistaken for rear axle problems. Snow treads or unevenly worn tires produce vibrations seeming to originate elsewhere. **Temporarily** inflating the tires to 40 lbs will significantly alter tire noise, but will have no effect on rear axle noises (which normally cease below about 30 mph).

Engine/Transmission Noise

Determine at what speed the noise is most pronounced, then stop the car in a quiet place. With the transmission in Neutral, run the engine through speeds corresponding to road speeds where the noise was noticed. Noises produced with the car standing still are coming from the engine or transmission.

Front Wheel Bearings

While holding the car speed steady, lightly apply the footbrake; this will often decease bearing noise, as some of the load is taken from the bearing.

Rear Axle Noises

Eliminating other possible sources can narrow the cause to the rear axle, which normally produces noise from worn gears or bearings. Gear noises tend to peak in a narrow speed range, while bearing noises will usually vary in pitch with engine speeds.

NOISE DIAGNOSIS

The Noise Is	Most Probably Produced By
· Identical under Drive or Coast · Different depending on road surface · Lower as the car speed is lowered · Similar with car standing or moving · A vibration	· Road surface, tires or front wheel bearings · Road surface or tires · Tires · Engine or transmission · Unbalanced tires, rear wheel bearing, unbalanced driveshaft or worn U-joint
· A knock or click about every 2 tire revolutions · Most pronounced on turns · A steady low-pitched whirring or scraping, starting at low speeds · A chattering vibration on turns	· Rear wheel bearing · Damaged differential gears · Damaged or worn pinion bearing · Wrong differential lubricant or worn clutch plates (limited slip rear axle)
· Noticed only in Drive, Coast or Float conditions	· Worn ring gear and/or pinion gear

REAR AXLE

Identification

➡Below is a list of the available rear axles and the years they were used.

1967
· Chrysler semi-floating 8¾" ring gear 100 series
· Dana 60 full-floating 9¾" ring gear 200, 300 series
· Chrysler full-floating 9⅝" ring gear 300 series
· Dana 70 full-floating 10½" ring gear 300 series

1968–71
· Chrysler semi-floating 8⅜" ring gear 100, 200 series
· Chrysler semi-floating 8¾" ring gear 200, 300 series
· Dana 60 full-floating 9¾" ring gear 200, 300 series
· Dana 70 full-floating 10½" ring gear 300 series

1972–78
· Chrysler semi-floating 8⅜" ring gear 100, 200 series
· Chrysler semi-floating 8¾" ring gear 100, 200 series
· Chrysler semi-floating 9¼" ring gear 100, 200 series
· Dana 60, 60HD full-floating 9¾" ring gear 300 series
· Dana 70 full-floating 10½" ring gear 300 series

1979
· Chrysler semi-floating 8⅜" ring gear 100, 200 series
· Chrysler semi-floating 9¼" ring gear 100, 200 series
· Dana 60, 60HD full-floating 9¾" ring gear 300 series
· Dana 70 full-floating 10½" ring gear 300 series

1980
· Chrysler semi-floating 8⅜" ring gear 100, 200 series
· Chrysler semi-floating 9¼" ring gear 100, 200 series
· Dana 60 full-floating 9¾" ring gear 200 series
· Dana 70 full-floating 10½" ring gear 300 series
· Dana 60HD full-floating 9¾" ring gear 300 series

1981–83
· Chrysler semi-floating 8⅜" ring gear 150, 250 series
· Chrysler semi-floating 9¼" ring gear 150, 250 series
· Dana 60 full-floating 9¾" ring gear 350 series
· Dana 60HD full-floating 9¾" ring gear 350 series

1984–88
· Chrysler semi-floating 8⅜" ring gear 150, 250 series
· Chrysler semi-floating 9¼" ring gear 150, 250, 350 series
· Chrysler semi-floating 9¼" HD ring gear 250, 350 series

· Dana 60 full-floating 9¾" ring gear 350 series
· Dana 60HD full-floating 9¾" ring gear 350 series

Axle Shafts and Bearings

Before servicing any axle shafts, be sure to jack and support the truck so that both rear wheels are off the ground. This will ensure that the vehicle will not roll off the supports if the vehicle is equipped with a limited slip rear axle and one wheel is turned inadvertently.

REMOVAL & INSTALLATION

Chrysler 8¾" Axle

➡Whenever this axle assembly is serviced, both the brake support plate gaskets and the inner axle shaft oil seal must be renewed.

1. Jack up the rear of the truck and remove the rear wheels.
2. Detach the clips which secure the brake drum to the axle shaft studs and remove the brake drum.
3. Through the access hole in the axle shaft flange, remove the axle shaft retaining nuts. The right-side axle shaft has a threaded adjuster in the retainer plate and a lock under one of its studs which should be removed at this time.
4. Remove the parking brake strut.
5. Attach a suitable puller to the axle shaft flange and remove the axle shaft.
6. Remove the brake assembly from the axle housing.
7. Remove the axle shaft oil seal from the axle housing.

✳✳ CAUTION

It is advisable to position some sort of protective sleeve over the axle shaft seal surface next to the bearing collar to protect the seal surface. Never use a torch or other heat source as an aid in removing any axle shaft components as this will result in serious damage to the axle assembly.

8. Wipe the axle housing seal bore clean. Install a new axle shaft oil seal.

9. Clean the axle shaft bearing cavity.

10. Grease and install the axle shaft bearing in the cavity. Be sure that the bearing is not cocked and that it is seated firmly against the shoulder.

11. Install the axle shaft bearing seal. It should be seated beyond the end of the flange face.

12. Insert the axle shaft, making sure that the splines do not damage the seal. Be sure that the splines are properly engaged with the differential side gear splines.

13. Remainder of installation is the reverse of removal.

Chrysler 8⅜″, 9¼″ and 9¼″ HD Axles

▶ **See Figures 74, 75, 76, 77 and 78**

➡**There is no provision for axle shaft end-play adjustment on these axles.**

1. Jack up the vehicle and remove the rear wheels.

2. Clean all dirt from the housing cover and remove the housing cover to drain the lubricant.

3. Remove the brake drum.

4. Rotate the differential case until the differential pinion shaft lockscrew can be removed. Remove the lockscrew and pinion shaft.

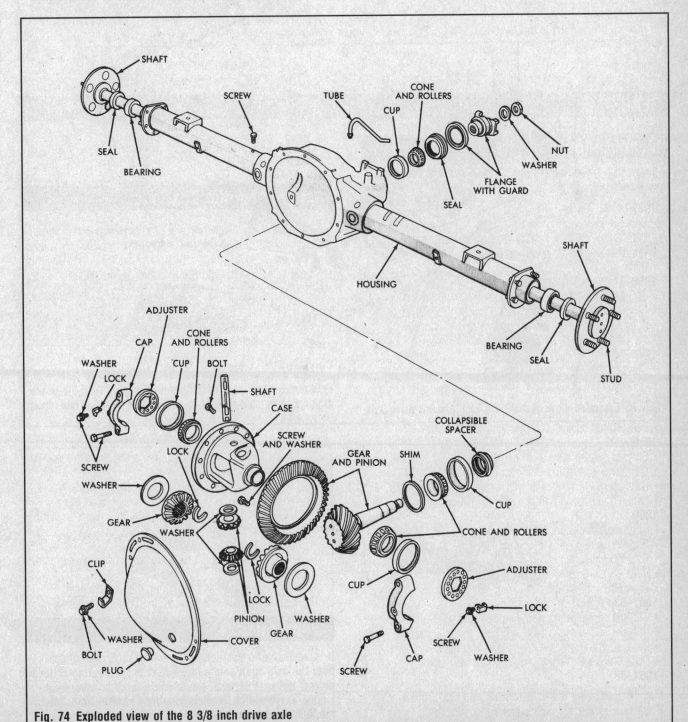

Fig. 74 Exploded view of the 8 3/8 inch drive axle

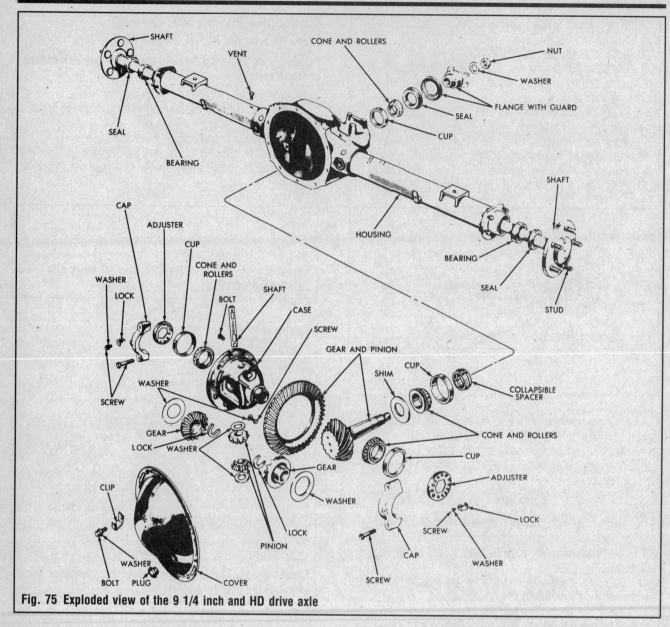

Fig. 75 Exploded view of the 9 1/4 inch and HD drive axle

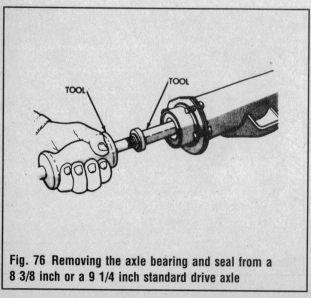

Fig. 76 Removing the axle bearing and seal from a 8 3/8 inch or a 9 1/4 inch standard drive axle

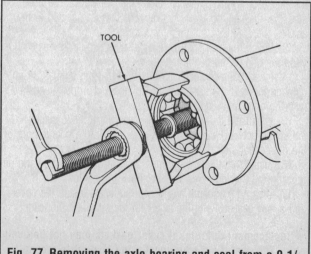

Fig. 77 Removing the axle bearing and seal from a 9 1/4 inch HD drive axle

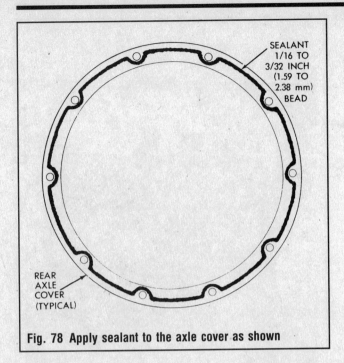

Fig. 78 Apply sealant to the axle cover as shown

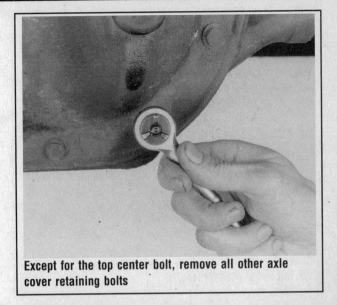

Except for the top center bolt, remove all other axle cover retaining bolts

5. Push the axle shafts toward the center of the vehicle and remove the C-locks from the grooves on the axle shafts.

6. Pull the axle shafts from the housing, being careful not to damage the bearing which remains in the housing.

7. Inspect the axle shaft bearings and replace any doubtful parts. Whenever the axle shaft is replaced, the bearings should also be replaced.

8. Remove the axle shaft seal from the bore in the housing, using the button end of the axle shaft.

9. Remove the axle shaft bearing from the housing. On the 8⅜″ and 9¼″ axle, use a slide hammer and adapter. On the 9¼″ HD axle, use a puller such as C-4828. Do not reuse the bearing or the seal.

10. Check the bearing shoulder in the axle housing for imperfections. These should be corrected with a file.

11. Clean the axle shaft bearing cavity.

12. Grease and install the axle shaft bearing in the cavity. An installer tool is recommended, although a driver can be used. Be sure that the bearing is not cocked and that it is seated firmly against the shoulder.

13. Install the axle shaft bearing seal. It should be seated beyond the end of the flange face.

14. Insert the axle shaft, making sure that the splines do not damage the seal. Be sure that the splines are properly engaged with the differential side gear splines.

15. Install the C-locks in the grooves on the axle shafts. Pull the shafts outward so that the C-locks seat in the counterbore of the differential side gears.

16. Install the differential pinion shaft through the case and pinions. Install the lockscrew and secure it in position.

17. Clean the housing and gasket surfaces. Install the cover and a new gasket. Refill the axle with the specified lubricant.

➥Replacement differential cover gaskets may not be available. The use of gel type nonsticking sealant is recommended.

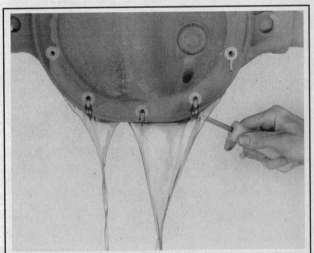

Loosen the top center bolt and gently pry the cover loose allowing the fluid to drain

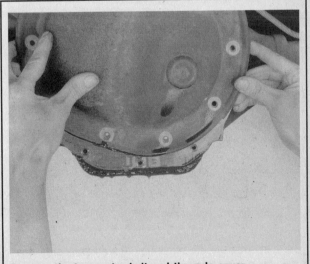

Remove the top center bolt and the axle cover

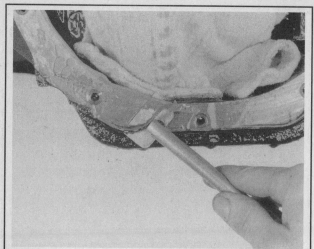

Cover the differential gears with a rag and scrape away the old cover gasket material

Rotate the differential around to gain access to the pinion shaft retaining screw. Loosen . . .

. . . and remove the screw from the differential to free the pinion shaft (arrows)

Slide the pinion shaft up, and remove it from the differential

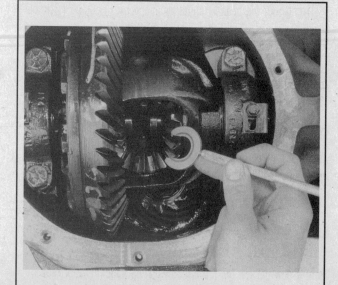

Push in on the axle, and using a magnet, withdraw the C-lock from the end of the axle

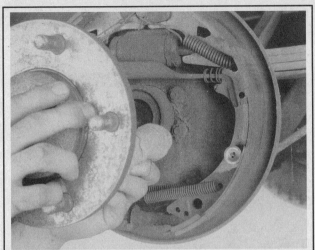

Slowly slide the axle out of the axle tube being careful not to damage the seal, if necessary

Use an axle seal puller to pry the old seal from the tube

View of the drive axle seal (arrow) with the axle shaft removed

Install the new axle seal using a seal installation driver of the proper size

Chrysler 9⅝″ Axle

1. Remove the axle shaft flange nuts.
2. Install puller screws in the threaded holes provided and tighten the screws to loosen the shaft.

➡**If threaded holes are not provided, rap the flange sharply with a soft mallet to loosen the shaft.**

3. Pull the shaft from the housing.
4. Installation is the reverse of removal. Always use a new gasket coated with sealer. Torque the flange nuts to 30–35 ft. lbs.

Dana 60, 60HD and 70 Axles
♦ **See Figure 79**

1967–84 MODELS

1. Remove the axle shaft flange nuts and washers.
2. Rap the axle shafts sharply in the center of the flange with a hammer to free the dowels.

3. Remove the tapered dowels and axle shafts. Some models are equipped with bolts rather than dowels.
4. Clean the gasket area with solvent and install a new flange gasket.
5. Install the axle shaft into the housing.
6. If the axle has an outer wheel bearing seal, install new gaskets on each side of the seal mounting flange.
7. Install the tapered dowels, lockwashers, and nuts. Torque the nuts to 40–70 ft.lbs. with 7/16″ studs and 65–105 ft.lbs. with ½″. Some axles have bolts instead of studs and tapered dowels. Bolt torque is 45–75 ft.lbs.

1985–88 MODELS

1. Remove the axle shaft flange locknuts and washers, or bolts.
2. On axles with locknuts, rap the axle shafts sharply in the center of the flange with a hammer to free the dowels.
3. Remove the tapered dowels and/or axle shafts.

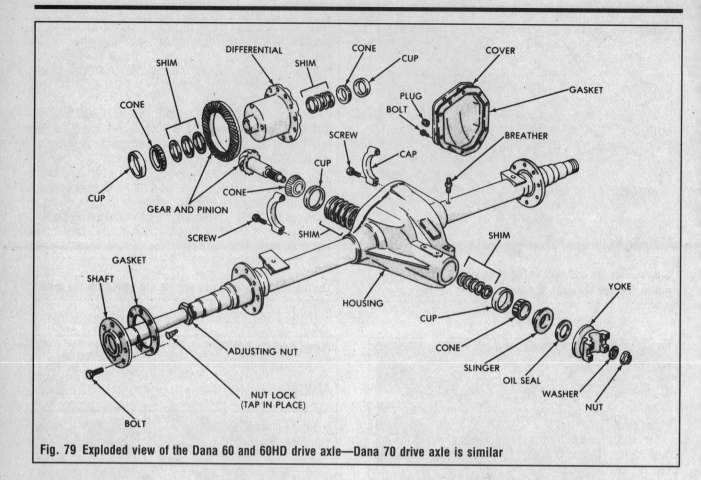

Fig. 79 Exploded view of the Dana 60 and 60HD drive axle—Dana 70 drive axle is similar

4. Clean the gasket area with solvent and install a new flange gasket.

5. Install the axle shaft into the housing.

6. If the axle has an outer wheel bearing seal, install new gaskets on each side of the seal mounting flange.

7. Install the tapered dowels, lockwashers, and nuts or Durlock® bolts. Torque the 7/16-20 nuts to 40–70 ft. lbs.; the 1/2-20 nuts to 65–105 ft. lbs.; the Durlock® bolts to 60 ft. lbs.

Full-Floating Axle Rear Wheel Bearings

REMOVAL, REPACKING, INSTALLATION & ADJUSTMENT

The wheel bearings on the 200 and 300 series full floating rear axles are packed with wheel bearing grease. Axle lubricant can also flow into the wheel hubs and bearings; however, wheel bearing grease is the primary lubricant. The wheel bearing grease provides lubrication until the axle lubricant reaches the bearings during normal operation.

1967–84 Vehicles

1. Set the parking brake and loosen the axle shaft bolts.

2. Raise the rear wheels off the floor and place jackstands under the rear axle housing so that the axle is parallel with the floor.

3. Remove the axle shaft bolts.

4. Remove the axle shaft and gaskets.

5. With the axle shaft removed, remove the gasket from the axle shaft flange studs.

6. Bend the lockwasher tab away from the locknut, and then remove the locknut, lockwasher, and the adjusting nut.

7. Remove the outer bearing cone and pull the wheel straight off the axle.

8. With a piece of hardwood or a brass drift which will just clear the outer bearing cup, drive the inner bearing cone and inner seal out of the wheel hub.

9. Wash all the old grease or axle lubricant out of the wheel hub, using a suitable solvent.

10. Wash the bearing cups and rollers and inspect them for pitting, galling, and uneven wear patterns. Inspect the roller for end wear.

11. If the bearing cups are to be replaced, drive them out with a brass drift. Install the new cups with a block of wood and hammer or press them in.

12. if the bearing cups are properly seated, a 0.0015″ (0.038mm) feeler gauge will not fit between the cup and the wheel hub. The gauge should not fit beneath the cup. Check several places to make sure the cups are squarely seated.

13. Pack each bearing cone and roller with a bearing packer or in the manner previously outlined for the front wheel bearings. Use a multipurpose wheel bearing grease.

14. Place the inner bearing cone and roller assembly in the wheel hub. Install a new inner seal in the hub with a seal installation tool.

15. Install the wheel.

16. Install the adjusting nut.

17. While rotating the wheel, tighten the adjusting nut until a slight drag is felt. Then, back off the nut ⅙ turn. This should give free rotation and little or no end-play.

18. Install the lock ring.

19. Install the outer nut. MAKE SURE THAT THE ADJUSTING NUT DOES NOT TURN WHILE TIGHTENING THE OUTER NUT! Tighten the outer nut to 35–65 ft. lbs.

20. Bend one tab of the lock ring inward to secure the adjusting nut and one tab outward to secure the outer nut. These tabs must be bent securely against a flat on each nut.

21. Install the axle shaft and new gasket or seal.

1985–88 Vehicles

1. Set the parking brake and loosen the axle shaft bolts.

2. Raise the rear wheels off the floor and place jackstands under the rear axle housing so that the axle is parallel with the floor.

3. Remove the axle shaft bolts.

4. Remove the axle shaft and gaskets.

5. With the axle shaft removed, remove the gasket from the axle shaft flange studs.

6. Bend the lockwasher tab away from the locknut, and then remove the locknut, lockwasher, and the adjusting nut.

7. Remove the outer bearing cone and pull the wheel straight off the axle.

8. With a piece of hardwood or a brass drift which will just clear the outer bearing cup, drive the inner bearing cone and inner seal out of the wheel hub.

9. Wash all the old grease or axle lubricant out of the wheel hub, using a suitable solvent.

10. Wash the bearing cups and rollers and inspect them for pitting, galling, and uneven wear patterns. Inspect the roller for end wear.

11. If the bearing cups are to be replaced, drive them out with a brass drift. Install the new cups with a block of wood and hammer or press them in.

12. If the bearing cups are properly seated, a 0.0015″ (0.038mm) feeler gauge will not fit between the cup and the wheel hub. The gauge should not fit beneath the cup. Check several places to make sure the cups are squarely seated.

13. Pack each bearing cone and roller with a bearing packer or in the manner previously outlined for the front wheel bearings. Use a multipurpose wheel bearing grease.

14. Place the inner bearing cone and roller assembly in the wheel hub. Install a new inner seal in the hub with a seal installation tool.

15. Install the wheel.

16. Install the adjusting nut.

17. While rotating the wheel, tighten the adjusting nut to 120–140 ft. lbs.

18. Back off the nut ⅓ turn (120°). This will provide 0.001–0.008″ end-play.

19. Install the lock ring onto the spindle keyway.

20. Install the axle shaft and new gasket.

ADJUSTMENT

▶ **See Figures 80 and 81**
1967–84

1. Raise and support the rear end on jackstands.

2. Remove the axle shaft.

3. Remove the outer nut and lock ring.

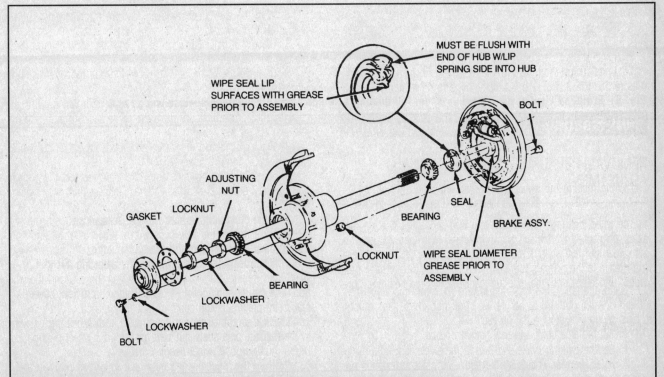

Fig. 80 Exploded view of the full floating axle and bearing components—locknut type

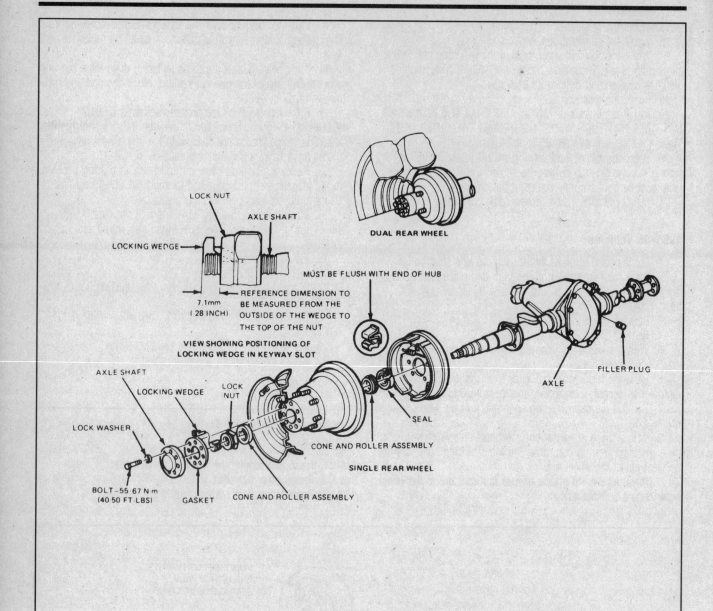

Fig. 81 Exploded view of the dual rear wheel full floating axle and related components—lock wedge type

4. While rotating the wheel, tighten the adjusting nut until a slight drag is felt. Then, back off the nut ⅙ turn. Tis should give free rotation and little or no end-play.

5. Install the lock ring.

6. Install the outer nut. MAKE SURE THAT THE ADJUSTING NUT DOES NOT TURN WHILE TIGHTENING THE OUTER NUT! Tighten the outer nut to 35–65 ft. lbs.

7. Bend one tab of the lock ring inward to secure the adjusting nut and one tab outward to secure the outer nut. These tabs must be bent securely against a flat on each nut.

8. Install the axle shaft and new gasket or seal.

1985–88

1. Raise and support the rear end on jackstands.

2. Remove the axle shaft.

3. Remove the lock ring and loosen the adjusting nut.

4. While rotating the wheel, tighten the adjusting nut to 120–140 ft. lbs.

5. Back off the nut ⅓ turn (120°). This will provide 0.001–0.008″ end-play.

6. Install the lock ring onto the spindle keyway.

7. Install the axle shaft and new gasket.

Pinion Seal

REMOVAL & INSTALLATION

Chrysler 8¾″ Axle

➡An inch-pound torque wrench and a torque wrench capable of at least 200 ft. lbs. are required for pinion seal installation.

1. Raise and safely support the vehicle with jackstands under the frame rails. Allow the axle to drop to rebound position for working clearance.
2. Remove the rear wheels and brake drums. No drag must be present on the axle.
3. Mark the companion flanges and U-joints for correct reinstallation position.
4. Remove the driveshaft.
5. Using an inch pound torque wrench and socket on the pinion yoke nut measure the amount of torque needed to maintain differential rotation through several clockwise revolutions. Record the measurement.
6. Use a suitable tool to hold the companion flange. Remove the pinion nut and washer.
7. Place a drain pan under the differential, clean the area around the seal, and mark the yoke-to-pinion relation.
8. Use a 2-jawed puller to remove the pinion.
9. Remove the seal with a small prybar.
10. Thoroughly clean the oil seal bore.

➡If you are not absolutely certain of the proper seal installation depth, the proper seal driver must be used. If the seal is misaligned or damaged during installation, it must be removed and a new seal installed.

11. Drive the new seal into place with a seal driver. Coat the seal ip with clean, waterproof wheel bearing grease.
12. Coat the splines with a small amount of wheel bearing grease and install the yoke, aligning the matchmarks. Never hammer the yoke onto the pinion!
13. Install a NEW nut on the pinion.
14. Hold the yoke with a holding tool. Tighten the pinion nut to 100 ft. lbs. Using the inch-pound torque wrench, take several readings. Continue tightening the nut until the original recorded preload reading is achieved.

➡Under no circumstances should the preload be more than 5 in. lbs. higher than the original reading.

15. Bearing preload should be uniform through several complete revolutions. If binding exists, the condition must be diagnosed and corrected. The assembly is unacceptable if the final pinion nut torque is below 170 ft. lbs. or pinion bearing preload is not correct.

✳✳ WARNING

Under no circumstances should the nut be backed off to reduce the preload reading! If the preload is exceeded, the yoke and bearing must be removed and a new collapsible spacer must be installed. The entire process of preload adjustment must be repeated.

16. Install the driveshaft using the matchmarks. Torque the nuts to 15 ft. lbs.

Chrysler 8⅜″ and 9¼″ Axles
▶ See Figures 82, 83 and 84

➡An inch-pound torque wrench and a torque wrench capable of at least 250 ft. lbs. are required for pinion seal installation.

1. Raise and safely support the vehicle with jackstands under the frame rails. Allow the axle to drop to rebound position for working clearance.
2. Remove the rear wheels and brake drums. No drag must be present on the axle.
3. Mark the companion flanges and U-joints for correct reinstallation position.
4. Remove the driveshaft.
5. Using an inch pound torque wrench and socket on the pinion yoke nut measure the amount of torque needed to maintain differential rotation through several clockwise revolutions. Record the measurement.
6. Use a suitable tool to hold the companion flange. Remove the pinion nut and washer.
7. Place a drain pan under the differential, clean the area around the seal, and mark the yoke-to-pinion relation.
8. Use a 2-jawed puller to remove the pinion.
9. Remove the seal with a small prybar.
10. Thoroughly clean the oil seal bore.

➡If you are not absolutely certain of the proper seal installation depth, the proper seal driver must be used. If the seal is misaligned or damaged during installation, it must be removed and a new seal installed.

11. Drive the new seal into place with a seal driver. Coat the seal ip with clean, waterproof wheel bearing grease.
12. Coat the splines with a small amount of wheel bearing grease and install the yoke, aligning the matchmarks. Never hammer the yoke onto the pinion!
13. Install a NEW nut on the pinion.
14. Hold the yoke with a holding tool. Tighten the pinion nut

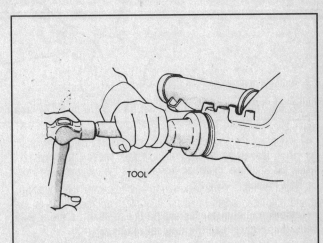

TOOL

Fig. 82 Installing the pinion seal on the 8 3/8 or 9 1/4 inch drive axle

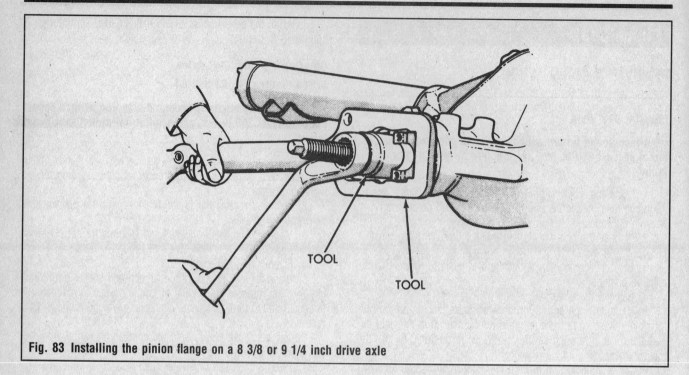

Fig. 83 Installing the pinion flange on a 8 3/8 or 9 1/4 inch drive axle

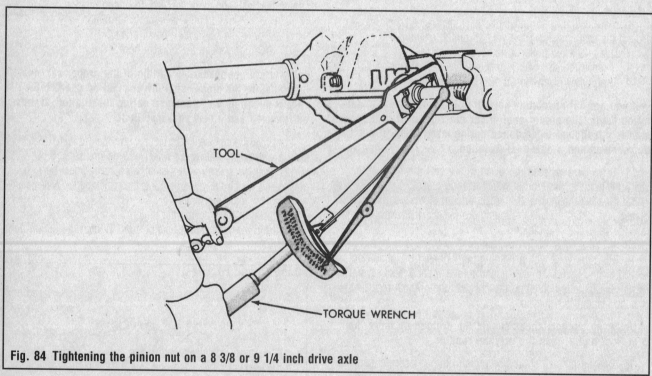

Fig. 84 Tightening the pinion nut on a 8 3/8 or 9 1/4 inch drive axle

to 210 ft. lbs. Using the inch-pound torque wrench, take several readings. Continue tightening the nut until the original recorded preload reading is achieved.

➡**Under no circumstances should the preload be more than 5 in. lbs. higher than the original reading.**

15. Bearing preload should be uniform through several complete revolutions. If binding exists, the condition must be diagnosed and corrected. The assembly is unacceptable if the final pin-

ion nut torque is below 210 ft. lbs. or pinion bearing preload is not correct.

✳✳ WARNING

Under no circumstances should the nut be backed off to reduce the preload reading! If the preload is exceeded, the yoke and bearing must be removed and a new collapsible spacer must be installed. The entire process of preload adjustment must be repeated.

16. Install the driveshaft using the matchmarks. Torque the nuts to 15 ft. lbs.

Chrysler 9⅝″ Axle

➡An inch-pound torque wrench and a torque wrench capable of at least 350 ft. lbs. are required for pinion seal installation.

1. Raise and safely support the vehicle with jackstands under the frame rails. Allow the axle to drop to rebound position for working clearance.
2. Remove the rear wheels and brake drums. No drag must be present on the axle.
3. Mark the companion flanges and U-joints for correct reinstallation position.
4. Remove the driveshaft.
5. Use a suitable tool to hold the companion flange. Remove the pinion nut and washer.
6. Place a drain pan under the differential, clean the area around the seal, and mark the yoke-to-pinion relation.
7. Use a 2-jawed puller to remove the pinion.
8. Remove the seal with a small prybar.
9. Thoroughly clean the oil seal bore.

➡If you are not absolutely certain of the proper seal installation depth, the proper seal driver must be used. If the seal is misaligned or damaged during installation, it must be removed and a new seal installed.

10. Drive the new seal into place with a seal driver. Coat the seal lip with clean, waterproof wheel bearing grease.
11. Coat the splines with a small amount of wheel bearing grease and install the yoke, aligning the matchmarks. Never hammer the yoke onto the pinion!
12. Install a NEW nut on the pinion.
13. Hold the yoke with a holding tool. Tighten the pinion nut to 325 ft. lbs. Install a new cotter pin.

✳✳ WARNING

Under no circumstances should the nut be backed off to align the cotter pin hole.

14. Install the driveshaft using the matchmarks.

Dana 60 and Dana 70 Axles

➡A torque wrench capable of at least 300 ft. lbs. is required for pinion seal installation.

1. Raise and support the truck on jackstands.
2. Allow the axle to hang freely.
3. Matchmark and disconnect the driveshaft from the front axle.
4. Using a holding tool, hold the pinion flange while removing the pinion nut.
5. Using a puller, remove the pinion flange.
6. Use a puller to remove the seal, or punch the seal out using a pin punch.
7. Thoroughly clean the seal bore and make sure that it is not damaged in any way. Coat the sealing edge of the new seal with a small amount of 80W/90 oil and drive the seal into the housing using a seal driver.

8. Coat the inside of the pinion flange with clean 80W/90 oil and install the flange onto the pinion shaft.
9. Install the nut on the pinion shaft and tighten it to 250–300 ft. lbs.
10. Connect the driveshaft.

Axle Unit

REMOVAL & INSTALLATION

▶ **See Figure 85**

Chrysler 8⅜″, 8¾″, 9¼″, 9⅝″ Axles

1. Raise and support the rear end on jackstands placed under the frame.
2. Prop the brake pedal in the UP position.
3. Remove the wheels and brake drums.
4. Disconnect the brake lines.
5. Disconnect the parking brake cables.
6. Matchmark the driveshaft and flange.
7. Disconnect the driveshaft at the flange and position it out of the way.
8. Disconnect the shock absorbers at the axle.
9. Position a floor jack under the axle to take up the weight.
10. Remove the spring U-bolt nuts and lower the axle.

To install:
11. Raise the axle into position.
12. Install the spring U-bolt nuts.
13. Connect the shock absorbers at the axle. Torque the nuts to 55 ft. lbs.
14. Connect the driveshaft at the flange.
15. Connect the parking brake cables.
16. Connect the brake lines.
17. Install the wheels and brake drums.
18. Bleed the brakes.
Observe the following torques for U-bolt nuts:
- ½-20: 62–70 ft. lbs.
- ¾-16: 175–225 ft. lbs.
- 9⁄16-18: 120–130 ft. lbs.
- ⅝-18: 175–200 ft. lbs.

Dana 60 and 70 Axles

1. Raise and support the rear end on jackstands placed under the frame.
2. Prop the brake pedal in the UP position.
3. Remove the axle shafts.
4. Remove the wheels and drums.
5. Disconnect the brake line and the flexible line connector.
6. Disconnect the parking brake cables.
7. Matchmark the driveshaft and flange.
8. Disconnect the driveshaft at the flange and position it out of the way.
9. Disconnect the shock absorbers at the axle.
10. Position a floor jack under the axle to take up the weight.
11. Remove the spring U-bolt nuts and lower the axle.

To install:
12. Raise the axle into position.
13. Install the spring U-bolt nuts. Torque the nuts to 200 ft. lbs.

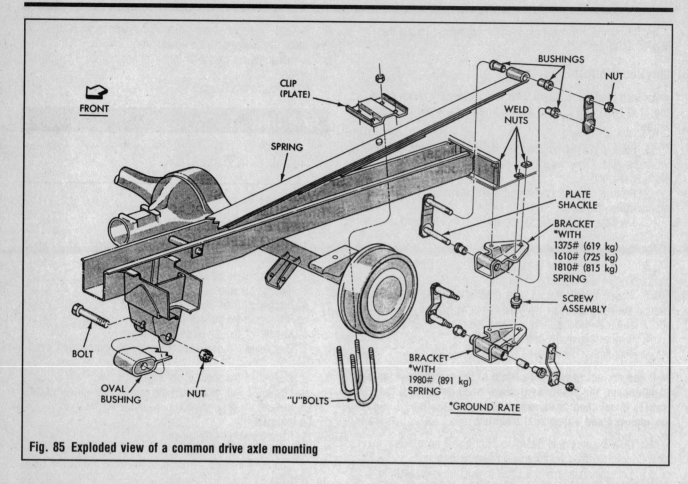

Fig. 85 Exploded view of a common drive axle mounting

14. Connect the shock absorbers at the axle. Torque the nuts to 55 ft. lbs.
15. Connect the driveshaft at the flange.
16. Connect the parking brake cables.
17. Connect the brake lines.
18. Install the drums and wheels. On 60 series axles, torque the lug nuts to 225 ft. lbs for cone-shaped nuts; 325 ft. lbs. for flanged nuts. On 70 series axles, torque the lug nuts to 400–450 ft. lbs.
19. Bleed the brakes.
20. Install the axle shafts.
21. Refill the housing with fluid.

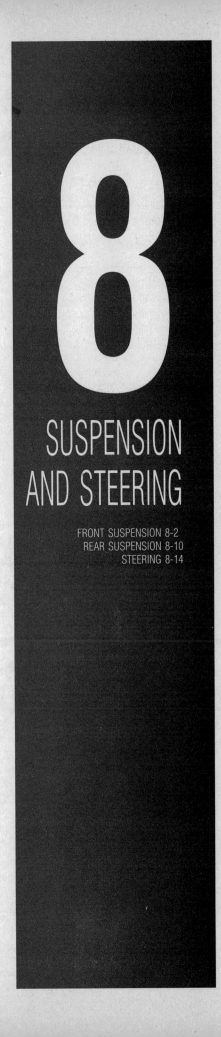

8

SUSPENSION
AND STEERING

FRONT SUSPENSION

Coil Springs

REMOVAL & INSTALLATION

♦ See Figures 1, 2 and 3

1970–73 Models

1. Raise the vehicle and support it with jackstands under the front ends of the frame rails.
2. Remove the wheel.
3. Remove the shock absorber and upper shock absorber bushing and sleeve.
4. If equipped, remove the sway bar.
5. Remove the lower control arm strut.
6. Install a spring compressor and tighten finger-tight.
7. Remove the cotter pins and ball joint nuts.
8. Install a ball joint breaker tool and turn the threaded portion of the tool to lock it against the lower stud.
9. Spread the tool to place the lower stud under pressure, then strike the steering knuckle sharply with a hammer to free the stud. Do not attempt to force the stud out of the steering knuckle with the tool.
10. Remove the tool. Slowly release the spring compressor until all tension is relieved from the spring.

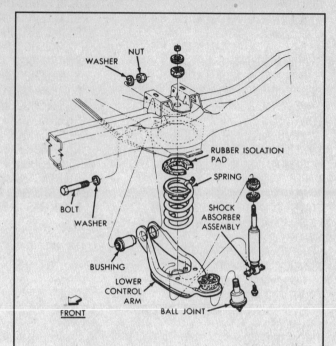

Fig. 2 Coil spring and lower control arm mounting details—1979–88 vehicles

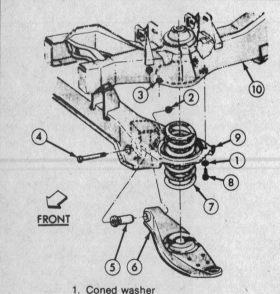

1. Coned washer
2. Nut
3. Weld nut
4. Bolt
5. Lower arm pivot bushing
6. Lower control arm assembly
7. Coil spring
8. Bolt
9. Crossmember assembly
10. Longitudinal rail

Fig. 1 Coil spring and lower control arm mounting details—1970–78 vehicles

Fig. 3 Freeing the lower ball joint with the ball joint taper breaker tool

To install:
11. Remove the spring compressor and spring.
12. Position the spring on the control arm and install the compressor.
13. Compress the spring until the ball joint is properly positioned.
14. Install the ball joint nuts and tighten them to 135 ft. lbs. for 100 and 200 series; 175 ft. lbs. for 300 series.
15. Install the strut. Tighten the mounting bolts to 85 ft. lbs.; the retainer nut to 50 ft. lbs.

16. Connect the sway bar and tighten the link to 100 in. lbs.
17. Remove the spring compressor.
18. Install the shock absorber. Tighten the upper end to 25 ft. lbs.; the lower end to 15 ft. lbs.
19. Install the wheels.

1974–84 Models

1. Block the brake pedal in the UP position.
2. Raise and support the front end on jackstands placed under the frame.
3. Remove the wheels.
4. Remove the brake calipers and suspend them out of the way. DO NOT DISCONNECT THE BRAKE LINE!
5. Remove the hub/rotor assembly.
6. Remove the brake splash shield.
7. Remove the shock absorbers.
8. Disconnect the sway bar.
9. Remove the lower control arm strut.
10. Install a spring compressor, such as tool DD-1278, tighten the nut finger-tight and back it off ½ turn.
11. Remove the ball joint nuts.
12. Using ball joint separator C-3564-A, or equivalent, spread the tool against the lower joint just endough to exert pressure then strike the knuckle sharply with a hammer to free the joint. NEVER ATTEMPT TO FORCE THE BALL JOINT OUT WITH TOOL PRESSURE ALONE! Remove the tool.
13. Slowly loosen the spring compressor until all tension is relieved from the coil.
14. Remove the compressor and spring.
To install:
15. Position the spring on the control arm and install the compressor.
16. Compress the spring until the ball joint is properly positioned.
17. Install the ball joint nuts and tighten them to 135 ft. lbs. for 100 and 200 series; 175 ft. lbs. for 300 series.
18. Install the strut. Tighten the mounting bolts to 85 ft. lbs.; the retainer nut to 50 ft. lbs.
19. Connect the sway bar and tighten the link to 100 in. lbs.
20. Remove the spring compressor.
21. Install the shock absorber. Tighten the upper end to 25 ft. lbs.; the lower end to 15 ft. lbs.
22. Install the brake splash shield. Tighten the bolts to 15 ft. lbs.
23. Install the rotor/hub assembly. Tighten the adjusting nut to 30–40 ft. lbs. while rotating the rotor. Back off the nut until it is loose. Finger-tighten the nut and install the locknut and new cotter pin.
24. Install the grease cap.
25. Install the brake caliper.
26. Install the wheels.

1985–88 Models

1. Raise and support the front end on jackstands placed under the frame.
2. Remove the wheels.
3. Remove the brake calipers and suspend them out of the way. DO NOT DISCONNECT THE BRAKE LINE! Remove the inner pad.
4. Remove the shock absorbers.
5. Disconnect the sway bar.

6. Remove the lower control arm strut.
7. Install a spring compressor, such as tool DD-1278, tighten the nut finger-tight and back it off ½ turn.
8. Remove the ball joint nuts.
9. Using ball joint separator C-3564-A, or equivalent, spread the tool against the lower joint just endough to exert pressure then strike the knuckle sharply with a hammer to free the joint. NEVER ATTEMPT TO FORCE THE BALL JOINT OUT WITH TOOL PRESSURE ALONE! Remove the tool.
10. Slowly loosen the spring compressor until all tension is relieved from the coil.
11. Remove the compressor and spring.
To install:
12. Position the spring on the control arm and install the compressor.
13. Compress the spring until the ball joint is properly positioned.
14. Install the ball joint nuts and tighten them to 135 ft. lbs.
15. Install the strut. Tighten the mounting bolts to 95 ft. lbs.; the retainer nut to 50 ft. lbs.
16. Connect the sway bar and tighten the link to 100 in. lbs.
17. Remove the spring compressor.
18. Install the shock absorber. Tighten the upper end to 25 ft. lbs.; the lower end to 15 ft. lbs.
19. Install the inboard brake pad and caliper. Tighten the retaining clips to 15 ft. lbs.
20. Install the wheels.

Leaf Springs

REMOVAL & INSTALLATION

▶ **See Figure 4**

1967–69 Models

1. Raise and support the front end on jackstands placed under the frame. The wheels should still be on the ground, but the weight should be off of the springs.
2. Remove the nuts, lockwashers and U-bolts securing the spring to the axle.
3. Remove the spring shackle bolts, shackles and front eye bolt.
4. Remove the spring.
5. Position the spring in place and install the eye bolt and nut. Do not tighten the bolt yet.
6. Install the shackles and bolts. Tighten them just enough to make them snug.
7. Make sure that the spring center bolt enters the locating hole in the axle pad.
8. Install the U-bolts, lockwashers and nuts. Make them just snug for now.
9. Lower the truck to its normal position with the weight back on the springs. Now tighten all bolts and nuts as follows:
- ½-20 U-bolt nuts: 60–70 ft. lbs.
- ¾-16 U-bolt nuts: 175–225 ft. lbs.
- 9/16-18 U-bolt nuts: 120–130 ft. lbs.
- 5/8-18 U-bolt nuts: 175–200 ft. lbs.
- 13/32-20 shackle bolts: 35–40 ft. lbs.
- 7/16-20 shackle bolts: 45–50 ft. lbs.
- Eye bolt: 150–175 ft. lbs.

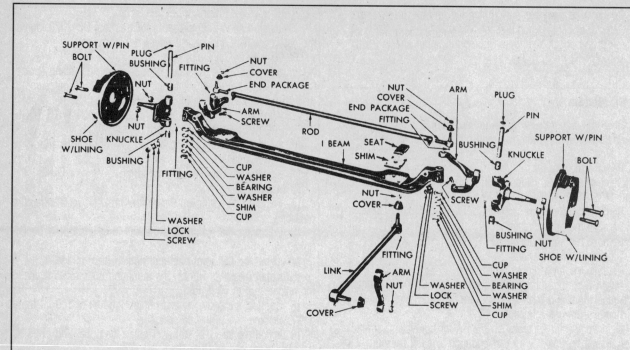

Fig. 4 Exploded view of the 1967–69 leaf spring front suspension

Shock Absorber

REMOVAL & INSTALLATION

Coil Spring Suspension

1. Raise and support the vehicle with jackstands positioned at the extreme front ends of the frame rails.
2. Remove the wheel.
3. Remove the upper nut and retainer.
4. Remove the two lower mounting bolts.
5. Remove the shock absorber.
6. When installing the shock absorber, make sure the upper

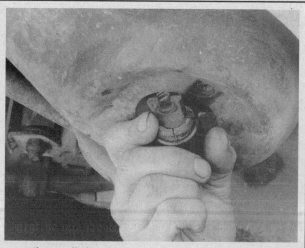

. . . then pull the shock absorber down through the opening in the control arm

busings are in the correct position. Replace any worn or cracked bushing. Tighten the top nut to 25 ft. lbs. Then, tighten the lower bolts to 15 ft. lbs.

Leaf Spring Suspension

1. Remove the two upper shock absorber bracket-to-frame bolts.
2. Remove the lower bracket nut and remove the shock absorber.
3. If new shocks are being installed, remove the upper bracket from the old shock.
4. Replace any worn or cracked bushing.
5. When installing the shock absorbers, tighten all fasteners to 50 ft. lbs.

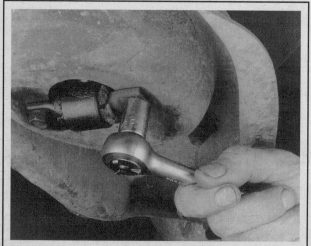

After unbolting the top shock absorber mount, remove the two lower mounting bolts . . .

Upper Control Arm

REMOVAL & INSTALLATION

▶ **See Figures 5, 6 and 7**

➡**Any time the control arm is removed, it is necessary to align the front end.**

1. Raise and support the vehicle with jackstands under the frame rails.
2. Remove the wheel.

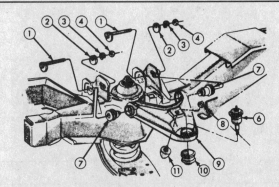

1. Cam and bolt assembly
2. Cam
3. Lock washer
4. Nut
6. Ball joint assembly
7. Bushing assembly
8. Lock nut
9. Upper control arm
10. Upper ball joint assembly
11. Bumper assembly

Fig. 5 Exploded view of the upper control arm on 1970–78 vehicles

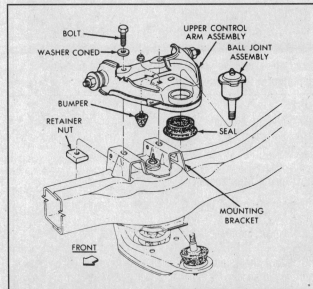

Fig. 6 Exploded view of the upper control arm on 1979–88 vehicles

Fig. 7 Freeing the upper ball joint with the ball joint taper breaker tool

3. Remove the shock absorber and shock absorber upper bushing and sleeve.
4. Install a spring compressor and tighten it finger-tight.
5. Remove the cotter pins and ball joint nuts.
6. Install a ball joint breaker and turn the threaded portion of the tool, locking it securely against the upper stud. Spread the tool enough to place the upper ball joint under pressure and strike the steering knuckle sharply to loosen the stud. Do not attempt to remove the stud from the steering knuckle with the tool.
7. Remove the tool.
8. Remove the eccentric pivot bolts, after marking their relative positions in the control arm.
9. Remove the upper control arm.
To install:
10. Install the upper control arm.
11. Install the pivot bolts and finger-tighten them for now.
12. Position the spring on the control arm and install the compressor.
13. Compress the spring until the ball joint is properly positioned.
14. Install the ball joint nuts and tighten them to 135 ft. lbs. For 1972–74 300 series trucks, the torque is 175 ft. lbs.
15. Install new cotter pins.
16. Remove the spring compressor.
17. Install the shock absorber. Tighten the upper end to 25 ft. lbs.; the lower end to 15 ft. lbs.
18. Install the wheels.
19. Lower the truck to the ground.
20. Tighten the pivot bolts to 70 ft. lbs.
21. Have the front end alignment checked.

Lower Control Arm

REMOVAL & INSTALLATION

1. Follow the procedure outlined under Coil Spring Removal and Installation.
2. Remove the mounting bolt from the crossmember.
3. Remove the lower control arm from the vehicle.

STEERING AND FRONT SUSPENSION COMPONENT LOCATIONS – COIL SPRING MODELS

1. Upper ball joint
2. Upper control arm
3. Outer tie rod end
4. Lower ball joint and grease fitting
5. Tie rod end clamp
6. Sway bar end link
7. Lower shock absorber mount
8. Front coil spring
9. Idler arm
10. Lower control arm
11. Inner tie rod end
12. Drag link
13. Center link

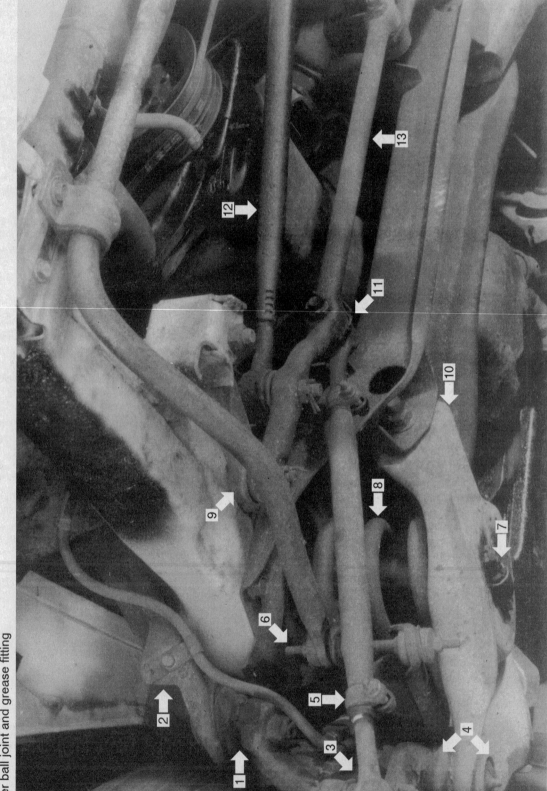

4. When installing the control arm, install the crossmember bolt finger-tight. After the vehicle has been lowered to the ground, tighten the mounting bolt to 225 ft. lbs.

Lower Ball Joint

REMOVAL & INSTALLATION

1. Remove the lower control arm.
2. Remove the ball joint seal.
3. Using tool C-4212 or an arbor press and a sleeve, press the ball joint from the control arm.
4. Installation is the reverse of removal. Be sure that the ball joint is fully seated. Install a new ball joint seal.
5. Install the lower control arm. Be sure to install the ball joint cotter pins.

Upper Ball Joint

REMOVAL & INSTALLATION

1. Install a jack under the outer end of the lower control arm and raise the vehicle.
2. Remove the wheel.
3. Remove the ball joint nuts. Using a ball joint breaker, loosen the upper ball joint.
4. Unscrew the ball joint from the control arm.
5. Screw a new ball joint into the control arm and tighten to 125 ft. lbs.
6. Install the new ball joint seal, using a 2 in. socket. Be sure that the seal is seated on the ball joint housing.
7. Insert the ball joint into the steering knuckle and install the ball joint nuts. Tighten the nuts to 135 ft. lbs. and install the cotter pins. On 1972–74 300 series, the torque is 175 ft. lbs.
8. Install the wheel and lower the truck to the ground.

Lower Control Arm Strut

REMOVAL & INSTALLATION

♦ **See Figures 8 and 9**

1. Raise and support the front end on jackstands.
2. Using a small drift and hammer, drive out the spring pin from the front end of the strut.
3. Remove the nut, retainer and bushing.
4. Remove the rear mounting bolts along with the jounce bumper and bracket.
5. Installation is the reverse of removal. Torque the mounting

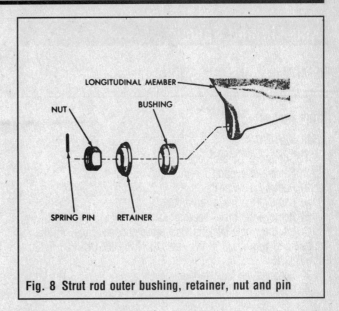

Fig. 8 Strut rod outer bushing, retainer, nut and pin

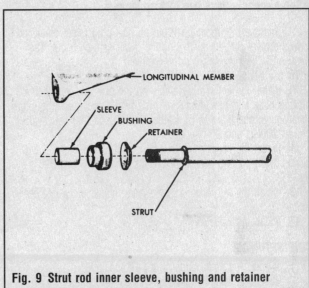

Fig. 9 Strut rod inner sleeve, bushing and retainer

bracket bolts to 85 ft. lbs. for 1972–76 models; 95 ft. lbs. for 1977–88 models. Torque the retainer nut to 50 ft. lbs.

Sway Bar

REMOVAL & INSTALLATION

1. Disconnect the bar at each end link.
2. Remove the bolts from the frame mounting brackets.
3. Remove the sway bar.
Installation is the reverse of removal. Tighten the frame bracket bolts to 23 ft. lbs.; the end links to 100 in. lbs.

Knuckle and Spindle

REMOVAL & INSTALLATION

Drum Brakes

LEAF SPRINGS

1. Support the brake pedal in the UP position.
2. Raise and support the front end on jackstands.
3. Remove the wheels.
4. Remove the brake drum/hub.
5. Remove the brake backing plate bolts.
6. Lift the whole backing plate/brake shoe assembly off the knuckle and wire it out of the way. DO NOT DISCONNECT THE BRAKE LINE!
7. Separate the knuckle and knuckle arm.
8. Remove the pivot pin locking screw or pin.

➡️**Some models have two locking screws.**

9. Remove the upper pivot pin oil seal plug (steel disc) and drive the pivot pin down, forcing the lower seal plug out. The pivot thrust bearing can now be removed.

To install:

10. Install the knuckle assembly on the axle and install the backing plate and new dust seal. Install the upper plate mounting bolts and torque them to 55 ft. lbs. on 100 and 200 series; 85 ft. lbs. on 200HD and 300 series.
11. Install the lower mounting bolts and torque them to 210 ft. lbs. on 100 and 200 series; 225 ft. lbs. on 200HD and 300 series.
12. Install the hub/drum assembly and adjust the wheel bearings.
13. Install the wheels.

COIL SPRINGS

1. support the brake pedal in the UP position.
2. Raise and support the front end on jackstands.
3. Remove the wheels.
4. Remove the brake drum/hub.
5. Support the lower control arm with a floor jack.
6. Disconnect the tie rod from the knuckle.
7. Remove the brake backing plate bolts.
8. Lift the whole backing plate/brake shoe assembly off the knuckle and wire it out of the way. DO NOT DISCONNECT THE BRAKE LINE!
9. Re-install and tighten the lower backing plate mounting bolts in the steering knuckle and knuckle arm.
10. Disconnect the ball joints from the knuckle and knuckle arm.
11. Separate the knuckle and knuckle arm.

To install:

12. Install the knuckle assembly on the control arms and install the backing plate and new dust seal. Install the upper plate mounting bolts and torque them to 55 ft. lbs. on 100 and 200 series; 85 ft. lbs. on 200HD and 300 series.
13. Install the lower mounting bolts and torque them to 210 ft. lbs. on 100 and 200 series; 225 ft. lbs. on 200HD and 300 series.
14. Connect the ball joints. Torque the nuts to 135 ft. lbs. on

100 and 200 series. On 300 series, the torque is 175 ft. lbs. Always use new cotter pins.

15. Connect the tie rod end and torque the nut to 45 ft. lbs. on the 100 and 200 series; 55 ft. lbs. on the 300 series. Install a new cotter pin.
16. Install the hub/drum assembly and adjust the wheel bearings.
17. Install the wheels.

Disc Brakes

1. Support the brake pedal in the UP position.
2. Raise and support the front end on jackstands.
3. Remove the wheels.
4. Remove the brake calipers and suspend them out of the way. DO NOT DISCONNECT THE BRAKE LINE! Remove the inner pad.
5. Remove the hub/rotor assembly.
6. Remove the brake splash shield.
7. Support the lower control arm with a floor jack.
8. Disconnect the tie rod from the knuckle.
9. Disconnect the ball joints from the knuckle.
10. Unbolt the brake adapter from the knuckle.

To install:

11. Install the adapter on the knuckle. Torque the bolts to 100 ft. lbs.
12. Align the knuckle arm and the knuckle. Torque the mounting bolts to 215 ft. lbs.
13. Install the knuckle assembly on the control arms and connect the ball joints. Torque the nuts to 135 ft. lbs. On 1972–74 300 series, the torque is 175 ft. lbs. Always use new cotter pins.
14. Connect the tie rod end and torque the nut to 45 ft. lbs. Install a new cotter pin.
15. Install the splash shield and new dust seal. Torque the bolts to 16 ft. lbs.
16. Install the hub/rotor assembly and adjust the wheel bearings.
17. Install the caliper and pads.
18. Install the wheels.

Front End Alignment

▶ **See Figure 10**

STEERING AXIS INCLINATION

➡️**Independent Front Suspension Only**

Steering axis inclination is the number of degrees that the spindle support centerline is tilted from the true vertical as viewed from the front. It has a fixed relationship with camber and does not change except in the event of damage to a spindle or ball joint. The angle is not adjustable and damaged parts must be replaced.

CAMBER

Camber is expressed as the number of degrees that the top of the wheel is tilted outward or inward from the true vertical when viewed from the front. Inward tilt is negative camber and outward

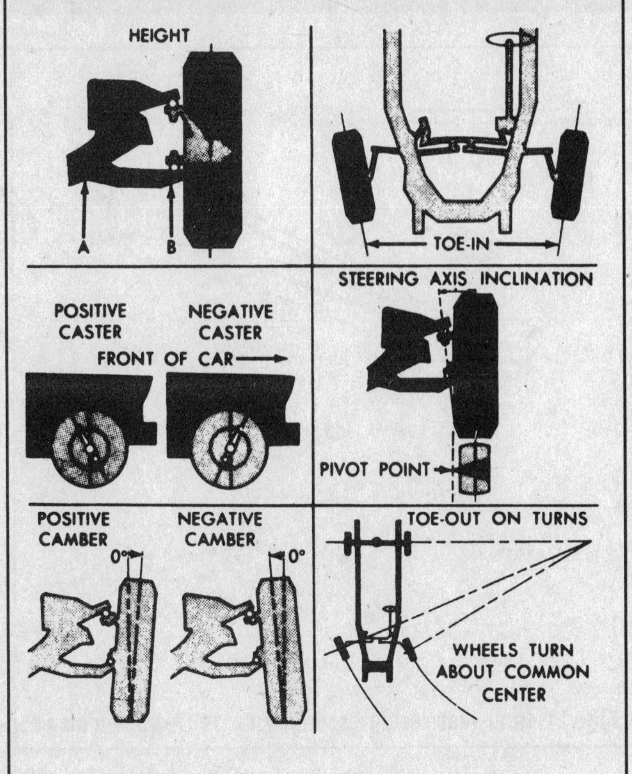

Fig. 10 Examples of the various alignment angles

tilt is positive camber. Excessive camber causes premature tire wear; negative camber causes wear on the inside of the tire and positive camber causes the tire to wear on the outside edge.

Camber is adjusted by means of eccentrics at the inner end of the upper control arms. Camber cannot be accurately measured without professional equipment.

CASTER

Caster is the backward or forward tilt from the vertical of the steering knuckle centerline at the top, measured in degrees. A steering knuckle centerline tilted backward has positive (+) caster, while one tilted forward has negative (−) caster. Positive caster produces greater directional stability and requires greater steering effort, since it increases the self-centering effect at the steering wheel.

Caster is adjusted by means of eccentrics at the inner end of the upper control arms. Caster cannot be measured accurately without professional equipment.

TOE-IN

Toe-in is the amount measured in inches, that the centerlines of the wheels are closer together at the front than at the rear. Toe-in must be checked after caster and camber have been adjusted, but it can be adjusted without disturbing the other two settings. You can make this adjustment without special equipment, if you make careful measurements. The adjustment is made at the tie-rod sleeves. The wheels must be straight-ahead.

1. Toe-in can be determined by measuring the distance between the centers of the tire treads, front and rear. If the tread pattern makes this impossible, you can measure between the edges of the wheel rims, but make sure to move the truck forward and measure in a couple of places to avoid errors caused by bent rims and wheel runout.
2. Loosen the clamp bolts on the tie rod sleeves.
3. Rotate the sleeves equally (in opposite directions) to obtain the correct measurement. If the sleeves are not adjusted equally, the steering will be crooked. If the steering wheel is already crooked, it can be straightened by turning the sleeves equally in the same direction.
4. When the adjustment is complete, tighten the clamps.

Wheel Alignment Specifications

Years	Model	Caster (deg.) Range	Caster (deg.) Pref.	Camber (deg.) Range	Camber (deg.) Pref.	Toe-in (in.)	Turning Angle (deg.)
1967–69	All	5½P to 6½P	6P	1¼P to 1¾P	1½P	1/16	①
1970–75	MS	0 to 1P	½P	0 to ½P	¼P	1/16	33
	PS	1¾P to 2¾P	2¼P	0 to ½P	¼P	1/16	33
1976–77	MS	0 to 1P	½P	¼P to ¾P	½P	1/16	35
	PS	1¾P to 2¾P	2¼P	¼P to ¾P	½P	1/16	33
1978–79	MS	½N to 1½P	½P	0 to 1P	½P	1/8	—
	PS	1¼P to 3¼P	2¼P	0 to 1P	½P	1/8	—
1980–83	All	1¼P to 3¼P	2¼P	0 to 1P	½P	1/8	—
1984–87	All	1¼P to 3¾P	2½P	¼N to 1P	3/8P	1/8	—
1988	All	1¼P to 3¾P	2½P	4/5N to 4/5P	0	0	—

MS: Manual Steering
PS: Power Steering
① 3,800 lb. GVW: 37
All others: 33

REAR SUSPENSION

Leaf Springs

REMOVAL & INSTALLATION

♦ **See Figures 11 thru 16**

1. Raise the truck and support the rear with jackstands under the frame. Be sure that the front wheels are chocked and that the parking brake is set. The wheels should be touching the floor, but the weight must be off of the springs.

2. Remove the nuts, lockwashers and U-bolts that hold the axle to the springs.

3. Remove the front pivot bolt.

4. Remove the rear shackle bolt nuts and the rear shackle plate.

5. Remove the spring.

To install:

6. Position the spring in place and install the eye bolt and nut. Do not tighten the bolt yet.

7. Install the shackles and bolts. Tighten them just enough to make them snug.

8. Make sure that the spring center bolt enters the locating hole in the axle pad. On headless-type spring bolts, install the

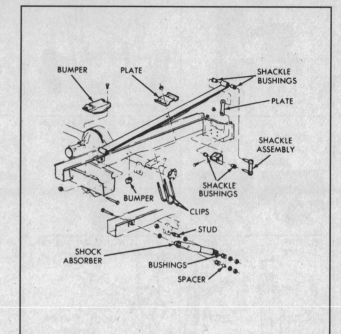

Fig. 11 Rear leaf spring assembly on 1967–69 vehicles

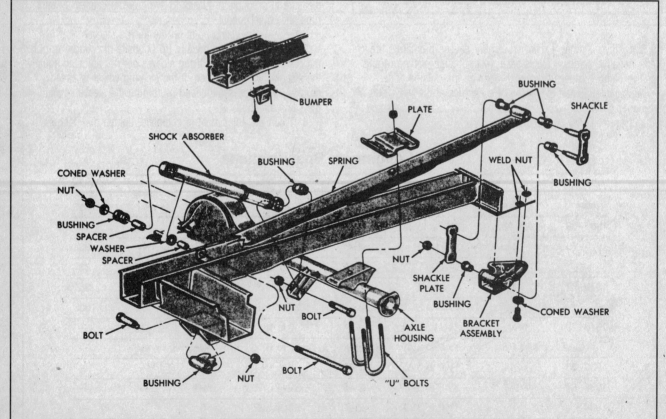

Fig. 12 Rear leaf spring assembly for 1970–78 vehicles—all models except 300 series

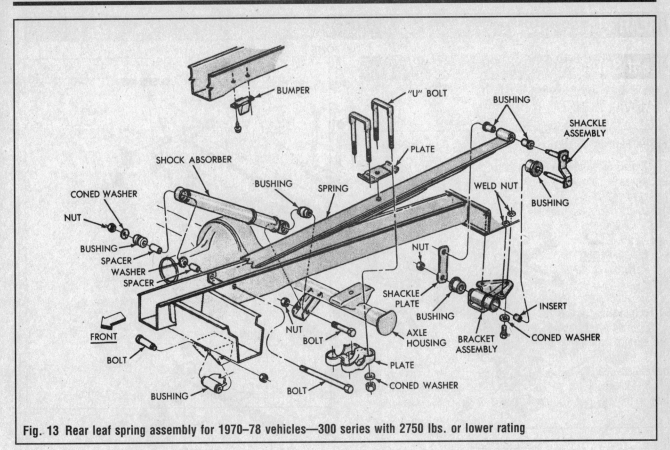

Fig. 13 Rear leaf spring assembly for 1970–78 vehicles—300 series with 2750 lbs. or lower rating

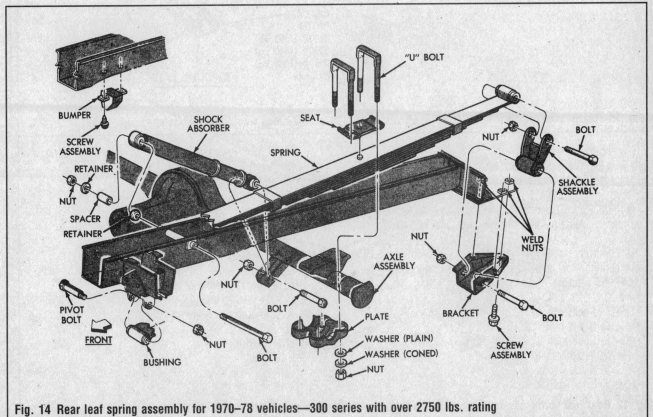

Fig. 14 Rear leaf spring assembly for 1970–78 vehicles—300 series with over 2750 lbs. rating

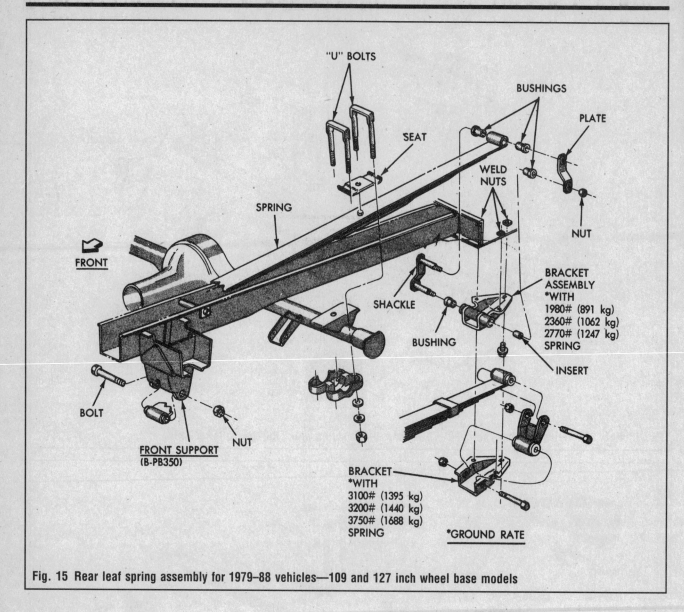

Fig. 15 Rear leaf spring assembly for 1979–88 vehicles—109 and 127 inch wheel base models

bolts with the lock groove lined up with the lockbolt hole in the bracket. Install the lockbolt and tighten the lockbolt nut. Install the lubrication fittings.

9. Install the U-bolts, lockwashers and nuts. Make them just snug for now. Align the auxiliary spring parallel with the main spring.

10. Lower the truck to its normal position with the weight back on the springs. Now tighten all bolts and nuts as follows:

1967–68 Models
- ½-20 U-bolt nuts: 60–70 ft. lbs.
- ¾-16 U-bolt nuts: 175–225 ft. lbs.
- ⁹⁄₁₆-18 U-bolt nuts: 120–130 ft. lbs.
- ⁵⁄₈-18 U-bolt nuts: 175–200 ft. lbs.
- ¹³⁄₃₂-20 shackle bolts: 35–40 ft. lbs.
- ⁷⁄₁₆-20 shackle bolts: 45–50 ft. lbs.
- Eye bolt: 150–175 ft. lbs.

1969–73 Models
- U-bolt nuts:
B100—50–80 ft. lbs.
All others—100–150 ft. lbs.

- Shackle bolts:
B100—65–105 ft. lbs.
All others—125–175 ft. lbs.
- Eye bolt:
B100—65–105 ft. lbs.
All others—125–175 ft. lbs.

1974 Models
- U-bolt nuts:
100 series—85 ft. lbs.
200/300—115 ft. lbs.
- Shackle bolts: 80 ft. lbs.
- Eye Bolt: 80 ft. lbs.

1975–78 Models
- U-bolt nuts:
½-20 nuts—65 ft. lbs.
⁹⁄₁₆-18 nuts—110 ft. lbs.
- Shackle bolts and eye bolts:
½-20—93 ft. lbs.
⁵⁄₈-18—160 ft. lbs.
¾-16—200 ft. lbs.

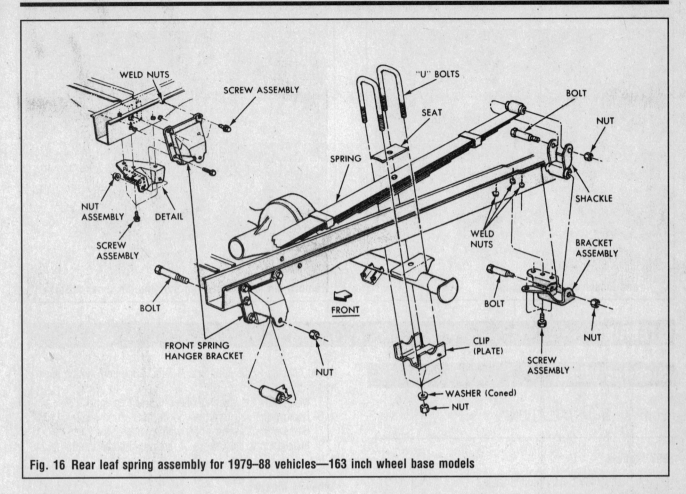

Fig. 16 Rear leaf spring assembly for 1979–88 vehicles—163 inch wheel base models

1979–88 Models

- U-bolt nuts:

$1/2$-20 nuts—65 ft. lbs.

$9/16$-18 nuts—110 ft. lbs.

- Shackle bolts and eye bolts:

$1/2$-20—95 ft. lbs.

$5/8$-18—125 ft. lbs.

$3/4$-16—155 ft. lbs.

Shock Absorbers

REMOVAL & INSTALLATION

1. Jack and support the truck.
2. Remove the nut from the stud or bolt at the upper end. Remove the stud or bolt from the upper end.
3. Remove the lower nut at the bushing end.
4. Pivot the shock absorber and washers from the lower stud.
5. Remove the shock absorber and washers from the lower stud.
6. Installation is the reverse of removal. Purge the new shock of air by extending it in its normal position and compressing it while inverted. Do this several times. It is normal for there to be more resistance to extension than to compression. Torque the nuts to 60 ft. lbs.

Unbolt the top shock absorber mount . . .

. . . and loosen the lower mount

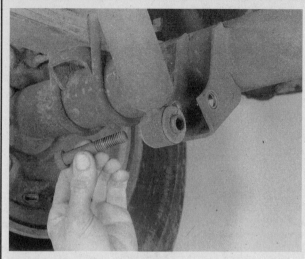

Remove the lower mounting bolt and the shock absorber

STEERING

Steering Wheel

REMOVAL & INSTALLATION

1967 Models

1. Disconnect the battery ground cable.
2. Rotate the horn button ¼ turn counterclockwise and remove the button, rubber grommet and horn contact ring.
3. Disconnect the horn wire.
4. Remove the three screws and spacers that attach the horn button housing to the column and remove the horn button and housing.
5. Matchmark the steering wheel hub and column.
6. Remove the nut from the end of the steering shaft.
7. Remove the steering wheel with a puller.
8. Installation is the reverse of removal. Tighten the nut to 24 ft. lbs.

1968–71 Models
▶ **See Figure 17**

1. Disconnect the battery ground cable.
2. Pull the horn button off its spring clips.

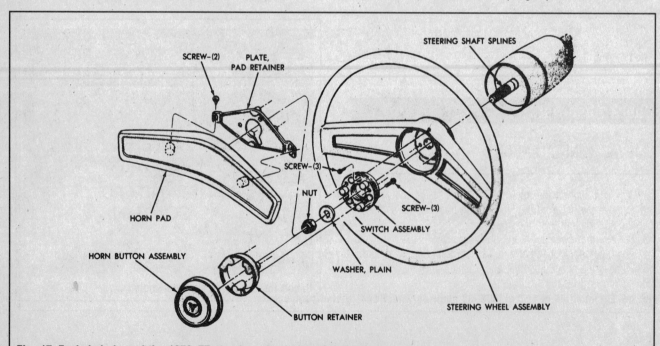

Fig. 17 Exploded view of the 1970–77 steering wheel and related components

3. Disconnect the horn wire.

4. Remove the 3 screws and lift out the horn switch.

5. Matchmark the steering wheel and shaft.

6. Remove the steering wheel retaining nut from the shaft.

7. Using a puller, remove the steering wheel.

8. When installing the steering wheel, align the matchmarks and torque the nut to 27 ft. lbs.

1972–77 Models

▶ **See Figure 17**

1. Disconnect the battery ground cable.

2. Remove the horn button by removing the two screws from underneath.

3. Disconnect the horn wire from the horn switch terminal.

4. Remove three screws and lift out the horn switch and button or pad retainer assembly.

5. Back the steering wheel retaining nut off the top of the shaft.

6. Install a steering wheel puller and draw the steering wheel from the steering shaft splines.

7. Remove the steering wheel nut and pull the steering wheel off the steering shaft.

8. Installation is the reverse of removal. Tighten the nut to 27 ft. lbs.

1978–88 Models

▶ **See Figure 18**

1. Disconnect the battery ground cable.

2. Working through the access holes in the back of the wheel, push the horn pad off. DO NOT PRY THE PAD OFF!

3. Disconnect the horn wire.

4. Matchmark the steering wheel and shaft.

5. Remove the steering wheel retaining nut.

6. Using a puller, remove the steering wheel from the shaft. NEVER HAMMER THE SHAFT TO FREE THE WHEEL!

7. Installation is the reverse of removal. Tighten the nut to 60 ft. lbs. on models through 1984; 45 ft. lbs. on 1985–88 models.

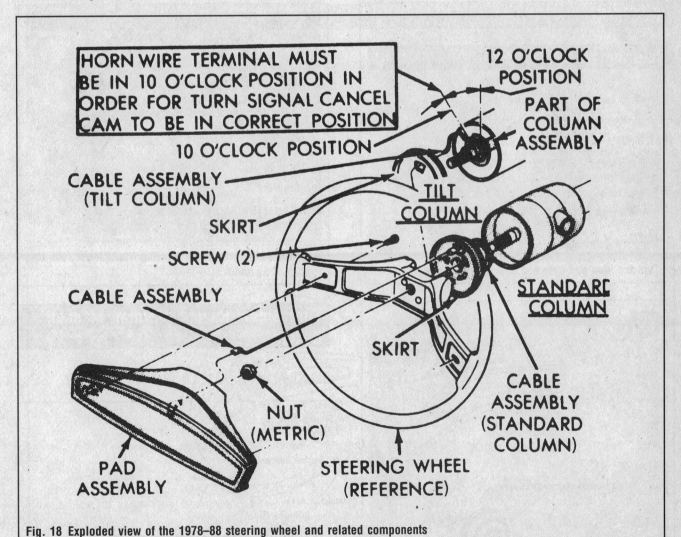

Fig. 18 Exploded view of the 1978–88 steering wheel and related components

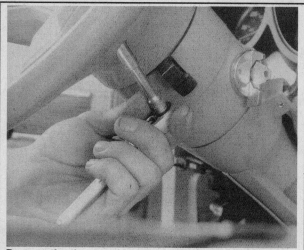

Remove the two steering wheel-to-horn pad retaining bolts

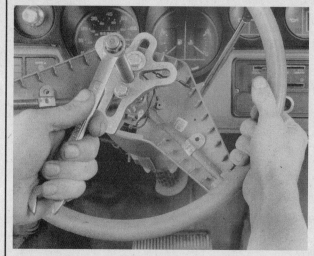

Using a puller, remove the steering wheel from the shaft

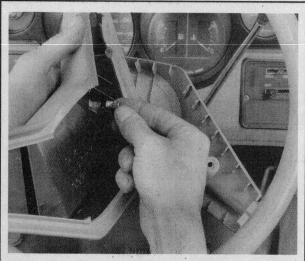

Turn the horn pad over and unplug the horn wire

Once the puller breaks the steering wheel loose, you can remove it by hand

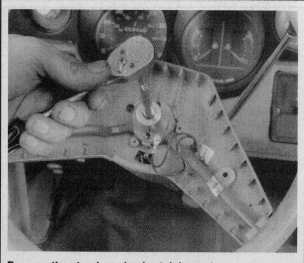

Remove the steering wheel retaining nut

Turn Signal/Hazard Warning Flasher Switch

REMOVAL & INSTALLATION

1967 Models

1. Remove the steering wheel.
2. Unscrew the turn signal lever.
3. Remove the column tube upper spring and spacer.
4. Disconnect the turn signal wires at the lower connector.
5. Remove the 2 switch hold-down screws and pull the switch and wiring from the column.
6. Installation is the reverse of removal.

1968–88 Models

◆ **See Figures 19, 20 and 21**

STANDARD COLUMNS

1. Remove the steering wheel.
2. Remove the turn signal lever retaining screw and remove the lever.
3. Disconnect the turn signal switch wiring at the lower connector.
4. Remove the wiring cover.
5. Remove the snapring from the upper end of the shaft.
6. Remove the screws retaining the turn signal switch and upper bearing.
7. Lift out the turn signal switch and wiring.
8. Installation is the reverse of removal.

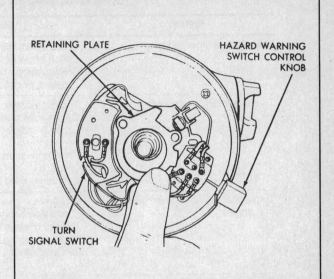

Fig. 21 Turning signal switch components—1983–88 models shown

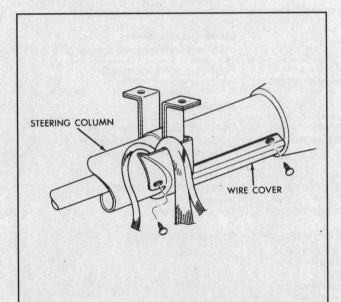

Fig. 19 Steering column wiring cover—1970–82 shown

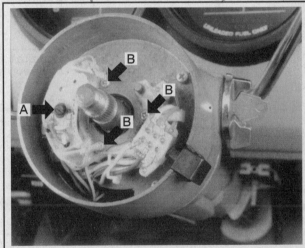

Turn signal lever retaining screw (A) and the three switch retaining screws (B) for standard columns

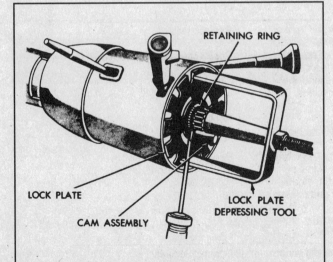

Fig. 20 Lock plate removal using the depressing tool

TILT COLUMNS

1. Remove the steering wheel.
2. Depress the lock plate with tool C-4156, or equivalent, just enough to remove the retaining ring, and pry the retaining ring out of the groove.
3. Remove the lock plate and upper bearing spring.
4. Place the turn signal switch in the right turn position.
5. Remove the screw which attaches the link between the turn signal switch and wiper/washer switch pivot.
6. Remove the screw which attaches the hazard switch knob.
7. Remove the 3 screws securing the turn signal switch.
8. Gently pull the switch and wiring from the column.
9. Installation is the reverse of removal.

Troubleshooting the Turn Signal Switch

Problem	Cause	Solution
Turn signal will not cancel	• Loose switch mounting screws • Switch or anchor bosses broken • Broken, missing or out of position detent, or cancelling spring	• Tighten screws • Replace switch • Reposition springs or replace switch as required
Turn signal difficult to operate	• Turn signal lever loose • Switch yoke broken or distorted • Loose or misplaced springs • Foreign parts and/or materials in switch • Switch mounted loosely	• Tighten mounting screws • Replace switch • Reposition springs or replace switch • Remove foreign parts and/or material • Tighten mounting screws
Turn signal will not indicate lane change	• Broken lane change pressure pad or spring hanger • Broken, missing or misplaced lane change spring • Jammed wires	• Replace switch • Replace or reposition as required • Loosen mounting screws, reposition wires and retighten screws
Turn signal will not stay in turn position	• Foreign material or loose parts impeding movement of switch yoke • Defective switch	• Remove material and/or parts • Replace switch
Hazard switch cannot be pulled out	• Foreign material between hazard support cancelling leg and yoke	• Remove foreign material. No foreign material impeding function of hazard switch—replace turn signal switch.
No turn signal lights	• Inoperative turn signal flasher • Defective or blown fuse • Loose chassis to column harness connector • Disconnect column to chassis connector. Connect new switch to chassis and operate switch by hand. If vehicle lights now operate normally, signal switch is inoperative • If vehicle lights do not operate, check chassis wiring for opens, grounds, etc.	• Replace turn signal flasher • Replace fuse • Connect securely • Replace signal switch • Repair chassis wiring as required
Instrument panel turn indicator lights on but not flashing	• Burned out or damaged front or rear turn signal bulb • If vehicle lights do not operate, check light sockets for high resistance connections, the chassis wiring for opens, grounds, etc. • Inoperative flasher • Loose chassis to column harness connection • Inoperative turn signal switch • To determine if turn signal switch is defective, substitute new switch into circuit and operate switch by hand. If the vehicle's lights operate normally, signal switch is inoperative.	• Replace bulb • Repair chassis wiring as required • Replace flasher • Connect securely • Replace turn signal switch • Replace turn signal switch
Stop light not on when turn indicated	• Loose column to chassis connection • Disconnect column to chassis connector. Connect new switch into system without removing old.	• Connect securely • Replace signal switch

Troubleshooting the Turn Signal Switch (cont.)

Problem	Cause	Solution
Stop light not on when turn indicated (cont.)	Operate switch by hand. If brake lights work with switch in the turn position, signal switch is defective.	
	• If brake lights do not work, check connector to stop light sockets for grounds, opens, etc.	• Repair connector to stop light circuits using service manual as guide
Turn indicator panel lights not flashing	• Burned out bulbs	• Replace bulbs
	• High resistance to ground at bulb socket	• Replace socket
	• Opens, ground in wiring harness from front turn signal bulb socket to indicator lights	• Locate and repair as required
Turn signal lights flash very slowly	• High resistance ground at light sockets	• Repair high resistance grounds at light sockets
	• Incorrect capacity turn signal flasher or bulb	• Replace turn signal flasher or bulb
	• If flashing rate is still extremely slow, check chassis wiring harness from the connector to light sockets for high resistance	• Locate and repair as required
	• Loose chassis to column harness connection	• Connect securely
	• Disconnect column to chassis connector. Connect new switch into system without removing old. Operate switch by hand. If flashing occurs at normal rate, the signal switch is defective.	• Replace turn signal switch
Hazard signal lights will not flash— turn signal functions normally	• Blow fuse	• Replace fuse
	• Inoperative hazard warning flasher	• Replace hazard warning flasher in fuse panel
	• Loose chassis-to-column harness connection	• Conect securely
	• Disconnect column to chassis connector. Connect new switch into system without removing old. Depress the hazard warning lights. If they now work normally, turn signal switch is defective.	• Replace turn signal switch
	• If lights do not flash, check wiring harness "K" lead for open between hazard flasher and connector. If open, fuse block is defective	• Repair or replace brown wire or connector as required

Ignition Switch

REMOVAL & INSTALLATION

Standard Columns

1. Remove the steering wheel.
2. Remove the turn signal switch.
3. Remove the retaining screw and lift the ignition lock cylinder lamp out of the way.
4. Remove the bearing housing.
5. Remove the coil spring.
6. Remove the lock plate from the shaft.

7. Remove the 2 retaining screws and lift the lock lever guide plate to expose the lock cylinder release hole.
8. Insert the key and place the lock cylinder in the **LOCK** position. Remove the key.
9. Insert a thin punch into the lock cylinder release hole and push inward to release the spring-loaded lock retainer. At the same time, pull the lock cylinder out of the column.
10. Remove the 3 retaining screws and lift out the ignition switch.

To install:

11. Position the ignition switch in the center detent position (OFF).
12. Place the shift lever in PARK.
13. Feed the wires down through the space between the hous-

ing and jacket. Position the switch in the housing and install the 3 retaining screws.

14. Place the lock cylinder in the **LOCK** position and press it into place in the column. It will snap into position.

15. The remainder of assembly is the reverse of disassembly.

Tilt Columns

1. Remove the steering wheel.
2. Remove the tilt lever and turn signal lever.
3. If equipped, remove the turn signal lever.
4. Remove the turn signal switch.
5. Using the key, place the lock cylinder in the **LOCK** position. Remove the key.
6. Insert a thin punch in the slot next to the switch mounting screw boss and depress the spring latch at the bottom of the slot. Hold the spring latch depressed and pull the lock cylinder out of the column.

7. Place the ignition switch in the **ACCESSORY** position and remove the mounting screws. Lift off the switch. The **ACCESSORY** position is the one opposite the spring-loaded end position.

To install:

8. First, install the lock cylinder. Place the cylinder in the LOCK position and push it into the housing. It will snap into place.

9. Rotate the lock cylinder to the **ACCESSORY** position.

10. Fit the actuator rod in the slider hole and position the switch on the column. Insert the mounting screws, but don't tighten them yet.

11. Push the switch gently down the column to remove all lash from the actuator rod. Tighten the mounting screws. Make sure that you didn't take the switch out of the **ACCESSORY** detent!

12. The remainder of installation is the reverse of removal.

Troubleshooting the Ignition Switch

Problem	Cause	Solution
Ignition switch electrically inoperative	· Loose or defective switch connector	· Tighten or replace connector
	· Feed wire open (fusible link)	· Repair or replace
	· Defective ignition switch	· Replace ignition switch
Engine will not crank	· Ignition switch not adjusted properly	· Adjust switch
Ignition switch wil not actuate mechanically	· Defective ignition switch	· Replace switch
	· Defective lock sector	· Replace lock sector
	· Defective remote rod	· Replace remote rod
Ignition switch cannot be adjusted correctly	· Remote rod deformed	· Repair, straighten or replace

Ignition Lock Cylinder

REMOVAL & INSTALLATION

Standard Columns

1. Remove the steering wheel.
2. Remove the turn signal switch.
3. Remove the retaining screw and lift the ignition lock cylinder lamp out of the way.
4. Remove the bearing housing.
5. Remove the coil spring.
6. Remove the lock plate from the shaft.
7. Remove the 2 retaining screws and lift the lock lever guide plate to expose the lock cylinder release hole.
8. Insert the key and place the lock cylinder in the **LOCK** position. Remove the key.
9. Insert a thin punch into the lock cylinder release hole and push inward to release the spring-loaded lock retainer.

At the same time, pull the lock cylinder out of the column.

10. When installing the lock cylinder, make sure it is in the **LOCK** position. Press it into the column. It will snap into place. The remainder of assembly is the reverse of disassembly.

Tilt Columns

1. Remove the steering wheel.
2. Remove the tilt lever and turn signal lever.
3. If equipped, remove the turn signal lever.
4. Remove the turn signal switch.
5. Using the key, place the lock cylinder in the **LOCK** position. Remove the key.
6. Insert a thin punch in the slot next to the switch mounting screw boss and depress the spring latch at the bottom of the slot. Hold the spring latch depressed and pull the lock cylinder out of the column.
7. Place the lock cylinder in the **LOCK** position and press it into place in the column. It will snap into position.
8. The remainder of assembly is the reverse of disassembly.

Steering Column

REMOVAL & INSTALLATION

1967–69 Models

◆ **See Figure 22**

1. Disconnect the battery ground cable.
2. Remove the grille.
3. Remove the nut and lockwasher from the end of the steering gear cross shaft.
4. Matchmark and remove the pitman arm from the cross shaft.
5. Remove the 3 steering gear mounting bolts.
6. On vans with manual transmission, disconnect the transmission control rods.
7. Remove the column access plate-to-floor screws.
8. Remove the column cap plate-to-access plate screws.
9. Disconnect the turn signal wiring.
10. Remove the steering column clamp at the instrument panel.
11. Lift the column and gear, as an assembly, from the van.
12. To remove the gear from the column, see Steering Gear Removal and Installation, below.

To install:

13. Position the assembly in the van.
14. Install the column clamp loosely.
15. Position the gear on the frame and loosely install the mounting bolts.
16. Rotate the gear to seat the column clamp in the instrument panel bracket. Torque the gear mounting bolts to 50 ft. lbs.

17. Adjust the column and clamp. Tighten the clamp bolts.
18. Center the gear and install the pitman arm. Torque the nut to 145 ft. lbs.
19. Connect the transmission rods.
20. Install the grille.
21. Connect the turn signal switch wiring.
22. Install the floor plate and access plate.
23. Install the steering wheel.
24. Connect the battery.

1970–77 Models

1. Disconnect the battery ground cable.
2. Turn the steering wheel to position the gear shaft coupling for removal of the roll pin.
3. Drive the roll pin from the pot joint (manual steering) or flexible coupling (power steering).
4. Disconnect the shift control linkage from the lower end of the column.
5. Loosen the 2 bolts at the floor plate O-ring retainer.
6. Remove the floor plate screws.
7. Unplug the column wiring connectors.
8. Loosen the column clamp-to-instrument panel bolts.
9. Pry the steering column shaft coupling from the steering gear.
10. Remove the column clamp bolts and lift the column from the van.

To install:

11. Position the column in the van.
12. Place the front wheel in the straight-ahead position.
13. Engage the wormshaft and coupling and install a *new* roll pin.
14. Install, but don't tighten, the column-to-instrument panel support bolts.

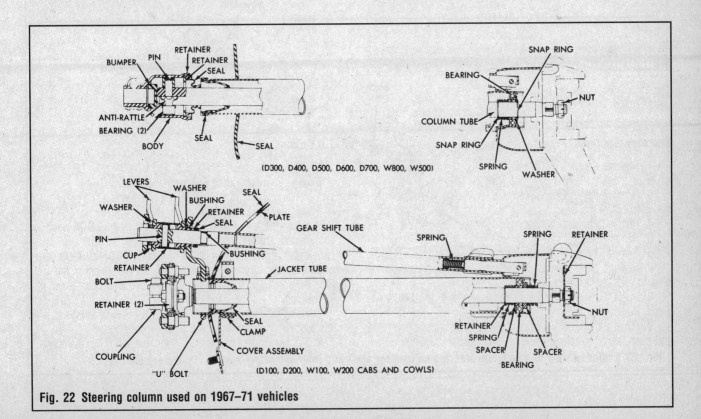

Fig. 22 Steering column used on 1967–71 vehicles

15. Center the floor pan plate around the column and install the screws snugly.

16. On vans with manual steering, the pot joint coupling and steering shaft must be adjusted so that the shaft is at its mid-point of travel in the joint. To do this, slide the column up and down in the column support clamp so that the dimension between the top of the coupling and the center of the gauge hole is $13/16''$. Tighten the column support clamp bolts to 30 ft. lbs.

17. Tighten the floor plate screws to 200 in. lbs., making sure that the column is centered around the shaft at the lower end.

18. Using rubber cement, install the dust seal.

19. Connect the shift linkage.

20. Connect the wiring.

21. Connect the battery.

1978–88 Models

◆ **See Figure 23**

1. Disconnect the battery ground cable.

2. On vans with a column shift, disconnect the link rod by prying the rod out of the grommet in the shift lever.

3. Remove the coupling roll pin.

4. Disconnect the wiring at the column.

5. Remove the steering wheel.

6. Remove the turn signal lever.

7. Remove the floor plate screws.

8. Remove the cluster bezel and panel lower reinforcement.

9. Disconnect the automatic shift indicator pointer from the shift housing.

10. Remove the column bracket-to-instrument panel nuts.

11. Carefully remove the coupling from the wormshaft and lift the column out of the truck.

To install:

12. Install a new shift grommet from the rod side of the lever using pliers and a back-up washer to snap the grommet into place. Coating the grommet with multi-purpose grease will aid in installation. A new grommet should be used whenever a rod is disconnected from the lever.

13. Position the column in the truck.

14. With the front wheels straight ahead and the master splines on the wormshaft and coupling aligned, engage the coupling and wormshaft and install the roll pin.

✳✳ WARNING

Never force the shaft down into position!

15. Install, but don't tighten, the bracket nuts.

16. Make sure that both plastic spacers are fully seated in their slots in the column support bracket, then, tighten the bracket nuts to 110 in. lbs.

17. Install the floor plate screws.

18. Install the steering wheel.

19. Connect the wiring.

20. Connect and adjust the shift linkage.

21. Connect the shift indicator pointer to the operating bracket in its original location. Slowly move the shift lever from **L** to **P**, pausing briefly at each position. The pointer must align with each selector position. If necessary, loosen the bolt and readjust the linkage to align the pointer correctly.

22. Install the panel lower reinforcement and cluster bezel.

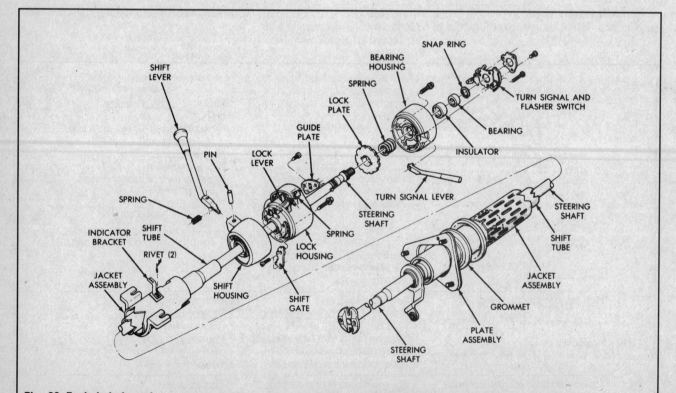

Fig. 23 Exploded view of a common steering column for 1981 and later vehicles—earlier models are similar

Troubleshooting the Steering Column

Problem	Cause	Solution
Will not lock	• Lockbolt spring broken or defective	• Replace lock bolt spring
High effort (required to turn ignition key and lock cylinder)	• Lock cylinder defective • Ignition switch defective • Rack preload spring broken or deformed • Burr on lock sector, lock rack, housing, support or remote rod coupling • Bent sector shaft • Defective lock rack • Remote rod bent, deformed • Ignition switch mounting bracket bent • Distorted coupling slot in lock rack (tilt column)	• Replace lock cylinder • Replace ignition switch • Replace preload spring • Remove burr • Replace shaft • Replace lock rack • Replace rod • Straighten or replace • Replace lock rack
Will stick in "start"	• Remote rod deformed • Ignition switch mounting bracket bent	• Straighten or replace • Straighten or replace
Key cannot be removed in "off-lock"	• Ignition switch is not adjusted correctly • Defective lock cylinder	• Adjust switch • Replace lock cylinder
Lock cylinder can be removed without depressing retainer	• Lock cylinder with defective retainer • Burr over retainer slot in housing cover or on cylinder retainer	• Replace lock cylinder • Remove burr
High effort on lock cylinder between "off" and "off-lock"	• Distorted lock rack • Burr on tang of shift gate (automatic column) • Gearshift linkage not adjusted	• Replace lock rack • Remove burr • Adjust linkage
Noise in column	• One click when in "off-lock" position and the steering wheel is moved (all except automatic column) • Coupling bolts not tightened • Lack of grease on bearings or bearing surfaces • Upper shaft bearing worn or broken • Lower shaft bearing worn or broken • Column not correctly aligned • Coupling pulled apart • Broken coupling lower joint • Steering shaft snap ring not seated • Shroud loose on shift bowl. Housing loose on jacket—will be noticed with ignition in "off-lock" and when torque is applied to steering wheel.	• Normal—lock bolt is seating • Tighten pinch bolts • Lubricate with chassis grease • Replace bearing assembly • Replace bearing. Check shaft and replace if scored. • Align column • Replace coupling • Repair or replace joint and align column • Replace ring. Check for proper seating in groove. • Position shroud over lugs on shift bowl. Tighten mounting screws.
High steering shaft effort	• Column misaligned • Defective upper or lower bearing • Tight steering shaft universal joint • Flash on I.D. of shift tube at plastic joint (tilt column only) • Upper or lower bearing seized	• Align column • Replace as required • Repair or replace • Replace shift tube • Replace bearings
Lash in mounted column assembly	• Column mounting bracket bolts loose • Broken weld nuts on column jacket • Column capsule bracket sheared	• Tighten bolts • Replace column jacket • Replace bracket assembly

Troubleshooting the Steering Column (cont.)

Problem	Cause	Solution
Lash in mounted column assembly (cont.)	• Column bracket to column jacket mounting bolts loose	• Tighten to specified torque
	• Loose lock shoes in housing (tilt column only)	• Replace shoes
	• Loose pivot pins (tilt column only)	• Replace pivot pins and support
	• Loose lock shoe pin (tilt column only)	• Replace pin and housing
	• Loose support screws (tilt column only)	• Tighten screws
Housing loose (tilt column only)	• Excessive clearance between holes in support or housing and pivot pin diameters	• Replace pivot pins and support
	• Housing support-screws loose	• Tighten screws
Steering wheel loose—every other tilt position (tilt column only)	• Loose fit between lock shoe and lock shoe pivot pin	• Replace lock shoes and pivot pin
Steering column not locking in any tilt position (tilt column only)	• Lock shoe seized on pivot pin	• Replace lock shoes and pin
	• Lock shoe grooves have burrs or are filled with foreign material	• Clean or replace lock shoes
	• Lock shoe springs weak or broken	• Replace springs
Noise when tilting column (tilt column only)	• Upper tilt bumpers worn	• Replace tilt bumper
	• Tilt spring rubbing in housing	• Lubricate with chassis grease
One click when in "off-lock" position and the steering wheel is moved	• Seating of lock bolt	• None. Click is normal characteristic sound produced by lock bolt as it seats.
High shift effort (automatic and tilt column only)	• Column not correctly aligned	• Align column
	• Lower bearing not aligned correctly	• Assemble correctly
	• Lack of grease on seal or lower bearing areas	• Lubricate with chassis grease
Improper transmission shifting—automatic and tilt column only	• Sheared shift tube joint	• Replace shift tube
	• Improper transmission gearshift linkage adjustment	• Adjust linkage
	• Loose lower shift lever	• Replace shift tube

Steering Linkage

REMOVAL & INSTALLATION

Tie Rod Ends

SOLID FRONT AXLE

1. Remove the cotter pin and loosen the nut.
2. Using a tie rod end separator, free the tie rod end from the knuckle.
3. Remove the nut and remove the tie rod end from the knuckle.
4. Count the exact number of threads visible between the tie rod end and the sleeve. Loosen the clamp bolts and unscrew the tie rod end.
5. To install the tie rod end, screw the end into the sleeve until the *exact* number of threads originally noted is showing.
6. Tighten the clamp bolts. Tighten the clamp bolts to 40–70 ft. lbs.; the tie rod end nut to:
   - ½-20: 40–80 ft. lbs.
   - ⅝-18: 50–90 ft. lbs.
   - ⁹⁄₁₆-18: 50–90 ft. lbs.
   - ⅞-18: 60–110 ft. lbs.

INDEPENDENT FRONT SUSPENSION

1. Raise and support the front end on jackstands.
2. Remove the cotter pin and nut from the tie rod end.
3. Using a separator, free the tie rod end from the knuckle arm or center link.
4. Count the exact number of threads visible between the tie rod end and the sleeve. Loosen the clamp bolts and unscrew the tie rod end.
5. To install the tie rod end, screw the end into the sleeve until the *exact* number of threads originally noted is showing.
6. Tighten the clamp bolts. Tighten the clamp bolts to 150–175 in. lbs on 100 and 200 series or 20–30 ft. lbs. on 300 series; the tie rod end nut to 40 ft. lbs.

Pitman Arm

1. Place the wheels in a straight-ahead position.
2. Disconnect the drag link at the pitman arm. You'll need a puller such as a tie rod end remover.
3. Remove the pitman arm-to-gear nut and washer.
4. Matchmark the pitman arm and gear housing for installation purposes.
5. Using a 2-jawed puller, remove the pitman arm from the gear.
6. Installation is the reverse of removal. Align the matchmarks when installing the pitman arm. Torque the pitman arm nut to:

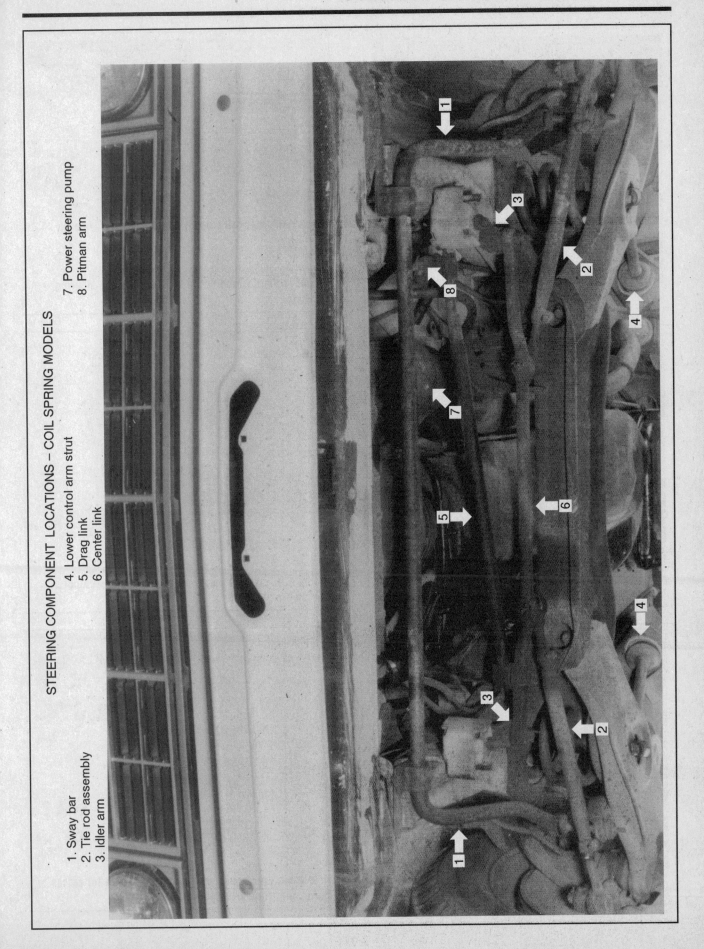

STEERING COMPONENT LOCATIONS – COIL SPRING MODELS

1. Sway bar
2. Tie rod assembly
3. Idler arm
4. Lower control arm strut
5. Drag link
6. Center link
7. Power steering pump
8. Pitman arm

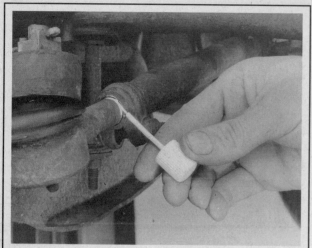

Before loosening the tie rod adjusting sleeve clamp, matchmark, or count the number of threads

Remove the castellated tie rod nut from the steering knuckle

Loosen the clamp on the tie rod adjusting sleeve

Using a tie rod separator, press the tie rod end out of the steering knuckle

Remove the cotter pin from the tie rod retaining nut

If re-using the tie rod, inspect the dust boot for cracks or hardening. If necessary, replace the boot

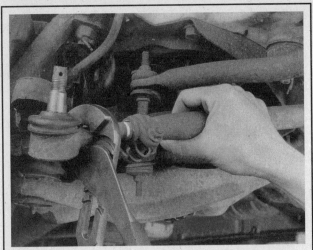

Unscrew the tie rod end from the adjusting sleeve—some tie rods use reverse threads

Remove the tie rod end from the adjusting sleeve

- 1967–69—145 ft. lbs.
- 1970–88—175 ft. lbs.

7. Torque the drag link ball stud nut to 40 ft. lbs., advancing the nut to align the cotter pin hole. Never back off the nut to align the hole.

Tie Rod and Drag Link

1. Place the wheels in a straight-ahead position.
2. Remove the cotter pins and nust from the drag link and tie rod ball studs.
3. Remove the drag link ball studs from the right-hand spindle and pitman arm.
4. Remove the tie rod ball studs from the left-hand spindle and drag link.
5. Installation is the reverse of removal. Seat the studs in the tapered hole before tightening the nuts. This will avoid wrap-up of the rubber grommets during tightening of the nuts. Torque the nuts to 40 ft. lb. Always use new cotter pins.
6. Have the front end alignment checked.

Connecting Rod

1. Raise and support the front end on jackstands.
2. Place the wheels in the straight-ahead position.
3. Disconnect the connecting rod from the drag link by removing the nut and separating the two with a tie rod end remover.
4. Loosen the bolts on the adjusting sleeve clamps. Count the number of turns it takes to remove the connecting rod from the adjuster sleeve and remove the rod.
5. Installation is the reverse of removal. Install the connecting rod the exact number of turns noted during removal. Torque the nuts to 40 ft. lb.
6. Have the front end alignment checked.

Manual Steering Gear

REMOVAL & INSTALLATION

1967–69 Models

1. Remove the steering column as outlined above.
2. Remove the steering wheel.
3. Remove the turn signal lever.
4. Loosen the turn signal switch clamp screw.
5. Tie a long piece of string to the end of the turn signal switch wiring. Pull the switch and wiring from the column, leaving enough of the string in the column to use in pulling the wiring back down inside the column.
6. Remove the snapring from the top of the steering shaft.
7. Slide the gear and shaft out of the column.
8. Installation is the reverse of removal.

1970–73 Models

1. Disconnect the drag link at the pitman arm.
2. Disconnect the battery.
3. Remove the windshield washer reservoir.
4. Remove the steering column.
5. Remove the bolts and nuts retaining the gear to the frame.
6. From under the left wheel well, remove the 2 bolts from the bottom of the splash shield. Force the splash shield away from the frame about ½″ and lift the gear off the mounting stud.
7. Installation is the reverse of removal. Tighten the mounting bolts and nut to 100 ft. lbs. Before connecting the drag link, make sure that the steering gear shaft is centered.

1974–78 Models

1. Place the wheels in a straight ahead position.
2. Matchmark the wormshaft coupling.
3. Remove the 2 wormshaft coupling bolts.
4. Disconnect the shift linkage at the column.
5. Matchmark the pitman arm and gear shaft.
6. Remove the pitman arm.
7. Remove the 3 gear mounting bolts.
8. Remove the steering column.
9. Remove the gear through the hole in the inboard side of the frame. It may be necessary to remove the 3 bolts from the left idler arm bracket and move the bracket out of the way.
10. Installation is the reverse of removal. Tighten the coupling bolts to 30 ft. lbs.; the pitman arm nut to 175 ft. lbs.; the steering gear mounting bolts to 100 ft. lbs.

1979–88 Models

1. Disconnect the battery ground.
2. Remove the steering column.
3. Disconnect the pitman arm from the gear.
4. Support the gear, remove the nuts and bolts and remove the gear.
5. Installation is the reverse of removal. Tighten the bolts/nuts to 100 ft. lbs. on 1979–83 vans; 150 ft. lbs. on 1984–88 models. Center the gear shaft before connecting the linkage.

ADJUSTMENTS

1967–69 Models

The worm bearing preload adjustment is performed with the gear out of the truck. The gear shaft adjustment can be performed with the gear in the truck. The worm bearing adjustment must be performed first, however.

Worm bearing preload can be checked with the gear in the truck as follows:
1. Place the wheels in a straight ahead position.
2. Matchmark and disconnect the pitman arm from the gear shaft.
3. Remove the horn button and spring.
4. Make sure that there is no binding in the steering column.
5. Place an inch-pound torque wrench on the steering wheel nut.
6. Turn the steering shaft with the torque wrench 2 full turns to wither side of center. and check the torque necessary to turn the shaft back over the center point. If the off-center torque (worm bearing preload) is 2–5½ in. lbs. the gear is properly adjusted.

WORM BEARING PRELOAD ADJUSTMENT

1. The pitman arm must be removed.
2. Loosen the cross shaft shaft adjuster locknut and back out the adjuster screw 2 turns.
3. Turn the steering wheel 2 complete turns to either side of center.

✳✳ WARNING

Never turn the steering wheel hard against either stop with the pitman arm disconnected. Damage to the gear will result!

4. With an inch-pound torque wrench, turn the steering shaft through the center point and note the turning torque. The torque should be 2–5½ in. lbs. If not, add or remove shims beneath the wormshaft cover. Shims are available in 0.0025", 0.0055" and 0.010" thicknesses.
5. Tighten the worm cover bolts to 20 ft. lbs.
6. Recheck the preload. If the preload has changed, redo the adjustment.

GEAR SHAFT (CROSS SHAFT) ADJUSTMENT

1. Disconnect the pitman arm.
2. Counting the number of complete turns, turn the steering wheel completely from one lock to the other. Turn it GENTLY!
3. Turn the wheel back from either stop, ½ the total number of turns.
4. Loosen the cross shaft adjusting screw locknut and turn the

adjusting screw in until all lash is removed. Tighten the locknut.
5. Turn the steering wheel 1 turn off of center.
6. Using an inch-pound torque wrench on the steering wheel nut, measure the torque needed to rotate the wheel over center. The torque reading should be 8–10 in. lbs. more than the worm bearing preload. If not, turn the adjusting screw until it is.
7. When the adjustment is complete, hold the adjusting screw and tighten the locknut to 20 ft. lbs.
8. Recheck the adjustment. If the load has changed, redo the adjustment.
9. Install the pitman arm.

1970–88 Models

WORM BEARING PRELOAD ADJUSTMENT

1. The pitman arm must be removed.
2. Loosen the sector shaft adjuster locknut and back out the adjuster screw 2 turns.
3. Remove the horn pad and spring.
4. Turn the steering wheel to the right stop and turn it back ½ turn.

✳✳ WARNING

Never turn the steering wheel hard against either stop with the pitman arm disconnected. Damage to the gear will result!

5. With an inch-pound torque wrench, turn the steering shaft at least 1 turn toward center and note the turning torque. The torque should be 1½–4½ in. lbs. If not, turn the adjuster screw clockwise to increase or counterclockwise to decrease, the preload.
6. Hold the adjuster screw and torque the locknut to 85 ft. lbs.
7. Recheck the preload. If the preload has changed, redo the adjustment.

BALL NUT AND SECTOR GEAR MESH ADJUSTMENT

1. Complete the worm bearing preload adjustment first.
2. Turn the steering wheel gently from one lock to the other. Count the number of turns. Turn the wheel back exactly to the midpoint of its travel.
3. Loosen the sector shaft adjuster locknut. Turn the sector shaft adjusting screw, which is located on the housing cover, clockwise until there is no lash present between the ball nut and sector teeth. Tighten the locknut to 24 ft. lbs.
4. Using and inch-pound torque wrench on the steering shaft nut, rotate the steering wheel ¼ turn away from the center. Note the torque required to turn the wheel through center. The reading should be 8¼–11¼ in. lbs. Turn the sector shaft adjustment screw, if required, to obtain the correct preload. Hold the adjusting nut and tighten the locknut to 24 ft. lbs.
5. Recheck the torque load. If the load has changed, redo the adjustment.
6. Once the adjustments are completed, straighten the front wheels and install the pitman arm.

➡ **Not only should the front wheels be straight-ahead, but both the steering gear and the steering wheel should be centered as well.**

7. Tighten the pitman arm securing nut to 180 ft. lbs.
8. Install the horn button, ring, or trim pad on the steering wheel.

Troubleshooting the Manual Steering Gear

Problem	Cause	Solution
Hard or erratic steering	• Incorrect tire pressure	• Inflate tires to recommended pressures
	• Insufficient or incorrect lubrication	• Lubricate as required (refer to Maintenance Section)
	• Suspension, or steering linkage parts damaged or misaligned	• Repair or replace parts as necessary
	• Improper front wheel alignment	• Adjust incorrect wheel alignment angles
	• Incorrect steering gear adjustment	• Adjust steering gear
	• Sagging springs	• Replace springs
Play or looseness in steering	• Steering wheel loose	• Inspect shaft spines and repair as necessary. Tighten attaching nut and stake in place.
	• Steering linkage or attaching parts loose or worn	• Tighten, adjust, or replace faulty components
	• Pitman arm loose	• Inspect shaft splines and repair as necessary. Tighten attaching nut and stake in place
	• Steering gear attaching bolts loose	• Tighten bolts
	• Loose or worn wheel bearings	• Adjust or replace bearings
	• Steering gear adjustment incorrect or parts badly worn	• Adjust gear or replace defective parts
Wheel shimmy or tramp	• Improper tire pressure	• Inflate tires to recommended pressures
	• Wheels, tires, or brake rotors out-of-balance or out-of-round	• Inspect and replace or balance parts
	• Inoperative, worn, or loose shock absorbers or mounting parts	• Repair or replace shocks or mountings
	• Loose or worn steering or suspension parts	• Tighten or replace as necessary
	• Loose or worn wheel bearings	• Adjust or replace bearings
	• Incorrect steering gear adjustments	• Adjust steering gear
	• Incorrect front wheel alignment	• Correct front wheel alignment
Tire wear	• Improper tire pressure	• Inflate tires to recommended pressures
	• Failure to rotate tires	• Rotate tires
	• Brakes grabbing	• Adjust or repair brakes
	• Incorrect front wheel alignment	• Align incorrect angles
	• Broken or damaged steering and suspension parts	• Repair or replace defective parts
	• Wheel runout	• Replace faulty wheel
	• Excessive speed on turns	• Make driver aware of conditions
Vehicle leads to one side	• Improper tire pressures	• Inflate tires to recommended pressures
	• Front tires with uneven tread depth, wear pattern, or different cord design (i.e., one bias ply and one belted or radial tire on front wheels)	• Install tires of same cord construction and reasonably even tread depth, design, and wear pattern
	• Incorrect front wheel alignment	• Align incorrect angles
	• Brakes dragging	• Adjust or repair brakes
	• Pulling due to uneven tire construction	• Replace faulty tire

Power Steering Gear

Power steering was introduced on Dodge vans in 1970.

REMOVAL & INSTALLATION

1970–73 Models

1. Disconnect the drag link at the pitman arm.
2. Disconnect the battery.
3. Remove the windshield washer reservoir.
4. Remove the steering column.
5. On models with heavy duty suspension, remove the pitman arm shield.
6. Place a drain pan under the gear and disconnect the fluid hoses from the steering gear.
7. Remove the bolts and nut retaining the gear to the frame.
8. From under the left wheel well, remove the 2 bolts from the bottom of the splash shield. Force the splash shield away from the frame about ½″ and lift the gear off the mounting stud.
9. Rotate the pitman arm to allow the gear to be lifted through the hood opening.
10. Installation is the reverse of removal. Tighten the mounting bolts and nut to 100 ft. lbs. Before connecting the drag link, make sure that the steering gear shaft is centered. Refill the reservoir, run the engine and check for leaks.

1974–78 Models

1. Remove the battery.
2. Remove the windshield washer reservoir.
3. Place a drain pan under the gear and disconnect the hoses.
4. Raise and support the front end on jackstands.
5. Disconnect the coupling at the steering gear, leaving the lower half on the wormshaft.
6. Disconnect the shift linkage at the steering column.
7. On heavy duty suspension models, remove the pitman arm shield.
8. Remove the pitman arm.
9. Remove the mounting bolt from the left side of the gear.
10. Remove one of the 2 remaining steering gear mounting bolts.
11. Remove the toe plate and column support bolts.
12. Unplug the wiring connectors at the column.
13. Remove the steering column.
14. Remove the 3 bolts from the left idler arm bracket and swing the bracket out of the way.
15. Remove the remaining bolt and remove the gear from the underside, through the opening in the inboard side of the frame.
   To install:
16. Position the gear on the frame and install one bolt.
17. Make sure that the coupling half is secured to the wormshaft with a roll pin.
18. Install the remaining 2 bolts and tighten all bolts to 100 ft. lbs.
19. Install the idler arm bracket.
20. Install the steering column.
21. Connect the wiring connectors at the column.
22. Install the toe plate and column support bolts.
23. Install the pitman arm.

24. On heavy duty suspension models, install the pitman arm shield.
25. Connect the shift linkage at the steering column.
26. Connect the coupling at the steering gear.
27. Connect the hoses.
28. Install the windshield washer reservoir.
29. Install the battery.
30. Fill the reservoir, run the engine and check for leaks.

1979–88 Models

1. Disconnect the battery ground cable.
2. Remove the steering column.
3. Place a drain pan under the gear and disconnect the hoses.
4. Remove the pitman arm.
5. Remove the 3 gear-to-frame bolts and remove the gear.
6. Installation is the reverse of removal. Torque the mounting bolts to 100 ft. lbs. Make sure that the steering gear shaft is centered before connecting the linkage.

ADJUSTMENTS

Preliminary Checks

1. Remove the gear from the truck.
2. Rotate the gear several times through its travel to expel all fluid from the gear.
3. Place a ¾″ 12-point socket on the stub shaft. Using an inch-pound torque wrench, check the torque ½ turn off the right stop, then ¼ turn off the left stop. Record these figures.
4. Center the gear and check the torque ½ turn to each side of center. Record these figures.
5. Turn the gear 90° to the right of center and turn the gear in a 180° arc to the left of center. Record the reading.

Worm Thrust Bearing Adjustment
▶ **See Figure 24**

1. Remove the adjuster plug locknut.
2. Turn the adjuster plug in until the plug and thrust bearing are fully bottomed. This takes about 20 ft. lbs. torque.
3. Matchmark the housing and one of the holes in the plug.

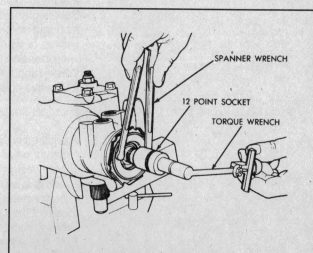

SPANNER WRENCH

12 POINT SOCKET

TORQUE WRENCH

Fig. 24 Adjusting the thrust bearing preload on power steering gear

4. Measure counterclockwise ¼″ from that mark and make another mark on the housing.

5. Rotate the plug counterclockwise until the marked hole aligns with the second housing mark.

6. Install the locknut and, while holding the adjuster plug, tighten the locknut securely.

7. Using an inch-pound torque wrench on the stub shaft, turn the shaft to the right stop then back ¼ turn. Note the reading. The reading should be 4–10 in. lbs. If not:

    a. Loosen the sector shaft preload adjuster screw locknut and turn the screw 1½ turns counterclockwise. If the screw bottoms, turn it back ½ turn.

    b. Retighten the locknut while holding the screw.

    c. Loosen the adjuster plug locknut.

    d. Turn the plug 1 turn counterclockwise.

    e. Turn the stub shaft to the right stop then back ¼ turn. Record the torque reading.

    f. Bottom the adjuster plug firmly with 20 ft. lbs. torque, then back it off until the stub shaft rotational torque is 3–4 in. lbs. more than the total torque reading with the adjuster plug tightened.

    g. Tighten the adjuster plug locknut securely.

➡**Preload torque tends to drop off when the locknut is tightened. Even so, the torque reading must be rechecked with the locknut tight and the torque must still be 3–4 in. lbs. more that total.**

Sector Shaft Overcenter Adjustment
◆ **See Figure 25**

1. Center the gear shaft.

2. Loosen the sector shaft adjusting screw locknut and tighten the sector shaft adjusting screw.

3. Tighten the locknut and, using an inch-pound torque wrench, rotate the sector shaft 90° to either side of center, noting the torque reading over center. The highest reading is what counts.

4. Continue adjusting and checking the preload until the preload is 4–8 in. lbs for a new gear not to exceed 18 in. lbs.; for a used gear (more than 400 miles), the preload should be 4–5 in. lbs. not to exceed 14 in. lbs.

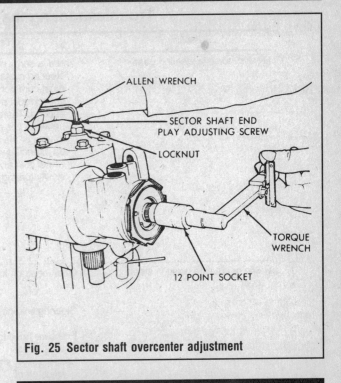

Fig. 25 Sector shaft overcenter adjustment

Power Steering Pump

REMOVAL & INSTALLATION

1. If the pump is to be replaced or disassembled, remove the pulley nut before removing the belt.

2. Remove the belt.

3. Place a drain pan under the pump and disconnect both hoses from the pump.

4. Remove the mounting and adjusting bolts and lift out the pump.

5. Installation is the reverse of removal. Torque the bolts to 30 ft. lbs. Make sure that the hoses are routed at least 1″ from all surfaces and at least 2″ from the exhaust manifold.

Troubleshooting the Power Steering Gear

Problem	Cause	Solution
Hissing noise in steering gear	• There is some noise in all power steering systems. One of the most common is a hissing sound most evident at standstill parking. There is no relationship between this noise and performance of the steering. Hiss may be expected when steering wheel is at end of travel or when slowly turning at standstill.	• Slight hiss is normal and in no way affects steering. Do not replace valve unless hiss is extremely objectionable. A replacement valve will also exhibit slight noise and is not always a cure. Investigate clearance around flexible coupling rivets. Be sure steering shaft and gear are aligned so flexible coupling rotates in a flat plane and is not distorted as shaft rotates. Any metal-to-metal contacts through flexible coupling will transmit valve hiss into passenger compartment through the steering column.
Rattle or chuckle noise in steering gear	• Gear loose on frame	• Check gear-to-frame mounting screws. Tighten screws to 88 N·m (65 foot pounds) torque.
	• Steering linkage looseness	• Check linkage pivot points for wear. Replace if necessary.
	• Pressure hose touching other parts of car	• Adjust hose position. Do not bend tubing by hand.
	• Loose pitman shaft over center adjustment	• Adjust to specifications
	NOTE: A slight rattle may occur on turns because of increased clearance off the "high point." This is normal and clearance must not be reduced below specified limits to eliminate this slight rattle.	
	• Loose pitman arm	• Tighten pitman arm nut to specifications
Squawk noise in steering gear when turning or recovering from a turn	• Damper O-ring on valve spool cut	• Replace damper O-ring
Poor return of steering wheel to center	• Tires not properly inflated	• Inflate to specified pressure
	• Lack of lubrication in linkage and ball joints	• Lube linkage and ball joints
	• Lower coupling flange rubbing against steering gear adjuster plug	• Loosen pinch bolt and assemble properly
	• Steering gear to column misalignment	• Align steering column
	• Improper front wheel alignment	• Check and adjust as necessary
	• Steering linkage binding	• Replace pivots
	• Ball joints binding	• Replace ball joints
	• Steering wheel rubbing against housing	• Align housing
	• Tight or frozen steering shaft bearings	• Replace bearings
	• Sticking or plugged valve spool	• Remove and clean or replace valve
	• Steering gear adjustments over specifications	• Check adjustment with gear out of car. Adjust as required.
	• Kink in return hose	• Replace hose

Troubleshooting the Power Steering Gear (cont.)

Problem	Cause	Solution
Car leads to one side or the other (keep in mind road condition and wind. Test car in both directions on flat road)	• Front end misaligned • Unbalanced steering gear valve **NOTE:** If this is cause, steering effort will be very light in direction of lead and normal or heavier in opposite direction	• Adjust to specifications • Replace valve
Momentary increase in effort when turning wheel fast to right or left	• Low oil level • Pump belt slipping • High internal leakage	• Add power steering fluid as required • Tighten or replace belt • Check pump pressure. (See pressure test)
Steering wheel surges or jerks when turning with engine running especially during parking	• Low oil level • Loose pump belt • Steering linkage hitting engine oil pan at full turn • Insufficient pump pressure • Pump flow control valve sticking	• Fill as required • Adjust tension to specification • Correct clearance • Check pump pressure. (See pressure test). Replace relief valve if defective. • Inspect for varnish or damage, replace if necessary
Excessive wheel kickback or loose steering	• Air in system • Steering gear loose on frame • Steering linkage joints worn enough to be loose • Worn poppet valve • Loose thrust bearing preload adjustment • Excessive overcenter lash	• Add oil to pump reservoir and bleed by operating steering. Check hose connectors for proper torque and adjust as required. • Tighten attaching screws to specified torque • Replace loose pivots • Replace poppet valve • Adjust to specification with gear out of vehicle • Adjust to specification with gear out of car
Hard steering or lack of assist	• Loose pump belt • Low oil level **NOTE:** Low oil level will also result in excessive pump noise • Steering gear to column misalignment • Lower coupling flange rubbing against steering gear adjuster plug • Tires not properly inflated	• Adjust belt tension to specification • Fill to proper level. If excessively low, check all lines and joints for evidence of external leakage. Tighten loose connectors. • Align steering column • Loosen pinch bolt and assemble properly • Inflate to recommended pressure
Foamy milky power steering fluid, low fluid level and possible low pressure	• Air in the fluid, and loss of fluid due to internal pump leakage causing overflow	• Check for leak and correct. Bleed system. Extremely cold temperatures will cause system aeriation should the oil level be low. If oil level is correct and pump still foams, remove pump from vehicle and separate reservoir from housing. Check welsh plug and housing for cracks. If plug is loose or housing is cracked, replace housing.

Troubleshooting the Power Steering Pump

Problem	Cause	Solution
Chirp noise in steering pump	• Loose belt	• Adjust belt tension to specification
Belt squeal (particularly noticeable at full wheel travel and stand still parking)	• Loose belt	• Adjust belt tension to specification
Growl noise in steering pump	• Excessive back pressure in hoses or steering gear caused by restriction	• Locate restriction and correct. Replace part if necessary.
Growl noise in steering pump (particularly noticeable at stand still parking)	• Scored pressure plates, thrust plate or rotor • Extreme wear of cam ring	• Replace parts and flush system • Replace parts
Groan noise in steering pump	• Low oil level • Air in the oil. Poor pressure hose connection.	• Fill reservoir to proper level • Tighten connector to specified torque. Bleed system by operating steering from right to left—full turn.
Rattle noise in steering pump	• Vanes not installed properly • Vanes sticking in rotor slots	• Install properly • Free up by removing burrs, varnish, or dirt
Swish noise in steering pump	• Defective flow control valve	• Replace part
Whine noise in steering pump	• Pump shaft bearing scored	• Replace housing and shaft. Flush system.
Hard steering or lack of assist	• Loose pump belt • Low oil level in reservoir **NOTE:** Low oil level will also result in excessive pump noise • Steering gear to column misalignment • Lower coupling flange rubbing against steering gear adjuster plug • Tires not properly inflated	• Adjust belt tension to specification • Fill to proper level. If excessively low, check all lines and joints for evidence of external leakage. Tighten loose connectors. • Align steering column • Loosen pinch bolt and assemble properly • Inflate to recommended pressure
Foaming milky power steering fluid, low fluid level and possible low pressure	• Air in the fluid, and loss of fluid due to internal pump leakage causing overflow	• Check for leaks and correct. Bleed system. Extremely cold temperatures will cause system aeration should the oil level be low. If oil level is correct and pump still foams, remove pump from vehicle and separate reservoir from body. Check welsh plug and body for cracks. If plug is loose or body is cracked, replace body.

Troubleshooting the Power Steering Pump (cont.)

Problem	Cause	Solution
Low pressure due to steering pump	• Flow control valve stuck or inoperative • Pressure plate not flat against cam ring	• Remove burrs or dirt or replace. Flush system. • Correct
Low pressure due to steering gear	• Pressure loss in cylinder due to worn piston ring or badly worn housing bore • Leakage at valve rings, valve body-to-worm seal	• Remove gear from car for disassembly and inspection of ring and housing bore • Remove gear from car for disassembly and replace seals
Low pump pressure	• Flow control valve stuck or inoperative • Pressure plate not flat against cam ring	• Remove burrs or dirt or replace. Flush system. • Correct
Momentary increase in effort when turning wheel fast to right or left	• Low oil level in pump • Pump belt slipping • High internal leakage	• Add power steering fluid as required • Tighten or replace belt • Check pump pressure. (See pressure test)
Steering wheel surges or jerks when turning with engine running especially during parking	• Low oil level • Loose pump belt • Steering linkage hitting engine oil pan at full turn • Insufficient pump pressure	• Fill as required • Adjust tension to specification • Correct clearance • Check pump pressure. (See pressure test). Replace flow control valve if defective.
Steering wheel surges or jerks when turning with engine running especially during parking (cont.)	• Sticking flow control valve	• Inspect for varnish or damage, replace if necessary
Excessive wheel kickback or loose steering	• Air in system	• Add oil to pump reservoir and bleed by operating steering. Check hose connectors for proper torque and adjust as required.
Low pump pressure	• Extreme wear of cam ring • Scored pressure plate, thrust plate, or rotor • Vanes not installed properly • Vanes sticking in rotor slots • Cracked or broken thrust or pressure plate	• Replace parts. Flush system. • Replace parts. Flush system. • Install properly • Freeup by removing burrs, varnish, or dirt • Replace part

Troubleshooting Basic Steering and Suspension Problems

Problem	Cause	Solution
Hard steering (steering wheel is hard to turn)	• Low or uneven tire pressure • Loose power steering pump drive belt • Low or incorrect power steering fluid • Incorrect front end alignment • Defective power steering pump • Bent or poorly lubricated front end parts	• Inflate tires to correct pressure • Adjust belt • Add fluid as necessary • Have front end alignment checked/adjusted • Check pump • Lubricate and/or replace defective parts
Loose steering (too much play in the steering wheel)	• Loose wheel bearings • Loose or worn steering linkage • Faulty shocks • Worn ball joints	• Adjust wheel bearings • Replace worn parts • Replace shocks • Replace ball joints
Car veers or wanders (car pulls to one side with hands off the steering wheel)	• Incorrect tire pressure • Improper front end alignment • Loose wheel bearings • Loose or bent front end components • Faulty shocks	• Inflate tires to correct pressure • Have front end alignment checked/adjusted • Adjust wheel bearings • Replace worn components • Replace shocks
Wheel oscillation or vibration transmitted through steering wheel	• Improper tire pressures • Tires out of balance • Loose wheel bearings • Improper front end alignment • Worn or bent front end components	• Inflate tires to correct pressure • Have tires balanced • Adjust wheel bearings • Have front end alignment checked/adjusted • Replace worn parts
Uneven tire wear	• Incorrect tire pressure • Front end out of alignment • Tires out of balance	• Inflate tires to correct pressure • Have front end alignment checked/adjusted • Have tires balanced

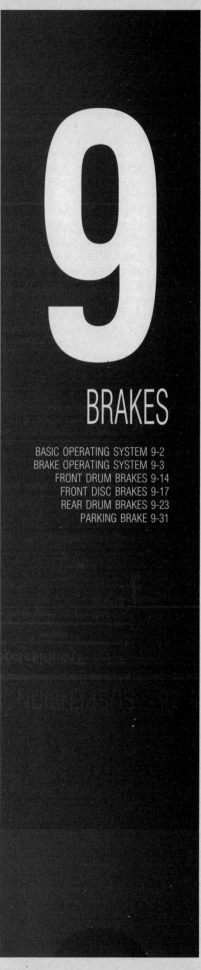

9
BRAKES

BASIC OPERATING SYSTEM

Basic Operating Principles

Hydraulic systems are used to actuate the brakes of all modern automobiles. The system transports the power required to force the frictional surfaces of the braking system together from the pedal to the individual brake units at each wheel. A hydraulic system is used for two reasons.

First, fluid under pressure can be carried to all parts of an automobile by small pipes and flexible hoses without taking up a significant amount of room or posing routing problems.

Second, a great mechanical advantage can be given to the brake pedal end of the system, and the foot pressure required to actuate the brakes can be reduced by making the surface area of the master cylinder pistons smaller than that of any of the pistons in the wheel cylinders or calipers.

The master cylinder consists of a fluid reservoir along with a double cylinder and piston assembly. Double type master cylinders are designed to separate the front and rear braking systems hydraulically in case of a leak. The master cylinder coverts mechanical motion from the pedal into hydraulic pressure within the lines. This pressure is translated back into mechanical motion at the wheels by either the wheel cylinder (drum brakes) or the caliper (disc brakes).

Steel lines carry the brake fluid to a point on the vehicle's frame near each of the vehicle's wheels. The fluid is then carried to the calipers and wheel cylinders by flexible tubes in order to allow for suspension and steering movements.

In drum brake systems, each wheel cylinder contains two pistons, one at either end, which push outward in opposite directions and force the brake shoe into contact with the drum.

In disc brake systems, the cylinders are part of the calipers. At least one cylinder in each caliper is used to force the brake pads against the disc.

All pistons employ some type of seal, usually made of rubber, to minimize fluid leakage. A rubber dust boot seals the outer end of the cylinder against dust and dirt. The boot fits around the outer end of the piston on disc brake calipers, and around the brake actuating rod on wheel cylinders.

The hydraulic system operates as follows: When at rest, the entire system, from the piston(s) in the master cylinder to those in the wheel cylinders or calipers, is full of brake fluid. Upon application of the brake pedal, fluid trapped in front of the master cylinder piston(s) is forced through the lines to the wheel cylinders. Here, it forces the pistons outward, in the case of drum brakes, and inward toward the disc, in the case of disc brakes. The motion of the pistons is opposed by return springs mounted outside the cylinders in drum brakes, and by spring seals, in disc brakes.

Upon release of the brake pedal, a spring located inside the master cylinder immediately returns the master cylinder pistons to the normal position. The pistons contain check valves and the master cylinder has compensating ports drilled in it. These are uncovered as the pistons reach their normal position. The piston check valves allow fluid to flow toward the wheel cylinders or calipers as the pistons withdraw. Then, as the return springs force the brake pads or shoes into the released position, the excess fluid reservoir through the compensating ports. It is during the time the pedal is in the released position that any fluid that has leaked out of the system will be replaced through the compensating ports.

Dual circuit master cylinders employ two pistons, located one behind the other, in the same cylinder. The primary piston is actuated directly by mechanical linkage from the brake pedal through the power booster. The secondary piston is actuated by fluid trapped between the two pistons. If a leak develops in front of the secondary piston, it moves forward until it bottoms against the front of the master cylinder, and the fluid trapped between the pistons will operate the rear brakes. If the rear brakes develop a leak, the primary piston will move forward until direct contact with the secondary piston takes place, and it will force the secondary piston to actuate the front brakes. In either case, the brake pedal moves farther when the brakes are applied, and less braking power is available.

All dual circuit systems use a switch to warn the driver when only half of the brake system is operational. This switch is usually located in a valve body which is mounted on the firewall or the frame below the master cylinder. A hydraulic piston receives pressure from both circuits, each circuit's pressure being applied to one end of the piston. When the pressures are in balance, the piston remains stationary. When one circuit has a leak, however, the greater pressure in that circuit during application of the brakes will push the piston to one side, closing the switch and activating the brake warning light.

In disc brake systems, this valve body also contains a metering valve and, in some cases, a proportioning valve. The metering valve keeps pressure from traveling to the disc brakes on the front wheels until the brake shoes on the rear wheels have contacted the drums, ensuring that the front brakes will never be used alone. The proportioning valve controls the pressure to the rear brakes to lessen the chance of rear wheel lock-up during very hard braking.

Warning lights may be tested by depressing the brake pedal and holding it while opening one of the wheel cylinder bleeder screws. If this does not cause the light to go on, substitute a new lamp, make continuity checks, and, finally, replace the switch as necessary.

The hydraulic system may be checked for leaks by applying pressure to the pedal gradually and steadily. If the pedal sinks very slowly to the floor, the system has a leak. This is not to be confused with a springy or spongy feel due to the compression of air within the lines. If the system leaks, there will be a gradual change in the position of the pedal with a constant pressure.

Check for leaks along all lines and at wheel cylinders. If no external leaks are apparent, the problem is inside the master cylinder.

DISC BRAKES

Instead of the traditional expanding brakes that press outward against a circular drum, disc brake systems utilize a disc (rotor) with brake pads positioned on either side of it. An easily-seen analogy is the hand brake arrangement on a bicycle. The pads squeeze onto the rim of the bike wheel, slowing its motion. Automobile disc brakes use the identical principle but apply the braking effort to a separate disc instead of the wheel.

The disc (rotor) is a casting, usually equipped with cooling fins between the two braking surfaces. This enables air to circulate between the braking surfaces making them less sensitive to heat buildup and more resistant to fade. Dirt and water do not drastically affect braking action since contaminants are thrown off by the centrifugal action of the rotor or scraped off the by the pads. Also, the equal clamping action of the two brake pads tends to ensure uniform, straight line stops. Disc brakes are inherently self-adjusting. There are three general types of disc brake:

1. A fixed caliper.
2. A floating caliper.
3. A sliding caliper.

The fixed caliper design uses two pistons mounted on either side of the rotor (in each side of the caliper). The caliper is mounted rigidly and does not move.

The sliding and floating designs are quite similar. In fact, these two types are often lumped together. In both designs, the pad on the inside of the rotor is moved into contact with the rotor by hydraulic force. The caliper, which is not held in a fixed position, moves slightly, bringing the outside pad into contact with the rotor. There are various methods of attaching floating calipers. Some pivot at the bottom or top, and some slide on mounting bolts. In any event, the end result is the same.

DRUM BRAKES

Drum brakes employ two brake shoes mounted on a stationary backing plate. These shoes are positioned inside a circular drum which rotates with the wheel assembly. The shoes are held in place by springs. This allows them to slide toward the drums (when they are applied) while keeping the linings and drums in alignment. The shoes are actuated by a wheel cylinder which is mounted at the top of the backing plate. When the brakes are applied, hydraulic pressure forces the wheel cylinder's actuating links outward. Since these links bear directly against the top of the brake shoes, the tops of the shoes are then forced against the inner side of the drum. This action forces the bottoms of the two shoes to contact the brake drum by rotating the entire assembly slightly (known as servo action). When pressure within the wheel cylinder is relaxed, return springs pull the shoes back away from the drum.

Most modern drum brakes are designed to self-adjust themselves during application when the vehicle is moving in reverse. This motion causes both shoes to rotate very slightly with the drum, rocking an adjusting lever, thereby causing rotation of the adjusting screw. Some drum brake systems are designed to self-adjust during application whenever the brakes are applied. This on-board adjustment system reduces the need for maintenance adjustments and keeps both the brake function and pedal feel satisfactory.

POWER BOOSTERS

Virtually all modern vehicles use a vacuum assisted power brake system to multiply the braking force and reduce pedal effort. Since vacuum is always available when the engine is operating, the system is simple and efficient. A vacuum diaphragm is located on the front of the master cylinder and assists the driver in applying the brakes, reducing both the effort and travel he must put into moving the brake pedal.

The vacuum diaphragm housing is normally connected to the intake manifold by a vacuum hose. A check valve is placed at the point where the hose enters the diaphragm housing, so that during periods of low manifold vacuum brakes assist will not be lost.

Depressing the brake pedal closes off the vacuum source and allows atmospheric pressure to enter on one side of the diaphragm. This causes the master cylinder pistons to move and apply the brakes. When the brake pedal is released, vacuum is applied to both sides of the diaphragm and springs return the diaphragm and master cylinder pistons to the released position.

If the vacuum supply fails, the brake pedal rod will contact the end of the master cylinder actuator rod and the system will apply the brakes without any power assistance. The driver will notice that much higher pedal effort is needed to stop the car and that the pedal feels harder than usual.

Vacuum Leak Test

1. Operate the engine at idle without touching the brake pedal for at least one minute.
2. Turn off the engine and wait one minute.
3. Test for the presence of assist vacuum by depressing the brake pedal and releasing it several times. If vacuum is present in the system, light application will produce less and less pedal travel. If there is no vacuum, air is leaking into the system.

System Operation Test

1. With the engine **OFF**, pump the brake pedal until the supply vacuum is entirely gone.
2. Put light, steady pressure on the brake pedal.
3. Start the engine and let it idle. If the system is operating correctly, the brake pedal should fall toward the floor if the constant pressure is maintained.

Power brake systems may be tested for hydraulic leaks just as ordinary systems are tested.

BRAKE OPERATING SYSTEM

✳✳ WARNING

Clean, high quality brake fluid is essential to the safe and proper operation of the brake system. You should always buy the highest quality brake fluid that is available. If the brake fluid becomes contaminated, drain and flush the system and fill the master cylinder with new fluid.

Never reuse any brake fluid. Any brake fluid that is removed from the system should be discarded.

Adjustments

DRUM BRAKES

♦ See Figure 1

The drum brakes are self-adjusting and require a manual adjustment only after the brake shoes have been replaced, or when the

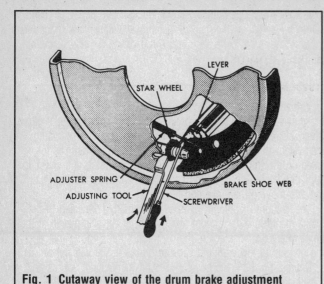

Fig. 1 Cutaway view of the drum brake adjustment

length of the adjusting screw has been changed while performing some other service operation, as i.e., taking off brake drums.

To adjust the brakes, follow the procedures given below:

Drum Installed

1. Raise and support the rear end on jackstands.
2. Remove the rubber plug from the adjusting slot on the backing plate.
3. Insert a brake adjusting spoon into the slot and engage the lowest possible tooth on the starwheel. Move the end of the brake spoon downward to move the starwheel upward and expand the adjusting screw. Repeat this operation until the brakes lock the wheels.
4. Insert a small screwdriver or piece of firm wire (coat hanger wire) into the adjusting slot and push the automatic adjusting lever out and free of the starwheel on the adjusting screw and hold it there.
5. Engage the topmost tooth possible on the starwheel with the brake adjusting spoon. Move the end of the adjusting spoon up-

ward to move the adjusting screw starwheel downward and contract the adjusting screw. Back off the adjusting screw starwheel until the wheel spins freely with a minimum of drag. Keep track of the number of turns that the starwheel is backed off, or the number of strokes taken with the brake adjusting spoon.

6. Repeat this operation for the other side. When backing off the brakes on the other side, the starwheel adjuster must be backed off the same number of turns to prevent side-to-side brake pull.
7. When the brakes are adjusted make several stops while backing the vehicle, to equalize the brakes at both of the wheels.
8. Remove the safety stands and lower the vehicle. Road test the vehicle.

Drum Removed

✳✳ CAUTION

Brake shoes may contain asbestos, which has been determined to be a cancer causing agent. Never clean the brake surfaces with compressed air! Avoid inhaling any dust from any brake surface! When cleaning brake surfaces, use a commercially available brake cleaning fluid.

1. Make sure that the shoe-to-contact pad areas are clean and properly lubricated.
2. Using and inside caliper check the inside diameter of the drum. Measure across the diameter of the assembled brake shoes, at their widest point.
3. Turn the adjusting screw so that the diameter of the shoes is 0.030" less than the brake drum inner diameter.
4. Install the drum.

Brake Light Switch

REMOVAL & INSTALLATION

The switch is mounted on a bracket above the brake pedal and is contacted by the brake pedal arm.

1. Disconnect the negative battery cable.
2. Disengage any connections from the switch.
3. Loosen the switch bracket.
4. Release the switch by sliding it away from the pedal arm.
To install:
5. Position a new switch to the bracket and secure any connections.
6. Adjust the switch.
7. Connect the negative battery cable and verify proper switch operation.

ADJUSTMENT

◆ **See Figure 2**

Without Speed Control

1. Loosen the switch-to-pedal bracket screw and slide the switch away from the pedal arm.
2. Push the pedal down by hand and allow it to return on its own to the free-hanging position. Do not pull it back!

Using a brake adjusting spoon through the backing plate access hole

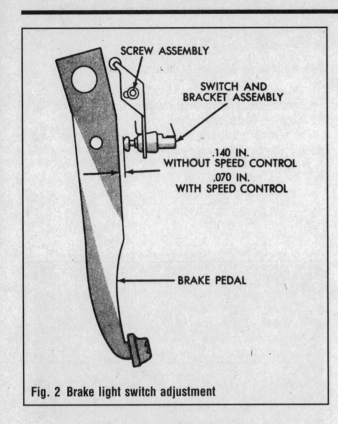

SCREW ASSEMBLY

SWITCH AND
BRACKET ASSEMBLY

.140 IN.
WITHOUT SPEED CONTROL
.070 IN.
WITH SPEED CONTROL

BRAKE PEDAL

Fig. 2 Brake light switch adjustment

3. Slide the switch towards the pedal until there is a gap of 0.140" between the plunger and pedal arm.

➡**The pedal must not move when measuring the gap.**

4. Tighten the switch screw to 82 inch lbs. Recheck the gap.

With Speed Control

1. Push the switch through the clip in the mounting bracket until it is seated against the bracket. The pedal will move forward slightly.

2. Gently pull back on the pedal as far as it will go. The switch will ratchet backwards to the correct position.

Master Cylinder

REMOVAL & INSTALLATION

1967–72 Models

B100

1. Disconnect the brake lines from the master cylinder.
2. Remove the master cylinder mounting nuts.
3. Disconnect the pushrod from the pedal.
4. Slide the master cylinder out.
5. Installation is the reverse of removal. Tighten the mounting nuts to 10 ft. lbs. Connect the pushrod. Bleed the master cylinder and brake system.

B200 AND B300

1. Disconnect the brake lines from the master cylinder.
2. Remove the master cylinder mounting nuts.

3. Slide the master cylinder out.
4. Installation is the reverse of removal. Tighten the mounting nuts to 10 ft. lbs. Connect the pushrod. Bleed the master cylinder and brake system.

1973–74 Models

B100

1. Disconnect the brake lines from the master cylinder.
2. Disconnect the pushrod from the pedal.
3. Remove the master cylinder mounting nuts.
4. Slide the master cylinder out.
5. Installation is the reverse of removal. Tighten the mounting nuts to 16 ft. lbs. Connect the pushrod. Bleed the master cylinder and brake system.

EXCEPT B100

1. Disconnect the brake lines from the master cylinder.
2. Remove the master cylinder mounting nuts.
3. Slide the master cylinder out.
4. Installation is the reverse of removal. Tighten the mounting nuts to 16 ft. lbs. Connect the pushrod. Bleed the master cylinder and brake system.

1975–78 Models

B100

1. Disconnect the brake lines from the master cylinder.
2. Disconnect the pushrod from the pedal.
3. Remove the master cylinder mounting nuts.
4. Slide the master cylinder out.
5. Installation is the reverse of removal. Tighten the mounting nuts to 16 ft. lbs. Connect the pushrod. Bleed the master cylinder and brake system.

EXCEPT B100

1. Disconnect the brake lines from the master cylinder.
2. Remove the bolt securing the pushrod to the pedal linkage.
3. Remove the master cylinder attaching nuts.
4. Slide the master cylinder from the van.
5. Installation is the reverse of removal. Tighten the mounting nuts to 16 ft. lbs. Connect the pushrod. Bleed the master cylinder and brake system.

1979–82 Models With an Aluminum Master Cylinder

WITHOUT POWER BRAKES

1. Disconnect the brake lines at the master cylinder.
2. Disconnect the stop lamp switch bracket and allow the switch to hang out of the way.
3. Pull the brake pedal backwards to disengage the pushrod from the master cylinder piston. This will require at least 50 lbs. of pull. It will also destroy the retention grommet.
4. Remove the master cylinder mounting nuts.
5. Slide the master cylinder straight away from the firewall. Remove all traces of the old grommet.
6. When installing the master cylinder, tighten the nuts to 16 ft. lbs. Moisten a new grommet with water, align the pushrod with the piston and, using the brake pedal, push the pushrod into the piston until it is fully seated. Install the boot.
7. Connect the stop lamp switch, adjust the switch, bleed the master cylinder and brake system.

WITH POWER BRAKES

1. Disconnect the brake lines from the master cylinder.
2. Remove the master cylinder mounting nuts.
3. Slide the master cylinder out.
4. Installation is the reverse of removal. Tighten the mounting nuts to 16 ft. lbs. Connect the pushrod. Bleed the master cylinder and brake system.

1979–88 Models With a Cast Iron Master Cylinder

1. Disconnect the brake lines from the master cylinder.
2. Remove the bolt securing the pushrod to the pedal linkage.
3. Remove the master cylinder attaching nuts.
4. Slide the master cylinder from the van.
5. Installation is the reverse of removal. Tighten the mounting

nuts to 16 ft. lbs. Connect the pushrod. Bleed the master cylinder and brake system.

1983–88 Models With an Aluminum Master Cylinder

1. Disconnect the brake lines from the master cylinder.
2. Remove the master cylinder mounting nuts.
3. Slide the master cylinder out.
4. Installation is the reverse of removal. Tighten the mounting nuts to 16 ft. lbs. Connect the pushrod. Bleed the master cylinder and brake system.

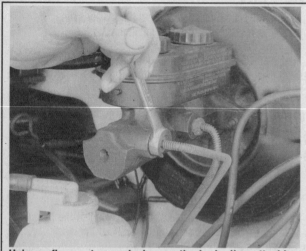

Using a flare nut wrench, loosen the brake line attaching nuts at the master cylinder . . .

Loosen and remove the master cylinder retaining nuts . . .

. . . and then carefully pull them out and away from the master cylinder

. . . then slide the master cylinder off of the mounting studs

OVERHAUL

♦ **See Figure 3**

1967–78 Chrysler Cast Iron Tandem Master Cylinder

1. Clean the outside of the cylinder. Remove the cover and drain the fluid.

2. Loosen the rear piston retainer screw from inside the reservoir, then remove the snapring from the outer end of the cylinder bore. Remove the primary piston.

3. Remove the secondary piston. If the piston sticks in the cylinder, air pressure may be used to remove it. Always use new rubber cups.

4. Note the position of the rubber cups and springs and remove them from the pistons and from the bore.

5. Remove the tube seats, using an easy out or a screw threaded into the seat. Unless the seat is damaged, it is not absolutely necessary to remove the seats.

6. Remove the residual pressure valves and springs found under the seats.

7. Clean the inside of the master cylinder with brake fluid or denatured alcohol.

8. Closely inspect the inside of the master cylinder. Polish the inside of the bore with crocus cloth. If there is rust or pitting, it will be necessary to use a hone. Discard the master cylinder if the scores or pitting cannot be eliminated by honing.

9. Do not reuse old rubber parts and be sure to use all the new parts supplied in the rebuilding kit.

10. Before assembly, thoroughly lubricate all parts with clean brake fluid.

11. Replace the primary cup on the front end of the piston with the lip away from the piston.

12. Carefully slide the second seal cup over the rear of the piston and into the second land. The cup lip must face the front of the piston.

13. Slowly work the rear secondary cup over the piston and position it in the rear land. The lip must face to the rear.

14. Slide the retainer cup over the front piston stem with the beveled side facing away from the piston cup.

15. Replace the small end of the pressure spring into the retainer.

16. Position the assembly in the bore. Be sure the cups are not canted.

17. Slowly work the secondary cup over the back of the rear piston with the cup lip facing forward.

18. Positing the spring retainer in the center of the rear piston assembly. It should be over the shoulder of the front piston. Position the piston assembly in the bore. Slowly work the cup lines into the bore. Slowly work the cup lines into the bore, then seat the piston assembly.

19. Hold the pistons in the seated position. Insert the piston retaining screw with the gasket, and tighten it securely.

20. Replace the residual pressure valves and spring. Position them in the front outlet and install the tube seats.

1967–78 Bendix Cast Iron Tandem Master Cylinder

1. Clean the outside of the cylinder and insert a screw extractor in the tube seat and tighten firmly. Tap gently on the tool and remove the seat.

2. Remove the cover and the gasket and drain the brake fluid from the cylinder.

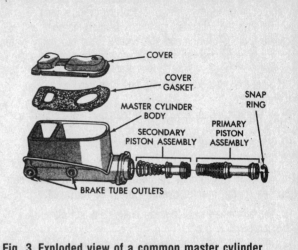

Fig. 3 Exploded view of a common master cylinder assembly—1984–88 cast iron model shown

3. Remove the snapring from the open end of the cylinder. Slide out the washer and carefully remove the primary piston then the secondary piston assembly from the master cylinder.

4. Clean all parts in a suitable solvent and blow dry with compressed air. Wash the cylinder bore with clean brake fluid and check for scoring or pitting. If the cylinder bore walls have light scratches or show signs of corrosion, it can be cleaned with a crocus cloth. Cylinder walls that have deep scratches or scoring may be honed, providing the diameter of the bore is not increased more than 0.002″.

✳✳ WARNING

Do not reuse any rubber parts! If you are using a brake cylinder rebuilding kit, use ALL the parts supplied with the kit!

5. Dip all component parts in clean brake fluid and coat the inside of the bore with brake fluid.

6. Carefully slide the front piston assembly into the cylinder body.

7. Slide the rear piston into the cylinder body.

8. Compress the pistons and install and tighten the front piston retainer screw.

9. Hold the washer in position and install the snapring.

10. Install the residual pressure valve and spring in the outlet port and firmly install the tube seats.

11. Bleed the master cylinder before installation.

1979–88 Aluminum Master Cylinder

1. Clean the outside of the master cylinder.

2. Remove the reservoir caps and empty the brake fluid from the reservoir.

3. With the master cylinder in a vise remove the reservoir from the master cylinder housing by grasping and moving from side to side.

4. Remove the reservoir grommets from the master cylinder.

5. Remove the secondary piston retainer pin from inside the master cylinder housing using a pair of needle nose pliers.

➡**This pin is not used on 1983–88 cylinders.**

6. Remove the snapring from the outer end of the cylinder bore and slide the primary piston out of the cylinder bore.

7. Remove the secondary piston by tapping the open end of the master cylinder on the end of a bench. If the secondary piston sticks it may be necessary to use air pressure to force the piston out.

8. Note the position of the cup lips then remove the cups from the piston.

9. If the brass tube seats are not reusable, replace them using an "easy out" tool.

10. Wash the inside of the bore with clean brake fluid and check for scoring, pitting or scratches.

➡**Do not hone the master cylinder. If any of the above conditions exist, the master cylinder must be replaced.**

11. Dip all components in clean brake fluid and place on a clean shop towel or paper.

12. Install the check flow washer and carefully work the primary cup on the end of the secondary piston with the lip away from the piston.

13. Slide the retainer cup over the front end of the piston followed by the piston spring.

14. Carefully work the secondary piston secondary cup over the rear end of the secondary piston, with the cup lip away from the piston.

15. Keep well lubricated with brake fluid and install the secondary piston assembly into the bore of the master cylinder.

16. Carefully work the second cup over the end of the primary piston with the larger lip of the cup toward the piston.

17. Center the spring retainer of the primary piston on the secondary piston. Push the piston assemblies into the bore up to the primary piston cup. Carefully work the cup into the bore then push the piston in up to the secondary seal. Carefully work the primary cup into the bore, then push in on the piston until seated.

18. Depress the piston with a brass or wood rod and install the snapring.

19. Position the secondary piston retainer pin in the housing and tap or press it until it is firmly seated.

20. Install new tube seats, firmly.

21. Install the reservoir grommets in the master cylinder housing.

22. Lubricate the reservoir mounting area, then with a rocking motion, install the reservoir into the master cylinder housing.

23. Before installation, bleed the master cylinder.

1979–88 Cast Iron Master Cylinder

1. Clean the outside of the cylinder and insert a screw extractor in the tube seat and tighten firmly. Tap gently on the tool and remove the seat.

2. Remove the cover and the gasket and drain the brake fluid from the cylinder.

3. Remove the snapring from the open end of the cylinder. Slide out the washer and carefully remove the primary piston then the secondary piston assembly from the master cylinder.

4. Clean all parts in a suitable solvent and blow dry with compressed air. Wash the cylinder bore with clean brake fluid and check for scoring or pitting. If the cylinder bore walls have light scratches or show signs of corrosion, it can be cleaned with a crocus cloth. Cylinder walls that have deep scratches or scoring may be honed, providing the diameter of the bore is not increased more than 0.002".

To disassemble the master cylinder, you must first remove the snapring

After removing the snapring, you can withdraw the piston assembly

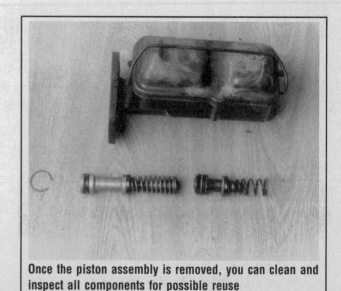

Once the piston assembly is removed, you can clean and inspect all components for possible reuse

5. Dip all component parts in clean brake fluid and coat the inside of the bore with brake fluid.

6. Carefully slide the front piston assembly into the cylinder body.

7. Slide the rear piston into the cylinder body.

8. Compress the pistons and install and tighten the front piston retainer screw.

9. Hold the washer in position and install the snapring.

10. Install the residual pressure valve and spring in the outlet port and firmly install the tube seats.

11. Bleed the master cylinder before installation.

Power Brake Booster

REMOVAL & INSTALLATION

Vacuum Assisted Booster

▶ **See Figures 4 and 5**

1. Remove the master cylinder.
2. Disconnect the vacuum hose from the power booster.

3. Disconnect the pushrod from the brake pedal.
4. Remove the power booster attaching nuts and remove the booster.
5. When installing the mounting nuts, tighten them to 16 ft. lbs. Connect the pushrod to the pedal. Coat the eyelet with Lubriplate® or equivalent.

Hydro-Boost

▶ **See Figure 6**

Some 1981 and later B350 school buses and all diesel engine equipped vans use the Bendix Hydro-Boost system.

The power steering pump provides the fluid pressure to operate both the brake booster and the power steering gear.

The hydro-boost assembly contains a valve which controls pump pressure while braking, a lever to control the position of the valve and a boost piston to provide the force to operate a conventional master cylinder attached to the front of the booster. The hydro-boost also has a reserve system, designed to store sufficient pressurized fluid to provide at least 2 brake applications in the event of insufficient fluid flow from the power steering pump. The brakes can also be applied unassisted if the reserve system is depleted.

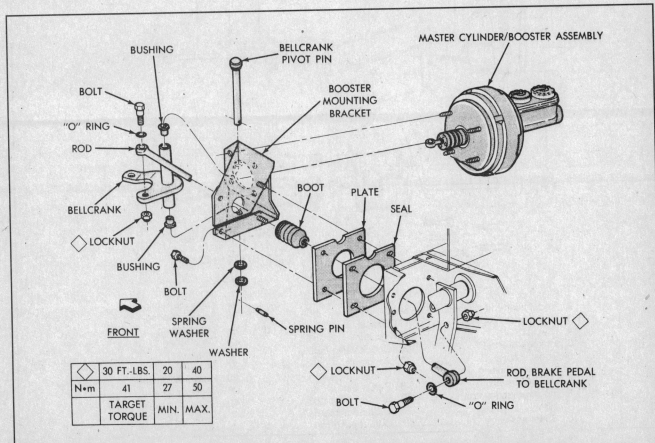

	30 FT.-LBS.	20	40
N•m	41	27	50
	TARGET TORQUE	MIN.	MAX.

Fig. 4 Transverse mounted power brake booster and related components—all models except B-350 school bus

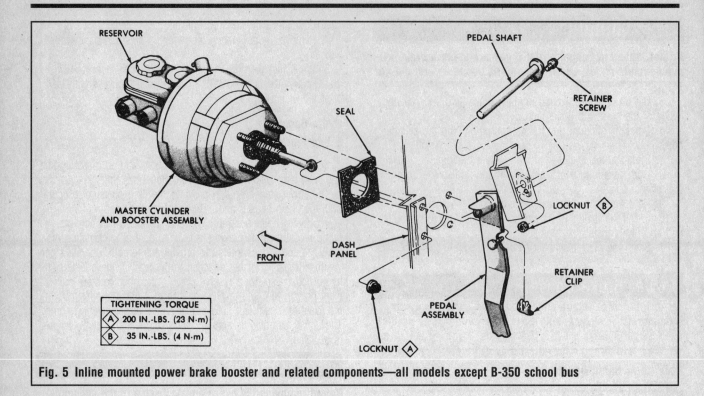

Fig. 5 Inline mounted power brake booster and related components—all models except B-350 school bus

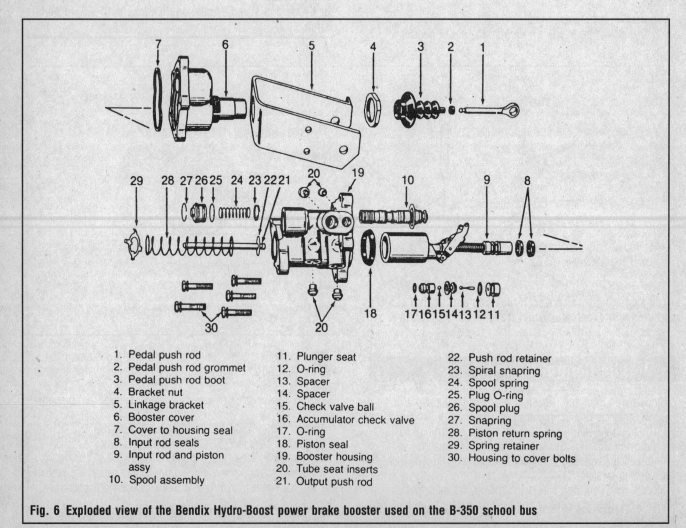

1. Pedal push rod
2. Pedal push rod grommet
3. Pedal push rod boot
4. Bracket nut
5. Linkage bracket
6. Booster cover
7. Cover to housing seal
8. Input rod seals
9. Input rod and piston assy
10. Spool assembly
11. Plunger seat
12. O-ring
13. Spacer
14. Spacer
15. Check valve ball
16. Accumulator check valve
17. O-ring
18. Piston seal
19. Booster housing
20. Tube seat inserts
21. Output push rod
22. Push rod retainer
23. Spiral snapring
24. Spool spring
25. Plug O-ring
26. Spool plug
27. Snapring
28. Piston return spring
29. Spring retainer
30. Housing to cover bolts

Fig. 6 Exploded view of the Bendix Hydro-Boost power brake booster used on the B-350 school bus

Do not depress the brake pedal with the master cylinder removed!

1. Remove the master cylinder from the Hydro-Boost unit. DO NOT DISCONNECT THE BRAKE LINES FROM THE MASTER CYLINDER!

Position the master cylinder out of the way.
2. Disconnect the 3 hydraulic lines from the Hydro-Boost unit.
3. Disconnect the pushrod from the brake pedal.
4. Remove the booster mounting nuts and lift the booster from the firewall.

The booster should never be carried by the accumulator. The accumulator contains high pressure nitrogen and can be dangerous if mishandled! If the accumulator is to be disposed of, do not expose it to fire or other forms of incineration! Gas pressure can be relieved by drilling a 1/16" hole in the end of the accumulator can. Always wear safety goggles during the drilling!

5. Installation is the reverse of removal. Torque the booster mounting nuts to 25 ft. lbs.; the master cylinder nuts to 25 ft. lbs.; connect the hydraulic lines, refill and bleed the booster as follows:

   a. Fill the pump reservoir with Dexron® II ATF.
   b. Disconnect the coil wires and crank the engine for several seconds.
   c. Check the fluid level and refill, if necessary.
   d. Connect the coil wires and start the engine.
   e. With the engine running, turn the steering wheel lock-to-lock twice. Shut off the engine.
   f. Depress the brake pedal several times to discharge the accumulator.
   g. Start the engine and repeat Step 5e.
   h. If foam appears in the reservoir, allow the foam to dissipate.
   i. Repeat Step e as often as necessary to expel all air from the system.

➡ **The system is, in effect, self-bleeding and normal vehicle operation will expel any further trapped air.**

Hydraulic Control Valves

Models with front and rear drum brakes are equipped with a brake warning light switch mounted in a housing on the frame rail. The front and rear brake lines are connected to the housing and a moving valve inside the housing reacts to changes in hydraulic pressure, warning the driver of excessively low pressure in either or both systems.

Models with front disc brakes incorporate the safety switch with either a metering valve or combination metering/proportioning valve

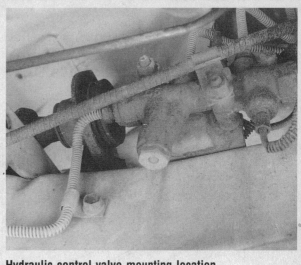

Hydraulic control valve mounting location

REMOVAL & INSTALLATION

▶ **See Figure 7**

Front Drum Brakes

1. Raise and support the front end on jackstands.
2. Remove the splash shield.
3. Disconnect the wiring at the warning light switch.
4. Disconnect the brake lines at the valve.
5. Unbolt and remove the valve from the frame.
6. Install the new valve and connect the lines and wiring.
7. Bleed the brake system.
8. Install the splash shield.

Front Disc Brakes

1. Raise and support the front end on jackstands.
2. Remove the splash shield.
3. Disconnect the wiring at the warning light switch.
4. Disconnect the brake lines at the valve.
5. Unbolt and remove the valve from the frame.
6. Install the new valve and connect the lines and wiring.
7. Bleed the brake system.
8. Install the splash shield.

CENTERING THE PROPORTIONING VALVE

After the brake system has been opened for any reason the warning light will remain on until the proportioning valve is centralized.

1985–88 valves are self-centering after the brakes are properly bled.

1. Raise and support the front end on jackstands.
2. Remove the splash shield.
3. Turn the ignition switch to ON.
4. Loosen the brake line at the valve for the part of the system that was not opened, or, if both sides were opened, loosen the line opposite the side that was bled last.
5. Depress the brake pedal slowly until the light goes out. If

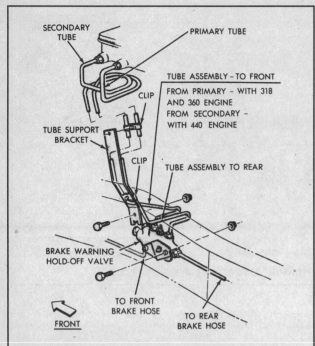

Fig. 7 Hydraulic control valve mounting details—1977–88 models shown, earlier years are similar

To remove the flexible brake hose, use a flare nut wrench and loosen the brake line attaching nut . . .

. . . then position it out of the way. Remove the brake hose bracket retaining bolt

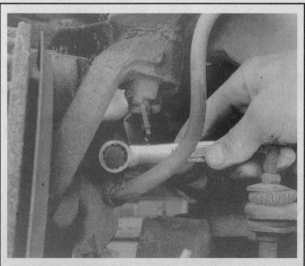

Unbolt the brake hose from the caliper . . .

both sides were opened, it may be necessary to repeat the procedure for another line at the valve.

6. Refill the master cylinder.

Brake Hoses and Lines

INSPECTION

The hydraulic brake lines and brake linings are to be inspected at the recommended intervals in the maintenance schedule. Follow the steel tubing from the master cylinder to the flexible hose fitting at each wheel. If a section of the tubing is found to be damaged, replace the entire section with tubing of the same type (steel, not copper), size, shape, and length. When installing a new section of brake tubing, flush clean brake fluid or denatured alcohol through to remove any dirt or foreign material from the line. Be sure to flare both ends to provide sound, leak-proof connections. When bending the tubing to fit the underbody contours, be careful not to kink or crack the line. Torque all hydraulic connections to 10–15 ft. lbs.

Check the flexible brake hoses that connect the steel tubing to each wheel cylinder. Replace the hose if it shows any signs of softening, cracking, or other damage. When installing a new front brake hose, position the hose to avoid contact with other chassis parts. Place a new copper gasket over the hose fitting and thread the hose assembly into the front wheel cylinder. A new rear brake hose must be positioned clear of the exhaust pipe or shock absorber. Thread the hose into the rear brake tube connector. When installing either a new front or rear brake hose, engage the opposite end of the hose to the bracket on the frame. Install the horseshoe type retaining clip and connect the tube to the hose with the tube fitting nut.

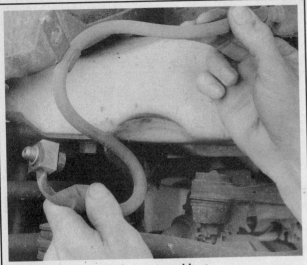

. . . and remove the hose assembly

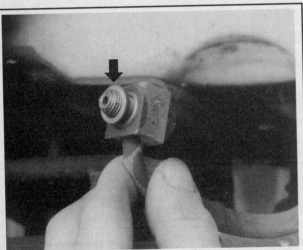

Always use new copper gaskets (arrow) when installing the brake hose

Always bleed the system after hose or line replacement. Before bleeding, make sure that the master cylinder is topped up with high temperature, extra heavy duty fluid of at least SAE 70R3 quality.

Bleeding the Brake System

When any part of the hydraulic system has been disconnected for repair or replacement, air may get into the lines and cause spongy pedal action (because air can be compressed and brake fluid cannot). To correct this condition, it is necessary to bleed the hydraulic system after it has been properly connected to be sure that all air is expelled from the brake cylinders and lines.

When bleeding the brake system, bleed one brake cylinder at a time, beginning at the cylinder with the longest hydraulic line (farthest from the master cylinder) first. Keep the master cylinder reservoir filled with brake fluid during bleeding operation. Never use brake fluid that has been drained from the hydraulic system, no matter how clean it is.

It will be necessary to centralize the pressure differential valve after a brake system failure has been corrected and the hydraulic system has been bled.

The primary and secondary hydraulic brake systems are individual systems and are bled separately. During the entire bleeding operation, do not allow the reservoir to run dry. Keep the master cylinder reservoirs filled with brake fluid.

WHEEL CYLINDERS AND CALIPERS

1. Clean all dirt from around the master cylinder fill cap, remove the cap and fill the master cylinder with brake fluid until the level is within ¼″ of the top of the edge of the reservoir.
2. Clean off the bleeder screws at the wheel cylinders and calipers.
3. Attach the length of rubber hose over the nozzle of the bleeder screw at the wheel to be done first. Place the other end of the hose in a glass jar, submerged in brake fluid.

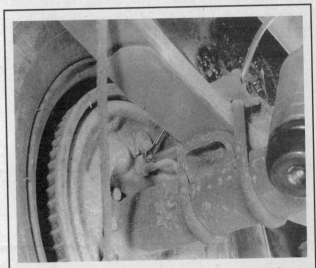

Wheel cylinder bleeding using a brake bleeder bottle

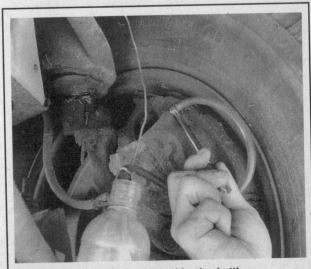

Caliper bleeding using a brake bleeder bottle

4. Open the bleed screw valve ½–¾ turn.

5. Have an assistant slowly depress the brake pedal. Close the bleeder screw valve and tell your assistant to allow the brake pedal to return slowly. Continue this pumping action to force any air out of the system. When bubbles cease to appear at the end of the bleeder hose, close the bleed valve and remove the hose.

6. Check the master cylinder fluid level and add fluid accordingly. Do this after bleeding each wheel.

7. Repeat the bleeding operation at the remaining 3 wheels, ending with the one closest to the master cylinder. Fill the master cylinder reservoir.

FRONT DRUM BRAKES

✳✳ CAUTION

Brake shoes may contain asbestos, which has been determined to be a cancer causing agent. Never clean the brake surfaces with compressed air! Avoid inhaling any dust from any brake surface! When cleaning brake surfaces, use a commercially available brake cleaning fluid.

There are two types of front drum brakes used on Dodge and Plymouth vans, a servo type with single anchor, and a Bendix Duo-Servo type. The servo type was used exclusively from 1967 to 70, and the Bendix Duo-Servo was added sometime in 1970 and was used occasionally from then on. The Bendix Duo-Servo type can be identified by the brake shoes which are marked **Pri**

MASTER CYLINDER

1. Fill the master cylinder reservoirs.

2. Place absorbent rags under the fluid lines at the master cylinder.

3. Have an assistant depress and hold the brake pedal.

4. With the pedal held down, slowly crack open the hydraulic line fitting, allowing the air to escape. Close the fitting and have the pedal released.

5. Repeat Steps 3 and 4 for each fitting until all the air is released.

(Primary) and **Sec** (Secondary) and "This Side Out", for easy identification.

Brake Drum

REMOVAL & INSTALLATION

Servo Type With Single Anchor

▶ See Figure 8

1. To aid in brake drum removal, loosen the brake adjusting star wheel.

2. Jack and support the vehicle.

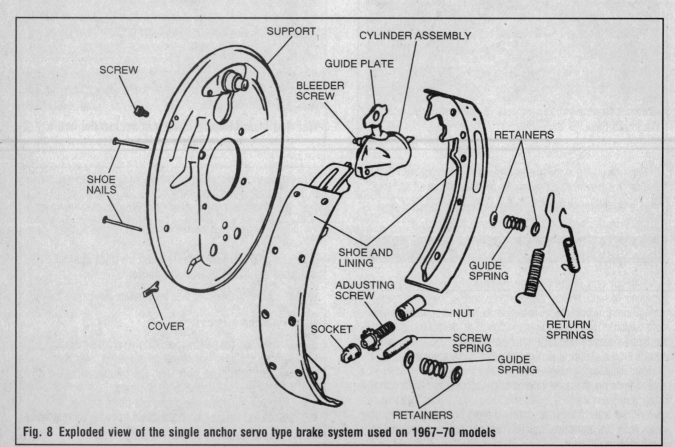

Fig. 8 Exploded view of the single anchor servo type brake system used on 1967–70 models

3. Insert a thin screwdriver into the adjusting hole after removing the plug. Push the adjusting lever away from the adjuster.

4. Release the brake adjustment by prying down against the star wheel with a brake adjusting spoon.

5. Remove the grease cap, cotter pin, lock, adjusting nut, and outer wheel bearing; remove the wheel and drum bearing; remove the wheel and drum assembly from the spindle or remove the wheel and then the drum.

6. Installation is the reverse of removal. Adjust the wheel bearings and readjust the brakes.

Bendix Duo-Servo Type

▶ See Figure 9

1. Raise and support the van on jackstands.
2. Remove the wheel and tire.
3. Remove the dust cover, cotter key, nut, locknut, washer, and outer bearing.
4. Carefully remove the drum.
5. If there is interference between the brake shoes and drum, release the brake shoes by applying a brake adjusting spoon to the star wheel adjuster.
6. Installation is the reverse of removal. Adjust the wheel bearings and then the brakes.

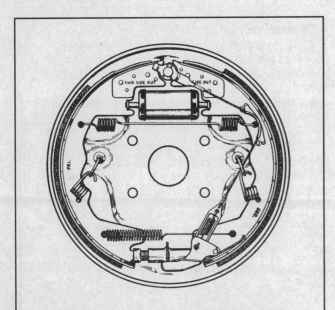

Fig. 9 Assembled view of the Bendix Duo-Servo front drum brakes used on 1970 and some later models

INSPECTION

1. Drum run out (out of round) and diameter should be measured. Each drum should be marked with its diameter. Drum diameter cannot exceed specification by more than 0.020″ and run out cannot exceed 0.006 in. Do not reface a drum more than 0.060″ over its standard diameter.

2. Check the drum for large cracks and scores. Replace the drum if necessary.

3. If the brake linings are wearing more on one edge than the other, then the drum may be "bell" shaped and will have to be replaced and resurfaced.

Brake Shoes

REMOVAL & INSTALLATION

Servo Type With Single Anchor

Remove the wheel and brake drum as outlined above, then proceed in the following manner:

1. Take off the shoe return springs. Detach the adjusting cable eye from the anchor and unhook the other end from the lever. Withdraw the cable, overload spring, and anchor plate.

2. Detach the adjusting lever from the spring and separate the spring from the pivot. Take the spring completely off from the secondary shoe web and unfasten it from the primary shoe web.

3. Remove the retainer springs and nails from the shoe. Extract both shoes from the pushrods and lift them out. Withdraw the star wheel assembly from the shoes.

To install:

4. Lightly lubricate the shoe tab contact area at six points on the support plate. Match both the primary and secondary brake shoes with each other.

5. Before installation in the van, fit the star wheel assembly between the shoes, with the star wheel next to the secondary shoe. The star wheels are stamped with an **L** or **R** to mark their location. Spread the anchor ends of the shoes apart to keep the star wheel assembly positioned.

6. Place the assembly on the support plate while attaching the shoe ends to the pushrods.

7. Install the shoe retaining nails, springs, and retainers. Place the anchor plate over the anchor.

8. Place the adjustment cable eye over the anchor so that it rests against the anchor plate. Attach the primary shoe return spring shoe web and fit the other end over the anchor.

9. Place the cable guide in the secondary shoe web and fit the end over the anchor. Hold this in position while engaging the secondary shoe return spring, through the guide and into the web. Put its other end over the anchor.

➡**See that the cable guide stays flat against the web and that the secondary shoe return spring overlaps that of the primary.**

10. Squeeze the ends of the spring loops, using pliers, until they are parallel, around the anchor.

11. The adjustment cable should be threaded over the guide and the end of the overload spring should be hooked into the lever.

➡**The eye of the adjuster cable must be tight against the anchor and parallel with the guide.**

12. Install the drum as previously detailed. Adjust the brakes.

Bendix Duo-Servo Type

1. Unhook and remove the adjusting lever return spring.
2. Remove the lever from the lever pivot pin.
3. Unhook the adjuster lever from the adjuster cable.
4. Unhook the upper shoe-to-shoe spring.
5. Unhook and remove the shoe hold-down springs.
6. Disconnect the parking brake cable from the parking brake lever.

7. Remove the shoes with the lower shoe-to-shoe spring and star wheel as an assembly.

To install:

8. The pivot screw and adjusting nut on the left side have left-hand threads and right-hand threads on the right side.

9. Lubricate and assemble the star wheel assembly. Lubricate the guide pads on the support plates.

10. Assemble the star wheel, lower shoe-to-shoe spring, and the primary and secondary shoes. Position this assembly on the support plate.

11. Install and hook the hold-down springs.

12. Install the upper shoe-to-shoe spring.

13. Install the cable and retaining clip.

14. Position the adjuster lever return spring on the pivot (green springs on left brakes and red springs on right brakes).

15. Install the adjuster lever. Route the adjuster cable and connect it to the adjuster.

16. Install the brake drum and adjust the brakes.

Wheel Cylinders

REMOVAL

▶ **See Figure 10**

When the brake drums are removed, carry out an inspection of the wheel cylinder boots for cuts, tears, cracks, or leaks. If any of these are present, the wheel cylinder should have a complete overhaul performed.

➡**Preservative fluid is used during assembly; its presence in small quantities does not indicate a problem.**

1. Remove the brake shoes and check them. Replace them if they are soaked with grease or brake fluid.

2. Detach the brake hose.

3. Unfasten the wheel cylinder attachment bolts and slide the wheel cylinder off its support.

OVERHAUL

1. Pry the boots off from either end of the wheel cylinder and withdraw the pushrods. Push in one of the pistons, to force out the other piston, its cup, the spring, the spring cup, and the piston, itself.

2. Wash the pistons, the wheel cylinder housing, and the spring in fresh brake fluid, or in denatured alcohol, and dry them off using compressed air.

✳✳ WARNING

Do not use a rag to dry them since the lint from it will stick to the surfaces.

3. Inspect the cylinder bore wall for signs of pitting, scoring, etc. If it is badly scored or pitted, the entire cylinder should be replaced. Light scratches or corrosion should be cleaned up with crocus cloth.

➡**Disregard the black stains from the piston cups that appear on the cylinder wall; they will do no damage.**

To assemble:

4. Dip the pistons and the cups in clean brake fluid. Replace the boots with new ones, if they show wear or deterioration. Coat the wall of the cylinder bore with clean brake fluid.

5. Place the spring in the cylinder bore. Position the cups in either end of the cylinder with the open end of the cups facing inward (toward each other).

6. Place the pistons in either end of the cylinder bore with the recessed ends facing outward (away from each other).

7. Install the boots over the ends of the cylinder and push down until each boot is seated, being careful not to damage either boot.

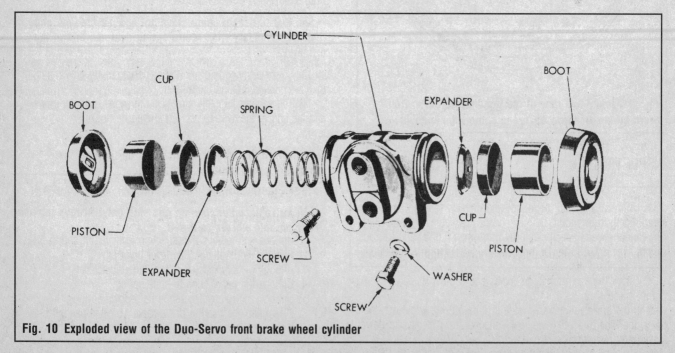

Fig. 10 Exploded view of the Duo-Servo front brake wheel cylinder

INSTALLATION

1. Install the wheel cylinder on its support.
2. Attach the jumper tube to the wheel cylinder. Install the

brake hose on the frame bracket. Connect the brake line to the hose. Connect the end of the brake hose. Connect the end of the brake hose through the end of the stand-off. Attach the jumper tube to the brake hose and attach the hose to the stand-off.

FRONT DISC BRAKES

✳✳ CAUTION

Brake shoes may contain asbestos, which has been determined to be a cancer causing agent. Never clean the brake surfaces with compressed air! Avoid inhaling any dust from any brake surface! When cleaning brake surfaces, use a commercially available brake cleaning fluid.

Application

♦ **See Figures 11 and 12**

On all models with disc brakes, the B100/150 series uses the Chrysler Sliding Caliper with 11.75″ rotor; the B200/250, and B300/350 uses the Chrysler Sliding Caliper with 12.82″ rotor.

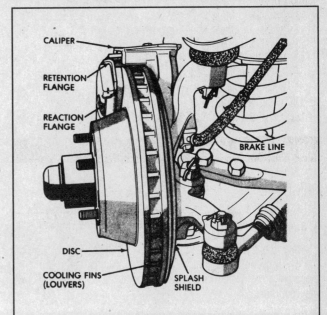

Fig. 12 Single piston Chrysler sliding caliper—front view

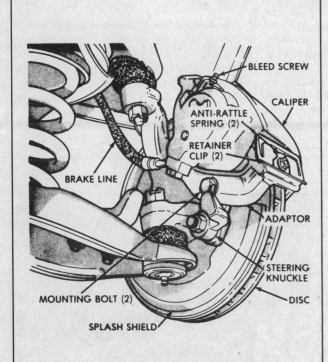

Fig. 11 Single piston Chrysler sliding caliper—rear view

Brake Pads

INSPECTION

Remove the brake pads as described below and measure the thickness of the lining. If the lining at any point on the pad assembly is less 0.0625″ (1/16″; 1.5mm) for LD brakes or 0.03125″ (1/32″; 0.794mm) for HD brakes, thick (above the backing plate or rivets), or there is evidence of the lining being contaminated by brake fluid or oil, replace the brake pad.

REMOVAL & INSTALLATION

♦ **See Figures 13, 14, 15, 16 and 17**

➡**Never replace the pads on one side only! Always replace pads on both wheels as a set!**

1. Raise and support the front end on jackstands.
2. Remove the wheels.

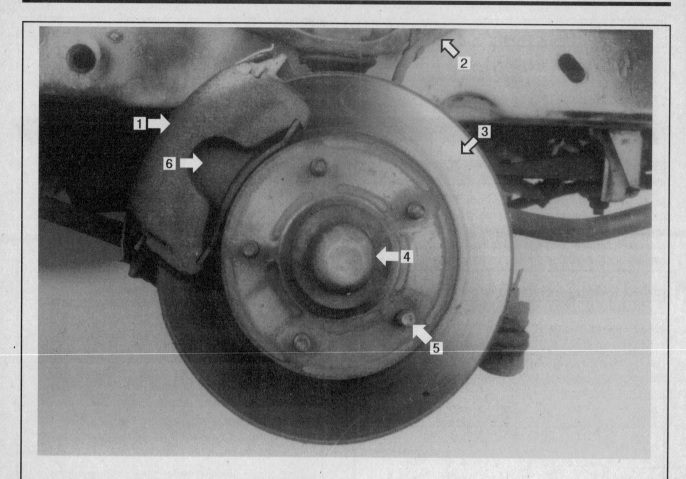

1. Brake caliper
2. Brake hose
3. Rotor
4. Wheel bearing dust cap
5. Wheel lug stud
6. Outboard brake pad/shoe

Front disc brake components

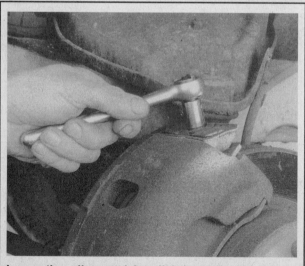

Loosen the caliper retaining clip's mounting bolt . . .

. . . then remove the bolt/clip assembly

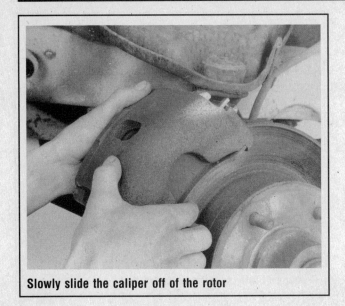

Slowly slide the caliper off of the rotor

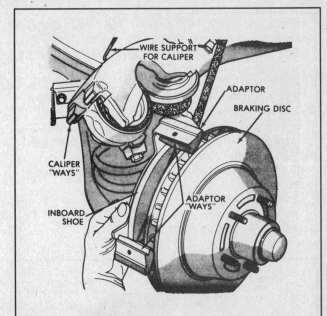

Fig. 14 Slide the inboard pad out of the caliper mount adaptor

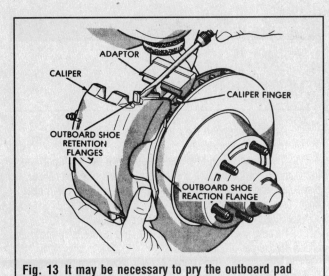

Fig. 13 It may be necessary to pry the outboard pad loose from the caliper

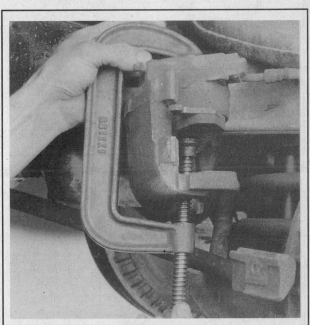

Use a C-clamp on the inboard pad to press the caliper piston into the caliper housing

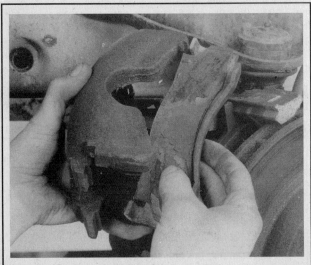

Remove the outboard pad from the caliper

3. Remove the caliper retaining clips and anti-rattle springs.

4. Remove the caliper from the disc by slowly sliding the caliper and brake pad assembly out and away from the disc. Do not damage the flexible brake hose.

5. Drain some of the fluid from the master cylinder.

6. Remove the outboard pad from the caliper by prying between the pad and the caliper fingers. Remove the inboard pad from the caliper support by the same method. DO NOT depress the brake pedal with the pads removed!

To install:

7. Push the pistons to the bottom of their bores. This may be done with a large C-clamp or a pair of large pliers by placing a flat metal bar against the pistons and depressing the pistons with a steady force. This operation will displace some of the fluid in the master cylinder.

8. Slide the new pads into the caliper and caliper support. The ears of the pad should rest on the bridges of the caliper.

9. Install the caliper on the disc and install the caliper retaining clips, pins and anti-rattle springs. Pump the brake pedal until it is firm.

10. Check the fluid level in the master cylinder and add fluid as needed.

11. Install the wheels.

12. Road test the van. The van may pull to one side, but the pull should disappear shortly as the pads wear in.

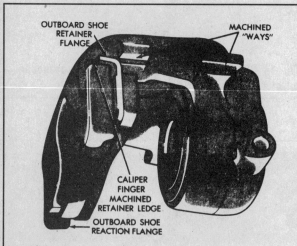

Fig. 15 The outboard pad should fit snugly on the caliper

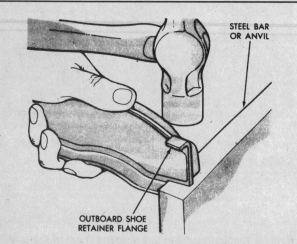

Fig. 16 Bend the outboard shoe retaining flanges if the pad is loose in the caliper

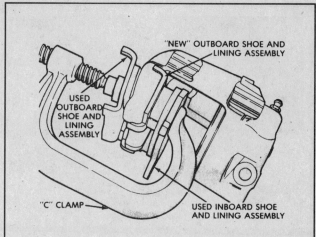

Fig. 17 If the pad is too tight to install by hand, use a C-clamp to fully seat the outboard pad

Brake Caliper

♦ See Figure 18

REMOVAL & INSTALLATION

1. Raise and support the front end on jackstands.
2. Remove the wheels.
3. Disconnect the rubber brake hose from the tubing at the frame mount. If the pistons are to be removed from the caliper, leave the brake hose connected to the caliper. Check the rubber hose for cracks or chafed spots.
4. Plug the brake line to prevent loss of fluid.
5. Remove the retaining screw, clip and antirattle spring that attach the caliper to the adaptor.
6. Carefully slide the caliper out and away from the disc. Check the pads to be sure that they are reinstalled in the same position.

To install:

7. Position the outboard shoe in the caliper. The shoe should not rattle in the caliper. If it does, or if any movement is obvious, bend the shoe tabs over the caliper to tighten the fit.

8. Install the inboard shoe.

9. Slide the caliper into position on the adaptor and over the rotor.

✳✳ WARNING

Take great care to avoid dislodging the piston dust boot!

10. Install the anti-rattle springs and retaining clips and torque the retaining screws to 16 ft. lbs.

➡The inboard shoe must always be installed on top of the retainer spring plate.

11. Fill the system with fresh fluid and bleed the brakes.

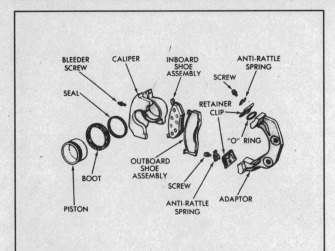

Fig. 18 Exploded view of the Chrysler sliding caliper and related components

OVERHAUL

1. Remove the caliper from the rotor.

2. If the pistons are to be removed, support the caliper on the upper control arm and surround it with towels to absorb the hydraulic fluid that will be lost.

3. Carefully depress the brake pedal to hydraulically push the piston from its bore. Prop the pedal at any position below the first inch of travel to prevent further loss of fluid.

4. Disconnect the plug and brake line after the first piston is removed.

5. Mount the caliper in a vise equipped with soft jaws.

6. Remove the dust boot.

7. Using a small wooden of plastic pointed tool, work the piston seal out of its groove in the piston bore.

8. Clean all parts in alcohol and allow to air dry.

9. Dip a new piston seal in the lubricant supplied with the factory rebuilding kit or in clean brake fluid. Install the seal in the groove in the bore.

10. Coat a new piston boot with lubricant and leave a generous amount inside the boot.

11. Install the piston seal into the caliper by working it into the groove with your fingers only. At first sight, the seal will appear larger than the bore, but will snap into place when properly seated.

12. Plug the high pressure inlet to the caliper and the bleeder screw hole and coat the piston with lubricant. Spread the boot with your fingers and work the piston into the boot, pressing down evenly.

13. Remove the plug and carefully push the piston down until it hits bottom.

14. Install the caliper on the vehicle, using the reverse order of removal.

15. Be sure to install the inboard pad anti-rattle spring on top of the retainer spring plate. Bleed the brakes. Road test the van making several stops to wear any foreign material off of the pads.

Brake Disc (Rotor)

REMOVAL & INSTALLATION

1. Jack up the front of the van and support it with jackstands. Remove the front wheel.

2. Remove the caliper assembly and support it to the frame with a piece of wire without disconnecting the brake fluid hose.

3. Remove the hub and rotor assembly as described in Chapter 1.

4. Install the rotor in the reverse order of removal, and adjust the wheel bearing as outlined in Section 1.

INSPECTION

If the rotor is deeply scarred or has shallow cracks, it may be refinished on a disc brake rotor lathe. Also, if the lateral run-out exceeds 0.010″ within a 6″ radius when measured with a dial indicator, with the stylus 1″ in from the edge of the rotor, the rotor should be refinished or replaced.

A maximum of 0.020″ of material may be removed equally from each friction surface of the rotor. If the damage cannot be corrected when the rotor has been machined to the minimum thickness shown on the rotor, it should be replaced.

The finished braking surfaces of the rotor must be parallel within 0.007″ and lateral run-out must not be more than 0.003″ on the inboard surface in a 5″ radius.

Remove the brake caliper and suspend it out of the way

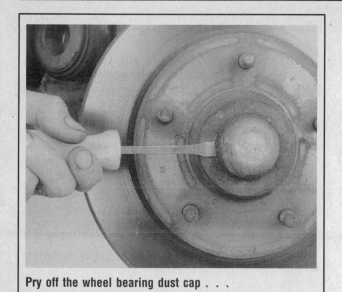

Pry off the wheel bearing dust cap . . .

. . . and the locknut ring

. . . and remove to gain access to the cotter pin

Remove the wheel bearing adjusting nut . . .

Remove the cotter pin . . .

. . . then pull the rotor off of the spindle

REAR DRUM BRAKES

❈❈ CAUTION

Brake shoes may contain asbestos, which has been determined to be a cancer causing agent. Never clean the brake surfaces with compressed air! Avoid inhaling any dust from any brake surface! When cleaning brake surfaces, use a commercially available brake cleaning fluid.

Brake Drum

INSPECTION

▶ **See Figure 19**

Check that there are no cracks or chips in the braking surface. Excessive bluing indicates overheating and a replacement drum is needed. The drum can be machined to remove minor damage and to establish a rounded braking surface on a warped drum. Never exceed the maximum oversize of the drum when machining the braking surface. The maximum inside diameter is stamped on the rim of the drum.

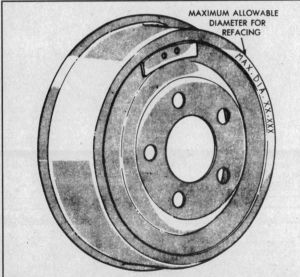

Fig. 19 Maximum allowable inside diameter dimensions are stamped on the rim of the brake drum

REMOVAL & INSTALLATION

Servo Type With Single Anchor

▶ **See Figure 20**

1. Jack and support the van.
2. Remove the plug from the brake adjustment access hole.

3. Insert a thin bladed screwdriver through the adjusting hole and hold the adjusting lever away from the star wheel.
4. Release the brake by prying down against the star wheel with a brake spoon.
5. Remove the rear wheel and clips from the wheel studs. Remove the brake drum.
6. Installation is the reverse of removal. Adjust the brakes.

Bendix Duo-Servo Type

1. Raise and support the vehicle.
2. Remove the rear wheel and tire.
3. Remove the axle shaft nuts, washers and cones. If the cones do not readily release, rap the axle shaft sharply in the center.
4. Remove the axle shaft.
5. Remove the outer hub nut.
6. Straighten the lockwasher tab and remove it along with the inner nut and bearing.
7. Carefully remove the drum.

To install:

8. Position the drum on the axle housing.
9. Install the bearing and inner nut. While rotating the wheel and tire, tighten the adjusting nut until a slight drag is felt.
10. Back off the adjusting nut 1/6 turn so that the wheel rotates freely without excessive end-play.
11. Install the lockrings and nut. Place a new gasket on the hub and install the axle shaft, cones, lockwashers and nuts.
12. Install the wheel and tire.
13. Road test the vehicle.

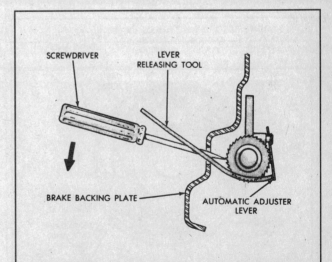

Fig. 20 Releasing the automatic adjuster lever from the starwheel

Brake Shoes

REMOVAL & INSTALLATION

Servo Type With Single Anchor

▶ **See Figures 21, 22, 23 and 24**

1. Raise and support the vehicle.

2. Remove the rear wheel, drum retaining clips and the brake drum.

3. Remove the brake shoe return springs, noting how the secondary spring overlaps the primary spring.

4. Remove the brake shoe retainer, springs and nails.

5. Disconnect the automatic adjuster cable from the anchor and unhook it from the lever. Remove the cable, cable guide, and anchor plate.

6. Remove the spring and lever from the shoe web.

7. Spread the anchor ends of the primary and secondary shoes and remove the parking brake spring and strut.

8. Disconnect the parking brake cable and remove the brake assembly.

9. Remove the primary and secondary brake shoe assemblies and the star adjuster as an assembly. Block the wheel cylinders to retain the pistons.

10. Measure the drum as described under Front Brakes.

To install:

11. Apply a thin coat of lubricant to the support platforms.

12. Attach the parking brake lever to the back side of the secondary shoe.

13. Place the primary and secondary shoes in their relative positions on a workbench.

14. Lubricate the adjuster screw threads. Install it between the primary and secondary shoes with the star wheel next to the secondary shoe. The star wheels are stamped with an **L** (left) and **R** (right).

15. Overlap the ends of the primary and second brake shoes and install the adjusting spring and lever at the anchor end.

16. Hold the shoes in position and install the parking brake cable into the lever.

17. Install the parking brake strut and spring between the parking brake lever and primary shoe.

18. Place the brake shoes on the support and install the retainer nails and springs.

19. Install the anchor pin plate.

20. Install the eye of the adjusting cable over the anchor pin and install the return spring between the anchor pin and primary shoe.

21. Install the cable guide in the secondary shoe and install the secondary return spring. Be sure that the primary spring overlaps the secondary spring.

22. Position the adjusting cable in the groove of the cable guide and engage the hook of the cable in the adjusting lever.

23. Install the brake drum and retaining clips. Install the wheel and tire.

24. Adjust the brakes and road test the van.

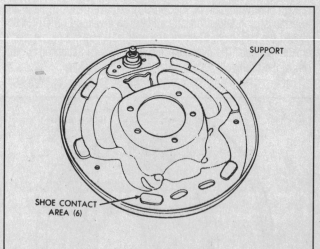

Fig. 22 Lubricate the shoe contact areas on the backing plate

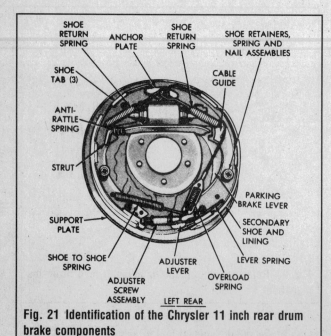

Fig. 21 Identification of the Chrysler 11 inch rear drum brake components

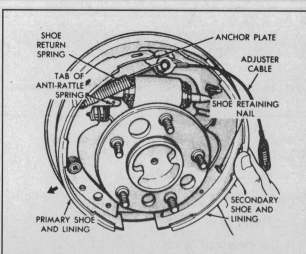

Fig. 23 The primary shoe always faces toward the front of the vehicle and has a shorter lining than the secondary shoe

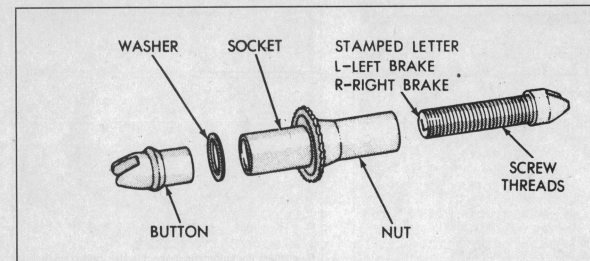

Fig. 24 Exploded view of the adjusting screw (starwheel)—lubricate the threads and the button/washer assembly

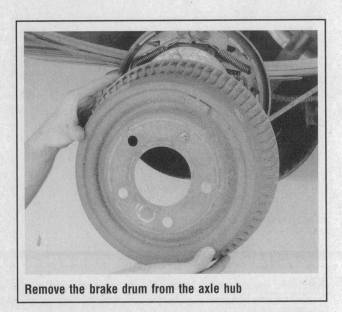

Remove the brake drum from the axle hub

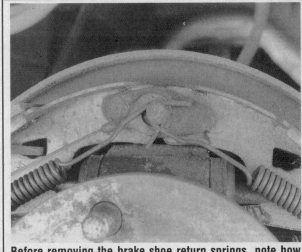

Before removing the brake shoe return springs, note how they overlap each other

If necessary, clean the brake assembly. Use an approved cleaner and follow all of its directions

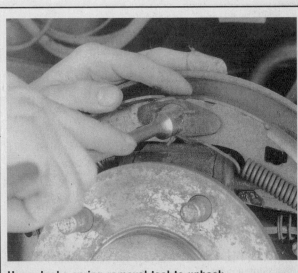

Use a brake spring removal tool to unhook . . .

. . . and remove both upper brake shoe return springs

Disconnect the automatic brake adjuster cable, cable guide and anchor plate

Push in and turn the shoe retainer 90 degrees . . .

Remove the automatic brake adjuster lever and spring

. . . and remove both retainer, spring and nail assemblies

Remove the upper pivot anchor plate

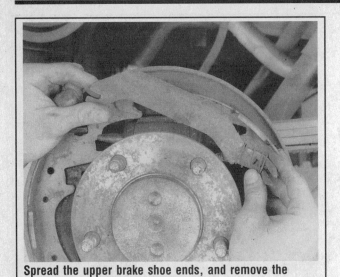

Spread the upper brake shoe ends, and remove the parking brake strut and spring

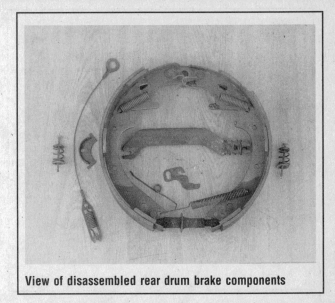

View of disassembled rear drum brake components

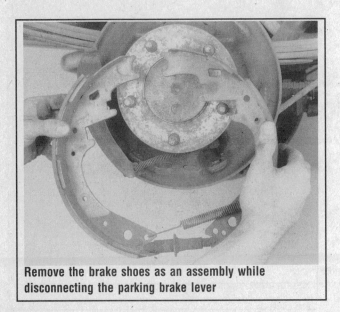

Remove the brake shoes as an assembly while disconnecting the parking brake lever

Overall view of properly installed brake shoes and components

Bendix Duo-Servo Type

▶ See Figures 25 thru 31

1. Unhook and remove the adjusting lever return spring.
2. Remove the lever from the lever pivot pin.
3. Unhook the adjuster lever from the adjuster cable.
4. Unhook the upper shoe-to-shoe spring.
5. Unhook and remove the shoe hold-down springs.
6. Disconnect the parking brake cable from the parking brake lever.
7. Remove the shoes with the lower shoe-to-shoe spring and star wheel as an assembly.

To install:

8. The pivot screw and adjusting nut on the left side have left-hand threads and right-hand threads on the right side.

9. Lubricate and assemble the star wheel assembly. Lubricate the guide pads on the support plates.
10. Assemble the star wheel, lower shoe-to-shoe spring, and the primary and secondary shoes. Position this assembly on the support plate.
11. Install and hook the hold-down springs.
12. Install the upper shoe-to-shoe spring.
13. Install the cable and retaining clip.
14. Position the adjuster lever return spring on the pivot (green springs on left brakes and red springs on right brakes).
15. Install the adjuster lever. Route the adjuster cable and connect it to the adjuster.
16. Install the brake drum and adjust the brakes.

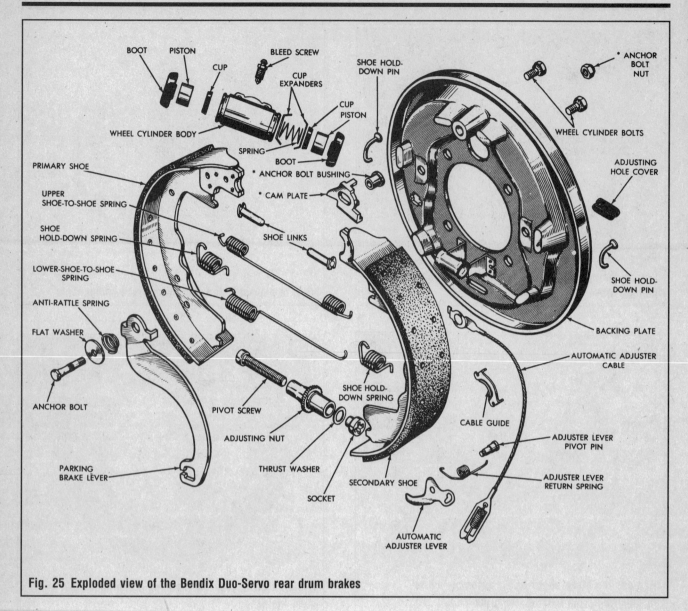

BOOT   PISTON   BLEED SCREW   SHOE HOLD-DOWN PIN   * ANCHOR BOLT NUT

CUP   CUP EXPANDERS

CUP PISTON   WHEEL CYLINDER BOLTS

WHEEL CYLINDER BODY

SPRING   BOOT   ADJUSTING HOLE COVER

PRIMARY SHOE   * ANCHOR BOLT BUSHING

UPPER SHOE-TO-SHOE SPRING   * CAM PLATE

SHOE HOLD-DOWN SPRING   SHOE LINKS   SHOE HOLD-DOWN PIN

LOWER-SHOE-TO-SHOE SPRING   BACKING PLATE

ANTI-RATTLE SPRING   AUTOMATIC ADJUSTER CABLE

FLAT WASHER

ANCHOR BOLT   PIVOT SCREW   SHOE HOLD-DOWN SPRING   CABLE GUIDE   ADJUSTER LEVER PIVOT PIN

ADJUSTING NUT   ADJUSTER LEVER RETURN SPRING

THRUST WASHER   SECONDARY SHOE

PARKING BRAKE LEVER   SOCKET   AUTOMATIC ADJUSTER LEVER

Fig. 25 Exploded view of the Bendix Duo-Servo rear drum brakes

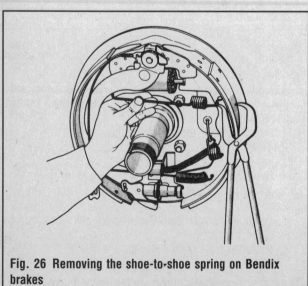

Fig. 26 Removing the shoe-to-shoe spring on Bendix brakes

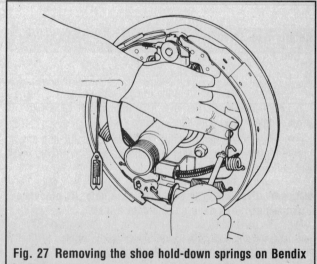

Fig. 27 Removing the shoe hold-down springs on Bendix brakes

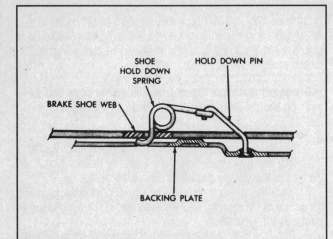

Fig. 28 View of the Bendix shoe hold-down spring and hold-down pin relationship

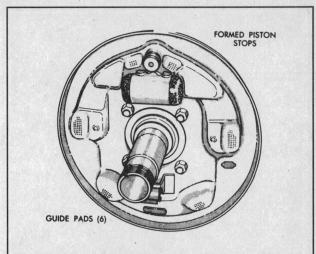

Fig. 30 View of the Bendix backing plate and guide pads—lubricate the guide pads (dotted areas)

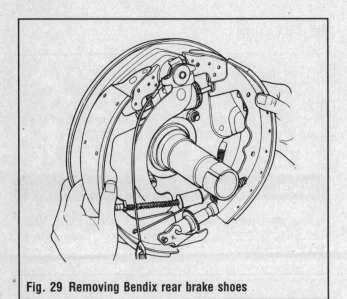

Fig. 29 Removing Bendix rear brake shoes

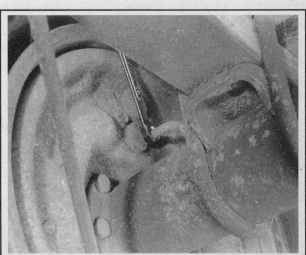

Fig. 31 View of a properly assembled Bendix rear drum brake

Wheel Cylinders

REMOVAL

When the brake drums are removed, carry out an inspection of the wheel cylinder boots for cuts, tears, cracks, or leaks. If any of these are present, the wheel cylinder should have a complete overhaul performed.

➡ **Preservative fluid is used during assembly; its presence in small quantities does not indicate a leak.**

1. Remove the brake shoes and check them. Replace them if they are soaked with grease or brake fluid.
2. Detach the brake hose.
3. Unfasten the wheel cylinder attachment bolts and slide the wheel cylinder off its support.

To remove the wheel cylinder, unfasten the brake line to the wheel cylinder

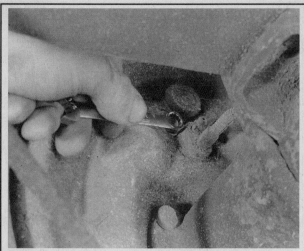

Remove the wheel cylinder attaching bolts and remove the wheel cylinder

OVERHAUL

▶ **See Figure 32**

1. Pry the boots off from either end of the wheel cylinder and withdraw the pushrods. Push in one of the pistons, to force out the other piston, its cup, the spring, the spring cup, and the piston, itself.

2. Wash the pistons, the wheel cylinder housing, and the spring in fresh brake fluid, or in denatured alcohol, and dry them off using compressed air.

✳✳ WARNING

Do not use a rag to dry them since the lint from it will stick to the surfaces.

3. Inspect the cylinder bore wall for signs of pitting, scoring, etc. If it is badly scored or pitted, the entire cylinder should be replaced. Light scratches or corrosion should be cleaned up with crocus cloth.

➡**Disregard the black stains from the piston cups that appear on the cylinder wall; they will do no damage.**

To assemble:

4. Dip the pistons and the cups in clean brake fluid. Replace the boots with new ones, if they show wear or deterioration. Coat the wall of the cylinder bore with clean brake fluid.

5. Place the spring in the cylinder bore. Position the cups in either end of the cylinder with the open end of the cups facing inward (toward each other).

6. Place the pistons in either end of the cylinder bore with the recessed ends facing outward (away from each other).

7. Install the boots over the ends of the cylinder and push down until each boot is seated, being careful not to damage either boot.

INSTALLATION

1. Install the wheel cylinder on its support.
2. Attach the jumper tube to the wheel cylinder. Install the brake hose on the frame bracket. Connect the brake line to the hose. Connect the end of the brake hose. Connect the end of the brake hose through the end of the stand-off. Attach the jumper tube to the brake hose and attach the hose to the stand-off.

Wheel Bearings

Rear wheel bearing adjustment (required only on Spicer 60 and 70 full-floating rear axles) is covered in Section 7 under Axle Shafts and Bearings.

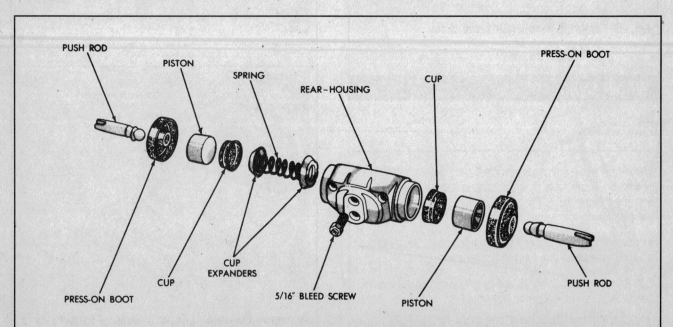

Fig. 32 Exploded view of a common rear wheel cylinder used on Chrysler brakes—Bendix style is similar

PARKING BRAKE

Front Cable

REMOVAL & INSTALLATION

▶ **See Figures 33, 34, 35, 36 and 37**

1967–72 Models

1. Raise and support the van on jackstands.
2. Disconnect the front cable return spring at the equalizer.
3. Remove the adjusting nut at the equalizer.
4. Disconnect the cable housing at the lower anchor point and remove the cable and housing from the bracket.

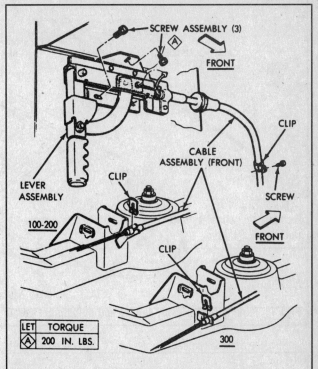

Fig. 34 Parking brake lever and cable for 1970–77 vehicles

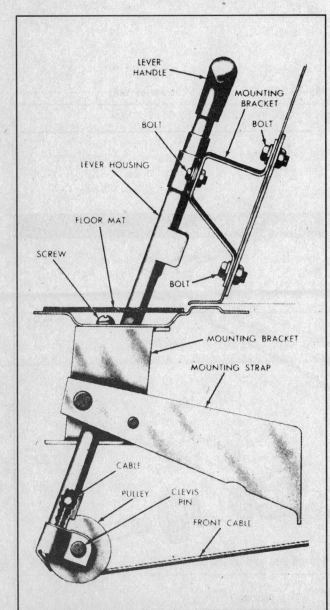

Fig. 33 Parking brake lever and cable for 1967–69 vehicles

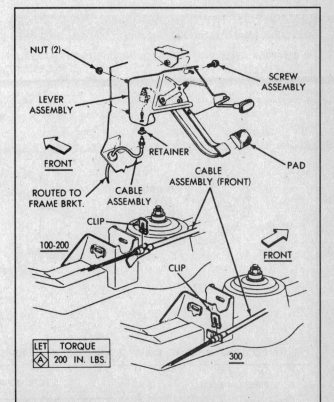

Fig. 35 Parking brake lever and cable for 1978–79 vehicles

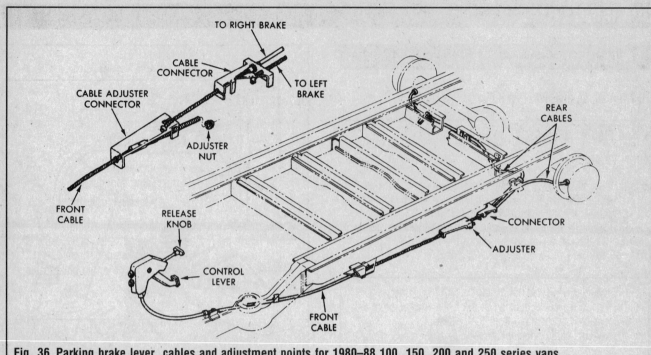

Fig. 36 Parking brake lever, cables and adjustment points for 1980–88 100, 150, 200 and 250 series vans

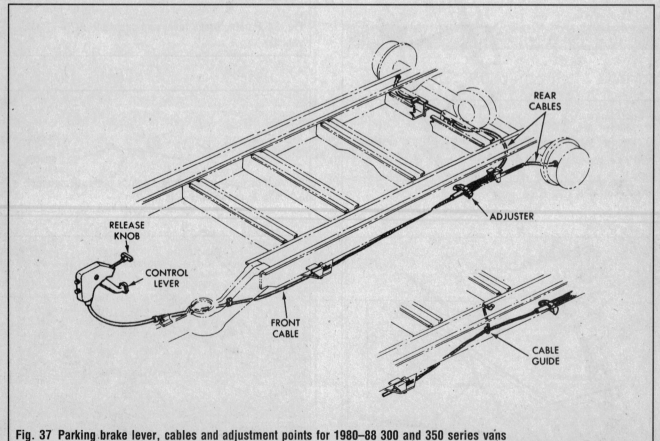

Fig. 37 Parking brake lever, cables and adjustment points for 1980–88 300 and 350 series vans

5. Remove the bolt from the cable housing anchor clip at the parking brake lever.

6. Remove the clevis pin at the lever.

7. Remove the anchor clip from the cable housing.

8. Remove the housing grommet from the firewall and cable assembly by pushing the grommet forward, towards the engine.

9. Install the housing grommet in the firewall.

10. Install the anchor clip on the cable housing.

11. Install the clevis pin at the lever.

12. Install the bolt from the cable housing anchor clip at the parking brake lever.

13. Install the cable and housing at the bracket. Connect the cable housing at the lower anchor point.

14. Install the adjusting nut at the equalizer.

15. Connect the front cable return spring at the equalizer.

16. Adjust the parking brake.

1973–88 Models

1. Raise and support the rear end on jackstands.

2. Remove the adjusting nut at the equalizer.

3. Disengage the cable housing at the lower anchor point and remove the cable and housing from the bracket.

4. Remove the cable housing anchor clip at the parking brake lever.

5. Remove the anchor clip from the lever.

6. Remove the housing grommet from the floor board.

7. Installation is the reverse of removal. Adjust the brakes.

Intermediate Cable

REMOVAL & INSTALLATION

▶ See Figure 38

1979–88 B100 and 200 Models With 12.12″ × 2″ Brakes

1. Remove the adjusting nut at the adjusting link.

2. Disengage the rear end of the cable from the ratio lever and remove the cable.

3. Installation is the reverse of removal. Adjust the brakes.

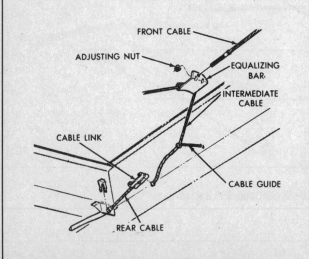

Fig. 38 Intermediate cable and adjustment point

Rear Cable

REMOVAL & INSTALLATION

1967–72 Models

1. Raise and support the vehicle.

2. Release the brake and remove the rear wheels.

3. Remove the brake drum.

4. Remove the brake shoe return springs.

5. Remove the brake shoe retaining springs.

6. Remove the brake shoes, strut and spring from the support plate.

7. Disconnect the brake cable from the operating arm.

8. Compress the retainers on the end of the brake cable housing and remove the cables from the brake support plate.

9. Remove the retaining bolt and nut from the brake cable bracket and clips at the front bracket.

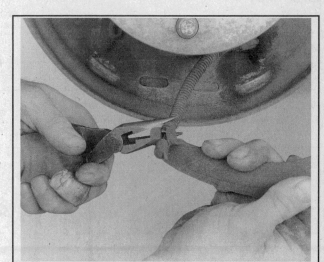

After removing all of the brake components, disconnect the cable from the operating arm

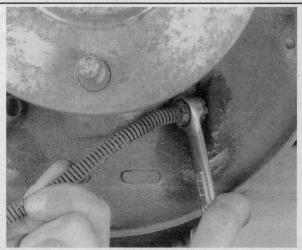

Compress the retaining fingers to remove the cable from the backing plate—a wrench works well

10. Disconnect the brake cable at the equalizer bar.
11. Remove the cable assembly.
12. Installation is the reverse of removal. Adjust the brakes.

1973–88 Models

1. Raise and support the rear end on jackstands.
2. Remove the rear wheels.
3. Remove the drums.
4. Remove the brake shoe return springs.
5. Remove the brake shoe retaining springs.
6. Remove the shoes, strut and spring from the support plate.
7. Disconnect the cable from the operating arm.
8. Compress the retainers on the end of the cable housing and remove the cable from the support plate.
9. Move the retaining clip out at the crossmember.
10. Disconnect the brake cable from the equalizer.
11. Installation is the reverse of removal. Adjust the brakes.

ADJUSTMENT

▶ **See Figure 36, 37 and 39**

All Models

1. Adjust the service brakes by making a few stops in reverse.
2. Raise and support the rear end on jackstands.

3. Release the parking brake lever and loosen the cable adjusting nut to be sure that the cable is slack.
4. Tighten the cable adjusting nut until a slight drag is felt while rotating the wheels.
5. Loosen the cable adjusting nut until the wheels can be rotated freely, then back off the cable adjusting nut two turns.
6. Apply the parking brake several times, then release it and check to be sure that the rear wheels rotate freely.

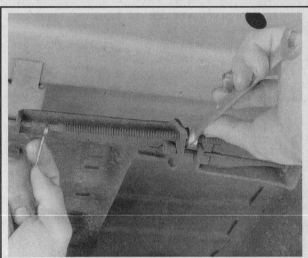

Hold the cable end while turning the adjusting screw on the parking brake cable

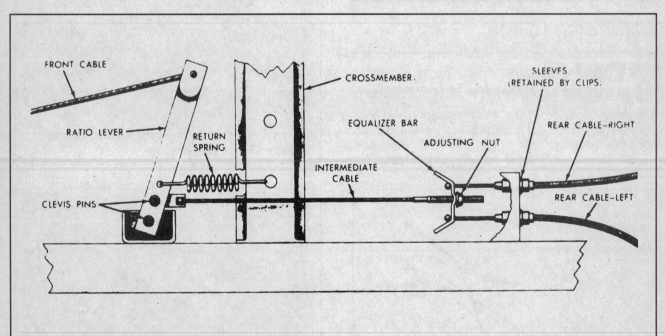

Fig. 39 Handbrake adjustment point for 1967–69 vehicles

Brake Specifications

All specifications in inches

Years	Models	Master Cyl. Bore	Brake Disc Minimum Thickness	Brake Disc Maximum Run-out	Brake Drum Orig. Inside Dia.	Brake Drum Max. Wear Limit	Wheel Cyl. or Caliper Bore Front	Wheel Cyl. or Caliper Bore Rear
1967	3800 GVW 4600 GVW	1.00	—	—	F10.00 R10.00	10.06	1⅛	13/16
	5200 GVW 5400 GVW	1.00	—	—	F11.00 R10.00	11.06 10.06	1⅛	13/16
1968–69	3800 GVW 4000 GVW 4600 GVW	1.00	—	—	F10.00 R10.00	10.06	1⅛	13/16
	4800 GVW 5200 GVW 5400 GVW	1.00	—	—	F11.00 R10.00	11.06 10.06	1⅛	13/16
1970–71	B100	1.00	—	—	F10.00 R10.00	10.06	1 3/16	⅞
	B200	1.00	—	—	F11.00 R10.00	11.06 10.06	1 3/16	⅞
	B300	1.125	—	—	F12.00 R12.00	12.06	1⅛	⅞
1972–75	B100	1.03	1.22	0.004	10.00	10.06	3.10	⅞
	B200	1.03	1.22	0.004	11.00	11.06	3.10	15/16
	B300 MB300	1.125	1.16	0.004	12.00	12.06	3.10	⅞
	CB300 MB300 w/DRW	1.125	1.16	0.004	12.00	12.06	3.10	1.00
1976–77	100	1.03	1.22	0.004	10.00	10.06	3.10	⅞
	200	1.03	1.22	0.004	11.00	11.06	3.10	15/16
	300	1.125	1.16	0.004	12.00	12.06	3.10	⅞
	300 w/DRW	1.125	1.16	0.004	12.00	12.06	3.10	1.00

Brake Specifications *(cont.)*
All specifications in inches

Years	Models	Master Cyl. Bore	Brake Disc		Brake Drum		Wheel Cyl. or Caliper Bore	
			Minimum Thickness	Maximum Run-out	Orig. Inside Dia.	Max. Wear Limit	Front	Rear
1978	100	1.03	1.22	0.004	10.00	10.06	3.10	7/8
	200	1.03	1.22	0.004	10.00	10.06	3.10	15/16
	300	1.125	1.16	0.004	12.00	12.06	3.10	7/8
	300 w/DRW	1.125	1.16	0.004	12.00	12.06	3.10	1.00
1979–80	100	1.125	1.22	0.004	10.00	10.06	3.10	15/16
	200	1.125	1.22	0.004	10.00	10.06	3.10	15/16
	300 w/3600 lb. FA	1.125	1.22	0.004	12.00	12.06	3.10	7/8
	300 w/4000 lb. FA	1.125	1.16	0.004	12.00	12.06	3.10	1.00
1981–83	150	1.125	1.22	0.004	10.00	10.06	3.10	15/16
	250	1.125	1.22	0.004	10.00	10.06	3.10	15/16
	350 w/3600 lb. FA	1.125	1.22	0.004	12.00	12.06	3.10	1.00
	350 w/4000 lb. FA	1.125	1.16	0.004	12.00	12.06	3.10	1.06
	350 school bus	1.310	1.16	0.004	12.00	12.06	3.10	1.06
1984	150	1.125	1.22	0.004	11.00	11.06	3.10	15/16
	250	1.125	1.22	0.004	11.00	11.06	3.10	15/16
	350 w/3600 lb. FA	1.125	1.22	0.004	12.00	12.06	3.10	1.00
	350 w/4000 lb. FA	1.125	1.16	0.004	12.00	12.06	3.10	1.06
	350 school bus	1.125	1.16	0.004	12.00	12.06	3.10	1.06
1985–88	150	1.125	1.22	0.004	11.00	11.06	3.10	15/16
	250	1.125	1.22	0.004	11.00	11.06	3.10	15/16
	350 w/3600 lb. FA	1.125	1.22	0.004	12.00	12.06	3.10	7/8
	350 w/4000 lb. FA	1.125	1.16	0.004	12.00	12.06	3.10	1.00
	350 school bus	1.125	1.16	0.004	12.00	12.06	3.10	1.00

DRW: dual rear wheels
FA: front axle

Troubleshooting the Brake System

Problem	Cause	Solution
Low brake pedal (excessive pedal travel required for braking action.)	• Excessive clearance between rear linings and drums caused by inoperative automatic adjusters	• Make 10 to 15 alternate forward and reverse brake stops to adjust brakes. If brake pedal does not come up, repair or replace adjuster parts as necessary.
	• Worn rear brakelining	• Inspect and replace lining if worn beyond minimum thickness specification
	• Bent, distorted brakeshoes, front or rear	• Replace brakeshoes in axle sets
	• Air in hydraulic system	• Remove air from system. Refer to Brake Bleeding.
Low brake pedal (pedal may go to floor with steady pressure applied.)	• Fluid leak in hydraulic system	• Fill master cylinder to fill line; have helper apply brakes and check calipers, wheel cylinders, differential valve tubes, hoses and fittings for leaks. Repair or replace as necessary.
	• Air in hydraulic system	• Remove air from system. Refer to Brake Bleeding.
	• Incorrect or non-recommended brake fluid (fluid evaporates at below normal temp).	• Flush hydraulic system with clean brake fluid. Refill with correct-type fluid.
	• Master cylinder piston seals worn, or master cylinder bore is scored, worn or corroded	• Repair or replace master cylinder
Low brake pedal (pedal goes to floor on first application—o.k. on subsequent applications.)	• Disc brake pads sticking on abutment surfaces of anchor plate. Caused by a build-up of dirt, rust, or corrosion on abutment surfaces	• Clean abutment surfaces
Fading brake pedal (pedal height decreases with steady pressure applied.)	• Fluid leak in hydraulic system	• Fill master cylinder reservoirs to fill mark, have helper apply brakes, check calipers, wheel cylinders, differential valve, tubes, hoses, and fittings for fluid leaks. Repair or replace parts as necessary.
	• Master cylinder piston seals worn, or master cylinder bore is scored, worn or corroded	• Repair or replace master cylinder
Decreasing brake pedal travel (pedal travel required for braking action decreases and may be accompanied by a hard pedal.)	• Caliper or wheel cylinder pistons sticking or seized	• Repair or replace the calipers, or wheel-cylinders
	• Master cylinder compensator ports blocked (preventing fluid return to reservoirs) or pistons sticking or seized in master cylinder bore	• Repair or replace the master cylinder
	• Power brake unit binding internally	• Test unit according to the following procedure: (a) Shift transmission into neutral and start engine (b) Increase engine speed to 1500 rpm, close throttle and fully depress brake pedal (c) Slow release brake pedal and stop engine (d) Have helper remove vacuum check valve and hose from power unit. Observe for backward movement of brake pedal. (e) If the pedal moves backward, the power unit has an internal bind—replace power unit

Troubleshooting the Brake System (cont.)

Problem	Cause	Solution
Spongy brake pedal (pedal has abnormally soft, springy, spongy feel when depressed.)	• Air in hydraulic system • Brakeshoes bent or distorted • Brakelining not yet seated with drums and rotors • Rear drum brakes not properly adjusted	• Remove air from system. Refer to Brake Bleeding. • Replace brakeshoes • Burnish brakes • Adjust brakes

Hard brake pedal (excessive pedal pressure required to stop vehicle. May be accompanied by brake fade.)	• Loose or leaking power brake unit vacuum hose
	• Incorrect or poor quality brakelining
	• Bent, broken, distorted brakeshoes
	• Calipers binding or dragging on mounting pins. Rear brakeshoes dragging on support plate.
	
	• Caliper, wheel cylinder, or master cylinder pistons sticking or seized
	• Power brake unit vacuum check valve malfunction
	
	• Power brake unit has internal bind
	
	• Master cylinder compensator ports (at bottom of reservoirs) blocked by dirt, scale, rust, or have small burrs (blocked ports prevent fluid return to reservoirs).
	• Brake hoses, tubes, fittings clogged or restricted
	• Brake fluid contaminated with improper fluids (motor oil, transmission fluid, causing rubber components to swell and stick in bores
	• Low engine vacuum
		• Tighten connections or replace leaking hose
		• Replace with lining in axle sets
		
		• Replace brakeshoes
		• Replace mounting pins and bushings. Clean rust or burrs from rear brake support plate ledges and lubricate ledges with molydisulfide grease.
		NOTE: If ledges are deeply grooved or scored, do not attempt to sand or grind them smooth—replace support plate.
		• Repair or replace parts as necessary
		
		• Test valve according to the following procedure:
		  (a) Start engine, increase engine speed to 1500 rpm, close throttle and immediately stop engine
		  (b) Wait at least 90 seconds then depress brake pedal
		  (c) If brakes are not vacuum assisted for 2 or more applications, check valve is faulty
		• Test unit according to the following procedure:
		  (a) With engine stopped, apply brakes several times to exhaust all vacuum in system
		  (b) Shift transmission into neutral, depress brake pedal and start engine
		  (c) If pedal height decreases with foot pressure and less pressure is required to hold pedal in applied position, power unit vacuum system is operating normally. Test power unit. If power unit exhibits a bind condition, replace the power unit.
		• Repair or replace master cylinder
		CAUTION: Do not attempt to clean blocked ports with wire, pencils, or similar implements. Use compressed air only.
		• Use compressed air to check or unclog parts. Replace any damaged parts.
		• Replace all rubber components, combination valve and hoses. Flush entire brake system with DOT 3 brake fluid or equivalent.
		
		• Adjust or repair engine

Troubleshooting the Brake System (cont.)

Problem	Cause	Solution
Grabbing brakes (severe reaction to brake pedal pressure.)	• Brakelining(s) contaminated by grease or brake fluid	• Determine and correct cause of contamination and replace brakeshoes in axle sets
	• Parking brake cables incorrectly adjusted or seized	• Adjust cables. Replace seized cables.
	• Incorrect brakelining or lining loose on brakeshoes	• Replace brakeshoes in axle sets
	• Caliper anchor plate bolts loose	• Tighten bolts
	• Rear brakeshoes binding on support plate ledges	• Clean and lubricate ledges. Replace support plate(s) if ledges are deeply grooved. Do not attempt to smooth ledges by grinding.
	• Incorrect or missing power brake reaction disc	• Install correct disc
	• Rear brake support plates loose	• Tighten mounting bolts
Dragging brakes (slow or incomplete release of brakes)	• Brake pedal binding at pivot	• Loosen and lubricate
	• Power brake unit has internal bind	• Inspect for internal bind. Replace unit if internal bind exists.
	• Parking brake cables incorrrectly adjusted or seized	• Adjust cables. Replace seized cables.
	• Rear brakeshoe return springs weak or broken	• Replace return springs. Replace brakeshoe if necessary in axle sets.
	• Automatic adjusters malfunctioning	• Repair or replace adjuster parts as required
	• Caliper, wheel cylinder or master cylinder pistons sticking or seized	• Repair or replace parts as necessary
	• Master cylinder compensating ports blocked (fluid does not return to reservoirs).	• Use compressed air to clear ports. Do not use wire, pencils, or similar objects to open blocked ports.
Vehicle moves to one side when brakes are applied	• Incorrect front tire pressure	• Inflate to recommended cold (reduced load) inflation pressure
	• Worn or damaged wheel bearings	• Replace worn or damaged bearings
	• Brakelining on one side contaminated	• Determine and correct cause of contamination and replace brakelining in axle sets
	• Brakeshoes on one side bent, distorted, or lining loose on shoe	• Replace brakeshoes in axle sets
	• Support plate bent or loose on one side	• Tighten or replace support plate
	• Brakelining not yet seated with drums or rotors	• Burnish brakelining
	• Caliper anchor plate loose on one side	• Tighten anchor plate bolts
	• Caliper piston sticking or seized	• Repair or replace caliper
	• Brakelinings water soaked	• Drive vehicle with brakes lightly applied to dry linings
	• Loose suspension component attaching or mounting bolts	• Tighten suspension bolts. Replace worn suspension components.
	• Brake combination valve failure	• Replace combination valve
Chatter or shudder when brakes are applied (pedal pulsation and roughness may also occur.)	• Brakeshoes distorted, bent, contaminated, or worn	• Replace brakeshoes in axle sets
	• Caliper anchor plate or support plate loose	• Tighten mounting bolts
	• Excessive thickness variation of rotor(s)	• Refinish or replace rotors in axle sets
Noisy brakes (squealing, clicking, scraping sound when brakes are applied.)	• Bent, broken, distorted brakeshoes	• Replace brakeshoes in axle sets
	• Excessive rust on outer edge of rotor braking surface	• Remove rust

Troubleshooting the Brake System (cont.)

Problem	Cause	Solution
Noisy brakes (squealing, clicking, scraping sound when brakes are applied.) (cont.)	• Brakelining worn out—shoes contacting drum of rotor	• Replace brakeshoes and lining in axle sets. Refinish or replace drums or rotors.
	• Broken or loose holdown or return springs	• Replace parts as necessary
	• Rough or dry drum brake support plate ledges	• Lubricate support plate ledges
	• Cracked, grooved, or scored rotor(s) or drum(s)	• Replace rotor(s) or drum(s). Replace brakeshoes and lining in axle sets if necessary.
	• Incorrect brakelining and/or shoes (front or rear).	• Install specified shoe and lining assemblies
Pulsating brake pedal	• Out of round drums or excessive lateral runout in disc brake rotor(s)	• Refinish or replace drums, re-index rotors or replace

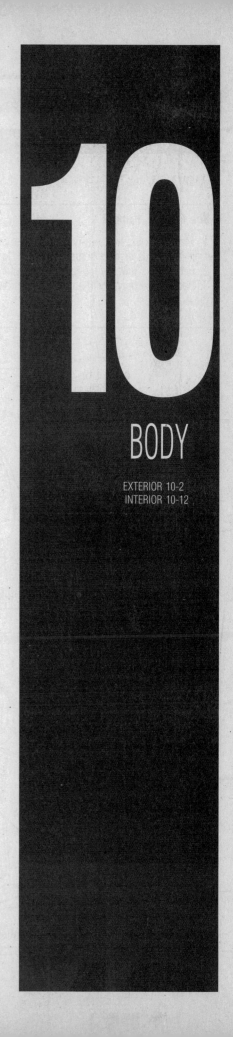

10

BODY

EXTERIOR

Front Doors

REMOVAL & INSTALLATION

♦ **See Figures 1 and 2**

1. Matchmark the hinge-to-body locations. Support the door either on jackstands or have somebody hold it for you.
2. Remove the lower hinge-to-frame bolts.
3. Remove the upper hinge-to-frame bolts and lift the door off of the body.

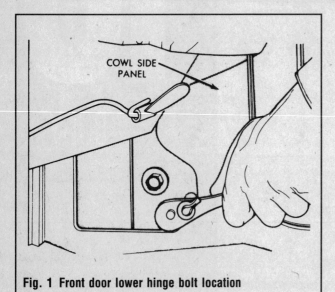

Fig. 1 Front door lower hinge bolt location

Fig. 2 Front door upper hinge bolt location

4. Install the door and hinges with the bolts finger-tight.
5. Adjust the door and torque the hinge bolts to 24 ft. lbs.

ADJUSTMENT

➡**Loosen the hinge-to-door bolts for lateral adjustment only. Loosen the hinge-to-body bolts for both lateral and vertical adjustment.**

1. Determine which hinge bolts are to be loosened and back them out just enough to allow movement.
2. To move the door safely, use a padded prybar. When the door is in the proper position, tighten the bolts to 24 ft. lbs. and check the door operation. There should be no binding interference when the door is closed and opened.
3. Door closing adjustment can also be affected by the position of the lock striker plate. Loosen the striker plate bolts and move the striker plate just enough to permit proper closing and locking of the door.

If necessary, loosen the striker bolt and adjust

Swing-Open Side Doors

♦ **See Figure 3**

REMOVAL & INSTALLATION

1. Matchmark the hinge-to-body locations. Support the door either on jackstands or have somebody hold it for you.
2. Remove the lower hinge-to-frame bolts.
3. Remove the upper hinge-to-frame bolts and lift the door off of the body.
4. Install the door and hinges with the bolts finger-tight.
5. Adjust the door and torque the hinge bolts to 24 ft. lbs.

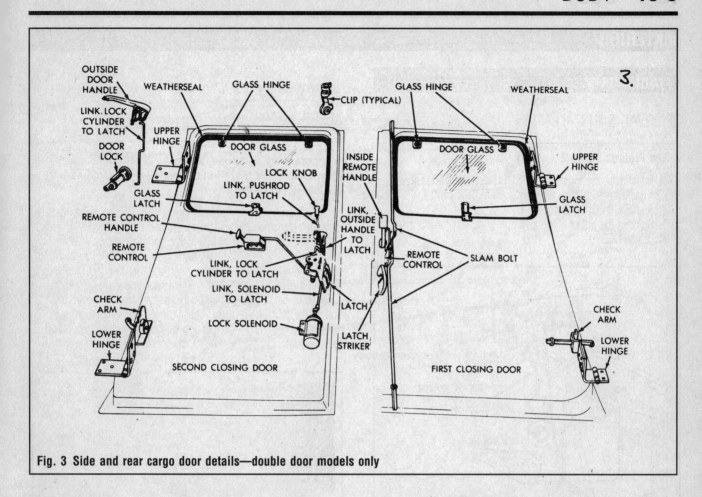

Fig. 3 Side and rear cargo door details—double door models only

ADJUSTMENT

➡Loosen the hinge-to-door bolts for lateral adjustment only. Loosen the hinge-to-body bolts for both lateral and vertical adjustment.

1. Determine which hinge bolts are to be loosened and back them out just enough to allow movement.

2. To move the door safely, use a padded prybar. When the door is in the proper position, tighten the bolts to 24 ft. lbs. and check the door operation. There should be no binding or interference when the door is closed and opened.

3. Door closing adjustment can also be affected by the position of the lock striker plate. Loosen the striker plate bolts and move the striker plate just enough to permit proper closing and locking of the door.

Sliding Side Doors

▶ **See Figure 4**

REMOVAL & INSTALLATION

---

1. Remove the lower rear screw from the roller track cover, body sheet metal side.

2. Remove the 2 bolts securing the upper hinge assembly mounting plate and remove the plate.

3. Remove the 2 screws securing the lower roller bracket to the door lower roller bracket support assembly.

4. Now, you'll need an assistant. Slide the door rearward, guiding the upper front and rear rollers out of the rails.

5. Installation is the reverse of removal. Adjust the door as described above.

ADJUSTMENT

1975–78 Models

VERTICAL ADJUSTMENT

1. Front fit is controlled at the lower roller support bracket. Loosen the 4 screws and adjust the door.

2. Rear fit is controlled at the upper hinge roller assembly. Loosen the 3 screws and adjust the door to maintain 0.04-0.06" clearance between the plastic guide on the roller and the track flang top surface by controlling the angle of the hinge door half relative to the body horizontal.

FORE AND AFT ADJUSTMENT

Loosen the 2 screws and adjust the hinge-roller assembly to control the door position.

IN-OUT ADJUSTMENT

1. Front lower fit is controlled at the lower roller bracket. Loosen the 2 screws and adjust the door.

2. Front upper fit is controlled at the upper hinge roller-to-

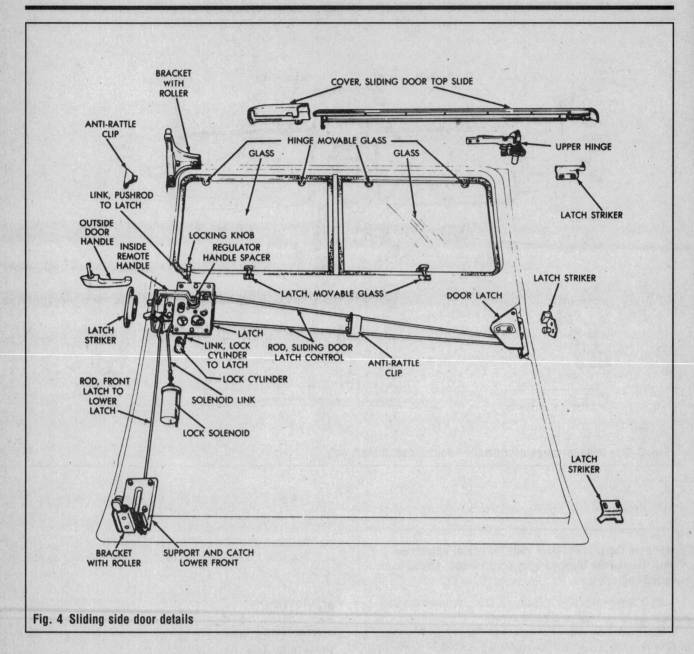

BRACKET WITH ROLLER

COVER, SLIDING DOOR TOP SLIDE

ANTI-RATTLE CLIP

HINGE MOVABLE GLASS

GLASS

GLASS

UPPER HINGE

LINK, PUSHROD TO LATCH

LATCH STRIKER

OUTSIDE DOOR HANDLE

LOCKING KNOB

INSIDE REMOTE HANDLE

REGULATOR HANDLE SPACER

LATCH, MOVABLE GLASS

DOOR LATCH

LATCH STRIKER

LATCH STRIKER

LATCH

LINK, LOCK CYLINDER TO LATCH

ROD, SLIDING DOOR LATCH CONTROL

ANTI-RATTLE CLIP

LATCH STRIKER

ROD, FRONT LATCH TO LOWER LATCH

LOCK CYLINDER

SOLENOID LINK

LOCK SOLENOID

BRACKET WITH ROLLER

SUPPORT AND CATCH LOWER FRONT

Fig. 4 Sliding side door details

bracket mounting stud. Loosen the 3 screws and adjust the door to maintain a 0.10" roller-to-track clearance.

3. Rear fit is adjusted at the rear striker.

1979–88 Models

FORE AND AFT ADJUSTMENT

1. Remove the outer covers.

2. Loosen the hinge-roller screws and move the assembly to the desired position.

3. Tighten the screws and check the fit.

4. If necessary, shim the front striker to make sure that the pin enters the striker by 12–15mm.

5. If it was necessary to shim the striker, loosen the striker screws so they are just snug, close the door and open it carefully so as not to move the striker. Tighten the screws.

VERTICAL ADJUSTMENT

1. Front edge fit:

a. Loosen the 3 upper roller bracket screws.

b. Loosen the 4 lower attaching screws.

c. Move the door to the correct position and tighten the lower bolts.

d. Make sure that there is 1.5mm clearance between the top roller and the top of the track.

2. Rear edge fit:

a. Loosen the rear center striker and move it up or down the amount the door is to be raised or lowered, and tighten the screws.

b. Close the door so that the rear latch is caught, but not fully closed.

c. Loosen the 3 hinge screws and fully close the door.

d. Push the front edge of the hinge up as far as it will go and snug down the front screw.

e. Pull down firmly on the swing arm and full tighten all 3 screws.

f. Make sure that there is 0.8mm clearance between the latch pawl and striker bar.

IN AND OUT ADJUSTMENT

1. Front upper corner adjustments are made by loosening the roller stud nut and moving the door to the correct position. Maintain a 1.5mm clearance between the rollers and the top of the track. Tighten the screws.

2. Front lower corner adjustments are made by loosening the 2 lower roller support bracket screws and moving the door to the desired position. Tighten the screws.

3. Rear adjustments are made by loosening the rear center striker and moving it to the desired position. Tighten the screws.

Rear Doors

▶ **See Figures 3, 5 and 6**

REMOVAL & INSTALLATION

1. Matchmark the hinge-to-body locations. Support the door either on jackstands or have somebody hold it for you.

2. Remove the lower hinge-to-frame bolts.

3. Remove the upper hinge-to-frame bolts and lift the door off of the body.

4. Install the door and hinges with the bolts finger-tight.

5. Adjust the door and torque the hinge bolts to 24 ft. lbs.

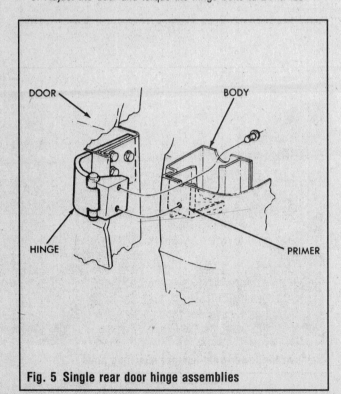

Fig. 5 Single rear door hinge assemblies

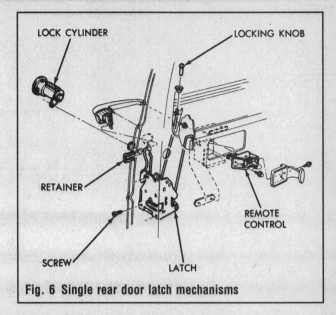

Fig. 6 Single rear door latch mechanisms

ADJUSTMENT

➡ **Loosen the hinge-to-door bolts for lateral adjustment only. Loosen the hinge-to-body bolts for both lateral and vertical adjustment.**

1. Determine which hinge bolts are to be loosened and back them out just enough to allow movement.

2. To move the door safely, use a padded prybar. When the door is in the proper position, tighten the bolts to 24 ft. lbs. and check the door operation. There should be no binding or interference when the door is closed and opened.

3. Door closing adjustment can also be affected by the position of the lock striker plate. Loosen the striker plate bolts and move the striker plate just enough to permit proper closing and locking of the door.

Exterior Hood

REMOVAL & INSTALLATION

▶ **See Figure 7**

1. Open and prop up the hood.

2. Remove the bolts from each hinge and lift off the hood.

3. Installation is the reverse of removal.

ALIGNMENT

The hood can be adjusted fore-aft and up-and-down to obtain a proper fit.

1. Loosen the hood-to-hinge bolts until they are finger-tight.

2. Reposition the hood as required.

3. Tighten the bolts.

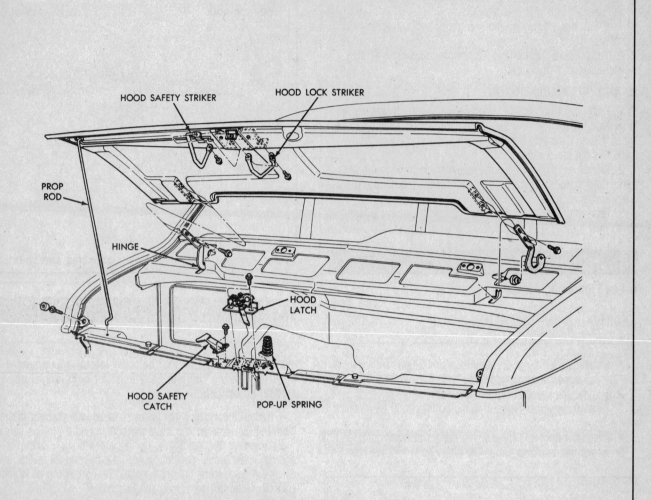

HOOD SAFETY STRIKER

HOOD LOCK STRIKER

PROP
ROD

HINGE

HOOD
LATCH

HOOD SAFETY
CATCH

POP-UP SPRING

Fig. 7 Common front hood assembly and related components

Front Bumpers

REMOVAL & INSTALLATION

1967–69 Models

1. Support the bumper.
2. Remove the nuts and bolts attaching the bumper to the frame and/or bumper arms.
3. Installation is the reverse of removal. Torque the bracket-to-frame bolts to 100 ft. lbs. on models with frame mounted bumpers.

1970–78 Models

1. Raise the hood.
2. Remove the grille.
3. Disconnect the parking light wiring.

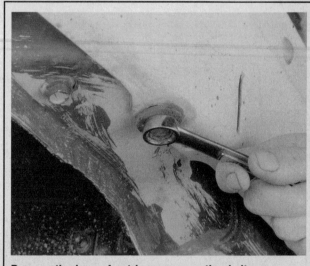

Remove the lower front bumper mounting bolts . . .

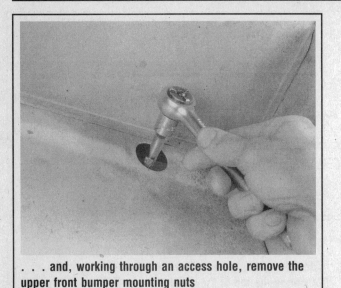

. . . and, working through an access hole, remove the upper front bumper mounting nuts

4. Support the bumper and remove the upper and lower mounting bolts.
5. Installation is the reverse of removal.

1979–88 Models

1. Remove the bumper guards.
2. Support the bumper and remove it from the brackets.
3. Installation is the reverse of removal.

Rear Bumpers

REMOVAL & INSTALLATION

1. Support the bumper.
2. Remove the nuts and bolts attaching the bumper to the frame and/or bumper arms.
3. Installation is the reverse of removal.

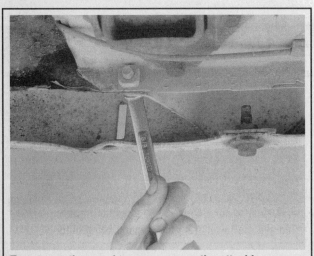

To remove the rear bumper, remove the attaching arm-to-frame bolts, or . . .

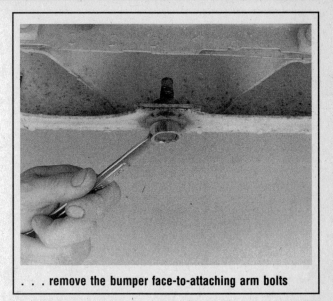

. . . remove the bumper face-to-attaching arm bolts

Grille

REMOVAL & INSTALLATION

1967–69 Models

The grille panel is a one piece stamped unit attached to the front sheet metal by 4 bolts at the bottom and 4 phillips screws at the top.

1970–74 Models

1. Remove the grille mounting bolts and nuts.
2. Disconnect the parking lamp wiring.
3. Installation is the reverse of removal.

1975–78 Models

1. Remove the headlamp trim.
2. Remove the grille mounting bolts and nuts.
3. Disconnect the parking lamp wiring.
4. Installation is the reverse of removal.

1979–88 Models

2 HEADLAMP SYSTEM

1. Remove the parking lamps.
2. Remove the grille mounting screws and lift out the grille.
3. Installation is the reverse of removal.

4 HEADLAMP SYSTEM

1. Remove the headlamp trim.
2. Remove the grille mounting bolts and nuts.
3. Remove the parking lamps.
4. Installation is the reverse of removal.

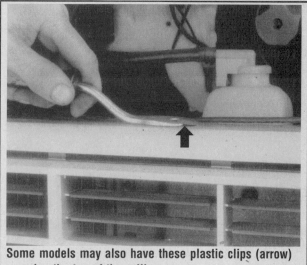

Remove the grille mounting screws along the center of the grille . . .

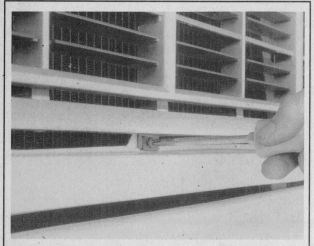

Some models may also have these plastic clips (arrow) securing the top of the grille

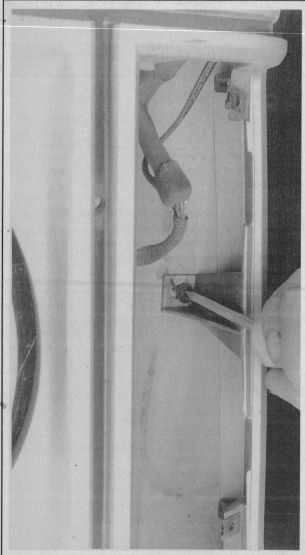

. . . as well as the ones hidden behind the parking lamp assemblies

Carefully remove the grille from the vehicle

Outside Mirrors

REMOVAL & INSTALLATION

All mirrors are removed by removing the mounting screws and lifting off the mirror and gasket.

Antenna

➡On 1967–77 vans, the antenna and cable can be removed separately. The antenna is easily unbolted from the body. The following procedures are for complete cable and mast removal.

REMOVAL & INSTALLATION

1967–69 Models

1. Disconnect the antenna cable at the radio by pulling it straight out of the set.
2. Working under the instrument panel, disengage the cable from its retainers.
3. Remove the mounting nut and mounting screw and lift off the antenna. At this point you can either unscrew the cable from the mast or pull it out with the mast.
4. Installation is the reverse of removal.

1970–74 Models

1. Disconnect the antenna lead from the back of the radio.
2. Remove the cable from the mounting clips.
3. Remove the mast mounting bolt and screw. They are accessible through the fresh air door in the right kick panel.
4. Installation is the reverse of removal.

1975–77 Models

1. Disconnect the battery ground cable.
2. Remove the windshield wiper arms.
3. Remove the cowl grille.
4. Disconnect the washer hoses from the nozzles.
5. On vans equipped with air conditioning, remove the lower panel cover.
6. Remove the radio bezel.
7. Unplug the antenna from the radio.
8. Open the right air door and unscrew the cable from the antenna.
9. Working under the hood, remove the cable grommet from the plenum chamber.
10. Remove the cable.
11. Remove the antenna mounting nuts and remove the antenna.
   To install:
12. Install the antenna.
13. Position the cable.
14. Install the cable grommet from the plenum chamber.
15. Screw the cable onto the antenna.
16. Plug the antenna into the radio.
17. Install the radio bezel.
18. On vans equipped with air conditioning, install the lower panel cover.
19. Connect the washer hoses to the nozzles.
20. Install the cowl grille.
21. Install the windshield wiper arms.
22. Connect the battery ground cable.

1978–88 Models

1. Disconnect the battery ground cable.
2. Remove the windshield wiper arms.
3. Remove the cowl grille.
4. Disconnect the washer hoses from the nozzles.
5. Remove the glove box. It snaps out.
6. On vans equipped with air conditioning, remove the right air duct.
7. Reaching through the glove box opening, unplug the antenna cable from the radio.

8. Working under the hood, remove the cable and grommet from the plenum chamber.
9. Unscrew the mast from the adapter.
10. Reach through the cowl opening and hold the antenna body.
11. Remove the adapter cap nut and pull the antenna from the sheet metal.
   To install:
12. Place the antenna in the sheet metal and install the adapter cap nut. Torque the capnut to 100–150 in. lbs.
13. Install the mast in the adapter.
14. Install the cable and grommet in the plenum chamber.
15. Plug the antenna cable into the radio.
16. On vans equipped with air conditioning, install the right air duct.
17. Install the glove box.
18. Connect the washer hoses at the nozzles.
19. Install the cowl grille.
20. Install the windshield wiper arms.
21. Connect the battery ground cable.

Windshield

REMOVAL & INSTALLATION

▶ **See Figure 8**

1967–69 Models

1. Remove the wiper arm and blade assemblies.
2. Pry off the center bar retainer starting at one end.
3. Pry up one end of the glass retainer and pull the retainer from around the weatherstripping.
4. Have a helper stand outside the windshield and, working from the inside, push the windshield and weatherstripping outward, starting at the upper left corner, working across the top.
5. Remove the weatherstripping from the glass.
   To install:
6. Clean the weatherstripping, glass and glass opening with solvent to remove all old sealer.
7. Apply liquid butyl sealer in the glass channel of the weatherstripping and install the weatherstripping on the glass.
8. Apply a bead of sealer to the opening flange and in the inner flange crevice of the weatherstripping lip.
9. Apply soapy water to the weatherstripping lip.
10. Have your assistant position the windshield assembly in the channel from the outside, applying firm inward pressure.
11. From inside, you guide the lip of the weatherstripping into place using a wood or fiberglass spatula, until the window is locked in place.
12. Install the glass retainer in the weatherstripping. You can push it into place with the spatula.
13. Install the center bar retainer.
14. Leak test the windshield.

1970–88 Models

1. Cover the cowl to protect the paint.
2. Remove the wiper arms.
3. Remove the windshield retainer strip from the weatherstripping. To remove the strip, pry up one end and carefully pull it

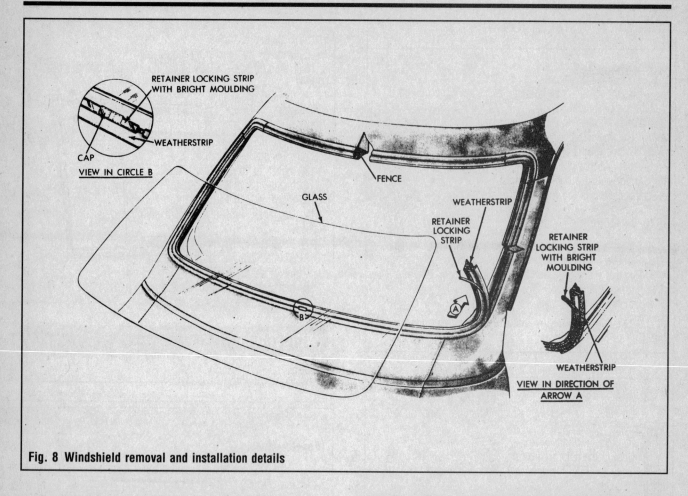

Fig. 8 Windshield removal and installation details

out. Later models have a bright cap over the retainer which must be pried out first.

4. Have a helper support the windshield from the outside while you push one corner of the glass out of the weatherstripping.

5. Once one corner is free, continue pushing *carefully* around the glass until the entire windshield is free.

6. The weatherstripping can then be removed from the frame. Replace any defective weatherstripping.

➡**Use only mineral spirits as a lubricant when installing the windshield!**

7. Install the weatherstripping in the frame. Make sure it's completely seated.

8. With your helper's assistance, slide one corner of the glass into the lower groove in the weatherstripping.

9. Move the glass into the groove as far as possible.

10. Using a fiberglass spatula, force the lip of the weatherstripping over the glass, working around the entire circumference.

11. Starting at one of the lower corners, force the retaining strip into its groove in the weatherstripping. DON'T STRETCH THE STRIP WHEN INSTALLING IT!

12. On later models, install the bright cap.

13. Using a hose, water-test the windshield.

14. Install the wiper arms.

Stationary Windows

REMOVAL & INSTALLATION

◆ **See Figures 9, 10 11 and 12**

➡**You'll need an assistant for this job.**

1. Have your assistant stand outside and support the glass.

2. Working from the inside truck, start at one upper corner and work the weatherstripping across the top of the glass, pulling the weatherstripping down and pushing outward on the glass until your assistant can grab the glass and lift it out.

3. Remove the moldings.

4. Remove the weatherstripping from the glass.

To install:

5. Clean the weatherstripping, glass and glass opening with solvent to remove all old sealer.

6. Apply liquid butyl sealer in the glass channel of the weatherstripping and install the weatherstripping on the glass.

7. Install the moldings.

8. Apply a bead of sealer to the opening flange and in the inner flange crevice of the weatherstripping lip.

9. Place a length of strong cord, such as butcher's twine, in

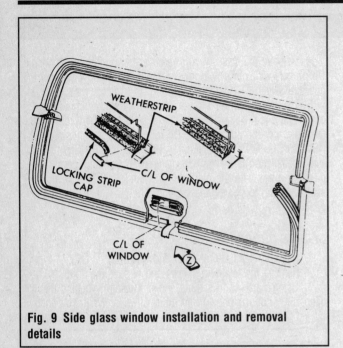

Fig. 9 Side glass window installation and removal details

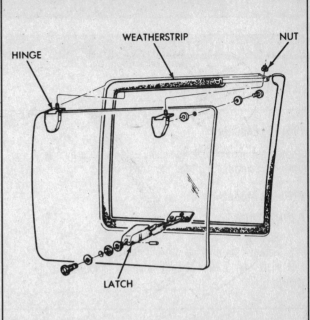

Fig. 11 Vented side glass mounting details—dual hinge models

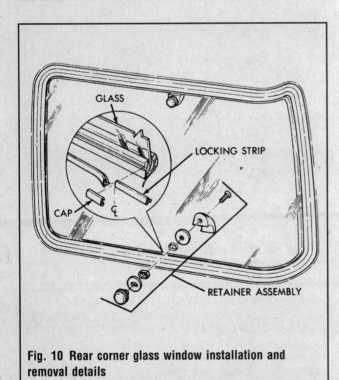

Fig. 10 Rear corner glass window installation and removal details

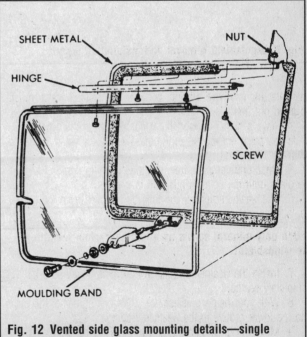

Fig. 12 Vented side glass mounting details—single hinge models

the flange crevice of the weatherstripping. The cord should go all the way around the weatherstripping with the ends, about 18" long each, hanging down together at the bottom center of the window.

10. Apply soapy water to the weatherstripping lip.

11. Have your assistant position the window assembly in the channel from the outside, applying firm inward pressure.

12. From inside, you guide the lip of the weatherstripping into place using the cord, working each end alternately, until the window is locked in place.

13. Remove the cord, clean the glass and weatherstripping of excess sealer and leak test the window.

Door Trim Panels

REMOVAL & INSTALLATION

1967–69 Models

The door access panel is simply held in place by screws. Remove the screws and lift out the panel.

1970–88 Models

FRONT DOORS

1. Remove the armrest.
2. Remove the door handle and trim cup.
3. If the van is equipped with a stereo radio, remove the speaker grille.

4. Remove the setscrew and remove the window crank handle. On models with power windows, remove the window switch trim cup and switch.
5. Using a flat wood spatula, insert it carefully behind the panel and slide it along to find the push-pins. When you encounter a pin, pry the pin outward. Do this until all the pins are out. NEVER PULL ON THE PANEL TO REMOVE THE PINS!
6. Installation is the reverse of removal. Carefully pound the pins into place with the palm of your hand. Be VERY careful to avoid missing the holes and breaking the pins or tearing the panel!

SLIDING DOORS

1. Carefully pry the pull-strap endcaps off.
2. Remove the retaining screws and remove the strap.
3. Using a flat wood spatula, insert it carefully behind the panel and slide it along to find the push-pins. When you encoun-

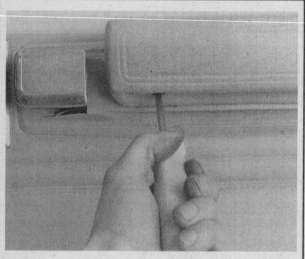

Remove the armrest attaching screws . . .

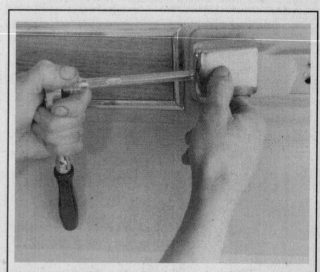

Unbolt the door handle—the bolt is behind the handle

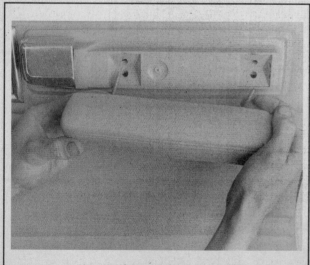

. . . and remove the armrest

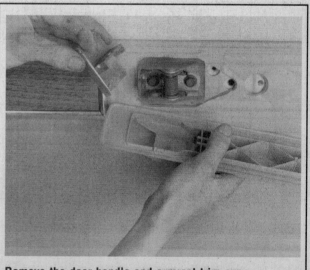

Remove the door handle and armrest trim cup

Loosen and remove the window crank setscrew . . .

Disconnect the door panel push-pins by prying the pin, not the panel, out of the door

. . . and remove the window crank handle and the round trim plate

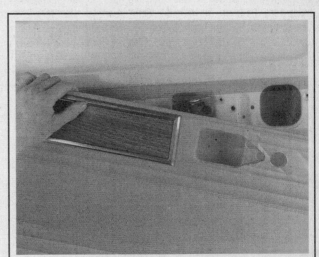

Once all push-pins have been unfastened, remove the door trim panel from the door

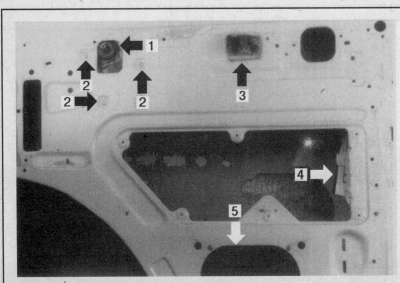

1. Window regulator
2. Window regulator attaching rivets
3. Door handle assembly
4. Window glass guide
5. Front door speaker

Door component locations for 1970–88 vehicles

ter a pin, pry the pin outward. Do this until all the pins are out. NEVER PULL ON THE PANEL TO REMOVE THE PINS!

4. Installation is the reverse of removal. Carefully pound the pins into place with the palm of your hand. Be VERY careful to avoid missing the holes and breaking the pins or tearing the panel!

Manual Door Locks

REMOVAL & INSTALLATION

Door Lock Cylinder

1. Raise the window all the way.
2. Remove the door trim panel.
3. Disconnect the lock actuating rod from the lock control clip.
4. Remove the lock cylinder retaining clip and pull the lock cylinder from the door. On the side doors, it will be necessary to loosen the inside lock control knob set screw and remove the knob.
5. Installation is the reverse of removal.

Power Door Locks

REMOVAL & INSTALLATION

▶ **See Figure 13**

Lock Solenoid

1. Raise the glass to the full UP position.
2. Remove the door trim panel.
3. Unplug the wiring from the solenoid.
4. Disconnect the linkage from the solenoid.
5. Remove the mounting screws and lift out the solenoid.
6. Installation is the reverse of removal.

Manual Door Glass and Regulator

REMOVAL & INSTALLATION

1. Remove the access or trim panel and watershield.
2. Lower the glass all the way.

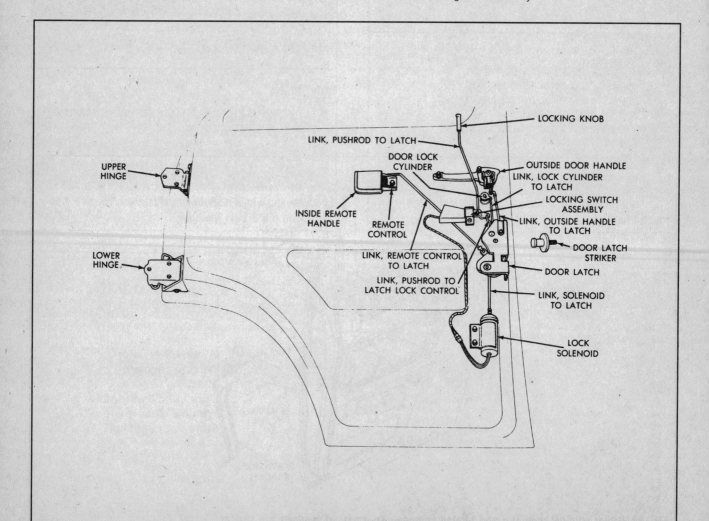

Fig. 13 Front door lock and latch assemblies—power locks shown, manual is similar

3. Remove the lower vent window support bolt.

4. Locate the vent window retaining clip screw through the weatherstripping and remove the screw.

5. Lower the door glass and tilt the vent window assembly rearward.

6. Remove the vent window.

7. Slide the door glass forward to disconnect it from the regulator.

8. Remove the inside weatherstripping from the glass opening.

9. Lift the glass from the door.

10. Unbolt and remove the regulator. Later models have the regulator secured with rivets. Drill these out.

11. Install the regulator. On later models, replace the rivets with $1/4$-$20 \times 1/2''$ bolts and nuts.

12. Lower the glass into the door.

13. Install the inside weatherstripping in the glass opening.

14. Slide the door glass rearward to connect it to the regulator.

15. Install the vent window.

16. Install the access panel and watershield.

Power Door Glass and Regulator

REMOVAL & INSTALLATION

◆ **See Figure 14**

1. Raise the glass to the full UP position.

2. Remove the trim panel and watershield.

3. Remove the down-stop bumper bracket.

4. Lower the glass all the way.

5. Remove the lower vent window support bolt.

6. Locate the vent window retaining clip screw through the weatherstripping and remove the screw.

7. Lower the door glass and tilt the vent window assembly rearward.

8. Remove the vent window.

9. Disconnect the regulator wiring from the harness.

10. Slide the door glass forward to disconnect it from the regulator.

11. Remove the inside weatherstripping from the glass opening.

12. Lift the glass from the door.

13. Drill out the regulator mounting rivets.

To install:

14. Install the regulator. Replace the rivets with $1/4$-$20 \times 1/2''$ bolts and nuts, torqued to 90 in. lbs.

15. Lower the glass into the door.

16. Install the inside weatherstripping in the glass opening.

17. Slide the door glass rearward to connect it to the regulator.

18. Connect the wiring.

19. Install the vent window.

20. Install the down-stop bumper.

21. Install the access panel and watershield.

Interior Engine Cover

REMOVAL & INSTALLATION

Early Models

To remove the cover, raise it, unbolt the support and remove the retaining pins from the hinges.

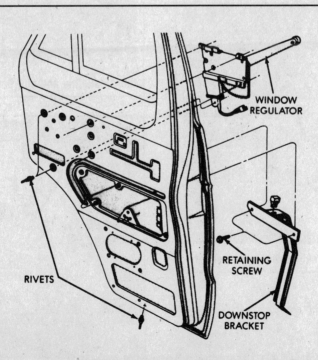

WINDOW REGULATOR

RETAINING SCREW

DOWNSTOP BRACKET

RIVETS

Fig. 14 Power window regulator and related components—manual windows are similar

Late Models

➡ **Depending on the option level of the vehicle, it may be necessary to remove some accessories that are fastened to the engine cover before it can be removed.**

To remove the cover, pull the floor covering back to expose the two hold-down bolts or latches. Remove the bolts and/or unhook the latches. There are two latches, located on either side of the cover (near the top), which must also be unhooked. Once the cover is loose, slide it rearward, then lift it up and pull it back. Remove the cover from the vehicle.

Holding the floor covering back, remove the lower hold-down bolts and hold-downs

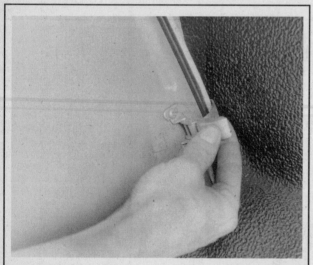

Unhook the two latches on the side of the engine cover

Lift up slightly and pull backwards on the cover . . .

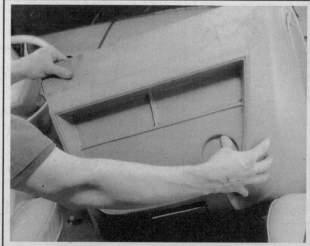

. . . and once it is clear of the dashboard, tilt the top of the cover up and remove it from the van

Inside Rear View Mirror

The mirror is held in place with a single setscrew. Loosen the screw and lift the mirror off. Repair kit for damaged mirrors are available at most auto parts stores.

Front Seat

REMOVAL & INSTALLATION

◈ **See Figures 15 and 16**

1967–88 Models

Remove the seat track-to-floor nuts and lift out the seat. Installation is the reverse of removal.

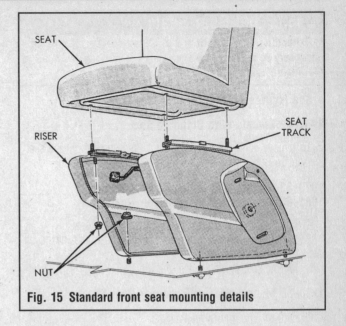

Fig. 15 Standard front seat mounting details

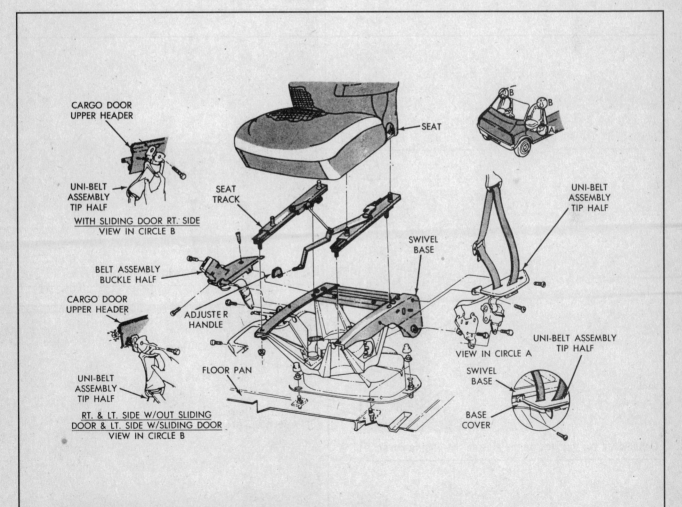

Fig. 16 Swivel front seat mounting details, including Uni-belt mounting

Center and Rear Seats

REMOVAL & INSTALLATION

▶ **See Figures 17 and 18**

1967–82 Models With Standard Seat

To remove either seat, remove the bolts/nuts. Lift out the seat. Installation is the reverse of removal.

1979–82 Models With Quick Release Seat
1983–88 Models With 3-Passenger Rear Seat

1. Lift up the release lever and push up on the seat.
2. While holding up the front of the seat, push rearward to unlatch the rear anchors.
3. Lift the seat up and out of the van.

1983–88 Models With 4-Passenger Rear Seat

1. Remove the hold-down bolts.
2. Remove the seat.

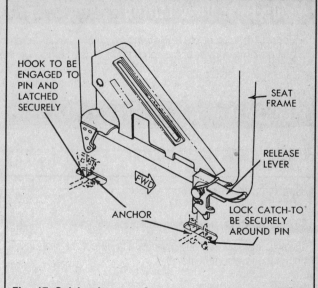

Fig. 17 Quick release or 3-passenger rear seat mounting details

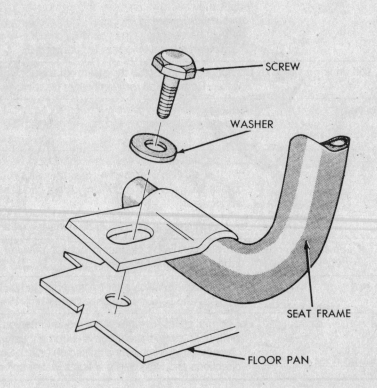

Fig. 18 Standard or 4-passenger rear seat mounting details

How to Remove Stains from Fabric Interior

For rest results, spots and stains should be removed as soon as possible. Never use gasoline, lacquer thinner, acetone, nail polish remover or bleach. Use a 3' x 3" piece of cheesecloth. Squeeze most of the liquid from the fabric and wipe the stained fabric from the outside of the stain toward the center with a lifting motion. Turn the cheesecloth as soon as one side becomes soiled. When using water to remove a stain, be sure to wash the entire section after the spot has been removed to avoid water stains. Encrusted spots can be broken up with a dull knife and vacuumed before removing the stain.

Type of Stain	How to Remove It
Surface spots	Brush the spots out with a small hand brush or use a commercial preparation such as K2R to lift the stain.
Mildew	Clean around the mildew with warm suds. Rinse in cold water and soak the mildew area in a solution of 1 part table salt and 2 parts water. Wash with upholstery cleaner.
Water stains	Water stains in fabric materials can be removed with a solution made from 1 cup of table salt dissolved in 1 quart of water. Vigorously scrub the solution into the stain and rinse with clear water. Water stains in nylon or other synthetic fabrics should be removed with a commercial type spot remover.
Chewing gum, tar, crayons, shoe polish (greasy stains)	Do not use a cleaner that will soften gum or tar. Harden the deposit with an ice cube and scrape away as much as possible with a dull knife. Moisten the remainder with cleaning fluid and scrub clean.
Ice cream, candy	Most candy has a sugar base and can be removed with a cloth wrung out in warm water. Oily candy, after cleaning with warm water, should be cleaned with upholstery cleaner. Rinse with warm water and clean the remainder with cleaning fluid.
Wine, alcohol, egg, milk, soft drink (non-greasy stains)	Do not use soap. Scrub the stain with a cloth wrung out in warm water. Remove the remainder with cleaning fluid.
Grease, oil, lipstick, butter and related stains	Use a spot remover to avoid leaving a ring. Work from the outisde of the stain to the center and dry with a clean cloth when the spot is gone.
Headliners (cloth)	Mix a solution of warm water and foam upholstery cleaner to give thick suds. Use only foam—liquid may streak or spot. Clean the entire headliner in one operation using a circular motion with a natural sponge.
Headliner (vinyl)	Use a vinyl cleaner with a sponge and wipe clean with a dry cloth.
Seats and door panels	Mix 1 pint upholstery cleaner in 1 gallon of water. Do not soak the fabric around the buttons.
Leather or vinyl fabric	Use a multi-purpose cleaner full strength and a stiff brush. Let stand 2 minutes and scrub thoroughly. Wipe with a clean, soft rag.
Nylon or synthetic fabrics	For normal stains, use the same procedures you would for washing cloth upholstery. If the fabric is extremely dirty, use a multi-purpose cleaner full strength with a stiff scrub brush. Scrub thoroughly in all directions and wipe with a cotton towel or soft rag.

GLOSSARY

AIR/FUEL RATIO: The ratio of air-to-gasoline by weight in the fuel mixture drawn into the engine.

AIR INJECTION: One method of reducing harmful exhaust emissions by injecting air into each of the exhaust ports of an engine. The fresh air entering the hot exhaust manifold causes any remaining fuel to be burned before it can exit the tailpipe.

ALTERNATOR: A device used for converting mechanical energy into electrical energy.

AMMETER: An instrument, calibrated in amperes, used to measure the flow of an electrical current in a circuit. Ammeters are always connected in series with the circuit being tested.

AMPERE: The rate of flow of electrical current present when one volt of electrical pressure is applied against one ohm of electrical resistance.

ANALOG COMPUTER: Any microprocessor that uses similar (analogous) electrical signals to make its calculations.

ARMATURE: A laminated, soft iron core wrapped by a wire that converts electrical energy to mechanical energy as in a motor or relay. When rotated in a magnetic field, it changes mechanical energy into electrical energy as in a generator.

ATMOSPHERIC PRESSURE: The pressure on the Earth's surface caused by the weight of the air in the atmosphere. At sea level, this pressure is 14.7 psi at 32°F (101 kPa at 0°C).

ATOMIZATION: The breaking down of a liquid into a fine mist that can be suspended in air.

AXIAL PLAY: Movement parallel to a shaft or bearing bore.

BACKFIRE: The sudden combustion of gases in the intake or exhaust system that results in a loud explosion.

BACKLASH: The clearance or play between two parts, such as meshed gears.

BACKPRESSURE: Restrictions in the exhaust system that slow the exit of exhaust gases from the combustion chamber.

BAKELITE: A heat resistant, plastic insulator material commonly used in printed circuit boards and transistorized components.

BALL BEARING: A bearing made up of hardened inner and outer races between which hardened steel balls roll.

BALLAST RESISTOR: A resistor in the primary ignition circuit that lowers voltage after the engine is started to reduce wear on ignition components.

BEARING: A friction reducing, supportive device usually located between a stationary part and a moving part.

BIMETAL TEMPERATURE SENSOR: Any sensor or switch made of two dissimilar types of metal that bend when heated or cooled due to the different expansion rates of the alloys. These types of sensors usually function as an on/off switch.

BLOWBY: Combustion gases, composed of water vapor and unburned fuel, that leak past the piston rings into the crankcase during normal engine operation. These gases are removed by the PCV system to prevent the buildup of harmful acids in the crankcase.

BRAKE PAD: A brake shoe and lining assembly used with disc brakes.

BRAKE SHOE: The backing for the brake lining. The term is, however, usually applied to the assembly of the brake backing and lining.

BUSHING: A liner, usually removable, for a bearing; an anti-friction liner used in place of a bearing.

CALIPER: A hydraulically activated device in a disc brake system, which is mounted straddling the brake rotor (disc). The caliper contains at least one piston and two brake pads. Hydraulic pressure on the piston(s) forces the pads against the rotor.

CAMSHAFT: A shaft in the engine on which are the lobes (cams) which operate the valves. The camshaft is driven by the crankshaft, via a belt, chain or gears, at one half the crankshaft speed.

CAPACITOR: A device which stores an electrical charge.

CARBON MONOXIDE (CO): A colorless, odorless gas given off as a normal byproduct of combustion. It is poisonous and extremely dangerous in confined areas, building up slowly to toxic levels without warning if adequate ventilation is not available.

CARBURETOR: A device, usually mounted on the intake manifold of an engine, which mixes the air and fuel in the proper proportion to allow even combustion.

CATALYTIC CONVERTER: A device installed in the exhaust system, like a muffler, that converts harmful byproducts of combustion into carbon dioxide and water vapor by means of a heat-producing chemical reaction.

CENTRIFUGAL ADVANCE: A mechanical method of advancing the spark timing by using flyweights in the distributor that react to centrifugal force generated by the distributor shaft rotation.

CHECK VALVE: Any one-way valve installed to permit the flow of air, fuel or vacuum in one direction only.

CHOKE: A device, usually a moveable valve, placed in the intake path of a carburetor to restrict the flow of air.

CIRCUIT: Any unbroken path through which an electrical current can flow. Also used to describe fuel flow in some instances.

CIRCUIT BREAKER: A switch which protects an electrical circuit from overload by opening the circuit when the current flow exceeds a predetermined level. Some circuit breakers must be reset manually, while most reset automatically.

COIL (IGNITION): A transformer in the ignition circuit which steps up the voltage provided to the spark plugs.

COMBINATION MANIFOLD: An assembly which includes both the intake and exhaust manifolds in one casting.

COMBINATION VALVE: A device used in some fuel systems that routes fuel vapors to a charcoal storage canister instead of venting them into the atmosphere. The valve relieves fuel tank pressure and allows fresh air into the tank as the fuel level drops to prevent a vapor lock situation.

COMPRESSION RATIO: The comparison of the total volume of the cylinder and combustion chamber with the piston at BDC and the piston at TDC.

CONDENSER: 1. An electrical device which acts to store an electrical charge, preventing voltage surges. 2. A radiator-like device in the air conditioning system in which refrigerant gas condenses into a liquid, giving off heat.

CONDUCTOR: Any material through which an electrical current can be transmitted easily.

CONTINUITY: Continuous or complete circuit. Can be checked with an ohmmeter.

COUNTERSHAFT: An intermediate shaft which is rotated by a mainshaft and transmits, in turn, that rotation to a working part.

CRANKCASE: The lower part of an engine in which the crankshaft and related parts operate.

CRANKSHAFT: The main driving shaft of an engine which receives reciprocating motion from the pistons and converts it to rotary motion.

CYLINDER: In an engine, the round hole in the engine block in which the piston(s) ride.

CYLINDER BLOCK: The main structural member of an engine in which is found the cylinders, crankshaft and other principal parts.

CYLINDER HEAD: The detachable portion of the engine, usually fastened to the top of the cylinder block and containing all or most of the combustion chambers. On overhead valve engines, it contains the valves and their operating parts. On overhead cam engines, it contains the camshaft as well.

DEAD CENTER: The extreme top or bottom of the piston stroke.

DETONATION: An unwanted explosion of the air/fuel mixture in the combustion chamber caused by excess heat and compression, advanced timing, or an overly lean mixture. Also referred to as "ping".

DIAPHRAGM: A thin, flexible wall separating two cavities, such as in a vacuum advance unit.

DIESELING: A condition in which hot spots in the combustion chamber cause the engine to run on after the key is turned off.

DIFFERENTIAL: A geared assembly which allows the transmission of motion between drive axles, giving one axle the ability to turn faster than the other.

DIODE: An electrical device that will allow current to flow in one direction only.

DISC BRAKE: A hydraulic braking assembly consisting of a brake disc, or rotor, mounted on an axle, and a caliper assembly containing, usually two brake pads which are activated by hydraulic pressure. The pads are forced against the sides of the disc, creating friction which slows the vehicle.

DISTRIBUTOR: A mechanically driven device on an engine which is responsible for electrically firing the spark plug at a predetermined point of the piston stroke.

DOWEL PIN: A pin, inserted in mating holes in two different parts allowing those parts to maintain a fixed relationship.

DRUM BRAKE: A braking system which consists of two brake shoes and one or two wheel cylinders, mounted on a fixed backing plate, and a brake drum, mounted on an axle, which revolves around the assembly.

DWELL: The rate, measured in degrees of shaft rotation, at which an electrical circuit cycles on and off.

ELECTRONIC CONTROL UNIT (ECU): Ignition module, module, amplifier or igniter. See Module for definition.

ELECTRONIC IGNITION: A system in which the timing and firing of the spark plugs is controlled by an electronic control unit, usually called a module. These systems have no points or condenser.

END-PLAY: The measured amount of axial movement in a shaft.

ENGINE: A device that converts heat into mechanical energy.

EXHAUST MANIFOLD: A set of cast passages or pipes which conduct exhaust gases from the engine.

FEELER GAUGE: A blade, usually metal, of precisely predetermined thickness, used to measure the clearance between two parts.

FIRING ORDER: The order in which combustion occurs in the cylinders of an engine. Also the order in which spark is distributed to the plugs by the distributor.

FLOODING: The presence of too much fuel in the intake manifold and combustion chamber which prevents the air/fuel mixture from firing, thereby causing a no-start situation.

FLYWHEEL: A disc shaped part bolted to the rear end of the crankshaft. Around the outer perimeter is affixed the ring gear. The starter drive engages the ring gear, turning the flywheel, which rotates the crankshaft, imparting the initial starting motion to the engine.

FOOT POUND (ft. lbs. or sometimes, ft.lb.): The amount of energy or work needed to raise an item weighing one pound, a distance of one foot.

FUSE: A protective device in a circuit which prevents circuit overload by breaking the circuit when a specific amperage is present. The device is constructed around a strip or wire of a lower amperage rating than the circuit it is designed to protect. When an amperage higher than that stamped on the fuse is present in the circuit, the strip or wire melts, opening the circuit.

GEAR RATIO: The ratio between the number of teeth on meshing gears.

GENERATOR: A device which converts mechanical energy into electrical energy.

HEAT RANGE: The measure of a spark plug's ability to dissipate heat from its firing end. The higher the heat range, the hotter the plug fires.

HUB: The center part of a wheel or gear.

HYDROCARBON (HC): Any chemical compound made up of hydrogen and carbon. A major pollutant formed by the engine as a byproduct of combustion.

HYDROMETER: An instrument used to measure the specific gravity of a solution.

INCH POUND (inch lbs.; sometimes in.lb. or in. lbs.): One twelfth of a foot pound.

INDUCTION: A means of transferring electrical energy in the form of a magnetic field. Principle used in the ignition coil to increase voltage.

INJECTOR: A device which receives metered fuel under relatively low pressure and is activated to inject the fuel into the engine under relatively high pressure at a predetermined time.

INPUT SHAFT: The shaft to which torque is applied, usually carrying the driving gear or gears.

INTAKE MANIFOLD: A casting of passages or pipes used to conduct air or a fuel/air mixture to the cylinders.

JOURNAL: The bearing surface within which a shaft operates.

KEY: A small block usually fitted in a notch between a shaft and a hub to prevent slippage of the two parts.

MANIFOLD: A casting of passages or set of pipes which connect the cylinders to an inlet or outlet source.

MANIFOLD VACUUM: Low pressure in an engine intake manifold formed just below the throttle plates. Manifold vacuum is highest at idle and drops under acceleration.

MASTER CYLINDER: The primary fluid pressurizing device in a hydraulic system. In automotive use, it is found in brake and hydraulic clutch systems and is pedal activated, either directly or, in a power brake system, through the power booster.

MODULE: Electronic control unit, amplifier or igniter of solid state or integrated design which controls the current flow in the ignition primary circuit based on input from the pick-up coil. When the module opens the primary circuit, high secondary voltage is induced in the coil.

NEEDLE BEARING: A bearing which consists of a number (usually a large number) of long, thin rollers.

OHM: (Ω) The unit used to measure the resistance of conductor-to-electrical flow. One ohm is the amount of resistance that limits current flow to one ampere in a circuit with one volt of pressure.

OHMMETER: An instrument used for measuring the resistance, in ohms, in an electrical circuit.

OUTPUT SHAFT: The shaft which transmits torque from a device, such as a transmission.

OVERDRIVE: A gear assembly which produces more shaft revolutions than that transmitted to it.

OVERHEAD CAMSHAFT (OHC): An engine configuration in which the camshaft is mounted on top of the cylinder head and operates the valve either directly or by means of rocker arms.

OVERHEAD VALVE (OHV): An engine configuration in which all of the valves are located in the cylinder head and the camshaft is located in the cylinder block. The camshaft operates the valves via lifters and pushrods.

OXIDES OF NITROGEN (NOx): Chemical compounds of nitrogen produced as a byproduct of combustion. They combine with hydrocarbons to produce smog.

OXYGEN SENSOR: Used with the feedback system to sense the presence of oxygen in the exhaust gas and signal the computer which can reference the voltage signal to an air/fuel ratio.

PINION: The smaller of two meshing gears.

PISTON RING: An open-ended ring which fits into a groove on the outer diameter of the piston. Its chief function is to form a seal between the piston and cylinder wall. Most automotive pistons have three rings: two for compression sealing; one for oil sealing.

PRELOAD: A predetermined load placed on a bearing during assembly or by adjustment.

PRIMARY CIRCUIT: The low voltage side of the ignition system which consists of the ignition switch, ballast resistor or resistance wire, bypass, coil, electronic control unit and pick-up coil as well as the connecting wires and harnesses.

PRESS FIT: The mating of two parts under pressure, due to the inner diameter of one being smaller than the outer diameter of the other, or vice versa; an interference fit.

RACE: The surface on the inner or outer ring of a bearing on which the balls, needles or rollers move.

REGULATOR: A device which maintains the amperage and/or voltage levels of a circuit at predetermined values.

RELAY: A switch which automatically opens and/or closes a circuit.

RESISTANCE: The opposition to the flow of current through a circuit or electrical device, and is measured in ohms. Resistance is equal to the voltage divided by the amperage.

RESISTOR: A device, usually made of wire, which offers a preset amount of resistance in an electrical circuit.

RING GEAR: The name given to a ring-shaped gear attached to a differential case, or affixed to a flywheel or as part of a planetary gear set.

ROLLER BEARING: A bearing made up of hardened inner and outer races between which hardened steel rollers move.

ROTOR: 1. The disc-shaped part of a disc brake assembly, upon which the brake pads bear; also called, brake disc. 2. The device mounted atop the distributor shaft, which passes current to the distributor cap tower contacts.

SECONDARY CIRCUIT: The high voltage side of the ignition system, usually above 20,000 volts. The secondary includes the ignition coil, coil wire, distributor cap and rotor, spark plug wires and spark plugs.

SENDING UNIT: A mechanical, electrical, hydraulic or electro-magnetic device which transmits information to a gauge.

SENSOR: Any device designed to measure engine operating conditions or ambient pressures and temperatures. Usually electronic in nature and designed to send a voltage signal to an on-board computer, some sensors may operate as a simple on/off switch or they may provide a variable voltage signal (like a potentiometer) as conditions or measured parameters change.

SHIM: Spacers of precise, predetermined thickness used between parts to establish a proper working relationship.

SLAVE CYLINDER: In automotive use, a device in the hydraulic clutch system which is activated by hydraulic force, disengaging the clutch.

SOLENOID: A coil used to produce a magnetic field, the effect of which is to produce work.

SPARK PLUG: A device screwed into the combustion chamber of a spark ignition engine. The basic construction is a conductive core inside of a ceramic insulator, mounted in an outer conductive base. An electrical charge from the spark plug wire travels along the conductive core and jumps a preset air gap to a grounding point or points at the end of the conductive base. The resultant spark ignites the fuel/air mixture in the combustion chamber.

SPLINES: Ridges machined or cast onto the outer diameter of a shaft or inner diameter of a bore to enable parts to mate without rotation.

TACHOMETER: A device used to measure the rotary speed of an engine, shaft, gear, etc., usually in rotations per minute.

THERMOSTAT: A valve, located in the cooling system of an engine, which is closed when cold and opens gradually in response to engine heating, controlling the temperature of the coolant and rate of coolant flow.

TOP DEAD CENTER (TDC): The point at which the piston reaches the top of its travel on the compression stroke.

TORQUE: The twisting force applied to an object.

TORQUE CONVERTER: A turbine used to transmit power from a driving member to a driven member via hydraulic action, providing changes in drive ratio and torque. In automotive use, it links the driveplate at the rear of the engine to the automatic transmission.

TRANSDUCER: A device used to change a force into an electrical signal.

TRANSISTOR: A semi-conductor component which can be actuated by a small voltage to perform an electrical switching function.

TUNE-UP: A regular maintenance function, usually associated with the replacement and adjustment of parts and components in the electrical and fuel systems of a vehicle for the purpose of attaining optimum performance.

TURBOCHARGER: An exhaust driven pump which compresses intake air and forces it into the combustion chambers at higher than atmospheric pressures. The increased air pressure allows more fuel to be burned and results in increased horsepower being produced.

VACUUM ADVANCE: A device which advances the ignition timing in response to increased engine vacuum.

VACUUM GAUGE: An instrument used to measure the presence of vacuum in a chamber.

VALVE: A device which control the pressure, direction of flow or rate of flow of a liquid or gas.

VALVE CLEARANCE: The measured gap between the end of the valve stem and the rocker arm, cam lobe or follower that activates the valve.

VISCOSITY: The rating of a liquid's internal resistance to flow.

VOLTMETER: An instrument used for measuring electrical force in units called volts. Voltmeters are always connected parallel with the circuit being tested.

WHEEL CYLINDER: Found in the automotive drum brake assembly, it is a device, actuated by hydraulic pressure, which, through internal pistons, pushes the brake shoes outward against the drums.

MASTER INDEX